W9-DGS-271

LITERATURE
The Power of Language
Instructor's Edition

Thomas Mc Laughlin
Appalachian State University

Harcourt Brace Jovanovich, Publishers

San Diego New York Chicago Austin Washington, D.C.
London Sydney Tokyo Toronto

Acknowledgments

This book is dedicated to my father, Tom, who gave me a space to write in and a model to follow.

For the time to write in, I owe thanks to my wife Joan and my children, Nora, Kate, and Julia. Thanks also for being glad I was doing this—it did keep me out of trouble—and to Joan for teaching me how to breathe.

Many of my colleagues were extremely helpful in suggesting readings for the anthology and in refining my thinking about criticism. I'd like especially to thank Jim Winders, Gene Miller, Melissa Barth, Chip Arnold, Emory Maiden, Leon Lewis, Edelma Huntley, George Gaston, Ron Coulthard, Jerry Williamson, and Bill Lightfoot. Thanks to Laurie Kirszner for teaching me how to get into this enterprise. And thanks to Frank Lentricchia, who has helped make two projects possible.

To the following reviewers of the completed book, I would like to express my appreciation for their comments and suggestions: Monika Brown, Pembroke State University; Cynthia Eby, James Madison University; Ed Folsom, University of Iowa; Jennifer Ginn, North Carolina State University; Donald Gray, Indiana University; Peter Maas, El Paso Community College; Steven Mailloux, Syracuse University; Robert McCoy, Kent State University; Scott McNabb, Grand Rapids Junior College; J. Hillis Miller, University of California, Irvine; Jim Mullican, Indiana State University; Robert Peterson, Middle Tennessee State University; Phillip Pierpont, Vincennes University.

Appalachian State University has supported this project by providing reduced time and many other resources. For this help I would like to thank Loyd Hilton, William Byrd, and Kenneth Webb.

I also received extensive help in the preparation of this manuscript and in the permissions process from student assistants: Michael Glenn, Carole Lassiter, and John Brown. Thanks also to Tim Cook and Susan Shoemaker for their essays. Janet Wellborn, Shannon Jackson, Rebecca Pierce-Ebdy, and Selena Martin helped with typing and photocopying.

I owe special thanks to my editors at Harcourt Brace Jovanovich, Marlane Miriello and David Dexter. Thanks also to Eleanor Garner for handling permissions, and to the rest of my book team: Mandy Van Dusen, production manager; Caty Van Housen, production editor; Gina Sample, designer; and Stacy Simpson, art editor.

ISBN: 0-15-551093-2 (Instructor's Edition)

Library of Congress Catalog Card Number: 88-81048

Printed in the United States of America

Foreword

Tom Mc Laughlin's *Literature: The Power of Language* is the introductory anthology we have all been waiting for. In as remarkable an act of translation as I have ever seen, Mc Laughlin brings the ideas of contemporary literary theory down to the earth of ordinary language. In so doing he brings to life for a broad audience, and in a strikingly vivid style, what a few advanced theorists have known for some time but have almost never been able to communicate beyond their own coterie: the proposition that—despite its generally forbidding, off-putting jargon—recent theory has the capacity to empower readers to become both active and responsible producers of their literary experience, and in such active reading to gain insight into how literature helps us make sense of ourselves in the world.

Mc Laughlin puts his aims across in a compelling way: this text is as teachable as those of his distinguished predecessors. Moreover, he honors the best literature of the past and the contemporary scene by gently guiding a fully engaged interaction with it. To use this book is not to forsake the critical methods we grew up with but to re-encounter them in a powerful new light. To use this book is also to learn how much common sense the newer methods can make when deployed by someone with Mc Laughlin's tact and wit.

After an encounter with *Literature: The Power of Language,* students will know that "literature" is no remote thing made by and for privileged people but an inescapable thing—a part of us, one of our paths to the world. Tom Mc Laughlin has created a book whose time has come.

Frank Lentricchia
Duke University

Preface

The premise of *Literature: The Power of Language* is that the insights and strategies of recent literary theory can and should be brought to bear on the Introduction to Literature classroom. Literary theory is not—or ought not to be—an arcane topic. Literary theory is in fact the study of the assumptions that readers put into play when they read. It maintains that those assumptions play an active role in the process by which readers produce meaning. In our time, which has been characterized by an extremely rich and controversial concern with theory, we have seen the most basic premises of literary studies brought under severe question. For many, this questioning has been disturbing; for others, it has been invigorating. But in addition to generating controversy, theory has also suggested a new set of assumptions that can enable powerful and productive reading.

Needless to say there is still plenty of controversy about what those premises should be, but I think it is possible to articulate some common ground, some shared strategies that have come out of recent theory and that can be useful for serious beginning critical readers. I have tried to lay out some of those strategies and assumptions in this anthology in a way that will be useful to students. A large part of that task, of course, involved making sure that the language of the book was accessible to students. One of the factors that has limited the usefulness of recent theory in the classroom has been its difficult language. The best of theory has used a language only as difficult as necessary for the task of challenging our understanding of language itself; but there has also been stylistic excess, which has allowed many faculty to ignore theory as obscurantist and self-indulgent. I am convinced that theory need not be obscure. Difficult and challenging, yes, but not obscure. In writing this book, I have worked to keep a first-year audience in mind. There is very little technical vocabulary or new terminology. What is different is the set of assumptions being offered for consideration—offered in language that the average first-year student can grasp.

Those assumptions, which serve as the framework on which this presentation rests, can be described as follows:

Readers are active. Most beginning readers work with a model of reading that pictures them as passive recipients of the author's message. I argue that passive readers are a contradiction in terms. Reading is productive work; it requires from readers an array of actions without which the work of literature can hardly be said to exist.

Readers are responsible for the readings they produce. Readers bring to the reading experience their own beliefs, values, and reading strategies, and they must therefore take responsibility for the meanings they find. This does not suggest that readers can produce any meaning they desire. They have to contend with the language of the literary text. Taking responsibility means showing how a particular reading makes sense of the text's language.

Reading literature is a way of understanding language. Literature won't let readers process language casually, as they do in daily life. It is often difficult, requiring a serious effort from readers if they are going to make sense of it at all. As a result, readers can and must attend closely to the language, observing how it functions and affects their response.

Language is a framework through which we all see the world and encounter experience. In our everyday use of language, we tend not to think about language at all, using it simply as a tool. But language is much more than a tool; it is the frame of reference through which we live, a system of meanings and values that shapes our experience of reality. So coming to understand language is a way of understanding how we operate as human beings, how we make meaning in our lives.

Writing about literature is an integral part of the reading process. Writing about literature allows readers to make sense of the literary work in much more detail and much more fully than would otherwise be possible. In writing, readers are forced to take responsibility for their readings. Writing about literature is a process of persuasion in which readers try to show the validity of their reading in terms of the language of the work.

In some ways, despite its emphasis on new theory, this book looks familiar. It is organized in a familiar way, by genre, beginning with poetry, which seems to me the best way to introduce the power of language. This organization allows students to encounter some of the necessary vocabulary of critical reading in a workable and familiar format. The literary works selected for the book are fairly traditional, on the conviction that new literary theory is not just useful with avant-garde works but also with some of the most familiar yet still powerful works of tradition. There has been a serious effort, though, to widen that tradition to include writers who have been unfairly eliminated from it in the past: women writers, minority writers, and contemporary writers.

Faculty often lament the passivity of their students, many of whom are products of TV and media culture. In *Literature: The Power of Language,* the goal is to remind student readers of their real powers and responsibilities. Reading simply does not allow passivity. Further, the experience of active, critical reading spills over into their experience of that media culture itself, allowing them to listen and view more critically, attaining the active stance that the media seem to want to deny them. Critical awareness—a questioning, skeptical habit of mind—is the goal toward which I hope the strategies of this book help students take a modest step.

To the Student

One of the messages that comes up frequently in this anthology is that poems and stories and plays do not exist only within the covers of schoolbooks. Stories get told all the time by ordinary people in conversation; dramatic works are the staples of TV and film; poetic language gets used in advertising and pop music. It is also important to remember that the critical skills that this text tries to encourage are useful not only in reading literature but also in "reading" cultural and social experience. If you learn how to read a poem well, you have learned skills that apply to almost all uses of language. If you learn how to make sense of a character in a story, you have learned something about how to "read" people in daily life. Being an active reader, that is, ought to be part of a larger project of learning to become a critical thinker. And there are people who want very much to deny you that status. Advertisers, some kinds of politicians, even some kinds of educators want you to accept what they are saying without question, as though their messages were the self-evident truth. The purpose of this text is to raise questions, and to help you to learn how to question those "truths" yourself, from a critical perspective that is as independent as possible.

Most directly, this text is concerned with asking questions about language. As you will see in all of these chapters, I am convinced that questions about language lead to the most basic questions about human life and behavior. Language carries along with it the basic concepts and values of our culture. It forms a framework through which we all encounter experience. So if we are to understand how we operate on and experience the world, we need to make sense of this powerful social structure. Literature is precisely the place to learn these lessons. Almost all literary works force us to think about language rather than just to use it. They make the processing of language difficult; they slow us down, allowing a clearer concentration on how the language is working. What we can get from literature, then, is a privileged glimpse into the nature and function of language, which in turn teaches us about our own identity as social beings.

This book also aims to give you as a reader the authority to produce your own reading of literary texts. It assumes that you will be writing about what you read, and that what you write will be an authentic expression of how you saw the text. But in order to write with that kind of freedom, you must first be confident that your reading makes sense in terms of the text's language. You have to do the hard work of reading before you can have the confidence to express your own opinion. After all, you can expect that others will see the text differently, and that your reading will be in competition with others. Can you make a case for your reading? Can you show where it came from and why it ought to be accepted? I hope that this book will provide you with some of the skills necessary to read well and to enter confidently into the battle of interpretations that most literary texts provoke.

Contents

Part One
Active Reading

Active Reading

Have you ever watched children watching TV? They do not move. If you pick them up they go slack on you. Their eyes widen and glaze over. You can almost see the stream of prepackaged images flow from the TV, into those glazed-over eyes, and then into the brain pan.

Television does seem to have this tranquilizing effect on many children—and, of course, on many adults. You don't have to concentrate much in order to watch TV; you just have to be in its presence. When you realize that the average American family has the TV on about seven hours a day—almost as much as they work or sleep—it's not surprising that some people have begun to call us a passive culture, a culture of consumption.

Many people have the same image when it comes to reading. They think of reading as a passive process in which only the author has done a productive piece of work. And since the author has put the words on the page, they think that the reader's job is simply to take the words in, to allow them to do their work on us. We are, according to this image, essentially passive as readers. Stories and poems and plays *happen to* us, have their effects on us. We are simply the consumers of what we read.

Nothing could be further from the truth. Readers are in fact engaged in a very active process. The very notion of a passive reader is a contradiction in terms. After all, when you sit down to read, all you have facing you are marks on a page, black figures against a white background. Whatever meaning they are going to have depends on your willingness to bring those marks to life. Reading is *work*. Readers bring their own knowledge and background to bear on what they read, using their experience of language and of human behavior to bring the meaning of those marks into existence.

In fact, reading is often *hard* work. So hard that, if you've spent a lot of time in the relatively passive role of TV consumer, reading may not seem worth the effort. In reading, the images are not delivered prepackaged to your mind. Readers have to exercise their own imaginations. Have you ever had the experience of seeing a movie based on a novel you've read? When you see the movie, the house that the story takes place in, for example, will be presented to you in a photographed image. But when you read the novel you have to make up that house, out of the words the author used to describe it. Following the words' cues, you have to use your own imagination in order to get a sense of what it looks like.

For some people, this effort of imagination is just too difficult. But it is precisely because reading requires this effort that it is so good for us as an antidote to TV and other forms of entertainment that allow us to be passive. In fact, one of the lessons that reading teaches us is that even TV should be watched with an active, critical mind. Good readers learn to be active in interpreting *all* of their experience.

The Power of Language

We will be spending much of our time in this book thinking about the kind of work readers have to do. But let me set up a preliminary description of the process. One of the most important jobs a reader has to perform, as I've suggested, is imagining the world that the story or poem or play allows us to bring to life. But there are other, less obvious, tasks that have to occur before we can exercise our visual imagination.

First of all, we have to be competent in the language. In order to turn those marks on the page into an imagined world, we have first to make sense of them, to construct their meaning. We can do this because we are part of a community of speakers of a certain language. We know what the words mean, and we know how they can be used together in meaningful combinations. We may or may not be able to express the rules of those combinations—the grammar—but as users of a language we recognize when a group of words makes sense and when it doesn't. This knowledge of the system makes it possible for us to make sense of the particular combination of words that a text provides. We, as readers, have to apply our knowledge of the system of language—its meanings and forms—before a work of literature can come to life.

The interesting thing about reading literature is that it often makes that process very difficult. In other kinds of reading, say for example when you're reading the directions in a product manual, you can make sense of the language very easily. The author has tried to put as few obstacles in the reader's way as possible. But when you're reading a poem or a story, you may encounter unusual words in unusual patterns, slowing you down and making the reading process difficult. As I've said, such reading is often *hard* work. One advantage of this fact, as I'll discuss later in the chapters on poetry, is that it teaches us about how language functions in our minds and our lives.

As an example of how literature can slow down the reading process, let's look at this famous poem by e. e. cummings:

[IN JUST-]

in Just-
spring   when the world is mud-

luscious the little
lame balloonman

whistles   far   and wee

and eddieandbill come
running from marbles and
piracies and it's
spring

when the world is puddle-wonderful

the queer
old balloonman whistles
far   and   wee
and bettyandisbel come dancing

from hop-scotch and jump-rope and

it's
spring
and

    the

    goat-footed

balloonMan   whistles
far
and
wee

There are no really difficult words here, but they are placed in some very unusual combinations. The usual syntax does not seem to apply; our expectations about how words follow words don't get fulfilled. Instead, words seem to jar against one another at random. Of course, the more time you spend trying to figure out the poem, the less random it seems. You become involved in a kind of game, a playing with the usual rules, a creative improvisation. And ultimately you can make sense of this poem; you can help to produce its quirky, playful insight.

Play is an important word in thinking about reading. What I've been calling the *work* of reading could also be thought of as the discipline that any game requires. Reading does call for work, but it is in the service of play. If you engage yourself fully in what you read, the difficulty of language can be pleasurable, an opportunity to play with meaning. All games have rules, just as language has rules, but playing a game also allows for creative innovation within the rules. In literature, language is used in a way that plays within but also plays with the rules of the system of meaning. As a result, reading literature increases our awareness of language.

In order to participate in the game of literature, you not only have to know the rules of language, but also the precise but flexible rules of literature itself. Each of the forms of literature imposes its own set of rules. A sonnet must be fourteen lines, for example, and a story should give some kind of resolution to its complications and conflicts. These rules are more flexible than the rules of language. They are not predicts that stories or poems or plays *must* follow, but they are predictable patterns that they do normally work through. Such patterns set up expectations in good readers, so that when the pattern is fulfilled, there is the pleasure of seeing a complex task well done, and when the pattern is disrupted, there is the pleasure of seeing a creative alteration of the rules—like hearing a jazz musician hit a note that can't be right but still manages to twist the tune into a whole new experience.

Readers can develop those expectations only if they learn how poems and stories and plays operate. We have to learn to ask good questions about literature. We need patterns to look for that will allow us to participate in the creation of meaning. It is the business of this text to introduce some of those questions, to develop a basic vocabulary for talking about literature, to allow us to get into the game.

We need to know what options were open to the author. Each move in a work of literature is a *choice*. To take some random examples, a character can be silent or talkative, a line of verse can be disciplined or loose, a conflict can be simple or complex. And we need to know what options are open to us as readers. What activities do we need to engage in if we are to participate in the literary experience as fully as possible? To continue our analogy of play, the more you learn about a game, the more you can enjoy it.

Here is A. E. Housman's classic poem about play and sport:

TO AN ATHLETE DYING YOUNG

The time you won your town the race
We chaired you through the market-place;
Man and boy stood cheering by,
And home we brought you shoulder-high.

To-day, the road all runners come,
Shoulder-high we bring you home,
And set you at your threshold down,
Townsman of a stiller town.

Smart lad, to slip betimes away
From fields where glory does not stay
And early though the laurel grows
It withers quicker than the rose.

Eyes the shady night has shut
Cannot see the record cut,
And silence sounds no worse than cheers
After earth has stopped the ears:

Now you will not swell the rout
Of lads that wore their honors out,
Runners whom renown outran
And the name died before the man.

So set, before its echoes fade,
The fleet foot on the sill of shade,
And hold to the low lintel up
The still-defended challenge-cup.

And round that early-laurelled head
Will flock to gaze the strengthless dead,
And find unwithered on its curls
The garland briefer than a girl's.

The speaker of this poem seems to understand the pleasure of mastering a game. The athlete who has died has had an experience of physical perfection, and the speaker consoles himself by noting that at least the athlete won't have to see his perfect skill deteriorate. His moment of mastery will live forever.

Part of Housman's tribute is that he has constructed a poem that reveals his own mastery of the game of poetry. The poem sets up strict rules for itself—four-line stanzas made up of rhyming pairs of lines, a four-beat rhythm with the accent on the second syllable of each unit—and it follows those rules expertly. The rhymes are neither predictable nor forced, the rhythm is consistent but varied at key points to provide emphasis. Housman has produced a highly formal poem, matching its very serious occasion. As readers we need to see how the poem builds up its form, and by anticipating the patterns we can appreciate how well-made but flexible the poem is. Housman's poem works as a tribute to an athlete because it is itself a successful play within its own rules. As readers we must be aware of those rules ourselves if we are to appreciate Housman's achievement.

Cultural Codes

There are other, less easy to define, rules that active readers must master—the patterns of human behavior. Poems and stories and plays are concerned with human beings. What they ask readers to imagine is a fictional world in which characters act and interact. Readers who can master the rules of language and the techniques of literature are then free to engage their imaginations in constructing the human reality that the marks on the page make possible. Literature relies on our knowledge of how people behave, so readers must also be competent in the rules of human behavior.

Now when I say "rules," I don't mean laws that people must follow, but typical patterns that they do seem to follow, at least as we make sense of their actions in our culture. Readers need to be aware of these patterns if they are to cooperate in creating the meaning of a character's actions. Of course many characters don't follow the expected patterns, but we need to know the typical so that we can recognize the unusual.

Human actions do have meanings. If you wear beach clothes to a formal dance, you are making a statement, sending a message of defiance or making a satirical comment. Those who saw you at the party would recognize the message because they know the "rules" of appropriate dress. There is, you could say, a "language" or "code" of clothing, in which various outfits can express formality or informality, business or pleasure, youth or age, even political affiliation. Couldn't you predict how a country-club Republican would dress, as opposed to a working-class Democrat?

Take another example—cars communicate meanings within our society. A "muscle car" *says* something different from a station wagon. Both cars tell us something about their owners: we could make good guesses about each driver's gender, age, marital status, income, and the like based on what the car communicates. To use the same terminology, there is a "code" or "language" of cars. Works of literature exist inside such codes, and assume we understand them as well. In literature, we are presented with human beings and their behavior. We can make sense of their actions, can give them a meaning, because we live inside these endlessly complicated codes or languages. The total system of those codes we call *culture,* and just as we need to know the rules of language and the rules of literature, we need to know the rules of culture.

In Joyce Carol Oates's 1966 story "Where Are You Going, Where Have You Been?" which is reprinted in the fiction chapters of this anthology, there is a spooky and dangerous character called *Arnold Friend*. We learn about him through cultural codes, to which Arnold has given a lot of thought. Here is a description of his car, for example:

> It was an open jalopy, painted a bright gold that caught the sunlight opaquely. . . . ARNOLD FRIEND was written in tarlike black letters on the side, with a drawing of a round, grinning face that reminded Connie of a pumpkin, except it wore sunglasses. . . . The left rear fender had been smashed and around it was written, on the gleaming gold background: DONE BY CRAZY WOMAN DRIVER.

What does this car with its decorations tell us about Arnold Friend

—what does it communicate? My sense of it is that the car is a desperate attempt to seem cool, to be with it, but that it is a failure. It is out of date and pathetically corny, the work of a man who is trying to create an identity for himself out of the cultural codes. Arnold also tries to communicate by his choice of music (again pathetic, last year's tunes), his dress, his hair, his facial expressions, his gestures. We as readers have to make sense of these efforts at communication, by means of our own understanding of these codes. The fact that, for me, Arnold's codes don't cohere together, don't communicate a unified message, is just part of what makes him seem to me a sinister character. As each reader goes through the story, he or she builds up a sense of Arnold, imagines what he looks like, tries to make sense of his actions.

Each reader builds meaning a little differently. To some readers, for example, the smile face that Arnold has painted on his car may seem cute and endearing, not silly and scary as it does to me. All of us in this culture live in the midst of the same codes, but all of us occupy a different position within the codes. Some of us are more competent in some codes than in others. There are some readers, for example, who would not recognize at all the music that Arnold likes to play, so that they would not be able to make full sense out of that message.

We might also *react* differently to these messages. Imagine the different reactions to Arnold's car that a protective parent might have, as opposed to those that a kid out for a joyride would have. The reactions differ because these people occupy different positions within the culture. They don't see the same event in the same way, so they each make different sense out of the story.

The Individual's Response

In a very real sense, everyone who reads the story will experience it differently. All readers do so much and such detailed work in order to bring the story into full existence, that it's inevitable for us to do the work in different ways. The result is that readers must take the responsibility for their reading of the story. The story doesn't have any meaning until readers go to work on it, so that each reader plays a vital role. We each bring to the story our own backgrounds and beliefs, as well as our own knowledge, and we impart our own design of meaning onto the story. Readings will always differ among good readers, and as we will see later, those differences are part of the fun. When we write or talk about literature, we have to have faith in our own reading, show how it came into being, explain why we believe what we believe about what we're reading. We have to be active readers and take responsibility for our actions.

However, this does not mean that we can make a poem or story or play mean whatever we want it to. The language rules, the literary rules, the cultural rules—all the systems of meaning that we bring to bear on our reading—all exist outside of our personal control. They are all social, interpersonal. We can play with and within the rules, but we can't ignore them. No one could legitimately claim that "To an Athlete Dying Young" was about a car, to take a bizarre example. The word *athlete* has a public meaning that you can't deny. Of course, *athlete* is a word with many meanings, and we could argue which meanings are relevant to the poem, but there are things that the word *doesn't* mean, and its range of meanings is set within the system of language. On another level of codes, no one could legitimately claim that Arnold Friend's jalopy means that he is a conservative businessman. We may have different reactions to what a "jalopy" represents, but we know what a jalopy is and what it means.

Our work as readers is therefore *constrained,* limited by the systems of meaning inside which both the story and we as readers dwell. One of the benefits of reading is that it allows us to learn about these systems. How does meaning come into existence? How do we make sense of the world we experience? What reading teaches us about these giant questions is that we live inside these codes of meaning. Our language provides us with a grid by which we categorize experience, and our knowledge of cultural codes allows us to make sense of human actions. We perceive the world through these codes, which it is the job of literature to bring to light. Literature forces us to work carefully within these systems, and in doing so we can learn their power.

Reading literature actively and critically draws our attention to these systems of meaning. Active readers are always aware of their response to what they are reading, and they always want to know why they are responding as they are. If I find Arnold Friend's pumpkin head smile face to be ominous, I want to know why. One reason why is that this particular detail of Arnold's characterization fits into a pattern of details that the story presents—his boots, his sunglasses—that point in the same direction. Elements of the text can often be pointed to as the source of our responses. But after all, those details cohere in a pattern because we look for such patterns. For me, and I think for most readers, there is an assumption that literature—and experience in general—does follow predictable patterns. I can make sense of Arnold Friend because I have an understanding of the systems of meaning that give him an identity. His identity is not easy to define because he seems to defy categorization. Is he young or old, lover or killer, human or demon? He doesn't fit in any classification very comfortably, but if we don't have these classifications, he wouldn't make any sense to us at all. His identity may challenge or even deny our usual assumptions (Connie, his victim in the story, certainly can't "make sense" of him), but in our attempt we learn something about the powers and limitations of how we look at the world.

What this approach to reading suggests is that in a very powerful way the study of literature is a tool for self-exploration. By examining how we respond to and make sense of texts, we can come to know more about ourselves, about how we look at the world. How did you respond to the message of cummings's "in Just-"? How did you help to construct the message itself? Answered carefully, these questions can lead to a self-understanding that is both deeply personal and thoroughly social. That is, what we learn about ourselves is how we live within socially defined systems of meaning. We have to examine the languages that allow us to look at the world, and to recognize that those languages are larger than the self, that they are not under our individual control. They are social structures, yet they live inside us.

These structures, these languages, can become invisible to us. Through constant, practical use, we can come to forget their existence, come to assume that the way we make sense of the world is just naturally right, completely self-evident. But reading literature disrupts this certainty. It shakes and stretches the structures of meaning so that they can't be ignored. We are therefore shown our commitment to *certain* systems of meaning, and can see how they affect our perception. To take the responsibility for our reading is thus also to take responsibility for ourselves.

Writing about Literature

In practical terms, taking responsibility for your reading means being able to justify the process by which you make sense of the story or poem or play. It does not mean claiming that yours is the *only* valid way of reading the text—there are always many possible valid readings, which emerge as competent readers go about their work. But it does mean claiming that your reading *is* valid, and that you can explain how you came up with it. This process of explaining and justifying your way of making sense of the text can occur in the classroom, for example, when a teacher asks why you responded to a character in a particular way. But the process happens most thoroughly when you write about literature.

Writing about literature, which we will discuss more fully in the last part of this text, is a natural outcome of the act of reading. Reading can be a very private experience, but most readers need to share their responses, to work together with other readers, in order to develop an *interpretation*. This function can be fulfilled in informal conversation and in class discussions, but the act of writing about literature allows for a very full development of the reader's point of view. When you write you are directing your efforts toward convincing other readers that your reading of the text is valid. Through this effort, you are forced to examine the text and your reading process very carefully.

In order to show that your reading is valid, you need to be able to point to details of the text that account for your interpretation. If you think, for example, that the speaker of Housman's "To an Athlete Dying Young" is more concerned about his own fate than the death of the athlete, you need to explain *why* you think so. What is there in the language of the poem, in the approach to the situation that the speaker takes, that makes you feel that way? Can you point to the elements of the text that gave rise to your reading in the first place? Perhaps it is the fact that the speaker spends so much time talking about the pains of aging, which the dead athlete won't experience but which the speaker perhaps is experiencing.

Explaining your reading of the poem also involves defining the systems of meaning that you brought to bear on the poem. Details don't speak for themselves. They are *given* a significance by the systems of meaning applied to them. In this case, I have used the literary assumption that a poem reveals the character of its speaker, and the larger cultural and psychological pattern that no one contemplates the death of another without reflecting on his or her own death. These are the patterns of thought that help me make my sense of the poem. If I am going to communicate my reading to others, I need to point to its language, but also to my own interpretive process.

Writing about literature is therefore not a matter of proving that you've found the right reading. Rather, it is showing how your reading makes sense. If you can make an effective case for your reading, that's all that's required. Of course it's possible to be wrong—to have misunderstood the language or to have made use of an irrelevant system of explanation—but there are still many valid readings. So as a reader you have the right to your point of view, as long as you take responsibility for your reading by engaging in a self-reflection, an analysis of your response to the text.

Writing about literature is therefore a matter of *rhetoric,* a process of convincing other readers that your opinion is worthy of consideration, that your account of things makes the most sense. You are constructing an argument in support of your point of view. In this sense, you are putting yourself on the line, taking the risk of revealing your own thought processes and claiming that they make strong sense of the text. Writing about literature is thus very personal. It reveals a lot about its writer, and the best critical writing reveals the most. Not that you're writing about yourself in a disguised autobiography. Rather, in the process of writing about the text you reveal how you make sense of it, and more generally how you look at the world.

Writing about literature is part of the process of active reading.

Reading the writing of another leads to a writing of your own. The urge to write about literature comes out of the effort you invest in reading. If you've done the work required by the text you're reading, it's only natural to want to explain that work, to share it with others.

Like any work, the process of reading must be driven by desire. If the work is going to be done well, it has to come out of a desire to understand what we read. Reading makes personal growth possible for the reader, but it requires a commitment of effort. Active reading means that readers have to get involved, to be aggressive in making sense of what they read. Readers have to search out and construct meaning—it isn't simply handed over to them. Almost no text says, "Here is what I mean. This is why I'm significant." That job is the responsibility of the reader.

Part Two
Poetry and the Power of Language

One
Introduction

Why does poetry have to be so difficult? Some poets seem to go out of their way to find difficult and unusual words; others use ordinary words but combine them in baffling ways. Reading poetry is always an effort. The poem never simply gives itself over to us, never allows readers to be passive consumers. For many readers these difficulties get in the way of the pleasure of poetry. If you have to read the poem again and again, disentangle complex sentences, look up unfamiliar words, and think in new patterns before you get the poem right, you might decide that the benefits aren't worth the effort.

I want to argue, of course, that the benefits *are* worth the effort. In fact, the effort is one of the benefits. Poems aren't difficult just to spite their readers. Poems are difficult because they are language used with precision and flair. Poems want to slow us down as readers, to make us explore how their language works. They require our active work, thus involving us in the process of producing the meaning and the emotion of the poem. A good reader of poetry has to start with its language, with the words on the page.

And that does require work. Poems are usually very compressed. Often a complex experience of meaning and emotion can come out of a few words. That means that each word of the poem counts heavily, so that it's absolutely necessary for a good reader to master *all* the words of the poem—to look them up if necessary, to think through all their meanings, to feel their emotional impact. In a sense, a poem is a field of potential meanings, a network of verbal relationships waiting to be brought to life, but it requires an active reader to realize that potential.

Becoming Aware of Language

One benefit an active reader can gain from the process of reading a poem is a heightened awareness of the power of language. In most of our uses of language, we don't pay much attention to it. Most of the time language is a tool, an instrument for accomplishing some goal. If you want a dinner in a restaurant, for example, there are verbal formulas that will get you one: "I'm ready to order now," or "Can you suggest something?" When you use such phrases you don't pay much attention to the words themselves, you just use them automatically. Your mind is on the goal, not the instrument. But when a poem plays with the meanings of words or puts them in odd combinations, readers have to *pay attention* to language itself rather than just make use of it.

When you pay attention to language an interesting change occurs. You become aware of the ways that language can shape your perceptions of the world. Language is not just an instrument but rather a framework through which we look at and make sense of the world. Through it we give meaning to experience. And by *we* I mean the social community of users of the language. We are all "located" in language, very specifically. That is, we have all learned *particular* words to name certain situations, so we each see the world through language in a different way. If you have grown up learning about war, for example, by means of words like *heroism* and *patriotism,* you will see war in just that way, unless events force you to find a new vocabulary. Such a vocabulary change seems to have occurred to the character who speaks "Anthem for Doomed Youth," a poem from World War I written by Wilfred Owen (1893–1918):

ANTHEM FOR DOOMED YOUTH

What passing-bells for these who die as cattle?
  —Only the monstrous anger of the guns.
  Only the stuttering rifles' rapid rattle
Can patter out their hasty orisons.
No mockeries now for them; no prayers nor bells;
  Nor any voice of mourning save the choirs,—
The shrill, demented choirs of wailing shells;
  And bugles calling for them from sad shires.

What candles may be held to speed them all?
  Not in the hands of boys but in their eyes
Shall shine the holy glimmers of goodbyes.
  The pallor of girls' brows shall be their pall;

Their flowers the tenderness of patient minds,
And each slow dusk a drawing-down of blinds.

When this poem describes soldiers as "cattle," a shift of meaning, a shaking of the usual framework of thought and language, occurs. To use the word *cattle* to describe soldiers is to see them as victims, not as heroes; as animals killed for another's profit, not as powerful individuals who control their own destiny. Owen's unusual use of this word startles us, upsets our ordinary responses. The same process occurs when he describes the traditional prayers for dead soldiers as "mockeries." This verges on the sacrilegious. Prayers are *tributes,* not *mockeries*. But Owen's experience of the technological mass murder that was World War I made the traditional words and their reassuring frameworks of thought useless. He had to come up with new words —or old words used in new contexts—that would allow his readers a new framework for thinking about war.

The power of this poem is a function of its masterful manipulation of language. It forces you to see an experience through words that will change your attitude toward it. Once you have thought about soldiers as *cattle,* your frame has been altered, and the word *hero* will never be the same for you. You may still hold to the emotions and values that *hero* produces, but those reactions have been challenged. They can't be as natural as before.

It is therefore by being difficult and challenging that poetry does its work. But only when the reader is willing to work as well does the poem come into its power. What follows in these chapters are explanations of some concepts that are useful in doing the work of reading. We will discuss how figures of speech work, how images are produced, and the like, because through these understandings of language we can help the poem come into existence. Readers need to make connections between words, to arrange them into meaningful patterns. They can do this only if they are informed readers who know how poetry operates, and active readers who will engage with the poem's language as fully as possible.

Benefiting from Poetry

Now, many readers may accept the existence of the benefits that I've been describing, but still complain that they aren't likely to spend any time dealing with poetry after they get out of school. That may be true, in the sense that they might not pick up Wordsworth or Frost on a quiet winter's night, but in a broader sense poetry is all around us. Writers of political slogans, advertising jingles, pop music lyrics—all recognize and put into practice in varying degrees the power of poetic language. "I Like Ike" and "All the Way with LBJ" play with the sound of words in order to insinuate an idea into our minds. Sometimes the poetry in these pop creations is very clever and subtle. For example, Swanson's frozen foods had a commercial that described the product as "home, home cookin'." Now, clearly, frozen food isn't home cooking, but just as clearly most of those who eat a lot of frozen foods are missing the warm family feeling that goes along with home-cooked food. What this jingle sets out to do is to replace our usual words for the product ("TV dinner") with a new phrase ("home, home cookin'") that will change our attitudes toward it. The ad operates on its own level just as Owen's poem operates. It changes our response by giving us a new framework through which we can look at the world.

Advertisers use such techniques because they recognize the power of language as a set of labels for our experience. If they can get at those labels, they can manipulate our responses. What makes advertising different from poetry is that ads try to hide their techniques inside glitter and imagery overkill, whereas poems invite us to analyze and understand their language. Poems take pleasure in their play with language; they show it off to us. And by displaying their techniques to us, poems can teach us to be critical about the power of all language.

READINGS

Each of the following poems presents a picture of war that tries to shape our response to death and heroism. How does each poem depict war? What attitude toward war does each poem represent? What is your own perspective on war? Do the poems challenge or reaffirm your beliefs?

Thomas Hardy (1840–1928)

THE MAN HE KILLED

"Had he and I but met
By some old ancient inn,
We should have sat us down to wet
Right many a nipperkin!

"But ranged as infantry,
And staring face to face,
I shot at him as he at me,
And killed him in his place.

"I shot him dead because—
Because he was my foe,
Just so: my foe of course he was;
That's clear enough; although

"He thought he'd 'list, perhaps,
Off-hand like—just as I—
Was out of work—had sold his traps—
No other reason why.

"Yes; quaint and curious war is!
You shoot a fellow down
You'd treat if met where any bar is,
Or help to half-a-crown."

Randall Jarrell (1914–1965)
THE DEATH OF THE BALL TURRET GUNNER

From my mother's sleep I fell into the State,
And I hunched in its belly till my wet fur froze.
Six miles from earth, loosed from its dream of life,
I woke to black flak and the nightmare fighters.
When I died they washed me out of the turret with a hose.

Yusef Komunyakaa (b. 1947)
STARLIGHT SCOPE MYOPIA

Gray-blue shadows lift
shadows onto an ox cart.

Making night work for us,
the starlight scope brings
men into killing range.

The river under Vi Bridge
takes the heart away

like the Water God
riding his dragon.
Smoke-colored

Viet Cong
move under our eyelids,

lords over loneliness
winding like coralvine through
sandalwood & lotus,

inside our skulls years
after this scene ends.

The brain closes down.
What looks like
one step into the trees,

they're lifting crates of ammo
and sacks of rice, swaying

under their shared weight.
Caught in the infrared,
what are they saying?

Are they talking about women
or calling the Americans

beaucoup dien cai dau?
One of them is laughing.
You want to place a finger

to his lips & say "shhhh."
You try reading ghost-talk

on their lips. They say
"up-up we go," lifting as one.
This one, old, bowlegged,

you feel you could reach out
& take him into your arms. You

peer down the sights of your M-16,
seeing the full moon
loaded on an ox cart.

Alfred, Lord Tennyson (1809–1892)
THE CHARGE OF THE LIGHT BRIGADE

1

Half a league, half a league,
Half a league onward,
All in the valley of Death
   Rode the six hundred.

"Forward the Light Brigade!
Charge for the guns!" he said.
Into the valley of Death
  Rode the six hundred.

2

"Forward, the Light Brigade!"
Was there a man dismayed?
Not though the soldier knew
  Someone had blundered.
Theirs not to make reply,
Theirs not to reason why,
Theirs but to do and die.
Into the valley of Death
  Rode the six hundred.

3

Cannon to right of them,
Cannon to left of them,
Cannon in front of them
  Volleyed and thundered;
Stormed at with shot and shell,
Boldly they rode and well,
Into the jaws of Death,
Into the mouth of hell
  Rode the six hundred.

4

Flashed all their sabers bare,
Flashed as they turned in air
Sab'ring the gunners there,
Charging an army, while
  All the world wondered.
Plunged in the battery smoke
Right through the line they broke;
Cossack and Russian
Reeled from the saber stroke
  Shattered and sundered.
Then they rode back, but not,
  Not the six hundred.

5

Cannon to right of them,
Cannon to left of them,

Cannon behind them
  Volleyed and thundered;
Stormed at with shot and shell,
While horse and hero fell,
They that had fought so well
Came through the jaws of Death,
Back from the mouth of hell,
All that was left of them,
  Left of six hundred.

6

When can their glory fade?
O the wild charge they made!
  All the world wondered.
Honor the charge they made!
Honor the Light Brigade,
  Noble six hundred!

Two

Denotation and Connotation

Poets don't invent a new language. They make use of the ordinary language of our daily lives. They may stretch it, put it into unusual combinations, tangle up the syntax, and make it difficult for an easy read, but they are working with and inside of our language. This may seem obvious, but sometimes poets are so creative in their use of words that we may feel they have left us behind and moved into another world of language.

But that's just not the case. Poems are part of our language. Difficult as they may be, they are ultimately accessible to us. Readers who are competent in the language can do the work that poems require, can cooperate in the production of poetic meaning and emotion.

In order to do the work of reading, a good reader has to have a sense of how meaning happens, how words do *their* work. This is a large topic, but I want to offer at least an outline of it so that we can begin to discuss how the language of poetry allows us to create meaning.

Dividing Up the World

First of all, words don't work in isolation. They work in *systems*. When we use the word *book,* for example, we identify a set of objects in the world. But *book* itself is part of a system of words like *newspaper, magazine,* and *newsletter,* all of which serve to categorize various kinds of printed matter. Together they act as a system that divides up a certain segment of the world. Similarly, the word *car* is part of a system of terms for motorized vehicles that includes *truck, motorcycle, bus,* and so on. We learn these systems of words before we have much experience with the objects themselves. There are, for instance, many children's picture and word books whose sole purpose is to set out these systems, so that when a child encounters a bus, he or she can fit it into the right linguistic category.

Taken together, all these systems of related words serve as a framework through which we make sense of the world. This is, in fact, the power of language that we discussed in the previous chapter. One proof of this power to divide up the world for us is that different languages divide it up differently. An easy example: in English we have five or six words to describe frozen precipitation—*snow, sleet, hail*—whereas in Eskimo languages there are dozens of terms. This suggests that the system through which Eskimos perceive the world is different from ours. Language is the embodiment of that system. It is through language that we perceive. We live inside it and so we must come to understand it if we are to understand ourselves.

Now, in dividing up the world language performs two distinct but related operations. It places objects and experiences into categories, and it expresses an attitude toward those objects and experiences. The categorizing function we call the **denotative** meaning of the word; the expression of an attitude we call the **connotative** meaning. These functions can best be illustrated by looking at two words with similar denotative but very different connotative meanings. I choose a controversial example because it illustrates how language has power. The words *gay* and *faggot* have similar denotative meanings —both place a person in the same category. But they obviously express different attitudes. And they both have power. The word *faggot* dehumanizes; the word *gay* reclaims human status. Both provide frameworks through which individuals and groups make sense of a human phenomenon. They express the values of the speaker who chooses one or the other. Both functions—denotation and connotation—are present in all language, but in poetry the combinations are often unusually complex.

Denotative meaning is obviously important to any poem. In fact, the poem hardly exists until it is read by a person who shares the framework of categories in language that the poem also relies on. When Wordsworth describes a girl's death as transforming her into an object "Rolled round in earth's diurnal course," he assumes that readers either know or are willing to find out what *diurnal* means (see "A slumber did my spirit seal"). Most poetry reflects very careful and precise word choices. The poem is engaged in giving a particular meaning to experience, so that the choice of a word is the choice of the precise framework that the reader is asked to bring to bear.

On this level readers have a basic duty to perform—they need to become competent in the language of the poem. This requires a simple willingness to look up unfamiliar words, a willingness that in turn depends on an openness to the unfamiliar. Many readers are distressed and even offended by unfamiliar language, but good poems include strange language only when it's the only language that will make the poem work. Some frameworks for looking at reality can be provided only by an unusual word. One of the benefits for readers in encountering a new word is that their framework is thereby expanded, their way of looking at the world is enriched.

The question of *connotative* meaning is more complex. Words don't just categorize experience, they evaluate it. They put an interpretation on it, they give an experience emotional coloration. Is someone who lives on skid row a *bum* or a *victim,* a *loser* or an *unfortunate*? Is someone who plants a bomb in an embassy a *terrorist* or a *freedom fighter*? What makes the connotative function of language complex is that different people would choose different answers to these questions in different situations. In each particular case the person's choice would reflect his or her value system, emotional makeup, and characteristic ways of interpreting experience.

Persuading the Reader

The language of a poem, then, is out to manipulate readers' emotional responses, to get them to evaluate the world in the same way it does. I use the word *manipulate* here, despite its negative connotations, because it suggests the emotional power of poetry. The great British poet John Milton's poem "On the Late Massacre in Piedmont" is a good example of a poem that wields the power of its language in a public and political context. The poem is a prayer in response to the deaths of a group of Italian Protestants at the hands of forces of the Catholic church. In seventeenth-century England, when Milton wrote the poem, conflicts between Protestants and Catholics were intense and violent. The poem's language characterizes the Protestant victims and the Catholic persecutors in precise but dramatic terms:

ON THE LATE MASSACRE IN PIEDMONT

Avenge, O Lord, thy slaughtered saints, whose bones
  Lie scattered on the Alpine mountains cold;
  Even them who kept thy truth so pure of old
  When all our fathers worshipped stocks and stones,
Forget not: in thy book record their groans
  Who were thy sheep and in their ancient fold
  Slain by the bloody Piemontese that rolled
  Mother with infant down the rocks. Their moans
The vales redoubled to the hills, and they
  To heaven. Their martyred blood and ashes sow
  O'er all th'Italian fields, where still doth sway

The triple tyrant: that from these may grow
  A hundredfold, who having learnt thy way
  Early may fly the Babylonian woe.

In this poem, Milton's interpretation of the event is powerfully expressed. The Protestants are "slaughtered saints," "thy sheep"; they spill their "martyred blood." The connotative force of these terms suggests the Protestants' purity, their innocence, their victimization. The Catholics are "the bloody Piemontese," "the triple tyrant," "the Babylonian woe"—all terms that suggest their violence, moral decay, and despotism. It is no criticism to call this poem propaganda—an attempt to sway opinion on a controversial issue. Milton wrote out of his own deep convictions, imposing on the event the meaning and feeling that made sense to him. A writer committed just as strongly to the Catholic cause would have seen and described the event differently, but that does not deny the power of Milton's view and his expression of it. Like all poets, Milton used language to make sense of experience, and the connotative power of his language exerts pressure on readers to make sense of it in the same way.

Negotiating with the Poem

But how should you as a reader respond to that pressure? After all, before you come to a poem you have your own values, your own framework for understanding and evaluating experience. Those values will affect how you would have viewed the situation that the poem depicts. Perhaps you would have seen it very differently. Let me return to Wilfred Owen's "Anthem for Doomed Youth" for an example. How should you respond to the poem if you don't and can't accept calling prayers for the dead "mockeries"? Two simple, but wrong, answers suggest themselves. One would be to reject the poem outright because you can't accept its values. The other would be to abandon your own values and simply accept those of the poem. Neither answer seems possible, or desirable. To reject a poem because it expresses values not your own is simply closed-minded. To accept a poem's values without thought would be to give up your own identity. The best course, as usual, lies somewhere in the middle.

Readers need to negotiate with the poem. They must be open to its language and values, but they must also retain their own values. Sometimes, of course, a poem will be so persuasive and dramatic that it will change a reader's values. After reading Owen's poem, "mockeries" may suddenly seem like the right word. But more typically, what a reader gets out of a poem is an encounter with another point of view, not an experience of conversion. By paying close attention to the poem's language, a reader can discover its values. That language, if it is well crafted, will have an effect on the reader—and the reader needs to be open to that effect. Poems demand active readers, not passive ones. A poem is a call to a reader to attend to language and to life. It assumes that the reader brings to the act of reading his or her own values and beliefs. The experience of poetry is the interchange between the poem and its readers, so readers must recognize and give value to their authentic responses. We can disagree with a poem's values and still see the integrity of its point of view and the power of its language.

What a poem needs from you as a reader is engagement. Experience the language, respond to it, try to make your own sense of the poem. This engagement with the poem has to begin with understanding the meanings of its words, but it must go on to a mature emotional response to those words. Language categorizes and interprets. Readers must understand and respond, relying on their own system of values.

READINGS

William Wordsworth (1770–1850)

A SLUMBER DID MY SPIRIT SEAL

A slumber did my spirit seal;
  I had no human fears:
She seemed a thing that could not feel
  The touch of earthly years.

No motion has she now, no force;
  She neither hears nor sees;
Rolled round in earth's diurnal course,
  With rocks, and stones, and trees.

1. What is the poem's attitude toward death?
2. How does the language of the poem express that attitude?

Stevie Smith (1902–1971)

HOW CRUEL IS THE STORY OF EVE

How cruel is the story of Eve
What responsibility

It has in history
For cruelty.

Touch, where the feeling is most vulnerable,
Unblameworthy—ah reckless—desiring children,
Touch there with a touch of pain?
Abominable.

Ah what cruelty,
In history
What misery.

Put up to barter
The tender feelings
Buy her a husband to rule her
Fool her to marry a master
She must or rue it
The Lord said it.

And man, poor man,
Is he fit to rule,
Pushed to it?
How can he carry it, the governance,
And not suffer for it
Insuffisance?
He must make woman lower then

So he can be higher then.
Oh what cruelty,
In history what misery.

Soon woman grows cunning
Masks her wisdom,
How otherwise will he
Bring food and shelter, kill enemies?
If he did not feel superior
It would be worse for her
And for the tender children
Worse for them.

Oh what cruelty,
In history what misery
Of falsity.

It is only a legend
You say? But what
Is the meaning of the legend
If not

To give blame to women most
And most punishment?

This is the meaning of a legend that colours
All human thought; it is not found among animals.

How cruel is the story of Eve,
What responsibility it has
In history
For misery.

Yet there is this to be said still:
Life would be over long ago
If men and women had not loved each other
Naturally, naturally,
Forgetting their mythology
They would have died of it else
Long ago, long ago,
And all would be emptiness now
And silence.

Oh dread Nature, for your purpose,
To have made them love so.

1. Describe in general the poem's interpretation of relations between the sexes.
2. Discuss the connotations of the following words as they function in context: *cruelty, barter, rue, cunning, tender, naturally, dread.*

Robinson Jeffers (1887–1962)
CARMEL POINT

The extraordinary patience of things!
This beautiful place defaced with a crop of suburban
  houses—
How beautiful when we first beheld it,
Unbroken field of poppy and lupin walled with clean cliffs;
No intrusion but two or three horses pasturing,
Or a few milch cows rubbing their flanks on the outcrop
  rock-heads—
Now the spoiler has come: does it care?
Not faintly. It has all time. It knows the people are a tide
That swells and in time will ebb, and all

Their works dissolve. Meanwhile the image of the pristine
  beauty
Lives in the very grain of the granite,
Safe as the endless ocean that climbs our cliff.—As for us:
We must uncenter our minds from ourselves;
We must unhumanize our views a little, and become
  confident
As the rock and ocean that we were made from.

1. What do the following words from the poem suggest about the natural world: *patience, pristine, confident*?
2. What do the following words suggest about human activity: *defaced, intrusion, the spoiler*?
3. Considering this language, what does the poem suggest about the relationship between man and nature?

Raymond Carver (1939–1988)

PHOTOGRAPH OF MY FATHER IN HIS TWENTY-SECOND YEAR

October. Here in this dank, unfamiliar kitchen
I study my father's embarrassed young man's face.
Sheepish grin, he holds in one hand a string
Of spiny yellow perch, in the other
A bottle of Carlsbad beer.

In jeans and denim shirt, he leans
Against the front fender of a Ford *circa* 1934.
He would like to pose bluff and hearty for his posterity,
Wear his old hat cocked over his ear, stick out his tongue . . .
All his life my father wanted to be bold.

But the eyes give him away, and the hands
That limply offer the string of dead perch
And the bottle of beer. Father, I loved you,
Yet how can I say thank you, I who cannot hold my liquor
  either
And do not even know the places to fish?

1. What words does Carver use to describe his father? What do they tell us about the man?
2. What words does Carver tell us do not apply to his father? What do these words tell us?

Heather McHugh (b. 1948)

LANGUAGE LESSON, 1976

When Americans say a man
takes liberties, they mean
he's gone too far. In Philadelphia

today a kid on a leash ordered
bicentennial burger,
hold the relish. Hold

is forget, in American.
On the courts of Philadelphia
the rich prepare

to serve, to fault.
The language is a game in which
love means nothing, doubletalk

means lie. I'm saying
doubletalk with me. I'm saying go
so far the customs are untold,

make nothing without words
and let me be
the one you never hold.

1. How do some ordinary words get "new" meanings in this poem?
2. What is the role of slang in the poem?
3. How do the new meanings get used at the end of the poem? Can you translate back?

Three
Figures of Speech

So far, our discussion of the language of poetry has been pretty straightforward. Words have meanings that make sense of experience, and poetry draws attention to the power of those words. But poetry is also a use of language in which meaning can be more indirect. For in poetry *figures of speech* abound—metaphors, similes, personifications—all the dazzling array of techniques by which ordinary meanings can be altered and by which readers can be forced into seeing the world in a whole new way.

What is a figure of speech? Let's begin with the Greek term for this kind of language: *trope,* which means "turn" or "twist." A figure of speech is a twisting of the normal meaning of a word. These twists are very common, even in ordinary conversation. If someone you work with makes a mistake at the job, and then says as a joke on himself, "I must have forgotten my brain today," you don't call his house to check if he left it there. You assume that he is using a figure of speech. His words can't be taken literally because they don't make any sense. Almost automatically we would recognize that he means that he isn't alert or can't concentrate, that it is *as if* he had forgotten his brain. We would recognize it as a figure of speech.

Figurative language isn't confined to poetry—you can find it in all uses of language. But poetry does make maximum use of the possibility for playing with meaning that figures of speech provide. As an example, let's look at a poem by William Shakespeare, a sonnet in which he reflects on old age:

SONNET 73

That time of year thou mayst in me behold
When yellow leaves, or none, or few, do hang
Upon those boughs which shake against the cold,
Bare ruined choirs where late the sweet birds sang.
In me thou see'st the twilight of such day
As after sunset fadeth in the west,
Which by and by black night doth take away,
Death's second self, that seals up all in rest.
In me thou see'st the glowing of such fire,
That on the ashes of his youth doth lie
As the deathbed whereon it must expire,
Consumed with that which it was nourished by.
  This thou perceivest, which makes thy love more strong,
  To love that well which thou must leave ere long.

In each four-line section of the poem, the speaker says something that doesn't make sense—"When you look at me you see autumn, or twilight, or a dying fire." Literally, of course, we don't. But the poem is an invitation to think figuratively, to ask, "How is a man like the autumn, like the twilight, like a dying fire?" I see the analogies as very straightforward. The autumn is near the end of the year or near winter, a common symbol of death; the twilight is near the night, which the speaker directly connects with death; and the dying fire has almost turned to ashes ("ashes to ashes, dust to dust"). The speaker of the poem asks the hearer to cooperate in making these analogies, and we get a picture of old age.

Readers of the poem do have to cooperate very actively in the making of such a meaning. Words like *autumn, twilight,* and *dying fire* are, like all language, terms that identify an experience as belonging to a certain category. But in the case of figurative language, two categories have to be superimposed in order to see what they have in common. Old age has in common with these events a sense of an ending coming, a diminishing of power, a sense of loss. Also, surprisingly, a bit of beauty in the yellow leaves, the diffuse light of twilight, the glowing of the coals. To me, this poem is therefore not simply an exercise in self-pity, it is a defiant claim that life is not over, that energy, though dimming, has not gone dark. The poem makes this claim by a very precise use of figurative language, which forces us to look at old age in a new and moving way.

Comparing the Categories

The simplest form of figurative language is a *simile,* in which the comparison of two terms is direct and explicit. Often a marker such as *like* or *as* or *as if* lets us know that our job is to work out the results of the comparison. Ordinary language is full of colorful similes—"sly as a fox," "smart as a whip," "eyes like diamonds," "a mind like a steel trap." In all of these cases the comparisons are easy enough to figure out. But in poems often the similes are based on odd or extreme comparisons. The first line of Richard Wilbur's poem "Mind" (reprinted later) claims, "Mind in its purest play is like some bat . . ." Now, how is the mind like a bat? A close reading of the rest of the poem suggests some answers, but the point is that this unusual simile stretches the reader's mind by a new exercise of thought.

Metaphor, perhaps the most important figure of speech, is sometimes the most difficult to detect. For example, I used one in the last sentence of the previous paragraph when I said that the reader's mind was "stretched," as if it were some kind of elastic container. That's a metaphor that is used very frequently, "to stretch your mind," but if you take it literally, it is a very strange thing to say. How can a mind be "stretched"? There is no possible literal answer, but if we think figuratively, we can make the phrase make sense. Metaphors such as this one are more difficult to detect than similes because there are no markers for them, no *like* or *as*.

In poetry, metaphors create verbal complexity. If each metaphor requires a comparison of categories, a poem like Gerard Manley Hopkins's "God's Grandeur" can produce for the reader an extremely rich experience of analogical thinking:

GOD'S GRANDEUR

The world is charged with the grandeur of God.
    It will flame out, like shining from shook foil;
    It gathers to a greatness, like the ooze of oil
Crushed. Why do men then now not reck his rod?
Generations have trod, have trod, have trod;
    And all is seared with trade; bleared, smeared with toil;
    And wears man's smudge and shares man's smell: the soil
Is bare now, nor can foot feel, being shod.

And for all this, nature is never spent;
    There lives the dearest freshness deep down things;

And though the last lights off the black West went
Oh, morning, at the brown brink eastward, springs—
Because the Holy Ghost over the bent
World broods with warm breast and with ah! bright wings.

The poem is built around a series of metaphors. The world is "charged" with God's grandeur, as though by an electric current; it is "seared" with human trade, as though burnt into obscurity; it is "smeared" by human toil, as though human work has blurred the beauty that God created: but at the end the world is saved by the spirit of God that still "broods" over the world, like a dove caring for its young. The metaphors in the poem are of course even more complex than I have just outlined. For a reader the figurative thinking here can be almost endless. There are so many comparisons and analogies called for by this poem that you must be a very active reader to keep up with it.

Metaphors and similies have similar functions, to apply one verbal category to another that resembles it, to say that "eyes" can be like "diamonds." There are some other figures of speech that are based on different manipulations of ordinary meaning. *Personification,* for example, is the use of human terms to describe nonhuman objects. When William Wordsworth says in "Lines Written in Early Spring" (reprinted later), "And 'tis my faith that every flower/Enjoys the air it breathes," he is giving to the flowers a human characteristic—perhaps the joy he feels himself when he sees them. Like all tropes, personification involves a mixing of categories. *Joy* defines a category that, at least to the rational mind, doesn't properly speaking belong to flowers but only to human beings. The technique of personification is very common in ordinary language as well, where we often speak, say, of a "vicious" wind (as if it were out to get us) or a "wise" old owl.

Another important figure of speech is *metonymy,* which is illustrated by the use of such phrases as "the crown" when speaking of the king. Metonymy, unlike metaphor, does not claim that the crown and the king are the same. Rather, it tries to characterize the complex reality of the king in one vivid detail that we associate with him.

Processing Reality

Some psychologists and linguists believe that figures of speech are characteristic human ways of looking at the world, such as comparison (metaphor) and association (metonymy). We have the mental habit of comparing things—"It's hot as hell"—and associating things—"This is a message from the front office." In the first case we have compared the weather with an example of unthinkable heat; in the second we have associated the chief officer of a company with his or her office. In poetry such mental operations come to the front of our awareness, rather than happening automatically as they often do in casual conversation.

The sheer frequency with which figures of speech occur in our ordinary language suggests how central they are to our thinking. We "dissect" a problem and "negotiate" traffic. We read "absorbing" books and listen to "electrifying" songs. Problems are "a drag"; good times "lift up" our spirits. Figures of speech are clearly a habit of mind for us. We tend to cross categories, to find the similarities under the verbal differences, to talk about one thing in terms of another.

The result of this habit is that our framework for "processing" reality is extremely complex. A word not only indicates the category of experience that it is normally associated with (for example, to dissect is to cut apart for scientific purposes), but it can also be used in other situations with which it shares some quality (namely, to dissect can mean to analyze, as in a problem). The ordinary meanings of a word can be twisted, and in fact they are *frequently* twisted, so that we often look at the world through a multiple framework. Figures of speech therefore have an effect on how we think and act. To characterize a problem as a thing that can be "dissected," for example, is to suggest that it can be divided into parts and studied, rather than to see a problem as a complex whole that must be experienced as such and not divided up. The figures of speech that we learn in our ordinary language, then, shape our perception of reality.

Poetry tends, as we have seen, to use difficult and unusual figures of speech. As active readers, we have to put in the effort to understand them. The result of that effort is an increased awareness of figures of speech in all language, even if they are used so frequently that they tend to disappear. Again we see that understanding poetry is understanding language, and understanding language is a path to understanding ourselves.

READINGS

John Donne (1572–1631)
HOLY SONNET 14

Batter my heart, three-personed God; for you
As yet but knock, breathe, shine, and seek to mend;
That I may rise and stand, o'erthrow me, and bend
Your force to break, blow, burn, and make me new.

I, like an usurped town, to another due,
Labor to admit you, but O, to no end;
Reason, your viceroy in me, me should defend,
But is captived, and proves weak or untrue.
Yet dearly I love you, and would be loved fain,
But am betrothed unto your enemy.
Divorce me, untie or break that knot again;
Take me to you, imprison me, for I,
Except you enthrall me, never shall be free,
Nor ever chaste, except you ravish me.

1. The figures of speech in this poem are extreme and violent. Why?
2. Some of the figures seem to be contradictory—overthrow me so that I may rise, ravish me so that I may be chaste. What is the logic of these complex figures?

William Wordsworth (1770–1850)

LINES WRITTEN IN EARLY SPRING

I heard a thousand blended notes,
While in a grove I sate reclined,
In that sweet mood when pleasant thoughts
Bring sad thoughts to the mind.

To her fair works did Nature link
The human soul that through me ran;
And much it grieved my heart to think
What man has made of man.

Through primrose tufts, in that green bower,
The periwinkle trailed its wreaths;
And 'tis my faith that every flower
Enjoys the air it breathes.

The birds around me hopped and played,
Their thoughts I cannot measure—
But the least motion which they made,
It seemed a thrill of pleasure.

The budding twigs spread out their fan,
To catch the breezy air;
And I must think, do all I can,
That there was pleasure there.

If this belief from heaven be sent,
If such be Nature's holy plan,

Have I not reason to lament
What man has made of man?

1. Identify and discuss the personifications in the poem.
2. How do these personifications relate to the poet's stated belief in a religion of nature?

Wallace Stevens (1878–1955)

THE DEATH OF A SOLDIER

Life contracts and death is expected,
As in a season of autumn.
The soldier falls.

He does not become a three-days personage,
Imposing his separation,
Calling for pomp.

Death is absolute and without memorial,
As in a season of autumn,
When the wind stops,

When the wind stops and, over the heavens,
The clouds go, nevertheless,
In their direction.

1. How is the death of a soldier like autumn?
2. What does the wind-and-weather image in the last five lines tell us about the death of a soldier?

Richard Wilbur (b. 1921)

MIND

Mind in its purest play is like some bat
That beats about in caverns all alone,
Contriving by a kind of senseless wit
Not to conclude against a wall of stone.

It has no need to falter or explore;
Darkly it knows what obstacles are there,
And so may weave and flitter, dip and soar
In perfect courses through the blackest air.

And has this simile a like perfection?
The mind is like a bat. Precisely. Save
That in the very happiest intellection
A graceful error may correct the cave.

1. The poem is based on an extended analogy between the mind and a bat. Following the logic of this analogy, what does the cave represent? What is the human equivalent of the bat's "senseless wit"? What are the "obstacles"?
2. Again following the analogy, what does it mean to "correct the cave"?
3. As a reader, do you find this analogy persuasive?

Sylvia Plath (1932–1963)
MORNING SONG

Love set you going like a fat gold watch.
The midwife slapped your footsoles, and your bald cry
Took its place among the elements.

Our voices echo, magnifying your arrival. New statue.
In a drafty museum, your nakedness
Shadows our safety. We stand round blankly as walls.

I'm no more your mother
Than the cloud that distils a mirror to reflect its own slow
Effacement at the wind's hand.

All night your moth-breath
Flickers among the flat pink roses. I wake to listen:
A far sea moves in my ear.

One cry, and I stumble from bed, cow-heavy and floral
In my Victorian nightgown.
Your mouth opens clean as a cat's. The window square

Whitens and swallows its dull stars. And now you try
Your handful of notes;
The clear vowels rise like balloons.

1. In this poem the speaker compares her child with a series of objects. What do these figures of speech tell us about her feelings for the child?
2. Do her feelings change over the course of the poem?

Four
Imagery

What does the word *image* mean? Let's look at two common uses of the word. First, an image is a reflection—not the thing itself, but a reproduction of its appearances in another form. We can see our image in a mirror, or hear an image of our voice on an audio tape. Second, in popular usage an image is a false version of the self, intended for a public audience. Movie stars and politicians have an image, which we would not be so naive as to mistake for their real selves. What these two uses of the word have in common is that an image is a fiction, something shaped by the human mind. It is a reflection of reality, either a distorted or a fairly accurate one, but by its very nature an image is *not* reality itself.

In traditional literary usage the term *image* refers to a poem's ability to evoke the experiences of the senses. An image is language that makes us imagine how an object or scene looks, sounds, smells, tastes, or feels. Images in poems try to make readers feel as though they are in the scene that the poem describes. What the popular meanings of the word remind us, though, is that images cannot *in fact* put us in the scene. They can do so only *in imagination*. Images are always only fictions. They don't give us reality directly, but rather through the frameworks of language and through a particular person's mind. An imagistic poem gives us someone else's version of reality. That's what makes this kind of poem fascinating: we see the world as another sees it.

As an example, look at this intense poem with a strange title by Imamu Amiri Baraka:

PREFACE TO A TWENTY VOLUME SUICIDE NOTE

Lately, I've become accustomed to the way
The ground opens up and envelops me
Each time I go out to walk the dog.
Or the broad edged silly music the wind
Makes when I run for a bus—

Things have come to that.

And now, each night I count the stars,
And each night I get the same number.
And when they will not come to be counted
I count the holes they leave.

Nobody sings anymore.

And then last night, I tiptoed up
To my daughter's room and heard her
Talking to someone, and when I opened
The door, there was no one there. . .
Only she on her knees,
Peeking into her own clasped hands.

This poem develops from a self-portrait of its speaker into a very specific description of a scene, the little girl kneeling in her room. Most readers see this little girl as praying, but it is not so clear how the speaker sees her. Does he feel that she is praying for his deliverance from madness, or does he fear that she has become as mad as him, muttering away to an empty room through her imprisoning, clasped hands? We cannot answer this question very confidently, precisely because the speaker doesn't tell us but only gives us a purely sensory report of the scene. He doesn't put a label on the girl's actions, calling them either prayer or madness. He just gives us the picture, and the sense that the speaker doesn't know *what* to make of it.

In this brief poem we see the issues that images force us to consider. The only depiction of the experience we get in the poem comes from a man who is suffering psychotic hallucinations and who is writing in order to stave off suicide. It is through his confused mind that we see the scene, yet most readers make the scene what *they* want it to mean, seeing the girl as praying, even if the speaker of the poem is unsure. Nevertheless, the speaker's disoriented viewpoint is disturbing. Once you realize his inability to make sense of the scene, you begin to doubt at least a little the sense that you have made out of it yourself.

Seeing through the Words

In poetry, the only medium for expressing an image is language, which further insures that the image does not present reality directly. From the poet's perspective the problem is this: that language is a system of categories that divide up reality, yet often the experience that the poet is trying to depict did not feel divided up, but rather felt like a complex and rich whole that cannot be explained completely within language. Words always seem to fail to capture exactly the texture of the moment of experience. As a result, an image in a poem is always a kind of failure. The poet can never feel completely satisfied that the words are adequate to the experience.

For the reader, an image presents a problem that becomes an opportunity. The words of a poem are all that readers have to go on. Those words can get readers started, can provoke readers' imaginations, but only readers can truly construct an image in their own minds. Readers follow the verbal hints and then build up their own imaginative version of the scene. No two readers will have the same picture of the little girl in "Preface to a Twenty Volume Suicide Note," for example. She will look different in each reader's mind, the room will look different, her words will sound different, her actions will take on a different meaning. The images that poems provoke happen only in the minds of readers, and readers must take an active role in filling in the picture in their own imagination.

But that is precisely what makes images fun. They are an invitation to use your imagination. Images in a sense challenge you to do your reader's job as well as possible. You must begin with the words. Take for example Ezra Pound's famous poem, often thought of as a prime example of imagistic poetry:

IN A STATION OF THE METRO

The apparition of these faces in the crowd;
Petals on a wet, black bough.

What do these lines ask us to do? The title, first of all, invites us to imagine ourselves in a scene. We have to call up any images of subways we have stored in our memories, either from our own experience or from films, TV, and the like. Within the scene we are then directed to a particularly striking visual experience, a sight of the faces in the crowd on the subway. The poem can invite us to do this, but we readers must provide those faces.

Yet more than a sensory experience is asked of us. We are also invited to feel the emotion of the scene, particularly through the word "apparition." This word has connotations of mystery, delusion, spookiness. Those faces seem unreal, beyond explanation. An image never depicts reality, remember, but an interpretation of it, a feeling about it.

The next line asks us to imagine a jarringly different scene—a close-up of a natural object, one that we usually think of as beautiful, though it is described here in understated language that does not evoke powerful emotion. A new, sharp, and clear image simply replaces the old one.

Now, despite the fact that I'm using *we* in this analysis, I'm obviously describing *my* own reading process. I'm using *we* because I feel that most readers would construct similar scenes, following the straightforward clues of this fairly simple language. Every reader will have different images, but most will be of a similar type, guided by the language of the poem.

When it comes to the next step, however, it's clear that readers will react in radically different ways. For we now have to consider how the two images are related to each other. Poems are usually pretty unified, so we would expect that although the images seem radically different, they must be related. Some possible connections: we are supposed to superimpose the two images—the spectral beauty of the faces recalls the beauty and fragility of the flowers, both faces and flowers light on a dark background; or, the second image crowds out the first, perhaps because the apparitions are frightening and are replaced by a more reassuring, peaceful, *normal* image. Is the metro a place of beauty or of fear, a place that evokes nature as a friend or as an escape?

The poem simply does not answer that question. It forces us to ask it, but then it doesn't answer. The poem leaves us with the images, not with abstract explanations. In fact, the images of this and other poems makes us question the adequacy of such explanations. Poems call our attention to the power of language as a framework for perception, but when their images return us to the complexities of experience, they suggest that those frameworks can limit our perception as well. As much as we may need to impose categories on experience, we also need to be reminded that they are *merely* categories.

Imagining the Experience

Images are always fictions. Reality is too complex in our experience to be captured fully by language—all language can do is *evoke* experience. But an image is a beginning for an active reader. It allows you to create a mental picture suggested by the language of the poem. Imagery puts you in an extremely powerful role, for without you even a poem's richest language remains inert. As an active reader, you will rise to the challenge of imagistic language, engaging your imagination in a very creative process. One pleasure of imagery is that language pushes you beyond language, into a sensory revery that is itself too complex to capture in words.

It is very difficult to find words that will do justice to our experience. In the exercises that follow, you are asked to try to express your responses to the imagery in each poem.

READINGS

John Keats (1795–1821)

TO AUTUMN

1

Season of mists and mellow fruitfulness,
  Close bosom-friend of the maturing sun;
Conspiring with him how to load and bless
  With fruit the vines that round the thatch-eves run;
To bend with apples the moss'd cottage-trees,
  And fill all fruit with ripeness to the core;
    To swell the gourd, and plump the hazel shells
  With a sweet kernel; to set budding more,
And still more, later flowers for the bees,
Until they think warm days will never cease,
    For summer has o'er-brimm'd their clammy cells.

2

Who hath not seen thee oft amid thy store?
  Sometimes whoever seeks abroad may find
Thee sitting careless on a granary floor,
  Thy hair soft-lifted by the winnowing wind;
Or on a half-reap'd furrow sound asleep,
  Drows'd with the fume of poppies, while thy hook
    Spares the next swath and all its twined flowers:
And sometimes like a gleaner thou dost keep
  Steady thy laden head across a brook;
  Or by a cyder-press, with patient look,
    Thou watchest the last oozings hours by hours.

3

Where are the songs of spring? Ay, where are they?
  Think not of them, thou hast thy music too,—
While barred clouds bloom the soft-dying day,

And touch the stubble-plains with rosy hue;
Then in a wailful choir the small gnats mourn
And touch the stubble-plains with rosy hue;

1. Try to describe your own image of the scene described in the last stanza.
2. What senses does the imagery of the poem appeal to?
3. What emotion does the poem express about the beauty of autumn?

William Carlos Williams (1883–1963)

YOUNG WOMAN AT A WINDOW

She sits with
tears on

her cheek
her cheek on

her hand
the child

in her lap
his nose

pressed
to the glass

1. What is your speculation about the causes behind the scene that the poem describes?
2. Does the poem express any attitude toward the woman and her child?

Emily Dickinson (1830–1886)

[A BIRD CAME DOWN THE WALK]

A bird came down the Walk—
He did not know I saw—
He bit an Angleworm in halves
And ate the fellow, raw,

And then he drank a Dew
From a convenient Grass—
And then hopped sidewise to the Wall
To let a Beetle pass—

He glanced with rapid eyes
That hurried all around—
They looked like frightened Beads, I thought—
He stirred his Velvet Head

Like one in danger, Cautious,
I offered him a Crumb
And he unrolled his feathers
And rowed him softer home—

Than Oars divide the Ocean,
Too silver for a seam—
Or Butterflies, off Banks of Noon
Leap, plashless as they swim.

1. What does the speaker of the poem notice about the bird? Why has it caught her attention?
2. How does the poem describe the flight of the bird?

Denise Levertov (b. 1923)

O TASTE AND SEE

The world is
not with us enough.
O taste and see

the subway Bible poster said,
meaning The Lord, meaning
if anything all that lives
to the imagination's tongue,

grief, mercy, language,
tangerine, weather, to
breathe them, bite,
savor, chew, swallow, transform

into our flesh our
deaths, crossing the street, plum, quince,
living in the orchard and being

hungry, and plucking
the fruit.

1. What does this poem suggest about how we should perceive our surroundings?
2. Discuss the lists of words in the third and fourth stanzas. Are the words in a particular order?

Gary Snyder (b. 1930)
HAY FOR THE HORSES

He had driven half the night
From far down San Joaquin
Through Mariposa, up the
Dangerous mountain roads,
And pulled in at eight a.m.
With his big truckload of hay behind the barn.
With winch and ropes and hooks
We stacked the bales up clean
To splintery redwood rafters
High in the dark, flecks of alfalfa
Whirling through shingle-cracks of light,
Itch of haydust in the sweaty shirt and shoes.
At lunchtime under Black oak
Out in the hot corral,
—The old mare nosing lunchpails,
Grasshoppers crackling in the weeds—
'I'm sixty-eight,' he said,
'I first bucked hay when I was seventeen.
I thought, that day I started,
I sure would hate to do this all my life.
And dammit, that's just what
I've gone and done.'

1. What is the speaker's attitude toward the job of loading hay? What does he notice?
2. What is the trucker's attitude? Why is it different?

Gary Soto (b. 1952)

THE ELEMENTS OF SAN JOAQUIN

Field

The wind sprays pale dirt into my mouth
The small, almost invisible scars
On my hands.
The pores in my throat and elbows
Have taken in a seed of dirt of their own.

After a day in the grape fields near Rolinda
A fine silt, washed by sweat,
Has settled into the lines
On my wrists and palms.

Already I am becoming the valley,
A soil that sprouts nothing
For any of us.

Wind

A dry wind over the valley
Peeled mountains, grain by grain,
To small slopes, loose dirt
Where red ants tunnel.

The wind strokes
The skulls and spines of cattle
To white dust, to nothing,

Covers the spiked tracks of beetles,
Of tumbleweed, of sparrows
That pecked the ground for insects.

Evenings, when I am in the yard weeding,
The wind picks up the breath of my armpits
Like dust, swirls it
Miles away

And drops it
On the ear of a rabid dog,
And I take on another life.

Wind

When you got up this morning the sun
Blazed an hour in the sky,

A lizard hid
Under the curled leaves of manzanita
And winked its dark lids.

Later, the sky grayed,
And the cold wind you breathed
Was moving under your skin and already far
From the small hives of your lungs.

Stars

At dusk the first stars appear.
Not one eager finger points toward them.
A little later the stars spread with the night
And an orange moon rises
To lead them, like a shepherd, toward dawn.

Sun

In June the sun is a bonnet of light
Coming up,
Little by little,
From behind a skyline of pine.

The pastures sway with fiddle-neck
Tassels of foxtail.

At Piedra
A couple fish on the river's edge,
Their shadows deep against the water.
Above, in the stubbled slopes,
Cows climb down
As the heat rises
In a mist of blond locusts,
Returning to the valley.

Rain

When autumn rains flatten sycamore leaves,
The tiny volcanos of dirt
Ants raised around their holes,
I should be out of work.

My silverware and stack of plates will go unused
Like the old, my two good slacks
Will smother under a growth of lint
And smell of the old dust
That rises
When the closet door opens or closes.

The skin of my belly will tighten like a belt
And there will be no reason for pockets.

Fog

If you go to your window
You will notice a fog drifting in.

The sun is no stronger than a flashlight.
Not all the sweaters
Hung in closets all summer

Could soak up this mist. The fog:
A mouth nibbling everything to its origin,
Pomegranate trees, stolen bicycles,

The string of lights at a used-car lot,
A Pontiac with scorched valves.

In Fresno the fog is passing
The young thief prying a window screen,
Graying my hair that falls
And goes unfound, my fingerprints
Slowly growing a fur of dust—

One hundred years from now
There should be no reason to believe
I lived.

Daybreak

In this moment when the light starts up
In the east and rubs
The horizon until it catches fire,

We enter the fields to hoe,
Row after row, among the small flags of onion,
Waving off the dragonflies
That ladder the air.

And tears the onions raise
Do not begin in your eyes but in ours,
In the salt blown
From one blister into another;

They begin in knowing
You will never waken to bear
The hour timed to a heart beat,
The wind pressing us closer to the ground.

When the season ends,
And the onions are unplugged from their sleep,
We won't forget what you failed to see,
And nothing will heal
Under the rain's broken fingers.

1. What is the speaker's emotional response to the landscape he describes?
2. Is there a coherent order to the sections of the poem?

Five
Poetic Form and Sound

One reason that the language of poetry has power is that it has been designed to delight and fascinate readers. Poets play with the language, listening to it for compelling sound patterns—rhythms and melodies, rhymes and harmonies. The sounds of spoken language have a music to them—listen to kids playing a game on the street, or neighbors gossiping over a fence. Poets try to bring out that music in written language. They want readers to *listen* to the poem for those musical patterns, so that they can learn to hear the powerful music of human speech.

Let's listen to those neighbors meeting over a fence. Mr. Smith is complaining to Mr. Jones that the new family in the neighborhood is letting its house get run down. He doesn't just say the words "They're dirty," he says them with a tone of voice, an emphasis that communicates the disgust he feels, the anger that he wants his neighbor to share. To hear that tone of voice would be to hear a verbal music. An emotion would come through. We could appreciate how the tone was performed—some gifted gossips could turn those two words into an aria—but we would also recognize that the tone of voice wasn't just a performance, but was part of a real communication, Mr. Smith's attempt to get his neighbor to see the situation the way he does. The music in language is fun to listen to, but it's also an important part of the meaning. *How* a thing is said is part of what's said.

Poets know how to construct a phrase that will get inside your head and refuse to be thrown out. You certainly have had the experience of some advertising jingle or pop lyric getting stuck in your brain. Advertisers know that a cleverly turned phrase can command people's attention. Think of the telephone company's "Reach out, reach out and touch someone," which in different commercials can be touching or funny or enthusiastic, depending on how the music of the phrase is performed. The rhythm and the melody of the words hold our attention, help to open us up to the message of the commercial.

The sound of a poem plays a similar role. There are phrases from poems that have stayed with me over many years, something about their sound, their rhythm, lodging them in my memory. One of the passages that has been with me the longest is from William Butler Yeats's "The Fisherman": "Before I am old / I shall have written him one / Poem maybe as cold / And passionate as the dawn." The context here is that Yeats is imagining his perfect audience, a "wise and simple" fisherman. But the context doesn't explain why the line stays with me. I think it has to do with how the poignancy of that "maybe" syncopates the rhythm of the line. For whatever reason, the phrase now has a permanent home in my neural circuitry. And for that reason, the emotion that the poem communicates—the sense of searching for an ideal but realizing that ideals are precisely what you can never find—has stayed with me as well.

Playing with Language

The sound of poetry has emotional power, but the process of crafting that sound seems often to come out of verbal *play*. Poets simply play with the verbal possibilities, trying various combinations until they hear the music they want. Part of this process involves the poet's awareness of already existing poetic forms. There are conventions in poetry, rules for combining the sounds of language, that a poet can use to produce verbal music. We'll be looking at some of these patterns later in this chapter, but for an example now, many American poets now enjoy writing in a Japanese form called the *haiku*, which requires that the poem be composed of seventeen syllables. Not sixteen, not eighteen, but seventeen. The point of writing in such a demanding form is for the poet to submit his or her idea to an external discipline. The limit on length obviously forces compression of expression, but it also makes for a predictable musical pattern.

Like all games, the verbal play of poetry has rules. Haikus are seventeen syllables, sonnets are fourteen lines. Poets get fascinated with the often intricate verbal patterns that language can take. Their impulse to write may come from deep emotional experience or from an almost meditative self-reflection, but poets also submit themselves to a verbal discipline, a craft of writing. Perhaps this discipline balances against their intensity of emotion or their urgency of thought. In either event, poets do often become fascinated by fitting their impulse to write into the patterns that the poetic forms demand.

There are basically two kinds of poetic form, closed forms and open forms. In a closed form the rules of the form pre-date the poet and the poem. A sonnet is always fourteen lines, and the craft of the poet involves a graceful play within the set rules. In an open form, the poet creates a form for the purposes of a single poem. Look again at this poem by William Carlos Williams:

YOUNG WOMAN AT A WINDOW

She sits with
tears on

her cheek
her cheek on

her hand
the child

in her lap
his nose

pressed
to the glass

This poem doesn't fit any recognized poetic form, it develops its own verbal rules, its own form. Each stanza is two lines long, each line has two or three syllables. The one place the pattern varies, in the ninth line, which has only one syllable, the word "pressed" gets emphasis and helps draw our attention to a particular detail of the image the poem is constructing. These verbal rules exist for this poem only—they will never be used again. But they *are* rules, they do produce a verbal pattern. An open form is not an absence of form, but a form that has been devised for the special occasion of the poem.

Listening for the Music

Now, so far we have been looking at form and sound from the author's perspective. What do these aspects of poetry demand of readers? First of all, they simply demand that we look and listen for them. Every poem deserves a reading out loud, so that the sense of the poem comes through, but also so that the sound of the poem has a chance to affect us. We need to learn what the possible patterns of sound are, so that we can participate in the verbal game. We need to build up expectations, depending on our knowledge of the form, so that when the formal pattern is completed we will feel the sense of resolution that comes from seeing any pattern come together. If we aren't *aware* of the musical possibilities of language, we can't hear them when they happen. If we don't know the rules of the verbal game, we can't appreciate a poem's formal success.

However, readers also need to be open to formal experimentation. Even in what I've called the "closed forms" the rules can be creatively revised. There are, after all, no penalties behind these rules. Poets play with them all the time. Poems do not typically have rigid sound patterns, but rather they set up a loose pattern that will allow improvisation within it. We need to know what the patterns are so we will develop expectations about what we will hear, and then if expectations are played with, we will notice the significant variation.

Readers also need to be alert to their own responses. Read the poem aloud. Listen to its music. What emotional response does the poem cause, just as a piece of sound? Is it slow and stately, or fast and enthusiastic? Is it brooding, or joyful, or stirring? Or is it repetitive and predictable? There are also questions to ask about the relationship between the sound of the poem and its meaning. How does the emotion produced by the poem's music go along with the meaning produced by its language?

Look at and listen to the following two poems from William Blake's *Songs of Innocence and of Experience*. "The Lamb" is a poem of Innocence in which the speaker is a child; the speaker of "The Tyger" is an adult who inhabits the state of the soul that Blake called Experience:

THE LAMB

Little Lamb, who made thee?
Dost thou know who made thee?
Gave thee life & bid thee feed,
By the stream & o'er the mead;
Gave thee clothing of delight,
Softest clothing wooly bright;
Gave thee such a tender voice,
Making all the vales rejoice!
Little Lamb who made thee?
Dost thou know who made thee?

Little Lamb I'll tell thee,
Little Lamb I'll tell thee!
He is calléd by thy name,
For he calls himself a Lamb:
He is meek & he is mild,
He became a little child:
I a child & thou a lamb,

We are calléd by his name.
  Little Lamb God bless thee.
  Little Lamb God bless thee.

THE TYGER

Tyger! Tyger! burning bright
In the forests of the night,
What immortal hand or eye
Could frame thy fearful symmetry?

In what distant deeps or skies
Burnt the fire of thine eyes?
On what wings dare he aspire?
What the hand dare sieze the fire?

And what shoulder, & what art,
Could twist the sinews of thy heart?
And when thy heart began to beat,
What dread hand? & what dread feet?

What the hammer? what the chain?
In what furnace was thy brain?
What the anvil? what dread grasp
Dare its deadly terrors clasp?

When the stars threw down their spears,
And water'd heaven with their tears,
Did he smile his work to see?
Did he who made the Lamb make thee?

Tyger! Tyger! burning bright
In the forests of the night,
What immortal hand or eye,
Dare frame thy fearful symmetry?

As I read these poems, they are meditations on God. The child's god is the Christ child, the Lamb of God, a benign god of peace. The adult's god is more frightening and harder to understand, like the Old Testament Jahweh or the powerful gods of Greek and Nordic mythology. And for me the sounds of the poems match their speakers' states of mind. "The Lamb" as music is simple and beautiful, childlike; "The Tyger" is rougher and more complex as music, it doesn't flow with the easy grace of "The Lamb." The music of "The Tyger" is suited to its troubled speaker, who has passed beyond the innocence of childhood and is beginning to see how difficult and confusing the world can be. In both these poems, the sound of the language helps me to make sense of the speaker's view of the world. If we are listening to the music, we are attending to one of the powers of language, the power to shape our emotions, to make us feel an experience as the speaker of the poem feels it.

Looking for the Patterns

Now let's turn to a discussion of some of the rules of poetic form, some of the techniques that poets can use to create the music of poetry for those who know how to listen. One of the most basic elements of the music of poetry comes from the fact that words sound like other words. Poets can take advantage of these similarities to create memorable phrases. Similarities in vowel sounds are called *assonance;* similarities in consonant sounds are called *alliteration. Go* and *know* are related by assonance; *go* and *get* are related by alliteration. Listen to the complex music that related sounds can make in this line from John Keats's "Eve of St. Agnes": "From silken Samarcand to cedar'd Lebanon." The repeated *s* sound and the various *o* and *a* sounds create a beautifully paced and complex music.

In Gerard Manley Hopkins's "The Windhover" the music is as complex as possible. The meaning of the poem can be constructed, but it is the alliterative and assonantal music that first catches our ear and our emotions.

THE WINDHOVER

To Christ Our Lord

I caught this morning morning's minion, king-
dom of daylight's dauphin, dapple-dawn-drawn Falcon, in his riding
Of the rolling level underneath him steady air, and striding
High there, how he rung upon the rein of a wimpling wing
In his ecstasy! then off, off forth on swing,
As a skate's heel sweeps smooth on a bow-bend: the hurl and gliding
Rebuffed the big wind. My heart in hiding
Stirred for a bird,—the achieve of, the mastery of the thing!

Brute beauty and valour and act, oh, air, pride, plume here
Buckle! AND the fire that breaks from thee then, a billion
Times told lovelier, more dangerous, O my chevalier!
No wonder of it: shéer plód makes plough down sillion

Shine, and blue-bleak embers, ah my dear,
  Fall, gall themselves, and gash gold-vermilion.

Certainly the most well known form of poetic music is *rhyme,* in which the last words of different lines of poetry end with the same vowel and consonant sounds. For some readers rhyme is what defines poetry, and rhyme does have very powerful effects. For example, it can give a phrase a strong finish, make it stand out as a self-contained, memorable phrase. In "Resolution and Independence" William Wordsworth says, "We Poets in our youth begin in gladness, / But thereof come in the end despondency and madness." The rhyme is part of the reason why the statement seems like a definitive description of the poetic temperament.

Not all rhymes are as perfect as "gladness" and "madness." Some poems employ *slant rhymes,* in which the last words of two lines recall each other but don't exactly repeat the sound. "My Last Duchess," by Robert Browning, is a fifty-six line poem made up of two-line, rhymed segments, called *couplets.* Now if each segment rhymed perfectly the poem would be fragmented, each segment would come to a conclusion and make the transition to the next difficult. But many of the rhymes are slant rhymes:

The bough of cherries some officious fool
Broke in the orchard for her, the white mule

"Fool" and "mule" are not exact rhymes, and the reader can therefore move more smoothly on to the next line.

Despite many readers' expectations, poems don't have to rhyme at all. At the beginning of this century many poets in the English language turned away from rhyme in search of a more natural sound. Rather than shape the sounds of language into a predetermined pattern, they wanted to allow the music of ordinary language to come through. The following poem by Allen Ginsberg isn't rhymed, but it has its own free-form music:

FIRST PARTY AT KEN KESEY'S WITH HELL'S ANGELS

Cool black night thru redwoods
cars parked outside in shade
behind the gate, stars dim above
the ravine, a fire burning by the side
porch and a few tired souls hunched over
in black leather jackets. In the huge

wooden house, a yellow chandelier
at 3 a.m. the blast of loudspeakers
hi-fi Rolling Stones Ray Charles Beatles
Jumping Joe Jackson and twenty youths
dancing to the vibration thru the floor,
a little weed in the bathroom, girls in scarlet
tights, one muscular smooth skinned man
sweating dancing for hours, beer cans
bent littering the yard, a hanged man
sculpture dangling from a high creek branch,
children sleeping softly in bedroom bunks,
And 4 police cars parked outside the painted
gate, red lights revolving in the leaves.

Lines 8–11 do an excellent job of suggesting the powerful sound of rock music. Anything as formal as rhyme would be wildly inappropriate, but the poem still achieves a music of its own.

There is a similar diversity of options open to the poet when it comes to the *rhythm* of a line of poetry. The rhythm of poetry in English depends on the fact that some syllables are spoken more loudly than others in the flow of speech, they receive more verbal *stress.* In the word *document,* for example, the first syllable is stressed and the other two are unstressed. Poets can take advantage of these patterns of stressed and unstressed syllables in order to form rhythmic combinations of words. These patterns can be very tightly organized, or they can be formed more loosely, allowing for rhythmic diversity.

The units of verbal rhythm are called metrical *feet.* Some of the distinctive feet have been given names, and, as we will see, some poetic forms demand a particular rhythmic unit.

iambic: unstressed, stressed ("de *cline*")
trochaic: stressed, unstressed ("*vi* tal")
anapestic: unstressed, unstressed, stressed ("en ter *tain*")
dactylic: stressed, unstressed, unstressed ("*lit* er ate")

These patterns can make use of more than one word to fill the rhythm: "on the stove," for example, is an anapestic rhythm.

The rhythm of poetry can also be varied by the number of feet in each line. Some lines are short and sharply rhythmic, others flow on in long patterns. There are also formal names from the ancient Greek for the lengths of lines:

monometer: one foot
dimeter: two feet
trimeter: three feet
tetrameter: four feet
pentameter: five feet
hexameter: six feet

Thus, a line of poetry that has five rhythmic units, each stressed on the second syllable, is called *iambic pentameter.* Here is a line of almost exact iambic pentameter: "That time of year thou mayst in me behold." The natural rhythm of the language has been transformed into a regular, musical pattern.

I should immediately say that very few poems utilize such regular rhythms in every line. In most successful poems that use traditional forms, the poem establishes a basic pattern that can then be varied subtly. A purely repetitive pattern can become singsong, overly predictable. The following lines from the same Shakespeare poem I just quoted are basically iambic pentameter, but they vary the rhythm beautifully: "Upon those boughs which shake against the cold / Bare, ruined choirs where late the sweet birds sang." The result of this variation is that the words that vary the pattern, "Bare, ruined choirs," attract our attention.

Rhythm can also be varied subtly by changes in the relationship between the rhythmic units and the units of meaning. When a unit of meaning ends at the end of a line, the line is called *end-stopped*: "Life contracts and death is expected, / As in a season of autumn. / The soldier falls." Each line ends as a unit of meaning ends. When a unit of meaning continues across into the next line, the technique is called *enjambment*: "I cannot rest from travel; I will drink / Life to the lees. All times I have enjoyed / Greatly, have suffered greatly." As lines of poetry are read aloud, units of meaning play off against units of rhythm, resulting almost always in a very intricate pattern that it is part of the craft of poetry to produce.

With recent poetry a different attitude about the line comes to the fore. Instead of predetermining a rhythmic pattern and fitting the language into it, many modern poems seem to be based on a rhythm that emerges from the words themselves. Similarly, the length of line can vary according to the needs of those emerging rhythmic patterns. There may be no set pattern, but rather an improvised rhythm and line. One recent American poet, Charles Olsen, has said that the line should be a unit of breath, but however you think of it, the line has become a much more fluid and variable unit.

Adrienne Rich's "Power" is an example of a poem that devises its own rhythmic patterns, particularly by varying the length of the line and by printing the poem to emphasize sound patterns within the line:

POWER

Living   in the earth-deposits   of our history

Today a backhoe divulged   out of a crumbling flank of
  earth

one bottle   amber   perfect   a hundred-year-old
cure for fever   or melancholy   a tonic
for living on this earth   in the winters of this climate

Today I was reading about Marie Curie:
she must have known she suffered   from radiation sickness
her body bombarded for years   by the element
she had purified
It seems she denied to the end
the source of the cataracts on her eyes
the cracked and suppurating skin   of her finger-ends
till she could no longer hold   a test-tube or a pencil

She died   a famous woman   denying
her wounds
denying
her wounds   came   from the same source as her power

Rich has created in this poem a rhythmic pattern that does not fit any definition and that will never be repeated, but an attentive reader will still feel its power.

The next larger level of organization of the sound of poetry is **stanza** forms. In some traditional poetry, a specified number of lines of verse are assembled in each stanza. A *couplet,* for example, is a two-line unit, often rhymed; a *quatrain* is a four-line unit. Often stanzas are characterized by a specific rhyme scheme, such as one in which the first and third lines rhyme, and the second and fourth lines rhyme. There are also longer units of lines for specific forms, such as the nine-line Spenserian stanza. This stanza form calls for eight lines of iambic pentameter, followed by a last line of hexameter, rhymed such that the first and third lines rhyme, the second, fourth, fifth and seventh lines rhyme, and the sixth, eighth, and ninth lines rhyme. I mention this form in order to indicate how complex and specific are the demands of some traditional stanza patterns.

Similar demands are made by the traditional forms that lie behind entire poems. At the beginning of this chapter, for example, I mentioned the *haiku,* which limits the entire poem to seventeen syllables. Some of the other formal conventions that define the shape of entire poems are the **sonnet,** the **ballad,** and the **villanelle.** In all of these cases the form imposes different disciplines and makes possible different effects.

The *sonnet* is a fourteen-line poem, usually with an iambic pentameter rhythm. There are in fact two sonnet forms. In the *Italian* or *Petrarchan sonnet,* there is an eight-line unit, or *octave,* and a six-line unit, or *sestet.* William Wordsworth's "It is a beauteous evening" is a Petrarchan sonnet:

[IT IS A BEAUTEOUS EVENING, CALM AND FREE]

It is a beauteous evening, calm and free,
The holy time is quiet as a Nun
Breathless with adoration; the broad sun
Is sinking down in its tranquillity;
The gentleness of heaven broods o'er the Sea:
Listen! the mighty Being is awake,
And doth with his eternal motion make
A sound like thunder—everlastingly.
Dear Child! dear Girl! that walkest with me here,
If thou appear untouched by solemn thought,
Thy nature is not therefore less divine:
Thou liest in Abraham's bosom all the year;
And worshipp'st at the Temple's inner shrine,
God being with thee when we know it not.

The division between the first eight lines and the last six is marked by the fact that the first eight describe the scene, whereas the last six deal with the little child who accompanies Wordsworth, and who lives unself-consciously within the beauties of the world Wordsworth describes.

The *English* or *Shakespearean sonnet* is organized differently, with three quatrains and a closing rhymed couplet. William Shakespeare is of course the master of the form, as we can see in the following poem:

SONNET 116

Let me not to the marriage of true minds
Admit impediments. Love is not love
Which alters when it alteration finds,
Or bends with the remover to remove.
Oh no! It is an ever-fixèd mark,
That looks on tempests and is never shaken.
It is the star to every wandering bark,
Whose worth's unknown, although his height be taken.
Love's not Time's fool, though rosy lips and cheeks
Within his bending sickle's compass come.
Love alters not with his brief hours and weeks,
But bears it out even to the edge of doom.
  If this be error and upon me proved,
  I never writ, nor no man ever loved.

In this poem each quatrain expresses a complete thought, so that the poem produces a very logical and orderly effect, in spite of its amorous subject. These sonnet forms, of course, can be varied and played with by the poet, but even in such a case the normal form of the sonnet serves as a set of expectations that the poet can work against.

A *ballad* is a looser form than the sonnet. It is composed of quatrains in which the second and fourth lines rhyme, and in which the first and third lines have four feet and the second and fourth have three feet. I say that it is a looser form because any number of these stanzas can be strung together in a ballad. This open-ended quality lends itself to storytelling in verse. The poet is free to string together ballad stanzas until the narrative is complete. There is an ancient tradition among the rural folk of England of singing ballads that have been passed down in the oral tradition from generation to generation. One such anonymous ballad is "Sir Patrick Spens," which tells the story of a knight who is sent to his death in the sea:

SIR PATRICK SPENS

The king sits in Dumferling toune,
  Drinking the blude-reid wine:
"O whar will I get guid sailor,
  To sail this schip of mine?"

Up and spak an eldern knicht,
  Sat at the kings richt kne:
"Sir Patrick Spens is the best sailor,
  That sails upon the se."

The king has written a braid letter,
  And signed it wi his hand,
And sent it to Sir Patrick Spens,
  Was walking on the sand.

The first line that Sir Patrick red,
  A loud lauch lauchéd he;
The next line that Sir Patrick red,
  The teir blinded his ee.

"O wha is this has done this deid,
  This ill deid don to me,
To send me out this time o' the yeir,
  To sail upon the se!

"Mak hast, make hast, my mirry men all
  Our guid schip sails the morne:"

"O say na sae, my master deir,
For I feir a deadlie storme.

"Late, late yestreen I saw the new moone,
Wi the auld moone in hir arme,
And I feir, I feir, my deir master,
That we will cum to harme."

O our Scots nobles wer richt laith
To weet their cork-heild schoone,
Bot lang owre a' the play wer playd,
Their hats they swam aboone.

O lang, lang may their ladies sit,
Wi thair fans into their hand,
Or eir they se Sir Patrick Spens
Cum sailing to the land.

O lang, lang may the ladies stand,
Wi thair gold kems in their hair
Waiting for thar ain deir lords,
For they'll se thame na mair.

Half owre, half owre to Aberdour,
It's fiftie fadom deip,
And thair lies guid Sir Patrick Spens,
Wi the Scots lords at his feit.

Individual poets have also used the ballad, again usually in the service of a story. In John Keats's "La Belle Dame sans Merci," for example, the poem tells the story of a knight who encounters an alluring but deadly woman of the fairy folk:

LA BELLE DAME SANS MERCI

1

O what can ail thee, knight at arms,
Alone and palely loitering?
The sedge has wither'd from the lake,
And no birds sing.

2

O what can ail thee, knight at arms,
So haggard and so woe-begone?
The squirrel's granary is full,
And the harvest's done.

3

I see a lily on thy brow
 With anguish moist and fever dew,
And on thy cheeks a fading rose
 Fast withereth too.

4

I met a lady in the meads,
 Full beautiful, a fairy's child;
Her hair was long, her foot was light,
 And her eyes were wild.

5

I made a garland for her head,
 And bracelets too, and fragrant zone;
She look'd at me as she did love,
 And made sweet moan.

6

I set her on my pacing steed,
 And nothing else saw all day long,
For sidelong would she bend, and sing
 A fairy's song.

7

She found me roots of relish sweet,
 And honey wild, and manna dew,
And sure in language strange she said—
 I love thee true.

8

She took me to her elfin grot,
 And there she wept, and sigh'd full sore,
And there I shut her wild wild eyes
 With kisses four.

9

And there she lulled me asleep,
 And there I dream'd—Ah! woe betide!
The latest dream I ever dream'd
 On the cold hill's side.

10

I saw pale kings, and princes too,
 Pale warriors, death pale were they all;

They cried—"La belle dame sans merci
  Hath thee in thrall!"

11

I saw their starv'd lips in the gloam
  With horrid warning gaped wide,
And I awoke and found me here
  On the cold hill's side.

12

And this is why I sojourn here,
  Alone and palely loitering,
Though the sedge is wither'd from the lake,
  And no birds sing.

In this poem the ballad form gives Keats the room to explore the complex psychology of the knight's obsession, and to describe in some detail the relationship between the knight and the woman of the fairy.

The *villanelle* is an example of a form that demands such complex verbal manipulations that the ingenuity of the poet is severely challenged. The villanelle consists of five three-line stanzas, all of which rhyme in the pattern *a b a,* and concludes with a quatrain that rhymes in the pattern *a b a a*—there are only two rhymes in the poem. In addition, line one is repeated in lines six, twelve, and eighteen, and line three is repeated in lines nine, fifteen, and nineteen. There are other restrictions, too. Faced with this kind of arbitrary complexity, why would a poet submit his or her impulse to what seems to be an almost excessive verbal discipline? Perhaps Dylan Thomas's villanelle "Do Not Go Gentle into That Good Night" will give us a clue. In the poem the speaker directs his words to his dying father, demanding that the father fight his death, not accept it:

DO NOT GO GENTLE INTO THAT GOOD NIGHT

Do not go gentle into that good night,
Old age should burn and rave at close of day;
Rage, rage against the dying of the light.

Though wise men at their end know dark is right,
Because their words had forked no lightning they
Do not go gentle into that good night.

Good men, the last wave by, crying how bright
Their frail deeds might have danced in a green bay,
Rage, rage against the dying of the light.

Wild men who caught and sang the sun in flight,
And learn, too late, they grieved it on its way,
Do not go gentle into that good night.

Grave men, near death, who see with blinding sight
Blind eyes could blaze like meteors and be gay,
Rage, rage against the dying of the light.

And you, my father, there on the sad height,
Curse, bless, me now with your fierce tears, I pray.
Do not go gentle into that good night.
Rage, rage against the dying of the light.

The speaker of this poem is obviously working from an intense emotional response to his father's death. The emotion is in fact so intense that it seems to scramble the syntax, making the meaning of the poem hard to figure out. But all that intensity is subject to the discipline of this ornery form, as though the speaker needed to control his emotions, to keep them from driving him mad. The meaning of the poem, then, is affected by the form, as the poem comes to be about the speaker's struggle to control yet express his powerful emotions.

In all poems, form and sound are worthy of attention. We need to hear the music of the poetry, feel how it affects us, think of how it affects the poem's meaning. Poems need readers who know the forms, so that they will feel the patterns being filled in or being revised. Poetry is a verbal craft as well as an exploration of meaning and feeling. The goal of that craft is to create language that will affect readers and that will draw their attention to the power of the poem's meaning.

Six

The Speaker of the Poem

To an active reader of poetry, the words of the poem are not just marks on a page. The experience of reading poetry does begin with those marks, but it does not end there. These marks activate a reading process—making sense of the language, unraveling the figures of speech, imagining the world that the poem suggests, anticipating the formal patterns. For an active reader there is a further consideration: What does all this work add up to? One answer for many readers is that it produces the sense of a mind at work making meaning in the world, the mind behind the poem. We can call this mind the *speaker* of the poem.

The speaker of the poem is not the poet, but rather the mind that the reader can construct out of the poem. As a principle of reading, it is safer to assume that the speaker is a fictional character created by the poet. There are poems in which the identity of the speaker is directly announced. In Robert Browning's "My Last Duchess" (reprinted later), the speaker is clearly a fictional character that Browning has created, a sixteenth-century Italian duke. Every word of the poem is his; we never hear the voice of the author. In fact, the duke exists only in and through the words of this poem. To read the "I" of the poem as the "I" of the author would be to miss out on Browning's creativity.

Browning's poem, like many others, asks us to construct a sense of the speaker out of his language. What kind of person would use the language as he does? What kind of mind would devise just these figures of speech, argue his case in just this way? We have to move from the verbal clues to a sense of a particular personality, a way of looking at the world. Many poems are like speeches from a play. Their speakers are like characters in a drama, finding themselves within a situation, speaking to another character, hoping to achieve some goal with that speech. A poem, often in a brief time, has to give readers hints so they can help construct this dramatic context. Poems, that is, don't just give us the speaker's mind, they give us that mind at work on a particular problem or event, so that we can see a very specific example of how that mind gives meaning to the world.

Even when a poem does not create an obviously fictional character as its speaker, readers should be asking the same question: what kind of mind created this poem? All poems have a speaker. It is always possible for readers to assemble the verbal evidence so that it points to an organizing intelligence, thus producing the personality of the speaker as they process the language of the poem. All of us are used to making judgments about others based on what they say and how they say it. If a person speaks crudely, in only the simplest words and in fragments of sentences, we might make some harsh judgments about that person's intelligence. Constructing the speaker of a poem involves exactly this kind of judgment—what kind of person expresses him- or herself in just this kind of language?

Let's look at a brief poem by William Carlos Williams that suggests a lot about its speaker:

THIS IS JUST TO SAY

I have eaten
the plums
that were in
the icebox

and which
you were probably
saving
for breakfast

Forgive me
they were delicious
so sweet
and so cold

This poem is written in the form of an apology. "Forgive me," it says. We can surmise from this that the speaker feels some guilt, especially since the plums were intended for someone else. Yet the last stanza seems to go in a different direction, lingering over the pleasure for which the speaker is supposed to feel guilty. He clearly wants to apologize and rub it in at the same time. And for me the pleasure he takes in describing the plums undercuts the apology. The speaker stands revealed as a petty hypocrite, apologizing but not really regretting.

Of course, this is *my* sense of the speaker. I tend to imagine this poem as part of a marriage relationship in which the speaker, the husband, is trying to manipulate his wife's feelings so that he can do as he wants. With a poem like this, any reader will construct some kind of context for this note. What each reader constructs will differ. Some readers feel that the apology still holds, that the description of the pleasure is part of his excuse.

Neither interpretation of the speaker's motives is obviously correct. Different readers will develop different senses of the speaker. We can only explain how the language of the poem leads to our image of the speaker, try to make an argument for how we read. It is important to remember that the speaker can only be brought into existence by a reader who puts together the clues of the poem in a particular way. The job of the reader is to construct an image of the speaker that accounts for as many of the details of the poem as possible.

Readers don't have to *like* the speakers they help to construct. In many cases the poet seems clearly to be creating a character who condemms himself in his own language. We are not supposed to like the duke in "My Last Duchess," for example. We are supposed to see through his self-explanation to his personal weaknesses. Readers have to make judgments about the speaker of the poem. By stating clearly how we feel about the speaker, and by explaining why the poem makes us feel this way, we can gain insight into our judgments about other people as well as come to understand the experience of the poem.

Without a concept like the speaker, a poem can seem abstract and dehumanized, language that we need to analyze but with which we cannot identify. The speaker humanizes a poem, and we need to work our way through the complexities of a poem in order to reach the mind behind it. How does that mind make sense of the world? How does it feel about and evaluate experience? We have before us the language that the speaker has used to make sense of a particular event. What that language can show us, as we have seen in previous chapters, is how a mind can impose a meaning and a feeling on the world.

Real people use language as well. So learning how to reconstruct the speaker is learning how we come to know other people through their language. It is an active process, a piece of work that each of us must do constantly, moving from the language of another person to an interpretation of who that person is. This will always be our own interpretation—that person might well see her- or himself differently than we do—because we are outside of and can only interpret that person's mind. In this way, poetry can teach us something about knowing other people.

READINGS

William Shakespeare (1564–1616)

SONNET 18

Shall I compare thee to a summer's day?
Thou art more lovely and more temperate.
Rough winds do shake the darling buds of May,
And summer's lease hath all too short a date.
Sometime too hot the eye of heaven shines,
And often is his gold complexion dimmed.
And every fair from fair sometimes declines,
By chance or nature's changing course untrimmed.
But thy eternal summer shall not fade,
Nor lose possession of that fair thou owest,
Nor shall Death brag thou wander'st in his shade
When in eternal lines to time thou grow'st.
So long as men can breathe, or eyes can see,
So long lives this, and this gives life to thee.

1. What verbal strategies does the speaker use in this poem to praise his beloved?
2. What will give eternal life to the person the speaker is complimenting?
3. What is the speaker's attitude toward himself in this poem?

Robert Browning (1812–1889)

MY LAST DUCHESS

Ferrara

That's my last Duchess painted on the wall,
Looking as if she were alive. I call
That piece a wonder, now: Frà Pandolf's hands
Worked busily a day, and there she stands.
Will't please you sit and look at her? I said
"Frà Pandolf" by design, for never read

Strangers like you that pictured countenance,
The depth and passion of its earnest glance,
But to myself they turned (since none puts by
The curtain I have drawn for you, but I)
And seemed as they would ask me, if they durst,
How such a glance came there; so, not the first
Are you to turn and ask thus. Sir, 'twas not
Her husband's presence only, called that spot
Of joy into the Duchess' cheek: perhaps
Frà Pandolf chanced to say "Her mantle laps
Over my lady's wrist too much," or "Paint
Must never hope to reproduce the faint
Half-flush that dies along her throat": such stuff
Was courtesy, she thought, and cause enough
For calling up that spot of joy. She had
A heart—how shall I say?—too soon made glad,
Too easily impressed; she liked whate'er
She looked on, and her looks went everywhere.
Sir, 'twas all one! My favor at her breast,
The dropping of the daylight in the West,
The bough of cherries some officious fool
Broke in the orchard for her, the white mule
She rode with round the terrace—all and each
Would draw from her alike the approving speech,
Or blush, at least. She thanked men—good! but thanked
Somehow—I know not how—as if she ranked
My gift of a nine-hundred-years-old name
With anybody's gift. Who'd stoop to blame
This sort of trifling? Even had you skill
In speech—(which I have not)—to make your will
Quite clear to such an one, and say, "Just this
Or that in you disgusts me; here you miss,
Or there exceed the mark"—and if she let
Herself be lessoned so, nor plainly set
Her wits to yours, forsooth, and made excuse
—E'en then would be some stooping; and I choose
Never to stoop. Oh sir, she smiled, no doubt,
Whene'er I passed her; but who passed without
Much the same smile? This grew; I gave commands;
Then all smiles stopped together. There she stands
As if alive. Will't please you rise? We'll meet
The company below, then. I repeat,
The Count your master's known munificence
Is ample warrant that no just pretense
Of mine for dowry will be disallowed;

Though his fair daughter's self, as I avowed
At starting, is my object. Nay, we'll go
Together down, sir. Notice Neptune, though,
Taming a sea horse, thought a rarity,
Which Claus of Innsbruck cast in bronze for me!

1. Describe the overall dramatic context of the poem. Who is speaking to whom about what for what reason?
2. How does the duke interpret his last wife's behavior? How do *you* interpret her behavior?
3. Is the duke insane? Would he be defined as insane in our current society? In his own?

Alfred, Lord Tennyson (1809–1892)
ULYSSES

It little profits that an idle king,
By this still hearth, among these barren crags,
Matched with an aged wife, I mete and dole
Unequal laws unto a savage race,
That hoard, and sleep, and feed, and know not me.

I cannot rest from travel; I will drink
Life to the lees. All times I have enjoyed
Greatly, have suffered greatly, both with those
That loved me, and alone; on shore, and when
Through scudding drifts the rainy Hyades
Vexed the dim sea. I am become a name;
For always roaming with a hungry heart
Much have I seen and known—cities of men
And manners, climates, councils, governments,
Myself not least, but honored of them all—
And drunk delight of battle with my peers,
Far on the ringing plains of windy Troy,
I am a part of all that I have met;
Yet all experience is an arch wherethrough
Gleams that untraveled world whose margin fades
Forever and forever when I move,
How dull it is to pause, to make an end,
To rust unburnished, not to shine in use!
As though to breathe were life! Life piled on life
Were all too little, and of one to me

Little remains; but every hour is saved
From that eternal silence, something more,
A bringer of new things; and vile it were
For some three suns to store and hoard myself,
And this gray spirit yearning in desire
To follow knowledge like a sinking star,
Beyond the utmost bound of human thought.

This is my son, mine own Telemachus,
To whom I leave the scepter and the isle—
Well-loved of me, discerning to fulfill
This labor, by slow prudence to make mild
A rugged people, and through soft degrees
Subdue them to the useful and the good.
Most blameless is he, centered in the sphere
Of common duties, decent not to fail
In offices of tenderness, and pay
Meet adoration to my household gods,
When I am gone. He works his work, I mine.

There lies the port; the vessel puffs her sail;
There gloom the dark, broad seas. My mariners,
Souls that have toiled, and wrought, and thought with me—
That ever with a frolic welcome took
The thunder and the sunshine, and opposed
Free hearts, free foreheads—you and I are old;
Old age hath yet his honor and his toil.
Death closes all; but something ere the end,
Some work of noble note, may yet be done,
Not unbecoming men that strove with Gods.
The lights begin to twinkle from the rocks;
The long day wanes; the slow moon climbs; the deep
Moans round with many voices. Come, my friends,
'Tis not too late to seek a newer world.
Push off, and sitting well in order smite
The sounding furrows; for my purpose holds
To sail beyond the sunset, and the baths
Of all the western stars, until I die.
It may be that the gulfs will wash us down;
It may be we shall touch the Happy Isles,
And see the great Achilles, whom we knew.
Though much is taken, much abides; and though
We are not now that strength which in old days
Moved earth and heaven, that which we are, we are—
One equal temper of heroic hearts,

Made weak by time and fate, but strong in will
To strive, to seek, to find, and not to yield.

1. What is Ulysses' attitude toward his current life?
2. Why is he attracted to adventure this late in his life?
3. How does he use language to appeal to the sailors?

Theodore Roethke (1908–1963)

MY PAPA'S WALTZ

The whiskey on your breath
Could make a small boy dizzy;
But I hung on like death:
Such waltzing was not easy.

We romped until the pans
Slid from the kitchen shelf;
My mother's countenance
Could not unfrown itself.

The hand that held my wrist
Was battered on one knuckle;
At every step you missed
My right ear scraped a buckle.

You beat time on my head
With a palm caked hard by dirt,
Then waltzed me off to bed
Still clinging to your shirt.

1. What is the speaker's attitude toward his father?
2. Judging by the language of the poem, is the speaker's memory of this event positive or negative?

Marnie Walsh

THE RED FOX

A winter day on the prairie
finds me in a bus
going nowhere

though a nowhere
of grey snow
the bus grey also
only the road ahead
real enough
to lead somewhere

It is cold
prairie cold
and the prairie runs grey
up hills not there
runs over the bus and down
crossing the dark windrow
following us

My breath is a wet
circle of existence
against the window
through which I glimpse
the fox
sitting in his singular sunset
the wind sleeking his fur

1. What is the speaker's emotional state before she sees the fox?
2. What effect does seeing the fox have on the speaker?

Seven
Poems in Relationship to Other Poems

Our study of poems in these chapters has focused very closely on how the individual poem operates, and on what the poem tells us about the role of language in our lives. We have looked at poems one by one, each outside the context of its place among other poems, outside the context of the career and life of its author, and outside the historical context of its time. The study of a poem's relationships with all its contexts brings a fuller understanding of the poem. Until now, we have been interested in developing the basic concepts necessary for active reading. But as the next step beyond the isolated poem, let us look at some of the ways a poem can relate to other poems.

Poems in a Book

Many poems are not published individually, but in a book of poems by the same author. Some of these books simply collect together recent poems that the poet has written, but in others the poems are tightly organized, clearly related to one another. In such a case, it's as though the entire book becomes one work of art, and each poem in it plays a part.

Such a collection is William Blake's *Songs of Innocence and of Experience: Shewing the Two Contrary States of the Human Soul*. First published together in 1794, the poems are divided into songs of Innocence and songs of Experience, which Blake thought of as the states of the soul that each person must go through on the way to achieving true selfhood. The poems are intricately related to one another, and in some cases there are matching poems in which a speaker from Innocence and a speaker from Experience consider the same issues. Both sections of the book, for example, contain poems called "Holy Thursday," which allow the two very different speakers to show how they view the same event, a procession of young children who live in orphanages run by the church. The two poems engage in a kind of debate that reveals the opposed states of mind of the speakers.

Poems within each state are also related to each other. In Innocence, for example, the speaker of each poem seems to be at a different stage of Innocence—the speaker of "The Lamb," is an almost purely innocent child; the speaker of "Holy Thursday" is an adult who seems to have held on to his innocence in defiance of experience.

All the poems together serve to define these two states, but in general you could say that Innocence is a trusting, positive view of the world as a benign place, whereas Experience is a more cynical, disillusioned view of the world as a complex place of sorrow, violence, and passion. Each of these poems deserves attention and can be studied in itself, but when they are read together, endless associations open up to the reader who is looking for them.

READINGS

William Blake (1757–1827)

SONGS OF INNOCENCE AND OF EXPERIENCE

Shewing the Two Contrary States of the Human Soul

SONGS OF INNOCENCE

Introduction

Piping down the valleys wild,
Piping songs of pleasant glee,
On a cloud I saw a child,
And he laughing said to me:

"Pipe a song about a Lamb!"
So I piped with merry chear.
"Piper, pipe that song again;"
So I piped: he wept to hear.

"Drop thy pipe, thy happy pipe;
Sing thy songs of happy chear:"
So I sung the same again,
While he wept with joy to hear.

"Piper, sit thee down and write
In a book, that all may read."
So he vanish'd from my sight,
And I pluck'd a hollow reed,

And I made a rural pen,
And I stain'd the water clear,
And I wrote my happy songs
Every child may joy to hear.

The Shepherd

How sweet is the Shepherd's sweet lot!
From the morn to the evening he strays;
He shall follow his sheep all the day,
And his tongue shall be filled with praise.

For he hears the lamb's innocent call,
And he hears the ewe's tender reply;
He is watchful while they are in peace,
For they know when their Shepherd is nigh.

The Ecchoing Green

The Sun does arise,
And make happy the skies;
The merry bells ring
To welcome the Spring;
The skylark and thrush,
The birds of the bush,
Sing louder around
To the bells' chearful sound,
While our sports shall be seen
On the Ecchoing Green.

Old John, with white hair,
Does laugh away care,
Sitting under the oak,
Among the old folk.
They laugh at our play,
And soon they all say:
"Such, such were the joys
When we all, girls & boys,
In our youth time were seen
On the Ecchoing Green."

Till the little ones, weary,
No more can be merry;
The sun does descend,

And our sports have an end.
Round the laps of their mothers
Many sisters and brothers,
Like birds in their nest,
Are ready for rest,
And sport no more seen
On the darkening Green.

The Lamb

Little Lamb, who made thee?
Dost thou know who made thee?
Gave thee life, & bid thee feed
By the stream & o'er the mead;
Gave thee clothing of delight,
Softest clothing, wooly, bright;
Gave thee such a tender voice,
Making all the vales rejoice?
Little Lamb, who made thee?
Dost thou know who made thee?

Little Lamb, I'll tell thee,
Little Lamb, I'll tell thee:
He is called by thy name,
For he calls himself a Lamb.
He is meek, & he is mild;
He became a little child.
I a child, & thou a lamb,
We are called by his name.
Little Lamb, God bless thee!
Little Lamb, God bless thee!

The Little Black Boy

My mother bore me in the southern wild,
And I am black, but O! my soul is white;
White as an angel is the English child,
But I am black, as if bereav'd of light.

My mother taught me underneath a tree,
And sitting down before the heat of day,
She took me on her lap and kissed me,
And pointing to the east, began to say:

"Look on the rising sun: there God does live,
And gives his light, and gives his heat away;
And flowers and trees and beasts and men receive
Comfort in morning, joy in the noonday.

"And we are put on earth a little space,
That we may learn to bear the beams of love;
And these black bodies and this sunburnt face
Is but a cloud, and like a shady grove.

"For when our souls have learn'd the heat to bear,
The cloud will vanish; we shall hear his voice,
Saying: 'Come out from the grove, my love & care,
And round my golden tent like lambs rejoice.' "

Thus did my mother say, and kissed me;
And thus I say to little English boy:
When I from black and he from white cloud free,
And round the tent of God like lambs we joy,

I'll shade him from the heat, till he can bear
To lean in joy upon our father's knee;
And then I'll stand and stroke his silver hair,
And be like him, and he will then love me.

The Blossom

Merry, Merry Sparrow!
Under leaves so green
A happy Blossom
Sees you swift as arrow
Seek your cradle narrow
Near my Bosom.

Pretty, Pretty Robin!
Under leaves so green
A happy Blossom
Hears you sobbing, sobbing,
Pretty, Pretty Robin,
Near my Bosom.

The Chimney Sweeper

When my mother died I was very young,
And my father sold me while yet my tongue
Could scarcely cry " 'weep! 'weep! 'weep! 'weep!"
So your chimneys I sweep, & in soot I sleep.

There's little Tom Dacre, who cried when his head,
That curl'd like a lamb's back, was shav'd: so I said
"Hush, Tom! never mind it, for when your head's bare
You know that the soot cannot spoil your white hair."

And so he was quiet, & that very night,
As Tom was a-sleeping, he had such a sight!

That thousands of sweepers, Dick, Joe, Ned, & Jack,
Were all of them lock'd up in coffins of black.

And by came an Angel who had a bright key,
And he open'd the coffins & set them all free;
Then down a green plain leaping, laughing, they run,
And wash in a river, and shine in the Sun.

Then naked & white, all their bags left behind,
They rise upon clouds and sport in the wind;
And the Angel told Tom, if he'd be a good boy,
He'd have God for his father, & never want joy.

And so Tom awoke; and we rose in the dark,
And got with our bags & our brushes to work.
Tho' the morning was cold, Tom was happy & warm;
So if all do their duty they need not fear harm.

The Little Boy Lost

"Father! father! where are you going?
O do not walk so fast.
Speak, father, speak to your little boy,
Or else I shall be lost."

The night was dark, no father was there;
The child was wet with dew;
The mire was deep, & the child did weep,
And away the vapour flew.

The Little Boy Found

The little boy lost in the lonely fen,
Led by the wand'ring light,
Began to cry; but God, ever nigh,
Appear'd like his father in white.

He kissed the child & by the hand led
And to his mother brought,
Who in sorrow pale, thro' the lonely dale,
Her little boy weeping sought.

Laughing Song

When the green woods laugh with the voice of joy,
And the dimpling stream runs laughing by;
When the air does laugh with our merry wit,
And the green hill laughs with the noise of it;

When the meadows laugh with lively green,
And the grasshopper laughs in the merry scene,

When Mary and Susan and Emily
With their sweet round mouths sing "Ha, Ha, He!"

When the painted birds laugh in the shade,
Where our table with cherries and nuts is spread,
Come live & be merry, and join with me,
To sing the sweet chorus of "Ha, Ha, He!"

A Cradle Song

Sweet dreams, form a shade
O'er my lovely infant's head;
Sweet dreams of pleasant streams
By happy, silent, moony beams.

Sweet sleep, with soft down
Weave thy brows an infant crown.
Sweet sleep, Angel mild,
Hover o'er my happy child.

Sweet smiles, in the night
Hover over my delight;
Sweet smiles, Mother's smiles,
All the livelong night beguiles.

Sweet moans, dovelike sighs,
Chase not slumber from thy eyes.
Sweet moans, sweeter smiles,
All the dovelike moans beguiles.

Sleep, sleep, happy child,
All creation slept and smil'd;
Sleep, sleep, happy sleep,
While o'er thee thy mother weep.

Sweet babe, in thy face
Holy image I can trace.
Sweet babe, once like thee,
Thy maker lay and wept for me,

Wept for me, for thee, for all,
When he was an infant small.
Thou his image ever see,
Heavenly face that smiles on thee,

Smiles on thee, on me, on all;
Who became an infant small.
Infant smiles are his own smiles;
Heaven & earth to peace beguiles.

The Divine Image

To Mercy, Pity, Peace, and Love
All pray in their distress;
And to these virtues of delight
Return their thankfulness.

For Mercy, Pity, Peace, and Love
Is God, our father dear,
And Mercy, Pity, Peace, and Love
Is Man, his child and care.

For Mercy has a human heart,
Pity a human face,
And Love, the human form divine,
And Peace, the human dress.

Then every man, of every clime,
That prays in his distress,
Prays to the human form divine,
Love, Mercy, Pity, Peace.

And all must love the human form,
In heathen, turk, or jew;
Where Mercy, Love, & Pity dwell
There God is dwelling too.

Holy Thursday

'Twas on a Holy Thursday, their innocent faces clean,
The children walking two & two, in red & blue & green,
Grey-headed beadles walk'd before, with wands as white as snow,
Till into the high dome of Paul's they like Thames' waters flow.

O what a multitude they seem'd, these flowers of London town!
Seated in companies they sit with radiance all their own.
The hum of multitudes was there, but multitudes of lambs,
Thousands of little boys & girls raising ther innocent hands.

Now like a mighty wind they raise to heaven the voice of song,
Or like harmonious thunderings the seats of Heaven among.

Beneath them sit the aged men, wise guardians of the poor;
Then cherish pity, lest you drive an angel from your door.

Night

The sun descending in the west,
The evening star does shine;
The birds are silent in their nest,
And I must seek for mine.
The moon like a flower
In heaven's high bower,
With silent delight
Sits and smiles on the night.

Farewell, green fields and happy groves,
Where flocks have took delight.
Where lambs have nibbled, silent moves
The feet of angels bright;
Unseen they pour blessing
And joy without ceasing,
On each bud and blossom,
And each sleeping bosom.

They look in every thoughtless nest,
Where birds are cover'd warm;
They visit caves of every beast,
To keep them all from harm.
If they see any weeping
That should have been sleeping,
They pour sleep on their head,
And sit down by their bed.

When wolves and tygers howl for prey,
They pitying stand and weep;
Seeking to drive their thirst away,
And keep them from the sheep;
But if they rush dreadful,
The angels, most heedful,
Receive each mild spirit,
New worlds to inherit.

And there the lion's ruddy eyes
Shall flow with tears of gold,
And pitying the tender cries,
And walking round the fold,
Saying "Wrath, by his meekness,

And by his health, sickness
Is driven away
From our immortal day.

"And now beside thee, bleating lamb,
I can lie down and sleep;
Or think on him who bore thy name,
Graze after thee and weep.
For, wash'd in life's river,
My bright mane for ever
Shall shine like the gold
As I guard o'er the fold."

Spring

Sound the Flute!
Now it's mute.
Birds delight
Day and Night;
Nightingale
In the dale,
Lark in Sky,
Merrily,
Merrily, Merrily, to welcome in the Year.

Little Boy,
Full of joy;
Little Girl,
Sweet and small;
Cock does crow,
So do you;
Merry voice,
Infant noise,
Merrily, Merrily, to welcome in the Year.

Little Lamb,
Here I am;
Come and lick
My white neck;
Let me pull
Your soft Wool;
Let me kiss
Your soft face:
Merrily, Merrily, we welcome in the Year.

Nurse's Song

When the voices of children are heard on the green
And laughing is heard on the hill,

My heart is at rest within my breast
    And everything else is still.

"Then come home, my children, the sun is gone down
And the dews of night arise;
Come, come, leave off play, and let us away
Till the morning appears in the skies."

"No, no, let us play, for it is yet day
And we cannot go to sleep;
Besides, in the sky the little birds fly
And the hills are all cover'd with sheep."

"Well, well, go & play till the light fades away
And then go home to bed."
The little ones leaped & shouted & laugh'd
    And all the hills ecchoed.

Infant Joy

"I have no name:
I am but two days old."
What shall I call thee?
"I happy am,
Joy is my name."
Sweet joy befall thee!

Pretty joy!
Sweet joy but two days old,
Sweet joy I call thee:
Thou dost smile,
I sing the while,
Sweet joy befall thee!

A Dream

Once a dream did weave a shade
O'er my Angel-guarded bed,
That an Emmet lost its way
Where on grass methought I lay.

Troubled, 'wilder'd, and forlorn,
Dark, benighted, travel-worn,
Over many a tangled spray,
All heart-broke I heard her say:

"O, my children! do they cry?
Do they hear their father sigh?
Now they look abroad to see:
Now return and weep for me."

Pitying, I drop'd a tear;
But I saw a glow-worm near,
Who replied: "What wailing wight
Calls the watchman of the night?

"I am set to light the ground,
While the beetle goes his round:
Follow now the beetle's hum;
Little wanderer, hie thee home."

On Another's Sorrow

Can I see another's woe
And not be in sorrow too?
Can I see another's grief,
And not seek for kind relief?

Can I see a falling tear,
And not feel my sorrow's share?
Can a father see his child
Weep, nor be with sorrow fill'd?

Can a mother sit and hear
An infant groan an infant fear?
No, no! never can it be!
Never, never can it be!

And can he who smiles on all
Hear the wren with sorrows small,
Hear the small bird's grief & care,
Hear the woes that infants bear,

And not sit beside the nest,
Pouring pity in their breast;
And not sit the cradle near,
Weeping tear on infant's tear;

And not sit both night & day,
Wiping all our tears away?
O, no! never can it be!
Never, never can it be!

He doth give his joy to all;
He becomes an infant small;
He becomes a man of woe;
He doth feel the sorrow too.

Think not thou canst sigh a sigh
And thy maker is not by;

Think not thou canst weep a tear
And thy maker is not near.

O! he gives to us his joy
That our grief he may destroy;
Till our grief is fled & gone
He doth sit by us and moan.

SONGS OF EXPERIENCE

Introduction

Hear the voice of the Bard!
Who Present, Past, & Future, sees;
Whose ears have heard
The Holy Word
That walk'd among the ancient trees,

Calling the lapsed Soul,
And weeping in the evening dew;
That might controll
The starry pole,
And fallen, fallen light renew!

"O Earth, O Earth, return!
Arise from out the dewy grass;
Night is worn,
And the morn
Rises from the slumberous mass.

"Turn away no more;
Why wilt thou turn away?
The starry floor,
The wat'ry shore,
Is giv'n thee till the break of day."

Earth's Answer

Earth rais'd up her head
From the darkness dread & drear.
Her light fled,
Stony dread!
And her locks cover'd with grey despair.

"Prison'd on wat'ry shore,
Starry Jealousy does keep my den:
Cold and hoar,
Weeping o'er,
I hear the father of the ancient men.

"Selfish father of men!
Cruel, jealous, selfish fear!
Can delight,
Chain'd in night,
The virgins of youth and morning bear?

"Does spring hide its joy
When buds and blossoms grow?
Does the sower
Sow by night,
Or the plowman in darkness plow?

"Break this heavy chain
That does freeze my bones around.
Selfish! vain!
Eternal bane!
That free Love with bondage bound."

The Clod and the Pebble

"Love seeketh not Itself to please,
Nor for itself hath any care,
But for another gives its ease,
And builds a Heaven in Hell's despair."

So sung a little Clod of Clay
Trodden with the cattle's feet,
But a Pebble of the brook
Warbled out these metres meet:

"Love seeketh only Self to please,
To bind another to Its delight,
Joys in another's loss of ease,
And builds a Hell in Heaven's despite."

Holy Thursday

Is this a holy thing to see
In a rich and fruitful land,
Babes reduc'd to misery,
Fed with cold and usurous hand?

Is that trembling cry a song?
Can it be a song of joy?
And so many children poor?
It is a land of poverty!

And their sun does never shine,
And their fields are bleak & bare,

And their ways are fill'd with thorns:
It is eternal winter there.

For where-e'er the sun does shine,
And where-e'er the rain does fall,
Babe can never hunger there,
Nor poverty the mind appall.

The Little Girl Lost

In futurity
I prophetic see
That the earth from sleep
(Grave the sentence deep)

Shall arise and seek
For her maker meek;
And the desart wild
Become a garden mild.

* * *

In the southern clime,
Where the summer's prime
Never fades away,
Lovely Lyca lay.

Seven summers old
Lovely Lyca told;
She had wander'd long
Hearing wild birds' song.

"Sweet sleep, come to me
Underneath this tree.
Do father, mother weep,
Where can Lyca sleep?

"Lost in desart wild
Is your little child.
How can Lyca sleep
If her mother weep?

"If her heart does ake
Then let Lyca wake;
If my mother sleep,
Lyca shall not weep.

"Frowning, frowning night,
O'er this desart bright

Let thy moon arise
While I close my eyes."

Sleeping Lyca lay
While the beasts of prey,
Come from caverns deep,
View'd the maid asleep.

The kingly lion stood
And the virgin view'd,
Then he gamboll'd round
O'er the hallow'd ground.

Leopards, tygers, play
Round her as she lay,
While the lion old
Bow'd his mane of gold

And her bosom lick,
And upon her neck
From his eyes of flame
Ruby tears there came;

While the lioness
Loos'd her slender dress,
And naked they convey'd
To caves the sleeping maid.

The Little Girl Found

All the night in woe
Lyca's parents go
Over vallies deep,
While the desarts weep.

Tired and woe-begone,
Hoarse with making moan,
Arm in arm seven days
They trac'd the desart ways.

Seven nights they sleep
Among shadows deep,
And dream they see their child
Starv'd in desart wild.

Pale, thro' pathless ways
The fancied image strays
Famish'd, weeping, weak,
With hollow piteous shriek.

Rising from unrest,
The trembling woman prest
With feet of weary woe:
She could no further go.

In his arms he bore
Her, arm'd with sorrow sore;
Till before their way
A couching lion lay.

Turning back was vain:
Soon his heavy mane
Bore them to the ground.
Then he stalk'd around,

Smelling to his prey;
But their fears allay
When he licks their hands,
And silent by them stands.

They look upon his eyes
Fill'd with deep surprise,
And wondering behold
A spirit arm'd in gold.

On his head a crown,
On his shoulders down
Flow'd his golden hair.
Gone was all their care.

"Follow me," he said;
"Weep not for the maid;
In my palace deep
Lyca lies asleep."

Then they followed
Where the vision led,
And saw their sleeping child
Among tygers wild.

To this day they dwell
In a lonely dell;
Nor fear the wolvish howl
Nor the lions' growl.

The Chimney Sweeper

A little black thing among the snow,
Crying "weep! 'weep!' in notes of woe!
"Where are thy father & mother? say?"
"They are both gone up to the church to pray.

"Because I was happy upon the heath,
And smil'd among the winter's snow,
They clothed me in the clothes of death,
And taught me to sing the notes of woe.

"And because I am happy & dance & sing,
They think they have done me no injury,
And are gone to praise God & his Priest & King,
Who make up a heaven of our misery."

Nurse's Song

When the voices of children are heard on the green
And whisp'rings are in the dale,
The days of my youth rise fresh in my mind,
My face turns green and pale.

Then come home, my children, the sun is gone down,
And the dews of night arise;
Your spring & your day are wasted in play,
And your winter and night in disguise.

The Sick Rose

O Rose, thou art sick!
The invisible worm
That flies in the night,
In the howling storm,

Has found out thy bed
Of crimson joy,
And his dark secret love
Does thy life destroy.

The Fly

Little Fly,
Thy summer's play
My thoughtless hand
Has brush'd away.

Am not I
A fly like thee?
Or art not thou
A man like me?

For I dance,
And drink, & sing,
Till some blind hand
Shall brush my wing.

If thought is life
And strength & breath,
And the want
Of thought is death;

Then am I
A happy fly,
If I live
Of if I die.

The Angel

I dreamt a Dream! what can it mean?
And that I was a maiden Queen,
Guarded by an Angel mild:
Witless woe was ne'er beguil'd!

And I wept both night and day,
And he wip'd my tears away,
And I wept both day and night,
And hid from him my heart's delight.

So he took his wings and fled;
Then the morn blush'd rosy red;
I dried my tears, & arm'd my fears
With ten thousand shields and spears.

Soon my Angel came again:
I was arm'd, he came in vain;
For the time of youth was fled,
And grey hairs were on my head.

The Tyger

Tyger! Tyger! burning bright
In the forests of the night,
What immortal hand or eye
Could frame thy fearful symmetry?

In what distant deeps or skies
Burnt the fire of thine eyes?
On what wings dare he aspire?
What the hand dare sieze the fire?

And what shoulder, & what art,
Could twist the sinews of thy heart?
And when thy heart began to beat,
What dread hand? & what dread feet?

What the hammer? what the chain?
In what furnace was thy brain?

What the anvil? what dread grasp
Dare its deadly terrors clasp?

When the stars threw down their spears,
And water'd heaven with their tears,
Did he smile his work to see?
Did he who made the Lamb make thee?

Tyger! Tyger! burning bright
In the forests of the night,
What immortal hand or eye,
Dare frame thy fearful symmetry?

My Pretty Rose-tree

A flower was offer'd to me,
Such a flower as May never bore;
But I said "I've a Pretty Rose-tree,"
And I passed the sweet flower o'er.

Then I went to my Pretty Rose-tree,
To tend her by day and by night;
But my Rose turn'd away with jealousy,
And her thorns were my only delight.

Ah! Sun-flower

Ah, Sun-flower! weary of time,
Who countest the steps of the Sun,
Seeking after that sweet golden clime
Where the traveller's journey is done:

Where the Youth pined away with desire,
And the pale Virgin shrouded in snow
Arise from their graves, and aspire
Where my Sun-flower wishes to go.

The Lilly

The modest Rose puts forth a thorn,
The humble Sheep a threat'ning horn;
While the Lilly white shall in Love delight,
Nor a thorn, nor a threat, stain her beauty bright.

The Garden of Love

I went to the Garden of Love,
And saw what I never had seen:
A Chapel was built in the midst,
Where I used to play on the green.

And the gates of this Chapel were shut,
And "Thou shalt not" writ over the door;
So I turn'd to the Garden of Love
That so many sweet flowers bore;

And I saw it was filled with graves,
And tomb-stones where flowers should be;
And Priests in black gowns were walking their rounds,
And binding with briars my joys & desires.

The Little Vagabond

Dear Mother, dear Mother, the Church is cold,
But the Ale-house is healthy & pleasant & warm;
Besides I can tell where I am used well,
Such usage in Heaven will never do well.

But if at the Church they would give us some Ale,
And a pleasant fire our souls to regale,
We'd sing and we'd pray all the live-long day,
Nor ever once wish from the Church to stray.

Then the Parson might preach, & drink, & sing,
And we'd be as happy as birds in the spring;
And modest Dame Lurch, who is always at Church,
Would not have bandy children, nor fasting, nor birch.

And God, like a father rejoicing to see
His children as pleasant and happy as he,
Would have no more quarrel with the Devil or the Barrel,
But kiss him, & give him both drink and apparel.

London

I wander thro' each charter'd street,
Near where the charter'd Thames does flow,
And mark in every face I meet
Marks of weakness, marks of woe.

In every cry of every Man,
In every Infant's cry of fear,
In every voice, in every ban,
The mind-forg'd manacles I hear.

How the Chimney-sweeper's cry
Every black'ning Church appalls;
And the hapless Soldier's sigh
Runs in blood down Palace walls.

But most thro' midnight streets I hear
How the youthful Harlot's curse

Blasts the new born Infant's tear,
And blights with plagues the Marriage hearse.

The Human Abstract

Pity would be no more
If we did not make somebody Poor;
And Mercy no more could be
If all were as happy as we.

And mutual fear brings peace,
Till the selfish loves increase:
Then Cruelty knits a snare,
And spreads his baits with care.

He sits down with holy fears,
And waters the ground with tears;
Then Humility takes its root
Underneath his foot.

Soon spreads the dismal shade
Of Mystery over his head;
And the Catterpiller and Fly
Feed on the Mystery.

And it bears the fruit of Deceit,
Ruddy and sweet to eat;
And the Raven his nest has made
In its thickest shade.

The Gods of the earth and sea
Sought thro' Nature to find this Tree;
But their search was all in vain:
There grows one in the Human Brain.

A Poison Tree

I was angry with my friend:
I told my wrath, my wrath did end.
I was angry with my foe:
I told it not, my wrath did grow.

And I water'd it in fears,
Night & morning with my tears;
And I sunned it with smiles,
And with soft deceitful wiles.

And it grew both day and night,
Till it bore an apple bright;
And my foe beheld it shine,
And he knew that it was mine,

And into my garden stole
When the night had veil'd the pole:
In the morning glad I see
My foe outstretch'd beneath the tree.

A Little Boy Lost

"Nought loves another as itself,
Nor venerates another so,
Nor is it possible to Thought
A greater than itself to know:

"And Father, how can I love you
Or any of my brothers more?
I love you like the little bird
That picks up crumbs around the door."

The Priest sat by and heard the child,
In trembling zeal he siez'd his hair:
He led him by his little coat,
And all admir'd the Priestly care.

And standing on the altar high,
"Lo! what a fiend is here!" said he,
"One who sets reason up for judge
Of our most holy Mystery."

The weeping child could not be heard,
The weeping parents wept in vain;
They strip'd him to his little shirt,
And bound him in an iron chain;

And burn'd him in a holy place,
Where many had been burn'd before:
The weeping parents wept in vain.
Are such things done on Albion's shore?

A Little Girl Lost

Children of the future Age
Reading this indignant page,
Know that in a former time
Love! sweet Love! was thought a crime.

In the Age of Gold,
Free from winter's cold,
Youth and maiden bright
To the holy light,
Naked in the sunny beams delight.

Once a youthful pair,
Fill'd with softest care,
Met in garden bright
Where the holy light
Had just remov'd the curtains of the night.

There, in rising day,
On the grass they play;
Parents were afar,
Strangers came not near,
And the maiden soon forgot her fear.

Tired with kisses sweet,
They agree to meet
When the silent sleep
Waves o'er heaven's deep,
And the weary tired wanderers weep.

To her father white
Came the maiden bright;
But his loving look,
Like the holy book,
All her tender limbs with terror shook.

"Ona! pale and weak!
To thy father speak:
O, the trembling fear!
O, the dismal care!
That shakes the blossoms of my hoary hair."

To Tirzah

Whate'er is Born of Mortal Birth
Must be consumed with the Earth
To rise from Generation free:
Then what have I to do with thee?

The Sexes sprung from Shame & Pride,
Blow'd in the morn; in evening died;
But Mercy chang'd Death into Sleep;
The Sexes rose to work & weep.

Thou, Mother of my Mortal part,
With cruelty didst mould my Heart,
And with false self-decieving tears
Didst bind my Nostrils, Eyes, & Ears:

Didst close my Tongue in senseless clay,
And me to Mortal Life betray.

The Death of Jesus set me free:
Then what have I to do with thee?

The Schoolboy

I love to rise in a summer morn
When the birds sing on every tree;
The distant huntsman winds his horn,
And the sky-lark sings with me.
O! what sweet company.

But to go to school in a summer morn,
O! it drives all joy away;
Under a cruel eye outworn,
The little ones spend the day
In sighing and dismay.

Ah! then at times I drooping sit,
And spend many an anxious hour,
Nor in my book can I take delight,
Nor sit in learning's bower,
Worn thro' with the dreary shower.

How can the bird that is born for joy
Sit in a cage and sing?
How can a child, when fears annoy,
But droop his tender wing,
And forget his youthful spring?

O! father & mother, if buds are nip'd
And blossoms blown away,
And if the tender plants are strip'd
Of their joy in the springing day,
By sorrow and care's dismay,

How shall the summer arise in joy,
Or the summer fruits appear?
Or how shall we gather what griefs destroy,
Or bless the mellowing year,
When the blasts of winter appear?

The Voice of the Ancient Bard

Youth of delight, come hither,
And see the opening morn,
Image of truth new born.
Doubt is fled, & clouds of reason,
Dark disputes & artful teazing.
Folly is an endless maze,
Tangled roots perplex her ways.

How many have fallen there!
They stumble all night over bones of the dead,
And feel they know not what but care,
And wish to lead others, when they should be led.

A Divine Image

Cruelty has a Human Heart,
And Jealousy a Human Face;
Terror the Human Form Divine,
And Secrecy the Human Dress.

The Human Dress is forged Iron,
The Human Form a fiery Forge,
The Human Face a Furnace seal'd,
The Human Heart its hungry Gorge.

Poems in a Career

Poems can also be related to one another because their authors have produced a career full of clearly related poems. All seem to come from the same mind, as it reacts to new circumstances over the span of a human life.

In this section are presented several poems from the career of an Irish poet of the late nineteenth and early twentieth centuries, William Butler Yeats, who many people feel is the greatest poet of this century. Yeats's poetry deals with a wide range of topics—love, politics, occult spirituality, death, aging, imagination. His poems also range over his entire life, from youth to old age, and the poems reflect attempts to deal with key events in human life—youthful passion, adult responsibility, the recognition of mortality, death.

But the poems also have much in common. The mind behind each poem seems similar to the mind behind all the others. They show a similar approach to language. Often they produce a similar music. Reading them together should point up both their similarities and their differences and help us produce meanings that we couldn't produce if we read them in isolation.

READINGS

William Butler Yeats (1865–1939)

THE STOLEN CHILD

Where dips the rocky highland
Of Sleuth Wood in the lake,

There lies a leafy island
Where flapping herons wake
The drowsy water-rats;
There we've hid our faery vats,
Full of berries
And of reddest stolen cherries.
Come away, O human child!
To the waters and the wild
With a faery, hand in hand,
For the world's more full of weeping than you can understand.

Where the wave of moonlight glosses
The dim grey sands with light,
Far off by furthest Rosses
We foot it all the night,
Weaving olden dances,
Mingling hands and mingling glances
Till the moon has taken flight;
To and fro we leap
And chase the frothy bubbles,
While the world is full of troubles
And is anxious in its sleep.
Come away, O human child!
To the waters and the wild
With a faery, hand in hand,
For the world's more full of weeping than you can understand.

Where the wandering water gushes
From the hills above Glen-Car,
In pools among the rushes
That scarce could bathe a star,
We seek for slumbering trout
And whispering in their ears
Give them unquiet dreams;
Leaning softly out
From ferns that drop their tears
Over the young streams.
Come away, O human child!
To the waters and the wild
With a faery, hand in hand,
For the world's more full of weeping than you can understand.

Away with us he's going,
The solemn-eyed:
He'll hear no more the lowing
Of the calves on the warm hillside
Or the kettle on the hob

Sing peace into his breast,
Or see the brown mice bob
Round and round the oatmeal-chest.
For he comes, the human child,
To the waters and the wild
With a faery, hand in hand,
From a world more full of weeping than he can understand.

THE LAKE ISLE OF INNISFREE

I will arise and go now, and go to Innisfree,
And a small cabin build there, of clay and wattles made;
Nine bean-rows will I have there, a hive for the honey-bee,
And live alone in the bee-loud glade.

And I shall have some peace there, for peace comes dropping slow,
Dropping from the veils of the morning to where the cricket sings;
There midnight's all a glimmer, and noon a purple glow,
And evening full of the linnet's wings.

I will arise and go now, for always night and day
I hear lake water lapping with low sounds by the shore;
While I stand on the roadway, or on the pavements grey,
I hear it in the deep heart's core.

WHO GOES WITH FERGUS?

Who will go drive with Fergus now,
And pierce the deep wood's woven shade,
And dance upon the level shore?
Young man, lift up your russet brow,
And lift your tender eyelids, maid,
And brood on hopes and fear no more.

And no more turn aside and brood
Upon love's bitter mystery;
For Fergus rules the brazen cars,
And rules the shadows of the wood,
And the white breast of the dim sea
And all dishevelled wandering stars.

EASTER 1916

I have met them at close of day
Coming with vivid faces
From counter or desk among grey
Eighteenth-century houses.
I have passed with a nod of the head
Or polite meaningless words,
Or have lingered awhile and said
Polite meaningless words,
And thought before I had done
Of a mocking tale or a gibe
To please a companion
Around the fire at the club,
Being certain that they and I
But lived where motley is worn:
All changed, changed utterly:
A terrible beauty is born.

That woman's days were spent
In ignorant good-will,
Her nights in argument
Until her voice grew shrill.
What voice more sweet than hers
When, young and beautiful,
She rode to harriers?
This man had kept a school
And rode our wingèd horse;
This other his helper and friend
Was coming into his force;
He might have won fame in the end,
So sensitive his nature seemed,
So daring and sweet his thought.
This other man I had dreamed
A drunken, vainglorious lout.
He had done most bitter wrong
To some who are near my heart,
Yet I number him in the song;
He, too, has resigned his part
In the casual comedy;
He, too, has been changed in his turn,
Transformed utterly:
A terrible beauty is born.

Hearts with one purpose alone
Through summer and winter seem

Enchanted to a stone
To trouble the living stream.
The horse that comes from the road,
The rider, the birds that range
From cloud to tumbling cloud,
Minute by minute they change;
A shadow of cloud on the stream
Changes minute by minute;
A horse-hoof slides on the brim,
And a horse plashes within it;
The long-legged moor-hens dive,
And hens to moor-cocks call;
Minute by minute they live:
The stone's in the midst of all.

Too long a sacrifice
Can make a stone of the heart.
O when may it suffice?
That is Heaven's part, our part
To murmur name upon name,
As a mother names her child
When sleep at last has come
On limbs that had run wild.
What is it but nightfall?
No, no, not night but death;
Was it needless death after all?
For England may keep faith
For all that is done and said.
We know their dream; enough
To know they dreamed and are dead;
And what if excess of love
Bewildered them till they died?
I write it out in a verse—
MacDonagh and MacBride
And Connolly and Pearse
Now and in time to be,
Wherever green is worn,
Are changed, changed utterly:
A terrible beauty is born.

THE FISHERMAN

Although I can see him still,
The freckled man who goes

To a grey place on a hill
In grey Connemara clothes
At dawn to cast his flies,
It's long since I began
To call up to the eyes
This wise and simple man.
All day I'd looked in the face
What I had hoped 'twould be
To write for my own race
And the reality;
The living men that I hate,
The dead man that I loved,
The craven man in his seat,
The insolent unreproved,
And no knave brought to book
Who has won a drunken cheer,
The witty man and his joke
Aimed at the commonest ear,
The clever man who cries
The catch-cries of the clown,
The beating down of the wise
And great Art beaten down.

Maybe a twelvemonth since
Suddenly I began,
In scorn of this audience,
Imagining a man,
And his sun-freckled face,
And grey Connemara cloth,
Climbing up to a place
Where stone is dark under froth,
And the down-turn of his wrist
When the flies drop in the stream;
A man who does not exist,
A man who is but a dream;
And cried, 'Before I am old
I shall have written him one
Poem maybe as cold
And passionate as the dawn.'

ADAM'S CURSE

We sat together at one summer's end,
That beautiful mild woman, your close friend,
And you and I, and talked of poetry.

I said: "A line will take us hours maybe;
Yet if it does not seem a moment's thought,
Our stitching and unstitching has been naught.
Better go down upon your marrow-bones
And scrub a kitchen pavement, or break stones
Like an old pauper, in all kinds of weather;
For to articulate sweet sounds together
Is to work harder than all these, and yet
Be thought an idler by the noisy set
Of bankers, schoolmasters, and clergymen
The martyrs call the world."

And thereupon
That beautiful mild woman for whose sake
There's many a one shall find out all heartache
On finding that her voice is sweet and low
Replied: "To be born woman is to know—
Although they do not talk of it at school—
That we must labour to be beautiful."

I said: "It's certain there is no fine thing
Since Adam's fall but needs much labouring.
There have been lovers who thought love should be
So much compounded of high courtesy
That they would sigh and quote with learned looks
Precedents out of beautiful old books;
Yet now it seems an idle trade enough."

We sat grown quiet at the name of love;
We saw the last embers of daylight die,
And in the trembling blue-green of the sky
A moon, worn as if it had been a shell
Washed by time's waters as they rose and fell
About the stars and broke in days and years.

I had a thought for no one's but your ears:
That you were beautiful, and that I strove
To love you in the old high way of love;
That it had all seemed happy, and yet we'd grown
As weary-hearted as that hollow moon.

THE FOLLY OF BEING COMFORTED

One that is ever kind said yesterday:
"Your well-belovèd's hair has threads of grey,
And little shadows come about her eyes;

Time can but make it easier to be wise
Though now it seem impossible, and so
All that you need is patience."
                                        Heart cries, "No,
I have not a crumb of comfort, not a grain.
Time can but make her beauty over again:
Because of that great nobleness of hers
The fire that stirs about her, when she stirs,
Burns but more clearly. O she had not these ways
When all the wild summer was in her gaze."

O heart! O heart! if she'd but turn her head,
You'd know the folly of being comforted.

THE WILD SWANS AT COOLE

The trees are in their autumn beauty,
The woodland paths are dry,
Under the October twilight the water
Mirrors a still sky;
Upon the brimming water among the stones
Are nine-and-fifty swans.

The nineteenth autumn has come upon me
Since I first made my count;
I saw, before I had well finished,
All suddenly mount
And scatter wheeling in great broken rings
Upon their clamorous wings.

I have looked upon those brilliant creatures,
And now my heart is sore.
All's changed since I, hearing at twilight,
The first time on this shore,
The bell-beat of their wings above my head,
Trod with a lighter tread.

Unwearied still, lover by lover,
They paddle in the cold
Companionable streams or climb the air;
Their hearts have not grown old;
Passion or conquest, wander where they will,
Attend upon them still.

But now they drift on the still water,
Mysterious, beautiful;

Among what rushes will they build,
By what lake's edge or pool
Delight men's eyes when I awake some day
To find they have flown away?

THE SECOND COMING

Turning and turning in the widening gyre
The falcon cannot hear the falconer;
Things fall apart; the center cannot hold;
Mere anarchy is loosed upon the world,
The blood-dimmed tide is loosed, and everywhere
The ceremony of innocence is drowned;
The best lack all conviction, while the worst
Are full of passionate intensity.

Surely some revelation is at hand;
Surely the Second Coming is at hand.
The Second Coming! Hardly are those words out
When a vast image out of *Spiritus Mundi*
Troubles my sight: somewhere in sands of the desert
A shape with lion body and the head of a man,
A gaze blank and pitiless as the sun,
Is moving its slow thighs, while all about it
Reel shadows of the indignant desert birds.
The darkness drops again; but now I know
That twenty centuries of stony sleep
Were vexed to nightmare by a rocking cradle,
And what rough beast, its hour come round at last,
Slouches towards Bethlehem to be born?

A PRAYER FOR MY DAUGHTER

Once more the storm is howling, and half hid
Under this cradle-hood and coverlid
My child sleeps on. There is no obstacle
But Gregory's wood and one bare hill
Whereby the haystack- and roof-levelling wind,
Bred on the Atlantic, can be stayed;
And for an hour I have walked and prayed
Because of the great gloom that is in my mind.

I have walked and prayed for this young child an hour
And heard the sea-wind scream upon the tower,
And under the arches of the bridge, and scream
In the elms above the flooded stream;
Imagining in excited reverie
That the future years had come,
Dancing to a frenzied drum,
Out of the murderous innocence of the sea.

May she be granted beauty and yet not
Beauty to make a stranger's eye distraught,
Or hers before a looking-glass, for such,
Being made beautiful overmuch,
Consider beauty a sufficient end,
Lose natural kindness and maybe
The heart-revealing intimacy
That chooses right, and never find a friend.

Helen being chosen found life flat and dull
And later had much trouble from a fool,
While that great Queen, that rose out of the spray,
Being fatherless could have her way
Yet chose a bandy-leggèd smith for man.
It's certain that fine women eat
A crazy salad with their meat
Whereby the Horn of Plenty is undone.

In courtesy I'd have her chiefly learned;
Hearts are not had as a gift but hearts are earned
By those that are not entirely beautiful;
Yet many, that have played the fool
For beauty's very self, has charm made wise,
And many a poor man that has roved,
Loved and thought himself beloved,
From a glad kindness cannot take his eyes.

May she become a flourishing hidden tree
That all her thoughts may like the linnet be,
And have no business but dispensing round
Their magnanimities of sound,
Not but in merriment begin a chase,
Nor but in merriment a quarrel.
O may she live like some green laurel
Rooted in one dear perpetual place.

My mind, because the minds that I have loved,
The sort of beauty that I have approved,

Prosper but little, has dried up of late,
Yet knows that to be choked with hate
May well be of all evil chances chief.
If there's no hatred in a mind
Assault and battery of the wind
Can never tear the linnet from the leaf.

An intellectual hatred is the worst,
So let her think opinions are accursed.
Have I not seen the loveliest woman born
Out of the mouth of Plenty's horn,
Because of her opinionated mind
Barter that horn and every good
By quiet natures understood
For an old bellows full of angry wind?

Considering that, all hatred driven hence,
The soul recovers radical innocence
And learns at last that it is self-delighting,
Self-appeasing, self-affrighting,
And that its own sweet will is Heaven's will;
She can, though every face should scowl
And every windy quarter howl
Or every bellows burst, be happy still.

And may her bridegroom bring her to a house
Where all's accustomed, ceremonious;
For arrogance and hatred are the wares
Peddled in the thoroughfares.
How but in custom and in ceremony
Are innocence and beauty born?
Ceremony's a name for the rich horn,
And custom for the spreading laurel tree.

SAILING TO BYZANTIUM

1

That is no country for old men. The young
In one another's arms, birds in the trees
—Those dying generations—at their song,
The salmon-falls, the mackerel-crowded seas,
Fish, flesh, or fowl, commend all summer long
Whatever is begotten, born, and dies.
Caught in that sensual music all neglect
Monuments of unageing intellect.

2

An aged man is but a paltry thing,
A tattered coat upon a stick, unless
Soul clap its hands and sing, and louder sing
For every tatter in its mortal dress,
Nor is there singing school but studying
Monuments of its own magnificence;
And therefore I have sailed the seas and come
To the holy city of Byzantium.

3

O sages standing in God's holy fire
As in the gold mosaic of a wall,
Come from the holy fire, perne in a gyre,
And be the singing-masters of my soul.
Consume my heart away; sick with desire
And fastened to a dying animal
It knows not what it is; and gather me
Into the artifice of eternity.

4

Once out of nature I shall never take
My bodily form from any natural thing,
But such a form as Grecian goldsmiths make
Of hammered gold and gold enamelling
To keep a drowsy Emperor awake;
Or set upon a golden bough to sing
To lords and ladies of Byzantium
Of what is past, or passing, or to come.

LEDA AND THE SWAN

A sudden blow: the great wings beating still
Above the staggering girl, her thighs caressed
By the dark webs, her nape caught in his bill,
He holds her helpless breast upon his breast.

How can those terrified vague fingers push
The feathered glory from her loosening thighs?
And how can body, laid in that white rush,
But feel the strange heart beating where it lies?

A shudder in the loins engenders there
The broken wall, the burning roof and tower

And Agamemnon dead.
                                        Being so caught up,
So mastered by the brute blood of the air,
Did she put on his knowledge with his power
Before the indifferent beak could let her drop?

CRAZY JANE TALKS WITH THE BISHOP

I met the Bishop on the road
And much said he and I.
"Those breasts are flat and fallen now,
Those veins must soon be dry;
Live in a heavenly mansion,
Not in some foul sty."

"Fair and foul are near of kin,
And fair needs foul," I cried.
"My friends are gone, but that's a truth
Nor grave nor bed denied,
Learned in bodily lowliness
And in the heart's pride.

"A woman can be proud and stiff
When on love intent;
But Love has pitched his mansion in
The place of excrement;
For nothing can be sole or whole
That has not been rent."

LAPIS LAZULI

(For Harry Clifton)

I have heard that hysterical women say
They are sick of the palette and fiddle-bow,
Of poets that are always gay,
For everybody knows or else should know
That if nothing drastic is done
Aeroplane and Zeppelin will come out,
Pitch like King Billy bomb-balls in
Until the town lie beaten flat.

All perform their tragic play,
There struts Hamlet, there is Lear,

That's Ophelia, that Cordelia;
Yet they, should the last scene be there,
The great stage curtain about to drop,
If worthy their prominent part in the play,
Do not break up their lines to weep.
They know that Hamlet and Lear are gay;
Gaiety transfiguring all that dread.
All men have aimed at, found and lost;
Black out; Heaven blazing into the head:
Tragedy wrought to its uttermost.
Though Hamlet rambles and Lear rages,
And all the drop-scenes drop at once
Upon a hundred thousand stages,
It cannot grow by an inch or an ounce.

On their own feet they came, or on shipboard,
Camel-back, horse-back, ass-back, mule-back,
Old civilisations put to the sword.
Then they and their wisdom went to rack:
No handiwork of Callimachus,
Who handled marble as if it were bronze,
Made draperies that seemed to rise
When sea-wind swept the corner, stands;
His long lamp-chimney shaped like the stem
Of a slender palm, stood but a day;
All things fall and are built again,
And those that build them again are gay.

Two Chinamen, behind them a third,
Are carved in lapis lazuli,
Over them flies a long-legged bird,
A symbol of longevity;
The third, doubtless a serving-man,
Carries a musical instrument.

Every discolouration of the stone,
Every accidental crack or dent,
Seems a water-course or an avalanche,
Or lofty slope where it still snows
Though doubtless plum or cherry-branch
Sweetens the little half-way house
Those Chinamen climb towards, and I
Delight to imagine them seated there;
There, on the mountain and the sky,
On all the tragic scene they stare.
One asks for mournful melodies;

Accomplished fingers begin to play.
Their eyes mid many wrinkles, their eyes,
Their ancient, glittering eyes, are gay.

THE WILD OLD WICKED MAN

'Because I am mad about women
I am mad about the hills,'
Said that wild old wicked man
Who travels where God wills.
'Not to die on the straw at home,
Those hands to close these eyes,
That is all I ask, my dear,
From the old man in the skies.
Daybreak and a candle-end.

'Kind are all your words, my dear,
Do not the rest withhold.
Who can know the year, my dear,
When an old man's blood grows cold?
I have what no young man can have
Because he loves too much.
Words I have that can pierce the heart,
But what can he do but touch?'
Daybreak and a candle-end.

Then said she to that wild old man,
His stout stick under his hand,
'Love to give or to withhold
Is not at my command.
I gave it all to an older man:
That old man in the skies.
Hands that are busy with His beads
Can never close those eyes.'
Daybreak and a candle-end.

'Go your ways, O go your ways,
I choose another mark,
Girls down on the seashore
Who understand the dark;
Bawdy talk for the fishermen;
A dance for the fisher-lads;
When dark hangs upon the water
They turn down their beds.
Daybreak and a candle-end.

'A young man in the dark am I,
But a wild old man in the light,
That can make a cat laugh, or
Can touch by mother wit
Things hid in their marrow-bones
From time long passed away,
Hid from all those warty lads
That by their bodies lay.
Daybreak and a candle-end.

'All men live in suffering,
I know as few can know,
Whether they take the upper road
Or stay content on the low,
Rower bent in his row-boat
Or weaver bent at his loom,
Horesman erect upon horseback
Or child hid in the womb.
Daybreak and a candle-end.

'That some stream of lightning
From the old man in the skies
Can burn out that suffering
No right-taught man denies.
But a coarse old man am I,
I choose the second-best,
I forget it all awhile
Upon a woman's breast.'
Daybreak and a candle-end.

LONG-LEGGED FLY

That civilisation may not sink,
Its great battle lost,
Quiet the dog, tether the pony
To a distant post;
Our master Caesar is in the tent
Where the maps are spread,
His eye fixed upon nothing,
A hand under his head.
Like a long-legged fly upon the stream
His mind moves upon silence.

That the topless towers be burnt
And men recall that face,

Move most gently if move you must
In this lonely place.
She thinks, part woman, three parts a child,
That nobody looks; her feet
Practice a tinker shuffle
Picked up on a street.
Like a long-legged fly upon the stream
Her mind moves upon silence.

That girls at puberty may find
The first Adam in their thought,
Shut the door of the Pope's chapel,
Keep those children out.
There on that scaffolding reclines
Michael Angelo.
With no more sound than the mice make
His hand moves to and fro.
Like a long-legged fly upon the stream
His mind moves upon silence.

Poems in Conversation

In a sense, all the poems in English are related to one another in that they share the same language. Of course English has changed over time, and it differs in various subcultures and geographical regions, but all who use the language share some basic frameworks for looking at the world. So we can think of poems as engaging in infinite conversations over time with other poems. They use the same words —even if their meanings have changed over time. They face the same issues—war or death or politics or spirituality—even if they do so each in a way unique to its own time and place. Earlier poems influence later ones. When a poet writes on a certain issue, he or she is aware that earlier poems have dealt with these issues as well, and in some ways their poems are answers to, or arguments with, those earlier poems.

Readers who spend a lot of time reading poetry begin to hear these conversations, and in fact enter into them. Since we readers play such a large role in producing the meaning of the poem, we are ourselves part of this web of relationships. We share the same language, we engage in this collective and often argumentative effort at making sense of the world.

The poems that follow are related to each other in this way. They are of course very different, written by poets of different times and places, but each seems an answer to the other, each seems to have the others in mind. Now, each of these poems is also very complex in itself. It takes a serious reading effort to participate in any one of them.

If we then ask how one of these is related to the others, we must be prepared for an extra effort as things get complicated.

To probe the relationships, we could ask such questions as these: Are their speakers in similar situations? Do they produce similar imagery? Are their figures of speech similar? Do they give similar or different meanings to the events and places they describe? What we can learn about the relationships among poems is limited only by our energy and imagination.

READINGS

William Wordsworth (1770–1850)

LINES
Composed a Few Miles above Tintern Abbey, on Revisiting the Banks of the Wye during a Tour, July 13, 1798

Five years have past; five summers, with the length
Of five long winters! and again I hear
These waters, rolling from their mountain-springs
With a soft inland murmur.—Once again
Do I behold these steep and lofty cliffs,
That on a wild secluded scene impress
Thoughts of more deep seclusion; and connect
The landscape with the quiet of the sky.
The day is come when I again repose
Here, under this dark sycamore, and view
These plots of cottage-ground, these orchard-tufts,
Which at this season, with their unripe fruits,
Are clad in one green hue, and lose themselves
'Mid groves and copses. Once again I see
These hedge-rows, hardly hedge-rows, little lines
Of sportive wood run wild: these pastoral farms,
Green to the very door; and wreaths of smoke
Sent up, in silence, from among the trees!
With some uncertain notice, as might seem
Of vagrant dwellers in the houseless woods,
Or of some Hermit's cave, where by his fire
The Hermit sits alone.

These beauteous forms,
Through a long absence, have not been to me
As is a landscape to a blind man's eye:
But oft, in lonely rooms, and 'mid the din

Of towns and cities, I have owed to them
In hours of weariness, sensations sweet,
Felt in the blood, and felt along the heart;
And passing even into my purer mind,
With tranquil restoration:—feelings too
Of unremembered pleasure: such, perhaps,
As have no slight or trivial influence
On that best portion of a good man's life,
His little, nameless, unremembered, acts
Of kindness and of love. Nor less, I trust,
To them I may have owed another gift,
Of aspect more sublime; that blessed mood,
In which the burthen of the mystery,
In which the heavy and the weary weight
Of all this unintelligible world,
Is lightened:—that serene and blessed mood,
In which the affections gently lead us on,—
Until, the breath of this corporeal frame
And even the motion of our human blood
Almost suspended, we are laid asleep
In body, and become a living soul:
While with an eye made quiet by the power
Of harmony, and the deep power of joy,
We see into the life of things.

If this
Be but a vain belief, yet, oh! how oft—
In darkness and amid the many shapes
Of joyless daylight; when the fretful stir
Unprofitable, and the fever of the world,
Have hung upon the beatings of my heart—
How oft, in spirit, have I turned to thee,
O sylvan Wye! thou wanderer thro' the woods,
How often has my spirit turned to thee!

And now, with gleams of half-extinguished thought,
With many recognitions dim and faint,
And somewhat of a sad perplexity,
The picture of the mind revives again:
While here I stand, not only with the sense
Of present pleasure, but with pleasing thoughts
That in this moment there is life and food
For future years. And so I dare to hope,
Though changed, no doubt, from what I was when first
I came among these hills; when like a roe
I bounded o'er the mountains, by the sides

Of the deep rivers, and the lonely streams,
Wherever nature led: more like a man
Flying from something that he dreads, than one
Who sought the thing he loved. For nature then
(The coarser pleasures of my boyish days,
And their glad animal movements all gone by)
To me was all in all.—I cannot paint
What then I was. The sounding cataract
Haunted me like a passion: the tall rock,
The mountain, and the deep and gloomy wood,
Their colours and their forms, were then to me
An appetite; a feeling and a love.
That had no need of a remoter charm,
By thought supplied, nor any interest
Unborrowed from the eye.—That time is past,
And all its aching joys are now no more,
And all its dizzy raptures. Not for this
Faint I, nor mourn nor murmur; other gifts
Have followed; for such loss, I would believe,
Abundant recompense. For I have learned
To look on nature, not as in the hour
Of thoughtless youth; but hearing oftentimes
The still, sad music of humanity,
Nor harsh nor grating, though of ample power
To chasten and subdue. And I have felt
A presense that disturbs me with the joy
Of elevated thoughts; a sense sublime
Of something far more deeply interfused,
Whose dwelling is the light of setting suns,
And the round ocean and the living air,
And the blue sky, and in the mind of man:
A motion and a spirit, that impels
All thinking things, all objects of all thought,
And rolls through all things. Therefore am I still
A lover of the meadows and the woods,
And mountains; and of all that we behold
From this green earth; of all the mighty world
Of eye, and ear,—both what they half create,
And what perceive; well pleased to recognise
In nature and the language of the sense,
The anchor of my purest thoughts, the nurse,
The guide, the guardian of my heart, and soul
Of all my moral being.

Nor perchance,

If I were not thus taught, should I the more
Suffer my genial spirits to decay:
For thou art with me here upon the banks
Of this fair river; thou my dearest Friend,
My dear, dear Friend; and in thy voice I catch
The language of my former heart, and read
My former pleasures in the shooting lights
Of thy wild eyes. Oh! yet a little while
May I behold in thee what I was once,
My dear, dear Sister! and this prayer I make,
Knowing that Nature never did betray
The heart that loved her; 'tis her privilege,
Through all the years of this our life, to lead
From joy to joy: for she can so inform
The mind that is within us, so impress
With quietness and beauty, and so feed
With lofty thoughts, that neither evil tongues,
Rash judgments, nor the sneers of selfish men,
Nor greetings where no kindness is, nor all
The dreary intercourse of daily life,
Shall e'er prevail against us, or disturb
Our cheerful faith, that all which we behold
Is full of blessings. Therefore let the moon
Shine on thee in thy solitary walk;
And let the misty mountain-winds be free
To blow against thee: and, in after years,
When these wild ecstasies shall be matured
Into a sober pleasure; when thy mind
Shall be a mansion for all lovely forms,
Thy memory be as a dwelling-place
For all sweet sounds and harmonies; oh! then,
If solitude, or fear, or pain, or grief,
Should be thy portion, with what healing thoughts
Of tender joy wilt thou remember me,
And these my exhortations! Nor, perchance—
If I should be where I no more can hear
Thy voice, nor catch from thy wild eyes these gleams
Of past existence—wilt thou then forget
That on the banks of this delightful stream
We stood together; and that I, so long
A worshipper of Nature, hither came
Unwearied in that service; rather say
With warmer love—oh! with far deeper zeal
Of holier love. Nor wilt thou then forget,
That after many wanderings, many years

Of absence, these steep woods and lofty cliffs,
And this green pastoral landscape, were to me
More dear, both for themselves and for thy sake!

John Keats (1795–1821)

ODE ON A GRECIAN URN

1

Thou still unravish'd bride of quietness,
  Thou foster-child of silence and slow time,
Sylvan historian, who canst thus express
  A flowery tale more sweetly than our rhyme:
What leaf-fring'd legend haunts about thy shape
  Of deities or mortals, or of both,
    In Tempe or the dales of Arcady?
  What men or gods are these? What maidens loth?
What mad pursuit? What struggle to escape?
    What pipes and timbrels? What wild ecstasy?

2

Heard melodies are sweet, but those unheard
  Are sweeter; therefore, ye soft pipes, play on;
Not to the sensual ear, but, more endear'd,
  Pipe to the spirit ditties of no tone:
Fair youth, beneath the trees, thou canst not leave
  Thy song, nor ever can those trees be bare;
    Bold lover, never, never canst thou kiss,
Though winning near the goal—yet, do not grieve;
    She cannot fade, though thou hast not thy bliss,
  For ever wilt thou love, and she be fair!

3

Ah, happy, happy boughs! that cannot shed
  Your leaves, nor ever bid the spring adieu;
And, happy melodist, unwearied,
  For ever piping songs for ever new;
More happy love! more happy, happy love!
  For ever warm and still to be enjoy'd,
    For ever panting, and for ever young;
All breathing human passion far above,
  That leaves a heart high-sorrowful and cloy'd,
    A burning forehead, and a parching tongue.

4

Who are these coming to the sacrifice?
  To what green altar, O mysterious priest,
Lead'st thou that heifer lowing at the skies,
  And all her silken flanks with garlands drest?
What little town by river or sea shore,
  Or mountain-built with peaceful citadel,
    Is emptied of this folk, this pious morn?
And, little town, thy streets for evermore
  Will silent be; and not a soul to tell
    Why thou art desolate, can e'er return.

5

O Attic shape! Fair attitude! with brede
  Of marble men and maidens overwrought,
With forest branches and the trodden weed;
  Thou, silent form, dost tease us out of thought
As doth eternity: Cold Pastoral!
  When old age shall this generation waste,
    Thou shalt remain, in midst of other woe
  Than ours, a friend to man, to whom thou say'st,
"Beauty is truth, truth beauty,"—that is all
    Ye know on earth, and all ye need to know.

Matthew Arnold (1822–1888)
DOVER BEACH

The sea is calm tonight.
The tide is full, the moon lies fair
Upon the straits—on the French coast the light
Gleams and is gone; the cliffs of England stand,
Glimmering and vast, out in the tranquil bay.
Come to the window, sweet is the night air!
Only, from the long line of spray
Where the sea meets the moon-blanched land,
Listen! you hear the grating roar
Of pebbles which the waves draw back, and fling,
At their return, up the high strand,
Begin, and cease, and then again begin,
With tremulous cadence slow, and bring
The eternal note of sadness in.

Sophocles long ago
Heard it on the Aegean, and it brought
Into his mind the turbid ebb and flow
Of human misery; we
Find also in the sound a thought,
Hearing it by this distant northern sea.

The Sea of Faith
Was once, too, at the full, and round earth's shore
Lay like the folds of a bright girdle furled.
But now I only hear
Its melancholy, long, withdrawing roar,
Retreating, to the breath
Of the night wind, down the vast edges drear
And naked shingles of the world.

Ah, love, let us be true
To one another! for the world, which seems
To lie before us like a land of dreams,
So various, so beautiful, so new,
Hath really neither joy, nor love, nor light,
Nor certitude, nor peace, nor help for pain;
And we are here as on a darkling plain
Swept with confused alarms of struggle and flight,
Where ignorant armies clash by night.

William Butler Yeats (1865–1939)

AMONG SCHOOL CHILDREN

1

I walk through the long schoolroom questioning;
A kind old nun in a white hood replies;
The children learn to cipher and to sing,
To study reading-books and history,
To cut and sew, be neat in everything
In the best modern way—the children's eyes
In momentary wonder stare upon
A sixty-year-old smiling public man.

2

I dream of a Ledaean body, bent
Above a sinking fire, a tale that she
Told of a harsh reproof, or trivial event
That changed some childish day to tragedy—

Told, and it seemed that our two natures blent
Into a sphere from youthful sympathy,
Or else, to alter Plato's parable,
Into the yolk and white of the one shell.

3

And thinking of that fit of grief or rage
I look upon one child or t'other there
And wonder if she stood so at that age—
For even daughters of the swan can share
Something of every paddler's heritage—
And had that colour upon cheek or hair,
And thereupon my heart is driven wild:
She stands before me as a living child.

4

Her present image floats into the mind—
Did Quattrocento finger fashion it
Hollow of cheek as though it drank the wind
And took a mess of shadows for its meat?
And I though never of Ledaean kind
Had pretty plumage once—enough of that,
Better to smile on all that smile, and show
There is a comfortable kind of old scarecrow.

5

What youthful mother, a shape upon her lap
Honey of generation had betrayed,
And that must sleep, shriek, struggle to escape
As recollection or the drug decide,
Would think her son, did she but see that shape
With sixty or more winters on its head,
A compensation for the pang of his birth,
Or the uncertainty of his setting forth?

6

Plato thought nature but a spume that plays
Upon a ghostly paradigm of things;
Solider Aristotle played the taws
Upon the bottom of a king of kings;
World-famous golden-thighed Pythagoras
Fingered upon a fiddle-stick or strings
What a star sang and careless Muses heard:
Old clothes upon old sticks to scare a bird.

7

Both nuns and mothers worship images,
But those the candles light are not as those
That animate a mother's reveries,
But keep a marble or a bronze repose.
And yet they too break hearts—O Presences
That passion, piety or affection knows,
And that all heavenly glory symbolise—
O self-born mockers of man's enterprise;

8

Labour is blossoming or dancing where
The body is not bruised to pleasure soul,
Nor beauty born out of its own despair,
Nor blear-eyed wisdom out of midnight oil.
O chestnut tree, great-rooted blossomer,
Are you the leaf, the blossom, or the bole?
O body swayed to music, O brightening glance,
How can we know the dancer from the dance?

Wallace Stevens (1878–1955)

THE IDEA OF ORDER AT KEY WEST

She sang beyond the genius of the sea.
The water never formed to mind or voice,
Like a body wholly body, fluttering
Its empty sleeves; and yet its mimic motion
Made constant cry, caused constantly a cry,
That was not ours although we understood,
Inhuman, of the veritable ocean.

The sea was not a mask. No more was she.
The song and water were not medleyed sound
Even if what she sang was what she heard,
Since what she sang was uttered word by word.
It may be that in all her phrases stirred
The grinding water and the gasping wind;
But it was she and not the sea we heard.

For she was the maker of the song she sang.
The ever-hooded, tragic-gestured sea
Was merely a place by which she walked to sing.
Whose spirit is this? we said, because we knew
It was the spirit that we sought and knew
That we should ask this often as she sang.

If it was only the dark voice of the sea
That rose, or even colored by many waves;
If it was only the outer voice of sky
And cloud, of the sunken coral water-walled,
However clear, it would have been deep air,
The heaving speech of air, a summer sound
Repeated in a summer without end
And sound alone. But it was more than that,
More even than her voice, and ours, among
The meaningless plungings of water and the wind,
Theatrical distances, bronze shadows heaped
On high horizons, mountainous atmospheres
Of sky and sea.
                It was her voice that made
The sky acutest at its vanishing.
She measured to the hour its solitude.
She was the single artificer of the world
In which she sang. And when she sang, the sea,
Whatever self it had, became the self
That was her song, for she was the maker. Then we,
As we beheld her striding there alone,
Knew that there never was a world for her
Except the one she sang and, singing, made.

Ramon Fernandez, tell me, if you know,
Why, when the singing ended and we turned
Toward the town, tell why the glassy lights,
The lights in the fishing boats at anchor there,
As the night descended, tilting in the air,
Mastered the night and portioned out the sea,
Fixing emblazoned zones and fiery poles,
Arranging, deepening, enchanting night.

Oh! Blessed rage for order, pale Ramon,
The maker's rage to order words of the sea,
Words of the fragrant portals, dimly-starred,
And of ourselves and of our origins,
In ghostlier demarcations, keener sounds.

A. R. Ammons (b. 1926)

CORSONS INLET

I went for a walk over the dunes again this morning
to the sea,

then turned right along
  the surf
                  rounded a naked headland
                  and returned

  along the inlet shore:

it was muggy sunny, the wind from the sea steady and high,
crisp in the running sand,
      some breakthroughs of sun
  but after a bit

continuous overcast:

the walk liberating, I was released from forms,
from the perpendiculars,
      straight lines, blocks, boxes, binds
of thought
into the hues, shadings, rises, flowing bends and blends
          of sight:

                    I allow myself eddies of meaning:
yield to a direction of significance
running
like a stream through the geography of my work:
  you can find
in my sayings
                  swerves of action
                  like the inlet's cutting edge:

        there are dunes of motion,
organizations of grass, white sandy paths of remembrance
in the overall wandering of mirroring mind:

but Overall is beyond me: is the sum of these events
I cannot draw, the ledger I cannot keep, the accounting
beyond the account:

in nature there are few sharp lines: there are areas of
primrose
      more or less dispersed;
disorderly orders of bayberry; between the rows
of dunes,
irregular swamps of reeds,
though not reeds alone, but grass, bayberry, yarrow,
  all . . .
predominantly reeds:

I have reached no conclusions, have erected no boundaries,

shutting out and shutting in, separating inside
        from outside: I have
        drawn no lines:
        as

manifold events of sand
change the dune's shape that will not be the same shape
tomorrow,

so I am willing to go along, to accept
the becoming
thought, to stake off no beginnings or ends, establish
        no walls:

by transitions the land falls from grassy dunes to creek
to undercreek: but there are no lines, though
        change in that transition is clear
        as any sharpness: but "sharpness" spread out,
allowed to occur over a wider range
than mental lines can keep:

the moon was full last night: today, low tide was low:
black shoals of mussels exposed to the risk
of air
and, earlier, of sun,
waved in and out with the waterline, waterline inexact,
caught always in the event of change:
        a young mottled gull stood free on the shoals
        and ate
to vomiting: another gull, squawking possession, cracked a
    crab,
picked out the entrails, swallowed the soft-shelled legs, a
    ruddy
turnstone running in to snatch leftover bits:

risk is full: every living thing in
siege: the demand is life, to keep life: the small
white blacklegged egret, how beautiful, quietly stalks and
    spears
            the shallows, darts to shore
                        to stab—what? I couldn't
see against the black mudflats—a frightened
fiddler crab?
            the news to my left over the dunes and
reeds and bayberry clumps was
            fall: thousands of tree swallows
            gathering for flight:
            an order held

in constant change: a congregation
rich with entropy: nevertheless, separable, noticeable
as one event,
not chaos: preparations for
flight from winter,
cheet, cheet, cheet, cheet, wings rifling the green clumps,
beaks
at the bayberries
a perception full of wind, flight, curve,
sound:
the possibility of rule as the sum of rulelessness:
the "field" of action
with moving, incalculable center:

in the smaller view, order tight with shape:
blue tiny flowers on a leafless weed: carapace of crab:
snail shell:
pulsations of order
in the bellies of minnows: orders swallowed,
broken down, transferred through membranes
to strengthen larger orders: but in the large view, no
lines or changeless shapes: the working in and out, together
and against, of millions of events: this,
so that I make
no form
formlessness:

orders as summaries, as outcomes of actions override
or in some way result, not predictably (seeing me gain
the top of a dune,
the swallows
could take flight—some other fields of bayberry
could enter fall
berryless) and there is serenity:

no arranged terror: no forcing of image, plan,
or thought:
no propaganda, no humbling of reality to precept:

terror pervades but is not arranged, all possibilities
of escape open: no route shut, except in
the sudden loss of all routes:

I see narrow orders, limited tightness, but will
not run to that easy victory:
still around the looser, wider forces work:
I will try

to fasten into order enlarging grasps of disorder, widening
scope, but enjoying the freedom that
Scope eludes my grasp, that there is no finality of vision,
that I have perceived nothing completely,
that tomorrow a new walk is a new walk.

ANTHOLOGY OF POETRY

Anonymous

GET UP AND BAR THE DOOR

It fell about the Martinmas time,
And a gay time it was then,
When our good wife got puddings to make,
And she's boild them in the pan.

The wind sae cauld blew south and north,
And blew into the floor;
Quoth our goodman to our goodwife,
"Gae out and bar the door."

"My hand is in my hussyfskap,
Goodman, as ye may see;
An it shoud nae be barrd this hundred year,
It's no be barrd for me."

They made a paction tween them twa,
They made it firm and sure,
That the first word whaeer shoud speak,
Shoud rise and bar the door.

Then by there came two gentlemen,
At twelve oclock at night,
And they could neither see house nor hall,
Nor coal nor candle-light.

"Now whether is this a rich man's house,
Or whether is it a poor?"
But neer a word wad ane o them speak,
For barring of the door.

And first they ate the white puddings,
And then they ate the black;
Tho muckle thought the goodwife to hersel,
Yet neer a word she spake.

Then said the one unto the other,
"Here, man, tak ye my knife;
Do ye tak aff the auld man's beard,
And I'll kiss the goodwife."

"But there's nae water in the house,
 And what shall we do than?"
"What ails ye at the pudding-broo,
 That boils into the pan?"

O up then started our goodman,
 An angry man was he:
"Will ye kiss my wife before my een,
 And scad me wi pudding-bree?"

Then up and started our goodwife,
 Gied three skips on the floor:
"Goodman, you've spoken the foremost word,
 Get up and bar the door."

Edmund Spenser (c. 1552–1599)
SONNET 75

One day I wrote her name upon the strand,
But came the waves and washèd it away:
Agayne I wrote it with a second hand,
But came the tyde, and made my paynes his pray.
"Vayne man," sayd she, "that doest in vaine assay,
A mortall thing so to immortalize,
For I my selve shall lyke to this decay,
And eek my name bee wypèd out lykewize."
"Not so," quod I, "let baser things devize,
To dy in dust, but you shall live by fame:
My verse your vertues rare shall eternize,
And in the heavens wryte your glorious name.
Where whenas death shall all the world subdew,
Our love shall live, and later life renew."

Christopher Marlowe (1564–1593)
THE PASSIONATE SHEPHERD TO HIS LOVE

Come live with me and be my love,
And we will all the pleasures prove
That valleys, groves, hills, and fields,
Woods, or steepy mountain yields.

And we will sit upon the rocks,
Seeing the shepherds feed their flocks,
By shallow rivers to whose falls
Melodious birds sing madrigals.

And I will make thee beds of roses
And a thousand fragrant posies,
A cap of flowers, and a kirtle
Embroidered all with leaves of myrtle;

A gown made of the finest wool
Which from our pretty lambs we pull;
Fair lined slippers for the cold,
With buckles of the purest gold;

A belt of straw and ivy buds,
With coral clasps and amber studs:
And if these pleasures may thee move,
Come live with me, and be my love.

The shepherds' swains shall dance and sing
For thy delight each May morning:
If these delights thy mind may move,
Then live with me and be my love.

William Shakespeare (1564–1616)
BLOW, BLOW, THOU WINTER WIND

Blow, blow, thou winter wind,
Thou art not so unkind
As man's ingratitude;
Thy tooth is not so keen,
Because thou art not seen,
Although thy breath be rude.
Heigh-ho! sing, heigh-ho! unto the green holly:
Most friendship is feigning, most loving mere folly:
Then, heigh-ho, the holly!
This life is most jolly.

Freeze, freeze, thou bitter sky,
That dost not bite so nigh
As benefits forgot:
Though thou the waters warp,
Thy sting is not so sharp
As friend remembered not.
Heigh-ho! sing, etc.

HARK! HARK! THE LARK

Hark, hark! the lark at heaven's gate sings,
  And Phoebus 'gins arise,
His steeds to water at those springs
  On chaliced flowers that lies;
And winking Mary-buds begin
  To ope their golden eyes:
With every thing that pretty is,
  My lady sweet, arise:
  Arise, arise!

Ben Jonson (1572/3–1637)

ON MY FIRST DAUGHTER

Here lies, to each her parents' ruth,
Mary, the daughter of their youth;
Yet all heaven's gifts being heaven's due,
It makes the father less to rue.
At six months' end she parted hence
With safety of her innocence;
Whose soul heaven's queen, whose name she bears,
In comfort of her mother's tears,
Hath placed amongst her virgin-train:
Where, while that severed doth remain,
This grave partakes the fleshly birth;
Which cover lightly, gentle earth!

John Donne (1572–1631)

THE CANONIZATION

For God's sake hold your tongue, and let me love,
  Or chide my palsy, or my gout,
My five gray hairs, or ruined fortune, flout,
  With wealth your state, your mind with arts improve,
    Take you a course, get you a place,
    Observe His Honor, or His Grace,
Or the King's real, or his stampèd face
  Contemplate; what you will, approve,
  So you will let me love.

Alas, alas, who's injured by my love?
What merchant's ships have my sighs drowned?
Who says my tears have overflowed his ground?
When did my colds a forward spring remove?
When did the heats which my veins fill
Add one man to the plaguy bill?
Soldiers find wars, and lawyers find out still
Litigious men, which quarrels move,
Though she and I do love.

Call us what you will, we are made such by love;
Call her one, me another fly,
We're tapers too, and at our own cost die,
And we in us find the eagle and the dove.
The phoenix riddle hath more wit
By us: we two being one, are it.
So, to one neutral thing both sexes fit.
We die and rise the same, and prove
Mysterious by this love.

We can die by it, if not live by love,
And if unfit for tombs and hearse
Our legend be, it will be fit for verse;
And if no piece of chronicle we prove,
We'll build in sonnets pretty rooms;
As well a well-wrought urn becomes
The greatest ashes, as half-acre tombs,
And by these hymns, all shall approve
Us canonized for love:

And thus invoke us: You whom reverend love
Made one another's hermitage;
You, to whom love was peace, that now is rage;
Who did the whole world's soul contract, and drove
Into the glasses of your eyes
(So made such mirrors, and such spies,
That they did all to you epitomize)
Countries, towns, courts: Beg from above
A pattern of your love!

HOLY SONNET 10

Death, be not proud, though some have callèd thee
Mighty and dreadful, for thou art not so;
For those whom thou think'st thou dost overthrow

Die not, poor Death, nor yet canst thou kill me.
From rest and sleep, which but thy pictures be,
Much pleasure; then from thee much more must flow,
And soonest our best men with thee do go,
Rest of their bones, and soul's delivery.
Thou art slave to fate, chance, kings, and desperate men,
And dost with poison, war, and sickness dwell,
And poppy or charms can make us sleep as well
And better than thy stroke; why swell'st thou then?
One short sleep past, we wake eternally
And death shall be no more; Death, thou shalt die.

Andrew Marvell (1621–1678)

TO HIS COY MISTRESS

Had we but world enough, and time,
This coyness, lady, were no crime.
We would sit down, and think which way
To walk, and pass our long love's day.
Thou by the Indian Ganges' side
Shouldst rubies find; I by the tide
Of Humber would complain. I would
Love you ten years before the Flood,
And you should, if you please, refuse
Till the conversion of the Jews.
My vegetable love should grow
Vaster than empires, and more slow;
An hundred years should go to praise
Thine eyes, and on thy forehead gaze;
Two hundred to adore each breast,
But thirty thousand to the rest;
An age at least to every part,
And the last age should show your heart.
For, lady, you deserve this state,
Nor would I love at lower rate.
But at my back I always hear
Time's wingèd chariot hurrying near;
And yonder all before us lie
Deserts of vast eternity.
Thy beauty shall no more be found,
Nor, in thy marble vault, shall sound
My echoing song; then worms shall try
That long-preserved virginity,

And your quaint honor turn to dust,
And into ashes all my lust:
The grave's a fine and private place,
But none, I think, do there embrace.
  Now therefore, while the youthful hue
Sits on thy skin like morning dew,
And while thy willing soul transpires
At every pore with instant fires,
Now let us sport us while we may,
And now, like amorous birds of prey,
Rather at once our time devour
Than languish in his slow-chapped power.
Let us roll all our strength and all
Our sweetness up into one ball,
And tear our pleasures with rough strife
Thorough the iron gates of life:
Thus, though we cannot make our sun
Stand still, yet we will make him run.

BERMUDAS

  Where the remote Bermudas ride,
In th' ocean's bosom unespied,
From a small boat that rowed along,
The listening winds received this song:

  "What should we do but sing his praise
That led us through the wat'ry maze
Unto an isle so long unknown,
And yet far kinder than our own?
Where he the huge sea monsters wracks,
That lift the deep upon their backs;
He lands us on a grassy stage,
Safe from the storms, and prelate's rage.
He gave us this eternal spring
Which here enamels everything,
And sends the fowls to us in care,
On daily visits through the air;
He hangs in shades the orange bright,
Like golden lamps in a green night,
And does in the pomegranates close
Jewels more rich than Ormus shows;
He makes the figs our mouths to meet,
And throws the melons at our feet;
But apples plants of such a price,

No tree could ever bear them twice;
With cedars, chosen by his hand,
From Lebanon, he stores the land;
And makes the hollow seas that roar
Proclaim the ambergris on shore;
He cast (of which we rather boast)
The Gospel's pearl upon our coast,
And in these rocks for us did frame
A temple, where to sound his name.
O let our voice his praise exalt
Till it arrive at heaven's vault,
Which, thence (perhaps) rebounding, may
Echo beyond the Mexique Bay."

Thus sung they in the English boat
An holy and a cheerful note;
And all the way, to guide their chime,
With falling oars they kept the time.

Robert Herrick (1591–1674)

DELIGHT IN DISORDER

A sweet disorder in the dress
Kindles in clothes a wantonness.
A lawn about the shoulders thrown
Into a fine distractiòn;
An erring lace, which here and there
Enthralls the crimson stomacher;
A cuff neglectful, and thereby
Ribbons to flow confusedly;
A winning wave, deserving note,
In the tempestuous petticoat;
A careless shoestring, in whose tie
I see a wild civility:
Do more bewitch me than when art
Is too precise in every part.

CORINNA'S GOING A-MAYING

Get up! get up for shame! the blooming morn
Upon her wings presents the god unshorn.
See how Aurora throws her fair

Fresh-quilted colors through the air:
Get up, sweet slug-a-bed, and see
The dew bespangling herb and tree.
Each flower has wept and bowed toward the east
Above an hour since, yet you not dressed;
Nay, not so much as out of bed?
When all the birds have matins said,
And sung their thankful hymns, 'tis sin,
Nay, profanation to keep in,
Whenas a thousand virgins on this day
Spring, sooner than the lark, to fetch in May.

Rise, and put on your foliage, and be seen
To come forth, like the springtime, fresh and green,
And sweet as Flora. Take no care
For jewels for your gown or hair;
Fear not; the leaves will strew
Gems in abundance upon you;
Besides, the childhood of the day has kept,
Against you come, some orient pearls unwept;
Come and receive them while the light
Hangs on the dew-locks of the night,
And Titan on the eastern hill
Retires himself, or else stands still
Till you come forth. Wash, dress, be brief in praying:
Few beads are best when once we go a-Maying.

Come, my Corinna, come; and, coming, mark
How each field turns a street, each street a park
Made green and trimmed with trees; see how
Devotion gives each house a bough
Or branch: each porch, each door ere this,
An ark, a tabernacle is,
Made up of whitethorn neatly interwove,
As if here were those cooler shades of love.
Can such delights be in the street
And open fields, and we not see't?
Come, we'll abroad; and let's obey
The proclamation made for May,
And sin no more, as we have done, by staying;
But, my Corinna, come, let's go a-Maying.

There's not a budding boy or girl this day
But is got up and gone to bring in May;
A deal of youth, ere this, is come

Back, and with whitethorn laden home.
Some have dispatched their cakes and cream
Before that we have left to dream;
And some have wept, and wooed, and plighted troth,
And chose their priest, ere we can cast off sloth.
Many a green-gown has been given,
Many a kiss, both odd and even;
Many a glance, too, has been sent
From out the eye, love's firmament;
Many a jest told of the keys betraying
This night, and locks picked; yet we're not a-Maying.

Come, let us go while we are in our prime,
And take the harmless folly of the time.
We shall grow old apace, and die
Before we know our liberty.
Our life is short, and our days run
As fast away as does the sun;
And, as a vapor or a drop of rain
Once lost, can ne'er be found again,
So when or you or I are made
A fable, song, or fleeting shade,
All love, all liking, all delight
Lies drowned with us in endless night.
Then while time serves, and we are but decaying,
Come, my Corinna, come, let's go a-Maying.

TO THE VIRGINS, TO MAKE MUCH OF TIME

Gather ye rosebuds while ye may,
Old time is still a-flying;
And this same flower that smiles today,
Tomorrow will be dying.

The glorious lamp of heaven, the sun,
The higher he's a-getting,
The sooner will his race be run,
And nearer he's to setting.

That age is best which is the first,
When youth and blood are warmer;
But being spent, the worse, and worst
Times still succeed the former.

Then be not coy, but use your time,
  And while ye may, go marry;
For having lost but once your prime,
  You may forever tarry.

NEUTRALITY LOATHSOME

God will have all or none; serve Him, or fall
Down before Baal, Bel, or Belial.
Either be hot or cold: God doth despise,
Abhor, and spew out all neutralities.

George Herbert (1593–1633)

EASTER WINGS

Lord, who createdst man in wealth and store,
  Though foolishly he lost the same,
    Decaying more and more
      Till he became
        Most poor:
        With thee
      O let me rise
    As larks, harmoniously,
  And sing this day thy victories:
Then shall the fall further the flight in me.

My tender age in sorrow did begin:
  And still with sicknesses and shame
    Thou didst so punish sin,
      That I became
        Most thin.
        With thee
      Let me combine,
    And feel this day thy victory;
  For, if I imp my wing on thine,
Affliction shall advance the flight in me.

VIRTUE

Sweet day, so cool, so calm, so bright,
The bridal of the earth and sky:

The dew shall weep thy fall tonight;
    For thou must die.

Sweet rose, whose hue, angry and brave,
Bids the rash gazer wipe his eye:
Thy root is ever in its grave,
    And thou must die.

Sweet spring, full of sweet days and roses,
A box where sweets compacted lie;
My music shows ye have your closes,
    And all must die.

Only a sweet and virtuous soul,
Like seasoned timber, never gives;
But though the whole world turn to coal,
    Then chiefly lives.

Thomas Carew (1594/5–1640)
A SONG

Ask me no more where Jove bestows,
When June is past, the fading rose;
For in your beauties orient deep,
These flowers, as in their causes, sleep.

Ask me no more whither do stray
The golden atoms of the day;
For in pure love heaven did prepare
Those powders to enrich your hair.

Ask me no more whither doth haste
The nightingale when May is past;
For in your sweet dividing throat
She winters, and keeps warm her note.

Ask me no more where those stars light,
That downwards fall in dead of night;
For in your eyes they sit, and there
Fixèd become; as in their sphere.

Ask me no more if east or west
The phoenix builds her spicy nest;
For unto you at last she flies,
And in your fragrant bosom dies.

Richard Lovelace (1618–1657/8)

TO ALTHEA, FROM PRISON

When Love with unconfinèd wings
  Hovers within my gates,
And my divine Althea brings
  To whisper at the grates;
When I lie tangled in her hair
  And fettered to her eye,
The gods that wanton in the air
  Know no such liberty.

When flowing cups run swiftly round,
  With no allaying Thames,
Our careless heads with roses bound,
  Our hearts with loyal flames;
When thirsty grief in wine we steep,
  When healths and draughts go free,
Fishes that tipple in the deep
  Know no such liberty.

When, like committed linnets, I
  With shriller throat shall sing
The sweetness, mercy, majesty,
  And glories of my King;
When I shall voice aloud how good
  He is, how great should be,
Enlargèd winds, that curl the flood,
  Know no such liberty.

Stone walls do not a prison make,
  Nor iron bars a cage;
Minds innocent and quiet take
  That for an hermitage.
If I have freedom in my love,
  And in my soul am free,
Angels alone, that soar above,
  Enjoy such liberty.

John Milton (1608–1674)

WHEN I CONSIDER HOW MY LIGHT IS SPENT

When I consider how my light is spent,
  Ere half my days, in this dark world and wide,

And that one talent which is death to hide,
Lodged with me useless, though my soul more bent
To serve therewith my Maker, and present
My true account, lest he returning chide;
"Doth God exact day-labor, light denied?"
I fondly ask; but Patience to prevent
That murmur, soon replies, "God doth not need
Either man's work or his own gifts; who best
Bear his mild yoke, they serve him best. His state
Is kingly. Thousands at his bidding speed
And post o'er land and ocean without rest:
They also serve who only stand and wait."

Aphra Behn (1640–1689)

THE WILLING MISTRESS

Amyntas led me to a grove,
Where all the trees did shade us;
The sun itself, though it had strove,
It could not have betrayed us.
The place secured from human eyes
No other fear allows
But when the winds that gently rise
Do kiss the yielding boughs.

Down there we sat upon the moss,
And did begin to play
A thousand amorous tricks, to pass
The heat of all the day.
A many kisses did he give
And I returned the same,
Which made me willing to receive
That which I dare not name.

His charming eyes no aid required
To tell their softening tale;
On her that was already fired,
'Twas easy to prevail.
He did but kiss and clasp me round,
Whilst those his thoughts expressed:
And laid me gently on the ground;
Ah who can guess the rest?

Anne Bradstreet (c. 1612–1672)

A LETTER TO HER HUSBAND ABSENT UPON PUBLIC EMPLOYMENT

My head, my heart, mine eyes, my life, nay, more,
My joy, my magazine of earthly store,
If two be one, as surely thou and I,
How stayest thou there, whilst I at Ipswich lie?
So many steps, head from the heart to sever,
If but a neck, soon should we be together.
I, like the Earth this season, mourn in black,
My sun is gone so far in's zodiac,
Whom wilst I 'joyed, nor storms, nor frost I felt,
His warmth such frigid colds did cause to melt.
My chilled limbs now numbed lie forlorn;
Return, return, sweet Sol, from Capricorn;
In this dead time, alas, what can I more
Than view those fruits which through thy heat I bore?
Which sweet contentment yield me for a space,
True living pictures of their father's face.
O strange effect! now thou art southward gone,
I weary grow the tedious day so long;
But when thou northward to me shall return,
I wish my Sun may never set, but burn
Within the Cancer of my glowing breast,
The welcome house of him my dearest guest.
Where ever, ever stay, and go not thence,
Till nature's sad decree shall call thee hence;
Flesh of thy flesh, bone of thy bone,
I here, thou there, yet both but one.

THE AUTHOR TO HER BOOK

Thou ill-formed offspring of my feeble brain,
Who after birth didst by my side remain,
Till snatched from thence by friends, less wise than true,
Who thee abroad, exposed to public view,
Made thee in rags, halting to th' press to trudge,
Where errors were not lessened (all may judge).
At thy return my blushing was not small,
My rambling brat (in print) should mother call,
I cast thee by as one unfit for light,

Thy visage was so irksome in my sight;
Yet being mine own, at length affection would
Thy blemishes amend, if so I could:
I washed thy face, but more defects I saw,
And rubbing off a spot still made a flaw.
I stretched thy joints to make thee even feet,
Yet still thou run'st more hobbling than is meet;
In better dress to trim thee was my mind,
But nought save homespun cloth i' th' house I find.
In this array 'mongst vulgars may'st thou roam.
In critic's hands beware thou dost not come,
And take thy way where yet thou art not known;
If for thy father asked, say thou hadst none;
And for thy mother, she alas is poor,
Which caused her thus to send thee out of door.

Edward Taylor (1644–1729)
UPON A SPIDER CATCHING A FLY

Thou sorrow, venom elf.
  Is this thy play,
To spin a web out of thyself
  To catch a fly?
    For why?

I saw a pettish wasp
  Fall foul therein,
Whom yet thy whorl pins did not clasp
  Lest he should fling
    His sting.

But as afraid, remote
  Didst stand hereat
And with thy little fingers stroke
  And gently tap
    His back.

Thus gently him didst treat
  Lest he should pet,
And in a froppish waspish heat
Should greatly fret
  Thy net.

Whereas the silly fly,
  Caught by its leg,

Thou by the throat took'st hastily,
  And 'hind the head
    Bite dead.

This goes to pot, that not
  Nature doth call.
Strive not above what strength hath got,
  Lest in the brawl
    Thou fall.

This fray seems thus to us:
  Hell's spider gets
His entrails spun to whipcords thus,
  And wove to nets
    And sets,

To tangle Adam's race
  In's strategems
To their destructions, spoiled, made base
  By venom things,
    Damned sins.

But mighty, gracious Lord,
  Communicate
Thy grace to break the cord; afford
  Us glory's gate
    And state.

We'll Nightingale sing like,
  When perched on high
In glory's cage, Thy glory, bright,
  And thankfully,
    For joy.

HUSWIFERY

Make me, O Lord, Thy spinning wheel complete.
  Thy holy word my distaff make for me.
Make mine affections Thy swift flyers neat,
  And make my soul Thy holy spool to be.
  My conversation make to be Thy reel,
  And reel the yarn thereon spun of Thy wheel.
Make me Thy loom then, knit therein this twine;
  And make Thy holy spirit, Lord, wind quills;
Then weave the web Thyself. The yarn is fine.
  Thine ordinances make my fulling mills.

Then dye the same in heavenly colors choice,
All pinked with varnished flowers of paradise.

Then clothe therewith mine understanding, will,
Affections, judgment, conscience, memory,
My words and actions, that their shine may fill
My ways with glory and Thee glorify.
Then mine apparel shall display before Ye
That I am clothed in holy robes for glory.

Anne Finch (1661–1720)

FRIENDSHIP BETWEEN EPHELIA AND ARDELIA

Eph. What friendship is, Ardelia, show.
Ard. 'Tis to love, as I love you.
Eph. This account, so short (though kind)
Suits not my inquiring mind.
Therefore farther now repeat:
What is friendship when complete?
Ard. 'Tis to share all joy and grief;
'Tis to lend all due relief
From the tongue, the heart, the hand;
'Tis to mortgage house and land;
For a friend be sold a slave;
'Tis to die upon a grave,
If a friend therein do lie.
Eph. This indeed, though carried high,
This, though more than e'er was done
Underneath the rolling sun,
This has all been said before.
Can Ardelia say no more?
Ard. Words indeed no more can show:
But 'tis to love, as I love you.

TO THE NIGHTINGALE

Exert thy voice, sweet harbinger of spring!
This moment is thy time to sing,
This moment I attend to praise,
And set my numbers to thy lays.

Free as thine shall be my song;
As thy music, short or long.
Poets, wild as thee, were born,
Pleasing best when unconfined,
When to please is least designed,
Soothing but their cares to rest;
Cares do still their thoughts molest,
And still th'unhappy poet's breast,
Like thine, when best he sings, is placed against a thorn.
She begins. Let all be still!
Muse, thy promise now fulfill!
Sweet, oh! sweet, still sweeter yet
Can thy words such accents fit,
Canst thou syllables refine,
Melt a sense that shall retain
Still some spirit of the brain,
Till with sounds like these it join.
'Twill not be! then change thy note;
Let division shake thy throat.
Hark! Division now she tries;
Yet as far the muse outflies.
Cease then, prithee, cease thy tune;
Trifler wilt thou sing till June?
Till thy business all lies waste,
And the time of building's past!
Thus we poets that have speech,
Unlike what thy forests teach,
If a fluent vein be shown
That's transcendent to our own,
Criticize, reform, or preach,
Or censure what we cannot reach.

Samuel Johnson (1709–1784)

ON THE DEATH OF DR. ROBERT LEVET

Condemned to Hope's delusive mine,
As on we toil from day to day,
By sudden blasts, or slow decline,
Our social comforts drop away.

Well tried through many a varying year,
See Levet to the grave descend;
Officious, innocent, sincere,
Of every friendless name the friend.

Yet still he fills Affection's eye,
  Obscurely wise, and coarsely kind;
Nor, lettered Arrogance, deny
  Thy praise to merit unrefined.

When fainting Nature called for aid,
  And hovering Death prepared the blow,
His vigorous remedy displayed
  The power of art without the show.

In Misery's darkest cavern known,
  His useful care was ever nigh,
Where hopeless Anguish poured his groan,
  And lonely Want retired to die.

No summons mocked by chill delay,
  No petty gain disdained by pride,
The modest wants of every day
  The toil of every day supplied.

His virtues walked their narrow round,
  Nor made a pause, nor left a void;
And sure the Eternal Master found
  The single talent well employed.

The busy day, the peaceful night,
  Unfelt, uncounted, glided by;
His frame was firm, his powers were bright,
  Though now his eightieth year was nigh.

Then with no throbbing fiery pain,
  No cold gradations of decay,
Death broke at once the vital chain,
  And freed his soul the nearest way.

Thomas Gray (1716–1771)
ELEGY WRITTEN IN A COUNTRY CHURCHYARD

The curfew tolls the knell of parting day,
  The lowing herd wind slowly o'er the lea,
The plowman homeward plods his weary way,
  And leaves the world to darkness and to me.

Now fades the glimmering landscape on the sight,
  And all the air a solemn stillness holds,
Save where the beetle wheels his droning flight,
  And drowsy tinklings lull the distant folds;

Save that from yonder ivy-mantled tower
  The moping owl does to the moon complain
Of such, as wandering near her secret bower,
  Molest her ancient solitary reign.

Beneath those rugged elms, that yew tree's shade,
  Where heaves the turf in many a moldering heap,
Each in his narrow cell forever laid,
  The rude forefathers of the hamlet sleep.

The breezy call of incense-breathing Morn,
  The swallow twittering from the straw-built shed,
The cock's shrill clarion, or the echoing horn,
  No more shall rouse them from their lowly bed.

For them no more the blazing hearth shall burn,
  Or busy housewife ply her evening care;
No children run to lisp their sire's return,
  Or climb his knees the envied kiss to share.

Oft did the harvest to their sickle yield,
  Their furrow oft the stubborn glebe has broke;
How jocund did they drive their team afield!
  How bowed the woods beneath their sturdy stroke!

Let not Ambition mock their useful toil,
  Their homely joys, and destiny obscure;
Nor Grandeur hear with a disdainful smile
  The short and simple annals of the poor.

The boast of heraldry, the pomp of power,
  And all that beauty, all that wealth e'er gave,
Awaits alike the inevitable hour.
  The paths of glory lead but to the grave.

Nor you, ye proud, impute to these the fault,
  If Memory o'er their tomb no trophies raise,
Where through the long-drawn aisle and fretted vault
  The pealing anthem swells the note of praise.

Can storied urn or animated bust
  Back to its mansion call the fleeting breath?
Can Honor's voice provoke the silent dust,
  Or Flattery soothe the dull cold ear of Death?

Perhaps in this neglected spot is laid
  Some heart once pregnant with celestial fire;
Hands that the rod of empire might have swayed,
  Or waked to ecstasy the living lyre.

But Knowledge to their eyes her ample page
  Rich with the spoils of time did ne'er unroll;
Chill Penury repressed their noble rage,
  And froze the genial current of the soul.

Full many a gem of purest ray serene,
  The dark unfathomed caves of ocean bear:
Full many a flower is born to blush unseen,
  And waste its sweetness on the desert air.

Some village Hampden, that with dauntless breast
  The little tyrant of his fields withstood;
Some mute inglorious Milton here may rest,
  Some Cromwell guiltless of his country's blood.

The applause of listening senates to command,
  The threats of pain and ruin to despise,
To scatter plenty o'er a smiling land,
  And read their history in a nation's eyes,

Their lot forbade: nor circumscribed alone
  Their growing virtues, but their crimes confined;
Forbade to wade through slaughter to a throne,
  And shut the gates of mercy on mankind,

The struggling pangs of conscious truth to hide,
  To quench the blushes of ingenuous shame,
Or heap the shrine of Luxury and Pride
  With incense kindled at the Muse's flame.

Far from the madding crowd's ignoble strife,
  Their sober wishes never learned to stray;
Along the cool sequestered vale of life
  They kept the noiseless tenor of their way.

Yet even these bones from insult to protect
  Some frail memorial still erected nigh,
With uncouth rhymes and shapeless sculpture decked,
  Implores the passing tribute of a sigh.

Their name, their years, spelt by the unlettered Muse,
  The place of fame and elegy supply:
And many a holy text around she strews,
  That teach the rustic moralist to die.

For who to dumb Forgetfulness a prey,
  This pleasing anxious being e'er resigned,
Left the warm precincts of the cheerful day,
  Nor cast one longing lingering look behind?

On some fond breast the parting soul relies,
  Some pious drops the closing eye requires;
Even from the tomb the voice of Nature cries,
  Even in our ashes live their wonted fires.

For thee, who mindful of the unhonored dead
  Dost in these lines their artless tale relate;
If chance, by lonely contemplation led,
  Some kindred spirit shall inquire thy fate,

Haply some hoary-headed swain may say,
  "Oft have we seen him at the peep of dawn
Brushing with hasty steps the dews away
  To meet the sun upon the upland lawn.

"There at the foot of yonder nodding beech
  That wreathes its old fantastic roots so high,
His listless length at noontide would he stretch,
  And pore upon the brook that babbles by.

"Hard by yon wood, now smiling as in scorn,
  Muttering his wayward fancies he would rove,
Now drooping, woeful wan, like one forlorn,
  Or crazed with care, or crossed in hopeless love.

"One morn I missed him on the customed hill,
  Along the heath and near his favorite tree;
Another came; nor yet beside the rill,
  Nor up the lawn, nor at the wood was he;

"The next with dirges due in sad array
  Slow through the churchway path we saw him borne.
Approach and read (for thou canst read) the lay,
  Graved on the stone beneath yon aged thorn."

The Epitaph

Here rests his head upon the lap of Earth
  A youth to Fortune and to Fame unknown.
Fair Science frowned not on his humble birth,
  And Melancholy marked him for her own.

Large was his bounty, and his soul sincere,
  Heaven did a recompense as largely send:
He gave to Misery all he had, a tear,
  He gained from Heaven ('twas all he wished) a friend.

No farther seek his merits to disclose,
  Or draw his frailties from their dread abode
(There they alike in trembling hope repose),
  The bosom of his Father and his God.

Phillis Wheatly (?1735–1784)

ON BEING BROUGHT FROM AFRICA TO AMERICA

'Twas mercy brought me from my *Pagan* land,
Taught my benighted soul to understand
That there's a God, that there's a *Saviour* too:
Once I redemption neither sought nor knew.
Some view our sable race with scornful eye,
"Their colour is a diabolic dye."
Remember, *Christians, Negroes,* black as *Cain,*
May be refined, and join th' angelic train.

Charlotte Smith (1748–1806)

PRESSED BY THE MOON, MUTE ARBITRESS OF TIDES

Written in the churchyard at Middleton in Sussex

Pressed by the moon, mute arbitress of tides,
  While the loud equinox its power combines,
  The sea no more its swelling surge confines,
But o'er the shrinking land sublimely rides.
The wild blast, rising from the western cave,
  Drives the huge billows from their heaving bed,
  Tears from their grassy tombs the village dead,
And breaks the silent sabbath of the grave!
With shells and seaweed mingled, on the shore
  Lo! their bones whiten in the frequent wave;
  But vain to them the winds and waters rave;
They hear the warring elements no more:
While I am doomed—by life's long storm oppressed,
To gaze with envy on their gloomy rest.

Robert Burns (1759–1796)

A RED, RED ROSE

O My Luve's like a red, red rose,
  That's newly sprung in June;
O My Luve's like the melodie
  That's sweetly played in tune.

As fair art thou, my bonnie lass,
  So deep in luve am I;
And I will luve thee still, my dear,
  Till a' the seas gang dry.

Till a' the seas gang dry, my dear,
  And the rocks melt wi' the sun:
O I will love thee still, my dear,
  While the sands o' life shall run.

And fare thee weel, my only luve,
  And fare thee weel awhile!
And I will come again, my luve,
  Though it were ten thousand mile.

William Wordsworth (1770–1850)
NUTTING

—————It seems a day
(I speak of one from many singled out)
One of those heavenly days that cannot die;
When, in the eagerness of boyish hope,
I left our cottage-threshold, sallying forth
With a huge wallet o'er my shoulder slung,
A nutting-crook in hand; and turned my steps
Tow'rd some far-distant wood, a Figure quaint,
Tricked out in proud disguise of cast-off weeds
Which for that service had been husbanded,
By exhortation of my frugal Dame—
Motley accoutrement, of power to smile
At thorns, and brakes, and brambles,—and, in truth,
More ragged than need was! O'er pathless rocks,
Through beds of matted fern, and tangled thickets,
Forcing my way, I came to one dear nook
Unvisited, where not a broken bough
Drooped with its withered leaves, ungracious sign
Of devastation; but the hazels rose
Tall and erect, with tempting clusters hung,
A virgin scene!—A little while I stood,
Breathing with such suppression of the heart
As joy delights in; and, with wise restraint
Voluptuous, fearless of a rival, eyed
The banquet;—or beneath the trees I sate

Among the flowers, and with the flowers I played;
A temper known to those, who, after long
And weary expectation, have been blest
With sudden happiness beyond all hope.
Perhaps it was a bower beneath whose leaves
The violets of five seasons re-appear
And fade, unseen by any human eye;
Where fairy water-breaks do murmur on
For ever; and I saw the sparkling foam,
And—with my cheek on one of those green stones
That, fleeced with moss, under the shady trees,
Lay round me, scattered like a flock of sheep—
I heard the murmur and the murmuring sound,
In that sweet mood when pleasure loves to pay
Tribute to ease; and, of its joy secure,
The heart luxuriates with indifferent things,
Wasting its kindliness on stocks and stones,
And on the vacant air. Then up I rose,
And dragged to earth both branch and bough, with crash
And merciless ravage: and the shady nook
Of hazels, and the green and mossy bower,
Deformed and sullied, patiently gave up
Their quiet being: and, unless I now
Confound my present feelings with the past;
Ere from the mutilated bower I turned
Exulting, rich beyond the wealth of kings,
I felt a sense of pain when I beheld
The silent trees, and the saw the intruding sky.—
Then, dearest Maiden, move along these shades
In gentleness of heart; with gentle hand
Touch—for there is a spirit in the woods.

RESOLUTION AND INDEPENDENCE

1

There was a roaring in the wind all night;
The rain came heavily and fell in floods;
But now the sun is rising calm and bright;
The birds are singing in the distant woods;
Over his own sweet voice the Stock-dove broods;
The Jay makes answer as the Magpie chatters;
And all the air is filled with pleasant noise of waters.

2

All things that love the sun are out of doors;
The sky rejoices in the morning's birth;
The grass is bright with rain-drops;—on the moors
The hare is running races in her mirth;
And with her feet she from the plashy earth
Raises a mist; that, glittering in the sun,
Runs with her all the way, wherever she doth run.

3

I was a Traveller then upon the moor;
I saw the hare that raced about with joy;
I heard the woods and distant waters roar;
Or heard them not, as happy as a boy:
The pleasant season did my heart employ:
My old remembrances went from me wholly;
And all the ways of men, so vain and melancholy.

4

But, as it sometimes chanceth, from the might
Of joy in minds that can no further go,
As high as we have mounted in delight
In our dejection do we sink as low;
To me that morning did it happen so;
And fears and fancies thick upon me came;
Dim sadness—and blind thoughts, I knew not, nor could name.

5

I heard the sky-lark warbling in the sky;
And I bethought me of the playful hare:
Even such a happy Child of earth am I;
Even as these blissful creatures do I fare;
Far from the world I walk, and from all care;
But there may come another day to me—
Solitude, pain of heart, distress, and poverty.

6

My whole life I have lived in pleasant thought,
As if life's business were a summer mood;
As if all needful things would come unsought
To genial faith, still rich in genial good;
But how can He expect that others should
Build for him, sow for him, and at his call
Love him, who for himself will take no heed at all?

7

I thought of Chatterton, the marvellous Boy,
The sleepless Soul that perished in his pride;
Of Him who walked in glory and in joy
Following his plough, along the mountain-side:
By our own spirits are we deified:
We Poets in our youth begin in gladness;

8

But thereof come in the end despondency and madness.
Now, whether it were by peculiar grace,
A leading from above, a something given,
Yet it befel, that, in this lonely place,
When I with these untoward thoughts had striven,
Beside a pool bare to the eye of heaven
I saw a Man before me unawares:
The oldest man he seemed that ever wore grey hairs.

9

As a huge stone is sometimes seen to lie
Couched on the bald top of an eminence;
Wonder to all who do the same espy,
By what means it could thither come, and whence;
So that it seems a thing endued with sense:
Like a sea-beast crawled forth, that on a shelf
Of rock or sand reposeth, there to sun itself;

10

Such seemed this Man, not all alive nor dead,
Nor all asleep—in his extreme old age:
His body was bent double, feet and head
Coming together in life's pilgrimage;
As if some dire constraint of pain, or rage
Of sickness felt by him in times long past,
A more than human weight upon his frame had cast.

11

Himself he propped, limbs, body, and pale face,
Upon a long grey staff of shaven wood:
And, still as I drew near with gentle pace,
Upon the margin of that moorish flood
Motionless as a cloud the old Man stood,
That heareth not the loud winds when they call;
And moveth all together, if it move at all.

12

At length, himself unsettling, he the pond
Stirred with his staff, and fixedly did look
Upon the muddy water, which he conned,
As if he had been reading in a book:
And now a stranger's privilege I took;
And, drawing to his side, to him did say,
"This morning gives us promise of a glorious day."

13

A gentle answer did the old Man make,
In courteous speech which forth he slowly drew:
And him with further words I thus bespake,
"What occupation do you there pursue?
This is a lonesome place for one like you."
Ere he replied, a flash of mild surprise
Broke from the sable orbs of his yet-vivid eyes.

14

His words came feebly, from a feeble chest,
But each in solemn order followed each,
With something of a lofty utterance drest—
Choice word and measured phrase, above the reach
Of ordinary men; a stately speech;
Such as grave Livers do in Scotland use,
Religious men, who give to God and man their dues.

15

He told, that to these waters he had come
To gather leeches, being old and poor:
Employment hazardous and wearisome!
And he had many hardships to endure:
From pond to pond he roamed, from moor to moor;
Housing, with God's good help, by choice or chance;
And in this way he gained an honest maintenance.

16

The old Man still stood talking by my side;
But now his voice to me was like a stream
Scarce heard; nor word from word could I divide;
And the whole body of the Man did seem
Like one whom I had met with in a dream;
Or like a man from some far region sent,
To give me human strength, by apt admonishment.

17

My former thoughts returned: the fear that kills;
And hope that is unwilling to be fed;
Cold, pain, and labour, and all fleshly ills;
And mighty Poets in their misery dead.
—Perplexed, and longing to be comforted,
My question eagerly did I renew,
"How is it that you live, and what is it you do?"

18

He with a smile did then his words repeat;
And said, that, gathering leeches, far and wide
He travelled; stirring thus about his feet
The waters of the pools where they abide.
"Once I could meet with them on every side;
But they have dwindled long by slow decay;
Yet still I persevere, and find them where I may."

19

While he was talking thus, the lonely place,
The old Man's shape, and speech—all troubled me:
In my mind's eye I seemed to see him pace
About the weary moors continually,
Wandering about alone and silently.
While I these thoughts within myself pursued,
He, having made a pause, the same discourse renewed.

20

And soon with this he other matter blended,
Cheerfully uttered, with demeanour kind,
But stately in the main; and when he ended,
I could have laughed myself to scorn to find
In that decrepit Man so firm a mind.
"God," said I, "be my help and stay secure;
I'll think of the Leech-gatherer on the lonely moor!"

Samuel Taylor Coleridge (1772–1834)

KUBLA KHAN

In Xanadu did Kubla Khan
A stately pleasure dome decree:
Where Alph, the sacred river, ran

Through caverns measureless to man
  Down to a sunless sea.
So twice five miles of fertile ground
With walls and towers were girdled round:
And there were gardens bright with sinuous rills,
Where blossomed many an incense-bearing tree;
And here were forests ancient as the hills,
Enfolding sunny spots of greenery.

But oh! that deep romantic chasm which slanted
Down the green hill athwart a cedarn cover!
A savage place! as holy and enchanted
As e'er beneath a waning moon was haunted
By woman wailing for her demon lover!
And from this chasm, with ceaseless turmoil seething,
As if this earth in fast thick pants were breathing,
A mighty fountain momently was forced:
Amid whose swift half-intermitted burst
Huge fragments vaulted like rebounding hail,
Or chaffy grain beneath the thresher's flail:
And 'mid these dancing rocks at once and ever
It flung up momently the sacred river.
Five miles meandering with a mazy motion
Through wood and dale the sacred river ran,
Then reached the caverns measureless to man,
And sank in tumult to a lifeless ocean:
And 'mid this tumult Kubla heard from far
Ancestral voices prophesying war!
  The shadow of the dome of pleasure
  Floated midway on the waves;
  Where was heard the mingled measure
  From the fountain and the caves.
It was a miracle of rare device,
A sunny pleasure dome with caves of ice!

  A damsel with a dulcimer
  In a vision once I saw:
  It was an Abyssinian maid,
  And on her dulcimer she played,
  Singing of Mount Abora.
  Could I revive within me
  Her symphony and song,
  To such a deep delight 'twould win me,
That with music loud and long,
I would build that dome in air,

That sunny dome! those caves of ice!
And all who heard should see them there,
And all should cry, Beware! Beware!
His flashing eyes, his floating hair!
Weave a circle round him thrice,
And close your eyes with holy dread,
For he on honeydew hath fed,
And drunk the milk of Paradise.

FROST AT MIDNIGHT

The Frost performs its secret ministry,
Unhelped by any wind. The owlet's cry
Came loud—and hark, again! loud as before.
The inmates of my cottage, all at rest,
Have left me to that solitude, which suits
Abstruser musings: save that at my side
My cradled infant slumbers peacefully.
'Tis calm indeed! so calm, that it disturbs
And vexes meditation with its strange
And extreme silentness. Sea, hill, and wood,
This populous village! Sea, and hill, and wood,
With all the numberless goings-on of life,
Inaudible as dreams! the thin blue flame
Lies on my low-burnt fire, and quivers not;
Only that film, which fluttered on the grate,
Still flutters there, the sole unquiet thing.
Methinks its motion in this hush of nature
Gives it dim sympathies with me who live,
Making it a companionable form,
Whose puny flaps and freaks the idling Spirit
By its own moods interprets, everywhere
Echo or mirror seeking of itself,
And makes a toy of Thought.

But O! how oft,
How oft, at school, with most believing mind,
Presageful, have I gazed upon the bars,
To watch that fluttering *stranger!* and as oft
With unclosed lids, already had I dreamt
Of my sweet birthplace, and the old church tower,
Whose bells, the poor man's only music, rang
From morn to evening, all the hot fair-day,

So sweetly, that they stirred and haunted me
With a wild pleasure, falling on mine ear
Most like articulate sounds of things to come!
So gazed I, till the soothing things, I dreamt,
Lulled me to sleep, and sleep prolonged my dreams!
And so I brooded all the following morn,
Awed by the stern preceptor's face, mine eye
Fixed with mock study on my swimming book:
Save if the door half opened, and I snatched
A hasty glance, and still my heart leaped up,
For still I hoped to see the *stranger's* face,
Townsman, or aunt, or sister more beloved,
My playmate when we both were clothed alike!

Dear Babe, that sleepest cradled by my side,
Whose gentle breathings, heard in this deep calm,
Fill up the interspersèd vacancies
And momentary pauses of the thought!
My babe so beautiful! it thrills my heart
With tender gladness, thus to look at thee,
And think that thou shalt learn far other lore,
And in far other scenes! For I was reared
On the great city, pent 'mid cloisters dim,
And saw nought lovely but the sky and stars.
But *thou*, my babe! shalt wander like a breeze
By lakes and sandy shores, beneath the crags
Of ancient mountain, and beneath the clouds,
Which image in their bulk both lakes and shores
And mountain crags: so shalt thou see and hear
The lovely shapes and sounds intelligible
Of that eternal language, which thy God
Utters, who from eternity doth teach
Himself in all, and all things in himself.
Great universal Teacher! he shall mold
Thy spirit, and by giving make it ask.

Therefore all seasons shall be sweet to thee,
Whether the summer clothe the general earth
With greenness, or the redbreast sit and sing
Betwixt the tufts of snow on the bare branch
Of mossy apple tree, while the nigh thatch
Smokes in the sun-thaw; whether the eave-drops fall
Heard only in the trances of the blast,
Or if the secret ministry of frost
Shall hang them up in silent icicles,
Quietly shining to the quiet Moon.

THE RIME OF THE ANCIENT MARINER

In Seven Parts

Facile credo, plures esse Naturas invisibiles quam visibiles in rerum universitate. Sed horum [sic] omnium familiam quis nobis enarrabit? et gradus et cognationes et discrimina et singulorum munera? Quid agunt? quae loca habitant? Harum rerum notitiam semper ambivit ingenium humanum, nunquam attigit. Juvat, interea, non diffiteor, quandoque in animo, tanquam in tabulâ, majoris et melioris mundi imaginem contemplari: ne mens assuefacta hodiernae vitae minutiis se contrahat nimis, et tota subsidat in pusillas cogitationes. Sed veritati interea invigilandum est, modusque servandus, ut certa ab incertis, diem a nocte, distinguamus.

T. Burnet, *Archaeol. Phil.* p. 68.

Argument

How a Ship, having first sailed to the Equator, was driven by storms to the cold Country towards the South Pole; how the Ancient Mariner cruelly and in contempt of the laws of hospitality killed a Seabird and how he was followed by many and strange Judgments: and in what manner he came back to his own Country.

Part 1

An ancient Mariner meeteth three Gallants bidden to a wedding feast, and detaineth one.

It is an ancient Mariner
And he stoppeth one of three.
—"By thy long gray beard and glittering eye,
Now wherefore stopp'st thou me?

The Bridegroom's doors are opened wide,
And I am next of kin;
The guests are met, the feast is set:
May'st hear the merry din."

He holds him with his skinny hand,
"There was a ship," quoth he.
"Hold off! unhand me, graybeard loon!"
Eftsoons his hand dropped he.

The Wedding-Guest is spellbound by the eye of the old seafaring man, and constrained to hear his tale.

He holds him with his glittering eye—
The Wedding-Guest stood still,
And listens like a three years' child:
The Mariner hath his will.

The Wedding-Guest sat on a stone:
He cannot choose but hear;
And thus spake on that ancient man,
The bright-eyed Mariner.

"The ship was cheered, the harbor cleared,
Merrily did we drop
Below the kirk, below the hill,
Below the lighthouse top.

The Mariner tells how the ship sailed southward with a good wind and fair weather, till it reached the Line.

The Sun came up upon the left,
Out of the sea came he!
And he shone bright, and on the right
Went down into the sea.

Higher and higher every day,
Till over the mast at noon—"
The Wedding-Guest here beat his breast,
For he heard the loud bassoon.

The Wedding-Guest heareth the bridal music; but the Mariner continueth his tale.

The bride hath paced into the hall,
Red as a rose is she;
Nodding their heads before her goes
The merry minstrelsy.

The Wedding-Guest he beat his breast,
Yet he cannot choose but hear;
And thus spake on that ancient man,
The bright-eyed Mariner.

The ship driven by a storm towards the south pole.

"And now the STORM-BLAST came, and he
Was tyrannous and strong;
He struck with his o'ertaking wings,
And chased us south along.

With sloping masts and dipping prow,
As who pursued with yell and blow
Still treads the shadow of his foe,
And forward bends his head,
The ship drove fast, loud roared the blast,
And southward aye we fled.

And now there came both mist and snow,
And it grew wondrous cold:
And ice, mast-high, came floating by,
As green as emerald.

The land of ice, and of fearful sounds where no living thing was to be seen.

And through the drifts the snowy clifts
Did send a dismal sheen:
Nor shapes of men nor beasts we ken—
The ice was all between.

The ice was here, the ice was there,
The ice was all around:

It cracked and growled, and roared and
  howled,
Like noises in a swound!

Till a great sea-bird, called the Albatross, came through the snow-fog, and was received with great joy and hospitality.

At length did cross an Albatross,
Thorough the fog it came;
As if it had been a Christian soul,
We hailed it in God's name.

It ate the food it ne'er had eat,
And round and round it flew.
The ice did split with a thunder-fit;
The helmsman steered us through!

And lo! the Albatross proveth a bird of good omen, and followeth the ship as it returned northward through fog and floating ice.

And a good south wind sprung up behind;
The Albatross did follow,
And every day, for food or play,
Came to the mariner's hollo!

In mist or cloud, on mast or shroud,
It perched for vespers nine;
Whiles all the night, through fog-smoke
  white,
Glimmered the white Moon-shine."

The ancient Mariner inhospitably killeth the pious bird of good omen.

"God save thee, ancient Mariner!
From the fiends, that plague thee thus!—
Why look'st thou so?"—With my crossbow
I shot the ALBATROSS.

Part 2

The Sun now rose upon the right:
Out of the sea came he,
Still hid in mist, and on the left
Went down into the sea.

And the good south wind still blew behind,
But no sweet bird did follow,
Nor any day for food or play
Came to the mariners' hollo!

His shipmates cry out against the ancient Mariner, for killing the bird of good luck.

And I had done a hellish thing,
And it would work 'em woe:
For all averred, I had killed the bird
That made the breeze to blow.
Ah wretch! said they, the bird to slay,
That made the breeze to blow!

But when the fog cleared off, they justify the same, and thus make themselves accomplices in the crime.

Nor dim nor red, like God's own head,
The glorious Sun uprist:
Then all averred, I had killed the bird
That brought the fog and mist.
'Twas right, said they, such birds to slay,
That bring the fog and mist.

The fair breeze continues; the ship enters the Pacific Ocean, and sails northward, even till it reaches the Line.

The fair breeze blew, the white foam flew,
The furrow followed free;
We were the first that ever burst
Into that silent sea.

The ship hath been suddenly becalmed.

Down dropped the breeze, the sails dropped
  down,
'Twas sad as sad could be;
And we did speak only to break
The silence of the sea!

All in a hot and copper sky,
The bloody Sun, at noon,
Right up above the mast did stand,
No bigger than the Moon.

Day after day, day after day,
We stuck, nor breath nor motion;
As idle as a painted ship
Upon a painted ocean.

And the Albatross begins to be avenged.

Water, water, everywhere,
And all the boards did shrink;
Water, water, everywhere,
Nor any drop to drink.

The very deep did rot: O Christ!
That ever this should be!
Yea, slimy things did crawl with legs
Upon the slimy sea.

A Spirit had followed them; one of the invisible inhabitants of this planet, neither departed souls nor angels; concerning whom the learned Jew, Josephus, and the Platonic Constantinopolitan, Michael Psellus, may be consulted. They are very numerous, and there is no climate or element without one or more.

About, about, in reel and rout
The death-fires danced at night;
The water, like a witch's oils,
Burnt green, and blue and white.

And some in dreams assurèd were
Of the Spirit that plagued us so;
Nine fathom deep he had followed us
From the land of mist and snow.

And every tongue, through utter drought,
Was withered at the root;

We could not speak, no more than if
We had been choked with soot.

The shipmates, in their sore distress, would fain throw the whole guilt on the ancient Mariner: in sign whereof they hang the dead sea bird round his neck.

Ah! well-a-day! what evil looks
Had I from old and young!
Instead of the cross, the Albatross
About my neck was hung.

Part 3

There passed a weary time. Each throat
Was parched, and glazed each eye.
A weary time! a weary time!
How glazed each weary eye,
When looking westward, I beheld
A something in the sky.

The ancient Mariner beholdeth a sign in the element afar off.

At first it seemed a little speck,
And then it seemed a mist;
It moved and moved, and took at last
A certain shape, I wist.

A speck, a mist, a shape, I wist!
And still it neared and neared:
As if it dodged a water-sprite,
It plunged and tacked and veered.

At its nearer approach, it seemeth him to be a ship; and at a dear ransom he freeth his speech from the bonds of thirst.

With throats unslaked, with black lips baked,
We could nor laugh nor wail;
Through utter drought all dumb we stood!
I bit my arm, I sucked the blood,
And cried, A sail! a sail!

A flash of joy;

With throats unslaked, with black lips baked,
Agape they heard me call:
Gramercy! they for joy did grin,
And all at once their breath drew in,
As they were drinking all.

And horror follows. For can it be a ship that comes onward without wind or tide?

See! see! (I cried) she tacks no more!
Hither to work us weal;
Without a breeze, without a tide,
She steadies with upright keel!

The western wave was all aflame.
The day was well nigh done!
Almost upon the western wave
Rested the broad bright Sun;
When that strange shape drove suddenly
Betwixt us and the Sun.

It seemeth him but the skeleton of a ship.

And straight the Sun was flecked with bars,
(Heaven's Mother send us grace!)
As if through a dungeon grate he peered
With broad and burning face.

And its ribs are seen as bars on the face of the setting Sun.

Alas! (thought I, and my heart beat loud)
How fast she nears and nears!
Are those *her* sails that glance in the Sun,
Like restless gossameres?

The Spectre-Woman and her Deathmate, and no other on board the skeleton ship.

Are those *her* ribs through which the Sun
Did peer, as through a grate?
And is that Woman all her crew?
Is that a DEATH? and are there two?
Is DEATH that woman's mate?

Like vessel, like crew!

Her lips were red, *her* looks were free,
Her locks were yellow as gold:
Her skin was as white as leprosy,
The Night-mare LIFE-IN-DEATH was she,
Who thicks man's blood with cold.

Death and Life-in-Death have diced for the ship's crew, and she (the latter) winneth the ancient Mariner.

The naked hulk alongside came,
And the twain were casting dice;
"The game is done! I've won! I've won!"
Quoth she, and whistles thrice.

No twilight within the courts of the Sun.

The Sun's rim dips; the stars rush out:
At one stride comes the dark;
With far-heard whisper, o'er the sea,
Off shot the spectre-bark.

At the rising of the Moon,

We listened and looked sideways up!
Fear at my heart, as at a cup,
My lifeblood seemed to sip!
The stars were dim, and thick the night,
The steersman's face by his lamp gleamed
  white;
From the sails the dew did drip—
Till clomb above the eastern bar
The hornèd Moon, with one bright star
Within the nether tip.

One after another,

One after one, by the star-dogged Moon,
Too quick for groan or sigh,
Each turned his face with a ghastly pang,
And cursed me with his eye.

His shipmates drop down dead.

Four times fifty living men,
(And I heard nor sigh nor groan)
With heavy thump, a lifeless lump,
They dropped down one by one.

But Life-in-Death begins her work on the ancient Mariner.

The souls did from their bodies fly—
They fled to bliss or woe!
And every soul, it passed me by,
Like the whizz of my crossbow!

Part 4

The Wedding-Guest feareth that a Spirit is talking to him;

"I fear thee, ancient Mariner!
I fear thy skinny hand!
And thou art long, and lank, and brown,
As is the ribbed sea-sand.

I fear thee and thy glittering eye,
And thy skinny hand, so brown."—

But the ancient Mariner assureth him of his bodily life, and proceedeth to relate his horrible penance.

Fear not, fear not, thou Wedding-Guest!
This body dropped not down.

Alone, alone, all, all alone,
Alone on a wide wide sea!
And never a saint took pity on
My soul in agony.

He despiseth the creatures of the calm,

The many men, so beautiful!
And they all dead did lie:
And a thousand thousand slimy things
Lived on; and so did I.

And envieth that they should live, and so many lie dead.

I looked upon the rotting sea,
And drew my eyes away;
I looked upon the rotting deck,
And there the dead men lay.

I looked to heaven, and tried to pray;
But or ever a prayer had gushed,
A wicked whisper came, and made
My heart as dry as dust.

I closed my lids, and kept them close,
And the balls like pulses beat;
For the sky and the sea, and the sea and the sky
Lay like a load on my weary eye,
And the dead were at my feet.

But the curse liveth for him in the eye of the dead men.

The cold sweat melted from their limbs,
Nor rot nor reek did they:
The look with which they looked on me
Had never passed away.

An orphan's curse would drag to hell
A spirit from on high;
But oh! more horrible than that
Is the curse in a dead man's eye!
Seven days, seven nights, I saw that curse,
And yet I could not die.

In his loneliness and fixedness he yearneth towards the journeying Moon, and the stars that still sojourn, yet still move onward; and every where the blue sky belongs to them, and is their appointed rest, and their native country and their own natural homes, which they enter unannounced, as lords that are certainly expected and yet there is a silent joy at their arrival.

The moving Moon went up the sky,
And nowhere did abide:
Softly she was going up,
And a star or two beside—

Her beams bemocked the sultry main,
Like April hoar-frost spread;
But where the ship's huge shadow lay,
The charmèd water burnt alway
A still and awful red.

By the light of the Moon he beholdeth God's creatures of the great calm.

Beyond the shadow of the ship,
I watched the water snakes:
They moved in tracks of shining white,
And when they reared, the elfish light
Fell off in hoary flakes.

Within the shadow of the ship
I watched their rich attire:
Blue, glossy green, and velvet black,
They coiled and swam; and every track
Was a flash of golden fire.

Their beauty and their happiness.

O happy living things! no tongue
Their beauty might declare:
A spring of love gushed from my heart,

He blesseth them in his heart.

And I blessed them unaware:
Sure my kind saint took pity on me,
And I blessed them unaware.

The spell begins to break.

The self-same moment I could pray;
And from my neck so free
The Albatross fell off, and sank
Like lead into the sea.

Part 5

Oh sleep! it is a gentle thing,
Beloved from pole to pole!

To Mary Queen the praise be given!
She sent the gentle sleep from Heaven,
That slid into my soul.

By grace of the holy Mother, the ancient Mariner is refreshed with rain.

The silly buckets on the deck,
That had so long remained,
I dreamt that they were filled with dew;
And when I awoke, it rained.

My lips were wet, my throat was cold,
My garments all were dank;
Sure I had drunken in my dreams,
And still my body drank.

I moved, and could not feel my limbs:
I was so light—almost
I thought that I had died in sleep,
And was a blessed ghost.

He heareth sounds and seeth strange sights and commotions in the sky and the element.

And soon I heard a roaring wind:
It did not come anear;
But with its sound it shook the sails,
That were so thin and sere.

The upper air burst into life!
And a hundred fire-flags sheen,
To and fro they were hurried about!
And to and fro, and in and out,
The wan stars danced between.

And the coming wind did roar more loud,
And the sails did sigh like sedge;
And the rain poured down from one black
  cloud;
The Moon was at its edge.

The thick black cloud was cleft, and still
The Moon was at its side:
Like waters shot from some high crag,
The lightning fell with never a jag,
A river steep and wide.

The bodies of the ship's crew are inspirited, and the ship moves on;

The loud wind never reached the ship,
Yet now the ship moved on!
Beneath the lightning and the Moon
The dead men gave a groan.

They groaned, they stirred, they all uprose,
Nor spake, nor moved their eyes;
It had been strange, even in a dream,
To have seen those dead men rise.

The helmsman steered, the ship moved on;
Yet never a breeze up-blew;
The mariners all 'gan work the ropes,
Where they were wont to do;
They raised their limbs like lifeless tools—
We were a ghastly crew.

The body of my brother's son
Stood by me, knee to knee:
The body and I pulled at one rope,
But he said nought to me.

But not by the souls of the men, nor by dæmons of earth or middle air, but by a blessed troop of angelic spirits, sent down by the invocation of the guardian saint.

"I fear thee, ancient Mariner!"
Be calm, thou Wedding Guest!
'Twas not those souls that fled in pain,
Which to their corses came again,
But a troop of spirits blest:

For when it dawned—they dropped their
 arms,
And clustered round the mast;
Sweet sounds rose slowly through their
 mouths,
And from their bodies passed.

Around, around, flew each sweet sound,
Then darted to the Sun;
Slowly the sounds came back again,
Now mixed, now one by one.

Sometimes a-dropping from the sky
I heard the sky-lark sing;
Sometimes all little birds that are,
How they seemed to fill the sea and air
With their sweet jargoning!

And now 'twas like all instruments,
Now like a lonely flute;
And now it is an angel's song.
That makes the heavens be mute.

It ceased; yet still the sails made on
A pleasant noise till noon,
A noise like of a hidden brook
In the leafy month of June,
That to the sleeping woods all night
Singeth a quiet tune.

Till noon we quietly sailed on,
Yet never a breeze did breathe:

Slowly and smoothly went the ship,
Moved onward from beneath.

The lonesome Spirit from the South Pole carries on the ship as far as the Line, in obedience to the angelic troop, but still requireth vengeance.

Under the keel nine fathom deep,
From the land of mist and snow,
The spirit slid: and it was he
That made the ship to go.
The sails at noon left off their tune,
And the ship stood still also.

The Sun, right up above the mast,
Had fixed her to the ocean:
But in a minute she 'gan stir,
With a short uneasy motion—
Backwards and forwards half her length
With a short uneasy motion.

Then like a pawing horse let go,
She made a sudden bound:
It flung the blood into my head,
And I fell down in a swound.

The Polar Spirit's fellow demons, the invisible inhabitants of the element, take part in his wrong; and two of them relate, one to the other, that penance long and heavy for the ancient Mariner hath been accorded to the Polar Spirit, who returneth southward.

How long in that same fit I lay,
I have not to declare;
But ere my living life returned,
I heard and in my soul discerned
Two voices in the air.

Is it he?" quoth one, "Is this the man?
By him who died on cross,
With his cruel bow he laid full low
The harmless Albatross.

The spirit who bideth by himself
In the land of mist and snow,
He loved the bird that loved the man
Who shot him with his bow."

The other was a softer voice,
As soft as honeydew:
Quoth he, "The man hath penance done,
And penance more will do."

Part 6

FIRST VOICE

"But tell me, tell me! speak again,
Thy soft response renewing—
What makes that ship drive on so fast?
What is the ocean doing?"

SECOND VOICE

"Still as a slave before his lord,
The ocean hath no blast;
His great bright eye most silently
Up to the Moon is cast—

If he may know which way to go;
For she guides him smooth or grim.
See, brother, see! how graciously
She looketh down on him."

FIRST VOICE

The Mariner hath been cast into a trance; for the angelic power causeth the vessel to drive northward faster than human life could endure.

"But why drives on that ship so fast,
Without or wave or wind?"

SECOND VOICE

"The air is cut away before,
And closes from behind.

Fly, brother, fly! more high, more high!
Or we shall be belated:
For slow and slow that ship will go,
When the Mariner's trance is abated."

The supernatural motion is retarded; the Mariner awakes, and his penance begins anew.

I woke, and we were sailing on
As in a gentle weather:
'Twas night, calm night, the moon was high;
The dead men stood together.

All stood together on the deck,
For a charnel-dungeon fitter:
All fixed on me their stony eyes,
That in the Moon did glitter.

The pang, the curse, with which they died,
Had never passed away:
I could not draw my eyes from theirs,
Nor turn them up to pray.

The curse is finally expiated.

And now this spell was snapped: once more
I viewed the ocean green,
And looked far forth, yet little saw
Of what had else been seen—

Like one, that on a lonesome road
Doth walk in fear and dread,
And having once turned round walks on,
And turns no more his head;

Because he knows, a frightful fiend
Doth close behind him tread.

But soon there breathed a wind on me,
Nor sound nor motion made:
Its path was not upon the sea,
In ripple or in shade.

It raised my hair, it fanned my cheek
Like a meadow-gale of spring—
It mingled strangely with my fears,
Yet it felt like a welcoming.

Swiftly, swiftly flew the ship,
Yet she sailed softly too:
Sweetly, sweetly blew the breeze—
On me alone it blew.

And the ancient Mariner beholdeth his native country.

Oh! dream of joy! is this indeed
The lighthouse top I see?
Is this the hill? is this the kirk?
Is this mine own countree?

We drifted o'er the harbor bar,
And I with sobs did pray—
O let me be awake, my God!
Or let me sleep alway.

The harbor bay was clear as glass,
So smoothly it was strewn!
And on the bay the moonlight lay,
And the shadow of the Moon.

The rock shone bright, the kirk no less,
That stands above the rock:
The moonlight steeped in silentness
The steady weathercock.

And the bay was white with silent light,
Till rising from the same,
Full many shapes, that shadows were,
In crimson colors came.

The angelic spirits leave the dead bodies.

And appear in their own forms of light.

A little distance from the prow
Those crimson shadows were:
I turned my eyes upon the deck—
Oh, Christ! what saw I there!

Each corse lay flat, lifeless and flat,
And, by the holy rood!

A man all light, a seraph man,
On every corse there stood.

This seraph band, each waved his hand:
It was a heavenly sight!
They stood as signals to the land,
Each one a lovely light;

This seraph band, each waved his hand,
No voice did they impart—
No voice; but oh! the silence sank
Like music on my heart.

But soon I heard the dash of oars,
I heard the Pilot's cheer;
My head was turned perforce away
And I saw a boat appear.

The Pilot and the Pilot's boy,
I heard them coming fast:
Dear Lord in Heaven! it was a joy
The dead men could not blast.

I saw a third—I heard his voice:
It is the Hermit good!
He singeth loud his godly hymns
That he makes in the wood.
He'll shrieve my soul, he'll wash away
The Albatross's blood.

Part 7

The Hermit of the Wood,

This Hermit good lives in that wood
Which slopes down to the sea.
How loudly his sweet voice he rears!
He loves to talk with marineres
That come from a far countree.

He kneels at morn, and noon, and eve—
He hath a cushion plump:
It is the moss that wholly hides
The rotted old oak-stump.

The skiff-boat neared: I hear them talk,
"Why, this is strange, I trow!
Where are those lights so many and fair,
That signal made but now?"

Approacheth the ship with wonder.

"Strange, by my faith!" the Hermit said—
"And they answered not our cheer!

The planks looked warped! and see those
sails,
How thin they are and sere!
I never saw aught like to them,
Unless perchance it were
Brown skeletons of leaves that lag
My forest-brook along;
When the ivy tod is heavy with snow,
And the owlet whoops to the wolf below,
That eats the she-wolf's young."

"Dear Lord! it hath a fiendish look,"
(The Pilot made reply)
"I am a-feared"—"Push on, push on!"
Said the Hermit cheerily.

The boat came closer to the ship,
But I nor spake nor stirred;
The boat came close beneath the ship,
And straight a sound was heard.

The ship suddenly sinketh.

Under the water it rumbled on,
Still louder and more dread:
It reached the ship, it split the bay;
The ship went down like lead.

The ancient Mariner is saved in the Pilot's boat.

Stunned by that loud and dreadful sound,
Which sky and ocean smote,
Like one that hath been seven days drowned
My body lay afloat;
But swift as dreams, myself I found
Within the Pilot's boat.

Upon the whirl, where sank the ship,
The boat spun round and round;
And all was still, save that the hill
Was telling of the sound.

I moved my lips—the Pilot shrieked
And fell down in a fit;
The holy Hermit raised his eyes,
And prayed where he did sit.

I took the oars: the Pilot's boy,
Who now doth crazy go,
Laughed loud and long, and all the while
His eyes went to and fro.
"Ha! ha!" quoth he, "full plain I see,
The Devil knows how to row."

And now, all in my own countree,
I stood on the firm land!
The Hermit stepped forth from the boat,
And scarcely he could stand.

The ancient Mariner earnestly entreateth the Hermit to shrieve him; and the penance of life falls on him.

"O shrieve me, shrieve me, holy man!"
The Hermit crossed his brow.
"Say quick," quoth he, "I bid thee say—
What manner of man art thou?"

Forthwith this frame of mine was wrenched
With a woeful agony,
Which forced me to begin my tale;
And then it left me free.

And ever and anon through out his future life an agony constraineth him to travel from land to land;

Since then, at an uncertain hour,
That agony returns:
And till my ghastly tale is told,
This heart within me burns.

I pass, like night, from land to land;
I have strange power of speech;
That moment that his face I see,
I know the man that must hear me:
To him my tale I teach.

What loud uproar bursts from that door!
The wedding-guests are there:
But in the garden-bower the bride
And bride-maids singing are:
And hark the little vesper bell,
Which biddeth me to prayer!

O Wedding-Guest! this soul hath been
Alone on a wide wide sea:
So lonely 'twas, that God himself
Scarce seemèd there to be.

O sweeter than the marriage feast,
'Tis sweeter far to me,
To walk together to the kirk
With a goodly company!—

To walk together to the kirk,
And all together pray,
While each to his great Father bends,
Old men, and babes, and loving friends
And youths and maidens gay!

And to teach, by his own example, love and reverence to all things that God made and loveth.

Farewell, farewell! but this I tell
To thee, thou Wedding-Guest!
He prayeth well, who loveth well
Both man and bird and beast.

He prayeth best, who loveth best
All things both great and small;
For the dear God who loveth us,
He made and loveth all.

The Mariner, whose eye is bright,
Whose beard with age is hoar,
Is gone: and now the Wedding-Guest
Turned from the bridegroom's door.

He went like one that hath been stunned,
And is of sense forlorn:
A sadder and a wiser man,
He rose the morrow morn.

Percy Bysshe Shelley (1792–1822)

OZYMANDIAS

I met a traveller from an antique land,
Who said—"Two vast and trunkless legs of stone
Stand in the desart. . . . Near them, on the sand,
Half sunk a shattered visage lies, whose frown,
And wrinkled lip, and sneer of cold command,
Tell that its sculptor well those passions read
Which yet survive, stamped on these lifeless things,
The hand that mocked them, and the heart that fed;
And on the pedestal, these words appear:
My name is Ozymandias, King of Kings,
Look on my Works, ye Mighty, and despair!
Nothing beside remains. Round the decay
Of that colossal Wreck, boundless and bare
The lone and level sands stretch far away."

A SONG: "MEN OF ENGLAND"

Men of England, wherefore plough
For the lords who lay ye low?

Wherefore weave with toil and care
The rich robes your tyrants wear?

Wherefore feed and clothe and save
From the cradle to the grave
Those ungrateful drones who would
Drain your sweat—nay, drink your blood?

Wherefore, Bees of England, forge
Many a weapon, chain, and scourge,
That these stingless drones may spoil
The forced produce of your toil?

Have ye leisure, comfort, calm,
Shelter, food, love's gentle balm?
Or what is it ye buy so dear
With your pain and with your fear?

The seed ye sow, another reaps;
The wealth ye find, another keeps;
The robes ye weave, another wears;
The arms ye forge, another bears.

Sow seed—but let no tyrant reap:
Find wealth—let no impostor heap:
Weave robes—let not the idle wear:
Forge arms—in your defence to bear.

Shrink to your cellars, holes, and cells—
In halls ye deck another dwells.
Why shake the chains ye wrought? Ye see
The steel ye tempered glance on ye.

With plough and spade and hoe and loom
Trace your grave and build your tomb
And weave your winding-sheet—till fair
England be your Sepulchre.

John Keats (1795–1821)

ON FIRST LOOKING INTO CHAPMAN'S HOMER

Much have I travell'd in the realms of gold,
   And many goodly states and kingdoms seen;
   Round many western islands have I been
Which bards in fealty to Apollo hold.
Oft of one wide expanse had I been told

That deep-brow'd Homer ruled as his demesne;
Yet did I never breathe its pure serene
Till I heard Chapman speak out loud and bold:
Then felt I like some watcher of the skies
When a new planet swims into his ken;
Or like stout Cortez when with eagle eyes
He star'd at the Pacific—and all his men
Look'd at each other with a wild surmise—
Silent, upon a peak in Darien.

Emily Brontë (1818–1848)

NO COWARD SOUL IS MINE

No coward soul is mine
No trembler in the world's storm-troubled sphere
I see Heaven's glories shine
And Faith shines equal arming me from Fear

O God within my breast
Almighty ever-present Deity
Life, that in me hast rest
As I Undying Life, have power in Thee

Vain are the thousand creeds
That move men's hearts, unutterably vain,
Worthless as withered weeds
Or idlest froth amid the boundless main

To waken doubt in one
Holding so fast by thy infinity
So surely anchored on
The steadfast rock of Immortality

With wide-embracing love
Thy spirit animates eternal years
Pervades and broods above,
Changes, sustains, dissolves, creates and rears

Though Earth and moon were gone
And suns and universes ceased to be
And thou wert left alone
Every Existence would exist in thee

There is not room for Death
Nor atom that his might could render void
Since thou art Being and Breath
And what thou art may never be destroyed.

[TELL ME, TELL ME, SMILING CHILD]

Tell me, tell me, smiling child,
What the past is like to thee?
"An Autumn evening soft and mild
With a wind that sighs mournfully."

Tell me, what is the present hour?
"A green and flowery spray
Where a young bird sits gathering its power
To mount and fly away."

And what is the future, happy one?
"A sea beneath a cloudless sun;
A mighty, glorious, dazzling sea
Stretching into infinity."

Ralph Waldo Emerson (1803–1882)

THE RHODORA:
On Being Asked, Whence Is the Flower?

In May, when sea-winds pierced our solitudes,
I found the fresh Rhodora in the woods,
Spreading its leafless blooms in a damp nook,
To please the desert and the sluggish brook.
The purple petals, fallen in the pool,
Made the black water with their beauty gay;
Here might the red-bird come his plumes to cool,
And court the flower that cheapens his array.
Rhodora! if the sages ask thee why
This charm is wasted on the earth and sky,
Tell them, dear, that if eyes were made for seeing,
Then Beauty is its own excuse for being:
Why thou wert there, O rival of the rose!
I never thought to ask, I never knew:
But, in my simple ignorance, suppose
The self-same Power that brought me there brought you.

THE SNOW-STORM

Announced by all the trumpets of the sky,
Arrives the snow, and, driving o'er the fields
Seems nowhere to alight: the whited air

Hides hills and woods, the river, and the heaven,
And veils the farm-house at the garden's end.
The sled and traveller stopped, the courier's feet
Delayed, all friends shut out, the housemates sit
Around the radiant fireplace, enclosed
In a tumultuous privacy of storm.

Come see the north wind's masonry.
Out of an unseen quarry evermore
Furnished with tile, the fierce artificer
Curves his white bastions with projected roof
Round every windward stake, or tree, or door.
Speeding, the myriad-handed, his wild work
So fanciful, so savage, nought cares he
For number or proportion. Mockingly,
On coop or kennel he hangs Parian wreaths;
A swan-like form invests the hidden thorn;
Fills up the farmer's lane from wall to wall,
Maugre the farmer's sighs; and at the gate
A tapering turret overtops the work.
And when his hours are numbered, and the world
Is all his own, retiring, as he were not,
Leaves, when the sun appears, astonished Art
To mimic in slow structures, stone by stone,
Built in an age, the mad wind's night-work,
The frolic architecture of the snow.

Alfred, Lord Tennyson (1809–1892)
BREAK, BREAK, BREAK

Break, break, break,
  On thy cold gray stones, O Sea!
And I would that my tongue could utter
  The thoughts that arise in me.

O, well for the fisherman's boy,
  That he shouts with his sister at play!
O, well for the sailor lad,
  That he sings in his boat on the bay!

And the stately ships go on
  To their haven under the hill;
But O for the touch of a vanished hand,
  And the sound of a voice that is still!

Break, break, break,
  At the foot of thy crags, O Sea!
But the tender grace of a day that is dead
  Will never come back to me.

TEARS, IDLE TEARS

Tears, idle tears, I know not what they mean,
Tears from the depth of some divine despair
Rise in the heart, and gather to the eyes,
In looking on the happy autumn-fields,
And thinking of the days that are no more.

Fresh as the first beam glittering on a sail,
That brings our friends up from the underworld,
Sad as the last which reddens over one
That sinks with all we love below the verge;
So sad, so fresh, the days that are no more.

Ah, sad and strange as in dark summer dawns
The earliest pipe of half-awakened birds
To dying ears, when unto dying eyes
The casement slowly grows a glimmering square;
So sad, so strange, the days that are no more.

Dear as remembered kisses after death,
And sweet as those by hopeless fancy feigned
On lips that are for others; deep as love,
Deep as first love, and wild with all regret;
O Death in Life, the days that are no more!

CROSSING THE BAR

Sunset and evening star,
  And one clear call for me!
And may there be no moaning of the bar,
  When I put out to sea,

But such a tide as moving seems asleep,
  Too full for sound and foam,
When that which drew from out the boundless deep
  Turns again home.

Twilight and evening bell,
  And after that the dark!

And may there be no sadness of farewell,
  When I embark;

For though from out our bourne of Time and Place
  The flood may bear me far,
I hope to see my Pilot face to face
  When I have crossed the bar.

Christina Rossetti (1830–1894)
SYMBOLS

I watched a rosebud very long
  Brought on by dew and sun and shower,
  Waiting to see the perfect flower:
Then, when I thought it should be strong,
  It opened at the matin hour
    And fell at evensong.

I watched a nest from day to day,
  A green nest full of pleasant shade,
  Wherein three speckled eggs were laid:
But when they should have hatched in May,
  The two old birds had grown afraid
    Or tired, and flew away.

Then in my wrath I broke the bough
  That I had tended so with care,
  Hoping its scent should fill the air;
I crushed the eggs, not heeding how
  Their ancient promise had been fair:
    I would have vengeance now.

But the dead branch spoke from the sod,
  And the eggs answered me again:
  Because we failed dost thou complain?
Is thy wrath just? And what if God,
  Who waiteth for thy fruits in vain,
    Should also take the rod?

IN AN ARTIST'S STUDIO

One face looks out from all his canvases,
  One selfsame figure sits or walks or leans:
  We found her hidden just behind those screens,

That mirror gave back all her loveliness.
A queen in opal or in ruby dress,
  A nameless girl in freshest summer-greens,
  A saint, an angel—every canvas means
The same one meaning, neither more nor less.
He feeds upon her face by day and night,
  And she with true kind eyes looks back on him,
Fair as the moon and joyful as the light:
  Not wan with waiting, not with sorrow dim;
Not as she is, but was when hope shone bright;
  Not as she is, but as she fills his dream.

Robert Browning (1812–1889)

PORPHYRIA'S LOVER

The rain set early in tonight,
    The sullen wind was soon awake,
It tore the elm-tops down for spite,
    And did its worst to vex the lake:
    I listened with heart fit to break.
When glided in Porphyria; straight
    She shut the cold out and the storm,
And kneeled and made the cheerless grate
    Blaze up, and all the cottage warm;
    Which done, she rose, and from her form
Withdrew the dripping cloak and shawl,
    And laid her soiled gloves by, untied
Her hat and let the damp hair fall,
    And, last, she sat down by my side
    And called me. When no voice replied,
She put my arm about her waist,
    And made her smooth white shoulder bare,
And all her yellow hair displaced,
    And, stooping, made my cheek lie there,
    And spread, o'er all, her yellow hair,
Murmuring how she loved me—she
    Too weak, for all her heart's endeavor,
To set its struggling passion free
    From pride, and vainer ties dissever,
    And give herself to me forever.
But passion sometimes would prevail,
    Nor could tonight's gay feast restrain
A sudden thought of one so pale

For love of her, and all in vain:
So, she was come through wind and rain.
Be sure I looked up at her eyes
Happy and proud; at last I knew
Porphyria worshiped me: surprise
Made my heart swell, and still it grew
While I debated what to do.
That moment she was mine, mine, fair,
Perfectly pure and good: I found
A thing to do, and all her hair
In one long yellow string I wound
Three times her little throat around,
And strangled her. No pain felt she;
I am quite sure she felt no pain.
As a shut bud that holds a bee,
I warily oped her lids: again
Laughed the blue eyes without a stain.
And I untightened next the tress
About her neck; her cheek once more
Blushed bright beneath my burning kiss:
I propped her head up as before,
Only, this time my shoulder bore
Her head, which droops upon it still:
The smiling rosy little head,
So glad it has its utmost will,
That all it scorned at once is fled,
And I, its love, am gained instead!
Porphyria's love: she guessed not how
Her darling one wish would be heard.
And thus we sit together now,
And all night long we have not stirred,
And yet God has not said a word!

Elizabeth Barrett Browning (1806–1861)

GRIEF

I tell you, hopeless grief is passionless;
That only men incredulous of despair,
Half-taught in anguish, through the midnight air
Beat upward to God's throne in loud access
Of shrieking and reproach. Full desertness,
In souls as countries, lieth silent-bare
Under the blanching, vertical eye-glare

Of the absolute heavens. Deep-hearted man, express
Grief for thy dead in silence like to death—
Most like a monumental statue set
In everlasting watch and moveless woe
Till itself crumble to the dust beneath.
Touch it; the marble eyelids are not wet:
If it could weep, it could arise and go.

HIRAM POWERS' "GREEK SLAVE"

They say ideal beauty cannot enter
The house of anguish. On the threshold stands
An alien image with enshackled hands,
Called the Greek Slave! as if the artist meant her
(That passionless perfection which he lent her,
Shadowed not darkened where the sill expands)
To so confront man's crimes in different lands
With man's ideal sense. Pierce to the centre,
Art's fiery finger, and break up ere long
The serfdom of this world. Appeal, fair stone,
From God's pure heights of beauty against man's wrong!
Catch up in thy divine face, not alone
East griefs but west, and strike and shame the strong,
By thunders of white silence, overthrown.

SONNET 22

When our two souls stand up erect and strong,
Face to face, silent, drawing nigh and nigher,
Until the lengthening wings break into fire
At either curvéd point,—what bitter wrong
Can the earth do to us, that we should not long
Be here contented? Think. In mounting higher,
The angels would press on us and aspire
To drop some golden orb of perfect song
Into our deep, dear silence. Let us stay
Rather on earth, Belovéd,—where the unfit
Contrarious moods of men recoil away
And isolate pure spirits, and permit
A place to stand and love in for a day,
With darkness and the death-hour rounding it.

A CURSE FOR A NATION

Prologue

I heard an angel speak last night,
  And he said "Write!
Write a Nation's curse for me,
And send it over the Western Sea."

I faltered, taking up the word:
  "Not so, my lord!
If curses must be, choose another
To send thy curse against my brother.

"For I am bound by gratitude,
  By love and blood,
To brothers of mine across the sea,
Who stretch out kindly hands to me."

"Therefore," the voice said, "shalt thou write
  My curse tonight.
From the summits of love a curse is driven,
As lightning is from the tops of heaven."

"Not so," I answered. "Evermore
  My heart is sore
For my own land's sins: for little feet
Of children bleeding along the street:

"For parked-up honors that gainsay
  The right of way:
For almsgiving through a door that is
Not open enough for two friends to kiss:

"For love of freedom which abates
  Beyond the Straits:
For patriot virtue starved to vice on
Self-praise, self-interest, and suspicion:

"For an oligarchic parliament,
  And bribes well-meant.
What curse to another land assign,
When heavy-souled for the sins of mine?"

"Therefore," the voice said, "shalt thou write
  My curse tonight.
Because thou hast strength to see and hate
A foul thing done *within* thy gate."

"Not so," I answered once again.
  "To curse, choose men.
For I, a woman, have only known
How the heart melts and the tears run down."

"Therefore," the voice said, "shalt thou write
  My curse tonight.
Some women weep and curse, I say
(And no one marvels), night and day.

"And thou shalt take their part tonight,
  Weep and write.
A curse from the depths of womanhood
Is very salt, and bitter, and good."

So thus I wrote, and mourned indeed,
  What all may read.
And thus, as was enjoined on me,
I send it over the Western Sea.

The Curse

I

Because ye have broken your own chain
  With the strain
Of brave men climbing a Nation's height,
Yet thence bear down with brand and thong
On souls of others,—for this wrong
  This is the curse. Write.

Because yourselves are standing straight
  In the state
Of Freedom's foremost acolyte,
Yet keep calm footing all the time
On writhing bond-slaves,—for this crime
  This is the curse. Write.

Because ye prosper in God's name,
  With a claim
To honor in the old world's sight,
Yet do the fiend's work perfectly
In strangling martyrs,—for this lie
  This is the curse. Write.

II

Ye shall watch while kings conspire
Round the people's smouldering fire
  And, warm for your part,
Shall never dare—O shame!

To utter the thought into flame
  Which burns at your heart.
  This is the curse. Write.

Ye shall watch while nations strive
With the bloodhounds, die or survive,
  Drop faint from their jaws,
Or throttle them backward to death;
And only under your breath
  Shall favour the cause.
  This is the curse. Write.

Ye shall watch while strong men draw
The nets of feudal law
  To strangle the weak;
And, counting the sin for a sin,
Your soul shall be sadder within
  Than the word ye shall speak.
  This is the curse. Write.

When good men are praying erect
That Christ may avenge his elect
  And deliver the earth,
The prayer in your ears, said low,
Shall sound like the tramp of a foe
  That's driving you forth.
  This is the curse. Write.

When wise men give you their praise,
They shall pause in the heat of the phrase,
  As if carried too far.
When ye boast your own charters kept true,
Ye shall blush; for the thing which ye do
  Derides what ye are.
  This is the curse. Write.

When fools cast taunts at your gate,
Your scorn ye shall somewhat abate
  As ye look o'er the wall;
For your conscience, tradition, and name
Explode with a deadlier blame
Than the worst of them all.
  This is the curse. Write.

Go, wherever ill deeds shall be done,
Go, plant your flag in the sun
  Beside the ill-doers!

And recoil from clenching the curse
Of God's witnessing Universe
With a curse of yours.
THIS is the curse. Write.

Emily Dickinson (1830–1886)

[I FELT A FUNERAL, IN MY BRAIN]

I felt a Funeral, in my Brain,
And Mourners to and fro
Kept treading—treading—till it seemed
That Sense was breaking through—

And when they all were seated,
A Service, like a Drum—
Kept beating—beating—till I thought
My Mind was going numb—

And then I heard them lift a Box
And creak across my Soul
With those same Boots of Lead, again,
Then Space—began to toll,

As all the Heavens were a Bell,
And Being, but an Ear,
And I, and Silence, some strange Race
Wrecked, solitary, here—

And then a Plank in Reason, broke,
And I dropped down, and down—
And hit a World, at every plunge,
And Finished knowing—then—

[MUCH MADNESS IS DIVINEST SENSE]

Much Madness is divinest Sense—
To a discerning Eye—
Much Sense—the starkest Madness—
'Tis the Majority
In this, as All, prevail—
Assent—and you are sane—
Demur—you're straightway dangerous—
And handled with a Chain—

[I LIKE A LOOK OF AGONY]

I like a look of Agony,
Because I know it's true—
Men do not sham Convulsion,
Nor simulate, a Throe—

The Eyes glaze once—and that is Death—
Impossible to feign
The Beads upon the Forehead
By homely Anguish strung.

[APPARENTLY WITH NO SURPRISE]

Apparently with no surprise
To any happy flower,
The frost beheads it at its play
In accidental power.

The blond assassin passes on,
The sun proceeds unmoved
To measure off another day
For an approving God.

[THE BRAIN—IS WIDER THAN THE SKY]

The Brain—is wider than the Sky—
For—put them side by side—
The one the other will contain
With ease—and You—beside—

The Brain is deeper than the sea—
For—hold them—Blue to Blue—
The one the other will absorb—
As Sponges—Buckets—do—

The Brain is just the weight of God—
For—Heft them—Pound for Pound—
And they will differ—if they do—
As Syllable from Sound—

[I NEVER LOST AS MUCH BUT TWICE]

I never lost as much but twice,
And that was in the sod.
Twice have I stood a beggar
Before the door of God!

Angels—twice descending
Reimbursed my store—
Burglar! Banker—Father!
I am poor once more!

[THESE ARE THE DAYS WHEN BIRDS COME BACK]

These are the days when Birds come back—
A very few—a Bird or two—
To take a backward look.

These are the days when skies resume
The old—old sophistries of June—
A blue and gold mistake.

Oh fraud that cannot cheat the Bee—
Almost thy plausibility
Induces my belief.

Till ranks of seeds their witness bear—
And softly thro' the altered air
Hurries a timid leaf.

Oh Sacrament of summer days,
Oh Last Communion in the Haze—
Permit a child to join.

Thy sacred emblems to partake—
Thy consecrated bread to take
And thine immortal wine!

Walt Whitman (1819–1892)

ONCE I PASS'D THROUGH A POPULOUS CITY

Once I pass'd through a populous city imprinting my brain
  for future use with its shows, architecture, customs,
  traditions,

Yet now of all that city I remember only a woman I casually
met there who detain'd me for love of me,
Day by day and night by night we were together—all else
has long been forgotten by me,
I remember I say only that woman who passionately clung
to me,
Again we wander, we love, we separate again,
Again she holds me by the hand, I must not go,
I see her close beside me with silent lips sad and tremulous.

WHEN I HEARD THE LEARN'D ASTRONOMER

When I heard the learn'd astronomer,
When the proofs, the figures, were ranged in columns before
me,
When I was shown the charts and diagrams, to add, divide,
and measure them,
When I sitting heard the astronomer where he lectured with
much applause in the lecture-room,
How soon unaccountable I became tired and sick,
Till rising and gliding out I wander'd off by myself,
In the mystical moist night-air, and from time to time,
Look'd up in perfect silence at the stars.

I SAW IN LOUISIANA A LIVE-OAK GROWING

I saw in Louisiana a live-oak growing,
All alone stood it and the moss hung down from the
branches,
Without any companion it grew there uttering joyous leaves
of dark green,
And its look, rude, unbending, lusty, made me think of
myself,
But I wonder'd how it could utter joyous leaves standing
alone there without its friend near, for I knew I could not,
And I broke off a twig with a certain number of leaves upon
it, and twined around it a little moss,
And brought it away, and I have placed it in sight in my
room,
It is not needed to remind me as of my own dear friends,
(For I believe lately I think of little else than of them,)

Yet it remains to be a curious token, it makes me think of
manly love;
For all that, and though the live-oak glistens there in
Louisiana solitary in a wide flat space,
Uttering joyous leaves all its life without a friend a lover
near,
I know very well I could not.

Lewis Carroll (1832–1898)

JABBERWOCKY

'Twas brillig, and the slithy toves
Did gyre and gimble in the wabe;
All mimsy were the borogoves,
And the mome raths outgrabe.

"Beware the Jabberwock, my son!
The jaws that bite, the claws that catch!
Beware the Jubjub bird, and shun
The frumious Bandersnatch!"

He took his vorpal sword in hand;
Long time the manxome foe he sought—
So rested he by the Tumtum tree,
And stood awhile in thought.

And, as in uffish thought he stood,
The Jabberwock, with eyes of flame,
Came whiffling through the tulgey wood,
And burbled as it came!

One, two! One, two! And through and through
The vorpal blade went snicker-snack!
He left it dead, and with its head
He went galumphing back.

"And hast thou slain the Jabberwock?
Come to my arms, my beamish boy!
O frabjous day! Callooh! Callay!"
He chortled in his joy.

'Twas brillig, and the slithy toves
Did gyre and gimble in the wabe;
All mimsy were the borogoves,
And the mome raths outgrabe.

Thomas Hardy (1840–1928)
HAP

If but some vengeful god would call to me
From up the sky, and laugh: "Thou suffering thing,
Know that thy sorrow is my ecstasy,
That thy love's loss is my hate's profiting!"

Then would I bear it, clench myself, and die,
Steeled by the sense of ire unmerited;
Half-eased in that a Powerfuller than I
Had willed and meted me the tears I shed.

But not so. How arrives it joy lies slain,
And why unblooms the best hope ever sown?
—Crass Casualty obstructs the sun and rain,
And dicing Time for gladness casts a moan. . . .
These purblind Doomsters had as readily strown
Blisses about my pilgrimage as pain.

Gerard Manley Hopkins (1844–1889)
SPRING AND FALL
To a Young Child

Márgarét, are you grieving
Over Goldengrove unleaving?
Leáves, like the things of man, you
With your fresh thoughts care for, can you?
Áh! ás the heart grows older
It will come to such sights colder
By and by, nor spare a sigh
Though worlds of wanwood leafmeal lie;
And yet you wíll weep and know why.
Now no matter, child, the name:
Sórrow's spríngs áre the same.
Nor mouth had, no nor mind, expressed
What heart heard of, ghost guessed:
It ís the blight man was born for,
It is Margaret you mourn for.

A. E. Housman (1859–1936)

WITH RUE MY HEART IS LADEN

With rue my heart is laden
 For golden friends I had,
For many a rose-lipt maiden
 And many a lightfoot lad.

By brooks too broad for leaping
 The lightfoot boys are laid;
The rose-lipt girls are sleeping
 In fields where roses fade.

EIGHT O'CLOCK

He stood, and heard the steeple
 Sprinkle the quarters on the morning town.
One, two, three, four, to market-place and people
 It tossed them down.

Strapped, noosed, nighing his hour,
 He stood and counted them and cursed his luck;
And then the clock collected in the tower
 Its strength, and struck.

LOVELIEST OF TREES, THE CHERRY NOW

Loveliest of trees, the cherry now
Is hung with bloom along the bough,
And stands about the woodland ride
Wearing white for Eastertide.

Now, of my threescore years and ten,
Twenty will not come again,
And take from seventy springs a score,
It only leaves me fifty more.

And since to look at things in bloom
Fifty springs are little room,
About the woodlands I will go
To see the cherry hung with snow.

Wilfred Owen (1893–1918)
FUTILITY

Move him into the sun—
Gently its touch awoke him once,
At home, whispering of fields unsown.
Always it woke him, even in France,
Until this morning and this snow.
If anything might rouse him now
The kind old sun will know.

Think how it wakes the seeds,—
Woke, once, the clays of a cold star.
Are limbs, so dear-achieved, are sides,
Full-nerved—still warm—too hard to stir?
Was it for this the clay grew tall?
—O what made fatuous sunbeams toil
To break earth's sleep at all?

T. S. Eliot (1888–1965)
THE LOVE SONG OF J. ALFRED PRUFROCK

S'io credesse che mia risposta fosse
A persona che mai tornasse al mondo,
Questa fiamma staria senza piu scosse.
Ma perciocche giammai di questo fondo
Non torno vivo alcun, s'i'odo il vero,
Senza tema d'infamia ti rispondo.

Let us go then, you and I,
When the evening is spread out against the sky
Like a patient etherized upon a table;
Let us go, through certain half-deserted streets,
The muttering retreats
Of restless nights in one-night cheap hotels
And sawdust restaurants with oyster shells:
Streets that follow like a tedious argument
Of insidious intent
To lead you to an overwhelming question . . .
Oh, do not ask, "What is it?"
Let us go and make our visit.

In the room the women come and go
Talking of Michelangelo.

The yellow fog that rubs its back upon the windowpanes,
The yellow smoke that rubs its muzzle on the windowpanes
Licked its tongue into the corners of the evening,
Lingered upon the pools that stand in drains,
Let fall upon its back the soot that falls from chimneys,
Slipped by the terrace, made a sudden leap,
And seeing that it was a soft October night,
Curled once about the house, and fell asleep.

And indeed there will be time
For the yellow smoke that slides along the street,
Rubbing its back upon the windowpanes;
There will be time, there will be time
To prepare a face to meet the faces that you meet;
There will be time to murder and create,
And time for all the works and days of hands
That lift and drop a question on your plate;
Time for you and time for me,
And time yet for a hundred indecisions,
And for a hundred visions and revisions,
Before the taking of a toast and tea.

In the room the women come and go
Talking of Michelangelo.

And indeed there will be time
To wonder, "Do I dare?" and, "Do I dare?"
Time to turn back and descend the stair,
With a bald spot in the middle of my hair—
(They will say: "How his hair is growing thin!")
My morning coat, my collar mounting firmly to the chin,
My necktie rich and modest, but asserted by a simple pin—
(They will say: "But how his arms and legs are thin!")
Do I dare
Disturb the universe?
In a minute there is time
For decisions and revisions which a minute will reverse.

For I have known them all already, known them all—
Have known the evenings, mornings, afternoons,
I have measured out my life with coffee spoons;
I know the voices dying with a dying fall
Beneath the music from a farther room.
So how should I presume?

And I have known the eyes already, known them all—
The eyes that fix you in a formulated phrase,

And when I am formulated, sprawling on a pin,
When I am pinned and wriggling on the wall,
Then how should I begin
To spit out all the butt-ends of my days and ways?
  And how should I presume?

  And I have known the arms already, known them all—
Arms that are braceleted and white and bare
(But in the lamplight, downed with light brown hair!)
Is it perfume from a dress
That makes me so digress?
Arms that lie along a table, or wrap about a shawl.
  And should I then presume?
  And how should I begin?

. . .

  Shall I say, I have gone at dusk through narrow streets
And watched the smoke that rises from the pipes
Of lonely men in shirt-sleeves, leaning out of
  windows? . . .

  I should have been a pair of ragged claws
Scuttling across the floors of silent seas.

. . .

  And the afternoon, the evening, sleeps so peacefully!
Smoothed by long fingers,
Asleep . . . tired . . . or it malingers,
Stretched on the floor, here beside you and me.
Should I, after tea and cakes and ices,
Have the strength to force the moment to its crisis?
But though I have wept and fasted, wept and prayed,
Though I have seen my head (grown slightly bald) brought
  in upon a platter,
I am no prophet—and here's no great matter;
I have seen the moment of my greatness flicker,
And I have seen the eternal Footman hold my coat, and
  snicker,
And in short, I was afraid.

  And would it have been worth it, after all,
After the cups, the marmalade, the tea,
Among the porcelain, among some talk of you and me,
Would it have been worth while,
To have bitten off the matter with a smile,
To have squeezed the universe into a ball

To roll it toward some overwhelming question,
To say: "I am Lazarus, come from the dead,
Come back to tell you all, I shall tell you all"—
If one, settling a pillow by her head,
  Should say: "That is not what I meant at all.
  That is not it, at all."

  And would it have been worth it, after all,
Would it have been worth while,
After the sunsets and the dooryards and the sprinkled streets,
After the novels, after the teacups, after the skirts that trail
  along the floor—
And this, and so much more?—
It is impossible to say just what I mean!
But as if a magic lantern threw the nerves in patterns on a
  screen:
Would it have been worth while
If one, settling a pillow or throwing off a shawl,
And turning toward the window, should say:
  "That is not it at all,
  That is not what I meant, at all."

. . .

  No! I am not Prince Hamlet, nor was meant to be;
Am an attendant lord, one that will do
To swell a progress start a scene or two,
Advise the prince; no doubt, an easy tool,
Deferential, glad to be of use,
Politic, cautious, and meticulous;
Full of high sentence, but a bit obtuse;
At times, indeed, almost ridiculous—
Almost, at times, the Fool.

  I grow old . . . I grow old . . .
I shall wear the bottoms of my trousers rolled.

  Shall I part my hair behind? Do I dare to eat a peach?
I shall wear white flannel trousers, and walk upon the beach.
I have heard the mermaids singing, each to each.

I do not think that they will sing to me.

I have seen them riding seaward on the waves
Combing the white hair of the waves blown back
When the wind blows the water white and black.

We have lingered in the chambers of the sea
By sea-girls wreathed with seaweed red and brown
Till human voices wake us, and we drown.

JOURNEY OF THE MAGI

"A cold coming we had of it,
Just the worst time of the year
For a journey, and such a long journey:
The ways deep and the weather sharp,
The very dead of winter."
And the camels galled, sore-footed, refractory,
Lying down in the melting snow.
There were times we regretted
The summer palaces on slopes, the terraces,
And the silken girls bringing sherbet.
Then the camel men cursing and grumbling
And running away, and wanting their liquor and women,
And the night-fires going out, and the lack of shelters,
And the cities hostile and the towns unfriendly
And the villages dirty and charging high prices:
A hard time we had of it.
At the end we preferred to travel all night,
Sleeping in snatches,
With the voices singing in our ears, saying
That this was all folly.

Then at dawn we came down to a temperate valley,
Wet, below the snow line, smelling of vegetation;
With a running stream and a water mill beating the darkenss,
And three trees on the low sky,
And an old white horse galloped away in the meadow.
Then we came to a tavern with vine-leaves over the lintel,
Six hands at an open door dicing for pieces of silver,
And feet kicking the empty wineskins.
But there was no information, and so we continued
And arrived at evening, not a moment too soon
Finding the place; it was (you may say) satisfactory.

All this was a long time ago, I remember,
And I would do it again, but set down
This set down
This: were we led all that way for
Birth or Death? There was a Birth, certainly,
We had evidence and no doubt. I had seen birth and death,
But had thought they were different; this Birth was
Hard and bitter agony for us, like Death, our death.
We returned to our places, these Kingdoms,
But no longer at ease here, in the old dispensation,
With an alien people clutching their gods.
I should be glad of another death.

D. H. Lawrence (1885–1930)

PIANO

Softly, in the dusk, a woman is singing to me;
Taking me back down the vista of years, till I see
A child sitting under the piano, in the boom of the tingling strings
And pressing the small, poised feet of a mother who smiles as she sings.

In spite of myself, the insidious mastery of song
Betrays me back, till the heart of me weeps to belong
To the old Sunday evenings at home, with winter outside
And hymns in the cozy parlor, the tinkling piano our guide.

So now it is vain for the singer to burst into clamor
With the great black piano appassionato. The glamor
Of childish days is upon me, my manhood is cast
Down in the flood of remembrance, I weep like a child for the past.

H. D. [Hilda Doolittle] (1886–1961)

HEAT

O wind, rend open the heat,
cut apart the heat,
rend it to tatters.

Fruit cannot drop
through this thick air—
fruit cannot fall into heat
that presses up and blunts
the points of pears
and rounds the grapes.

Cut the heat—
plough through it,
turning it on either side
of your path.

SEA ROSE

Rose, harsh rose,
marred and with stint of petals,
meager flower, thin,
sparse of leaf,

more precious
than a wet rose
single on a stem—
you are caught in the drift.

Stunted, with small leaf,
you are flung on the sand,
you are lifted
in the crisp sand
that drives in the wind.

Can the spice-rose
drip such acrid fragrance
hardened in a leaf?

SEA POPPIES

Amber husk
fluted with gold,
fruit on the sand
marked with a rich grain,

treasure
spilled near the shrub-pines
to bleach on the boulders:

your stalk has caught root
among wet pebbles
and drift flung by the sea
and grated shells
and split conch-shells.

Beautiful, wide-spread,
fire upon leaf,
what meadow yields
so fragrant a leaf
as your bright leaf?

Robert Frost (1874–1963)

STOPPING BY WOODS ON A SNOWY EVENING

Whose woods these are I think I know,
His house is in the village, though;
He will not see me stopping here
To watch his woods fill up with snow.

My little horse must think it queer
To stop without a farmhouse near
Between the woods and frozen lake
The darkest evening of the year.

He gives his harness bells a shake
To ask if there is some mistake.
The only other sound's the sweep
Of easy wind and downy flake.

The woods are lovely, dark, and deep,
But I have promises to keep,
And miles to go before I sleep,
And miles to go before I sleep.

DESIGN

I found a dimpled spider, fat and white,
On a white heal-all, holding up a moth
Like a white piece of rigid satin cloth—
Assorted characters of death and blight
Mixed ready to begin the morning right,
Like the ingredients of a witches' broth—
A snow-drop spider, a flower like a froth,
And dead wings carried like a paper kite.

What had that flower to do with being white,
The wayside blue and innocent heal-all?
What brought the kindred spider to that height,
Then steered the white moth thither in the night?
What but design of darkness to appall?—
If design govern in a thing so small.

"OUT, OUT—"

The buzz saw snarled and rattled in the yard
And made dust and dropped stove-length sticks of wood.
Sweet-scented stuff when the breeze drew across it.
And from there those that lifted eyes could count
Five mountain ranges one behind the other
Under the sunset far into Vermont.
And the saw snarled and rattled, snarled and rattled,

As it ran light, or had to bear a load.
And nothing happened: day was all but done.
Call it a day, I wish they might have said
To please the boy by giving him the half hour
That a boy counts so much when saved from work.
His sister stood beside them in her apron
To tell them "Supper." At the word, the saw,
As if to prove saws knew what supper meant,
Leaped out at the boy's hand, or seemed to leap—
He must have given the hand. However it was,
Neither refused the meeting. But the hand!
The boy's first outcry was a rueful laugh,
As he swung toward them holding up the hand
Half in appeal, but half as if to keep
The life from spilling. Then the boy saw all—
Since he was old enough to know, big boy
Doing a man's work, though a child at heart—
He saw all spoiled. "Don't let him cut my hand off—
The doctor, when he comes. Don't let him, sister!"
So. But the hand was gone already.
The doctor put him in the dark of ether.
He lay and puffed his lips out with his breath.
And then—the watcher at his pulse took fright.
No one believed. They listened at his heart.
Little—less—nothing!—and that ended it.
No more to build on there. And they, since they
Were not the one dead, turned to their affairs.

AFTER APPLE-PICKING

My long two-pointed ladder's sticking through a tree
Toward heaven still,
And there's a barrel that I didn't fill
Beside it, and there may be two or three
Apples I didn't pick upon some bough.
But I am done with apple-picking now.
Essence of winter sleep is on the night,
The scent of apples: I am drowsing off.
I cannot rub the strangeness from my sight
I got from looking through a pane of glass
I skimmed this morning from the drinking trough
And held against the world of hoary grass.
It melted, and I let it fall and break.

But I was well
Upon my way to sleep before it fell,
And I could tell
What form my dreaming was about to take.
Magnified apples appear and disappear,
Stem end and blossom end,
And every fleck of russet showing clear.
My instep arch not only keeps the ache,
It keeps the pressure of a ladder-round.
I feel the ladder sway as the boughs bend.
And I keep hearing from the cellar bin
The rumbling sound
Of load on load of apples coming in.
For I have had too much
Of apple-picking: I am overtired
Of the great harvest I myself desired.
There were ten thousand thousand fruit to touch,
Cherish in hand, lift down, and not let fall.
For all
That struck the earth,
No matter if not bruised or spiked with stubble,
Went surely to the cider-apple heap
As of no worth.
One can see what will trouble
This sleep of mine, whatever sleep it is.
Were he not gone,
The woodchuck could say whether it's like his
Long sleep, as I describe its coming on,
Or just some human sleep.

Wallace Stevens (1878–1955)

THE SNOW MAN

One must have a mind of winter
To regard the frost and the boughs
Of the pine-trees crusted with snow;

And have been cold a long time
To behold the junipers shagged with ice,
The spruces rough in the distant glitter

Of the January sun; and not to think
Of any misery in the sound of the wind,
In the sound of a few leaves,

Which is the sound of the land
Full of the same wind
That is blowing in the same bare place

For the listener, who listens in the snow,
And, nothing himself, beholds
Nothing that is not there and the nothing that is.

ANECDOTE OF THE JAR

I placed a jar in Tennessee,
And round it was, upon a hill.
It made the slovenly wilderness
Surround that hill.

The wilderness rose up to it,
And sprawled around, no longer wild.
The jar was round upon the ground
And tall and of a port in air.

It took dominion everywhere.
The jar was gray and bare.
It did not give of bird or bush,
Like nothing else in Tennessee.

William Carlos Williams (1883–1963)

A SORT OF A SONG

Let the snake wait under
his weed
and the writing
be of words, slow and quick, sharp
to strike, quiet to wait,
sleepless.

—through metaphor to reconcile
the people and the stones.
Compose. (No ideas
but in things) Invent!
Saxifrage is my flower that splits
the rocks.

QUEEN-ANN'S-LACE

Her body is not so white as
anemone petals nor so smooth—nor
so remote a thing. It is a field
of the wild carrot taking
the field by force; the grass
does not raise above it.
Here is no question of whiteness,
white as can be, with a purple mole
at the center of each flower.
Each flower is a hand's span
of her whiteness. Wherever
his hand has lain there is
a tiny purple blemish. Each part
is a blossom under his touch
to which the fibres of her being
stem one by one, each to its end,
until the whole field is a
white desire, empty, a single stem,
a cluster, flower by flower,
a pious wish to whiteness gone over—
or nothing.

THE RED WHEEL BARROW

so much depends
upon

a red wheel
barrow

glazed with rain
water

beside the white
chickens

NANTUCKET

Flowers through the window
lavender and yellow

changed by white curtains—
Smell of cleanliness—

Sunshine of late afternoon—
On the glass tray

a glass pitcher, the tumbler
turned down, by which

a key is lying—And the
immaculate white bed

SPRING AND ALL

By the road to the contagious hospital
under the surge of the blue
mottled clouds driven from the
northeast—a cold wind. Beyond, the
waste of broad, muddy fields
brown with dried weeds, standing and fallen

patches of standing water
the scattering of tall trees

All along the road the reddish
purplish, forked, upstanding, twiggy
stuff of bushes and small trees
with dead, brown leaves under them
leafless vines—

Lifeless in appearance, sluggish
dazed spring approaches—

They enter the new world naked,
cold, uncertain of all
save that they enter. All about them
the cold, familiar wind—

Now the grass, tomorrow
the stiff curl of wildcarrot leaf
One by one objects are defined—
It quickens: clarity, outline of leaf

But now the stark dignity of
entrance—Still, the profound change
has come upon them: rooted, they
grip down and begin to awaken

Marianne Moore (1887–1972)

TO A SNAIL

If "compression is the first grace of style,"
you have it. Contractility is a virtue
as modesty is a virtue.
It is not the acquisition of any one thing
that is able to adorn,
or the incidental quality that occurs
as a concomitant of something well said,
that we value in style,
but the principle that is hid:
in the absence of feet, "a method of conclusions";
"a knowledge of principles,"
in the curious phenomenon of your occipital horn.

POETRY

I, too, dislike it: there are things that are important beyond
all this fiddle.
Reading it, however, with a perfect contempt for it, one
discovers in
it after all, a place for the genuine.
Hands that can grasp, eyes
that can dilate, hair that can rise
if it must, these things are important not because a

high-sounding interpretation can be put upon them but
because they are
useful. When they become so derivative as to become
unintelligible,
the same thing may be said for all of us, that we
do not admire what
we cannot understand: the bat
holding on upside down or in quest of something to

eat, elephants pushing, a wild horse taking a roll, a tireless
wolf under a tree, the immovable critic twitching
his skin
like a horse that feels a flea, the baseball fan, the statistician—
nor is it valid
to discriminate against 'business documents and

school-books'; all these phenomena are important. One must
make a distinction
however: when dragged into prominence by half poets,
the result is not poetry,
nor till the poets among us can be
'literalists of
the imagination'—above
insolence and triviality and can present

for inspection, imaginary gardens with real toads in them,
shall we have
it. In the meantime, if you demand on the one hand,
the raw material of poetry in
all its rawness and
that which is on the other hand
genuine, then you are interested in poetry.

AN EGYPTIAN PULLED GLASS BOTTLE IN THE SHAPE OF A FISH

Here we have thirst
and patience, from the first,
and art, as in a wave held up for us to see
in its essential perpendicularity;

not brittle but
intense—the spectrum, that
spectacular and nimble animal the fish,
whose scales turn aside the sun's sword by their polish.

THE MIND IS AN ENCHANTING THING

is an enchanted thing
like the glaze on a
katydid-wing
subdivided by sun
till the nettings are legion.
Like Gieseking playing Scarlatti;

like the apteryx-awl
as a beak, or the
kiwi's rain-shawl

of haired feathers, the mind
feeling its way as though blind,
walks along with its eyes on the ground.

It has memory's ear
that can hear without
having to hear.
Like the gyroscope's fall,
truly unequivocal
because trued by regnant certainty,

it is a power of
strong enchantment. It
is like the dove-
neck animated by
sun; it is memory's eye;
it's conscientious inconsistency.

It tears off the veil; tears
the temptation, the
mist the heart wears,
from its eyes,—if the heart
has a face; it takes apart
dejection. It's fire in the dove-neck's

iridescence; in the
inconsistencies
of Scarlatti.
Unconfusion submits
its confusion to proof; it's
not a Herod's oath that cannot change.

e. e. cummings (1894–1962)
[BUFFALO BILL'S]

Buffalo Bill's
defunct
who used to
ride a watersmooth-silver
stallion
and break onetwothreefourfive pigeons justlikethat
Jesus
he was a handsome man
and what i want to know is
how do you like your blueeyed boy
Mister Death

W. H. Auden (1907–1973)

[FOR WHAT AS EASY]

For what as easy
For what though small,
For what is well
Because between,
To you simply
From me I mean.

Who goes with who
The bedclothes say,
As I and you
Go kissed away,
The data given,
The senses even.

Fate is not late,
Nor the speech rewritten,
Nor one word forgotten,
Said at the start
About heart,
By heart, for heart.

LAW LIKE LOVE

Law, say the gardeners, is the sun,
Law is the one
All gardeners obey
Tomorrow, yesterday, today.

Law is the wisdom of the old
The impotent grandfathers feebly scold;
The grandchildren put out a treble tongue,
Law is the senses of the young.

Law, says the priest with a priestly look,
Expounding to an unpriestly people,
Law is the words in my priestly book,
Law is my pulpit and my steeple.

Law, says the judge as he looks down his nose,
Speaking clearly and most severely,
Law is as I've told you before,
Law is as you know I suppose,
Law is but let me explain it once more,
Law is The Law.

Yet law-abiding scholars write;
Law is neither wrong nor right,
Law is only crimes
Punished by places and by times,
Law is the clothes men wear
Anytime, anywhere,
Law is Goodmorning and Goodnight.

Others say, Law is our Fate;
Others say, Law is our State;
Others say, others say
Law is no more
Law has gone away.

And always the loud angry crowd
Very angry and very loud
Law is We,
And always the soft idiot softly Me.

If we, dear, know we know no more
Than they about the Law,
If I no more than you
Know what we should and should not do
Except that all agree
Gladly or miserably
That the Law is
And that all know this,
If therefore thinking it absurd
To identify Law with some other word,
Unlike so many men
I cannot say Law is again,
No more than they can we suppress
The universal wish to guess
Or slip out of our own position
Into an unconcerned condition.
Although I can at least confine
Your vanity and mine
To stating timidly
A timid similarity,
We shall boast anyway:
Like love I say.

Like love we don't know where or why,
Like love we can't compel or fly,
Like love we often weep,
Like love we seldom keep.

MUSÉE DES BEAUX ARTS

About suffering they were never wrong,
The Old Masters: how well they understood
Its human position; how it takes place
While someone else is eating or opening a window or just
  walking dully along;
How, when the aged are reverently, passionately waiting
For the miraculous birth, there always must be
Children who did not specially want it to happen, skating
On a pond at the edge of the wood:
They never forgot
That even the dreadful martyrdom must run its course
Anyhow in a corner, some untidy spot
Where the dogs go on with their doggy life and the
  torturer's horse
Scratches its innocent behind on a tree.

In Brueghel's *Icarus,* for instance: how everything turns away
Quite leisurely from the disaster; the ploughman may
Have heard the splash, the forsaken cry,
But for him it was not an important failure; the sun shone
As it had to on the white legs disappearing into the green
Water; and the expensive delicate ship that must have seen
Something amazing, a boy falling out of the sky,
Had somewhere to get to and sailed calmly on.

THE SHIELD OF ACHILLES

She looked over his shoulder
  For vines and olive trees,
Marble well-governed cities
  And ships upon untamed seas,
But there on the shining metal
  His hands had put instead
An artificial wilderness
  And a sky like lead.

A plain without a feature, bare and brown,
  No blade of grass, no sign of neighborhood,
Nothing to eat and nowhere to sit down,
  Yet, congregated on its blankness, stood

  An unintelligible multitude,
A million eyes, a million boots in line,
Without expression, waiting for a sign.

Out of the air a voice without a face
  Proved by statistics that some cause was just
In tones as dry and level as the place:
  No one was cheered and nothing was discussed;
  Column by column in a cloud of dust
They marched away enduring a belief
Whose logic brought them, somewhere else, to grief.

She looked over his shoulder
  For ritual pieties,
White flower-garlanded heifers,
  Libation and sacrifice,
But there on the shining metal
  Where the altar should have been,
She saw by his flickering forge-light
  Quite another scene.

Barbed wire enclosed an arbitrary spot
  Where bored officials lounged (one cracked a joke)
And sentries sweated for the day was hot:
  A crowd of ordinary decent folk
  Watched from without and neither moved nor spoke
As three pale figures were led forth and bound
To three posts driven upright in the ground.

The mass and majesty of this world, all
  That carries weight and always weighs the same
Lay in the hands of others; they were small
  And could not hope for help and no help came:
  What their foes liked to do was done, their shame
Was all the worst could wish; they lost their pride
And died as men before their bodies died.

She looked over his shoulder
  For athletes at their games,
Men and women in a dance
  Moving their sweet limbs
Quick, quick, to music,
  But there on the shining shield
His hands had set no dancing-floor
  But a weed-choked field.

A ragged urchin, aimless and alone,
  Loitered about that vacancy; a bird
Flew up to safety from his well-aimed stone:
  That girls are raped, that two boys knife a third,
  Were axioms to him, who'd never heard
Of any world where promises were kept,
Or one could weep because another wept.

The thin-lipped armorer,
  Hephaestos, hobbled away,
Thetis of the shining breasts
  Cried out in dismay
At what the god had wrought
  To please her son, the strong
Iron-hearted man-slaying Achilles
  Who would not live long.

Dylan Thomas (1914–1953)

FERN HILL

Now as I was young and easy under the apple boughs
About the lilting house and happy as the grass was green,
  The night above the dingle starry,
    Time let me hail and climb
  Golden in the heydays of his eyes,
And honored among wagons I was prince of the apple
  towns
And once below a time I lordly had the trees and leaves
    Trail with daisies and barley
  Down the rivers of the windfall light.

And as I was green and carefree, famous among the barns
About the happy yard and singing as the farm was home,
  In the sun that is young once only,
    Time let me play and be
  Golden in the mercy of his means,
And green and golden I was huntsman and herdsman, the
  calves
Sang to my horn, the foxes on the hills barked clear and
  cold,
    And the sabbath rang slowly
  In the pebbles of the holy streams.

All the sun long it was running, it was lovely, the hay
Fields high as the house, the tunes from the chimneys, it was
  air
    And playing, lovely and watery
      And fire green as grass.
    And nightly under the simple stars
As I rode to sleep the owls were bearing the farm away,
All the moon long I heard, blessed among stables, the night-
  jars
    Flying with the ricks, and the horses
      Flashing into the dark.

And then to awake, and the farm, like a wanderer white
With the dew, come back, the cock on his shoulder: it was
  all
    Shining, it was Adam and maiden,
      The sky gathered again
    And the sun grew round that very day.
So it must have been after the birth of the simple light
In the first, spinning place, the spellbound horses walking
  warm
    Out of the whinnying green stable
      On to the fields of praise.

And honored among foxes and pheasants by the gay house
Under the new made clouds and happy as the heart was
  long,
    In the sun born over and over,
      I ran my heedless ways,
    My wishes raced through the house high hay
And nothing I cared, at my sky blue trades, that time allows
In all his tuneful turning so few and such morning songs
    Before the children green and golden
      Follow him out of grace,

Nothing I cared, in the lamb white days, that time would
  take me
Up to the swallow thronged loft by the shadow of my hand,
    In the moon that is always rising,
      Nor that riding to sleep
    I should hear him fly with the high fields
And wake to the farm forever fled from the childless land.
Oh as I was young and easy in the mercy of his means,
      Time held me green and dying
    Though I sang in my chains like the sea.

Langston Hughes (1902–1967)
DREAM VARIATION

To fling my arms wide
In some place of the sun,
To whirl and to dance
Till the white day is done.
Then rest at cool evening
Beneath a tall tree
While night comes on gently,
    Dark like me—
That is my dream!

To fling my arms wide
In the face of the sun,
Dance! Whirl! Whirl!
Till the quick day is done.
Rest at pale evening . . .
A tall, slim tree . . .
Night coming tenderly
    Black like me.

Louise Bogan (1897–1970)
CARTOGRAPHY

As you lay in sleep
I saw the chart
Of artery and vein
Running from your heart,

Plain as the strength
Marked upon the leaf
Along the length,
Mortal and brief,

Of your gaunt hand.
I saw it clear:
The wiry brand
Of the life we bear

Mapped like the great
Rivers that rise
Beyond our fate
And distant from our eyes.

Theodore Roethke (1908–1963)

CUTTINGS

Sticks-in-a-drowse droop over sugary loam,
Their intricate stem-fur dries;
But still the delicate slips keep coaxing up water;
The small cells bulge;

One nub of growth
Nudges a sand-crumb loose,
Pokes through a musty sheath
Its pale tendrilous horn.

CUTTINGS
(later)

This urge, wrestle, resurrection of dry sticks,
Cut stems struggling to put down feet,
What saint strained so much,
Rose on such lopped limbs to a new life?

I can hear, underground, that sucking and sobbing,
In my veins, in my bones I feel it,—
The small waters seeping upward,

The tight grains parting at last.
When sprouts break out,
Slippery as fish,
I quail, lean to beginnings, sheath-wet.

Gwendolyn Brooks (b. 1917)

KITCHENETTE BUILDING

We are things of dry hours and the involuntary plan,
Grayed in, and gray. "Dream" makes a giddy sound, not strong
Like "rent," "feeding a wife," "satisfying a man."

But could a dream send up through onion fumes
Its white and violet, fight with fried potatoes
And yesterday's garbage ripening in the hall,
Flutter, or sing an aria down these rooms

Even if we were willing to let it in,
Had time to warm it, keep it very clean,
Anticipate a message, let it begin?

We wonder. But not well! not for a minute!
Since Number Five is out of the bathroom now,
We think of lukewarm water, hope to get in it.

Randall Jarrell (1914–1965)

EIGHTH AIR FORCE

If, in an odd angle of the hutment,
A puppy laps the water from a can
Of flowers, and the drunk sergeant shaving
Whistles *O Paradiso!*—shall I say that man
Is not as men have said: a wolf to man?

The other murderers troop in yawning;
Three of them play Pitch, one sleeps, and one
Lies counting missions, lies there sweating
Till even his heart beats: One; One; One.
O murderers! . . . Still, this is how it's done:

This is war. . . . But since these play, before they die,
Like puppies with their puppy; since, a man,
I did as these have done, but did not die—
I will content the people as I can
And give up these to them: Behold the man!

I have suffered, in a dream, because of him,
Many things; for this last saviour, man,
I have lied as I lie now. But what is lying?
Men wash their hands, in blood, as best they can:
I find no fault in this just man.

Robinson Jeffers (1887–1962)

HURT HAWKS

I

The broken pillar of the wing jags from the clotted shoulder,
The wing trails like a banner in defeat,
No more to use the sky forever but live with famine

And pain a few days: cat nor coyote
Will shorten the week of waiting for death, there is game
without talons
He stands under the oak-bush and waits
The lame feet of salvation; at night he remembers freedom
And flies in a dream, the dawns ruin it.
He is strong and pain is worse to the strong, incapacity is
worse.
The curs of the day come and torment him
At distance, no one but death the redeemer will humble that
head,
The intrepid readiness, the terrible eyes.
The wild God of the world is sometimes merciful to those
That ask mercy, not often to the arrogant,
You do not know him, you communal people, or you have
forgotten him;
Intemperate and savage, the hawk remembers him;
Beautiful and wild, the hawks, and men that are dying,
remember him.

II

I'd sooner, except the penalties, kill a man than a hawk; but
the great redtail
Had nothing left but unable misery
From the bone too shattered for mending, the wing that
trailed under his talons when he moved.
We had fed him six weeks, I gave him freedom,
He wandered over the foreland hill and returned in the
evening, asking for death,
Not like a beggar, still eyed with the old
Implacable arrogance. I gave him the lead gift in the
twilight. What fell was relaxed,
Owl-downy, soft feminine feathers; but what
Soared: the fierce rush: the night-herons by the flooded river
cried fear at its rising
Before it was quite unsheathed from reality.

Robert Lowell (1917–1977)

THE PUBLIC GARDEN

Burnished, burned-out, still burning as the year
you lead me to our stamping ground.
The city and its cruising cars surround

the Public Garden. All's alive—
the children crowding home from school at five,
punting a football in the bricky air,
the sailors and their pick-ups under trees
with Latin labels. And the jaded flock
of swanboats paddles to its dock.
The park is drying.
Dead leaves thicken to a ball
inside the basin of a fountain, where
the heads of four stone lions stare
and suck on empty fawcets. Night
deepens. From the arched bridge, we see
the shedding park-bound mallards, how they keep
circling and diving in the lanternlight,
searching for something hidden in the muck.
And now the moon, earth's friend, that cared so much
for us, and cared so little, comes again—
always a stranger! As we walk,
it lies like chalk
over the waters. Everything's aground.
Remember summer? Bubbles filled
the fountain, and we splashed. We drowned
in Eden, while Jehovah's grass-green lyre
was rustling all about us in the leaves
that gurgled by us, turning upside down . . .
The fountain's failing waters flash around
the garden. Nothing catches fire.

Richard Wilbur (b. 1921)

THE DEATH OF A TOAD

A toad the power mower caught,
Chewed and clipped of a leg, with a hobbling hop has got
To the garden verge, and sanctuaried him
Under the cineraria leaves, in the shade
Of the ashen heartshaped leaves, in a dim,
Low, and a final glade.

The rare original heartsblood goes,
Spends on the earthen hide, in the folds and wizening, flows
In the gutters of the banked and staring eyes. He lies
As still as if he would return to stone,
And soundlessly attending, dies
Toward some deep monotone,

Toward misted and ebullient seas
And cooling shores, toward lost Amphibia's emperies.
Day dwindles, drowning, and at length is gone
In the wide and antique eyes, which still appear
To watch, across the castrate lawn,
The haggard daylight steer.

Denise Levertov (b. 1923)

THE WORLD OUTSIDE

I

On the kitchen wall a flash
of shadow:
swift pilgrimage
of pigeons, a spiral
celebration of air, of sky-deserts.
And on tenement windows
a blaze
of lustred watermelon:
stain of the sun
westering somewhere back of Hoboken.

II

The goatherd upstairs! Music
from his sweet flute
roves from summer to summer
in the dusty air of airshafts
and among the flakes
of soot that float
in a daze from chimney
to chimney—notes
remote, cool, speaking of slender
shadows under olive-leaves. A silence.

III

Groans, sighs, in profusion,
with coughing, muttering, orchestrate
solitary grief: the crash of glass, a low voice
repeating over and over, 'No.
No, I want my key. No you did not.
No,'—a commonplace.
And in counterpoint, from other windows,

the effort to be merry—ay, maracas!
—sibilant, intricate—the voices wailing pleasure,
arriving perhaps at joy, late, after sets
have been switched off, and silences
are dark windows?

IN MIND

There's in my mind a woman
of innocence, unadorned but

fair-featured, and smelling of
apples or grass. She wears

a utopian smock or shift, her hair
is light brown and smooth, and she

is kind and very clean without
ostentation—
but she has
no imagination.
And there's a
turbulent moon-ridden girl

or old woman, or both,
dressed in opals and rags, feathers

and torn taffeta,
who knows strange songs—

but she is not kind.

STEPPING WESTWARD

What is green in me
darkens, muscadine.

If woman is inconstant,
good, I am faithful to

ebb and flow, I fall
in season and now

is a time of ripening.
If her part

is to be true,
a north star,

good, I hold steady
in the black sky

and vanish by day,
yet burn there

in blue or above
quilts of cloud.

There is no savor
more sweet, more salt

than to be glad to be
what, woman,

and who, myself,
I am, a shadow

that grows longer as the sun
moves, drawn out

on a thread of wonder.
If I bear burdens

they begin to be remembered
as gifts, goods, a basket

of bread that hurts
my shoulders but closes me

in fragrance. I can
eat as I go.

Sylvia Plath (1932–1963)
LADY LAZARUS

I have done it again.
One year in every ten
I manage it—

A sort of walking miracle, my skin
Bright as a Nazi lampshade,
My right foot

A paperweight,
My face a featureless, fine
Jew linen.

Peel off the napkin
O my enemy.
Do I terrify?—

The nose, the eye pits, the full set of teeth?
The sour breath
Will vanish in a day.

Soon, soon the flesh
The grave cave ate will be
At home on me

And I a smiling woman.
I am only thirty.
And like the cat I have nine times to die.

This is Number Three.
What a trash
To annihilate each decade.

What a million filaments.
The peanut-crunching crowd
Shoves in to see

Them unwrap me hand and foot—
The big strip tease.
Gentlemen, ladies

These are my hands
My knees.
I may be skin and bone,

Nevertheless, I am the same, identical woman.
The first time it happened I was ten.
It was an accident.

The second time I meant
To last it out and not come back at all.
I rocked shut

As a seashell.
They had to call and call
And pick the worms off me like sticky pearls.

Dying
Is an art, like everything else.
I do it exceptionally well.

I do it so it feels like hell.
I do it so it feels real.
I guess you could say I've a call.

It's easy enough to do it in a cell.
It's easy enough to do it and stay put.
It's the theatrical

Comeback in broad day
To the same place, the same face, the same brute
Amused shout:

"A miracle!"
That knocks me out.
There is a charge

For the eyeing of my scars, there is a charge
For the hearing of my heart—
It really goes.

And there is a charge, a very large charge
For a word or a touch
Or a bit of blood

Or a piece of my hair or my clothes.
So, so, Herr Doktor.
So, Herr Enemy.

I am your opus,
I am your valuable,
The pure gold baby

That melts to a shriek.
I turn and burn.
Do not think I underestimate your great concern.

Ash, ash—
You poke and stir.
Flesh, bone, there is nothing there—

A cake of soap,
A wedding ring,
A gold filling.

Herr God, Herr Lucifer
Beware
Beware.

Out of the ash
I rise with my red hair
And I eat men like air.

EDGE

The woman is perfected.
Her dead

Body wears the smile of accomplishment,
The illusion of a Greek necessity

Flows in the scrolls of her toga,
Her bare

Feet seem to be saying:
We have come so far, it is over.

Each dead child coiled, a white serpent,
One at each little

Pitcher of milk, now empty.
She has folded

Them back into ther body as petals
Of a rose close when the garden

Stiffens and odors bleed
From the sweet, deep throats of the night flower.

The moon has nothing to be sad about,
Staring from her hood of bone.

She is used to this sort of thing.
Her blacks crackle and drag.

Allen Ginsberg (b. 1926)

A SUPERMARKET IN CALIFORNIA

What thoughts I have of you tonight, Walt Whitman, for I
walked down the sidestreets under the trees with a
headache self-conscious looking at the full moon.
In my hungry fatigue, and shopping for images, I went
into the neon fruit supermarket, dreaming of your
enumerations!

What peaches and what penumbras! Whole families shopping at night! Aisles full of husbands! Wives in the avocados, babies in the tomatoes!—and you, Garcia Lorca, what were you doing down by the watermelons?

I saw you, Walt Whitman, childless, lonely old grubber, poking among the meats in the refrigerator and eyeing the grocery boys.
I heard you asking questions of each: Who killed the pork chops? What price bananas? Are you my Angel?
I wandered in and out of the brilliant stacks of cans following you, and followed in my imagination by the store detective.
We strode down the open corridors together in our solitary fancy tasting artichokes, possessing every frozen delicacy, and never passing the cashier.

Where are we going, Walt Whitman? The doors close in an hour. Which way does your beard point tonight?
(I touch your book and dream of our odyssey in the supermarket and feel absurd.)
Will we walk all night through solitary streets? The trees add shade to shade, lights out in the houses, we'll both be lonely.

Will we stroll dreaming of the lost America of love past blue automobiles in driveways, home to our silent cottage?
Ah, dear father, graybeard, lonely old courage-teacher, what America did you have when Charon quit poling his ferry and you got out on a smoking bank and stood watching the boat disappear on the black waters of Lethe?

A STRANGE NEW COTTAGE IN BERKELEY

All afternoon cutting bramble blackberries off a tottering brown fence
under a low branch with its rotten old apricots miscellaneous under the leaves,
fixing the drip in the intricate gut machinery of a new toilet;
found a good coffeepot in the vines by the porch, rolled a big tire out of the scarlet bushes, hid my marijuana;

wet the flowers, playing the sunlit water each to
each, returning for godly extra drops for the stringbeans
and daisies;
three times walked round the grass and sighed
absently:
my reward, when the garden fed me its plums from
the form of a small tree in the corner,
an angel thoughtful of my stomach, and my dry
and lovelorn tongue.

Robert Creeley (b. 1926)

THE LANGUAGE

Locate *I*
love you some-
where in

teeth and
eyes, bite
it but

take care not
to hurt, you
want so

much so
little. Words
say everything.

I
love you
again,

then what
is emptiness
for. To

fill, fill.
I heard words
and words full

of holes
aching. Speech
is a mouth.

SOME ECHOES

Some echoes,
little pieces,
falling, a dust,

sunlight, by
the window, in
the eyes. Your

hair as
you brush
it, the light

behind
the eyes,
what is left of it.

PLACE

There was a path
through the field
down to the river,

from the house
a walk of
a half an hour.

Like that—
walking,
still,

to go swimming,
but only
if someone's there.

THE WORLD

I wanted so ably
to reassure you, I wanted
the man you took to be me,

to comfort you, and got
up, and went to the window,
pushed back, as you asked me to,

the curtain, to see
the outline of the trees
in the night outside.

The light, love,
the light we felt then,
greyly, was it, that

came in, on us, not
merely my hands or yours,
or a wetness so comfortable,

but in the dark then
as you slept, the grey
figure came so close

and leaned over,
between us, as you
slept, restless, and

my own face had to
see it, and be seen by it,
the man it was, your

grey lost tired bewildered
brother, unused, untaken—
hated by love, and dead,

but not dead, for an
instant, saw me, myself
the intruder, as he was not.

I tried to say, it is
all right, she is
happy, you are no longer

needed. I said,
he is dead, and he
went as you shifted

and woke, at first afraid,
then knew by my own knowing
what had happened—

and the light then
of the sun coming
for another morning
in the world.

Ted Hughes (b. 1930)

EXAMINATION AT THE WOMB-DOOR

Who owns these scrawny little feet? *Death.*
Who owns this bristly scorched-looking face? *Death.*
Who owns these still-working lungs? *Death.*
Who owns this utility coat of muscles? *Death.*
Who owns these unspeakable guts? *Death.*
Who owns these questionable brains? *Death.*
All this messy blood? *Death.*
These minimum-efficiency eyes? *Death.*
This wicked little tongue? *Death.*
This occasional wakefulness? *Death.*

Given, stolen, or held pending trial?
Held.

Who owns the whole rainy, stony earth? *Death.*
Who owns all of space? *Death.*

Who is stronger than hope? *Death.*
Who is stronger than the will? *Death.*
Stronger than love? *Death.*
Stronger than life? *Death.*

But who is stronger than death?
Me, evidently.

Pass, Crow.

CROW ALIGHTS

Crow saw the herded mountains, steaming in the morning.
And he saw the sea
Dark-spined, with the whole earth in its coils.
He saw the stars, fuming away into the black, mushrooms
of the nothing forest, clouding their spores, the virus of
God.
And he shivered with the horror of Creation.

In the hallucination of the horror
He saw this shoe, with no sole, rain-sodden,
Lying on a moor.
And there was this garbage can, bottom rusted away,

A playing place for the wind, in a waste of puddles.
There was this coat, in the dark cupboard,
in the silent room, in the silent house.
There was this face, smoking its cigarette between the dusk
window and the fire's embers.

Near the face, this hand, motionless.

Near the hand, this cup.

Crow blinked. He blinked. Nothing faded.

He stared at the evidence.

Nothing escaped him. (Nothing could escape.)

THE THOUGHT-FOX

I imagine this midnight moment's forest:
Something else is alive
Beside the clock's loneliness
And this blank page where my fingers move.

Through the window I see no star:
Something more near
Though deeper within darkness
Is entering the loneliness:

Cold, delicately as the dark snow,
A fox's nose touches twig, leaf;
Two eyes serve a movement, that now
And again now, and now, and now

Sets neat prints into the snow
Between trees, and warily a lame
Shadow lags by stump and in hollow
Of a body that is bold to come

Across clearings, an eye,
A widening deepening greenness,
Brilliantly, concentratedly,
Coming about its own business

Till, with a sudden sharp hot stink of fox
It enters the dark hole of the head.
The window is starless still; the clock ticks,
The page is printed.

Stevie Smith (1902–1971)

NOT WAVING BUT DROWNING

Nobody heard him, the dead man,
But still he lay moaning:
I was much further out than you thought
And not waving but drowning.

Poor chap, he always loved larking
And now he's dead
It must have been too cold for him his heart gave way,
They said.

Oh, no no no, it was too cold always
(Still the dead one lay moaning)
I was much too far out all my life
And not waving but drowning.

Imamu Amiri Baraka (b. 1934)

A POEM FOR BLACK HEARTS

For Malcolm's eyes, when they broke
the face of some dumb white man, For
Malcolm's hands raised to bless us
all black and strong in his image
of ourselves, For Malcolm's words
fire darts, the victor's tireless
thrusts, words hung above the world
change as it may, he said it, and
for this he was killed, for saying,
and feeling, and being/change, all
collected hot in his heart, For Malcolm's
heart, raising us above our filthy cities,
for his stride, and his beat, and his address
to the grey monsters of the world, For Malcolm's
pleas for your dignity, black men, for your life,
black man, for the filling of your minds
with righteousness, For all of him dead and
gone and vanished from us, and all of him which
clings to our speech black god of our time.
For all of him, and all of yourself, look up,

black man, quit stuttering and shuffling, look up,
black man, quit whining and stooping, for all of him,
For Great Malcolm a prince of the earth, let nothing in us
  rest
until we avenge ourselves for his death, stupid animals
that killed him, let us never breathe a pure breath if
we fail, and white men call us faggots till the end of
the earth.

Anne Sexton (1928–1974)

THE MOSS OF HIS SKIN

Young girls in old Arabia were often buried alive next to their dead fathers, apparently as sacrifice to the goddesses of the tribes.
Harold Feldman, "Children of the Desert," *Psychoanalysis and Psychoanalytic Review*, Fall 1958

It was only important
to smile and hold still,
to lie down beside him
and to rest awhile,
to be folded up together
as if we were silk,
to sink from the eyes of mother
and not to talk.
The black room took us
like a cave or a mouth
or an indoor belly.
I held my breath
and daddy was there,
his thumbs, his fat skull,
his teeth, his hair growing
like a field or a shawl.
I lay by the moss
of his skin until
it grew strange. My sisters
will never know that I fall
out of myself and pretend
that Allah will not see
how I hold my daddy
like an old stone tree.

Adrienne Rich (b. 1929)

THE KNIGHT

A knight rides into the noon,
and his helmet points to the sun,
and a thousand splintered suns
are the gaiety of his mail.
The soles of his feet glitter
and his palms flash in reply,
and under his crackling banner
he rides like a ship in sail.

A knight rides into the noon,
and only his eye is living,
a lump of bitter jelly
set in a metal mask,
betraying rags and tatters
that cling to the flesh beneath
and wear his nerves to ribbons
under the radiant casque.

Who will unhorse this rider
and free him from between
the walls of iron, the emblems
crushing his chest with their weight?
Will they defeat him gently,
or leave him hurled on the green,
his rags and wounds still hidden
under the great breastplate?

AUNT JENNIFER'S TIGERS

Aunt Jennifer's tigers prance across a screen,
Bright topaz denizens of a world of green.
They do not fear the men beneath the tree;
They pace in sleek chivalric certainty.

Aunt Jennifer's fingers fluttering through her wool
Find even the ivory needle hard to pull.
The massive weight of Uncle's wedding band
Sits heavily upon Aunt Jennifer's hand.

When Aunt is dead, her terrified hands will lie
Still ringed with ordeals she was mastered by.
The tigers in the panel that she made
Will go on prancing, proud and unafraid.

FROM A SURVIVOR

The pact that we made was the ordinary pact
of men & women in those days

I don't know who we thought we were
that our personalities
could resist the failures of the race

Lucky or unlucky, we didn't know
the race had failures of that order
and that we were going to share them

Like everbody else, we thought of ourselves as special

Your body is as vivid to me
as it ever was: even more

since my feeling for it is clearer:
I know what it could and could not do

it is no longer
the body of a god
or anything with power over my life

Next year it would have been 20 years
and you are wastefully dead
who might have made the leap
we talked, too late, of making

which I live now
not as a leap
but a succession of brief, amazing movements

each one making possible the next

Thomas Kinsella (b. 1928)

HEN WOMAN

The noon heat in the yard
smelled of stillness and coming thunder.
A hen scratched and picked at the shore.
It stopped, its body crouched and puffed out.
The brooding silence seemed to say 'Hush . . .'

The cottage door opened,
a black hole
in a whitewashed wall so bright
the eyes narrowed.
Inside, a clock murmured 'Gong . . .'

(I had felt all this before . . .)

She hurried out in her slippers
muttering, her face dark with anger,
and gathered the hen up jerking
languidly. Her hand fumbled.
Too late. Too late.

It fixed me with its pebble eyes
(seeing what mad blur?).
A white egg showed in the sphincter;
mouth and beak opened together;
and time stood still.

Nothing moved: bird or woman,
fumbled or fumbling—locked there
(as I must have been) gaping.

*

There was a tiny movement at my feet,
tiny and mechanical; I looked down.
A beetle like a bronze leaf
was inching across the cement,
clasping with small tarsi
a ball of dung bigger than its body.
The serrated brow pressed the ground humbly,
lifted in a short stare, bowed again;
the dung-ball advanced minutely,
losing a few fragments,
specks of staleness and freshness.

*

A mutter of thunder far off
—time not quite stopped.
I saw the egg had moved a fraction:
a tender blank brain
under torsion, a clean new world.
As I watched, the mystery completed.

The black zero of the orifice
closed to a point
and the white zero of the egg hung free,
flecked with greenish brown oils.

It slowly turned and fell.
Dreamlike, fussed by her splayed fingers,
it floated outward, moon-white,
leaving no trace in the air,
and began its drop to the shore.

*

I feed upon it still, as you see;
there is no end to that which,
not understood, may yet be noted
and hoarded in the imagination,
in the yolk of one's being, so to speak,
there to undergo its (quite animal) growth,
dividing blindly,
twitching, packed with will,
searching in its own tissue
for the structure
in which it may wake.
Something that had—clenched
in its cave—not been
now was: an egg of being.
Through what seemed a whole year it fell
—as it still falls, for me,
solid and light, the red gold beating
in its silvery womb,
alive as the yolk and white
of my eye; as it will continue
to fall, probably, until I die,
through the vast indifferent spaces
with which I am empty.

*

It smashed against the grating
and slipped down quickly out of sight.
It was over in a comical flash.
The soft mucous shell clung a little longer,
then drained down.

She stood staring, in blank anger.
Then her eyes came to life, and she laughed
and let the bird flap away.
'It's all the one.
There's plenty more where that came from!'

Hen to pan!
It was a simple world.

Elizabeth Bishop (1911–1979)
IN THE WAITING ROOM

In Worcester, Massachusetts,
I went with Aunt Consuelo
to keep her dentist's appointment
and sat and waited for her
in the dentist's waiting room.
It was winter. It got dark
early. The waiting room
was full of grown-up people,
arctics and overcoats,
lamps and magazines.
My aunt was inside
what seemed like a long time
and while I waited I read
the *National Geographic*
(I could read) and carefully
studied the photographs:
the inside of a volcano,
black, and full of ashes;
then it was spilling over
in rivulets of fire.
Osa and Martin Johnson
dressed in riding breeches,
laced boots, and pith helmets.
A dead man slung on a pole
—"Long Pig," the caption said.
Babies with pointed heads
wound round and round with string;
black, naked women with necks
wound round and round with wire
like the necks of light bulbs.
Their breasts were horrifying.
I read it right straight through.
I was too shy to stop.

And then I looked at the cover:
the yellow margins, the date.

Suddenly, from inside,
came an *oh!* of pain
—Aunt Consuelo's voice—
not very loud or long.
I wasn't at all surprised;
even then I knew she was
a foolish, timid woman.
I might have been embarrassed,
but wasn't. What took me
completely by surprise
was that it was *me:*
my voice, in my mouth.
Without thinking at all
I was my foolish aunt,
I—we—were falling, falling,
our eyes glued to the cover
of the *National Geographic,*
February, 1918.

I said to myself: three days
and you'll be seven years old.
I was saying it to stop
the sensation of falling off
the round, turning world
into cold, blue-black space.
But I felt: you are an *I,*
you are an *Elizabeth,*
you are one of *them.*
Why should you be one, too?
I scarcely dared to look
to see what it was I was.
I gave a sidelong glance
—I couldn't look any higher—
at shadowy gray knees,
trousers and skirts and boots
and different pairs of hands
lying under the lamps.
I knew that nothing stranger
had ever happened, that nothing
stranger could ever happen.

Why should I be my aunt,
or me, or anyone?
What similarities—

boots, hands, the family voice
I felt in my throat, or even
the *National Geographic*
and those awful hanging breasts—
held us all together
or made us all just one?
How—I didn't know any
word for it—how "unlikely" . . .
How had I come to be here,
like them, and overhear
a cry of pain that could have
got loud and worse but hadn't?

The waiting room was bright
and too hot. It was sliding
beneath a big black wave,
another, and another.

Then I was back in it.
The War was on. Outside,
in Worcester, Massachusetts,
were night and slush and cold,
and it was still the fifth
of February, 1918.

THE FISH

I caught a tremendous fish
and held him beside the boat
half out of water, with my hook
fast in a corner of his mouth.
He didn't fight.
He hadn't fought at all.
He hung a grunting weight,
battered and venerable
and homely. Here and there
his brown skin hung in strips
like ancient wallpaper,
and its pattern of darker brown
was like wallpaper:
shapes like full-blown roses
stained and lost through age.
He was speckled with barnacles,
fine rosettes of lime,

and infested
with tiny white sea-lice,
and underneath two or three
rags of green weed hung down.
While his gills were breathing in
the terrible oxygen
—the frightening gills,
fresh and crisp with blood,
that can cut so badly—
I thought of the coarse white flesh
packed in like feathers,
the big bones and the little bones,
the dramatic reds and blacks
of his shiny entrails,
and the pink swim-bladder
like a big peony.
I looked into his eyes
which were far larger than mine
but shallower, and yellowed,
the irises backed and packed
with tarnished tinfoil
seen through the lenses
of old scratched isinglass.
They shifted a little, but not
to return my stare.
—It was more like the tipping
of an object toward the light.
I admired his sullen face,
the mechanism of his jaw,
and then I saw
that from his lower lip
—if you could call it a lip—
grim, wet, and weaponlike,
hung five old pieces of fish-line,
or four and a wire leader
with the swivel still attached,
with all their five big hooks
grown firmly in his mouth.
A green line, frayed at the end
where he broke it, two heavier lines,
and a fine black thread
still crimped from the strain and snap
when it broke and he got away.
Like medals with their ribbons
frayed and wavering,

a five-haired beard of wisdom
trailing from his aching jaw.
I stared and stared
and victory filled up
the little rented boat,
from the pool of bilge
where oil had spread a rainbow
around the rusted engine
to the bailer rusted orange,
the sun-cracked thwarts,
the oarlocks on their strings,
the gunnels—until everything
was rainbow, rainbow, rainbow!
And I let the fish go.

James Dickey (b. 1923)

A DOG SLEEPING ON MY FEET

Being his resting place,
I do not even tense
The muscles of a leg
Or I would seem to be changing.
Instead, I turn the page
Of the notebook, carefully not

Remembering what I have written,
For now, with my feet beneath him
Dying like embers,
The poem is beginning to move
Up through my pine-prickling legs
Out of the night wood,

Taking hold of the pen by my fingers.
Before me the fox floats lightly,
On fire with his holy scent.
All, all are running.
Marvelous is the pursuit,
Like a dazzle of nails through the ankles,

Like a twisting shout through the trees
Sent after the flying fox
Through the holes of logs, over streams
Stock-still with the pressure of moonlight.

My killed legs,
My legs of a dead thing, follow,

Quick as pins, through the forest,
And all rushes on into dark
And ends on the brightness of paper.
When my hand, which speaks in a daze
The hypnotized language of beasts,
Shall falter, and fail

Back into the human tongue,
And the dog gets up and goes out
To wander the dawning yard,
I shall crawl to my human bed
And lie there smiling at sunrise,
With the scent of the fox

Burning my brain like an incense,
Floating out of the night wood,
Coming home to my wife and my sons
From the dream of an animal,
Assembling the self I must wake to,
Sleeping to grow back my legs.

Robert Bly (b. 1926)

WAKING FROM SLEEP

Inside the veins there are navies setting forth,
Tiny explosions at the water lines,
And seagulls weaving in the wind of the salty blood.

It is the morning. The country has slept the whole winter.
Window seats were covered with fur skins, the yard was full
Of stiff dogs, and hands that clumsily held heavy books.

Now we wake, and rise from bed, and eat breakfast!—
Shouts rise from the harbor of the blood,
Mist, and masts rising, the knock of wooden tackle in the sunlight.

Now we sing, and do tiny dances on the kitchen floor.
Our whole body is like a harbor at dawn;
We know that our master has left us for the day.

Charles Simic (b. 1938)

FORK

This strange thing must have crept
Right out of hell.
It resembles a bird's foot
Worn around the cannibal's neck.

As you hold it in your hand,
As you stab with it into a piece of meat,
It is possible to imagine the rest of the bird:
Its head which like your fist
Is large, bald, beakless and blind.

Peter Porter (b. 1929)

A CONSUMER'S REPORT

The name of the product I tested is *Life,*
I have completed the form you sent me
and understand that my answers are confidential.
I had it as a gift,
I didn't feel much while using it,
in fact I think I'd have liked to be more excited.
It seemed gentle on the hands
but left an embarrassing deposit behind.
It was not economical
and I have used much more than I thought
(I suppose I have about half left
but it's difficult to tell)—
although the instructions are fairly large
there are so many of them
I don't know which to follow, especially
as they seem to contradict each other.
I'm not sure such a thing
should be put in the way of children—
It's difficult to think of a purpose
for it. One of my friends says
it's just to keep its maker in a job.
Also the price is much too high.
Things are piling up so fast,
after all, the world got by
for a thousand million years

without this, do we need it now?
(Incidentally, please ask your man
to stop calling me 'the respondent',
I don't like the sound of it.)
There seems to be a lot of different labels,
sizes and colours should be uniform,
the shape is awkward, it's waterproof
but not heat resistant, it doesn't keep
yet it's very difficult to get rid of:
whenever they make it cheaper they seem
to put less in—if you say you don't
want it, then it's delivered anyway.
I'd agree it's a popular product,
it's got into the language; people
even say they're on the side of it.
Personally I think it's overdone,
a small thing people are ready
to behave badly about. I think
we should take it for granted. If its
experts are called philosophers or market
researchers or historians, we shouldn't
care. We are the consumers and the last
law makers. So finally, I'd buy it.
But the question of a 'best buy'
I'd like to leave until I get
the competitive product you said you'd send.

Seamus Heaney (b. 1939)

MAKING STRANGE

I stood between them,
the one with his travelled intelligence
and tawny containment,
his speech like the twang of a bowstring,

and another, unshorn and bewildered
in the tubs of his wellingtons,
smiling at me for help,
faced with this stranger I'd brought him.

Then a cunning middle voice
came out of the field across the road
saying, 'Be adept and be dialect,
tell of this wind coming past the zinc hut,

call me sweetbriar after the rain
or snowberries cooled in the fog.
But love the cut of this travelled one
and call me also the cornfield of Boaz.

Go beyond what's reliable
in all that keeps pleading and pleading,
these eyes and puddles and stones,
and recollect how bold you were

when I visited you first
with departures you cannot go back on.'
A chaffinch flicked from an ash and next thing
I found myself driving the stranger

through my own country, adept
at dialect, reciting my pride
in all that I knew, that began to make strange
at that same recitation.

James Merrill (b. 1926)
AFTER GREECE

Light into the olive entered
And was oil. Rain made the huge pale stones
Shine from within. The moon turned his hair white
Who next stepped from between the columns,
Shielding his eyes. All through
The countryside were old ideas
Found lying open to the elements.
Of the gods' houses only
A minor premise here and there
Would be balancing the heaven of fixed stars
Upon a Doric capital. The rest
Lay spilled, their fluted drums half sunk in cyclamen
Or deep in water's biting clarity
Which just barely upheld me
The next week, when I sailed for home.
But where is home—these walls?
These limbs? The very spaniel underfoot
Races in sleep, toward what?
It is autumn. I did not invite
Those guests, windy and brittle, who drink my liquor.
Returning from a walk I find
The bottles filled with spleen, my room itself

Smeared by reflection on to the far hemlocks.
I some days flee in dream
Back to the exposed porch of the maidens
Only to find my great-great-grandmothers
Erect there, peering
Into a globe of red Bohemian glass.
As it swells and sinks, I call up
Graces, Furies, Fates, removed
To my country's warm, lit halls, with rivets forced
Through drapery, and nothing left to bear.
They seem anxious to know
What holds up heaven nowadays.
I start explaining how in that vast fire
Were other irons—well, Art, Public Spirit,
Ignorance, Economics, Love of Self,
Hatred of Self, a hundred more,
Each burning to be felt, each dedicated
To sparing us the worst; how I distrust them
As I should have done those ladies; how I want
Essentials: salt, wine, olive, the light, the scream—
No! I have scarcely named you,
And look, in a flash you stand full-grown before me,
Row upon row, Essentials,
Dressed like your sister caryatids
Or tombstone angels jealous of their dead,
With undulant coiffures, lips weathered, cracked by grime,
And faultless eyes gone blank beneath the immense
Zinc and gunmetal northern sky . . .
Stay then. Perhaps the system
Calls for spirits. This first glass I down
To the last time
I ate and drank in that old world. May I
Also survive its meanings, and my own.

Gary Snyder (b. 1930)

MID-AUGUST AT SOURDOUGH MOUNTAIN LOOKOUT

Down valley a smoke haze
Three days heat, after five days rain
Pitch glows on the fir-cones
Across rocks and meadows
Swarms of new flies.

I cannot remember things I once read
A few friends, but they are in cities.
Drinking cold snow-water from a tin cup
Looking down for miles
Through high still air.

Wendell Berry (b. 1934)

THE WILD GEESE

Horseback on Sunday morning,
harvest over, we taste persimmon
and wild grape, sharp sweet
of summer's end. In time's maze
over the fall fields, we name names
that went west from here, names
that rest on graves. We open
a persimmon seed to find the tree
that stands in promise,
pale, in the seed's marrow.
Geese appear high over us,
pass, and the sky closes. Abandon,
as in love or sleep, holds
them to their way, clear,
in the ancient faith: what we need
is here. And we pray, not
for new earth or heaven, but to be
quiet in heart, and in eye
clear. What we need is here.

James Wright (1927–1980)

A BLESSING

Just off the highway to Rochester, Minnesota,
Twilight bounds softly forth on the grass.
And the eyes of those two Indian ponies
Darken with kindness.
They have come gladly out of the willows
To welcome my friend and me.
We step over the barbed wire into the pasture
Where they have been grazing all day, alone.

They ripple tensely, they can hardly contain their happiness
That we have come.
They bow shyly as wet swans. They love each other.
There is no loneliness like theirs.
At home once more,
They begin munching the young tufts of spring in the darkness.
I would like to hold the slenderer one in my arms,
For she has walked over to me
And nuzzled my left hand.
She is black and white,
Her mane falls wild on her forehead,
And the light breeze moves me to caress her long ear
That is delicate as the skin over a girl's wrist.
Suddenly I realize
That if I stepped out of my body I would break
Into blossom.

John Ashbery (b. 1927)

DECOY

We hold these truths to be self-evident:
That ostracism, both political and moral, has
Its place in the twentieth-century scheme of things;
That urban chaos is the problem we have been seeing into and seeing into,
For the factory, deadpanned by its very existence into a
Descending code of values, has moved right across the road from total financial upheaval
And caught regression head-on. The descending scale does not imply
A corresponding deterioration of moral values, punctuated
By acts of corporate vandalism every five years,
Like a bunch of violets pinned to a dress, that knows and ignores its own standing.
There is every reason to rejoice with those self-styled prophets of commercial disaster, those harbingers of gloom,
Over the imminent lateness of the denouement that, advancing slowly, never arrives,
At the same time keeping the door open to a tongue-and-cheek attitude on the part of the perpetrators,

The men who sit down to their vast desks on Monday to begin planning the week's notations, jotting memoranda that take
Invisible form in the air, like flocks of sparrows
Above the city pavements, turning and wheeling aimlessly
But on the average directed by discernible motives.

To sum up: We are fond of plotting itineraries
And our pyramiding memories, alert as dandelion fuzz, dart from one pretext to the next
Seeking in occasions new sources of memories, for memory is profit
Until the day it spreads out all its accumulation, delta-like, on the plain
For that day no good can come of remembering, and the anomalies cancel each other out.
But until then foreshortened memories will keep us going, alive, one to the other.

There was never any excuse for this and perhaps there need be none,
For kicking out into the morning, on the wide bed,
Waking far apart on the bed, the two of them:
Husband and wife
Man and wife

Audre Lorde (b. 1934)

NOW THAT I AM FOREVER WITH CHILD

How the days went
while you were blooming within me
I remember each upon each—
the swelling changed planes of my body
and how you first fluttered, then jumped
and I thought it was my heart.

How the days wound down
and the turning of winter
I recall, with you growing heavy
against the wind. I thought
now her hands
are formed, and her hair
has started to curl
now her teeth are done

now she sneezes.
Then the seed opened
I bore you one morning just before spring
My head rang like a fiery piston
my legs were towers between which
A new world was passing.

Since then
I can only distinguish
one thread within running hours
You, flowing through selves
toward You.

Michael Harper (b. 1938)
DEAR JOHN, DEAR COLTRANE

a love supreme, a love supreme
a love supreme, a love supreme

Sex fingers toes
in the marketplace
near your father's church
in Hamlet, North Carolina—
witness to this love
in this calm fallow
of these minds,
there is no substitute for pain:
genitals gone or going,
seed burned out,
you tuck the roots in the earth,
turn back, and move
by river through the swamps,
singing: *a love supreme, a love supreme;*
what does it all mean?

Loss, so great each black
woman expects your failure
in mute change, the seed gone.
You plod up into the electric city—
your song now crystal and
the blues. You pick up the horn
with some will and blow
into the freezing night:
a love supreme, a love supreme—

Dawn comes and you cook
up the thick sin 'tween
impotence and death, fuel
the tenor sax cannibal
heart, genitals and sweat
that makes you clean—
a love supreme, a love supreme—

Why you so black?
cause I am
why you so funky?
cause I am
why you so black?
cause I am
why you so sweet?
cause I am
why you so black?
cause I am
a love supreme, a love supreme:

So sick
you couldn't play *Naima,*
so flat we ached
for song you'd concealed
with your own blood,
your diseased liver gave
out its purity,
the inflated heart
pumps out, the tenor kiss,
tenor love:
a love supreme, a love supreme—
a love supreme, a love supreme—

May Swenson (b. 1927)
BLEEDING

Stop bleeding   said the knife.
I would if I   could said the cut.
Stop bleeding   you make me messy with this blood.
I'm sorry said   the cut.
Stop or I will   sink in farther said the knife.

Don't said the   cut.
The knife did   not say it couldn't help it but it sank
in farther.
If only you   didn't bleed said the knife I wouldn't have to
do this.
I know said   the cut I bleed too easily I hate that I can't
help it I   wish I were a knife like you and didn't have
to bleed.
Meanwhile   stop bleeding will you said the knife.
Yes you   are a mess and sinking in farther said the cut I will
have to   stop.
Have you   stopped by now said the knife.
I've almost   stopped I think
Why must you   bleed in the first place said the knife.
For the reason   maybe that you must do what you must
do said the cut.
I can't stand   bleeding said the knife and sank in farther.
I hate it too   said the cut I know it isn't you it's me
you're lucky to   be a knife you ought to be glad
about that.
Too many cuts   around said the knife they're messy I
don't know
how they stand   themselves
They don't said   the cut.
You're bleeding   again.
No I've stopped   said the cut. See you're coming out
now the
blood is drying   it will rub off you'll be shiny again
and clean.
If only cuts   wouldn't bleed so much said the knife
coming out a little.
But then knives   might become dull said the cut.
Aren't you bleeding   a little said the knife.
I hope not said the   cut.
I feel you are just   a little.
Maybe just a little   but I can stop now.
I feel a little   wetness still said the knife sinking in
a little but then   coming out a little.
Just a little maybe   just enough said the cut.
That's enough now   stop now do you feel better now
said the knife.
I feel I have to   bleed to feel I think said the cut.
I don't I don't have   to feel said the knife drying now
becoming shiny.

Jody Aliesan (b. 1943)
RADIATION LEAK

I come from farm folk:
we know about trouble,
settle near a stream
in case the well runs dry,
plant enough to store
so we'll eat through the winter.
we learn about the signs of spring,
how to watch the sky.

but the radio says
all our food jars are poison.
everywhere. overnight.
don't touch them at all.
and the stream only looks clear;
you can't see the death in it.
if you drank a cup of it
you'd rot from inside.

helicopters came,
people in them wearing space suits.
they dropped us food pills, books
on how to stay alive.
waves on the lakeshore
slap up with fishbellies.
evergreen needles
are turning yellow,
needles and feathers falling

I hold my head in my hands
and bring away hair.

Galway Kinnell (b. 1927)
THE FUNDAMENTAL PROJECT OF TECHNOLOGY

"A flash! A white flash sparkled!"
Tatsuichiro Akizuki, *Concentric Circles of Death*

Under glass: glass dishes which changed
in color; pieces of transformed beer bottles;
a household iron; bundles of wire become solid

lumps of iron; a pair of pliers; a ring of skull-
bone fused to the inside of a helmet; a pair of eyeglasses
taken off the eyes of an eyewitness, without glass,
which vanished, when a white flash sparkled.

An old man, possibly a soldier back then,
now reduced down to one who soon will die,
sucks at the cigaret dangling from his lip, peers
at the uniform, scorched, of some tiniest schoolboy,
sighs out bluish mists of his own ashes over
a pressed tin lunch box well crushed back then when
the word *future* first learned, in a white flash, to jerk tears.

On the bridge outside, in navy black, a group
of schoolchildren line up, hold it, grin at a flash-pop,
swoop in a flock across grass, see a stranger, cry,
hello! hello! hello! and soon, *goodbye! goodbye! goodbye!*
having pecked up the greetings that fell half unspoken
and the going-sayings that those who went the morning
it happened a white flash sparkled did not get to say.

If all a city's faces were to shrink back all at once
from their skulls, would a new sound come into existence,
audible above moans eaves extract from wind that smoothes
the grass on graves; or raspings heart's-blood greases still;
or wails infants trill born already skillful at the grandpa's rattle;
or intra-screams bitter-knowledge's speechlessness
memorized, at that white flash, inside closed-forever mouths?

To de-animalize human mentality, to purge it of obsolete
evolutionary characteristics, in particular of death,
which foreknowledge terrorizes the contents of skulls with,
is the fundamental project of technology; however,
pseudologica fantastica's mechanisms require:
if you would establish deathlessness you must eliminate
those who die; a task attempted, when a white flash sparkled.

Unlike the trees of home, which continually evaporate
along the skyline, the trees here have been enticed down
toward world-eternity. No one knows which gods they enshrine.
Does it matter? Awareness of ignorance is as devout
as knowledge of knowledge. Or more so. Even though not knowing,

sometimes we weep, from surplus of gratitude, even though knowing,
twice already on earth sparkled a flash, a white flash.

The children go away. By nature they do. And by memory—
in scorched uniforms, holding tiny crushed lunch tins.
All the pleasure-groans of each night call them to return, satori
their ghostliness back into the ashes, in the momentary shrines,
the thankfulness of arms, from which they will go
again and again, until the day flashes and no one lives
to look back and say, a flash, a white flash sparkled.

Stephen Dunn (b. 1939)

BEACHED WHALES OFF MARGATE

One day they just started rolling up,
six pilot whales from way out.
Two hundred people pushed three of them back, oh
it took hours. I tell you all this
because two hundred people usually hurt
what they touch. But not this time.
After it was done, they all stood around
for a while, like the humans they used to be,
lamenting the three who were dead.
Separateness set in slowly; an aerial shot
would have shown a group moving away
from its center, leaving in ones and twos
toward their large, inconsiderate houses.

Edward Hirsch (b. 1950)

DAWN WALK

Some nights when you're asleep
Deep under the covers, far away,
Slowly curling yourself back
Into a childhood no one
Living will ever remember

Now that your parents touch hands
Under the ground
As they always did upstairs
In the master bedroom, only more
Distant now, deaf to the nightmares,
The small cries that no longer
Startle you awake but still
Terrify me so that
I do get up, some nights, restless
And anxious to walk through
The first trembling blue light
Of dawn in a calm snowfall.
It's soothing to see the houses
Asleep in their own large bodies,
The dreamless fences, the courtyards
Unscarred by human footprints,
The huge clock folding its hands
In the forehead of the skyscraper
Looming downtown. In the park
The benches are layered in
White, the statue out of history
Is an outline of blue snow. Cars,
Too, are rimmed and motionless
Under a thin blanket smoothed down
By the smooth maternal palm
Of the wind. So thanks to the
Blue morning, to the blue spirit
Of winter, to the soothing blue gift
Of powdered snow! And soon
A few scattered lights come on
In the houses, a motor coughs
And starts up in the distance, smoke
Raises its arms over the chimneys.
Soon the trees suck in the darkness
And breathe out the light
While black drapes open in silence.
And as I turn home where
I know you are already awake,
Wandering slowly through the house
Searching for me, I can suddenly
Hear my own footsteps crunching
The simple astonishing news
That we are here,
Yes, we are still here.

FAST BREAK

(In Memory of Dennis Turner, 1946–1984)

A hook shot kisses the rim and
hangs there, helplessly, but doesn't drop

and for once our gangly starting center
boxes out his man and times his jump

perfectly, gathering the orange leather
from the air like a cherished possession

and spinning around to throw a strike
to the outlet who is already shoveling

an underhand pass toward the other guard
scissoring past a flat-footed defender

who looks stunned and nailed to the floor
in the wrong direction, turning to catch sight

of a high, gliding dribble and a man
letting the play develop in front of him

in slow motion, almost exactly
like a coach's drawing on the blackboard,

both forwards racing down the court
the way that forwards should, fanning out

and filling the lanes in tandem, moving
together as brothers passing the ball

between them without a dribble, without
a single bounce hitting the hardwood

until the guard finally lunges out
and commits to the wrong man

while the power-forward explodes past them
in a fury, taking the ball into the air

by himself now and laying it gently
against the glass for a layup,

but losing his balance in the process,
inexplicably falling, hitting the floor

with a wild, headlong motion
for the game he loved like a country

and swiveling back to see an orange blur
floating perfectly through the net.

Gregory Orr (b. 1947)

MORNING SONG

Sun on his face wakes him.
The boy makes his way down
through the spidery dark
of stairs to his breakfast
of cereal in a blue bowl.
He carries to the barn
a pie plate heaped
with vegetable scraps
for the three-legged deer.
As a fawn it stood still
and alone in high hay
while the red tractor
spiraled steadily inward,
mowing its precise swaths.
"I lived" is the song
the boy hears as the deer
hobbles toward him.
In the barn's huge gloom
light falls through cracks
the way swordblades
pierce a magician's box.

Bruce Weigl (b. 1949)

HOMAGE TO ELVIS, HOMAGE TO THE FATHERS

All night the pimp's cars slide past the burning mill
Where I've come back
To breathe the slag stink air of home.
Without words the gray workers trade shifts,
The serious drinkers fill the bar
To dull the steel
Ringing their brains.

As I remember, as I want it to be,
The buick was pastel, pale
In the light burning out of the city's dirty side
Where we lived out our life
Sentences in a company house.

Good people to love and fight, matters
Of the lucky heart that doesn't stop.

Beyond the mill street
Slag heaps loom up like dunes, almost beautiful.
Once we played our war games there
And a boy from the block ran screaming
He's here, it's him at the record store
And we slid down the sooty waste of the mill
And black and grimy we stood outside
Behind the screaming older sisters
And saw him, his hair puffed up and shiny, his gold
Bracelets catching light.

He changed us somehow; we cleaned up.
We spun his 45's in the basement,
Danced on the cool concrete and plastered
Our hair back like his and twisted
Our forbidden hips.
Across the alley our fathers died
Piece by piece among the blast furnace rumble.
They breathed the steel rifted air
As if it were good.

Unwelcome, I stand outside the mill gates
And watch the workers pass like ghosts.
I close my eyes and it all makes sense:
I believe I will live forever.
I believe the world will rip apart
From the inside
Of our next moment alive.

William Matthews (b. 1942)
AN ELEGY FOR BOB MARLEY

In an elegy for a musician,
one talks a lot about music,
which is a way to think about time
instead of death or Marley,

and isn't poetry itself about time?
But death is about death and not time.
Surely the real fuel for elegy
is anger to be mortal.

No wonder Marley sang so often
of an ever-arriving future, that verb tense
invented by religion and political rage.
Soon come. Readiness is all,

and not enough. From the urinous
dust and sodden torpor
of Trenchtown, from the fruitpeels
and imprecations, from cunning,

from truculence, from the luck
to be alive, however, cruelly,
Marley made a brave music—
a rebel music, he called it,

though music calls us together,
however briefly—and a fortune.
One is supposed to praise the dead
in elegies for leaving us their songs,

though they had not choice; nor could
the dead bury the dead if we could pay
them to. This is something else we can't
control, another loss, which is, as someone

said in hope of consolation,
only temporary, though the same phrase
could be used of our lives and bodies
and all that we hope survives them.

Albert Goldbarth (b. 1948)

A FILM

1.

It's strangely like a man
and a display of toy cars. It is,
in a sense. Collected by the hundred
at the base of the drive-in

movie screen, we're toyed
before the larger life—its anguishes
and joys—that's our life
given grandiosity

of size to match our feelings.
And we come down from the mountains,

down from the keeping of stars,
to watch: a single beam of light

become a world—the oldest story.
Now a woman's joined the man. The second
oldest story is going to start now,
jumbo, with butter, with salt.

2.

The story's thin: some little
aspiration, flawed and baubled.
The dialogue's thin: "I never
thought . . ." "Why, you . . ." A house

is a sheet of cannily painted plywood,
propped by rods. "Inside,"
our days and nights
are taking place on a kind of scale

so enormous, their height and width
must be a function of flattenings like
the cats and dogs receive,
in cartoons, from steamrollers. Maybe

these actors' real lives are convoluted
and fecund . . . All I know is everything,
people, house, a background extending to outer
space, is a coating of white paint.

3.

Out in the mountains around us
tonight, if the paper's correct, a couple
of dozen believers have come to wait
for the end of the world, and their

select ascension—"the Rapture,"
they call it—to some new world.
They have candles. They sing. Their knees
are naked on rock. The date has been

ordained for a decade . . . any minute now,
"the Testament of Fire." And when tomorrow
comes, is snoozy, is crumpled
popcorn boxes like always? Won't their

disappointment be blinding, be the fierce sun
as it rises and covers the lake, covers
it completely, a film
over water that's deep and abiding.

Ai (b. 1947)

SHE DIDN'T EVEN WAVE

For Marilyn Monroe

I buried Mama in her wedding dress
and put gloves on her hands,
but I couldn't do much about her face,
blue-black and swollen,
so I covered it with a silk scarf.
I hike my dress up to my thighs
and rub them,
watching you tip the mortuary fan back and forth.
Hey. Come on over. Cover me all up
like I was never here. Just never.
Come on. I don't know why I talk like that.
It was a real nice funeral. Mama's.
I touch the rhinestone heart pinned to my blouse.
Honey, let's look at it again.
See. It's bright like the lightning that struck her.

I walk outside
and face the empty house.
You put your arms around me. Don't.
Let me wave goodbye.
Mama never got a chance to do it.
She was walking toward the barn
when it struck her. I didn't move;
I just stood at the screen door.
Her whole body was light.
I'd never seen anything so beautiful.

I remember how she cried in the kitchen
a few minutes before.
She said, *God. Married.*
I don't believe it, Jean, I won't.
He takes and takes and you just give.
At the door, she held out her arms
and I ran to her.
She squeezed me so tight:

I was all short of breath.
And she said, *don't do it.*
In ten years, your heart will be eaten out
and you'll forgive him, or some other man, even that

and it will kill you.
Then she walked outside.
And I kept saying, I've got to, Mama,
hug me again. Please don't go.

Sharon Olds (b. 1942)

THE DEATH OF MARILYN MONROE

The ambulance men touched her cold
body, lifted it, heavy as iron,
onto the stretcher, tried to close the
mouth, closed the eyes, tied the
arms to the sides, moved a caught
strand of hair, as if it mattered,
saw the shape of her breasts, flattened by
gravity, under the sheet,
carried her, as if it were she,
down the steps.

These men were never the same. They went out
afterwards, as they always did,
for a drink or two, but they could not meet
each other's eyes.

Their lives took
a turn—one had nightmares, strange
pains, impotence, depression. One did not
like his work, his wife looked
different, his kids. Even death
seemed different to him—a place where she
would be waiting,

and one found himself standing at night
in the doorway to a room of sleep, listening to a
woman breathing, just an ordinary
woman
breathing.

Susan Tichy (b. 1952)

IN AN ARAB TOWN
West Bank

The fat, pale proprietor
stands at his plateglass window
while we drink tea
with sugar, tea with rum

from our pockets—
none of the men refuse.
It makes them
brave, so they reach out,
delicately at first,
for my white skin,
for whose sake also
two Israeli soldiers
loiter in the street. In fact

we don't talk politics
but Persian verse. I learn,
fighting fingers off my knee,
that no poem should be read
in haste, or carried in a pocket
close to the body's heat. The poet
is the tongue of God's voice. His words
should be recorded in script,
and not by a woman
because her hand will shake.

Then one boy, whose manhood
barely shadows his lip,
recites the perfect letters
which he has placed in my lap.
They teach us *mabrook,*
"you are blessed,"
and *fucka,* because all things
are pure to the tongue.

And two girls
who won't come into the teahouse,
who wear so many colors
their men go blind,
pass fruit through the kitchen windows
for us, giggling. Sisters.
We're told they can't read.

But women, we've been warned,
are most dangerous.
Men lose their tempers, their cool,
spread talk, get caught.
Women are perfectly capable
of riding buses,
arms full of chickens and bombs,
giggling all the way
about some fat unmarried neighbor
or some poor man's cock.

Katha Pollitt (b. 1949)
ARCHAEOLOGY

"Our real poems are already in us
and all we can do is dig."
—Jonathan Galassi

You knew the odds on failure from the start,
that morning you first saw, or thought you saw,
beneath the heatstruck plains of a second-rate country
the outline of buried cities. A thousand to one
you'd turn up nothing more than the rubbish heap
of a poor Near Eastern backwater:
a few chipped beads,
splinters of glass and pottery, broken tablets
whose secret lore, laboriously deciphered,
would prove to be only a collection of ancient grocery lists.
Still, the train moved away from the station without you.

How many lives ago
was that? How many choices?
Now that you've got your bushelful of shards
do you say, *give me back my years*
or wrap yourself in the distant
glitter of desert stars,
telling yourself it was foolish after all
to have dreamed of uncovering
some fluent vessel, the bronze head of a god?
Pack up your fragments. Let the simoom
flatten the digging site. Now come
the passionate midnights in the museum basement
when out of that random rubble you'll invent
the dusty market smelling of sheep and spices,
streets, palmy gardens, courtyards set with wells
to which, in the blue of evening, one by one
come strong veiled women, bearing their pefect jars.

Norman H. Russell (b. 1921)
indian school

in the darkness
of the house of the white brother
i go alone and am frightened
strange things touch me

i cannot breathe his air
or eat his tasteless food

on his walls
are pictures of the world
that his walls shut out
in his hands are leaves of words
from dead mens mouths

he speaks to me with only
the sounds of his mouth
for he is dumb and blind
as the staggering old bear
filled with many arrows
as the rocks that lie on the mountain

and in his odd robes
uglier
than any other creature i have ever seen

i am not wise enough to know
gods purpose in him.

Rita Dove (b. 1952)

DUSTING

Everyday a wilderness—no
shade in sight. Beulah
patient among knickknacks,
the solarium a rage
of light, a grainstorm
as her gray cloth brings
dark wood to life.

Under her hand scrolls
and crests gleam
darker still. What
was his name, that
silly boy at the fair with
the rifle booth? And his kiss and
the clear bowl with one bright
fish, rippling
wound!

Not Michael—
something finer. Each dust

stroke a deep breath and
the canary in bloom.
Wavery memory: home
from a dance, the front door
blown open and the parlor
in snow, she rushed
the bowl to the stove, watched
as the locket of ice
dissolved and he
swam free.

That was years before
Father gave her up
with her name, years before
her name grew to mean
Promise, then
Desert-in-Peace.
Long before the shadow and
sun's accomplice, the tree.

Maurice.

Teresa Anderson (b. 1944)
DELPHINE

In every direction from here
the land is flat and merciless,
horizons painfully stark,
trees spaced wide apart
and ponds too often dry;
Louis Desaire chose a cruel
and inconstant homestead,
known for blizzards and
duststorms, locusts and
withering blight in the wheat;
his children have headed for
the certainty of towns,
abandoning the farm to the
windmill dismantled, the
well overgrown with sunflowers
and the front porch sagging
under the weight of a sleeping cat.
Delphine's kitchen is used as a

feed shed for cattle who have
broken in the door, and the
iron stove is now a nesting
place for prairie hens and mice;
thistle-topped grasses cover the cellar
out back, and the barn has long since
lost its battle with searing winds.
But at night when the house shifts
under the flying shadows of clouds,
they come back, the man
with his bawdy laugh,
hands reaching for
sweet, home-made wine
and eyes following the
woman, a diminutive,
green-eyed girl now,
just come from the wedding dance,
who stands uncertainly at
the parlor door, wondering
at the crude sound of his English,
picturing a cradle by the stove
and wishing he would remove
the pins from her heavy, dark hair.

Jay Parini (b. 1948)

THE MISSIONARY VISITS OUR CHURCH IN SCRANTON

He came to us every other summer
from the jungles of Brazil,
his gabardine suit gone shiny in the knees
from so much praying.

He came on the hottest Sunday, mid-July,
holding up a spear before our eyes,
the very instrument, we were told,
which impaled a brace of his Baptist colleagues.

The congregation wheezed in unison,
waiting for the slides: the savage women
dandling their breasts on tawny knees,
the men with painted buttocks
dancing in a ring.

The congregation loosened their collars,
mopped their brows, all praying
that the Lord would intervene.

Always, at the end, one saw the chapel:
its white-baked walls, the circle of women
in makeshift bras, the men in shirts.

They were said to be singing a song of Zion.
They were said to be wishing us well in Scranton.

Robert Morgan (b. 1944)

BRICKING THE CHURCH

At the foot of Meetinghouse Hill
where once the white chapel
pointed among junipers and pulled
a wash of gravestones west,

they've buried the wooden snow that
answered sarvis in bloom
and early morning fogs, in brick,
a crust the same dull red

as clay in nearby gullies.
The little churchhouse now looks more
like a post office or school.
It's hard to find

among the brown winter slopes
or plowed fields of spring.
Brick was prestigious back when
they set their minds and savings to it.

They wanted to assert its form
and presence if not in stone
at least in hardened earth, urban weight,
as the white clapboards replaced

unpainted lumber which replaced
the logs of the original
where men brought their guns to preaching
and wolves answered the preacher.

The structure grows successive rings,
and as its doctrine softens
puts on a hard shell
for weathering this world.

William Pitt Root (b. 1941)

SOMETIMES HEAVEN IS A MEAN MACHINE

For Wayne Sloan

It is like riding Death and not dying.

It shudders, snarls and roars like an iron lion.
It shines like the chromed bones of a bull.

At night its single headlight
rakes across the highway like the lowered horn
of a charging unicorn.

It looks like Death waiting for a taker.

You take it, you ride.

All day, all night for years
while the bright arcs of your breath flex
into curves repeating earthshapes
you ride, the road informing you.

You ride
your own death and you do not die.

It shines and you ride its shining.

Marilyn Waniek (b. 1946)

OLD BIBLES

I throw things away
usually, but there's
this whole shelf
of Bibles in my house.
Old Bibles, with pages missing
or scribbled by children
and black covers chewed by puppies.
I believe in euthanasia,
but I can't get rid of them.
It's a sin,
like stepping on a crack
or not crossing your fingers
or dropping the flag.
I did that once,
and for weeks
a gaunt bearded stranger

in tricolored clothes
came to get me,
moaning,
Give me my flag.
And Bibles are worse,
they maybe have souls
like little birds fluttering
over the dump
when the wind blows their pages.
Bibles are holy, blessed,
they're like
kosher.

So I keep them,
a row of solemn apostles
doomed to life,
and I wait for the great collection
and conflagration,
when they'll all burn together
with a sound like the wings
of a flock of doves:
little ash ascensions
of the Word.

Diana O Hehir (b. 1922)

LEARNING TO TYPE

A laboratory chimpanzee has been taught to communicate by means of a symbol-keyed typewriter.

The sign for anger could be a felled pine tree.
Arbitrarily, love is a glass of orange juice.

On this machine you can type only declarative sentences:
My eyes hurt;
I have two tears sliding down the ridges of my nose;
My father lies on his hospital bed. His eyes are open.

A chimpanzee has no voice-box
And a machine must teach it the difference between make
  and give.
Make me a heart for giving; give me time.

I am sitting now at a machine like a middle aged woman.
Its panel is intricate and garbled; there are symbols for leave-
  takings:

Pictures of the crowd praying outside the cathedral,
Of the red train moving slowly off down the station.

If I study long enough I can find out how:
Machine, make me fingers to manage the dangerous keys.

Stan Rice (b. 1942)

METAPHYSICAL SHOCK WHILE WATCHING A TV CARTOON

Things come from nothing.
The lawnmower
the bulldog uses
to shave the cat
in the cartoon I am watching:
from nothing.
The startled duck bursts
from nothing; drags its feet in the water;
doubles the blaze.
Suddenly, where there was nothing,
there is a lawnmower.
In the next scene the cat is not shaved.
Its hair has returned spontaneously,
and the bulldog's jowls are overlapping
a big naked bone which then
is a stick of dynamite which explodes the dog's head.
In the next scene the dog's head is a dog's head again.
Nothing did it, and nothing
made it ok. The logic of the cartoon
overwhelms me. I watch the TV in the mirror
over the fireplace to get some perspective. But this just
doubles the nothing. *I* came
from where that lawnmower came from.
Jesus, I whisper. Im frightened; and write down
on the telephone messagepad the first line
of this poem; itself, especially, suddenly,
from nothing.

Star Black (b. 1946)

REALLY

I've been everywhere and done everthing except Europe
and I don't know, I feel spaced out most of the time.

I'd like to see Turkey and take a boat down the Rhine
before the war, the first war, the war of the roses,

but just talking about the States and all, it seems
to me I could make you feel a whole lot better when
you start counting your losses and twisting in your
sleep. You get so weird then, contorted, and if you

stick with me I can watch you shave in the morning,
Albert, shy as Victoria. I hurt inside, too, always
hold my breath when I drive past a graveyard, have to,
no choice. Somebody said if you hold your breath when

you drive past a graveyard everthing would be nice,
must have meant for a little while but I like lies.

Jorie Graham (b. 1951)
HISTORY

Into whose ear the deeds are spoken. The only
listener. So I believed
he would remember everything, the murmuring trees,
the sunshine's zealotry, its deep
unevenness. For history
is the opposite
of the eye
for whom, for instance, six million bodies in portions
of hundreds and
the flowerpots broken by a sudden wind stand as
equivalent. What more
is there
than fact? *I'll give 10,000 dollars to the man*
who proves the holocaust really
occurred said the exhausted solitude
in San Francisco in 1980.
Far in the woods, in a faded
photograph, in 1942 the man with his own genitalia
in his mouth and hundreds of
slow holes
a pitchfork has opened
over his face
grows beautiful. The ferns and deepwood
lilies catch
the eye. Three men in ragged uniforms

with guns keep laughing
nervously. They share the day
with him. A bluebird
sings. The feathers of the shade touch every inch
of skin—the hand holding down the delicate gun,
the hands holding down the delicate
hips. And the sky
is visible between the men, between
the trees, a blue spirit
enveloping
anything. Late in the story, in Northern Italy,
a man cuts down some trees for winter
fuel. We read this in the evening
news. Watching the fire burn late
one night, watching it change and change, a hand grenade,
lodged in the pulp the young tree
grew around, explodes, blinding the man, killing
his wife. Now who
will tell the children
fairytales? The ones where simple
crumbs over the forest
floor endure
to help us home?

READING PLATO

This is the story
    of a beautiful
lie, what slips
    through my fingers,
your fingers. It's winter,
    it's far

in the lifespan
    of man.
Bareheaded, in a soiled
    shirt,
speechless, my friend
    is making

lures, his hobby. Flies
    so small
he works with tweezers and
    a magnifying glass.

They must be
so believable

they're true—feelers,
antennae,
quick and frantic
as something
drowning. His heart
beats wildly

in his hands. It is
blinding
and who will forgive him
in his tiny
garden? He makes them
out of hair,

deer hair, because it's hollow
and floats.
Past death, past sight,
this is
his good idea, what drives
the silly days

together. Better than memory. Better
than love.
Then they are done, a hook
under each pair
of wings, and it's Spring,
and the men

wade out into the riverbed
at dawn. Above,
the stars still connect-up
their hungry animals.
Soon they'll be satisfied
and go. Meanwhile

upriver, downriver, imagine, quick
in the air,
in flesh, in a blue
swarm of
flies, our knowledge of
the graceful

deer skips easily across
the surface.

Dismembered, remembered,
    it's finally
alive. Imagine
    the body

they were all once
    a part of,
these men along the lush
    green banks
trying to slip in
    and pass

for the natural world.

Pattiann Rogers (b. 1940)

CONCEPTS AND THEIR BODIES
(The Boy in the Field Alone)

Staring at the mud turtle's eye
Long enough, he sees *concentricity* there
For the first time, as if it possessed
Pupil and iris and oracular lid,
As if it grew, forcing its own gene of circularity.
The concept is definitely
The cellular arrangement of sight.

The five amber grasses maintaining their seedheads
In the breeze against the sky
Have borne *latitude* from the beginning,
Secure *civility* like leaves in their folds.
He discovers *persistence* in the mouth
Of the caterpillar in the same way
As he discovers clear syrup
On the broken end of the dayflower,
Exactly as he comes accidently upon
The mud crown of the crawfish.

The spotted length of the bullfrog leaping
Lakeward just before the footstep
Is not bullfrog, spread and sailing,
But the body of *initiative* with white glossy belly.
Departure is the wing let loose
By the dandelion, and it does possess
A sparse down and will not be thought of,

Even years later, even in the station
At midnight among the confusing lights,
As separate from that white twist
Of filament drifting.

Nothing is sharp enough to disengage
The butterfly's path from *erraticism.*

And *freedom* is this September field
Covered this far by tree shadows
Through which this child chooses to run
Until he chooses to stop,
And it will be so hereafter.

Kay Smith

ANNUNCIATION

for Kathy

In all the old paintings
The Virgin is reading—
No one knows what,
When she is disturbed
By an angel with a higher mission,
Beyond books.

She looks up reluctantly,
Still marking the place with her finger.
The angel is impressive,
With red shoes and just
A hint of wing and shine everywhere.
Listening to the measured message
The Virgin bows her head,
Her eyes aslant
Between the angel and the book.

At the Uffizi
We stood
Before a particularly beautiful angel
And a hesitant Sienese Virgin,
We two sometimes women.
Believing we could ignore
All messages,
Unobliged to wings or words,
We laughed in the vibrant space
Between the two,

Somewhere in the angled focus
Of the Virgin's eye.

Now, in the harder times,
I do not laugh so often;
Still the cheap postcard in my room
Glints with the angel's robe.
I look with envy
At the angel and the book,
Wishing I had chosen
One or the other,
Anything but the space between.

Simon Ortiz (b. 1941)

A STORY OF HOW A WALL STANDS

At Acu, there is a wall almost 400 years old which supports hundreds of tons of dirt and bones—it's a graveyard built on a steep incline—and it looks like it's about to fall down the incline but will not for a long time.

My father, who works with stone,
says, "That's just the part you see,
the stones which seem to be
just packed in on the outside,"
and with his hands put the stone and mud
in place. "Underneath
what looks like loose stone,
there is stone woven together."
He ties one hand over the other,
fitting like the bones of his hands
and fingers. "That's what is
holding it together."

"It is built that carefully,"
he says, "the mud mixed
to a certain texture," patiently
"with the fingers," worked
in the palm of his hand. "So that
placed between the stones, they hold
together for a long, long time."

He tells me those things,
the story of them worked
with his fingers, in the palm

of his hands, working the stone
and the mud until they become
the wall that stands a long, long time.

David Baker (b. 1954)

RUNNING THE RIVER LINES

For Tim Gaines

Tonight, on a bank line strung
for catfish, a crawdad hooked through the tail
and dangled scarcely an inch
in the murky water, we catch a loon.

It must have seen our bait, scouting
overhead for something to eat, a school of minnows
or a washed-up mussel to pick apart,
and somehow snagged itself. No wonder

we haven't caught any fish,
the way it flaps there splashing and crying
its hideous cry, hurt
by the small hook at the corner of its beak

but more utterly amazed
that its wings will not bear it away from the bank.
It shrieks and splashes as we draw close,
straining against the willow pole

until it finally rips itself loose, beats its way
low over the water,
lifting at last, disappearing
into the depth of the river evening,

its cry still strung between us like a fine line.

Raymond Carver (1939–1988)

THE RIVER

I waded, deepening, into the dark water.
Evening, and the push
and swirl of the river as it closed
around my legs and held on.
Young grisle broke water.
Parr darted one way, smolt another.

Gravel turned under my boots as I edged out.
Watched by the furious eyes of king salmon.
Their immense heads turned slowly,
eyes burning with fury, as they hung
in the deep current.
They were there. I felt them there,
and my skin prickled. But
there was something else.
I braced with the wind on my neck.
Felt the hair rise
as something touched my boot.
Grew afraid at what I couldn't see.
Then of everthing that filled my eyes—
that other shore hung with heavy branches,
the dark mountain range behind.
And this river that had suddenly
grown black and swift.
I drew breath and cast anyway.
Prayed nothing would strike.

Christopher Gilbert (b. 1949)

CHARGE

Gimme the ball, Willie is saying
throughout this 2-on-2 pick-up game.
Winners are the ones who play, being
at the sidelines is ridiculous.
So what happens here is a history
won not by the measure of points,
but by simply getting into it.
Willie plays like it could all be gone
at once, like his being is at stake.
Gimme the ball, he cusses.
Gwen Brooks' player from the streets.
The game is wherever there's a chance.
It is nothing easy he's after,
but the rapture gained with presence.
His catalogue of moves represents
his life. Recognize its stance.
So alive to be the steps
in whose mind the symbol forms,
miraculous to be the feeling
which threads these steps to dance.

The other side is very serious—
they want to play him 2-on-1.
Messrs. Death and Uniformity.
He's got a move to make them smile.
Gimme the ball, Willie says again
and again, *"Gimme the goddamn ball."*

William Heyen (b. 1940)

MANTLE

Mantle ran so hard, they said,
he tore his legs to pieces.
What is this but spirit?

52 homers in '56, the triple crown.
I was a high school junior, batting
fourth behind him in a dream.

I prayed for him to quit, before
his lifetime dropped below .300.
But he didn't, and it did.

He makes Brylcreem commercials now,
models with open mouths draped around him
as they never were in Commerce, Oklahoma,

where the sandy-haired, wide-shouldered boy
stood up against his barn,
lefty for an hour (Ruth, Gehrig),

then righty (DiMaggio),
as his father winged them in,
and the future blew toward him

now a fastball, now a slow
curve hanging
like a model's smile.

David Bottoms (b. 1949)

UNDER THE BOATHOUSE

Out of my clothes, I ran past the boathouse
to the edge of the dock
and stood before the naked silence of the lake,

on the drive behind me, my wife
rattling keys, calling for help with the grill,
the groceries wedged into the trunk.
Near the tail end of her voice, I sprang
from the homemade board, bent body
like a hinge, and speared the surface,
cut through water I would not open my eyes in,
to hear the junked depth pop in both ears
as my right hand dug into silt and mud,
my left clawed around a pain.
In a fog of rust I opened my eyes to see
what had me, and couldn't, but knew
the fire in my hand and the weight of the thing
holding me under, knew the shock of all
things caught by the unknown
as I kicked off the bottom like a frog,
my limbs doing fearfully strange strokes,
lungs collapsed in a confusion of bubbles,
all air rising back to its element.
I flailed after it, rose toward the bubbles
breaking on light, then felt down my arm
a tug running from a taut line.
Halfway between the bottom of the lake
and the bottom of the sky, I hung like a buoy
on a short rope, an effigy
flown in an underwater parade,
and imagined myself hanging there forever,
a curiosity among fishes, a bait hanging up
instead of down. In the lung-ache,
in the loud pulsing of the temples, what gave first
was something in my head, a burst
of colors like the blind see, and I saw
against the surface a shadow like an angel
quivering in a dead-man's float,
then a shower of plastic knives and forks
spilling past me in the lightened water, a can
of barbequed beans, a bottle of A.1., napkins
drifting down like white leaves,
heavenly litter from the world I struggled toward.
What gave then was something on the other end,
and my hand rose on its own and touched my face.
Into the splintered light under the boathouse,
the loved, suffocating air hovering over the lake,
the cry of my wife leaning dangerously
over the dock, empty grocery bags at her feet,
I bobbed with a hook through the palm of my hand.

SIGN FOR MY FATHER, WHO STRESSED THE BUNT

On the rough diamond,
the hand-cut field below the dog lot and barn,
we rehearsed the strict technique
of bunting. I watched from the infield,
the mound, the backstop
as your left hand climbed the bat, your legs
and shoulders squared toward the pitcher.
You could drop it like a seed
down either base line. I admired your style,
but not enough to take my eyes off the bank
that served as our center-field fence.

Years passed, three leagues of organized ball,
no few lives. I could homer
into the garden beyond the bank,
into the left-field lot of Carmichael Motors,
and still you stressed the same technique,
the crouch and spring, the lead arm absorbing
just enough impact. That whole tiresome pitch
about basics never changing,
and I never learned what you were laying down.

Like a hand brushed across the bill of a cap,
let this be the sign
I'm getting a grip on the sacrifice.

Jim Webb

GET IN, JESUS

I stood
  the sawed off
    hours you stand
    when you're
      outside of
        Jenkins
    hitch-hikin home.

The Letcher-Pike
    line
    ain't no place

for a hippie
to catch a ride

Long hair, hairy beard,
blue jeans, back packed
makes it too crowded
for the church goers
whose front plate
proclaims
God Is My Co-Pilot,
too crowded
for those who
eat more possum,
for coal trucks,
county mounties,
& countless
others

Till,
as in the numb
dumb dreams you
have when there's
nothing else,

a wore out 57 Chevy
210 two door
screams & stops,
the door flies open
& a mountain crazy
says,
"Get in Jesus"

Knowing even saints
appear at Halloween,
& knowing no others
are likely,

I climb in
the back seat.

Up front
Two card carryin
sad lost eyed
burned out
John Greenleaf
in Detroit Citiers

& now two in back
settle down with
the floor's dust

The car spins off,
the Boone's Farm
is passed,
I drink

The only one who talks
looks back &
says,
"Where you goin
Jesus?"

"Mingo County
West Virginia,"
I say.
"West Virginia? Have
another drink"

I drink again. "Almost
Heaven" I say
watchin
the green spring
fly by

He says
"I ain't never rode
with Jesus before"
I say
"neither have I"

"Aw come on now Jesus, you
can tell
us, we
won't tell
no one"
& they all cackle
& I laugh too &
take another swig,
the wine is sweet
& terrible
as the God I've
heard about
all my days.

They're ridin crazy
so Jesus crosses
my mind
& I think about it,
about bein Jesus
& savin souls
by losin mine
A body could do worse,
bein Jesus might be
better'n I'll be,
"Pour the coal to it, boys"
Jesus says &
they howl, the driver
squeals a curve away.
We're flyin
bout as high as
the earth
can stand
Saints all. Martyrs
to wars, whores, pieces
of silver
Saints
lost & dying
"Hey Jesus,
tell us something,
What's it like to be
hung up
on a cross?"
"It ain't for shit"
I say
"What'd you let 'em
do it for, Jesus?"
"Just couldn't
help myself" I say
& laugh
We all laugh &
they're tickled
that God would
ride with them
& drink sweet
cheap wine
without even
wipin
the bottle
As for me,
when they cut off

just the other side
of Virgie,
I got out—
the door stood open
"Are you really Jesus?"
he says with a sawmill smile
I smile back
"If I was Jesus
you think I'd be
thumbin?"
We all grin,
wheels spin,
gravels fly,
the dust
settles

Philip Booth (b. 1925)

PICK-UP

Riding high.
Over the blunt hood,
the headlights flat out. Gunrack
in the back window, radio scanning from
country to rock.
I don't wanna let you
stop now.
Joey, black CAT cap over
a thin spot, nestles his up, door to
door with the 4x4 Ram, in from
Nine Mile Corner.
Do it, Baby, do it,
one more time.
They talk options:
dual tube bumpers, lift kits,
Holley carbs. Maybe, after getting off
Friday, Daylite Off-Roaders. Or
fog lights.
Bye, bye, Miss American Pie . . .
Joey punches the scan, and gets back
Wheeling.
They talk low-end power,
desert radials, Hooker roll-bars,
the whole catalogue. Everything's far
except here: the glow of the panel,

the surge of the tach as they diddle,
idle, and then back off.
                There are girls
out there, from here to Iowa,
                waiting.

Nikki Giovanni (b. 1943)

EGO TRIPPING
(There May Be A Reason Why)

I was born in the congo
I walked to the fertile crescent and built
    the sphinx
I designed a pyramid so tough that a star
    that only glows every one hundred years falls
    into the center giving divine perfect light
I am bad

I sat on the throne
    drinking nectar with allah
I got hot and sent an ice age to europe
    to cool my thirst
My oldest daughter is nefertiti
    the tears from my birth pains
    created the nile
I am a beautiful woman

I gazed on the forest and burned
    out the sahara desert
    with a packet of goat's meat
    and a change of clothes
I crossed it in two hours
I am a gazelle so swift
    so swift you can't catch me

    For a birthday present when he was three
I gave my son hannibal an elephant
    He gave me rome for mother's day
My strength flows ever on
My son noah built new/ark and
I stood proudly at the helm
    as we sailed on a soft summer day
I turned myself into myself and was
    jesus

men intone my loving name
All praises All praises
I am the one who would save

I sowed diamonds in my back yard
My bowels deliver uranium
the filings from my fingernails are
semi-precious jewels
On a trip north
I caught a cold and blew
My nose giving oil to the arab world
I am so hip even my errors are correct
I sailed west to reach east and had to round off
the earth as I went
The hair from my head thinned and gold was laid
across three continents
I am so perfect so divine so ethereal so surreal
I cannot be comprehended
except by my permission

I mean . . . I . . . can fly
like a bird in the sky . . .

Louise Glück (b. 1943)
THE MIRROR

Watching you in the mirror I wonder
what it is like to be so beautiful
and why you do not love
but cut yourself, shaving
like a blind man. I think you let me stare
so you can turn against yourself
with greater violence,
needing to show me how you scrape the flesh away
scornfully and without hestitation
until I see you correctly,
as a man bleeding, not
the reflection I desire.

Elizabeth Spires (b. 1952)
WIDOW'S WALK

When he visited Nantucket, Crevecoeur noted, "A singular custom prevails here among the women. . . . They have adopted these

> *many years the Asiatic custom of taking a dose of opium every morning; and so deeply rooted is it, that they would be at a loss how to live without this indulgence."*
>
> —Walter Teller,
> *Cape Cod and the Offshore Islands*

Captain: the weathervane's rusted.
Iron-red, its coxcomb leans into the easterly wind
as I do every afternoon swinging
a blind eye out to sea. The light
fails, day closes around me, a vast oceanic whirlpool . . .
I can still see your eyes, those monotonic palettes,
smell your whiskeyed kisses!
Still feel the eelgrass of embrace—
the ocean pounds outside the heart's door.
Dearest, the lamps are going on. I'm caught
in the smell of whales burning! Vaporous and drowsy,
I spiral down the staircase in my wrapper,
a shadow among many shadows in Nantucket Town.
Out in the yard, the chinaberry tree
turns amber. A hymn spreads through the deepening air—
the church steeple's praying for the people. Last night
I dreamed you waved farewell.
I stood upon the pier, the buoys tolling
a warning knell. Trussed in my whalebone,
I grew away from you, fluttering in the twilight,
a cutout, a fancy French silhouette.

Garret Kaoru Hongo (b. 1951)

WHAT FOR

At six I lived for spells:
how a few Hawaiian words could call
up the rain, could hymn like the sea
in the long swirl of chambers
curling in the nautilus of a shell,
how Amida's ballads of the Buddhaland
in the drone of the priest's liturgy
could conjure money from the poor
and give them nothing but mantras,
the strange syllables that healed desire.

I lived for stories about the war
my grandfather told over *hana* cards,

slapping them down on the mats
with a sharp Japanese *kiai*.

I lived for songs my grandmother sang
stirring curry into a thick stew,
weaving a calligraphy of Kannon's love
into grass mats and straw sandals.

I lived for the red volcano dirt
staining my toes, the salt residue
of surf and sea wind in my hair,
the arc of a flat stone skipping
in the hollow trough of a wave.

I lived a child's world, waited
for my father to drag himself home,
dusted with blasts of sand, powdered rock,
and the strange ash of raw cement,
his deafness made worse by the clang
of pneumatic drills, sore in his bones
from the buckings of a jackhammer.

He'd hand me a scarred lunchpail,
let me unlace the hightop G.I. boots,
call him the new name I'd invented
that day in school, write it for him
on his newspaper. He'd rub my face
with hands that felt like gravel roads,
tell me to move, go play, and then he'd
walk to the laundry sink to scrub,
rinse the dirt of his long day
from a face brown and grained as koa wood.

I wanted to take away the pain
in his legs, the swelling in his joints,
give him back his hearing,
clear and rare as crystal chimes,
the fins of glass that wrinkled
and sparked the air with their sound.

I wanted to heal the sores that work
and war had sent to him,
let him play catch in the backyard
with me, tossing a tennis ball
past papaya trees without the shoulders
of pain shrugging back his arms.

I wanted to become a doctor of pure magic,
to string a necklace of sweet words
fragrant as pine needles and plumeria,
fragrant as the bread my mother baked,
place it like a lei of cowrie shells
and *pikake* flowers around my father's neck,
and chant him a blessing, a sutra.

Margaret Atwood (b. 1939)

SPELLING

My daughter plays on the floor
with plastic letters,
red, blue & hard yellow,
learning how to spell,
spelling,
how to make spells

*

and I wonder how many women
denied themselves daughters,
closed themselves in rooms,
drew the curtains
so they could mainline words.

*

A child is not a poem,
a poem is not a child.
There is no either/or.
However.

*

I return to the story
of the woman caught in the war
& in labor, her thighs tied
together by the enemy
so she could not give birth.
Ancestress: the burning witch,
her mouth covered by leather
to strangle words.

A word after a word
after a word is power.

*

At the point where language falls away
from the hot bones, at the point
where the rock breaks open and darkness
flows out of it like blood, at
the melting point of granite
when the bones know
they are hollow & the word
splits & doubles & speaks
the truth & the body
itself becomes a mouth.

This is a metaphor.

*

How do you learn to spell?
Blood, sky & the sun,
your own name first,
your first naming, your first name,
your first word.

Leon Stokesbury (b. 1945)

UNSENT MESSAGE TO MY BROTHER IN HIS PAIN

Please do not die now. Listen.
Yesterday, storm clouds rolled
out of the west like thick muscles.
Lightning bloomed. Such a sideshow
of colors. You should have seen it.
A woman watched with me, then we slept.
Then, when I woke first, I saw
in her face that rest is possible.
The sky, it suddenly seems
important to tell you, the sky
was pink as a shell. Listen
to me. People orbit the moon now.
They must look like flies around

Fatty Arbuckle's head, that new
and that strange. My fellow American,
I bought a French cookbook. In it
are hundreds and hundreds of recipes.
If you come to see me, I shit you not,
we will cook with wine. Listen
to me. Listen to me, my brother,
please don't go. Take a later flight,
a later train. Another look around.

W. S. Di Piero (b. 1945)

FOUR BROTHERS

1.

Pino the Lizard in his patent leather shoes
wears cologne none of us ever heard of,
though he must have told us a dozen times
Pinaud, you dopes. It's French. Who cares?
Everything we know is hearsay, and what we see
depends on what we know. Pino's the one
who made it big, the only brother of three.
There would have been a fourth, but for something
Mrs. Pino did one night to the lastborn
because she felt too old, too tired. Nobody
talks about it. That was years ago. Now Pino
works outdoors, selling nickel bags to blacks,
writing numbers, lending money to men
outside the neighborhood. He doesn't know
how short his life is going to be, how one day
he'll blink and won't be there anymore to see
himself the way we see ourselves in how we act.
The first time men in good suits came
and took him to jail, in a big honest afternoon
while everybody stood outside watching, Mrs. Pino
stayed in her doorway, silent, and the cardoor closed
as if a stranger's hand had touched a pillow pressed
on an infant's face, then held it, held it there.

2.

Out of respect, maybe out of danger, people refuse
to talk about Frankie, the oldest, as if he were
religion. I don't understand his story, but it
loiters in its mystery the way most stories do.

The morning after the youngest died, Frankie
locked himself inside his upstairs room.
He's lived there ever since. His mother
delivers papers, cigarets, food,
while Frankie listens to the radio
and draws those faces, all big names,
Carole Lombard, Rita Hayworth, Marilyn Monroe,
sending sketches out with half-eaten meals.
All gifts to his mother, a vengeance,
to punish her with images of ladies
who love wild light, real stars who never
have to remember anything. Frankie
isn't crazy, but he needs certain things.
Sometimes I catch myself waiting for him to die
as if I knew he'd leave me his charcoal
or ruffled pads or picture of himself. The worst
would be to find he left nothing, cared nothing
about remembering or being remembered.
If he needs to draw, he must need memory too.

3.

Sally may be trucking through pine barrens
or selling taffy to Camden Puerto Ricans.
Hating both his brothers, snorting what's left of love
while he drinks with the Strongman in Toms River
or buys thread with the Blockhead in Wilmington.
He watched Frankie go upstairs, saw skinny Pino
driven off to prison, and he knew even more.
So he signed on with the carnival. I saw the ad
in a Jersey paper: SEE STRANGE SALVATORE EAT WILD FIRE!
I try to see the strange places he must love
passing through, his mouth his only real house,
every night those knots of fire, big fists between
his lips, past his teeth, down the tunnel to his belly,
all fire in the center of him, then to save it all
at the last minute. *Pull out the fire. Pull it out!*
Later, closing the show in mud and fog, he hauls
canvas with a midget and runaway murderer.
Everbody knows the carnival always brings rain.
Sally remembers everything, so he doesn't need
memory, only his mouth deep in a pillow, breath
trapped in a fire deep inside his throat
while he sleeps with two women, or a man,
owing himself only the need to go and go.

Lynn Emanuel (b. 1949)

FRYING TROUT WHILE DRUNK

Mother is drinking to forget a man
Who could fill the woods with invitations:
Come with me he whispered and she went
In his Nash Rambler, its dash
Where her knees turned green
In the radium dials of the '50s.
When I drink it is always 1953,
Bacon wilting in the pan on Cook Street
And mother, wrist deep in red water,
Laying a trail from the sink
To a glass of gin and back.
She is a beautiful, unlucky woman
In love with a man of lechery so solid
You could build a table on it
And when you did the blues would come to visit.
I remember all of us awkwardly at dinner,
The dark slung across the porch,
And then mother's dress falling to the floor,
Buttons ticking like seeds spit on a plate.
When I drink I am too much like her—
The knife in one hand and in the other
The trout with a belly white as my wrist.
I have loved you all my life
She told him and it was true
In the same way that all her life
She drank, dedicated to the act itself,
She stood at this stove
And with the care of the very drunk
Handed him the plate.

Daniel Mark Epstein (b. 1948)

MIAMI

After years of stock-car racing, running
rifles to Cuba, money from Rio, high
diving from helicopters into the Gulf;
after a life at gunpoint, on a dare,
my father can't make the flight out of Miami.

Turbojets roar and sing, the ground crew
scatters out of the shadow of the plane.
My father undoes his seat belt, makes his way
up the aisle, dead-white and sweating,
ducks out the hatchway, mumbling
luggage was left at the dock, his watch
in the diner. Head down
he lurches through the accordion boarding tube,
strides the shining wing of the airport, past
windows full of planes and sky, past bars,
candy machines and posters for Broadway shows.
Gasping in the stratosphere of terror, he
bursts through the glass doors and runs
to a little garden near the rental cars.
He sits among the oleanders and palms.

It started with the Bay Bridge.
He couldn't take that steel vault into the blue
above the blue, so much horizon!
Then it was the road itself, the rise and fall,
the continual blind curve.
He hired a chauffeur, he took the train.
Then it was hotels, so many rooms
the same, he had to sleep with the light on.
His courage has shrunk to the size of a windowbox.

Father who scared the witches and vampires
from my childhood closets, father
who walked before me like a hero's shield
through neighborhoods where hoodlums honed their knives
on concrete, where nerve was law,
who will drive you home from Miami?
You're broke and I'm a thousand miles away
with frightened children of my own.
Who will rescue you from the garden
where jets flash like swords above your head?

Robert A. Fink

MOTHER'S DAY

Tornado humid
and still as an elderly couple
in a car about to spin the highway:

an oak tree comes into focus,
an anonymous field of white-faced cows.

Outside my window, new pecan leaves
droop green as if the scene were underwater
or a lost world cut off from explanation.
A cardinal flashes past, complicates the scheme.
Memory is a fickle teacher

never satisfied with any one position,
so I turn seven and snug between a V
of sycamore limbs swaying green
between the sky, one fist of blue above my head,
and the ground thirty feet below

where my mother waits
holding her apron like a net
making promises we both know
she cannot keep.

Don Johnson (b. 1942)

THE SERGEANT

When others mustered out in '46, you soldiered
on, commanding a squad that buried box
after narrow box the Army sent home from abroad.

For a year the wind off the Kasserine,
peasants mudded to their knees on Mindanao
and oceans being oceans all over the world
kept turning up dead West Virginians.

You brought all the known soldiers home,
to Coal Fork, Seth, Clendinin,
to the smudged daguerreotypes of company shacks
that lay beyond slick rivers without bridges.

Your honor guard traveled the state that year
making heroes.
                    You and your men were heroes—
the War ceremonially perfect—
in hills the newsreels never reached.

Sometimes twice a day you stiffened
against the world's first standing order:
assigning remains to the last slit trenches

they would hold, awarding the widows flags
they would bundle away under cedar
or hang on the wall of the child
conceived a month before Pearl Harbor.

*

You were occupied with death
and mother ironed
ten uniforms a week to keep you creased
and properly rigid. Starch drifted
like dry snow in parlor corners where I etched
stick figures in the dust—
my own command.
And I learned to fold the flags
into tight blue parcels of stars, to execute
the manual of arms with the snap
of a garrison corporal.
But you never said
"Death" or took me along to the hills.

Coming in to the warm laundry smells of your room,
I'd find you silently polishing brass or trying to coax
from your boots the last bright sheen the leather
remembered. And I knew I would rise the next morning
in darkness, roused by the small-bore crack
of your clothes—your limbs forcing open shined khaki—
to watch you go quietly off to your men.

*

One summer night you had the neighbors in the yard
for home-made peach ice cream and army films
projected on the flaking wall of the hen-house.

G.I.'s bridged the Rhine at Remagen; Jap bodies
spilled like sun-struck worms from a pill box,
their faces scaled like snakes in the old wall's
peeling paint.
And I wondered who buried them
but lay in the sweet summer grass unafraid
until the black-and-white war was done. Barrages
stopped. Helmeted winners of medals marched home.

Still the film reeled on, to Buchenwald, Dachau,
where bulldozers shoved gray bones into pits

without ritual, where the living were mute
fluoroscopic ghosts you called D.P.'s, real stick people
crushed into huts like our mildewed sheds.

Out of your sight, in the dark, I cried
for them all, and for the man with a child
thinner than any mountain stray. His face,
framed in a single paint chip, leaned into the yard
and, with eyes like the half-blind bank mules'
at the mines, he seemed to stare at the light
from my bedroom window.

After the films
had run out, while your friends were gathering plates
or whispering good-night, I sat by your polished
brown shoes, wanting to say,
"The man . . . ,"

that he held that child in his coat-hanger arms
then shoved him through the warp in the lapped boards
covering our coop. That the boy was in there
huddled in the dung and feathers, waiting.

But you never knew how he clung
to those humid walls with the hens
or how the flung door's slicing trapezoid of light
cornered him in shadow.

You were occupied with death,
while every day I trooped the darkened rows of nests,
gathering the still-warm eggs with held breath.

Marie Boroff (b. 1923)
UNDERSTANDING POETRY

Death be not proud . . . How proud we were, how tough,
You my arch-poet, I your paraphrase!
Our pyrotechnics set their wits ablaze:
Logic, trope, scheme, theme, structure, all that stuff.
I met them, matched them, made them call my bluff;
We thrashed it out, rehashed it forty ways;
Strutting that little scene, I played for praise
And won my share—oh yes, I had enough.

Death be not proud . . . When did the clapping stop?
Standing in that still house, remembering how
We sojourned there in joy, the joy that was,
I hear, Jack Donne, beneath your razzmatazz,
A quieter music. "If it be not now,
Yet it will come." Teach that, or shut up shop.

Carolyn Forché (b. 1950)
THE COLONEL

What you have heard is true. I was in his house. His wife carried a tray of coffee and sugar. His daughter filed her nails, his son went out for the night. There were daily papers, pet dogs, a pistol on the cushion beside him. The moon swung bare on its black cord over the house. On the television was a cop show. It was in English. Broken bottles were embedded in the walls around the house to scoop the kneecaps from a man's legs or cut his hands to lace. On the windows there were gratings like those in liquor stores. We had dinner, rack of lamb, good wine, a gold bell was on the table for calling the maid. The maid brought green mangoes, salt, a type of bread. I was asked how I enjoyed the country. There was a brief commercial in Spanish. His wife took everything away. There was some talk then of how difficult it had become to govern. The parrot said hello on the terrace. The colonel told it to shut up, and pushed himself from the table. My friend said to me with his eyes: say nothing. The colonel returned with a sack used to bring groceries home. He spilled many human ears on the table. They were like dried peach halves. There is no other way to say this. He took one of them in his hands, shook it in our faces, dropped it into a water glass. It came alive there. I am tired of fooling around he said. As for the rights of anyone, tell your people they can go fuck themselves. He swept the ears to the floor with his arm and held the last of his wine in the air. Something for your poetry, no? he said. Some of the ears on the floor caught this scrap of his voice. Some of the ears on the floor were pressed to the gound.

Part Three
Fiction and Cultural Codes

One
The Function of Fiction

Because we learn about stories in school, we might tend to think that stories exist only in textbooks and libraries. They could sometimes seem like just one more academic subject that has to be mastered. But in fact, stories surround us in our daily lives, and they affect us on a very deep level. They are one of the ways we learn how to deal with the world—the stories we read sink deep into our memories and become part of our self-identity. Think back and recall your favorite story from childhood. It probably remains with you in detail, more vivid than some real-life events. We begin hearing stories in our infancy. Parents tell them to their little children as entertainment, and as pleasant ways of teaching moral lessons. And that begins a fascination that continues to attract us to stories as adults, a fact that all kinds of speakers and writers realize. Preachers tell stories from the pulpit to illustrate their sermons, politicians tell stories to humanize the issues, advertisers tell them to hold the audience's attention while the sell takes hold. In our own lives we tell stories in casual gossip, pass family stories on to our children, tell the story of our day when we get home from work.

Why all these stories? Clearly, the basic structure of a story appeals to us. A story follows actions over a period of time, and in a story, we always learn the consequences of actions, effect always follows cause. Stories make sense out of events, simplifying and clarifying why things happen. For those of us caught in a complicated and confusing world, the order and logic of stories are appealing. In the real world, for example, crime is a complex problem that most of us feel powerless to deal with. But to Sherlock Holmes a crime is a puzzle that will be solved within the hour needed to read the story. A traditional story has a beginning, a middle, and an end, a neatness that we don't encounter much in life. Stories appeal to readers because they do away with the mess of ordinary experience, paring down to the essentials of an action, making the meaning of an event stand clear.

Getting the Point

It is important to realize that stories do have meanings. Hardly ever is a story told simply for the pleasure of its telling. There is, of course, great pleasure in a good story, but the pleasure is usually in service of some point that the teller wants to make. And even if the teller isn't trying to pass on a lesson, the listener or reader may still receive one. For example, as a nighttime story, "Little Red-Cap" (or "Little Red Riding Hood") appeals to many parents and children. They may choose the story because it's entertaining—funny and scary and satisfying at the same time—yet there is no denying that the story teaches some lessons. It shows the results of disobeying parents, of trusting strangers, of straying off the straight-and-narrow path. Neither the parent nor the child may be paying attention to these lessons, but the message still gets communicated.

Societies use stories like this to communicate their values to the young. When we read a fairy tale or folk story we are learning how a group of people look at the world, how they make sense of their experience, and the same is true in a modern short story. Throughout the history of fiction, stories have served this function. They pass on the values of the group, the values that explain how the world works. The earliest stories we know of, the ancient myths of our culture and of cultures around the world, do this job most directly. Myths are stories about the beginnings of things, fictions told precisely because no one *knows* about the beginnings. Myths make sense of mysterious realities; they provide the structures through which groups of people look at the world. If a children's story teaches a child how to behave, a myth is a story that teaches a culture how to see and think.

In most modern stories the point behind the narrative is complex. Very few stories today can be reduced to neat moral statements the way "Little Red-Cap" can. These stories usually reflect a clear understanding of the complexity of modern life, and the values they communicate are adequate to that complexity. But there are still values being communicated; a particular view of the world is still being passed on. In Chekhov's "The Bet," for example, the story clearly exists in order to make a statement about the value of life, but that statement is not simple. What that story communicates about how to deal with experience can't be reduced to a formula—it is more like a set of questions being raised, rather than a set of answers being offered.

Taking It Seriously

Which brings us to the reader of fiction. If fiction is a way that our culture communicates and questions its values, how are its readers to behave as they read? In a child's story, the child who hears it is assumed to enjoy it and take in the moral almost without realizing it. In a folktale, the values being communicated are assumed by all the audience and seem just the natural way to look at the world. But actually in these situations the reader is active. The child or the audience of a tale still has to make sense of the story, still has to process the meanings that the story offers.

The modern short story, even more, *demands* that the reader be active and questioning. Modern stories almost never express directly the values they communicate. The reader must work through the story as an active participant in the creation of meaning. As a reader learns how stories are put together—how plots work, how characters develop, how the language of fiction works—he or she becomes more adept at making sense of the story, at helping to produce its values. But readers always have values of their own as well, which they don't simply give up when a story's values are very different from their own. So beyond producing meaning, readers also have to *evaluate* the message of the story. A story almost always has a point to make—it is crucial that readers work to become aware of it and to decide how they will respond to it.

Even stories based on values other than our own can be enjoyed and benefited from. It is always healthy to have our values challenged, particularly by a story that causes us pleasure. Fiction often forces us to examine our own values—not to reject them, but to recognize that other value systems, other ways of making sense of the world, exist around us. Fiction reminds us of the complexity of the world. It forces us to remember that different people make sense of the world differently, depending on the value system that they have learned to live by. Fiction won't let us believe that our own values are the only ones possible. The very experience of reading forces us to explore other perspectives on reality. It forces us to get out of our own perspective for a while, and it asks us to look at ourselves critically.

What this process requires from you as a reader is an active participation in the creation of meaning. You need to know how stories are constructed and to know the basic critical terms that help us make sense of stories. You also need to commit yourself to taking the challenge of fiction seriously. There is tremendous pleasure in seeing the world from a new angle. And only readers who learn how to read actively and who are willing to risk a serious response can experience this pleasure.

Despite all the serious work that stories do, pleasure is still the reason why we read them. Even the most moral tales of childhood would not survive unless children enjoyed them. All good stories give pleasure in their offer to the reader to explore an imaginary world, to learn about complex characters, to experience dramatic action, to appreciate the power of language. But good readers—active readers—also can gain the pleasure of self-discovery. By accepting the challenge of fiction, by allowing the story's values to question the reader's own views, the active reader can gain self-knowledge. Fiction may deal with stories that occur only in the imagination, but those stories have very real effects on readers—on those who are willing to take fiction seriously.

READINGS

Myth from Togoland
THE EYE OF THE GIANT

Long, long ago there was a great famine in the world, and a certain young man whilst wandering in search of food strayed into a part of the bush where he had never been before. Presently he perceived a strange mass lying on the ground. He approached and saw that it was the body of a giant whose hair resembled that of white men in that it was silky rather than woolly. It was of an incredible length and stretched as far as from Krachi to Salaga. The young man was properly awed at the spectacle, and wished to withdraw, but the giant noticing him asked what he wanted.

The young man explained and begged the giant to give him some food. The latter agreed on condition that the youth would serve him for a while. This matter having been arranged, the giant said his name was Owuo or Death, and then gave the boy some meat.

Never before had the latter tasted such fine food, and he was well pleased with his bargain. He served his master for a long time and received plenty of meat, but one day he grew homesick, and begged his master to give him a short holiday. The latter agreed if the youth would promise to bring another boy in his place. So the youth returned to his village and there persuaded his brother to go with him into the bush and gave him to Owuo.

In course of time the youth got hungry again and longed for the meat which Owuo had taught him to like so much. So one day he made up his mind to return to his master, and leaving the village made his way back to the giant's abode. The latter asked him what he wanted, and when the youth told him that he wanted to taste once more of the good meat, the giant told him to enter the hut and take as much as he liked, but he would have to work for him again.

The youth agreed and entered the hut. He ate as much as he could, and set to at the task his master set him. The work continued for a long time and the boy ate his fill every day. But to his surprise he never saw anything of his brother, and whenever he asked about him the giant told him that the lad was away on his business.

Once more the youth grew homesick and asked for leave to return to his village. The giant agreed on condition that he would bring a girl for him, Owuo, to wed. So the youth went home and there persuaded his sister to go into the bush and marry the giant. The girl agreed, and took with her a slave companion, and they all repaired to the giant's abode. There the youth left the two girls and went back to the village.

It was not very long after that he again grew hungry and longed for the taste of the meat. So he made his way once more into the bush and found the giant. The giant did not seem overpleased to see the boy and grumbled at being bothered a fourth time. However, he told the boy to go into the inner chamber of his hut and take what he wanted. The youth did so and took up a bone which he began to devour. To his horror he recognized it at once as being the bone of his sister. He looked around at all the rest of the meat and saw that it was that of his sister and her slave girl.

Thoroughly frightened he escaped from the house and ran back into the village. There he told the elders what he had done and the awful thing he had seen. At once the alarm was sounded and all the people went out into the bush to see for themselves the dread thing they had heard about. When they drew near to the giant, they grew afraid at the sight of so evil a monster. They went back to the village and consulted among themselves what best they should do. At least it was agreed to go to Salaga where the giant's hair finished and set light to it. This was done, and when the hair was burning well, they returned to the bush and watched the giant.

Presently the latter began to toss about and sweat. It was quite evident that he was beginning to feel the heat. The nearer the flames advanced the more he tossed and grumbled. At last the fire reached his head, and for the moment the giant was dead.

The villagers approached him cautiously, and the young man noticed "medicine" which had been concealed in the roots of the giant's hair. He took it and called the others to come and see what he had found. No one could say what power this medicine might have, but an old man suggested that no harm would be done if they took some and sprinkled it on the bones and meat in the hut. This idea was carried out, and to the surprise of every one, the girls and the boy returned to life at once.

The youth who had still some of the medicine left proposed to put it on the giant. But at this there was a great uproar, as the people feared Owuo might come to life again. The boy therefore by way of compromise sprinkled it into the eye of the dead giant. At once the eye opened and the people all fled away in terror. But it is from that eye that death comes; for every time that Owuo shuts that eye a man dies, and unfortunately for us he is for ever blinking and winking.

Edited by Ada Cardinall

1. What does this story tell us about this society's concept of death?
2. Why is the giant white in an African myth?
3. What is the significance of the meat the youth desires?
4. How is medicine understood in this culture?
5. What are the limits of understanding this story for an outsider to the culture?

Jakob and Wilhelm Grimm (pub. 1812–1815)
LITTLE RED-CAP

There was once a sweet little maid, much beloved by everybody, but most of all by her grandmother, who never knew how to make enough of her. Once she sent her a little cap of red velvet, and as it was very becoming to her, and she never wore anything else, people called her Little Red-Cap. One day her mother said to her,

"Come, Little Red-Cap, here are some cakes and a flask of wine for you to take to grandmother; she is weak and ill, and they will do her good. Make haste and start before it grows hot, and walk properly and nicely, and don't run, or you might fall and break the flask of wine, and there would be none left for grandmother. And when you go into her room, don't forget to say, Good morning, instead of staring about you."

"I will be sure to take care," said Little Red-Cap to her mother, and gave her hand upon it. Now the grandmother lived away in the wood, half-an-hour's walk from the village; and when Little Red-Cap had reached the wood, she met the wolf; but as she did not know what a bad sort of animal he was, she did not feel frightened.

"Good day, Little Red-Cap," said he.

"Thank you kindly, Wolf," answered she.

"Where are you going so early, Little Red-Cap?"

"To my grandmother's."

"What are you carrying under your apron?"

"Cakes and wine; we baked yesterday; and my grandmother is very weak and ill, so they will do her good, and strengthen her."

"Where does your grandmother live, Little Red-Cap?"

"A quarter of an hour's walk from here; her house stands beneath the three oak trees, and you may know it by the hazel bushes," said Little Red-Cap. The wolf thought to himself,

"That tender young thing would be a delicious morsel, and would taste better than the old one; I must manage somehow to get both of them."

Then he walked by Little Red-Cap a little while, and said,

"Little Red-Cap, just look at the pretty flowers that are growing all round you, and I don't think you are listening to the song of the birds; you are posting along just as if you were going to school, and it is so delightful out here in the wood."

Little Red-Cap glanced round her, and when she saw the sunbeams darting here and there through the trees, and lovely flowers everywhere, she thought to herself,

"If I were to take a fresh nosegay to my grandmother she would be very pleased, and it is so early in the day that I shall reach her in plenty of time"; and so she ran about in the wood, looking for flowers. And as she picked one she saw a still prettier one a little farther off, and so she went farther and farther into the wood. But the wolf went straight to the grandmother's house and knocked at the door.

"Who is there?" cried the grandmother.

"Little Red-Cap," he answered, "and I have brought you some cake and wine. Please open the door."

"Lift the latch," cried the grandmother; "I am too feeble to get up."

So the wolf lifted the latch, and the door flew open, and he fell on the grandmother and ate her up without saying one word. Then he drew on her clothes, put on her cap, lay down in her bed, and drew the curtains.

Little Red-Cap was all this time running about among the flowers, and when she had gathered as many as she could hold, she remembered her grandmother, and set off to go to her. She was surprised to find the door standing open, and when she came inside she felt very strange, and thought to herself,

"Oh, dear, how uncomfortable I feel, and I was so glad this morning to go to my grandmother!"

And when she said, "Good morning," there was no answer. Then she went up to the bed and drew back the curtains; there lay the grandmother with her cap pulled over her eyes, so that she looked very odd.

"O grandmother, what large ears you have got!"

"The better to hear with."

"O grandmother, what great eyes you have got!"

"The better to see with."

"O grandmother, what large hands you have got!"

"The better to take hold of you with."

"But, grandmother, what a terrible large mouth you have got!"

"The better to devour you!" And no sooner had the wolf said it than he made one bound from the bed, and swallowed up poor Little Red-Cap.

Then the wolf, having satisfied his hunger, lay down again in the bed, went to sleep, and began to snore loudly. The huntsman heard him as he was passing by the house, and thought.

"How the old woman snores—I had better see if there is anything the matter with her."

Then he went into the room, and walked up to the bed, and saw the wolf lying there.

"At last I find you, you old sinner!" said he; "I have been looking for you a long time." And he made up his mind that the wolf had swallowed the grandmother whole, and that she might yet be saved. So he did not fire, but took a pair of shears and began to slit up the wolf's body. When he made a few snips Little Red-Cap appeared, and after a few more snips she jumped out and cried, "Oh dear, how frightened I have been! it is so dark inside the wolf." And then out came the old grandmother, still living and breathing. But Little Red-Cap went and quickly fetched some large stones, with which she filled the wolf's body, so that when he waked up, and was going to rush away, the stones were so heavy that he sank down and fell dead.

They were all three very pleased. The huntsman took off the wolf's skin, and carried it home. The grandmother ate the cakes, and drank the wine, and held up her head again, and Little Red-Cap said to herself that she would never more stray about in the wood alone, but would mind what her mother told her.

It must also be related how a few days afterwards, when Little Red-Cap was again taking cakes to her grandmother, another wolf spoke to her, and wanted to tempt her to leave the path; but she was on her guard, and went straight on her way, and told her grandmother how that the wolf had met her, and wished her good-day, but had looked so wicked about the eyes that she thought if it had not been on the high road he would have devoured her.

"Come," said the grandmother, "we will shut the door, so that he may not get in."

Soon after came the wolf knocking at the door, and calling out, "Open the door, grandmother, I am Little Red-Cap, bringing you cakes." But they remained still, and did not open the door. After that the wolf slunk by the house, and got at last upon the roof to wait until

Little Red-Cap should return home in the evening; then he meant to spring down upon her, and devour her in the darkness. But the grandmother discovered his plot. Now there stood before the house a great stone trough, and the grandmother said to the child, "Little Red-Cap, I was boiling sausages yesterday, so take the bucket, and carry away the water they were boiled in, and pour it into the trough."

And Little Red-Cap did so until the great trough was quite full. When the smell of the sausages reached the nose of the wolf he snuffed it up, and looked round, and stretched out his neck so far that he lost his balance, and began to slip, and he slipped down off the roof straight into the great trough, and was drowned. Then Little Red-Cap went cheerfully home, and came to no harm.

1. What values does this tale communicate to children?
2. Is the violence in the tale too extreme? What makes it acceptable to children?
3. What role does the huntsman play in the story?
4. How is Little Red-Cap different at the end of the story?
5. Are the values the story teaches appropriate for children in our society?
6. What does the story teach about sex roles?
7. What accounts for the continuing popularity of the story?

Geoffrey Chaucer (c. 1343–1400)

THE PARDONER

THE WORDS OF THE HOST TO THE PHYSICIAN AND THE PARDONER: Our Host started swearing as if he were crazy. "Help! By Christ's nails and blood," he said, "that was a false fellow and a false judge. May such judges and their witnesses find deaths as shameful as the heart can imagine! All the same, this poor virgin was killed, alas! She paid too dearly for her beauty! Therefore, I always say that you can see that gifts of Fortune and of Nature are the cause of death for many a creature. Her beauty was the death of her, I dare say. Alas, she was slain so piteously! From both these gifts I spoke of just now, people very often get more harm than profit.

"But truly, my own dear master, that was a sad tale to hear—nevertheless, let it pass, it doesn't matter. I pray God to save your noble body, and also your urinals and chamberpots, your syrups and medicines, and also every box full of your remedies; God and our Lady St. Mary bless them! As I hope to prosper, you are a proper man, and like a prelate, by St. Ronyan! Didn't I say that well? I can't say the medical terms, but I do know that your story has so pierced my heart that I have almost caught a bad pain. By God's bones, unless

I have some medicine or a draught of moist and malty ale, or else hear a merry story at once, my heart will break with pity for this poor maiden. You fine friend, you Pardoner," said he, "tell us some gay stories or jokes immediately."

"It shall be done," said the Pardoner, "by St. Ronyan! But first," he said, "I must have a drink and eat a cake here at this alehouse."

But at once the gentlefolk objected. "No, don't let him tell us any ribaldry! Tell us some moral thing so that we can be instructed, and then we shall be glad to listen."

"I agree, certainly," said the Pardoner. "But I must think up some honest piece while I drink."

PROLOGUE

HERE FOLLOWS THE PROLOGUE OF THE PARDONER'S TALE: *Radix malorum est cupiditas.* "Ladies and gentlemen," he said, when I preach in churches, I strive to have a haughty speech and ring out the words as round as a bell; for I know all that I say by heart. My text is always the same, and ever has been—Greed is the root of all evil.

"In the beginning I announce where I come from, and then I show my papal bulls, one and all. First I show our bishop's seal on my license to protect myself, so that no one, priest or cleric, will be so bold as to interrupt me as I do Christ's holy work. And after that I tell my tales. I show bulls of popes, cardinals, patriarchs, and bishops, and I speak a few words in Latin to flavor my preaching and to stir the congregation to devotion. Then I show my long glass cases, crammed full of rags and bones—they are relics, everybody thinks. Then I have a shoulder bone from a holy Jew's sheep set in metal. 'Good men,' I say, "pay attention to my words: if this bone is dipped into any well, and if a cow, or calf, or sheep, or ox is swollen from eating a worm or from being stung by an insect, take some water from that well and wash his tongue; he will at once be cured. Furthermore, any sheep which takes a drink from that well will be cured of pox and scabs and of every other sore. Take heed of what I say: if the farmer who owns the livestock will take a drink from this well every week, after fasting, before the cock crows, just as this holy Jew taught our ancestors, his livestock and his goods will multiply. And, sirs, it also cures jealousy; for even if a man is in a jealous rage, let him make his soup with this water and he shall nevermore distrust his wife, though he knows it to be true that she has been so unfaithful as to have had two or three priests.

" 'Here is a mitten which you can also look at. The man who puts his hand into this mitten will see his grain multiply, after he has sown it, no matter whether it is oats or wheat, if he contributes pennies or else groats.

" 'Good men and women, I warn you about one thing: if there is any man now in this church who has done a horrible sin and who is afraid and ashamed to be shriven of it, or any woman old or young who has made her husband a cuckold—such folk shall have no power or grace to make an offering to my relics in this church. But if whoever finds himself free from such fault will come up and make an offering in the name of God, I shall absolve him by the authority which was granted to me by papal bull.'

"By this trick I have gained a hundred marks year after year since I became a pardoner. I stand in my pulpit like a cleric and, when the ignorant people have taken their seats, I preach as you have just heard and tell a hundred other false tales. Then I take pains to stretch my neck out and nod east and west over the congregation, like a dove sitting on a barn. My hands and tongue go so fast that it is a joy to see me at work. All my preaching is about avarice and similar sins, in order to make the people generous in contributing their pennies, especially to me. For my purpose is nothing but profit, and not at all the correction of sin. I don't care if their souls go wandering when they are buried! Certainly, many a sermon grows out of an evil purpose: sometimes to please and flatter folk, to get advancement by hypocrisy, and sometimes for vanity and sometimes for hatred. For when I am afraid to quarrel in other ways, then I sting a fellow so sharply with my tongue in preaching that he can't escape being falsely defamed, if he has been rude to my brethren or to me. Even though I don't call him by name, everyone knows by signs and other circumstances who it is I mean. Thus I get even with folk who mistreat us; in this fashion I spit out my venom in the guise of holiness, to appear holy and true.

"But I shall explain my purpose briefly. I preach for nothing but avarice; therefore, my theme is now and always was: *Radix malorum est cupiditas*. In this way I am able to preach against the same vice which I practice: avarice. Yet, though I am guilty of that sin myself, I can still make other folk turn away from it and bitterly repent. But that's not my main purpose; I preach only for avarice. That ought to be enough about this subject.

"Then I tell them many samples of old stories about ancient times. For ignorant people love old stories; they can easily remember and repeat such things. Why, do you think that I would willingly live in poverty as long as I can preach and win gold and silver by my teaching? No, no, I never really considered that! For I will preach and beg in various countries, but I will do no labor with my hands, or live by making baskets to keep from being an idle beggar. I will not copy any one of the apostles; I will have money, wool, cheese, and wheat, even though it's given to me by the poorest page or widow in a village, whose children will consequently starve. No, I'll drink liquor from the vine and have a jolly wench in every town. But listen, ladies and gentlemen, in conclusion: your desire is that I tell a story. Now that

I have drunk a draught of malty ale, I hope, by God, that I can tell you something which you will like reasonably well. For, though I am a very vicious man myself, I can tell you a moral tale which I am accustomed to preach when I am working. Now hold your peace! I shall begin my tale."

THE PARDONER'S TALE

HERE BEGINS THE PARDONER'S TALE: Once upon a time in Flanders there was a group of young people much given to dissipation, such as riotous living, gambling, and frequenting brothels and taverns, where they danced and played dice both night and day, to the music of harps, lutes, and guitars, and also ate and drank beyond their capacities. In this way they wickedly performed the devil's work within these devil's temples through abominable excesses. Their oaths were so great and so damnable that it was terrifying to hear them swear. They tore apart the body of our blessed Lord—it seemed to them that the Jews had not tortured him enough—and each of them laughed at the others' sins. And then small and shapely dancing girls would enter, and young girls selling fruit, singers with harps, bawds, and cake-sellers—all the confirmed agents of the devil—to kindle and blow the fire of lust that goes hand in hand with gluttony.

I take Holy Writ as my witness that licentiousness results from wine and drunkenness. Look how drunken Lot, against the laws of nature, slept with his two daughters without knowing it; he was so drunk that he did not know what he was doing. Herod, as anyone who reads the stories knows, when he was full of wine at his own feast, gave the order right at his own table for innocent John the Baptist to be slain. Seneca was without doubt correct when he said that he could see no difference between a man who is out of his mind and a man who is drunk, except that insanity, when it occurs in an ill-tempered man, lasts longer than drunkenness.

Oh, gluttony, filled with wickedness! Oh, first cause of our ruin! Oh, origin of our damnation, until Christ redeemed us with His blood! To come to the point, see how dearly this cursed wickedness was paid for! All this world was corrupted by gluttony. Our father Adam and also his wife were driven from Paradise to labor and suffer because of that sin. There is no doubt about that, for as long as Adam fasted he was in Paradise, so I read, but when he ate of the forbidden fruit on the tree, he was at once cast out into trouble and pain. Oh, gluttony, well should we complain of you! Oh, if a man only knew how many illnesses follow excess and gluttony, he would be more moderate in his diet at the table. Alas, the short throat and the tender mouth; they cause men—east, west, south, and north—to labor hard in earth, air, and water to provide a glutton with his rare food and drink! Oh, Paul, you treated this subject well: "Meat for the belly and the belly for meat; God shall destroy both." So says Paul. Alas, it is an ugly thing, by my faith, to say these words, but uglier is the deed, when a man so drinks of the white and red wines that he makes a privy of his throat through such wicked excess.

The Apostle, weeping, says movingly: "There are many of those people about whom I told you—I say it now weeping, with a piteous voice: they are enemies of the cross of Christ; their end is death; the belly is their God!" Oh, stomach! Oh, belly! Oh, stinking gut, filled with dung and corruption! From either end of you, foul noises come forth. How great is the labor and cost to feed you! How these cooks stamp and strain and grind to turn substance into accident in order to satisfy your gluttonous appetite! They knock the marrow out of the hard bones, for they throw away nothing which will slide softly and sweetly down the gullet. The glutton's sauce is made tasty by spices of leaves, bark, and roots, to give him still a keener appetite. But, truly, the man who makes a habit of such delicacies is dead even while he lives in those vices.

Wine is a lecherous thing, and drunkenness is full of strife and wretchedness. Oh, drunken man, your face is distorted, your breath is sour, you are a foul thing to embrace, and a sound seems to come from your drunken nose as if you kept repeating "Samson, Samson!" And yet, God knows, Samson never drank wine. You fall down like a stuck pig; your tongue is lost, and all your self-respect. For drunkenness is the true tomb of a man's wit and discretion. That man who is dominated by drink cannot keep a secret; that is sure. Therefore, hold yourself aloof from the white and the red, and especially from the white wine of Lepe, which is sold in Fish Street or in Cheapside. This Spanish wine is secretly blended with other wines in stock, and from it rise fumes so powerful that a man who takes three drinks, though he believes himself at home in Cheapside, finds he is in Spain at the town of Lepe—not at La Rochelle or Bordeaux. And then he will say, "Samson, Samson!"

But listen to one word, ladies and gentlemen, I beg you. All the great deeds and victories in the Old Testament, I swear, were accomplished through the true and omnipotent God by abstinence and prayer. Read the Bible, and you will learn this. Look at Attila, the great conqueror; he died shamefully and dishonorably in his sleep, bleeding steadily from the nose because of drunkenness. A military leader should live soberly. And more important still, consider very carefully what God commanded Lemuel—I mean Lemuel, not Samuel; read the Bible and see what is expressly stated about giving wine to those charged with the dispensation of justice. No more of this matter, for that much should suffice.

Now that I have spoken of gluttony, I shall next forbid your gambling. Gambling is the true mother of lies, deceit, cursed perjury, blasphemy of Christ, and manslaughter, and also a waste of time and money. Furthermore, it is a reproof and a dishonor to be considered a common gambler. And, always, the higher the rank of the gambler, the more despicable is he considered. If a prince gambles, his governing and policy are held in low repute by general opinion. Stilbon, who was a wise ambassador, was sent from Sparta to Corinth, in great pomp, to make an alliance. And when he arrived, it happened by chance that he found all the highest officials of that land gambling. Therefore, as soon as possible, he stole home to his country, and said, "I will not lose my reputation there and so lay myself open to defamation as to ally you with gamblers. Send other wise ambassadors, for I swear that I had rather die than make an alliance for you with gamblers. For you who are so glorious in honor shall not be allied with gamblers by my efforts or treaties." So said this wise philosopher.

Observe also that the King of Parthia, as the book tells us, scornfully sent a pair of golden dice to King Demetrius because he was so accustomed to gamble; his glory or renown was utterly without value for him. Lords can find other kinds of games honest enough to pass the time.

I shall now speak a word or two in the manner of the old books about great and small oaths. Violent swearing is an abominable thing, and false swearing is even more to be reproved. The high God forbade all swearing—witness Matthew; but holy Jeremiah says this particularly about swearing: "You shall swear true oaths and not lie; swear discreetly and also righteously." But idle swearing is a sin. Observe that in the first table of the high God's illustrious commandments, the second of His commandments is: "Take not my name amiss or in vain." You see, He forbade such swearing ahead of homicide or many other cursed sins; I say it stands in that order. Be sure of this fact if you understand His commandments; that is the second commandment. Later I shall show you clearly that vengeance shall not leave the house of the man who is too outrageous in his swearing. "By God's precious heart," and "by His nails," and "by the blood of Christ that is at Hailes, seven is my number and yours is five and three!" "By God's arms, if you cheat, I will run this dagger through your heart!"—such is the fruit which comes from the two bitchy bones: swearing, anger, falsehood, homicide. Now, for the love of Christ who died for us, give up your oaths, both large and small. But now, sirs, I shall tell my tale.

These three rioters of whom I tell were seated in a tavern drinking, long before any bell rang for nine o'clock. And as they drank, they heard a bell toll before a corpse which was being carried to its grave.

One of them called to his servant: "Boy, hurry and ask at once whose corpse it was that just passed by. And see that you get his name straight."

"Sir," replied the boy, "that's not at all necessary. I was told that two hours before you arrived. He was, by God, an old crony of yours, and last night he was suddenly killed as he sat straight up on his bench completely drunk. A stealthy thief, whom men call Death, who kills all the people in this country, came and cut his heart in two with a spear, and went away without a word. During this plague, he has slain a thousand. And, master, before you go into his presence, it seems to me that it will be necessary for you to be wary of such an opponent. Always be ready to meet him; my mother taught me that. I'll say no more."

"By St. Mary," said the tavern-keeper, "the boy speaks true, for this year Death has slain the men, women, children, laborers, and servants in a large village over a mile from here. I think he must live there. It would make great sense to be warned before he did you any harm."

"Yes, by God's arms!" said this rioter. "Is it so dangerous to meet him? I shall seek him out by roads and paths, I swear by God's worthy bones! Listen, friends, we three are of one mind; let's each of us give his hand to the other two, and each of us will become the other's brother. Then we shall slay this false traitor Death. He who has slain so many shall himself be slain, by God's worthiness, before night!"

These three pledged their faith together, each to live and die for the other two, as though they had been born brothers. And they jumped up in a drunken rage and went out towards the village which the tavern-keeper had told them about. And they swore many a horrible oath, completely tearing Christ's blessed body apart—Death shall be slain, if they can catch him!

When they had gone not quite half a mile, just as they were about to cross a fence, they met a poor old man. This old man greeted them very humbly and said, "Now, lords, God save you!"

The proudest of these three rioters replied, "Hey, bad luck to you, fellow! Why are you all covered up except for your face? Why have you lived so long and grown so old?"

The old man stared into his face and said: "Because I cannot find a man in any city or any village, though I walked to India, who wishes to change his youth for my age. And, therefore, I must continue to have my age for as long a time as it is God's will. Alas, not even Death will take my life. And so I walk about like a restless prisoner and knock both early and late with my stick upon the earth, which is my mother's door, saying, 'Dear mother, let me in; look how I shrink, flesh, skin, and blood! Alas, when shall my bones find rest? Mother, I will trade my strongbox, which for so long has been in my bedroom, for a hair shirt to wrap myself in!' Yet she will not do me that favor, and my face is therefore pale and wrinkled.

"But, sirs, it is discourteous of you to speak rudely to an old man, unless he does or says something wrong. You can read for yourselves in Holy Writ: 'You should rise before an old white-haired man.' Therefore, I shall give you some advice: do no harm now to an old man, any more than you would like people to do to you when you are old, if you live that long. And may God be with you, wherever you walk or ride! I must go where I have to go."

"No, old one, by God, you shall not go," the second gambler said at once. "You won't get off so lightly, by St. John! Just now you spoke of that same traitor Death, who kills all our friends in this country. Take my word, you are his spy; so tell where he is or you shall regret it, by God and by the holy sacrament! For, truly, you are in his plot to slay us young folk, you false thief!"

"Now, sirs," the old man answered, "if you are so eager to find Death, turn up this crooked path; for I left him in that wood, by my faith, under a tree. He will stay there; he won't conceal himself because of your boasting. You see that oak? You shall find him right there. May God, who redeemed mankind, save you and amend you!"

The old man spoke thus, and all the rioters ran until they reached the oak tree. And there they found what seemed to them almost eight bushels of fine round florins of coined gold. Then they looked for Death no longer. Each of them was so happy at the sight of the bright, shining florins that they sat down by this precious hoard. The worst of them spoke the first word.

"Brothers," he said, "listen to what I say. I have a great deal of sense, even though I joke and scoff. Fortune has given us this treasure so that we can live our lives in mirth and gaiety, and we shall spend it as easily as it came. Aye, God's precious worth! Who would have thought we should have such luck today? If we could only carry this gold from here home to my house or to yours—you realize, of course, that all this gold is ours—then we would have the highest happiness. Yet we really cannot do it by daylight. People would say that we were obviously highwaymen and would have us hanged because of our own treasure. This money must be transported by night, as carefully and quietly as possible. Therefore, I suggest that we draw straws among us and see where the cut falls. The one who draws the cut must willingly run into town as quickly as possible, and secretly bring bread and wine for us. Meanwhile, two of us will guard the treasure diligently, and, if he doesn't take too long, we shall be able at nightfall to carry the money wherever we agree is best."

He held the straws in his fist, and told the others to draw to see where the cut would fall. It fell to the youngest of the three, and he at once set out for town. But, as soon as he had left, one of the other two spoke to the second: "You know very well that you are my sworn brother; I shall now tell you something to your advantage. You see that our companion is gone, and this great heap of gold, which is to be divided among the three of us, is still here. But if I could so arrange matters that the gold would be divided between us two alone, would I not have done you a friendly turn?"

The second answered: "I don't see how that can be; he knows very well that the gold was left with the two of us. What shall we do? What shall we say to him?"

"Shall it be a secret?" asked the first scoundrel. "If so, I'll tell you in a few words what we can do to accomplish this."

"I agree not to betray you," said the second, "upon my word."

"Now," said the first, "you know that we are two, and the two of us are stronger than one. When he returns and sits down, you get up at once as if to tussle with him, and I will run him through the sides while you scuffle with him as if in sport, and you be sure to stab him with your dagger also. Then, all this gold, my dear friend, can be divided between you and me. Both of us will be able to fulfill all our desires and to play dice whenever we like." Thus these two scoundrels agreed to murder the third, as you have heard me say.

The youngest, who went into town, kept turning over in his mind the beauty of the bright new florins. "Oh, Lord!" he said, "if it only were possible for me to have all this treasure for myself alone, no man living under God's throne would live so merrily as I!"

And at last the devil, our enemy, put into his mind the idea of buying poison with which he could kill his two companions. For the fiend found his way of life such that he wished to bring him into trouble. The fellow's clear purpose was to kill both the others and never to repent. He went on into town, without any more loitering, to the shop of an apothecary, whom he begged to sell him some poison to kill his rats; there was a polecat in his yard, also, he said, which had killed his capons, and he was eager to get revenge, if possible, upon vermin which harassed him at night.

The apothecary answered, "You shall have such a mixture, God save my soul, that no creature in this world who eats or drinks of it, even the equivalent of a grain of wheat, shall fail to die at once. Yes, he shall die in less time than it takes you to walk a mile, this poison is so strong and violent."

This wicked man grabbed up the box of poison and ran quickly to a man in the next street from whom he borrowed three large bottles. He poured his poison into two; the third he kept clean for his own drink; for he planned to work hard all night transporting the gold from its place. When this rioter—bad luck to him!—had filled his three large bottles with wine, he returned to his companions.

What need is there to make a longer sermon of this? They quickly killed him just as they had already planned, and, when that was done,

one said, "Now let's sit and drink and make merry. Afterwards we'll bury his body." It happened that with these words he took up a bottle in which there was poison, and drank, giving his friend a drink from the same bottle. As a result, both immediately died.

Truly, I doubt that Avicenna ever wrote a treatise or chapter in which there were more amazing symptoms of poisoning than these two wretches evidenced before they died. That was the end of these two murderers, as well as of the false poisoner.

Oh, cursed sin of all evil! Oh, treacherous murder, oh, wickedness! Oh, gluttony, luxury, and gambling! You blasphemer of Christ with vulgarity and large oaths, born of habit and pride! Alas, mankind, how can it be that you are so false and so unkind to your Creator, who made you and redeemed you with His precious heart's blood?

Now, good men, may God forgive you your trespasses and keep you from the sin of avarice! My holy pardon can cure you all, so long as you offer nobles, or silver pennies, or else silver brooches, spoons, or rings. Bow your head before this holy document! Come on up, you wives, offer some of your wool! I will at once enter your names here on my roll, and you shall go into the bliss of heaven. I absolve you by my great power—you who will offer—as clean and as white as you were born.—And there, ladies and gentlemen, that's the way I preach. And may Jesus Christ, who is our soul's physician, grant that you receive His pardon, for that is the best; I will not deceive you.

But, sirs, I forgot one word in my tale: I have relics and pardons in my bag, as fine as any man's in England, which were given to me by the Pope's own hand. If any of you wish, out of piety, to make an offering and to receive my absolution, come up at once, kneel down here, and humbly receive my pardon. Or else you can accept pardon as you travel, fresh and new at the end of every mile, just so you make another offering each time of nobles or pennies which are good and genuine. It is an honor to everyone here that you have available a pardoner with sufficient power to absolve you as you ride through the country, in case of accidents which might happen. Perhaps one or two of you will fall off your horses and break your necks. See what security it is to all of you that I happen to be in your group and can absolve you, both high and low, when the soul passes from the body. I suggest that our Host, here, shall be first; for he is most enveloped in sin. Come on, Sir Host, make the first offering right now, and you can kiss each one of the relics. Yes, for just a groat! Unbuckle your purse at once.

"No, no!" said the Host. "Then I would be under Christ's curse! Stop this, it won't do, as I hope to prosper! You would make me kiss your old breeches, and swear they were the relic of a saint, though they were foully stained by your bottom! But, by the cross that St. Helen found, I wish I had your testicles in my hand instead of relics or holy objects. Cut them off; I'll help you carry them. They shall be enshrined in hog's dung!"

The Pardoner answered not a word; he was so angry he would not say anything.

"Now," said our Host, "I will joke no longer with you or with any other angry man."

But at once the worthy Knight, when he saw everybody laughing, said, "No more of this; that's enough! Sir Pardoner, cheer up and be merry; and you, Sir Host, who are so dear to me, I beg you to kiss the Pardoner. And Pardoner, I pray you, come near. Let's laugh and play as we did before."

At once they kissed and rode ahead on their way. HERE ENDS THE PARDONER'S TALE.

1. Why does the Pardoner make the message of his story so explicit?
2. What function does the story play in the Pardoner's occupation?
3. How does the story reveal the Pardoner's character?
4. Does the story make for an effective sermon?

Anton Chekhov (1860–1904)
THE BET

I

It was a dark autumn night. The old banker was pacing from corner to corner of his study, recalling to his mind the party he gave in the autumn fifteen years ago. There were many clever people at the party and much interesting conversation. They talked among other things of capital punishment. The guests, among them not a few scholars and journalists, for the most part disapproved of capital punishment. They found it obsolete as a means of punishment, unfitted to a Christian State and immoral. Some of them thought that capital punishment should be replaced universally by life-imprisonment.

"I don't agree with you," said the host. "I myself have experienced neither capital punishment nor life-imprisonment, but if one may judge *a priori,* then in my opinion capital punishment is more moral and more human than imprisonment. Execution kills instantly, life-imprisonment kills by degrees. Who is the more humane executioner, one who kills you in a few seconds or one who draws the life out of you incessantly, for years?"

"They're both equally immoral," remarked one of the guests, "because their purpose is the same, to take away life. The State is not God. It has no right to take away that which it cannot give back, if it should so desire."

Among the company was a lawyer, a young man of about twenty-five. On being asked his opinion, he said:

"Capital punishment and life-imprisonment are equally immoral; but if I were offered the choice between them, I would certainly choose the second. It's better to live somehow than not to live at all."

There ensued a lively discussion. The banker who was then younger and more nervous suddenly lost his temper, banged his fist on the table, and turning to the young lawyer, cried out:

"It's a lie. I bet you two millions you wouldn't stick in a cell even for five years."

"If you're serious," replied the lawyer, "then I bet I'll stay not five but fifteen."

"Fifteen! Done!" cried the banker. "Gentlemen, I stake two millions."

"Agreed. You stake two millions, I my freedom," said the lawyer.

So this wild, ridiculous bet came to pass. The banker, who at that time had too many millions to count, spoiled and capricious, was beside himself with rapture. During supper he said to the lawyer jokingly:

"Come to your senses, young man, before it's too late. Two millions are nothing to me, but you stand to lose three or four of the best years of your life. I say three or four, because you'll never stick it out any longer. Don't forget either, you unhappy man, that voluntary is much heavier than enforced imprisonment. The idea that you have the right to free yourself at any moment will poison the whole of your life in the cell. I pity you."

And now the banker, pacing from corner to corner, recalled all this and asked himself:

"Why did I make this bet? What's the good? The lawyer loses fifteen years of his life and I throw away two millions. Will it convince people that capital punishment is worse or better than imprisonment for life. No, No! all stuff and rubbish. On my part, it was the caprice of a well-fed man; on the lawyer's, pure greed of gold."

He recollected further what happened after the evening party. It was decided that the lawyer must undergo his imprisonment under the strictest observation, in a garden-wing of the banker's house. It was agreed that during the period he would be deprived of the right to cross the threshold, to see living people, to hear human voices, and to receive letters and newspapers. He was permitted to have a musical instrument, to read books, to write letters, to drink wine and smoke tobacco. By the agreement he could communicate, but only in silence, with the outside world through a little window specially constructed for this purpose. Everything necessary, books, music, wine, he could receive in any quantity by sending a note through the window. The agreement provided for all the minutest details, which made the confinement strictly solitary, and it obliged the lawyer to remain exactly fifteen years from twelve o'clock of November 14th, 1870, to twelve o'clock of November 14th, 1885. The least attempt on his part to violate the conditions, to escape if only for two minutes before the time freed the banker from the obligation to pay him the two millions.

During the first year of imprisonment, the lawyer, as far as it was possible to judge from his short notes, suffered terribly from loneliness and boredom. From his wing day and night came the sound of the piano. He rejected wine and tobacco. "Wine," he wrote, "excites desires, and desires are the chief foes of a prisoner; besides, nothing is more boring than to drink good wine alone," and tobacco spoiled the air in his room. During the first year the lawyer was sent books of a light character; novels with a complicated love interest, stories of crime and fantasy, comedies, and so on.

In the second year the piano was heard no longer and the lawyer asked only for classics. In the fifth year, music was heard again, and the prisoner asked for wine. Those who watched him said that during the whole of that year he was only eating, drinking, and lying on his bed. He yawned often and talked angrily to himself. Books he did not read. Sometimes at nights he would sit down to write. He would write for a long time and tear it all up in the morning. More than once he was heard to weep.

In the second half of the sixth year, the prisoner began zealously to study languages, philosophy, and history. He fell on these subjects so hungrily that the banker hardly had time to get books enough for him. In the space of four years about six hundred volumes were bought at his request. It was while that passion lasted that the banker received the following letter from the prisoner: "My dear gaoler, I am writing these lines in six languages. Show them to experts. Let them read them. If they do not find one single mistake, I beg you to give orders to have a gun fired off in the garden. By the noise I shall know that my efforts have not been in vain. The geniuses of all ages and countries speak in different languages; but in them all burns the same flame. Oh, if you knew my heavenly happiness now that I can understand them!" The prisoner's desire was fulfilled. Two shots were fired in the garden by the banker's order.

Later on, after the tenth year, the lawyer sat immovable before his table and read only the New Testament. The banker found it strange that a man who in four years had mastered six hundred erudite volumes, should have spent nearly a year in reading one book, easy to understand and by no means thick. The New Testament was then replaced by the history of religions and theology.

During the last two years of his confinement the prisoner read an extraordinary amount, quite haphazardly. Now he would apply himself to the natural sciences, then would read Byron or Shakespeare. Notes used to come from him in which he asked to be sent at the same time a book on chemistry, a text-book of medicine, a novel, and some treatise on philosophy or theology. He read as though he were swimming in the sea among broken pieces of wreckage, and in his desire to save his life was eagerly grasping one piece after another.

II

The banker recalled all this, and thought:

"To-morrow at twelve o'clock he receives his freedom. Under the agreement, I shall have to pay him two millions. If I pay, it's all over with me. I am ruined for ever . . ."

Fifteen years before he had too many millions to count, but now he was afraid to ask himself which he had more of, money or debts. Gambling on the Stock-Exchange, risky speculation, and the recklessness of which he could not rid himself even in old age, had gradually brought his business to decay; and the fearless, self-confident, proud man of business had become an ordinary banker, trembling at every rise and fall in the market.

"That cursed bet," murmured the old man clutching his head in despair . . . "Why didn't the man die? He's only forty years old. He will take away my last penny, marry, enjoy life, gamble on the Exchange, and I will look on like an envious beggar and hear the same words from him every day: 'I'm obliged to you for the happiness of my life. Let me help you.' No, it's too much! The only escape from bankruptcy and disgrace—is that the man should die."

The clock had just struck three. The banker was listening. In the house everyone was asleep, and one could hear only the frozen trees whining outside the windows. Trying to make no sound, he took out of his safe the key of the door which had not been opened for fifteen years, put on his overcoat, and went out of the house. The garden was dark and cold. It was raining. A keen damp wind hovered howling over the garden and gave the trees no rest. Though he strained his eyes, the banker could see neither the ground, nor the white statues, nor the garden-wing, nor the trees. Approaching the place where the garden-wing stood, he called the watchman twice. There was no answer. Evidently the watchman had taken shelter from the bad weather and was now asleep somewhere in the kitchen or the greenhouse.

"If I have the courage to fulfil my intention," thought the old man, "the suspicion will fall on the watchman first of all."

In the darkness he groped for the stairs and the door and entered the hall of the garden-wing, then poked his way into a narrow passage and struck a match. Not a soul was there. Someone's bed, with no bedclothes on it, stood there, and an iron stove was dark in the corner.

The seals on the door that led into the prisoner's room were unbroken.

When the match went out, the old man, trembling from agitation, peeped into the little window.

In the prisoner's room a candle was burning dim. The prisoner himself sat by the table. Only his back, the hair on his head and his hands were visible. On the table, the two chairs, and on the carpet by the table, open books were strewn.

Five minutes passed and the prisoner never once stirred. Fifteen years' confinement had taught him to sit motionless. The banker tapped on the window with his finger, but the prisoner gave no movement in reply. Then the banker cautiously tore the seals from the door and put the key into the lock. The rusty lock gave a hoarse groan and the door creaked. The banker expected instantly to hear a cry of surprise and the sound of steps. Three minutes passed and it was as quiet behind the door as it had been before. He made up his mind to enter.

Before the table sat a man, unlike an ordinary human being. It was a skeleton, with tight-drawn skin, with a woman's long curly hair, and a shaggy beard. The colour of his face was yellow, of an earthy shade; the cheeks were sunken, the back long and narrow, and the hand upon which he leaned his hairy head was so lean and skinny that it was painful to look upon. His hair was already silvering with grey, and no one who glanced at the senile emaciation of the face would have believed that he was only forty years old. On the table, before his bended head, lay a sheet of paper on which something was written in a tiny hand.

"Poor devil," thought the banker, "he's asleep and probably seeing millions in his dreams. I have only to take and throw this half-dead thing on the bed, smother him a moment with the pillow, and the most careful examination will find no trace of unnatural death. But, first, let us read what he has written here."

The banker took the sheet from the table and read:

"To-morrow at twelve o'clock midnight, I shall obtain my freedom and the right to mix with people. But before I leave this room and see the sun I think it necessary to say a few words to you. On my own clear conscience and before God who sees me I declare to you that I despise freedom, life, health, and all that your books call the blessings of the world.

"For fifteen years I have diligently studied earthly life. True, I saw neither the earth nor the people, but in your books I drank fragrant wine, sang songs, hunted deer and wild boar in the forests, loved women . . . . And beautiful women, like clouds ethereal, created by the magic of your poets' genius, visited me by night and whispered to me wonderful tales, which made my head drunken. In your books I climbed the summits of Elbruz and Mont Blanc and saw from there how the sun rose in the morning, and in the evening overflowed the sky, the ocean and the mountain ridges with a purple gold. From there I saw how above me lightnings glimmered, cleaving the clouds; I saw green forests, fields, rivers, lakes, cities; I heard sirens singing, and the playing of the pipes of Pan; I touched the wings of beautiful devils who came flying to me to speak of God . . . In your books I cast myself into bottomless abysses, worked miracles, burned cities to the ground, preached new religions, conquered whole countries . . .

"Your books gave me wisdom. All that unwearying human thought created in the centuries is compressed to a little lump in my skull. I know that I am more clever than you all.

"And I despise your books, despise all worldly blessings and wisdom. Everything is void, frail, visionary and delusive as a mirage. Though you be proud and wise and beautiful, yet will death wipe you from the face of the earth like the mice underground; and your posterity, your history, and the immortality of your men of genius will be as frozen slag, burnt down together with the terrestrial globe.

"You are mad, and gone the wrong way. You take lie for truth and ugliness for beauty. You would marvel if by certain conditions frogs and lizards should suddenly grow on apple and orange trees, instead of fruit, and if roses should begin to breathe the odour of a sweating horse. So do I marvel at you, who have bartered heaven for earth. I do not want to understand you.

"That I may show you in deed my contempt for that by which you live, I waive the two millions of which I once dreamed of as paradise, and which I now despise. That I may deprive myself of my right to them, I shall come out from here five minutes before the stipulated term, and thus shall violate the agreement."

When he had read, the banker put the sheet on the table, kissed the head of the strange man, and began to weep. He went out of the wing. Never at any other time, not even after his terrible losses on the Exchange, had he felt such contempt for himself as now. Coming home, he lay down on his bed, but agitation and tears kept him long from sleep . . .

The next morning the poor watchman came running to him and told him that they had seen the man who lived in the wing climbing through the window into the garden. He had gone to the gate and disappeared. With his servants the banker went instantly to the wing and established the escape of his prisoner. To avoid unnecessary rumours he took the paper with the renunciation from the table and, on his return, locked it in his safe.

1. What is the nature of the bet between the banker and the lawyer?
2. What does the lawyer do with his years in imprisonment?

3. What is his attitude toward mankind at the end of his experience?
4. Why does he reject the money he would win from the bet?
5. How is the banker changed by what the lawyer has done?
6. Is the story believable? Can you imagine such a bet?

Sherwood Anderson (1876–1941)

I WANT TO KNOW WHY

We got up at four in the morning, that first day in the East. On the evening before, we had climbed off a freight train at the edge of town and with the true instinct of Kentucky boys had found our way across town and to the race track and the stables at once. Then we knew we were all right. Hanley Turner right away found a nigger we knew. It was Bildad Johnson, who in the winter works at Ed Becker's livery barn in our home town, Beckersville. Bildad is a good cook as almost all our niggers are and of course he, like everyone in our part of Kentucky who is anyone at all, likes the horses. In the spring Bildad begins to scratch around. A nigger from our country can flatter and wheedle anyone into letting him do most anything he wants. Bildad wheedles the stablemen and the trainers from the horse farms in our country around Lexington. The trainers come into town in the evening to stand around and talk and maybe get into a poker game. Bildad gets in with them. He is always doing little favors and telling about things to eat, chicken browned in a pan, and how is the best way to cook sweet potatoes and corn bread. It makes your mouth water to hear him.

When the racing season comes on and the horses go to the races and there is all the talk on the streets in the evenings about the new colts, and everyone says when they are going over to Lexington or to the spring meeting at Churchill Downs or to Latonia, and the horsemen that have been down to New Orleans or maybe at the winter meeting at Havana in Cuba come home to spend a week before they start out again, at such a time when everything talked about in Beckersville is just horses and nothing else and the outfits start out and horse racing is in every breath of air you breathe, Bildad shows up with a job as cook for some outfit. Often when I think about it, his always going all season to the races and working in the livery barn in the winter where horses are and where men like to come and talk about horses, I wish I was a nigger. It's a foolish thing to say, but that's the way I am about being around horses, just crazy. I can't help it.

Well, I must tell you about what we did and let you in on what I'm talking about. Four of us boys from Beckersville, all whites and sons of men who live in Beckersville regular, made up our minds we were going to the races, not just to Lexington or Louisville, I don't mean, but to the big Eastern track we were always hearing our Beckersville men talk about, to Saratoga. We were all pretty young then. I was just turned fifteen and I was the oldest of the four. It was my scheme. I admit that, and I talked the others into trying it. There was Hanley Turner and Henry Rieback and Tom Tumberton and myself. I had thirty-seven dollars I had earned during the winter working nights and Saturdays in Enoch Myer's grocery. Henry Rieback had eleven dollars and the others, Hanley and Tom, had only a dollar or two each. We fixed it all up and laid low until the Kentucky spring meetings were over and some of our men, the sportiest ones, the ones we envied the most, had cut out. Then we cut out too.

I won't tell you the trouble we had beating our way on freights and all. We went through Cleveland and Buffalo and other cities and saw Niagara Falls. We bought things there, souvenirs and spoons and cards and shells with pictures of the falls on them for our sisters and mothers, but thought we had better not send any of the things home. We didn't want to put the folks on our trail and maybe be nabbed.

We got into Saratoga as I said at night and went to the track. Bildad fed us up. He showed us a place to sleep in hay over a shed and promised to keep still. Niggers are all right about things like that. They won't squeal on you. Often a white man you might meet, when you had run away from home like that, might appear to be all right and give you a quarter or a half dollar or something, and then go right and give you away. White men will do that, but not a nigger. You can trust them. They are squarer with kids. I don't know why.

At the Saratoga meeting that year there were a lot of men from home. Dave Williams and Arthur Mulford and Jerry Myers and others. Then there was a lot from Louisville and Lexington Henry Rieback knew but I didn't. They were professional gamblers and Henry Rieback's father is one too. He is what is called a sheet writer and goes away most of the year to tracks. In the winter when he is home in Beckersville he don't stay there much but goes away to cities and deals faro. He is a nice man and generous, is always sending Henry presents, a bicycle and a gold watch and a boy scout suit of clothes and things like that.

My own father is a lawyer. He's all right, but don't make much money and can't buy me things, and anyway I'm getting so old now I don't expect it. He never said nothing to me against Henry, but Hanley Turner and Tom Tumberton's fathers did. They said to their boys that money so come by is no good and they didn't want their boys brought up to hear gamblers' talk and be thinking about such things and maybe embrace them.

That's all right and I guess the men know what they are talking about, but I don't see what it's got to do with Henry or with horses either. That's what I'm writing this story about. I'm puzzled. I'm getting to be a man and want to think straight and be O.K., and there's something I saw at the race meeting at the Eastern track I can't figure out.

I can't help it, I'm crazy about thoroughbred horses, I've always been that way. When I was ten years old and saw I was growing to be big and couldn't be a rider I was so sorry I nearly died. Harry Hellinfinger in Beckersville, whose father is Postmaster, is grown up and too lazy to work, but likes to stand around in the street and get up jokes on boys like sending them to a hardware store for a gimlet to bore square holes and other jokes like that. He played one on me. He told me that if I would eat a half a cigar I would be stunted and not grow any more and maybe could be a rider. I did it. When Father wasn't looking I took a cigar out of his pocket and gagged it down some way. It made me awful sick and the doctor had to be sent for, and then it did no good. I kept right on growing. It was a joke. When I told what I had done and why, most fathers would have whipped me, but mine didn't.

Well, I didn't get stunted and didn't die. It serves Harry Hellinfinger right. Then I made up my mind I would like to be a stableboy, but had to give that up too. Mostly niggers do that work and I knew Father wouldn't let me go into it. No use to ask him.

If you've never been crazy about thoroughbreds, it's because you've never been around where they are much and don't know any better. They're beautiful. There isn't anything so lovely and clean and full of spunk and honest and everything as some race horses. On the big horse farms that are all around our town Beckersville there are tracks, and the horses run in the early morning. More than a thousand times I've got out of bed before daylight and walked two or three miles to the tracks. Mother wouldn't of let me go, but Father always says, "Let him alone." So I got some bread out of the breadbox and some butter and jam, gobbled it and lit out.

At the tracks you sit on the fence with men, whites and niggers, and they chew tobacco and talk, and then the colts are brought out. It's early and the grass is covered with shiny dew and in another field a man is plowing and they are frying things in a shed where the track niggers sleep, and you know how a nigger can giggle and laugh and say things that make you laugh. A white man can't do it and some niggers can't, but a track nigger can every time.

And so the colts are brought out and some are just galloped by stable boys, but almost every morning on a big track owned by a rich man who lives maybe in New York, there are always, nearly every morning, a few colts and some of the old race horses and geldings and mares that are cut loose.

It brings a lump into my throat when a horse runs. I don't mean all horses, but some. I can pick them nearly every time. It's in my blood like in the blood of race track niggers and trainers. Even when they just go slop-jogging along with a little nigger on their backs, I can tell a winner. If my throat hurts and it's hard for me to swallow, that's him. He'll run like Sam Hill when you let him out. If he don't win every time it'll be a wonder and because they've got him in a pocket behind another or he was pulled or got off bad at the post or something. If I wanted to be a gambler like Henry Rieback's father I could get rich. I know I could and Henry says so too. All I would have to do is to wait till that hurt comes when I see a horse and then bet every cent. That's what I would do if I wanted to be a gambler, but I don't.

When you're at the tracks in the morning—not the race tracks but the training tracks around Beckersville—you don't see a horse, the kind I've been talking about, very often, but it's nice anyway. Any thoroughbred, that is sired right and out of a good mare and trained by a man that knows how, can run. If he couldn't what would he be there for and not pulling a plow?

Well, out of the stables they come and the boys are on their backs and it's lovely to be there. You hunch down on top of the fence and itch inside you. Over in the sheds the niggers giggle and sing. Bacon is being fried and coffee made. Everything smells lovely. Nothing smells better than coffee and manure and horses and niggers and bacon frying and pipes being smoked out of doors on a morning like that. It just gets you, that's what it does.

But about Saratoga. We was there six days and not a soul from home seen us and everything came off just as we wanted it to, fine weather and horses and races and all. We beat our way home and Bildad gave us a basket with fried chicken and bread and other eatables in, and I had eighteen dollars when we got back to Beckersville. Mother jawed and cried, but Pop didn't say much. I told everything we done, except one thing. I did and saw that alone. That's what I'm writing about. It got me upset. I think about it at night. Here it is.

At Saratoga we laid up nights in the hay in the shed Bildad had showed us and ate with the niggers early and at night when the race people had all gone away. The men from home stayed mostly in the grandstand and betting field and didn't come out around the places where the horses are kept except to the paddocks just before a race when the horses are saddled. At Saratoga they don't have paddocks under an open shed as at Lexington and Churchill Downs and other tracks down in our country, but saddle the horses right out in an open place under trees on a lawn as smooth and nice as Banker Bohon's front yard here in Beckersville. It's lovely. The horses are sweaty and nervous and shine and the men come out and smoke cigars and look at them and the trainers are there and the owners, and your heart thumps so you can hardly breathe.

Then the bugle blows for post and the boys that ride come running out with their silk clothes on and you run to get a place by the fence with the niggers.

I always am wanting to be a trainer or owner, and at the risk of being seen and caught and sent home I went to the paddocks before every race. The other boys didn't, but I did.

We got to Saratoga on a Friday, and on Wednesday the next week the big Mullford Handicap was to be run. Middlestride was in it and Sunstreak. The weather was fine and the track fast. I couldn't sleep the night before.

What had happened was that both these horses are the kind it makes my throat hurt to see. Middlestride is long and looks awkward and is a gelding. He belongs to Joe Thompson, a little owner from home who only has a half dozen horses. The Mullford Handicap is for a mile and Middlestride can't untrack fast. He goes away slow and is always 'way back at the half, then he begins to run and if the race is a mile and a quarter he'll just eat up everything and get there.

Sunstreak is different. He is a stallion and nervous and belongs on the biggest farm we've got in our country, the Van Riddle place that belongs to Mr. Van Riddle of New York. Sunstreak is like a girl you think about sometimes but never see. He is hard all over and lovely too. When you look at his head you want to kiss him. He is trained by Jerry Tillford who knows me and has been good to me lots of times, lets me walk into a horse's stall to look at him close and other things. There isn't anything as sweet as that horse. He stands at the post quiet and not letting on, but he is just burning up inside. Then when the barrier goes up he is off like his name, Sunstreak. It makes you ache to see him. It hurts you. He just lays down and runs like a bird dog. There can't anything I ever see run like him except Middlestride when he gets untracked and stretches himself.

Gee! I ached to see that race and those two horses run, ached and dreaded it too. I didn't want to see either of our horses beaten. We had never sent a pair like that to the races before. Old men in Beckersville said so and the niggers said so. It was a fact.

Before the race, I went over to the paddocks to see. I looked a last look at Middlestride, who isn't such a much standing in a paddock that way, then I went to see Sunstreak.

It was his day. I knew when I see him. I forgot all about being seen myself and walked right up. All the men from Beckersville were there and no one noticed me except Jerry Tillford. He saw me and something happened. I'll tell you about that.

I was standing looking at that horse and aching. In some way, I can't tell how, I knew just how Sunstreak felt inside. He was quiet and letting the niggers rub his legs and Mr. Van Riddle himself put the saddle on, but he was just a raging torrent inside. He was like the water in the river at Niagara Falls just before it goes plunk down. That horse wasn't thinking about running. He don't have to think about that. He was just thinking about holding himself back till the time for the running came. I knew that. I could just in a way see right inside him. He was going to do some awful running and I knew it. He wasn't bragging or letting on much or prancing or making a fuss, but just waiting. I knew it and Jerry Tillford his trainer knew. I looked up, and then that man and I looked into each other's eyes. Something happened to me. I guess I loved the man as much as I did the horse because he knew what I knew. Seemed to me there wasn't anything in the world but that man and the horse and me. I cried and Jerry Tillford had a shine in his eyes. Then I came away to the fence to wait for the race. The horse was better than me, more steadier and, now I know, better than Jerry. He was the quietest and he had to do the running.

Sunstreak ran first of course and he busted the world's record for a mile. I've seen that if I never see anything more. Everything came out just as I expected. Middlestride got left at the post and was 'way back and closed up to be second, just as I knew he would. He'll get a world's record too some day. They can't skin the Beckersville country on horses.

I watched the race calm because I knew what would happen. I was sure. Hanley Turner and Henry Rieback and Tom Tumberton were all more excited than me.

A funny thing had happened to me. I was thinking about Jerry Tillford the trainer and how happy he was all through the race. I liked him that afternoon even more than I ever liked my own father. I almost forgot the horses thinking that way about him. It was because of what I had seen in his eyes as he stood in the paddocks beside Sunstreak before the race started. I knew he had been watching and working with Sunstreak since the horse was a baby colt, had taught him to run and be patient and when to let himself out and not to quit, never. I knew that for him it was like a mother seeing her child do something brave or wonderful. It was the first time I ever felt for a man like that.

After the race that night I cut out from Tom and Hanley and Henry. I wanted to be by myself and I wanted to be near Jerry Tillford if I could work it. Here is what happened.

The track in Saratoga is near the edge of town. It is all polished up and trees around, the evergreen kind, and grass and everything painted and nice. If you go past the track you get to a hard road made of asphalt for automobiles, and if you go along this for a few miles there is a road turns off to a little rummy-looking farmhouse set in a yard.

That night after the race I went along that road because I had seen Jerry and some other men go that way in an automobile. I didn't expect to find them. I walked for a ways and then sat down by a fence to think. It was the direction they went in. I wanted to be as near Jerry as I could. I felt close to him. Pretty soon I went up the side road—I don't know why—and came to the rummy farmhouse. I was just lonesome to see Jerry, like wanting to see your father at night when you are a young kid. Just then an automobile came along and turned in. Jerry was in it and Henry Rieback's father, and Arthur Bedford from home, and Dave Williams and two other men I didn't know. They got out of the car and went into the house, all but Henry Rieback's father who quarreled with them and said he wouldn't go. It was only about nine o'clock, but they were all drunk and the rummy-looking farmhouse was a place for bad women to stay in. That's what it was. I crept up along a fence and looked through a window and saw.

It's what gave me the fantods. I can't make it out. The women in the house were all ugly mean-looking women, not nice to look at or be near. They were homely too, except one who was tall and looked a little like the gelding Middlestride, but not clean like him, but with a hard ugly mouth. She had red hair. I saw everything plain. I got up by an old rosebush by an open window and looked. The women had on loose dresses and sat around in chairs. The men came in and some sat on the women's laps. The place smelled rotten and there was rotten talk, the kind a kid hears around a livery stable in a town like Beckersville in the winter but don't ever expect to hear talked when there are women around. It was rotten. A nigger wouldn't go into such a place.

I looked at Jerry Tillford. I've told you how I had been feeling about him on account of his knowing what was going on inside of Sunstreak in the minute before he went to the post for the race in which he made a world's record.

Jerry bragged in that bad woman house as I knew Sunstreak wouldn't never have bragged. He said that he made that horse, that it was him that won the race and made the record. He lied and bragged like a fool. I never heard such silly talk.

And then, what do you suppose he did! He looked at the woman in there, the one that was lean and hard-mouthed and looked a little like the gelding Middlestride but not clean like him, and his eyes began to shine just as they did when he looked at me and at Sunstreak in the paddocks at the track in the afternoon. I stood there by the window—gee!—but I wished I hadn't gone away from the tracks, but had stayed with the boys and the niggers and the horses. The tall rotten-looking woman was between us just as Sunstreak was in the paddocks in the afternoon.

Then, all of a sudden, I began to hate that man. I wanted to scream and rush in the room and kill him. I never had such a feeling before.

I was so mad clean through that I cried and my fists were doubled up so my fingernails cut my hands.

And Jerry's eyes kept shining and he waved back and forth, and then he went and kissed that woman and I crept away and went back to the tracks and to bed and didn't sleep hardly any, and then next day I got the other kids to start home with me and never told them anything I seen.

I been thinking about it ever since. I can't make it out. Spring has come again and I'm nearly sixteen and go to the tracks mornings same as always, and I see Sunstreak and Middlestride and a new colt named Strident I'll bet will lay them all out, but no one thinks so but me and two or three niggers.

But things are different. At the tracks the air don't taste as good or smell as good. It's because a man like Jerry Tillford, who knows what he does, could see a horse like Sunstreak run, and kiss a woman like that the same day. I can't make it out. Darn him, what did he want to do like that for? I keep thinking about it and it spoils looking at horses and smelling things and hearing niggers laugh and everything. Sometimes I'm so mad about it I want to fight someone. It gives me the fantods. What did he do it for? I want to know why.

1. Why is the boy attracted to horse racing? What values does it represent?
2. What do the boy and Jerry Tillford have in common?
3. Why do Tillford's actions upset the boy so deeply?
4. How does this incident affect the boy's value system?
5. How do you respond to the event? Does it seem as serious to you as it did to the boy?

Two
Plot

One of the appeals of fiction is that it organizes and unifies events. Most of us experience life as a complex succession of events in which it is difficult to find simple patterns. What is the cause, for example, of an adolescent's tragic suicide? We can search in every facet of his life and find what seem to be reasons, but they hardly ever add up to a satisfying explanation. Or we may find no plausible reasons at all. In most stories, however, the causes of an event are clearly dramatized. If a character is troubled to the point of suicide, the story can take us back to *the moment* when he experienced the trauma that led him to his desperation. Fiction satisfies our urge to find the explanations that link the past to the present by direct cause and effect. Stories make sense. In a well-made story it is never merely "first this happened, then this happened," it is "this happened, and that caused this to happen." This organization of events over time we call **plot.** Because the plot makes sense of events in a way that reflects the values that the story stands for, it is one of the most important concepts for readers to grasp.

Producing the Structure

The typical structure of events in most stories in our culture concerns an individual's conflict with some opposing force. The central individual is called the *hero,* or more objectively the **protagonist.** The plot usually brings this protagonist into conflict with some opposing force, called the **antagonist.** This force may be another character (a villain or competitor, for example), a force of nature (a storm to master or a mountain to climb), or a force within the protagonist (an addiction, for example, or a hidden, evil side to his or her character). The plot is then the series of events that deepen the conflict to a point of crisis, a confrontation between the opposing forces. The crisis is then resolved, and the consequences for each of the forces are made clear. This is a tightly logical form—the initial conflict brings about the point of crisis, which causes the logical consequences. The plots of most stories are a particular variation of this basic structure.

This basic plot structure is most clearly visible in pop culture stories. In a typical Western, for example, the sheriff is the protagonist, the heroic individual who brings order to the town. His antagonist is the outlaw, who threatens that order in a series of outrages that lead to a final battle with the sheriff, who defeats the outlaw and makes the town safe. Each step in the plot leads logically to the next. Very few plots are this simple, though, and the basic structure can be varied endlessly. The sheriff might be less than a hero—a drunk, say—or the outlaw may be charming and attractive. The events that lead to the climax can be anything from a verbal challenge to a murder, depending on the characters. The final conflict may be a moment's explosion or an elaborate battle, and the consequences can be as complex as desired. The hero can even lose. The basic plot, in other words, lies underneath any story, which can elaborate on it in a huge variety of ways.

Stories are written on the assumption that readers are aware of this basic plot, and that they have built up expectations about how a story should progress. Good readers anticipate the outcome of the plot as they read, projecting into the future a logical extension of the pattern they have perceived so far in the story. Many times these expectations are fulfilled. A villain, for example, may get just the punishment he deserves. But many times even very logical expectations are confounded by the story. There are, for example, detective stories that do not solve the mystery but rather open up a darker and deeper mystery. Especially in modern fiction, the reader's expectations for a logical plot may not be fulfilled. Many modern stories are built on the premise that such plots oversimplify experience, that they falsify the complexity we all live in. Such stories frustrate all expectations. They may even have no coherent plot at all. Rather than reduce events to simple cause and effect, they may try to reproduce the complex and murky world of experience, in which events seldom take on a simple shape.

Nevertheless, it is important that readers approach stories with the basic plot pattern in mind. For traditional stories, the pattern will allow readers to participate in the developing logic of the story. For the modern story that confounds expectations, readers must at least *have* expectations if this effect of the story is to be felt. Stories like this are out to shake readers up, to make them question their expectations and see that the logic of the basic plot is not the only possible way of making sense. This effect requires an active reader, and one who is open to new forms of experience.

Proceeding to the Values

The structure of the plot appeals to us on a very deep level. Some critics even say it is built into our language, that the sentence is a little story (or that the story is an expanded sentence): the subject of the sentence is like the hero of the story, the verb is the action he takes, the object the opponent he acts on. The logic that holds a story together is as basic to a culture as the logic of its language. We can see in the basic plot some of the central values and beliefs of our culture. The hero, for example, is a striking *individual,* just as we are a culture that worships the individual. The action he engages in almost always involves a *conflict,* just as we are a culture based on competition. And the hero is traditionally a *male,* just as we are a culture that associates males with assertive action.

There is nothing universal about any of these cultural associations; they are simply characteristics of stories in our culture. Many recent stories have tried to go against these assumptions, trying to reveal them as limits on our thinking about human experience. In many modern stories, for example, there is no dramatic conflict, no satisfying resolution—just a moment carefully considered, without the contrivance of a definitive conclusion. Some stories bring the dominance of the individual into question, depicting the protagonist as part of a social world rather than as an isolated individual. Other stories are centered on female protagonists, powerfully demonstrating that the association of assertive action only with males is false and limiting. In all of these cases, the values of our culture as expressed in the traditional plot structure are brought into question.

As an active reader, then, you need to attend to how the actions of the story are structured. Plot reveals character and embodies the values of the story. You must also participate in the development of the story by using imagination and logic to project the outcome of the plot. If the story fulfills your expectations, you can feel the pleasure of a pattern working itself out. But if the story doesn't follow the lines you project, as a good reader you will ask *why.*

READINGS

Nathaniel Hawthorne (1804–1864)

YOUNG GOODMAN BROWN

Young Goodman Brown came forth at sunset into the street at Salem village; but put his head back, after crossing the threshold, to exchange a parting kiss with his young wife. And Faith, as the wife was aptly named, thrust her own pretty head into the street, letting the wind play with the pink ribbons of her cap while she called to Goodman Brown.

"Dearest heart," whispered she, softly and rather sadly, when her lips were close to his ear, "prithee put off your journey until sunrise and sleep in your own bed to-night. A lone woman is troubled with such dreams and such thoughts that she's afeared of herself sometimes. Pray tarry with me this night, dear husband, of all nights in the year."

"My love and my Faith," replied young Goodman Brown, "of all nights in the year, this one night must I tarry away from thee. My journey, as thou callest it, forth and back again, must needs be done 'twixt now and sunrise. What, my sweet, pretty wife, dost thou doubt me already, and we but three months married?"

"Then God bless you!" said Faith, with the pink ribbons; "and may you find all well when you come back."

"Amen!" cried Goodman Brown. "Say thy prayers, dear Faith, and go to bed at dusk, and no harm will come to thee."

So they parted; and the young man pursued his way until, being about to turn the corner by the meeting-house, he looked back and saw the head of Faith still peeping after him with a melancholy air in spite of her pink ribbons.

"Poor little Faith!" thought he, for his heart smote him. "What a wretch am I to leave her on such an errand! She talks of dreams, too. Methought as she spoke there was trouble in her face, as if a dream had warned her what work is to be done to-night. But no, no; 'twould kill her to think it. Well, she's a blessed angel on earth; and after this one night I'll cling to her skirts and follow her to heaven."

With this excellent resolve for the future, Goodman Brown felt himself justified in making more haste on his present evil purpose. He had taken a dreary road, darkened by all the gloomiest trees of the forest, which barely stood aside to let the narrow path creep through, and closed immediately behind. It was all as lonely as could be; and there is this peculiarity in such a solitude, that the traveller knows not who may be concealed by the innumerable trunks and the thick boughs overhead; so that with lonely footsteps he may yet be passing through an unseen multitude.

"There may be a devilish Indian behind every tree," said Goodman Brown to himself; and he glanced fearfully behind him as he added, "What if the devil himself should be at my very elbow!"

His head being turned back, he passed a crook of the road, and, looking forward again, beheld the figure of a man, in grave and decent attire, seated at the foot of an old tree. He arose at Goodman Brown's approach and walked onward side by side with him.

"You are late, Goodman Brown," said he. "The clock of the Old

South was striking as I came through Boston, and that is full fifteen minutes agone."

"Faith kept me back a while," replied the young man, with a tremor in his voice, caused by the sudden appearance of his companion, though not wholly unexpected.

It was now deep dusk in the forest, and deepest in that part of it where these two were journeying. As nearly as could be discerned, the second traveller was about fifty years old, apparently in the same rank of life as Goodman Brown, and bearing a considerable resemblance to him, though perhaps more in expression than features. Still they might have been taken for father and son. And yet, though the elder person was as simply clad as the younger, and as simple in manner too, he had an indescribable air of one who knew the world, and who would not have felt abashed at the governor's dinner table or in King William's court, were it possible that his affairs should call him thither. But the only thing about him that could be fixed upon as remarkable was his staff, which bore the likeness of a great black snake, so curiously wrought that it might almost be seen to twist and wriggle itself like a living serpent. This, of course, must have been an ocular deception, assisted by the uncertain light.

"Come, Goodman Brown," cried his fellow-traveller, "this is a dull place for the beginning of a journey. Take my staff, if you are so soon weary."

"Friend," said the other, exchanging his slow pace for a full stop, "having kept covenant by meeting thee here, it is my purpose now to return whence I came. I have scruples touching the matter thou wot'st of."

"Sayest thou so?" replied he of the serpent, smiling apart. "Let us walk on, nevertheless, reasoning as we go; and if I convince thee not thou shalt turn back. We are but a little way in the forest yet."

"Too far! too far!" exclaimed the goodman, unconsciously resuming his walk. "My father never went into the woods on such an errand, nor his father before him. We have been a race of honest men and good Christians since the days of the martyrs; and shall I be the first of the name of Brown that ever took this path and kept—"

"Such company, thou wouldst say," observed the elder person, interpreting his pause. "Well said, Goodman Brown! I have been as well acquainted with your family as with ever a one among the Puritans; and that's no trifle to say. I helped your grandfather, the constable, when he lashed the Quaker woman so smartly through the streets of Salem; and it was I that brought your father a pitch-pine knot, kindled at my own hearth, to set fire to an Indian village, in King Philip's war. They were my good friends, both; and many a pleasant walk have we had along this path, and returned merrily after midnight. I would fain be friends with you for their sake."

"If it be as thou sayest," replied Goodman Brown. "I marvel they never spoke of these matters; or, verily, I marvel not, seeing that the least rumor of the sort would have driven them from New England. We are a people of prayer, and good works to boot, and abide no such wickedness."

"Wickedness or not," said the traveller with the twisted staff, "I have a very general acquaintance here in New England. The deacons of many a church have drunk the communion wine with me; the selectmen of divers towns make me their chairman; and a majority of the Great and General Court are firm supporters of my interest. The governor and I, too—But these are state secrets."

"Can this be so?" cried Goodman Brown, with a stare of amazement at his undisturbed companion. "Howbeit, I have nothing to do with the governor and council; they have their own ways, and are no rule for a simple husbandman like me. But, were I to go on with thee, how should I meet the eye of that good old man, or minister, at Salem village? Oh, his voice would make me tremble both Sabbath day and lecture day."

Thus far the elder traveller had listened with due gravity; but now burst into a fit of irrepressible mirth, shaking himself so violently that his snakelike staff actually seemed to wriggle in sympathy.

"Ha! ha! ha!" shouted he again and again; then composing himself, "Well, go on, Goodman Brown, go on; but, prithee, don't kill me with laughing."

"Well, then, to end the matter at once," said Goodman Brown, considerably nettled, "there is my wife, Faith. It would break her dear little heart; and I'd rather break my own."

"Nay, if that be the case," answered the other, "e'en go thy ways, Goodman Brown. I would not for twenty old women like the one hobbling before us that Faith should come to any harm."

As he spoke he pointed his staff at a female figure on the path, in whom Goodman Brown recognized a very pious and exemplary dame, who had taught him his catechism in youth, and was still his moral and spiritual adviser, jointly with the minister and Deacon Gookin.

"A marvel, truly, that Goody Cloyse should be so far in the wilderness at nightfall," said he. "But with your leave, friend, I shall take a cut through the woods until we have left this Christian woman behind. Being a stranger to you, she might ask whom I was consorting with and whither I was going."

"Be it so," said his fellow-traveller. "Betake you the woods, and let me keep the path."

Accordingly the young man turned aside, but took care to watch his companion, who advanced softly along the road until he had come within a staff's length of the old dame. She, meanwhile, was making the best of her way, with singular speed for so aged a woman, and mumbling some indistinct words—a prayer, doubtless—as she went. The traveller put forth his staff and touched her withered neck with what seemed the serpent's tail.

"The devil!" screamed the pious old lady.

"Then Goody Cloyse knows her old friend?" observed the traveller, confronting her and leaning on his writhing stick.

"Ah, forsooth, and is it your worship indeed?" cried the good dame. "Yea, truly it is, and in the very image of my old gossip, Goodman Brown, the grandfather of the silly fellow that now is. But—would your worship believe it?—my broomstick hath strangely disappeared, stolen, as I suspect, by that unhanged witch, Goody Cory, and that, too, when I was all anointed with the juice of smallage, and cinquefoil, and wolf's bane—"

"Mingled with fine wheat and the fat of a new-born babe," said the shape of old Goodman Brown.

"Ah, your worship knows the recipe," cried the old lady, cackling aloud. "So, as I was saying, being all ready for the meeting, and no horse to ride on, I made up my mind to foot it; for they tell me there is a nice young man to be taken into communion to-night. But now your good worship will lend me your arm, and we shall be there in a twinkling."

"That can hardly be," answered her friend. "I may not spare you my arm, Goody Cloyse; but here is my staff, if you will."

So saying, he threw it down at her feet, where, perhaps, it assumed life, being one of the rods which its owner had formerly lent to the Egyptian magi. Of this fact, however, Goodman Brown could not take cognizance. He had cast up his eyes in astonishment, and, looking down again, beheld neither Goody Cloyse nor the serpentine staff, but his fellow-traveller alone, who waited for him as calmly as if nothing had happened.

"That old woman taught me my catechism," said the young man; and there was a world of meaning in this simple comment.

They continued to walk onward, while the elder traveller exhorted his companion to make good speed and persevere in the path, discoursing so aptly that his arguments seemed rather to spring up in the bosom of his auditor than to be suggested by himself. As they went, he plucked a branch of maple to serve for a walking stick, and began to strip it of the twigs and little boughs, which were wet with evening dew. The moment his fingers touched them they became strangely withered and dried up as with a week's sunshine. Thus the pair proceeded, at a good free pace, until suddenly, in a gloomy hollow of the road, Goodman Brown sat himself down on the stump of a tree and refused to go any farther.

"Friend," said he, stubbornly, "my mind is made up. Not another step will I budge on this errand. What if a wretched old woman do choose to go to the devil when I thought she was going to heaven; is that any reason why I should quit my dear Faith and go after her?"

"You will think better of this by and by," said his acquaintance, composedly. "Sit here and rest yourself a while; and when you feel like moving again, there is my staff to help you along."

Without more words, he threw his companion the maple stick, and was as speedily out of sight as if he had vanished into the deepening gloom. The young man sat a few moments by the roadside, applauding himself greatly, and thinking with how clear a conscience he should meet the minister in his morning walk, nor shrink from the eye of good old Deacon Gookin. And what calm sleep would be his that very night, which was to have been spent so wickedly, but so purely and sweetly now, in the arms of Faith! Amidst these pleasant and praiseworthy meditations, Goodman Brown heard the tramp of horses along the road, and deemed it advisable to conceal himself within the verge of the forest, conscious of the guilty purpose that had brought him thither, though now so happily turned from it.

On came the hoof tramps and the voices of the riders, two grave old voices, conversing soberly as they drew near. These mingled sounds appeared to pass along the road, within a few yards of the young man's hiding-place; but, owing doubtless to the depth of the gloom at that particular spot, neither the travellers nor their steeds were visible. Though their figures brushed the small boughs by the wayside, it could not be seen that they intercepted, even for a moment, the faint gleam from the strip of bright sky athwart which they must have passed. Goodman Brown alternately crouched and stood on tiptoe, pulling aside the branches and thrusting forth his head as far as he durst without discerning so much as a shadow. It vexed him the more, because he could have sworn, were such a thing possible, that he recognized the voices of the minister and Deacon Gookin, jogging along quietly, as they were wont to do, when bound to some ordination or ecclesiastical council. While yet within hearing, one of the riders stopped to pluck a switch.

"Of the two, reverend sir," said the voice like the deacon's, "I had rather miss an ordination dinner than to-night's meeting. They tell me that some of our community are to be here from Falmouth and beyond, and others from Connecticut and Rhode Island, besides several of the Indian powwows, who, after their fashion, know almost as much deviltry as the best of us. Moreover, there is a goodly young woman to be taken into communion."

"Mighty well, Deacon Gookin!" replied the solemn old tones of the minister. "Spur up, or we shall be late. Nothing can be done, you know, until I get on the ground."

The hoofs clattered again; and the voices talking so strangely in the empty air, passed on through the forest, where no church had ever been gathered or solitary Christian prayed. Whither, then, could these holy men be journeying so deep into the heathen wilderness? Young Goodman Brown caught hold of a tree for support, being ready to sink down on the ground, faint and overburdened with the heavy sickness of his heart. He looked up to the sky, doubting whether there really was a heaven above him. Yet there was the blue arch, and the stars brightening in it.

"With heaven above and Faith below, I will yet stand firm against the devil!" cried Goodman Brown.

While he still gazed upward into the deep arch of the firmament and had lifted his hands to pray, a cloud, though no wind was stirring, hurried across the zenith and hid the brightening stars. The blue sky was still visible, except directly overhead, where this black mass of cloud was sweeping swiftly northward. Aloft in the air, as if from the depths of the cloud, came a confused and doubtful sound of voices. Once the listener fancied that he could distinguish the accents of townspeople of his own, men and women, both pious and ungodly, many of whom he had met at the communion table, and had seen others rioting at the tavern. The next moment, so indistinct were the sounds, he doubted whether he had heard aught but the murmur of the old forest, whispering without a wind. Then came a stronger swell of those familiar tones, heard daily in the sunshine at Salem village, but never until now from a cloud of night. There was one voice, of a young woman, uttering lamentations, yet with an uncertain sorrow, and entreating for some favor, which, perhaps, it would grieve her to obtain; and all the unseen multitude, both saints and sinners, seemed to encourage her onward.

"Faith!" shouted Goodman Brown, in a voice of agony and desperation; and the echoes of the forest mocked him, crying, "Faith! Faith!" as if bewildered wretches were seeking her all through the wilderness.

The cry of grief, rage, and terror was yet piercing the night, when the unhappy husband held his breath for a response. There was a scream, drowned immediately in a louder murmur of voices, fading into far-off laughter, as the dark cloud swept away, leaving the clear and silent sky above Goodman Brown. But something fluttered lightly down through the air and caught on the branch of a tree. The young man seized it, and beheld a pink ribbon.

"My Faith is gone!" cried he, after one stupefied moment. "There is no good on earth, and sin is but a name. Come, devil, for to thee is this world given."

And, maddened with despair, so that he laughed loud and long, did Goodman Brown grasp his staff and set forth again, at such a rate that he seemed to fly along the forest path rather than to walk or run.

The road grew wilder and drearier and more faintly traced, and vanished at length, leaving him in the heart of the dark wilderness, still rushing onward with the instinct that guides mortal man to evil. The whole forest was peopled with frightful sounds—the creaking of the trees, the howling of wild beasts, and the yell of Indians; while sometimes the wind tolled like a distant church bell, and sometimes gave a broad roar around the traveller, as if all Nature were laughing him to scorn. But he was himself the chief horror of the scene, and shrank not from its other horrors.

"Ha! ha! ha!" roared Goodman Brown when the wind laughed at him. "Let us hear which will laugh loudest. Think not to frighten me with your deviltry. Come witch, come wizard, come Indian powwow, come devil himself, and here comes Goodman Brown. You may as well fear him as he fear you."

In truth, all through the haunted forest there could be nothing more frightful than the figure of Goodman Brown. On he flew among the black pines, brandishing his staff with frenzied gestures, now giving vent to an inspiration of horrid blasphemy, and now shouting forth such laughter as set all the echoes of the forest laughing like demons around him. The fiend in his own shape is less hideous than when he rages in the breast of man. Thus sped the demoniac on his course, until, quivering among the trees, he saw a red light before him, as when the felled trunks and branches of a clearing have been set on fire, and throw up their lurid blaze against the sky, at the hour of midnight. He paused, in a lull of the tempest that had driven him onward, and heard the swell of what seemed a hymn, rolling solemnly from a distance with the weight of many voices. He knew the tune; it was a familiar one in the choir of the village meeting-house. The verse died heavily away, and was lengthened by a chorus, not of human voice, but of all the sounds of the benighted wilderness pealing in awful harmony together. Goodman Brown cried out, and his cry was lost to his own ear by its unison with the cry of the desert.

In the interval of silence he stole forward until the light glared full upon his eyes. At one extremity of an open space, hemmed in by the dark wall of the forest, arose a rock, bearing some rude, natural resemblance either to an altar or a pulpit, and surrounded by four blazing pines, their tops aflame, their stems untouched, like candles at an evening meeting. The mass of foliage that had overgrown the summit of the rock was all on fire, blazing high into the night and fitfully illuminating the whole field. Each pendent twig and leafy festoon was in a blaze. As the red light arose and fell, a numerous congregation alternately shone forth, then disappeared in shadow, and again grew, as it were, out of the darkness, peopling the heart of the solitary woods at once.

"A grave and dark-clad company," quoth Goodman Brown.

In truth they were such. Among them, quivering to and fro between gloom and splendor, appeared faces that would be seen next day at the council board of the province, and others which, Sabbath after Sabbath, looked devoutly heavenward, and benignantly over the crowded pews, from the holiest pulpits in the land. Some affirm that the lady of the governor was there. At least there were high dames well known to her, and wives of honored husbands, and widows, a great multitude, and ancient maidens, all of excellent repute, and fair young girls, who trembled lest their mothers should espy them. Either the sudden gleams of light flashing over the obscure field bedazzled Goodman Brown, or he recognized a score of the church members of Salem village famous for their especial sanctity. Good old Deacon Gookin had arrived, and waited at the skirts of that venerable saint, his revered pastor. But, irreverently consorting with these grave, reputable, and pious people, these elders of the church, these chaste dames and dewy virgins, there were men of dissolute lives and women of spotted fame, wretches given over to all mean and filthy vice, and suspected even of horrid crimes. It was strange to see that the good shrank not from the wicked, nor were the sinners abashed by the saints. Scattered also among their pale-faced enemies were the Indian priests, or powwows, who had often scared their native forest with more hideous incantations than any known to English witchcraft.

"But where is Faith?" thought Goodman Brown; and, as hope came into his heart, he trembled.

Another verse of the hymn arose, a slow and mournful strain, such as the pious love, but joined to words which expressed all that our nature can conceive of sin, and darkly hinted at far more. Unfathomable to mere mortals is the lore of fiends. Verse after verse was sung; and still the chorus of the desert swelled between like the deepest tone of a mighty organ; and with the final peal of that dreadful anthem there came a sound, as if the roaring wind, the rushing streams, the howling beasts, and every other voice of the unconcerted wilderness were mingling and according with the voice of guilty man in homage to the prince of all. The four blazing pines threw up a loftier flame, and obscurely discovered shapes and visages of horror on the smoke wreaths above the impious assembly. At the same moment the fire on the rock shot redly forth and formed a glowing arch above its base, where now appeared a figure. With reverence be it spoken, the figure bore no slight similitude, both in garb and manner, to some grave divine of the New England churches.

"Bring forth the converts!" cried a voice that echoed through the field and rolled into the forest.

At the word, Goodman Brown stepped forth from the shadow of the trees and approached the congregation, with whom he felt a loathful brotherhood by the sympathy of all that was wicked in his heart.

He could have well-nigh sworn that the shape of his own dead father beckoned him to advance, looking downward from a smoke wreath, while a woman, with dim features of despair, threw out her hand to warn him back. Was it his mother? But he had no power to retreat one step, nor to resist, even in thought, when the minister and good old Deacon Gookin seized his arms and led him to the blazing rock. Thither came also the slender form of a veiled female, led between Goody Cloyse, that pious teacher of the catechism, and Martha Carrier, who had received the devil's promise to be queen of hell. A rampant hag was she. And there stood the proselytes beneath the canopy of fire.

"Welcome, my children," said the dark figure, "to the communion of your race! Ye have found thus young your nature and your destiny. My children, look behind you!"

They turned; and flashing forth, as it were, in a sheet of flame, the fiend worshippers were seen; the smile of welcome gleamed darkly on every visage.

"There," resumed the sable form, "are all whom ye have reverenced from youth. Ye deemed them holier than yourselves, and shrank from your own sin, contrasting it with their lives of righteousness and prayerful aspirations heavenward. Yet here are they all in my worshipping assembly. This night it shall be granted you to know their secret deeds; how hoary-bearded elders of the church have whispered wanton words to the young maids of their households; how many a woman, eager for widows' weeds, has given her husband a drink at bedtime and let him sleep his last sleep in her bosom; how beardless youths have made haste to inherit their fathers' wealth; and how fair damsels—blush not, sweet ones—have dug little graves in the garden, and bidden me, the sole guest, to an infant's funeral. By the sympathy of your human hearts for sin ye shall scent out all the places—whether in church, bed-chamber, street, field, or forest—where crime has been committed, and shall exult to behold the whole earth one stain of guilt, one mighty blood spot. Far more than this. It shall be yours to penetrate, in every bosom, the deep mystery of sin, the fountain of all wicked arts, and which inexhaustibly supplies more evil impulses than human power—than my power at its utmost—can make manifest in deeds. And now, my children, look upon each other."

They did so; and, by the blaze of the hell-kindled torches, the wretched man beheld his Faith, and the wife her husband, trembling before that unhallowed altar.

"Lo, there ye stand, my children," said the figure, in a deep and solemn tone, almost sad with its despairing awfulness, as if his once angelic nature could yet mourn for our miserable race. "Depending upon one another's hearts, ye had still hoped that virtue were not all a dream. Now are ye undeceived. Evil is the nature of mankind. Evil must be your only happiness. Welcome again, my children, to the communion of your race."

"Welcome," repeated the fiend worshippers, in one cry of despair and triumph.

And there they stood, the only pair, as it seemed, who were yet hesitating on the verge of wickedness in this dark world. A basin was hollowed, naturally, in the rock. Did it contain water, reddened by the lurid light? or was it blood? or, perchance, a liquid flame? Herein did the shape of evil dip his hand and prepare to lay the mark of baptism upon their foreheads, that they might be partakers of the mystery of sin, more conscious of the secret guilt of others, both in deed and thought, than they could now be of their own. The husband cast one look at his pale wife, and Faith at him. What polluted wretches would the next glance show them to each other, shuddering alike at what they disclosed and what they saw!

"Faith! Faith!" cried the husband, "look up to heaven, and resist the wicked one."

Whether Faith obeyed he knew not. Hardly had he spoken when he found himself amid calm night and solitude, listening to a roar of the wind which died heavily away through the forest. He staggered against the rock, and felt it chill and damp; while a hanging twig, that had been all on fire, besprinkled his cheek with the coldest dew.

The next morning young Goodman Brown came slowly into the street of Salem village, staring around him like a bewildered man. The good old minister was taking a walk along the graveyard to get an appetite for breakfast and meditate his sermon, and bestowed a blessing, as he passed, on Goodman Brown. He shrank from the venerable saint as if to avoid an anathema. Old Deacon Gookin was at domestic worship, and the holy words of his prayer were heard through the open window. "What God doth the wizard pray to?" quoth Goodman Brown. Goody Cloyse, that excellent old Christian, stood in the early sunshine at her own lattice, catechizing a little girl who had brought her a pint of morning's milk. Goodman Brown snatched away the child as from the grasp of the fiend himself. Turning the corner by the meeting-house, he spied the head of Faith, with the pink ribbons, gazing anxiously forth, and bursting into such joy at sight of him that she skipped along the street and almost kissed her husband before the whole village. But Goodman Brown looked sternly and sadly into her face, and passed on without a greeting.

Had Goodman Brown fallen asleep in the forest and only dreamed a wild dream of a witch-meeting?

Be it so if you will; but, alas! it was a dream of evil omen for young Goodman Brown. A stern, a sad, a darkly meditative, a distrustful, if not a desperate man did he become from the night of that fearful dream. On the Sabbath day, when the congregation were singing a holy psalm, he could not listen because an anthem of sin rushed loudly upon his ear and drowned all the blessed strain. When the minister spoke from the pulpit with power and fervid eloquence, and, with his hand on the open Bible, of the sacred truths of our religion, and of saint-like lives and triumphant deaths, and of future bliss or misery unutterable, then did Goodman Brown turn pale, dreading lest the roof should thunder down upon the gray blasphemer and his hearers. Often, awaking suddenly at midnight, he shrank from the bosom of Faith; and at morning or eventide, when the family knelt down at prayer, he scowled and muttered to himself, and gazed sternly at his wife, and turned away. And when he had lived long, and was borne to his grave a hoary corpse, followed by Faith, an aged woman, and children and grandchildren, a goodly procession, besides neighbors not a few, they carved no hopeful verse upon his tombstone, for his dying hour was gloom.

1. What do we know about Young Goodman Brown at the beginning of the story?
2. What values does he represent?
3. What is his antagonist? How does he come into contact with it?
4. Why is Young Goodman Brown so attracted to what he sees in the forest?
5. What is the moment of final conflict between the hero and his antagonist?
6. Is the plot resolved in the way you expected?

Frank O'Connor (1903–1966)
GUESTS OF THE NATION

I

At dusk the big Englishman, Belcher, would shift his long legs out of the ashes and say "Well, chums, what about it?" and Noble or me would say "All right, chum" (for we had picked up some of their curious expressions), and the little Englishman, Hawkins, would light the lamp and bring out the cards. Sometimes Jeremiah Donovan would come up and supervise the game and get excited over Hawkin's cards, which he always played badly, and shout at him as if he was one of our own "Ah, you divil, you, why didn't you play the tray?"

But ordinarily Jeremiah was a sober and contented poor devil like the big Englishman, Belcher, and was looked up to only because he was a fair hand at documents, though he was slow enough even with them. He wore a small cloth hat and big gaiters over his long pants, and you seldom saw him with his hands out of his pockets. He reddened when you talked to him, tilting from toe to heel and back, and looking down all the time at his big farmer's feet. Noble and me used to make fun of his broad accent, because we were from the town.

I couldn't at the time see the point of me and Noble guarding Belcher and Hawkins at all, for it was my belief that you could have planted that pair down anywhere from this to Claregalway and they'd have taken root there like a native weed. I never in my short experience seen two men to take to the country as they did.

They were handed on to us by the Second Battalion when the search for them became too hot, and Noble and myself, being young, took over with a natural feeling of responsibility, but Hawkins made us look like fools when he showed that he knew the country better than we did.

"You're the bloke they calls Bonaparte," he says to me. "Mary Brigid O'Connell told me to ask you what you done with the pair of her brother's socks you borrowed."

For it seemed, as they explained it, that the Second used to have little evenings and some of the girls of the neighbourhood turned in, and, seeing they were such decent chaps, our fellows couldn't leave the two Englishmen out of them. Hawkins learned to dance "The Walls of Limerick," "The Siege of Ennis," and "The Waves of Tory" as well as any of them, though, naturally, he couldn't return the compliment, because our lads at that time did not dance foreign dances on principle.

So whatever privileges Belcher and Hawkins had with the Second they just naturally took with us, and after the first day or two we gave up all pretence of keeping a close eye on them. Not that they could have got far, for they had accents you could cut with a knife and wore khaki tunics and overcoats with civilian pants and boots. But it's my belief that they never had any idea of escaping and were quite content to be where they were.

It was a treat to see how Belcher got off with the old woman of the house where we were staying. She was a great warrant to scold, and cranky even with us, but before ever she had a chance of giving our guests, as I may call them, a lick of her tongue, Belcher had made her his friend for life. She was breaking sticks, and Belcher, who hadn't been more than ten minutes in the house, jumped up from his seat and went over to her.

"Allow me, madam," he says, smiling his queer little smile, "please allow me"; and he takes the bloody hatchet. She was struck too paralytic to speak, and after that, Belcher would be at her heels, carrying a bucket, a basket, or a load of turf, as the case might be. As Noble said, he got into looking before she leapt, and hot water, or any little thing she wanted, Belcher would have it ready for her. For such a huge man (and though I am five foot ten myself I had to look up at him) he had an uncommon shortness—or should I say lack?—of speech. It took us some time to get used to him, walking in and out, like a ghost, without a word. Especially because Hawkins talked enough for a platoon, it was strange to hear big Belcher with his toes in the ashes come out with a solitary "Excuse me, chum," or "That's right, chum." His one and only passion was cards, and I will say for him that he was a good card-player. He could have fleeced myself and Noble, but whatever we lost to him Hawkins lost to us, and Hawkins played with the money Belcher gave him.

Hawkins lost to us because he had too much old gab, and we probably lost to Belcher for the same reason. Hawkins and Noble would spit at one another about religion into the early hours of the morning, and Hawkins worried the soul out of Noble, whose brother was a priest, with a string of questions that would puzzle a cardinal. To make it worse even in treating of holy subjects, Hawkins had a deplorable tongue. I never in all my career met a man who could mix such a variety of cursing and bad language into an argument. He was a terrible man, and a fright to argue. He never did a stroke of work, and when he had no one else to talk to, he got stuck in the old woman.

He met his match in her, for one day when he tried to get her to complain profanely of the drought, she gave him a great comedown by blaming it entirely on Jupiter Pluvius (a deity neither Hawkins nor I had ever heard of, though Noble said that among the pagans it was believed that he had something to do with the rain). Another day he was swearing at the capitalists for starting the German war when the old lady laid down her iron, puckered up her little crab's mouth, and said: "Mr. Hawkins, you can say what you like about the war, and think you'll deceive me because I'm only a simple poor countrywoman, but I know what started the war. It was the Italian Count that stole the heathen divinity out of the temple in Japan. Believe me, Mr. Hawkins, nothing but sorrow and want can follow the people that disturb the hidden powers."

A queer old girl, all right.

II

We had our tea one evening, and Hawkins lit the lamp and we all sat into cards. Jeremiah Donovan came in too, and sat down and watched us for a while, and it suddenly struck me that he had no great love for the two Englishmen. It came as a great surprise to me, because I hadn't noticed anything about him before.

Late in the evening a really terrible argument blew up between Hawkins and Noble, about capitalists and priests and love of your country.

"The capitalists," says Hawkins with an angry gulp, "pays the priests to tell you about the next world so as you won't notice what the bastards are up to in this."

"Nonsense, man!" says Noble, losing his temper. "Before ever a capitalist was thought of, people believed in the next world."

Hawkins stood up as though he was preaching a sermon.

"Oh, they did, did they?" he says with a sneer. "They believed all the things you believe, isn't that what you mean? And you believe that God created Adam, and Adam created Shem, and Shem created Jehoshophat. You believe all that silly old fairytale about Eve and Eden and the apple. Well, listen to me, chum. If you're entitled to hold a silly belief like that, I'm entitled to hold my silly belief—which is that the first thing your God created was a bleeding capitalist, with morality and Rolls-Royce complete. Am I right, chum?" he says to Belcher.

"You're right, chum," says Belcher with his amused smile, and got up from the table to stretch his long legs into the fire and stroke his moustache. So, seeing that Jeremiah Donovan was going, and that there was no knowing when the argument about religion would be over, I went out with him. We strolled down to the village together, and then he stopped and started blushing and mumbling and saying I ought to be behind, keeping guard on the prisoners. I didn't like the tone he took with me, and anyway I was bored with life in the cottage, so I replied by asking him what the hell we wanted guarding them at all for. I told him I'd talked it over with Noble, and that we'd both rather be out with a fighting column.

"What use are those fellows to us?" says I.

He looked at me in surprise and said: "I thought you knew we were keeping them as hostages."

"Hostages?" I said.

"The enemy have prisoners belonging to us," he says, "and now they're talking of shooting them. If they shoot our prisoners, we'll shoot theirs."

"Shoot them?" I said

"What else did you think we were keeping them for?" he says.

"Wasn't it very unforeseen of you not to warn Noble and myself of that in the beginning?" I said.

"How was it?" says he. "You might have known it."

"We couldn't know it, Jeremiah Donovan," says I. "How could we when they were on our hands so long?"

"The enemy have our prisoners as long and longer," says he.

"That's not the same thing at all," says I.

"What difference is there?" says he.

I couldn't tell him, because I knew he wouldn't understand. If it was only an old dog that was going to the vet's, you'd try and not get too fond of him, but Jeremiah Donovan wasn't a man that would ever be in danger of that.

"And when is this thing going to be decided?" says I.

"We might hear tonight," he says. "Or tomorrow or the next day at latest. So if it's only hanging round here that's a trouble to you, you'll be free soon enough."

It wasn't the hanging round that was a trouble to me at all by this time. I had worse things to worry about. When I got back to the cottage the argument was still on. Hawkins was holding forth in his best style, maintaining that there was no next world, and Noble was maintaining that there was; but I could see that Hawkins had had the best of it.

"Do you know what, chum?" he was saying with a saucy smile. "I think you're just as big a bleeding unbeliever as I am. You say you believe in the next world, and you know just as much about the next world as I do, which is sweet damn-all. What's heaven? You don't know. Where's heaven? You don't know. You know sweet damn-all! I ask you again, do they wear wings?"

"Very well, then," says Noble, "they do. Is that enough for you? They do wear wings."

"Where do they get them, then? Who makes them? Have they a factory for wings? Have they a sort of store where you hands in your chit and takes your bleeding wings?"

"You're an impossible man to argue with," says Noble. "Now, listen to me—" And they were off again.

It was long after midnight when we locked up and went to bed. As I blew out the candle I told Noble what Jeremiah Donovan was after telling me. Noble took it very quietly. When we'd been in bed about an hour he asked me did I think we ought to tell the Englishmen. I didn't think we should, because it was more than likely that the English wouldn't shoot our men, and even if they did, the brigade officers, who were always up and down with the Second Battalion and knew the Englishmen well, wouldn't be likely to want them plugged. "I think so too," says Noble. "It would be great cruelty to put the wind up them now."

"It was very unforeseen of Jeremiah Donovan anyhow," says I.

It was next morning that we found it so hard to face Belcher and Hawkins. We went about the house all day scarcely saying a word. Belcher didn't seem to notice; he was stretched into the ashes as usual, with his usual look of waiting in quietness for something unforeseen to happen, but Hawkins noticed and put it down to Noble's being beaten in the argument of the night before.

"Why can't you take a discussion in the proper spirit?" he says severely. "You and your Adam and Eve! I'm a Communist, that's what I am. Communist or anarchist, it all comes to much the same thing." And for hours he went round the house, muttering when the fit took him. "Adam and Eve! Adam and Eve! Nothing better to do with their time than picking bleeding apples!"

III

I don't know how we got through that day, but I was very glad when it was over, the tea things were cleared away, and Belcher said in his peaceable way: "Well, chums, what about it?" We sat round the table and Hawkins took out the cards, and just then I heard Jeremiah Donovan's footstep on the path and a dark presentiment crossed my mind. I rose from the table and caught him before he reached the door:

"What do you want?" I asked.

"I want those two soldier friends of yours," he says, getting red.

"Is that the way, Jeremiah Donovan?" I asked.

"That's the way. There were four of our lads shot this morning, one of them a boy of sixteen."

"That's bad," I said.

At that moment Noble followed me out, and the three of us walked down the path together, talking in whispers. Feeney, the local intelligence officer, was standing by the gate.

"What are you going to do about it?" I asked Jeremiah Donovan.

"I want you and Noble to get them out; tell them they're being shifted again; that'll be the quietest way."

"Leave me out of that," says Noble under his breath.

Jeremiah Donovan looks at him hard.

"All right," he says. "You and Feeney get a few tools from the shed and dig a hole by the far end of the bog. Bonaparte and myself will be after you. Don't let anyone see you with the tools. I wouldn't like it to go beyond ourselves."

We saw Feeney and Noble go round to the shed and went in ourselves. I left Jeremiah Donovan to do the explanations. He told them that he had orders to send them back to the Second Battalion. Hawkins let out a mouthful of curses, and you could see that though Belcher didn't say anything, he was a bit upset too. The old woman was for having them stay in spite of us, and she didn't stop advising them until Jeremiah Donovan lost his temper and turned on her. He had a nasty temper, I noticed. It was pitch-dark in the cottage by this time, but no one thought of lighting the lamp, and in the darkness the two Englishmen fetched their topcoats and said good-bye to the old woman.

"Just as a man makes a home of a bleeding place, some bastard at headquarters thinks you're too cushy and shunts you off," says Hawkins, shaking her hand.

"A thousand thanks, madam," says Belcher. "A thousand thanks for everything"—as though he'd made it up.

We went round to the back of the house and down towards the bog. It was only then that Jeremiah Donovan told them. He was shaking with excitement.

"There were four of our fellows shot in Cork this morning and now you're to be shot as a reprisal."

"What are you talking about?" snaps Hawkins. "It's bad enough being mucked about as we are without having to put up with your funny jokes."

"It isn't a joke," says Donovan. "I'm sorry, Hawkins, but it's true," and begins on the usual rigmarole about duty and how unpleasant it is.

I never noticed that people who talk a lot about duty find it much of a trouble to them.

"Oh, cut it out!" says Hawkins.

"Ask Bonaparte," says Donovan, seeing that Hawkins isn't taking him seriously. "Isn't it true, Bonaparte?"

"It is," I say, and Hawkins stops.

"Ah, for Christ's sake, chum!"

"I mean it, chum," I say.

"You don't sound as if you meant it."

"If he doesn't mean it, I do," says Donovan, working himself up.

"What have you against me, Jeremiah Donovan?"

"I never said I had anything against you. But why did your people take out four of our prisoners and shoot them in cold blood?"

He took Hawkins by the arm and dragged him on, but it was impossible to make him understand that we were in earnest. I had the Smith and Wesson in my pocket and I kept fingering it and wondering what I'd do if they put up a fight for it or ran, and wishing to God they'd do one or the other. I knew if they did run for it, that I'd never fire on them. Hawkins wanted to know was Noble in it, and when we said yes, he asked us why Noble wanted to plug him. Why did any of us want to plug him? What had he done to us? Weren't we all chums? Didn't we understand him and didn't he understand us? Did we imagine for an instant that he'd shoot us for all the so-and-so officers in the so-and-so British Army?

By this time we'd reached the bog, and I was so sick I couldn't even answer him. We walked along the edge of it in the darkness, and every now and then Hawkins would call a halt and begin all over again, as if he was wound up, about our being chums, and I knew that nothing but the sight of the grave would convince him that we had to do it. And all the time I was hoping that something would happen; that they'd run for it or that Noble would take over the responsibility from me. I had the feeling that it was worse on Noble than on me.

IV

At last we saw the lantern in the distance and made towards it. Noble was carrying it, and Feeney was standing somewhere in the darkness behind him, and the picture of them so still and silent in the bogland brought it home to me that we were in earnest, and banished the last bit of hope I had.

Belcher, on recognizing Noble, said: "Hallo, chum," in his quiet way, but Hawkins flew at him at once, and the argument began all over again, only this time Noble had nothing to say for himself and stood with his head down, holding the lantern between his legs.

It was Jeremiah Donovan who did the answering. For the twentieth time, as though it was haunting his mind, Hawkins asked if anybody thought he'd shoot Noble.

"Yes, you would," says Jeremiah Donovan.

"No, I wouldn't, damn you!"

"You would, because you'd know you'd be shot for not doing it."

"I wouldn't, not if I was to be shot twenty times over. I wouldn't shoot a pal. And Belcher wouldn't—isn't that right, Belcher?"

"That's right, chum," Belcher said, but more by way of answering the question than of joining in the argument. Belcher sounded as though whatever unforeseen thing he'd always been waiting for had come at last.

"Anyway, who says Noble would be shot if I wasn't? What do you think I'd do if I was in his place, out in the middle of a blasted bog?"

"What would you do?" asks Donovan.

"I'd go with him wherever he was going, of course. Share my last bob with him and stick by him through thick and thin. No one can ever say of me that I let down a pal."

"We had enough of this," says Jeremiah Donovan, cocking his revolver. "Is there any message you want to send?"

"No, there isn't."

"Do you want to say your prayers?"

Hawkins came out with a cold-blooded remark that even shocked me and turned on Noble again.

"Listen to me, Noble," he says. "You and me are chums. You can't come over to my side, so I'll come over to your side. That show you I mean what I say? Give me a rifle and I'll go along with you and the other lads."

Nobody answered him. We knew that was no way out.

"Hear what I'm saying?" he says. "I'm through with it. I'm a deserter or anything else you like. I don't believe in your stuff, but it's no worse than mine. That satisfy you?"

Noble raised his head, but Donovan began to speak and he lowered it again without replying.

"For the last time, have you any messages to send?" says Donovan in a cold, excited sort of voice.

"Shut up, Donovan! You don't understand me, but these lads do. They're not the sort to make a pal and kill a pal. They're not the tools of any capitalist."

I alone of the crowd saw Donovan raise his Webley to the back of Hawkins's neck, and as he did so I shut my eyes and tried to pray. Hawkins had begun to say something else when Donovan fired, and as I opened my eyes at the bang, I saw Hawkins stagger at the knees and lie out flat at Noble's feet, slowly and as quiet as a kid falling asleep, with the lantern-light on his lean legs and bright farmer's boots. We all stood very still, watching him settle out in the last agony.

Then Belcher took out a handkerchief and began to tie it about his own eyes (in our excitement we'd forgotten to do the same for Hawkins), and, seeing it wasn't big enough, turned and asked for the loan of mine. I gave it to him and he knotted the two together and pointed with his foot at Hawkins.

"He's not quite dead," he says. "Better give him another."

Sure enough, Hawkins's left knee is beginning to rise. I bend down and put my gun to his head; then, recollecting myself, I get up again. Belcher understands what's in my mind.

"Give him his first," he says. "I don't mind. Poor bastard, we don't know what's happening to him now."

I knelt and fired. By this time I didn't seem to know what I was doing. Belcher, who was fumbling a bit awkwardly with the handkerchiefs, came out with a laugh as he heard the shot. It was the first time I heard him laugh and it sent a shudder down my back; it sounded so unnatural.

"Poor bugger!" he said quietly. "And last night he was so curious about it all. It's very queer, chums, I always think. Now he knows as much about it as they'll ever let him know, and last night he was all in the dark."

Donovan helped him to tie the handkerchiefs about his eyes. "Thanks, chum," he said. Donovan asked if there were any messages he wanted sent.

"No, chum," he says. "Not for me. If any of you would like to write to Hawkins's mother, you'll find a letter from her in his pocket. He and his mother were great chums. But my missus left me eight years ago. Went away with another fellow and took the kid with her. I like the feeling of a home, as you may have noticed, but I couldn't start again after that."

It was an extraordinary thing, but in those few minutes Belcher said more than in all the weeks before. It was just as if the sound of the shot had started a flood of talk in him and he could go on the whole night like that, quite happily, talking about himself. We stood round like fools now that he couldn't see us any longer. Donovan looked at Noble, and Noble shook his head. Then Donovan raised his Webley, and at that moment Belcher gives his queer laugh again. He may have thought we were talking about him, or perhaps he noticed the same thing I'd noticed and couldn't understand it.

"Excuse me, chums," he says. "I feel I'm talking the hell of a lot, and so silly, about my being so handy about a house and things like that. But this thing came on me suddenly. You'll forgive me, I'm sure."

"You don't want to say a prayer?" asks Donovan.

"No, chum," he says. "I don't think it would help. I'm ready, and you boys want to get it over."

"You understand that we're only doing our duty?" says Donovan.

Belcher's head was raised like a blind man's, so that you could only see his chin and the tip of his nose in the lantern-light.

"I never could make out what duty was myself," he said. "I think you're all good lads, if that's what you mean. I'm not complaining."

Noble, just as if he couldn't bear any more of it, raised his fist at Donovan, and in a flash Donovan raised his gun and fired. The big man went over like a sack of meal, and this time there was no need of a second shot.

I don't remember much about the burying, but that it was worse than all the rest because we had to carry them to the grave. It was all mad lonely with nothing but a patch of lantern-light between ourselves and the dark, and birds hooting and screeching all round, disturbed by the guns. Noble went through Hawkins's belongings to find the letter from his mother, and then joined his hands together. He did the same with Belcher. Then, when we'd filled in the grave, we separated from Jeremiah Donovan and Feeney and took our tools back to the shed. All the way we didn't speak a word. The kitchen was dark and cold as we'd left it, and the old woman was sitting over the hearth, saying her beads. We walked past her into the room, and Noble struck a match to light the lamp. She rose quietly and came to the doorway with all her cantankerousness gone.

"What did ye do with them?" she asked in a whisper, and Noble started so that the match went out in his hand.

"What's that?" he asked without turning round.

"I heard ye," she said.

"What did you hear?" asked Noble.

"I heard ye. Do ye think I didn't hear ye, putting the spade back in the houseen?"

Noble struck another match and this time the lamp lit for him.

"Was that what ye did to them?" she asked.

Then, by God, in the very doorway, she fell on her knees and began praying, and after looking at her for a minute or two Noble did the same by the fireplace. I pushed my way out past her and left them at it. I stood at the door, watching the stars and listening to the shrieking of the birds dying out over the bogs. It is so strange what you feel at times like that that you can't describe it. Noble says he saw everything ten times the size, as though there were nothing in the whole world but the little patch of bog with the two Englishmen stiffening into it, but with me it was as if the patch of bog where the Englishmen were was a million miles away, and even Noble and the old woman, mumbling behind me, and the birds and the bloody stars were all far away, and I was somehow very small and very lost and lonely like a child astray in the snow. And anything that happened to me afterwards, I never felt the same about again.

1. What conflict does the protagonist of the story face?
2. How is the story affected by the fact that the protagonist tells his own story?
3. Why does he have a problem with the captives he is guarding?
4. How does he make his decision?
5. What is the outcome of events for the protagonist? Does it flow logically from the plot?

Doris Lessing (b. 1919)
THROUGH THE TUNNEL

Going to the shore on the first morning of the vacation, the young English boy stopped at a turning of the path and looked down at a wild and rocky bay, and then over to the crowded beach he knew so well from other years. His mother walked on in front of him, carrying a bright striped bag in one hand. Her other arm, swinging loose, was very white in the sun. The boy watched that white, naked arm, and turned his eyes, which had a frown behind them, toward the bay and back again to his mother. When she felt he was not with her, she swung around. "Oh, there you are, Jerry!" she said. She looked impatient, then smiled. "Why, darling, would you rather not come with me? Would you rather—" She frowned, conscientiously worrying over what amusements he might secretly be longing for, which she had been too busy or too careless to imagine. He was very familiar with that anxious, apologetic smile. Contrition sent him running after her. And yet, as he ran, he looked back over his shoulder at the wild bay; and all morning, as he played on the safe beach, he was thinking of it.

Next morning, when it was time for the routine of swimming and sunbathing, his mother said, "Are you tired of the usual beach, Jerry? Would you like to go somewhere else?"

"Oh, no!" he said quickly, smiling at her out of that unfailing impulse of contrition—a sort of chivalry. Yet, walking down the path with her, he blurted out, "I'd like to go and have a look at those rocks down there."

She gave the idea her attention. It was a wild-looking place, and there was no one there; but she said, "Of course, Jerry. When you've had enough, come to the big beach. Or just go straight back to the villa, if you like." She walked away, that bare arm, now slightly reddened from yesterday's sun, swinging. And he almost ran after her again, feeling it unbearable that she should go by herself, but he did not.

She was thinking, Of course he's old enough to be safe without me. Have I been keeping him too close? He mustn't feel he ought to be with me. I must be careful.

He was an only child, eleven years old. She was a widow. She was determined to be neither possessive nor lacking in devotion. She went worrying off to her beach.

As for Jerry, once he saw that his mother had gained her beach, he began the steep descent to the bay. From where he was, high up among red-brown rocks, it was a scoop of moving bluish green fringed with white. As he went lower, he saw that it spread among small promontories and inlets of rough, sharp rock, and the crisping, lapping surface showed stains of purple and darker blue. Finally, as he ran sliding and scraping down the last few yards, he saw an edge of white surf and the shallow, luminous movement of water over white sand, and, beyond that, a solid, heavy blue.

He ran straight into the water and began swimming. He was a good swimmer. He went out fast over the gleaming sand, over a middle region where rocks lay like discolored monsters under the surface, and then he was in the real sea—a warm sea where irregular cold currents from the deep water shocked his limbs.

When he was so far out that he could look back not only on the little bay but past the promontory that was between it and the big beach, he floated on the buoyant surface and looked for his mother. There she was, a speck of yellow under an umbrella that looked like a slice of orange peel. He swam back to shore, relieved at being sure she was there, but all at once very lonely.

On the edge of a small cape that marked the side of the bay away from the promontory was a loose scatter of rocks. Above them, some boys were stripping off their clothes. They came running, naked, down to the rocks. The English boy swam toward them, but kept his distance at a stone's throw. They were of that coast; all of them were burned smooth dark brown and speaking a language he did not understand. To be with them, of them, was a craving that filled his whole body. He swam a little closer; they turned and watched him with narrowed, alert dark eyes. Then one smiled and waved. It was enough. In a minute, he had swum in and was on the rocks beside them, smiling with a desperate, nervous supplication. They shouted cheerful greetings at him; and then, as he preserved his nervous, uncomprehending smile, they understood that he was a foreigner strayed from his own beach, and they proceeded to forget him. But he was happy. He was with them.

They began diving again and again from a high point into a well of blue sea between rough, pointed rocks. After they had dived and come up, they swam around, hauled themselves up, and waited their turn to dive again. They were big boys—men, to Jerry. He dived, and they watched him; and when he swam around to take his place, they made way for him. He felt he was accepted and he dived again, carefully, proud of himself.

Soon the biggest of the boys poised himself, shot down into the water, and did not come up. The others stood about, watching. Jerry, after waiting for the sleek brown head to appear, let out a yell of warning; they looked at him idly and turned their eyes back toward the water. After a long time, the boy came up on the other side of a big dark rock, letting the air out of his lungs in a sputtering gasp and a shout of triumph. Immediately the rest of them dived in. One moment, the morning seemed full of chattering boys; the next, the air and the surface of the water were empty. But through the heavy blue, dark shapes could be seen moving and groping.

Jerry dived, shot past the school of underwater swimmers, saw a black wall of rock looming at him, touched it, and bobbed up at once to the surface, where the wall was a low barrier he could see across. There was no one visible; under him, in the water, the dim shapes of the swimmers had disappeared. Then one, and then another of the boys came up on the far side of the barrier of rock, and he understood that they had swum through some gap or hole in it. He plunged down again. He could see nothing through the stinging salt water but the blank rock. When he came up the boys were all on the diving rock, preparing to attempt the feat again. And now, in a panic of failure, he yelled up, in English, "Look at me! Look!" and he began splashing and kicking in the water like a foolish dog.

They looked down gravely, frowning. He knew the frown. At moments of failure, when he clowned to claim his mother's attention, it was with just this grave, embarrassed inspection that she rewarded him. Through his hot shame, feeling the pleading grin on his face like a scar that he could never remove, he looked up at the group of big brown boys on the rock and shouted, *"Bonjour! Merci! Au revoir! Monsieur, monsieur!"* while he hooked his fingers round his ears and waggled them.

Water surged into his mouth; he choked, sank, came up. The rock, lately weighted with boys, seemed to rear up out of the water as their weight was removed. They were flying down past him, now, into the water; the air was full of falling bodies. Then the rock was empty in the hot sunlight. He counted one, two, three. . . .

At fifty, he was terrified. They must all be drowning beneath him, in the watery caves of the rock! At a hundred, he stared around him at the empty hillside, wondering if he should yell for help. He counted faster, faster, to hurry them up, to bring them to the surface quickly, to drown them quickly—anything rather than the terror of counting on and on into the blue emptiness of the morning. And then, at a hundred and sixty, the water beyond the rock was full of boys blowing like brown whales. They swam back to the shore without a look at him.

He climbed back to the diving rock and sat down, feeling the hot roughness of it under his thighs. The boys were gathering up their bits of clothing and running off along the shore to another promontory. They were leaving to get away from him. He cried openly, fists in his eyes. There was no one to see him, and he cried himself out.

It seemed to him that a long time had passed, and he swam out to where he could see his mother. Yes, she was still there, a yellow spot under an orange umbrella. He swam back to the big rock, climbed up, and dived into the blue pool among the fanged and angry boulders. Down he went, until he touched the wall of rock again. But the salt was so painful in his eyes that he could not see.

He came to the surface, swam to shore and went back to the villa to wait for his mother. Soon she walked slowly up the path, swinging her striped bag, the flushed, naked arm dangling beside her. "I want some swimming goggles," he panted, defiant and beseeching.

She gave him a patient, inquisitive look as she said casually, "Well, of course, darling."

But now, now, now! He must have them this minute, and no other time. He nagged and pestered until she went with him to a shop. As soon as she had bought the goggles, he grabbed them from her hand as if she were going to claim them for herself, and was off, running down the steep path to the bay.

Jerry swam out to the big barrier rock, adjusted the goggles, and dived. The impact of the water broke the rubber-enclosed vacuum, and the goggles came loose. He understood that he must swim down to the base of the rock from the surface of the water. He fixed the goggles tight and firm, filled his lungs, and floated, face down, on the water. Now, he could see. It was as if he had eyes of a different kind—fish eyes that showed everything clear and delicate and wavering in the bright water.

Under him, six or seven feet down, was a floor of perfectly clean, shining white sand, rippled firm and hard by the tides. Two grayish shapes steered there, like long, rounded pieces of wood or slate. They were fish. He saw them nose toward each other, poise motionless, make a dart forward, swerve off, and come around again. It was like a water dance. A few inches above them the water sparkled as if sequins were dropping through it. Fish again—myriads of minute fish, the length of his fingernail, were drifting through the water, and in a moment he could feel the innumerable tiny touches of them against his limbs. It was like swimming in flaked silver. The great rock the big boys had swum through rose sheer out of the white sand—black, tufted lightly with greenish weed. He could see no gap in it. He swam down to its base.

Again and again he rose, took a big chestful of air, and went down. Again and again he groped over the surface of the rock, feeling it, almost hugging it in the desperate need to find the entrance. And then, once, while he was clinging to the black wall, his knees came up and he shot his feet out forward and they met no obstacle. He had found the hole.

He gained the surface, clambered about the stones that littered the barrier rock until he found a big one, and, with this in his arms, let himself down over the side of the rock. He dropped, with the weight, straight to the sandy floor. Clinging tight to the anchor of stone, he lay on his side and looked in under the dark shelf at the place where his feet had gone. He could see the hole. It was an irregular, dark gap; but he could not see deep into it. He let go of his anchor, clung with his hands to the edges of the hole, and tried to push himself in.

He got his head in, found his shoulders jammed, moved them in sidewise, and was inside as far as his waist. He could see nothing ahead. Something soft and clammy touched his mouth; he saw a dark frond moving against the grayish rock, and panic filled him. He thought of octopuses, of clinging weed. He pushed himself out backward and caught a glimpse, as he retreated, of a harmless tentacle of seaweed drifting in the mouth of the tunnel. But it was enough. He reached the sunlight, swam to shore, and lay on the diving rock. He looked down into the blue well of water. He knew he must find his way through that cave, or hole, or tunnel, and out the other side.

First, he thought, he must learn to control his breathing. He let himself down into the water with another big stone in his arms, so that he could lie effortlessly on the bottom of the sea. He counted. One, two, three. He counted steadily. He could hear the movement of blood in his chest. Fifty-one, fifty-two. . . . His chest was hurting. He let go of the rock and went up into the air. He saw that the sun was low. He rushed to the villa and found his mother at her supper. She said only "Did you enjoy yourself?" and he said "Yes."

All night the boy dreamed of the water-filled cave in the rock, and as soon as breakfast was over he went to the bay.

That night, his nose bled badly. For hours he had been underwater, learning to hold his breath, and now he felt weak and dizzy. His mother said, "I shouldn't overdo things, darling, if I were you."

That day and the next, Jerry exercised his lungs as if everything, the whole of his life, all that he would become, depended upon it. Again his nose bled at night, and his mother insisted on his coming with her the next day. It was a torment to him to waste a day of his careful self-training, but he stayed with her on that other beach, which now seemed a place for small children, a place where his mother might lie safe in the sun. It was not his beach.

He did not ask for permission, on the following day, to go to his beach. He went, before his mother could consider the complicated rights and wrongs of the matter. A day's rest, he discovered, had improved his count by ten. The big boys had made the passage while he counted a hundred and sixty. He had been counting fast, in his fright. Probably now, if he tried, he could get through that long tunnel, but he was not going to try yet. A curious, most unchildlike persistence, a controlled impatience, made him wait. In the meantime, he lay underwater on the white sand, littered now by stones he had brought down from the upper air, and studied the entrance to the tunnel. He knew every jut and corner of it, as far as it was possible to see. It was as if he already felt its sharpness about his shoulders.

He sat by the clock in the villa, when his mother was not near, and checked his time. He was incredulous and then proud to find he could hold his breath without strain for two minutes. The words "two minutes," authorized by the clock, brought close the adventure that was so necessary to him.

In another four days, his mother said casually one morning, they must go home. On the day before they left, he would do it. He would do it if it killed him, he said defiantly to himself. But two days before they were to leave—a day of triumph when he increased his count by fifteen—his nose bled so badly that he turned dizzy and had to lie limply over the big rock like a bit of seaweed, watching the thick red blood flow on to the rock and trickle slowly down to the sea. He was frightened. Supposing he died there, trapped? Supposing—his head went around, in the hot sun, and he almost gave up. He thought he would return to the house and lie down, and next summer, perhaps, when he had another year's growth in him—*then* he would go through the hole.

But even after he had made the decision, or thought he had, he found himself sitting up on the rock and looking down into the water; and he knew that now, this moment, when his nose had only just stopped bleeding, when his head was still sore and throbbing—this was the moment when he would try. If he did not do it now, he never would. He was trembling with fear that he would not go; and he was trembling with horror at that long, long tunnel under the rock, under the sea. Even in the open sunlight, the barrier rock seemed very wide and very heavy; tons of rock pressed down on where he would go. If he died there, he would lie until one day—perhaps not before next year—those big boys would swim into it and find it blocked.

He put on his goggles, fitted them tight, tested the vacuum. His hands were shaking. Then he chose the biggest stone he could carry and slipped over the edge of the rock until half of him was in the cool, enclosing water and half in the hot sun. He looked up once at the empty sky, filled his lungs once, twice, and then sank fast to the bottom with the stone. He let it go and began to count. He took the edges of the hole in his hands and drew himself into it, wriggling his shoulders in sidewise as he remembered he must, kicking himself along with his feet.

Soon he was clear inside. He was in a small rock-bound hole filled with yellowish-gray water. The water was pushing him up against the roof. The roof was sharp and pained his back. He pulled himself along with his hands—fast, fast—and used his legs as levers. His head knocked against something; a sharp pain dizzied him. Fifty, fifty-one, fifty-two. . . . He was without light, and the water seemed to press upon him with the weight of rock. Seventy-one, seventy-two. . . . There was no strain on his lungs. He felt like an inflated balloon, his lungs were so light and easy, but his head was pulsing.

He was being continually pressed against the sharp roof, which felt slimy as well as sharp. Again he thought of octopuses, and wondered if the tunnel might be filled with weed that could tangle him. He gave himself a panicky, convulsive kick forward, ducked his head, and swam. His feet and hands moved freely, as if in open water. The hole must have widened out. He thought he must be swimming fast, and he was frightened of banging his head if the tunnel narrowed.

A hundred, a hundred and one. . . . The water paled. Victory filled him. His lungs were beginning to hurt. A few more strokes and he would be out. He was counting wildly; he said a hundred and fifteen, and then, a long time later, a hundred and fifteen again. The water was a clear jewel-green all around him. Then he saw, above his head, a crack running up through the rock. Sunlight was falling through it, showing the clean, dark rock of the tunnel, a single mussel shell, and darkness ahead.

He was at the end of what he could do. He looked up at the crack as if it were filled with air and not water, as if he could put his mouth to it to draw in air. A hundred and fifteen, he heard himself say inside his head—but he had said that long ago. He must go on into the blackness ahead, or he would drown. His head was swelling, his lungs cracking. A hundred and fifteen, a hundred and fifteen pounded through his head, and he feebly clutched at rocks in the dark, pulling himself forward, leaving the brief space of sunlit water behind. He felt he was dying. He was no longer quite conscious. He struggled on in the darkness between lapses into unconsciousness. An immense, swelling pain filled his head, and then the darkness cracked with an explosion of green light. His hands, groping forward, met nothing; and his feet, kicking back, propelled him out into the open sea.

He drifted to the surface, his face turned up to the air. He was gasping like a fish. He felt he would sink now and drown; he could not swim the few feet back to the rock. Then he was clutching it and pulling himself up on to it. He lay face down, gasping. He could see nothing but a red-veined, clotted dark. His eyes must have burst, he thought; they were full of blood. He tore off his goggles and a gout of blood went into the sea. His nose was bleeding, and the blood had filled the goggles.

He scooped up handfuls of water from the cool, salty sea, to splash on his face, and did not know whether it was blood or salt water he tasted. After a time, his heart quieted, his eyes cleared, and he sat up. He could see the local boys diving and playing half a mile away. He did not want them. He wanted nothing but to get back home and lie down.

In a short while, Jerry swam to shore and climbed slowly up the path to the villa. He flung himself on his bed and slept, waking at the sound of feet on the path outside. His mother was coming back. He rushed to the bathroom, thinking she must not see his face with bloodstains, or tearstains, on it. He came out of the bathroom and met her as she walked into the villa, smiling, her eyes lighting up.

"Have a nice morning?" she asked, laying her hand on his warm brown shoulder a moment.

"Oh, yes, thank you," he said.

"You look a bit pale." And then, sharp and anxious, "How did you bang your head?"

"Oh, just banged it," he told her.

She looked at him closely. He was strained; his eyes were glazed-looking. She was worried. And then she said to herself, Oh, don't fuss! Nothing can happen. He can swim like a fish.

They sat down to lunch together.

"Mummy," he said, "I can stay under water for two minutes —three minutes, at least." It came bursting out of him.

"Can you, darling?" she said. "Well, I shouldn't overdo it. I don't think you ought to swim any more today."

She was ready for a battle of wills, but he gave in at once. It was no longer of the least importance to go to the bay.

1. What is the boy's antagonist in the story?
2. Why does the boy decide to take on the challenge of swimming through the tunnel?
3. What role does his mother play in the decision? The local boys?
4. Why is the swim itself described in so much detail?
5. How is the boy changed by his experience?

Three
Character

Character is the term for the people in fiction, the heroes and villains, allies and enemies, love interests and comic reliefs. Plot, in fact, can be thought of as character in action. Often the key to understanding a story is learning the motivation of a particular character—why did he or she perform an action, react in a certain way? As analysts of character, readers behave like amateur psychologists, trying to imagine the inner workings of the characters' minds, based on their behavior and appearance. For many readers, getting to know fictional characters is the very purpose of reading stories. Characters are the human element in the story; they appeal to our curiosity and our sympathy.

Characters in fiction vary greatly, depending on the roles they play in the story. Some are presented very superficially. All we get is a quick glimpse of them, from the outside, so that we see only surface, not interior life. These characters usually play minor roles. Other characters, usually the main agents of the action, we get to know in great depth, as layer after layer of psychological complexity is revealed. These are the great characters of traditional, realistic fiction. They are so richly portrayed that they often seem to be more real and more memorable than the living people we know. In contrast, some contemporary fiction presents even main characters as only a surface, in the conviction that the surfaces of others are all we have available to us in the real world and may be all that exists anyway. Characters also differ in their ability to change. Some are completely static—once they are pegged as a personality at the beginning of the story, they will never change. Others change radically—in fact, the point of many stories is a dramatic change that a character experiences.

In traditional stories there is a typical hierarchy of characters, based on how much of our interest and sympathy they demand. *Central characters* are those whose fates we observe. They are the protagonist or the antagonist, or are otherwise central to the plot. As the action of the story progresses, we are watching how they behave, how the consequences of actions change them. Often readers identify with these characters very closely, so that the death or destruction of a character seems to the reader like the loss of a personal friend. Central characters are sometimes accompanied by *foil characters,* whose function is to bring out some trait in the main character. For example, in a Western the hero often has a sidekick, usually a comic character who brings out the hero's human side. *Minor characters* provide needed functions, such as local color, reminding us of the social and regional setting of the story. Others are mere pawns in the game of the plot, necessary only to the movement of the action. A taxi, for example, needs a driver, who might appear in one sentence of the story. Minor characters are not developed nearly as fully as the central characters, and thus do not demand our sympathy and curiosity.

Reading the Signs

For many readers, curiosity fuels their interest in characters. Stories provide almost laboratory conditions for thinking about how we get to know others. In reading a story we encounter a great deal of information about characters, from which we have to achieve a grasp of their personalities. We move from a character's looks, movements, facial expressions, clothing, and possessions, to a judgment about inner qualities. Some stories do much of this work for us, describing those inner qualities directly, but more frequently we must do virtually all of the work. The story will provide details of action and appearance, and ask us to fill in the larger pattern. Readers, then, cooperate in the creation of the characters, actively imagining what the story only suggests. Most readers, for example, form a detailed visual image of important characters, even if the story doesn't describe them at all.

Every detail about a character is potentially significant. In our relationships with other people we judge their personality on the basis of observation. The same is true in fiction. The way a character walks, for example, is important—some people stride with authority, some shamble in fear. Dress is significant—we guess at social class, income, and personality on the basis of clothing. The kind of car a character drives, the kind of home he or she lives in, all are signs that suggest the kind of person we are dealing with. Even the movement of an eyebrow in the midst of a conversation can show us how a character is responding. Perhaps most important of all, we rely on speech, or as it is called in fiction, **dialogue,** to point us to the character's inner life. As readers we need to make sense of these signs, to see if they fit together into a coherent pattern or if they suggest contradictions in the character's personality.

How do we do this? How are actions, gestures, styles of speech meaningful? When we see a man in a checked hunting jacket, we assume that he is an outdoorsman, a rugged guy. We have in our mind the differences between that coat and a car coat, or a tailored wool topcoat, and each of those coats suggests the kind of person who would wear it. That is to say that coats are a kind of social code that all of us in our culture know. Each kind of coat can be a sign for a kind of person, and if we know the code we can make the judgment. Now, these signs are extremely specific and complex. That checked hunting jacket may be on someone who is also wearing a shirt and tie, dress slacks, and city shoes. In this case we wouldn't think "hunter," but we might guess that we're looking at a yuppie who buys from an L. L. Bean catalog and comes no closer to nature than his front lawn. That guess would come from the fact that "shirt and tie" is a sign for professional work and status. Whenever we are trying to get to know someone, many such codes are at work, making sense of the huge numbers of signs that a person displays.

These codes are specific to a given culture. Only those who know the codes can read the signs. If an African writer describes a certain combination of traditional and modern clothes, those of us outside the culture can only guess at the meanings they convey. To turn it around, it would be hard for anyone but an American of our time to judge what kind of person would wear a Yankees cap in California, or what kind of person owns a Jeep Wrangler. But those of us who know the codes can assemble the signs into a portrait of the person. The signs may or may not add up to a coherent, unified personality. They may point in contradictory directions. But they are always suggestive, always pointing to a meaning, a personal style.

Understanding the Codes

In addition to these outward signs, fiction also presents its readers with a way of knowing that doesn't exist in our real-world relationships. It can give us the inner life of the characters directly. The story can tell us what the characters are thinking or feeling even if they cannot express it themselves. It can tell us their dreams in great detail, for example, even if the characters cannot remember the next morning. We can experience characters as if we lived within their minds and bodies, while in reality we are always on the outside, guessing at what's going on inside the minds of other people. Even if people tell us what they are feeling, they may not be able to express it all or even understand themselves well. In fiction, though, the story is capable of total knowledge. The interior of a character can be open to us directly. Even in this case, however, we cannot overlook the role of cultural codes in our understanding. For example, we will still fit the characters into one of the systems of personality types that we have learned through our own experience and education. They might be introverted or extroverted, schizophrenic or neurotic. These labels are products of our society's thinking, codes that shape the way we make sense of people and characters.

Cultural codes are very powerful. Although we think we treat people as unique individuals, the actual process of coming to know them, at least at first, requires putting them into categories according to the signs they send out. Even readers who consider themselves passive are involved in this process. We can do this in a clumsy way, simply labeling people or characters without paying attention to subtle details, or we can realize that the signs are always complex and often contradictory. The guy who drives a Porsche may also dress like a nerd. In all but the simplest characters the signs have this kind of complexity, and they resist simple labeling. Great characters are elusive. We can't pin them down and fit them into easy categories. They keep surprising us, overturning our expectations about them and sending out so many signs that their complexity can't be reduced.

The process of characterization requires an active role for readers. The writer can decide which signs the character should communicate, but you must make sense of those signs, by means of the cultural codes you have taken in. That does not mean that you can create a character in any shape you want. The codes always restrain you. But it does mean that different readers will fill in the patterns that the signs suggest in different ways. Making sense of the signs is a complex task, one that does not have an objective standard of truth to judge it by. After all, a character does not exist outside of someone's reading experience; we can't check our reading against the character's objective nature. So part of the job of active readers is to explain their interpretation of a character. What are the signs you have noticed? What codes make sense of them? What sense of the character's personality emerges from the signs? In explaining how you constructed your vision of the character, you can see into the heart of the story, see how words on a page can evoke the subtle reality of a complex being. Words have that power, but only when active readers perform their task.

READINGS

John Steinbeck (1902–1968)

THE CHRYSANTHEMUMS

The high grey-flannel fog of winter closed off the Salinas Valley from the sky and from all the rest of the world. On every side it sat like a lid on the mountains and made of the great valley a closed pot. On the broad, level land floor the gang ploughs bit deep and left the black earth shining like metal where the shares had cut. On the foot-hill ranches across the Salinas River, the yellow stubble fields seemed to be bathed in pale cold sunshine, but there was no sunshine in the valley now in December. The thick willow scrub along the river flamed with sharp and positive yellow leaves.

It was a time of quiet and of waiting. The air was cold and tender. A light wind blew up from the southwest so that the farmers were mildly hopeful of a good rain before long; but fog and rain do not go together.

Across the river, on Henry Allen's foot-hill ranch there was little work to be done, for the hay was cut and stored and the orchards were ploughed up to receive the rain deeply when it should come. The cattle on the higher slopes were becoming shaggy and rough-coated.

Elisa Allen, working in her flower garden, looked down across the yard and saw Henry, her husband, talking to two men in business suits. The three of them stood by the tractor-shed, each man with one foot on the side of the little Fordson. They smoked cigarettes and studied the machine as they talked.

Elisa watched them for a moment and then went back to her work. She was thirty-five. Her face was lean and strong and her eyes were as clear as water. Her figure looked blocked and heavy in her gardening costume, a man's black hat pulled low down over her eyes, clod-hopper shoes, a figured print dress almost completely covered by a big corduroy apron with four big pockets to hold the snips, the trowel and scratcher, the seeds and the knife she worked with. She wore heavy leather gloves to protect her hands while she worked.

She was cutting down the old year's chrysanthemum stalks with a pair of short and powerful scissors. She looked down toward the men by the tractor-shed now and then. Her face was eager and mature and handsome; even her work with the scissors was over-eager, over-powerful. The chrysanthemum stems seemed too small and easy for her energy.

She brushed a cloud of hair out of her eyes with the back of her glove, and left a smudge of earth on her cheek in doing it. Behind her stood the neat white farmhouse with red geraniums close-banked around it as high as the windows. It was a hard-swept-looking little house, with hard-polished windows, and a clean mud-mat on the front steps.

Elisa cast another glance toward the tractor-shed. The strangers were getting into their Ford coupé. She took off a glove and put her strong fingers down into the forest of new green chrysanthemum sprouts that were growing around the old roots. She spread the leaves and looked down among the close-growing stems. No aphids were there, no sow bugs or snails or cutworms. Her terrier fingers destroyed such pests before they could get started.

Elisa started at the sound of her husband's voice. He had come near quietly, and he leaned over the wire fence that protected her flower garden from cattle and dogs and chickens.

"At it again," he said. "You've got a strong new crop coming."

Elisa straightened her back and pulled on the gardening glove again. "Yes. They'll be strong this coming year." In her tone and on her face there was a little smugness.

"You've got a gift with things," Henry observed. "Some of those yellow chrysanthemums you had this year were ten inches across. I wish you'd work out in the orchard and raise some apples that big."

Her eyes sharpened. "Maybe I could do it, too. I've a gift with things, all right. My mother had it. She could stick anything in the ground and make it grow. She said it was having planters' hands that knew how to do it."

"Well, it sure works with flowers," he said.

"Henry, who were those men you were talking to?"

"Why, sure, that's what I came to tell you. They were from the Western Meat Company. I sold those thirty head of three-year-old steers. Got nearly my own price, too."

"Good," she said. "Good for you."

"And I thought," he continued, "I thought how it's Saturday afternoon, and we might go into Salinas for dinner at a restaurant, and then to a picture show—to celebrate, you see."

"Good," she repeated. "Oh, yes. That will be good."

Henry put on his joking tone. "There's fights tonight. How'd you like to go to the fights?"

"Oh, no," she said breathlessly. "No, I wouldn't like fights."

"Just fooling, Elisa. We'll go to a movie. Let's see. It's two now. I'm going to take Scotty and bring down those steers from the hill. It'll take us maybe two hours. We'll go in town about five and have a dinner at the Cominos Hotel. Like that?"

"Of course I'll like it. It's good to eat away from home."

"All right, then. I'll go get up a couple of horses."

She said: "I'll have plenty of time to transplant some of these sets, I guess."

She heard her husband calling Scotty down by the barn. And a little later she saw the two men ride up the pale yellow hillside in search of the steers.

There was a little square sandy bed kept for rooting the chrysanthemums. With her trowel she turned the soil over and over, and smoothed it and patted it firm. Then she dug ten parallel trenches to receive the sets. Back at the chrysanthemum bed she pulled out the little crisp shoots, trimmed off the leaves of each one with her scissors and laid it on a small orderly pile.

A squeak of wheels and plod of hoofs came from the road. Elisa looked up. The country road ran along the dense bank of willows and cottonwoods that bordered the river, and up this road came a curious vehicle, curiously drawn. It was an old spring-wagon, with a round canvas top on it like the cover of a prairie schooner. It was drawn by an old bay horse and a little grey-and-white burro. A big stubble-bearded man sat between the cover flaps and drove the crawling team. Underneath the wagon, between the hind wheels, a lean and rangy mongrel dog walked sedately. Words were painted on the canvas, in clumsy, crooked letters. "Pots, pans, knives, sisors, lawn mores, Fixed." Two rows of articles, and the triumphantly definitive "Fixed" below. The black paint had run down in little sharp points beneath each letter.

Elisa, squatting on the ground, watched to see the crazy, loose-jointed wagon pass by. But it didn't pass. It turned into the farm road in front of her house, crooked old wheels skirling and squeaking. The rangy dog darted from between the wheels and ran ahead. Instantly, the two ranch shepherds flew out at him. Then all three stopped, and with stiff and quivering tails, with taut straight legs, with ambassadorial dignity, they slowly circled, sniffing daintily. The caravan pulled up to Elisa's wire fence and stopped. Now the newcomer dog, feeling outnumbered, lowered his tail and retired under the wagon with raised hackles and bared teeth.

The man on the wagon seat called out: "That's a bad dog in a fight when he gets started."

Elisa laughed. "I see he is. How soon does he generally get started?"

The man caught up her laughter and echoed it heartily. "Sometimes not for weeks and weeks," he said. He climbed stiffly down, over the wheel. The horse and the donkey drooped like unwatered flowers.

Elisa saw that he was a very big man. Although his hair and beard were greying, he did not look old. His worn black suit was wrinkled and spotted with grease. The laughter had disappeared from his face and eyes the moment his laughing voice ceased. His eyes were dark, and they were full of the brooding that gets in the eyes of teamsters and of sailors. The calloused hands he rested on the wire fence were cracked, and every crack was a black line. He took off his battered hat.

"I'm off my general road, ma'am," he said. "Does this dirt road cut over across the river to the Los Angeles highway?"

Elisa stood up and shoved the thick scissors in her apron pocket. "Well, yes, it does, but it winds around and then fords the river. I don't think your team could pull through the sand."

He replied with some asperity: "It might surprise you what them beasts can pull through."

"When they get started?" she asked.

He smiled for a second. "Yes. When they get started."

"Well," said Elisa, "I think you'll save time if you go back to the Salinas road and pick up the highway there."

He drew a big finger down the chicken wire and made it sing. "I ain't in any hurry, ma'am. I go from Seattle to San Diego and back every year. Takes all my time. About six months each way. I aim to follow nice weather."

Elisa took off her gloves and stuffed them in the apron pocket with the scissors. She touched the under edge of her man's hat, searching for fugitive hairs. "That sounds like a nice kind of way to live," she said.

He leaned confidentially over the fence. "Maybe you noticed the writing on my wagon. I mend pots and sharpen knives and scissors. You got any of them things to do?"

"Oh, no," she said quickly. "Nothing like that." Her eyes hardened with resistance.

"Scissors is the worst thing," he explained. "Most people just ruin scissors trying to sharpen 'em, but I know how. I got a special tool. It's a little bobbit kind of thing, and patented. But it sure does the trick."

"No. My scissors are all sharp."

"All right, then. Take a pot," he continued earnestly, "a bent pot, or a pot with a hole. I can make it like new so you don't have to buy no new ones. That's a saving for you."

"No," she said shortly. "I tell you I have nothing like that for you to do."

His face fell to an exaggerated sadness. His voice took on a whining undertone. "I ain't had a thing to do today. Maybe I won't have no supper tonight. You see I'm off my regular road. I know folks on the highway clear from Seattle to San Diego. They save their things for me to sharpen up because they know I do it so good and save them money."

"I'm sorry," Elisa said irritably. "I haven't anything for you to do."

His eyes left her face and fell to searching the ground. They roamed about until they came to the chrysanthemum bed where she had been working. "What's them plants, ma'am?"

The irritation and resistance melted from Elisa's face. "Oh, those are chrysanthemums, giant whites and yellows. I raise them every year, bigger than anybody around here."

"Kind of a long-stemmed flower? Looks like a quick puff of colored smoke?" he asked.

"That's it. What a nice way to describe them."

"They smell kind of nasty till you get used to them," he said.

"It's a good bitter smell," she retorted, "not nasty at all."

He changed his tone quickly. "I like the smell myself."

"I had ten-inch blooms this year," she said.

The man leaned farther over the fence. "Look. I know a lady down the road a piece, has got the nicest garden you ever seen. Got nearly every kind of flower but no chrysanthemums. Last time I was mending a copper-bottom washtub for her (that's a hard job but I do it good), she said to me: 'If you ever run acrost some nice chrysanthemums I wish you'd try to get me a few seeds.' That's what she told me."

Elisa's eyes grew alert and eager. "She couldn't have known much about chrysanthemums. You can raise them from seed, but it's much easier to root the little sprouts you see there."

"Oh," he said. "I s'pose I can't take none to her, then."

"Why yes you can," Elisa cried. "I can put some in damp sand, and you can carry them right along with you. They'll take root in the pot if you keep them damp. And then she can transplant them."

"She'd sure like to have some, ma'am. You say they're nice ones?"

"Beautiful," she said. "Oh, beautiful." Her eyes shone. She tore off the battered hat and shook out her dark pretty hair. "I'll put them in a flowerpot, and you can take them right with you. Come into the yard."

While the man came through the picket gate Elisa ran excitedly along the geranium-bordered path to the back of the house. And she returned carrying a big red flowerpot. The gloves were forgotten now. She kneeled on the ground by the starting bed and dug up the sandy soil with her fingers and scooped it into the bright new flowerpot. Then she picked up the little pile of shoots she had prepared. With her strong fingers she pressed them into the sand and tamped around them with her knuckles. The man stood over her. "I'll tell you what to do," she said. "You remember so you can tell the lady."

"Yes. I'll try to remember."

"Well, look. These will take root in about a month. Then she must set them out, about a foot apart in good rich earth like this, see?" She lifted a handful of dark soil for him to look at. "They'll grow fast and tall. Now remember this: In July tell her to cut them down, about eight inches from the ground."

"Before they bloom?" he asked.

"Yes, before they bloom." Her face was tight with eagerness. "They'll grow right up again. About the last of September the buds will start."

She stopped and seemed perplexed. "It's the budding that takes the most care," she said hesitantly. "I don't know how to tell you." She looked deep into his eyes, searchingly. Her mouth opened a little, and she seemed to be listening. "I'll try to tell you," she said. "Did you ever hear of planting hands?"

"Can't say I have, ma'am."

"Well, I can only tell you what it feels like. It's when you're picking off the buds you don't want. Everything goes right down into your fingertips. You watch your fingers work. They do it themselves. You can feel how it is. They pick and pick the buds. They never make a mistake. They're with the plant. Do you see? Your fingers and the plant. You can feel that, right up your arm. They know. They never make a mistake. You can feel it. When you're like that you can't do anything wrong. Do you see that? Can you understand that?"

She was kneeling on the ground looking up at him. Her breast swelled passionately.

The man's eyes narrowed. He looked away self-consciously. "Maybe I know," he said. "Sometimes in the night in the wagon there—"

Elisa's voice grew husky. She broke in on him: "I've never lived as you do, but I know what you mean. When the night is dark—why, the stars are sharp-pointed, and there's quiet. Why, you rise up and up! Every pointed star gets driven into your body. It's like that. Hot and sharp and—lovely."

Kneeling there, her hand went out toward his legs in the greasy black trousers. Her hesitant fingers almost touched the cloth. Then her hand dropped to the ground. She crouched low like a fawning dog.

He said: "It's nice, just like you say. Only when you don't have no dinner, it ain't."

She stood up then, very straight, and her face was ashamed. She held the flowerpot out to him and placed it gently in his arms. "Here. Put it in your wagon, on the seat, where you can watch it. Maybe I can find something for you to do."

At the back of the house she dug in the can pile and found two old and battered aluminum saucepans. She carried them back and gave them to him. "Here, maybe you can fix these."

His manner changed. He became professional. "Good as new I can fix them." At the back of his wagon he set a little anvil, and out of an oily toolbox dug a small machine hammer. Elisa came through the gate to watch him while he pounded out the dents in the kettles. His mouth grew sure and knowing. At a difficult part of the work he sucked his underlip.

"You sleep right in the wagon?" Elisa asked.

"Right in the wagon, ma'am. Rain or shine. I am dry as a cow in there."

"It must be nice," she said. "It must be very nice. I wish women could do such things."

"It ain't the right kind of a life for a woman."

Her upper lip raised a little, showing her teeth. "How do you know? How can you tell?" she said.

"I don't know, ma'am," he protested. "Of course I don't know. Now here's your kettles, done. You don't have to buy no new ones."

"How much?"

"Oh, fifty cents'll do. I keep my prices down and my work good. That's why I have all them satisfied customers up and down the highway."

Elisa brought him a fifty-cent piece from the house and dropped it in his hand. "You might be surprised to have a rival some time. I can sharpen scissors, too. And I can beat the dents out of little pots. I could show you what a woman might do."

He put his hammer back in the oily box and shoved the little anvil out of sight. "It would be a lonely life for a woman, ma'am, and a scarey life, too, with animals creeping under the wagon all night." He climbed over the single-tree, steadying himself with a hand on the burro's white rump. He settled himself in the seat, picked up the lines. "Thank you kindly ma'am," he said. "I'll do like you told me; I'll go back and catch the Salinas road."

"Mind," she called, "if you're long in getting there, keep the sand damp."

"Sand, ma'am? . . . Oh, sure. You mean around the chrysanthemums. Sure I will." He clucked his tongue. The beasts leaned luxuriously into their collars. The mongrel dog took his place between the back wheels. The wagon turned and crawled out the entrance road and back the way it had come, along the river.

Elisa stood in front of her wire fence watching the slow progress of the caravan. Her shoulders were straight, her head thrown back, her eyes half-closed, so that the scene came vaguely into them. Her lips moved silently, forming the words "Good-bye—good-bye."

Then she whispered: "That's a bright direction. There's a glowing there." The sound of her whisper startled her. She shook herself free and looked about to see whether anyone had been listening. Only the dogs had heard. They lifted their heads toward her from their sleeping in the dust, and then stretched out their chins and settled asleep again. Elisa turned and ran hurriedly into the house.

In the kitchen she reached behind the stove and felt the water tank. It was full of hot water from the noonday cooking. In the bathroom she tore off her soiled clothes and flung them into the corner. And then she scrubbed herself with a little block of pumice, legs and thighs, loins and chest and arms, until her skin was scratched and red. When she had dried herself she stood in front of a mirror in her bedroom and looked at her body. She tightened her stomach and threw out her chest. She turned and looked over her shoulder at her back.

After a while she began to dress, slowly. She put on her newest underclothing and her nicest stockings and the dress which was the symbol of her prettiness. She worked carefully on her hair, pencilled her eyebrows and rouged her lips.

Before she was finished she heard the little thunder of hoofs and the shouts of Henry and his helper as they drove the red steers into the corral. She heard the gate bang shut and set herself for Henry's arrival.

His step sounded on the porch. He entered the house calling: "Elisa, where are you?"

"In my room, dressing. I'm not ready. There's hot water for your bath. Hurry up. It's getting late."

When she heard him splashing in the tub, Elisa laid his dark suit on the bed, and shirt and socks and tie beside it. She stood his polished shoes on the floor beside the bed. Then she went to the porch and sat primly and stiffly down. She looked toward the river road where the willow-line was still yellow with frosted leaves so that under the high grey fog they seemed a thin band of sunshine. This was the only color in the grey afternoon. She sat unmoving for a long time. Her eyes blinked rarely.

Henry came banging out of the door, shoving his tie inside his vest as he came. Elisa stiffened and her face grew tight. Henry stopped short and looked at her. "Why—why, Elisa. You look so nice!"

"Nice? You think I look nice? What do you mean by 'nice'?"

Henry blundered on. "I don't know. I mean you look different, strong and happy."

"I am strong? Yes, strong. What do you mean 'strong'?"

He looked bewildered. "You're playing some kind of a game," he said helplessly. "It's a kind of a play. You look strong enough to break a calf over your knee, happy enough to eat it like a watermelon."

For a second she lost her rigidity. "Henry! Don't talk like that.

You didn't know what you said." She grew complete again. "I'm strong," she boasted. "I never knew before how strong."

Henry looked down toward the tractor-shed, and when he brought his eyes back to her, they were his own again. "I'll get out the car. You can put on your coat while I'm starting."

Elisa went into the house. She heard him drive to the gate and idle down his motor, and then she took a long time to put on her hat. She pulled it here and pressed it there. When Henry turned the motor off she slipped into her coat and went out.

The little roadster bounced along on the dirt road by the river, raising the birds and driving the rabbits into the brush. Two cranes flapped heavily over the willowline and dropped into the river-bed.

Far ahead on the road Elisa saw a dark speck. She knew.

She tried not to look as they passed it, but her eyes would not obey. She whispered to herself sadly: "He might have thrown them off the road. That wouldn't have been much trouble, not very much. But he kept the pot," she explained. "He had to keep the pot. That's why he couldn't get them off the road."

The roadster turned a bend and she saw the caravan ahead. She swung full around toward her husband so she could not see the little covered wagon and the mis-matched team as the car passed them.

In a moment it was over. The thing was done. She did not look back.

She said loudly, to be heard above the motor: "It will be good, tonight, a good dinner."

"Now you've changed again," Henry complained. He took one hand from the wheel and patted her knee. "I ought to take you in to dinner oftener. It would be good for both of us. We get so heavy out on the ranch."

"Henry," she asked, "could we have wine at dinner?"

"Sure we could. Say! That will be fine."

She was silent for a while; then she said: "Henry, at those prize-fights, do the men hurt each other very much?"

"Sometimes a little, not often. Why?"

"Well, I've read how they break noses, and blood runs down their chests. I've read how the fighting gloves get heavy and soggy with blood."

He looked around at her. "What's the matter, Elisa? I didn't know you read things like that." He brought the car to a stop, then turned to the right over the Salinas River bridge.

"Do any women ever go to the fights?" she asked.

"Oh, sure, some. What's the matter, Elisa? Do you want to go? I don't think you'd like it, but I'll take you if you really want to go."

She relaxed limply in the seat. "Oh, no. No, I don't want to go. I'm sure I don't." Her face was turned away from him. "It will be enough if we can have wine. It will be plenty." She turned up her coat collar so he could not see that she was crying weakly—like an old woman.

1. Elisa is the main character of the story. How does the story get us to feel sympathy for her?
2. What problems does she face?
3. Why does she react so strongly to the actions of the tinker?
4. The tinker could be thought of as a foil character. What does he reveal to us about Elisa?
5. What role does Henry play in the story?
6. Why does seeing the flowers on the road affect Elisa so deeply?
7. How is she changed by the whole experience?

Virginia Woolf (1882–1941)

MOMENTS OF BEING
"Slater's Pins Have No Points"

"Slater's pins have no points—don't you always find that?" said Miss Craye, turning round as the rose fell out of Fanny Wilmot's dress, and Fanny stooped, with her ears full of the music, to look for the pin on the floor.

The words gave her an extraordinary shock, as Miss Craye struck the last chord of the Bach fugue. Did Miss Craye actually go to Slater's and buy pins then, Fanny Wilmot asked herself, transfixed for a moment. Did she stand at the counter waiting like anybody else, and was she given a bill with coppers wrapped in it, and did she slip them into her purse and then, an hour later, stand by her dressing table and take out the pins? What need had she of pins? For she was not so much dressed as cased, like a beetle compactly in its sheath, blue in winter, green in summer. What need had she of pins—Julia Craye—who lived, it seemed, in the cool glassy world of Bach fugues, playing to herself what she liked, and only consenting to take one or two pupils at the Archer Street College of Music (so the Principal, Miss Kingston, said) as a special favour to herself, who had "the greatest admiration for her in every way." Miss Craye was left badly off, Miss Kingston was afraid, at her brother's death. Oh, they used to have such lovely things, when they lived at Salisbury, and her brother Julius was, of course, a very well-known man: a famous archaeologist. It was a great privilege to stay with them, Miss Kingston said ("My family had always known them—they were regular Canterbury people," Miss Kingston said), but a little frightening for a child;

one had to be careful not to slam the door or bounce into the room unexpectedly. Miss Kingston, who gave little character sketches like this on the first day of term while she received cheques and wrote out receipts for them, smiled here. Yes, she had been rather a tomboy; she had bounced in and set all those green Roman glasses and things jumping in their case. The Crayes were not used to children. The Crayes were none of them married. They kept cats; the cats, one used to feel, knew as much about the Roman urns and things as anybody.

"Far more than I did!" said Miss Kingston brightly, writing her name across the stamp in her dashing, cheerful, full-bodied hand, for she had always been practical. That was how she made her living, after all.

Perhaps then, Fanny Wilmot thought, looking for the pin, Miss Craye said that about "Slater's pins having no points," at a venture. None of the Crayes had ever married. She knew nothing about pins—nothing whatever. But she wanted to break the spell that had fallen on the house; to break the pane of glass which separated them from other people. When Polly Kingston, that merry little girl, had slammed the door and made the Roman vases jump, Julius, seeing that no harm was done (that would be his first instinct) looked, for the case was stood in the window, at Polly skipping home across the fields; looked with the look his sister often had, that lingering, driving look.

"Stars, sun, moon," it seemed to say, "the daisy in the grass, fires, frost on the window-pane, my heart goes out to you. But," it always seemed to add, "you break, you pass, you go." And simultaneously it covered the intensity of both these states of mind with "I can't reach you—I can't get at you," spoken wistfully, frustratedly. And the stars faded, and the child went. That was the kind of spell that was the glassy surface, that Miss Craye wanted to break by showing, when she had played Bach beautifully as a reward to a favourite pupil (Fanny Wilmot knew that she was Miss Craye's favourite pupil), that she, too, knew, like other people, about pins. Slater's pins had no points.

Yes, the "famous archaeologist" had looked like that too. "The famous archaeologist"—as she said that, endorsing cheques, ascertaining the day of the month, speaking so brightly and frankly, there was in Miss Kingston's voice an indescribable tone which hinted at something odd; something queer in Julius Craye; it was the very same thing that was odd perhaps in Julia too. One could have sworn, thought Fanny Wilmot, as she looked for the pin, that at parties, meetings (Miss Kingston's father was a clergyman), she had picked up some piece of gossip, or it might only have been a smile, or a tone when his name was mentioned, which had given her "a feeling" about Julius Craye. Needless to say, she had never spoken about it to anybody. Probably she scarcely knew what she meant by it. But whenever she spoke of Julius, or heard him mentioned, that was the first thing that came to mind; and it was a seductive thought; there was something odd about Julius Craye.

It was so that Julia looked too, as she sat half turned on the music stool, smiling. It's on the field, it's on the pane, it's in the sky —beauty; and I can't get at it; I can't have it—I, she seemed to add, with that little clutch of the hand which was so characteristic, who adore it so passionately, would give the whole world to possess it! And she picked up the carnation which had fallen on the floor, while Fanny searched for the pin. She crushed it, Fanny felt, voluptuously in her smooth veined hands stuck about with water-coloured rings set in pearls. The pressure of her fingers seemed to increase all that was most brilliant in the flower; to set it off; to make it more frilled, fresh, immaculate. What was odd in her, and perhaps in her brother, too, was that this crush and grasp of the finger was combined with a perpetual frustration. So it was even now with the carnation. She had her hands on it; she pressed it; but she did not possess it, enjoy it, not entirely and altogether.

None of the Crayes had married, Fanny Wilmot remembered. She had in mind how one evening when the lesson had lasted longer than usual and it was dark, Julia Craye had said "it's the use of men, surely, to protect us," smiling at her that same odd smile, as she stood fastening her cloak, which made her, like the flower, conscious to her finger tips of youth and brilliance, but, like the flower, too, Fanny suspected, made her feel awkward.

"Oh, but I don't want protection," Fanny had laughed, and when Julia Craye, fixing on her that extraordinary look, had said she was not so sure of that, Fanny positively blushed under the admiration in her eyes.

It was the only use of men, she had said. Was it for that reason then, Fanny wondered, with her eyes on the floor, that she had never married? After all, she had not lived all her life in Salisbury. "Much the nicest part of London," she had said once, "(but I'm speaking of fifteen or twenty years ago) is Kensington. One was in the Gardens in ten minutes—it was like the heart of the country. One could dine out in one's slippers without catching cold. Kensington—it was like a village then, you know," she had said.

Here she broke off, to denounce acridly the draughts in the Tubes.

"It was the use of men," she had said, with a queer wry acerbity. Did that throw any light on the problem why she had not married? One could imagine every sort of scene in her youth, when with her good blue eyes, her straight firm nose, her air of cool distinction, her piano playing, her rose flowering with chaste passion in the bosom of her muslin dress, she had attracted first the young men to whom such things, the china tea cups and the silver candlesticks and the inlaid table, for the Crayes had such nice things, were wonderful; young men not sufficiently distinguished; young men of the cathedral town with ambitions. She had attracted them first, and then her brother's friends from Oxford or Cambridge. They would come down in the summer; row her on the river; continue the argument about Browning by letter; and arrange perhaps, on the rare occasions when she stayed in London, to show her—Kensington Gardens?

"Much the nicest part of London—Kensington (I'm speaking of fifteen or twenty years ago)," she had said once. One was in the Gardens in ten minutes—in the heart of the country. One could make that yield what one liked, Fanny Wilmot thought, single out, for instance, Mr. Sherman, the painter, an old friend of hers; make him call for her, by appointment, one sunny day in June; take her to have tea under the trees. (They had met, too, at those parties to which one tripped in slippers without fear of catching cold.) The aunt or other elderly relative was to wait there while they looked at the Serpentine. They looked at the Serpentine. He may have rowed her across. They compared it with the Avon. She would have considered the comparison very furiously. Views of rivers were important to her. She sat hunched a little, a little angular, though she was graceful then, steering. At the critical moment, for he had determined that he must speak now—it was his only chance of getting her alone—he was speaking with his head turned at an absurd angle, in his great nervousness, over his shoulder—at that very moment she interrupted fiercely. He would have them into the Bridge, she cried. It was a moment of horror, of disillusionment, of revelation, for both of them. I can't have it, I can't possess it, she thought. He could not see why she had come then. With a great splash of his oar he pulled the boat round. Merely to snub him? He rowed her back and said good-bye to her.

The setting of that scene could be varied as one chose, Fanny Wilmot reflected. (Where had that pin fallen?) It might be Ravenna; or Edinburgh, where she had kept house for her brother. The scene could be changed; and the young man and the exact manner of it all, but one thing was constant—her refusal, and her frown, and her anger with herself afterwards, and her argument, and her relief—yes, certainly her immense relief. The very next day, perhaps, she would get up at six, put on her cloak, and walk all the way from Kensington to the river. She was so thankful that she had not sacrificed her right to go and look at things when they are at their best—before people are up, that is to say she could have her breakfast in bed if she liked. She had not sacrificed her independence.

Yes, Fanny Wilmot smiled, Julia had not endangered her habits. They remained safe; and her habits would have suffered if she had married. "They're ogres," she had said one evening, half laughing, when another pupil, a girl lately married, suddenly bethinking her that she would miss her husband, had rushed off in haste.

"They're ogres," she had said, laughing grimly. An ogre would have interfered perhaps with breakfast in bed; with walks at dawn down to the river. What would have happened (but one could hardly conceive this) had she had children? She took astonishing precautions against chills, fatigue, rich food, the wrong food, draughts, heated rooms, journeys in the Tube, for she could never determine which of these it was exactly that brought on those terrible headaches that gave her life the semblance of a battlefield. She was always engaged in outwitting the enemy, until it seemed as if the pursuit had its interest; could she have beaten the enemy finally she would have found life a little dull. As it was, the tug-of-war was perpetual—on the one side the nightingale or the view which she loved with passion—yes, for views and birds she felt nothing less than passion; on the other the damp path or the horrid long drag up a steep hill which would certainly make her good for nothing next day and bring on one of her headaches. When, therefore, from time to time, she managed her forces adroitly and brought off a visit to Hampton Court the week the crocuses—those glossy bright flowers were her favourite—were at their best, it was a victory. It was something that lasted; something that mattered for ever. She strung the afternoon on the necklace of memorable days, which was not too long for her to be able to recall this one or that one; this view, that city; to finger it, to feel it, to savour, sighing, the quality that made it unique.

"It was so beautiful last Friday," she said, "that I determined I must go there." So she had gone off to Waterloo on her great undertaking—to visit Hampton Court—alone. Naturally, but perhaps foolishly, one pitied her for the thing she never asked pity for (indeed she was reticent habitually, speaking of her health only as a warrior might speak of his foe)—one pitied her for always doing everything alone. Her brother was dead. Her sister was asthmatic. She found the climate of Edinburgh good for her. It was too bleak for Julia. Perhaps, too, she found the associations painful, for her brother, the famous archaeologist, had died there; and she had loved her brother. She lived in a little house off the Brompton Road entirely alone.

Fanny Wilmot saw the pin; she picked it up. She looked at Miss Craye. Was Miss Craye so lonely? No, Miss Craye was steadily, blissfully, if only for that moment, a happy woman. Fanny had surprised her in a moment of ecstasy. She sat there, half turned away from the piano, with her hands clasped in her lap holding the carnation upright, while behind her was the sharp square of the window, uncurtained, purple in the evening, intensely purple after the brilliant electric lights which burnt unshaded in the bare music room. Julia Craye, sitting hunched and compact holding her flower, seemed to emerge out of the London night, seemed to fling it like a cloak behind her, it seemed, in its bareness and intensity, the effluence of her spirit, something she had made which surrounded her. Fanny stared.

All seemed transparent, for a moment, to the gaze of Fanny Wilmot, as if looking through Miss Craye, she saw the very fountain of her being spurting its pure silver drops. She saw back and back into the past behind her. She saw the green Roman vases stood in their case; heard the choristers playing cricket; saw Julia quietly descend the curving steps on to the lawn; then saw her pour out tea beneath the cedar tree; softly enclosed the old man's hand in hers; saw her going round and about the corridors of that ancient Cathedral dwelling place with towels in her hand to mark them; lamenting, as she went, the pettiness of daily life; and slowly ageing, and putting away clothes when summer came, because at her age they were too bright to wear; and tending her father's sickness; and cleaving her way ever more definitely as her will stiffened towards her solitary goal; travelling frugally; counting the cost and measuring out of her tight shut purse the sum needed for this journey or for that old mirror; obstinately adhering, whatever people might say, in choosing her pleasures for herself. She saw Julia—

Julia blazed. Julia kindled. Out of the night she burnt like a dead white star. Julia opened her arms. Julia kissed her on the lips. Julia possessed it.

"Slater's pins have no points," Miss Craye said, laughing queerly and relaxing her arms, as Fanny Wilmot pinned the flower to her breast with trembling fingers.

1. What does Fanny know about Miss Craye's life? How does she create her images of Miss Craye?
2. How does Fanny move from observation to speculation about Miss Craye?
3. What is the significance of the phrase, "Slater's pins have no points"?
4. What is the "moment of ecstasy" that Fanny sees in Miss Craye at the end of the story?
5. Do you agree that Fanny sees the essence of Miss Craye's being?
6. What is the significance of Miss Craye's kiss?

Joyce Carol Oates (b. 1938)
WHERE ARE YOU GOING, WHERE HAVE YOU BEEN?

For Bob Dylan

Her name was Connie. She was fifteen and she had a quick, nervous giggling habit of craning her neck to glance into mirrors or checking other people's faces to make sure her own was all right. Her mother, who noticed everything and knew everything and who hadn't much reason any longer to look at her own face, always scolded Connie about it. "Stop gawking at yourself. Who are you? You think you're so pretty?" she would say. Connie would raise her eyebrows at these familiar old complaints and look right through her mother into a shadowy vision of herself as she was right at that moment: she knew she was pretty and that was everything. Her mother had been pretty once too, if you could believe those old snapshots in the album, but now her looks were gone and that was why she was always after Connie.

"Why don't you keep your room clean like your sister? How've you got your hair fixed—what the hell stinks? Hair spray? You don't see your sister using that junk."

Her sister June was twenty-four and still lived at home. She was a secretary in the high school Connie attended, and if that wasn't bad enough—with her in the same building—she was so plain and chunky and steady that Connie had to hear her praised all the time by her mother and her mother's sisters. June did this, June did that, she saved money and helped clean the house and cooked and Connie couldn't do a thing, her mind was all filled with trashy daydreams. Their father was away at work most of the time and when he came home he wanted supper and he read the newspaper at supper and after supper he went to bed. He didn't bother talking much to them, but around his bent head Connie's mother kept picking at her until Connie wished her mother was dead and she herself was dead and it was all over. "She makes me want to throw up sometimes," she complained to her friends. She had a high, breathless, amused voice that made everything she said sound a little forced, whether it was sincere or not.

There was one good thing: June went places with girl friends of hers, girls who were just as plain and steady as she, and so when Connie wanted to do that her mother had no objections. The father of Connie's best friend drove the girls the three miles to town and left them at a shopping plaza so they could walk through the stores or go to a movie, and when he came to pick them up at eleven he never bothered to ask what they had done.

They must have been familiar sights, walking around the shopping plaza in their shorts and flat ballerina slippers that always scuffed the sidewalk, with charm bracelets jingling on their thin wrists; they would lean together to whisper and laugh secretly if someone passed who amused or interested them. Connie had long dark blond hair that drew everyone's eye to it, and she wore part of it pulled up on her head and puffed out and the rest of it she let fall down her back. She wore a pull-over jersey blouse that looked one way when she was at home and another way when she was away from home. Everything about her had two sides to it, one for home and one for anywhere that was not home: her walk, which could be childlike and bobbing, or languid enough to make anyone think she was hearing music in her head; her mouth, which was pale and smirking most of the time, but bright and pink on these evenings out; her laugh, which was cynical and drawling at home—"Ha, ha, very funny,"—but high-pitched and nervous anywhere else, like the jingling of the charms on her bracelet.

Sometimes they did go shopping or to a movie, but sometimes they went across the highway, ducking fast across the busy road, to a drive-in restaurant where older kids hung out. The restaurant was shaped like a big bottle, though squatter than a real bottle, and on its cap was a revolving figure of a grinning boy holding a hamburger aloft. One night in midsummer they ran across, breathless with daring, and right away someone leaned out a car window and invited them over, but it was just a boy from high school they didn't like. It made them feel good to be able to ignore him. They went up through the maze of parked and cruising cars to the bright-lit, fly-infested restaurant, their faces pleased and expectant as if they were entering a sacred building that loomed up out of the night to give them what haven and blessing they yearned for. They sat at the counter and crossed their legs at the ankles, their thin shoulders rigid with excitement, and listened to the music that made everything so good: the music was always in the background, like music at a church service; it was something to depend upon.

A boy named Eddie came in to talk with them. He sat backwards on his stool, turning himself jerkily around in semicircles and then stopping and turning back again, and after a while he asked Connie if she would like something to eat. She said she would and so she tapped her friend's arm on the way out—her friend pulled her face up into a brave, droll look—and Connie said she would meet her at eleven, across the way. "I just hate to leave her like that," Connie said earnestly, but the boy said that she wouldn't be alone for long. So they went out to his car, and on the way Connie couldn't help but let her eyes wander over the windshields and faces all around her, her face gleaming with a joy that had nothing to do with Eddie or even this place; it might have been the music. She drew her shoulders up and sucked in her breath with the pure pleasure of being alive, and just at that moment she happened to glance at a face just a few feet from hers. It was a boy with shaggy black hair, in a convertible jalopy painted gold. He stared at her and then his lips widened into a grin. Connie slit her eyes at him and turned away, but she couldn't help glancing back and there he was, still watching her. He wagged a finger and laughed and said, "Gonna get you, baby," and Connie turned away again without Eddie noticing anything.

She spent three hours with him, at the restaurant where they ate hamburgers and drank Cokes in wax cups that were always sweating, and then down an alley a mile or so away, and when he left her off at five to eleven only the movie house was still open at the plaza. Her girl friend was there, talking with a boy. When Connie came up, the two girls smiled at each other and Connie said, "How was the movie?" and the girl said, "*You* should know." They rode off with the girl's father, sleepy and pleased, and Connie couldn't help but look back at the darkened shopping plaza with its big empty parking lot and its signs that were faded and ghostly now, and over at the drive-in restaurant where cars were still circling tirelessly. She couldn't hear the music at this distance.

Next morning June asked her how the movie was and Connie said, "So-so."

She and that girl and occasionally another girl went out several times a week, and the rest of the time Connie spent around the house—it was summer vacation—getting in her mother's way and thinking, dreaming about the boys she met. But all the boys fell back and dissolved into a single face that was not even a face but an idea, a feeling, mixed up with the urgent insistent pounding of the music and the humid night air of July. Connie's mother kept dragging her back to the daylight by finding things for her to do or saying suddenly, "What's this about the Pettinger girl?"

And Connie would say nervously, "Oh, her. That dope." She always drew thick clear lines between herself and such girls, and her mother was simple and kind enough to believe it. Her mother was so simple, Connie thought, that it was maybe cruel to fool her so much. Her mother went scuffling around the house in old bedroom slippers and complained over the telephone to one sister about the other, then the other called up and the two of them complained about the third one. If June's name was mentioned her mother's tone was approving, and if Connie's name was mentioned it was disapproving. This did not really mean she disliked Connie, and actually Connie thought that her mother preferred her to June just because she was prettier, but the two of them kept up a pretense of exasperation, a sense that they were tugging and struggling over something of little value to either of them. Sometimes, over coffee, they were almost friends, but something would come up—some vexation that was like a fly buzzing suddenly around their heads—and their faces went hard with contempt.

One Sunday Connie got up at eleven—none of them bothered with church—and washed her hair so it could dry all day long in the sun. Her parents and sister were going to a barbecue at an aunt's house and Connie said no, she wasn't interested, rolling her eyes to let her mother know just what she thought of it. "Stay home alone then," her mother said sharply. Connie sat out back in a lawn chair and watched them drive away, her father quiet and bald, hunched around so that he could back the car out, her mother with a look that was still angry and not at all softened through the windshield, and in the back seat poor old June, all dressed up as if she didn't know what a barbecue was, with all the running yelling kids and the flies. Connie sat with her eyes closed in the sun, dreaming and dazed with the warmth about her as if this were a kind of love, the caresses of love, and her mind slipped over onto thoughts of the boy she had been with the night before and how nice he had been, how sweet it always was, not the way someone like June would suppose but sweet, gentle, the way it was in movies and promised in songs; and when she opened her eyes she hardly knew where she was, the back yard ran off into weeds and a fence-like line of trees and behind it the sky was perfectly blue and still. The asbestos "ranch house" that was now three years old startled her—it looked small. She shook her head as if to get awake.

It was too hot. She went inside the house and turned on the radio to drown out the quiet. She sat on the edge of her bed, barefoot, and listened for an hour and a half to a program called XYZ Sunday Jamboree, record after record of hard, fast, shrieking songs she sang along with, interspersed by exclamations from "Bobby King": "An' look here, you girls at Napoleon's—Son and Charley want you to pay real close attention to this song coming up!"

And Connie paid close attention herself, bathed in a glow of slow-pulsed joy that seemed to rise mysteriously out of the music itself and lay languidly about the airless little room, breathed in and breathed out with each gentle rise and fall of her chest.

After a while she heard a car coming up the drive. She sat up at once, startled, because it couldn't be her father so soon. The gravel kept crunching all the way in from the road—the driveway was long—and Connie ran to the window. It was a car she didn't know. It was an open jalopy, painted a bright gold that caught the sunlight opaquely. Her heart began to pound and her fingers snatched at her hair, checking it, and she whispered, "Christ. Christ," wondering how bad she looked. The car came to a stop at the side door and the horn sounded four short taps, as if this were a signal Connie knew.

She went into the kitchen and approached the door slowly, then hung out the screen door, her bare toes curling off the step. There were two boys in the car and now she recognized the driver: he had shaggy, shabby black hair that looked crazy as a wig and he was grinning at her.

"I ain't late, am I?" he said.

"Who the hell do you think you are?" Connie said.

"Toldja I'd be out, didn't I?"

"I don't even know who you are."

She spoke sullenly, careful to show no interest or pleasure, and he spoke in a fast, bright monotone. Connie looked past him to the other boy, taking her time. He had fair brown hair, with a lock that fell onto his forehead. His sideburns gave him a fierce, embarrassed look, but so far he hadn't even bothered to glance at her. Both boys wore sunglasses. The driver's glasses were metallic and mirrored everything in miniature.

"You wanta come for a ride?" he said.

Connie smirked and let her hair fall loose over one shoulder.

"Don'tcha like my car? New paint job," he said. "Hey."

"What?"

"You're cute."

She pretended to fidget, chasing flies away from the door.

"Don'tcha believe me, or what?" he said.

"Look, I don't even know who you are," Connie said in disgust.

"Hey, Ellie's got a radio, see. Mine broke down." He lifted his friend's arm and showed her the little transistor radio the boy was holding, and now Connie began to hear the music. It was the same program that was playing inside the house.

"Bobby King?" she said.

"I listen to him all the time. I think he's great."

"He's kind of great," Connie said reluctantly.

"Listen, that guy's *great*. He knows where the action is."

Connie blushed a little, because the glasses made it impossible for her to see just what this boy was looking at. She couldn't decide if she liked him or if he was just a jerk, and so she dawdled in the doorway and wouldn't come down or go back inside. She said, "What's all that stuff painted on your car?"

"Can'tcha read it?" He opened the door very carefully, as if he were afraid it might fall off. He slid out just as carefully, planting his feet firmly on the ground, the tiny metallic world in his glasses slowing down like gelatine hardening, and in the midst of it Connie's bright green blouse. "This here is my name, to begin with," he said. ARNOLD FRIEND was written in tarlike black letters on the side, with a drawing of a round, grinning face that reminded Connie of a pumpkin, except it wore sunglasses. "I wanta introduce myself, I'm Arnold Friend and that's my real name and I'm gonna be your friend, honey, and inside the car's Ellie Oscar, he's kinda shy." Ellie brought his transistor radio up to his shoulder and balanced it there. "Now, these numbers are a secret code, honey," Arnold Friend explained. He read off the numbers 33, 19, 17 and raised his eyebrows at her to see what she thought of that, but she didn't think much of it. The left rear fender had been smashed and around it was written, on the gleaming gold background: DONE BY CRAZY WOMAN DRIVER. Connie had to laugh at that. Arnold Friend was pleased at her laughter and looked up at her. "Around the other side's a lot more—you wanta come and see them?"

"No."

"Why not?"

"Why should I?"

"Don'tcha wanta see what's on the car? Don'tcha wanta go for a ride?"

"I don't know."

"Why not?"

"I got things to do."

"Like what?"

"Things."

He laughed as if she had said something funny. He slapped his thighs. He was standing in a strange way, leaning back against the car as if he were balancing himself. He wasn't tall, only an inch or so taller than she would be if she came down to him. Connie liked the way he was dressed, which was the way all of them dressed: tight faded jeans stuffed into black, scuffed boots, a belt that pulled his waist in and showed how lean he was, and a white pull-over shirt that was a little soiled and showed the hard small muscles of his arms and shoulders. He looked as if he probably did hard work, lifting and carrying things. Even his neck looked muscular. And his face was a familiar face, somehow: the jaw and chin and cheeks slightly darkened because he hadn't shaved for a day or two, and the nose long and hawklike, sniffling as if she were a treat he was going to gobble up and it was all a joke.

"Connie, you ain't telling the truth. This is your day set aside for a ride with me and you know it" he said, still laughing. The way he straightened and recovered from his fit of laughing showed that it had been all fake.

"How do you know what my name is?" she said suspiciously.

"It's Connie."

"Maybe and maybe not."

"I know my Connie," he said, wagging his finger. Now she remembered him even better, back at the restaurant, and her cheeks warmed at the thought of how she had sucked in her breath just at the moment she passed him—how she must have looked to him. And he had remembered her. "Ellie and I come out here especially for you," he said. "Ellie can sit in back. How about it?"

"Where?"

"Where what?"

"Where're we going?"

He looked at her. He took off the sunglasses and she saw how pale the skin around his eyes was, like holes that were not in shadow but instead in light. His eyes were like chips of broken glass that catch the light in an amiable way. He smiled. It was as if the idea of going for a ride somewhere, to someplace, was a new idea to him.

"Just for a ride, Connie sweetheart."

"I never said my name was Connie," she said.

"But I know what it is. I know your name and all about you, lots of things," Arnold Friend said. He had not moved yet but stood still leaning back against the side of his jalopy. "I took a special interest in you, such a pretty girl, and found out all about you—like I know your parents and sister are gone somewheres and I know where and how long they're going to be gone, and I know who you were with last night, and your best girl friend's name is Betty. Right?"

He spoke in a simple lilting voice, exactly as if he were reciting the words to a song. His smile assured her that everything was fine. In the car Ellie turned up the volume on his radio and did not bother to look around at them.

"Ellie can sit in the back seat," Arnold Friend said. He indicated his friend with a casual jerk of his chin, as if Ellie did not count and she should not bother with him.

"How'd you find out all that stuff?" Connie said.

"Listen: Betty Schultz and Tony Fitch and Jimmy Pettinger and Nancy Pettinger," he said in a chant. "Raymond Stanley and Bob Hunter—"

"Do you know all those kids?"

"I know everybody."

"Look, you're kidding. You're not from around here."

"Sure."

"But—how come we never saw you before?"

"Sure you saw me before," he said. He looked down at his boots, as if he were a little offended. "You just don't remember."

"I guess I'd remember you," Connie said.

"Yeah?" He looked up at this, beaming. He was pleased. He began to mark time with the music from Ellie's radio, tapping his fists lightly together. Connie looked away from his smile to the car, which was painted so bright it almost hurt her eyes to look at it. She looked at the name, ARNOLD FRIEND. And up at the front fender was an expression that was familiar—MAN THE FLYING SAUCERS. It was an expression kids had used the year before but didn't use this year. She looked at it for a while as if the words meant something to her that she did not yet know.

"What're you thinking about? Huh?" Arnold Friend demanded. "Not worried about your hair blowing around in the car, are you?"

"No."

"Think I maybe can't drive good?"

"How do I know?"

"You're a hard girl to handle. How come?" he said. "Don't you know I'm your friend? Didn't you see me put my sign in the air when you walked by?"

"What sign?"

"My sign." And he drew an X in the air, leaning out toward her. They were maybe ten feet apart. After his hand fell back to his side the X was still in the air, almost visible. Connie let the screen door close and stood perfectly still inside it, listening to the music from her radio and the boy's blended together. She stared at Arnold Friend. He stood there so stiffly relaxed, pretending to be relaxed, with one hand idly on the door handle as if he were keeping himself up that way and had no intention of ever moving again. She recognized most things about him, the tight jeans that showed his thighs and buttocks and the greasy leather boots and the tight shirt, and even that slippery friendly smile of his, that sleepy dreamy smile that all the boys used to get across ideas they didn't want to put into words. She recognized all this and also the singsong way he talked, slightly mocking, kidding, but serious and a little melancholy, and she recognized the way he tapped one fist against the other in homage to the perpetual music behind him. But all these things did not come together.

She said suddenly, "Hey, how old are you?"

His smile faded. She could see then that he wasn't a kid, he was much older—thirty, maybe more. At this knowledge her heart began to pound faster.

"That's a crazy thing to ask. Can'tcha see I'm your own age?"

"Like hell you are."

"Or maybe a coupla years older. I'm eighteen."

"Eighteen?" she said doubtfully.

He grinned to reassure her and lines appeared at the corners of his mouth. His teeth were big and white. He grinned so broadly his eyes became slits and she saw how thick the lashes were, thick and black as if painted with a black tarlike material. Then, abruptly, he seemed to become embarrassed and looked over his shoulder at Ellie. "*Him,* he's crazy," he said. "Ain't he a riot? He's a nut, a real character." Ellie was still listening to the music. His sunglasses told nothing about what he was thinking. He wore a bright orange shirt unbuttoned halfway to show his chest, which was a pale, bluish chest and not muscular like Arnold Friend's. His shirt collar was turned up all around and the very tips of the collar pointed out past his chin as if they were protecting him. He was pressing the transistor radio up against his ear and sat there in a kind of daze, right in the sun.

"He's kinda strange," Connie said.

"Hey, she says you're kinda strange! Kinda strange!" Arnold Friend cried. He pounded on the car to get Ellie's attention. Ellie turned for the first time and Connie saw with shock that he wasn't a kid either—he had a fair, hairless face, cheeks reddened slightly as if the veins grew too close to the surface of his skin, the face of a forty-year-old baby. Connie felt a wave of dizziness rise in her at this sight and she stared at him as if waiting for something to change the shock of the moment, make it all right again. Ellie's lips kept shaping words, mumbling along with the words blasting in his ear.

"Maybe you two better go away," Connie said faintly.

"What? How come?" Arnold Friend cried. "We come out here to take you for a ride. It's Sunday." He had the voice of the man on the radio now. It was the same voice, Connie thought. "Don'tcha know it's Sunday all day? And honey, no matter who you were with last night, today you're with Arnold Friend and don't you forget it! Maybe you better step out here," he said, and this last was in a different voice. It was a little flatter, as if the heat was finally getting to him.

"No. I got things to do."

"Hey."

"You two better leave."

"We ain't leaving until you come with us."

"Like hell I am—"

"Connie, don't fool around with me. I mean—I mean, don't fool *around,*" he said, shaking his head. He laughed incredulously. He placed his sunglasses on top of his head, carefully, as if he were indeed wearing a wig, and brought the stems down behind his ears. Connie stared at him, another wave of dizziness and fear rising in her so that for a moment he wasn't even in focus but was just a blur standing there against his gold car, and she had the idea that he had driven up the driveway all right but had come from nowhere before that and belonged nowhere and that everything about him and even about the music that was so familiar to her was only half real.

"If my father comes and sees you—"

"He ain't coming. He's at a barbecue."

"How do you know that?"

"Aunt Tillie's. Right now they're—uh—they're drinking. Sitting around," he said vaguely, squinting as if he were staring all the way to town and over to Aunt Tillie's back yard. Then the vision seemed to get clearer and he nodded energetically. "Yeah. Sitting around. There's your sister in a blue dress, huh? And high heels, the poor sad bitch—nothing like you, sweetheart! And your mother's helping some fat woman with the corn, they're cleaning the corn—husking the corn—"

"What fat woman?" Connie cried.

"How do I know what fat woman, I don't know every goddamn fat woman in the world!" Arnold Friend laughed.

"Oh, that's Mrs. Hornsby. . . . Who invited her?" Connie said. She felt a little lightheaded. Her breath was coming quickly.

"She's too fat. I don't like them fat. I like them the way you are, honey," he said, smiling sleepily at her. They stared at each other for a while, through the screen door. He said softly, "Now, what you're going to do is this: you're going to come out that door. You're going to sit up front with me and Ellie's going to sit in the back, the hell with Ellie, right? This isn't Ellie's date. You're my date. I'm your lover, honey."

"What? You're crazy—"

"Yes, I'm your lover. You don't know what that is but you will," he said. "I know that too. I know all about you. But look: it's real nice and you couldn't ask for nobody better than me, or more polite. I always keep my word. I'll tell you how it is, I'm always nice at first, the first time. I'll hold you so tight you won't think you have to try to get away or pretend anything because you'll know you can't. And I'll come inside you where it's all secret and you'll give in to me and you'll love me—"

"Shut up! You're crazy!" Connie said. She backed away from the door. She put her hands up against her ears as if she'd heard something terrible, something not meant for her. "People don't talk like that, you're crazy," she muttered. Her heart was almost too big now for her chest and its pumping made sweat break out all over her. She looked out to see Arnold Friend pause and then take a step toward the porch, lurching. He almost fell. But, like a clever drunken man, he managed to catch his balance. He wobbled in his high boots and grabbed hold of one of the porch posts.

"Honey?" he said. "You still listening?"

"Get the hell out of here!"

"Be nice, honey. Listen."

"I'm going to call the police—"

He wobbled again and out of the side of his mouth came a fast spat curse, an aside not meant for her to hear. But even this "Christ!" sounded forced. Then he began to smile again. She watched this smile come, awkward as if he were smiling from inside a mask. His whole face was a mask, she thought wildly, tanned down to his throat but then running out as if he had plastered make-up on his face but had forgotten about his throat.

"Honey—? Listen, here's how it is. I always tell the truth and I promise you this: I ain't coming in that house after you."

"You better not! I'm going to call the police if you—if you don't—"

"Honey," he said, talking right through her voice, "honey, I'm not coming in there but you are coming out here. You know why?"

She was panting. The kitchen looked like a place she had never seen before, some room she had run inside but that wasn't good enough, wasn't going to help her. The kitchen window had never had a curtain, after three years, and there were dishes in the sink for her to do—probably—and if you ran your hand across the table you'd probably feel something sticky there.

"You listening, honey? Hey?"

"—going to call the police—"

"Soon as you touch the phone I don't need to keep my promise and can come inside. You won't want that."

She rushed forward and tried to lock the door. Her fingers were shaking. "But why lock it," Arnold Friend said gently, talking right into her face. "It's just a screen door. It's just nothing." One of his boots was at a strange angle, as if his foot wasn't in it. It pointed out to the left, bent at the ankle. "I mean, anybody can break through a screen door and glass and wood and iron or anything else if he needs to, anybody at all, and specially Arnold Friend. If the place got lit up with a fire, honey, you'd come runnin' out into my arms, right into my arms an' safe at home—like you knew I was your lover and'd stopped fooling around. I don't mind a nice shy girl but I don't like no fooling around." Part of those words were spoken with a slight rhythmic lilt, and Connie somehow recognized them—the echo of a song from last year, about a girl rushing into her boy friend's arms and coming home again—

Connie stood barefoot on the linoleum floor, staring at him. "What do you want?" she whispered.

"I want you," he said.

"What?"

"Seen you that night and thought, that's the one, yes sir. I never needed to look anymore."

"But my father's coming back. He's coming to get me. I had to wash my hair first—" She spoke in a dry, rapid voice, hardly raising it for him to hear.

"No, your daddy is not coming and yes, you had to wash your hair and you washed it for me. It's nice and shining and all for me. I thank you sweetheart," he said with a mock bow, but again he almost lost his balance. He had to bend and adjust his boots. Evidently his feet did not go all the way down; the boots must have been stuffed with something so that he would seem taller. Connie stared out at him and behind him at Ellie in the car, who seemed to be looking off toward Connie's right into nothing. This Ellie said, pulling the words out of the air one after another as if he were just discovering them, "You want me to pull out the phone?"

"Shut your mouth and keep it shut," Arnold Friend said, his face red from bending over or maybe from embarrassment because Connie had seen his boots. "This ain't none of your business."

"What—what are you doing? What do you want?" Connie said. "If I call the police they'll get you, they'll arrest you—"

"Promise was not to come in unless you touch that phone, and I'll keep that promise," he said. He resumed his erect position and tried to force his shoulders back. He sounded like a hero in a movie, declaring something important. But he spoke too loudly and it was as if he were speaking to someone behind Connie. "I ain't made plans for coming in that house where I don't belong but just for you to come out to me, the way you should. Don't you know who I am?"

"You're crazy," she whispered. She backed away from the door but did not want to go into another part of the house, as if this would give him permission to come through the door. "What do you . . . you're crazy, you. . . ."

"Huh? What're you saying, honey?"

Her eyes darted everywhere in the kitchen. She could not remember what it was, this room.

"This is how it is, honey: you come out and we'll drive away, have a nice ride. But if you don't come out we're gonna wait till your people come home and then they're all going to get it."

"You want that telephone pulled out?" Ellie said. He held the radio away from his ear and grimaced, as if without the radio the air was too much for him.

"I toldja shut up, Ellie," Arnold Friend said, "you're deaf, get a hearing aid, right? Fix yourself up. This little girl's no trouble and's gonna be nice to me, so Ellie keep to yourself, this ain't your date—right? Don't hem in on me, don't hog, don't crush, don't bird dog, don't trail me," he said in a rapid, meaningless voice, as if he were running through all the expressions he'd learned but was no longer sure which of them was in style, then rushing on to new ones, making them up with his eyes closed. "Don't crawl under my fence, don't squeeze in my chipmunk hole, don't sniff my glue, suck my popsicle, keep your own greasy fingers on yourself!" He shaded his eyes and peered in at Connie, who was backed against the kitchen table. "Don't mind him, honey, he's just a creep. He's a dope. Right? I'm the boy for you and like I said, you come out here nice like a lady and give me your hand, and nobody else gets hurt, I mean, your nice old bald-headed daddy and your mummy and your sister in her high heels. Because listen: why bring them in this?"

"Leave me alone," Connie whispered.

"Hey, you know that old woman down the road, the one with the chickens and stuff—you know her?"

"She's dead!"

"Dead? What? You know her?" Arnold Friend said.

"She's dead—"

"Don't you like her?"

"She's dead—she's—she isn't here any more—"

"But don't you like her, I mean, you got something against her?

Some grudge or something?" Then his voice dipped as if he were conscious of a rudeness. He touched the sunglasses perched up on top of his head as if to make sure they were still there. "Now, you be a good girl."

"What are you going to do?"

"Just two things, or maybe three," Arnold Friend said. "But I promise it won't last long and you'll like me the way you get to like people you're close to. You will. It's all over for you here, so come on out. You don't want your people in any trouble, do you?"

She turned and bumped against a chair or something, hurting her leg, but she ran into the back room and picked up the telephone. Something roared in her ear, a tiny roaring, and she was so sick with fear that she could do nothing but listen to it—the telephone was clammy and very heavy and her fingers groped down to the dial but were too weak to touch it. She began to scream into the phone, into the roaring. She cried out, she cried for her mother, she felt her breath start jerking back and forth in her lungs as if it were something Arnold Friend was stabbing her with again and again with no tenderness. A noisy sorrowful wailing rose all about her and she was locked inside it the way she was locked inside this house.

After a while she could hear again. She was sitting on the floor with her wet back against the wall.

Arnold Friend was saying from the door, "That's a good girl. Put the phone back.

She kicked the phone away from her.

"No, honey. Pick it up. Put it back right."

She picked it up and put it back. The dial tone stopped.

"That's a good girl. Now, you come outside."

She was hollow with what had been fear but what was now just an emptiness. All that screaming had blasted it out of her. She sat, one leg cramped under her, and deep inside her brain was something like a pinpoint of light that kept going and would not let her relax. She thought, I'm not going to see my mother again. She thought, I'm not going to sleep in my bed again. Her bright green blouse was all wet.

Arnold Friend said, in a gentle-loud voice that was like a stage voice, "The place where you came from ain't there any more, and where you had in mind to go is cancelled out. This place you are now—inside your daddy's house—is nothing but a cardboard box I can knock down any time. You know that and always did know it. You hear me?"

She thought, I have got to think. I have got to know what to do.

"We'll go out to a nice field, out in the country here where it smells so nice and it's sunny," Arnold Friend said. "I'll have my arms tight around you so you won't need to try to get away and I'll show you what love is like, what it does. The hell with this house! It looks solid all right," he said. He ran a fingernail down the screen and the noise did not make Connie shiver, as it would have the day before. "Now, put your hand on your heart, honey. Feel that? That feels solid too but we know better. Be nice to me, be sweet like you can because what else is there for a girl like you but to be sweet and pretty and give in?—and get away before her people come back?"

She felt her pounding heart. Her hand seemed to enclose it. She thought for the first time in her life that it was nothing that was hers, that belonged to her, but just a pounding, living thing inside this body that wasn't really hers either.

"You don't want them to get hurt," Arnold Friend went on. "Now, get up, honey. Get up all by yourself."

She stood.

"Now, turn this way. That's right. Come over here to me.—Ellie, put that away, didn't I tell you? You dope. You miserable creepy dope," Arnold Friend said. His words were not angry but only part of an incantation. The incantation was kindly. "Now, come out through the kitchen to me, honey, and let's see a smile, try it, you're a brave, sweet little girl and now they're eating corn and hot dogs cooked to bursting over an outdoor fire, and they don't know one thing about you and never did and honey, you're better than them because not one of them would have done this for you."

Connie felt the linoleum under her feet; it was cool. She brushed her hair back out of her eyes. Arnold Friend let go of the post tentatively and opened his arms for her, his elbows pointing in toward each other and his wrists limp, to show that this was an embarrassed embrace and a little mocking, he didn't want to make her self-conscious.

She put out her hand against the screen. She watched herself push the door slowly open as if she were back safe somewhere in the other doorway, watching this body and this head of long hair moving out into the sunlight where Arnold Friend waited.

"My sweet little blue-eyed girl," he said in a half-sung sigh that had nothing to do with her brown eyes but was taken up just the same by the vast, sunlit reaches of the land behind him and on all sides of him—so much land that Connie had never seen before and did not recognize except to know that she was going to it.

1. What signs does Connie communicate? How do we get to know her?
2. How does Arnold Friend use pop culture codes to construct his own character?
3. Arnold Friend becomes a symbolic character. What does he symbolize?
4. What is the effect of his supernatural qualities on his status as a character?

Four
Setting

How does an action have meaning in human relationships? What does it mean, for example, when someone drinks a beer? First off we might think it doesn't *mean* anything, that it's just a physical act. But it's also an act that always takes place within a specific social context and so it communicates something. For a seventeen-year-old at the prom it's a sign of defiance of authority. For a bunch of guys watching a football game it's a gesture of group feeling. For an alcoholic trying to dry out, it may be a betrayal of family and career. In all these cases the same action has a different meaning because it is part of a different situation. Think of the differences between drinking a beer at a bar and drinking a beer at a church picnic. In this case, where you are makes all the difference—where you are physically, and where you are socially.

In fiction, this concern for context and surroundings is described by the term **setting.** The setting of a story establishes a fictional world in which the characters act. Some stories are very careful to describe the natural surroundings, especially when they are exotic or beautiful. Other stories emphasize the interior spaces, houses and rooms, in which a story will develop. Describing the room a character lives in, for example, can tell the reader a lot about the character. Stories can also describe in great detail the social context in which an action occurs. A careful examination of the setting of the story can help us to see the significance of actions and understand the development of character.

Many stories are very careful to define the context in which an action occurs. An action doesn't take on meaning until we understand how it fits into the situation. In Flannery O'Connor's "Parker's Back," for example, a man has the face of Christ tattooed onto his back. Parker feels a strong religious emotion because of this action, but his wife sees it as a blasphemy. The plot pivots around the difference between what the act means to Parker and what it means within his family and social surroundings. O'Connor is careful to define exactly the religious and social context in which Parker finds himself. In this sense, a story like "Parker's Back" can teach us how difficult it is to understand an action fully. We need to know as much as possible about what surrounds an action in order to understand what it means, and this can be an enormous task. We can look at the social relationships of the characters, the exact situation in which the action occurs, the place it occurs, the history of the relationships between the characters, and so on. Actions always occur within a very complicated world of social and interpersonal forces.

Setting can also be crucial for understanding character formation. The question of how a character has become who he or she is can often be answered by looking at the family and social surroundings. In our society, we tend to think that each individual is solely responsible for his or her own development—but in fact there are many external factors that shape personality. The setting of a story can depict those factors in a way that makes clear how the character is affected by environment. It can show how family life shapes a child, how education affects a student, how the social class a character is born into limits or expands experience. Even the codes by which we all understand experience are themselves part of the social environment. None of these factors is chosen; they are simply given in an individual's life. Character development can, in fact, be thought of as the process by which the character succeeds or fails in coming to terms with these important, surrounding influences.

In a story like James Joyce's "Eveline," the character has been brought up in a very restrictive environment, and the crisis of the story concerns her reaction when she is offered the opportunity to escape it. Her action is the result of a choice, but she is deciding within a social situation in which she has been born and bred. For her, as for many characters, her surroundings are crucial for understanding her motives and her actions.

In some stories the setting is so powerful that it almost becomes a character itself. Especially in stories with a detailed and realistic natural setting, the characters may encounter nature as their antagonist, the force they must struggle against. In a story like Stephen Crane's "The Open Boat," the natural setting plays this role, and we watch the various characters respond to the changing role of the sea in their story. Nature, of course, is not always an antagonist. In many cases it is a source of comfort and calm, or it serves as a test of the characters' sensitivity. Characters experience nature in various ways, and seeing them deal with nature often tells us a lot about their personalities. Do they want to dominate nature or cooperate with it? Do they fear it or love it? Natural settings tend to reveal the basic elements of characters. Rather than adjusting to shifting social circumstances, characters often reveal hidden truths about themselves in the ways they deal with the natural world.

Creating the World

But setting is not just an aid to understanding plot and character. It is an important fictional element in its own right. For the term *setting* describes nothing less basic than the fictional world that the story creates. Stories ask readers to enter into a world that exists only in the story. The rules that organize that world may be quite similar to those of our world, but they may also be radically different. To take an obvious example, science fiction stories often ask us to imagine worlds that no human has ever seen. Fantasy stories ask us to imagine a world in which animals speak or dreams come to life. As readers, we make an agreement with the story that we will accept the premises of the world it creates, even if we know them to be impossible in our reality. If you're reading a fairy tale and when the princess pricks her finger and falls asleep for a hundred years your reaction is that such a thing can't happen, you are failing to accept the world of that story—and you will miss the pleasure of experiencing that different world and all you might learn from it.

In realistic fiction, the rules of our world work pretty well. We expect realistic fiction to remain within the real world and these expectations are not challenged. The realistic story may present us with unsettling actions or bizarre characters, but they exist in what we think of as the normal world. In fantastic fiction, however, our normal expectations don't do us any good. We have to build up new expectations, based on the rules of this new world. In these stories, we as readers need to suspend our own assumptions if we are to live imaginatively within the fictional world. There are even extreme cases in which the fictional world seems to have almost no rules, in which anything goes. In Donald Barthelme's "The Indian Uprising," the world of the story seems absurd. There may be some rules, but they are foreign to us. Faced with this kind of story, you can try desperately to make sense of the absurd, or you can sit back and enjoy the chaos. As we begin any story we have to orient ourselves to the new world, and be willing to cooperate with the story in imagining another reality.

Clearly, one of the reasons we read fiction is because it seems to take us out of our own world and into worlds that exist only in the imagination. In successful stories, that world is fully realized, so that we believe it is possible while we are reading it, even if we know it's absurd. Good readers can get absorbed into the world of the story, learning to enjoy the feel of a new terrain. Because of this experience of an alternate world, readers can gain a fresh view of their own surroundings, just as we can appreciate home better when we've traveled to other places. Many times we take our physical surroundings for granted. They are so familiar to us that we almost don't see them, and aren't aware of how they affect us. The rooms we live in, for example, affect our emotions and our outlook. Workspaces can support or undercut productivity. Our cities can become environments that promote fear and hopelessness. Reading stories and entering new worlds can make us aware of how these environmental factors affect us in our daily lives.

The same effect occurs on a larger social level. The social setting of a story is often very different from our own, so that it's a stretch of the mind for us to understand all the messages being flashed back and forth in the social scene. We have to imagine ourselves into another social class, or another country, or another time. And when we return we might have a different view of our own social situation. How much are we a product of our social circumstances? Do we realize how much they shape the ways we think? By experiencing other social situations and other ways of thinking we can come to know our own. As active readers, we can turn words on a page into an imaginary world as we read, and the experience of that fictional world can affect how we see our own world. Fiction helps us understand reality.

READINGS

Flannery O'Connor (1925–1964)

PARKER'S BACK

Parker's wife was sitting on the front porch floor, snapping beans. Parker was sitting on the step, some distance away, watching her sullenly. She was plain, plain. The skin on her face was thin and drawn as tight as the skin on an onion and her eyes were grey and sharp like the points of two icepicks. Parker understood why he had married her—he couldn't have got her any other way—but he couldn't understand why he stayed with her now. She was pregnant and pregnant women were not his favorite kind. Nevertheless, he stayed as if she had him conjured. He was puzzled and ashamed of himself.

The house they rented sat alone save for a single tall pecan tree on a high embankment overlooking a highway. At intervals a car would shoot past below and his wife's eyes would swerve suspiciously after the sound of it and then come back to rest on the newspaper full of beans in her lap. One of the things she did not approve of was automobiles. In addition to her other bad qualities, she was forever sniffing up sin. She did not smoke or dip, drink whiskey, use bad language or paint her face, and God knew some paint would have improved it, Parker thought. Her being against color, it was the more remarkable she had married him. Sometimes he supposed that she had married him because she meant to save him. At other times he had a suspicion that she actually liked everything she said she didn't. He could account for her one way or another; it was himself he could not understand.

She turned her head in his direction and said, "It's no reason you can't work for a man. It don't have to be a woman."

"Aw shut your mouth for a change," Parker muttered.

If he had been certain she was jealous of the woman he worked for he would have been pleased but more likely she was concerned with the sin that would result if he and the woman took a liking to each other. He had told her that the woman was a hefty young blond; in fact she was nearly seventy years old and too dried up to have an interest in anything except getting as much work out of him as she could. Not that an old woman didn't sometimes get an interest in a young man, particularly if he was as attractive as Parker felt he was, but this old woman looked at him the same way she looked at her old tractor—as if she had to put up with it because it was all she had. The tractor had broken down the second day Parker was on it and she had set him at once to cutting bushes, saying out of the side of her mouth to the nigger, "Everything he touches, he breaks." She also asked him to wear his shirt when he worked; Parker had removed it even though the day was not sultry; he put it back on reluctantly.

This ugly woman Parker married was his first wife. He had had other women but he had planned never to get himself tied up legally. He had first seen her one morning when his truck broke down on the highway. He had managed to pull it off the road into a neatly swept yard on which sat a peeling two-room house. He got out and opened the hood of the truck and began to study the motor. Parker had an extra sense that told him when there was a woman nearby watching him. After he had leaned over the motor a few minutes, his neck began to prickle. He cast his eye over the empty yard and porch of the house. A woman he could not see was either nearby beyond a clump of honeysuckle or in the house, watching him out the window.

Suddenly Parker began to jump up and down and fling his hand about as if he had mashed it in the machinery. He doubled over and held his hand close to his chest. "God dammit!" he hollered, "Jesus Christ in hell! Jesus God Almighty damn! God dammit to hell!" he went on, flinging out the same few oaths over and over as loud as he could.

Without warning a terrible bristly claw slammed the side of his face and he fell backwards on the hood of the truck. "You don't talk no filth here!" a voice close to him shrilled.

Parker's vision was so blurred that for an instant he thought he had been attacked by some creature from above, a giant hawk-eyed angel wielding a hoary weapon. As his sight cleared, he saw before him a tall raw-boned girl with a broom.

"I hurt my hand," he said. "I HURT my hand." He was so incensed that he forgot that he hadn't hurt his hand. "My hand may be broke," he growled although his voice was still unsteady.

"Lemme see it," the girl demanded.

Parker stuck out his hand and she came closer and looked at it. There was no mark on the palm and she took the hand and turned it over. Her own hand was dry and hot and rough and Parker felt himself jolted back to life by her touch. He looked more closely at her. I don't want nothing to do with this one, he thought.

The girl's sharp eyes peered at the back of the stubby reddish hand she held. There emblazoned in red and blue was a tattooed eagle perched on a cannon. Parker's sleeve was rolled to the elbow. Above the eagle a serpent was coiled about a shield and in the spaces between the eagle and the serpent there were hearts, some with arrows through them. Above the serpent there was a spread hand of cards. Every space on the skin of Parker's arm, from wrist to elbow, was covered in some loud design. The girl gazed at this with an almost stupefied smile of shock, as if she had accidentally grasped a poisonous snake; she dropped the hand.

"I got most of my other ones in foreign parts," Parker said. "These here I mostly got in the United States. I got my first one when I was only fifteen year old."

"Don't tell me," the girl said, "I don't like it. I ain't got any use for it."

"You ought to see the ones you can't see," Parker said and winked.

Two circles of red appeared like apples on the girl's cheeks and softened her appearance. Parker was intrigued. He did not for a minute think that she didn't like the tattoos. He had never yet met a woman who was not attracted to them.

Parker was fourteen when he saw a man in a fair, tattooed from head to foot. Except for his loins which were girded with a panther hide, the man's skin was patterned in what seemed from Parker's distance—he was near the back of the tent, standing on a bench—a single intricate design of brilliant color. The man, who was small and sturdy, moved about on the platform, flexing his muscles so that the arabesque of men and beasts and flowers on his skin appeared to have a subtle motion of its own. Parker was filled with emotion, lifted up as some people are when the flag passes. He was a boy whose mouth habitually hung open. He was heavy and earnest, as ordinary as a loaf of bread. When the show was over, he had remained standing on the bench, staring where the tattooed man had been, until the tent was almost empty.

Parker had never before felt the least motion of wonder in himself. Until he saw the man at the fair, it did not enter his head that there was anything out of the ordinary about the fact that he existed. Even then it did not enter his head, but a peculiar unease settled in him. It was as if a blind boy had been turned so gently in a different direction that he did not know his destination had been changed.

He had his first tattoo some time after—the eagle perched on the cannon. It was done by a local artist. It hurt very little, just enough to make it appear to Parker to be worth doing. This was peculiar too for before he had thought that only what did not hurt was worth doing. The next year he quit school because he was sixteen and could. He went to the trade school for a while, then he quit the trade school and worked for six months in a garage. The only reason he worked at all was to pay for more tattoos. His mother worked in a laundry and could support him, but she would not pay for any tattoo except her name on a heart, which he had put on, grumbling. However, her name was Betty Jean and nobody had to know it was his mother. He found out that the tattoos were attractive to the kind of girls he liked but who had never liked him before. He began to drink beer and get in fights. His mother wept over what was becoming of him. One night she dragged him off to a revival with her, not telling him where they were going. When he saw the big lighted church, he jerked out of her grasp and ran. The next day he lied about his age and joined the navy.

Parker was large for the tight sailor's pants but the silly white cap, sitting low on his forehead, made his face by contrast look thoughtful and almost intense. After a month or two in the navy, his mouth ceased to hang open. His features hardened into the features of a man. He stayed in the navy five years and seemed a natural part of the grey mechanical ship, except for his eyes, which were the same pale slate-color as the ocean and reflected the immense spaces around him as if they were a microcosm of the mysterious sea. In port Parker wandered about comparing the run-down places he was in to Birmingham, Alabama. Everywhere he went he picked up more tattoos.

He had stopped having lifeless ones like anchors and crossed rifles. He had a tiger and a panther on each shoulder, a cobra coiled about a torch on his chest, hawks on his thighs, Elizabeth II and Philip over where his stomach and liver were respectively. He did not care much what the subject was so long as it was colorful; on his abdomen he had a few obscenities but only because that seemed the proper place for them. Parker would be satisfied with each tattoo about a month, then something about it that had attracted him would wear off. Whenever a decent-sized mirror was available, he would get in front of it and study his overall look. The effect was not of one intricate arabesque of colors but of something haphazard and botched. A huge dissatisfaction would come over him and he would go off and find another tattooist and have another space filled up. The front of Parker was almost completely covered but there were no tattoos on his back. He had no desire for one anywhere he could not readily see it himself. As the space on the front of him for tattoos decreased, his dissatisfaction grew and became general.

After one of his furloughs, he didn't go back to the navy but remained away without official leave, drunk, in a rooming house in a city he did not know. His dissatisfaction, from being chronic and latent, had suddenly become acute and raged in him. It was as if the panther and the lion and the serpents and the eagles and the hawks had penetrated his skin and lived inside him in a raging warfare. The navy caught up with him, put him in the brig for nine months and then gave him a dishonorable discharge.

After that Parker decided that country air was the only kind fit to breathe. He rented the shack on the embankment and bought the old truck and took various jobs which he kept as long as it suited him. At the time he met his future wife, he was buying apples by the bushel and selling them for the same price by the pound to isolated homesteaders on back country roads.

"All that there," the woman said, pointing to his arm, "is no better than what a fool Indian would do. It's a heap of vanity." She seemed to have found the word she wanted. "Vanity of vanities," she said.

Well what the hell do I care what she thinks of it? Parker asked himself, but he was plainly bewildered. "I reckon you like one of these better than another anyway," he said, dallying until he thought of something that would impress her. He thrust the arm back at her. "Which you like best?"

"None of them," she said, "but the chicken is not as bad as the rest."

"What chicken?" Parker almost yelled.

She pointed to the eagle.

"That's an eagle," Parker said. "What fool would waste their time having a chicken put on themself?"

"What fool would have any of it?" the girl said and turned away. She went slowly back to the house and left him there to get going. Parker remained for almost five minutes, looking agape at the dark door she had entered.

The next day he returned with a bushel of apples. He was not one to be outdone by anything that looked like her. He liked women with meat on them, so you didn't feel their muscles, much less their old bones. When he arrived, she was sitting on the top step and the yard was full of children, all as thin and poor as herself; Parker remembered it was Saturday. He hated to be making up to a woman when there were children around, but it was fortunate he had brought the bushel of apples off the truck. As the children approached him to see what he carried, he gave each child an apple and told it to get lost; in that way he cleared out the whole crowd.

The girl did nothing to acknowledge his presence. He might have been a stray pig or goat that had wandered into the yard and she too tired to take up the broom and send it off. He set the bushel of apples down next to her on the step. He sat down on a lower step.

"Hep yourself," he said, nodding at the basket; then he lapsed into silence.

She took an apple quickly as if the basket might disappear if she didn't make haste. Hungry people made Parker nervous. He had always had plenty to eat himself. He grew very uncomfortable. He reasoned he had nothing to say so why should he say it? He could not think now why he had come or why he didn't go before he wasted another bushel of apples on the crowd of children. He supposed they were her brothers and sisters.

She chewed the apple slowly but with a kind of relish of concentration, bent slightly but looking out ahead. The view from the porch stretched off across a long incline studded with iron weed and across the highway to a vast vista of hills and one small mountain. Long views depressed Parker. You look out into space like that and you begin to feel as if someone were after you, the navy or the government or religion.

"Who them children belong to, you?" he said at length.

"I ain't married yet," she said. "They belong to momma." She said it as if it were only a matter of time before she would be married.

Who in God's name would marry her? Parker thought.

A large barefooted woman with a wide gap-toothed face appeared in the door behind Parker. She had apparently been there for several minutes.

"Good evening," Parker said.

The woman crossed the porch and picked up what was left of the bushel of apples. "We thank you," she said and returned with it into the house.

"That your old woman?" Parker muttered.

The girl nodded. Parker knew a lot of sharp things he could have said like "You got my sympathy," but he was gloomily silent. He just sat there, looking at the view. He thought he must be coming down with something.

"If I pick up some peaches tomorrow I'll bring you some," he said.

"I'll be much obliged to you," the girl said.

Parker had no intention of taking any basket of peaches back there but the next day he found himself doing it. He and the girl had almost nothing to say to each other. One thing he did say was, "I ain't got any tattoo on my back."

"What you got on it?" the girl said.

"My shirt," Parker said. "Haw."

"Haw, haw," the girl said politely.

Parker thought he was losing his mind. He could not believe for a minute that he was attracted to a woman like this. She showed not the least interest in anything but what he brought until he appeared the third time with two cantaloups. "What's your name?" she asked.

"O. E. Parker," he said.

"What does the O. E. stand for?"

"You can just call me O. E.," Parker said. "Or Parker. Don't nobody call me by my name."

"What's it stand for?" she persisted.

"Never mind," Parker said. "What's yours?"

"I'll tell you when you tell me what them letters are the short of," she said. There was just a hint of flirtatiousness in her tone and it went rapidly to Parker's head. He had never revealed the name to any man or woman, only to the files of the navy and the government, and it was on his baptismal record which he got at the age of a month; his mother was a Methodist. When the name leaked out of the navy files, Parker narrowly missed killing the man who used it.

"You'll go blab it around," he said.

"I'll swear I'll never tell anybody," she said. "On God's holy word I swear it."

Parker sat for a few minutes in silence. Then he reached for the girl's neck, drew her ear close to his mouth and revealed the name in a low voice.

"Obadiah," she whispered. Her face slowly brightened as if the name came as a sign to her. "Obadiah," she said.

The name still stank in Parker's estimation.

"Obadiah Elihue," she said in a reverent voice.

"If you call me that aloud, I'll bust your head open," Parker said. "What's yours?"

"Sarah Ruth Cates," she said.

"Glad to meet you, Sarah Ruth," Parker said.

Sarah Ruth's father was a Straight Gospel preacher but he was away, spreading it in Florida. Her mother did not seem to mind his attention to the girl so long as he brought a basket of something with him when he came. As for Sarah Ruth herself, it was plain to Parker after he had visited three times that she was crazy about him. She liked him even though she insisted that pictures on the skin were vanity of vanities and even after hearing him curse, and even after she had asked him if he was saved and he had replied that he didn't see it was anything in particular to save him from. After that, inspired, Parker had said, "I'd be saved enough if you was to kiss me."

She scowled. "That ain't being saved," she said.

Not long after that she agreed to take a ride in his truck. Parker parked it on a deserted road and suggested to her that they lie down together in the back of it.

"Not until after we're married," she said—just like that.

"Oh that ain't necessary," Parker said and as he reached for her, she thrust him away with such force that the door of the truck came off and he found himself flat on his back on the ground. He made up his mind then and there to have nothing further to do with her.

They were married in the County Ordinary's office because Sarah Ruth thought churches were idolatrous. Parker had no opinion about that one way or the other. The Ordinary's office was lined with cardboard file boxes and record books with dusty yellow slips of paper hanging on out of them. The Ordinary was an old woman with red hair who had held office for forty years and looked as dusty as her books. She married them from behind the iron-grill of a stand-up desk and when she finished, she said with a flourish, "Three dollars and fifty cents and till death do you part!" and yanked some forms out of a machine.

Marriage did not change Sarah Ruth a jot and it made Parker gloomier than ever. Every morning he decided he had had enough and would not return that night; every night he returned. Whenever Parker couldn't stand the way he felt, he would have another tattoo, but the only surface left on him now was his back. To see a tattoo on his own back he would have to get two mirrors and stand between them in just the correct position and this seemed to Parker a good way to make an idiot of himself. Sarah Ruth who, if she had had better sense, could have enjoyed a tattoo on his back, would not even look at the ones he had elsewhere. When he attempted to point out especial details of them, she would shut her eyes tight and turn her back as well. Except in total darkness, she preferred Parker dressed and with his sleeves rolled down.

"At the judgement seat of God, Jesus is going to say to you, 'What you been doing all your life besides have pictures drawn all over you?' " she said.

"You don't fool me none," Parker said, "you're just afraid that hefty girl I work for'll like me so much she'll say, 'Come on, Mr. Parker, let's you and me . . .' "

"You're tempting sin," she said, "and at the judgement seat of

God you'll have to answer for that too. You ought to go back to selling the fruits of the earth."

Parker did nothing much when he was at home but listen to what the judgement seat of God would be like for him if he didn't change his ways. When he could, he broke in with tales of the hefty girl he worked for. " 'Mr. Parker,' " he said she said, 'I hired you for your brains.' " (She had added, "So why don't you use them?")

"And you should have seen her face the first time she saw me without my shirt," he said. " 'Mr. Parker,' she said, 'you're a walking panner-rammer!' " This had, in fact, been her remark but it had been delivered out of one side of her mouth.

Dissatisfaction began to grow so great in Parker that there was no containing it outside of a tattoo. It had to be his back. There was no help for it. A dim half-formed inspiration began to work in his mind. He visualized having a tattoo put there that Sarah Ruth would not be able to resist—a religious subject. He thought of an open book with HOLY BIBLE tattooed under it and an actual verse printed on the page. This seemed just the thing for a while; then he began to hear her say, "Ain't I already got a real Bible? What you think I want to read the same verse over and over for when I can read it all?" He needed something better even than the Bible! He thought about it so much that he began to lose sleep. He was already losing flesh—Sarah Ruth just threw food in the pot and let it boil. Not knowing for certain why he continued to stay with a woman who was both ugly and pregnant and no cook made him generally nervous and irritable, and he developed a little tic in the side of his face.

Once or twice he found himself turning around abruptly as if someone were trailing him. He had had a granddaddy who had ended in the state mental hospital, although not until he was seventy-five, but as urgent as it might be for him to get a tattoo, it was just as urgent that he get exactly the right one to bring Sarah Ruth to heel. As he continued to worry over it, his eyes took on a hollow preoccupied expression. The old woman he worked for told him that if he couldn't keep his mind on what he was doing, she knew where she could find a fourteen-year-old colored boy who could. Parker was too preoccupied even to be offended. At any time previous, he would have left her then and there, saying drily, "Well, you go ahead and get him then."

Two or three mornings later he was baling hay with the old woman's sorry baler and her broken down tractor in a large field, cleared save for one enormous old tree standing in the middle of it. The old woman was the kind who would not cut down a large old tree because it was a large old tree. She had pointed it out to Parker as if he didn't have eyes and told him to be careful not to hit it as the machine picked up hay near it. Parker began at the outside of the field and made circles inward toward it. He had to get off the tractor every now and then and untangle the baling cord or kick a rock out of the way. The old woman had told him to carry the rocks to the edge of the field, which he did when she was there watching. When he thought he could make it, he ran over them. As he circled the field his mind was on a suitable design for his back. The sun, the size of a golf ball, began to switch regularly from in front to behind him, but he appeared to see it both places as if he had eyes in the back of his head. All at once he saw the tree reaching out to grasp him. A ferocious thud propelled him into the air, and he heard himself yelling in an unbelievably loud voice, "GOD ABOVE!"

He landed on his back while the tractor crashed upsidedown into the tree and burst into flame. The first thing Parker saw were his shoes, quickly being eaten by the fire; one was caught under the tractor, the other was some distance away, burning by itself. He was not in them. He could feel the hot breath of the burning tree on his face. He scrambled backwards, still sitting, his eyes cavernous, and if he had known how to cross himself he would have done it.

His truck was on a dirt road at the edge of the field. He moved toward it, still sitting, still backwards, but faster and faster; halfway to it he got up and began a kind of forward-bent run from which he collapsed on his knees twice. His legs felt like two old rusted rain gutters. He reached the truck finally and took off in it, zigzagging up the road. He drove past his house on the embankment and straight for the city, fifty miles distant.

Parker did not allow himself to think on the way to the city. He only knew that there had been a great change in his life, a leap forward into a worse unknown, and that there was nothing he could do about it. It was for all intents accomplished.

The artist had two large cluttered rooms over a chiropodist's office on a back street. Parker, still barefooted, burst silently in on him at a little after three in the afternoon. The artist, who was about Parker's own age—twenty-eight—but thin and bald, was behind a small drawing table, tracing a design in green ink. He looked up with an annoyed glance and did not seem to recognize Parker in the hollow-eyed creature before him.

"Let me see the book you got with all the pictures of God in it," Parker said breathlessly. "The religious one."

The artist continued to look at him with his intellectual, superior stare. "I don't put tattoos on drunks," he said.

"You know me!" Parker cried indignantly. "I'm O. E. Parker! You done work for me and I always paid!"

The artist looked at him another moment as if he were not altogether sure. "You've fallen off some," he said. "You must have been in jail."

"Married," Parker said.

"Oh," said the artist. With the aid of mirrors the artist had tattooed on the top of his head a miniature owl, perfect in every detail. It was about the size of a half-dollar and served him as a show piece. There were cheaper artists in town but Parker had never wanted anything but the best. The artist went over to a cabinet at the back of the room and began to look over some art books. "Who are you interested in?" he said, "saints, angels, Christs or what?"

"God," Parker said.

"Father, Son or Spirit?"

"Just God," Parker said impatiently. "Christ. I don't care. Just so it's God."

The artist returned with a book. He moved some papers off another table and put the book down on it and told Parker to sit down and see what he liked. "The up-t-date ones are in the back," he said.

Parker sat down with the book and wet his thumb. He began to go through it, beginning at the back where the up-to-date pictures were. Some of them he recognized—The Good Shepherd, Forbid Them Not, The Smiling Jesus, Jesus the Physician's Friend, but he kept turning rapidly backwards and the pictures became less and less reassuring. One showed a gaunt green dead face streaked with blood. One was yellow with sagging purple eyes. Parker's heart began to beat faster and faster until it appeared to be roaring inside him like a great generator. He flipped the pages quickly, feeling that when he reached the one ordained, a sign would come. He continued to flip through until he had almost reached the front of the book. On one of the pages a pair of eyes glanced at him swiftly. Parker sped on, then stopped. His heart too appeared to cut off; there was absolute silence. It said as plainly as if silence were a language itself, GO BACK.

Parker returned to the picture—the haloed head of a flat stern Byzantine Christ with all-demanding eyes. He sat there trembling; his heart began slowly to beat again as if it were being brought to life by a subtle power.

"You found what you want?" the artist asked.

Parker's throat was too dry to speak. He got up and thrust the book at the artist, opened at the picture.

"That'll cost you plenty," the artist said. "You don't want all those little blocks though, just the outline and some better features."

"Just like it is," Parker said, "just like it is or nothing."

"It's your funeral," the artist said, "but I don't do that kind of work for nothing."

"How much?" Parker asked.

"It'll take maybe two days work."

"How much?" Parker said.

"On time or cash?" the artist asked. Parker's other jobs had been on time, but he had paid.

"Ten down and ten for every day it takes," the artist said.

Parker drew ten dollar bills out of his wallet; he had three left in.

"You come back in the morning," the artist said, putting the money in his own pocket. "First I'll have to trace that out of the book."

"No no!" Parker said. "Trace it now or gimme my money back," and his eyes blared as if he were ready for a fight.

The artist agreed. Anyone stupid enough to want a Christ on his back, he reasoned, would be just as likely as not to change his mind the next minute, but once the work was begun he could hardly do so.

While he worked on the tracing, he told Parker to go wash his back at the sink with the special soap he used there. Parker did it and returned to pace back and forth across the room, nervously flexing his shoulders. He wanted to go look at the picture again but at the same time he did not want to. The artist got up finally and had Parker lie down on the table. He swabbed his back with ethyl chloride and then began to outline the head on it with his iodine pencil. Another hour passed before he took up his electric instrument. Parker felt no particular pain. In Japan he had had a tattoo of the Buddha done on his upperarm with ivory needles; in Burma, a little brown root of a man had made a peacock on each of his knees using thin pointed sticks, two feet long; amateurs had worked on him with pins and soot. Parker was usually so relaxed and easy under the hand of the artist that he often went to sleep, but this time he remained awake, every muscle taut.

At midnight the artist said he was ready to quit. He propped one mirror, four feet square, on a table by the wall and took a smaller mirror off the lavatory wall and put it in Parker's hands. Parker stood with his back to the one on the table and moved the other until he saw a flashing burst of color reflected from his back. It was almost completely covered with little red and blue and ivory and saffron squares; from them he made out the lineaments of the face—a mouth, the beginning of heavy brows, a straight nose, but the face was empty; the eyes had not yet been put in. The impression for the moment was almost as if the artist had tricked him and done the Physician's Friend.

"It don't have eyes," Parker cried out.

"That'll come," the artist said, "in due time. We have another day to go on it yet."

Parker spent the night on a cot at the Haven of Light Christian Mission. He found these the best places to stay in the city because they were free and included a meal of sorts. He got the last available cot and because he was still barefooted, he accepted a pair of second-hand shoes which, in his confusion, he put on to go to bed; he was still shocked from all that had happened to him. All night he lay awake in the long dormitory of cots with lumpy figures on them. The only light was from a phosphorescent cross glowing at the end of the room. The tree reached out to grasp him again, then burst into flame; the shoe burned quietly by itself; the eyes in the book said to him distinctly GO BACK and at the same time did not utter a sound. He wished that he were not in this city, not in this Haven of Light Mission, not in a bed by himself. He longed miserably for Sarah Ruth. Her sharp tongue and icepick eyes were the only comfort he could bring to mind. He decided he was losing it. Her eyes appeared soft and dilatory compared with the eyes in the book, for even though he could not summon up the exact look of those eyes, he could still feel their penetration. He felt as though, under their gaze, he was as transparent as the wing of a fly.

The tattooist had told him not to come until ten in the morning, but when he arrived at that hour, Parker was sitting in the dark hallway on the floor, waiting for him. He had decided upon getting up that, once the tattoo was on him, he would not look at it, that all his sensations of the day and night before were those of a crazy man and that he would return to doing things according to his own sound judgement.

The artist began where he left off. "One thing I want to know," he said presently as he worked over Parker's back, "why do you want this on you? Have you gone and got religion? Are you saved?" he asked in a mocking voice.

Parker's throat felt salty and dry. "Naw," he said, "I ain't got no use for none of that. A man can't save his self from whatever it is he don't deserve none of my sympathy." These words seemed to leave his mouth like wraiths and to evaporate at once as if he had never uttered them.

"Then why . . ."

"I married this woman that's saved," Parker said. "I never should have done it. I ought to leave her. She's done gone and got pregnant."

"That's too bad," the artist said. "Then it's her making you have this tattoo."

"Naw," Parker said, "she don't know nothing about it. It's a surprise for her."

"You think she'll like it and lay off you a while?"

"She can't hep herself," Parker said. "She can't say she don't like the looks of God." He decided he had told the artist enough of his business. Artists were all right in their place but he didn't like them poking their noses into the affairs of regular people. "I didn't get no sleep last night," he said. "I think I'll get some now."

That closed the mouth of the artist but it did not bring him any sleep. He lay there, imagining how Sarah Ruth would be struck speechless by the face on his back and every now and then this would be interrupted by a vision of the tree of fire and his empty shoe burning beneath it.

The artist worked steadily until nearly four o'clock, not stopping to have lunch, hardly pausing with the electric instrument except to wipe the dripping dye off Parker's back as he went along. Finally he finished. "You can get up and look at it now," he said.

Parker sat up but he remained on the edge of the table.

The artist was pleased with his work and wanted Parker to look at it at once. Instead Parker continued to sit on the edge of the table, bent forward slightly but with a vacant look. "What ails you?" the artist said. "Go look at it."

"Ain't nothing ail me," Parker said in a sudden belligerent voice. "That tattoo ain't going nowhere. It'll be there when I get there." He reached for his shirt and began gingerly to put it on.

The artist took him roughly by the arm and propelled him between the two mirrors. "Now *look,*" he said, angry at having his work ignored.

Parker looked, turned white and moved away. The eyes in the reflected face continued to look at him—still, straight, all-demanding, enclosed in silence.

"It was your idea, remember," the artist said. "I would have advised something else."

Parker said nothing. He put on his shirt and went out the door while the artist shouted, "I'll expect all of my money!"

Parker headed toward a package shop on the corner. He bought a pint of whiskey and took it into a nearby alley and drank it all in five minutes. Then he moved on to a pool hall nearby which he frequented when he came to the city. It was a well-lighted barn-like place with a bar up one side and gambling machines on the other and pool tables in the back. As soon as Parker entered, a large man in a red and black checkered shirt hailed him by slapping him on the back and yelling, "Yeyyyyyy boy! O. E. Parker!"

Parker was not yet ready to be struck on the back. "Lay off," he said, "I got a fresh tattoo there."

"What you got this time?" the man asked and then yelled to a few at the machines. "O. E.'s got him another tattoo."

"Nothing special this time," Parker said and slunk over to a machine that was not being used.

"Come on," the big man said, "let's have a look at O. E.'s tattoo," and while Parker squirmed in their hands, they pulled up his shirt. Parker felt all the hands drop away instantly and his shirt fell again like a veil over the face. There was a silence in the pool room which seemed to Parker to grow from the circle around him until it extended to the foundations under the building and upward through the beams in the roof.

Finally some one said, "Christ!" Then they all broke into noise at once. Parker turned around, an uncertain grin on his face.

"Leave it to O. E. !" the man in the checkered shirt said. "That boy's a real card!"

"Maybe he's gone and got religion," some one yelled.

"Not on your life," Parker said.

"O. E.'s got religion and is witnessing for Jesus, ain't you, O. E.?" a little man with a piece of cigar in his mouth said wryly. "An o-riginal way to do it if I ever saw one."

"Leave it to Parker to think of a new one!" the fat man said.

"Yyeeeeeeyyyyyyy boy!" someone yelled and they all began to whistle and curse in compliment until Parker said, "Aaa shut up."

"What'd you do it for?" somebody asked.

"For laughs," Parker said. "What's it to you?"

"Why ain't you laughing then?" somebody yelled. Parker lunged into the midst of them and like a whirlwind on a summer's day there began a fight that raged amid overturned tables and swinging fists until two of them grabbed him and ran to the door with him and threw him out. Then a calm descended on the pool hall as nerve shattering as if the long barn-like room were the ship from which Jonah had been cast into the sea.

Parker sat for a long time on the ground in the alley behind the pool hall, examining his soul. He saw it as a spider web of facts and lies that was not at all important to him but which appeared to be necesary in spite of his opinion. The eyes that were now forever on his back were eyes to be obeyed. He was as certain of it as he had ever been of anything. Throughout his life, grumbling and sometimes cursing, often afraid, once in rapture, Parker had obeyed whatever instinct of this kind had come to him—in rapture when his spirit had lifted at the sight of the tattooed man at the fair, afraid when he had joined the navy, grumbling when he had married Sarah Ruth.

The thought of her brought him slowly to his feet. She would know what he had to do. She would clear up the rest of it, and she would at least be pleased. It seemed to him that, all along, that was what he wanted, to please her. His truck was still parked in front of the building where the artist had his place, but it was not far away. He got in it and drove out of the city and into the country night. His head was almost clear of liquor and he observed that his dissatisfaction was gone, but he felt not quite like himself. It was as if he were himself but a stranger to himself, driving into a new country though everything he saw was familiar to him, even at night.

He arrived finally at the house on the embankment, pulled the truck under the pecan tree and got out. He made as much noise as possible to assert that he was still in charge here, that his leaving her for a night without word meant nothing except it was the way he did things. He slammed the car door, stamped up the two steps and across the porch and rattled the door knob. It did not respond to his touch. "Sarah Ruth!" he yelled, "let me in."

There was no lock on the door and she had evidently placed the back of a chair against the knob. He began to beat on the door and rattle the knob at the same time.

He heard the bed springs screak and bent down and put his head to the keyhole, but it was stopped up with paper. "Let me in!" he hollered, bamming on the door again. "What you got me locked out for?"

A sharp voice close to the door said, "Who's there?"

"Me, Parker said, "O. E."

He waited a moment.

"Me," he said impatiently, "O. E."

Still no sound from inside.

He tried once more. "O. E.," he said, bamming the door two or three more times. "O. E. Parker. You know me."

There was a silence. Then the voice said slowly, "I don't know no O. E."

"Quit fooling," Parker pleaded. "You ain't got any business doing me this way. It's me, old O. E., I'm back. You ain't afraid of me."

"Who's there?" the same unfeeling voice said.

Parker turned his head as if he expected someone behind him to give him the answer. The sky had lightened slightly and there were two or three streaks of yellow floating above the horizon. Then as he stood there, a tree of light burst over the skyline.

Parker fell back against the door as if he had been pinned there by a lance.

"Who's there?" the voice from inside said and there was a quality about it now that seemed final. The knob rattled and the voice said peremptorily, "Who's there, I ast you?"

Parker bent down and put his mouth near the stuffed keyhole. "Obadiah," he whispered and all at once he felt the light pouring through him, turning his spider web soul into a perfect arabesque of colors, a garden of trees and birds and beasts.

"Obadiah Elihue!" he whispered.

The door opened and he stumbled in. Sarah Ruth loomed there, hands on her hips. She began at once, "That was no hefty blond woman you was working for and you'll have to pay her every penny on her tractor you busted up. She don't keep insurance on it. She came here and her and me had us a long talk and I . . ."

Trembling, Parker set about lighting the kerosene lamp.

"What's the matter with you, wasting that keresene this near daylight?" she demanded. "I ain't got to look at you."

A yellow glow enveloped them. Parker put the match down and began to unbutton his shirt.

"And you ain't going to have none of me this near morning," she said.

"Shut your mouth," he said quietly. "Look at this and then I don't want to hear no more out of you." He removed the shirt and turned his back to her.

"Another picture," Sarah Ruth growled. "I might have known you was off after putting some more trash on yourself."

Parker's knees went hollow under him. He wheeled around and cried, "Look at it! Don't just say that! *Look* at it!"

"I done looked," she said.

"Don't you know who it is?" he cried in anguish.

"No, who is it?" Sarah Ruth said. "It ain't anybody I know."

"It's him," Parker said.

"Him who?"

"God!" Parker cried.

"God? God don't look like that!"

"What do you know how he looks?" Parker moaned. "You ain't seen him."

"He don't *look,*" Sarah Ruth said. "He's a spirit. No man shall see his face."

"Aw listen," Parker groaned, "this is just a picture of him."

"Idolatry!" Sarah Ruth screamed. "Idolatry! Enflaming yourself with idols under every green tree! I can put up with lies and vanity but I don't want no idolator in this house!" and she grabbed up the broom and began to thrash him across the shoulders with it.

Parker was too stunned to resist. He sat there and let her beat him until she had nearly knocked him senseless and large welts had formed on the face of the tattooed Christ. Then he staggered up and made for the door.

She stamped the broom two or three times on the floor and went to the window and shook it out to get the taint of him off it. Still gripping it, she looked toward the pecan tree and her eyes hardened still more. There he was—who called himself Obadiah Elihue—leaning against the tree, crying like a baby.

1. How is Parker's background different from his wife's?
2. Why is Parker attracted to her?
3. Why does he get the tattoo? How does it affect him?
4. Why does his wife react so violently?
5. What does the story have to say about understanding an action within its context?

James Joyce (1882–1941)
EVELINE

She sat at the window watching the evening invade the avenue. Her head was leaned against the window curtains and in her nostrils was the odour of dusty cretonne. She was tired.

Few people passed. The man out of the last house passed on his way home; she heard his footsteps clacking along the concrete pavement and afterwards crunching on the cinder path before the new red houses. One time there used to be a field there in which they used to play every evening with other people's children. Then a man from Belfast bought the field and built houses in it—not like their little brown houses but bright brick houses with shining roofs. The children of the avenue used to play together in that field—the Devines, the Waters, the Dunns, little Keogh the cripple, she and her brothers and sisters. Ernest, however, never played: he was too grown up. Her father used often to hunt them in out of the field with his blackthorn stick; but usually little Keogh used to keep *nix* and call out when he saw her father coming. Still they seemed to have been rather happy then. Her father was not so bad then; and besides, her mother was alive. That was a long time ago; she and her brothers and sisters were all grown up; her mother was dead. Tizzie Dunn was dead, too, and the Waters had gone back to England. Everything changes. Now she was going to go away like the others, to leave her home.

Home! She looked round the room, reviewing all its familiar objects which she had dusted once a week for so many years, wondering where on earth all the dust came from. Perhaps she would never see again those familiar objects from which she had never dreamed of being divided. And yet during all those years she had never found out the name of the priest whose yellowing photograph hung on the wall above the broken harmonium beside the coloured print of the promises made to Blessed Margaret Mary Alacoque. He had been a school friend of her father. Whenever he showed the photograph to a visitor her father used to pass it with a casual word:

—He is in Melbourne now.

She had consented to go away, to leave her home. Was that wise? She tried to weigh each side of the question. In her home anyway she had shelter and food; she had those whom she had known all her life about her. Of course she had to work hard both in the house and at business. What would they say of her in the Stores when they found out that she had run away with a fellow? Say she was a fool, perhaps; and her place would be filled up by advertisement. Miss Gavan would be glad. She had always had an edge on her, especially whenever there were people listening.

—Miss Hill, don't you see these ladies are waiting?

—Look lively, Miss Hill, please.

She would not cry many tears at leaving the Stores.

But in her new home, in a distant unknown country, it would not be like that. Then she would be married—she, Eveline. People would treat her with respect then. She would not be treated as her mother had been. Even now, though she was over nineteen, she sometimes felt herself in danger of her father's violence. She knew it was that that had given her the palpitations. When they were growing up he had never gone for her, like he used to for Harry and Ernest, because she was a girl; but latterly he had begun to threaten her and say what he would do to her only for her dead mother's sake. And now she had nobody to protect her. Ernest was dead and Harry, who was in the church decorating business, was nearly always down somewhere in the country. Besides, the invariable squabble for money on Saturday nights had begun to weary her unspeakably. She always gave her entire wages—seven shillings—and Harry always sent up what he could but the trouble was to get any money from her father. He said she used to squander the money, that she had no head, that he wasn't going to give her his hard-earned money to throw about the streets, and much more, for he was usually fairly bad of a Saturday night. In the end he would give her the money and ask her had she any intention of buying Sunday's dinner. Then she had to rush out as quickly as she could and do her marketing, holding her black leather purse tightly in her hand as she elbowed her way through the crowds and returning home late under her load of provisions. She had hard work to keep the house together and to see that the two young children who had been left to her charge went to school regularly and got their meals regularly. It was hard work—a hard life—but now that she was about to leave it she did not find it a wholly undesirable life.

She was about to explore another life with Frank. Frank was very kind, manly, open-hearted. She was to go away with him by the night-boat to be his wife and to live with him in Buenos Ayres where he had a home waiting for her. How well she remembered the first time she had seen him; he was lodging in a house on the main road where she used to visit. It seemed a few weeks ago. He was standing at the gate, his peaked cap pushed back on his head and his hair tumbled forward over a face of bronze. Then they had come to know each other. He used to meet her outside the Stores every evening and see her home. He took her to see *The Bohemian Girl* and she felt elated as she sat in an unaccustomed part of the theatre with him. He was awfully fond of music and sang a little. People knew that they were courting and, when he sang about the lass that loves a sailor, she always felt pleasantly confused. He used to call her Poppens out of fun. First of all it had been an excitement for her to have a fellow and then she had begun to like him. He had tales of distant countries. He had started as a deck boy at a pound a month on a ship of the Allan Line going out to Canada. He told her the names of the ships he had been on and the names of the different services. He had sailed through the Straits of Magellan and he told her stories of the terrible Patagonians. He had fallen on his feet in Buenos Ayres, he said, and had come over to the old country just for a holiday. Of course, her father had found out the affair and had forbidden her to have anything to say to him.

—I know these sailor chaps, he said.

One day he had quarrelled with Frank and after that she had to meet her lover secretly.

The evening deepened in the avenue. The white of two letters in her lap grew indistinct. One was to Harry; the other was to her father. Ernest had been her favourite but she liked Harry too. Her father was becoming old lately, she noticed; he would miss her. Sometimes he could be very nice. Not long before, when she had been laid up for a day, he had read her out a ghost story and made toast for her at the fire. Another day, when her mother was alive, they had all gone for a picnic to the Hill of Howth. She remembered her father putting on her mother's bonnet to make the children laugh.

Her time was running out but she continued to sit by the window, leaning her head against the window curtain, inhaling the odour of dusty cretonne. Down far in the avenue she could hear a street organ playing. She knew the air. Strange that it should come that very night to remind her of the promise to her mother, her promise to keep the home together as long as she could. She remembered the last night of her mother's illness; she was again in the close dark room at the other side of the hall and outside she heard a melancholy air of Italy. The organ-player had been ordered to go away and given sixpence. She remembered her father strutting back into the sickroom saying:

—Damned Italians! coming over here!

As she mused the pitiful vision of her mother's life laid its spell on the very quick of her being—that life of commonplace sacrifices closing in final craziness. She trembled as she heard again her mother's voice saying constantly with foolish insistence:

—Derevaun Seraun! Derevaun Seraun!

She stood up in a sudden impulse of terror. Escape! She must escape! Frank would save her. He would give her life, perhaps love, too. But she wanted to live. Why should she be unhappy? She had a right to happiness. Frank would take her in his arms, fold her in his arms. He would save her.

. . .

She stood among the swaying crowd in the station at the North Wall. He held her hand and she knew that he was speaking to her, saying something about the passage over and over again. The station was full of soldiers with brown baggages. Through the wide doors of the sheds she caught a glimpse of the black mass of the boat, lying in beside the quay wall, with illumined portholes. She answered nothing. She felt her cheek pale and cold and, out of a maze of distress, she prayed to God to direct her, to show her what was her duty. The boat blew a long mournful whistle into the mist. If she went, to-morrow she would be on the sea with Frank, steaming towards Buenos Ayres. Their passage had been booked. Could she still draw back after all he had done for her? Her distress awoke a nausea in her body and she kept moving her lips in silent fervent prayer.

A bell clanged upon her heart. She felt him seize her hand:

—Come!

All the seas of the world tumbled about her heart. He was drawing her into them: he would drown her. She gripped with both hands at the iron railing.

—Come!

No! No! No! It was impossible. Her hands clutched the iron in frenzy. Amid the seas she sent a cry of anguish!

—Eveline! Evvy!

He rushed beyond the barrier and called to her to follow. He was shouted at to go on but he still called to her. She set her white face to him, passive, like a helpless animal. Her eyes gave him no sign of love or farewell or recognition.

1. What do we find out about Eveline's physical surroundings?
2. What do they suggest about her life?
3. What do we know about her family and social situation?
4. What does Eveline's late mother mean to her?
5. What does the sailor, Frank, mean to her? Why does she reject him?

Stephen Crane (1871–1900)
THE OPEN BOAT
A Tale Intended to Be After the Fact. Being the Experience of Four Men from the Sunk Steamer "Commodore."

1

None of them knew the color of the sky. Their eyes glanced level, and were fastened upon the waves that swept toward them. These waves were of the hue of slate, save for the tops, which were of foaming white, and all of the men know the colors of the sea. The horizon narrowed and widened, and dipped and rose, and at all times its edge was jagged with waves that seemed thrust up in points like rocks. Many a man ought to have a bath-tub larger than the boat which here rode upon the sea. These waves were most wrongfully and barbarously abrupt and tall, and each froth-top was a problem in small-boat navigation.

The cook squatted in the bottom and looked with both eyes at the six inches of gunwale which separated him from the ocean. His sleeves were rolled over his fat forearms, and the two flaps of his unbuttoned vest dangled as he bent to bail out the boat. Often he said: "Gawd! That was a narrow clip." As he remarked it he invariably gazed eastward over the broken sea.

The oiler, steering with one of the two oars in the boat, sometimes raised himself suddenly to keep clear of water that swirled in over the stern. It was a thin little oar and it seemed often ready to snap.

The correspondent, pulling at the other oar, watched the waves and wondered why he was there.

The injured captain, lying in the bow, was at this time buried in that profound dejection and indifference which comes, temporarily at least, to even the bravest and most enduring when, willy nilly, the firm fails, the army loses, the ship goes down. The mind of the master of a vessel is rooted deep in the timbers of her, though he commands for a day or a decade, and this captain had on him the stern impression of a scene in the greys of dawn of seven turned faces, and later a stump of a top-mast with a white ball on it that slashed to and fro at the waves, went low and lower, and down. Thereafter there was something strange in his voice. Although steady, it was deep with mourning, and of a quality beyond oration or tears.

"Keep'er a little more south, Billie," said he.

" 'A little more south,' sir," said the oiler in the stern.

A seat in this boat was not unlike a seat upon a bucking broncho, and by the same token, a broncho is not much smaller. The craft pranced and reared, and plunged like an animal. As each wave came, and she rose for it, she seemed like a horse making at a fence outrageously high. The manner of her scramble over these walls of water is a mystic thing, and, moreover, at the top of them were ordinarily these problems in white water, the foam racing down from the summit of each wave, requiring a new leap, and a leap from the air. Then, after scornfully bumping a crest, she would slide, and race, and splash down a long incline, and arrive bobbing and nodding in front of the next menace.

A singular disadvantage of the sea lies in the fact that after successfully surmounting one wave you discover that there is another behind it just as important and just as nervously anxious to do something effective in the way of swamping boats. In a ten-foot dinghy one can get an idea of the resources of the sea in the line of waves that is not probable to the average experience which is never at sea in a dinghy. As each slatey wall of water approached, it shut all else from the view of the men in the boat, and it was not difficult to imagine that this particular wave was the final outburst of the ocean, the last effort of the grim water. There was a terrible grace in the move of the waves, and they came in silence, save for the snarling of the crests.

In the wan light, the faces of the men must have been grey. Their eyes must have glinted in strange ways as they gazed steadily astern. Viewed from a balcony, the whole thing would doubtless have been weirdly picturesque. But the men in the boat had no time to see it, and if they had had leisure there were other things to occupy their minds. The sun swung steadily up the sky, and they knew it was broad day because the color of the sea changed from slate to emerald-green, streaked with amber lights, and the foam was like tumbling snow. The process of the breaking day was unknown to them. They were aware only of this effect upon the color of the waves that rolled toward them.

In disjointed sentences the cook and the correspondent argued as to the difference between a life-saving station and a house of refuge. The cook had said: "There's a house of refuge just north of the Mosquito Inlet Light, and as soon as they see us, they'll come off in their boat and pick us up."

"As soon as who see us?" said the correspondent.

"The crew," said the cook.

"Houses of refuge don't have crews," said the correspondent. "As I understand them, they are only places where clothes and grub are stored for the benefit of shipwrecked people. They don't carry crews."

"Oh, yes, they do," said the cook.

"No, they don't," said the correspondent.

"Well, we're not there yet, anyhow," said the oiler, in the stern.

"Well," said the cook, "perhaps it's not a house of refuge that I'm thinking of as being near Mosquito Inlet Light. Perhaps it's a life-saving station."

"We're not there yet," said the oiler, in the stern.

2

As the boat bounced from the top of each wave, the wind tore through the hair of the hatless men, and as the craft plopped her stern down again the spray splashed past them. The crest of each of these waves was a hill, from the top of which the men surveyed, for a moment, a broad tumultuous expanse, shining and wind-riven. It was probably splendid. It was probably glorious, this play of the free sea, wild with lights of emerald and white and amber.

"Bully good thing it's an on-shore wind," said the cook. "If not, where would we be? Wouldn't have a show."

"That's right," said the correspondent.

The busy oiler nodded his assent.

Then the captain, in the bow, chuckled in a way that expressed humor, contempt, tragedy, all in one. "Do you think we've got much of a show now, boys?" said he.

Whereupon the three were silent, save for a trifle of hemming and hawing. To express any particular optimism at this time they felt to be childish and stupid, but they all doubtless possessed this sense of the situation in their mind. A young man thinks doggedly at such times. On the other hand, the ethics of their condition was decidedly against any open suggestions of hopelessness. So they were silent.

"Oh, well," said the captain, soothing his children, "we'll get ashore all right."

But there was that in his tone which made them think, so the oiler quoth: "Yes! If this wind holds!"

The cook was bailing: "Yes! If we don't catch hell in the surf."

Canton flannel gulls flew near and far. Sometimes they sat down on the sea, near patches of brown seaweed that rolled on the waves with a movement like carpets on a line in a gale. The birds sat comfortably in groups, and they were envied by some in the dinghy, for the wrath of the sea was no more to them than it was to a covey of prairie chickens a thousand miles inland. Often they came very close and stared at the men with black bead-like eyes. At these times they were uncanny and sinister in their unblinking scrutiny, and the men hooted angrily at them, telling them to be gone. One came, and evidently decided to alight on the top of the captain's head. The bird flew parallel to the boat and did not circle, but made short sidelong jumps in the air in chicken-fashion. His black eyes were wistfully fixed upon the captain's head. "Ugly brute," said the oiler to the bird. "You look as if you were made with a jacknife." The cook and the correspondent swore darkly at the creature. The captain naturally wished to knock it away with the end of the heavy painter; but he did not dare do it, because anything resembling an emphatic gesture would have capsized this freighted boat, and so with his open hand, the captain gently and carefully waved the gull away. After it had been discouraged from the pursuit the captain breathed easier on account of his hair, and others breathed easier because the bird struck their minds at this time as being somehow gruesome and ominous.

In the meantime the oiler and the correspondent rowed. And also they rowed.

They sat together in the same seat, and each rowed an oar. Then the oiler took both oars; then the correspondent took both oars; then the oiler; then the correspondent. They rowed and they rowed. The very ticklish part of the business was when the time came for the reclining one in the stern to take his turn at the oars. By the very last star of truth, it is easier to steal eggs from under a hen than it was to change seats in the dinghy. First the man in the stern slid his hand along the thwart and moved with care, as if he were of Sèvres. Then the man in the rowing seat slid his hand along the other thwart. It was all done with the most extraordinary care. As the two sidled past each other, the whole party kept watchful eyes on the coming wave, and the captain cried: "Look out now! Steady there!"

The brown mats of seaweed that appeared from time to time were like islands, bits of earth. They were traveling, apparently, neither one way nor the other. They were, to all intents, stationary. They informed the men in the boat that it was making progress slowly toward the land.

The captain, rearing cautiously in the bow, after the dinghy soared on a great swell, said that he had seen the lighthouse at Mosquito Inlet. Presently the cook remarked that he had seen it. The correspondent was at the oars then, and for some reason he too wished to look at the lighthouse, but his back was toward the far shore and the waves were important, and for some time he could not seize an opportunity to turn his head. But at last there came a wave more gentle than the others, and when at the crest of it he swiftly scoured the western horizon.

"See it?" said the captain.

"No," said the correspondent slowly, "I didn't see anything."

"Look again," said the captain. He pointed. "It's exactly in that direction."

At the top of another wave, the correspondent did as he was bid, and this time his eyes chanced on a small still thing on the edge of the swaying horizon. It was precisely like the point of a pin. It took an anxious eye to find a lighthouse so tiny.

"Think we'll make it, captain?"

"If this wind holds and the boat don't swamp, we can't do much else," said the captain.

The little boat, lifted by each towering sea, and splashed viciously by the crests, made progress that in the absence of seaweed was not apparent to those in her. She seemed just a wee thing wallowing, miraculously top-up, at the mercy of five oceans. Occasionally, a great spread of water, like white flames, swarmed into her.

"Bail her, cook," said the captain serenely.

"All right, captain," said the cheerful cook.

3

It would be difficult to describe the subtle brotherhood of men that was here established on the seas. No one said that it was so. No one mentioned it. But it dwelt in the boat, and each man felt it warm him. They were a captain, an oiler, a cook, and a correspondent, and they were friends, friends in a more curiously iron-bound degree than may be common. The hurt captain, lying against the water-jar in the bow, spoke always in a low voice and calmly, but he could never command a more ready and swiftly obedient crew than the motley three of the dinghy. It was more than a mere recognition of what was best for the common safety. There was surely in it a quality that was personal and heartfelt. And after this devotion to the commander of the boat there was this comradeship that the correspondent, for instance, who had been taught to be cynical of men, knew even at the time was the best experience of his life. But no one said that it was so. No one mentioned it.

"I wish we had a sail," remarked the captain. "We might try my overcoat on the end of an oar and give you two boys a chance to rest." So the cook and the correspondent held the mast and spread wide the overcoat. The oiler steered, and the little boat made good way with her new rig. Sometimes the oiler had to scull sharply to keep a sea from breaking into the boat, but otherwise sailing was a success.

Meanwhile the lighthouse had been growing slowly larger. It had now almost assumed color, and appeared like a little grey shadow on the sky. The man at the oars could not be prevented from turning his head rather often to try for a glimpse of this little grey shadow.

At last, from the top of each wave the men in the tossing boat could see land. Even as the lighthouse was an upright shadow on the sky, this land seemed but a long black shadow on the sea. It certainly was thinner than paper. "We must be about opposite New Smyrna," said the cook, who had coasted this shore often in schooners. "Captain, by the way, I believe they abandoned that life-saving station there about a year ago."

"Did they?" said the captain.

The wind slowly died away. The cook and the correspondent were not now obliged to slave in order to hold high the oar. But the waves continued their old impetuous swooping at the dinghy, and the little craft, no longer under way, struggled woundily over them. The oiler or the correspondent took the oars again.

Shipwrecks are *à propos* of nothing. If men could only train for them and have them occur when the men had reached pink condition, there would be less drowning at sea. Of the four in the dinghy none had slept any time worth mentioning for two days and two nights previous to embarking the dinghy, and in the excitement of clambering about the deck of a foundering ship they had also forgotten to eat heartily.

For these reasons, and for others, neither the oiler nor the correspondent was fond of rowing at this time. The correspondent wondered ingenuously how in the name of all that was sane could there be people who thought it amusing to row a boat. It was not an amusement; it was a diabolical punishment, and even a genius of mental aberrations could never conclude that it was anything but a horror to the muscles and a crime against the back. He mentioned to the boat in general how the amusement of rowing struck him, and the weary-faced oiler smiled in full sympathy. Previously to the foundering, by the way, the oiler had worked double-watch in the engine-room of the ship.

"Take her easy, now, boys," said the captain. "Don't spend yourselves. If we have to run a surf you'll need all your strength, because we'll sure have to swim for it. Take your time."

Slowly the land arose from the sea. From a black line it became a line of black and a line of white, trees and sand. Finally, the captain said that he could make out a house on the shore. "That's the house of refuge, sure," said the cook. "They'll see us before long, and come out after us."

The distant lighthouse reared high. "The keeper ought to be able to make us out now, if he's looking through a glass," said the captain. "He'll notify the life-saving people."

"None of those other boats could have got ashore to give word of the wreck," said the oiler, in a low voice. "Else the lifeboat would be out hunting us."

Slowly and beautifully the land loomed out of the sea. The wind came again. It had veered from the north-east to the south-east. Finally, a new sound struck the ears of the men in the boat. It was the low thunder of the surf on the shore. "We'll never be able to make the lighthouse now," said the captain. "Swing her head a little more north, Billie," said he.

" 'A little more north,' sir," said the oiler.

Whereupon the little boat turned her nose once more down the wind, and all but the oarsman watched the shore grow. Under the influence of this expansion doubt and direful apprehension was leaving the minds of the men. The management of the boat was still most absorbing, but it could not prevent a quiet cheerfulness. In an hour, perhaps, they would be ashore.

Their backbones had become thoroughly used to balancing in the boat, and they now rode this wild colt of a dinghy like circus men. The correspondent thought that he had been drenched to the skin, but happening to feel in the top pocket of his coat, he found therein eight cigars. Four of them were soaked with sea-water; four were perfectly scathless. After a search, somebody produced three dry matches, and thereupon the four waifs rode impudently in their little boat, and with an assurance of an impending rescue shining in their eyes, puffed at the big cigars and judged well and ill of all men. Everybody took a drink of water.

4

"Cook," remarked the captain, "there don't seem to be any signs of life about your house of refuge."

"No," replied the cook. "Funny they don't see us!"

A broad stretch of lowly coast lay before the eyes of the men. It was of dunes topped with dark vegetation. The roar of the surf was plain, and sometimes they could see the white lip of a wave as it spun up the beach. A tiny house was blocked out black upon the sky. Southward, the slim lighthouse lifted its little gray length.

Tide, wind, and waves were swinging the dinghy northward. "Funny they don't see us," said the men.

The surf's roar was here dulled, but its tone was, nevertheless, thunderous and mighty. As the boat swam over the great rollers, the men sat listening to this roar. "We'll swamp sure," said everybody.

It is fair to say here that there was not a life-saving station within twenty miles in either direction, but the men did not know this fact, and in consequence they made dark and opprobrious remarks concerning the eyesight of the nation's life-savers. Four scowling men sat in the dinghy and surpassed records in the invention of epithets.

"Funny they don't see us."

The lightheartedness of a former time had completely faded. To their sharpened minds it was easy to conjure pictures of all kinds of incompetency and blindness and, indeed, cowardice. There was the shore of the populous land, and it was bitter and bitter to them that from it came no sign.

"Well," said the captain, ultimately, "I suppose we'll have to make a try for ourselves. If we stay out here too long, we'll none of us have strength left to swim after the boat swamps."

And so the oiler, who was at the oars, turned the boat straight for the shore. There was a sudden tightening of muscle. There was some thinking.

"If we don't all get ashore—" said the captain. "If we don't all get ashore, I suppose you fellows know where to send news of my finish?"

They then briefly exchanged some addresses and admonitions. As for the reflections of the men, there was a great deal of rage in them. Perchance they might be formulated thus: "If I am going to be drowned—if I am going to be drowned—if I am going to be drowned, why in the name of the seven mad gods who rule the sea, was I allowed to come thus far and contemplate sand and trees? Was I brought here merely to have my nose dragged away as I was about to nibble the sacred cheese of life? It is preposterous. If this old ninny-woman, Fate, cannot do better than this, she should be deprived of the management of men's fortunes. She is an old hen who knows not her intention. If she has decided to drown me, why did she not do it in the beginning and save me all this trouble? The whole affair is absurd . . . . But no, she cannot mean to drown me. She dare not drown me. She cannot drown me. Not after all this work." Afterward the man might have had an impulse to shake his fist at the clouds: "Just you drown me, now, and then hear what I call you!"

The billows that came at this time were more formidable. They seemed always just about to break and roll over the little boat in a turmoil of foam. There was a preparatory and long growl in the speech of them. No mind unused to the sea would have concluded that the dingy could ascend these sheer heights in time. The shore was still afar. The oiler was a wily surfman. "Boys," he said swiftly, "she won't live three minutes more, and we're too far out to swim. Shall I take her to sea again, captain?"

"Yes! Go ahead!" said the captain.

This oiler, by a series of quick miracles, and fast and steady oarmanship, turned the boat in the middle of the surf and took her safely to sea again.

There was a considerable silence as the boat bumped over the furrowed sea to deeper water. Then somebody in gloom spoke. "Well, anyhow, they must have seen us from the shore by now."

The gulls went in slanting flight up the wind toward the grey desolate east. A squall, marked by dingy clouds, and clouds brick-red, like smoke from a burning building, appeared from the south-east.

"What do you think of those life-saving people? Ain't they peaches?"

"Funny they haven't seen us."

"Maybe they think we're out here for sport! Maybe they think we're fishin'. Maybe they think we're damned fools."

It was a long afternoon. A changed tide tried to force them southward, but the wind and wave said northward. Far ahead, where coastline, sea, and sky formed their mighty angle, there were little dots which seemed to indicate a city on the shore.

"St. Augustine?"

The captain shook his head. "Too near Mosquito Inlet."

And the oiler rowed, and then the correspondent rowed. Then the oiler rowed. It was a weary business. The human back can become the seat of more aches and pains than are registered in books for the composite anatomy of a regiment. It is a limited area, but it can become the theatre of innumerable muscular conflicts, tangles, wrenches, knots, and other comforts.

"Did you ever like to row, Billie?" asked the correspondent.

"No," said the oiler. "Hang it!"

When one exchanged the rowing-seat for a place in the bottom of the boat, he suffered a bodily depression that caused him to be careless of everything save an obligation to wiggle one finger. There was cold sea-water swashing to and fro in the boat, and he lay in it. His head, pillowed on a thwart, was within an inch of the swirl of a wave crest, and sometimes a particularly obstreperous sea came in-board and drenched him once more. But these matters did not annoy him. It is almost certain that if the boat had capsized he would have tumbled comfortably out upon the ocean as if he felt sure that it was a great soft mattress.

"Look! There's a man on the shore!"

"Where?"

"There! See 'im? See 'im?"

"Yes, sure! He's walking along."

"Now he's stopped. Look! He's facing us!"

"He's waving at us!"

"So he is! By thunder!"

"Ah, now we're all right! Now we're all right! There'll be a boat out here for us in half-an-hour."

"He's going on. He's running. He's going up to that house there."

The remote beach seemed lower than the sea, and it required a searching glance to discern the little black figure. The captain saw a floating stick and they rowed to it. A bath-towel was by some weird chance in the boat, and tying this on the stick, the captain waved it. The oarsman did not dare turn his head, so he was obliged to ask questions.

"What's he doing now?"

"He's standing still again. He's looking, I think. . . . There he goes again. Toward the house. . . . Now he's stopped again."

"Is he waving at us?"

"No, not now! He was, though."

"Look! There comes another man!"

"He's running."

"Look at him go, would you."

"Why, he's on a bicycle. Now he's met the other man. They're both waving at us. Look!"

"There comes something up the beach."

"What the devil is that thing?"

"Why, it looks like a boat."

"Why, certainly, it's a boat."

"No; it's on wheels."

"Yes, so it is. Well, that must be the life-boat. They drag them along shore on a wagon."

"That's the life-boat sure."

"No, by—, it's—it's an omnibus."

"I tell you it's a life-boat."

"It is not! It's an omnibus. I can see it plain. See? One of these big hotel omnibuses."

"By thunder, you're right. It's an omnibus, sure as fate. What do you suppose they are doing with an omnibus? Maybe they are going around collecting the life-crew, hey?"

"That's it, likely. Look! There's a fellow waving a little black flag.

He's standing on the steps of the omnibus. There come those other two fellows. Now they're all talking together. Look at the fellow with the flag. Maybe he ain't waving it!"

"That ain't a flag, is it? That's his coat: Why, certainly, that's his coat."

"So it is; it's his coat. He's taken it off and is waving it around his head. But would you look at him swing it!"

"Oh, say, there isn't any life-saving station there. That's just a winter-resort hotel omnibus that has brought over some of the boarders to see us drown."

"What's that idiot with the coat mean? What's he signaling, anyhow?"

"It looks as if he were trying to tell us to go north. There must be a life-saving station up there."

"No; he thinks we're fishing. Just giving us a merry hand. See? Ah, there, Willie."

"Well, I wish I could make something out of those signals. What do you suppose he means?"

"He don't mean anything; he's just playing."

"Well, if he'd just signal us to try the surf again, or to go to sea and wait, or go north, or go south, or go to hell, there would be some reason in it. But look at him! He just stands there and keeps his coat revolving like a wheel! The ass!"

"There come more people."

"Now there's quite a mob. Look! Isn't that a boat?"

"Where? Oh, I see where you mean. No, that's no boat."

"That fellow is still waving his coat."

"He must think we like to see him do that. Why don't he quit it? It don't mean anything."

"I don't know. I think he is trying to make us go north. It must be that there's a life-saving station there somewhere."

"Say, he ain't tired yet. Look at 'im wave!"

"Wonder how long he can keep that up. He's been revolving his coat ever since he caught sight of us. He's an idiot. Why aren't they getting men to bring a boat out? A fishing boat—one of those big yawls—could come out here all right. Why don't he do something?"

"Oh, it's all right now."

"They'll have a boat out here for us in less than no time, now that they've seen us."

A faint yellow tone came into the sky over the low land. The shadows on the sea slowly deepened. The wind bore coldness with it, and the men began to shiver.

"Holy smoke!" said one, allowing his voice to express his impious mood, "if we keep on monkeying out here! If we've got to flounder out here all night!"

"Oh, we'll never have to stay here all night! Don't you worry.

They've seen us now, and it won't be long before they'll come chasing out after us."

The shore grew dusky. The man waving a coat blended gradually into this gloom, and it swallowed in the same manner the omnibus and the group of people. The spray, when it dashed uproariously over the side, made the voyagers shrink and swear like men who were being branded.

"I'd like to catch the chump who waved the coat. I feel like soaking him one, just for luck."

"Why? What did he do?"

"Oh, nothing, but then he seemed so damned cheerful."

In the meantime the oiler rowed, and then the correspondent rowed, and then the oiler rowed. Gray-faced and bowed forward, they mechanically, turn by turn, plied the leaden oars. The form of the lighthouse had vanished from the southern horizon, but finally a pale star appeared, just lifting from the sea. The streaked saffron in the west passed before the all-merging darkness, and the sea to the east was black. The land had vanished, and was expressed only by the low and drear thunder of the surf.

"If I am going to be drowned—if I am going to be drowned—if I am going to be drowned, why, in the name of the seven mad gods who rule the sea, was I allowed to come thus far and contemplate sand and trees? Was I brought here merely to have my nose dragged away as I was about to nibble the sacred cheese of life?"

The patient captain, drooped over the water-jar, was sometimes obliged to speak to the oarsman.

"Keep her head up! Keep her head up!"

"Keep her head up, sir." The voices were weary and low.

This was surely a quiet evening. All save the oarsman lay heavily and listlessly in the boat's bottom. As for him, his eyes were just capable of noting the tall black waves that swept forward in a most sinister silence, save for an occasional subdued growl of a crest.

The cook's head was on a thwart, and he looked without interest at the water under his nose. He was deep in other scenes. Finally he spoke. "Billie," he murmured dreamfully, "what kind of pie do you like best?"

5

"Pie!" said the oiler and the correspondent, agitatedly. "Don't talk about those things, blast you!"

"Well," said the cook, "I was just thinking about ham sandwiches, and—"

A night on the seas in an open boat is a long night. As darkness settled finally, the shine of the light, lifting from the sea in the south, changed to full gold. On the northern horizon a new light appeared, a small bluish gleam on the edge of the waters. These two lights were the furniture of the world. Otherwise there was nothing but waves.

Two men huddled in the stern, and distances were so magnificent in the dinghy that the rower was enabled to keep his feet partly warm by thrusting them under his companions. Their legs indeed extended far under the rowing-seat until they touched the feet of the captain forward. Sometimes, despite the efforts of the tired oarsman, a wave came piling into the boat, an icy wave of the night, and the chilling water soaked them anew. They would twist their bodies for a moment and groan, and sleep the dead sleep once more, while the water in the boat gurgled about them as the craft rocked.

The plan of the oiler and the correspondent was for one to row until he lost the ability, and then arouse the other from his sea-water couch in the bottom of the boat.

The oiler plied the oars until his head drooped forward and the overpowering sleep blinded him; and he rowed yet afterward. Then he touched a man in the bottom of the boat, and called his name. "Will you spell me for a little while?" he said meekly.

"Sure, Billie," said the correspondent, awaking and dragging himself to a sitting position. They exchanged places carefully, and the oiler, cuddling down in the sea-water at the cook's side, seemed to go to sleep instantly.

The particular violence of the sea had ceased. The waves came without snarling. The obligation of the man at the oars was to keep the boat headed so that the tilt of the rollers would not capsize her, and to preserve her from filling when the crests rushed past. The black waves were silent and hard to be seen in the darkness. Often one was almost upon the boat before the oarsman was aware.

In a low voice the correspondent addressed the captain. He was not sure that the captain was awake, although this iron man seemed to be always awake. "Captain, shall I keep her making for that light north, sir?"

The same steady voice answered him. "Yes. Keep it about two points off the port bow."

The cook had tied a life-belt around himself in order to get even the warmth which this clumsy cork contrivance could donate, and he seemed almost stovelike when a rower, whose teeth invariably chattered wildly as soon as he ceased his labor, dropped down to sleep.

The correspondent, as he rowed, looked down at the two men sleeping underfoot. The cook's arm was around the oiler's shoulders, and, with their fragmentary clothing and haggard faces, they were the babes of the sea—a grotesque rendering of the old babes in the wood.

Later he must have grown stupid at his work, for suddenly there was a growling of water, and a crest came with a roar and a swash into the boat, and it was a wonder that it did not set the cook afloat in his life-belt. The cook continued to sleep, but the oiler sat up, blinking his eyes and shaking with the new cold.

"Oh, I'm awful sorry, Billie," said the correspondent, contritely.

"That's all right, old boy," said the oiler, and lay down again and was asleep.

Presently it seemed that even the captain dozed, and the correspondent thought that he was the one man afloat on all the oceans. The wind had a voice as it came over the waves, and it was sadder than the end.

There was a long, loud swishing astern of the boat, and a gleaming trail of phosphorescence, like blue flame, was furrowed on the back waters. It might have been made by a monstrous knife.

Then there came a stillness, while the correspondent breathed with the open mouth and looked at the sea.

Suddenly there was another long flash of bluish light, and this time it was alongside the boat, and might almost have been reached with an oar. The correspondent saw an enormous fin speed like a shadow through the water, hurling the crystalline spray and leaving the long glowing trail.

The correspondent looked over his shoulder at the captain. His face was hidden, and he seemed to be asleep. He looked at the babes of the sea. They certainly were asleep. So, being bereft of sympathy, he leaned a little way to one side and swore softly into the sea.

But the thing did not then leave the vicinity of the boat. Ahead or astern, on one side or the other, at intervals long or short, fled the long sparkling streak, and there was to be heard the whiroo of the dark fin. The speed and power of the thing was greatly to be admired. It cut the water like a gigantic and keen projectile.

The presence of this biding thing did not affect the man with the same horror that it would if he had been a picnicker. He simply looked at the sea dully and swore in an undertone.

Nevertheless, it is true that he did not wish to be alone with the thing. He wished one of his companions to awake by chance and keep him company with it. But the captain hung motionless over the water-jar, and the oiler and the cook in the bottom of the boat were plunged in slumber.

6

"If I am going to be drowned—if I am going to be drowned—if I am going to be drowned, why, in the name of the seven mad gods who rule the sea, was I allowed to come thus far and contemplate sand and trees?"

During this dismal night, it may be remarked that a man would conclude that it was really the intention of the seven mad gods to drown him, despite the abominable injustice of it. For it was certainly an abominable injustice to drown a man who had worked so hard, so hard. The man felt it would be a crime most unnatural. Other people had drowned at sea since galleys swarmed with painted sails, but still—

When it occurs to a man that nature does not regard him as important, and that she feels she would not maim the universe by disposing of him, he at first wishes to throw bricks at the temple, and he hates deeply the fact that there are no bricks and no temples. Any visible expression of nature would surely be pelleted with his jeers.

Then, if there be no tangible thing to hoot, he feels, perhaps, the desire to confront a personification and indulge in pleas, bowed to one knee, and with hands supplicant, saying, "Yes, but I love myself."

A high cold star on a winter's night is the word he feels that she says to him. Thereafter he knows the pathos of his situation.

The men in the dinghy had not discussed these matters, but each had, no doubt, reflected upon them in silence and according to his mind. There was seldom any expression upon their faces save the general one of complete weariness. Speech was devoted to the business of the boat.

To chime the notes of his emotion, a verse mysteriously entered the correspondent's head. He had even forgotten that he had forgotten this verse, but it suddenly was in his mind.

A soldier of the Legion lay dying in
Algiers;
There was a lack of woman's nursing,
there was dearth of woman's tears;
But a comrade stood beside him, and he
took that comrade's hand.
And he said, "I never more shall see my
own, my native land.

In his childhood the correspondent had been made acquainted with the fact that a soldier of the Legion lay dying in Algiers, but he had never regarded it as important. Myriads of his school-fellows had informed him of the soldier's plight, but the dinning had naturally ended by making him perfectly indifferent. He had never considered it his affair that a soldier of the Legion lay dying in Algiers, nor had it appeared to him as a matter of sorrow. It was less to him than the breaking of a pencil's point.

Now, however, it quaintly came to him as a human, living thing. It was no longer merely a picture of a few throes in the breast of a poet, meanwhile drinking tea and warming his feet at the grate; it was an actuality—stern, mournful, and fine.

The correspondent plainly saw the soldier. He lay on the sand with his feet out straight and still. While his pale left hand was upon his chest in an attempt to thwart the going of his life, the blood came between his fingers. In the far Algerian distance, a city of low square forms was set against a sky that was faint with the last sunset hues. The correspondent, plying the oars and dreaming of the slow and slower movement of the lips of the soldier, was moved by a profound and perfectly impersonal comprehension. He was sorry for the soldier of the Legion who lay dying in Algiers.

The thing which had followed the boat and waited had evidently grown bored at the delay. There was no longer to be heard the slash of the cutwater, and there was no longer the flame of the long trail. The light in the north still glimmered, but it was apparently no nearer to the boat. Sometimes the beam of the surf rang in the correspondent's ears, and he turned the craft seaward then and rowed harder. Southward, some one had evidently built a watch-fire on the beach. It was too low and too far to be seen, but it made a shimmering, roseate reflection upon the bluff back of it, and this could be discerned from the boat. The wind came stronger, and sometimes a wave suddenly raged out like a mountain-cat, and there was to be seen the sheen and sparkle of a broken crest.

The captain, in the bow, moved on his water-jar and sat erect. "Pretty long night," he observed to the correspondent. He looked at the shore. "Those life-saving people take their time."

"Did you see that shark playing around?"

"Yes, I saw him. He was a big fellow, all right."

"Wish I had known you were awake."

Later the correspondent spoke into the bottom of the boat.

"Billie!" There was a slow and gradual disentanglement. "Billie, will you spell me?"

"Sure," said the oiler.

As soon as the correspondent touched the cold, comfortable sea-water in the bottom of the boat and had huddled close to the cook's life-belt he was deep in sleep, despite the fact that his teeth played all the popular airs. This sleep was so good to him that it was but a moment before he heard a voice call his name in a tone that demonstrated the last stages of exhaustion. "Will you spell me?"

"Sure, Billie."

The light in the north had mysteriously vanished, but the correspondent took his course from the wide-awake captain.

Later in the night they took the boat farther out to sea, and the captain directed the cook to take one oar at the stern and keep the boat facing the seas. He was to call out if he should hear the thunder of the surf. This plan enabled the oiler and the correspondent to get respite together. "We'll give those boys a chance to get into shape again," said the captain. They curled down and after a few preliminary chatterings and trembles, slept once more the dead sleep. Neither knew they had bequeathed to the cook the company of another shark, or perhaps the same shark.

As the boat caroused on the waves, spray occasionally bumped over the side and gave them a fresh soaking, but this had no power to break their repose. The ominous slash of the wind and the water affected them as it would have affected mummies.

"Boys," said the cook, with the notes of every reluctance in his voice, "she's drifted in pretty close. I guess one of you had better take her to sea again." The correspondent, aroused, heard the crash of the toppled crests.

As he was rowing, the captain gave him some whiskey and water, and this steadied the chills out of him. "If I ever get ashore and anybody shows me even a photograph of an oar—"

At last there was a short conversation.

"Billie!. . . Billie, will you spell me?"

"Sure," said the oiler.

7

When the correspondent again opened his eyes, the sea and the sky were each of the gray hue of the dawning. Later, carmine and gold was painted upon the waters. The morning appeared finally, in its splendor, with a sky of pure blue, and the sunlight flamed on the tips of the waves.

On the distant dunes were set many little black cottages, and a tall white windmill reared above them. No man, nor dog, nor bicycle appeared on the beach. The cottages might have formed a deserted village.

The voyagers scanned the shore. A conference was held in the boat. "Well," said the captain, "if no help is coming, we might better try a run through the surf right away. If we stay out here much longer we will be too weak to do anything for ourselves at all." The others silently acquiesced in this reasoning. The boat was headed for the beach. The correspondent wondered if none ever ascended the tall wind-tower, and if then they never looked seaward. This tower was a giant, standing with its back to the plight of the ants. It represented in a degree, to the correspondent, the serenity of nature amid the struggles of the individual—nature in the wind, and nature in the vision of men. She did not seem cruel to him then, nor beneficent, nor treacherous, nor wise. But she was indifferent, flatly indifferent. It is, perhaps, plausible that a man in this situation, impressed with the unconcern of the universe, should see the innumerable flaws of his life and have them taste wickedly in his mind and wish for another chance. A distinction between right and wrong seems absurdly clear to him, then, in this new ignorance of the grave-edge, and he understands that if he were given another opportunity he would mend his conduct and his words, and be better and brighter during an introduction or at a tea.

"Now, boys," said the captain, "she is going to swamp sure. All we can do is to work her in as far as possible, and then when she swamps, pile out and scramble for the beach. Keep cool now, and don't jump until she swamps sure."

The oiler took the oars. Over his shoulders he scanned the surf. "Captain," he said, "I think I'd better bring her about, and keep her head-on to the seas, and back her in."

"All right, Billie," said the captain. "Back her in." The oiler swung the boat then, and seated in the stern, the cook and the correspondent were obliged to look over their shoulders to contemplate the lonely and indifferent shore.

The monstrous inshore rollers heaved the boat high until the men were again enabled to see the white sheets of water scudding up the slanted beach. "We won't get in very close," said the captain. Each time a man could wrest his attention from the rollers, he turned his glance toward the shore, and in the expression of the eyes during this contemplation there was a singular quality. The correspondent, observing the others, knew that they were not afraid, but the full meaning of their glances was shrouded.

As for himself, he was too tired to grapple fundamentally with the fact. He tried to coerce his mind into thinking of it, but the mind was dominated at this time by the muscles, and the muscles said they did not care. It merely occurred to him that if he should drown it would be a shame.

There was no hurried words, no pallor, no plain agitation. The men simply looked at the shore. "Now, remember to get well clear of the boat when you jump," said the captain.

Seaward the crest of a roller suddenly fell with a thundererous crash, and the long white comber came roaring down upon the boat.

"Steady now," said the captain. The men were silent. They turned their eyes from the shore to the comber and waited. The boat slid up the incline, leaped at the furious top, bounced over it, and swung down the long back of the wave. Some water had been shipped, and the cook bailed it out.

The next crest crashed also. The tumbling, boiling flood of white water caught the boat and whirled it almost perpendicular. Water swarmed in from all sides. The correspondent had his hands on the gunwale at this time, and when the water entered at that place he swiftly withdrew his fingers, as if he objected to wetting them.

The little boat, drunken with this weight of water, reeled and snuggled deeper into the sea.

"Bail her out, cook! Bail her out!" said the captain.

"All right, Captain," said the cook.

"Now, boys, the next one will do for us sure," said the oiler. "Mind to jump clear of the boat."

The third wave moved forward, huge, furious, implacable. It fairly swallowed the dinghy, and almost simultaneously the men tumbled into the sea. A piece of life-belt had lain in the bottom of the boat, and as the correspondent went overboard he held this to his chest with his left hand.

The January water was icy, and he reflected immediately that it was colder than he had expected to find it off the coast of Florida. This appeared to his dazed mind as a fact important enough to be noted at the time. The coldness of the water was sad; it was tragic. This fact was somehow mixed and confused with his opinion of his own situation so that it seemed almost a proper reason for tears. The water was cold.

When he came to the surface he was conscious of little but the noisy water. Afterward he saw his companions in the sea. The oiler was ahead in the race. He was swimming strongly and rapidly. Off to the correspondent's left, the cook's great white and corked back bulged out of the water, and in the rear the captain was hanging with his one good hand to the keel of the overturned dinghy.

There is a certain immovable quality to a shore, and the correspondent wondered at it amid the confusion of the sea.

It seemed also very attractive; but the correspondent knew that it was a long journey, and he paddled leisurely. The piece of life-preserver lay under him, and sometimes he whirled down the incline of a wave as if he were on a hand-sled.

But finally he arrived at a place in the sea where travel was beset with difficulty. He did not pause swimming to inquire what manner of current had caught him, but there his progress ceased. The shore was set before him like a bit of scenery on a stage, and he looked at it, and understood with his eyes each detail of it.

As the cook passed, much farther to the left, the captain was calling to him, "Turn over on your back, cook! Turn over on your back and use the oar."

"All right, sir." The cook turned on his back, and, paddling with an oar, went ahead as if he were a canoe.

Presently the boat also passed to the left of the correspondent, with the captain clinging with one hand to the keel. He would have appeared like a man raising himself to look over a board fence if it were not for the extraordinary gymnastics of the boat. The correspondent marveled that the captain could still hold to it.

They passed on nearer to shore—the oiler, the cook, the captain—and following them went the water-jar, bouncing gaily over the seas.

The correspondent remained in the grip of this strange new enemy, a current. The shore, with its white slope of sand and its green bluff, topped with little silent cottages, was spread like a picture before him. It was very near to him then, but he was impressed as one who, in a gallery, looks at a scene from Brittany or Algiers.

He thought: "I am going to drown? Can it be possible? Can it be possible? Can it be possible?" Perhaps an individual must consider his own death to be the final phenomenon of nature.

But later a wave perhaps whirled him out of this small deadly current, for he found suddenly that he could again make progress toward the shore. Later still he was aware that the captain, clinging with one hand to the keel of the dinghy, had his face turned away from the shore and toward him, and was calling his name. "Come to the boat! Come to the boat!"

In his struggle to reach the captain and the boat, he reflected that when one gets properly wearied drowning must really be a comfortable arrangement—a cessation of hostilities accompanied by a large degree of relief; and he was glad of it, for the main thing in his mind for some moment had been horror of the temporary agony: he did not wish to be hurt.

Presently he saw a man running along the shore. He was undressing with most remarkable speed. Coat, trousers, shirt, everything flew magically off him.

"Come to the boat!" called the captain.

"All right, Captain." As the correspondent paddled, he saw the captain let himself down to bottom and leave the boat. Then the correspondent performed his one little marvel of the voyage. A large wave caught him and flung him with ease and supreme speed completely over the boat and far beyond it. It struck him even then as an event in gymnastics and a true miracle of the sea. An overturned boat in the surf is not a plaything to a swimming man.

The correspondent arrived in water that reached only to his waist, but his condition did not enable him to stand for more than a moment. Each wave knocked him into a heap, and the under-tow pulled at him.

Then he saw the man who had been running and undressing, and undressing and running, come bounding into the water. He dragged ashore the cook, and then waded towards the captain, but the captain waved him away, and sent him to the corespondent. He was naked, naked as a tree in winter, but a halo was about his head, and he shone like a saint. He gave a strong pull, and a long drag, and a bully heave at the correspondent's hand. The correspondent, schooled in the minor formulae, said: "Thanks, old man." But suddenly the man cried: "What's that?" He pointed a swift finger. The correspondent said: "Go."

In the shallows, face downward, lay the oiler. His forehead touched sand that was periodically, between each wave, clear of the sea.

The correspondent did not know all that transpired afterward. When he achieved safe ground he fell, striking the sand with each particular part of his body. It was as if he had dropped from a roof, but the thud was grateful to him.

It seemed that instantly the beach was populated with men with blankets, clothes, and flasks, and women with coffeepots and all the remedies sacred to their minds. The welcome of the land to the men from the sea was warm and generous, but a still and dripping shape was carried slowly up the beach, and the land's welcome for it could only be the different and sinister hospitality of the grave.

When it came night, the white waves paced to and fro in the moonlight, and the wind brought the sound of the great sea's voice to the men on shore, and they felt that they could then be interpreters.

1. Crane describes "a terrible grace in the movement of the waves." What is the reaction of the men to that beauty?
2. The sea is the antagonist in this story, but at one point the men realize that "nature does not regard [them] as important." What does this passage say about the relationship between man and nature?
3. What is the significance of the fact that the oiler dies whereas the others survive?

Donald Barthelme (b. 1933)

THE INDIAN UPRISING

We defended the city as best we could. The arrows of the Comanches came in clouds. The war clubs of the Comanches clattered on the soft, yellow pavements. There were earthworks along the Boulevard Mark Clark and the hedges had been laced with sparkling wire. People were trying to understand. I spoke to Sylvia. "Do you think this is a good life?" The table held apples, books, long-playing records. She looked up. "No."

Patrols of paras and volunteers with armbands guarded the tall, flat buildings. We interrogated the captured Comanche. Two of us forced his head back while another poured water into his nostrils. His body jerked, he choked and wept. Not believing a hurried, careless, and exaggerated report of the number of casualties in the outer districts where trees, lamps, swans had been reduced to clear fields of fire we issued entrenching tools to those who seemed trustworthy and turned the heavy-weapons companies so that we could not be surprised from that direction. And I sat there getting drunker and more in love and more in love. We talked.

"Do you know Fauré's 'Dolly'?"

"Would that be Gabriel Fauré?"

"It would."

"Then I know it," she said. "May I say that I play it at certain times, when I am sad, or happy, although it requires four hands."

"How is that managed?"

"I accelerate," she said, "ignoring the signature."

And when they shot the scene in the bed I wondered how you felt under the eyes of the cameramen, grips, juicers, men in the mixing booth: excited? stimulated? And when they shot the scene in the shower I sanded a hollow-core door working carefully against the illustrations in texts and whispered instructions from one who had already solved the problem. I had made after all other tables, one while living with Nancy, one while living with Eunice, one while living with Marianne.

Red men in waves like people scattering in a square startled by something tragic or a sudden, loud noise accumulated against the barricades we had made of window dummies, silk, thoughtfully planned job descriptions (including scales for the orderly progress of other colors), wine in demijohns, and robes. I analyzed the composition of the barricade nearest me and found two ashtrays, ceramic, one dark brown and one dark brown with an orange blur at the lip; a tin frying pan; two-litre bottles of red wine; three-quarter-litre bottles of Black & White, aquavit, cognac, vodka, gin, Fad #6 sherry; a hollow-core door in birch veneer on black wrought-iron legs; a blanket, red-orange with faint blue stripes, a red pillow and a blue pillow; a woven straw wastebasket; two glass jars for flowers; corkscrews and can openers; two plates and two cups, ceramic, dark brown; a yellow-and-purple poster; a Yugoslavian carved flute, wood, dark brown; and other items. I decided I knew nothing.

The hospitals dusted wounds with powders the worth of which was not quite established, other supplies having been exhausted early in the first day. I decided I knew nothing. Friends put me in touch with a Miss R., a teacher, unorthodox they said, excellent they said, successful with difficult cases, steel shutters on the windows made the house safe. I had just learned via an International Distress Coupon that Jane had been beaten up by a dwarf in a bar on Tenerife but Miss R. did not allow me to speak of it. "You know nothing," she said, "you feel nothing, you are locked in a most savage and terrible ignorance, I despise you, my boy, *mon cher*, my heart. You may attend but you must not attend now, you must attend later, a day or a week or an hour, you are making me ill . . . " I nonevaluated these remarks as Korzybski instructed. But it was difficult. Then they pulled back in a feint near the river and we rushed into that sector with a reinforced battalion hastily formed among the Zouaves and cabdrivers. This unit was crushed in the afternoon of a day that began with spoons and letters in hallways and under windows where men tested the history of the heart, cone-shaped muscular organ that maintains *circulation of the blood.*

But it is you I want now, here in the middle of this Uprising, with the streets yellow and threatening, short, ugly lances with fur at the throat and inexplicable shell money lying in the grass. It is when I am with you that I am happiest, and it is for you that I am making this hollow-core door table with black wrought-iron legs. I held Sylvia by her bear-claw necklace. "Call off your braves," I said. "We have many years left to live." There was a sort of muck running in the gutters, yellowish, filthy stream suggesting excrement, or nervousness, a city that does not know what it has done to deserve baldness, errors, infidelity. "With luck you will survive until matins," Sylvia said. She ran off down the Rue Chester Nimitz, uttering shrill cries.

Then it was learned that they had infiltrated our ghetto and that the people of the ghetto instead of resisting had joined the smooth, well-coordinated attack with zipguns, telegrams, lockets, causing that portion of the line held by the I.R.A. to swell and collapse. We sent more heroin into the ghetto, and hyacinths, ordering another hundred thousand of the pale, delicate flowers. On the map we considered the situation with its strung-out inhabitants and merely personal emotions. Our parts were blue and their parts were green. I showed the blue-and-green map to Sylvia. "Your parts are green," I said. "You gave me heroin first a year ago," Sylvia said. She ran off down George C. Marshall Allée, uttering shrill cries. Miss R. pushed me into a large room painted white (jolting and dancing in the soft light, and I was excited! and there were people watching!) in which there were two chairs. I sat in one chair and Miss R. sat in the other. She wore a blue dress containing a red figure. There was nothing exceptional about her. I was disappointed by her plainness, by the bareness of the room, by the absence of books.

The girls of my quarter wore long blue mufflers that reached to their knees. Sometimes the girls hid Comanches in their rooms, the blue mufflers together in a room creating a great blue fog. Block opened the door. He was carrying weapons, flowers, loaves of bread. And he was friendly, kind, enthusiastic, so I related a little of the history of torture, reviewing the technical literature quoting the best modern sources, French, German, and American, and pointing out the flies which had gathered in anticipation of some new, cool color.

"What is the situation?" I asked.

"The situation is liquid," he said. "We hold the south quarter and they hold the north quarter. The rest is silence."

"And Kenneth?"

"That girl is not in love with Kenneth." Block said frankly. "She is in love with his coat. When she is not wearing it she is huddling under it. Once I caught it going down the stairs by itself. I looked inside. Sylvia."

Once I caught Kenneth's coat going down the stairs by itself but the coat was a trap and inside a Comanche who made a thrust with his short, ugly knife at my leg which buckled and tossed me over the balustrade through a window and into another situation. Not believing that your body brilliant as it was and your fat, liquid spirit distinguished and angry as it was were stable quantities to which one could return on wires more than once, twice, or another number of times I said: "See the table?"

In Skinny Wainwright Square the forces of green and blue swayed and struggled. The referees ran out on the field trailing chains. And then the blue part would be enlarged, the green diminished. Miss R. began to speak. "A former king of Spain, a Bonaparte, lived for a time in Bordentown, New Jersey. But that's no good." She paused. "The ardor aroused in men by the beauty of women can only be satisfied by God. That is *very* good (it is Valéry) but it is now what I have to teach you, goat, muck, filth, heart of my heart." I showed the table to Nancy. "See the table?" She stuck out her tongue red as a cardinal's hat. "I made such a table once," Block said frankly. "People all over America have made such tables. I doubt very much whether one can enter an American home without finding at least one such table, or traces of its having been there, such as faded places in the carpet." And afterward in the garden the men of the 7th Cavalry played Gabrieli, Albinoni, Marcello, Vivaldi, Boccherini. I saw Sylvia. She wore a yellow ribbon, under a long blue muffler. "Which side are you on," I cried, "after all?"

"The only form of discourse of which I approve," Miss R. said in her dry, tense voice, "is the litany. I believe our masters and teachers as well as plain citizens should confine themselves to what can safely be said. Thus when I hear the words *pewter, snake, tea, Fad #6 sherry, serviette, fenestration, crown, blue* coming from the mouth of some public official, or some raw youth, I am not disappointed. Vertical organization is also possible," Miss R. said, "as in

pewter
snake
tea
Fad #6 sherry
serviette
fenestration
crown
blue

I run to liquids and colors," she said, "but you, you may run to something else, my virgin, my darling, my thistle, my poppet, my own. Young people," Miss R. said, "run to more and more unpleasant combinations as they sense the nature of our society. Some people," Miss R. said, "run to conceits or wisdom but I hold to the hard, brown, nutlike word. I might point out that there is enough aesthetic excitement here to satisfy anyone but a damned fool." I sat in solemn silence.

Fire arrows lit my way to the post office in Patton Place where members of the Abraham Lincoln Brigade offered their last, exhausted letters, postcards, calendars. I opened a letter but inside was a Comanche flint arrowhead play by Frank Wedekind in an elegant gold chain and congratulations. Your earring rattled against my spectacles when I leaned forward to touch the soft, ruined place where the hearing aid had been. "Pack it in! Pack it in!" I urged, but the men in charge of the Uprising refused to listen to reason or to understand that it was real and that our water supply had evaporated and that our credit was no longer what it had been, once.

We attached wires to the testicles of the captured Comanche. And I sat there getting drunker and drunker and more in love and more in love. When we threw the switch he spoke. His name, he said, was Gustave Aschenbach. He was born at L——, a country town in the province of Silesia. He was the son of an upper official in the judicature, and his forebears had all been officers, judges, departmental functionaries . . . And you can never touch a girl in the same way more than once, twice, or another number of times however much you may wish to hold, wrap, or otherwise fix her hand, or look, or some other quality, or incident, known to you previously. In Sweden the little Swedish children cheered when we managed nothing more remarkable than getting off a bus burdened with packages, bread and liver-paste and beer. We went to an old church and sat in the royal box. The organist was practicing. And then into the graveyard next to the church. *Here lies Anna Pedersen, a good woman.* I threw a mushroom on the grave. The officer commanding the garbage dump reported by radio that the garbage had begun to move.

Jane! I heard via an International Distress Coupon that you were beaten up by a dwarf in a bar on Tenerife. That doesn't sound like you, Jane. Mostly you kick the dwarf in his little dwarf groin before he can get his teeth into your tasty and nice-looking leg, don't you, Jane? Your affair with Harold is reprehensible, you know that, don't you, Jane? Harold is married to Nancy. And there is Paula to think about (Harold's kid), and Billy (Harold's other kid). I think your values are peculiar, Jane! Strings of language extend in every direction to bind the world into a rushing, ribald whole.

And you can never return to felicities in the same way, the brilliant body, the distinguished spirit recapitulating moments that occur once, twice, or another number of times in rebellions, or water. The rolling consensus of the Comanche nation smashed our inner defenses on three sides. Block was firing a greasegun from the upper floor of a building designed by Emery Roth & Sons. "See the table?" "Oh, pack it in with your bloody table!" The city officials were tied to trees.

Dusky warriors padded with their forest tread into the mouth of the mayor. "Who do you want to be?" I asked Kenneth and he said he wanted to be Jean-Luc Godard but later when time permitted conversations in large lighted rooms, whispering galleries with black-and-white Spanish rugs and problematic sculpture on calm, red catafalques. The sickness of the quarrel lay thick in the bed. I touched your back, the white, raised scars.

We killed a great many in the south suddenly with helicopters and rockets but we found that those we had killed were children and more come from the north and from the east and from other places where there are children preparing to live. "Skin," Miss R. said softly in the white, yellow room. "This is the Clemency Committee. And would you remove your belt and shoelaces." I removed my belt and shoelaces and looked (rain shattering from a great height the prospects of silence and clear, neat rows of houses in the subdivisions) into their savage black eyes, paint; feathers, beads.

1. How is the world of this story different from our own? How is it similar?
2. Is the world of the story consistent within itself?
3. What is the significance of the lists of objects that occur throughout the story?
4. Does the story convince you that a world like this could exist?

Five
Narration

So far we have been concentrating on the elements of the story being told—the action, the people, the situation that surrounds them. Now we turn our attention to the telling of the story, the process by which the story is presented. The same basic plot, characters, and setting can be conveyed in an infinite variety of ways. To take just one variable, the story could be told as if it were going on right before us in the present, or it could be narrated as a long-ago memory. The choice is up to the author, as are a huge number of other choices, all of which together constitute the **narrative style** of the story. In seeing how the story is handled, the reader gains a very strong clue to the meaning of the story. Stories teach us ways of looking at the world, and the way the story presents its own materials will tell us a lot about its values.

First of all, it is important to remember that a story always has a teller. By this I don't mean the author, but rather the fictional character who tells the story, the **narrator.** This is the voice within the story that tells the tale. By attending closely to the handling of the story, we can build up a sense of this fictional person who arranges the presentation of actions, characters, and situations. Sometimes the narrator seems to be very close to the author, but most often the narrator is a truly independent being, existing only within the story. There are some distinctions about kinds of narrators and how they function.

Identifying the Narrator

The most basic distinction in types of narrators is based on how involved the narrator is in the story. In some cases the narrator is completely outside the action of the story, simply a voice telling a story that happened to other people. This is called a **third-person narrator** —the story told is concerned only with others; the narrator is not involved. A **first-person narrator,** however, is directly involved in the action of the story—an "I" speaking out of personal experience. First-person narrators are sometimes only minor agents in the story, telling us what they observed rather than what they did, but sometimes the main character tells the story, so that the plot is an event in his or her life.

The choice of the kind of narrator is crucial to the story and depends on a number of factors. Third-person narration tends to be detached and objective, whereas first-person is involved and judgmental. Third-person tends to be reliable and totally informed; first-person, because the narrator is more personally involved in the story, is less reliable and more limited in information. Third-person narration tends to give light; first person, heat. Of course, these distinctions are not pure and simple, and we'll give each more attention.

One of the most basic questions about narrators is, How much do they know? The narrator who is a character in the story is *limited* in what he or she knows. Such a narrator cannot know directly what other characters are thinking, for example, only what they express in their speech and appearance. A first-person narrator can't know directly about actions he or she did not actually observe. What this narrator *can* know—and know very intensely—is what he or she has seen and experienced. First-person narrators can provide a tremendous amount of the detail they have observed. They can communicate the lived *feel* of an event and put the reader into the experience. Imagine a person telling about an accident he was involved in. He can probably recount every second of the event and every response he went through, but he cannot give a clear overall picture of the event, since he saw it only from his own angle. First-person narrators capture our sympathy as readers—we see things through their eyes, hear their judgments. We may finally dislike them, but they control our point of view.

In the opposite case, if the narrator is external to the events of the story, he or she is capable of fuller explanations. Some stories with third-person narrators ask the reader to accept the convention that the narrator knows *everything* relevant to the story. **Omniscient narrators,** as they are called, have access to the thoughts of all the characters, and can narrate events that have covered generations and continents. They can even narrate two actions occurring simultaneously. It is as if someone could see an accident as both drivers saw it, experience each of their thoughts and feelings, and also occupy a perfect vantage point for seeing objectively exactly how the crash occurred. Obviously, this is not a kind of knowledge available to real human beings. As the term *omniscient* suggests, it is a godlike quality that we as readers agree to grant to the story as a convention that allows the whole story to be told. Some omniscient narrators make judgments about actions and characters, but most remain impartial and objective, presenting the story without commentary and without overtly directing our sympathy.

To see how the wrong choice of narrative approach can undo a story, let's think about what these two techniques ask of readers. First-person narration asks the reader to be involved in the story, and to adopt the narrator's perspective. We can try to see the action from our own perspective, make our own judgments, but to do so we have to struggle against the power the first-person narrator holds over us. First-person narration also asks us to live, as readers, within the limitations of its knowledge. We have to behave as we do in real life, making judgments about other characters from the outside, following the external signs into a speculation about internal states. Third-person omniscient narration, however, asks us to stand back from the action. It gives us enough information to make our own judgments, although even an omniscient narrator often has a point to make. If a story requires for its success that readers feel sympathy for a character, making that character the first-person narrator would ensure that response. If a story is trying to explain a complex event as fully as possible, an omniscient narrator could obviously provide the necessary information. The wrong choice would ask readers to engage in the wrong set of activities, in which case they couldn't cooperate in the making of the world of the story.

Notice, for example, John Cheever's "The Chaste Clarissa," which is narrated in third-person style. If Baxter, the main character, was allowed to narrate his own story, we would sympathize with him more than Cheever desires. We would not have the detachment we need to be able to judge him properly. In Ralph Ellison's "Battle Royal," however, a third-person narrator would lose the sense of immediacy we get as the boy describes his experiences in the fight.

One trick that a story can play is to place the narration in the hands of an **unreliable narrator.** This is a first-person narrator who does not have access to information, or who does not understand the events or characters he or she describes. All first-person narrators are limited to some degree in what they can know, but an unreliable narrator cannot be trusted at all. Stories like this remind us of the complexity of human knowing. As readers, we tend to believe what a narrator tells us, and stories with unreliable narrators shake that confidence, reminding us that all descriptions of human actions involve judgments based on limited knowledge and are therefore not to be trusted completely.

Controlling the Story

The narrator, the storyteller within the story, is also responsible for how the action is handled. Every action can be narrated at a different pace, and with different emphases, expanded or compressed as the narrator chooses. Let's say, for example, that a character is entering a room. This can be handled in a brief phrase. Or the narrator may choose to attend to every step in the action: we may hear about how the character reaches for the doorknob, slowly inches the door back, moves her right shoulder through the doorway, glances around the door, steps carefully into the room, then pivots to face the room full front. This simple action of entering a room has been broken down into its elements, perhaps in order to increase suspense or to show how deliberate and careful the character is. The narrator is faced with the question of handling detail at every step. The decisions in each case come together to comprise the story's pace, or *narrative rhythm*.

The narrator has control over how time is experienced in the story. We have all had the experience of how time can expand and contract. A week of vacation seems to go by in a flash; a moment of intense concentration can seem to last forever. These same effects can be achieved in fiction. Narrators can make years go by in a phrase, or they can spend pages describing an event that took only a moment. These manipulations of time occur for many reasons. A narrator might want to connect immediately an action to its consequences years later, or might want to dramatize how all the characters involved in a story reacted to the same momentary event. Fiction is capable of playing with time, and the narrator is responsible for these choices in the story.

It is also the narrator who *interprets* the action of the story. Some narrators do very little interpretation, giving the facts of the action without trying to explain their significance. Even in this case, however, they are making sense of the action by how they handle and observe it, and this is communicated to us. Narrators can choose among all the options we have discussed—pace, timing, perspective on the action, and degree of involvement. These choices indicate how they think about the meanings of the action, even if they don't state their opinions directly. Mostly, narrators interpret action openly, telling us what they think of what they observe. But with their control of language, they also can label actions and characters in a way that more subtly indicates their value judgments. Narrators are always working to control readers' interpretations of events, using fictional techniques and language to manipulate our responses. Even so, you as a reader make your own interpretation, and it may be quite different from the narrator's. A character's signs and gestures that the narrator reports are open to many interpretations of which the narrator's is only one. An active reader can enter into a debate with the narrator, if he or she does not share the narrator's opinion. Narrators are a powerful force in fiction, but that does not mean that you will give up your own separate judgment.

The relationship between the reader and the narrator is complicated. The narrator seems to be in control, with the reader choosing either to accept or reject the narrator's interpretations. But narrators themselves are products of readers' activities. Each narrator is one of the characters in the story, and like all characters is constructed by the reader out of signs and codes. With most characters, the signs that offer themselves to interpretation are gestures, appearances, dialogue, and actions. In the case of the narrator, the signs are his or her narrative decisions. The reader builds up an image of the narrator by observing how the narrative process is handled and then translates those decisions into signs of a personality. What kind of person pays close attention, for example, to even the most ordinary actions? What kind of person detaches himself or herself to a vast distance from all experience?

So just who is in control? Does the narrator's viewpoint dominate the reader's, or is the narrator a product of the reader's imaginative work? There is no simple answer. Both questions point to a truth. The reader has power, but so does the narrator. Stories ask us to enter into this realm of relationships between reader and story, where there are no easy answers, no certain truths. What is required of the active reader is to enter into the process of making sense of the story. You must hold on to your own values and still be open to understanding those of the narrator. In the interaction between the two, the meaning of the story will emerge.

READINGS

Ralph Ellison (b. 1914)

BATTLE ROYAL

It goes a long way back, some twenty years. All my life I had been looking for something, and everywhere I turned someone tried to tell me what it was. I accepted their answers too, though they were often in contradiction and even self-contradictory. I was naïve. I was looking for myself and asking everyone except myself questions which I, and only I, could answer. It took me a long time and much painful boomeranging of my expectations to achieve a realization everyone else appears to have been born with. That I am nobody but myself. But first I had to discover that I am an invisible man!

And yet I am no freak of nature, nor of history. I was in the cards, other things having been equal (or unequal) eighty-five years ago. I am not ashamed of my grandparents for having been slaves. I am only ashamed of myself for having at one time been ashamed. About eighty-five years ago they were told that they were free, united with others of our country in everything pertaining to the common good, and, in everything social, separate like the fingers of the hand. And they believed it. They exulted in it. They stayed in their place, worked hard, and brought up my father to do the same. But my grandfather is the one. He was an odd old guy, my grandfather, and I am told I take after him. It was he who caused the trouble. On his deathbed he called my father to him and said, "Son, after I'm gone I want you to keep up the fight. I never told you, but our life is a war and I have been a traitor all my born days, a spy in the enemy's country ever since I give up my gun back in the Reconstruction. Live with your head in the lion's mouth. I want you to overcome 'em with yeses, undermine 'em with grins, agree 'em to death and destruction, let 'em swoller you till they vomit or bust wide open." They thought the old man had gone out of his mind. He had been the meekest of men. The younger children were rushed from the room, the shades drawn and the flame of the lamp turned so low that it sputtered on the wick like the old man's breathing. "Learn it to the younguns," he whispered fiercely; then he died.

But my folks were more alarmed over his last words than over his dying. It was as though he had not died at all, his words caused so much anxiety. I was warned emphatically to forget what he had said and, indeed, this is the first time it has been mentioned outside the family circle. It had a tremendous effect upon me, however. I could never be sure of what he meant. Grandfather had been a quiet old man who never made any trouble, yet on his deathbed he had called himself a traitor and a spy, and he had spoken of his meekness as a dangerous activity. It became a constant puzzle which lay unanswered in the back of my mind. And whenever things went well for me I remembered my grandfather and felt guilty and uncomfortable. It was as though I was carrying out his advice in spite of myself. And to make matters worse, everyone loved me for it. I was praised by the most lilywhite men of the town. I was considered an example of desirable conduct—just as my grandfather had been. And what puzzled me was that the old man had defined it as *treachery*. When I was praised for my conduct I felt a guilt that in some way I was doing something that was really against the wishes of the white folks, that if they had understood they would have desired me to act just the opposite, that I should have been sulky and mean, and that that really would have been what they wanted, even though they were fooled and thought they wanted me to act as I did. It made me afraid that some day they would look upon me as a traitor and I would be lost. Still I was more afraid to act any other way because they didn't like that at all. The old man's words were like a curse. On my graduation day I delivered an oration in which I showed that humility was the secret, indeed, the very essence of progress. (Not that I believed this—how could I, remembering my grandfather?—I only believed that it worked.) It was a great success. Everyone praised me and I was invited to give the speech at a gathering of the town's leading white citizens. It was a triumph for our whole community.

It was in the main ballroom of the leading hotel. When I got there I discovered that it was on the occasion of a smoker, and I was told that since I was to be there anyway I might as well take part in the battle royal to be fought by some of my schoolmates as part of the entertainment. The battle royal came first.

All of the town's big shots were there in their tuxedos, wolfing down the buffet foods, drinking beer and whiskey and smoking black cigars. It was a large room with a high ceiling. Chairs were arranged in neat rows around three sides of a portable boxing ring. The fourth side was clear, revealing a gleaming space of polished floor. I had some misgivings over the battle royal, by the way. Not from a distaste for fighting, but because I didn't care too much for the other fellows who were to take part. They were tough guys who seemed to have no grandfather's curse worrying their minds. No one could mistake their toughness. And besides, I suspected that fighting a battle royal might detract from the dignity of my speech. In those pre-invisible days I visualized myself as a potential Booker T. Washington. But the other fellows didn't care too much for me either, and there were nine of them. I felt superior to them in my way, and I didn't like the manner in which we were all crowded together into the servants' elevator. Nor did they like my being there. In fact, as the warmly lighted floors flashed past the elevator we had words over the fact that I, by taking part in the fight, had knocked one of their friends out of a night's work.

We were led out of the elevator through a rococo hall into an anteroom and told to get into our fighting togs. Each of us was issued a pair of boxing gloves and ushered out into the big mirrored hall, which we entered looking cautiously about us and whispering, lest we might accidentally be heard above the noise of the room. It was foggy with cigar smoke. And already the whiskey was taking effect. I was shocked to see some of the most important men of the town quite tipsy. They were all there—bankers, lawyers, judges, doctors, fire chiefs, teachers, merchants. Even one of the more fashionable pastors. Something we could not see was going on up front. A clarinet was vibrating sensuously and the men were standing up and moving eagerly forward. We were a small tight group, clustered together, our bare upper bodies touching and shining with anticipatory sweat; while up front the big shots were becoming increasingly excited over something we still could not see. Suddenly I heard the school superintendent, who had told me to come, yell, "Bring up the shines, gentlemen! Bring up the little shines!"

We were rushed up to the front of the ballroom, where it smelled even more strongly of tobacco and whiskey. Then we were pushed into place. I almost wet my pants. A sea of faces, some hostile, some amused, ringed around us, and in the center, facing us, stood a magnificent blonde—stark naked. There was a dead silence. I felt a blast of cold air chill me. I tried to back away, but they were behind me and around me. Some of the boys stood with lowered heads, trembling. I felt a wave of irrational guilt and fear. My teeth chattered, my skin turned to goose flesh, my knees knocked. Yet I was strongly attracted and looked in spite of myself. Had the price of looking been blindness, I would have looked. The hair was yellow like that of a circus kewpie doll, the face heavily powdered and rouged, as though to form an abstract mask, the eyes hollow and smeared a cool blue, the color of a baboon's butt. I felt a desire to spit upon her as my eyes brushed slowly over her body. Her breasts were firm and round as the domes of East Indian temples, and I stood so close as to see the fine skin texture and beads of pearly perspiration glistening like dew around the pink and erected buds of her nipples. I wanted at one and the same time to run from the room, to sink through the floor, or to go to her and cover her from my eyes and the eyes of the others with my body; to feel the soft thighs, to caress her and destroy her, to love her and murder her, to hide from her, and yet to stroke where below the small American flag tatooed upon her belly her thighs formed a capital V. I had a notion that of all in the room she saw only me with her impersonal eyes.

And then she began to dance, a slow sensuous movement; the smoke of a hundred cigars clinging to her like the thinnest of veils. She seemed like a fair bird-girl girdled in veils calling to me from the angry surface of some gray and threatening sea. I was transported. Then I became aware of the clarinet playing and the big shots yelling at us. Some threatened us if we looked and others if we did not. On my right I saw one boy faint. And now a man grabbed a silver pitcher from a table and stepped close as he dashed ice water upon him and stood him up and forced two of us to support him as his head hung and moans issued from his thick bluish lips. Another boy began to plead to go home. He was the largest of the group, wearing dark red fighting trunks much too small to conceal the erection which projected from him as though in answer to the insinuating low-registered moaning of the clarinet. He tried to hide himself with his boxing gloves.

And all the while the blond continued dancing, smiling faintly at the big shots who watched her with fascination, and faintly smiling at our fear. I noticed a certain merchant who followed her hungrily, his lips loose and drooling. He was a large man who wore diamond studs in a shirtfront which swelled with the ample paunch underneath, and each time the blond swayed her undulating hips he ran his hand through the hair of his bald head and, with his arms upheld, his posture clumsy like that of an intoxicated panda, wound his belly in a slow and obscene grind. This creature was completely hypnotized. The music had quickened. As the dancer flung herself about with a detached expression on her face, the men began reaching out to touch her. I could see their beefy fingers sink into the soft flesh. Some of the others tried to stop them and she began to move around the floor in graceful circles, as they gave chase, slipping and sliding over the polished floor. It was mad. Chairs went crashing, drinks were spilt, as they ran laughing and howling after her. They caught her just as she reached a door, raised her from the floor, and tossed her as college boys are tossed at a hazing, and above her red, fixed-smiling lips I saw the terror and disgust in her eyes, almost like my own terror and that which I saw in some of the other boys. As I watched, they tossed her twice and her soft breasts seemed to flatten against the air and her legs flung wildly as she spun. Some of the more sober ones helped her to escape. And I started off the floor, heading for the anteroom with the rest of the boys.

Some were still crying and in hysteria. But as we tried to leave we were stopped and ordered to get into the ring. There was nothing to do but what we were told. All ten of us climbed under the ropes and allowed ourselves to be blindfolded with broad bands of white cloth. One of the men seemed to feel a bit sympathetic and tried to cheer us up as we stood with our backs against the ropes. Some of us tried to grin. "See that boy over there?" one of the men said. "I want you to run across at the bell and give it to him right in the belly. If you don't get him, I'm going to get you. I don't like his looks." Each of us was told the same. The blindfolds were put on. Yet even then I had been going over my speech. In my mind each word was as bright as flame. I felt the cloth pressed into place, and frowned so that it would be loosened when I relaxed.

But now I felt a sudden fit of blind terror. I was unused to darkness. It was as though I had suddenly found myself in a dark room filled with poisonous cottonmouths. I could hear the bleary voices yelling insistently for the battle royal to begin.

"Get going in there!"

"Let me at the big nigger!"

I strained to pick up the school superintendent's voice, as though to squeeze some security out of that slightly more familiar voice.

"Let me at those black sonsabitches!" someone yelled.

"No, Jackson, no!" another voiced yelled. "Here, somebody, help me hold Jack."

"I want to get at that ginger-colored nigger. Tear him limb from limb," the first voice yelled.

I stood against the ropes trembling. For in those days I was what they called ginger-colored, and he sounded as though he might crunch me between his teeth like a crisp ginger cookie.

Quite a struggle was going on. Chairs were being kicked about and I could hear voices grunting as with a terrific effort. I wanted to see, to see more desperately than ever before. But the blindfold was as tight as a thick skin-puckering scab and when I raised my gloved hands to push the layers of white aside a voice yelled, "Oh, no you don't, black bastard! Leave that alone!"

"Ring the bell before Jackson kills him a coon!" someone boomed in the sudden silence. And I heard the bell clang and the sound of scuffling forward.

A glove smacked against my head. I pivoted, striking out stiffly as someone went past, and felt the jar ripple along the length of my arm to my shoulder. Then it seemed as though all nine of the boys had turned upon me at once. Blows pounded me from all sides while I struck out as best I could. So many blows landed upon me that I wondered if I were not the only blindfolded fighter in the ring, or if the man called Jackson hadn't succeeded in getting me after all.

Blindfolded, I could no longer control my motions. I had no dignity. I stumbled about like a baby or a drunken man. The smoke had become thicker and with each new blow it seemed to sear and further restrict my lungs. My saliva became like hot bitter glue. A glove connected with my head, filling my mouth with warm blood. It was everywhere. I could not tell if the moisture I felt upon my body was sweat or blood. A blow landed hard against the nape of my neck. I felt myself going over, my head hitting the floor. Streaks of blue light filled the black world behind the blindfold. I lay prone, pretending that I was knocked out, but felt myself seized by hands and yanked to my feet. "Get going, black boy! Mix it up!" My arms were like lead, my head smarting from blows. I managed to feel my way to the ropes and held on, trying to catch my breath. A glove landed in my midsection and I went over again, feeling as though the smoke had become a knife jabbed into my guts. Pushed this way and that by the legs milling around me, I finally pulled erect and discovered that I could see the black, sweat-washed forms weaving in the smoky-blue atmosphere like drunken dancers weaving to the rapid drumlike thuds of blows.

Everyone fought hysterically. It was complete anarchy. Everybody fought everybody else. No group fought together for long. Two, three, four, fought one, then turned to fight each other, were themselves attacked. Blows landed below the belt and in the kidney, with the gloves open as well as closed, and with my eye partly opened now there was not so much terror. I moved carefully, avoiding blows, although not too many to attract attention, fighting from group to group. The boys groped about like blind, cautious crabs crouching to protect their mid-sections, their heads pulled in short against their shoulders, their arms stretched nervously before them, with their fists testing the smoke-filled air like the knobbed feelers of hypersensitive snails. In the corner I glimpsed a boy violently punching the air and heard him scream in pain as he smashed his hand against a ring post. For a second I saw him bent over holding his hand, then going down as a blow caught his unprotected head. I played one group against the other, slipping in and throwing a punch then stepping out of range while pushing the others into the melee to take the blows blindly aimed at me. The smoke was agonizing and there were no rounds, no bells at three minute intervals to relieve our exhaustion. The room spun around me, a swirl of lights, smoke, sweating bodies surrounded by tense white faces. I bled from both nose and mouth, the blood spattering upon my chest.

The men kept yelling. "Slug him, black boy! Knock his guts out!"

"Uppercut him! Kill him! Kill that big boy!"

Taking a fake fall, I saw a boy going down heavily beside me as though we were felled by a single blow, saw a sneaker-clad foot shoot into his groin as the two who had knocked him down stumbled upon him. I rolled out of range, feeling a twinge of nausea.

The harder we fought the more threatening the men became. And yet, I had begun to worry about my speech again. How would it go? Would they recognize my ability? What would they give me?

I was fighting automatically when suddenly I noticed that one after another of the boys was leaving the ring. I was surprised, filled with panic, as though I had been left alone with an unknown danger. Then I understood. The boys had arranged it among themselves. It was custom for the two men left in the ring to slug it out for the winner's prize. I discovered this too late. When the bell sounded two men in tuxedos leaped into the ring and removed the blindfold. I found myself facing Tatlock, the biggest of the gang. I felt sick at my stomach. Hardly had the bell stopped ringing in my ears than it clanged again and I saw him moving swiftly toward me. Thinking of nothing else to do I hit him smash on the nose. He kept coming, bringing the rank sharp violence of stale sweat. His face was a black blank of a face, only his eyes alive—with hate of me and aglow with a feverish terror from what had happened to us all. I became anxious. I wanted to deliver my speech and he came at me as though he meant to beat it out of me. I smashed him again and again, taking his blows as they came. Then on a sudden impulse I struck him lightly and as we clinched, I whispered, "Fake like I knocked you out, you can have the prize."

"I'll break your behind," he whispered hoarsely.

"For *them?*"

"For *me*, sonofabitch."

They were yelling for us to break it up and Tatlock spun me half around with a blow, and as a joggled camera sweeps in a reeling scene, I saw the howling red faces crouching tense beneath the cloud of blue-gray smoke. For a moment the world wavered, unraveled, flowed, then my head cleared and Tatlock bounced before me. The fluttering shadow before my eyes was his jabbing left hand. Then falling forward, my head against his damp shoulder, I whispered.

"I'll make it five dollars more."

"Go to hell."

But his muscles relaxed a trifle beneath my pressure and I breathed, "Seven?"

"Give it to your ma," he said, ripping me beneath the heart.

And while I still held him I butted him and moved away. I felt myself bombarded with punches. I fought back with hopeless desperation. I wanted to deliver my speech more than anything else in the world, because I felt only these men could judge truly my ability, and now this stupid clown was ruining my chances. I began fighting carefully now, moving in to punch him and out again with my greater speed. A lucky blow to his chin and I had him going too—until I heard a loud voice yell, "I got my money on the big boy."

Hearing this, I almost dropped my guard. I was confused. Should I try to win against the voice out there? Would not this go against my speech, and was not this a moment for humility, for nonresistance? A blow to my head as I danced about sent my right eye popping like a jack-in-the-box and settled my dilemma. The room went red as I fell. It was a dream fall, my body languid and fastidious as to where to land, until the floor became impatient and smashed up to meet me. A moment later I came to. An hypnotic voice said FIVE emphatically. And I lay there, hazily watching a dark red spot of my own blood shaping itself into a butterfly, glistening and soaking into the soiled gray world of the canvas.

When the voice drawled TEN I was lifted up and dragged to a chair. I sat dazed. My eye pained and swelled with each throb of my pounding heart and I wondered if now I would be allowed to speak. I was wringing wet, my mouth still bleeding. We were grouped along the wall now. The other boys ignored me as they congratulated Tatlock and speculated as to how much they would be paid. One boy whimpered over his smashed hand. Looking up front, I saw attendants in white jackets rolling the portable ring away and placing a small square rug in the vacant space surrounded by chairs. Perhaps, I thought, I will stand on the rug to deliver my speech.

Then the M.C. called to us, "Come on up here boys and get your money."

We ran forward to where the men laughed and talked in their chairs, waiting. Everyone seemed friendly now.

"There it is on the rug" the man said. I saw the rug covered with coins of all dimensions and a few crumpled bills. But what excited me, scattered here and there, were the gold pieces.

"Boys, it's all yours," the man said. "You get all you grab."

"That's right, Sambo," a blond man said, winking at me confidentially.

I trembled with excitement, forgetting my pain. I would get the gold and the bills, I thought. I would use both hands. I would throw my body against the boys nearest me to block them for the gold.

"Get down around the rug now," the man commanded, "and don't anyone touch it until I give the signal."

"This ought to be good," I heard.

As told, we got around the square rug on our knees. Slowly the man raised his freckled hand as we followed it upward with our eyes.

I heard, "These niggers look like they're about to pray!"

Then. "Ready," the man said. "Go!"

I lunged for a yellow coin lying on the blue design on the carpet, touching it and sending a surprised shriek to join those rising around me. I tried frantically to remove my hand but could not let go. A hot, violent force tore through my body, shaking me like a wet rat. The rug was electrified. The hair bristled up on my head as I shook myself free. My muscles jumped, my nerves jangled, writhed. But I saw that this was not stopping the other boys. Laughing in fear and embarrassment, some were holding back and scooping up the coins knocked off by the painful contortions of the others. The men roared above us as we struggled.

"Pick it up, goddamnit, pick it up!" someone called like a bass-voiced parrot. "Go on, get it!"

I crawled rapidly around the floor, picking up the coins, trying to avoid the coppers and to get greenbacks and the gold. Ignoring the shock by laughing, as I brushed the coins off quickly, I discovered that I could contain the electricity—a contradiction, but it works. Then the men began to push us onto the rug. Laughing embarrassedly, we struggled out of their hands and kept after the coins. We were all wet and slippery and hard to hold. Suddenly I saw a boy lifted into the air, glistening with sweat like a circus seal, and dropped, his wet back landing flush upon the charged rug, heard him yell and saw him literally dance upon his back, his elbows became a frenzied tattoo upon the floor, his muscles twitching like the flesh of a horse stung by many flies. When he finally rolled off, his face was gray and no one stopped him when he ran from the floor amid booming laughter.

"Get the money," the M.C. called. "That's good hard American cash!"

And we snatched and grabbed, snatched and grabbed. I was careful not to come too close to the rug now, and when I felt the hot whiskey breath descend upon me like a cloud of foul air I reached out and grabbed the leg of a chair. It was occupied and I held on desperately.

"Leggo nigger! Leggo!"

The huge face wavered down to mine as he tried to push me free. But my body was slippery and he was too drunk. It was Mr. Colcord, who owned a chain of movie houses and "entertainment palaces." Each time he grabbed me I slipped out of his hands. It became a real struggle. I feared the rug more than I did the drunk, so I held on, surprising myself for a moment by trying to topple *him* upon the rug. It was such an enormous idea that I found myself actually carrying it out. I tried not to be obvious, yet when I grabbed his leg, trying to tumble him out of the chair, he raised up roaring with laughter, and looking at me with soberness dead in the eye, kicked me viciously in the chest. The chair leg flew out of my hand and I felt myself going and rolled. It was as though I had rolled through a bed of hot coals. It seemed a whole century would pass before I would roll free, a century in which I was seared through the deepest levels of my body to the fearful breath within me and the breath seared and heated to the point of explosion. It'll all be over in a flash, I thought as I rolled clear. It'll all be over in a flash.

But not yet, the men on the other side were waiting, red faces swollen as though from apoplexy as they bent forward in their chairs. Seeing their fingers coming toward me I rolled away as a fumbled football rolls off the receiver's fingertips, back into the coals. That time I luckily sent the rug sliding out of place and heard the coins ringing against the floor and the boys scuffling to pick them up and the M.C. calling, "All right boys, that's all. Go get dressed and get your money."

I was limp as a dish rag. My back felt as though it had been beaten with wires.

When we had dressed the M.C. came in and gave us each five dollars, except Tatlock, who got more for being last in the ring. Then he told us to leave. I was not to get a chance to deliver my speech, I thought. I was going out into the dim alley in despair when I was stopped and told to go back. I returned to the ballroom, where the men were pushing back their chairs and gathering in groups to talk.

The M.C. knocked on a table for quiet. "Gentlemen," he said, "we almost forgot an important part of the program. A most serious part, gentlemen. This boy was brought here to deliver a speech which he made at his graduation yesterday . . ."

"Bravo!"

"I'm told that he is the smartest boy we've got out there in Greenwood. I'm told that he knows more big words than a pocket-sized dictionary."

Much applause and laughter.

"So now, gentlemen, I want you to give him your attention."

There was still laughter as I faced them, my mouth dry, my eye throbbing. I began slowly, but evidently my throat was tense, because they began shouting, "Louder! Louder!"

"We of the younger generation extol the wisdom of that great leader and educator," I shouted, "who first spoke these flaming words of wisdom. 'A ship lost at sea for many days suddenly sighted a friendly vessel. From the mast of the unfortunate vessel was seen a signal: "Water, water; we die of thirst!" The answer from the friendly vessel came back: "Cast down your bucket where you are." The captain of the distressed vessel, at last heeding the injunction, cast down his bucket, and it came up full of fresh sparkling water from the mouth of the Amazon River.' And like him I say, and in his words, 'To those of my race who depend upon bettering their condition in a foreign land, or who underestimate the importance of cultivating friendly relations with the Southern white man, who is his next-door neighbor, I would say: "Cast down your bucket where you are"—cast it down in making friends in every manly way of the people of all races by whom we are surrounded . . .' "

I spoke automatically and with such fervor that I did not realize that the men were still talking and laughing until my dry mouth, filling up with blood from the cut, almost strangled me. I coughed, wanting to stop and go to one of the tall brass, sand-filled spittoons to relieve myself, but a few of the men, especially the superintendent, were listening and I was afraid. So I gulped it down, blood, saliva, and all, and continued. (What powers of endurance I had during those days! What enthusiasm! What a belief in the rightness of things!) I spoke even louder in spite of the pain. But still they talked and still they laughed, as though deaf with cotton in dirty ears. So I spoke with greater emotional emphasis. I closed my ears and swallowed blood until I was nauseated. The speech seemed a hundred times as long as before, but I could not leave out a single word. All had to be said, each memorized nuance considered, rendered. Nor was that all. Whenever I uttered a word of three or more syllables a group of voices would yell for me to repeat it. I used the phrase "social responsibility" and they yelled:

"What's that word you say, boy?"

"Social responsibility," I said.

"What?"

"Social . . ."

"Louder."

" . . . responsibility."

"More!"

"Respon—"

"Repeat!"

"—sibility."

The room filled with the uproar of laughter until, no doubt, distracted by having to gulp down my blood, I made a mistake and yelled a phrase I had often seen denounced with newspaper editorials, heard debated in private.

"Social . . ."

"What?" they yelled.

". . . equality—"

The laughter hung smokelike in the sudden stillness. I opened my eyes, puzzled. Sounds of displeasure filled the room. The M.C. rushed forward. They shouted hostile phrases at me. But I did not understand.

A small dry mustached man in the front blared out, "Say that slowly, son!"

"What sir?"

"What you just said!"

"Social responsibility, sir," I said.

"You weren't being smart, were you, boy?" he said, not unkindly.

"No, sir!"

"You sure that about 'equality' was a mistake?"

"Oh, yes, sir," I said. "I was swallowing blood."

"Well, you had better speak more slowly so we can understand. We mean to do right by you, but you've got to know your place at all times. All right, now, go on with your speech."

I was afraid. I wanted to leave but I wanted also to speak and I was afraid they'd snatch me down.

"Thank you, sir," I said, beginning where I had left off, and having them ignore me as before.

Yet when I finished there was a thunderous applause. I was surprised to see the superintendent come forth with a package wrapped in white tissue paper, and, gesturing for quiet, address the men.

"Gentlemen, you see that I did not overpraise this boy. He makes a good speech and some day he'll lead his people in the proper paths. And I don't have to tell you that that is important in these days and times. This is a good, smart boy, and so to encourage him in the right direction, in the name of the Board of Education I wish to present him a prize in the form of this . . ."

He paused, removing the tissue paper and revealing a gleaming calfskin brief case.

". . . in the form of this first-class article from Shad Whitmore's shop."

"Boy," he said, addressing me, "take this prize and keep it well. Consider it a badge of office. Prize it. Keep developing as you are and some day it will be filled with important papers that will help shape the destiny of your people."

I was so moved that I could hardly express my thanks. A rope of bloody saliva forming a shape like an undiscovered continent drooled upon the leather and I wiped it quickly away. I felt an importance that I had never dreamed.

"Open it and see what's inside," I was told.

My fingers a-tremble, I complied, smelling the fresh leather and finding an official-looking document inside. It was a scholarship to the state college for Negroes. My eyes filled with tears and I ran awkwardly off the floor.

I was so overjoyed; I did not even mind when I discovered that the gold pieces I had scrambled for were brass pocket tokens advertising a certain make of automobile.

When I reached home everyone was excited. Next day the neighbors came to congratulate me. I even felt safe from grandfather, whose deathbed curse usually spoiled my triumphs. I stood beneath his photograph with my brief case in hand and smiled triumphantly into his stolid black peasant's face. It was a face that fascinated me. The eyes seemed to follow everywhere I went.

That night I dreamed I was at a circus with him and that he refused to laugh at the clowns no matter what they did. Then later he told me to open my brief case and read what was inside and I did, finding an official envelope stamped with the state seal; and inside the envelope I found another and another, endlessly, and I thought I would fall of weariness. "Them's years," he said. "Now open that one." And I did and in it I found an engraved document containing a short message in letters of gold. "Read it," my grandfather said. "Out loud."

"To Whom It May Concern," I intoned. "Keep This Nigger-Boy Running."

I awoke with the old man's laughter ringing in my ears.

(It was a dream I was to remember and dream again for many years. But at that time I had no insight into its meaning. First I had to attend college.)

1. Why does Ellison choose to have the boy tell his own story?
2. How does the boy distinguish himself from the others in the fight?
3. What kind of detail does the boy provide in his description of the fight?
4. What is the significance of the grandfather's message and the boy's dream?

Arthur C. Clarke (b. 1917)
THE STAR

It is three thousand light years to the Vatican. Once, I believed that space could have no power over faith, just as I believed that the heavens declared the glory of God's handiwork. Now I have seen that handiwork, and my faith is sorely troubled. I stare at the crucifix that hangs on the cabin wall above the Mark VI Computer, and for the first time in my life I wonder if it is no more than an empty symbol.

I have told no one yet, but the truth cannot be concealed. The facts are there for all to read, recorded on the countless miles of magnetic tape and the thousands of photographs we are carrying back to Earth. Other scientists can interpret them as easily as I can, and I am not one who would condone that tampering with the truth which often gave my order a bad name in the olden days.

The crew are already sufficiently depressed: I wonder how they will take this ultimate irony. Few of them have any religious faith, yet they will not relish using this final weapon in their campaign against me—that private, good-natured, but fundamentally serious, war which lasted all the way from Earth. It amused them to have a Jesuit as chief astrophysicist: Dr. Chandler, for instance, could never get over it (why are medical men such notorious atheists?). Sometimes he would meet me on the observation deck, where the lights are always low so that the stars shine with undiminished glory. He would come up to me in the gloom and stand staring out of the great oval port, while the heavens crawled slowly around us as the ship turned end over end with the residual spin we had never bothered to correct.

"Well, Father," he would say at last, "it goes on forever and forever, and perhaps *Something* made it. But how you can believe that Something has a special interest in us and our miserable little world—that just beats me." Then the argument would start, while the stars and nebulae would swing around us in silent, endless arcs beyond the flawlessly clear plastic of the observation port.

It was, I think, the apparent incongruity of my position that caused most amusement to the crew. In vain I would point to my three papers in the *Astrophysical Journal*, my five in the *Monthly Notices of the Royal Astronomical Society*. I would remind them that my order has long been famous for its scientific works. We may be few now, but ever since the eighteenth century we have made contributions to astronomy and geophysics out of all proportion to our numbers. Will my report on the Phoenix Nebula end our thousand years of history? It will end, I fear, much more than that.

I do not know who gave the nebula its name, which seems to me a very bad one. If it contains a prophecy, it is one that cannot be verified for several billion years. Even the word nebula is misleading: this is a far smaller object than those stupendous clouds of mist—the stuff of unborn stars—that are scattered throughout the length of the Milky Way. On the cosmic scale, indeed, the Phoenix Nebula is a tiny thing—a tenuous shell of gas surrounding a single star.

Or what is left of a star . . .

The Rubens engraving of Loyola seems to mock me as it hangs there above the spectrophotometer tracings. What would *you*, Father, have made of this knowledge that has come into my keeping, so far from the little world that was all the universe you knew? Would your faith have risen to the challenge, as mine has failed to do?

You gaze into the distance, Father, but I have traveled a distance beyond any that you could have imagined when you founded our order a thousand years ago. No other survey ship has been so far from Earth: we are at the very frontiers of the explored universe. We set out to reach the Phoenix Nebula, we succeeded, and we are homeward bound with our burden of knowledge. I wish I could lift that burden from my shoulders, but I call to you in vain across the centuries and the light-years that lie between us.

On the book you are holding the words are plain to read. AD MAJOREM DEI GLORIAM, the message runs, but it is a message I can no longer believe. Would you still believe it, if you could see what we have found?

We knew, of course, what the Phoenix Nebula was. Every year, in our galaxy alone, more than a hundred stars explode, blazing for a few hours or days with thousands of times their normal brilliance before they sink back into death and obscurity. Such are the ordinary novae—the commonplace disasters of the universe. I have recorded the spectrograms and light curves of dozens since I started working at the Lunar Observatory.

But three or four times in every thousand years occurs something beside which even a nova pales into total insignificance.

When a star becomes a *supernova,* it may for a little while outshine all the massed suns of the galaxy. The Chinese astronomers watched this happen in A.D. 1054, not knowing what it was they saw. Five centuries later, in 1572, a supernova blazed in Cassiopeia so brilliantly that it was visible in the daylight sky. There have been three more in the thousand years that have passed since then.

Our mission was to visit the remnants of such a catastrophe, to reconstruct the events that led up to it, and if possible, to learn its cause. We came slowly in through the concentric shells of gas that had been blasted out six thousand years before, yet were expanding still. They were immensely hot, radiating even now with a fierce violet light, but were far too tenuous to do us any damage. When the star had exploded, its outer layers had been driven upward with such speed that they had escaped completely from its gravitational field. Now they formed a hollow shell large enough to engulf a thousand solar systems, and at its center burned the tiny, fantastic object which the star had now become—a White Dwarf, smaller than the Earth, yet weighing a million times as much.

The glowing gas shells were all around us, banishing the normal night of interstellar space. We were flying into the center of a cosmic bomb that had detonated millennia ago and whose incandescent fragments were still hurtling apart. The immense scale of the explosion, and the fact that the debris already covered a volume of space many billions of miles across, robbed the scene of any visible movement. It would take decades before the unaided eye could detect any motion in these tortured wisps and eddies of gas, yet the sense of turbulent expansion was overwhelming.

We had checked our primary drive hours before, and were drifting slowly toward the fierce little star ahead. Once it had been a sun like our own, but it had squandered in a few hours the energy that should have kept it shining for a million years. Now it was a shrunken miser, hoarding its resources as if trying to make amends for its prodigal youth.

No one seriously expected to find planets. If there had been any before the explosion, they would have been boiled into puffs of vapor, and their substance lost in the greater wreckage of the star itself. But we made the automatic search, as we always do when approaching an unknown sun, and presently we found a single small world circling the star at an immense distance. It must have been the Pluto of this vanished solar system, orbiting on the frontiers of the night. Too far from the central sun ever to have known life, its remoteness had saved it from the fate of all its lost companions.

The passing fires had seared its rocks and burned away the mantle of frozen gas that must have covered it in the days before the disaster. We landed, and we found the Vault.

Its builders had made sure that we should. The monolithic marker that stood above the entrance was now a fused stump, but even the first long-range photographs told us that here was the work of intelligence. A little later we detected the continent-wide pattern of radioactivity that had been buried in the rock. Even if the pylon above the Vault had been destroyed, this would have remained, an immovable and all but eternal beacon calling to the stars. Our ship fell toward this gigantic bull's-eye like an arrow into its target.

The pylon must have been a mile high when it was built, but now it looked like a candle that had melted down into a puddle of wax. It took us a week to drill through the fused rock, since we did not have the proper tools for a task like this. We were astronomers, not archaeologists, but we could improvise. Our original purpose was forgotten: this lonely monument, reared with such labor at the greatest possible distance from the doomed sun, could have only one meaning. A civilization that knew it was about to die had made its last bid for immortality.

It will take us generations to examine all the treasures that were placed in the Vault. They had plenty of time to prepare, for their sun must have given its first warnings many years before the final detonation. Everything that they wished to preseve, all the fruit of their genius, they brought here to this distant world in the days before the end, hoping that some other race would find it and that they would not be utterly forgotten. Would we have done as well, or would we have been too lost in our own misery to give thought to a future we could never see or share?

If only they had had a little more time! They could travel freely enough between the planets of their own sun, but they had not yet learned to cross the interstellar gulfs, and the nearest solar system was a hundred light-years away. Yet even had they possessed the secret of the Transfinite Drive, no more than a few millions could have been saved. Perhaps it was better thus.

Even if they had not been so disturbingly human as their sculpture shows, we could not have helped admiring them and grieving for their fate. They left thousands of visual records and the machines for projecting them, together with elaborate pictorial instructions from which it will not be difficult to learn their written language. We have examined many of these records, and brought to life for the first time in six thousand years the warmth and beauty of a civilization that in many ways must have been superior to our own. Perhaps they only showed us the best, and one can hardly blame them. But their words were very lovely, and their cities were built with a grace that matches anything of man's. We have watched them at work and play, and listened to their musical speech sounding across the centuries. One scene is still before my eyes—a group of children on a beach of strange blue sand, playing in the waves as children play on Earth. Curious whiplike trees line the shore, and some very large animal is wading in the shadows yet attracting no attention at all.

And sinking into the sea, still warm and friendly and life-giving, is the sun that will soon turn traitor and obliterate all this innocent happiness.

Perhaps if we had not been so far from home and so vulnerable to loneliness, we should not have been so deeply moved. Many of us had seen the ruins of ancient civilizations on other worlds, but they had never affected us so profoundly. This tragedy was unique. It is one thing for a race to fail and die, as nations and cultures have done on Earth. But to be destroyed so completely in the full flower of its achievement, leaving no survivors—how could that be reconciled with the mercy of God?

My colleagues have asked me that, and I have given what answers I can. Perhaps you could have done better, Father Loyola, but I have found nothing in the *Exercitia Spiritualia* that helps me here. They were not an evil people: I do not know what gods they worshiped, if indeed they worshiped any. But I have looked back at them across the centuries, and have watched while the loveliness they used their last strength to preserve was brought forth again into the light of their shrunken sun. They could have taught us much: why were they destroyed?

I know the answers that my colleagues will give when they get back to Earth. They will say that the universe has no purpose and no plan, that since a hundred suns explode every year in our galaxy, at this very moment some race is dying in the depths of space. Whether that race has done good or evil during its lifetime will make no difference in the end: there is no divine justice, for there is no God.

Yet, of course, what we have seen proves nothing of the sort. Anyone who argues thus is being swayed by emotion, not logic. God has no need to justify His actions to man. He who built the universe can destroy it when He chooses. It is arrogance—it is perilously near blasphemy—for us to say what He may or may not do.

This I could have accepted, hard though it is to look upon whole worlds and peoples thrown into the furnace. But there comes a point when even the deepest faith must falter, and now, as I look at the calculations lying before me, I know I have reached that point at last.

We could not tell, before we reached the nebula, how long ago the explosion took place. Now, from the astronomical evidence and the record in the rocks of that one surviving planet, I have been able to date it very exactly. I know in what year the light of this colossal conflagration reached our Earth. I know how brilliantly the supernova whose corpse now dwindles behind our speeding ship once shone in terrestrial skies. I know how it must have blazed low in the east before sunrise, like a beacon in that oriental dawn.

There can be no reasonable doubt: the ancient mystery is solved at last. Yet, oh God, there were so many stars you could have used. What was the need to give these people to the fire, that the symbol of their passing might shine above Bethlehem?

1. What do we learn about the priest who is our narrator? What was his state before he learned about the star?
2. How does he reconcile science and faith?
3. What is the significance of this supernova in human history?
4. What does this discovery do to the priest?

Honoré de Balzac (1799–1850)
SARRASINE

I was deep in one of those daydreams which overtake even the shallowest of men, in the midst of the most tumultuous parties. Midnight had just sounded from the clock of the Elysée-Bourbon. Seated in a window recess and hidden behind the sinuous folds of a silk curtain, I could contemplate at my leisure the garden of the mansion where I was spending the evening. The trees, partially covered with snow, stood out dimly against the grayish background of a cloudy sky, barely whitened by the moon. Seen amid these fantastic surroundings, they vaguely resembled ghosts half out of their shrouds, a gigantic representation of the famous Dance of the Dead. Then, in turning in the other direction, I could admire the Dance of the Living! a splendid salon decorated in silver and gold, with glittering chandeliers, sparkling with candles. There, milling about, whirling around, flitting here and there, were the most beautiful women of Paris, the richest, the noblest, dazzling, stately, resplendent with diamonds, flowers in their hair, on their bosoms, on their heads, strewn over dresses or in garlands at their feet. Light, rustling movements, voluptuous steps, made the laces, the silk brocades, the gauzes, float around their delicate forms. Here and there, some overly animated glances darted forth, eclipsing the lights, the fire of the diamonds, and stimulated anew some too-ardent hearts. One might also catch movements of the head meaningful to lovers, and negative gestures for husbands. The sudden outbursts of the gamblers' voices at each unexpected turn of the dice, the clink of gold, mingled with the music and the murmur of conversation, and to complete the giddiness of this mass of people intoxicated by everything seductive the world can hold, a haze of perfume and general inebriation played upon the fevered mind. Thus, on my right, the dark and silent image of death; on my left, the seemly bacchanalias of life: here, cold nature, dull, in mourning; there, human beings enjoying themselves. On the borderline between these two so different scenes, which, a thousand times repeated in various guises, make Paris the world's most amusing and most philosophical city, I was making for myself a moral macédoine, half pleasant, half funereal. With my left foot I beat time, and I felt as though the other were in the grave. My leg was in fact chilled by one of those insidious drafts which freeze half our bodies while the other half feels the humid heat of rooms, an occurrence rather frequent at balls.

"Monsieur de Lanty hasn't owned this house for very long, has he?"

"Oh yes. Maréchal Carigliano sold it to him nearly ten years ago."

"Ah!"

"These people must have a huge fortune."

"They must have."

"What a party! It's shockingly elegant."

"Do you think they're as rich as M. de Nucingen or M. de Gondreville?"

"You mean you don't know?"

I stuck my head out and recognized the two speakers as members of that strange race which, in Paris, deals exclusively with "whys" and "hows," with "Where did they come from?" "What's happening?" "What has she done?" They lowered their voices and walked off to talk in greater comfort on some isolated sofa. Never had a richer vein been offered to seekers after mystery. Nobody knew what country the Lanty family came from, or from what business, what plunder, what piratical activity, or what inheritance derived a fortune estimated at several millions. All the members of the family spoke Italian, French, Spanish, English, and German perfectly enough to create the belief that they must have spent a long time among these various peoples. Were they gypsies? Were they freebooters?

"Even if it's the devil," some young politicians said, "they give a marvelous party."

"Even if the Count de Lanty had robbed a bank, I'd marry his daughter any time!" cried a philosopher.

Who wouldn't have married Marianina, a girl of sixteen whose beauty embodied the fabled imaginings of the Eastern poets! Like the sultan's daughter, in the story of the Magic Lamp, she should have been kept veiled. Her singing put into the shade the partial talents of Malibran, Sontag, and Fodor, in whom one dominant quality has always excluded over-all perfection; whereas Marianina was able to bring to the same level purity of sound, sensibility, rightness of movement and pitch, soul and science, correctness and feeling. This girl was the embodiment of that secret poetry, the common bond among all the arts, which always eludes those who search for it. Sweet and modest, educated and witty, no one could eclipse Marianina, save her mother.

Have you ever encountered one of those women whose striking beauty defies the inroads of age and who seem at thirty-six more desirable than they could have been fifteen years earlier? Their visage is a vibrant soul, it glows; each feature sparkles with intelligence; each pore has a special brilliance, especially in artificial light. Their seductive eyes refuse, attract, speak or remain silent; their walk is innocently knowledgeable; their voices employ the melodious wealth of the most coquettishly soft and tender notes. Based on comparisons, their praises flatter the self-love of the most sentient. A movement of their eyebrows, the least glance, their pursed lips, fill with a kind of terror those whose life and happiness depend upon them. Inexperienced in love and influenced by words, a young girl can be seduced; for this kind of woman, however, a man must know, like M. de Jaucourt, not to cry out when he is hiding in a closet and the maid breaks two of his fingers as she shuts the door on them. In loving these powerful sirens, one gambles with one's life. And this, perhaps, is why we love them so passionately. Such was the Countess de Lanty.

Filippo, Marianina's brother, shared with his sister in the Countess's marvelous beauty. To be brief, this young man was a living image of Antinous, even more slender. Yet how well these thin, delicate proportions are suited to young people when an olive complexion, strongly defined eyebrows, and the fire of velvet eyes give promise of future male passion, of brave thoughts! If Filippo resided in every girl's heart as an ideal, he also resided in the memory of every mother as the best catch in France.

The beauty, the fortune, the wit, the charms of these two children, came solely from their mother. The Count de Lanty was small, ugly, and pock-marked; dark as a Spaniard, dull as a banker. However, he was taken to be a deep politician, perhaps because he rarely laughed, and was always quoting Metternich or Wellington.

This mysterious family had all the appeal of one of Lord Byron's poems, whose difficulties each person in the fashionable world interpreted in a different way: an obscure and sublime song in every strophe. The reserve maintained by M. and Mme de Lanty about their origin, their past life, and their relationship with the four corners of the globe had not lasted long as a subject of astonishment in Paris. Nowhere perhaps is Vespasian's axiom better understood. There, even bloodstained or filthy money betrays nothing and stands for everything. So long as high society knows the amount of your fortune, you are classed among those having an equal amount, and no one asks to see your family tree, because everyone knows how much it cost. In a city where social problems are solved like algebraic equations, adventurers have every opportunity in their favor. Even supposing this family were of gypsy origin, it was so wealthy, so attractive, that society had no trouble in forgiving its little secrets. Unfortunately, however, the mystery of the Lantys presented a continuing source of curiosity, rather like that contained in the novels of Ann Radcliffe.

Observers, people who make it a point to know in what shop you buy your candlesticks, or who ask the amount of your rent when they find your apartment attractive, had noticed, now and then, in the midst of the Countess's parties, concerts, balls, and routs, the appearance of a strange personage. It was a man. The first time he had appeared in the mansion was during a concert, when he seemed to have been drawn to the salon by Marianina's enchanting voice.

"All of a sudden, I'm cold," a lady had said who was standing with a friend by the door.

The stranger, who was standing next to the women, went away.

"That's odd! I'm warm now," she said, after the stranger had gone. "And you'll say I'm mad, but I can't help thinking that my neighbor, the man dressed in black who just left, was the cause of my chill."

Before long, the exaggeration native to those in high society gave birth to and accumulated the most amusing ideas, the most outrageous expressions, the most ridiculous anecdotes about this mysterious personage. Although not a vampire, a ghoul, or an artificial man, a kind of Faust or Robin Goodfellow, people fond of fantasy said he had something of all these anthropomorphic natures about him. Here and there, one came across some Germans who accepted as fact these clever witticisms of Parisian scandal mongering. The stranger was merely an old man. Many of the young men who were in the habit of settling the future of Europe every morning in a few elegant phrases would have liked to see in this stranger some great criminal, the possessor of vast wealth. Some storytellers recounted the life of this old man and provided really curious details about the atrocities he had committed while in the service of the Maharaja of Mysore. Some bankers, more positive by nature, invented a fable about money. "Bah," they said, shrugging their shoulders in pity, "this poor old man is a *tête génoise*!"

"Sir, without being indiscreet, could you please tell me what you mean by a *tête génoise*?"

"A man, sir, with an enormous lifetime capital and whose family's income doubtless depends on his good health."

I remember having heard at Mme d'Espard's a hypnotist proving on highly suspect historical data that this old man, preserved under glass, was the famous Balsamo, known as Cagliostro. According to this contemporary alchemist, the Sicilian adventurer had escaped death and passed his time fabricating gold for his grandchildren. Last, the bailiff of Ferette maintained that he had recognized this odd personage as the Count of Saint-Germain. These stupidities, spoken in witty accents, with the mocking air characteristic of atheistic society in our day, kept alive vague suspicions about the Lanty family. Finally, through a strange combination of circumstances, the members of this family justified everyone's conjectures by behaving somewhat mysteriously toward this old man, whose life was somehow hidden from all investigation.

Whenever this person crossed the threshold of the room he was supposed to inhabit in the Lanty mansion, his appearance always created a great sensation among the family. One might have called it an event of great importance. Filippo, Marianina, Mme de Lanty, and an old servant were the only persons privileged to assist the old man in walking, arising, sitting down. Each of them watched over his slightest movement. It seemed that he was an enchanted being upon whom depended the happiness, the life, or the fortune of them all. Was it affection or fear? Those in society were unable to discover any clue to help them solve this problem. Hidden for whole months in the depths of a secret sanctuary, this family genie would suddenly come forth, unexpectedly, and would appear in the midst of the salons like those fairies of bygone days who descended from flying dragons to interrupt the rites to which they had not been invited. Only the most avid onlookers were then able to perceive the uneasiness of the heads of the house, who could conceal their feelings with unusual skill. Sometimes, however, while dancing a quadrille, Marianina, naive as she was, would cast a terrified glance at the old man when she spied him among the crowd. Or else Filippo would slip quickly through the throng to his side and would stay near him, tender and attentive, as though contact with others or the slightest breath would destroy this strange creature. The Countess would make a point of drawing near, without seeming to have any intention of joining them; then, assuming a manner and expression of servitude mixed with tenderness, submission, and power, she would say a few words, to which the old man nearly always deferred, and he would disappear, led off, or, more precisely, carried off, by her. If Mme de Lanty were not present, the Count used a thousand stratagems to reach his side; however, he seemed to have difficulty making himself heard, and treated him like a spoiled child whose mother gives in to his whims in order to avoid a scene. Some bolder persons having thoughtlessly ventured to question the Count de Lanty, this cold, reserved man had appeared never to understand them. And so, after many tries, all futile because of the circumspection of the entire family, everyone stopped trying to fathom such a well-kept secret. Weary of trying, the companionable spies, the idly curious, and the politic all gave up bothering about this mystery.

However, even now perhaps in these glittering salons there were some philosophers who, while eating an ice or a sherbet, or placing their empty punch glass on a side table, were saying to each other: "It wouldn't surprise me to learn that those people are crooks. The old man who hides and only makes his appearance on the first day of spring or winter, or at the solstices, looks to me like a killer . . ."

"Or a confidence man . . ."

"It's almost the same thing. Killing a man's fortune is sometimes worse than killing the man."

"Sir, I have bet twenty louis, I should get back forty."

"But, sir, there are only thirty on the table."

"Ah well, you see how mixed the crowd is, here. It's impossible to play."

"True . . . But it's now nearly six months since we've seen the Spirit. Do you think he's really alive?"

"Hah! at best . . ."

These last words were spoken near me by people I did not know, as they were moving off, and as I was resuming, in an afterthought, my mixed thoughts of white and black, life and death. My vivid imagination as well as my eyes looked back and forth from the party, which had reached the height of its splendor, and the somber scene in the gardens. I do not know how long I meditated on these two faces of the human coin; but all at once I was awakened by the stifled laugh of a young woman. I was stunned by the appearance of the image which arose before me. By one of those tricks of nature, the half-mournful thought turning in my mind had emerged, and it appeared living before me, it had sprung like Minerva from the head of Jove, tall and strong, it was at once a hundred years old and twenty-two years old; it was alive and dead. Escaped from his room like a lunatic from his cell, the little old man had obviously slipped behind a hedge of people who were listening to Marianina's voice, finishing the cavatina from *Tancredi*. He seemed to have come out from underground, impelled by some piece of stage machinery. Motionless and somber, he stood for a moment gazing at the party, the noises of which had perhaps reached his ears. His almost somnambulatory preoccupation was so concentrated on things that he was in the world without seeing it. He had unceremoniously sprung up next to one of the most ravishing women in Paris, a young and elegant dancer, delicately formed, with one of those faces as fresh as that of a child, pink and white, so frail and transparent that a man's glance seems to penetrate it like a ray of sunlight going though ice. They were both there before me, together, united, and so close that the stranger brushed against her, her gauzy dress, her garlands of flowers, her softly curled hair, her floating sash.

I had brought this young woman to Mme de Lanty's ball. Since this was her first visit to the house, I forgave her her stifled laugh, but I quickly gave her a signal which completely silenced her and filled her with awe for her neighbor. She sat down next to me. The old man did not want to leave this lovely creature, to whom he had attached himself with that silent and seemingly baseless stubbornness to which the extremely old are prone, and which makes them appear childish. In order to sit near her, he had to take a folding chair. His slightest movements were full of that cold heaviness, the stupid indecision, characteristic of the gestures of a paralytic. He sat slowly down on his seat, with circumspection, muttering some unintelligible words. His worn-out voice was like the sound made by a stone falling down a well. The young woman held my hand tightly, as if seeking protection on some precipice, and she shivered when this man at whom she was looking turned upon her two eyes without warmth, glaucous eyes which could only be compared to dull mother-of-pearl.

"I'm afraid," she said, leaning toward my ear.

"You can talk," I answered. "He is very hard of hearing."

"Do you know him?"

"Yes."

Thereupon, she gathered up enough courage to look for a moment at this creature for which the human language had no name, a form without substance, a being without life, or a life without action. She was under the spell of that timorous curiosity which leads women to seek out dangerous emotions, to go see chained tigers, to look at boa constrictors, frightening themselves because they are separated from them only by weak fences. Although the little old man's back was stooped like a laborer's, one could easily tell that he must have had at one time a normal shape. His excessive thinness, the delicacy of his limbs, proved that he had always been slender. He was dressed in black silk trousers which fell about his bony thighs in folds, like an empty sail. An anatomist would have promptly recognized the symptoms of galloping consumption by looking at the skinny legs supporting this strange body. You would have said they were two bones crossed on a tombstone.

A feeling of profound horror for mankind gripped the heart when one saw the marks that decrepitude had left on this fragile machine. The stranger was wearing an old-fashioned gold-embroidered white waistcoat, and his linen was dazzlingly white. A frill of somewhat yellowed lace, rich enough for a queen's envy, fell into ruffles on his breast. On him, however, this lace seemed more like a rag than like an ornament. Centered on it was a fabulous diamond which glittered like the sun. This outmoded luxury, this particular and tasteless jewel, made the strange creature's face even more striking. The setting was worthy of the portrait. This dark face was angular and all sunk in. The chin was sunken, the temples were sunken; the eyes were lost in yellowish sockets. The jawbones stood out because of his indescribable thinness, creating cavities in the center of each cheek. These deformations, more or less illuminated by the candles, produced shadows and strange reflections which succeeded in erasing any human characteristics from his face. And the years had glued the thin, yellow skin of his face so closely to his skull that it was covered all over with a multitude of circular wrinkles, like the ripples on a pond into which a child has thrown a pebble, or star-shaped, like a cracked windowpane, but everywhere deep and close-set as the edges of pages in a closed book. Some old people have presented more hideous portraits; what contributed the most, however, in lending the appearance of an artificial creature to the specter which had risen up before us was the red and white with which he glistened. The eyebrows of his mask took from the light a luster which revealed that they were painted on. Fortunately for the eye depressed by the sight of such ruin, his cadaverous skull was covered by a blond wig whose innumerable curls were evidence of an extraordinary pretension. For the rest, the feminine coquetry of this phantasmagorical personage was rather strongly emphasized by the gold ornaments hanging from his ears, by the rings whose fine stones glittered on his bony fingers, and by a watch chain which shimmered like the brilliants of a choker around a woman's neck. Finally, this sort of Japanese idol had on his bluish lips a fixed and frozen smile, implacable and mocking, like a skull. Silent and motionless as a statue, it exuded the musty odor of old clothes which the heirs of some duchess take out for inventory. Although the old man turned his eyes toward the crowd, it seemed that the movements of those orbs, incapable of sight, were accomplished only by means of some imperceptible artifice; and when the eyes came to rest on something, anyone looking at them would have concluded that they had not moved at all. To see, next to this human wreckage, a young woman whose neck, bosom, and arms were bare and white, whose figure was in the full bloom of its beauty, whose hair rose from her alabaster forehead and inspired love, whose eyes did not receive but gave off light, who was soft, fresh, and whose floating curls and sweet breath seemed too heavy, too hard, too powerful for this shadow, for this man of dust: ah! here were death and life indeed, I thought, in a fantastic arabesque, half hideous chimera, divinely feminine from the waist up.

"Yet there are marriages like that often enough in the world," I said to myself.

"He smells like a graveyard," cried the terrified young woman, pressing against me for protection, and whose uneasy movements told me she was frightened. "What a horrible sight," she went on. "I can't stay here any longer. If I look at him again, I shall believe that death itself has come looking for me. Is he alive?"

She reached out to the phenomenon with that boldness women can summon up out of the strength of their desires; but she broke into a cold sweat, for no sooner had she touched the old man than she heard a cry like a rattle. This sharp voice, if voice it was, issued from a nearly dried up throat. Then the sound was quickly followed by a little, convulsive, childish cough of a peculiar sonorousness. At this sound, Marianina, Filippo, and Mme de Lanty looked in our direction, and their glances were like bolts of lightning. The young woman wished she were at the bottom of the Seine. She took my arm and led me into a side room. Men, women, everyone made way for us. At the end of the public rooms, we came into a small, semicircular chamber. My companion threw herself onto a divan, trembling with fright, oblivious to her surroundings.

"Madame, you are mad," I said to her.

"But," she replied, after a moment's silence, during which I gazed at her in admiration, "is it my fault? Why does Mme de Lanty allow ghosts to wander about in her house?"

"Come," I replied, "you are being ridiculous, taking a little old man for a ghost."

"Be still," she said, with that forceful and mocking air all women so easily assume when they want to be in the right. "What a pretty room!" she cried, looking around. "Blue satin always makes such wonderful wall hangings. How refreshing it is! Oh! what a beautiful painting!" she went on, getting up and going to stand before a painting in a magnificent frame.

We stood for a moment in contemplation of this marvel, which seemed to have been painted by some supernatural brush. The picture was of Adonis lying on a lion's skin. The lamp hanging from the ceiling of the room in an alabaster globe illuminated this canvas with a soft glow which enabled us to make out all the beauties of the painting.

"Does such a perfect creature exist?" she asked me, after having, with a soft smile of contentment, examined the exquisite grace of the contours, the pose, the color, the hair; in short, the entire picture.

"He is too beautiful for a man," she added, after an examination such as she might have made of some rival.

Oh! how jealous I then felt: something in which a poet had vainly tried to make me believe, the jealously of engravings, of pictures, wherein artists exaggerate human beauty according to the doctrine which leads them to idealize everything.

"It's a portrait," I replied, "the product of the talent of Vien. But that great painter never saw the original and maybe you'd admire it less if you knew that this daub was copied from the statue of a woman."

"But who is it?"

I hesitated.

"I want to know," she added, impetuously.

"I believe," I replied, "that this Adonis is a . . . a relative of Mme de Lanty."

I had the pain of seeing her rapt in the contemplation of this figure. She sat in silence; I sat down next to her and took her hand without her being aware of it! Forgotten for a painting! At this moment, the light footsteps of a woman in a rustling dress broke the silence. Young Marianina came in, and her innocent expression made her even more alluring than did her grace and her lively dress; she was walking slowly and escorting with maternal care, with filial solicitude, the costumed specter who had made us flee from the music room and whom she was leading, watching with what seemed to be concern as he slowly advanced on his feeble feet. They went together with some difficulty to a door hidden behind a tapestry. There, Marianina knocked softly. At once, as if by magic, a tall, stern man, a kind of family genie, appeared. Before entrusting the old man to the care of his mysterious guardian, the child respectfully kissed the walking corpse, and her chaste caress was not devoid of that graceful cajolery of which some privileged women possess the secret.

"Addio, addio," she said, with the prettiest inflection in her youthful voice.

She added to the final syllable a marvelously well-executed trill, but in a soft voice, as if to give poetic expresion to the emotions in her heart. Suddenly struck by some memory, the old man stood on the threshold of this secret hideaway. Then, through the silence, we heard the heavy sigh that came from his chest: he took the most beautiful of rings which adorned his skeletal fingers, and placed it in Marianina's bosom. The young girl broke into laughter, took the ring, and slipped it onto her finger over her glove; then she walked quickly toward the salon, from which there could be heared the opening measures of a quadrille. She saw us:

"Ah, you were here," she said blushing.

After having seemed as if about to question us, she ran to her partner with the careless petulance of youth.

"What did that mean?" my young companion asked me. "Is he her husband? I must be dreaming. Where am I?"

"You," I replied, "you, madame, superior as you are, you who understand so well the most hidden feelings, who know how to inspire in a man's heart the most delicate of feelings without blighting it, without breaking it at the outset, you who pity heartache and who combine the wit of a Parisienne with a passionate soul worthy of Italy or Spain—"

She perceived the bitter irony of my speech; then without seeming to have heard, she interrupted me: "Oh, you fashion me to your own taste. What tyranny! You don't want me for myself!"

"Ah, I want nothing," I cried, taken aback by her severity. "Is it true, at least, that you enjoy hearing stories of those vivid passions that ravishing Southern women inspire in our hearts?"

"Yes, so?"

"So, I'll call tomorrow around nine and reveal this mystery to you."

"No," she replied, "I want to know now."

"You haven't yet given me the right to obey you when you say: I want to."

"At this moment," she replied with maddening coquetry, "I have the most burning desire to know the secret. Tomorrow, I might not even listen to you . . ."

She smiled and we parted; she just as proud, just as forbidding, and I just as ridiculous as ever. She had the audacity to waltz with a young aide-de-camp; and I was left in turn angry, pouting, admiring, loving, jealous.

"Till tomorrow," she said, around two in the morning, as she left the ball.

"I won't go," I thought to myself. "I'll give you up. You are more capricious, perhaps a thousand times more fanciful . . . than my imagination."

The next evening, we were both seated before a good fire in a small, elegant salon, she on a low sofa, I on cushions almost at her feet, and my eyes below hers. The street was quiet. The lamp shed a soft light. It was one of those evenings pleasing to the soul, one of those never-to-be-forgotten moments, one of those hours spent in peace and desire whose charm, later on, is a matter for constant regret, even when we may be happier. Who can erase the vivid imprint of the first feelings of love?

"Well," she said, "I'm listening."

"I don't dare begin. The story has some dangerous passages for its teller. If I become too moved, you must stop me."

"Tell."

"I will obey."

Ernest-Jean Sarrasine was the only son of a lawyer in the Franche-Comté, I went on, after a pause. His father had amassed six or eight thousand livres of income honestly enough, a professional's fortune which at that time in the provinces, was considered to be colossal. The elder Sarrasine, having but one child and anxious to overlook nothing where his education was concerned, hoped to make a magistrate of him, and to live long enough to see, in his old age, the grandson of Matthieu Sarrasine, farmer of Saint-Dié, seated beneath the lilies and napping through some trial for the greater glory of the law; however, heaven did not hold this pleasure in store for the lawyer.

The younger Sarrasine, entrusted to the Jesuits at an early age, evidenced an unusual turbulence. He had the childhood of a man of talent. He would study only what pleased him, frequently rebelled, and sometimes spent hours on end plunged in confused thought, occupied at times in watching his comrades at play, at times dreaming of Homeric heroes. Then, if he made up his mind to amuse himself, he threw himself into games with an extraordinary ardor. When a fight broke out between him and a friend, the battle rarely ended without bloodshed. If he was the weaker of the two, he would bite. Both active and passive by turns, without aptitude and not overly intelligent, his bizarre character made his teachers as wary of him as were his classmates. Instead of learning the elements of Greek, he drew the Reverend Father as he explained a passage in Thucydides to them, sketched the mathematics teacher, the tutors, the Father in charge of discipline, and he scribbled shapeless designs on the walls. Instead of singing the Lord's praises in church, he distracted himself during services by whittling on a pew; or when he had stolen a piece of wood, he carved some holy figure. If he had no wood, paper, or pencil, he reproduced his ideas with bread crumbs. Whether copying the characters in the pictures that decorated the choir, or improvising, he always left behind him some gross sketches whose licentiousness shocked the youngest Fathers; evil tongues maintained that the older Jesuits were amused by them. Finally, if we are to believe school gossip, he was expelled for having, while awaiting his turn at the confessional on Good Friday, shaped a big stick of wood into the form of Christ. The impiety with which this statue was endowed was too blatant not to have merited punishment of the artist. Had he not had the audacity to place this somewhat cynical figure on top of the tabernacle!

Sarrasine sought in Paris a refuge from the effects of a father's curse. Having one of those strong wills that brook no obstacle, he obeyed the commands of his genius and entered Bouchardon's studio. He worked all day, and in the evening went out to beg for his living. Astonished at the young artist's progress and intelligence, Bouchardon soon became aware of his pupil's poverty; he helped him, grew fond of him, and treated him like his own son. Then, when Sarrasine's genius was revealed in one of those works in which future talent struggles with the effervescence of youth, the warmhearted Bouchardon endeavored to restore him to the old lawyer's good graces. Before the authority of the famous sculptor, the parental anger subsided. All Besançon rejoiced at having given birth to a great man of the future. In the first throes of the ecstasy produced by his flattered vanity, the miserly lawyer gave his son the means to cut a good figure in society. For a long time, the lengthy and laborious studies demanded by sculpture tamed Sarrasine's impetuous nature and wild genius. Bouchardon, foreseeing the violence with which the passions would erupt in this young soul, which was perhaps as predisposed to them as Michelangelo's had been, channeled his energy into constant labor. He succeeded in keeping Sarrasine's extraordinary impetuosity within limits by forbidding him to work; by suggesting distractions when he saw him being carried away by the fury of some idea, or by entrusting him with important work when he seemed on the point of abandoning himself to dissipation. However, gentleness was always the most powerful of weapons where this passionate soul was concerned, and the master had no greater control over his student than when he inspired his gratitude through paternal kindness.

At twenty-two, Sarrasine was necessarily removed from the salutary influence Bouchardon had exercised over his morals and his habits. He reaped the fruits of his genius by winning the sculpture prize established by the Marquis de Marigny, the brother of Mme de Pompadour, who did so much for the arts. Diderot hailed the statue by Bouchardon's pupil as a masterpiece. The King's sculptor, not without great sorrow, saw off to Italy a young man whom he had kept, as a matter of principle, in total ignorance of the facts of life.

For six years, Sarrasine had boarded with Bouchardon. As fanatic in his art as Canova was later to be, he arose at dawn, went to the studio, did not emerge until nightfall, and lived only with his Muse. If he went to the Comédie-Française, he was taken by his master. He felt so out of place at Mme Geoffrin's and in high society, into which Bouchardon tried to introduce him, that he preferred to be alone, and shunned the pleasures of that licentious era. He had no other mistress but sculpture and Clotilde, one of the luminaries of the Opéra. And even this affair did not last. Sarrasine was rather ugly, always badly dressed, and so free in his nature, so irregular in his private life, that the celebrated nymph, fearing some catastrophe, soon relinquished the sculptor to his love of the Arts. Sophie Arnould made one of her witticisms on this subject. She confessed her surprise, I believe, that her friend had managed to triumph over statuary.

Sarrasine left for Italy in 1758. During the journey, his vivid imagination caught fire beneath a brilliant sky and at the sight of the wonderful monuments which are to be found in the birthplace of the Arts. He admired the statues, the frescoes, the paintings, and thus inspired, he came to Rome, filled with desire to carve his name between Michelangelo's and M. Bouchardon's. Accordingly, at the beginning, he divided his time between studio tasks and examining the works of art in which Rome abounds. He had already spent two weeks in the ecstatic state which overwhelms young minds at the sight of the queen of ruins, when he went one evening to the Teatro Argentina, before which a huge crowd was assembled. He inquired as to the causes of this gathering and everyone answered with two names: Zambinella! Jomelli! He entered and took a seat in the orchestra, squeezed between two notably fat *abbati*; however, he was lucky enough to be fairly close to the stage. The curtain rose. For the first time in his life, he heard that music whose delights M. Jean-Jacques Rousseau had so eloquently praised to him at one of Baron d'Holbach's evenings. The young sculptor's senses were, so to speak, lubricated by the accents of Jomelli's sublime harmony. The languorous novelties of these skillfully mingled Italian voices plunged him into a delicious ecstasy. He remained speechless, motionless, not even feeling crowded by the two priests. His soul passed into his ears and eyes. He seemed to hear through every pore. Suddenly a burst of applause which shook the house greeted the prima donna's entrance. She came coquettishly to the front of the stage and greeted the audience with infinite grace. The lights, the general enthusiasm, the theatrical illusion, the glamour of a style of dress which in those days was quite attractive, all conspired in favor of this woman. Sarrasine cried out with pleasure.

At that instant he marveled at the ideal beauty he had hitherto sought in life, seeking in one often unworthy model the roundness of a perfect leg; in another, the curve of a breast; in another, white shoulders, finally taking some girl's neck, some woman's hands, and some child's smooth knees, without ever having encountered under the cold Parisian sky the rich, sweet creations of ancient Greece. La Zambinella displayed to him, united, living, and delicate, those exquisite female forms he so ardently desired, of which a sculptor is at once the severest and the most passionate judge. Her mouth was expressive, her eyes loving, her complexion dazzlingly white. And along with these details, which would have enraptured a painter, were all the wonders of those images of Venus revered and rendered by the chisels of the Greeks. The artist never wearied of admiring the inimitable grace with which the arms were attached to the torso, the marvelous roundness of the neck, the harmonious lines drawn by the eyebrows, the nose, and the perfect oval of the face, the purity of its vivid contours and the effect of the thick, curved lashes which lined her heavy and voluptuous eyelids. This was more than a woman, this was a masterpiece! In this unhoped-for creation could be found a love to enrapture any man, and beauties worthy of satisfying a critic. With his eyes, Sarrasine devoured Pygmalion's statue, come down from its pedestal. When La Zambinella sang, the effect was delirium. The artist felt cold; then he felt a heat which suddenly began to prickle in the innermost depth of his being, in what we call the heart, for lack of any other word! He did not applaud, he said nothing, he experienced an impulse of madness, a kind of frenzy which overcomes us only when we are at the age when desire has something frightening and infernal about it. Sarrasine wanted to leap onto the stage and take possession of this woman: his strength, increased a hundredfold by a moral depression impossible to explain, since these phenomena occur in an area hidden from human observation, seemed to manifest itself with painful violence. Looking at him, one would have thought him a cold and senseless man. Fame, knowledge, future, existence, laurels, everything collapsed.

"To be loved by her, or die!" Such was the decree Sarrasine passed upon himself. He was so utterly intoxicated that he no longer saw the theater, the spectators, the actors, or heard the music. Moreover, the distance between himself and La Zambinella had ceased to exist, he possessed her, his eyes were riveted upon her, he took her for his own. An almost diabolical power enabled him to feel the breath of this voice, to smell the scented powder covering her hair, to see the planes of her face, to count the blue veins shadowing her satin skin. Last, this agile voice, fresh and silvery in timbre, supple as a thread shaped by the slightest breath of air, rolling and unrolling, cascading and scattering, this voice attacked his soul so vividly that several times he gave vent to involuntary cries torn from him by convulsive feelings of pleasure which are all too rarely vouchsafed by human passions. He was presently obliged to leave the theater. His trembling legs almost refused to support him. He was limp, weak as a sensitive man who has given way to overwhelming anger. He had experienced such pleasure, or perhaps he had suffered so keenly, that his life had drained away like water from a broken vase. He felt empty inside, a prostration similar to the debilitation that overcomes those convalescing from serious illness.

Overcome by an inexplicable sadness, he sat down on the steps of a church. There, leaning back against a pillar, he fell into a confused meditation, as in a dream. He had been smitten by passion. Upon returning to his lodgings, he fell into one of those frenzies of activity which disclose to us the presence of new elements in our lives. A prey to this first fever of love derived equally from both pleasure and pain, he tried to appease his impatience and his delirium by drawing La Zambinella from memory. It was a kind of embodied meditation. On one page, La Zambinella appeared in that apparently calm and cool pose favored by Raphael, Giorgione, and every great painter. On another, she was delicately turning her head after having finished a trill, and appeared to be listening to herself. Sarrasine sketched his mistress in every pose: he drew her unveiled, seated, standing, lying down, chaste or amorous, embodying through the delirium of his pencils every capricious notion that can enter our heads when we think intently about a mistress. However, his fevered thoughts went beyond drawing. He saw La Zambinella, spoke to her, beseeched her, he passed a thousand years of life and happiness with her by placing her in every imaginable position; in short, by sampling the future with her. On the following day, he sent his valet to rent a box next to the stage for the entire season. Then, like all young people with lusty souls, he exaggerated to himself the difficulties of his undertaking and first fed his passion with the pleasure of being able to admire his mistress without obstruction. This golden age of love, during which we take pleasure in our own feeling and in which we are happy almost by ourselves, was not destined to last long in Sarrasine's case. Nevertheless, events took him by surprise while he was still under the spell of this vernal hallucination, as naive as it was voluptuous. In a week he lived a lifetime, spending the mornings kneeding the clay by which he would copy La Zambinella, despite the veils, skirts, corsets, and ribbons which concealed her from him. In the evenings, installed in his box early, alone, lying on a sofa like a Turk under the influence of opium, he created for himself a pleasure as rich and varied as he wished it to be. First, he gradually familiarized himself with the overly vivid emotions his mistress's singing afforded him, he then trained his eyes to see her, and finally he could contemplate her without fearing an outburst of the wild frenzy which had seized him on the first day. As his passion became calmer, it grew deeper. For the rest, the unsociable sculptor did not allow his friends to intrude upon his solitude, which was peopled with images, adorned with fantasies of hope, and filled with happiness. His love was so strong, so naive, that he experienced all the innocent scruples that assail us when we love for the first time. As he began to realize that he would soon have to act, to plot, to inquire where La Zambinella lived, whether she had a mother, uncle, teacher, family, to ponder, in short, on ways to see her, speak to her, these great, ambitious thoughts made his heart swell so painfully that he put them off until later, deriving as much satisfaction from his physical suffering as he did from his intellectual pleasures.

"But," Mme de Rochefide interrupted me, "I still don't see anything about either Marianina or her little old man."

"You are seeing nothing but him!" I cried impatiently, like an author who is being forced to spoil a theatrical effect.

For several days, I resumed after a pause, Sarrasine had reappeared so faithfully in his box and his eyes had expressed such love that his passion for La Zambinella's voice would have been common knowledge throughout Paris, had this adventure happened there; however, in Italy, madame, everyone goes to the theater for himself, with his own passions, and with a heartfelt interest which precludes spying through opera glasses. Nevertheless, the sculptor's enthusiasm did not escape the attention of the singers for long. One evening, the Frenchman saw that they were laughing at him in the wings. It is hard to know what extreme actions he might not have taken had La Zambinella not come onto the stage. She gave Sarrasine one of those eloquent glances which often reveal much more than women intend them to. This glance was a total revelation. Sarrasine was loved!

"If it's only a caprice," he thought, already accusing his mistress of excessive ardor, "she doesn't know what she is subjecting herself to. I am hoping her caprice will last my whole life."

At that moment, the artist's attention was distracted by three soft knocks on the door of his box. He opened it. An old woman entered with an air of mystery.

"Young man," she said, "if you want to be happy, be prudent. Put on a cape, wear a hat drawn down over your eyes; then, around ten in the evening, be in the Via del Corso in front of the Hotel di Spagna."

"I'll be there," he replied, placing two louis in the duenna's wrinkled hand.

He left his box after having given a signal to La Zambinella, who timidly lowered her heavy eyelids, like a woman pleased to be understood at last. Then he ran home to dress himself as seductively as he could. As he was leaving the theater, a strange man took his arm.

"Be on your guard, Frenchman," he whispered in his ear. "This is a matter of life and death. Cardinal Cicognara is her protector and doesn't trifle."

At that moment, had some demon set the pit of hell between Sarrasine and La Zambinella, he would have crossed it with one leap. Like the horses of the gods described by Homer, the sculptor's love had traversed vast distances in the twinkling of an eye.

"If death itself were waiting for me outside the house, I would go even faster," he replied.

"*Poverino!*" the stranger cried as he disappeared.

Speaking of danger to a lover is tantamount to selling him pleasures, is it not? Sarrasine's valet had never seen his master take so much care over his toilette. His finest sword, a gift from Bouchardon, the sash Clotilde had given him, his embroidered coat, his silver-brocade waistcoat, his gold snuffbox, his jeweled watches, were all taken from their coffers, and he adorned himself like a girl about to appear before her first love. At the appointed hour, drunk with love and seething with hope, Sarrasine, concealed in his cape, sped to the rendezvous the old woman had given him. The duenna was waiting for him.

"You took a long time," she said. "Come."

She led the Frenchman along several back streets and stopped before a rather handsome mansion. She knocked. The door opened. She led Sarrasine along a labyrinth of stairways, galleries, and rooms which were lit only by the feeble light of the moon, and soon came to a door through whose cracks gleamed bright lights and from behind which came the joyful sounds of several voices. When at a word from the old women he was admitted to this mysterious room, Sarrasine was suddenly dazzled at finding himself in a salon as brilliantly lighted as it was sumptuously furnished, in the center of which stood a table laden with venerable bottles and flashing flagons sparkling with ruby facets. He recognized the singers from the theater, along with some charming women, all ready to begin an artists' orgy as soon as he was among them. Sarrasine suppressed a feeling of disappointment and put on a good face. He had expected a dim room, his mistress seated by the fire, some jealous person nearby, death and love, an exchange of confidences in low voices, heart to heart, dangerous kisses and faces so close that La Zambinella's hair would have caressed his forehead throbbing with desire, feverish with happiness.

"*Vive la folie!*" he cried. "*Signori e belle donne,* you will allow me to take my revenge later and to show you my gratitude for the way you have welcomed a poor sculptor."

Having been greeted warmly enough by most of those present, whom he knew by sight, he sought to approach the armchair on which La Zambinella was casually reclining. Ah! how his heart beat when he spied a delicate foot shod in one of those slippers which in those days, may I say, madame, gave women's feet such a coquettish and voluptuous look that I don't know how men were able to resist them. The well-fitting white stockings with green clocks, the short skirts, the slippers with pointed toes, and the high heels of Louis XV's reign may have contributed something to the demoralization of Europe and the clergy.

"Something?" the Marquise replied. "Have you read nothing?"

La Zambinella, I continued, smiling, had impudently crossed her legs and was gently swinging the upper one with a certain attractive indolence which suited her capricious sort of beauty. She had removed her costume and was wearing a bodice that accentuated her narrow waist and set off the satin panniers of her dress, which was embroidered with blue flowers. Her bosom, the treasures of which were concealed, in an excess of coquetry, by a covering of lace, was dazzling white. Her hair arranged something like that of Mme du Barry, her face, though it was partially hidden under a full bonnet, appeared only the more delicate, and powder suited her. To see her thus was to adore her. She gave the sculptor a graceful smile. Unhappy at not being able to speak to her without witnesses present, Sarrasine politely sat down next to her and talked about music, praising her extraordinary talent; but his voice trembled with love, with fear and hope.

"What are you afraid of?" asked Vitagliani, the company's most famous singer. "Go ahead; you need fear no rivals here." Having said this, the tenor smiled without another word. This smile was repeated on the lips of all the guests, whose attention contained a hidden malice a lover would not have noticed. Such openness was like a dagger thrust in Sarrasine's heart. Although endowed with a certain strength of character, and although nothing could change his love, it had perhaps not yet occurred to him that La Zambinella was virtually a courtesan, and that he could not have both the pure pleasure that make a young girl's love so delicious and the tempestuous transports by which the hazardous possession of an actress must be purchased. He reflected and resigned himself. Supper was served. Sarrasine and La Zambinella sat down informally side by side. For the first half of the meal, the artists preserved some decorum, and the sculptor was able to chat with the singer. He found her witty, acute, but astonishingly ignorant, and she revealed herself to be weak and superstitious. The delicacy of her organs was reflected in her understanding. When Vitagliani uncorked the first bottle of champagne, Sarrasine read in his companion's eyes a start of terror at the tiny explosion caused by the escaping gas. The love-stricken artist interpreted the involuntary shudder of this feminine constitution as the sign of an excessive sensitivity. The Frenchman was charmed by this weakness. How much is protective in a man's love!

"My strength your shield!" Is this not written at the heart of all declarations of love? Too excited to shower the beautiful Italian with compliments, Sarrasine, like all lovers, was by turns serious, laughing, or reflective. Although he seemed to be listening to the other guests, he did not hear a word they were saying, so absorbed was he in the pleasure of finding himself beside her, touching her hand as he served her. He bathed in a secret joy. Despite the eloquence of a few mutual glances, he was astonished at the reserve La Zambinella maintained toward him. Indeed, she had begun by pressing his foot and teasing him with the flirtatiousness of a woman in love and free to show it; but she suddenly wrapped herself in the modesty of a young girl, after hearing Sarrasine describe a trait which revealed the excessive violence of his character. When the supper became an orgy, the guests broke into song under the influence of the Peralta and the Pedro-Ximenes. There were ravishing duets, songs from Calabria, Spanish seguidillas, Neapolitan canzonettas. Intoxication was in every eye, in the music, in hearts and voices alike. Suddenly an enchanting vivacity welled up, a gay abandon, an Italian warmth of feeling inconceivable to those acquainted only with Parisian gatherings, London routs, or Viennese circles. Jokes and words of love flew like bullets in a battle through laughter, profanities, and invocations to the Holy Virgin or *il Bambino*. Someone lay down on a sofa and fell asleep. A girl was listening to a declaration of love unaware that she was spilling sherry on the tablecloth. In the midst of this disorder, La Zambinella remained thoughtful, as though terrorstruck. She refused to drink, perhaps she ate a bit too much; however, it is said that greediness in a woman is a charming quality. Admiring his mistress's modesty, Sarrasine thought seriously about the future.

"She probably wants to be married," he thought. He then turned his thoughts to the delights of this marriage. His whole life seemed too short to exhaust the springs of happiness he found in the depths of his soul. Vitagliani, who was sitting next to him, refilled his glass so often that, toward three in the morning, without being totally drunk, Sarrasine could no longer control his delirium. Impetuously, he picked up the woman, escaping into a kind of boudoir next to the salon, toward the door of which he had glanced more than once. The Italian woman was armed with a dagger.

"If you come any closer," she said, "I will be forced to plunge this weapon into your heart. Let me go! You would despise me. I have conceived too much respect for your character to surrender in this fashion. I don't want to betray the feeling you have for me."

"Oh no!" cried Sarrasine. "You cannot stifle a passion by stimulating it! Are you already so corrupt that, old in heart, you would act like a young courtesan who whets the emotions by which she plies her trade?"

"But today is Friday," she replied, frightened at the Frenchman's violence.

Sarrasine, who was not devout, broke into laughter. La Zambinella jumped up like a young deer and ran toward the salon. When Sarrasine appeared in her pursuit, he was greeted by an infernal burst of laughter.

He saw La Zambinella lying in a swoon upon a sofa. She was pale and drained by the extraordinary effort she had just made.

Although Sarrasine knew little Italian, he heard his mistress saying in a low voice to Vitagliani: "But he will kill me!"

The sculptor was utterly confounded by this strange scene. He regained his senses. At first he stood motionless; then he found his voice, sat down next to his mistress, and assured her of his respect. He was able to divert his passion by addressing the most high-minded phrases to this woman; and in depicting his love, he used all the resources of that magical eloquence, that inspired intermediary which women rarely refuse to believe. When the guests were surprised by the first gleams of morning light, a woman suggested they go to Frascati. Everyone enthusiastically fell in with the idea of spending the day at the Villa Ludovisi. Vitagliani went down to hire some carriages. Sarrasine had the pleasure of leading La Zambinella to a phaeton. Once outside Rome, the gaiety which had been momentarily repressed by each person's battle with sleepiness suddenly revived. Men and women alike seemed used to this strange life, these ceaseless pleasures, this artist's impulsiveness which turns life into a perpetual party at which one laughed unreservedly. The sculptor's companion was the only one who seemed downcast.

"Are you ill?" Sarrasine asked her. "Would you rather go home?"

"I'm not strong enough to stand all these excesses," she replied. "I must be very careful; but with you I feel so well! Had it not been for you, I would never have stayed for supper; a sleepless night and I lose whatever bloom I have."

"You are so delicate," Sarrasine said, looking at the charming creature's pretty face.

"Orgies ruin the voice."

"Now that we're alone," the artist cried, "and you no longer need fear the outbursts of my passion, tell me that you love me."

"Why?" she replied. "What would be the use? I seemed pretty to you. But you are French and your feelings will pass. Ah, you would not love me as I long to be loved."

"How can you say that?"

"Not to satisfy any vulgar passion; purely. I abhor men perhaps even more than I hate women. I need to seek refuge in friendship. For me, the world is a desert. I am an accursed creature, condemned to understand happiness, to feel it, to desire it, and like many others, forced to see it flee from me continually. Remember, sir, that I will not have deceived you. I forbid you to love me. I can be your devoted friend, for I admire your strength and your character. I need a brother, a protector. Be all that for me, but no more."

"Not love you!" Sarrasine cried. "But my dearest angel, you are my life, my happiness!"

"If I were to say one word, you would repulse me with horror."

"Coquette! Nothing can frighten me. Tell me you will cost my future, that I will die in two months, that I will be damned merely for having kissed you."

He kissed her, despite La Zambinella's efforts to resist this passionate embrace.

"Tell me you are a devil, that you want my money, my name, all my fame! Do you want me to give up being a sculptor? Tell me."

"And if I were not a woman?" La Zambinella asked in a soft silvery voice.

"What a joke!" Sarrasine cried. "Do you think you can deceive an artist's eye? Haven't I spent ten days devouring, scrutinizing, admiring your perfection? Only a woman could have this round, soft arm, these elegant curves. Oh, you want compliments."

She smiled at him sadly, and raising her eyes heavenward, she murmured: "Fatal beauty!"

At that moment her gaze had an indescribable expression of horror, so powerful and vivid that Sarrasine shuddered.

"Frenchman," she went on, "forget this moment of madness forever. I respect you, but as for love, do not ask it of me; that feeling is smothered in my heart. I have no heart!" she cried, weeping. "The stage where you saw me, that applause, that music, that fame I am condemned to, such is my life, I have no other. In a few hours you will not see me in the same way, the woman you love will be dead."

The sculptor made no reply. He was overcome with a dumb rage which oppressed his heart. He could only gaze with enflamed, burning eyes at this extraordinary woman. La Zambinella's weak voice, her manner, her movements and gestures marked with sorrow, melancholy, and discouragement, awakened all the wealth of passion in his soul. Each word was a goad. At that moment they reached Frascati. As the artist offered his mistress his arm to assist her in alighting, he felt her shiver.

"What is wrong? You would kill me," he cried, seeing her grow pale, "if I were even an innocent cause of your slightest unhappiness."

"A snake," she said, pointing to a grass snake which was sliding along a ditch. "I am afraid of those horrid creatures." Sarrasine crushed the snake's head with his heel.

"How can you be so brave?" La Zambinella continued, looking with visible horror at the dead reptile.

"Ah," the artist replied, smiling, "now do you dare deny you are a woman?"

They rejoined their companions and strolled through the woods of the Villa Ludovisi, which in those days belonged to Cardinal Cicognara. That morning fled too quickly for the enamored sculptor, but it was filled with a host of incidents which revealed to him the coquetry, the weakness, and the delicacy of this soft and enervated being. This was woman herself, with her sudden fears, her irrational whims, her instinctive worries, her impetuous boldness, her fussings, and her delicious sensibility. It happened that as they were wandering in the open countryside, the little group of merry singers saw in the distance some heavily armed men whose manner of dress was far from reassuring. Someone said, "They must be highwaymen," and everyone quickened his pace toward the refuge of the Cardinal's grounds. At this critical moment, Sarrasine saw from La Zambinella's pallor that she no longer had the strength to walk; he took her up in his arms and carried her for a while, running. When he came to a nearby arbor, he put her down.

"Explain to me," he said, "how this extreme weakness, which I would find hideous in any other woman, which would displease me and whose slightest indication would be almost enough to choke my love, pleases and charms me in you? Ah, how I love you," he went on. "All your faults, your terrors, your resentments, add an indefinable grace to your soul. I think I would detest a strong woman, a Sappho, a courageous creature, full of energy and passion. Oh, soft, frail creature, how could you be otherwise? That angelic voice, that delicate voice would be an anomaly coming from any body but yours."

"I cannot give you any hope," she said. "Stop speaking to me in this way, because they will make a fool of you. I cannot stop you from coming to the theater; but if you love me or if you are wise, you will come there no more. Listen, monsieur," she said in a low voice.

"Oh, be still," the impassioned artist said. "Obstacles make my love more ardent."

La Zambinella's graceful and modest attitude did not change, but she fell silent as though a terrible thought had revealed some misfortune to her. When it came time to return to Rome, she got into the four-seated coach, ordering the sculptor with imperious cruelty to return to Rome alone in the carriage. During the journey, Sarrasine resolved to kidnap La Zambinella. He spent the entire day making plans, each more outrageous than the other. At nightfall, as he was going out to inquire where his mistress's palazzo was located, he met one of his friends on the threshold.

"My dear fellow," he said, "our ambassador has asked me to

invite you to his house tonight. He is giving a magnificent concert, and when I tell you that Zambinella will be there . . ."

"Zambinella," cried Sarrasine, intoxicated by the name, "I'm mad about her!"

"You're like everyone else," his friend replied.

"If you are my friends, you, Vien, Lauterbourg, and Allegrain, will you help me do something after the party?" Sarrasine asked.

"It's not some cardinal to be killed? . . . not . . . ?"

"No, no," Sarrasine said, "I'm not asking you to do anything an honest person couldn't do."

In a short time, the sculptor had arranged everything for the success of his undertaking. He was one of the last to arrive at the ambassador's, but he had come in a traveling carriage drawn by powerful horses and driven by one of the most enterprising *vetturini* of Rome. The ambassador's palazzo was crowded; not without some difficulty, the sculptor, who was a stranger to everyone present, made his way to the salon where Zambinella was singing at that very moment.

"Is it out of consideration for the cardinals, bishops, and abbés present," Sarrasine asked, "that *she* is dressed like a man, that she is wearing a snood, kinky hair, and a sword?"

"She? What she?" asked the old nobleman to whom Sarrasine had been speaking. "La Zambinella." "La Zambinella!" the Roman prince replied. "Are you joking? Where are you from? Has there ever been a woman on the Roman stage? And don't you know about the creatures who sing female roles in the Papal States? I am the one, monsieur, who gave Zambinella his voice. I paid for everything that scamp ever had, even his singing teacher. Well, he has so little gratitude for the service I rendered him that he has never consented to set foot in my house. And yet, if he makes a fortune, he will owe it all to me."

Prince Chigi may well have gone on talking for some time; Sarrasine was not listening to him. A horrid truth had crept into his soul. It was as though he had been struck by lightning. He stood motionless, his eyes fixed on the false singer. His fiery gaze exerted a sort of magnetic influence on Zambinella, for the *musico* finally turned to look at Sarrasine, and at that moment his heavenly voice faltered. He trembled! An involuntary murmur escaping from the audience he had kept hanging on his lips completed his discomfiture; he sat down and cut short his aria. Cardinal Cicognara, who had glanced out the corner of his eye to see what had attracted his protégé's attention, then saw the Frenchman: he leaned over to one of his ecclesiastical aides-de-camp and appeared to be asking the sculptor's name. Having obtained the answer he sought, he regarded the artist with great attention and gave an order to an abbé, who quickly disappeared.

During this time, Zambinella, having recovered himself, once more began the piece he had so capriciously interrupted; but he sang it badly, and despite all the requests made to him, he refused to sing anything else. This was the first time he displayed that capricious tyranny for which he would later be as celebrated as for his talent and his vast fortune, due, as they said, no less to his voice than to his beauty.

"It is a woman," Sarrasine said, believing himself alone. "There is some hidden intrigue here. Cardinal Cicognara is deceiving the Pope and the whole city of Rome!"

The sculptor thereupon left the salon, gathered his friends together, and posted them out of sight in the courtyard of the palazzo. When Zambinella was confident that Sarrasine had departed, he appeared to regain his composure. Around midnight, having wandered through the rooms like a man seeking some enemy, the *musico* departed. As soon as he crossed the threshold of the palazzo, he was adroitly seized by men who gagged him with a handkerchief and drew him into the carriage Sarrasine had hired. Frozen with horror, Zambinella remained in a corner, not daring to move. He saw before him the terrible face of the artist, who was silent as death.

The journey was brief. Carried in Sarrasine's arms, Zambinella soon found himself in a dark, empty studio. Half dead, the singer remained in a chair, without daring to examine the statue of a woman in which he recognized his own features. He made no attempt to speak, but his teeth chattered. Sarrasine paced up and down the room. Suddenly he stopped in front of Zambinella.

"Tell me the truth," he pleaded in a low, altered voice. "You are a woman? Cardinal Cicognara . . ."

Zambinella fell to his knees, and in reply lowered his head.

"Ah, you are a woman," the artist cried in a delirium, "for even a . . . " He broke off. "No," he continued, "*he* would not be so cowardly."

"Ah, do not kill me," cried Zambinella, bursting into tears. "I only agreed to trick you to please my friends, who wanted to laugh."

"Laugh!" the sculptor replied in an infernal tone. "Laugh! Laugh! You dared play with a man's feelings, you?"

"Oh, have mercy!" Zambinella replied.

"I ought to kill you,"Sarrasine cried, drawing his sword with a violent gesture. "However," he went on, in cold disdain, "were I to scour your body with this blade, would I find there one feeling to stifle, one vengeance to satisfy? You are nothing. If you were a man or a woman, I would kill you, but . . ."

Sarrasine made a gesture of disgust which forced him to turn away, whereupon he saw the statue.

"And it's an illusion," he cried. Then, turning to Zambinella: "A woman's heart was a refuge for me, a home. Have you any sisters who resemble you? Then die! But no, you shall live. Isn't leaving you alive condemning you to something worse than death? It is neither my blood nor my existence that I regret, but the future and my heart's fortune. Your feeble hand has destroyed my happiness. What hope can I strip from you for all those you have blighted? You have dragged me down to your level. *To love, to be loved*! are henceforth meaningless words for me, as they are for you. I shall forever think of this imaginary woman when I see a real woman." He indicated the statue with a gesture of despair. "I shall always have the memory of a celestial harpy who thrusts its talons into all my manly feelings, and who will stamp all other women with a seal of imperfection! Monster! You who can give life to nothing. For me, you have wiped women from the earth."

Sarrasine sat down before the terrified singer. Two huge tears welled from his dry eyes, rolled down his manly cheeks, and fell to the ground: two tears of rage, two bitter and burning tears.

"No more love! I am dead to all pleasure, to every human emotion."

So saying, he seized a hammer and hurled it at the statue with such extraordinary force that he missed it. He thought he had destroyed this monument to his folly, and then took up his sword and brandished it to kill the singer. Zambinella uttered piercing screams. At that moment, three men entered and at once the sculptor fell, stabbed by three stiletto thrusts.

"On behalf of Cardinal Cicognara," one of them said.

"It is a good deed worthy of a Christian," replied the Frenchman as he died. These sinister messengers informed Zambinella of the concern of his protector, who was waiting at the door in a closed carriage, to take him away as soon as he had been rescued.

"But," Mme de Rochefide asked me, "what connection is there between this story and the little old man we saw at the Lantys'?"

"Madame, Cardinal Cicognara took possession of Zambinella's statue and had it executed in marble; today it is in the Albani Museum. There, in 1791, the Lanty family found it and asked Vien to copy it. The portrait in which you saw Zambinella at twenty, a second after having seen him at one hundred, later served for Girodet's *Endymion*; you will have recognized its type in the Adonis."

"But this Zambinella—he or she?"

"He, madame, is none other than Marianina's great uncle. Now you can readily see what interest Mme de Lanty has in hiding the source of a fortune which comes from—"

"Enough!" she said, gesturing to me imperiously. We sat for a moment plunged in the deepest silence.

"Well?" I said to her.

"Ah," she exclaimed, standing up and pacing up and down the room. She looked at me and spoke in an altered voice. "You have given me a disgust for life and for passions that will last a long time. Excepting for monsters, don't all human feelings come down to the same thing, to horrible disappointments? Mothers, our children kill us either by their bad behavior or by their lack of affection. Wives, we are deceived. Mistresses, we are forsaken, abandoned. Does friendship even exist? I would become a nun tomorrow did I not know that I can remain unmoved as a rock amid the storms of life. If the Christian's future is also an illusion, at least it is not destroyed until after death. Leave me."

"Ah," I said, "you know how to punish."

"Am I wrong?"

"Yes," I replied, with a kind of courage. "In telling this story, which is fairly well known in Italy, I have been able to give you a fine example of the progress made by civilization today. They no longer create these unfortunate creatures."

"Paris is a very hospitable place," she said. "It accepts everything, shameful fortunes and bloodstained fortunes. Crime and infamy can find asylum here; only virtue has no altars here. Yes, pure souls have their home in heaven! No one will have known me. I am proud of that!"

And the Marquise remained pensive.

Paris, November 1830

1. The narrator of the story tells his own story, and tells that of Sarrasine. How does his role change as he tells each story?
2. What does he hope to accomplish by telling the story? What does he actually accomplish?
3. How does he control the narrative pace of the story of Sarrasine? What moments get the greatest attention?

John Cheever (b. 1912)

THE CHASTE CLARISSA

The evening boat for Vineyard Haven was loading freight. In a little while, the warning whistle would separate the sheep from the goats—that's the way Baxter thought of it—the islanders from the tourists wandering through the streets of Woods Hole. His car, like all the others ticketed for the ferry, was parked near the wharf. He sat on the front bumper, smoking. The noise and movement of the small port seemed to signify that the spring had ended and that the shores of West Chop, across the Sound, were the shores of summer, but the implications of the hour and the voyage made no impression on Baxter at all. The delay bored and irritated him. When someone called his name, he got to his feet with relief.

It was old Mrs. Ryan. She called to him from a dusty station wagon, and he went over to speak to her. "I knew it," she said. "I knew that I'd see someone here from Holly Cove. I had that feeling in my bones. We've been traveling since nine this morning. We had trouble with the brakes outside Worcester. Now I'm wondering if Mrs. Talbot will have cleaned the house. She wanted seventy-five dollars for opening it last summer and I told her I wouldn't pay her that again, and I wouldn't be surprised if she's thrown all my letters away. Oh, I hate to have a journey end in a dirty house, but if worse comes to worst, we can clean it outselves. Can't we, Clarissa?" she asked, turning to a young woman who sat beside her on the front seat. "Oh, excuse me, Baxter!" she exclained. "You haven't met Clarissa, have you? This is Bob's wife, Clarissa Ryan."

Baxter's first thought was that a girl like that shouldn't have to ride in a dusty station wagon: she should have done much better. She was young. He guessed that she was about twenty-five. Red-headed, deep-breasted, slender, and indolent, she seemed to belong to a different species from old Mrs. Ryan and her large-boned, forthright daughters. "The Cape Cod girls, they have no combs. They comb their hair with codfish bones,' " he said to himself but Clarissa's hair was well groomed. Her bare arms were perfectly white. Woods Hole and the activity on the wharf seemed to bore her and she was not interested in Mrs. Ryan's insular gossip. She lighted a cigarette.

At a pause in the old lady's monologue, Baxter spoke to her daughter-in-law. "When is Bob coming down, Mrs. Ryan?" he asked.

"He isn't coming at all," the beautiful Clarissa said. "He's in France. He's—"

"He's gone there for the government," old Mrs. Ryan interrupted, as if her daughter-in-law could not be entrusted with this simple explanation. "He's working on this terribly interesting project. He won't be back until autumn. I'm going abroad myself. I'm leaving Clarissa alone. Of course," she added forcefully. "I expect that she will *love* the island. Everyone does. I expect that she will be kept very busy. I expect that she—"

The warning signal from the ferry cut her off. Baxter said goodbye. One by one, the cars drove aboard, and the boat started to cross the shoal water from the mainland to the resort. Baxter drank a beer in the cabin and watched Clarissa and old Mrs. Ryan, who were sitting on deck. Since he had never seen Clarissa before, he supposed that Bob Ryan must have married her during the past winter. He did not understand how this beauty had ended up with the Ryans. They were a family of passionate amateur geologists and bird-watchers. "We're all terribly keen about birds and rocks," they said when they were introduced to strangers. Their cottage was a couple of miles from any other and had, as Mrs. Ryan often said, "been thrown together out of a barn in 1922." They sailed, hiked, swam in the surf, and organized expeditions to Cuttyhunk and Tarpaulin Cove. They were people who emphasized *corpore sano* unduly, Baxter thought, and they shouldn't leave Clarissa alone in the cottage. The wind had blown a strand of her flame-colored hair across her cheek. Her long legs were crossed. As the ferry entered the harbor, she stood up and made her way down the deck against the light salt wind, and Baxter, who had returned to the island indifferently, felt that the summer had begun.

Baxter knew that in trying to get some information about Clarissa Ryan he had to be careful. He was accepted in Holly Cove because he had summered there all his life. He could be pleasant and he was a good-looking man, but his two divorces, his promiscuity, his stinginess, and his Latin complexion had left with his neighbors a vague feeling that he was unsavory. He learned that Clarissa had married Bob Ryan in November and that she was from Chicago. He heard people say that she was beautiful and stupid. That was all he did find out about her.

He looked for Clarissa on the tennis courts and the beaches. He didn't see her. He went several times to the beach nearest the Ryans' cottage. She wasn't there. When he had been on the island only a short time, he received from Mrs. Ryan, in the mail, an invitation to tea. It was an invitation that he would not ordinarily have accepted, but he drove eagerly that afternoon over to the Ryans' cottage. He was late. The cars of most of his friends and neighbors were parked in Mrs. Ryan's field. Their voices drifted out of the open windows into the garden, where Mrs. Ryan's climbing roses were in bloom. "Welcome aboard!" Mrs. Ryan shouted when he crossed the porch. "This is my farewell party. I'm going to Norway." She led him into a crowded room.

Clarissa sat behind the teacups. Against the wall at her back was a glass cabinet that held the Ryans' geological specimens. Her arms were bare. Baxter watched them while she poured his tea. "Hot? . . . Cold? Lemon? . . . Cream?" seemed to be all she had to say, but her red hair and her white arms dominated that end of the room. Baxter ate a sandwich. He hung around the table.

"Have you ever been to the island before, Clarissa?" he asked.

"Yes."

"Do you swim at the beach at Holly Cove?"

"It's too far away."

"When your mother-in-law leaves," Baxter said, "you must let me drive you there in the mornings. I go down at eleven."

"Well, thank you." Clarissa lowered her green eyes. She seemed uncomfortable, and the thought that she might be susceptible crossed Baxter's mind exuberantly. "Well, thank you," she repeated, "but I have a car of my own and—well, I don't know. I don't—"

"What are *you* two talking about?" Mrs. Ryan asked, coming between them and smiling wildly in an effort to conceal some of the force of her interference. "I know it isn't geology," she went on, "and I know that it isn't birds, and I know that it can't be books or music, because those are all things that Clarissa doesn't like, aren't they, Clarissa? Come with me, Baxter," and she led him to the other side of the room and talked to him about sheep raising. When the conversation had ended, the party itself was nearly over. Clarissa's chair was empty. She was not in the room. Stopping at the door to thank Mrs. Ryan and say goodbye, Baxter said that he hoped she wasn't leaving for Europe immediately.

"Oh, but I am," Mrs. Ryan said. "I'm going to the mainland on the six-o'clock boat and sailing from Boston at noon tomorrow."

At half past ten the next morning, Baxter drove up to the Ryans' cottage. Mrs. Talbot, the local woman who helped the Ryans with their housework, answered the door. She said that young Mrs. Ryan was home, and let him in. Clarissa came downstairs. She looked more beautiful than ever, although she seemed put out at finding him there. She accepted his invitation to go swimming, but she accepted it unenthusiastically. "Oh, all right," she said.

When she came downstairs again, she had on a bathrobe over her bathing suit, and a broad-brimmed hat. On the drive to Holly Cove, he asked about her plans for the summer. She was noncommittal. She seemed preoccupied and unwilling to talk. They parked the car and walked side by side over the dunes to the beach, where she lay in the sand with her eyes closed. A few of Baxter's friends and neighbors stopped to pass the time, but they didn't stop for long. Baxter noticed Clarissa's unresponsiveness made it difficult to talk. He didn't care.

He went swimming. Clarissa remained on the sand, bundled in her wrap. When he came out of the water, he lay down near her. He watched his neighbors and their children. The weather had been fair. The women were tanned. They were all married women and, unlike Clarissa, women with children, but the rigors of marriage and childbirth had left them all pretty, agile, and contented. While he was admiring them, Clarissa stood up and took off her bathrobe.

Here was something else, and it took his breath away. Some of the inescapable power of her beauty lay in the whiteness of her skin, some of it in the fact that, unlike the other women, who were at ease in bathing suits, Clarissa seemed humiliated and ashamed to find herself wearing so little. She walked down toward the water as if she were naked. When she first felt the water, she stopped short, for, again unlike the others, who were sporting around the pier like seals, Clarissa didn't like the cold. Then, caught for a second between nakedness and the cold, Clarissa waded in and swam a few feet. She came out of the water, hastily wrapped herself in the robe, and lay down in the sand. Then she spoke, for the first time that morning—for the first time in Baxter's experience—with warmth and feeling.

"You know, those stones on the point have grown a lot since I was here last," she said.

"What?" Baxter said.

"Those stones on the point," Clarissa said. "They've grown a lot."

"Stones don't grow." Baxter said.

"Oh yes they do," Clarissa said. "Didn't you know that? Stones grow. There's a stone in Mother's rose garden that's grown a foot in the last few years."

"I didn't know that stones grew," Baxter said.

"Well, they do," Clarissa said. She yawned, she shut her eyes. She seemed to fall asleep. When she opened her eyes again, she asked Baxter the time.

"Twelve o'clock," he said.

"I have to go home," she said. "I'm expecting guests."

Baxter could not contest this. He drove her home. She was unresponsive on the ride, and when he asked her if he could drive her to the beach again, she said no. It was a hot, fair day and most of the doors on the island stood open, but when Clarissa said goodbye to Baxter, she closed the door in his face.

Baxter got Clarissa's mail and newspapers from the post office the next day, but when he called with them at the cottage, Mrs. Talbot said that Mrs. Ryan was busy. He went that week to two large parties that she might have attended, but she was not at either. On Saturday night, he went to a barn dance, and late in the evening—they were dancing "Lady of the Lake"—he noticed Clarissa, sitting against the wall.

She was a striking wallflower. She was much more beautiful than any other woman there, but her beauty seemed to have intimidated the men. Baxter dropped out of the dance when he could and went to her. She was sitting on a packing case. It was the first thing she complained about. "There isn't even anything to sit on," she said.

"Don't you want to dance?" Baxter asked.

"Oh, I love to dance," she said. "I could dance all night, but I don't think *that's* dancing." She winced at the music of the fiddle and the piano. "I came with the Hortons. They just told me there was going to be a dance. They didn't tell me it was going to be this kind of a dance. I don't like all that skipping and hopping."

"Have your guests left?" Baxter asked.

"What guests?" Clarissa said.

"You told me you were expecting guests on Tuesday. When we were at the beach."

"I didn't say they were coming on Tuesday, did I?" Clarissa asked. "They're coming tomorrow."

"Can't I take you home?" Baxter asked.

"All right."

He brought the car around to the barn and turned on the radio. She got in and slammed the door with spirit. He raced the car over the back roads, and when he brought it up to the Ryans' cottage, he turned off the lights. He watched her hands. She folded them on her purse. "Well, thank you very much," she said. "I was having an awful time and you saved my life. I just don't understand this place, I guess. I've always had plenty of partners, but I sat on that hard box for nearly an hour and nobody even spoke to me. You saved my life."

"You're lovely, Clarissa," Baxter said.

"Well," Clarissa said, and she sighed. "That's just my outward self. Nobody knows the real me."

That was it, Baxter thought, and if he could only adjust his flattery to what she believed herself to be her scruples would dissolve. Did she think of herself as an actress, he wondered, a Channel swimmer, an heiress? The intimations of susceptibility that came from her in the summer night were so powerful, so heady, that they convinced Baxter that here was a woman whose chastity hung by a thread.

"I think I know the real you," Baxter said.

"Oh no you don't," Clarissa said. "Nobody does."

The radio played some lovelorn music from a Boston hotel. By the calendar, it was still early in the summer, but it seemed, from the stillness and the hugeness of the dark trees, to be much later. Baxter put his arms around Clarissa and planted a kiss on her lips.

She pushed him away violently and reached for the door. "Oh, now you've spoiled everything," she said as she got out of the car. "Now you've spoiled everything. I know what you've been thinking. I know you've been thinking it all along." She slammed the door and spoke to him across the window. "Well, you needn't come around here any more, Baxter," she said. "My girl friends are coming down from New York tomorrow on the morning plane and I'll be too busy to see you for the rest of the summer. Good night."

Baxter was aware that he had only himself to blame; he had moved too quickly. He knew better. He went to bed feeling angry and sad, and slept poorly. He was depressed when he woke, and his depression was deepened by the noise of a sea rain, blowing in from the northeast. He lay in bed listening to the rain and the surf. The storm would metamorphose the island. The beaches would be empty. Drawers would stick. Suddenly he got out of bed, went to the telephone, called the airport. The New York plane had been unable to land, they told him, and no more planes were expected that day. The storm seemed to be playing directly into his hands. At noon, he drove in to the village and bought a Sunday paper and a box of candy. The candy was for Clarissa, but he was in no hurry to give it to her.

She would have stocked the icebox, put out the towels, and planned the picnic, but now the arrival of her friends had been postponed, and the lively day that she had anticipated had turned out to be rainy and idle. There were ways, of course, for her to overcome her disappointment, but on the evidence of the barn dance he felt that she was lost without her husband or mother-in-law, and that there were few, if any, people on the island who would pay her a chance call or ask her over for a drink. It was likely that she would spend the day listening to the radio and the rain and that by the end of it she would be ready to welcome anyone, including Baxter. But as long as the forces of loneliness and idleness were working on his side, it was shrewder, Baxter knew, to wait. It would be best to come just before dark, and he waited until then. He drove to the Ryans' with his box of candy. The windows were lighted. Clarissa opened the door.

"I wanted to welcome your friends to the island," Baxter said. "I—"

"They didn't come," Clarissa said. "The plane couldn't land. They went back to New York. They telephoned me. I had planned such a nice visit. Now everything's changed."

"I'm sorry, Clarissa," Baxter said. "I've brought you a present."

"Oh!" She took the box of candy. "What a beautiful box! What a lovely present! What—" Her face and her voice were, for a minute, ingenuous and yielding and then he saw the force of resistance transform them. "You shouldn't have done it," she said.

"May I come in?" Baxter asked.

"Well, I don't know," she said. "You can't come in if you're just going to sit around."

"We could play cards," Baxter said.

"I don't know how," she said.

"I'll teach you," Baxter said.

"No," she said. "No, Baxter, you'll have to go. You just don't understand the kind of woman I am. I spent all day writing a letter to Bob. I wrote and told him that you kissed me last night. I can't let you come in." She closed the door.

From the look on Clarissa's face when he gave her the box of candy, Baxter judged that she liked to get presents. An inexpensive gold bracelet or even a bunch of flowers might do it, he knew, but Baxter was an extremely stingy man, and while he saw the usefulness of a present, he could not bring himself to buy one. He decided to wait.

The storm blew all Monday and Tuesday. It cleared on Tuesday night, and by Wednesday afternoon the tennis courts were dry and

Baxter played. He played until late. Then, when he had bathed and changed his clothes, he stopped at a cocktail party to pick up a drink. Here one of his neighbors, a married woman with four children, sat down beside him and began a general discussion of the nature of married love.

It was a conversation, with its glances and innuendoes, that Baxter had been through many times, and he knew roughly what it promised. His neighbor was one of the pretty mothers that Baxter had admired on the beach. Her hair was brown. Her arms were thin and tanned. Her teeth were sound. But while he appeared to be deeply concerned with her opinion on love, the white image of Clarissa loomed up in his mind, and he broke off the conversation and left the party. He drove to the Ryans'.

From a distance, the cottage looked shut. The house and the garden were perfectly still. He knocked and then rang. Clarissa spoke to him from an upstairs window.

"Oh, hello, Baxter," she said.

"I've come to say goodbye, Clarissa," Baxter said. He couldn't think of anything better.

"Oh, dear," Clarissa said. "Well, wait just a minute. I'll be down."

"I'm going away, Clarissa," Baxter said when she opened the door. "I've come to say goodbye."

"Where are you going?"

"I don't know." He said this sadly.

"Well, come in, then," she said hesitantly. "Come in for a minute. This is the last time that I'll see you, I guess, isn't it? Please excuse the way the place looks. Mr. Talbot got sick on Monday and Mrs. Talbot had to take him to the hospital on the mainland, and I haven't had anybody to help me. I've been all alone."

He followed her into the living room and sat down. She was more beautiful than ever. She talked about the problems that had been presented by Mrs. Talbot's departure. The fire in the stove that heated the water had died. There was a mouse in the kitchen. The bathtub wouldn't drain. She hadn't been able to get the car started.

In the quiet house, Baxter heard the sound of a leaky water tap and a clock pendulum. The sheet of glass that protected the Ryans' geological specimens reflected the fading sky outside the window. The cottage was near the water, and he could hear the surf. He noted these details dispassionately and for what they were worth. When Clarissa finished her remarks about Mrs. Talbot, he waited a full minute before he spoke.

"The sun is in your hair," he said.

"What?"

"The sun is in your hair. It's a beautiful color."

"Well, it isn't as pretty as it used to be," she said. "Hair like mine gets dark. But I'm not going to dye it. I don't think that women should dye their hair."

"You're so intelligent," he murmured

"You don't mean that?"

"Mean what?"

"Mean that I'm intelligent."

"Oh, but I do," he said. "You're intelligent. You're beautiful. I'll never forget that night I met you at the boat. I hadn't wanted to come to the island. I'd made plans to go out West."

"I can't be intelligent," Clarissa said miserably. "I must be stupid. Mother Ryan says that I'm stupid, and Bob says that I'm stupid, and even Mrs. Talbot says that I'm stupid, and—" She began to cry. She went to a mirror and dried her eyes. Baxter followed. He put his arms around her. "Don't put your arms around me," she said, more in despair than in anger. "Nobody ever takes me seriously until they get their arms around me." She sat down again and Baxter sat near her. "But you're not stupid, Clarissa," he said. "You have a wonderful intelligence, a wonderful mind. I've often thought so. I've often felt that you must have a lot of very interesting opinions."

"Well, that's funny," she said, "because I do have a lot of opinions. Of course, I never dare say them to anyone, and Bob and Mother Ryan don't ever let me speak. They always interrupt me, as if they were ashamed of me. But I do have these opinions. I mean, I think we're like cogs in a wheel. I've concluded that we're like cogs in a wheel. Do you think we're like cogs in a wheel?"

"Oh, yes," he said. "Oh, yes, I do!"

"I think we're like cogs in a wheel," she said. "For instance, do you think that women should work? I've given that a lot of thought. My opinion is that I don't think married women should work. I mean, unless they have a lot of money, of course, but even then I think it's a full-time job to take care of a man. Or do you think that women should work?"

"What do you think?" he asked. "I'm terribly interested in knowning what you think."

"Well, my opinion is," she said timidly, "that you just have to hoe your row. I don't think that working or joining the church is going to change everything, or special diets, either. I don't put much stock in fancy diets. We have a friend who cuts a quarter of a pound of meat at every meal. He has a scales right on the table and he weighs the meat. It makes the table look awful and I don't see what good it's going to do him. I buy what's reasonable. If ham is reasonable, I buy ham. If lamb is reasonable, I buy lamb. Don't you think that's intelligent?"

"I think that's very intelligent."

"And progressive education." she said. "I don't have a good opinion of progressive education. When we go to the Howards' for dinner, the children ride their tricycles around the table all the time, and it's my opinion that they get this way from progressive schools, and that children ought to be told what's nice and what isn't."

The sun that had lighted her hair was gone, but there was still enough light in the room for Baxter to see that she aired her opinions, her face suffused with color and her pupils dilated. Baxter listened patiently, for he knew by then that she merely wanted to be taken for something that she was not—that the poor girl was lost. "You're very intelligent," he said, now and then. "You're so intelligent."

It was as simple as that.

1. What kind of narrator is used in this story?
2. Whose mind does the narrator have access to?
3. What is the narrator's judgment of Baxter? How is it communicated?
4. What is the significance of the last line?
5. Does the narrator agree with Baxter's analysis of Clarissa? Do you?
6. How does it feel to see the events through Baxter's eyes?

Six
Language and Fiction

When we analyze poetry, we are accustomed to looking closely at its language. When it comes to fiction, we often tend to concentrate on larger structures in the story, such as plot and character, and to neglect the story's language. But in fact language makes all the other elements possible. For the reader, the story exists before all else as marks on a page, as written language. At this level there are no plots, no characters, no meanings. All these will come into existence only after the reader has dealt with those meaningful marks. Written language is the material with which readers, and writers, begin their work.

How do readers turn those marks into the elements of fiction? The process is complex, but so familiar to us through years of practice that it seems simple, and it happens for many readers unconsciously. At a basic level, certain combinations of marks (words) are signs for certain ideas or meanings. The marks DOG for example, are connected to our mental image of a dog. The combination ODG, conversely, is not significant to us. It doesn't connect to any idea or image. These connections are not natural but social. A sign points to a certain idea because we have agreed on it as members of this language community. Through learning within our system of language we come to associate words with ideas. In other words, we learn a complex code of signs and meanings. If we are competent in the language code, the sight of the sign will call up the meaning.

At the next level, we have rules for combining those words (signs) into meaningful phrases and sentences. "The dog is coming down the street" makes sense within the system, whereas "Is down the coming the street dog" doesn't because such a word order violates the rules of combination in our language. Those of us who are inside the system know those rules, so we can make sense of combinations of words. We can combine words into sentences, sentences into paragraphs, paragraphs into a story.

On top of these systems, at the highest level, we are aware of the rules for literary writing. We know, for example, that stories describe action over time. We know that characters will be constructed, that settings will be sketched in. Being aware of these conventions, active readers know what to do with the words and sentences they encounter. In fact, the purpose of our discussions of plot, character, and so on, is to increase our expectations as readers, to make us more aware of the conventions of literature, so that we can participate in the making of these larger patterns of meaning. Readers who are aware of all these systems do a better job in working along with the language of the story.

Assembling the Meanings

The meaning of a word is not simply a matter of a sign referring to an idea; words also communicate a feeling, an attitude toward the idea. As we discussed in the chapter "Denotation and Connotation" (Chapter Two, Part Two), the *connotative* meaning of a word puts a value on the idea or image it refers to. For example, imagine a story about a football coach who stresses discipline. If the narrator calls him a "dictator," he obviously puts a negative value on his actions. But if he calls him a "motivator," the word imparts a positive value. The two words have in this context the same *denotative* meaning—they refer to the same idea—but they express completely different values. In describing characters and actions, the words of a story always communicate value, shaping our response to people and events. Throughout a story we encounter these value-laden words, and as we assemble these values we are constructing the overall message of the story.

It is important to remember that these values are part of the meaning of a word. The author does not create them, but the author deploys them in appropriate places in the story. The meanings of words, including the values they express, pre-exist the story, since they are the verbal environment that both the author and the reader live in. Language is not just a tool that the author uses, it is a system of thinking and interpreting through which we look at the world. That system embodies the values of our culture, and through these values we make sense of experience and of a story.

Although the rules of language exert a tremendous constraint on the author, he or she is not passive or at their mercy. The conventions of literary language allow—in fact encourage—an innovative approach. Stories abound in strange combinations of words and unusual word choices that stretch the rules of language. In Ernest Hemingway's "The Undefeated," for example, the bull in a bullfight is described as "moving softly in a fast gallop." A phrase like this does not break the rules of combination in our language, but is does stretch them. "Softly" and "fast gallop" don't seem at first to go together, one suggesting grace, the other power. The combination makes us slow down the reading process, think of how these two elements might go together. And on reflection, we see how; it is precisely the combination of grace and power that Hemingway wants us to see in the bull, as a worthy opponent for his hero. Still, as readers we have been slowed down, forced to think through the language, to explore how it makes its meaning.

That slowing down is exactly the purpose of *literary language*. We normally use language without much thought, off the top of the head. But literary language makes us reflect on itself, and on the codes by which it gains meaning. It reminds us that language is never merely natural; it is always crafted by human desires. An individual writer tries to shape language to fit his or her desires. A whole culture constructs a language that reflects its desires. Literary language reminds us that all language and values are human products. Language provides us with the framework through which we see the world, but once we become aware of that frame, we realize that other frames are possible.

Recognizing the Style

An author's characteristic use of language is called his or her **style.** If this word seems to suggest something superficial, we need to revise our understanding of the word. Choices of language are expressions of values, and by looking closely at a story's language, we can build up a sense of its values. On a basic level, we can see how various characters and situations are described, in words with either positive or negative connotations. We can also think about the pattern of word choices the author has made. Are the words familiar or unusual? Are they combined in simple sentences or in elaborate, complex sentences? In a writer like Hemingway, the spare and straightforward style communicates Hemingway's commitment to the values of honesty, directness, and a clear vision of reality. In a writer like Poe, however, the unusual words and complex sentences suggest his vision of the world as a shadowy and complex place. Language is the framework through which we look at the world, so your giving close attention to the language of a story is a way to get to the heart of its values.

READINGS

Ernest Hemingway (1898–1961)
THE UNDEFEATED

Manuel Garcia climbed the stairs to Don Miguel Retana's office. He set down his suitcase and knocked on the door. There was no answer. Manuel, standing in the hallway, felt there was some one in the room. He felt it through the door.

"Retana," he said, listening.

There was no answer.

He's there, all right, Manuel thought.

"Retana," he said and banged the door.

"Who's there?" said some one in the office.

"Me, Manolo," Manuel said.

"What do you want?" asked the voice.

"I want to work," Manuel said.

Something in the door clicked several times and it swung open. Manuel went in, carrying his suitcase.

A little man sat behind a desk at the far side of the room. Over his head was a bull's head, stuffed by a Madrid taxidermist; on the walls were framed photographs and bull-fight posters.

The little man sat looking at Manuel.

"I thought they'd killed you," he said.

Manuel knocked with his knuckles on the desk. The little man sat looking at him across the desk.

"How many corridas you had this year?" Retana asked.

"One," he answered.

"Just that one?" the little man asked.

"That's all."

"I read about it in the papers," Retana said. He leaned back in the chair and looked at Manuel.

Manuel looked up at the stuffed bull. He had seen it often before. He felt a certain family interest in it. It had killed his brother, the promising one, about nine years ago. Manuel remembered the day. There was a brass plate on the oak shield the bull's head was mounted on. Manuel could not read it, but he imagined it was in memory of his brother. Well, he had been a good kid.

The plate said: "The Bull 'Mariposa' of the Duke of Veragua, which accepted 9 varas for 7 caballos, and caused the death of Antonio Garcia, Novillero, April 27, 1909."

Retana saw him looking at the stuffed bull's head.

"The lot the Duke sent me for Sunday will make a scandal," he said. "They're all bad in the legs. What do they say about them at the Café?"

"I don't know," Manuel said. "I just got in."

"Yes," Retana said. "You still have your bag."

He looked at Manuel, leaning back behind the big desk.

"Sit down," he said. "Take off your cap."

Manuel sat down; his cap off, his face was changed. He looked pale, and his coleta pinned forward on his head, so that it would not show under the cap, gave him a strange look.

"You don't look well," Retana said.

"I just got out of the hospital," Manuel said.

"I heard they'd cut your leg off," Retana said.

"No," said Manuel. "It got all right."

Retana leaned forward across the desk and pushed a wooden box of cigarettes toward Manuel.

"Have a cigarette," he said.

"Thanks."

Manuel lit it.

"Smoke?" he said, offering the match to Retana.

"No," Retana waved his had, "I never smoke."

Retana watched him smoking.

"Why don't you get a job and go to work?" he said.

"I don't want to work," Manuel said. "I am a bull-fighter."

"There aren't any bull-fighters any more," Retana said.

"I'm a bull-fighter," Manuel said.

"Yes, while you're in there," Retana said.

Manuel laughed.

Retana sat, saying nothing and looking at Manuel.

"I'll put you in a nocturnal if you want," Retana offered.

"When?" Manuel asked.

"Tomorrow night."

"I don't like to substitute for anybody," Manuel said. That was the way they all got killed. That was the way Salvador got killed. He tapped with his knuckles on the table.

"It's all I've got," Retana said.

"Why don't you put me on next week?" Manuel suggested.

"You wouldn't draw," Retana said. "All they want is Litri and Rubito and La Torre. Those kids are good."

"They'd come to see me get it," Manuel said, hopefully.

"No, they wouldn't. They don't know who you are any more."

"I've got a lot of stuff," Manuel said.

"I'm offering to put you on tomorrow night," Retana said. "You can work with young Hernandez and kill two novillos after the Charlots."

"Whose novillos?" Manuel asked.

"I don't know. Whatever stuff they've got in the corrals. What the veterinaries won't pass in the daytime."

"I don't like to substitute," Manuel said.

"You can take it or leave it," Retana said. He leaned forward over the papers. He was no longer interested. The appeal that Manuel had made to him for a moment when he thought of the old days was gone. He would like to get him to substitute for Larita because he could get him cheaply. He could get others cheaply too. He would like to help him though. Still he had given him the chance. It was up to him.

"How much do I get?" Manuel asked. He was still playing with the idea of refusing. But he knew he could not refuse.

"Two hundred and fifty pesetas," Retana said. He had thought of five hundred, but when he opened his mouth it said two hundred and fifty.

"You pay Villalta seven thousand," Manuel said.

"You're not Villalta," Retana said.

"I know it," Manuel said.

"He draws it, Manolo," Retana said in explanation.

"Sure," said Manuel. He stood up. "Give me three hundred, Retana."

"All right," Retana agreed. He reached in the drawer for a paper.

"Can I have fifty now?" Manuel asked.

"Sure," said Retana. He took a fifty-peseta note out of his pocketbook and laid it, spread out flat, on the table.

Manuel picked it up and put it in his pocket.

"What about a cuadrilla?" he asked.

"There's the boys that always work for me nights," Retana said. "They're all right."

"How about picadors?" Manuel asked.

"They're not much," Retana admitted.

"I've got to have one good pic," Manuel said.

"Get him then," Retana said. "Go and get him."

"Not out of this," Manuel said. "I'm not paying for any cuadrilla out of sixty duros."

Retana said nothing but looked at Manuel across the big desk.

"You know I've got to have one good pic," Manuel said.

Retana said nothing but looked at Manuel from a long way off.

"It's isn't right," Manuel said.

Retana was still considering him, leaning back in his chair, considering him from a long way away.

"There're the regular pics," he offered.

"I know," Manuel said. "I know your regular pics."

Retana did not smile. Manuel knew it was over.

"All I want is an even break," Manuel said reasoningly.

"When I go out there I want to be able to call my shots on the bull. It only takes one good picador."

He was talking to a man who was no longer listening.

"If you want something extra," Retana said, "go and get it. There will be a regular cuadrilla out there. Bring as many of your own pics as you want. The charlotada is over by 10.30."

"All right," Manuel said. "If that's the way you feel about it."

"That's the way," Retana said.

"I'll see you tomorrow night," Manuel said.

"I'll be out there," Retana said.

Manuel picked up his suitcase and went out.

"Shut the door," Retana called.

Manuel looked back. Retana was sitting forward looking at some papers. Manuel pulled the door tight until it clicked.

He went down the stairs and out of the door into the hot brightness of the street. It was very hot in the street and the light on the white buildings was sudden and hard on his eyes. He walked down the shady side of the steep street toward the Puerta del Sol. The shade felt solid and cool as running water. The heat came suddenly as he crossed the intersecting streets. Manuel saw no one he knew in all the people he passed.

Just before the Puerta del Sol he turned into a café.

It was quiet in the café. There were a few men sitting at tables against the wall. At one table four men played cards. Most of the men sat against the wall smoking, empty coffee-cups and liqueur-glasses before them on the tables. Manuel went through the long room to a small room in back. A man sat at a table in the corner asleep. Manuel sat down at one of the tables.

A waiter came in and stood beside Manuel's table.

"Have you seen Zurito?" Manuel asked him.

"He was in before lunch," the waiter answered. "He won't be back before five o'clock."

"Bring me some coffee and milk and a shot of the ordinary," Manuel said.

The waiter came back into the room carrying a tray with a big coffee-glass and a liqueur-glass on it. In his left hand he held a bottle of brandy. He swung these down to the table and a boy who had followed him poured coffee and milk into the glass from two shiny, spouted pots with long handles.

Manuel took off his cap and the waiter noticed his pigtail pinned forward on his head. He winked at the coffee-boy as he poured out the brandy into the little glass beside Manuel's coffee. The coffee-boy looked at Manuel's pale face curiously.

"You fighting here?" asked the waiter, corking up the bottle.

"Yes," Manuel said. "Tomorrow."

The waiter stood there, holding the bottle on one hip.

"You in the Charlie Chaplins?" he asked.

The coffee-boy looked away, embarrassed.

"No. In the ordinary."

"I thought they were going to have Chaves and Hernandez," the waiter said.

"No. Me and another."

"Who? Chaves or Hernandez?"

"Hernandez, I think."

"What's the matter with Chaves?"

"He got hurt."

"Where did you hear that?"

"Retana."

"Hey, Looie," the waiter called to the next room, "Chaves got cogida."

Manuel had taken the wrapper off the lumps of sugar and dropped them into his coffee. He stirred it and drank it down, sweet, hot, and warming in his empty stomach. He drank off the brandy.

"Give me another shot of that," he said to the waiter.

The waiter uncorked the bottle and poured the glass full, slopping another drink into the saucer. Another waiter had come up in front of the table. The coffee-boy was gone.

"Is Chaves hurt bad?" the second waiter asked Manuel.

"I don't know," Manuel said, "Retana didn't say."

"A hell of a lot he cares," the tall waiter said. Manuel had not seen him before. He must have just come up.

"If you stand in with Retana in this town, you're a made man," the tall waiter said. "If you aren't in with him, you might just as well go out and shoot yourself."

"You said it," the other waiter who had come in said. "You said it then."

"You're right I said it," said the tall waiter. "I know what I'm talking about when I talk about that bird."

"Look what he's done for Villalta," the first waiter said.

"And that ain't all," the tall waiter said. "Look what he's done for Marcial Lalanda. Look what he's done for Nacional."

"You said it, kid," agreed the short waiter.

Manuel looked at them, standing talking in front of his table. He had drunk his second brandy. They had forgotten about him. They were not interested in him.

"Look at that bunch of camels," the tall waiter went on. "Did you ever see this Nacional II?"

"I seen him last Sunday didn't I?" the original waiter said.

"He's a giraffe," the short waiter said.

"What did I tell you?" the tall waiter said. "Those are Retana's boys."

"Say, give me another shot of that," Manuel said. He had poured the brandy the waiter had slopped over in the saucer into his glass and drank it while they were talking.

The original waiter poured his glass full mechanically, and the three of them went out of the room talking.

In the far corner the man was still asleep, snoring slightly on the intaking breath, his head back against the wall.

Manuel drank his brandy. He felt sleepy himself. It was too hot to go out into the town. Besides there was nothing to do. He wanted to see Zurito. He would go to sleep while he waited. He kicked his suitcase under the table to be sure it was there. Perhaps it would be better to put it back under the seat, against the wall. He leaned down and shoved it under. Then he leaned forward on the table and went to sleep.

When he woke there was some one sitting across the table from him. It was a big man with a heavy brown face like an Indian. He had been sitting there some time. He had waved the waiter away and sat reading the paper and occasionally looking down at Manuel, asleep, his head on the table. He read the paper laboriously, forming the words with his lips as he read. When it tired him he looked at Manuel. He sat heavily in the chair, his black Cordoba hat tipped forward.

Manuel sat up and looked at him.

"Hello, Zurito," he said.

"Hello, kid," the big man said.

"I've been asleep." Manuel rubbed his forehead with the back of his fist.

"I thought maybe you were."

"How's everything?"

"Good. How is everything with you?"

"Not so good."

They were both silent. Zurito, the picador, looked at Manuel's white face. Manuel looked down at the picador's enormous hands folding the paper to put away in his pocket.

"I got a favor to ask you, Manos," Manuel said.

Manosduros was Zurito's nickname. He never heard it without thinking of his huge hands. He put them forward on the table self-consciously.

"Let's have a drink," he said.

"Sure," said Manuel.

The waiter came and went and came again. He went out of the room looking back at the two men at the table.

"What's the matter, Manolo?" Zurito set down his glass.

"Would you pic two bulls for me tomorrow night?" Manuel asked, looking up at Zurito across the table.

"No," said Zurito. "I'm not pic-ing."

Manuel looked down at his glass. He had expected that answer; now he had it. Well, he had it.

"I'm sorry, Manolo, but I'm not pic-ing." Zurito looked at his hands.

"That's all right," Manuel said.

"I'm too old," Zurito said.

"I just asked you," Manuel said.

"Is it the nocturnal tomorrow?"

"That's it. I figured if I had just one good pic, I could get away with it."

"How much are you getting?"

"Three hundred pesetas."

"I get more than that for pic-ing."

"I know," said Manuel. "I didn't have any right to ask you."

"What do you keep on doing it for?" Zurito asked. "Why don't you cut off your coleta, Manolo?"

"I don't know," Manuel said.

"You're pretty near as old as I am," Zurito said.

"I don't know," Manuel said. "I got to do it. If I can fix it so that I get an even break, that's all I want. I got to stick with it, Manos."

"No, you don't."

"Yes, I do. I've tried keeping away from it."

"I know how you feel. But it isn't right. You ought to get out and stay out."

"I can't do it. Besides, I've been going good lately."

Zurito looked at his face.

"You've been in the hospital."

"But I was going great when I got hurt."

Zurito said nothing. He tipped the cognac out of his saucer into his glass.

"The papers said they never saw a better faena," Manuel said.

Zurito looked at him.

"You know when I get going I'm good," Manuel said.

"You're too old," the picador said.

"No," said Manuel. "You're ten years older than I am."

"With me it's different."

"I'm not too old," Manuel said.

They sat silent, Manuel watching the picador's face.

"I was going great till I got hurt," Manuel offered.

"You ought to have seen me, Manos," Manuel said, reproachfully.

"I don't want to see you," Zurito said. "It makes me nervous."

"You haven't seen me lately."

"I've seen you plenty."

Zurito looked at Manuel, avoiding his eyes.

"You ought to quit it, Manolo."

"I can't," Manuel said. "I'm going good now, I tell you."

Zurito leaned forward, his hands on the table.

"Listen. I'll pic for you and if you don't go big tomorrow night, you'll quit. See? Will you do that?"

"Sure."

Zurito leaned back, relieved.

"You got to quit," he said. "No monkey business. You got to cut the coleta."

"I won't have to quit," Manuel said. "You watch me. I've got the stuff."

Zurito stood up. He felt tired from arguing.

"You got to quit," he said. "I'll cut your coleta myself."

"No, you won't," Manuel said. "You won't have a chance."

Zurito called the waiter.

"Come on," said Zurito. "Come on up to the house."

Manuel reached under the seat for his suitcase. He was happy. He knew Zurito would pic for him. He was the best picador living. It was all simple now.

"Come on up to the house and we'll eat," Zurito said.

Manuel stood in the patio de caballos waiting for the Charlie Chaplins to be over. Zurito stood beside him. Where they stood it was dark. The high door that led into the bull-ring was shut. Above them they heard a shout, then another shout of laughter. Then there was silence. Manuel liked the smell of the stables about the patio de caballos. It smelt good in the dark. There was another roar from the arena and then applause, prolonged applause, going on and on.

"You ever seen these fellows?" Zurito asked, big and looming beside Manuel in the dark.

"No," Manuel said.

"They're pretty funny," Zurito said. He smiled to himself in the dark.

The high, double, tight-fitting door into the bull-ring swung open and Manuel saw the ring in the hard light of the arc-lights, the plaza, dark all the way around, rising high; around the edge of the ring were running and bowing two men dressed like tramps, followed by a third in the uniform of a hotel bell-boy who stooped and picked up the hats and canes thrown down onto the sand and tossed them back up into the darkness.

The electric light went on in the patio.

"I'll climb onto one of those ponies while you collect the kids," Zurito said.

Behind them came the jingle of the mules, coming out to go into the arena and be hitched onto the dead bull.

The members of the cuadrilla, who had been watching the burlesque from the runway between the barrera and the seats, came walking back and stood in a group talking, under the electric light in the patio. A good-looking lad in a silver-and-orange suit came up to Manuel and smiled.

"I'm Hernandez," he said and put out his hand.

Manuel shook it.

"They're regular elephants we've got tonight," the boy said cheerfully.

"They're big ones with horns," Manuel agreed.

"You drew the worst lot," the boy said.

"That's all right," Manuel said. "The bigger they are, the more meat for the poor."

"Where did you get that one?" Hernandez grinned.

"That's an old one," Manuel said. "You line up your cuadrilla, so I can see what I've got."

"You've got some good kids," Hernandez said. He was very cheerful. He had been on twice before in nocturnals and was beginning to get a following in Madrid. He was happy the fight would start in a few minutes.

"Where are the pics?" Manuel asked.

"They're back in the corrals fighting about who gets the beautiful horses," Hernandez grinned.

The mules came through the gate in a rush, the whips snapping, bells jangling and the young bull ploughing a furrow of sand.

They formed up for the paseo as soon as the bull had gone through.

Manuel and Hernandez stood in front. The youths of the cuadrillas were behind, their heavy capes furled over their arms. In back, the four picadors, mounted, holding their steel-tipped push-poles erect in the half-dark of the corral.

"It's a wonder Retana wouldn't give us enough light to see the horses by," one picador said.

"He knows we'll be happier if we don't get too good a look at these skins," another pic answered.

"This thing I'm on barely keeps me off the ground," the first picador said.

"Well, they're horses."

"Sure, they're horses."

They talked, sitting their gaunt horses in the dark.

Zurito said nothing. He had the only steady horse of the lot. He had tried him, wheeling him in the corrals and he responded to the bit and the spurs. He had taken the bandage off his right eye and cut the strings where they had tied his ears tight shut at the base. He was a good, solid horse, solid on his legs. That was all he needed. He intended to ride him all through the corrida. He had already, since he had mounted, sitting in the half-dark in the big, quilted saddle, waiting for the paseo, pic-ed through the whole corrida in his mind. The other picadors went on talking on both sides of him. He did not hear them.

The two matadors stood together in front of their three peones, their capes furled over their left arms in the same fashion. Manuel was thinking about the three lads in back of him. They were all three Madrilenos, like Hernandez, boys about nineteen. One of them, a gypsy, serious, aloof, and dark-faced, he liked the look of. He turned.

"What's your name, kid?" he asked the gypsy.

"Fuentes," the gypsy said.

"That's a good name," Manuel said.

The gypsy smiled, showing his teeth.

"You take the bull and give him a little run when he comes out," Manuel said.

"All right," the gypsy said. His face was serious. He began to think about just what he would do.

"Here she goes," Manuel said to Hernandez.

"All right. We'll go."

Heads up, swinging with the music, their right arms swinging free, they stepped out, crossing the sanded arena under the arc-lights, the cuadrillas opening out behind, the picadors riding after, behind came the bull-ring servants and the jingling mules. The crowd applauded Hernandez as they marched across the arena. Arrogant, swinging, they looked straight ahead as they marched.

They bowed before the president, and the procession broke up into its component parts. The bull-fighters went over to the barrera and changed their heavy mantles for the light fighting capes. The mules went out. The picadors galloped jerkily around the ring, and two rode out the gate they had come in by. The servants swept the sand smooth.

Manuel drank a glass of water poured for him by one of Retana's deputies, who was acting as his manager and sword-handler. Hernandez came over from speaking with his own manager.

"You got a good hand, kid," Manuel complimented him.

"They like me," Hernandez said happily.

"How did the paseo go?" Manuel asked Retana's man.

"Like a wedding," said the handler. "Fine. You came out like Joselito and Belmonte."

Zurito rode by, a bulky equestrian statue. He wheeled his horse and faced him toward the toril on the far side of the ring where the bull would come out. It was strange under the arc-light. He pic-ed in the hot afternoon sun for big money. He didn't like this arc-light business. He wished they would get started.

Manuel went up to him.

"Pic him, Manos," he said. "Cut him down to size for me."

"I'll pic him, kid," Zurito spat on the sand. "I'll make him jump out of the ring."

"Lean on him, Manos," Manuel said.

"I'll lean on him," Zurito said. "What's holding it up?"

"He's coming now," Manuel said.

Zurito sat there, his feet in the box-stirrups, his great legs in the buck-skin-covered armor gripping the horse, the reins in his left hand, the long pic held in his right hand, his broad hat well down over his eyes to shade them from the lights, watching the distant door of the toril. His horse's ears quivered. Zurito patted him with his left hand.

The red door of the toril swung back and for a moment Zurito looked into the empty passageway far across the arena. Then the bull came out in a rush, skidding on his four legs as he came out under the lights, then charging in a gallop, moving softly in a fast gallop, silent except as he woofed through wide nostrils as he charged, glad to be free after the dark pen.

In the first row of seats, slightly bored, leaning forward to write on the cement wall in front of his knees, the substitute bull-fight critic of *El Heraldo* scribbled: "Campagnero, Negro, 42, came out at 90 miles an hour with plenty of gas—"

Manuel, leaning against the barrera, watching the bull, waved his hand and the gypsy ran out, trailing his cape. The bull, in full gallop, pivoted and charged the cape, his head down, his tail rising. The gypsy moved in a zigzag, and as he passed, the bull caught sight of him and abandoned the cape to charge the man. The gyp sprinted and vaulted the red fence of the barrera as the bull struck it with his horns, banging into the wood blindly.

The critic of *El Heraldo* lit a cigarette and tossed the match at the bull, then wrote in his note-book, "large and with enough horns to satisfy the cash customers, Campagnero showed a tendency to cut into the terrain of the bull-fighters."

Manuel stepped out on the hard sand as the bull banged into the fence. Out of the corner of his eye he saw Zurito sitting the white horse close to the barrera, about a quarter of the way around the ring to the left. Manuel held the cape close in front of him, a fold in each hand, and shouted at the bull. "Huh! Huh!" The bull turned, seemed to brace against the fence as he charged in a scramble, driving into the cape as Manuel side-stepped, pivoted on his heels with the charge of the bull, and swung the cape just ahead of the horns. At the end of the swing he was facing the bull again and held the cape in the same position close in front of his body, and pivoted again as the bull recharged. Each time, as he swung, the crowd shouted.

Four times he swung with the bull, lifting the cape so it billowed full, and each time bringing the bull around to charge again. Then, at the end of the fifth swing, he held the cape against his hip and pivoted, so the cape swung out like a ballet dancer's skirt and wound the bull around himself like a belt, to step clear, leaving the bull facing Zurito on the white horse, come up and planted firm, the horse facing the bull, its ears forward, its lips nervous, Zurito, his hat over his eyes, leaning forward, the long pole sticking out before and behind in a sharp angle under his right arm, held half-way down, the triangular iron point facing the bull.

El Heraldo's second-string critic, drawing on his cigarette, his eyes on the bull, wrote: "the veteran Manolo designed a series of acceptable veronicas, ending in a very Belmontistic recorte that earned applause from the regulars, and we entered the tercio of the cavalry."

Zurito sat his horse, measuring the distance between the bull and the end of the pic. As he looked, the bull gathered himself together and charged, his eyes on the horse's chest. As he lowered his head to hook, Zurito sunk the point of the pic in the swelling hump of muscle above the bull's shoulder, leaned all his weight on the shaft, and with his left hand pulled the white horse into the air, front hoofs pawing, and swung him to the right as he pushed the bull under and through so the horns passed safely under the horse's belly and the horse came down, quivering, the bull's tail brushing his chest as he charged the cape Hernandez offered him.

Hernandez ran sideways, taking the bull out and away with the cape, toward the other picador. He fixed him with a swing of the cape, squarely facing the horse and rider, and stepped back. As the bull saw the horse he charged. The picador's lance slid along his back, and as the shock of the charge lifted the horse, the picador was already half-way out of the saddle, lifting his right leg clear as he missed with the lance and falling to the left side to keep the horse between him and the bull. The horse, lifted and gored, crashed over with the bull driving into him, the picador gave a shove with his boots against the horse and lay clear, waiting to be lifted and hauled away and put on his feet.

Manuel let the bull drive into the fallen horse; he was in no hurry, the picador was safe; besides, it did a picador like that good to worry. He'd stay on longer next time. Lousy pics! He looked across the sand at Zurito a little way out from the barrera, his horse rigid, waiting.

"Huh!" he called to the bull, "Tomar!" holding the cape in both hands so it would catch his eye. The bull detached himself from the horse and charged the cape, and Manuel, running sideways and holding the cape spread wide, stopped, swung on his heels, and brought the bull sharply around facing Zurito.

"Campagnero accepted a pair of varas for the death of one rosinante, with Hernandez and Manolo at the quites," *El Heraldo's* critic wrote. "He pressed on the iron and clearly showed he was no horse-lover. The veteran Zurito resurrected some of his old stuff with the pike-pole, notably the suerte—"

"Olé! Olé!" the man sitting beside him shouted. The shout was lost in the roar of the crowd, and he slapped the critic on the back. The critic looked up to see Zurito, directly below him, leaning far out over his horse, the length of the pic rising in a sharp angle under his armpit, holding the pic almost by the point, bearing down with all his weight, holding the bull off, the bull pushing and driving to get at the horse, and Zurito, far out, on top of him, holding him, holding him, and slowly pivoting the horse against the pressure, so that at last he was clear. Zurito felt the moment when the horse was clear and the bull could come past, and relaxed the absolute steel lock of his resistance, and the triangular steel point of the pic ripped in the bull's hump of shoulder muscle as he tore loose to find Hernandez's cape before his muzzle. He charged blindly into the cape and the boy took him out into the open arena.

Zurito sat patting his horse and looking at the bull charging the cape that Hernandez swung for him out under the bright light while the crowd shouted.

"You see that one?" he said to Manuel.

"It was a wonder," Manuel said.

"I got him that time," Zurito said. "Look at him now."

At the conclusion of a closely turned pass of the cape the bull slid to his knees. He was up at once, but far out across the sand Manuel and Zurito saw the shine of the pumping flow of blood, smooth against the black of the bull's shoulder.

"I got him that time," Zurito said.

"He's a good bull," Manuel said.

"If they gave me another shot at him, I'd kill him," Zurito said.

"They'll change the thirds on us," Manuel said.

"Look at him now," Zurito said.

"I got to go over there," Manuel said, and started on a run for the other side of the ring, where the monos were leading a horse out by the bridle toward the bull, whacking him on the legs with rods and all, in a procession, trying to get him toward the bull, who stood, dropping his head, pawing, unable to make up his mind to charge.

Zurito, sitting his horse, walking him toward the scene, not missing any detail, scowled.

Finally the bull charged, the horse leaders ran for the barrera, the picador hit too far back, and the bull got under the horse, lifted him, threw him onto his back.

Zurito watched. The monos, in their red shirts, running out to drag the picador clear. The picador, now on his feet, swearing and flopping his arms. Manuel and Heranadez standing ready with their capes. And the bull, the great, black bull, with a horse on his back, hooves dangling, the bridle caught in the horns. Black bull with a horse on his back, staggering short-legged, then arching his neck and lifting, thrusting, charging to slide the horse off, horse sliding down. Then the bull into a lunging charge at the cape Manuel spread for him.

The bull was slower now, Manuel felt. He was bleeding badly. There was a sheen of blood all down his flank.

Manuel offered him the cape again. There he came, eyes open, ugly, watching the cape. Manuel stepped to the side and raised his arms, tightening the cape ahead of the bull for the veronica.

Now he was facing the bull. Yes, his head was going down a little. He was carrying it lower. That was Zurito.

Manuel flopped the cape; there he comes; he side-stepped and swung in another veronica. He's shooting awfully accurately, he thought. He's had enough fight, so he's watching now. He's hunting now. Got his eye on me. But I always give him the cape.

He shook the cape at the bull; there he comes; he side-stepped. Awful close that time. I don't want to work that close to him.

The edge of the cape was wet with blood where it had swept along the bull's back as he went by.

All right, here's the last one.

Manuel, facing the bull, having turned with him each charge, offered the cape with his two hands. The bull looked at him. Eyes watching, horns straight forward, the bull looked at him, watching.

"Huh!" Manuel said, "Toro!" and leaning back, swung the cape forward. Here he comes. He side-stepped, swung the cape in back of him, and pivoted, so the bull followed a swirl of cape and then was left with nothing, fixed by the pass, dominated by the cape. Manuel swung the cape under his muzzle with one hand, to show the bull was fixed, and walked away.

There was no applause.

Manuel walked across the sand toward the barrera, while Zurito rode out of the ring. The trumpet had blown to change the act to the planting of the banderillos while Manuel had been working with the bull. He had not consciously noticed it. The monos were spreading canvas over the two dead horses and sprinkling sawdust around them.

Manuel came up to the barrera for a drink of water. Retana's man handed him the heavy porous jug.

Fuentes, the tall gypsy, was standing holding a pair of banderillos, holding them together, slim, red sticks, fish-hook points out. He looked at Manuel.

"Go on out there," Manuel said.

The gypsy trotted out. Manuel set down the jug and watched. He wiped his face with his handkerchief.

The critic of *El Heraldo* reached for the bottle of warm champagne that stood between his feet, took a drink, and finished his paragraph.

"— the aged Manolo rated no applause for a vulgar series of lances with the cape and we entered the third of the palings."

Alone in the center of the ring the bull stood, still fixed. Fuentes, tall, flat-backed, walking toward him arrogantly, his arms spread out, the two slim, red sticks, one in each hand, held by the fingers, points straight forward. Fuentes walked forward. Back of him and to one side was a peon with a cape. The bull looked at him and was no longer fixed.

His eyes watched Fuentes, now standing still. Now he leaned back, calling to him. Fuentes twitched the two banderillos and the light on the steel points caught the bull's eye.

His tail went up and he charged.

He came straight, his eyes on the man. Fuentes stood still, leaning back, the banderillos pointing forward. As the bull lowered his head to hook, Fuentes leaned backward, his arms came together and rose, his two hands touching, the banderillos two descending red lines, and leaning forward drove the points into the bull's shoulder, leaning far in over the bull's horns and pivoting on the two upright sticks, his legs tight together, his body curving to one side to let the bull pass.

"Olé!" from the crowd.

The bull was hooking wildly, jumping like a trout, all four feet off the ground. The red shaft of the banderillos tossed as he jumped.

Manuel, standing at the barrera, noticed that he looked always to the right.

"Tell him to drop the next pair on the right," he said to the kid who started to run out to Fuentes with the new banderillos.

A heavy hand fell on his shoulder. It was Zurito.

"How do you feel, kid?" he asked.

Manuel was watching the bull.

Zurito leaned forward on the barrera, leaning the weight of his body on his arms. Manuel turned to him.

"You're going good," Zurito said.

Manuel shook his head. He had nothing to do now until the next third. The gypsy was very good with the banderillos. The bull would come to him in the next third in good shape. He was a good bull. It had all been easy up to now. The final stuff with the sword was all he worried over. He did not really worry. He did not even think about it. But standing there he had a heavy sense of apprehension. He looked out at the bull, planning his faena, his work with the red cloth that was to reduce the bull, to make him manageable.

The gypsy was walking out toward the bull again, walking heel-and-toe, insultingly, like a ballroom dancer, the red shafts of the banderillos twitching with his walk. The bull watched him, not fixed now, hunting him, but waiting to get close enough so he could be sure of getting him, getting the horns into him.

As Fuentes walked forward the bull charged. Fuentes ran across the quarter of a circle as the bull charged and, as he passed running backward, stopped, swung forward, rose on his toes, arm straight out, and sunk the banderillos straight down into the tight of the big shoulder muscles as the bull missed him.

The crowd were wild about it.

"That kid won't stay in this night stuff long," Retana's man said to Zurito.

"He's good," Zurito said.

"Watch him now."

They watched.

Fuentes was standing with his back against the barrera. Two of the caudrilla were back of him, with their capes ready to flop over the fence to distract the bull.

The bull, with his tongue out, his barrel heaving, was watching the gypsy. He thought he had him now. Back against the red planks. Only a short charge away. The bull watched him.

The gypsy bent back, drew back his arms, the banderillos pointing at the bull. He called to the bull, stamped one foot. The bull was suspicious. He wanted the man. No more barbs in the shoulder.

Fuentes walked a little closer to the bull. Bent back. Called again. Somebody in the crowd shouted a warning.

"He's too damn close," Zurito said.

"Watch him," Retana's man said.

Leaning back, inciting the bull with the banderillos, Fuentes jumped, both feet off the ground. As he jumped the bull's tail rose and he charged. Fuentes came down on his toes, arms straight out, whole body arching forward, and drove the shafts straight down as he swung his body clear of the right horn.

The bull crashed into the barrera where the flopping capes had attracted his eye as he lost the man.

The gypsy came running along the barrera toward Manuel, taking the applause of the crowd. His vest was ripped where he had not quite cleared the point of the horn. He was happy about it, showing it to the spectators. He made the tour of the ring. Zurito saw him go by, smiling, pointing at his vest. He smiled.

Somebody else was planting the last pair of banderillos. Nobody was paying any attention.

Retana's man tucked a baton inside the red cloth of a muleta, folded the cloth over it, and handed it over the barrera to Manuel. He reached in the leather sword-case, took out a sword, and holding it by its leather scabbard, reached it over the fence to Manuel. Manuel pulled the blade out by the red hilt and the scabbard fell limp.

He looked at Zurito. The big man saw he was sweating.

"Now you get him, kid," Zurito said.

Manuel nodded.

"He's in good shape," Zurito said.

"Just like you want him," Retana's man assured him.

Manuel nodded.

The trumpeter, up under the roof, blew for the final act, and Manuel walked across the arena toward where, up in the dark boxes, the president must be.

In the front row of seats the substitute bull-fight critic of *El Heraldo* took a long drink of the warm champagne. He had decided it was not worth while to write a running story and would write up the corrida back in the office. What the hell was it anyway? Only a nocturnal. If he missed anything he would get it out of the morning papers. He took another drink of the champagne. He had a date at Maxim's at twelve. Who were these bull-fighters anyway? Kids and bums. A bunch of bums. He put his pad of paper in his pocket and looked over toward Manuel, standing very much alone in the ring, gesturing with his hat in a salute toward a box he could not see high up in the dark plaza. Out in the ring the bull stood quiet, looking at nothing.

"I dedicate this bull to you, Mr. President, and to the public of Madrid, the most intelligent and generous of the world," was what Manuel was saying. It was a formula. He said it all. It was a little long for nocturnal use.

He bowed at the dark, straightened, tossed his hat over his shoulder, and, carrying the muleta in his left hand and the sword in his right, walked out toward the bull.

Manuel walked toward the bull. The bull looked at him; his eyes were quick. Manuel noticed the way the banderillos hung down on his left shoulder and the steady sheen of blood from Zurito's pic-ing. He noticed the way the bull's feet were. As he walked forward, holding the muleta in his left hand and the sword in his right, he watched the bull's feet. The bull could not charge without gathering his feet together. Now he stood square on them, dully.

Manuel walked toward him, watching his feet. This was all right. He could do this. He must work to get the bull's head down, so he could go in past the horns and kill him. He did not think about the sword, not about killing the bull. He thought about one thing at a time. The coming things oppressed him, though. Walking forward, watching the bull's feet, he saw successively his eyes, his wet muzzle, and the wide, forward-pointing spread of his horns. The bull had light circles about his eyes. His eyes watched Manuel. He felt he was going to get this little one with the white face.

Standing still now and spreading the red cloth of the muleta with the sword, pricking the point into the cloth so that the sword, now held in his left hand, spread the red flannel like the jib of a boat, Manuel noticed the points of the bull's horns. One of them was splintered from banging against the barrera. The other was sharp as a porcupine quill. Manuel noticed while spreading the muleta that the white base of the horn was stained red. While he noticed these things he did not lose sight of the bull's feet. The bull watched Manuel steadily.

He's on the defensive now, Manuel thought. He's reserving himself. I've got to bring him out of that and get his head down. Always get his head down. Zurito had his head down once, but he' s come back. He'll bleed when I start him going and that will bring it down.

Holding the muleta, with the sword in his left hand widening it in front of him, he called to the bull.

The bull looked at him.

He leaned back insultingly and shook the wide-spread flannel.

The bull saw the muleta. It was a bright scarlet under the arc-light. The bull's legs tightened.

Here he comes. Whoosh! Manuel turned as the bull came and raised the muleta so that it passed over the bull's horns and swept down his broad back from head to tail. The bull had gone clean up in the air with the charge. Manuel had not moved.

At the end of the pass the bull turned like a cat coming around a corner and faced Manuel.

He was on the offensive again. His heaviness was gone. Manuel noted the fresh blood shining down the black shoulder and dripping down the bull's leg. He drew the sword out of the muleta and held it in his right hand. The muleta held low down in his left hand, leaning toward the left, he called to the bull. The bull's legs tightened, his eyes on the muleta. Here he comes, Manuel thought. Yuh!

He swung with the charge, sweeping the muleta ahead of the bull, his feet firm, the sword following the curve, a point of light under the arcs.

The bull recharged as the pase natural finished and Manuel raised the muleta for a pase de pecho. Firmly planted, the bull came by his chest under the raised muleta. Manuel leaned his head back to avoid the clattering banderillo shafts. The hot, black bull body touched his chest as it passed.

Too damn close, Manuel thought. Zurito, leaning on the barrera, spoke rapidly to the gypsy, who trotted out toward Manuel with a cape. Zurito pulled his hat down low and looked out across the arena at Manuel.

Manuel was facing the bull again, the muleta held low and to the left. The bull's head was down as he watched the muleta.

"If it was Belmonte doing that stuff, they'd go crazy," Retana's man said.

Zurito said nothing. He was watching Manuel out in the center of the arena.

"Where did the boss dig this fellow up?" Retana's man asked.

"Out of the hospital," Zurito said.

"That's where he's going damn quick," Retana's man said.

Zurito turned on him.

"Knock on that," he said, pointing to the barrera.

"I was just kidding, man," Retana's man said.

"Knock on the wood."

Retana's man leaned forward and knocked three times on the barrera.

"Watch the faena," Zurito said.

Out in the center of the ring, under the lights, Manuel was kneeling, facing the bull, and as he raised the muleta in both hands the bull charged, tail up.

Manuel swung his body clear and, as the bull recharged, brought around the muleta in a half-circle that pulled the bull to his knees.

"Why, that one's a great bull-fighter," Retana's man said.

"No, he's not," said Zurito.

Manuel stood up and, the muleta in his left hand, the sword in his right, acknowledged the applause from the dark plaza.

The bull had humped himself up from his knees and stood waiting, his head hung low.

Zurito spoke to two of the other lads of the cuadrilla and they ran out to stand back of Manuel with their capes. There were four men back of him now. Hernandez had followed him since he first came out with the muleta. Fuentes stood watching, his cape held against his body, tall, in repose, watching lazy-eyed. Now the two came up. Hernandez motioned them to stand one at each side. Manuel stood alone, facing the bull.

Manuel waved back the men with the capes. Stepping back cautiously, they saw his face was white and sweating.

Didn't they know enough to keep back? Did they want to catch the bull's eye with the capes after he was fixed and ready? He had enough to worry about without that kind of thing.

The bull was standing, his four feet square, looking at the muleta. Manuel furled the muleta in his left hand. The bull's eyes watched it. His body was heavy on his feet. He carried his head low, but not too low.

Manuel lifted the muleta at him. The bull did not move. Only his eyes watched.

He's all lead, Manuel thought. He's all square. He's framed right. He'll take it.

He thought in bull-fight terms. Sometimes he had a thought and the particular piece of slang would not come into his mind and he could not realize the thought. His instincts and his knowledge worked automatically, and his brain worked slowly and in words. He knew all about bulls. He did not have to think about them. He just did the right thing. His eyes noted things and his body performed the necessary measures without thought. If he thought about it, he would be gone.

Now, facing the bull, he was conscious of many things at the same time. There were the horns, the one splintered, the other smoothly sharp, the need to profile himself toward the left horn, lance himself short and straight, lower the muleta so the bull would follow it, and, going in over the horns, put the sword all the way into a little spot about as big as a five-peseta piece straight in back of the neck, between the sharp pitch of the bull's shoulders. He must do all this and must then come out from between the horns. He was conscious he must do all this, but his only thought was in words: "Corto y derecho."

"Corto y derecho," he thought, furling the muleta. Short and straight. Corto y derecho, he drew the sword out of the muleta, profiled on the splintered left horn, dropped the muleta across his body, so his right hand with the sword on the level with his eye made the sign of the cross, and, rising on his toes, sighted along the dipping blade of the sword at the spot high up between the bull's shoulders.

Corto y derecho he launched himself on the bull.

There was a shock, and he felt himself go up in the air. He pushed on the sword as he went up and over, and it flew out of his hand. He hit the ground and the bull was on him. Manuel, lying on the ground, kicked at the bull's muzzle with his slippered feet. Kicking, kicking, the bull after him, missing him in his excitement, bumping him with his head, driving the horns into the sand. Kicking like a man keeping a ball in the air, Manuel kept the bull from getting a clean thrust at him.

Manuel felt the wind on his back from the capes flopping at the bull, and then the bull was gone, gone over him in a rush. Dark, as his belly went over. Not even stepped on.

Manuel stood up and picked up the muleta. Fuentes handed him the sword. It was bent where it had struck the shoulder-blade. Manuel straightened it on his knee and ran toward the bull, standing now beside one of the dead horses. As he ran, his jacket flopped where it had been ripped under his armpit.

"Get him out of there," Manuel shouted to the gypsy. The bull had smelled the blood of the dead horse and ripped into the canvas-cover with his horns. He charged Fuentes's cape, with the canvas hanging from his splintered horn, and the crowd laughed. Out in the ring, he tossed his head to rid himself of the canvas. Hernandez, running up from behind him, grabbed the end of the canvas and neatly lifted it off the horn.

The bull followed it in a half-charge and stopped still. He was on the defensive again. Manuel was walking toward him with the sword and muleta. Manuel swung the muleta before him. The bull would not charge.

Manuel profiled toward the bull, sighting along the dipping blade of the sword. The bull was motionless, seemingly dead on his feet, incapable of another charge.

Manuel rose to his toes, sighting along the steel, and charged.

Again there was the shock and he felt himself being borne back in a rush, to strike hard on the sand. There was no chance of kicking this time. The bull was on top of him. Manuel lay as though dead, his head on his arms, and the bull bumped him. Bumped his back, bumped his face in the sand. He felt the horn go into the sand between his folded arms. The bull hit him in the small of the back. His face drove into the sand. The horn drove through one of his sleeves and the bull ripped it off. Manuel was tossed clear and the bull followed the capes.

Manuel got up, found the sword and muleta, tried the point of the sword with his thumb, and then ran toward the barrera for a new sword.

Retana's man handed him the sword over the edge of the barrera.

"Wipe off your face," he said.

Manuel, running again toward the bull, wiped his bloody face with his handkerchief. He had not seen Zurito. Where was Zurito?

The cuadrilla had stepped away from the bull and waited with their capes. The bull stood, heavy and dull again after the action.

Manuel walked toward him with the muleta. He stopped and shook it. The bull did not respond. He passed it right and left, left and right before the bull's muzzle. The bull's eyes watched it and turned with the swing, but he would not charge. He was waiting for Manuel.

Manuel was worried. There was nothing to do but go in. Corto y derecho. He profiled close to the bull, crossed the muleta in front of his body and charged. As he pushed in the sword, he jerked his body to the left to clear the horn. The bull passed him and the sword shot up in the air, twinkling under the arc-lights, to fall red-hilted on the sand.

Manuel ran over and picked it up. It was bent and he straightened it over his knee.

As he came running toward the bull, fixed again now, he passed Hernandez standing with his cape.

"He's all bone," the boy said encouragingly.

Manuel nodded, wiping his face. He put the bloody handkerchief in his pocket.

There was the bull. He was close to the barrera now. Damn him. Maybe he was all bone. Maybe there was not any place for the sword to go in. The hell there wasn't! He'd show them.

He tried a pass with the muleta and the bull did not move. Manuel chopped the muleta back and forth in front of the bull. Nothing doing.

He furled the muleta, drew the sword out, profiled and drove in on the bull. He felt the sword buckle as he shoved it in, leaning his weight on it, and then it shot high in the air, end-over-ending into the crowd. Manuel had jerked clear as the sword jumped.

The first cushions thrown down out of the dark missed him. Then one hit him in the face, his bloody face looking toward the crowd. They were coming down fast. Spotting the sand. Somebody threw an empty champagne-bottle from close range. It hit Manuel on the foot. He stood there watching the dark, where the things were coming from. Then something whished through the air and struck by him. Manuel leaned over and picked it up. It was his sword. He straightened it over his knee and gestured with it to the crowd.

"Thank you," he said. "Thank you."

Oh, the dirty bastards! Dirty bastards! Oh, the lousy, dirty bastards! He kicked into a cushion as he ran.

There was the bull. The same as ever. All right, you dirty, lousy bastard!

Manuel passed the muleta in front of the bull's black muzzle.

Nothing doing.

You won't! All right. He stepped close and jammed the sharp peak of the muleta into the bull's damp muzzle.

The bull was on him as he jumped back and as he tripped on a cushion he felt the horn go into him, into his side. He grabbed the horn with his two hands and rode backward, holding tight onto the place. The bull tossed him and he was clear. He lay still. It was all right. The bull was gone.

He got up coughing and feeling broken and gone. The dirty bastards!

"Give me the sword," he shouted. "Give me the stuff."

Fuentes came up with the muleta and the sword.

Hernandez put his arm around him.

"Go on to the infirmary, man," he said. "Don't be a damn fool."

"Get away from me," Manuel said. "Get to hell away from me."

He twisted free. Hernandez shrugged his shoulders. Manuel ran toward the bull.

There was the bull standing, heavy, firmly planted.

All right, you bastard! Manuel drew the sword out of the muleta, sighted with the same movement, and flung himself onto the bull. He felt the sword go in all the way. Right up to the guard. Four fingers and his thumb into the bull. The blood was hot on his knuckles, and he was on top of the bull.

The bull lurched with him as he lay on, and seemed to sink; then he was standing clear. He looked at the bull going down slowly over on his side, then suddenly four feet in the air.

Then he gestured at the crowd, his hand warm from the bull blood.

All right, you bastards! He wanted to say something, but he started to cough. It was hot and choking. He looked down for the muleta. He must go over and salute the president. President hell! He was sitting down looking at something. It was the bull. His four feet up. Thick tongue out. Things crawling around on his belly and under his legs. Crawling where the hair was thin. Dead bull. To hell with the bull! To hell with them all! He started to get to his feet and commenced to cough. He sat down again, coughing. Somebody came and pushed him up.

They carried him across the ring to the infirmary, running with him across the sand, standing blocked at the gate as the mules came in, then around under the dark passageway, men grunting as they took him up the stairway, and then laid him down.

The doctor and two men in white were waiting for him. They laid him out on the table. They were cutting away his shirt. Manuel felt tired. His whole chest felt scalding inside. He started to cough and they held something to his mouth. Everybody was very busy.

There was an electric light in his eyes. He shut his eyes.

He heard someone coming very heavily up the stairs. Then he did not hear it. Then he heard a noise far off. That was the crowd. Well, somebody would have to kill his other bull. They had cut away all his shirt. The doctor smiled at him. There was Retana.

"Hello, Retana!" Manuel said. He could not hear his voice.

Retana smiled at him and said something. Manuel could not hear it.

Zurito stood beside the table, bending over where the doctor was working. He was in his picador clothes, without his hat.

Zurito said something to him. Manuel could not hear it.

Zurito was speaking to Retana. One of the men in white smiled and handed Retana a pair of scissors. Retana gave them to Zurito. Zurito said something to Manuel. He could not hear it.

To hell with this operating-table. He'd been on plenty of operating-tables before. He was not going to die. There would be a priest if he was going to die.

Zurito was saying something to him. Holding up the scissors.

That was it. They were going to cut off his coleta. They were going to cut off his pigtail.

Manuel sat up on the operating-table. The doctor stepped back, angry. Some one grabbed him and held him.

"You couldn't do a thing like that, Manos," he said.

He heard suddenly, clearly, Zurito's voice.

"That's all right," Zurito said. "I won't do it. I was joking."

"I was going good," Manuel said. "I didn't have any luck. That was all."

Manuel lay back. They had put something over his face. It was all familiar. He inhaled deeply. He felt very tired. He was very, very tired. They took the thing away from his face.

"I was going good," Manuel said weakly. "I was going great."

Retana looked at Zurito and started for the door.

"I'll stay here with him," Zurito said.

Retana shrugged his shoulders.

Manuel opened his eyes and looked at Zurito.

"Wasn't I going good, Manos?" he asked, for confirmation.

"Sure," said Zurito. "You were going great."

The doctor's assistant put the cone over Manuel's face and he inhaled deeply. Zurito stood awkwardly, watching.

1. Choose a passage from the story and examine its word choice and sentence structure.
2. How do the characters speak? Is their speech similar to or different from the narrator's?
3. What values do the characters represent? Why is Zurito such a perfect example of these values?
4. Do the values of the story match its language?

Edgar Allan Poe (1809–1849)
THE FALL OF THE HOUSE OF USHER

Son cœur est un luth suspendu;
Sitôt qu'on le touche il résonne.
De Béranger

During the whole of a dull, dark, and soundless day in the autumn of the year, when the clouds hung oppressively low in the heavens, I had been passing alone, on horseback, through a singularly dreary tract of country; and at length found myself, as the shades of the evening drew on, within view of the melancholy House of Usher. I know not how it was—but, with the first glimpse of the building, a sense of insufferable gloom pervaded my spirit. I say insufferable; for the feeling was unrelieved by any of that half-pleasurable, because poetic, sentiment, with which the mind usually receives even the sternest natural images of the desolate or terrible. I looked upon the scene before me—upon the mere house, and the simple landscape features of the domain, upon the bleak walls, upon the vacant eye-like windows, upon a few rank sedges, and upon a few white trunks of decayed trees—with an utter depression of soul which I can compare to no earthly sensation more properly than to the after-dream of the reveller upon opium: the bitter lapse into everyday life, the hideous dropping off of the veil. There was an iciness, a sinking, a sickening of the heart, an unredeemed dreariness of thought which no goading of the imagination could torture into aught of the sublime. What was it—I paused to think—what was it that so unnerved me in the contemplation of the House of Usher? It was a mystery all insoluble; nor could I grapple with the shadowy fancies that crowded upon me as I pondered. I was forced to fall back upon the unsatisfactory conclusion, that while, beyond doubt, there *are* combinations of very simple natural objects which have the power of thus affecting us, still the analysis of this power lies among considerations beyond our depth. It was possible, I reflected, that a mere different arrangement of the particulars of the scene, of the details of the picture, would be sufficient to modify, or perhaps to annihilate its capacity for sorrowful impression; and, acting upon this idea, I reined my horse to the precipitous brink of a black and lurid tarn that lay in unruffled lustre by the dwelling, and gazed down—but with a shudder even more thrilling than before—upon the remodelled and inverted images of the gray sedge, and the ghastly tree-stems, and the vacant and eye-like windows.

Nevertheless, in this mansion of gloom I now proposed to myself a sojourn of some weeks. Its proprietor, Roderick Usher, had been one of my boon companions in boyhood; but many years had elapsed since our last meeting. A letter, however, had lately reached me in a distant part of the country—a letter from him—which, in its wildly importunate nature, had admitted of no other than a personal reply. The MS. gave evidence of nervous agitation. The writer spoke of acute bodily illness, of a mental disorder which oppressed him, and of an earnest desire to see me, as his best, and indeed his only personal friend, with a view of attempting, by the cheerfulness of my society, some alleviation of his malady. It was the manner in which all this, and much more, was said—it was the apparent *heart* that went with his request—which allowed me no room for hesitation; and I accordingly obeyed forthwith what I still considered a very singular summons.

Although, as boys, we had been even intimate associates, yet I really knew little of my friend. His reserve had been always excessive and habitual. I was aware, however, that his very ancient family had been noted, time out of mind, for a peculiar sensibility of temperament, displaying itself, through long ages, in many works of exalted art, and manifested, of late, in repeated deeds of munificent yet unobtrusive charity, as well as in a passionate devotion to the intricacies, perhaps even more than to the orthodox and easily recognizable beauties, of musical science. I had learned, too, the very remarkable fact, that the stem of the Usher race, all time-honored as it was, had put forth, at no period, any enduring branch; in other words, that the entire family lay in the direct line of descent, and had always, with very trifling and very temporary variation, so lain. It was this deficiency, I considered, while running over in thought the perfect keeping of the character of the premises with the accredited character of the people, and while speculating upon the possible influence which the one, in the long lapse of centuries, might have exercised upon the other—it was this deficiency, perhaps, of collateral issue, and the consequent undeviating transmission, from sire to son, of the patrimony with the name, which had, at length, so identified the two as to merge the original title of the estate in the quaint and equivocal appellation of the "House of Usher"—an appellation which seemed to include, in the minds of the peasantry who used it, both the family and the family mansion.

I have said that the sole effect of my somewhat childish experiment, that of looking down within the tarn, had been to deepen the first singular impression. There can be no doubt that the consciousness of the rapid increase of my superstition—for why should I not so term it?—served mainly to accelerate the increase itself. Such, I have long known, is the paradoxical law of all sentiments having terror as a basis. And it might have been for this reason only, that, when I again uplifted my eyes to the house itself, from its image in the pool, there grew in my mind a strange fancy—a fancy so ridiculous, indeed, that I but mention it to show the vivid force of the sensations which oppressed me. I had so worked upon my imagination as really to believe that about the whole mansion and domain there hung an atmosphere peculiar to themselves and their immediate vicinity: an atmosphere which had no affinity with the air of heaven, but which had reeked up from the decayed trees, and the gray wall, and the silent tarn: a pestilent and mystic vapor, dull, sluggish, faintly discernible, and leaden-hued.

Shaking off from my spirit what *must* have been a dream, I scanned more narrowly the real aspect of the building. Its principal feature seemed to be that of an excessive antiquity. The discoloration of ages had been great. Minute fungi overspread the whole exterior, hanging in a fine tangled webwork from the eaves. Yet all this was apart from any extraordinary dilapidation. No portion of the masonry had fallen; and there appeared to be a wild inconsistency between its still perfect adaptation of parts and the crumbling condition of the individual stones. In this there was much that reminded me of the specious totality of old wood-work which has rotted for long years in some neglected vault, with no disturbance from the breath of the external air. Beyond this indication of extensive decay, however, the fabric gave little token of instability. Perhaps the eye of a scrutinizing observer might have discovered a barely perceptible fissure, which, extending from the roof of the building in front, made its way down the wall in a zigzag direction, until it became lost in the sullen waters of the tarn.

Noticing these things, I rode over a short causeway to the house. A servant in waiting took my horse, and I entered the Gothic archway of the hall. A valet, of stealthy step, thence conducted me, in silence, through many dark and intricate passages in my progress to the *studio* of his master. Much that I encountered on the way contributed, I know not how, to heighten the vague sentiments of which I have already spoken. While the objects around me—while the carvings of the ceilings, the sombre tapestries of the walls, the ebon blackness of the floors, and the phantasmagoric armorial trophies which rattled as I strode, were but matters to which, or to such as which, I had been accustomed from my infancy—while I hesitated not to acknowledge how familiar was all this—I still wondered to find how unfamiliar were the fancies which ordinary images were stirring up. On one of the staircases, I met the physician of the family. His countenance, I thought, wore a mingled expression of low cunning and perplexity. He accosted me with trepidation and passed on. The valet now threw open a door and ushered me into the presence of his master.

The room in which I found myself was very large and lofty. The windows were long, narrow, and pointed, and at so vast a distance from the black oaken floor as to be altogether inaccessible from within. Feeble gleams of encrimsoned light made their way through the trellised panes, and served to render sufficiently distinct the more prominent objects around; the eye, however, struggled in vain to reach the remoter angles of the chamber, or the recesses of the vaulted and fretted ceiling. Dark draperies hung upon the walls. The general furniture was profuse, comfortless, antique, and tattered. Many books and musical instruments lay scattered about, but failed to give any vitality to the scene. I felt that I breathed an atmosphere of sorrow. An air of stern, deep, and irredeemable gloom hung over and pervaded all.

Upon my entrance, Usher arose from a sofa on which he had been lying at full length, and greeted me with a vivacious warmth which had much in it, I at first thought, of an overdone cordiality—of the constrained effort of the *ennuye* man of the world. A glance, however, at his countenance, convinced me of his perfect sincerity. We sat down; and for some moments, while he spoke not, I gazed upon him with a feeling half of pity, half of awe. Surely, man had never before so terribly altered, in so brief a period, as had Roderick Usher! It was with difficulty that I could bring myself to admit the identity of the wan being before me with the companion of my early boyhood. Yet the character of his face had been at all times remarkable. A cadaverousness of complexion; an eye large, liquid, and luminous beyond comparison, lips somewhat thin and very pallid, but of a surpassingly beautiful curve; a nose of a delicate Hebrew model, but with a breadth of nostril unusual in similar formations; a finely moulded chin, speaking, in its want of prominence, of a want of moral energy; hair of a more than web-like softness and tenuity; these features, with an inordinate expansion above the regions of the temple, made up altogether a countenance not easily to be forgotten. And now in the mere exaggeration of the prevailing character of these features, and of the expression they were wont to convey, lay so much of change that I doubted to whom I spoke. The now ghastly pallor of the skin, and the now miraculous lustre of the eye, above all things startled and even awed me. The silken hair, too, had been suffered to grow all unheeded, and as, in its wild gossamer texture, it floated rather than fell about the face, I could not, even with effort, connect its Arabesque expression with any idea of simple humanity.

In the manner of my friend I was at once struck with an incoherence, an inconsistency; and I soon found this to arise from a series of feeble and futile struggles to overcome an habitual trepidancy, an excessive nervous agitation. For something of this nature I had indeed been prepared, no less by his letter, than by reminiscences of certain boyish traits, and by conclusions deduced from his peculiar physical conformation and temperament. His action was alternately vivacious and sullen. His voice varied rapidly from a tremulous indecision (when the animal spirits seemed utterly in abeyance) to that species of energetic concision—that abrupt, weighty, unhurried, and hollow-sounding enunciation—that leaden, self-balanced and perfectly modulated guttural utterance, which may be observed in the lost drunkard, or the irreclaimable eater of opium, during the periods of his most intense excitement.

It was thus that he spoke of the object of my visit, of his earnest desire to see me, and of the solace he expected me to afford him. He entered, at some length, into what he conceived to be the nature of his malady. It was, he said, a constitutional and a family evil, and one for which he despaired to find a remedy—a mere nervous affection, he immediately added, which would undoubtedly soon pass off. It displayed itself in a host of unnatural sensations. Some of these, as he detailed them, interested and bewildered me; although, perhaps, the terms, and the general manner of the narration had their weight. He suffered much from a morbid acuteness of the senses; the most insipid food was alone endurable; he could wear only garments of certain texture; the odors of all flowers were oppressive; his eyes were tortured by even a faint light; and there were but peculiar sounds, and these from stringed instruments, which did not inspire him with horror.

To an anomolous species of terror I found him a bounden slave. 'I shall perish,' said he, 'I *must* perish in this deplorable folly. Thus, thus, and not otherwise, shall I be lost. I dread the events of the future, not in themselves, but in their results. I shudder at the thought of any, even the most trivial, incident, which may operate upon this intolerable agitation of soul. I have, indeed, no abhorrence of danger, except in its absolute effect—in terror. In this unnerved—in this pitiable condition, I feel that the period will sooner or later arrive when I must abandon life and reason together, in some struggle with the grim phantasm, FEAR.'

I learned, moreover, at intervals, and through broken and equivocal hints, another singular feature of his mental condition. He was enchained by certain superstitious impressions in regard to the dwelling which he tenanted, and whence, for many years, he had never ventured forth—in regard to an influence whose suppositious force was conveyed in terms too shadowy here to be re-stated—an influence which some peculiarities in the mere form and substance of his family mansion, had, by dint of long sufferance, he said, obtained over his spirit—an effect which the *physique* of the gray walls and turrets, and of the dim tarn into which they all looked down, had, at length, brought about upon the *morale* of his existence.

He admitted, however, although with hesitation, that much of the peculiar gloom which thus afflicted him could be traced to a more natural and far more palpable origin—to the severe and long-continued illness, indeed to the evidently approaching dissolution, of a tenderly beloved sister—his sole companion for long years, his last and only relative on earth. 'Her decease,' he said, with a bitterness which I can never forget, 'would leave him (him the hopeless and the frail) the last of the ancient race of the Ushers.' While he spoke, the lady Madeline (for so was she called) passed slowly through a remote portion of the apartment, and, without having noticed my presence, disappeared. I regarded her with an utter astonishment not unmingled with dread, and yet I found it impossible to account for such feelings. A sensation of stupor oppressed me, as my eyes followed her retreating steps. When a door, at length, closed upon her, my glance sought instinctively and eagerly the countenance of the brother; but he had buried his face in his hands, and I could only perceive that a far more than ordinary wanness had overspread the emaciated fingers through which trickled many passionate tears.

The disease of the lady Madeline had long baffled the skill of her physicians. A settled apathy, a gradual wasting away of the person, and frequent although transient affections of a partially cataleptical character, were the unusual diagnosis. Hitherto she had steadily borne up against the pressure of her malady, and had not betaken herself finally to bed; but, on the closing in of the evening of my arrival at the house, she succumbed (as her brother told me at night with inexpressible agitation) to the prostrating power of the destroyer; and I learned that the glimpse I had obtained of her person would thus probably be the last I should obtain—that the lady, at least while living, would be seen by me no more.

For several days ensuing, her name was unmentioned by either Usher or myself: and during this period I was busied in earnest endeavors to alleviate the melancholy of my friend. We painted and read together; or I listened, as if in a dream, to the wild improvisations of his speaking guitar. And thus, as a closer and still closer intimacy admitted me more unreservedly into the recesses of his spirit, the more bitterly did I perceive the futility of all attempt at cheering a mind from which darkness, as if an inherent positive quality, poured forth upon all objects of the moral and physical universe, in one unceasing radiation of gloom.

I shall ever bear about me a memory of the many solemn hours I thus spent alone with the master of the House of Usher. Yet I should fail in any attempt to convey an idea of the exact character of the studies, or of the occupations, in which he involved me, or led me the way. An excited and highly distempered ideality threw a sulphureous lustre over all. His long improvised dirges will ring forever in my ears. Among other things, I hold painfully in mind a certain singular perversion and amplification of the wild air of the last waltz of Von Weber. From the paintings over which his elaborate fancy brooded, and which grew, touch by touch, into vaguenesses at which I shuddered the more thrillingly, because I shuddered knowing not why;—from these paintings (vivid as their images now are before me) I would in vain endeavor to educe more than a small portion which should lie within the compass of merely written words. By the utter simplicity, by the nakedness of his designs, he arrested and over-awed attention. If ever mortal painted an idea, that mortal was Roderick Usher. For me at least, in the circumstances then surrounding me, there arose out of the pure abstractions which the hypochondriac contrived to throw upon his canvas, an intensity of intolerable awe, no shadow of which felt I ever yet in the contemplation of the certainly glowing yet too concrete reveries of Fuseli.

One of the phantasmagoric conceptions of my friend, partaking not so rigidly of the spirit of abstraction, may be shadowed forth, although feebly, in words. A small picture presented the interior of an immensely long and rectangular vault or tunnel, with low walls, smooth, white, and without interruption or device. Certain accessory points of the design served well to convey the idea that this excavation lay at an exceeding depth below the surface of the earth. No outlet was observed in any portion of its vast extent, and no torch, or other artificial source of light was discernible; yet a flood of intense rays rolled throughout, and bathed the whole in a ghastly and inappropriate splendor.

I have just spoken of that morbid condition of the auditory nerve which rendered all music intolerable to the sufferer, with the exception of certain effects of stringed instruments. It was, perhaps, the narrow limits to which he thus confined himself upon the guitar, which gave birth, in great measure, to the fantastic character of his performances. But the fervid *facility* of his *impromptus* could not be so accounted for. They must have been, and were, in the notes, as well as in the words of his wild fantasias (for he not unfrequently accompanied himself with rhymed verbal improvisations), the result of that intense mental collectedness and concentration to which I have previously alluded as observable only in particular moments of the highest artificial excitement. The words of one of these rhapsodies I have easily remembered. I was, perhaps, the more forcibly impressed with it, as he gave it, because, in the under or mystic current of its meaning, I fancied that I perceived, and for the first time, a full consciousness on the part of Usher, of the tottering of his lofty reason upon her throne. The verses, which were entitled 'The Haunted Palace,' ran very nearly, if not accurately, thus:

In the greenest of our valleys
By good angels tenanted,
Once a fair and stately palace—
Radiant palace—reared its head.
In the monarch Thought's dominion,
It stood there!
Never seraph spread a pinion
Over fabric half so fair!

Banners yellow, glorious, golden,
On its roof did float and flow
(This—all this—was in the olden
Time long ago)
And every gentle air that dallied,
In that sweet day,
Along the ramparts plumed and pallid,
A wingèd odor went away.

Wanderers in that happy valley,
Through two luminous windows, saw
Spirits moving musically
To a lute's well-tunèd law,
Round about a throne where, sitting,
Porphyrogene!
In state his glory well befitting,
The ruler of the realm was seen.

And all with pearl and ruby glowing
Was the fair palace door,
Through which came flowing, flowing, flowing,
And sparkling evermore,
A troop of Echoes, whose sweet duty
Was but to sing,
In voices of surpassing beauty,
The wit and wisdom of their king.

But evil things, in robes of sorrow,
Assailed the monarch's high estate;
(Ah, let us mourn!—for never morrow
Shall dawn upon him, desolate!)
And round about his home the glory
That blushed and bloomed
Is but a dim-remembered story
Of the old time entombed.

And travellers, now, within that valley,
Through the red-litten windows see
Vast forms that move fantastically
To a discordant melody;
While, like a ghastly rapid river,
Through the pale door
A hideous throng rush out forever,
And laugh—but smile no more.

I well remember that suggestions arising from this ballad led us into a train of thought wherein there became manifest an opinion of Usher's which I mention not so much on account of its novelty, (for other men have thought thus), as on account of the pertinacity with which he maintained it. This opinion, in its general form, was that of the sentience of all vegetable things. But, in his disordered fancy, the idea had assumed a more daring character, and trespassed, under certain conditions, upon the kingdom of inorganization. I lack words to express the full extent, or the earnest *abandon* of his persuasion. The belief, however, was connected (as I have previously hinted) with the gray stones of the home of his forefathers. The conditions of the sentience had been here, he imagined, fulfilled in the method of collocation of these stones—in the order of their arrangement, as well as in that of the many *fungi* which overspread them, and of the decayed trees which stood around—above all, in the long undisturbed endurance of this arrangement, and in its reduplication in the still waters of the tarn. Its evidence—the evidence of the sentience—was to be seen, he said, (and I here started as he spoke), in the gradual yet certain condensation of an atmosphere of their own about the waters and the walls. The result was discoverable, he added, in that silent, yet importunate and terrible influence which for centuries had moulded the destinies of his family, and which made *him* what I now saw him—what he was. Such opinions need no comment, and I will make none.

Our books—the books which, for years, had formed no small portion of the mental existence of the invalid—were, as might be supposed, in strict keeping with this character of phantasm. We pored together over such works as the *Ververt et Chartreuse* of Gresset; the

Belphegor of Machiavelli; the *Heaven and Hell of* Swedenborg; the *Subterranean Voyage of Nicholas Klimm* by Holberg; the *Chiromancy* of Robert Flud, of Jean D'Indaginé, and of De la Chambre; the *Journey into the Blue Distance* of Tieck; and the *City of the Sun* of Campanella. One favorite volume was a small octavo edition of the *Directorium Inquisitorum,* by the Dominican Eymeric de Gironne; and there were passages in Pomponius Mela, about the old African Satyrs and Aegipans, over which Usher would sit dreaming for hours. His chief delight, however, was found in the perusal of an exceedingly rare and curious book in quarto Gothic—the manual of a forgotten church—the *Vigila Mortuorum Secundum Chorum Ecclesia Maguntinæn.*

I could not help thinking of the wild ritual of this work, and of its probable influence upon the hypochondriac, when, one evening, having informed me abruptly that the lady Madeline was no more, he stated his intention of preserving her corpse for a fortnight, (previously to its final interment), in one of the numerous vaults within the main walls of the building. The worldly reason, however, assigned for this singular proceeding, was one which I did not feel at liberty to dispute. The brother had been led to his resolution (so he told me) by consideration of the unusual character of the malady of the deceased, of certain obtrusive and eager inquiries on the part of her medical men, and of the remote and exposed situation of the burial-ground of the family. I will not deny that when I called to mind the sinister countenance of the person whom I met upon the staircase, on the day of my arrival at the house, I had no desire to oppose what I regarded as at best but a harmless, and by no means an unnatural, precaution.

At the request of Usher, I personally aided him in the arrangements for the temporary entombment. The body having been encoffined, we two alone bore it to its rest. The vault in which we placed it (and which had been so long unopened that our torches, half smothered in its oppressive atmosphere, gave us little opportunity for investigation) was small, damp, and entirely without means of admission for light; lying, at great depth, immediately beneath that portion of the building in which was my own sleeping apartment. It had been used, apparently, in remote feudal times, for the worst purposes of a donjon-keep, and, in later days, as a place of deposit for powder, or some other highly combustible substance, as a portion of its floor, and the whole interior of a long archway through which we reached it, were carefully sheathed with copper. The door, of massive iron, had been, also, similarly protected. Its immense weight caused an unusually sharp grating sound, as it moved upon its hinges.

Having deposited our mournful burden upon tressels within this region of horror, we partially turned aside the yet unscrewed lid of the coffin, and looked upon the face of the tenant. A striking similitude between the brother and sister now first arrested my attention; and

Usher, divining, perhaps, my thoughts, murmured out some few words from which I learned that the deceased and himself had been twins, and that sympathies of a scarcely intelligible nature had always existed between them. Our glances, however, rested not long upon the dead—for we could not regard her unawed. The disease which had thus entombed the lady in the maturity of youth, had left, as usual in all maladies of a strictly cataleptical character, the mockery of a faint blush upon the bosom and the face, and that suspiciously lingering smile upon the lip which is so terrible in death. We replaced and screwed down the lid, and, having secured the door of iron, made our way, with toil, into the scarcely less gloomy apartments of the upper portion of the house.

And now, some days of bitter grief having elapsed, an observable change came over the features of the mental disorder of my friend. His ordinary manner had vanished. His ordinary occupations were neglected or forgotten. He roamed from chamber to chamber with hurried, unequal, and objectless step. The pallor of his countenance had assumed, if possible, a more ghastly hue—but the luminousness of his eye had utterly gone out. The once occasional huskiness of his tone was heard no more; and a tremulous quaver, as if of extreme terror, habitually characterized his utterance. There were times, indeed, when I thought his unceasingly agitated mind was laboring with some oppressive secret, to divulge which he struggled for the necessary courage. At times, again, I was obliged to resolve all into the mere inexplicable vagaries of madness, for I beheld him gazing upon vacancy for long hours, in an attitude of the profoundest attention, as if listening to some imaginary sound. It was no wonder that his condition terrified—that it infected me. I felt creeping upon me, by slow yet certain degrees, the wild influences of his own fantastic yet impressive superstitions.

It was, especially, upon retiring to bed late in the night of the seventh or eighth day after the placing of the lady Madeline within the donjon, that I experienced the full power of such feelings. Sleep came not near my couch, while the hours waned and waned away. I struggled to reason off the nervousness which had dominion over me. I endeavored to believe that much, if not all of what I felt, was due to the bewildering influence of the gloomy furniture of the room—of the dark and tattered draperies, which, tortured into motion by the breath of a rising tempest, swayed fitfully to and fro upon the walls, and rustled uneasily about the decorations of the bed. But my efforts were fruitless. An irrepressible tremor gradually pervaded my frame; and, at length, there sat upon my very heart an incubus of utterly causeless alarm. Shaking this off with a gasp and a struggle, I uplifted myself upon the pillows, and, peering earnestly within the intense darkness of the chamber, hearkened—I know not why, except that an instinctive spirit prompted me—to certain low and indefinite sounds which came, through the pauses of the storm, at long intervals I knew not whence. Overpowered by an intense sentiment of horror, unaccountable yet unendurable, I threw on my clothes with haste (for I felt that I should sleep no more during the night), and endeavored to arouse myself from the pitiable condition into which I had fallen, by pacing rapidly to and fro through the apartment.

I had taken but few turns in this manner, when a light step on an adjoining staircase arrested my attention. I presently recognized it as that of Usher. In an instant afterward he rapped, with a gentle touch, at my door, and entered, bearing a lamp. His countenance was, as usual, cadaverously wan—but, moreover, there was a species of mad hilarity in his eyes—an evidently restrained *hysteria* in his whole demeanor. His air appalled me—but anything was preferable to the solitude which I had so long endured, and I even welcomed his presence as a relief.

'And you have not seen it?' he said abruptly, after having stared about him for some moments in silence—'you have not then seen it?—but, stay! you shall.' Thus speaking, and having carefully shaded his lamp, he hurried to one of the casements and threw it freely open to the storm.

The impetuous fury of the entering gust nearly lifted us from our feet. It was, indeed, a tempestuous yet sternly beautiful night, and one wildly singular in its terror and its beauty. A whirlwind had apparently collected its force in our vicinity; for there were frequent and violent alterations in the direction of the wind; and the exceeding density of the clouds (which hung so low as to press upon the turrets of the house) did not prevent our perceiving the life-like velocity with which they flew careering from all points against each other, without passing away into the distance. I say that even their exceeding density did not prevent our perceiving this; yet we had no glimpse of the moon or stars, nor was there any flashing forth of the lightning. But the under surfaces of the huge masses of agitated vapor, as well as all terrestrial objects immediately around us, were glowing in the unnatural light of a faintly luminous and distinctly visible gaseous exhalation which hung about and enshrouded the mansion.

'You must not—you shall not behold this!' said I, shudderingly, to Usher, as I led him, with a gentle violence, from the window to a seat. 'These appearances, which bewilder you, are merely electrical phenomena not uncommon—or it may be that they have their ghastly origin in the rank miasma of the tarn. Let us close this casement; the air is chilling and dangerous to your frame. Here is one of your favorite romances. I will read, and you shall listen;—and so we will pass away this terrible night together.'

The antique volume which I had taken up was the *Mad Trist* of Sir Launcelot Canning; but I had called it a favorite of Usher's more in sad jest than in earnest; for, in truth, there is little in its uncouth and unimaginative prolixity which could have had interest for the lofty and spiritual ideality of my friend. It was, however, the only book immediately at hand; and I indulged a vague hope that the excitement which now agitated the hypochondriac might find relief (for the history of mental disorder is full of similar anomalies) even in the extremeness of the folly which I should read. Could I have judged, indeed, by the wild overstrained air of vivacity with which he hearkened, or apparently hearkened, to the words of the tale, I might well have congratulated myself upon the success of my design.

I had arrived at that well-known portion of the story where Ethelred, the hero of the *Trist,* having sought in vain for peaceable admission into the dwelling of the hermit, proceeds to make good an entrance by force. Here, it will be remembered, the words of the narrative run thus:

> And Ethelred, who was by nature of a doughty heart, and who was now mighty withal, on account of the powerfulness of the wine which he had drunken, waited no longer to hold parley with the hermit, who, in sooth, was of an obstinate and maliceful turn, but, feeling the rain upon his shoulders, and fearing the rising of the tempest, uplifted his mace outright, and, with blows, made quickly room in the plankings of the door for his gauntleted hand; and now pulling therewith sturdily, he so cracked, and ripped, and tore all asunder, that the noise of the dry and hollow-sounding wood alarumed and reverberated throughout the forest.

At the termination of this sentence I started, and for a moment, paused; for it appeared to me (although I at once concluded that my excited fancy had deceived me)—it appeared to me that, from some very remote portion of the mansion, there came, indistinctly, to my ears, what might have been, in its exact similarity of character, the echo (but a stifled and dull one certainly) of the very cracking and ripping sound which Sir Launcelot had so particularly described. It was, beyond doubt, the coincidence alone which had arrested my attention; for, amid the rattling of the sashes of the casements, and the ordinary commingled noises of the still increasing storm, the sound, in itself, had nothing, surely, which should have interested or disturbed me. I continued the story:

> But the good champion Ethelred, now entering within the door, was sore enraged and amazed to perceive no signal of the maliceful hermit; but, in the stead thereof, a dragon of a scaly and prodigious demeanor, and of a fiery tongue, which sate in guard before a palace of gold, with a floor of silver; and upon the wall there hung a shield of shining brass with this legend enwritten—
>
> *Who entereth herein, a conqueror hath bin;*
> *Who slayeth the dragon, the shield he shall win;*

> And Ethelred uplifted his mace, and struck upon the head of the dragon, which fell before him, and gave up his pesty breath, with a shriek so horrid and harsh, and withal so piercing, that Ethelred had fain to close his ears with his hands against the dreadful noise of it, the like whereof was never before heard.

Here again I paused abruptly, and now with a feeling of wild amazement—for there could be no doubt whatever that, in this instance, I did actually hear (although from what direction it proceeded I found it impossible to say) a low and apparently distant, but harsh, protracted, and most unusual screaming or grating sound—the exact counterpart of what my fancy had already conjured up for the dragon's unnatural shriek as described by the romancer.

Oppressed, as I certainly was, upon the occurrence of the second and most extraordinary coincidence, by a thousand conflicting sensations, in which wonder and extreme terror were predominant, I still retained sufficient presence of mind to avoid exciting, by any observation, the sensitive nervousness of my companion. I was by no means certain that he had noticed the sounds in question; although, assuredly, a strange alteration had, during the last few minutes, taken place in his demeanor. From a position fronting my own, he had gradually brought round his chair, so as to sit with his face to the door of the chamber; and thus I could but partially perceive his features, although I saw that his lips trembled as if he were murmuring inaudibly. His head had dropped upon his breast—yet I knew that he was not asleep, from the wide and rigid opening of the eye as I caught a glance of it in profile. The motion of his body, too, was at variance with this idea—for he rocked from side to side with a gentle yet constant and uniform sway. Having rapidly taken notice of all this, I resumed the narrative of Sir Launcelot, which thus proceeded:

> And now, the champion, having escaped from the terrible fury of the dragon, bethinking himself of the brazen shield, and of the breaking up of the enchantment which was upon it, removed the carcass from out of the way before him, and approached valorously over the silver pavement of the castle to where the shield was upon the wall; which in sooth tarried not for his full coming, but fell down at his feet upon the silver floor, with a mighty great and terrible ringing sound.

No sooner had these syllables passed my lips, than—as if a shield of brass had indeed, at the moment, fallen heavily upon a floor of silver—I became aware of a distinct, hollow, metallic and clangorous yet apparently muffled reverberation. Completely unnerved, I leaped to my feet; but the measured rocking movement of Usher was undisturbed. I rushed to the chair in which he sat. His eyes were bent fixedly before him, and throughout his whole countenance there reigned a stony rigidity. But as I placed my hand upon his shoulder, there came a strong shudder over his whole person; a sickly smile quivered about his lips; and I saw that he spoke in a low, hurried, and gibbering murmur, as if unconscious of my presence. Bending closely over him, I at length drank in the hideous import of his words.

'Not hear it?—yes, I hear it, and *have* heard it. Long—long—long—many minutes, many hours, many days, have I heard it—yet I dared not— oh, pity me, miserable wretch that I am!—I dared not—I *dared* not speak! *We have put her living in the tomb!* Said I not that my senses were acute? I *now* tell you that I heard her first feeble movements in the hollow coffin. I heard them—many, many days ago—yet I dared not—*I dared not speak!* And now—to-night—Ethelred—ha! ha!—the breaking of the hermit's door, and the death-cry of the dragon, and the clangor of the shield!—say, rather, the rending of her coffin, and the grating of the iron hinges of her prison, and her struggles within the coppered archway of the vault! Oh whither shall I fly? Will she not be here anon? Is she not hurrying to upbraid me for my haste? Have I not heard her footstep on the stair? Do I not distinguish that heavy and horrible beating of her heart? MADMAN!' here he sprang furiously to his feet, and shrieked out his syllables, as if in the effort he were giving up his soul—*'Madman! I tell you that she now stands without the door!'*

As if in the superhuman energy of his utterance there had been found the potency of a spell, the huge antique panels to which the speaker pointed, threw slowly back, upon the instant, their ponderous and ebony jaws. It was the work of the rushing gust—but then without those doors there DID stand the lofty and enshrouded figure of the lady Madeline of Usher. There was blood upon her white robes, and the evidence of some bitter struggle upon every portion of her emaciated frame. For a moment she remained trembling and reeling to and fro upon the threshold—then, with a low moaning cry, fell heavily inward upon the person of her brother, and in her violent and now final death-agonies, bore him to the floor a corpse, and a victim to the terrors he had anticipated.

From that chamber, and from that mansion, I fled aghast. The storm was still abroad in all its wrath as I found myself crossing the old causeway. Suddenly there shot along the path a wild light, and I turned to see whence a gleam so unusual could have issued; for the vast house and its shadows were alone behind me. The radiance was that of the full, setting, and blood-red moon which now shone vividly through that once barely-discernible fissure of which I have before spoken as extending from the roof of the building, in a zigzag direction, to the base. While I gazed, this fissure rapidly widened—there came a fierce breath of the whirlwind—the entire orb of the satellite burst at once upon my sight—my brain reeled as I saw the mighty walls rushing asunder—there was a long tumultuous shouting sound like the voice of a thousand waters—and the deep and dank tarn at my feet closed sullenly and silently over the fragments of the HOUSE OF USHER.

1. How does Poe's vocabulary affect your reading?
2. What kind of sentences does he use most frequently?
3. What does the language of the story tell us about its narrator?
4. What is the narrator's way of dealing with the mysterious events he observes?
5. What does Usher's poem tell us about his character?

James Baldwin (1924–1988)

THE ROCKPILE

Across the street from their house, in an empty lot between two houses, stood the rockpile. It was a strange place to find a mass of natural rock jutting out of the ground; and someone, probably Aunt Florence, had once told them that the rock was there and could not be taken away because without it the subway cars underground would fly apart, killing all the people. This, touching on some natural mystery concerning the surface and the center of the earth, was far too intriguing an explanation to be challenged, and it invested the rockpile, moreover, with such mysterious importance that Roy felt it to be his right, not to say his duty, to play there.

Other boys were to be seen there each afternoon after school and all day Saturday and Sunday. They fought on the rockpile. Sure footed, dangerous, and reckless, they rushed each other and grappled on the heights, sometimes disappearing down the other side in a confusion of dust and screams and upended, flying feet. "It's a wonder they don't kill themselves," their mother said, watching sometimes from the fire escape. "You children stay away from there, you hear me?" Though she said "children" she was looking at Roy, where he sat beside John on the fire escape. "The good Lord knows," she continued, "I don't want you to come home bleeding like a hog every day the Lord sends." Roy shifted impatiently, and continued to stare at the street, as though in this gazing he might somehow acquire wings. John said nothing. He had not really been spoken to: he was afraid of the rockpile and of the boys who played there.

Each Saturday morning John and Roy sat on the fire escape and watched the forbidden street below. Sometimes their mother sat in the room behind them, sewing, or dressing their younger sister, or nursing the baby, Paul. The sun fell across them and across the fire escape with a high, benevolent indifference; below them, men and women, and boys and girls, sinners all, loitered; sometimes one of the church-members passed and saw them and waved. Then, for the moment that they waved decorously back, they were intimidated. They watched the saint, man or woman, until he or she had disappeared from sight. The passage of one of the redeemed made them consider, however vacantly, the wickedness of the street, their own latent wickedness in sitting where they sat; and made them think of their father, who came home early on Saturdays and who would soon be turning this corner and entering the dark hall below them.

But until he came to end their freedom, they sat, watching and longing above the street. At the end of the street nearest their house was the bridge which spanned the Harlem River and led to a city called the Bronx; which was where Aunt Florence lived. Nevertheless, when they saw her coming, she did not come from the bridge, but from the opposite end of the street. This, weakly, to their minds, she explained by saying that she had taken the subway, not wishing to walk, and that, besides, she did not live in *that* section of the Bronx. Knowing that the Bronx was across the river, they did not believe this story ever, but, adopting toward her their father's attitude, assumed that she had just left some sinful place which she dared not name, as, for example, a movie palace.

In the summertime boys swam in the river, diving off the wooden dock, or wading in from the garbage-heavy bank. Once a boy, whose name was Richard, drowned in the river. His mother had not known where he was; she had even come to their house, to ask if he was there. Then, in the evening, at six o'clock, they had heard from the street a woman screaming and wailing; and they ran to the windows and looked out. Down the street came the woman, Richard's mother, screaming, her face raised to the sky and tears running down her face. A woman walked beside her, trying to make her quiet and trying to hold her up. Behind them walked a man, Richard's father, with Richard's body in his arms. There were two white policemen walking in the gutter, who did not seem to know what should be done. Richard's father and Richard were wet, and Richard's body lay across his father's arms like a cotton baby. The woman's screaming filled all the street; cars slowed down and the people in the cars stared; people opened their windows and looked out and came rushing out of doors to stand in the gutter, watching. Then the small procession disappeared within the house which stood beside the rockpile. Then, *"Lord, Lord, Lord!"* cried Elizabeth, their mother, and slammed the window down.

One Saturday, an hour before his father would be coming home, Roy was wounded on the rockpile and brought screaming upstairs. He and John had been sitting on the fire escape and their mother had gone into the kitchen to sip tea with Sister McCandless. By and by

Roy became bored and sat beside John in restless silence; and John began drawing into his school-book a newspaper advertisement which featured a new electric locomotive. Some friends of Roy passed beneath the fire escape and called him. Roy began to fidget, yelling down to them through the bars. Then a silence fell. John looked up. Roy stood looking at him.

"I'm going downstairs," he said.

"You better stay where you is, boy. You know Mama don't want you going downstairs."

"I be right *back*. She won't even know I'm gone, less you run and tell her."

"I ain't *got* to tell her. What's going to stop her from coming in here and looking out the window?"

"She's talking," Roy said. He started into the house.

"But Daddy's going to be home soon!"

"I be back before *that*. What you all the time got to be so *scared* for?"

He was already in the house and he now turned, leaning on the windowsill, to swear impatiently, "I be back in *five* minutes."

John watched him sourly as he carefully unlocked the door and disappeared. In a moment he saw him on the sidewalk with his friends. He did not dare to go and tell his mother that Roy had left the fire escape because he had practically promised not to. He started to shout, *Remember, you said five minutes!* but one of Roy's friends was looking up at the fire escape. John looked down at his schoolbook: he became engrossed again in the problem of the locomotive.

When he looked up again he did not know how much time had passed, but now there was a gang fight on the rockpile. Dozens of boys fought each other in the harsh sun: clambering up the rocks and battling hand to hand, scuffed shoes sliding on the slippery rock; filling the bright air with curses and jubilant cries. They filled the air, too, with flying weapons: stones, sticks, tin cans, garbage, whatever could be picked up and thrown. John watched in a kind of absent amazement—until he remembered that Roy was still downstairs, and that he was one of the boys on the rockpile. Then he was afraid; he could not see his brother among the figures in the sun; and he stood up, leaning over the fire- escape railing. Then Roy appeared from the other side of the rocks; John saw that his shirt was torn; he was laughing. He moved until he stood at the very top of the rockpile. Then, something, an empty tin can, flew out of the air and hit him on the forehead, just above the eye. Immediately, one side of Roy's face ran with blood, he fell and rolled on his face down the rocks. Then for a moment there was no movement at all, no sound; the sun, arrested, lay on the street and the sidewalk and the arrested boys. Then some-one screamed or shouted; boys began to run away, down the street, toward the bridge. The figure on the ground, having caught its breath and felt its own blood, began to shout. John cried, "Mama! Mama!" and ran inside.

"Don't fret, don't fret," panted Sister McCandless as they rushed down the dark, narrow, swaying stairs, "don't fret. Ain't a boy been born don't get his knocks every now and again. *Lord!"* they hurried into the sun. A man had picked Roy up and now walked slowly toward them. One or two boys sat silent on the stoops; at either end of the street there was a group of boys watching. "He ain't hurt bad," the man said, "wouldn't be making this kind of noise if he was hurt real bad."

Elizabeth, trembling, reached out to take Roy, but Sister McCandless, bigger, calmer, took him from the man and threw him over her shoulder as she once might have handled a sack of cotton. "God bless you," she said to the man, "God bless you, son." Roy was still screaming. Elizabeth stood behind Sister McCandless to stare at his bloody face.

"It's just a flesh wound," the man kept saying, "just broke the skin, that's all." They were moving across the sidewalk, toward the house. John, not now afraid of the staring boys, looked toward the corner to see if his father was yet in sight.

Upstairs, they hushed Roy's crying. They bathed the blood away, to find, just above the left eyebrow, the jagged, superficial scar. "Lord, have mercy," murmured Elizabeth, "another inch and it would've been his eye." And she looked with apprehension toward the clock. "Ain't it the truth," said Sister McCandless, busy with bandages and iodine.

"When did he go downstairs?" his mother asked at last.

Sister McCandless now sat fanning herself in the easy chair, at the head of the sofa where Roy lay, bound and silent. She paused for a moment to look sharply at John. John stood near the window, holding the newspaper advertisement and the drawing he had done.

"We was sitting on the fire escape," he said. "Some boys he knew called him."

"When?"

"He said he'd be back in five minutes."

"Why didn't you tell me he was downstairs?"

He looked at his hands, clasping his notebook, and did not answer.

"Boy," said Sister McCandles, "you hear your mother a-talking to you?"

He looked at his mother. He repeated:

"He said he'd be back in five minutes."

"He said he'd be back in five minutes," said Sister McCandless with scorn, "don't look to me like that's no right answer. You's the man of the house, you supposed to look after your baby brothers and sisters—you ain't supposed to let them run off and get half-killed. But I expect," she added, rising from the chair, dropping the cardboard fan, "your Daddy'll make you tell the truth. Your Ma's way too soft with you."

He did not look at her, but at the fan where it lay in the dark red, depressed seat where she had been. The fan advertised a pomade for the hair and showed a brown woman and her baby, both with glistening hair, smiling happily at each other.

"Honey," said Sister McCandless, "I got to be moving along. Maybe I drop in later tonight. I don't reckon you going to be at Tarry Service tonight?"

Tarry Service was the prayer meeting held every Saturday night at church to strengthen believers and prepare the church for the coming of the Holy Ghost on Sunday.

"I don't reckon," said Elizabeth. She stood up; she and Sister McCandless kissed each other on the cheek. "But you be sure to remember me in your prayers."

"I surely will do that." She paused, with her hand on the door knob, and looked down at Roy and laughed. "Poor little man," she said, "reckon he'll be content to sit on the fire escape *now*."

Elizabeth laughed with her. "It sure ought to be a lesson to him. You don't reckon," she asked nervously, still smiling, "he going to keep that scar, do you?"

"Lord, no," said Sister McCandless, "ain't nothing but a scratch. I declare, Sister Grimes, you worse than a child. Another couple of weeks and you won't be able to *see* no scar. No, you go on about your housework, honey, and thank the Lord it weren't no worse." She opened the door; they heard the sound of feet on the stairs. "I expect that's the Reverend," said Sister McCandless, placidly, "I *bet* he going to raise cain."

"Maybe it's Florence," Elizabeth said. "Sometimes she get here about this time." They stood in the doorway, staring, while the steps reached the landing below and began again climbing to their floor. "No," said Elizabeth then, "that ain't her walk. That's Gabriel."

"Well, I'll just go on," said Sister McCandless, "and kind of prepare his mind." She pressed Elizabeth's hand as she spoke and started into the hall, leaving the door behind her slightly ajar. Elizabeth turned slowly back into the room. Roy did not open his eyes, or move; but she knew that he was not sleeping; he wished to delay until the last possible moment any contact with his father. John put his newspaper and his notebook on the table and stood, leaning on the table, staring at her.

"It wasn't my fault," he said. "I couldn't stop him from going downstairs."

"No," she said, "you ain't got nothing to worry about. You just tell your Daddy the truth."

He looked directly at her, and she turned to the window, staring into the street. What was Sister McCandless saying? Then from her bedroom she heard Delilah's thin wail and she turned, frowning, looking toward the bedroom and toward the still open door. She knew that John was watching her. Delilah continued to wail, she thought, angrily, *Now that girl's getting too big for that,* but she feared that Delilah would awaken Paul and she hurried into the bedroom. She tried to soothe Delilah back to sleep. Then she heard the front door open and close—too loud, Delilah raised her voice, with an exasperated sigh Elizabeth picked the child up. Her child and Gabriel's, her children and Gabriel's: Roy, Delilah, Paul. Only John was nameless and a stranger, living unalterable testimony to his mother's days in sin.

"What happened?" Gabriel demanded. He stood, enormous, in the center of the room, his black lunchbox dangling from his hand, staring at the sofa where Roy lay. John stood just before him, it seemed to her astonished vision just below him, beneath his fist, his heavy shoe. The child stared at the man in fascination and terror—when a girl down home she had seen rabbits stand so paralyzed before the barking dog. She hurried past Gabriel to the sofa, feeling the weight of Delilah in her arms like the weight of a shield, and stood over Roy, saying:

"Now, ain't a thing to get upset about, Gabriel. This boy sneaked downstairs while I had my back turned and got hisself hurt a little. He's alright now."

Roy, as though in confirmation, now opened his eyes and looked gravely at his father. Gabriel dropped his lunchbox with a clatter and knelt by the sofa.

"How you feel, son? Tell your Daddy what happened?"

Roy opened his mouth to speak and then, relapsing into panic, began to cry. His father held him by the shoulder.

"You don't want to cry. You's Daddy's little man. Tell your Daddy what happened.

"He went downstairs," said Elizabeth, "where he didn't have no business to be, and got to fighting with them bad boys playing on that rockpile. That's what happened and it's a mercy it weren't nothing worse."

He looked up at her. "Can't you let this boy answer me for hisself?"

Ignoring this, she went on, more gently: "He got cut on the forehead, but it ain't nothing to worry about."

"You call a doctor? How you know it ain't nothing to worry about?"

"Is you got money to be throwing away on doctors? No, I ain't called no doctor. Ain't nothing wrong with my eyes that I can't tell whether he's hurt bad or not. He got a fright more'n anything else, and you ought to pray God it teaches him a lesson."

"You got a lot to say *now,*" he said, "but I'll have *me* something to say in a minute. I'll be wanting to know when all this happened, what you was doing with your eyes *then.*" He turned back to Roy, who had lain quietly sobbing eyes wide open and body held rigid: and who now, at his father's touch, remembered the height, the sharp, sliding rock beneath his feet, the sun, the explosion of the sun, his plunge into darkness and his salty blood; and recoiled, beginning to scream, as his father touched his forehead. "Hold still, hold still," crooned his father, shaking, "hold still. Don't cry. Daddy ain't going to hurt you, he just wants to see this bandage, see what they've done to his little man." But Roy continued to scream and would not be still and Gabriel dared not lift the bandage for fear of hurting him more. And he looked at Elizabeth in fury: "Can't you put that child down and help me with this boy? John, take your baby sister from your mother—don't look like neither of you got good sense."

John took Delilah and sat down with her in the easy chair. His mother bent over Roy, and held him still, while his father, carefully—but still Roy screamed—lifted the bandage and stared at the wound. Roy's sob began to lessen. Gabriel readjusted the bandage. "You see," said Elizabeth, finally, "he ain't nowhere near dead."

"It sure ain't your fault that he ain't dead." He and Elizabeth considered each other for a moment in silence. "He came mightly close to losing an eye. Course, his eyes ain't as big as your'n, so I reckon you don't think it matters so much." At this her face hardened; he smiled. "Lord, have mercy," he said, "you think you ever going to learn to do right? Where was you when all this happened? Who let him go downstairs?"

"Ain't nobody let him go downstairs, he just went. He got a head just like his father, it got to be broken before it'll bow. I was in the kitchen."

"Where was Johnnie?"

"He was in here?"

"Where?"

"He was on the fire escape."

"Didn't he know Roy was downstairs?"

"I reckon."

"What you mean, you reckon? He ain't got your big eyes for nothing, does he?" He looked over at John. "Boy, you see your brother go downstairs?"

"Gabriel, ain't no sense in trying to blame Johnnie. You know right well if you have trouble making Roy behave, he ain't going to listen to his brother. He don't hardly listen to me."

"How come you didn't tell your mother Roy was downstairs?"

John said nothing, staring at the blanket which covered Delilah.

"Boy, you hear me? You want me to take a strap to you?"

"No, you ain't," she said. "You ain't going to take no strap to this boy, not today you ain't. Ain't a soul to blame for Roy's lying up there now but you—you because you done spoiled him so that he thinks he can do just anything and get away with it. I'm here to tell you that ain't no way to raise no child. You don't pray to the Lord to help you do better than you been doing, you going to live to shed bitter tears that the Lord didn't take his soul today." And she was trembling. She moved, unseeing, toward John and took Delilah from his arms. She looked back at Gabriel, who had risen, who stood near the sofa, staring at her. And she found in his face not fury alone, which would not have surprised her; but hatred so deep as to become insupportable in its lack of personality. His eyes were struck alive, unmoving, blind with malevolence—she felt, like the pull of the earth at her feet, his longing to witness her perdition. Again, as though it might be propitiation, she moved the child in her arms. And at this his eyes changed, he looked at Elizabeth, the mother of his children, the helpmeet given by the Lord. Then her eyes clouded; she moved to leave the room; her foot struck the lunchbox lying on the floor.

"John," she said, "pick up your father's lunchbox like a good boy."

She heard, behind her, his scrambling movement as he left the easy chair, the scrape and jangle of the lunchbox as he picked it up, bending his dark head near the toe of his father's heavy shoe.

1. Describe the kind of language used by the characters in the story.
2. Describe the kind of language used by the narrator.
3. What role does John, the brother of the boy injured on the rockpile, play in the story?
4. What values do the parents in the story hold? Does the narrator hold the same values?

Seven
Fiction and Society

For many people, reading fiction is an escape. Harlequin romances or pulp science fiction or hard-boiled detective novels seem to take them out of their own lives, which may seem humdrum in comparison. Fiction for them is like a forgetfulness drug; they can escape their own identity for a while by identifying with the characters in the story. There is also a more sophisticated form of escapism among readers who believe that the world of art is an ideal universe, far above our ordinary experience. For these readers, the pleasure of great fiction is its orderliness, its sense of unity and structure. They tend to see the world as a chaotic place, and they treat fiction as an escape into a perfected world.

What these two kinds of readers have in common is a recognition of how absorbing a story can be. Good readers can get so caught up in a story that when reality interrupts their reading they feel that they are coming back from a far place, totally unrelated to their ordinary experience. In spite of this feeling, however, fiction is never completely separate from our world. It may give us a *feeling* of escape, but as we read we are still the same people who live in the real world. And we can *learn about* that real world from fiction—a story can give us powerful insight into our own experience.

Learning from Fiction

The feeling of being absorbed in a fictional world is very compelling. Reading about an exotic character in a strange land in another time makes us feel like a part of that new world, especially because we have actively participated in creating it. But even during the act of reading, the person who reads is still the person who lives a life in the real world. When we go to a fictional world we bring our world with us, in the values and ways of understanding that we have learned in our own time and place. It is impossible for us to experience a character like Mark Twain's Huck Finn, for example, as one of Twain's contemporaries would have. We can learn about Huck's world, but we cannot become a part of it, leaving our own behind us. Our Huck Finn will always be the Huck that can be comprehended by a late-twentieth-century reader. This is why the way a story is received changes in succeeding generations, as each time brings its own values to bear. As readers, we may be deeply affected by a story, but our habits of value and perception are transforming the story into an experience we can make sense of.

Another link between fiction and reality is suggested by the fact that readers often feel that even the most fantastic stories teach them something about their own real-life situations. Many readers will see their lives reflected in the plot of a story, or a character will bring some trait of their own into sharp view. None of us, presumably, has had the experience of sleeping for years like Rip Van Winkle, but all of us have had some version of the experience Rip has when he wakes up and finds the world changed. Rip feels like an outsider in his own home place, and he feels this so dramatically that a reader is reminded of his or her own feelings of alienation. Stories dramatize and bring the essence of actions into clear relief, so that we can study them and perhaps see similar patterns in our lives.

If fiction is not an escape from real life, then what role does it play in the lives of individuals and societies? We have been stressing throughout this part of the book that fiction deals with values. It allows readers to examine their relationship to the values of their society. Some stories reinforce social values; others question or challenge cherished beliefs. In reading some stories, readers can work comfortably with their own values in making sense of the story; in other cases, readers' values encounter resistance in the story, causing discomfort and self-reflection. A character, for example, may cohere understandably, with all the signs pointing in the same direction, or a character may never satisfy our desire for unity, with signs pointing in contradictory directions. In this latter case, our very notion of human identity may come into question. The story may suggest that there is no such thing as a stable identity, but rather that all human beings are subject to internal divisions and contradictions. If you try to reduce Miss Emily, from Faulkner's "A Rose for Emily," to a coherent unity, you are underestimating the complexity of the details that portray her. Fiction, then, can touch basic systems of belief, and even the slightest story has the power to unsettle an attentive reader.

One indication of the power of stories to affect values is that societies often want to control or censor stories. Whether it is a repressive government that will not allow stories to appear that challenge its ideology, or whether it's an outraged parents' group that is disturbed about the stories their children read in school, social powers have long realized that stories have real effects on readers. In our society, for example, many parents want to limit children's access to stories (whether in print or on film or video) that present promiscuous sex or drug use in a positive way. These parents realize that people learn from the stories they encounter, learn not just that certain kinds of behavior exist but also an attitude toward that behavior.

The problem with censorship is the notion that certain stories can be legislated out of existence. They might as well legislate against the dawn. If a particular point of view exists in a society, it will always find its way into stories. And if the publication of such stories is banned, they will find their way into folklore, be told in the schoolyard, get distributed by underground presses. Stories are so central to our way of thinking that they cannot be controlled by social directives.

Utilizing Fiction

In many cases stories are written with a political purpose in mind. That is, they are stories about issues of power and domination in society. Many writers are motivated by their political conscience, writing stories that address their moral and social concerns. In Mukherjee's "Angela," for example, the problems of an immigrant adjusting to a new culture and recovering from past injustices are examined. Authors often want to appeal to readers on the personal level of the story, where the abstractions of political discourse can become concrete and emotionally effective.

The simplest form of political commitment in fiction is outright **propaganda,** in which the story exists only to illustrate some political idea. In stories used for propaganda, the plot and characters must be kept simple so that the political point won't become obscured. In an anti-Soviet propaganda story, for example, the Soviets would all be evil sadists, while the Americans would be idealistic heroes. Needless to say, many popular films are built around stories of this kind. Most propaganda is so crude that you can see right through it, but since it also appeals to gut emotions there is the danger that your clear thinking can be overcome.

A more sophisticated kind of political fiction deals with complex characters and actions that are entangled in social issues. In Joseph Conrad's "Outpost of Progress," there are two believable characters whose fates tell us something about the moral costs of colonialism.

They are not simply puppets who serve Conrad's political point. Conrad is out to tell a good story, but the story also comments on a political issue. Even stories that appear to be strictly personal will often have a political concern. John Steinbeck's "The Chrysanthemums," a story included in the "Character" chapter, deals very closely with the personal concerns of a farm wife. But her conflicts can also be understood in terms of how her society defined the role of women, limiting them to domestic work within the family. Steinbeck considers a large social issue in the process of telling an effective story about a believable character.

Stories, then, are connected to real life. Even the most fantastic story that takes us to an alien world can teach us something about our own lives. Stories are never really an escape. The pleasure they give may seem like a break from your daily life, but you bring your life in society with you when you read, so the social world is never excluded from the experience of fiction. Fiction is concerned with people in action. We can learn from fiction, even if what we learn in many cases disturbs rather than satisfies us.

READINGS

Joseph Conrad (1857–1924)

AN OUTPOST OF PROGRESS

I

There were two white men in charge of the trading station. Kayerts, the chief, was short and fat; Carlier, the assistant, was tall with a large head and a very broad trunk perched upon a long pair of thin legs. The third man on the staff was a Sierra Leone nigger, who maintained that his name was Henry Price. However, for some reason or other, the natives down the river had given him the name of Makola, and it stuck to him through all his wanderings about the country. He spoke English and French with a warbling accent, wrote a beautiful hand, understood bookkeeping, and cherished in his innermost heart the worship of evil spirits. His wife was a negress from Loanda, very large and very noisy. Three children rolled about in sunshine before the door of his low, shed-like dwelling. Makola, taciturn and impenetrable, despised the two white men. He had charge of a small clay storehouse with a dried-grass roof, and pretended to keep a correct account of beads, cotton cloth, red kerchiefs, brass wire, and other trade goods it contained. Besides the storehouse and Makola's hut, there was only one large building in the cleared ground of the station. It was built neatly of reeds, with a verandah on all the four sides. There were three rooms in it. The one in the middle was the living-room, and had two rough tables and a few stools in it. The other two were the bedrooms for the white men. Each had a bedstead and a mosquito net for all furniture. The plank floor was littered with the belongings of the white men; open half-empty boxes, torn wearing apparel, old boots; all the things dirty and all the things broken, that accumulate mysteriously round untidy men. There was also another dwelling-place some distance away from the buildings. In it, under a tall cross much out of the perpendicular, slept the man who had seen the beginning of all this; who had planned and had watched the construction of this outpost of progress. He had been, at home, an unsuccessful painter who, weary of pursuing fame on an empty stomach, had gone out there through high protections. He had been the first chief of that station. Makola had watched the energetic artist die of fever in the just finished house with his usual kind of "I told you so" indifference. Then, for a time, he dwelt alone with his family, his account books, and the Evil Spirit that rules the lands under the equator. He got on very well with his god. Perhaps he had propitiated him by a promise of more white men to play with, by and by. At any rate the director of the Great Trading Company, coming up in a steamer that resembled an enormous sardine box with a flat-roofed shed erected on it, found the station in good order, and Makola as usual quietly diligent. The director had the cross put up over the first agent's grave, and appointed Kayerts to the post. Carlier was told off as second in charge. The director was a man ruthless and efficient, who at times, but very imperceptibly, indulged in grim humour. He made a speech to Kayerts and Carlier, pointing out to them the promising aspect of this station. The nearest trading-post was about three hundred miles away. It was an exceptional opportunity for them to distinguish themselves and to earn pecentages on the trade. This appointment was a favour done to beginners. Kayerts was moved almost to tears by his director's kindness. He would, he said, by doing his best, try to justify the flattering confidence, &c., &c. Kayerts had been in the Administration of the Telegraphs, and knew how to express himself correctly. Carlier, an ex-non-commissioned officer of cavalry in an army guaranteed from harm by several European Powers, was less impressed. If there were commissions to get, so much the better; and, trailing a sulky glance over the river, the forests, the impenetrable bush that seemed to cut off the station from the rest of the world, he muttered between his teeth, "We shall see, very soon."

Next day, some bales of cotton goods and a few cases of provisions having been thrown on shore, the sardine-box steamer went off, not to return for another six months. On the deck the director touched his cap to the two agents, who stood on the bank waving their hats, and turning to an old servant of the Company on his passage to headquarters, said, "Look at those two imbeciles. They must be mad at home to send me such specimens. I told those fellows to plant a vegetable garden, build new storehouses and fences, and construct a landing-stage. I bet nothing will be done! They won't know how to begin. I always thought the station on this river useless, and they just fit the station!"

"They will form themselves there," said the old stager with a quiet smile.

"At any rate, I am rid of them for six months," retorted the director.

The two men watched the steamer round the bend, then, ascending arm in arm the slope of the bank, returned to the station. They had been in this vast and dark country only a very short time, and as yet always in the midst of other white men, under the eye and guidance of their superiors. And now, dull as they were to the subtle influences of surroundings, they felt themselves very much alone, when suddenly left unassisted to face the wilderness; a wilderness rendered more strange, more incomprehensible by the mysterious glimpses of the vigorous life it contained. They were two perfectly insignificant and incapable individuals, whose existence is only rendered possible through the high organization of civilized crowds. Few men realize that their life, the very essence of their character, their capabilities and their audacities, are the only expression of their belief in the safety of their surroundings. The courage, the composure, the confidence; the emotions and principles; every great and every insignificant thought belongs not to the individual but to the crowd: to the crowd that believes blindly in the irresistible force of its institutions and of its morals, in the power of its police and of its opinion. But the contact with pure unmitigated savagery, with primitive nature and primitive man, brings sudden and profound trouble into the heart. To the sentiment of being alone of one's kind, to the clear perception of the loneliness of one's thoughts, of one's sensations—to the negation of the habitual, which is safe, there is added the affirmation of the unusual, which is dangerous; a suggestion of things vague, uncontrollable, and repulsive, whose discomposing intrusion excites the imagination and tries the civilized nerves of the foolish and the wise alike.

Kayerts and Carlier walked arm in arm, drawing close to one another as children do in the dark; and they had the same, not altogether unpleasant, sense of danger which one half suspects to be imaginary. They chatted persistently in familiar tones. "Our station is prettily situated," said one. The other assented with enthusiasm, enlarging volubly on the beauties of the situation. Then they passed near the grave. "Poor devil!" said Kayerts. "He died of fever, didn't he?" muttered Carlier, stopping short. "Why," retorted Kayerts, with indignation, "I've been told that the fellow exposed himself recklessly to the sun. The climate here, everybody says, is not all worse than at home, as long as you keep out of the sun. Do you hear that, Carlier? I am chief here, and my orders are that you should not expose yourself to the sun!" He assumed his superiority jocularly, but his meaning was serious. The idea that he would, perhaps, have to bury Carlier and remain alone, gave him an inward shiver. He felt suddenly that this Carlier was more precious to him here, in the centre of Africa, than a brother could be anywhere else. Carlier, entering into the spirit of the thing, made a military salute and answered in a brisk tone, "Your orders shall be attended to, chief!" Then he burst out laughing, slapped Kayerts on the back and shouted, "We shall let life run easily here! Just sit still and gather in the ivory those savages will bring. This country has its good points, after all!" They both laughed loudly while Carlier thought: "That poor Kayerts; he is so fat and unhealthy. It would be awful if I had to bury him here. He is a man I respect." . . . Before they reached the verandah of their house they called one another "my dear fellow."

The first day they were very active, pottering about with hammers and nails and red calico, to put up curtains, make their house habitable and pretty; resolved to settle down comfortably to their new life. For them an impossible task. To grapple effectually with even purely material problems requires more serenity of mind and more lofty courage than people generally imagine. No two beings could have been more unfitted for such a struggle. Society, not from any tenderness, but because of its strange needs, had taken care of those two men, forbidding them all independent thought, all initiative, all departure from routine; and forbidding it under pain of death. They could only live on condition of being machines. And now, released from the fostering care of men with pens behind the ears, or of men with gold lace on the sleeves, they were like those lifelong prisoners who, liberated after many years, do not know what use to make of their freedom. They did not know what use to make of their faculties, being both, through want of practice, incapable of independent thought.

At the end of two months Kayerts often would say, "If it was not for my Melie, you wouldn't catch me here." Melie was his daughter. He had thrown up his post in the Administration of the Telegraphs, though he had been for seventeen years perfectly happy there, to earn a dowry for his girl. His wife was dead, and the child was being brought up by his sisters. He regretted the streets, the pavements, the cafés, his friends of many years; all the things he used to see, day after day; all the thoughts suggested by familiar things—the thoughts effortless, monotonous, and soothing of a Government clerk; he regretted all the gossip, the small enmities, the mild venom, and the little jokes of Government offices. "If I had had a decent brother-in-law," Carlier would remark, "a fellow with a heart, I would not be here."

He had left the army and had made himself so obnoxious to his family by his laziness and impudence, that an exasperated brother-in-law had made superhuman efforts to procure him an appointment in the Company as a second-class agent. Having not a penny in the world he was compelled to accept this means of livelihood as soon as it became quite clear to him that there was nothing more to squeeze out of his relations. He, like Kayerts, regretted his old life. He regretted the clink of sabre and spurs on a fine afternoon, the barrack-room witticisms, the girls of garrison towns; but, besides, he had also a sense of grievance. He was evidently a much ill-used man. This made him moody, at times. But the two men got on well together in the fellowship of their stupidity and laziness. Together they did nothing, absolutely nothing, and enjoyed the sense of the idleness for which they were paid. And in time they came to feel something resembling affection for one another.

They lived like blind men in a large room, aware only of what came in contact with them (and of that only imperfectly), but unable to see the general aspect of things. The river, the forest, all the great land throbbing with life, were like a great emptiness. Even the brilliant sunshine disclosed nothing intelligible. Things appeared and disappeared before their eyes in an unconnected and aimless kind of way. The river seemed to come from nowhere and flow nowhither. It flowed through a void. Out of that void, at times, came canoes, and men with spears in their hands would suddenly crowd the yard of the station. They were naked, glossy black, ornamented with snowy shells and glistening brass wire, perfect of limb. They made an uncouth babbling noise when they spoke, moved in a stately manner, and sent quick, wild glances out of their startled, never-resting eyes. Those warriors would squat in long rows, four or more deep, before the verandah, while their chiefs bargained for hours with Makola over an elephant tusk. Kayerts sat on his chair and looked down on the proceedings, understanding nothing. He stared at them with his round blue eyes, called out to Carlier, "Here look! look at that fellow there—and that other one, to the left. Did you ever see such a face? Oh, the funny brute!"

Carlier, smoking native tobacco in a short wooden pipe, would swagger up twirling his moustaches, and surveying the warriors with haughty indulgence, would say—

"Fine animals. Brought any bone? Yes? It's not any too soon. Look at the muscles of that fellow—third from the end. I wouldn't care to get a punch on the nose from him. Fine arms, but legs no good below the knee. Couldn't make cavalry men of them." And after glancing down complacently at his own shanks, he always concluded: "Pah! Don't they stink! You, Makola! Take that herd over to the fetish" (the storehouse was in every station called the fetish, perhaps because of the spirit of civilization it contained) "and give them up some of the rubbish you keep there. I'd rather see it full of bone than full of rags."

Kayerts approved.

"Yes, yes! Go and finish that palaver over there, Mr. Makola. I will come round when you are ready, to weigh the tusk. We must be careful." Then turning to his companion: "This is the tribe that lives down the river; they are rather aromatic. I remember, they had been once before here. D'ye hear that row? What a fellow has got to put up with in this dog of a country! My head is split."

Such profitable visits were rare. For days the two pioneers of trade and progress would look on their empty courtyard in the vibrating brilliance of vertical sunshine. Below the high bank, the silent river flowed on glittering and steady. On the sands in the middle of the stream, hippos and alligators sunned themselves side by side. And stretching away in all directions, surrounding the insignificant cleared spot of the trading post, immense forests, hiding fateful complications of fantastic life, lay in the eloquent silence of mute greatness. The two men understood nothing, cared for nothing but for the passage of days that separated them from the steamer's return. Their predecessor had left some torn books. They took up these wrecks of novels, and, as they had never read anything of the kind before, they were surprised and amused. Then during long days there were interminable and silly discussions about plots and personages. In the centre of Africa they made acquaintance of Richelieu and of d'Artagnan, of Hawk's Eye and of Father Goriot, and of many other people. All these imaginary personages became subjects for gossip as if they had been living friends. They discounted their virtues, suspected their motives, decried their successes; were scandalized at their duplicity or were doubtful about their courage. The accounts of crimes filled them with indignation, while tender or pathetic passages moved them deeply. Carlier cleared his throat and said in a soldierly voice, "What nonsense!" Kayerts, his round eyes suffused with tears, his fat cheeks quivering, rubbed his bald head, and declared, "This is a splendid book. I had no idea there were such clever fellows in the world." They also found some old copies of a home paper. That print discussed what it was pleased to call "Our Colonial Expansion" in high-flown language. It spoke much of the rights and duties of civilization, of the sacredness of the civilizing work, and extolled the merits of those who went about bringing light, and faith and commerce to the dark places of the earth. Carlier and Kayerts read, wondered, and began to think better of themselves. Carlier said one evening, waving his hand about, "In a hundred years, there will be perhaps a town here. Quays, and warehouses, and barracks, and—and—billiard-rooms. Civilization, my boy, and virtue—and all. And then, chaps will read that two good fellows, Kayerts and Carlier, were the first civilized men to live in this very spot!" Kayerts nodded, "Yes, it is a consolation to think of that." They seemed to forget their dead predecessor; but, early one day, Carlier went out and replanted the cross firmly. "It used to make me squint whenever I walked that way," he explained to Kayerts over the morning coffee. "It made me squint, leaning over so much. So I planted it upright. And solid, I promise you! I suspended myself with both hands to the cross-piece. Not a move. Oh, I did that properly."

At times Gobila came to see them. Gobila was the chief of the neighboring villages. He was a gray-headed savage, thin and black, with a white cloth round his loins and a mangy panther skin hanging over his back. He came up with long strides of his skeleton legs, swinging a staff as tall as himself, and, entering the common room of the station, would squat on his heels to the left of the door. There he sat, watching Kayerts, and now and then making a speech which the other did not understand. Kayerts, without interrupting his occupation, would from time to time say in a friendly manner: "How goes it, you old image?" and they would smile at one another. The two whites had a liking for that old and incomprehensible creature, and called him Father Gobila. Gobila's manner was paternal, and he seemed really to love all white men. They all appeared to him very young, indistinguishably alike (except for stature), and he knew that they were all brothers, and also immortal. The death of the artist, who was the first white man whom he knew intimately, did not disturb this belief, because he was firmy convinced that the white stranger had pretended to die and got himself buried for some mysterious purpose of his own, into which it was useless to inquire. Perhaps it was his way of going home to his own country? At any rate, these were his brothers, and he transferred his absurd affection to them. They returned it in a way. Carlier slapped him on the back, and recklessly struck off matches for his amusement. Kayerts was always ready to let him have a sniff at the ammonia bottle. In short, they behaved just like that other white creature that had hidden itself in a hole in the ground. Gobila considered them attentively. Perhaps they were the same being with the other—or one of them was. He couldn't decide—clear up that mystery; but he remained always very friendly. In consequence of that friendship the women of Gobila's village walked in single file through the reedy grass, bringing every morning to the station, fowls, and sweet potatoes, and palm wine, and sometimes a goat. The Company never provisions the stations fully, and the agents required those local supplies to live. They had them through the good-will of Gobila, and lived well. Now and then one of them had a bout with fever, and the other nursed him with gentle devotion. They did not think much of it. It left them weaker, and their appearance changed for the worse.

Carlier was hollow-eyed and irritable. Kayerts showed a drawn, flabby face above the rotundity of his stomach, which gave him a weird aspect. But being constantly together, they did not notice the change that took place gradually in their appearance, and also in their dispositions.

Five months passed in that way.

Then, one morning, as Kayerts and Carlier, lounging in their chairs under the verandah, talked about the approaching visit of the steamer, a knot of armed men came out of the forest and advanced towards the station. They were strangers to that part of the country. They were tall, slight, draped classically from neck to heel in blue fringed cloths, and carried percussion muskets over their bare right shoulders. Makola showed signs of excitement, and ran out of the storehouse (where he spent all his days) to meet these visitors. They came into the courtyard and looked about them with steady, scornful glances. Their leader, a powerful and determined-looking negro with bloodshot eyes, stood in front of the verandah and made a long speech. He gesticulated much, and ceased very suddenly.

There was something in his intonation, in the sounds of the long sentences he used, that startled the two whites. It was like a reminiscence of something not exactly familiar, and yet resembling the speech of civilized men. It sounded like one of those impossible languages which sometimes we hear in our dreams.

"What lingo is that?" said the amazed Carlier. "In the first moment I fancied the fellow as going to speak French. Anyway, it is a different kind of gibberish to what we ever heard."

"Yes," replied Kayerts. "Hey, Makola, what does he say? Where do they come from? Who are they?"

But Makola, who seemed to be standing on hot bricks, answered hurriedly, "I don't know. They come from very far. Perhaps Mrs. Price will understand. They are perhaps bad men."

The leader, after waiting for a while, said something sharply to Makola, who shook his head. Then the man, after looking round, noticed Makola's hut and walked over there. The next moment Mrs. Makola was heard speaking with great volubility. The other strangers—they were six in all—strolled about with an air of ease, put their heads through the door of the storeroom, congregated round the grave, pointed understanding at the cross, and generally made themselves at home.

"I don't like those chaps—and, I say, Kayerts, they must be from the coast; they've got firearms," observed the sagacious Carlier.

Kayerts also did not like those chaps. They both, for the first time, became aware that they lived in conditions where the unusual may be dangerous, and that there was no power on earth outside of themselves to stand between them and the unusual. They became uneasy, went in and loaded their revolvers. Kayerts said, "We must order Makola to tell them to go away before dark."

The strangers left in the afternoon, after eating a meal prepared for them by Mrs. Makola. The immense woman was excited, and talked much with the visitors. She rattled away shrilly, pointing here and there at the forests and at the river. Makola sat apart and watched. At times he got up and whispered to his wife. He accompanied the strangers across the ravine at the back of the station-ground, and returned slowly looking very thoughtful. When questioned by the white men he was very strange, seemed not to understand, seemed to have forgotten French—seemed to have forgotten how to speak altogether. Kayerts and Carlier agreed that the nigger had had too much palm wine.

There was some talk about keeping a watch in turn, but in the evening everything seemed so quiet and peaceful that they retired as usual. All night they were disturbed by a lot of drumming in the villages. A deep, rapid roll near by would be followed by another far off—then all ceased. Soon short appeals would rattle out here and there, then all mingle together, increase, become vigorous and sustained, would spread out over the forest, roll through the night, unbroken and ceaseless, near and far, as if the whole land had been one immense drum booming out steadily an appeal to heaven. And through the deep and tremendous noise sudden yells that resembled snatches of songs from a madhouse darted shrill and high in discordant jets of sound which seemed to rush far above the earth and drive all peace from under the stars.

Carlier and Kayerts slept badly. They both thought they had heard shots fired during the night—but they could not agree as to the direction. In the morning Makola was gone somewhere. He returned about noon with one of yesterday's strangers, and eluded all Kayerts' attempts to close with him: had become deaf apparently. Kayerts wondered. Carlier, who had been fishing off the bank, came back and remarked while he showed his catch, "The niggers seem to be in a deuce of a stir; I wonder what's up. I saw about fifteen canoes cross the river during the two hours I was there fishing." Kayerts, worried, said, "Isn't this Makola very queer to-day?" Carlier advised, "Keep all our men together in case of some trouble.

II

There were ten station men who had been left by the Director. Those fellows, having engaged themselves to the Company for six months (without having any idea of a month in particular and only a very faint notion of time in general), had been serving the cause of progress for upwards of two years. Belonging to a tribe from a very distant part of the land of darkness and sorrow, they did not run away, naturally supposing that as wandering strangers they would be killed by the inhabitants of the country; in which they were right. They lived in straw huts on the slope of a ravine over-grown with reedy grass, just behind the station buildings. They were not happy, regretting the festive incantations, the sorceries, the human sacrifices of their own land; where they also had parents, brothers, sisters, admired chiefs, respected magicians, loved friends, and other ties supposed generally to be human. Besides, the rice rations served out by the Company did not agree with them, being a food unknown to their land, and to which they could not get used. Consequently they were unhealthy and miserable. Had they been of any other tribe they would have made up their minds to die—for nothing is easier to certain savages than suicide—and so have escaped from the puzzling difficulties of existence. But belonging, as they did, to a warlike tribe with filed teeth, they had more grit, and went on stupidly living through disease and sorrow. They did very little work, and had lost their splendid physique. Carlier and Kayerts doctored them assiduously without being able to bring them back into condition again. They were mustered every morning and told off to different tasks—grass-cutting, fence-building, tree-felling, &c., &c., which no power on earth could induce them to execute efficiently. The two whites had practically very little control over them.

In the afternoon Makola came over to the big house and found Kayerts watching three heavy columns of smoke rising above the forests. "What is that?" asked Kayerts. "Some villages burn," answered Makola, who seemed to have regained his wits. Then he said abruptly: "We have got very little ivory; bad six months' trading. Do you like get a little more ivory?"

"Yes," said Kayerts, eagerly. He thought of percentages which were low.

"Those men who came yesterday are traders from Loanda who have got more ivory than they can carry home. Shall I buy? I know their camp."

"Certainly," said Kayerts. "What are those traders?"

"Bad fellows," said Makola, indifferently. "They fight with people, and catch women and children. They are bad men, and got guns. There is a great disturbance in the country. Do you want ivory?"

"Yes," said Kayerts. Makola said nothing for a while. Then: "Those workmen of ours are no good at all," he muttered, looking round. "Station in very bad order, sir. Director will growl. Better get a fine lot of ivory, then he say nothing."

"I can't help it; the men won't work," said Kayerts. "When will you get that ivory?"

"Very soon," said Makola. "Perhaps to-night. You leave it to me, and keep indoors, sir. I think you had better give some palm wine to our men to make a dance this evening. Enjoy themselves. Work better tomorrow. There's plenty palm wine—gone a little sour."

Kayerts said "yes," and Makola, with his own hands carried big calabashes to the door of his hut. They stood there till the evening, and Mrs. Makola looked into every one. The men got them at sunset. When Kayerts and Carlier retired, a big bonfire was flaring before the men's huts. They could hear their shouts and drumming. Some men from Gobila's village had joined the station hands, and the entertainment was a great success.

In the middle of the night, Carlier waking suddenly, heard a man shout loudly; then a shot was fired. Only one. Carlier ran out and met Kayerts on the verandah. They were both startled. As they went across the yard to call Makola, they saw shadows moving in the night. One of them cried, "Don't shoot! It's me, Price." Then Makola appeared close to them. "Go back, go back, please," he urged, "you spoil all." "There are strange men about," said Carlier. "Never mind; I know," said Makola. Then he whispered, "All right. Bring ivory. Say nothing! I know my business." The two white men reluctantly went back to the house, but did not sleep. They heard footsteps, whispers, some groans. It seemed as if a lot of men came in, dumped heavy things on the ground, squabbled a long time, then went away. They lay on their hard beds and thought: "This Makola is invaluable." In the morning Carlier came out, very sleepy, and pulled at the cord of the big bell. The station hands mustered every morning to the sound of the bell. That morning nobody came. Kayerts turned out also, yawning. Across the yard they saw Makola come out of his hut, a tin basin of soapy water in his hand. Makola, a civilized nigger, was very neat in his person. He threw the soapsuds skillfully over a wretched little yellow cur he had, then turning his face to the agent's house, he shouted from the distance, "All the men gone last night!"

They heard him plainly, but in their surprise they both yelled out together: "What!" Then they stared at one another. "We are in a proper fix now," growled Carlier. "It's incredible!" muttered Kayerts. "I will go to the huts and see," said Carlier, striding off. Makola coming up found Kayerts standing alone.

"I can hardly believe it," said Kayerts, tearfully. "We took care of them as if they had been our children."

"They went with the coast people," said Makola after a moment of hesitation.

"What do I care with whom they went—the ungrateful brutes!" claimed the other. Then with sudden suspicion, and looking hard Makola, he added: "What do you know about it?"

Makola moved his shoulders, looking down on the ground. "What do I know? I think only. Will you come and look at the ivory I've got there? It is a fine lot. You never saw such."

He moved towards the store. Kayerts followed him mechanically, thinking about the incredible desertion of the men. On the ground before the door of the fetish lay six splendid tusks.

"What did you give for it?" asked Kayerts, after surveying the lot with satisfaction.

"No regular trade," said Makola. "They brought the ivory and gave it to me. I told them to take what they most wanted in the station. It is a beautiful lot. No station can show such tusks. Those traders wanted carriers badly, and our men were no good here. No trade, no entry in books; all correct."

Kayerts nearly burst with indignation. "Why!" he shouted, "I believe you have sold our men for these tusks!" Makola stood impassive and silent. "I—I—will—I," stuttered Kayerts. "You fiend!" he yelled out.

"I did the best for you and the Company," said Makola, imperturbably. "Why you shout so much? Look at this tusk."

"I dismiss you! I will report you—I won't look at the tusk. I forbid you to touch them. I order you to throw them into the river. You—you!"

"You very red, Mr. Kayerts. If you are so irritable in the sun, you will get fever and die—like the first chief!" pronounced Makola impressively.

They stood still, contemplating one another with intense eyes, as if they had been looking with effort across immense distances. Kayerts shivered. Makola had meant no more than he said, but his words seemed to Kayerts full of ominous menace! He turned sharply and went away to the house. Makola retired into the bosom of his family; and the tusks, left lying before the store, looked very large and valuable in the sunshine.

Carlier came back on the verandah. "They're all gone, hey?" asked Kayerts from the far end of the common room in a muffled voice. "You did not find anybody?"

"Oh, yes," said Carlier, "I found one of Gobila's people lying dead before the huts—shot through the body. We heard that shot last night."

Kayerts came out quickly. He found his companion staring grimly over the yard at the tusks, away by the store. They both sat in silence for a while. Then Kayerts related his conversation with Makola. Carlier said nothing. At the midday meal they ate very little. They hardly exchanged a word that day. A great silence seemed to lie heavily over the station and press on their lips. Makola did not open the store; he spent the day playing with his children. He lay full-length on a mat outside his door, and the youngsters sat on his chest and clambered all over him. It was a touching picture. Mrs. Makola was busy cooking all day as usual. The white men made a somewhat better meal in the evening. Afterwards, Carlier smoking his pipe strolled over to the store; he stood for a long time over the tusks, touched one or two with his foot, even tried to lift the largest one by its small end. He came back to his chief, who had not stirred from the verandah, threw himself in the chair and said—

"I can see it! They were pounced upon while they slept heavily after drinking all that palm wine you've allowed Makola to give them. A put-up job! See? The worst is, some of Gobila's people were there, and got carried off too, no doubt. The least drunk woke up, and got shot for his sobriety. This is a funny country. What will you do now?"

"We can't touch it, of course," said Kayerts.

"Of course not," assented Carlier.

"Slavery is an awful thing," stammered out Kayerts in an unsteady voice.

"Frightful—the sufferings," grunted Carlier with conviction.

They believed their words. Everybody shows a respectful deference to certain sounds that he and his fellows can make. But about feelings people really know nothing. We talk with indignation or enthusiasm; we talk about oppression, cruelty, crime, devotion, self-sacrifice, virtue, and we know nothing real beyond the words. Nobody knows what suffering or sacrifice mean—except perhaps the victims of the mysterious purpose of these illusions.

Next morning they saw Makola very busy setting up in the yard the big scales used for weighing ivory. By and by Carlier said: "What's that filthy scoundrel up to?" and lounged out into the yard. Kayerts followed. They stood watching. Makola took no notice. When the balance was swung true, he tried to lift a tusk into the scale. It was too heavy. He looked up helplessly without a word, and for a minute they stood round that balance as mute and still as three statues. Suddenly Carlier said: "Catch hold of the other end, Makola—you beast!" and together they swung the tusk up. Kayerts trembled in every limb. He muttered, "I say! O! I say!" and putting his hand in his pocket found there a dirty bit of paper and the stump of a pencil. He turned his back on the others, as if about to do something tricky, and noted stealthily the weights which Carlier shouted out to him with unnecessary loudness. When all was over Makola whispered to himself: "The sun's very strong here for the tusks." Carlier said to Kayerts in a careless tone: "I say, chief, I might just as well give him a lift with this lot into the store."

As they were going back to the house Kayerts observed with a sigh: "It had to be done." And Carlier said: "It's deplorable, but, the men being Company's men the ivory is Company's ivory. We must look after it." "I will report to the Director, of course," said Kayerts. "Of course, let him decide," approved Carlier.

At midday they made a hearty meal. Kayerts sighed from time to time. Whenever they mentioned Makola's name they always added to it an opprobrious epithet. It eased their conscience. Makola gave himself a half-holiday, and bathed his children in the river. No one from Gobila's villages came near the station that day. No one came the next day, and the next, nor for a whole week. Gobila's people might have been dead and buried for any sign of life they gave. But they were only mourning for those they had lost by the witchcraft of white men, who had brought wicked people into their country. The wicked people were gone, but fear remained. Fear always remains. A man may destroy everything within himself, love and hate and belief, and even doubt; but as long as he clings to life he cannot destroy fear: the fear, subtle, indestructible, and terrible, that pervades his being; that tinges his thoughts; that lurks in his heart; that watches on his lips the struggle of his last breath. In his fear, the mild old Gobila offered extra human sacrifices to all the Evil Spirits that had taken possession of his white friends. His heart was heavy. Some warriors spoke about burning and killing, but the cautious old savage dissuaded them. Who could foresee the woe those mysterious creatures, if irritated, might bring? They should be left alone. Perhaps in time they would disappear into the earth as the first one had disappeared. His people must keep away from them, and hope for the best.

Kayerts and Carlier did not disappear, but remained above on this earth, that, somehow, they fancied had become bigger and very empty. It was not the absolute and dumb solitude of the post that impressed them so much as an inarticulate feeling that something from within them was gone, something that worked for their safety, and had kept the wilderness from interfering with their hearts. The images of home, the memory of people like them, of men that thought and felt as they used to think and feel, receded into distances made indistinct by the glare of unclouded sunshine. And out of the great silence of the surrounding wilderness, its very hopelessness and savagery seemed to approach them nearer, to draw them gently, to look upon them, to envelop them with a solicitude irresistible, familiar, and disgusting.

Days lengthened into weeks, then into months. Gobila's people drummed and yelled to every new moon, as of yore, but kept away from the station. Makola and Carlier tried once in a canoe to open communications, but were received with a shower of arrows, and had to fly back to the station for dear life. That attempt set the country up and down the river into an uproar that could be very distinctly heard for days. The steamer was late. At first they spoke of delay jauntily, then anxiously, then gloomily. The matter was becoming serious. Stores were running short. Carlier cast his lines off the bank, but the river was low, and the fish kept out in the stream. They dared not stroll far way from the station to shoot. Moreover, there was no game in the impenetrable forest. Once Carlier shot a hippo in the river. They had no boat to secure it, and it sank. When it floated up it drifted away, and Gobila's people secured the carcase. It was the occasion for a national holiday, but Carlier had a fit of rage over it and talked about the necessity of exterminating all the niggers before the country could be made habitable. Kayerts mooned about silently; spent hours looking at the portrait of his Melie. It represented a little girl with long bleached tresses and a rather sour face. His legs were much swollen, and he could hardly walk. Carlier, undermined by fever, could not swagger any more, but kept tottering about, still with a devil-may-care air, as became a man who remembered his crack regiment. He had become hoarse, sarcastic, and inclined to say unpleasant things. He called it "being frank with you." They had long ago reckoned their percentages on trade, including in them that last deal of "this infamous Makola." They had also concluded not to say anything about it. Kayerts hesitated at first—was afraid of the Director.

"He has seen worse things done on the quiet," maintained Carlier, with a horse laugh. "Trust him! He won't thank you if you blab. He is no better than you or me. Who will talk if we hold our tongues? There is nobody here."

That was the root of the trouble! There was nobody there; and being left there alone with their weakness, they became daily more like a pair of accomplices than like a couple of devoted friends. They had heard nothing from home for eight months. Every evening they said. "Tomorrow we shall see the steamer." But one of the Company's steamers had been wrecked, and the Director was busy with the other, relieving very distant and important stations on the main river. He thought that the useless station, and the useless men, could wait. Meantime Kayerts and Carlier lived on rice boiled without salt, and cursed the Company, all Africa, and the day they were born. One must have lived on such diet to discover what ghastly trouble the necessity of swallowing one's food may become. There was literally nothing else in the station but rice and coffee; they drank the coffee without sugar. The last fifteen lumps Kayerts had solemenly locked away in his box, together with a half-bottle of Cognâc, "in case of sickness," he explained. Carlier approved. "When one is sick," he said, "any little extra like that is cheering."

They waited. Rank grass began to sprout over the courtyard. The bell never rang now. Days passed, silent, exasperating, and slow. When the two men spoke, they snarled, and their silences were bitter, as if tinged by the bitterness of their thoughts.

One day after a lunch of boiled rice, Carlier put down his cup untasted, and said: "Hang it all! Let's have a decent cup of coffee for once. Bring out that sugar, Kayerts!"

"For the sick," muttered Kayerts, without looking up.

"For the sick," mocked Carlier. "Bosh! . . . Well! I am sick."

"You are no more sick than I am, and I go without," said Kayerts in a peaceful tone.

"Come! out with that sugar, you stingy old slave-dealer."

Kayerts looked up quickly. Carlier was smiling with marked insolence. And suddenly it seemed to Kayerts that he had never seen that man before. Who was he? He knew nothing about him. What was he capable of? There was a surprising flash of violent emotion within him, as if in the presence of something undreamt-of, dangerous, and final. But he managed to pronounce with composure—

"That joke is in very bad taste. Don't repeat it."

"Joke!" said Carlier, hitching himself forward on his seat. "I am hungry—I am sick—I don't joke! I hate hypocrites. You are a hypocrite. You are a slave-dealer. I am a slave-dealer. There's nothing but slave-dealers in this cursed country. I mean to have sugar in my coffee to-day, anyhow!"

"I forbid you to speak to me in that way," said Kayerts with a fair show of resolution.

"You!—What?" shouted Carlier, jumping up.

Kayerts stood up also. "I am your chief," he began, trying to master the shakiness of his voice.

"What?" yelled the other. "Who's chief? There's no chief here. There's nothing here: there's nothing but you and I. Fetch the sugar—you potbellied ass."

"Hold your tongue. Go out of this room," screamed Kayerts. "I dismiss you—you scoundrel!"

Carlier swung a stool. All at once he looked dangerously in earnest. "You flabby, good-for-nothing civilian—take that!" he howled.

Kayerts dropped under the table, and the stool struck the grass inner wall of the room. Then, as Carlier was trying to upset the table, Kayerts in desperation made a blind rush, head low, like a cornered pig would do, and over-turning his friend, bolted along the verandah, and into his room. He locked the door, snatched his revolver, and stood panting. In less than a minute Carlier was kicking at the door furiously, howling, "If you don't bring out that sugar, I will shoot you at sight, like a dog. Now then—one—two—three. You won't? I will show you who's the master."

Kayerts thought the door would fall in, and scrambled through the square hole that served for a window in his room. There was then the whole breadth of the house between them. But the other was apparently not strong enough to break in the door, and Kayerts heard him running round. Then he also began to run laboriously on his swollen legs. He ran as quickly as he could, grasping the revolver, and unable yet to understand what was happening to him. He saw in succession Makola's house, the store, the river, the ravine, and the low bushes; and he saw all those things again as he ran for the second time around the house. Then again they flashed past him. That morning he could not have walked a yard without a groan.

And now he ran. He ran fast enough to keep out of sight of the other man.

Then as, weak and desperate, he thought, "Before I finish the next round I shall die," he heard the other man stumble heavily, then stop. He stopped also. He had the back and Carlier the front of the house, as before. He heard him drop into a chair cursing, and suddenly his own legs gave way, and he slid down into a sitting posture with his back to the wall. His mouth was as dry as a cinder, and his face was wet with perspiration—and tears. What was it all about? He thought it must be a horrible illusion; he thought he was dreaming; he thought he was going mad! After a while he collected his senses. What did they quarrel about? That sugar! How absurd! He would give it to him—didn't want it himself. And he began scrambling to his feet with a sudden feeling of security. But before he had fairly stood upright, a commonsense reflection occurred to him and drove him back into despair. He thought: "If I give way now to that brute of a soldier, he will begin this horror again tomorrow—and the day after—every day—raise other pretensions, trample on me, torture me, make me his slave—and I will be lost! Lost! The steamer may not come for days—may never come." He shook so that he had to sit down on the floor again. He shivered forlornly. He felt he could not, would not move any more. He was completely distracted by the sudden perception that the position was without issue—that death and life had in a moment become equally difficult and terrible.

All at once he heard the other push his chair back; and he leaped to his feet with extreme facility. He listened and got confused. Must run again! Right or left? He heard footsteps. He darted to the left, grasping his revolver, and at the very same instant, as it seemed to him, they came into violent collision. Both shouted with surprise. A loud explosion took place between them; a roar of red fire, thick smoke; and Kayerts, deafened and blinded, rushed back thinking: "I am hit—it's all over." He expected the other to come round—to gloat over his agony. He caught hold of an upright of the roof—"All over!" Then he heard a crashing fall on the other side of the house, as if somebody had tumbled headlong over a chair—then silence. Nothing more happened. He did not die. Only his shoulder felt as if it had been badly wrenched, and he had lost his revolver. He was disarmed and helpless! He waited for his fate. The other man made no sound. It was a strategem. He was stalking him now! Along what side? Perhaps he was taking aim this very minute!

After a few moments of an agony frightful and absurd, he decided to go and meet his doom. He was prepared for every surrender. He turned the corner, steadying himself with one hand on the wall; made a few paces, and nearly swooned. He had seen on the floor, protruding past the other corner, a pair of turned-up feet. A pair of white naked feet in red slippers. He felt deadly sick, and stood for a time in profound darkness. Then Makola appeared before him, saying quietly: "Come along, Mr. Kayerts. He is dead." He burst into tears of gratitude; a loud, sobbing fit of crying. After a time he found himself sitting in a chair and looking at Carlier, who lay stretched on his back. Makola was kneeling over the body.

"Is this your revolver?" asked Makola, getting up.

"Yes," said Kayerts; then he added very quickly, "He ran after me to shoot me—you saw!"

"Yes, I saw," said Makola. "There is only one revolver; where's his?"

"Don't know," whispered Kayerts in a voice that had become suddenly very faint.

"I will go and look for it," said the other, gently. He made the round along the verandah, while Kayerts sat still and looked at the corpse. Makola came back empty-handed, stood in deep thought, then stepped quietly into the dead man's room, and came out directly with a revolver, which he held up before Kayerts. Kayerts shut his eyes. Everything was going round. He found life more terrible and difficult than death. He had shot an unarmed man.

After meditating for a while, Makola said softly, pointing at the dead man who lay there with his right eye blown out—

"He died of fever." Kayerts looked at him with a stony stare. "Yes," repeated Makola, thoughtfully, stepping over the corpse, "I think he died of fever. Bury him to-morrow."

And he went away slowly to his expectant wife, leaving the two white men alone on the verandah.

Night came, and Kayerts sat unmoving on his chair. He sat quiet as if he had taken a dose of opium. The violence of the emotions he had passed through produced a feeling of exhausted serenity. He had plumbed in one short afternoon the depths of horror and despair, and now found repose in the conviction that life had no more secrets for him; neither had death! He sat by the corpse thinking; thinking very actively, thinking very new thoughts. He seemed to have broken loose from himself altogether. His old thoughts, convictions, likes and dislikes, things he respected and things he abhorred, appeared in their true light at last! Appeared contemptible and childish, false and ridiculous. He revelled in his new wisdom while he sat by the man he had killed. He argued with himself about all things under heaven with that kind of wrong-headed lucidity which may be observed in some lunatics. Incidentally he reflected that the fellow dead there had been a noxious beast anyway; that men died every day in thousands; perhaps in hundreds of thousands—who could tell?—and that in the number, that one death could not possibly make any difference; couldn't have any importance, at least to a thinking creature. He, Kayerts, was a thinking creature. He had been all his life, till that moment, a believer in a lot of nonsense like the rest of mankind —who are fools; but now he thought! He knew! He was at peace; he was familiar with the highest wisdom! Then he tried to imagine himself dead, and Carlier sitting in his chair watching him; and his attempt met with such unexpected success, that in a very few moments he became not at all sure who was dead and who was alive. This extraordinary achievement of his fancy startled him, however, and by a clever and timely effort of mind he saved himself just in time from becoming Carlier. His heart thumped, and he felt hot all over at the thought of that danger. Carlier! What a beastly thing! To compose his now disturbed nerves—and no wonder!—he tried to whistle a little. Then, suddenly, he fell asleep, or thought he had slept; but at any rate there was a fog, and somebody had whistled in the fog.

He stood up. The day had come, and a heavy mist had descended upon the land: the mist penetrating, enveloping, and silent; the morning mist of tropical lands; the mist that clings and kills; the mist white and deadly, immaculate and poisonous. He stood up, saw the body, and threw his arms above his head with a cry like that of a man who, waking from a trance, finds himself immured forever in a tomb. *"Help! . . . . My God!*

A shriek inhuman, vibrating and sudden, pierced like a sharp dart the white shroud of that land of sorrow. Three short, impatient screeches followed, and then, for a time, the fog-wreaths rolled on, undisturbed, through a formidable silence. Then many more shrieks, rapid and piercing, like the yells of some exasperated and ruthless creature, rent the air. Progress was calling to Kayerts from the river. Progress and civilization and all the virtues. Society was calling to its accomplished child to come, to be taken care of, to be instructed, to be judged, to be condemned; it called him to return to that rubbish heap from which he had wandered away, so that justice could be done.

Kayerts heard and understood. He stumbled out of the verandah, leaving the other man quite alone for the first time since they had been thrown there together. He groped his way through the fog, calling in his ignorance upon the invisible heaven to undo its work. Makola flitted by in the mist, shouting as he ran—

"Steamer! Steamer! They can't see. They whistle for the station. I go ring the bell. Go down to the landing, sir. I ring."

He disappeared. Kayerts stood still. He looked upwards; the fog rolled low over his head. He looked round like a man who has lost his way; and he saw a dark smudge, a cross-shaped stain, upon the shifting purity of the mist. As he began to stumble toward it, the station bell rang in a tumultuous peal its answer to the impatient clamour of the steamer.

The Managing Director of the Great Civilizing Company (since we know that civilization follows trade) landed first, and incontinently lost sight of the steamer. The fog down by the river was exceedingly dense; above, at the station, the bell rang unceasing and brazen.

The Director shouted loudly to the steamer:

"There is nobody down to meet us; there may be something wrong, though they are ringing. You had better come, too!"

And he began to toil up the steep bank. The captain and the engine-driver of the boat followed behind. As they scrambled up the fog thinned, and they could see their Director a good way ahead. Suddenly they saw him start forward, calling to them over his shoulder; "Run! Run to the house! I've found one of them. Run, look for the other!"

He had found one of them! And even he, the man of varied and startling experience, was somewhat discomposed by the manner of this finding. He stood and fumbled in his pockets (for a knife) while he faced Kayerts, who was hanging by a leather strap from the cross. He had evidently climbed the grave, which was high and narrow, and after tying the end of the strap to the arm, had swung himself off. His toes were only a couple of inches above the ground; his arms hung stiffly down; he seemed to be standing rigidly at attention, but with one purple cheek playfully posed on the shoulder. And, irreverently, he was putting out a swollen tongue at his Managing Director.

1. How do Kayerts and Carlier react to being in the wilderness?
2. What do these two men suggest as representatives of "progress and civilization"?
3. What role does Makola play in the story?
4. How do Kayerts and Carlier react when their men are taken into slavery? How do their reactions change over time?
5. What makes the two men so violent in the end?
6. What does the story suggest about colonialism?

Bharati Mukherjee

ANGELA

Orrin and I are in Delia's hospital room. There's no place to sit because we've thrown our parkas, caps, and scarves on the only chair. The sides of Delia's bed have metal railings so we can't sit on her bed as we did on Edith's when Edith was here to have her baby last November. The baby, if a girl, was supposed to be named Darlene, after Mother, but Edith changed her mind at the last minute. She changed her mind while she was being shaved by the nurse. She picked "Desirée" out of a novel.

My sisters are hopeless romantics.

Orrin loves Delia and brings her little gifts. Yesterday he brought her potted red flowers from Hy-Vee and jangly Mexican earrings I can't quite see Delia wearing; the day before he tied a pair of big, puffy dice to the bedrails. Today he's carrying *One Hundred Years of Solitude.* Delia can't read. She's in a coma, but any day she might come out of it.

He's so innocent! I want to hold his head in my hands, I want to stop up his ears with my fingers so he can't hear Dr. Menezies speak. The doctor is a heavy, gloomy man from Goa, India. Hard work got him where he is. He dismisses Orrin's optimism as frivolous and childish.

"We could read twenty or thirty pages a day to her." Orrin pokes me through my sweater. "You want to start reading?" It's a family joke that I hate to read—my English isn't good enough yet—and Orrin's almost family. "It's like *Dynasty,* only more weird."

"You read. I'll get us some coffee."

"A Diet Coke for me."

Dr. Vinny Menezies lies in wait for me by the vending machines. "Hullo, hullo." He jerks his body into bows as I get myself coffee. "You brighten my day." He's an old-fashioned suitor, an unmarried immigrant nearing forty. He has put himself through medical school in Bombay and Edinburgh, and now he's ready to take a wife, preferably a younger woman who is both affectionate and needy. We come from the same subcontinent of hunger and misery: that's a bonus, he told me.

I feel in the pockets of my blue jeans for quarters, and the coffee slops out of the paper cup.

"I'm making you nervous, Angie?" Dr. Menezies extracts a large, crisp handkerchief from his doctor's white jacket, and blots my burning finger tips. "You're so shy, so sensitive."

He pronounces the *s* in *sensitive* as a *z.*

"Do you have a nickel for five pennies? I need to get a Coke for poor Orrin."

"Of course." He holds a shiny nickel out to me. He strokes my palm as I count out the pennies. "That boyfriend of Delia's, he's quite mental with grief. no?"

"He loves her," I mumble.

"And I you."

But Dr. Menezies lightens the gravity of his confession by choosing that moment to kick the stuck candy machine.

A week before the accident, Orrin asked Delia to marry him. Delia told me this. I've been her sister for less than two years, but we tell each other things. Bad and good. I told her about the cook at the orphanage, how he'd chop wings off crows with his cleaver so I could sew myself a sturdy pair of angel wings. He said I was as good as an angel and the wings would be my guarantee. He'd sit me on the kitchen floor and feed me curried mutton and rich, creamy custards meant for the Bishop Pymm. Delia told me about her black moods. Nobody knows about the black moods; they don't show, she's always so sweet-tempered. She's afraid she's going crazy. Most of the time she loves Orrin, but she doesn't want him to marry a nut.

Orrin calls me by name, his special name for me. "Angel," he says. "Tell me, was she going to say yes?"

I pull open the flip-top of his Diet Coke. He needs looking after, especially now.

"You've come to know her better than any of us." He sits on the windowsill, his feet on the chair. His shoes squash our winter things. "Please, I can handle the truth."

"Of course she loves you, Orrin." In the dry heat of Delia's hospital room, even my smile is charged with static.

Delia's eyes are open. We can't tell what she sees or hears. It would have been easier on us if she'd look as though she were sleeping. Orrin chats to her and holds her hand. He makes plans. He'll quit his job with the United Way. He'll move back from Des Moines. When Delia gets out, they'll fly to Nicaragua and work on a farm side by side with Sandinistas. Orrin's an idealist.

I believe in miracles, not chivalry.

Grace makes my life spin. How else does a girl left for dead in Dacca get to the Brandons' farmhouse in Van Buren County?

When I was six, soldiers with bayonets cut off my nipples. "They left you poor babies for dead," Sister Stella at the orphanage would tell me, the way I might tell Desiree bedtime stories. "They left you for dead, but the Lord saved you. Now it's your turn to do Him credit."

We are girls with special missions. Some day soon, the mysteries will be revealed. When Sister Stella was my age, she was a Muslim, the daughter of a man who owned jute mills. Then she fell in love with a tourist from Marseilles, and when he went home she saw him for what he was: the Lord's instrument for calling her to Christianity. Reading portents requires a special kind of literacy.

Mrs. Grimlund, the nurse, steals into the room with her laced, rubber-soled shoes. Dr. Menezies is with her. "Hullo, again." At the end of a long afternoon, his white doctor jacket looks limp, but his voice is eager. "Don't look so glum. Delia isn't dying." He doesn't actually ignore Orrin, but it's me he wants to talk to.

Orrin backs off to the window. "We aren't looking glum," he mutters.

Dr. Menezies fusses with Delia's chart. "We're giving her our best. Not to worry, please."

Mrs. Grimlund, deferential, helps out Dr. Menezies. "My, my," she says in a loud, throaty voice, "we're looking a lot livelier today, aren't we?" She turns her blue watchful eyes on Orrin. As a nurse and a good Christian she wants to irradiate the room with positive thinking. She marches to the window and straightens a bent shutter. Then she eases the empty Coke can out of Orrin's hand and drops it into the wastebasket. She can always find things that need doing. When I first got to Iowa, she taught me to skate on the frozen lake behind our church.

Dr. Menezies plucks Delia's left hand out from under the blanket and times her pulse. His watch is flat, a gold wafer on a thick, hairy wrist. It looks expensive. His silk tie, the band of shirt that shows between the lapels of his jacket, even the fountain pen with gold clip look very expensive. He's a spender. Last Christmas he gave me a choker of freshwater pearls he'd sent for from a Macy's catalog.

"Splendid," he agrees. But it's me he's looking at. "Very satisfactory indeed." In spite of my bony scarred body and plain face.

Sometimes I visualize grace as a black, tropical bat, cutting through dusk on blunt, ugly wings.

"You wonder why a thing like this happens," Mrs. Grimlund whispers. She lacks only imagnation. She tucks Delia's hand back under the blanket and tidies up Orrin's gifts on the night table. I brought a bag of apples. For Orrin, not Delia. Someone has to make him keep up his energies. "She's such a sweet, loving Christian person."

Orrin turns on her. "Don't look for the hand of Providence in this! It was an accident. Delia hit an icy patch and lost control of the wheel." He twists and twists the shutter control.

"Let me get you another Coke," I beg.

"Stop mothering me!"

Orrin needs to move around. He walks from the window to the bed, where Dr. Menezies is holding his flashlight like a lorgnette, then back to the window. He sits on the chair, on top of our parkas. I hate to see him this lost.

"Delia always carries her witness," Mrs. Grimlund goes on. "I never once saw her upset or angry." She's known Delia all of Delia's life. She told me that it was Delia who asked specifically for a sister from Bangladesh. She was dropping me off after choir practice last week and she said, "Delia said, 'I have everything, so I want a sister who has nothing. I want a sister I can really share my things with.' "

I never once saw her angry, either. I did see her upset. The moods came on her very suddenly. She'd read the papers, a story about bad stuff in a day-care center maybe, about little kids being fondled and photographed, then she'd begin to cry. The world's sins weighed on her.

Orrin can't seem to stay in the chair. He stumbles toward the door. He isn't trying to leave Delia's room, he's just trying to get hold of himself.

Once Orrin goes out of the room, Mrs. Grimlund lets go a little of her professional cheeriness. "It just pulls the rug from under you, doesn't it? You wonder why."

I was in the back seat, that's how I got off with a stiff neck. I have been blessed. The Lord keeps saving me.

Delia was driving and little Kim was in the bucket seat, telling a funny story about Miss Wendt, his homeroom teacher. Mother says that when Kim first got here, he didn't speak a word of anything, not even Korean. He was four. She had to teach him to eat lunch slowly. Kim was afraid the kids at school might snatch it if he didn't eat real fast.

He braced himself when we went into that spin. He broke his wrist and sprained his ankle, and the attendant said probably nothing would have happened if he'd just relaxed and sort of collapsed when he saw it coming.

"There's no telling, is there?" The world's mysteries have ravaged Mrs. Grimlund. Her cap has slipped slightly off-center. "Who'll be taken and who'll be saved, I mean."

Dr. Menezies gives her a long, stern look. "Our job is not to wonder, but to help." He reaches across Delia to touch my arm.

Mrs. Grimlund reddens. What was meant as rebuke comes off as a brisk, passionate outburst. The dingy thicknesses of coat and shirt envelop a wild, raw heart. In the hospital he seems a man of circumspect feelings, but on Sunday afternoons when we drive around and around in his Scirocco, his manner changes. He seems raw, aimless, lost.

"I didn't mean anything wicked," Mrs. Grimlund whispers. "I wasn't questioning the Lord's ways."

I calm her with my smile. My winning smile, that's what the Brandons call it. "Of course you didn't." I am Angela the Angel. Angela was Sister Stella's name for me. The name I was born with is lost to me, the past is lost to me. I must have seen a lot of wickedness when I was six, but I can't remember any of it. The rapes, the dogs chewing on dead bodies, the soldiers. Nothing.

Orrin rushes us from the hall. Dr. Menezies, his passion ebbed, guides Orrin to the chair and I grab the parkas so Orrin will have more room to sit. He needs looking after. I imagine him among Sandinista farmers. He tells slight, swarthy men carrying machetes about rootworms and cutworms. His eyes develop a savior's glittery stare.

"We shouldn't be just standing around and chattering," he shouts. "We're chattering in front of her as though she's dead."

He's all wired up with grief. He was up most of last night, but he doesn't look tired. He looks angry, crazy, stunned, but not tired. He can be with Delia two more days, then he has to go back to Des Moines.

"Take him home." Dr. Menezies is at his best now. He takes charge. He helps Orrin into his jacket and hands him his scarf, cap, mittens. "He isn't doing Delia any good in this state. We have our hands full as it is."

Mrs. Grimlund watches me pull a glove on with my teeth. "I didn't mean it should have been you, Angie." Her lower lip's chewed so deep that there's blood.

Then Dr. Menezies' heavy arm rests on my shoulder. If his watch were any closer to my ear, I'd hear it hum. "Give my regards to your dear parents," he says. He makes a courtly, comical bow. "I shall be seeing you on Sunday? Yes, please?"

On Sunday, after church, we sit down to a huge pork roast—pigs aren't filthy creatures here as they are back home—and applesauce, mashed potatoes and gravy, candied carrots, hot rolls. My older sister Edith and Mary Wellman, the widow from two farms over have brought dessert: two fruit pies, a chocolate cake, and a small jar of macaroons. My brother Bill's wife, Judy, is studying for her master's in library science, so she usually brings something simple, like tossed salad.

I love these Sunday dinners. Company isn't formal and wearying as it was in the orphanage. The days that the trustees in their silk saris and high heels sat at our tables were headachy and endless. The Brandons talk about everything: what the Reverend Gertz said about the Salvadoran refugees, the blizzard we've just gone through, the tardy bank officers who still haven't authorized the loan for this season's plantings. Dad's afraid that if the money doesn't come through by the end of March, he and a whole lot of farmers in the county will be in trouble.

"It'll come through." Mother's the Rock of Gibraltar in our house. She forks carrot slivers delicately and leans her head a wee bit toward Judy, who is telling us about her first husband. "I wouldn't let him near the children, I don't care what the judge says." Bill just melts away from conversations about Judy's first husband. Mother wanted to be a schoolteacher, Delia told me. She wanted to help kids with learning difficulties. Delia wants to be a physical therapist.

"I shouldn't be so sanguine," Ron says. Ron is Edith's husband. He worked for John Deere until the big layoff, but he's not waiting for recall. He's training himself for computers at the community college, and during the day he sits in a cubicle in a hall full of cubicles and makes phone calls for a mail-order firm. The firm sells diet pills and offers promotional gifts. Ron thinks the whole thing's a scam to misuse credit cards.

"Oh, you always look on the negative side," Edith scolds. She eats at the small table—to the left of the dining table—with Kim and Fred. Fred is Judy's six-year-old. She's expecting a baby with Bill in the spring. Desirée is propped up and strapped into her white plastic feeding seat. Edith lifts teaspoonfuls of mashed potatoes to Desirée's full, baby lips. "She really goes for your gravy, Mom. Don't you, darling?"

Ron reaches into the basket of rolls. "Well, life hasn't been too upscale lately for any of us!"

Dr. Menezies bobs and weaves in his chair, passing the plate of butter curls and the gravy boat. He's clearly the most educated, the most traveled man at the table but he talks the least. He is polite, too polite, passing platters and tureens, anticipating and satisfying. This Sunday his hair springs in two big, glossy waves from a thin parting, and his mustache has a neat droop. He tries to catch my eye as he passes the butter.

"I don't know what we'd have done without you, Vinny," Dad says. Dad looks away at the yard, and beyond it at the fields that may not get planted this season.

We have deep feelings, but we aren't a demonstrative family. Fellowship is what we aim for. A parent's grieving would be a spectacle in Bangladesh.

Dr. Menezies tugs at his mustache. It could be a pompous gesture, but somehow he manages to make it seem gracious. "It was my duty only, sir."

I can tell he is thrilled with Dad's praise.

Around 3:30, after Edith and her family and Bill and his family have driven away, and Mary Wellman, Mother, and I have washed and dried the dishes, I play Mozart on the piano for Dr. Menezies. He likes to watch me play, he says. He's tone-deaf, but he says he likes the way the nuns taught me to sit, straight and elegant, on the piano bench. A little civility is how he thinks of this Sunday afternoon ritual. It's one more civility that makes the immense, snowy Midwest less alarming, less ambiguous.

I throw myself into the Fantasy in C Minor. The music, gliding on scarred fingers, transports me to the assembly hall of the orphanage. The bishop sits in the front row, flanked by the trustees in their flowered saris, and a row or two behind, blissful Sister Stella, my teacher. The air in the hall is sweet and lustrous. Together, pianist and audience, we have triumphed over sin, rapacity, war, all that's shameful in human nature.

"Bravo!" the doctor shouts, forgetting himself, forgetting we're in a farmhouse parlor in the middle of America, only Mary Wellman, my parents, and himself to listen. He claps his soft hands, and his gold watch reflects, a pure white flame, on a window pane. "Bravo, bravo!"

When I've lowered the lid, Mary Wellman gathers up her coat and cake pan. I've wrapped what was left of the chocolate cake in tin foil and she carries the small, shiny package breast-high as if it is a treasure. Then Mother excuses herself and goes up to her room to crochet an afghan for Christmas. She doesn't know whom she's making it for, yet. She knits, she crochets. On Sundays, she doesn't read, not even the Des Moines *Register*.

Dad joins Kim in the basement for basketball. Dr. Menezies doesn't care for basketball. Or football or baseball. He came to America as a professional, too old to pick up on some things. The trivia and the madness elude him. He approaches the New World with his stethoscope drawn; he listens to its scary gurgles. He leaves the frolicking to natives. Kim and I are forced to assimilate. A girl with braids who used to race through wet, leechy paddy fields now skates on frozen water: that surely is a marvel. And the marvels replicate. The coach has put me on the varsity cheerleading squad. To make me feel wanted. I'm grateful. I am wanted. Love is waving big, fluffy pompoms with the school colors; it's wearing new Nikes and leaping into the air. I'd never owned shoes in Bangladesh. All last spring, when Delia played—they said, she was tough on the boards, she was intimidating, awesome, second team all-state, from a school of only 200—I shook my pompoms fiercely from the court's edge. I screamed my sisterly love. Delia sent for me from Dacca. She knew what her special mission was when she was just in tenth grade. I could die not knowing, not being able even to guess.

"We're alone. At last."

Dr. Menezies floats toward me in squeaky new leather shoes. He's the acquisitor. His voice is hoarse, but his face is radiant. He should not alarm me now. After 3:30 on Sunday afternoons the Brandons leave the front room to us, and nothing untoward ever happens.

I retreat to the upright piano. Shockingly, my body trembles. "Where did everyone go? We seem to be the only idle ones around here."

The doctor laughs. "Idleness is the devil's workshop, no?"

I suggest a walk. But my suitor does not want to walk or go for a drive. He wants to sit beside me on the piano bench and whimper from the fullness of love.

I hold my shoulders pressed back, my spine taut and straight, so straight, the way Sister Stella taught me. Civilities to see us through minor crises.

"You must be worrying all the time about your future, no?" He strokes my hair, my neck. His inflection is ardent. "Your school will be over in May."

"In June."

"May, June, OK. But then what?" He rubs the lump scars between my shoulder blades.

There's a new embarrassing twitchiness to my body. My thighs squeezed tight, begin to hurt.

"In America, grown-up children are expected to fly the coop," my suitor explains. "You will have to fly, Angie. Make your own life. No shilly-shally, no depending on other people here."

"I thought I'd go to Iowa City. Study physical therapy, like Delia."

"Delia will never study physical therapy, Angie." His voice is deep, but quiet, though we are alone. "You are the strong one. I can tell you."

Mrs. Grimlund dances a sad, savage dance on weightless feet. There's no telling who'll be taken and who'll be saved. I wait for some sign. I've been saved for a purpose.

"Anyway, you're going to make the Brandons shell out three or four thousand? I don't think you're so selfish." He gives a shy giggle, but his face is intense. "I think when school is over, you'll be wanting to find a full-time job. Yes. You'll want to find a job. Or a husband. If it is the latter, I'm a candidate putting in an early word."

He slips a trembling arm around my waist and pulls me close. A wet, shy kiss falls like a blow on the side of my head.

Tomorrow when I visit Delia, I'll stop by the personnel department. They know me, my family. I'll work well with handicapped children. With burn-center children. I'll not waste my life.

But that night, in the room with two beds, Dr. Menezies lies on Delia's pink chenille bedspread. His dark, ghostly face rests on pillow shams trimmed with pink lace. He offers me intimacy, fellowship. He tempts with domesticity. Phantom duplexes, babies tucked tight into cribs, dogs running playfully off with the barbequed steaks.

What am I to do?

Only a doctor could love this body.

Then it is the lavender dusk of tropics. Delinquents and destitutes rush me. Legless kids try to squirm out of ditches. Packs of pariah dogs who have learned to gorge on dying infant flesh, soldiers with silvery bayonets, they keep coming at me, plunging their knives through my arms and shoulders. I dig my face into the muddy walls of a trough too steep to climb. Leeches, I can feel leeches gorging on the blood of my breasts.

1. What is Angela's relationship with her American family?
2. How much has she been Americanized? How is she adjusting to American society?
3. What does the proposal of the Indian doctor mean to her?
4. How does the last paragraph relate to the rest of the story?

Alice Walker (b. 1944)
EVERYDAY USE

for your grandmama

I will wait for her in the yard that Maggie and I made so clean and wavy yesterday afternoon. A yard like this is more comfortable than most people know. It is not just a yard. It is like an extended living room. When the hard clay is swept clean as a floor and the fine sand around the edges lined with tiny, irregular grooves, anyone can come and sit and look up into the elm tree and wait for the breezes that never come inside the house.

Maggie will be nervous until after her sister goes: she will stand hopelessly in corners, homely and ashamed of the burn scars down her arms and legs, eying her sister with a mixture of envy and awe. She thinks her sister has held life always in the palm of one hand, that "no" is a word the world never learned to say to her.

You've no doubt seen those TV shows where the child who has "made it" is confronted, as a surprise, by her own mother and father, tottering in weakly from backstage. (A pleasant surprise, of course: What would they do if parent and child came on the show only to curse out and insult each other?) On TV mother and child embrace and smile into each other's faces. Sometimes the mother and father weep, the child wraps them in her arms and leans across the table to tell how she would not have made it without their help. I have seen these programs.

Sometimes I dream a dream in which Dee and I are suddenly brought together on a TV program of this sort. Out of a dark and soft-seated limousine I am ushered into a bright room filled with many people. There I meet a smiling, gray, sporty man like Johnny

Carson who shakes my hand and tells me what a fine girl I have. Then we are on the stage and Dee is embracing me with tears in her eyes. She pins on my dress a large orchid, even though she has told me once that she thinks orchids are tacky flowers.

In real life I am a large, big-boned woman with rough, man-working hands. In the winter I wear flannel nightgowns to bed and overalls during the day. I can kill and clean a hog as mercilessly as a man. My fat keeps me hot in zero weather. I can work outside all day, breaking ice to get water for washing: I can eat pork liver cooked over the open fire minutes after it comes steaming from the hog. One winter I knocked a bull calf straight in the brain between the eyes with a sledge hammer and had the meat hung up to chill before nightfall. But of course all this does not show on television. I am the way my daughter would want me to be: a hundred pounds lighter, my skin like an uncooked barley pancake. My hair glistens in the hot bright lights. Johnny Carson has much to do to keep up with my quick and witty tongue.

But that is a mistake. I know even before I wake up. Who ever knew a Johnson with a quick tongue? Who can even imagine me looking a strange white man in the eye? It seems to me I have talked to them always with one foot raised in flight, with my head turned in whichever way is farthest from them. Dee, though. She would always look anyone in the eye. Hesitation was no part of her nature.

"How do I look, Mama?" Maggie says, showing just enough of her thin body enveloped in pink skirt and red blouse for me to know she's there, almost hidden by the door.

"Come out into the yard," I say.

Have you ever seen a lame animal, perhaps a dog run over by some careless person rich enough to own a car, sidle up to someone who is ignorant enough to be kind to him? That is the way my Maggie walks. She has been like this, chin on chest, eyes on ground, feet in shuffle, ever since the fire that burned the other house to the ground.

Dee is lighter than Maggie, with nicer hair and a fuller figure. She's a woman now, though sometimes I forget. How long ago was it that the other house burned? Ten, twelve years? Sometimes I can still hear the flames and feel Maggie's arms sticking to me, her hair smoking and her dress falling off her in little black papery flakes. Her eyes seemed stretched open, blazed open by the flames reflected in them. And Dee. I see her standing off under the sweet gum tree she used to dig gum out of; a look of concentration on her face as she watched the last dingy gray board of the house fall in toward the red-hot brick chimney. Why don't you do a dance around the ashes? I'd wanted to ask her. She had hated the house that much.

I used to think she hated Maggie, too. But that was before we raised the money, the church and me, to send her to Augusta to school. She used to read to us without pity; forcing words, lies, other folks' habits, whole lives upon us two, sitting trapped and ignorant underneath her voice. She washed us in a river of make-believe, burned us with a lot of knowledge we didn't necessarily need to know. Pressed us to her with the serious way she read, to shove us away at just the moment, like dimwits, we seemed about to understand.

Dee wanted nice things. A yellow organdy dress to wear to her graduation from high school; black pumps to match a green suit she'd made from an old suit somebody gave me. She was determined to stare down any disaster in her efforts. Her eyelids would not flicker for minutes at a time. Often I fought off the temptation to shake her. At sixteen she had a style of her own: and knew what style was.

I never had an education myself. After second grade the school was closed down. Don't ask me why: in 1927 colored asked fewer questions than they do now. Sometimes Maggie reads to me. She stumbles along good-naturedly but can't see well. She knows she is not bright. Like good looks and money, quickness passed her by. She will marry John Thomas (who has mossy teeth in an earnest face) and then I'll be free to sit here and I guess just sing church songs to myself. Although I never was a good singer. Never could carry a tune. I was always better at a man's job. I used to love to milk till I was hooked in the side in '49. Cows are soothing and slow and don't bother you, unless you try to milk them the wrong way.

I have deliberately turned my back on the house. It is three rooms, just like the one that burned, except the roof is tin; they don't make shingle roofs any more. There are no real windows, just some holes cut in the sides, like the portholes in a ship, but not round and not square, with rawhide holding the shutters up on the outside. This house is in a pasture, too, like the other one. No doubt when Dee sees it she will want to tear it down. She wrote me once that no matter where we "choose" to live, she will manage to come see us. But she will never bring her friends. Maggie and I thought about this and Maggie asked me, "Mama, when did Dee ever *have* any friends?"

She had a few. Furtive boys in pink shirts hanging about on washday after school. Nervous girls who never laughed. Impressed with her they worshiped the well-turned phrase, the cute shape, the scalding humor that erupted like bubbles in lye. She read to them.

When she was courting Jimmy T she didn't have much time to pay to us, but turned all her faultfinding power on him. He *flew* to marry a cheap city girl from a family of ignorant flashy people. She hardly had time to recompose herself.

When she comes I will meet—but there they are!

Maggie attempts to make a dash for the house, in her shuffling way, but I stay her with my hand. "Come back here," I say. And she stops and tries to dig a well in the sand with her toe.

It is hard to see them clearly through the strong sun. But even the first glimpse of leg out of the car tells me it is Dee. Her feet were always neat-looking, as if God himself had shaped them with a certain style. From the other side of the car comes a short, stocky man. Hair is all over his head a foot long and hanging from his chin like a kinky mule tail. I hear Maggie suck in her breath. "Uhnnnh," is what it sounds like. Like when you see the wriggling end of a snake just in front of your foot on the road. "Uhnnnh."

Dee next. A dress down to the ground, in this hot weather. A dress so loud it hurts my eyes. There are yellows and oranges enough to throw back the light of the sun. I feel my whole face warming from the heat waves it throws out. Earrings gold, too, and hanging down to her shoulders. Bracelets dangling and making noises when she moves her arm up to shake the folds of the dress out of her armpits. The dress is loose and flows, and as she walks closer, I like it. I hear Maggie go "Uhnnnh" again. It is her sister's hair. It stands straight up like the wool on a sheep. It is black as night and around the edges are two long pigtails that rope about like small lizards disappearing behind her ears.

"Wa-su-zo-Tean-o!" she says, coming on in that gliding way the dress makes her move. The short stocky fellow with the hair to his navel is all grinning and he follows up with "Asalamalakim, my mother and sister!" He moves to hug Maggie but she falls back, right up against the back of my chair. I feel her trembling there and when I look up I see the perspiration falling off her chin.

"Don't get up," says Dee. Since I am stout it takes something of a push. You can see me trying to move a second or two before I make it. She turns, showing white heels through her sandals, and goes back to the car. Out she peeks next with a Polaroid. She stoops down quickly and lines up picture after picture of me sitting there in front of the house with Maggie cowering behind me. She never takes a shot without making sure the house is included. When a cow comes nibbling around the edge of the yard she snaps it and me and Maggie *and* the house. Then she puts the Polaroid in the back seat of the car, and comes up and kisses me on the forehead.

Meanwhile Asalamalakim is going through motions with Maggie's hand. Maggie's hand is as limp as a fish, and probably as cold, despite the sweat, and she keeps trying to pull it back. It looks like Asalamalakim wants to shake hands but wants to do it fancy. Or maybe he don't know how people shake hands. Anyhow, he soon gives up on Maggie.

"Well," I say. 'Dee."

"No, Mama," she says. "Not 'Dee.' Wangero Leewanika Kemanjo!"

"What happened to 'Dee'?" I wanted to know.

"She's dead," Wangero said. 'I couldn't bear it any longer, being named after the people who oppress me."

"You know as well as me you was named after your aunt Dicie," I said. Dicie is my sister. She named Dee. We called her "Big Dee" after Dee was born.

"But who was *she* named after?" asked Wangero.

"I guess after Grandma Dee," I said.

"And who was she named after?" asked Wangero.

"Her mother," I said, and saw Wangero was getting tired. "That's about as far back as I can trace it," I said. Though, in fact, I probably could have carried it back beyond the Civil War through the branches.

"Well," said Asalamalakim, "there you are."

"Uhnnnh." I heard Maggie say.

"There I was not," I said, "before 'Dicie' cropped up in our family, so why should I try to trace it that far back?"

He just stood there grinning, looking down on me like somebody inspecting a Model A car. Every once in a while he and Wangero sent eye signals over my head.

"How do you pronounce this name?" I asked.

"You don't have to call me by it if you don't want to," said Wangero.

"Why shouldn't I?" I asked. "If that's what you want us to call you, we'll call you."

"I know it might sound awkward at first," said Wangero.

"I'll get used to it," I said. "Ream it out again."

Well, soon we got the name out of the way. Asalamalakim had a name twice as long and three times as hard. After I tripped over it two or three times he told me to just call him Hakim-a-barber. I wanted to ask him was he a barber, but I didn't really think he was, so I didn't ask.

"You must belong to those beef-cattle peoples down the road," I said. They said "Asalamalakim" when they met you, too, but they didn't shake hands. Always too busy: feeding the cattle, fixing the fences, putting up salt-lick shelters, throwing down hay. When the white folks poisoned some of the herd the men stayed up all night with rifles in their hands. I walked a mile and a half just to see the sight.

Hakim-a-barber said, "I accept some of their doctrines, but farming and raising cattle is not my style." (They didn't tell me, and I didn't ask, whether Wangero [Dee] had really gone and married him.)

We sat down to eat and right away he said he didn't eat collards and pork was unclean. Wangero, though, went on through the chitlins and corn bread, the greens and everything else. She talked a blue streak over the sweet potatoes. Everything delighted her. Even the fact that we still used the benches her daddy made for the table when we couldn't afford to buy chairs.

"Oh, Mama!" she cried. Then turned to Hakim-a-barber. "I never knew how lovely these benches are. You can feel the rump prints," she said, running her hands underneath her and along the bench. Then she gave a sigh and her hand closed over Grandma Dee's butter dish. "That's it!" she said. "I knew there was something I wanted to ask you if I could have." She jumped up from the table and went over in the corner where the churn stood, the milk in it clabber by now. She looked at the churn and looked at it.

"This churn top is what I need," she said. "Didn't Uncle Buddy whittle it out of a tree you all used to have?"

"Yes," I said.

"Uh huh," she said happily. "And I want the dasher, too."

"Uncle Buddy whittle that, too?" asked the barber.

Dee (Wangero) looked up at me.

"Aunt Dee's first husband whittled the dash," said Maggie so low you almost couldn't hear her. "His name was Henry, but they called him Stash."

"Maggie's brain is like an elephant's," Wangero said, laughing. "I can use the churn top as a centerpiece for the alcove table," she said, sliding a plate over the churn, "and I'll think of something artistic to do with the dasher."

When she finished wrapping the dasher the handle stuck out. I took it for a moment in my hands. You didn't even have to look close to see where hands pushing the dasher up and down to make butter had left a kind of sink in the wood. In fact, there were a lot of small sinks; you could see where thumbs and fingers had sunk into the wood. It was beautiful light yellow wood, from a tree that grew in the yard where Big Dee and Stash had lived.

After dinner Dee (Wangero) went to the trunk at the foot of my bed and started rifling through it. Maggie hung back in the kitchen over the dishpan. Out came Wangero with two quilts. They had been pieced by Grandma Dee and then Big Dee and me had hung them on the quilt frames on the front porch and quilted them. One was in the Lone Star pattern. The other was Walk Around the Mountain. In both of them were scraps of dresses Grandma Dee had worn fifty and more years ago. Bits and pieces of Grandpa Jarrell's Paisley shirts. And one teeny faded blue piece, about the size of a penny matchbox, that was from Great Grandpa Ezra's uniform that he wore in the Civil War.

"Mama," Wangero said sweet as a bird. "Can I have these old quilts?"

I heard something fall in the kitchen, and a minute later the kitchen door slammed.

"Why don't you take one or two of the others?" I asked. "These old things was just done by me and Big Dee from some tops your grandma pieced before she died."

"No," said Wangero. "I don't want those. They are stitched around the borders by machine."

"That'll make them last better," I said.

"That's not the point," said Wangero. "These are all pieces of dresses Grandma used to wear. She did all this stitching by hand. Imagine!" She held the quilts securely in her arms, stroking them.

"Some of the pieces, like those lavender ones, come from old clothes her mother handed down to her," I said, moving up to touch the quilts. Dee (Wangero) moved back just enough so that I couldn't reach the quilts. They already belonged to her.

"Imagine!" she breathed again, clutching them closely to her bosom.

"The truth is," I said, "I promised to give them quilts to Maggie, for when she marries John Thomas."

She gasped like a bee had stung her.

"Maggie can't appreciate these quilts!" she said. "She'd probably be backward enough to put them to everyday use."

"I reckon she would," I said. "God knows I been saving 'em for long enough with nobody using 'em. I hope she will!" I didn't want to bring up how I had offered Dee (Wangero) a quilt when she went away to college. Then she had told me they were old-fashioned, out of style.

"But they're *priceless*!" she was saying now, furiously; for she has a temper. "Maggie would put them on the bed and in five years they'd be in rags. Less than that!"

"She can always make some more," I said. "Maggie knows how to quilt."

Dee (Wangero) looked at me with hatred. "You will not understand. The point is these quilts, *these* quilts!"

"Well," I said, stumped. "What would *you* do with them?"

"Hang them," she said. As if that was the only thing you *could* do with quilts.

Maggie by now was standing in the door. I could almost hear the sound her feet made as they scraped over each other.

"She can have them, Mama," she said, like somebody used to never winning anything, or having anything reserved for her. "I can 'member Grandma Dee without the quilts."

I looked at her hard. She had filled her bottom lip with checkerberry snuff and it gave her face a kind of dopey, hangdog look. It was Grandma Dee and Big Dee who taught her how to quilt herself. She stood there with her scarred hands hidden in the folds of her skirt. She looked at her sister with something like fear but she wasn't mad at her. This was Maggie's portion. This was the way she knew God to work.

When I looked at her like that something hit me in the top of my head and ran down to the soles of my feet. Just like when I'm in church and the spirit of God touches me and I get happy and shout. I did something I never had done before: hugged Maggie to me, then dragged her on into the room, snatched the quilts out of Miss Wangero's hands and dumped them into Maggie's lap. Maggie just sat there on my bed with her mouth open.

"Take one or two of the others," I said to Dee.

But she turned without a word and went out to Hakim-a- barber.

"You just don't understand," she said, as Maggie and I came out to the car.

"What don't I understand?" I wanted to know.

"Your heritage," she said. And then she turned to Maggie, kissed her, and said, "You ought to try to make something of yourself, too, Maggie. It's really a new day for us. But from the way you and Mama still live you'd never know it."

She put on some sunglasses that hid everything above the tip of her nose and her chin.

Maggie smiled; maybe at the sunglasses. But a real smile, not scared.

After we watched the car dust settle I asked Maggie to bring me a dip of snuff. And then the two of us sat there just enjoying, until it was time to go in the house and go to bed.

1. Why has Dee changed her name to Wangero?
2. What is the history of the name *Dee* in her family?
3. What does her sister Maggie represent in the story?
4. Why is the mother the narrator of the story?
5. What is the significance of the quilt that Wangero wants to take with her?
6. What is Alice Walker suggesting about the importance of black history?

Margaret Atwood (b. 1939)

RAPE FANTASIES

The way they're going on about it in the magazines you'd think it was just invented, and not only that but it's something terrific, like a vaccine for cancer. They put it in capital letters on the front cover, and inside they have these questionnaires like the ones they used to have about whether you were a good enough wife or an endomorph or an ectomorph, remember that? with the scoring upside down on page 73, and then these numbered do-it-yourself dealies, you know? RAPE, TEN THINGS TO DO ABOUT IT, like it was ten new hairdos or something. I mean, what's so new about it?

So at work they all have to talk about it because no matter what magazine you open, there it is, staring you right between the eyes, and they're beginning to have it on the television, too. Personally I'd prefer a June Allyson movie anytime but they don't make them any more and they don't even have them that much on the Late Show. For instance, day before yesterday, that would be Wednesday, thank god it's Friday as they say, we were sitting around in the women's lunch room—the *lunch* room, I mean you'd think you could get some peace and quiet in there—and Chrissy closes up the magazine she's been reading and says, 'How about it, girls, do you have rape fantasies?"

The four of us were having our game of bridge the way we always do, and I had a bare twelve points counting the singleton with not that much of a bid in anything. So I said one club, hoping Sondra would remember about the one club convention, because the time before when I used that she thought I really meant clubs and she bid us up to three, and all I had was four little ones with nothing higher than a six, and we went down two and on top of that we were vulnerable. She is not the world's best bridge player. I mean, neither am I but there's a limit.

Darlene passed but the damage was done, Sondra's head went round like it was on ball bearings and she said, "*What* fantasies?"

"Rape fantasies," Chrissy said. She's a receptionist and she looks like one; she's pretty but cool as a cucumber, like she's been painted all over with nail polish, if you know what I mean. Varnished. "It says here all women have rape fantasies."

"For Chrissake, I'm eating an egg sandwich," I said, "and I bid one club and Darlene passed."

"You mean, like some guy jumping you in an alley or something," Sondra said. She was eating her lunch, we all eat our lunches during the game, and she bit into a piece of that celery she always brings and started to chew away on it with this thoughtful expression in her eyes and I knew we might as well pack it in as far as the game was concerned.

"Yeah, sort of like that," Chrissy said. She was blushing a little, you could see it even under her makeup.

"I don't think you should go out alone at night," Darlene said, "you put yourself in a position," and I may have been mistaken but she was looking at me. She's the oldest, she's forty-one though you wouldn't know it and neither does she, but I looked it up in the employees' file. I like to guess a person's age and then look it up to see if I'm right. I let myself have an extra pack of cigarettes if I am, though I'm trying to cut down. I figure it's harmless as long as you don't tell. I mean, not everyone has access to that file, it's more or less confidential. But it's all right if I tell you, I don't expect you'll ever meet her, though you never know, it's a small world. Anyway.

"For *heaven's* sake, it's only *Toronto,*" Greta said. She worked in Detroit for three years and she never lets you forget it, it's like she thinks she's a war hero or something, we should all admire her just for the fact that she's still walking this earth, though she was really living in Windsor the whole time, she just worked in Detroit. Which for me doesn't really count. It's where you sleep, right?

"Well, do you?" Chrissy said. She was obviously trying to tell us about hers but she wasn't about to go first, she's cautious, that one.

"I certainly don't," Darlene said, and she wrinkled up her nose, like this, and I had to laugh. "I think it's disgusting." She's divorced, I read that in the file too, she never talks about it. It must've been years ago anyway. She got up and went over to the coffee machine and turned her back on us as though she wasn't going to have anything more to do with it.

"Well," Greta said. I could see it was going to be between her and Chrissy. They're both blondes. I don't mean that in a bitchy way but they do try to outdress each other. Greta would like to get out of Filing, she'd like to be a receptionist too so she could meet more people. You don't meet much of anyone in Filing except other people in Filing. Me, I don't mind it so much, I have outside interests.

"Well," Greta said. "I sometimes think about, you know my apartment? It's got this little balcony, I like to sit out there in the summer and I have a few plants out there. I never bother that much about locking the door to the balcony, it's one of those sliding glass ones, I'm on the eighteenth floor for heaven's sake, I've got a good view of the lake and the CN Tower and all. But I'm sitting around one night in my housecoat, watching TV with my shoes off, you know how you do, and I see this guy's feet, coming down past the window, and the next thing you know he's standing on the balcony, he's let himself down by a rope with a hook on the end of it from the floor above, that's the nineteenth, and before I can even get up off the chesterfield he's inside the apartment. He's all dressed in black with black gloves on"—I knew right away what show she got the black gloves off because I saw the same one—"and then he, well, you know."

"You know what?" Chrissy said, but Greta said, "And afterwards he tells me that he goes all over the outside of the apartment building like that, from one floor to another, with his rope and his hook . . .

and then he goes out to the balcony and tosses his rope, and he climbs up it and disappears."

"Just like Tarzan," I said, but nobody laughed.

"Is that all?" Chrissy said. "Don't you ever think about, well, I think about being in the bathtub, with no clothes on . . . ."

"So who takes a bath in their clothes?" I said, you have to admit it's stupid when you come to think of it, but she just went on, ". . . with lots of bubbles, what I use is Vitabath, it's more expensive but it's so relaxing, and my hair pinned up, and the door opens and this fellow's standing there . . . ."

"How'd he get in?" Greta said.

"Oh, I don't know, through a window or something. Well, I can't very well get out of the bathtub, the bathroom's too small and besides he's blocking the doorway, so I just *lie* there, and he starts to very slowly take his own clothes off, and then he gets into the bathtub with me."

"Don't you scream or anything?" said Darlene. She'd come back with her cup of coffee, she was getting really interested. "I'd scream like bloody murder."

"Who'd hear me?" Chrissy said. "Besides, all the articles say it's better not to resist, that way you don't get hurt."

"Anyway you might get bubbles up your nose," I said, "from the deep breathing," and I swear all four of them looked at me like I was in bad taste, like I'd insulted the Virgin Mary or something. I mean, I don't see what's wrong with a little joke now and then. Life's too short, right?

"Listen," I said, "those aren't *rape* fantasies. I mean, you aren't getting *raped,* it's just some guy you haven't met formally who happens to be more attractive than Derek Cummins"—he's the Assistant Manager, he wears elevator shoes or at any rate they have these thick soles and he has this funny way of talking, we call him Derek Duck—"and you have a good time. Rape is when they've got a knife or something and you don't want to."

"So what about you, Estelle," Chrissy said, she was miffed because I laughed at her fantasy, she thought I was putting her down. Sondra was miffed too, by this time she'd finished her celery and she wanted to tell about hers, but she hadn't got in fast enough.

"All right, let me tell you one," I said. "I'm walking down this dark street at night and this fellow comes up and grabs my arm. Now it so happens that I have a plastic lemon in my purse, you know how it always says you should carry a plastic lemon in your purse? I don't really do it. I tried it once but the darn thing leaked all over my chequebook, but in this fantasy I have one, and I say to him, "You're intending to rape me, right?" and he nods, so I open my purse to get the plastic lemon, and I can't find it! My purse is full of all this junk,

Kleenex and cigarettes and my change purse and my lipstick and my driver's license, you know the kind of stuff; so I ask him to hold out his hands, like this, and I pile all this junk into them and down at the bottom there's the plastic lemon, and I can't get the top off. So I hand it to him and he's very obliging, he twists the top off and hands it back to me, and I squirt him in the eye."

I hope you don't think that's too vicious. Come to think of it, it is a bit mean, especially when he was so polite and all.

"*That's* your rape fantasy?" Chrissy says. "I don't believe it."

"She's a card," Darlene says, she and I are the ones that've been here the longest and she never will forget the time I got drunk at the office party and insisted I was going to dance under the table instead of on top of it, I did a sort of Cossack number but then I hit my head on the bottom of the table—actually it was a desk—when I went to get up, and I knocked myself out cold. She's decided that's the mark of an original mind and she tells everyone new about it and I'm not sure that's fair. Though I did do it.

"I'm being totally honest," I say. I always am and they know it. There's no point in being anything else, is the way I look at it, and sooner or later the truth will out so you might as well not waste the time, right? "You should hear the one about the Easy-Off Oven Cleaner."

But that was the end of the lunch hour, with one bridge game shot to hell, and the next day we spent most of the time arguing over whether to start a new game or play out the hands we had left over from the day before, so Sondra never did get a chance to tell about her rape fantasy.

It started me thinking though, about my own rape fantasies. Maybe I'm abnormal or something, I mean I have fantasies about handsome strangers coming in through the window too, like Mr. Clean, I wish one would, please god somebody without flat feet and big sweat marks on his shirt, and over five feet five, believe me being tall is a handicap though it's getting better, tall guys are starting to like someone whose nose reaches higher than their belly button. But if you're being totally honest you can't count those as rape fantasies. In a real rape fantasy, what you should feel is this anxiety, like when you think about your apartment building catching on fire and whether you should use the elevator or the stairs or maybe just stick your head under a wet towel, and you try to remember everything you've read about what to do but you can't decide.

For instance, I'm walking along this dark street at night and this short, ugly fellow comes up and grabs my arm, and not only is he ugly, you know, with a sort of puffy nothing face, like those fellows you have to talk to in the bank when your account's overdrawn—of course I don't mean they're all like that—but he's absolutely covered in pimples. So he gets me pinned against the wall, he's short but he's heavy, and he starts to undo himself and the zipper gets stuck. I mean, one of the most significant moments in a girl's life, it's almost like getting married or having a baby or something, and he sticks the zipper.

So I say, kind of disgusted, "Oh for Chrissake," and he starts to cry. He tells me he's never been able to get anything right in his entire life, and this is the last straw, he's going to go jump off a bridge.

"Look," I say, I feel so sorry for him, in my rape fantasies I always end up feeling sorry for the guy, I mean there has to be something *wrong* with them, if it was Clint Eastwood it'd be different but worse luck it never is. I was the kind of little girl who buried dead robins, know what I mean? It used to drive my mother nuts, she didn't like me touching them, because of the germs I guess. So I say, "Listen, I know how you feel. You really should do something about those pimples, if you got rid of them you'd be quite good looking, honest; then you wouldn't have to go around doing stuff like this. I had them myself once," I say, to comfort him, but in fact I did, and it ends up I give him the name of my old dermatologist, the one I had in high school, that was back in Leamington, except I used to go to St. Catharine's for the dermatologist. I'm telling you, I was really lonely when I first came here; I thought it was going to be such a big adventure and all, but it's a lot harder to meet people in a city. But I guess it's different for a guy.

Or I'm lying in bed with this terrible cold, my face is all swollen up, my eyes are red and my nose is dripping like a leaky tap, and this fellow comes in through the window and *he* has a terrible cold too, it's a new kind of flu that's been going around. So he says, "I'b goig do rabe you"—I hope you don't mind me holding my nose like this but that's the way I imagine it—and he lets out this terrific sneeze, which slows him down a bit, also I'm no object of beauty myself, you'd have to be some kind of pervert to want to rape someone with a cold like mine, it'd be like raping a bottle of LePages mucilage the way my nose is running. He's looking wildly around the room, and I realize it's because he doesn't have a piece of Kleenex! "Id's ride here," I say, and I pass him the Kleenex, god knows why he even bothered to get out of bed, you'd think if you were going to go around climbing in windows you'd wait till you were healthier, right? I mean, that takes a certain amount of energy. So I ask him why doesn't he let me fix him a NeoCitran and scotch, that's what I always take, you still have the cold but you don't feel it, so I do and we end up watching the Late Show together. I mean, they aren't all sex maniacs, the rest of the time they must lead a normal life. I figure they enjoy watching the Late Show just like anybody else.

I do have a scarier one though . . . where the fellow says he's hearing angel voices that're telling him he's got to kill me, you know, you read about things like that all the time in the papers. In this one I'm not in the apartment where I live now, I'm back in my mother's house in Leamington and the fellow's been hiding in the cellar, he grabs my arm when I go downstairs to get a jar of jam and he's got hold of the axe too, out of the garage, that one is really scary. I mean, what do you say to a nut like that?

So I start to shake but after a minute I get control of myself and I say, is he sure the angel voices have got the right person, because I hear the same angel voices and they've been telling me for some time that I'm going to give birth to the reincarnation of St. Anne who in turn has the Virgin Mary and right after that comes Jesus Christ and the end of the world, and he wouldn't want to interfere with that, would he? So he gets confused and listens some more, and then he asks for a sign and I show him my vaccination mark, you can see it's sort of an odd-shaped one, it got infected because I scratched the top off, and that does it, he apologizes and climbs out the coal chute again, which is how he got in in the first place, and I say to myself there's some advantage in having been brought up a Catholic even though I haven't been to church since they changed the service into English, it just isn't the same, you might as well be a Protestant. I must write to Mother and tell her to nail up that coal chute, it always has bothered me. Funny, I couldn't tell you at all what this man looks like but I know exactly what kind of shoes he's wearing, because that's the last I see of him, his shoes going up the coal chute, and they're the old-fashioned kind that lace up the ankles, even though he's a young fellow. That's strange, isn't it?

Let me tell you though I really sweat until I see him safely out of there and I go upstairs right away and make myself a cup of tea. I don't think about that one much. My mother always said you shouldn't dwell on unpleasant things and I generally agree with that, I mean, dwelling on them doesn't make them go away. Though not dwelling on them doesn't make them go away either, when you come to think of it.

Sometimes I have these short ones where the fellow grabs my arm but I'm really a Kung-Fu expert, can you believe it, in real life I'm sure it would just be a conk on the head and that's that, like getting your tonsils out, you'd wake up and it would be all over except for the sore places, and you'd be lucky if your neck wasn't broken or something. I could never even hit the volleyball in gym and a volleyball is fairly large, you know?—and I just go *zap* with my fingers into his eyes and that's it, he falls over, or I flip him against a wall or something. But I could never really stick my fingers in anyone's eyes, could you? It would feel like hot jello and I don't even like cold jello, just thinking about it gives me the creeps. I feel a bit guilty about that one, I mean how would you like walking around knowing someone's been blinded for life because of you?

But maybe it's different for a guy.

The most touching one I have is when the fellow grabs my arm and I say, sad and kind of dignified, "You'd be raping a corpse." That pulls him up short and I explain that I've just found out I have leukaemia and the doctors have only given me a few months to live. That's why I'm out pacing the streets alone at night, I need to think, you know, come to terms with myself. I don't really have leukaemia but in the fantasy I do. I guess I chose that particular disease because a girl in my grade-four class died of it, the whole class sent her flowers when she was in the hospital. I didn't understand then that she was going to die and I wanted to have leukaemia too so I could get flowers. Kids are funny, aren't they? Well, it turns out that he has leukaemia himself, and *he* only has a few months to live, that's why he's going around raping people, he's very bitter because he's so young and his life is being taken from him before he's really lived it. So we walk along gently under the street lights, it's spring and sort of misty, and we end up going for coffee, we're happy we've found the only other person in the world who can understand what we're going through, it's almost like fate, and after a while we just sort of look at each other and our hands touch, and he comes back with me and moves into my apartment and we spend our last months together before we die, we just sort of don't wake up in the morning though I've never decided which one of us gets to die first. If it's him I have to go on and fantasize about the funeral, if it's me I don't have to worry about that, so it just about depends on how tired I am at the time. You may not believe this but sometimes I even start crying. I cry at the ends of movies, even the ones that aren't all that sad, so I guess it's the same thing. My mother's like that too.

The funny thing about these fantasies is that the man is always someone I don't know, and the statistics in the magazines, well, most of them anyway, they say it's often someone you do know, at least a little bit, like your boss or something—I mean, it wouldn't be *my* boss, he's over sixty and I'm sure he couldn't rape his way out of a paper bag, poor old thing, but it might be someone like Derek Duck, in his elevator shoes, perish the thought—or someone you just met, who invites you up for a drink, it's getting so you can hardly be sociable any more, and how are you supposed to meet people if you can't trust them even that basic amount? You can't spend your whole life in the Filing Department or cooped up in your own apartment with all the doors and windows locked and the shades down. I'm not what you would call a drinker but I like to go out now and then for a drink or two in a nice place, even if I am by myself, I'm with Women's Lib on that even though I can't agree with a lot of the other things they say. Like here for instance, the waiters all know me and if anyone, you know, bothers me . . . I don't know why I'm telling you all this, except I think it helps you get to know a person, especially at first, hearing some of the things they think about. At work they call me the office worry wart, but it isn't so much like worrying, it's more like figuring out what you should do in an emergency, like I said before.

Anyway, another thing about it is that there's a lot of conversation, in fact I spend most of my time, in the fantasy that is, wondering what I'm going to say and what he's going to say, I think it would be better if you could get a conversation going. Like, how could a fellow do that to a person he's just had a long conversation with, once you let them know you're human, you have a life too. I don't see how they could go ahead with it, right? I mean, I know it happens but I just don't understand it, that's the part I really don't understand.

1. What are the characteristics of Estelle's rape fantasies?
2. Is the humor of the story appropriate to its subject?
3. What is the effect of finding out at the end of the story that Estelle is talking to a man?
4. What point is Atwood making about women and rape?

ANTHOLOGY OF FICTION

Washington Irving (1783–1859)

RIP VAN WINKLE

A Posthumous Writing of Diedrich Knickerbocker

By Woden, God of Saxons,
From whence comes Wensday, that is Wodensday,
Truth is a thing that ever I will keep
Unto thylke day in which I creep into
My sepulchre—

Cartwright

[The following Tale was found among the papers of the late Diedrich Knickerbocker, an old gentleman of New York, who was very curious in the Dutch history of the province, and the manners of the descendants from its primitive settlers. His historical researches, however, did not lie so much among books as among men; for the former are lamentably scanty on his favorite topics, whereas he found the old burghers, and still more their wives, rich in that legendary lore, so invaluable to true history. Whenever, therefore, he happened upon a genuine Dutch family, snugly shut up in its low-roofed farmhouse, under a spreading sycamore, he looked upon it as a little clasped volume of black-letter, and studied it with the zeal of a book-worm.

The result of all these researches was a history of the province during the reign of the Dutch governors, which he published some years since. There have been various opinions as to the literary character of his work, and, to tell the truth, it is not a whit better than it should be. Its chief merit is its scrupulous accuracy, which indeed was a little questioned on its first appearance, but has since been completely established; and it is now admitted into all historical collections, as a book of unquestionable authority.

The old gentleman died shortly after the publication of his work, and now that he is dead and gone, it cannot do much harm to his memory to say that his time might have been much better employed in weightier labors. He, however, was apt to ride his hobby his own way; and though it did now and then kick up the dust a little in the eyes of his neighbors, and grieve the spirit of some friends, for whom he felt the truest deference and affection; yet his errors and follies are remembered "more in sorrow than in anger," and it begins to be suspected, that he never intended to injure or offend. But however his memory may be appreciated by critics, it is still held dear by many folks, whose good opinion is well worth having; particularly by certain biscuit-bakers, who have gone so far as to imprint his likeness on their new-year cakes; and have thus given him a chance for immortality, almost equal to the being stamped on a Waterloo Medal, or a Queen Anne's Farthing.]

Whoever has made a voyage up the Hudson must remember the Kaatskill mountains. They are a dismembered branch of the great Appalachian family, and are seen away to the west of the river, swelling up to a noble height, and lording it over the surrounding country. Every change of season, every change of weather, indeed, every hour of the day, produces some change in the magical hues and shapes of these mountains, and they are regarded by all the good wives, far and near, as perfect barometers. When the weather is fair and settled, they are clothed in blue and purple, and print their bold outlines on the clear evening sky; but, sometimes, when the rest of the landscape is cloudless, they will gather a hood of gray vapors about their summits, which, in the last rays of the setting sun, will glow and light up like a crown of glory.

At the foot of these fairy mountains, the voyager may have descried the light smoke curling up from a village, whose shingle-roofs gleam among the trees, just where the blue tints of the upland melt away into the fresh green of the nearer landscape. It is a little village of great antiquity, having been founded by some of the Dutch colonists, in the early times of the province, just about the beginning of the government of the good Peter Stuyvesant, (may he rest in peace!) and there were some of the houses of the original settlers standing within a few years, built of small yellow bricks brought from Holland, having latticed windows and gable fronts, surmounted with weather-cocks.

In that same village, and in one of these very houses (which, to tell the precise truth, was sadly time-worn and weather-beaten), there lived many years since, while the country was yet a province of Great Britain, a simple good-natured fellow of the name of Rip Van Winkle. He was a descendant of the Van Winkles who figured so gallantly in the chivalrous days of Peter Stuyvesant, and accompanied him to the siege of Fort Christina. He inherited, however, but little of the martial character of his ancestors. I have observed that he was a simple good-natured man; he was, moreover, a kind neighbor, and an obedient hen-pecked husband. Indeed, to the latter circumstance might be owing that meekness of spirit which gained him such universal popularity; for those men are most apt to be obsequious and conciliating abroad, who are under the discipline of shrews at home. Their tempers, doubtless, are rendered pliant and malleable in the fiery furnace of domestic tribulation; and a curtain lecture is worth all the sermons in the world for teaching the virtues of patience and long-suffering. A termagant wife may, therefore, in some respects, be considered a tolerable blessing; and if so, Rip Van Winkle was thrice blessed.

Certain it is, that he was a great favorite among all the good wives of the village, who, as usual with the amiable sex, took his part in all family squabbles; and never failed, whenever they talked those matters over in their evening gossipings, to lay all the blame on Dame Van Winkle. The children of the village, too, would shout with joy whenever he approached. He assisted at their sports, made their playthings, taught them to fly kites and shoot marbles, and told them long stories of ghosts, witches, and Indians. Whenever he went dodging about the village, he was surrounded by a troop of them, hanging on his skirts, clambering on his back, and playing a thousand tricks on him with impunity; and not a dog would bark at him throughout the neighborhood.

The great error in Rip's composition was an insuperable aversion to all kinds of profitable labor. It could not be from the want of assiduity or perseverance; for he would sit on a wet rock, with a rod as long and heavy as a Tartar's lance, and fish all day without a murmur, even though he should not be encouraged by a single nibble. He would carry a fowling-piece on his shoulder for hours together, trudging through woods and swamps, and up hill and down dale, to shoot a few squirrels or wild pigeons. He would never refuse to assist a neighbor even in the roughest toil, and was a foremost man at all country frolics for husking Indian corn, or building stone-fences; the women of the village, too, used to employ him to run their errands, and to do such little odd jobs as their less obliging husbands would not do for them. In a word Rip was ready to attend to anybody's business but his own; but as to doing family duty, and keeping his farm in order, he found it impossible.

In fact, he declared it was of no use to work on his farm; it was the most pestilent little piece of ground in the whole country; every thing about it went wrong, and would go wrong, in spite of him. His fences were continually falling to pieces; his cow would either go astray, or get among the cabbages; weeds were sure to grow quicker in his fields than anywhere else; the rain always made a point of setting in just as he had some out-door work to do; so that though his patrimonial estate had dwindled away under his management, acre by acre, until there was little more left than a mere patch of Indian corn and potatoes, yet it was the worst conditioned farm in the neighborhood.

His children, too, were as ragged and wild as if they belonged to nobody. His son Rip, an urchin begotten in his own likeness, promised to inherit the habits with the old clothes of his father. He was generally seen trooping like a colt at his mother's heels, equipped in a pair of his father's cast-off galligaskins, which he had much ado to hold up with one hand, as a fine lady does her train in bad weather.

Rip Van Winkle, however, was one of those happy mortals, of foolish, well-oiled dispositions, who take the world easy, eat white bread or brown, whichever can be got with least thought or trouble, and would rather starve on a penny than work for a pound. If left to himself, he would have whistled life away in perfect contentment; but his wife kept continually dinning in his ears about his idleness, his carelessness, and the ruin he was bringing on his family. Morning, noon, and night, her tongue was incessantly going, and everything he said or did was sure to produce a torrent of household eloquence. Rip had but one way of replying to all lectures of the kind, and that, by frequent use, had grown into a habit. He shrugged his shoulders, shook his head, cast up his eyes, but said nothing. This, however, always provoked a fresh volley from his wife; so that he was fain to draw off his forces, and take to the outside of the house—the only side which, in truth, belongs to a hen-pecked husband.

Rip's sole domestic adherent was his dog Wolf, who was as much henpecked as his master; for Dame Van Winkle regarded them as companions in idleness, and even looked upon Wolf with an evil eye, as the cause of his master's going so often astray. True it is, in all points of spirit befitting an honorable dog, he was as courageous an animal as ever scoured the woods—but what courage can withstand the ever-during and all-besetting terrors of a woman's tongue? The moment Wolf entered the house his crest fell, his tail drooped to the ground, or curled between his legs, he sneaked about with a gallows air, casting many a sidelong glance at Dame Van Winkle, and at the least flourish of a broomstick or ladle, he would fly to the door with yelping precipitation.

Times grew worse and worse with Rip Van Winkle as years of matrimony rolled on; a tart temper never mellows with age, and a sharp tongue is the only edged tool that grows keener with constant use. For a long while he used to console himself, when driven from home, by frequenting a kind of perpetual club of the sages, philosophers, and other idle personages of the village; which held its sessions on a bench before a small inn, designated by a rubicund portrait of His Majesty George the Third. Here they used to sit in the shade through a long lazy summer's day, talking listlessly over village gossip, or telling endless sleepy stories about nothing. But it would have been worth any statesman's money to have heard the profound discussions that sometimes took place, when by chance an old newspaper fell into their hands from some passing traveller. How solemnly they would listen to the contents, as drawled out by Derrick Van Bummel, the schoolmaster, a dapper learned little man, who was not to be daunted by the most gigantic word in the dictionary; and how sagely they would deliberate upon public events some months after they had taken place.

The opinions of this junto were completely controlled by Nicholas Vedder, a patriarch of the village, and landlord of the inn, at the door of which he took his seat from morning till night, just moving sufficiently to avoid the sun and keep in the shade of a large tree; so that the neighbors could tell the hour by his movements as accurately as by a sun-dial. It is true he was rarely heard to speak, but smoked his pipe incessantly. His adherents, however (for every great man has his adherents), perfectly understood him, and knew how to gather his opinions. When any thing that was read or related displeased him, he was observed to smoke his pipe vehemently, and to send forth short, frequent and angry puffs; but when pleased, he would inhale the smoke slowly and tranquilly, and emit it in light and placid clouds; and sometimes, taking the pipe from his mouth, and letting the fragrant vapor curl about his nose, would gravely nod his head in token of perfect approbation.

From even this stronghold the unlucky Rip was at length routed by his termagant wife, who would suddenly break in upon the tranquillity of the assemblage and call the members all to naught; nor was that august personage, Nicholas Vedder himself, sacred from the daring tongue of this terrible virago, who charged him outright with encouraging her husband in habits of idleness.

Poor Rip was at last reduced almost to despair; and his only alternative, to escape from the labor of the farm and clamor of his wife, was to take gun in hand and stroll away into the woods. Here he would sometimes seat himself at the foot of a tree, and share the contents of his wallet with Wolf, with whom he sympathized as a fellow-sufferer in persecution. "Poor Wolf," he would say, "thy mistress leads thee a dog's life of it; but never mind, my lad, whilst I live thou shalt never want a friend to stand by thee!" Wolf would wag his tail, look wistfully in his master's face, and if dogs can feel pity I verily believe he reciprocated the sentiment with all his heart.

In a long ramble of the kind on a fine autumnal day, Rip had unconsciously scrambled to one of the highest parts of the Kaatskill mountains. He was after his favorite sport of squirrel shooting, and the still solitudes had echoed and re-echoed with the reports of his gun. Panting and fatigued, he threw himself, late in the afternoon, on a green knoll, covered with mountain herbage, that crowned the brow of a precipice. From an opening between the trees he could overlook all the lower country for many a mile of rich woodland. He saw at a distance the lordly Hudson, far, far below him, moving on its silent but majestic course, with the reflection of a purple cloud, or the sail of a lagging bark, here and there sleeping on its glassy bosom, and at last losing itself in the blue highlands.

On the other side he looked down into a deep mountain glen, wild, lonely, and shagged, the bottom filled with fragments from the impending cliffs, and scarcely lighted by the reflected rays of the setting sun. For some time Rip lay musing on this scene; evening was gradually advancing; the mountains began to throw their long blue shadows over the valleys; he saw that it would be dark long before he could reach the village, and he heaved a heavy sigh when he thought of encountering the terrors of Dame Van Winkle.

As he was about to descend, he heard a voice from a distance, hallooing, "Rip Van Winkle! Rip Van Winkle!" He looked round, but could see nothing but a crow winging its solitary flight across the mountain. He thought his fancy must have deceived him, and turned again to descend, when he heard the same cry ring through the still evening air: "Rip Van Winkle! Rip Van Winkle!"—at the same time Wolf bristled up his back, and giving a low growl, skulked to his master's side, looking fearfully down into the glen. Rip now felt a vague apprehension stealing over him; he looked anxiously in the same direction, and perceived a strange figure slowly toiling up the rocks, and bending under the weight of something he carried on his back. He was surprised to see any human being in this lonely and unfrequented place, but supposing it to be some one of the neighborhood in need of his assistance, he hastened down to yield it.

On nearer approach he was still more surprised at the singularity of the stranger's appearance. He was a short square-built old fellow, with thick bushy hair, and a grizzled beard. His dress was of the antique Dutch fashion—a cloth jerkin strapped round the waist—several pair of breeches, the outer one of ample volume, decorated with rows of buttons down the sides, and bunches at the knees. He bore on his shoulder a stout keg, that seemed full of liquor, and made signs for Rip to approach and assist him with the load. Though rather shy and distrustful of this new acquaintance, Rip complied with his usual alacrity; and mutually relieving one another, they clambered up a narrow gully, apparently the dry bed of a mountain torrent. As they ascended, Rip every now and then heard long rolling peals, like distant thunder, that seemed to issue out of a deep ravine, or rather cleft, between lofty rocks, toward which their rugged path conducted. He paused for an instant, but supposing it to be the muttering of one of those transient thunder-showers which often take place in mountain heights, he proceeded. Passing through the ravine, they came to a hollow, like a small amphitheatre, surrounded by perpendicular precipices, over the brinks of which impending trees shot their branches, so that you only caught glimpses of the azure sky and the bright evening cloud. During the whole time Rip and his companion had labored on in silence; for though the former marvelled greatly what could be the object of carrying a keg of liquor up this wild mountain, yet there was something strange and incomprehensible about the unknown, that inspired awe and checked familiarity.

On entering the amphitheatre, new objects of wonder presented themselves. On a level spot in the center was a company of odd-looking personages playing at nine-pins. They were dressed in a quaint outlandish fashion; some wore short doublets, other jerkins, with long knives in their belts, and most of them had enormous breeches, of similar style with that of the guide's. Their visages, too, were peculiar: one had a large head, broad face, and small piggish eyes: the face of another seemed to consist entirely of nose, and was surmounted by a white sugar-loaf hat set off with the little red cock's tail. They all had beards, of various shapes and colors. There was one who seemed to be the commander. He was a stout old gentleman, with a weather-beaten countenance; he wore a laced doublet, broad belt and hanger, high-crowned hat and feather, red stockings, and high-heeled shoes, with roses in them. The whole group reminded Rip of the figures in an old Flemish painting, in the parlor of Dominie Van Shaick, the village parson, and which had been brought over from Holland at the time of the settlement.

What seemed particularly odd to Rip was, that though these folks were evidently amusing themselves, yet they maintained the gravest faces, the most mysterious silence, and were, withal, the most melancholy party of pleasure he had ever witnessed. Nothing interrupted the stillness of the scene but the noise of the balls, which, whenever they were rolled, echoed along the mountains like rumbling peals of thunder.

As Rip and his companion approached them, they suddenly desisted from their play, and stared at him with such fixed statue-like gazes, and such strange, uncouth, lack-luster countenances, that his heart turned within him, and his knees smote together. His companion now emptied the contents of the keg into large flagons, and made signs to him to wait upon the company. He obeyed with fear and trembling; they quaffed the liquor in profound silence, and then returned to their game.

By degrees Rip's awe and apprehension subsided. He even ventured, when no eye was fixed upon him, to taste the beverage, which he found had much of the flavor of excellent Hollands. He was naturally a thirsty soul, and was soon tempted to repeat the draught. One taste provoked another; and he reiterated his visits to the flagon so often that at length his senses were overpowered, his eyes swam in his head, his head gradually declined, and he fell into a deep sleep.

On waking, he found himself on the green knoll whence he had first seen the old man of the glen. He rubbed his eyes—it was a bright sunny morning. The birds were hopping and twittering among the bushes, and the eagle was wheeling aloft, and breasting the pure mountain breeze. "Surely," thought Rip, "I have not slept here all night." He recalled the occurrences before he fell asleep. The strange man with a keg of liquor—the mountain ravine—the wild retreat among the rocks—the woe-begone party at nine-pins—the flagon—"Oh! that flagon! that wicked flagon!" thought Rip—"what excuse shall I make to Dame Van Winkle!"

He looked round for his gun, but in place of the clean well-oiled fowling-piece, he found an old firelock lying by him, the barrel incrusted with rust, the lock falling off, and the stock worm-eaten. He now suspected that the grave roysters of the mountain had put a trick upon him, and, having dosed him with liquor, had robbed him of his gun. Wolf, too, had disappeared, but he might have strayed away after a squirrel or partridge. He whistled after him and shouted his name, but all in vain; the echoes repeated his whistle and shout, but no dog was to be seen.

He determined to revisit the scene of the last evening's gambol, and if he met with any of the party, to demand his dog and gun. As he rose to walk, he found himself stiff in the joints, and wanting in his usual activity. "These mountain beds do not agree with me," thought Rip, "and if this frolic should lay me up with a fit of the rheumatism, I shall have a blessed time with Dame Van Winkle." With some difficulty he got down into the glen; he found the gully up which he and his companion had ascended the preceding evening; but to his astonishment a mountain stream was now foaming down it, leaping from rock to rock, and filling the glen with babbling murmurs. He, however, made shift to scramble up its sides, working his toilsome way through thickets of birch, sassafras, and witch-hazel, and sometimes tripped up or entangled by the wild grapevines that twisted their coils or tendrils from tree to tree, and spread a kind of network in his path.

At length he reached to where the ravine had opened through the cliffs to the amphitheatre; but no traces of such opening remained. The rocks presented a high impenetrable wall over which the torrent came tumbling in a sheet of feathery foam, and fell into a broad deep basin, black from the shadows of the surrounding forest. Here, then, poor Rip was brought to a stand. He again called and whistled after his dog; he was only answered by the cawing of a flock of idle crows, sporting high in air about a dry tree that overhung a sunny precipice; and who, secure in their elevation, seemed to look down and scoff at the poor man's perplexities. What was to be done—the morning was passing away, and Rip felt famished for want of his breakfast. He grieved to give up his dog and gun; he dreaded to meet his wife; but it would not do to starve among the mountains. He shook his head, shouldered the rusty firelock, and, with a heart full of trouble and anxiety, turned his steps homeward.

As he approached the village he met a number of people, but none whom he knew, which somewhat surprised him, for he had thought himself acquainted with every one in the country round. Their dress, too, was of a different fashion from that to which he was accustomed. They all stared at him with equal marks of surprise, and whenever they cast their eyes upon him, invariably stroked their chins. The constant recurrence of this gesture induced Rip, involuntarily, to do the same, when, to his astonishment, he found his beard had grown a foot long!

He had now entered the skirts of the village. A troop of strange children ran at his heels, hooting after him, and pointing at his gray beard. The dogs, too, not one of which he recognized for an old acquaintance, barked at him as he passed. The very village was altered; it was larger and more populous. There were rows of houses which he had never seen before, and those which had been his familiar haunts had disappeared. Strange names were over the doors—strange faces at the windows—every thing was strange. His mind now misgave him; he began to doubt whether both he and the world around him were not bewitched. Surely this was his native village, which he had left but the day before. There stood the Kaatskill mountains—there ran the silver Hudson at a distance—there was every hill and dale precisely as it had always been—Rip was sorely perplexed—"That flagon last night," thought he, "has addled my poor head sadly!"

It was with some difficulty that he found the way to his own house, which he approached with silent awe, expecting every moment to hear the shrill voice of Dame Van Winkle. He found the house gone to decay—the roof fallen in, the windows shattered, and the doors off the hinges. A half-starved dog that looked like Wolf was skulking about it. Rip called him by name, but the cur snarled, showed his teeth, and passed on. This was an unkind cut indeed—"My very dog," sighed poor Rip, "has forgotten me!"

He entered the house, which, to tell the truth, Dame Van Winkle had always kept in neat order. It was empty, forlorn, and apparently abandoned. This desolateness overcame all his connubial fears—he called loudly for his wife and children—the lonely chambers rang for a moment with his voice, and then all again was silence.

He now hurried forth, and hastened to his old resort, the village inn—but it too was gone. A large rickety wooden building stood in its place, with great gaping windows, some of them broken and mended with old hats and petticoats, and over the door was painted, "the Union Hotel, by Jonathan Doolittle." Instead of the great tree that used to shelter the quiet little Dutch inn of yore, there now was reared a tall naked pole, with something on the top that looked like a red night-cap, and from it was fluttering a flag, on which was a singular assemblage of stars and stripes—all this was strange and incomprehensible. He recognized on the sign, however, the ruby face of King George, under which he had smoked so many a peaceful pipe; but even this was singularly metamorphosed. The red coat was changed for one of blue and buff, a sword was held in the hand instead of a sceptre, the head was decorated with a cocked hat, and underneath was painted in large characters, GENERAL WASHINGTON.

There was, as usual, a crowd of folk about the door, but none that Rip recollected. The very character of the people seemed changed. There was a busy, bustling, disputatious tone about it, instead of the accustomed phlegm and drowsy tranquillity. He looked in vain for the sage Nicholas Vedder, with his broad face, double chin, and fair long pipe, uttering clouds of tobacco-smoke instead of idle speeches; or Van Bummel, the schoolmaster, doling forth the contents of an ancient newspaper. In place of these, a lean, bilious-looking fellow, with his pockets full of handbills, was haranguing vehemently about rights of citizens—elections—members of congress—liberty—Bunker's Hill—heroes of seventy-six—and other words, which were a perfect Babylonish jargon to the bewildered Van Winkle.

The appearance of Rip, with his long grizzled beard, his rusty fowlingpiece, his uncouth dress, and an army of women and children at his heels, soon attracted the attention of the tavern politicians. They crowded round him, eyeing him from head to foot with great curiosity. The orator bustled up to him, and, drawing him partly aside, inquired "on which side he voted?" Rip stared in vacant stupidity. Another short but busy little fellow pulled him by the arm, and, rising on tiptoe, inquired in his ear, "Whether he was Federal or Democrat?" Rip was equally at a loss to comprehend the question; when a knowing, self-important old gentleman, in a sharp cocked hat, made his way through the crowd, putting them to the right and left with his elbows as he passed, and planting himself before Van Winkle, with one arm akimbo, the other resting on his cane, his keen eyes and sharp hat penetrating, as it were, into his very soul, demanded in an austere tone, "what brought him to the election with a gun on his shoulder, and a mob at his heels, and whether he meant to breed a riot in the village?"—"Alas! gentlemen," cried Rip, somewhat dismayed, "I am a poor quiet man, a native of the place, and a loyal subject of the king, God bless him!"

Here a general shout burst from the by-standers—"A tory! a tory! a spy! a refugee! hustle him! away with him!" It was with great difficulty that the self-important man in the cocked hat restored order; and, having assumed a tenfold austerity of brow, demanded again of the unknown culprit, what he came there for, and whom he was seeking? The poor man humbly assured him that he meant no harm, but merely came there in search of some of his neighbors, who used to keep about the tavern.

"Well—who are they?—name them."

Rip bethought himself a moment, and inquired, "Where's Nicholas Vedder?"

There was a silence for a little while, when an old man replied, in a thin piping voice, "'Nicholas Vedder! why, he is dead and gone these eighteen years! There was a wooden tombstone in the churchyard that used to tell all about him, but that's rotten and gone too."

"Where's Brom Dutcher?"

"Oh, he went off to the army in the beginning of the war; some say he was killed at the storming of Stony Point—others say he was drowned in a squall at the foot of Antony's Nose. I don't know—he never came back again."

"Where's Van Bummel, the schoolmaster?"

"He went off to the wars too, was a great militia general, and is now in congress."

Rip's heart died away at hearing of these sad changes in his home and friends, and finding himself thus alone in the world. Every answer puzzled him too, by treating of such enormous lapses of time, and of matters which he could not understand: war—congress—Stony Point;—he had no courage to ask after any more friends, but cried out in despair, "Does nobody here know Rip Van Winkle?"

"Oh, Rip Van Winkle!" exclaimed two or three, "Oh, to be sure! that's Rip Van Winkle yonder, leaning against the tree."

Rip looked, and beheld a precise counterpart of himself, as he went up the mountain: apparently as lazy, and certainly as ragged. The poor fellow was now completely confounded. He doubted his own identity, and whether he was himself or another man. In the midst of his bewilderment, the man in the cocked hat demanded who he was, and what was his name?

"God knows," exclaimed he, at his wit's end; "I'm not myself—I'm somebody else—that's me yonder—no—that's somebody else got into my shoes—was myself last night, but I fell asleep on the mountain, and they've changed my gun, and every thing's changed, and I'm changed, and I can't tell what's my name, or who I am!"

The by-standers began now to look at each other, nod, wink significantly, and tap their fingers against their foreheads. There was a whisper, also, about securing the gun, and keeping the old fellow from doing mischief, at the very suggestion of which the self-important man in the cocked hat retired with some precipitation. At this critical moment a fresh comely woman pressed through the throng to get a peep at the gray-bearded man. She had a chubby child in her arms, which, frightened at his looks, began to cry. "Hush,

Rip," cried she, "hush, you little fool; the old man won't hurt you." The name of the child, the air of the mother, the tone of her voice, all awakened a train of recollections in his mind. "What is your name, my good woman?" asked he.

"Judith Gardenier."

"And your father's name?"

"Ah, poor man, Rip Van Winkle was his name, but it's twenty years since he went away from home with his gun, and never has been heard of since—his dog came home without him; but whether he shot himself, or was carried away by the Indians, nobody can tell. I was then but a little girl."

Rip had but one question more to ask; but he put it with a faltering voice:

"Where's your mother?"

"Oh, she too had died but a short time since; she broke a blood-vessel in a fit of passion at a New England peddler."

There was a drop of comfort, at least, in this intelligence. The honest man could contain himself no longer. He caught his daughter and her child in his arms. "I am your father!" cried he—"Young Rip Van Winkle once—old Rip Van Winkle now!—Does nobody know poor Rip Van Winkle?"

All stood amazed, until an old woman, tottering out from among the crowd, put her hand to her brow, and peering under it in his face for a moment, exclaimed, "Sure enough! it is Rip Van Winkle—it is himself! Welcome home again, old neighbor—Why, where have you been these twenty long years?"

Rip's story was soon told, for the whole twenty years had been to him but as one night. The neighbors stared when they heard it; some were seen to wink at each other, and put their tongues in their cheeks: and the self-important man in the cocked hat, who, when the alarm was over had returned to the field, screwed down the corners of his mouth, and shook his head—upon which there was a general shaking of the head throughout the assemblage.

It was determined, however, to take the opinion of old Peter Vanderdonk, who was seen slowly advancing up the road. He was a descendant of the historian of that name, who wrote one of the earliest accounts of the province. Peter was the most ancient inhabitant of the village, and well versed in all the wonderful events and traditions of the neighborhood. He recollected Rip at once, and corroborated his story in the most satisfactory manner. He assured the company that it was a fact, handed down from his ancestor the historian, that the Kaatskill mountains had always been haunted by strange beings. That it was affirmed that the great Hendrick Hudson, the first discoverer of the river and country, kept a kind of vigil there every twenty years, with his crew of the Half-moon; being permitted in this way to revisit the scenes of his enterprise, and keep a guardian eye upon the river, and the great city called by his name. That his father had once seen them in their old Dutch dresses playing at nine-pins in a hollow of the mountain; and that he himself had heard, one summer afternoon, the sound of their balls, like distant peals of thunder.

To make a long story short, the company broke up, and returned to the more important concerns of the election. Rip's daughter took him home to live with her; she had a snug, well-furnished house, and a stout cheery farmer for a husband, whom Rip recollected for one of the urchins that used to climb upon his back. As to Rip's son and heir, who was the ditto of himself, seen leaning against the tree, he was employed to work on the farm; but evinced an hereditary disposition to attend to any thing else but his business.

Rip now resumed his old walks and habits; he soon found many of his former cronies, though all rather the worse for the wear and tear of time; and preferred making friends among the rising generation, with whom he soon grew into great favor.

Having nothing to do at home, and being arrived at that happy age when a man can be idle with impunity, he took his place once more on the bench at the inn door, and was reverenced as one of the patriarchs of the village, and a chronicle of the old times "before the war." It was some time before he could get into the regular track of gossip, or could be made to comprehend the strange events that had taken place during his torpor. How that there had been a revolutionary war—that the country had thrown off the yoke of old England—and that, instead of being a subject of his Majesty George the Third, he was now a free citizen of the United States. Rip, in fact, was no politician; the changes of states and empires made but little impression on him; but there was one species of despotism under which he had long groaned, and that was—petticoat government. Happily that was at an end; he had got his neck out of the yoke of matrimony, and could go in and out whenever he pleased, without dreading the tyranny of Dame Van Winkle. Whenever her name was mentioned, however, he shook his head, shrugged his shoulders, and cast up his eyes; which might pass either for an expression of resignation to his fate, or joy at his deliverance.

He used to tell his story to every stranger that arrived at Mr. Doolittle's hotel. He was observed, at first, to vary on some points every time he told it, which was, doubtless, owing to his having so recently awaked. It at last settled down precisely to the tale I have related, and not a man, woman, or child in the neighborhood, but knew it by heart. Some always pretended to doubt the reality of it, and insisted that Rip had been out of his head, and that this was one point on which he always remained flighty. The old Dutch inhabitants, however, almost universally gave it full credit. Even to this day they never hear a thunderstorm of a summer afternoon about the

Kaatskill, but they say Hendrick Hudson and his crew are at their game of nine-pins; and it is a common wish of all hen-pecked husbands in the neighborhood, when life hangs heavy on their hands, that they might have a quieting draught out of Rip Van Winkle's flagon.

Mary Shelley (1797–1851)

THE MORTAL IMMORTAL
A Tale

July 16, 1833.—This is a memorable anniversary for me; on it I complete my three hundred and twenty-third year!

The Wandering Jew?—certainly not. More than eighteen centuries have passed over his head. In comparison with him, I am a very young immortal.

Am I, then, immortal? This is a question which I have asked myself, by day and night, for now three hundred and three years, and yet cannot answer it. I detected a gray hair amidst my brown locks this very day—that surely signifies decay. Yet it may have remained concealed there for three hundred years—for some persons have become entirely white-headed before twenty years of age.

I will tell my story, and my reader shall judge for me. I will tell my story, and so contrive to pass some few hours of a long eternity, become so wearisome to me. For ever! Can it be? to live for ever! I have heard of enchantments, in which the victims were plunged into a deep sleep, to wake, after a hundred years, as fresh as ever: I have heard of the Seven Sleepers—thus to be immortal would not be so burthensome: but, oh! the weight of never-ending time—the tedious passage of the still-succeeding hours! How happy was the fabled Nourjahad!—But to my task.

All the world has heard of Cornelius Agrippa. His memory is as immortal as his arts have made me. All the world has also heard of his scholar, who, unawares, raised the foul fiend during his master's absence, and was destroyed by him. The report, true or false, of this accident, was attended with many inconveniences to the renowned philosopher. All his scholars at once deserted him—his servants disappeared. He had no one near him to put coals on his ever-burning fires while he slept, or to attend to the changeful colours of his medicines while he studied. Experiment after experiment failed, because one pair of hands was insufficient to complete them; the dark spirits laughed at him for not being able to retain a single mortal in his service.

I was then very young—very poor—and very much in love. I had been for about a year the pupil of Cornelius, though I was absent when this accident took place. On my return, my friends implored me not to return to the alchymist's abode. I trembled as I listened to the dire tale they told: I required no second warning; and when Cornelius came and offered me a purse of gold if I would remain under his roof, I felt as if Satan himself tempted me. My teeth chattered—my hair stood on end:—I ran off as fast as my trembling knees would permit.

My failing steps were directed whither for two years they had every evening been attracted,—a gently bubbling spring of pure living waters, beside which lingered a dark-haired girl, whose beaming eyes were fixed on the path I was accustomed each night to tread. I cannot remember the hour when I did not love Bertha; we had been neighbours and playmates from infancy—her parents, like mine, were of humble life, yet respectable—our attachment had been a source of pleasure to them. In an evil hour, a malignant fever carried off both her father and mother, and Bertha became an orphan. She would have found a home beneath my paternal roof, but, unfortunately, the old lady of the near castle, rich, childless, and solitary, declared her intention to adopt her. Henceforth Bertha was clad in silk—inhabited a marble palace—and was looked on as being highly favoured by fortune. But in her new situation among her new associates, Bertha remained true to the friend of her humbler days; she often visited the cottage of my father, and when forbidden to go thither, she would stray towards the neighbouring wood, and meet me beside its shady fountain.

She often declared that she owed no duty to her new protectress equal in sanctity to that which bound us. Yet still I was too poor to marry, and she grew weary of being tormented on my account. She had a haughty but an impatient spirit, and grew angry at the obstacles that prevented our union. We met now after an absence, and she had been sorely beset while I was away; she complained bitterly, and almost reproached me for being poor. I replied hastily,—

"I am honest, if I am poor!—were I not, I might soon become rich!"

This exclamation produced a thousand questions. I feared to shock her by owning the truth, but she drew it from me; and then, casting a look of disdain on me, she said—

"You pretend to love, and you fear to face the Devil for my sake!"

I protested that I had only dreaded to offend her;—while she dwelt on the magnitude of the reward that I should receive. Thus encouraged—shamed by her—led on by love and hope, laughing at my late fears, with quick steps and a light heart, I returned to accept the offers of the alchymist, and was instantly installed in my office.

A year passed away. I became possessed of no insignificant sum of money. Custom had banished my fears. In spite of the most painful vigilance, I had never detected the trace of a cloven foot: nor was the studious silence of our abode ever disturbed by demoniac howls. I still continued my stolen interviews with Bertha, and Hope dawned on me—Hope—but not perfect joy; for Bertha fancied that love and security were enemies, and her pleasure was to divide them in my bosom. Though true of heart, she was somewhat of a coquette in manner; and I was jealous as a Turk. She slighted me in a thousand ways, yet would never acknowledge herself to be in the wrong. She would drive me mad with anger, and then force me to beg her pardon. Sometimes she fancied that I was not sufficiently submissive, and then she had some story of a rival, favoured by her protectress. She was surrounded by silk-clad youths—the rich and gay—What chance had the sad-robed scholar of Cornelius compared with these?

On one occasion, the philosopher made such large demands upon my time, that I was unable to meet her as I was wont. He was engaged in some mighty work, and I was forced to remain, day and night, feeding his furnaces and watching his chemical preparations. Bertha waited for me in vain at the fountain. Her haughty spirit fired at this neglect; and when at last I stole out during the few short minutes allotted to me for slumber, and hoped to be consoled by her, she received me with disdain, dismissed me in scorn, and vowed that any man should possess her hand rather than he who could not be in two places at once for her sake. She would be revenged!—And truly she was. In my dingy retreat I heard that she had been hunting, attended by Albert Hoffer. Albert Hoffer was favoured by her protectress, and the three passed in cavalcade before my smoky window. Methought that they mentioned my name—it was followed by a laugh of derision, as her dark eyes glanced contemptuously towards my abode.

Jealousy, with all its venom, and all its misery, entered my breast. Now I shed a torrent of tears, to think that I should never call her mine; and, anon, I imprecated a thousand curses on her inconstancy. Yet, still I must stir the fires of the alchymist, still attend on the changes of his unintelligible medicines.

Cornelius had watched for three days and nights, nor closed his eyes. The progress of his alembics was slower than he expected; in spite of his anxiety, sleep weighed upon his eyelids. Again and again he threw off drowsiness with more than human energy; again and again it stole away his senses. He eyed his crucibles wistfully. "Not ready yet," he murmured: "will another night pass before the work is accomplished? Winzy, you are vigilant—you are faithful—you have slept, my boy—you slept last night. Look at that glass vessel. The liquid it contains is of a soft rose-colour: the moment it begins to change its hue, awaken me—till then I may close my eyes. First, it will turn white, and then emit golden flashes; but wait not till then; when the rose-colour fades, rouse me." I scarcely heard the last words, muttered, as they were, in sleep. Even then he did not quite yield to nature. "Winzy, my boy," he again said, "do not touch the vessel—do not put it to your lips; it is a philter—a philter to cure love; you would not cease to love your Bertha—beware to drink!"

And he slept. His venerable head sunk on his breast, and I scarce heard his regular breathing. For a few minutes I watched the vessel—the rosy hue of the liquid remained unchanged. Then my thoughts wandered—they visited the fountain, and dwelt on a thousand charming scenes never to be renewed—never! Serpents and adders were in my heart as the word "Never!" half formed itself on my lips. False girl!—false and cruel! Never more would she smile on me as that evening she smiled on Albert. Worthless, detested woman! I would not remain unrevenged—she should see Albert expire at her feet—she should die beneath my vengeance. She had smiled in disdain and triumph—she knew my wretchedness and her power. Yet what power had she?—the power of exciting my hate—my utter scorn—my—oh, all but indifference! Could I attain that—could I regard her with careless eyes, transferring my rejected love to one fairer and more true, that were indeed a victory!

A bright flash darted before my eyes. I had forgotten the medicine of the adept; I gazed on it with wonder: flashes of admirable beauty, more bright than those which the diamond emits when the sun's rays are on it, glanced from the surface of the liquid; an odour the most fragrant and grateful stole over my sense; the vessel seemed one globe of living radiance, lovely to the eye, and most inviting to the taste. The first thought, instinctively inspired by the grosser sense, was, I will—I must drink. I raised the vessel to my lips. "It will cure me of love—of torture!" Already I had quaffed half of the most delicious liquor ever tasted by the palate of man, when the philosopher stirred. I started—I dropped the glass—the fluid flamed and glanced along the floor, while I felt Cornelius's grip at my throat, as he shrieked aloud, "Wretch! you have destroyed the labour of my life!"

The philosopher was totally unaware that I had drunk any portion of his drug. His idea was, and I gave a tacit assent to it, that I had raised the vessel from curiosity, and that, frighted at its brightness, and the flashes of intense light it gave forth, I had let it fall. I never undeceived him. The fire of the medicine was quenched—the fragrance died away—he grew calm, as a philosopher should under the heaviest trials, and dismissed me to rest.

I will not attempt to describe the sleep of glory and bliss which bathed my soul in paradise during the remaining hours of that memorable night. Words would be faint and shallow types of my enjoyment, or of the gladness that possessed my bosom when I woke. I trod air—my thoughts were in heaven. Earth appeared heaven, and my inheritance upon it was to be one trance of delight. "This it is to be cured of love," I thought; "I will see Bertha this day, and she will find her lover cold and regardless; too happy to be disdainful, yet how utterly indifferent to her!"

The hours danced away. The philosopher, secure that he had once succeeded, and believing that he might again, began to concoct the same medicine once more. He was shut up with his books and drugs, and I had a holiday. I dressed myself with care; I looked in an old but polished shield, which served me for a mirror; methought my good looks had wonderfully improved. I hurried beyond the precincts of the town, joy in my soul, the beauty of heaven and earth around me. I turned my steps towards the castle—I could look on its lofty turrets with lightness of heart, for I was cured of love. My Bertha saw me afar off, as I came up the avenue. I know not what sudden impulse animated her bosom, but at the sight, she sprung with a light fawn-like bound down the marble steps, and was hastening towards me. But I had been perceived by another person. The old high-born hag, who called herself her protectress, and was her tyrant, had seen me, also; she hobbled, panting, up the terrace; a page, as ugly as herself, held up her train, and fanned her as she hurried along, and stopped my fair girl with a "How, now, my bold mistress? whither so fast? Back to your cage—hawks are abroad!"

Bertha clasped her hands—her eyes were still bent on my approaching figure. I saw the contest. How I abhorred the old crone who checked the kind impulses of my Bertha's softening heart. Hitherto, respect for her rank had caused me to avoid the lady of the castle; now I disdained such trivial considerations. I was cured of love, and lifted above all human fears; I hastened forwards, and soon reached the terrace. How lovely Bertha looked! her eyes flashing fire, her cheeks glowing with impatience and anger, she was a thousand times more graceful and charming than ever—I no longer loved—Oh, no, I adored—worshipped—idolized her!

She had that morning been persecuted, with more than usual vehemence, to consent to an immediate marriage with my rival. She was reproached with the encouragement that she had shown him—she was threatened with being turned out of doors with disgrace and shame. Her proud spirit rose in arms at the threat; but when she remembered the scorn that she had heaped upon me, and how, perhaps, she had thus lost one whom she now regarded as her only friend, she wept with remorse and rage. At that moment I appeared. "O Winzy!" she exclaimed, "take me to your mother's cot; swiftly let me leave the detested luxuries and wretchedness of this noble dwelling—take me to poverty and happiness."

I clasped her in my arms with transport. The old lady was speechless with fury, and broke forth into invective only when we were far on our road to my natal cottage. My mother received the fair fugitive, escaped from a gilt cage to nature and liberty, with tenderness and joy; my father, who loved her, welcomed her heartily; it was a day of rejoicing, which did not need the addition of the celestial potion of the alchymist to steep me in delight.

Soon after this eventful day, I became the husband of Bertha. I ceased to be the scholar of Cornelius, but I continued his friend. I always felt grateful to him for having, unawares, procured me that delicious draught of a divine elixir, which, instead of curing me of love (sad cure! solitary and joyless remedy for evils which seem blessings to the memory), had inspired me with courage and resolution, thus winning for me an inestimable treasure in my Bertha.

I often called to mind that period of trance-like inebriation with wonder. The drink of Cornelius had not fulfilled the task for which he affirmed that it had been prepared, but its effects were more potent and blissful than words can express. They had faded by degrees, yet they lingered long—and painted life in hues of splendour. Bertha often wondered at my lightness of heart and unaccustomed gaiety; for, before, I had been rather serious, or even sad, in my disposition. She loved me the better for my cheerful temper, and our days were winged by joy.

Five years afterwards I was suddenly summoned to the bedside of the dying Cornelius. He had sent for me in haste, conjuring my instant presence. I found him stretched on his pallet, enfeebled even to death; all of life that yet remained animated his piercing eyes, and they were fixed on a glass vessel, full of a roseate liquid.

"Behold," he said, in a broken and inward voice, "the vanity of human wishes! a second time my hopes are about to be crowned, a second time they are destroyed. Look at that liquor—you remember five years ago I had prepared the same, with the same success;—then, as now, my thirsting lips expected to taste the immortal elixir—you dashed it from me! and at present it is too late."

He spoke with difficulty, and fell back on his pillow. I could not help saying,—

"How, revered master, can a cure for love restore you to life?"

A faint smile gleamed across his face as I listened earnestly to his scarcely intelligible answer.

"A cure for love and for all things—the Elixir of Immortality. Ah! if now I might drink, I shall live for ever!"

As he spoke, a golden flash gleamed from the fluid; a well-remembered fragrance stole over the air; he raised himself, all weak as he was—strength seemed miraculously to re-enter his frame—he stretched forth his hand—a loud explosion startled me—a ray of fire shot up from the elixir, and the glass vessel which contained it was shivered to atoms! I turned my eyes towards the philosopher; he had fallen back—his eyes were glassy—his features rigid—he was dead!

But I lived, and was to live for ever! So said the unfortunate alchymist, and for a few days I believed his words. I remembered the glorious drunkenness that had followed my stolen draught. I reflected on the change I had felt in my frame—in my soul. The bounding elasticity of the one—the buoyant lightness of the other. I surveyed myself in a mirror, and could perceive no change in my features during the space of the five years which had elapsed. I remembered the radiant hues and grateful scent of that delicious beverage—worthy the gift it was capable of bestowing—I was, then, IMMORTAL!

A few days after I laughed at my credulity. The old proverb, that "a prophet is least regarded in his own country," was true with respect to me and my defunct master. I loved him as a man—I respected him as a sage—but I derided the notion that he could command the powers of darkness, and laughed at the superstitious fears with which he was regarded by the vulgar. He was a wise philosopher, but had no acquaintance with any spirits but those clad in flesh and blood. His science was simply human; and human science, I soon persuaded myself, could never conquer nature's laws so far as to imprison the soul for ever within its carnal habitation. Cornelius had brewed a soul-refreshing drink—more inebriating than wine—sweeter and more fragrant than any fruit: it possessed probably strong medicinal powers, imparting gladness to the heart and vigor to the limbs; but its effects would wear out; already were they diminished in my frame. I was a lucky fellow to have quaffed health and joyous spirits, and perhaps long life, at my master's hands; but my good fortune ended there: longevity was far different from immortality.

I continued to entertain this belief for many years. Sometimes a thought stole across me—Was the alchymist indeed deceived? But my habitual credence was, that I should meet the fate of all the children of Adam at my appointed time—a little late, but still at a natural age. Yet it was certain that I retained a wonderfully youthful look. I was laughed at for my vanity in consulting the mirror so often, but I consulted it in vain—my brow was untrenched—my cheeks—my eyes—my whole person continued as untarnished as in my twentieth year.

I was troubled. I looked at the faded beauty of Bertha—I seemed more like her son. By degrees our neighbours began to make similar observations, and I found at last that I went by the name of the Scholar bewitched. Bertha herself grew uneasy. She became jealous and peevish, and at length she began to question me. We had no children; we were all in all to each other; and though, as she grew older, her vivacious spirit became a little allied to ill-temper, and her beauty sadly diminished, I cherished her in my heart as the mistress I had idolized, the wife I had sought and won with such perfect love.

At last our situation became intolerable: Bertha was fifty—I twenty years of age. I had, in very shame, in some measure adopted the habits of a more advanced age: I no longer mingled in the dance among the young and gay, but my heart bounded along with them while I restrained my feet; and a sorry figure I cut among the Nestors of our village. But before the time I mention, things were altered—we were universally shunned; we were—at least, I was—reported to have kept up an iniquitous acquaintance with some of my former master's supposed friends. Poor Bertha was pitied, but deserted. I was regarded with horror and detestation.

What was to be done? we sat by our winter fire—poverty had made itself felt, for none would buy the produce of my farm; and often I had been forced to journey twenty miles, to some place where I was not known, to dispose of our property. It is true we had saved something for an evil day—that day was come.

We sat by our lone fireside—the old-hearted youth and his antiquated wife. Again Bertha insisted on knowing the truth; she recapitulated all she had ever heard said about me, and added her own observations. She conjured me to cast off the spell; she described how much more comely gray hairs were than my chestnut locks; she descanted on the reverence and respect due to age—how preferable to the slight regard paid to mere children: could I imagine that the despicable gifts of youth and good looks outweighed disgrace, hatred, and scorn? Nay, in the end I should be burnt as a dealer in the black art, while she, to whom I had not deigned to communicate any portion of my good fortune, might be stoned as my accomplice. At length she insinuated that I must share my secret with her, and bestow on her like benefits to those I myself enjoyed, or she would denounce me—and then she burst into tears.

Thus beset, methought it was the best way to tell the truth. I revealed it as tenderly as I could, and spoke only of a *very long life,* not of immortality—which representation, indeed, coincided best with my own ideas. When I ended, I rose and said,

"And now, my Bertha, will you denounce the lover of your youth?—You will not, I know. But it is too hard, my poor wife, that you should suffer from my ill-luck and the accursed arts of Cornelius. I will leave you—you have wealth enough, and friends will return in my absence. I will go; young as I seem, and strong as I am, I can work and gain my bread among strangers, unsuspected and unknown. I loved you in youth; God is my witness that I would not desert you in age, but that your safety and happiness require it."

I took my cap and moved towards the door; in a moment Bertha's arms were round my neck, and her lips were pressed to mine. "No, my husband, my Winzy," she said, "you shall not go alone—take me with you; we will remove from this place, and, as you say, among strangers we shall be unsuspected and safe. I am not so very old as quite to shame you, my Winzy; and I dare say the charm will soon wear off, and, with the blessing of God, you will become more elderly-looking, as is fitting; you shall not leave me."

I returned the good soul's embrace heartily. "I will not, my Bertha; but for your sake I had not thought of such a thing. I will be your true, faithful husband while you are spared to me, and do my duty by you to the last."

The next day we prepared secretly for our emigration. We were obliged to make great pecuniary sacrifices—it could not be helped. We realised a sum sufficient, at least, to maintain us while Bertha lived; and, without saying adieu to any one, quitted our native country to take refuge in a remote part of western France.

It was a cruel thing to transport poor Bertha from her native village, and the friends of her youth, to a new country, new language, new customs. The strange secret of my destiny rendered this removal immaterial to me; but I compassionated her deeply, and was glad to perceive that she found compensation for her misfortunes in a variety of little ridiculous circumstances. Away from all tell-tale chroniclers, she sought to decrease the apparent disparity of our ages by a thousand feminine arts—rouge, youthful dress, and assumed juvenility of manner. I could not be angry—Did not I myself wear a mask? Why quarrel with hers, because it was less successful? I grieved deeply when I remembered that this was my Bertha, whom I had loved so fondly, and won with such transport—the dark-eyed, dark-haired girl, with smiles of enchanting archness and a step like a fawn—this mincing, simpering, jealous old woman. I should have revered her gray locks and withered cheeks; but thus!— It was my work, I knew; but I did not the less deplore this type of human weakness.

Her jealousy never slept. Her chief occupation was to discover that, in spite of outward appearances, I was myself growing old. I verily believe that the poor soul loved me truly in her heart, but never had woman so tormenting a mode of displaying fondness. She would discern wrinkles in my face and decrepitude in my walk, while I bounded along in youthful vigour, the youngest looking of twenty youths. I never dared address another woman: on one occasion, fancying that the belle of the village regarded me with favouring eyes, she bought me a gray wig. Her constant discourse among her acquaintances was, that though I looked so young, there was ruin at work within my frame; and she affirmed that the worst symptom about me was my apparent health. My youth was a disease, she said, and I ought at all times to prepare, if not for a sudden and awful death, at least to awake some morning white-headed, and bowed down with all the marks of advanced years. I let her talk—I often joined in her conjectures. Her warnings chimed in with my never-ceasing speculations concerning my state, and I took an earnest, thought painful, interest in listening to all that her quick wit and excited imagination could say on the subject.

Why dwell on these minute circumstances? We lived on for many long years. Bertha became bed-rid and paralytic: I nursed her as a mother might a child. She grew peevish, and still harped upon one string—of how long I should survive her. It has ever been a source of consolation to me, that I performed my duty scrupulously towards her. She had been mine in youth, she was mine in age, and at last, when I heaped the sod over her corpse, I wept to feel that I had lost all that really bound me to humanity.

Since then how many have been my cares and woes, how few and empty my enjoyments! I pause here in my history—I will pursue it no further. A sailor without rudder or compass, tossed on a stormy sea—a traveller lost on a wide-spread heath, without landmark or star to guide him—such have I been: more lost, more hopeless than either. A nearing ship, a gleam from some far cot, may save them; but I have no beacon except the hope of death.

Death! mysterious, ill-visaged friend of weak humanity! Why alone of all mortals have you cast me from your sheltering fold? O, for the peace of the grave! the deep silence of the iron-bound tomb! that thought would cease to work in my brain, and my heart beat no more with emotions varied only by new forms of sadness!

Am I immortal? I return to my first question. In the first place, is it not more probable that the beverage of the alchymist was fraught rather with longevity than eternal life? Such is my hope. And then be it remembered, that I only drank *half* of the potion prepared by him. Was not the whole necessary to complete the charm? To have drained half the Elixir of Immortality is but to be half immortal—my Forever is thus truncated and null.

But again, who shall number the years of the half of eternity? I often try to image by what rule the infinite may be divided. Sometimes I fancy age advancing upon me. One gray hair I have found. Fool! do I lament? Yes, the fear of age and death often creeps coldly into my heart; and the more I live, the more I dread death, even while I abhor life. Such an enigma is man—born to perish—when he wars, as I do, against the established laws of his nature.

But for this anomaly of feeling surely I might die: the medicine of the alchymist would not be proof against fire—sword—and the strangling waters. I have gazed upon the blue depths of many a placid lake, and the tumultuous rushing of many a mighty river, and have said, peace inhabits those waters; yet I have turned my steps away, to live yet another day. I have asked myself, whether suicide would be a crime in one to whom thus only the portals of the other world could be opened. I have done all, except presenting myself as a soldier or duellist, an object of destruction to my—no, *not* my fellow-mortals, and therefore I have shrunk away. They are not my fellows. The inextinguishable power of life in my frame, and their ephemeral existence, place us wide as the poles asunder. I could not raise a hand against the meanest or the most powerful among them.

Thus I have lived on for many a year—alone, and weary of myself—desirous of death, yet never dying—a mortal immortal. Neither ambition nor avarice can enter my mind, and the ardent love that gnaws at my heart, never to be returned—never to find an equal on which to expend itself—lives there only to torment me.

This very day I conceived a design by which I may end all —without self-slaughter, without making another man a Cain—an expedition, which mortal frame can never survive, even endued with the youth and strength that inhabits mine. Thus I shall put my immortality to the test, and rest for ever—or return, the wonder and benefactor of the human species.

Before I go, a miserable vanity has caused me to pen these pages. I would not die, and leave no name behind. Three centuries have passed since I quaffed the fatal beverage: another year shall not elapse before, encountering gigantic dangers—warring with the powers of frost in their home—beset by famine, toil, and tempest—I yield this body, too tenacious a cage for a soul which thirsts for freedom, to the destructive elements of air and water—or, if I survive, my name shall be recorded as one of the most famous among the sons of men; and, my task achieved, I shall adopt more resolute means, and, by scattering and annihilating the atoms that compose my frame, set at liberty the life imprisoned within, and so cruelly prevented from soaring from this dim earth to a sphere more congenial to its immortal essence.

Nathaniel Hawthorne (1804–1864)

RAPPACCINI'S DAUGHTER
(From the Writings of Aubépine)

A young man, named Giovanni Guasconti, came, very long ago, from the more southern region of Italy, to pursue his studies at the University of Padua. Giovanni, who had but a scanty supply of gold ducats in his pocket, took lodgings in a high and gloomy chamber of an old edifice which looked not unworthy to have been the palace of a Paduan noble, and which, in fact, exhibited over its entrance the armorial bearings of a family long since extinct. The young stranger, who was not unstudied in the great poem of his country, recollected that one of the ancestors of this family, and perhaps an occupant of this very mansion, had been pictured by Dante as a partaker of the immortal agonies of his Inferno. These reminiscences and associations, together with the tendency to heartbreak natural to a young man for the first time out of his native sphere, caused Giovanni to sigh heavily as he looked around the desolate and ill-furnished apartment.

"Holy Virgin, signor!" cried old Dame Lisabetta, who, won by the youth's remarkable beauty of person, was kindly endeavoring to give the chamber a habitable air, "what a sigh was that to come out of a young man's heart! Do you find this old mansion gloomy? For the love of Heaven, then, put your head out of the window, and you will see as bright sunshine as you have left in Naples."

Guasconti mechanically did as the old woman advised, but could not quite agree with her that the Paduan sunshine was as cheerful as that of southern Italy. Such as it was, however, it fell upon a garden beneath the window and expended its fostering influences on a variety of plants, which seemed to have been cultivated with exceeding care.

"Does this garden belong to the house?" asked Giovanni.

"Heaven forbid, signor, unless it were fruitful of better pot herbs than any that grow there now," answered old Lisabetta. "No; that garden is cultivated by the own hands of Signor Giacomo Rappaccini, the famous doctor, who, I warrant him, has been heard of as far as Naples. It is said that he distils these plants into medicines that are as potent as a charm. Oftentimes you may see the signor doctor at work, and perchance the signora, his daughter, too, gathering the strange flowers that grow in the garden."

The old woman had now done what she could for the aspect of the chamber; and, commending the young man to the protection of the saints, took her departure.

Giovanni still found no better occupation than to look down into the garden beneath his window. From its appearance, he judged it to be one of those botanic gardens which were of earlier date in Padua than elsewhere in Italy or in the world. Or, not improbably, it might once have been the pleasure-place of an opulent family; for there was the ruin of a marble fountain in the center, sculptured with rare art, but so wofully shattered that it was impossible to trace the original design from the chaos of remaining fragments. The water, however, continued to gush and sparkle into the sunbeams as cheerfully as ever. A little gurgling sound ascended to the young man's window and made him feel as if the fountain were an immortal spirit, that sung its song unceasingly and without heeding the vicissitudes around it, while one century embodied it in marble and another scattered the perishable garniture on the soil. All about the pool into which the water subsided grew various plants, that seemed to require a plentiful supply of moisture for the nourishment of gigantic leaves, and, in some instances, flowers gorgeously magnificent. There was one shrub in particular, set in a marble vase in the midst of the pool, that bore a profusion of purple blossoms, each of which had the lustre and richness of a gem; and the whole together made a show so resplendent that it seemed enough to illuminate the garden, even had there been no sunshine. Every portion of the soil was peopled with plants and herbs, which, if less beautiful, still bore tokens of assiduous care, as if all had their individual virtues, known to the scientific mind that fostered them. Some were placed in urns, rich with old carving, and others in common garden pots; some crept serpent-like along the ground or climbed on high, using whatever means of ascent was offered them. One plant had wreathed itself round a statue of Vertumnus, which was thus quite veiled and shrouded in a drapery of hanging foliage, so happily arranged that it might have served a sculptor for a study.

While Giovanni stood at the window he heard a rustling behind a screen of leaves, and became aware that a person was at work in the garden. His figure soon emerged into view, and showed itself to be that of no common laborer, but a tall, emaciated, sallow, and sickly-looking man, dressed in a scholar's garb of black. He was beyond the middle term of life, with gray hair, a thin, gray beard, and a face singularly marked with intellect and cultivation, but which could never, even in his more youthful days, have expressed much warmth of heart.

Nothing could exceed the intentness with which this scientific gardener examined every shrub which grew in his path: it seemed as if he was looking into their inmost nature, making observations in regard to their creative essence, and discovering why one leaf grew in this shape and another in that, and wherefore such and such flowers differed among themselves in hue and perfume. Nevertheless, in spite of this deep intelligence on his part, there was no approach to intimacy between himself and these vegetable existences. On the contrary, he avoided their actual touch or the direct inhaling of their odors with a caution that impressed Giovanni most disagreeably; for the man's demeanor was that of one walking among malignant influences, such as savage beasts, or deadly snakes, or evil spirits, which, should he allow them one moment of license, would wreak upon him some terrible fatality. It was strangely frightful to the young man's imagination to see this air of insecurity in a person cultivating a garden, that most simple and innocent of human toils, and which had been alike the joy and labor of the unfallen parents of the race. Was the garden, then, the Eden of the present world? And this man with such perception of harm in what his own hands caused to grow—was he the Adam?

The distrustful gardener, while plucking away the dead leaves or pruning the too luxuriant growth of the shrubs, defended his hands with a pair of thick gloves. Nor were these his only armor. When, in his walk through the garden, he came to the magnificent plant that hung its purple gems beside the marble fountain, he placed a kind of mask over his mouth and nostrils, as if all this beauty did but conceal a deadlier malice; but, finding his task still too dangerous, he drew back, removed the mask, and called loudly, but in the infirm voice of a person affected with inward disease—

"Beatrice! Beatrice!"

"Here am I, my father. What would you?" cried a rich and youthful voice from the window of the opposite house—a voice as rich as a tropical sunset, and which made Giovanni, though he knew not why, think of deep hues of purple or crimson and of perfumes heavily delectable, "Are you in the garden?"

"Yes, Beatrice," answered the gardener, "and I need your help."

Soon there emerged from under a sculptured portal the figure of a young girl, arrayed with as much richness of taste as the most splendid of the flowers, beautiful as the day, and with a bloom so deep and vivid that one shade more would have been too much. She looked redundant with life, health, and energy; all of which attributes were bound down and compressed, as it were, and girdled tensely, in their luxuriance, by her virgin zone. Yet Giovanni's fancy must have grown morbid while he looked down into the garden; for the impression which the fair stranger made upon him was as if here were another flower, the human sister of those vegetable ones, as beautiful as they, more beautiful than the richest of them, but still to be touched only with a glove, nor to be approached without a mask. As Beatrice came down the garden path, it was observable that she handled and inhaled the odor of several of the plants which her father had most sedulously avoided.

"Here, Beatrice," said the latter, "see how many needful offices require to be done to our chief treasure. Yet, shattered as I am, my life might pay the penalty of approaching it so closely as circumstances demand. Henceforth, I fear, this plant must be consigned to your sole charge."

"And gladly will I undertake it," cried again the rich tones of the young lady, as she bent towards the magnificent plant and opened her arms as if to embrace it. "Yes, my sister, my splendor, it shall be Beatrice's task to nurse and serve thee; and thou shalt reward her with thy kisses and perfumed breath, which to her is as the breath of life."

Then, with all the tenderness in her manner that was so strikingly expressed in her words, she busied herself with such attentions as the plant seemed to require; and Giovanni, at his lofty window, rubbed his eyes, and almost doubted whether it were a girl tending her favorite flower, or one sister performing the duties of affection to another. The scene soon terminated. Whether Dr. Rappaccini had finished his labors in the garden, or that his watchful eye had caught the stranger's face, he now took his daughter's arm and retired. Night was already closing in; oppressive exhalations seemed to proceed from the plants and steal upward past the open window; and Giovanni, closing the lattice, went to his couch and dreamed of a rich flower and beautiful girl. Flower and maiden were different, and yet the same, and fraught with some strange peril in either shape.

But there is an influence in the light of morning that tends to rectify whatever errors of fancy, or even of judgment, we may have incurred during the sun's decline, or among the shadows of the night, or in the less wholesome glow of moonshine. Giovanni's first movement, on starting from sleep, was to throw open the window and gaze down into the garden which his dreams had made so fertile of mysteries. He was surprised, and a little ashamed, to find how real and matter-of-fact an affair it proved to be, in the first rays of the sun which gilded the dewdrops that hung upon leaf and blossom, and, while giving a brighter beauty to each rare flower, brought everything within the limits of ordinary experience. The young man rejoiced that, in the heart of the barren city, he had the privilege of overlooking this spot of lovely and luxuriant vegetation. It would serve, he said to himself, as symbolic language to keep him in communion with Nature. Neither the sickly and thoughtworn Dr. Giacomo Rappaccini, it is true, nor his brilliant daughter, were now visible; so that Giovanni could not determine how much of the singularity which he attributed to both was due to their own qualities and how much to his wonder-working fancy; but he was inclined to take a most rational view of the whole matter.

In the course of the day he paid his respects to Signor Pietro Baglioni, professor of medicine in the university, a physician of eminent repute, to whom Giovanni had brought a letter of introduction. The professor was an elderly personage, apparently of genial nature and habits that might almost be called jovial. He kept the young man to dinner, and made himself very agreeable by the freedom and liveliness of his conversation, especially when warmed by a flask or two of Tuscan wine. Giovanni, conceiving that men of science, inhabitants of the same city, must needs be on familiar terms with one another, took an opportunity to mention the name of Dr. Rappaccini. But the professor did not respond with so much cordiality as he had anticipated.

"Ill would it become a teacher of the divine art of medicine," said Professor Pietro Baglioni, in answer to a question of Giovanni, "to withhold due and well-considered praise of a physician so eminently skilled as Rappaccini; but, on the other hand, I should answer it but scantily to my conscience were I to permit a worthy youth like yourself, Signor Giovanni, the son of an ancient friend, to imbibe erroneous ideas respecting a man who might hereafter chance to hold your life and death in his hands. The truth is, our worshipful Dr. Rappaccini has as much science as any member of the faculty—with perhaps one single exception—in Padua, or all Italy; but there are certain grave objections to his professional character."

"And what are they?" asked the young man.

"Has my friend Giovanni any disease of body or heart, that he is so inquisitive about physicians?" said the professor, with a smile.

"But as for Rappaccini, it is said of him—and I, who know the man well, can answer for its truth—that he cares infinitely more for science than for mankind. His patients are interesting to him only as subjects for some new experiment. He would sacrifice human life, his own among the rest, or whatever else was dearest to him, for the sake of adding so much as a grain of mustard seed to the great heap of his accumulated knowledge."

"Methinks he is an awful man indeed," remarked Guasconti, mentally recalling the cold and purely intellectual aspect of Rappaccini. "And yet, worshipful professor, is it not a noble spirit? Are there many men capable of so spiritual a love of science?"

"God forbid," answered the professor, somewhat testily; "at least, unless they take sounder views of the healing art than those adopted by Rappaccini. It is his theory that all medicinal virtues are comprised within those substances which we term vegetable poisons. These he cultivates with his own hands, and is said even to have produced new varieties of poison, more horribly deleterious than Nature, without the assistance of this learned person, would ever have plagued the world withal. That the signor doctor does less mischief than might be expected with such dangerous substances is undeniable. Now and then, it must be owned, he has effected, or seemed to effect, a marvellous cure; but, to tell you my private mind, Signor Giovanni, he should receive little credit for such instances of success—they being probably the work of chance—but should be held strictly accountable for his failures, which may justly be considered his own work."

The youth might have taken Baglioni's opinions with many grains of allowance had he known that there was a professional warfare of long continuance between him and Dr. Rappaccini, in which the latter was generally thought to have gained the advantage. If the reader be inclined to judge for himself, we refer him to certain black-letter tracts on both sides, preserved in the medical department of the University of Padua.

"I know not, most learned professor," returned Giovanni, after musing on what had been said of Rappaccini's exclusive zeal for science—"I know not how dearly this physician may love his art; but surely there is one object more dear to him. He has a daughter."

"Aha!" cried the professor, with a laugh. "So now our friend Giovanni's secret is out. You have heard of this daughter, whom all the young men in Padua are wild about, though not half a dozen have ever had the good hap to see her face. I know little of the Signora Beatrice save that Rappaccini is said to have instructed her deeply in his science, and that, young and beautiful as fame reports her, she is already qualified to fill a professor's chair. Perchance her father destines her for mine! Other absurd rumors there be, not worth talking about or listening to. So now, Signor Giovanni, drink off your glass of lachryma."

Guasconti returned to his lodgings somewhat heated with the wine he had quaffed, and which caused his brain to swim with strange fantasies in reference to Dr. Rappaccini and the beautiful Beatrice. On his way, happening to pass by a florist's, he bought a fresh bouquet of flowers.

Ascending to his chamber, he seated himself near the window, but within the shadow thrown by the depth of the wall, so that he could look down into the garden with little risk of being discovered. All beneath his eye was a solitude. The strange plants were basking in the sunshine, and now and then nodding gently to one another, as if in acknowledgment of sympathy and kindred. In the midst, by the shattered fountain, grew the magnificent shrub, with its purple gems clustering all over it; they glowed in the air, and gleamed back again out of the depths of the pool, which thus seemed to overflow with colored radiance from the rich reflection that was steeped in it. At first, as we have said, the garden was a solitude. Soon, however—as Giovanni had half hoped, half feared, would be the case—a figure appeared beneath the antique sculptured portal, and came down between the rows of plants, inhaling their various perfumes as if she were one of those beings of old classic fable that lived upon sweet odors. On again beholding Beatrice, the young man was even startled to perceive how much her beauty exceeded his recollection of it; so brilliant, so vivid, was its character, that she glowed amid the sunlight, and, as Giovanni whispered to himself, positively illuminated the more shadowy intervals of the garden path. Her face being now more revealed than on the former occasion, he was struck by its expression of simplicity and sweetness—qualities that had not entered into his idea of her character, and which made him ask anew what manner of mortal she might be. Nor did he fail again to observe, or imagine, an analogy between the beautiful girl and the gorgeous shrub that hung its gemlike flowers over the fountain—a resemblance which Beatrice seemed to have indulged a fantastic humor in heightening, both by the arrangement of her dress and the selection of its hues.

Approaching the shrub, she threw open her arms, as with a passionate ardor, and drew its branches into an intimate embrace—so intimate that her features were hidden in its leafy bosom and her glistening ringlets all intermingled with the flowers.

"Give me thy breath, my sister," exclaimed Beatrice; "for I am faint with common air. And give me this flower of thine, which I separate with gentlest fingers from the stem and place it close beside my heart."

With these words the beautiful daughter of Rappaccini plucked one of the richest blossoms of the shrub, and was about to fasten it in her bosom. But now, unless Giovanni's draughts of wine had bewildered his senses, a singular incident occurred. A small orange-colored reptile, of the lizard or chameleon species, chanced to be creeping along the path, just at the feet of Beatrice. It appeared to Giovanni—but, at the distance from which he gazed, he could scarcely have seen anything so minute—it appeared to him, however, that a drop or two of moisture from the broken stem of the flower descended upon the lizard's head. For an instant the reptile contorted itself violently, and then lay motionless in the sunshine. Beatrice observed this remarkable phenomenon, and crossed herself, sadly, but without surprise; not did she therefore hesitate to arrange the fatal flower in her bosom. There it blushed, and almost glimmered with the dazzling effect of a precious stone, adding to her dress and aspect the one appropriate charm which nothing else in the world could have supplied. But Giovanni, out of the shadow of his window, bent forward and shrank back, and murmured and trembled.

"Am I awake? Have I my senses?" said he to himself. "What is this being? Beautiful shall I call her, or inexpressibly terrible?"

Beatrice now strayed carelessly through the garden, approaching closer beneath Giovanni's window, so that he was compelled to thrust his head quite out of its concealment in order to gratify the intense and painful curiosity which she excited. At this moment there came a beautiful insect over the garden wall: it had, perhaps, wandered through the city, and found no flowers or verdure among those antique haunts of men until the heavy perfumes of Dr. Rappaccini's shrubs had lured it from afar. Without alighting on the flowers, this winged brightness seemed to be attracted by Beatrice, and lingered in the air and fluttered about her head. Now, here it could not be but that Giovanni Guasconti's eyes deceived him. Be that as it might, he fancied that, while Beatrice was gazing at the insect with childish delight, it grew faint and fell at her feet; its bright wings shivered; it was dead—from no cause that he could discern, unless it were the atmosphere of her breath. Again Beatrice crossed herself and sighed heavily as she bent over the dead insect.

An impulsive movement of Giovanni drew her eyes to the window. There she beheld the beautiful head of the young man—rather a Grecian than an Italian head, with fair, regular features, and a glistening of gold among his ringlets—gazing down upon her like a being that hovered in mid air. Scarcely knowing what he did, Giovanni threw down the bouquet which he had hitherto held in his hand.

"Signora," said he, "there are pure and healthful flowers. Wear them for the sake of Giovanni Guasconti."

"Thanks, signor," replied Beatrice, with her rich voice, that came forth as it were like a gush of music, and with a mirthful expression half childish and half womanlike. "I accept your gift, and would fain recompense it with this precious purple flower; but, if I toss it into the air, it will not reach you. So Signor Guasconti must even content himself with my thanks."

She lifted the bouquet from the ground, and then, as if inwardly ashamed at having stepped aside from her maidenly reserve to respond to a stranger's greeting, passed swiftly homeward through the garden. But few as the moments were, it seemed to Giovanni, when she was on the point of vanishing beneath the sculptured portal, that his beautiful bouquet was already beginning to wither in her grasp. It was an idle thought; there could be no possibility of distinguishing a faded flower from a fresh one at so great a distance.

For many days after this incident the young man avoided the window that looked into Dr. Rappaccini's garden, as if something ugly and monstrous would have blasted his eyesight had he been betrayed into a glance. He felt conscious of having put himself, to a certain extent, within the influence of an unintelligible power by the communication which he had opened with Beatrice. The wisest course would have been, if his heart were in any real danger, to quit his lodgings and Padua itself at once; the next wiser, to have accustomed himself, as far as possible, to the familiar and daylight view of Beatrice—thus bringing her rigidly and systematically within the limits of ordinary experience. Least of all, while avoiding her sight, ought Giovanni to have remained so near this extraordinary being that the proximity and possibility even of intercourse should give a kind of substance and reality to the wild vagaries which his imagination ran riot continually in producing. Guasconti had not a deep heart—or, at all events, its depths were not sounded now; but he had a quick fancy, and an ardent southern temperament, which rose every instant to a higher fever pitch. Whether or not Beatrice possessed those terrible attributes, that fatal breath, the affinity with those so beautiful and deadly flowers which were indicated by what Giovanni had witnessed, she had at least instilled a fierce and subtle poison into his system. It was not love, although her rich beauty was a madness to him; nor horror, even while he fancied her spirit to be imbued with the same baneful essence that seemed to pervade her physical fame; but a wild offspring of both love and horror that had each parent in it, and burned like one and shivered like the other. Giovanni knew not what to dread; still less did he know what to hope; yet hope and dread kept a continual warfare in his breast, alternately vanquishing one another and starting up afresh to renew the contest. Blessed are all simple emotions, be they dark or bright! It is the lurid intermixture of the two that produces the illuminating blaze of the infernal regions.

Sometimes he endeavored to assuage the fever of his spirit by a rapid walk through the streets of Padua or beyond its gates: his footsteps kept time with the throbbings of his brain, so that the walk was apt to accelerate itself to a race. One day he found himself arrested; his arm was seized by a portly personage, who had turned back on recognizing the young man and expended much breath in overtaking him.

"Signor Giovanni! Stay, my young friend!" cried he. "Have you forgotten me? That might well be the case if I were as much altered as yourself."

It was Baglioni, whom Giovanni had avoided ever since their first meeting, from a doubt that the professor's sagacity would look too deeply into his secrets. Endeavoring to recover himself, he started forth wildly from his inner world into the outer one and spoke like a man in a dream.

"Yes; I am Giovanni Guasconti. You are Professor Pietro Baglioni. Now let me pass!"

"Not yet, not yet, Signor Giovanni Guasconti," said the professor, smiling, but at the same time scrutinizing the youth with an earnest glance. "What! did I grow up side by side with your father? and shall his son pass me like a stranger in these old streets of Padua? Stand still, Signor Giovanni; for we must have a word or two before we part."

"Speedily, then, most worshipful professor, speedily," said Giovanni, with feverish impatience. "Does not your worship see that I am in haste?"

Now, while he was speaking there came a man in black along the street, stooping and moving feebly like a person in inferior health. His face was all overspread with a most sickly and sallow hue, but yet so pervaded with an expression of piercing and active intellect that an observer might easily have overlooked the merely physical attributes and have seen only this wonderful energy. As he passed, this person exchanged a cold and distant salutation with Baglioni, but fixed his eyes upon Giovanni with an intentness that seemed to bring out whatever was within him worthy of notice. Nevertheless, there was a peculiar quietness in the look, as if taking merely a speculative, not human, interest in the young man.

"It is Dr. Rappaccini!" whispered the professor when the stranger had passed. "Has he ever seen your face before?"

"Not that I know," answered Giovanni, starting at the name.

"He *has* seen you! he must have seen you!" said Baglioni, hastily. "For some purpose or other, this man of science is making a study of you. I know that look of his! It is the same that coldly illuminates his face as he bends over a bird, a mouse, or a butterfly, which, in pursuance of some experiment, he has killed by the perfume of a flower; a look as deep as Nature itself, but without Nature's warmth of love. Signor Giovanni, I will stake my life upon it, you are the subject of one of Rappaccini's experiments!"

"Will you make a fool of me?" cried Giovanni, passionately, "*That,* signor professor, were an untoward experiment."

"Patience! patience!" replied the imperturbable professor. "I tell thee, my poor Giovanni, that Rappaccini has a scientific interest in thee. Thou hast fallen into fearful hands! And the Signora Beatrice,—what part does she act in this mystery?"

But Guasconti, finding Baglioni's pertinacity intolerable, here broke away, and was gone before the professor could again seize his arm. He looked after the young man intently and shook his head.

"This must not be," said Baglioni to himself. "The youth is the son of my old friend, and shall not come to any harm from which the arcana of medical science can preserve him. Besides, it is too insufferable an impertinence in Rappaccini thus to snatch the lad out of my own hands, as I may say, and make use of him for his infernal experiments. This daughter of his! It shall be looked to. Perchance, most learned Rappaccini, I may foil you where you little dream of it!"

Meanwhile Giovanni had pursued a circuitous route, and at length found himself at the door of his lodgings. As he crossed the threshold he was met by old Lisabetta, who smirked and smiled, and was evidently desirous to attract his attention; vainly, however, as the ebullition of his feelings had momentarily subsided into a cold and dull vacuity. He turned his eyes full upon the withered face that was puckering itself into a smile, but seemed to behold it not. The old dame, therefore, laid her grasp upon his cloak.

"Signor! signor!" whispered she, still with a smile over the whole breadth of her visage, so that it looked not unlike a grotesque carving in wood, darkened by centuries. "Listen, signor! There is a private entrance into the garden!"

"What do you say?" exclaimed Giovanni, turning quickly about, as if an inanimate thing should start into feverish life. "A private entrance into Dr. Rappaccini's garden?"

"Hush! hush! not so loud!" whispered Lisabetta, putting her hand over his mouth. "Yes, into the worshipful doctor's garden, where you may see all his fine shrubbery. Many a young man in Padua would give gold to be admitted among those flowers."

Giovanni put a piece of gold into her hand.

"Show me the way," said he.

A surmise, probably excited by his conversation with Baglioni, crossed his mind, that this interposition of old Lisabetta might perchance be connected with the intrigue, whatever were its nature, in which the professor seemed to suppose that Dr. Rappaccini was involving him. But such a suspicion, though it disturbed Giovanni, was inadequate to restrain him. The instant that he was aware of the possibility of approaching Beatrice, it seemed an absolute necessity of his existence to do so. It mattered not whether she were angel or demon; he was irrevocably within her sphere, and must obey the law that whirled him onward, in ever-lessening circles, towards a result which he did not attempt to foreshadow; and yet, strange to say, there came across him a sudden doubt whether this intense interest on his part were not delusory; whether it were really of so deep and positive a nature as to justify him in now thrusting himself into an incalculable position; whether it were not merely the fantasy of a young man's brain, only slightly or not at all connected with his heart.

He paused, hesitated, turned half about, but again went on. His withered guide led him along several obscure passages, and finally undid a door, through which, as it was opened, there came the sight and sound of rustling leaves, with the broken sunshine glimmering among them. Giovanni stepped forth, and, forcing himself through the entanglement of a shrub that wreathed its tendrils over the hidden entrance, stood beneath his own window in the open area of Dr. Rappaccini's garden.

How often is it the case that, when impossibilities have come to pass and dreams have condensed their misty substance into tangible realities, we find outselves calm, and even coldly self-possessed, amid circumstances which it would have been a delirium of joy or agony to anticipate! Fate delights to thwart us thus. Passion will choose his own time to rush upon the scene, and lingers sluggishly behind when an appropriate adjustment of events would seem to summon his appearance. So was it now with Giovanni. Day after day his pulses had throbbed with feverish blood at the improbable idea of an interview with Beatrice, and of standing with her, face to face, in this very garden, basking in the Oriental sunshine of her beauty, and snatching from her full gaze the mystery which he deemed the riddle of his own existence. But now there was a singular and untimely equanimity within his breast. He threw a glance around the garden to discover if Beatrice or her father were present, and, perceiving that he was alone, began a critical observation of the plants.

The aspect of one and all of them dissatisfied him; their gorgeousness seemed fierce, passionate, and even unnatural. There was hardly an individual shrub which a wanderer, straying by himself through a forest, would not have been startled to find growing wild, as if an unearthly face had glared at him out of the thicket. Several also would have shocked a delicate instinct by an appearance of artificialness indicating that there had been such commixture, and, as it were, adultery, of various vegetable species, that the production was no longer of God's making, but the monstrous offspring of man's depraved fancy, glowing with only an evil mockery of beauty. They were probably the result of experiment, which in one or two cases had succeeded in mingling plants individually lovely into a compound possessing the questionable and ominous character that distinguished the whole growth of the garden. In fine, Giovanni recognized but two or three plants in the collection, and those of a kind that he well knew to be poisonous. While busy with these contemplations he heard the rustling of a silken garment, and turning, beheld Beatrice emerging from beneath the sculptured portal.

Giovanni had not considered with himself what should be his deportment; whether he should apologize for his intrusion into the garden, or assume that he was there with the privity at least, if not by the desire, of Dr. Rappaccini or his daughter; but Beatrice's manner placed him at his ease, though leaving him still in doubt by what agency he had gained admittance. She came lightly along the path and met him near the broken fountain. There was surprise in her face, but brightened by a simple and kind expression of pleasure.

"You are a connoisseur in flowers, signor," said Beatrice, with a smile, alluding to the bouquet which he had flung her from the window. "It is no marvel, therefore, if the sight of my father's rare collection has tempted you to take a nearer view. If he were here, he could tell you many strange and interesting facts as to the nature and habits of these shrubs; for he has spent a lifetime in such studies, and this garden is his world."

"And yourself, lady," observed Giovanni, "if fame says true,—you likewise are deeply skilled in the virtues indicated by these rich blossoms and these spicy perfumes. Would you deign to be my instructress, I should prove an apter scholar than if taught by Signor Rappaccini himself."

"Are there such idle rumors?" asked Beatrice, with the music of a pleasant laugh. "Do people say that I am skilled in my father's science of plants? What a jest is there! No; though I have grown up among these flowers, I know no more of them than their hues and perfume; and sometimes methinks I would fain rid myself of even that small knowledge. There are many flowers here, and those not the least brilliant, that shock and offend me when they meet my eye. But pray, signor, do not believe these stories about my science. Believe nothing of me save what you see with your own eyes."

"And must I believe all that I have seen with my own eyes?" asked Giovanni, pointedly, while the recollection of former scenes made him shrink. "No, signora, you demand too little of me. Bid me believe nothing save what comes from your own lips."

It would appear that Beatrice understood him. There came a deep flush to her cheek; but she looked full into Giovanni's eyes, and responded to his gaze of uneasy suspicion with a queenlike haughtiness.

"I do so bid you, signor," she replied. "Forget whatever you may have fancied in regard to me. If true to the outward senses, still it may be false in its essence; but the words of Beatrice Rappaccini's lips are true from the depths of the heart outward. Those you may believe."

A fervor glowed in her whole aspect and beamed upon Giovanni's consciousness like the light of truth itself; but while she spoke there was a fragrance in the atmosphere around her, rich and delightful, though evanescent, yet which the young man, from an indefinable reluctance, scarcely dared to draw into his lungs. It might be the odor of the flowers. Could it be Beatrice's breath which thus embalmed her words with a strange richness, as if by steeping them in her heart? A faintness passed like a shadow over Giovanni and flitted away; he seemed to gaze through the beautiful girl's eyes into her transparent soul, and felt no more doubt or fear.

The tinge of passion that had colored Beatrice's manner vanished; she became gay, and appeared to derive a pure delight from her communion with the youth not unlike what the maiden of a lonely island might have felt conversing with a voyager from the civilized world. Evidently her experience of life had been confined within the limits of that garden. She talked now about matters as simple as the daylight or summer clouds, and now asked questions in reference to the city, or Giovanni's distant home, his friends, his mother, and his sister—questions indicating such seclusion, and such lack of familiarity with modes and forms, that Giovanni responded as if to an infant. Her spirit gushed out before him like a fresh rill that was just catching its first glimpse of the sunlight and wondering at the reflections of earth and sky which were flung into its bosom. There came thoughts, too, from a deep source, and fantasies of a gemlike brilliancy, as if diamonds and rubies sparkled upward among the bubbles of the fountain. Ever and anon there gleamed across the young man's mind a sense of wonder that he should be walking side by side with the being who had so wrought upon his imagination, whom he had idealized in such hues of terror, in whom he had positively witnessed such manifestations of dreadful attributes—that he should be conversing with Beatrice like a brother, and should find her so human and so maidenlike. But such reflections were only momentary; the effect of her character was too real not to make itself familiar at once.

In this free intercourse they had strayed through the garden, and now, after many turns among its avenues, were come to the shattered fountain, besides which grew the magnificent shrub, with its treasury of glowing blossoms. A fragrance was diffused from it which Giovanni recognized as identical with that which he had attributed to Beatrice's breath, but incomparably more powerful. As her eyes fell upon it, Giovanni beheld her press her hand to her bosom as if her heart were throbbing suddenly and painfully.

"For the first time in my life," murmured she, addressing the shrub, "I had forgotten thee."

"I remember, signora," said Giovanni, "that you once promised to reward me with one of these living gems for the bouquet which I had the happy boldness to fling to your feet. Permit me now to pluck it as a memorial of this interview."

He made a step towards the shrub with extended hand; but Beatrice darted forward, uttering a shriek that went through his heart like a dagger. She caught his hand and drew it back with the whole force of her slender figure. Giovanni felt her touch thrilling through his fibres.

"Touch it not!" exclaimed she, in a voice of agony. "Not for thy life! It is fatal!"

Then, hiding her face, she fled from him and vanished beneath the sculptured portal. As Giovanni followed her with his eyes, he beheld the emaciated figure and pale intelligence of Dr. Rappaccini, who had been watching the scene, he knew not how long, within the shadow of the entrance.

No sooner was Guasconti alone in his chamber than the image of Beatrice came back to his passionate musings, invested with all the witchery that had been gathering around it ever since his first glimpse of her, and now likewise imbued with a tender warmth of girlish womanhood. She was human; her nature was endowed with all gentle and feminine qualities; she was worthiest to be worshipped; she was capable, surely, on her part, of the height and heroism of love. Those tokens which he had hitherto considered as proofs of a frightful peculiarity in her physical and moral system were now either forgotten or by the subtle sophistry of passion transmitted into a golden crown of enchantment, rendering Beatrice the more admirable by so much as she was the more unique. Whatever had looked ugly was now beautiful; or, if incapable of such a change, it stole away and hid itself among those shapeless half ideas which throng the dim region beyond the daylight of our perfect consciousness. Thus did he spend the night, nor fell asleep until the dawn had begun to awake the slumbering flowers in Dr. Rappaccini's garden, whither Giovanni's dreams doubtless led him. Up rose the sun in his due season, and, flinging his beams upon the young man's eyelids, awoke him to a sense of pain. When thoroughly aroused, he became sensible of a burning and tingling agony in his hand—in his right hand—the very hand which Beatrice had grasped in her own when he was on the point of plucking one of the gemlike flowers. On the back of that hand there was now a purple print like that of four small fingers, and the likeness of a slender thumb upon his wrist.

O, how stubbornly does love,—or even that cunning semblance of love which flourishes in the imagination, but strikes no depth of root into the heart,—how stubbornly does it hold its faith until the moment comes when it is doomed to vanish into thin mist! Giovanni wrapped a handkerchief about his hand and wondered what evil thing had stung him, and soon forgot his pain in a reverie of Beatrice.

After the first interview, a second was in the inevitable course of what we call fate. A third; a fourth; and a meeting with Beatrice in the garden was no longer an incident in Giovanni's daily life, but the whole space in which he might be said to live; for the anticipation and memory of that ecstatic hour made up the remainder. Nor was it otherwise with the daughter of Rappaccini. She watched for the youth's appearance and flew to his side with confidence as unreserved as if they had been playmates from early infancy—as if they were such playmates still. If, by any unwonted chance, he failed to come at the appointed moment, she stood beneath the window and sent up the rich sweetness of her tones to float around him in his chamber and echo and reverberate throughout his heart: "Giovanni! Giovanni! Why tarriest thou? Come down!" And down he hastened into that Eden of poisonous flowers.

But, with all this intimate familiarity, there was still a reserve in Beatrice's demeanor, so rigidly and invariably sustained that the idea of infringing it scarcely occurred to his imagination. By all appreciable signs, they loved; they had looked love with eyes that conveyed the holy secret from the depths of one soul into the depths of the other, as if it were too sacred to be whispered by the way; they had even spoken love in those gushes of passion when their spirits darted forth in articulated breath like tongues of long hidden flame; and yet there had been no seal of lips, no clasp of hands, nor any slightest caress such as love claims and hallows. He had never touched one of the gleaming ringlets of her hair; her garment—so marked was the physical barrier between them—had never been waved against him by a breeze. On the few occasions when Giovanni had seemed tempted to overstep the limit, Beatrice grew so sad, so stern, and withal wore such a look of desolate separation, shuddering at itself, that not a spoken word was requisite to repel him. At such times he was startled at the horrible suspicions that rose, monster-like, out of the caverns of his heart and stared him in the face; his love grew thin and faint as the morning mist; his doubts alone had substance. But, when Beatrice's face brightened again after the momentary shadow, she was transformed at once from the mysterious, questionable being whom he had watched with so much awe and horror; she was now the beautiful and unsophisticated girl whom he felt that his spirit knew with a certainty beyond all other knowledge.

A considerable time had now passed since Giovanni's last meeting with Baglioni. One morning, however, he was disagreeably surprised by a visit from the professor, whom he had scarcely thought of for whole weeks, and would willingly have forgotten still longer. Given up as he had long been to a pervading excitement, he could tolerate no companions except upon condition of their perfect sympathy with his present state of feeling. Such sympathy was not to be expected from professor Baglioni.

The visitor chatted carelessly for a few moments about the gossip of the city and the university, and then took up another topic.

"I have been reading an old classic author lately," said he, "and met with a story that strangely interested me. Possibly you may remember it. It is of an Indian prince, who sent a beautiful woman as a present to Alexander the Great. She was as lovely as the dawn and gorgeous as the sunset; but what especially distinguished her was a certain rich perfume in her breath—richer than a garden of Persian roses. Alexander, as was natural to a youthful conqueror, fell in love at first sight with this magnificent stranger; but a certain sage physician, happening to be present, discovered a terrible secret in regard to her."

"And what was that?" asked Giovanni, turning his eyes downward to avoid those of the professor.

"That this lovely woman," continued Baglioni, with emphasis, "had been nourished with poisons from her birth upward, until her whole nature was so imbued with them that she herself had become the deadliest poison in existence. Poison was her element of life. With that rich perfume of her breath she blasted the very air. Her love would have been poison—her embrace death. Is not this a marvellous tale?"

"A childish fable," answered Giovanni, nervously starting from his chair. "I marvel how your worship finds time to read such nonsense among your graver studies."

"By the by," said the professor, looking uneasily about him, "what singular fragrance is this in your apartment? Is it the perfume of your gloves? It is faint, but delicious; and yet, after all, by no means agreeable. Were I to breathe it long, methinks it would make me ill. It is like the breath of a flower; but I see no flowers in the chamber."

"Nor are there any," replied Giovanni, who had turned pale as the professor spoke; "nor, I think, is there any fragrance except in your worship's imagination. Odors, being a sort of element combined of the sensual and the spiritual, are apt to deceive us in this manner. The recollection of a perfume, the bare idea of it, may easily be mistaken for a present reality."

"Ay; but my sober imagination does not often play such tricks," said Baglioni; "and, were I to fancy any kind of odor, it would be that of some vile apothecary drug, wherewith my fingers are likely enough to be imbued. Our worshipful friend Rappaccini, as I have heard, tinctures his medicaments with odors richer than those of Araby. Doubtless, likewise, the fair and learned Signora Beatrice would minister to her patients with draughts as sweet as a maiden's breath; but woe to him that sips them!"

Giovanni's face evinced many contending emotions. The tone in which the professor alluded to the pure and lovely daughter of Rappaccini was a torture to his soul; and yet the intimation of a view of her character, opposite to his own, gave instantaneous distinctness to a thousand dim suspicions, which now grinned at him like so many demons. But he strove hard to quell them and to respond to Baglioni with a true lover's perfect faith.

"Signor professor," said he, "you were my father's friend; perchance, too, it is your purpose to act a friendly part towards his son. I would fain feel nothing towards you save respect and deference; but I pray you to observe, signor, that there is one subject on which we must not speak. You know not the Signora Beatrice. You cannot, therefore, estimate the wrong—the blasphemy, I may even say—that is offered to her character by a light or injurious word."

"Giovanni! my poor Giovanni!" answered the professor, with a calm expression of pity. "I know this wretched girl far better than yourself. You shall hear the truth in respect to the poisoner Rappaccini and his poisonous daughter; yes, poisonous as she is beautiful. Listen; for, even should you do violence to my gray hairs, it shall not silence me. That old fable of the Indian woman has become a truth by the deep and deadly science of Rappaccini and in the person of the lovely Beatrice."

Giovanni groaned and hid his face.

"Her father," continued Baglioni, "was not restrained by natural affection from offering up his child in this horrible manner as the victim of his insane zeal for science; for, let us do him justice, he is as true a man of science as ever distilled his own heart in an alembic. What, then, will be your fate? Beyond a doubt you are selected as the material of some new experiment. Perhaps the result is to be death; perhaps a fate more awful still. Rappaccini, with what he calls the interest of science before his eyes, will hesitate at nothing."

"It is a dream," muttered Giovanni to himself; "surely it is a dream."

"But," resumed the professor, "be of good cheer, son of my friend. It is not yet too late for the rescue. Possibly we may even succeed in bringing back this miserable child within the limits of ordinary nature, from which her father's madness has estranged her. Behold this little silver vase! It was wrought by the hands of the renowned Benvenuto Cellini, and is well worthy to be a love gift to the fairest dame in Italy. But its contents are invaluable. One little sip of this antidote would have rendered the most virulent poisons of the Borgias innocuous. Doubt not that it will be as efficacious against those of Rappaccini. Bestow the vase, and the precious liquid within it, on your Beatrice, and hopefully await the result."

Baglioni laid a small, exquisitely wrought silver vial on the table and withdrew, leaving what he had said to produce its effects upon the young man's mind.

"We will thwart Rappaccini yet," thought he, chuckling to himself, as he descended the stairs; "but, let us confess the truth of him, he is a wonderful man—a wonderful man indeed; a vile empiric, however, in his practice, and therefore not to be tolerated by those who respect the good old rules of the medical profession."

Throughout Giovanni's whole acquaintance with Beatrice, he had occasionally, as we have said, been haunted by dark surmises as to her character; yet so thoroughly had she made herself felt by him as a simple, natural, most affectionate, and guileless creature, that the image now held up by Professor Baglioni looked as strange and incredible as if it were not in accordance with his own original conception. True, there were ugly recollections connected with his first glimpses of the beautiful girl; he could not quite forget the bouquet that withered in her grasp, and the insect that perished amid the sunny air, by no ostensible agency save the fragrance of her breath. These incidents, however, dissolving in the pure light of her character, had no longer the efficacy of facts, but were acknowledged as mistaken fantasies, by whatever testimony of the senses they might appear to be substantiated. There is something truer and more real than what we can see with the eyes and touch with the finger. On such better evidence had Giovanni founded his confidence in Beatrice, though rather by the necessary force of her high attributes than by any deep and generous faith on his part. But now his spirit was incapable of sustaining itself at the height to which the early enthusiasm of passion had exalted it; he fell down, grovelling among earthly doubts, and defiled therewith the pure whiteness of Beatrice's image. Not that he gave her up; he did but distrust. He resolved to institute some decisive test that should satisfy him, once for all, whether there were those dreadful peculiarities in her physical nature which could not be supposed to exist without some corresponding monstrosity of soul. His eyes, gazing down afar, might have deceived him as to the lizard, the insect, and the flowers; but if he could witness, at the distance of a few paces, the sudden blight of one fresh and healthful flower in Beatrice's hand, there would be room for no further question. With this idea he hastened to the florist's and purchased a bouquet that was still gemmed with the morning dewdrops.

It was now the customary hour of his daily interview with Beatrice. Before descending into the garden, Giovanni failed not to look at his figure in the mirror—a vanity to be expected in a beautiful young man, yet, as displaying itself at that troubled and feverish moment, the token of a certain shallowness of feeling and insincerity of character. He did gaze, however, and said to himself that his features had never before possessed so rich a grace, nor his eyes such vivacity, nor his cheeks so warm a hue of super-abundant life.

"At least," thought he, "her poison has not yet insinuated itself into my system. I am no flower to perish in her grasp."

With that thought he turned his eyes on the bouquet, which he had never once laid aside from his hand. A thrill of indefinable horror shot through his frame on perceiving that those dewy flowers were already beginning to droop; they wore the aspect of things that had been fresh and lovely yesterday. Giovanni grew white as marble, and stood motionless before the mirror, staring at his own reflection there as at the likeness of something frightful. He remembered Baglioni's remark about the fragrance that seemed to pervade the chamber. It must have been the poison in his breath! Then he shuddered—shuddered at himself. Recovering from his stupor, he began to watch with curious eye a spider that was busily at work hanging its web from the antique cornice of the apartment, crossing and recrossing the artful system of interwoven lines—as vigorous and active a spider as ever dangled from an old ceiling. Giovanni bent towards the insect, and emitted a deep, long breath. The spider suddenly ceased its toil; the web vibrated with a tremor originating in the body of the small artisan. Again Giovanni sent forth a breath, deeper, longer, and imbued with a venomous feeling out of his heart: he knew not whether he were wicked, or only desperate. The spider made a convulsive gripe with his limbs and hung dead across the window.

"Accursed! accursed!" muttered Giovanni, addressing himself. "Hast thou grown so poisonous that this deadly insect perishes by thy breath?"

At that moment a rich, sweet voice came floating up from the garden.

"Giovanni! Giovanni! It is past the hour! Why tarriest thou? Come down!"

"Yes," muttered Giovanni again. "She is the only being whom my breath may not slay! Would that it might!"

He rushed down, and in an instant was standing before the bright and loving eyes of Beatrice. A moment ago his wrath and despair had been so fierce that he could have desired nothing so much as to wither

her by a glance; but with her actual presence there came influences which had too real an existence to be at once shaken off; recollections of the delicate and benign power of her feminine nature, which had so often enveloped him in a religious calm; recollections of many a holy and passionate outgush of her heart, when the pure fountain had been unsealed from its depths and made visible in its transparency to his mental eye; recollections which, had Giovanni known how to estimate them, would have assured him that all this ugly mystery was but an earthly illusion, and that, whatever mist of evil might seem to have gathered over her, the real Beatrice was a heavenly angel. Incapable as he was of such high faith, still her presence had not utterly lost its magic. Giovanni's rage was quelled into an aspect of sullen insensibility. Beatrice, with a quick spiritual sense, immediately felt that there was a gulf of blackness between them which neither he nor she could pass. They walked on together, sad and silent, and came thus to the marble fountain and to its pool of water on the ground, in the midst of which grew the shrub that bore gemlike blossoms. Giovanni was affrighted at the eager enjoyment—the appetite, as it were—with which he found himself inhaling the fragrance of the flowers.

"Beatrice," asked he, abruptly, "whence came this shrub?"

"My father created it," answered she, with simplicity.

"Created it! created it!" repeated Giovanni. "What mean you, Beatrice?"

"He is a man fearfully acquainted with the secrets of Nature," replied Beatrice; "and at the hour when I first drew breath, this plant sprang from the soil, the offspring of his science, of his intellect, while I was but his earthly child. Approach it not!" continued she, observing with terror that Giovanni was drawing nearer to the shrub. "It has qualities that you little dream of. But I, dearest Giovanni,—I grew up and blossomed with the plant and was nourished with its breath. It was my sister, and I loved it with a human affection; for, alas!—hast thou not suspected it?—there was an awful doom."

Here Giovanni frowned so darkly upon her that Beatrice paused and trembled. But her faith in his tenderness reassured her, and made her blush that she had doubted for an instant.

"There was an awful doom," she continued, "the effect of my father's fatal love of science, which estranged me from all society of my kind. Until Heaven sent thee, dearest Giovanni, O, how lonely was thy poor Beatrice!"

"Was it a hard doom?" asked Giovanni fixing his eyes upon her.

"Only of late have I known how hard it was," answered she, tenderly. "O, yes; but my heart was torpid, and therefore quiet."

Giovanni's rage broke forth from his sullen gloom like a lightning flash out of a dark cloud.

"Accursed one!" cried he, with venomous scorn and anger. "And, finding thy solitude wearisome, thou has severed me likewise from all the warmth of life and enticed me into thy region of unspeakable horror!"

"Giovanni!" exclaimed Beatrice, turning her large bright eyes upon his face. The force of his words had not found its way into her mind; she was merely thunderstruck.

"Yes, poisonous thing!" repeated Giovanni, beside himself with passion. "Thou hast done it! Thou hast blasted me! Thou hast filled my veins with poison! Thou hast made me as hateful, as ugly, as loathsome and deadly a creature as thyself—a world's wonder of hideous monstrosity! Now, if our breath be happily as fatal to ourselves as to all others, let us join our lips in one kiss of unutterable hatred, and so die!"

"What has befallen me?" murmured Beatrice, with a low moan out of her heart. "Holy Virgin, pity me, a poor heart-broken child!"

"Thou—dost thou pray?" cried Giovanni, still with the same fiendish scorn. "Thy very prayers, as they come from thy lips, taint the atmosphere with death. Yes, yes; let us pray! Let us to church and dip our fingers in the holy water at the portal! They that come after us will perish as by a pestilence! Let us sign crosses in the air! It will be scattering curses abroad in the likeness of holy symbols!"

"Giovanni," said Beatrice, calmly, for her grief was beyond passion, "why doest thou join thyself with me thus in those terrible words? I, it is true, am the horrible thing thou namest me. But thou, —what hast thou to do, save with one other shudder at my hideous misery to go forth out of the garden and mingle with thy race, and forget that there ever crawled on earth such a monster as poor Beatrice?"

"Dost thou pretend ignorance?" asked Giovanni, scowling upon her. "Behold! this power have I gained from the pure daughter of Rappaccini."

There was a swarm of summer insects flitting through the air in search of the food promised by the flower odors of the fatal garden. They circled round Giovanni's head, and were evidently attracted towards him by the same influence which had drawn them for an instant within the sphere of several of the shrubs. He sent forth a breath among them, and smiled bitterly at Beatrice as at least a score of the insects fell dead upon the ground.

"I see it! I see it!" shrieked Beatrice. "It is my father's fatal science! No, no, Giovanni; it was not I! Never! never! I dreamed only to love thee and be with thee a little time, and so to let thee pass away, leaving but thine image in my heart; for, Giovanni, believe it, though my body be nourished with poison, my spirit is God's creature, and craves love as its daily food. But my father,—he has united us in this fearful sympathy. Yes; spurn me, tread upon me, kill me! O, what is death after such words as thine? But it was not I. Not for a world of bliss would I have done it."

Giovanni's passion had exhausted itself in its outburst from his lips. There now came across him a sense, mournful, and not without tenderness, of the intimate and peculiar relationship between Beatrice and himself. They stood, as it were, in an utter solitude, which would be made none the less solitary by the densest throng of human life. Ought not, then, the desert of humanity around them to press this insulated pair closer together? If they should be cruel to one another, who was there to be kind to them? Besides, thought Giovanni, might there not still be a hope of his returning within the limits of ordinary nature, and leading Beatrice, the redeemed Beatrice, by the hand? O, weak, and selfish, and unworthy spirit, that could dream of an earthly union and earthly happiness as possible, after such deep love had been so bitterly wronged as was Beatrice's love by Giovanni's blighting words! No, no; there could be no such hope. She must pass heavily, with that broken heart, across the borders of Time—she must bathe her hurts in some fount of paradise, and forget her grief in the light of immortality, and *there* be well.

But Giovanni did not know it.

"Dear Beatrice," said he approaching her, while she shrank as always at his approach, but now with a different impulse, "dearest Beatrice, our fate is not yet so desperate. Behold! there is a medicine, potent as a wise physician has assured me, and almost divine in its efficacy. It is composed of ingredients the most opposite to those by which thy awful father has brought this calamity upon thee and me. It is distilled of blessed herbs. Shall we not quaff it together, and thus be purified from evil?"

"Give it me!" said Beatrice, extending her hand to receive the little silver vial which Giovanni took from his bosom. She added, with a peculiar emphasis, "I will drink; but do thou await the result."

She put Baglioni's antidote to her lips; and, at the same moment, the figure of Rappaccini emerged from the portal and came slowly towards the marble fountain. As he drew near, the pale man of science seemed to gaze with a triumphant expression at the beautiful youth and maiden, as might an artist who should spend his life in achieving a picture or a group of statuary and finally be satisfied with his success. He paused; his bent form grew erect with conscious power; he spread out his hands over them in the attitude of a father imploring a blessing upon his children; but those were the same hands that had thrown poison into the stream of their lives. Giovanni trembled. Beatrice shuddered nervously, and pressed her hand upon her heart.

"My daughter," said Rappaccini, "thou art no longer lonely in the world. Pluck one of those precious gems from thy sister shrub and bid thy bridegroom wear it in his bosom. It will not harm him now. My science and the sympathy between thee and him have so wrought within his system that he now stands apart from common men, as thou dost, daughter of my pride and triumph, from ordinary women. Pass on, then, through the world, most dear to one another and dreadful to all besides!"

"My father," said Beatrice, feebly—and still as she spoke she kept her hand upon her heart—"wherefore didst thou inflict this miserable doom upon thy child?"

"Miserable!" exclaimed Rappaccini. "What mean you, foolish girl? Dost thou deem it misery to be endowed with marvelous gifts against which no power nor strength could avail an enemy—misery, to be able to quell the mightiest with a breath—misery, to be as terrible as thou art beautiful? Wouldst thou, then, have preferred the condition of a weak woman, exposed to all evil and capable of none?"

"I would fain have been loved, not feared," murmured Beatrice, sinking down upon the ground. "But now it matters not. I am going, father, where the evil which thou hast striven to mingle with my being will pass away like a dream—like the fragrance of these poisonous flowers, which will no longer taint my breath among the flowers of Eden. Farewell, Giovanni! Thy words of hatred are like lead within my heart; but they, too, will fall away as I ascend. O, was there not, from the first, more poison in thy nature than in mine?"

To Beatrice—so radically had her earthly part been wrought upon by Rappaccini's skill—as poison had been life, so the powerful antidote was death; and thus the poor victim of man's ingenuity and of thwarted nature, and of the fatality that attends all such efforts of perverted wisdom, perished there, at the feet of her father and Giovanni. Just at that moment Professor Pietro Baglioni looked forth from the window, and called loudly, in a tone of triumph mixed with horror, to the thunderstricken man of science—

"Rappaccini! Rappaccini! and is *this* the upshot of your experiment!"

Edgar Allan Poe (1809–1849)

THE PURLOINED LETTER

Nil sapientiæ odiosius acumine nimio.
[Nothing is more troublesome than too much keenness of discernment.]
Seneca

At Paris, just after dark one gusty evening in the autumn of 18–, I was enjoying the twofold luxury of meditation and a meerschaum, in company with my friend C. Auguste Dupin, in his little back library, or book-closet, *au troisième, No. 33 Rue Dunôt, Faubourg St. Germain.* For one hour at least we had maintained a profound silence; while each, to any casual observer, might have seemed intently and exclusively occupied with the curling eddies of smoke that oppressed the atmosphere of the chamber. For myself, however, I was mentally discussing certain topics which had formed matter for conversation between us at an earlier period of the evening; I mean the affair of the Rue Morgue, and the mystery attending the murder of Marie Rogêt. I looked upon it, therefore, as something of a coincidence, when the door of our apartment was thrown open and admitted our old acquaintance, Monsieur G——, the Prefect of the Parisian police.

We gave him a hearty welcome; for there was nearly half as much of the entertaining as of the contemptible about the man, and we had not seen him for several years. We had been sitting in the dark, and Dupin now arose for the purpose of lighting a lamp, but sat down again, without doing so, upon G.'s saying that he had called to consult us, or rather to ask the opinion of my friend, about some official business which had occasioned a great deal of trouble.

"If it is any point requiring reflection," observed Dupin, as he forbore to enkindle the wick, "we shall examine it to better purpose in the dark."

"That is another of your odd notions," said the Prefect, who had a fashion of calling every thing "odd" that was beyond his comprehension, and thus lived amid an absolute legion of "oddities."

"Very true," said Dupin, as he supplied his visitor with a pipe, and rolled towards him a comfortable chair.

"And what is the difficulty now?" I asked. "Nothing more in the assassination way, I hope?"

"Oh no; nothing of that nature. The fact is, the business is *very* simple indeed, and I make no doubt that we can manage it sufficiently well ourselves; but then I thought Dupin would like to hear the details of it, because it is so excessively *odd.*"

"Simple and odd," said Dupin.

"Why, yes; and not exactly that either. The fact is, we have all been a good deal puzzled because the affair *is* so simple, and yet baffles us altogether."

"Perhaps it is the very simplicity of the thing which puts you at fault," said my friend.

"What nonsense you *do* talk!" replied the Prefect, laughing heartily.

"Perhaps the mystery is a little *too* plain," said Dupin.

"Oh, good heavens! who ever heard of such an idea?"

"A little *too* self-evident."

"Ha! ha! ha!—ha! ha! ha!—ho! ho! ho"—roared our visitor, profoundly amused, "oh, Dupin, you will be the death of me yet!"

"And what, after all, *is* the matter on hand?" I asked.

"Why, I will tell you," replied the Prefect, as he gave a long, steady, and contemplative puff, and settled himself in his chair. "I will tell you in a few words; but, before I begin, let me caution you that this is an affair demanding the greatest secrecy, and that I should most probably lose the position I now hold, were it known that I confided it to any one."

"Proceed," said I.

"Or not," said Dupin.

"Well, then; I have received personal information, from a very high quarter, that a certain document of the last importance, has been purloined from the royal apartments. The individual who purloined it is known; this beyond a doubt; he was seen to take it. It is known, also, that it still remains in his possession."

"How is this known?" asked Dupin.

"It is clearly inferred," replied the Prefect, "from the nature of the document, and from the non-appearance of certain results which would at once arise from its passing *out* of the robber's possession;—that is to say, from his employing it as he must design in the end to employ it."

"Be a little more explicit," I said.

"Well, I may venture so far as to say that the paper gives its holder a certain power in a certain quarter where such power is immensely valuable." The Prefect was fond of the cant of diplomacy.

"Still I do not quite understand," said Dupin.

"No? Well; the disclosure of the document to a third person, who shall be nameless, would bring in question the honor of a personage of most exalted station; and this fact gives the holder of the document an ascendancy over the illustrious personage whose honor and peace are so jeopardized."

"But this ascendancy," I interposed, "would depend upon the robber's knowledge of the loser's knowledge of the robber. Who would dare—"

"The thief," said G., "is the Minister D——, who dares all things, those unbecoming as well as those becoming a man. The method of the theft was not less ingenious than bold. The document in question—a letter, to be frank—had been received by the personage robbed while alone in the royal *boudoir*. During its perusal she was suddenly interrupted by the entrance of the other exalted personage from whom especially it was her wish to conceal it. After a hurried and vain endeavor to thrust it in a drawer, she was forced to place it, open as it was, upon a table. The address, however, was uppermost, and, the contents thus unexposed, the letter escaped notice. At this juncture enters the Minister D——. His lynx eye immediately perceives the paper, recognizes the handwriting of the address, observes the confusion of the personage addressed, and fathoms her secret. After some business transactions, hurried through in his ordinary manner, he produces a letter somewhat similar to the one in question, opens it, pretends to read it, and then places it in close juxtaposition to the other. Again he converses, for some fifteen minutes, upon the public affairs. At length, in taking leave, he takes also from the table the letter to which he had no claim. Its rightful owner saw, but, of course, dared not call attention to the act, in the presence of the third personage who stood at her elbow. The minister decamped; leaving his own letter—one of no importance—upon the table."

"Here, then," said Dupin to me, "you have precisely what you demand to make the ascendancy complete—the robber's knowledge of the loser's knowledge of the robber."

"Yes," replied the Prefect; "and the power thus attained has, for some months past, been wielded, for political purposes, to a very dangerous extent. The personage robbed is more thoroughly convinced, every day, of the necessity of reclaiming her letter. But this, or course, cannot be done openly. In fine, driven to despair, she has committed the matter to me."

"Than whom," said Dupin, amid a perfect whirlwind of smoke, "no more sagacious agent could, I suppose, be desired, or even imagined."

"You flatter me," replied the Prefect; "but it is possible that some such opinion may have been entertained."

"It is clear," said I, "as you observe, that the letter is still in the possession of the minister; since it is this possession, and not any employment of the letter, which bestows the power. With the employment the power departs."

"True," said G.; "and upon this conviction I proceeded. My first care was to make thorough search of the minister's hotel; and here my chief embarrassment lay in the necessity of searching without his knowledge. Beyond all things, I have been warned of the danger which would result from giving him reason to suspect our design."

"But," said I, "you are quite *au fait* in these investigations. The Parisian police have done this thing often before."

"O yes; and for this reason I did not despair. The habits of the minister gave me, too, a great advantage. He is frequently absent from home all night. His servants are by no means numerous. They sleep at a distance from their master's apartment, and being chiefly Neapolitans, are readily made drunk. I have keys, as you know, with which I can open any chamber or cabinet in Paris. For three months a night has not passed, during the greater part of which I have not been engaged, personally, in ransacking the D—— Hôtel. My honor is interested, and, to mention a great secret, the reward is enormous. So I did not abandon the search until I had become fully satisfied that the thief is a more astute man than myself. I fancy that I have investigated every nook and corner of the premises in which it is possible that the paper can be concealed."

"But is it not possible," I suggested, "that although the letter may be in possession of the minister, as it unquestionably is, he may have concealed it elsewhere than upon his own premises?"

"This is barely possible," said Dupin. "The present peculiar condition of affairs at court, and especially of those intrigues in which D—— is known to be involved, would render the instant availability of the document—its susceptibility of being produced at a moment's notice—a point of nearly equal importance with its possession."

"Its susceptibility of being produced?" said I.

"That is to say, of being *destroyed,"* said Dupin.

"True," I observed; "the paper is clearly then upon the premises. As for its being upon the person of the minister, we may consider that as out of the question."

"Entirely," said the Prefect. "He had been twice waylaid, as if by foot-pads, and his person rigorously searched under my own inspection."

"You might have spared yourself this trouble," said Dupin. "D——, I presume, is not altogether a fool, and, if not, must have anticipated these waylayings, as a matter of course."

"Not *altogether* a fool," said G., "but then he is a poet, which I take to be only one remove from a fool."

"True," said Dupin, after a long and thoughtful whiff from his meerschaum, "although I have been guilty of certain doggerel myself."

"Suppose you detail," said I, "the particulars of your search."

"Why the fact is, we took our time, and we searched *every where.* I have had long experience in these affairs. I took the entire building, room by room; devoting the nights of a whole week to each. We examined, first, the furniture of each apartment. We opened every possible drawer; and I presume you know that, to a properly trained police agent, such a thing as a *secret* drawer is impossible. Any man is a dolt who permits a 'secret' drawer to escape him in a search of this kind. The thing is *so* plain. There is a certain amount of bulk—of space—to be accounted for in every cabinet. Then we have accurate rules. The fiftieth part of a line could not escape us. After the cabinets we took the chairs. The cushions we probed with the fine long needles you have seen me employ. From the tables we removed the tops."

"Why so?"

"Sometimes the top of a table, or other similarly arranged piece of furniture, is removed by the person wishing to conceal an article;

then the leg is excavated, the article deposited within the cavity, and the top replaced. The bottoms and tops of bedposts are employed in the same way."

"But could not the cavity be detected by sounding?" I asked.

"By no means, if, when the article is deposited, a sufficient wadding of cotton be placed around it. Besides, in our case, we were obliged to proceed without noise."

"But you could not have removed—you could not have taken to pieces *all* articles of furniture in which it would have been possible to make a deposit in the manner you mention. A letter may be compressed into a thin spiral roll, not differing much in shape or bulk from a large knitting-needle, and in this form it might be inserted into the rung of a chair, for example. You did not take to pieces all the chairs?"

"Certainly not; but we did better—we examined the rungs of every chair in the hotel, and indeed the jointings of every description of furniture, by the aid of a most powerful microscope. Had there been any traces of recent disturbance we should not have failed to detect it instantly. A single grain of gimlet-dust, for example, would have been as obvious as an apple. Any disorder in the glueing—any unusual gaping in the joints—would have sufficed to insure detection."

"I presume you looked to the mirrors, between the boards and the plates, and you probed the beds and the bed-clothes, as well as the curtains and carpets."

"That of course; and when we had absolutely completed every particle of the furniture in this way, then we examined the house itself. We divided its entire surface into compartments, which we numbered, so that none might be missed; then we scrutinized each individual square inch throughout the premises, including the two houses immediately adjoining, with the microscope as before."

"The two houses adjoining!" I exclaimed; "you must have had a great deal of trouble."

"We had; but the reward offered is prodigious."

"You include the *grounds* about the houses?"

"All the grounds are paved with brick. They gave us comparatively little trouble. We examined the moss between the bricks, and found it undisturbed."

"You looked among D——'s papers, of course, and into the books of the library?"

"Certainly; we opened every package and parcel; we not only opened every book, but we turned over every leaf in each volume, not contenting ourselves with a mere shake, according to the fashion of some of our police officers. We also measured the thickness of every book-*cover,* with the most accurate admeasurement, and applied to each the most jealous scrutiny of the microscope. Had any of the bindings been recently meddled with, it would have been utterly impossible that the fact should have escaped observation. Some five or six volumes, just from the hands of the binder, we carefully probed, longitudinally, with the needles."

"You explored the floors beneath the carpets?"

"Beyond doubt. We removed every carpet, and examined the boards with the microscope."

"And the paper on the walls?"

"Yes."

"You looked into the cellars?"

"We did."

"Then," I said, "you have been making a miscalculation, and the letter is *not* upon the premises as you suppose."

"I fear you are right there," said the Prefect. "And now, Dupin, what would you advise me to do?"

"To make a thorough re-search of the premises."

"That is absolutely needless," replied G——. "I am not more sure that I breathe than I am that the letter is not at the Hôtel."

"I have no better advice to give you," said Dupin. "You have, of course, an accurate description of the letter?"

"Oh, yes!"—And here the Prefect, producing a memorandum-book, proceeded to read aloud a minute account of the internal, and especially of the external, appearance of the missing document. Soon after finishing the perusal of this description, he took his departure, more entirely depressed in spirits than I had ever known the good gentleman before.

In about a month afterward he paid us another visit, and found us occupied very nearly as before. He took a pipe and a chair and entered into some ordinary conversation. At length I said;—

"Well, but G——, what of the purloined letter? I presume you have at last made up your mind that there is no such thing as over-reaching the Minister?"

"Confound him, say I—yes; I made the reexamination, however, as Dupin suggested—but it was all labor lost, as I knew it would be."

"How much was the reward offered, did you say?" asked Dupin.

"Why, a very great deal—a *very* liberal reward—I don't like to say how much, precisely; but one thing I *will* say, that I wouldn't mind giving my individual check for fifty thousand francs to any one who could obtain me that letter. The fact is, it is becoming of more and more importance every day; and the reward has been lately doubled. If if were trebled, however, I could do no more than I have done."

"Why, yes," said Dupin, drawlingly, between the whiffs of his meerschaum, "I really—think, G——, you have not exerted yourself—to the utmost in this matter. You might—do a little more, I think, eh?"

"How?—in what way?"

"Why—puff, puff—you might—puff, puff—employ counsel in the matter, eh?—puff, puff, puff. Do you remember the story they tell of Abernethy?"

"No; hang Abernethy!"

"To be sure! hang him and welcome. But, once upon a time, a certain rich miser conceived the design of spunging upon this Abernethy for a medical opinion. Getting up, for this purpose, an ordinary conversation in a private company, he insinuated his case to the physician, as that of an imaginary individual.

" 'We will suppose,' said the miser, 'that his symptoms are such and such; now, doctor, what would *you* have directed him to take?'

" 'Take! said Abernethy, 'why, take *advice,* to be sure.' "

"But," said the Prefect, a little discomposed, "I am *perfectly* willing to take advice, and to pay for it. I would *really* give fifty thousand francs to any one who would aid me in the matter."

"In that case," replied Dupin, opening a drawer, and producing a check-book, "you may as well fill me up a check for the amount you mentioned. When you have signed it, I will hand you the letter."

I was astounded. The Prefect appeared absolutely thunder-stricken. For some minutes he remained speechless and motionless, looking incredulously at my friend with open mouth, and eyes that seemed starting from their sockets; then, apparently recovering himself in some measure, he seized a pen, and after several pauses and vacant stares, finally filled up and signed a check for fifty thousand francs, and handed it across the table to Dupin. The latter examined it carefully and deposited it in his pocket-book; then, unlocking an *escritoire,* took thence a letter and gave it to the Prefect. This functionary grasped it in a perfect agony of joy, opened it with a trembling hand, cast a rapid glance at its contents, and then, scrambling and struggling to the door, rushed at length unceremoniously from the room and from the house, without having uttered a syllable since Dupin had requested him to fill up the check.

When he had gone, my friend entered into some explanations.

"The Parisian police," he said, "are exceedingly able in their way. They are persevering, ingenious, cunning, and thoroughly versed in the knowledge which their duties seem chiefly to demand. Thus, when G—— detailed to us his mode of searching the premises at the Hôtel D——, I felt entire confidence in his having made a satisfactory investigation—so far as his labors extended."

"So far as his labors extended?" said I.

"Yes," said Dupin. "The measures adopted were not only the best of their kind, but carried out to absolute perfection. Had the letter been deposited within the range of their search, these fellows would, beyond a question, have found it."

I merely laughed—but he seemed quite serious in all that he said.

"The measures, then," he continued, "were good in their kind, and well executed; their defect lay in their being inapplicable to the case, and to the man. A certain set of highly ingenious resources are, with the Prefect, a sort of Procrustean bed, to which he forcibly adapts his designs. But he perpetually errs by being too deep or too shallow, for the matter in hand; and many a schoolboy is a better reasoner than he. I knew one about eight years of age, whose success at guessing in the game of 'even and odd' attracted universal admiration. This game is simple, and is played with marbles. One player holds in his hand a number of these toys, and demands of another whether that number is even or odd. If the guess is right, the guesser wins one; if wrong, he loses one. The boy to whom I allude won all the marbles of the school. Of course he had some principle of guessing; and this lay in mere observation and admeasurement of the astuteness of his opponents. For example, an arrant simpleton is his opponent, and, holding up his closed hand, asks: 'Are they even or odd?' Our schoolboy replies, 'Odd,' and loses; but upon the second trial he wins, for he then says to himself, 'The simpleton had them even upon the first trial, and his amount of cunning is just sufficient to make him have them odd upon the second; I will therefore guess odd;'—he guesses odd, and wins. Now, with a simpleton a degree above the first, he would have reasoned thus: 'This fellow finds that in the first instance I guessed odd, and, in the second, he will propose to himself upon the first impulse, a simple variation from even to odd, as did the first simpleton; but then a second thought will suggest that this is too simple a variation, and finally he will decide upon putting it even as before. I will therefore guess even;'—he guesses even, and wins. Now this mode of reasoning in the schoolboy, whom his fellows termed 'lucky,'—what, in its last analysis, is it?"

"It is merely," I said, "an identification of the reasoner's intellect with that of his opponent."

"It is," said Dupin; "and, upon inquiring of the boy by what means he effected the *thorough* identification in which his success consisted, I received answer as follows: 'When I wish to find out how wise, or how stupid, or how good, or how wicked is any one, or what are his thoughts at the moment, I fashion the expression on my face, as accurately as possible, in accordance with the expression of his, and then wait to see what thoughts or sentiments arise in my mind or heart, as if to match or correspond with the expression.' This response of the schoolboy lies at the bottom of all the spurious profundity which has been attributed to Rochefoucault, to La Bougive, to Machiavelli, and to Campanella."

"And the identification," I said, "of the reasoner's intellect with that of his opponent, depends, if I understand you aright, upon the accuracy with which the opponent's intellect is admeasured."

"For its practical value it depends upon this," replied Dupin; "and the Prefect and his cohort fail so frequently, first, by ill-admeasurement, or rather through non-admeasurement, of the intellect with which they are engaged. They consider only their *own* ideas of ingenuity; and, in searching for anything hidden, advert only to the modes in which *they* would have hidden it. They are right in this much—that their own ingenuity is a faithful representative of that of *the mass;* but when the cunning of the individual felon is diverse in character from their own, the felon foils them, of course. This always happens when it is above their own, and very usually when it is below. They have no variation of principle in their investigations; at best, when urged by some unusual emergency—by some extraordinary reward—they extend or exaggerate their old modes of *practice,* without touching their principles. What, for example, in this case of D——, has been done to vary the principle of action? What is all this boring, and probing, and sounding, and scrutinizing with the microscope, and dividing the surface of the building into registered square inches—what is it all but an exaggeration of *the application* of one principle or set of principles of search, which are based upon the one set of notions regarding human ingenuity, to which the Prefect, in the long routine of his duty, has been accustomed? Do you not see he has taken it for granted that *all* men proceed to conceal a letter,—not exactly in a gimlet-hole bored in a chair-leg—but, at least, in *some* out-of-the-way hole or corner suggested by the same tenor of thought which would urge a man to secrete a letter in a gimlet-hole bored in a chair-leg? And do you not see also, that such *recherchés* nooks for concealment are adapted only for ordinary occasions, and would be adopted only by ordinary intellects; for, in all cases of concealment, a disposal of the article concealed—a disposal of it in this *recherché* manner—is, in the very first instance, presumable and presumed; and thus its discovery depends, not at all upon the acumen, but altogether upon the mere care, patience, and determination of the seekers; and where the case is of importance—or, what amounts to the same thing in the policial eyes, when the reward is of magnitude,—the qualities in question have *never* been known to fail. You will now understand what I meant in suggesting that, had the purloined letter been hidden anywhere within the limits of the Prefect's examination—in other words, had the principle of its concealment been comprehended within the principles of the Prefect—its discovery would have been a matter altogether beyond question. This functionary, however, has been thoroughly mystified; and the remote source of his defeat lies in the supposition that the Minister is a fool, because he has acquired renown as a poet. All fools are poets; this the Prefect *feels;* and he is merely guilty of a *non distributio medii* [a failure of logic] in thence inferring that all poets are fools."

"But is this really the poet?" I asked. "There are two brothers, I know; and both have attained reputation in letters. The Minister I believe has written learnedly on the Differential Calculus. He is a mathematician, and no poet."

"You are mistaken; I know him well; he is both. As poet *and* mathematician, he would reason well; as mere mathematician, he could not have reasoned at all, and thus would have been at the mercy of the Prefect."

"You surprise me," I said, "by these opinions, which have been contradicted by the voice of the world. You do not mean to set at naught the well-digested idea of centuries. The mathematical reason has long been regarded as *the* reason *par excellence.*"

"*'Il y a à parier,'*" replied Dupin, quoting from Chamfort, "*'que toute idée publique, toute convention reçue, est une sottise, car elle a convenue au plus grand nombre.'* [One could wager that every public idea, every accepted convention is a piece of foolishness for the very fact of its having been conceived by the masses.] The mathematicians, I grant you, have done their best to promulgate the popular error to which you allude, and which is none the less an error for its promulgation as truth. With an art worthy a better cause, for example, they have insinuated the term 'analysis' into application to algebra. The French are the originators of this particular deception; but if a term is of any importance—if words derive any value from applicability—then 'analysis' conveys 'algebra' about as much as, in Latin, '*ambitus*' implies 'ambition,' '*religio*' 'religion,' or '*homines honesti,*' a set of *honorable* men."

"You have a quarrel on hand, I see," said I, "with some of the algebraists of Paris; but proceed."

"I dispute the availability, and thus the value, of that reason which is cultivated in any especial form other than the abstractly logical. I dispute, in particular, the reason educed by mathematical study. The mathematics are the science of form and quantity; mathematical reasoning is merely logic applied to observation upon form and quantity. The great error lies in supposing that even the truths of what is called *pure* algebra, are abstract or general truths. And this error is so egregious that I am confounded at the universality with which it has been received. Mathematical axioms are *not* axioms of general truth. What is true of *relation*—of form and quantity—is often grossly false in regard to morals, for example. In this latter science it is very usually *un*true that the aggregated parts are equal to the whole. In chemistry also the axiom fails. In the consideration of motive it fails; for two motives, each of a given value, have not, necessarily, a value when united, equal to the sum of their values apart. There are numerous other mathematical truths which are only truths within the limits of *relation*. But the mathematician argues from his *finite truths,* through habit, as if they were of an absolutely general applicability—as the world indeed imagines them to be. Bryant, in his very learned 'Mythology,' mentions an analogous source of error, when he says that 'although the Pagan fables are not believed, yet we forget ourselves continually, and make inferences from them as existing realities.' With the algebraists, however, who are Pagans themselves, the 'Pagan fables' *are* believed, and the inferences are made, not so much through lapse of memory as through an unaccountable addling of the brains. In short, I never yet encountered the mere mathematician who would be trusted out of equal roots, or one who did not clandestinely hold it as a point of his faith that $x^2 + px$ was absolutely and unconditionally equal to q. Say to one of these gentlemen, by way of experiment, if you please, that you believe occasions may occur where $x^2 + px$ is *not* altogether equal to q, and, having made him understand what you mean, get out of his reach as speedily as convenient, for, beyond doubt, he will endeavor to knock you down.

"I mean to say," continued Dupin, while I merely laughed at his last observations, "that if the Minister had been no more than a mathematician, the Prefect would have been under no necessity of giving me this check. I knew him, however, as both mathematician and poet, and my measures were adapted to his capacity, with reference to the circumstances by which he was surrounded. I knew him as a courtier, too, and as a bold *intriguant*. Such a man, I considered, could not fail to be aware of the ordinary policial modes of action. He could not have failed to anticipate—and events have proved that he did not fail to anticipate—the waylayings to which he was subjected. He must have foreseen, I reflected, the secret investigations of his premises. His frequent absences from home at night, which were hailed by the Prefect as certain aids to his success, I regarded only as *ruses,* to afford opportunity for thorough search to the police, and thus the sooner to impress them with the conviction to which G——, in fact, did finally arrive—the conviction that the letter was not upon the premises. I felt, also, that the whole train of thought, which I was at some pains in detailing to you just now, concerning the invariable principle of policial action in searches for articles concealed—I felt that this whole train of thought would necessarily pass through the mind of the Minister. It would imperatively lead him to despise all the ordinary *nooks* of concealment. He could not, I reflected, be so weak as not to see that the most intricate and remote recess of his hotel would be as open as his commonest closets to the eyes, to the probes, to the gimlets, and to the microscopes of the Prefect. I saw, in fine, that he would be driven, as a matter of course, to simplicity, if not deliberately induced as a matter of choice. You will remember, perhaps, how desperately the Prefect laughed when I suggested, upon our first interview, that it was just possible this mystery troubled him so much on account of its being so *very* self-evident."

"Yes," said I, "I remember his merriment well. I really thought he would have fallen into convulsions."

"The material world," continued Dupin, "abounds with very strict analogies to the immaterial; and thus some color or truth has been given to the rhetorical dogma, that metaphor, or simile, may be made to strengthen an argument as well as to embellish a description. The principle of the *vis inertiæ,* for example, seems to be identical in physics and metaphysics. It is not more true in the former, that a large body is with more difficulty set in motion than a smaller one, and that its subsequent *momentum* is commensurate with this difficulty, than it is, in the latter, that intellects of the vaster capacity, while more forcible, more constant, and more eventful in their movements than those of inferior grade, are yet the less readily moved, and more embarrassed and full of hesitation in the first few steps of their progress. Again: have you ever noticed which of the street signs, over the shop doors, are the most attractive of attention?"

"I have never given the matter a thought," I said.

"There is a game of puzzles," he resumed, "which is played upon a map. One party playing requires another to find a given word—the name of town, river, state or empire—any word, in short, upon the motley and perplexed surface of the chart. A novice in the game generally seeks to embarrass his opponents by giving them the most minutely lettered names; but the adept selects such words as stretch, in large characters, from one end of the chart to the other. These, like the over-largely lettered signs and placards of the street, escape observation by dint of being excessively obvious; and here the physical oversight is precisely analogous with the moral inapprehension by which the intellect suffers to pass unnoticed those considerations which are too obtrusively and too palpably self-evident. But this is a point, it appears, somewhat above or beneath the understanding of the Prefect. He never once thought is probable, or possible, that the Minister had deposited the letter immediately beneath the nose of the whole world, by way of best preventing any portion of that world from perceiving it.

"But the more I reflected upon the daring, dashing, and discriminating ingenuity of D——; upon the fact that the document must always have been *at hand,* if he intended to use it to good purpose; and upon the decisive evidence, obtained by the Prefect, that it was not hidden within the limits of that dignitary's ordinary search—the more satisfied I became that, to conceal this letter, the Minister had resorted to the comprehensive and sagacious expedient of not attempting to conceal it at all.

"Full of these ideas, I prepared myself with a pair of green spectacles, and called one fine morning, quite by accident, at the ministerial hotel. I found D—— at home, yawning, lounging, and dawdling, as usual, and pretending to be in the last extremity of *ennui*. He is, perhaps, the most really energetic human being now alive—but that is only when nobody sees him.

"To be even with him, I complained of my weak eyes, and lamented the necessity of the spectacles, under cover of which I cautiously and thoroughly surveyed the whole apartment, while seemingly intent only upon the conversation of my host.

"I paid especial attention to a large writing-table near which he sat, and upon which lay confusedly, some miscellaneous letters and other papers, with one or two musical instruments and a few books. Here, however, after a long and very deliberate scrutiny, I saw nothing to excite particular suspicion.

"At length my eyes, in going the circuit of the room, fell upon a trumpery filigree card-rack of pasteboard, that hung dangling by a dirty blue ribbon, from a little brass knob just beneath the middle of the mantle-piece. In this rack, which had three or four compartments, were five or six visiting cards and a solitary letter. This last was much soiled and crumpled. It was torn nearly in two, across the middle—as if a design, in the first instance, to tear it entirely up as worthless, had been altered, or stayed, in the second. It has a large black seal, bearing the D—— cipher *very* conspicuously, and was addressed, in a diminutive female hand, to D——, the minister, himself. It was thrust carelessly, and even, as it seemed, contemptuously, into one of the upper divisions of the rack.

"No sooner had I glanced at this letter than I concluded it to be that of which I was in search. To be sure, it was, to all appearance, radically different from the one of which the Prefect had read us so minute a description. Here the seal was large and black, with the D—— cipher; there it was small and red, with the ducal arms of the S—— family. Here, the address, to the Minister, was diminutive and feminine; there the superscription, to a certain royal personage, was markedly bold and decided; the size alone formed a point of correspondence. But, then, the *radicalness* of these differences, which was excessive; the dirt; the soiled and torn condition of the paper, so inconsistent with the *true* methodical habits of D——, and so suggestive of a design to delude the beholder into an idea of the worthlessness of the document; these things, together with the hyperobtrusive situation of this document, full in the view of every visitor, and thus exactly in accordance with the conclusions to which I had previously arrived; these things, I say, were strongly corroborative of suspicion, in one who came with the intention to suspect.

"I protracted my visit as long as possible, and, while I maintained a most animated discussion with the Minister, upon a topic which I knew well had never failed to interest and excite him, I kept my attention really riveted upon the letter. In this examination, I committed to memory its external appearance and arrangement in the rack; and also fell, at length, upon a discovery which set at rest whatever trivial doubt I might have entertained. In scrutinizing the edges of the paper, I observed them to be more *chafed* than seemed necessary. They presented the *broken* appearance which is manifested when a stiff paper, having been once folded and pressed with a folder, is refolded in a reversed direction, in the same creases or edges which had formed the original fold. This discovery was sufficient. It was clear to me that the letter had been turned, as a glove, inside out, re-directed, and re-sealed. I bade the Minister good morning, and took my departure at once, leaving a gold snuff-box upon the table.

"The next morning I called for the snuff-box, when we resumed, quite eagerly, the conversation of the preceding day. While thus engaged, however, a loud report, as if of a pistol, was heard immediately beneath the windows of the hotel, and was succeeded by a series of fearful screams, and the shoutings of a mob. D—— rushed to a casement, threw it open, and looked out. In the meantime I stepped to the card-rack, took the letter, put it in my pocket, and replaced it by a *fac-simile,* (so far as regards externals) which I had carefully prepared at my lodgings; imitating the D—— cipher, very readily, by means of a seal formed of bread.

"The disturbance in the street had been occasioned by the frantic behavior of a man with a musket. He had fired it among a crowd of women and children. It proved, however, to have been without ball, and the fellow was suffered to go his way as a lunatic or a drunkard. When he had gone, D—— came from the window, whither I had followed him immediately upon securing the object in view. Soon afterward I bade him farewell. The pretented lunatic was a man in my own pay."

"But what purpose had you," I asked, "in replacing the letter by a *fac-simile?* Would it not have been better, at the first visit, to have seized it openly, and departed?"

"D——," replied Dupin, "is a desperate man, and a man of nerve. His hotel, too, is not without attendants devoted to his interests. Had I made the wild attempt you suggest, I might never have left the Ministerial presence alive. The good people of Paris might have heard of me no more. But I had an object apart from these considerations.

You know my political prepossessions. In this matter, I act as a partisan of the lady concerned. For eighteen months the Minister has had her in his power. She has now him in hers; since, being unaware that the letter is not in his possession, he will proceed with his exactions as if it was. Thus will he inevitably commit himself, at once, to his political destruction. His downfall, too, will not be more precipitate than awkward. It is all very well to talk about the *facilis descensus Averni;* but in all kinds of climbing, as Catalani said of singing, it is far more easy to get up than to come down. In the present instance I have no sympathy—at least no pity—for him who descends. He is that *monstrum horrendum,* an unprincipled man of genius. I confess, however, that I should like very well to know the precise character of his thoughts, when, being defied by her whom the Prefect terms 'a certain personage,' he is reduced to opening the letter which I left for him in the card-rack."

"How? did you put any thing particular in it?"

"Why—it did not seem altogether right to leave the interior blank—that would have been insulting. D——, at Vienna once, did me an evil turn, which I told him, quite good-humoredly, that I should remember. So, as I knew he would feel some curiosity in regard to the identity of the person who had outwitted him, I thought it a pity not to give him a clue. He is well acquainted with my MS., and I just copied into the middle of the blank sheet the words—

——Un dessein si funeste,
S'il n'est digne d'Atrée, est digne de Thyeste.
[Such a dreadful plan.
If not worthy of Atreus, it is worthy of Thyestes.]

They are to be found in Crébillon's 'Atrée.' "

Herman Melville (1819–1891)

BARTLEBY THE SCRIVENER
A Story of Wall Street

I am a rather elderly man. The nature of my avocations, for the last thirty years, has brought me into more than ordinary contact with what would seem an interesting and somewhat singular set of men, of whom, as yet, nothing that I know of, has ever been written—I mean, the law-copyists, or scriveners. I have known very many of them, professionally and privately, and, if I pleased, could relate divers histories, at which good-natured gentlemen might smile, and sentimental souls might weep. But I waive the biographies of all other scriveners, for a few passages in the life of Bartleby, who was a scrivener, the strangest I ever saw, or heard of. While, of other law-copyists, I might write the complete life, of Bartleby nothing of that sort can be done. I believe that no materials exist, for a full and satisfactory biography of this man. It is an irreparable loss to literature. Bartleby was one of those beings of whom nothing is ascertainable, except from the original sources, and, in his case, those are very small. What my own astonished eyes saw of Bartleby, *that* is all I know of him, except, indeed, one vague report, which will appear in the sequel.

Ere introducing the scrivener, as he first appeared to me, it is fit I make some mention of myself, my employés, my business, my chambers, and general surroundings; because some such description is indispensable to an adequate understanding of the chief character about to be presented. Imprimis: I am a man who, from his youth upward, has been filled with a profound conviction that the easiest way of life is the best. Hence, though I belong to a profession proverbially energetic and nervous, even to turbulence, at times, yet nothing of that sort have I ever suffered to invade my peace. I am one of those unambitious lawyers who never addresses a jury, or in any way draws down public applause; but, in the cool tranquillity of a snug retreat, do a snug business among rich men's bonds, and mortgages, and title-deeds. All who know me, consider me an eminently *safe* man. The late John Jacob Astor, a personage little given to poetic enthusiasm, had no hesitation in pronouncing my first grand point to be prudence; my next, method. I do not speak it in vanity, but simply record the fact, that I was not unemployed in my profession by the late John Jacob Astor; a name which, I admit, I love to repeat; for it hath a rounded and orbicular sound to it, and rings like unto bullion. I will freely add, that I was not insensible to the late John Jacob Astor's good opinion.

Some time prior to the period at which this little history begins, my avocations had been largely increased. The good old office, now extinct in the State of New York, of a Master in Chancery, had been conferred upon me. It was not a very arduous office, but very pleasantly remunerative. I seldom lose my temper; much more seldom indulge in dangerous indignation at wrongs and outrages; but, I must be permitted to be rash here, and declare, that I consider the sudden and violent abrogation of the office of Master in Chancery, by the new Constitution, as a—premature act; inasmuch as I had counted upon a life-lease of the profits, whereas I only received those of a few short years. But this is by the way.

My chambers were upstairs, at No. —Wall Street. At one end, they looked upon the white wall of the interior of a spacious skylight shaft, penetrating the building from top to bottom.

This view might have been considered rather tame than otherwise, deficient in what landscape painters call 'life.' But, if so, the view from the other end of my chambers offered, at least, a contrast, if nothing more. In that direction, my windows commanded an unobstructed view of a lofty brick wall, black by age and everlasting shade; which wall required no spy-glass to bring out its lurking beauties, but, for the benefit of all near-sighted spectators, was pushed up to within ten feet of my window panes. Owing to the great height of the surrounding buildings, and my chambers being on the second floor, the interval between this wall and mine not a little resembled a huge square cistern.

At the period just preceding the advent of Bartleby, I had two persons as copyists in my employment, and a promising lad as an office-boy. First, Turkey; second, Nippers, third, Ginger Nut. These may seem names, the like of which are not usually found in the Directory. In truth, they were nicknames, mutually conferred upon each other by my three clerks, and were deemed expressive of their respective persons or characters. Turkey was a short, pursy Englishman, of about my own age—that is, somewhere not far from sixty. In the morning, one might say, his face was of a fine florid hue, but after twelve o'clock, meridian—his dinner hour—it blazed like a grate full of Christmas coals; and continued blazing—but, as it were, with a gradual wane—till six o'clock, P.M., or thereabouts; after which, I saw no more of the proprietor of the face, which, gaining its meridian with the sun, seemed to set with it, to rise, culminate, and decline the following day, with the like regularity and undiminished glory. There are many singular coincidences I have known in the course of my life, not the least among which was the fact, that, exactly when Turkey displayed his fullest beams from his red and radiant countenance, just then, too, at that critical moment, began the daily period when I considered his business capacities as seriously disturbed for the remainder of the twenty-four hours. Not that he was absolutely idle, or averse to business, then; far from it. The difficulty was, he was apt to be altogether too energetic. There was a strange, inflamed, flurried, flighty recklessness of activity about him. He would be incautious in dipping his pen into his inkstand. All his blots upon my documents were dropped there after twelve o'clock, meridian. Indeed, not only would he be reckless, and sadly given to making blots in the afternoon, but, some days, he went further, and was rather noisy. At such times, too, his face flamed with augmented blazonry, as if cannel coal had been heaped on anthracite. He made an unpleasant racket with his chair; spilled his sandbox; in mending his pens, impatiently split them all to pieces, and threw them on the floor in a sudden passion; stood up, and leaned over his table, boxing his papers about in a most indecorous manner, very sad to behold in an elderly man like him. Nevertheless, as he was in many ways a most valuable person to me, and all the time before twelve o'clock, meridian, was the quickest, steadiest creature, too, accomplishing a great deal of work in a style not easily to be matched—for these reasons, I was willing to overlook his eccentricities, though, indeed, occasionally, I remonstrated with him. I did this very gently, however, because, though the civilest, nay, the blandest and most reverential of men in the morning, yet, in the afternoon, he was disposed, upon provocation, to be slightly rash with his tongue—in act, insolent. Now, valuing his morning services as I did, and resolved not to lose them—yet, at the same time, made uncomfortable by his inflamed ways after twelve o'clock—and being a man of peace, unwilling by my admonitions to call forth unseemly retorts from him, I took upon me, one Saturday noon (he was always worse on Saturdays) to hint to him, very kindly, that, perhaps, now that he was growing old, it might be well to abridge his labours; in short, he need not come to my chambers after twelve o'clock, but, dinner over, had best go home to his lodgings, and rest himself till tea-time. But no; he insisted upon his afternoon devotions. His countenance became intolerably fervid, as he oratorically assured me—gesticulating with a long ruler at the other end of the room—that if his services in the morning were useful, how indispensable, then, in the afternoon?

'With submission, sir,' said Turkey, on this occasion, 'I consider myself your right-hand man. In the morning I but marshal and deploy my columns; but in the afternoon I put myself at their head, and gallantly charge the foe, thus'—and he made a violent thrust with the ruler.

'But the blots, Turkey,' intimated I.

'True; but, with submission, sir, behold these hairs! I am getting old. Surely, sir, a blot or two of a warm afternoon is not to be severely urged against gray hairs. Old age—even if it blot the page—is honourable. With submission, sir, we *both* are getting old.'

This appeal to my fellow-feeling was hardly to be resisted. At all events, I saw that go he would not. So, I made up my mind to let him stay, resolving, nevertheless, to see to it that, during the afternoon, he had to do with my less important papers.

Nippers, the second on my list, was a whiskered, sallow, and upon the whole, rather piratical-looking young man, of about five-and-twenty. I always deemed him the victim of two evil powers—ambition and indigestion. The ambition was evinced by a certain impatience of the duties of a mere copyist, and unwarrantable usurpation of strictly professional affairs, such as the original drawing up of legal documents. The indigestion seemed betokened in an occasional nervous testiness and grinning irritability, causing the teeth to audibly grind together over mistakes committed in copying; unnecessary maledictions, hissed, rather than spoken, in the heat of business; and especially by a continual discontent with the height of the table where he worked. Though of a very ingenious mechanical turn, Nippers could never get this table to suit him. He put chips under it, blocks of various sorts, bits of pasteboard, and at last went so far as to attempt an exquisite adjustment, by final pieces of folded blotting-paper. But no invention would answer. If, for the sake of easing his back, he brought the table lid at a sharp angle well up toward his chin, and wrote there like a man using the steep roof of a Dutch house for his desk, then he declared that it stopped the circulation in his arms. If now he lowered the table to his waistbands, and stooped over it in writing, then there was a sore aching in his back. In short, the truth of the matter was, Nippers knew not what he wanted. Or, if he wanted anything, it was to be rid of a scrivener's table altogether. Among the manifestations of his diseased ambition was a fondness he had for receiving visits from certain ambiguous-looking fellows in seedy coats, whom he called his clients. Indeed, I was aware that not only was he, at times, considerable of a ward-politician, but he occasionally did a little business at the Justices' courts, and was not unknown on the steps of the Tombs. I have good reason to believe, however, that one individual who called upon him at my chambers, and who, with a grand air, he insisted was his client, was no other than a dun, and the alleged title-deed, a bill. But, with all his failings, and the annoyances he caused me, Nippers, like his compatriot Turkey, was a very useful man to me; wrote a neat, swift hand; and, when he chose, was not deficient in a gentlemanly sort of deportment. Added to this, he always dressed in a gentlemanly sort of way; and so, incidentally, reflected credit upon my chambers. Whereas, with respect to Turkey, I had much ado to keep him from being a reproach to me. His clothes were apt to look oily, and smell of eating-houses. He wore his pantaloons very loose and baggy in summer. His coats were execrable; his hat not to be handled. But while the hat was a thing of indifference to me, inasmuch as his natural civility and deference, as a dependent Englishman, always led him to doff it the moment he entered the room, yet his coat was another matter. Concerning his coats, I reasoned with him; but with no effect. The truth was, I suppose, that a man with so small an income could not afford to sport such a lustrous face and a lustrous coat at one and the same time. As Nippers once observed, Turkey's money went chiefly for red ink. One winter day, I presented Turkey with a highly respectable-looking coat of my own—a padded gray coat, of a most comfortable warmth, and which buttoned straight up from the knee to the neck. I thought Turkey would appreciate the favour, and abate his rashness and obstreperousness of afternoons. But no; I verily believe that buttoning himself up in so downy and blanket-like a coat had a pernicious effect upon him—upon the same principle that too much oats are bad for horses. In fact, precisely as a rash, restive horse is said to feel his oats, so Turkey felt his coat. It made him insolent. He was a man whom prosperity harmed.

Though, concerning the self-indulgent habits of Turkey, I had my own private surmises, yet, touching Nippers, I was well persuaded that, whatever might be his faults in other respects, he was, at least, a temperate young man. But, indeed, nature herself seemed to have been his vintner, and, at his birth, charged him so thoroughly with an irritable, brandy-like disposition, that all subsequent potations were needless. When I consider how, amid the stillness of my chambers, Nippers would sometimes impatiently rise from his seat, and stooping over his table, spread his arms wide apart, seize the whole desk, and move it, and jerk it, with a grim, grinding motion on the floor, as if the table were a perverse voluntary agent, intent on thwarting and vexing him, I plainly perceive that, for Nippers, brandy-and-water were altogether superfluous.

It was fortunate for me that, owing to its peculiar cause—indigestion—the irritability and consequent nervousness of Nippers were mainly observable in the morning, while in the afternoon he was comparatively mild. So that, Turkey's paroxysms only coming on about twelve o'clock, I never had to do with their eccentricities at one time. Their fits relieved each other, like guards. When Nippers's was on, Turkey's was off; and *vice versa*. This was a good natural arrangement, under the circumstances.

Ginger Nut, the third on my list, was a lad, some twelve years old. His father was a carman, ambitious of seeing his son on the bench instead of a cart, before he died. So he sent him to my office, as student at law, errand-boy, cleaner and sweeper, at the rate of one dollar a week. He had a little desk to himself, but he did not use it much. Upon inspection, the drawer exhibited a great array of the shells of various sorts of nuts. Indeed, to this quick-witted youth, the whole noble science of the law was contained in a nut-shell. Not the least among the employments of Ginger Nut, as well as one which he discharged with the most alacrity, was his duty as cake and apple purveyor for Turkey and Nippers. Copying law-papers being proverbially a dry, husky sort of business, my two scriveners were fain to moisten their mouths very often with Spitzenbergs, to be had at the numerous stalls nigh the Custom House and Post Office. Also, they sent Ginger Nut very frequently for that peculiar cake—small, flat, round, and very spicy—after which he had been named by them. Of a cold morning, when business was but dull, Turkey would gobble up scores of these cakes, as if they were mere wafers—indeed, they sell them at the rate of six or eight for a penny—the scrape of his pen blending with the crunching of the crisp particles in his mouth. Of all the fiery afternoon blunders and flurried rashnesses of Turkey, was his once moistening a ginger-cake between his lips, and clapping it on to a mortgage, for a seal. I came within an ace of dismissing him then. But he mollified me by making an oriental bow, and saying—'With submission, sir, it was generous of me to find you in stationery on my own account.'

Now my original business—that of a conveyancer and title-hunter, and drawer-up of recondite documents of all sorts—was considerably increased by receiving the master's office. There was now great work for scriveners. Not only must I push the clerks already with me, but I must have additional help.

In answer to my advertisement, a motionless young man one morning stood upon my office threshold, the door being open, for it was summer. I can see that figure now—pallidly neat, pitiably respectable, incurably forlorn! It was Bartleby.

After a few words touching his qualifications, I engaged him, glad to have among my corps of copyists a man of so singularly sedate an aspect, which I thought might operate beneficially upon the flighty temper of Turkey, and the fiery one of Nippers.

I should have stated before that ground-glass folding-doors divided my premises into two parts, one of which was occupied by my scriveners, the other by myself. According to my humour, I threw open these doors, or closed them. I resolved to assign Bartleby a corner by the folding-doors, but on my side of them, so as to have this quiet man within easy call, in case any trifling thing was to be done. I placed his desk close up to a small side-window in that part of the room, a window which originally had afforded a lateral view of certain grimy back-yards and bricks, but which, owing to subsequent erections, commanded at present no view at all, though it gave some light. Within three feet of the panes was a wall, and the light came down from far above, between two lofty buildings, as from a very small opening in a dome. Still further to a satisfactory arrangement, I procured a high green folding-screen, which might entirely isolate Bartleby from my sight, though not remove him from my voice. And thus, in a manner, privacy and society were conjoined.

At first, Bartleby did an extraordinary quantity of writing. As if long famishing for something to copy, he seemed to gorge himself on my documents. There was no pause for digestion. He ran a day and night line, copying by sunlight and by candle-light. I should have been quite delighted with his application, had he been cheerfully industrious. But he wrote on silently, palely, mechanically.

It is, of course, an indispensable part of a scrivener's business to verify the accuracy of his copy, word by word. Where there are two or more scriveners in an office, they assist each other in this examination, one reading from the copy, the other holding the original. It is a very dull, wearisome, and lethargic affair. I can readily imagine that, to some sanguine temperaments, it would be altogether intolerable. For example, I cannot credit that the mettlesome poet, Byron, would have contentedly sat down with Bartleby to examine a law document of, say five hundred pages, closely written in a crimpy hand.

Now and then, in the haste of business, it had been my habit to assist in comparing some brief document myself, calling Turkey or Nippers for this purpose. One object I had, in placing Bartleby so handy to me behind the screen, was, to avail myself of his services on such trivial occasions. It was on the third day, I think, of his being with me, and before any necessity had arisen for having his own writing examined, that, being much hurried to complete a small affair I had in hand, I abruptly called to Bartleby. In my haste and natural expectancy of instant compliance, I sat with my head bent over the original on my desk, and my right hand sideways, and somewhat nervously extended with the copy, so that, immediately upon emerging from his retreat, Bartleby might snatch it and proceed to business without the least delay.

In this very attitude did I sit when I called to him, rapidly stating what it was I wanted him to do—namely, to examine a small paper with me. Imagine my surprise, nay, my consternation, when, without moving from his privacy, Bartleby, in a singularly mild, firm voice, replied, 'I would prefer not to.'

I sat a while in perfect silence, rallying my stunned faculties. Immediately it occurred to me that my ears had deceived me, or Bartleby had entirely misunderstood my meaning. I repeated my request in the clearest tone I could assume; but in quite as clear a one came the previous reply, 'I would prefer not to.'

'Prefer not to,' echoed I, rising in high excitement, and crossing the room with a stride. 'What do you mean? Are you moon-struck? I want you to help me compare this sheet here—take it,' and I thrust it toward him.

'I would prefer not to,' said he.

I looked at him steadfastly. His face was leanly composed; his gray eye dimly calm. Not a wrinkle of agitation rippled him. Had there been the least uneasiness, anger, impatience, or impertinence in his manner; in other words, had there been anything ordinarily human about him, doubtless I should have violently dismissed him from the premises. But as it was, I should have as soon thought of turning my pale plaster-of-paris bust of Cicero out of doors. I stood gazing at him a while, as he went on with his own writing, and then reseated myself at my desk. This is very strange, thought I. What had one best do? But my business hurried me. I concluded to forget the matter for the present, reserving it for my future leisure. So calling Nippers from the other room, the paper was speedily examined.

A few days after this, Bartleby concluded four lengthy documents, being quadruplicates of a week's testimony taken before me in my High Court of Chancery. It became necessary to examine them. It was an important suit, and great accuracy was imperative. Having all things arranged, I called Turkey, Nippers, and Ginger Nut, from the next room, meaning to place the four copies in the hands of my four clerks, while I should read from the original. Accordingly, Turkey, Nippers, and Ginger Nut had taken their seats in a row, each with his document in his hand, when I called to Bartleby to join this interesting group.

'Bartleby! quick, I am waiting.'

I heard a slow scrape of his chair legs on the uncarpeted floor, and soon he appeared standing at the entrance of his hermitage.

'What is wanted?' said he mildly.

'The copies, the copies,' said I, hurriedly. 'We are going to examine them. There'—and I held toward him the fourth quadruplicate.

'I would prefer not to,' he said, and gently disappeared behind the screen.

For a few moments I was turned into a pillar of salt, standing at the head of my seated column of clerks. Recovering myself, I advanced toward the screen, and demanded the reason for such extraordinary conduct.

'*Why* do you refuse?'

'I would prefer not to.'

With any other man I should have flown outright into a dreadful passion, scorned all further words, and thrust him ignominiously from my presence. But there was something about Bartleby that not only strangely disarmed me, but, in a wonderful manner, touched and disconcerted me. I began to reason with him.

'These are your own copies we are about to examine. It is labour saving to you, because one examination will answer for your four papers. It is common usage. Every copyist is bound to help examine his copy. Is it not so? Will you not speak? Answer!'

'I prefer not to,' he replied in a flute-like tone. It seemed to me that, while I had been addressing him, he carefully revolved every statement that I made; fully comprehended the meaning; could not gainsay the irresistible conclusion; but, at the same time, some paramount consideration prevailed with him to reply as he did.

'You are decided, then, not to comply with my request—a request made according to common usage and common sense?'

He briefly gave me to understand, that on that point my judgment was sound. Yes: his decision was irreversible.

It is not seldom the case that, when a man is brow–beaten in some unprecedented and violently unreasonable way, he begins to stagger in his own plainest faith. He begins, as it were, vaguely to surmise that, wonderful as it may be, all the justice and all the reason is on the other side. Accordingly, if any disinterested persons are present, he turns to them for some reinforcement for his own faltering mind.

'Turkey,' said I, 'what do you think of this? Am I not right?'

'With submission, sir,' said Turkey, in his blandest tone, 'I think that you are.'

'Nippers,' said I, 'What do *you* think of it?'

'I think I should kick him out of the office.'

(The reader, of nice perceptions, will here perceive that, it being morning, Turkey's answer is couched in polite and tranquil terms, but Nippers's replies in ill-tempered ones. Or, to repeat a previous sentence, Nippers's ugly mood was on duty, and Turkey's off.)

'Ginger Nut,' said I, willing to enlist the smallest suffrage in my behalf, 'what do *you* think of it?'

'I think, sir, he's a little *luny,*' replied Ginger Nut, with a grin.

'You hear what they say,' said I, turning toward the screen, 'come forth and do your duty.'

But he vouchsafed no reply. I pondered a moment in sore perplexity. But once more business hurried me. I determined again to postpone the consideration of this dilemma to my future leisure. With a little trouble we made out to examine the papers without Bartleby, though at every page or two Turkey deferentially dropped his opinion, that this proceeding was quite out of the common; while Nippers, twitching in his chair with a dyspeptic nervousness, ground out, between his set teeth, occasional hissing maledictions against the stubborn oaf behind the screen. And for his (Nippers's) part, this was the first and the last time he would do another man's business without pay.

Meanwhile Bartleby sat in his hermitage, oblivious to everything but his own peculiar business there.

Some days passed, the scrivener being employed upon another lengthy work. His late remarkable conduct led me to regard his ways narrowly. I observed that he never went to dinner; indeed, that he never went anywhere. As yet I had never, of my personal knowledge, known him to be outside of my office. He was a perpetual sentry in the corner. At about eleven o'clock though, in the morning, I noticed that Ginger Nut would advance toward the opening in Bartleby's screen, as if silently beckoned thither by a gesture invisible to me where I sat. The boy would then leave the office, jingling a few pence, and reappear with a handful of ginger nuts, which he delivered in the hermitage, receiving two of the cakes for his trouble.

He lives, then, on ginger-nuts, thought I; never eats a dinner, properly speaking; he must be a vegetarian, then; but no, he never eats even vegetables, he eats nothing but ginger-nuts. My mind then ran on in reveries concerning the probable effects upon the human constitution of living entirely on ginger-nuts. Ginger-nuts are so called, because they contain ginger as one of their peculiar constituents, and the final flavoring one. Now, what was ginger? A hot, spicy thing. Was Bartleby hot and spicy? Not at all. Ginger, then, had no effect upon Bartleby. Probably he preferred it should have none.

Nothing so aggravates an earnest person as a passive resistance. If the individual so resisted be of a not inhumane temper, and the resisting one perfectly harmless to his passivity, then, in the better moods of the former, he will endeavor charitably to construe to his imagination what proves impossible to be solved by his judgment. Even so, for the most part, I regarded Bartleby and his ways. Poor fellow! thought I, he means no mischief; it is plain he intends no insolence; his aspect sufficiently evinces that his eccentricities are involuntary. He is useful to me. I can get along with him. If I turn him away, the chances are he will fall in with some less-indulgent employer, and then he will be rudely treated, and perhaps driven forth miserably to starve. Yes. Here I can cheaply purchase a delicious self-approval. To befriend Bartleby; to humour him in his strange wilfulness, will cost me little or nothing, while I lay up in my soul what will eventually prove a sweet morsel for my conscience. But this mood was not invariable with me. The passiveness of Bartleby sometimes irritated me. I felt strangely goaded on to encounter him in new opposition—to elicit some angry spark from him answerable to my own. But, indeed, I might as well have essayed to strike fire with my knuckles against a bit of Windsor soap. But one afternoon the evil impulse in me mastered me, and the following little scene ensued:—

'Bartleby,' said I, 'when those papers are all copied, I will compare them with you.'

'I would prefer not to.'

'How? Surely you do not mean to persist in that mulish vagary?'

No answer.

I threw open the folding-doors near by, and, turning upon Turkey and Nippers, exclaimed:

'Bartleby a second time says, he won't examine his papers. What do you think of it, Turkey?'

It was afternoon, be it remembered. Turkey sat glowing like a brass boiler; his bald head steaming; his hands reeling among his blotted papers.

'Think of it?' roared Turkey; 'I think I'll just step behind the screen, and black his eyes for him!'

So saying, Turkey rose to his feet and threw his arms into a pugilistic position. He was hurrying away to make good his promise, when I detained him, alarmed at the effect of incautiously rousing Turkey's combativeness after dinner.

'Sit down, Turkey,' said I, 'and hear what Nippers has to say. What do you think of it, Nippers? Would I not be justified in immediately dismissing Bartleby?'

'Excuse me, that is for you to decide, sir. I think his conduct quite unusual, and, indeed, unjust, as regards Turkey and myself. But it may only be a passing whim.'

'Ah,' exclaimed I, 'you have strangely changed your mind, then—you speak very gently of him now.'

'All beer,' cried Turkey; 'gentleness is effects of beer—Nippers and I dined together to-day. You see how gentle *I* am, sir. Shall I go and black his eyes?'

'You refer to Bartleby, I suppose. No, not to-day, Turkey,' I replied; 'pray, put up your fists.'

I closed the doors, and again advanced toward Bartleby. I felt additional incentives tempting me to my fate. I burned to be rebelled against again. I remembered that Bartleby never left the office.

'Bartleby,' said I. 'Ginger Nut is away; just step around to the Post Office, won't you? (it was but a three minutes' walk), and see if there is anything for me.'

'I would prefer not to.'

'You *will* not?'

'I *prefer* not.'

I staggered to my desk, and sat there in a deep study. My blind inveteracy returned. Was there any other thing in which I could procure myself to be ignominiously repulsed by this lean, penniless wight?—my hired clerk? What added thing is there, perfectly reasonable, that he will be sure to refuse to do?

'Bartleby!'

No answer.

'Bartleby,' in a louder tone.

No answer.

'Bartleby,' I roared.

Like a very ghost, agreeably to the laws of magical invocation, at the third summons, he appeared at the entrance of his hermitage.

'Go to the next room, and tell Nippers to come to me.'

'I prefer not to,' he respectfully and slowly said, and mildly disappeared.

'Very good, Bartleby,' said I, in a quiet sort of serenely-severe self-possessed tone, intimating the unalterable purpose of some terrible retribution very close at hand. At the moment I half intended something of the kind. But upon the whole, as it was drawing toward my dinner-hour, I thought it best to put on my hat and walk home for the day, suffering much from perplexity and distress of mind.

Shall I acknowledge it? The conclusion of this whole business was, that it soon became a fixed fact of my chambers, that a pale young scrivener, by the name of Bartleby, had a desk there; that he copied for me at the usual rate of four cents a folio (one hundred words); but he was permanently exempt from examining the work done by him, that duty being transferred to Turkey and Nippers, out of compliment, doubtless, to their superior acuteness; moreover, said Bartleby was never, on any account, to be dispatched on the most trivial errand of any sort; and that even if entreated to take upon him such a matter, it was generally understood that he would 'prefer not to'—in other words, that he would refuse point-blank.

As days passed on, I became considerably reconciled to Bartleby. His steadiness, his freedom from all dissipation, his incessant industry (except when he chose to throw himself into a standing revery behind his screen), his great stillness, his unalterableness of demeanour under all circumstances, made him a valuable acquisition. One prime thing was this—*he was always there*—first in the morning, continually through the day, and the last at night. I had a singular confidence in his honesty. I felt my most precious papers perfectly safe in his hands. Sometimes, to be sure, I could not, for the very soul of me, avoid falling into sudden spasmodic passions with him. For it was exceeding difficult to bear in mind all the time those strange peculiarities, privileges, and unheard-of exemptions, forming the tacit stipulations on Bartleby's part under which he remained in my office. Now and then, in the eagerness of dispatching pressing business, I would inadvertently summon Bartleby, in a short, rapid tone, to put his finger, say, on the incipient tie of a bit of red tape with which I was about compressing some papers. Of course, from behind the screen the usual answer, 'I prefer not to,' was sure to come; and then, how could a human creature, with the common infirmities of our nature, refrain from bitterly exclaiming upon such perverseness—such unreasonableness. However, every added repulse of this sort which I received only tended to lessen the probability of my repeating the inadvertence.

Here it must be said, that according to the custom of most legal gentlemen occupying chambers in densely populated law-buildings, there were several keys to my door. One was kept by a woman residing in the attic, which person weekly scrubbed and daily swept and dusted my apartments. Another was kept by Turkey for convenience sake. The third I sometimes carried in my own pocket. The fourth I knew not who had.

Now, one Sunday morning I happened to go to Trinity Church, to hear a celebrated preacher, and finding myself rather early on the ground I thought I would walk round to my chambers for a while.

Luckily I had my key with me; but upon applying it to the lock, I found it resisted by something inserted from the inside. Quite surprised, I called out; when to my consternation a key was turned from within; and thrusting his lean visage at me, and holding the door ajar, the apparition of Bartleby appeared, in his shirt-sleeves, and otherwise in a strangely tattered dishabille, saying quietly that he was sorry, but he was deeply engaged just then, and—preferred not admitting me at present. In a brief word or two, he moreover added, that perhaps I had better walk round the block two or three times, and by that time he would probably have concluded his affairs.

Now, the utterly unsurmised appearance of Bartleby, tenanting my law-chambers of a Sunday morning, with his cadaverously gentlemanly nonchalance, yet withal firm and self-possessed, had such a strange effect upon me, that incontinently I slunk away from my own door, and did as desired. But not without sundry twinges of impotent rebellion against the mild effrontery of this unaccountable scrivener. Indeed, it was his wonderful mildness chiefly, which not only disarmed me, but unmanned me as it were. For I consider that one, for the time, is a sort of unmanned when he tranquilly permits his hired clerk to dictate to him, and order him away from his own premises. Furthermore, I was full of uneasiness as to what Bartleby could possibly be doing in my office in his shirt-sleeves, and in an otherwise dismantled condition of a Sunday morning. Was anything amiss going on? Nay, that was out of the question. It was not to be thought of for a moment that Bartleby was an immoral person. But what could he be doing there?—copying? Nay again, whatever might be his eccentricities, Bartleby was an eminently decorous person. He would be the last man to sit down at his desk in any state approaching to nudity. Besides, it was Sunday; and there was something about Bartleby that forbade the supposition that he would by any secular occupation violate the proprieties of the day.

Nevertheless, my mind was not pacified; and full of a restless curiosity, at last I returned to the door. Without hindrance I inserted my key, opened it, and entered. Bartleby was not to be seen. I looked round anxiously, peeped behind his screen; but it was very plain that he was gone. Upon more closely examining the place, I surmised that for an indefinite period Bartleby must have ate, dressed, and slept in my office, and that, too, without plate, mirror, or bed. The cushioned seat of a rickety old sofa in one corner bore the faint impress of a lean, reclining form. Rolled away under his desk, I found a blanket; under the empty grate a blacking box and brush; on a chair, a tin basin, with soap and a ragged towel; in a newspaper a few crumbs of ginger-nuts and a morsel of cheese. Yes, thought I, it is evident enough that Bartleby has been making his home here, keeping bachelor's hall all by himself. Immediately then the thought came sweeping across me, what miserable friendlessness and loneliness are here revealed! His poverty is great; but his solitude, how horrible! Think of it. Of a Sunday, Wall Street is deserted as Petra; and every night of every day it is an emptiness. This building, too, which of week-days hums with industry and life, at nightfall echoes with sheer vacancy, and all through Sunday is forlorn. And here Bartleby makes his home; sole spectator of a solitude which he has seen all-populous—a sort of innocent and transformed Marius brooding among the ruins of Carthage!

For the first time in my life a feeling of overpowering stinging melancholy seized me. Before, I had never experienced aught but a not unpleasing sadness. The bond of a common humanity now drew me irresistibly to gloom. A fraternal melancholy! For both I and Bartleby were sons of Adam. I remembered the bright silks and sparkling faces I had seen that day, in gala trim, swan-like sailing down the Mississippi of Broadway; and I contrasted them with the pallid copyist, and thought to myself, Ah, happiness courts the light, so we deem the world is gay; but misery hides aloof, so we deem that misery there is none. These sad fancyings—chimeras, doubtless, of a sick and silly brain—led on to other and more special thoughts, concerning the eccentricities of Bartleby. Presentiments of strange discoveries hovered round me. The scrivener's pale form appeared to me laid out, among uncaring strangers, in its shivering winding-sheet.

Suddenly I was attracted by Bartleby's closed desk, the key in open sight left in the lock.

I mean no mischief, seek the gratification of no heartless curiosity, thought I; besides, the desk is mine, and its contents, too, so I will make bold to look within. Everything was methodically arranged, the papers smoothly placed. The pigeon-holes were deep, and removing the files of documents, I groped into their recesses. Presently I felt something there, and dragged it out. It was an old bandana handkerchief, heavy and knotted. I opened it, and saw it was a savings-bank.

I now recalled all the quiet mysteries which I had noted in the man. I remembered that he never spoke but to answer; that, though at intervals he had considerable time to himself, yet I had never seen him reading—no, not even a newspaper; that for long periods he would stand looking out, at his pale window behind the screen, upon the dead brick wall; I was quite sure he never visited any refectory or eating-house; while his pale face clearly indicated that he never drank beer like Turkey, or tea and coffee even, like other men; that he never went anywhere in particular that I could learn; never went out for a walk, unless, indeed, that was the case at present; that he had declined telling who he was, or whence he came, or whether he had any relatives in the world; that though so thin and pale, he never complained of ill health. And more than all, I remembered a certain unconscious air of pallid—how shall I call it?—of pallid haughtiness, say, or rather an austere reserve about him, which had positively awed me into my tame compliance with his eccentricities, when I had feared to ask him to do the slightest incidental thing for me, even though I might know, from his long-continued motionlessness, that behind his screen he must be standing in one of those dead-wall reveries of his.

Revolving all these things, and coupling them with the recently discovered fact, that he made my office his constant abiding-place and home, and not forgetful of his morbid moodiness; revolving all these things, a prudential feeling began to steal over me. My first emotions had been those of pure melancholy and sincerest pity; but just in proportion as the forlornness of Bartleby grew and grew to my imagination, did that same melancholy merge into fear, that pity into repulsion. So true it is, and so terrible, too, that up to a certain point the thought or sight of misery enlists our best affections; but, in certain special cases, beyond that point it does not. They err who would assert that invariably this is owing to the inherent selfishness of the human heart. It rather proceeds from a certain hopelessness of remedying excessive and organic ill. To a sensitive being, pity is not seldom pain. And when at last it is perceived that such pity cannot lead to effectual succour, common-sense bids the soul be rid of it. What I saw that morning persuaded me that the scrivener was the victim of innate and incurable disorder. I might give alms to his body; but his body did not pain him; it was his soul that suffered, and his soul I could not reach.

I did not accomplish the purpose of going to Trinity Church that morning. Somehow, the things I had seen disqualified me for the time from church-going. I walked homeward, thinking what I would do with Bartleby. Finally, I resolved upon this—I would put certain calm questions to him the next morning, touching his history, etc., and if he declined to answer them openly and unreservedly (and I supposed he would prefer not), then to give him a twenty–dollar bill over and above whatever I might owe him, and tell him his services were no longer required; but that if in any other way I could assist him, I would be happy to do so, especially if he desired to return to his native place, wherever that might be, I would willingly help to defray the expenses. Moreover, if, after reaching home, he found himself at any time in want of aid, a letter from him would be sure of a reply.

The next morning came.

'Bartleby,' said I, gently calling to him behind his screen.

No reply.

'Bartleby,' said I, in a still gentler tone, 'come here; I am not going to ask you to do anything you would prefer not to do—I simply wish to speak to you.'

Upon this he noiselessly slid into view.

'Will you tell me, Bartleby, where you were born?'

'I would prefer not to.'

'Will you tell me *anything* about yourself?'

'I would prefer not to.'

'But what reasonable objection can you have to speak to me? I feel friendly toward you.'

He did not look at me while I spoke, but kept his glance fixed upon my bust of Cicero, which, as I then sat, was directly behind me, some six inches above my head.

'What is your answer, Bartleby?' said I, after waiting a considerable time for a reply, during which his countenance remained immovable, only there was the faintest conceivable tremor of the white attenuated mouth.

'At present I prefer to give no answer,' he said, and retired into his hermitage.

It was rather weak in me, I confess, but his manner, on this occasion, nettled me. Not only did there seem to lurk in it a certain calm disdain, but his perverseness seemed ungrateful, considering the undeniable good usage and indulgence he had received from me.

Again I sat ruminating what I should do. Mortified as I was at his behaviour, and resolved as I had been to dismiss him when I entered my office, nevertheless I strangely felt something superstitious knocking at my heart, and forbidding me to carry out my purpose, and denouncing me for a villain if I dared to breathe one bitter word against this forlornest of mankind. At last, familiarly drawing my chair behind his screen, I sat down and said: 'Bartleby, never mind, then, about revealing your history; but let me entreat you, as a friend, to comply as far as may be with the usages of this office. Say now, you will help to examine papers to-morrow or next day: in short, say now, that in a day or two you will begin to be a little reasonable:—say so, Bartleby.'

'At present I would prefer not to be a little reasonable,' was his mildly cadaverous reply.

Just then the folding-doors opened, and Nippers approached. He seemed suffering from an unusually bad night's rest, induced by severer indigestion than common. He overheard those final words of Bartleby.

'*Prefer not,* eh?' gritted Nippers—'I'd *prefer* him, if I were you, sir,' addressing me—'I'd *prefer* him; I'd give him preferences, the stubborn mule! What is it, sir, pray, that he *prefers* not to do now?'

Bartleby moved not a limb.

'Mr. Nippers,' said I, 'I'd prefer that you would withdraw for the present.'

Somehow, of late, I had got into the way of involuntarily using this word 'prefer' upon all sorts of not exactly suitable occasions. And I trembled to think that my contact with the scrivener had already and seriously affected me in a mental way. And what further and deeper aberration might it not yet produce? This apprehension had not been without efficacy in determining me to summary measures.

As Nippers, looking very sour and sulky, was departing, Turkey blandly and deferentially approached.

'With submission, sir,' said he, 'yesterday I was thinking about Bartleby here, and I think that if he would but prefer to take a quart of good ale every day, it would do much toward mending him, and enabling him to assist in examining his papers.'

'So you have got the word too,' said I, slightly excited.

'With submission, what word, sir,' asked Turkey, respectfully crowding himself into the contracted space behind the screen, and by so doing, making me jostle the scrivener. 'What word, sir?'

'I would prefer to be left alone here,' said Bartleby, as if offended at being mobbed in his privacy.

'*That's* the word, Turkey,' said I—'*that's* it.'

'Oh, *prefer?* oh yes—queer word. I never use it myself. But, sir, as I was saying, if he would but prefer—,'

'Turkey,' interrupted I, 'you will please withdraw.'

'Oh certainly, sir, if you prefer that I should.'

As he opened the folding-door to retire, Nippers at his desk caught a glimpse of me, and asked whether I would prefer to have a certain paper copied on blue paper or white. He did not in the least roguishly accent the word prefer. It was plain that it involuntarily rolled from his tongue. I thought to myself, surely I must get rid of a demented man, who already has in some degree turned the tongues, if not the heads of myself and clerks. But I thought it prudent not to break the discussion at once.

The next day I noticed that Bartleby did nothing but stand at his window in his dead-wall revery. Upon asking him why he did not write, he said that he had decided upon doing no more writing.

'Why, how now? what next?' exclaimed I, 'do no more writing?'

'No more.'

'And what is the reason?'

'Do you not see the reason for yourself?' he indifferently replied.

I looked steadfastly at him, and perceived that his eyes looked dull and glazed. Instantly it occurred to me, that his unexampled diligence in copying by his dim window for the first few weeks of his stay with me might have temporarily impaired his vision.

I was touched. I said something in condolence with him. I hinted that of course he did wisely in abstaining from writing for a while; and urged him to embrace that opportunity of taking wholesome exercise in the open air. This, however, he did not do. A few days after this, my other clerks being absent, and being in a great hurry to dispatch certain letters by the mail, I thought that having nothing else earthly to do, Bartleby would surely be less inflexible than usual, and carry these letters to the Post Office. But he blankly declined. So, much to my inconvenience, I went myself.

Still added days went by. Whether Bartleby's eyes improved or not, I could not say. To all appearance, I thought they did. But when I asked him if they did, he vouchsafed no answer. At all events, he would do no copying. At last, in reply to my urgings, he informed me that he had permanently given up copying.

'What!' exclaimed I; 'suppose your eyes should get entirely well —better than ever before—would you not copy then?'

'I have given up copying,' he answered, and slid aside.

He remained as ever, a fixture in my chamber. Nay—if that were possible—he became still more of a fixture than before. What was to be done? He would do nothing in the office; why should he stay there? In plain fact, he had now become a millstone to me, not only useless as a necklace, but afflictive to bear. Yet I was sorry for him. I speak less than truth when I say that, on his own account, he occasioned me uneasiness. If he would but have named a single relative or friend, I would instantly have written, and urged their taking the poor fellow away to some convenient retreat. But he seemed alone, absolutely alone in the universe. A bit of wreck in the mid-Atlantic. At length, necessities connected with my business tyrannized over all other considerations. Decently as I could, I told Bartleby that in six days time he must unconditionally leave the office. I warned him to take measures, in the interval, for procuring some other abode. I offered to assist him in this endeavour, if he himself would but take the first step toward a removal. 'And when you finally quit me, Bartleby,' added I, 'I shall see that you go not away entirely unprovided. Six days from this hour, remember.'

At the expiration of that period, I peeped behind the screen, and lo! Bartleby was there.

I buttoned up my coat, balanced myself; advanced slowly toward him, touched his shoulder, and said, 'The time has come; you must quit this place; I am sorry for you; here is money; but you must go.'

'I would prefer not,' he replied, with his back still toward me.

'You *must*.'

He remained silent.

Now I had an unbounded confidence in this man's common honesty. He had frequently restored to me sixpences and shillings carelessly dropped upon the floor, for I am apt to be very reckless in such shirt-button affairs. The proceeding, then, which followed will not be deemed extraordinary.

'Bartleby,' said I, 'I owe you twelve dollars on account; here are thirty-two; the odd twenty are yours—Will you take it?' and I handed the bills toward him.

But he made no motion.

'I will leave them here, then,' putting them under a weight on the table. Then taking my hat and cane and going to the door, I tranquilly turned and added—'After you have removed your things from these offices, Bartleby, you will of course lock the door—since every one is now gone for the day but you—and if you please, slip your key underneath the mat, so that I may have it in the morning. I shall not see you again; so good-by to you. If, hereafter, in your new place of abode, I can be of any service to you, do not fail to advise me by letter. Good-by, Bartleby, and fare you well.'

But he answered not a word; like the last column of some ruined temple, he remained standing mute and solitary in the middle of the otherwise deserted room.

As I walked home in a pensive mood, my vanity got the better of my pity. I could not but highly plume myself on my masterly management in getting rid of Bartleby. Masterly I call it, and such it must appear to any dispassionate thinker. The beauty of my procedure seemed to consist in its perfect quietness. There was no vulgar bullying, no bravado of any sort, no choleric hectoring, and striding to and fro across the apartment, jerking out vehement commands for Bartleby to bundle himself off with his beggarly traps. Nothing of the kind. Without loudly bidding Bartleby depart—as an inferior genius might have done—I *assumed* the ground that depart he must; and upon that assumption built all I had to say. The more I thought over my procedure, the more I was charmed with it. Nevertheless, next morning upon awakening, I had my doubts—I had somehow slept off the fumes of vanity. One of the coolest and wisest hours a man has, is just after he awakes in the morning. My procedure seemed as sagacious as ever—but only in theory. How it would prove in practice—there was the rub. It was truly a beautiful thought to have assumed Bartleby's departure; but, after all, that assumption was simply my own, and none of Bartleby's. The great point was, not whether I had assumed that he would quit me, but whether he would prefer so to do. He was more a man of preferences than assumptions.

After breakfast, I walked down town, arguing the probabilities *pro* and *con*. One moment I thought it would prove a miserable failure, and Bartleby would be found all alive at my office as usual; the next moment it seemed certain that I should find his chair empty. And so I kept veering about. At the corner of Broadway and Canal Street, I saw quite an excited group of people standing in earnest conversation.

'I'll take odds he doesn't,' said a voice as I passed.

'Doesn't go?—done!' said I; 'put up your money.'

I was instinctively putting my hand in my pocket to produce my own, when I remembered that this was an election day. The words I had overheard bore no reference to Bartleby, but to the success or non-success of some candidate for the mayoralty. In my intent frame of mind, I had, as it were, imagined that all Broadway shared in my excitement, and were debating the same question with me. I passed on, very thankful that the uproar of the street screened my momentary absent-mindedness.

As I had intended, I was earlier than usual at my office door. I stood listening for a moment. All was still. He must be gone. I tried the knob. The door was locked. Yes, my procedure had worked to a charm; he indeed must be vanished. Yet a certain melancholy mixed with this: I was almost sorry for my brilliant success. I was fumbling under the door-mat for the key, which Bartleby was to have left there for me, when accidentally my knee knocked against a panel, producing a summoning sound, and in response a voice came to me from within—'Not yet; I am occupied.'

It was Bartleby.

I was thunderstruck. For an instant I stood like the man who, pipe in mouth, was killed one cloudless afternoon long ago in Virginia, by summer lightning; at his own warm open window he was killed, and remained leaning out there upon the dreamy afternoon, till some one touched him, when he fell.

'Not gone!' I murmured at last. But again obeying that wondrous ascendancy which the inscrutable scrivener had over me, and from which ascendancy, for all my chafing, I could not completely escape, I slowly went downstairs and out into the street, and while walking round the block, considered what I should next do in this unheard-of perplexity. Turn the man out by an actual thrusting I could not; to drive him away by calling him hard names would not do; calling in the police was an unpleasant idea; and yet, permit him to enjoy his cadaverous triumph over me—this, too, I could not think of. What was to be done? or, if nothing could be done, was there anything further that I could *assume* in the matter? Yes, as before I had prospectively assumed that Bartleby would depart, so now I might retrospectively assume that departed he was. In the legitimate carrying out of this assumption, I might enter my office in a great hurry, and pretending not to see Bartleby at all, walk straight against him as if he were air. Such a proceeding would in a singular degree have the appearance of a home-thrust. It was hardly possible that Bartleby could withstand such an application of the doctrine of assumptions. But upon second thoughts the success of the plan seemed rather dubious. I resolved to argue the matter over with him again.

'Bartleby,' said I, entering the office, with a quietly severe expression, 'I am seriously displeased. I am pained, Bartleby. I had thought better of you. I had imagined you of such a gentlemanly organisation, that in any delicate dilemma a slight hint would suffice—in short, an assumption. But it appears I am deceived. Why,' I added, unaffectedly starting, 'you have not even touched that money yet,' pointing to it, just where I had left it the evening previous.

He answered nothing.

'Will you, or will you not, quit me?' I now demanded in a sudden passion, advancing close to him.

'I would prefer *not* to quit you,' he replied, gently emphasizing the *not*.

'What earthly right have you to stay here? Do you pay any rent? Do you pay my taxes? Or is this property yours?'

He answered nothing.

'Are you ready to go on and write now? Are your eyes recovered? Could you copy a small paper for me this morning? or help examine a few lines? or step round to the Post Office? In a word, will you do anything at all, to give a colouring to your refusal to depart the premises?'

He silently retired into his hermitage.

I was now in such a state of nervous resentment that I thought it but prudent to check myself at present from further demonstrations. Bartleby and I were alone. I remembered the tragedy of the unfortunate Adams and the still more unfortunate Colt in the solitary office of the latter; and how poor Colt, being dreadfully incensed by Adams, and imprudently permitting himself to get wildly excited, was at unawares hurried into his fatal act—an act which certainly no man could possibly deplore more than the actor himself. Often it had occurred to me in my ponderings upon the subject, that had that altercation taken place in the public street, or at a private residence, it would not have terminated as it did. It was the circumstance of being alone in a solitary office, upstairs, of a building entirely unhallowed by humanising domestic associations—an uncarpeted office, doubtless, of a dusty, haggard sort of appearance—this it must have been, which greatly helped to enhance the irritable desperation of the hapless Colt.

But when this old Adam of resentment rose in me and tempted me concerning Bartleby, I grappled him and threw him. How? Why, simply by recalling the divine injunction: 'A new commandment give I unto you, that ye love one another.' Yes, this it was that saved me. Aside from higher considerations, charity often operates as a vastly wise and prudent principle—a great safeguard to its possessor. Men have committed murder for jealousy's sake, and anger's sake, and hatred's sake, and selfishness' sake, and spiritual pride's sake; but no man, that ever I heard of, ever committed a diabolical murder for sweet charity's sake. Mere self-interest, then, if no better motive can be enlisted, should, especially with high-tempered men, prompt all beings to charity and philanthropy. At any rate, upon the occasion in question, I strove to drown my exasperated feelings toward the scrivener by benevolently construing his conduct. Poor fellow, poor fellow! thought I, he don't mean anything; and besides, he has seen hard times, and ought to be indulged.

I endeavored, also, immediately to occupy myself, and at the same time to comfort my despondency. I tried to fancy, that in the course of the morning, at such time as might prove agreeable to him, Bartleby, of his own free accord, would emerge from his hermitage and take up some decided line of march in the direction of the door. But no. Half-past twelve o'clock came; Turkey began to glow in the face, overturn his inkstand, and become generally obstreperous; Nippers abated down into quietude and courtesy; Ginger Nut munched his noon apple; and Bartleby remained standing at his window in one of his profoundest dead-wall reveries. Will it be credited? Ought I to acknowledge it? That afternoon I left the office without saying one further word to him.

Some days now passed, during which, at leisure intervals, I looked a little into 'Edwards on the Will,' and 'Priestley on Necessity.' Under the circumstances, those books induced a salutary feeling. Gradually I slid into the persuasion that these troubles of mine, touching the scrivener, had been all predestinated from eternity, and Bartleby was billeted upon me for some mysterious purpose of an all-wise Providence, which it was not for a mere mortal like me to fathom. Yes, Bartleby, stay there behind your screen, thought I; I shall persecute you no more; you are harmless and noiseless as any of these old chairs; in short, I never feel so private as when I know you are here. At last I see it, I feel it; I penetrate to the predestinated purpose of my life. I am content. Others may have loftier parts to enact; but my mission in this world, Bartleby, is to furnish you with office-room for such period as you may see fit to remain.

I believe that this wise and blessed frame of mind would have continued with me, had it not been for the unsolicited and uncharitable remarks obtruded upon me by my professional friends who visited the rooms. But thus it often is, that the constant friction of illiberal minds wears out at last the best resolves of the more generous. Though to be sure, when I reflected upon it, it was not strange that people entering my office should be struck by the peculiar aspect of the unaccountable Bartleby, and so be tempted to throw out some sinister observations concerning him. Sometimes an attorney, having business with me, and calling at my office, and finding no one but the scrivener there, would undertake to obtain some sort of precise information from him touching my whereabouts; but without heeding his idle talk, Bartleby would remain standing immovable in the middle of the room. So after contemplating him in that position for a time, the attorney would depart, no wiser than he came.

Also, when a reference was going on, and the room full of lawyers and witnesses, and business driving fast, some deeply-occupied legal gentleman present, seeing Bartleby wholly unemployed, would request him to run round to his (the legal gentleman's) office and fetch some papers for him. Thereupon, Bartleby would tranquilly decline, and yet remain idle as before. Then the lawyer would give a great stare, and turn to me. And what could I say? At last I was made aware that all through the circle of my professional acquaintance, a whisper of wonder was running round, having reference to the strange creature I kept at my office. This worried me very much. And as the idea came upon me of his possibly turning out a long-lived man, and keep occupying my chambers, and denying my authority; and perplexing my visitors; and scandalising my professional reputation; and casting a general gloom over the premises; keeping soul and body together to the last upon his savings (for doubtless he spent but half a dime a day), and in the end perhaps outlive me, and claim possession of my office by right of his perpetual occupancy: as all these dark anticipations crowded upon me more and more, and my friends continually intruded their relentless remarks upon the apparition in my room; a great change was wrought in me. I resolved to gather all my faculties together, and forever rid me of this intolerable incubus.

Ere revolving any complicated project, however, adapted to this end, I first simply suggested to Bartleby the propriety of his permanent departure. In a calm and serious tone, I commended the idea to his careful and mature consideration. But, having taken three days to meditate upon it, he apprised me, that his original determination remained the same; in short, that he still preferred to abide with me.

What shall I do? I now said to myself, buttoning up my coat to the last button. What shall I do? what ought I to do? what does conscience say I *should* do with this man, or rather, ghost. Rid myself of him, I must; go, he shall. But how? You will not thrust him, the poor, pale, passive mortal—you will not thrust such a helpless creature out of your door? you will not dishonour yourself by such cruelty? No, I will not. I cannot do that. Rather would I let him live and die here, and then mason up his remains in the wall. What, then, will you do? For all your coaxing, he will not budge. Bribes he leaves under your own paperweight on your table; in short, it is quite plain that he prefers to cling to you.

Then something severe, something unusual must be done. What! surely you will not have him collared by a constable, and commit his innocent pallor to the common jail? And upon what ground could you procure such a thing to be done?—a vagrant, is he? What! he a vagrant, a wanderer, who refuses to budge? It is because he will *not* be a vagrant, then, that you seek to count him *as* a vagrant. That is too absurd. No visible means of support; there I have him. Wrong again: for indubitably he *does* support himself, and that is the only unanswerable proof that any man can show of his possessing the means so to do. No more, then. Since he will not quit me, I must quit him. I will change my offices; I will move elsewhere, and give him fair notice, that if I find him on my new premises I will then proceed against him as a common trespasser.

Acting accordingly, next day I thus addressed him: "I find these chambers too far from the City Hall; the air is unwholesome. In a word, I propose to remove my offices next week, and shall no longer require your services. I tell you this now, in order that you may seek another place."

He made no reply, and nothing more was said.

On the appointed day I engaged carts and men, proceeded to my chambers, and, having but little furniture, everything was removed in a few hours. Throughout, the scrivener remained standing behind the screen, which I directed to be removed the last thing. It was withdrawn; and, being folded up like a huge folio, left him the motionless occupant of a naked room. I stood in the entry watching him a moment, while something from within me upbraided me.

I re-entered, with my hand in my pocket—and—and my heart in my mouth.

'Good-by, Bartleby; I am going—good-bye, and God some way bless you; and take that,' slipping something in his hand. But it dropped upon the floor, and then—strange to say—I tore myself from him whom I had so longed to be rid of.

Established in my new quarters, for a day or two I kept the door locked, and started at every footfall in the passages. When I returned to my rooms, after any little absence, I would pause at the threshold for an instant, and attentively listen ere applying my key. But these fears were needless. Bartleby never came nigh me.

I thought all was going well, when a perturbed-looking stranger visited me, inquiring whether I was the person who had recently occupied rooms at No.— Wall Street.

Full of forebodings, I replied that I was.

'Then, sir,' said the stranger, who proved a lawyer, 'you are responsible for the man you left there. He refuses to do any copying; he refuses to do anything; he says he prefers not to; and he refuses to quit the premises.'

'I am very sorry, sir,' said I, with assumed tranquillity, but an inward tremor, 'but, really, the man you allude to is nothing to me—he is no relation or apprentice of mine, that you should hold me responsible for him.'

'In mercy's name, who is he?'

'I certainly cannot inform you. I know nothing about him. Formerly I employed him as a copyist; but he has done nothing for me now for some time past.'

'I shall settle him, then—good morning, sir.'

Several days passed, and I heard nothing more; and, though I often felt a charitable prompting to call at the place and see poor Bartleby, yet a certain squeamishness, of I know not what, withheld me.

All is over with him, by this time, thought I, at last, when, through another week, no further intelligence reached me. But, coming to my room the day after, I found several persons waiting at my door in a high state of nervous excitement.

'That's the man—here he comes,' cried the foremost one, whom I recognised as the lawyer who had previously called upon me alone.

'You must take him away, sir, at once,' cried a portly person among them, advancing upon me, and whom I knew to be the landlord of No.—Wall Street. 'These gentlemen, my tenants, cannot stand it any longer; Mr. B——,' pointing to the lawyer, 'has turned him out of his room, and he now persists in haunting the building generally, sitting upon the banisters of the stairs by day, and sleeping in the entry by night. Everybody is concerned; clients are leaving the offices; some fears are entertained of a mob; something you must do, and that without delay.'

Aghast at this torrent, I fell back before it, and would fain have locked myself in my new quarters. In vain I persisted that Bartleby was nothing to me—no more than to anyone else. In vain—I was the last person known to have anything to do with him, and they held me to the terrible account. Fearful, then, of being exposed in the papers (as one person present obscurely threatened), I considered the matter, and, at length, said, that if the lawyer would give me a confidential interview with the scrivener, in his (the lawyer's) own room, I would, that afternoon, strive my best to rid them of the nuisance they complained of.

Going upstairs to my old haunt, there was Bartleby silently sitting upon the banister at the landing.

'What are you doing here, Bartleby?' said I.

'Sitting upon the banister,' he mildly replied.

I motioned him into the lawyer's room, who then left us.

'Bartleby,' said I, 'are you aware that you are the cause of great tribulation to me, by persisting in occupying the entry after being dismissed from the office?'

No answer.

'Now one of two things must take place. Either you must do something, or something must be done to you. Now what sort of business would you like to engage in? Would you like to re-engage in copying for someone?'

'No, I would prefer not to make any change.'

'Would you like a clerkship in a dry-goods store?'

'There is too much confinement about that. No, I would not like a clerkship; but I am not particular.'

'Too much confinement,' I cried, 'why, you keep yourself confined all the time!'

'I would prefer not to take a clerkship,' he rejoined, as if to settle that little item at once.

'How would a bar-tender's business suit you? There is no trying of the eyesight in that.'

'I would not like it at all; though, as I said before, I am not particular.'

His unwonted wordiness inspirited me. I returned to the charge.

'Well, then would you like to travel through the country collecting bills for the merchants? That would improve your health.'

'No, I would prefer to be doing something else.'

'How, then would going as a companion to Europe, to entertain some young gentleman with your conversation—How would that suit you?'

'Not at all. It does not strike me that there is anything definite about that. I like to be stationary. But I am not particular.'

'Stationary you shall be, then,' I cried, now losing all patience, and, for the first time in all my exasperating connection with him, fairly flying into a passion. 'If you do not go away from these premises before night, I shall feel bound—indeed, I *am* bound—to—to quit the premises myself!' I rather absurdly concluded, knowing not with what possible threat to try to frighten his immobility into compliance. Despairing of all further efforts, I was precipitately leaving him, when a final thought occurred to me—one which had not been wholly unindulged before.

'Bartleby,' said I, in the kindest tone I could assume under such exciting circumstances, 'will you go home with me now—not to my office, but my dwelling—and remain there till we can conclude upon some convenient arrangement for you at our leisure? Come, let us start now, right away.'

'No; at present I would prefer not to make any change at all.'

I answered nothing; but, effectually dodging everyone by the suddenness and rapidity of my flight, rushed from the building, ran up Wall Street toward Broadway, and, jumping into the first omnibus, was soon removed from pursuit. As soon as tranquillity returned, I distinctly perceived that I had now done all that I possibly could, both in respect to the demands of the landlord and his tenants, and with regard to my own desire and sense of duty, to benefit Bartleby, and shield him from rude persecution. I now strove to be entirely carefree and quiescent; and my conscience justified me in the attempt; though, indeed, it was not so successful as I could have wished. So fearful was I of being again hunted out by the incensed landlord and his exasperated tenants, that, surrendering my business to Nippers, for a few days, I drove about the upper part of the town and through the suburbs, in my rockaway; crossed over to Jersey City and Hoboken, and paid fugitive visits to Manhattanville and Astoria. In fact, I almost lived in my rockaway for the time.

When again I entered my office, lo, a note from the landlord lay upon the desk. I opened it with trembling hands. It informed me that the writer had sent to the police, and had Bartleby removed to the Tombs as a vagrant. Moreover, since I knew more about him than anyone else, he wished me to appear at the place, and make a suitable statement of the facts. These tidings had a conflicting effect upon me. At first I was indignant; but, at last, almost approved. The landlord's energetic, summary disposition had led him to adopt a procedure which I do not think I would have decided upon myself; and yet, as a last resort, under such peculiar circumstances, it seemed the only plan.

As I afterward learned, the poor scrivener, when told that he must be conducted to the Tombs, offered not the slightest obstacle, but, in his pale, unmoving way, silently acquiesced.

Some of the compassionate and curious bystanders joined the party; and headed by one of the constables arm in arm with Bartleby, the silent procession filed its way through all that noise, and heat, and joy of the roaring thoroughfares at noon.

The same day I received the note, I went to the Tombs, or, to speak more properly, the Halls of Justice. Seeking the right officer, I stated the purpose of my call, and was informed that the individual I described was, indeed, within. I then assured the functionary that Bartleby was a perfectly honest man, and greatly to be compassionated, however unaccountably eccentric. I narrated all I knew, and closed by suggesting the idea of letting him remain in as indulgent confinement as possible, till something less harsh might be done—though, indeed, I hardly knew what. At all events, if nothing else could be decided upon, the almshouse must receive him. I then begged to have an interview.

Being under no disgraceful charge, and quite serene and harmless in all his ways, they had permitted him freely to wander about the prison, and, especially, in the enclosed grass-platted yards thereof. And so I found him there, standing all alone in the quietest of the yards, his face toward a high wall, while all around, from the narrow slits of the jail windows, I thought I saw peering out upon him the eyes of murderers and thieves.

'Bartleby!'

'I know you,' he said, without looking round—'and I want nothing to say to you.'

'It was not I that brought you here, Bartleby,' said I, keenly pained at his implied suspicion. 'And to you, this should not be so vile a place. Nothing reproachful attaches to you by being here. And see, it is not so sad a place as one might think. Look, there is the sky, and here is the grass.'

'I know where I am,' he replied, but would say nothing more, and so I left him.

As I entered the corridor again, a broad meat-like man, in an apron, accosted me, and jerking his thumb over his shoulder, said, 'Is that your friend?'

'Yes.'

'Does he want to starve? If he does; let him live on the prison fare, that's all.'

'Who are you?' asked I, not knowing what to make of such an unofficially speaking person in such a place.

'I am the grub-man. Such gentlemen as have friends here, hire me to provide them with something good to eat.'

'Is this so?' said I, turning to the turnkey.

He said it was.

'Well, then,' said I, slipping some silver into the grub-man's hands (for so they called him), 'I want you to give particular attention to my friend there; let him have the best dinner you can get. And you must be as polite to him as possible.'

'Introduce me, will you?' said the grub-man, looking at me with an expression which seemed to say he was all impatience for an opportunity to give a specimen of his breeding.

Thinking it would prove of benefit to the scrivener, I acquiesced; and, asking the grub-man his name, went up with him to Bartleby.

'Bartleby, this is a friend; you will find him very useful to you.'

'Your sarvant, sir, your sarvant,' said the grub-man, making a low salutation behind his apron. 'Hope you find it pleasant here, sir; nice grounds—cool apartments—hope you'll stay with us some time—try to make it agreeable. What will you have for dinner today?'

'I prefer not to dine to-day,' said Bartleby, turning away. 'It would disagree with me; I am unused to dinners.' So saying, he slowly moved to the other side of the enclosure, and took up a position fronting the dead-wall.

'How's this?' said the grub-man, addressing me with a stare of astonishment. 'He's odd, ain't he?'

'I think he is a little deranged,' said I sadly.

'Deranged? deranged is it? Well, now, upon my word, I thought that friend of yourn was a gentleman forger; they are always pale and genteel-like, them forgers. I can't help pity 'em—can't help it, sir. Did you know Monroe Edwards?' he added touchingly, and paused. Then, laying his hand piteously on my shoulder, sighed, 'he died of consumption at Sing Sing. So you weren't acquainted with Monroe?'

'No, I was never socially acquainted with any forgers. But I cannot stop longer. Look to my friend yonder. You will not lose by it. I will see you again.'

Some few days after this, I again obtained admission to the Tombs, and went through the corridors in quest of Bartleby; but without finding him.

'I saw him coming from his cell not long ago,' said a turnkey, 'maybe he's gone to loiter in the yards.'

So I went in that direction.

'Are you looking for the silent man?' said another turnkey, passing me. 'Yonder he lies—sleeping in the yard there. 'Tis not twenty minutes since I saw him lie down.'

The yard was entirely quiet. It was not accessible to the common prisoners. The surrounding walls, of amazing thickness, kept off all sounds behind them. The Egyptian character of the masonry weighed upon me with its gloom. But a soft imprisoned turf grew under foot. The heart of the eternal pyramids, it seemed, wherein, by some strange magic, through the clefts, grass-seed, dropped by birds, had sprung.

Strangely huddled at the base of the wall, his knees drawn up, and lying on his side, his head touching the cold stones, I saw the wasted Bartleby. But nothing stirred. I paused; then went close up to him; stooped over, and saw that his dim eyes were open; otherwise he seemed profoundly sleeping. Something prompted me to touch him. I felt his hand, when a tingling shiver ran up my arm and down my spine to my feet.

The round face of the grub-man peered upon me now. 'His dinner is ready. Won't he dine to-day, either? Or does he live without dining?'

'Lives without dining,' said I, and closed the eyes.

'Eh!—He's asleep, ain't he?'

'With kings and counsellors,' murmured I.

* * *

There would seem little need for proceeding further in this history. Imagination will readily supply the meagre recital of poor Bartleby's interment. But, ere parting with the reader, let me say, that if this little narrative has sufficiently interested him, to awaken curiosity as to who Bartleby was, and what manner of life he led prior to the present narrator's making his acquaintance, I can only reply, that in such curiosity I fully share, but am wholly unable to gratify it. Yet here I hardly know whether I should divulge one little item of rumour, which came to my ear a few months after the scrivener's decease. Upon what basis it rested I could never ascertain; and hence, how true it is I cannot now tell. But, inasmuch as this vague report has not been without a certain suggestive interest to me, however sad, it may prove the same with some others; and so I will briefly mention it. The report was this: that Bartleby had been a subordinate clerk in the Dead Letter Office at Washington, from which he had been suddenly removed by a change in the administration. When I think over this rumour, hardly can I express the emotions which seize me. Dead letters! does it not sound like dead men? Conceive a man by nature and misfortune prone to a pallid hopelessness, can any business seem more fitted to heighten it than that of continually handling these dead letters, and assorting them for the flames? For by the cartload they are annually burned. Sometimes from out the folded paper the pale clerk takes a ring—the finger it was meant for, perhaps, moulders in the grave; a bank-note sent in swiftest charity—he whom it would relieve, nor eats nor hungers any more; pardon for those died despairing; hope for those who died unhoping; good tidings for those who died stifled by unrelieved calamities. On errands of life, these letters speed to death.

Ah, Bartleby! Ah, humanity!

D. H. Lawrence (1885–1930)

THE BLIND MAN

Isabel Pervin was listening for two sounds—for the sound of wheels on the drive outside and for the noise of her husband's footsteps in the hall. Her dearest and oldest friend, a man who seemed almost indispensable to her living, would drive up in the rainy dusk of the closing November day. The trap had gone to fetch him from the station. And her husband, who had been blinded in Flanders, and who had a disfiguring mark on his brow, would be coming in from the outhouses.

He had been home for a year now. He was totally blind. Yet they had been very happy. The Grange was Maurice's own place. The back was a farmstead, and the Wernhams, who occupied the rear premises, acted as farmers. Isabel lived with her husband in the handsome rooms in front. She and he had been almost entirely alone together since he was wounded. They talked and sang and read together in a wonderful and unspeakable intimacy. Then she reviewed books for a Scottish newspaper, carrying on her old interest, and he occupied himself a good deal with the farm. Sightless, he could still discuss everything with Wernham, and he could also do a good deal of work about the place—menial work, it is true, but it gave him satisfaction. He milked the cows, carried in the pails, turned the separator, attended to the pigs and horses. Life was still very full and strangely serene for the blind man, peaceful with the almost incomprehensible peace of immediate contact in darkness. With his wife he had a whole world, rich and real and invisible.

They were newly and remotely happy. He did not even regret the loss of his sight in these times of dark, palpable joy. A certain exultance swelled his soul.

But as time wore on, sometimes the rich glamor would leave them. Sometimes, after months of this intensity, a sense of burden overcame Isabel, a weariness, a terrible ennui, in that silent house approached between a colonnade of tall-shafted pines. Then she felt she would go mad, for she could not bear it. And sometimes he had devastating fits of depression, which seemed to lay waste his whole being. It was worse than depression—a black misery, when his own life was a torture to him, and when his presence was unbearable to his wife. The dread went down to the roots of her soul as these black days recurred. In a kind of panic she tried to wrap herself up still further in her husband. She forced the old spontaneous cheerfulness and joy to continue. But the effort it cost her was almost too much. She knew she could not keep it up. She felt she would scream with the strain, and would give anything, anything, to escape. She longed to possess her husband utterly; it gave her inordinate joy to have him entirely to herself. And yet, when again he was gone in a black and massive misery, she could not bear him, she could not bear herself; she wished she could be snatched away off the earth altogether, anything rather than live at this cost.

Dazed, she schemed for a way out. She invited friends, she tried to give him some further connection with the outer world. But it was no good. After all their joy and suffering, after their dark, great year of blindness and solitude and unspeakable nearness, other people seemed to them both shallow, rattling, rather impertinent. Shallow prattle seemed presumptuous. He became impatient and irritated, she was wearied. And so they lapsed into their solitude again. For they preferred it.

But now, in a few weeks' time, her second baby would be born. The first had died, an infant, when her husband first went out to France. She looked with joy and relief to the coming of the second. It would be her salvation. But also she felt some anxiety. She was thirty years old, her husband was a year younger. They both wanted the child very much. Yet she could not help feeling afraid. She had her husband on her hands, a terrible joy to her, and a terrifying burden. The child would occupy her love and attention. And then, what of Maurice? What would he do? If only she could feel that he, too, would be at peace and happy when the child came! She did so want to luxuriate in a rich, physical satisfaction of maternity. But the man, what would he do? How could she provide for him, how avert those shattering black moods of his, which destroyed them both?

She sighed with fear. But at this time Bertie Reid wrote to Isabel. He was her old friend, a second or third cousin, a Scotchman, as she was a Scotchwoman. They had been brought up near to one another, and all her life he had been her friend, like a brother, but better than her own brothers. She loved him—though not in the marrying sense. There was a sort of kinship between them, an affinity. They understood one another instinctively. But Isabel would never have thought of marrying Bertie. It would have seemed like marrying in her own family.

Bertie was a barrister and a man of letters, a Scotchman of the intellectual type, quick, ironical, sentimental, and on his knees before the woman he adored but did not want to marry. Maurice Pervin was different. He came of a good old country family—the Grange was not a very great distance from Oxford. He was passionate, sensitive, perhaps over-sensitive, wincing—a big fellow with heavy limbs and a forehead that flushed painfully. For his mind was slow, as if drugged by the strong provincial blood that beat in his veins. He was very sensitive to his own mental slowness, his feelings being quick and acute. So that he was just the opposite to Bertie, whose mind was much quicker than his emotions, which were not so very fine.

From the first the two men did not like each other. Isabel felt that they *ought* to get on together. But they did not. She felt that if only each could have the clue to the other there would be such a rare understanding between them. It did not come off, however. Bertie adopted a slightly ironical attitude, very offensive to Maurice, who returned the Scotch irony with English resentment, a resentment which deepened sometimes into stupid hatred.

This was a little puzzling to Isabel. However, she accepted it in the course of things. Men were made freakish and unreasonable. Therefore, when Maurice was going out to France for the second time, she felt that, for her husband's sake, she must discontinue her friendship with Bertie. She wrote to the barrister to this effect. Bertram Reid simply replied that in this, as in all other matters, he must obey her wishes, if these were indeed her wishes.

For nearly two years nothing had passed between the two friends. Isabel rather gloried in the fact; she had no compunction. She had one great article of faith, which was, that husband and wife should be so important to one another, that the rest of the world simply did not count. She and Maurice were husband and wife. They loved one another. They would have children. Then let everybody and everything else fade into insignificance outside this connubial felicity. She professed herself quite happy and ready to receive Maurice's friends. She was happy and ready: the happy wife, the ready woman in possession. Without knowing why, the friends retired abashed, and came no more. Maurice, of course, took as much satisfaction in this connubial absorption as Isabel did.

He shared in Isabel's literary activities, she cultivated a real interest in agriculture and cattle-raising. For she, being at heart perhaps an emotional enthusiast, always cultivated the practical side of life and prided herself on her mastery of practical affairs. Thus the husband and wife had spent the five years of their married life. The last had been one of blindness and unspeakable intimacy. And now Isabel felt a great indifference coming over her, a sort of lethargy. She wanted to be allowed to bear her child in peace, to nod by the fire and drift vaguely, physically, from day to day. Maurice was like an ominous thunder-cloud. She had to keep waking up to remember him.

When a little note came from Bertie, asking if he were to put up a tombstone to their dead friendship, and speaking of the real pain he felt on account of her husband's loss of sight, she felt a pang, a fluttering agitation of re-awakening. And she read the letter to Maurice.

"Ask him to come down," he said.

"Ask Bertie to come here!" she reechoed.

"Yes—if he wants to."

Isabel paused for a few moments.

"I know he wants to—he'd only be too glad," she replied. "But what about you, Maurice? How would you like it?"

"I should like it."

"Well—in that case—But I thought you didn't care for him—"

"Oh, I don't know. I might think differently of him now," the blind man replied. It was rather abstruse to Isabel.

"Well, dear," she said, "if you're quite sure—"

"I'm sure enough. Let him come," said Maurice.

So Bertie was coming, coming this evening, in the November rain and darkness. Isabel was agitated, racked with her old restlessness and indecision. She had always suffered from this pain of doubt, just an agonizing sense of uncertainty. It had begun to pass off, in the lethargy of maternity. Now it returned, and she resented it. She struggled as usual to maintain her calm, composed, friendly bearing, a sort of mask she wore over all her body.

A woman had lighted a tall lamp beside the table and spread the cloth. The long dining room was dim, with its elegant but rather severe pieces of old furniture. Only the round table glowed softly under the light. It had a rich, beautiful effect. The white cloth glistened and dropped its heavy, pointed lace corners almost to the carpet, the china was old and handsome, creamy-yellow, with a blotched pattern of harsh red and deep blue, the cups large and bell-shaped, the teapot gallant. Isabel looked at it with superficial appreciation.

Her nerves were hurting her. She looked automatically again at the high, uncurtained windows. In the last dusk she could just perceive outside a huge fir-tree swaying its boughs: it was as if she thought it rather than saw it. The rain came flying on the window panes. Ah, why had she no peace? These two men, why did they tear at her? Why did they not come—why was there this suspense?

She sat in a lassitude that was really suspense and irritation. Maurice, at least, might come in—there was nothing to keep him out. She rose to her feet. Catching sight of her reflection in a mirror, she glanced at herself with a slight smile of recognition, as if she were an old friend to herself. Her face was oval and calm, her nose a little arched. Her neck made a beautiful line down to her shoulder. With hair knotted loosely behind, she had something of a warm, maternal look. Thinking this of herself, she arched her eyebrows and her rather heavy eyelids, with a little flicker of a smile, and for a moment her gray eyes looked amused and wicked, a little sardonic, out of her transfigured Madonna face.

Then, resuming her air of womanly patience—she was really fatally self-determined—she went with a little jerk towards the door. Her eyes were slightly reddened.

She passed down the wide hall and through a door at the end. Then she was in the farm premises. The scent of dairy, and of a farm-kitchen, and of farm-yard and of leather almost overcame her: but particularly the scent of dairy. They had been scalding out the pans. The flagged passage in front of her was dark, puddled, and wet. Light came out from the open kitchen door. She went forward and stood in the doorway. The farm-people were at tea, seated at a little distance from her, round a long, narrow table, in the center of which stood a white lamp. Ruddy faces, ruddy hands holding food, red mouths working, heads bent over the tea-cups: men, land-girls, boys: it was tea-time, feeding-time. Some faces caught sight of her. Mrs. Wernham, going round behind the chairs with a large black teapot, halting slightly in her walk, was not aware of her for a moment. Then she turned suddenly.

"Oh, is it Madam!" she exclaimed. "Come in, then, come in! We're at tea." And she dragged forward a chair.

"No, I won't come in," said Isabel. "I'm afraid I interrupt your meal."

"No—no—not likely, Madam, not likely."

"Hasn't Mr. Pervin come in, do you know?"

"I'm sure I couldn't say! Missed him, have you, Madam?"

"No, I only wanted him to come in," laughed Isabel, as if shyly.

"Wanted him, did ye? Get up, boy—get up, now—"

Mrs. Wernham knocked one of the boys on the shoulder. He began to scrape to his feet, chewing largely.

"I believe he's in top stable," said another face from the table.

"Ah! No, don't get up. I'm going myself," said Isabel.

"Don't you go out of a dirty night like this. Let the lad go. Get along wi' ye, boy," said Mrs. Wernham.

"No, no," said Isabel, with a decision that was always obeyed. "Go on with your tea, Tom. I'd like to go across to the stable, Mrs. Wernham."

"Did ever you hear tell!" exclaimed the woman.

"Isn't the trap late?" asked Isabel.

"Why, no," said Mrs. Wernham, peering into the distance at the tall, dim clock. "No, Madam—we can give it another quarter or twenty minutes yet, good—yes, every bit of a quarter."

"Ah! It seems late when darkness falls so early," said Isabel.

"It do, that it do. Bother the days, that they draw in so," answered Mrs. Wernham. "Proper miserable!"

"They are," said Isabel, withdrawing.

She pulled on her overshoes, wrapped a large tartan shawl around her, put on a man's felt hat, and ventured out along the causeways of the first yard. It was very dark. The wind was roaring in the great elms behind the outhouses. When she came to the second yard the darkness seemed deeper. She was unsure of her footing. She wished she had brought a lantern. Rain blew against her. Half she liked it, half she felt unwilling to battle.

She reached at last the just visible door of the stable. There was no sign of a light anywhere. Opening the upper half, she looked in: into a simple well of darkness. The smell of horses, and ammonia, and of warmth was startling to her, in that full night. She listened with all her ears but could hear nothing save the night, and the stirring of a horse.

"Maurice!" she called, softly and musically, though she was afraid. "Maurice—are you there?"

Nothing came from the darkness. She knew the rain and wind blew in upon the horses, the hot animal life. Feeling it wrong, she entered the stable and drew the lower half of the door shut, holding the upper part close. She did not stir, because she was aware of the presence of the dark hind-quarters of the horses, though she could not see them, and she was afraid. Something wild stirred in her heart.

She listened intensely. Then she heard a small noise in the distance—far away, it seemed—the chink of a pan, and a man's voice speaking a brief word. It would be Maurice, in the other part of the stable. She stood motionless, waiting for him to come through the partition door. The horses were so terrifyingly near to her, in the invisible.

The loud jarring of the inner door-latch made her start; the door was opened. She could hear and feel her husband entering and invisibly passing among the horses near to her, darkness as they were, actively intermingled. The rather low sound of his voice as he spoke to the horses came velvety to her nerves. How near he was, and how invisible! The darkness seemed to be in a strange swirl of violent life, just upon her. She turned giddy.

Her presence of mind made her call, quietly and musically:

"Maurice! Maurice—dea-ar!"

"Yes," he answered. "Isabel?"

She saw nothing, and the sound of his voice seemed to touch her.

"Hello!" she answered cheerfully, straining her eyes to see him. He was still busy, attending to the horses near her, but she saw only darkness. It made her almost desperate.

"Won't you come in, dear?" she said.

"Yes, I'm coming. Just half a minute. *Stand over—now!* Trap's not come, has it?"

"Not yet," said Isabel.

His voice was pleasant and ordinary, but it had a slight suggestion of the stable to her. She wished he would come away. Whilst he was so utterly invisible, she was afraid of him.

"How's the time?" he asked.

"Not yet six," she replied. She disliked to answer into the dark. Presently he came very near to her, and she retreated out of doors.

"The weather blows in here," he said, coming steadily forward, feeling for the doors. She shrank away. At last she could dimly see him.

"Bertie won't have much of a drive," he said, as he closed the doors.

"He won't indeed!" said Isabel calmly, watching the dark shape at the door.

"Give me your arm, dear," she said.

She pressed his arm close to her, as she went. But she longed to see him, to look at him. She was nervous. He walked erect, with face rather lifted, but with a curious tentative movement of his powerful muscular legs. She could feel the clever, careful, strong contact of his feet with the earth, as she balanced against him. For a moment he was a tower of darkness to her, as if he rose out of the earth.

In the house-passage he wavered and went cautiously, with a curious look of silence about him as he felt for the bench. Then he sat down heavily. He was a man with rather sloping shoulders, but with heavy limbs, powerful legs that seemed to know the earth. His head was small, usually carried high and light. As he bent down to unfasten his gaiters and boots he did not look blind. His hair was brown and crisp, his hands were large, reddish, intelligent, the veins stood out in the wrists; and his thighs and knees seemed massive. When he stood up his face and neck were surcharged with blood, the veins stood out on his temples. She did not look at his blindness.

Isabel was always glad when they had passed through the dividing door into their own regions of repose and beauty. She was a little afraid of him, out there in the animal grossness of the back. His bearing also changed, as he smelt the familiar indefinable odor that pervaded his wife's surroundings, a delicate, refined scent, very faintly spicy. Perhaps it came from the potpourri bowls.

He stood at the foot of the stairs, arrested, listening. She watched him, and her heart sickened. He seemed to be listening to fate.

"He's not here yet," he said. "I'll go up and change."

"Maurice," she said, "you're not wishing he wouldn't come, are you?"

"I couldn't quite say," he answered. "I feel myself rather on the *qui vive*."

"I can see you are," she answered. And she reached up and kissed his cheek. She saw his mouth relax into a slow smile.

"What are you laughing at?" she said roguishly.

"You consoling me," he answered.

"Nay," she answered. "Why should I console you? You know we love each other—you know *how* married we are! What does anything else matter?"

"Nothing at all, my dear."

He felt for her face and touched it, smiling.

"*You're* all right, aren't you?" he asked anxiously.

"I'm wonderfully all right, love," she answered. "It's you I am a little troubled about, at times."

"Why me?" he said, touching her cheeks delicately with the tips of his fingers. The touch had an almost hypnotizing effect on her.

He went away upstairs. She saw him mount into the darkness, unseeing and unchanging. He did not know that the lamps on the upper corridor were unlighted. He went on into the darkness with unchanging step. She heard him in the bathroom.

Pervin moved about almost unconsciously in his familiar surroundings, dark though everything was. He seemed to know the presence of objects before he touched them. It was a pleasure to him to rock thus through a world of things, carried on the flood in a sort of blood-prescience. He did not think much or trouble much. So long as he kept his sheer immediacy of blood-contact with the substantial world he was happy, he wanted no intervention of visual consciousness. In this state there was a certain rich positivity, bordering sometimes on rapture. Life seemed to move in him like a tide lapping, lapping, and advancing, enveloping all things darkly. It was a pleasure to stretch forth the hand and meet the unseen object, clasp it, and possess it in pure contact. He did not try to remember, to visualize. He did not want to. The new way of consciousness substituted itself in him.

The rich suffusion of this state generally kept him happy, reaching its culmination in the consuming passion for his wife. But at times the flow would seem to be checked and thrown back. Then it would beat inside him like a tangled sea, and he was tortured in the shattered chaos of his own blood. He grew to dread this arrest, this throw-back, this chaos inside himself, when he seemed merely at the mercy of his own powerful and conflicting elements. How to get some measure of control or surety, this was the question. And when the question rose maddening in him, he would clench his fists as if he would *compel* the whole universe to submit to him. But it was in vain. He could not even compel himself.

Tonight, however, he was still serene, though little tremors of unreasonable exasperation ran through him. He had to handle the razor very carefully, as he shaved, for it was not at one with him, he was afraid of it. His hearing also was too much sharpened. He heard the woman lighting the lamps on the corridor, and attending to the fire in the visitor's room. And then, as he went to his room, he heard the trap arrive. Then came Isabel's voice, lifted and calling, like a bell ringing:

"Is it you, Bertie? Have you come?"

And a man's voice answered out of the wind:

"Hello, Isabel! There you are."

"Have you had a miserable drive? I'm so sorry we couldn't send a closed carriage. I can't see you at all, you know."

"I'm coming. No, I liked the drive—it was like Porthshire. Well, how are you? You're looking fit as ever, as far as I can see."

"Oh, yes," said Isabel. "I'm wonderfully well. How are you? Rather thin, I think—"

"Worked to death—everybody's old cry. But I'm all right, Ciss. How's Pervin?—isn't he here?"

'Oh, yes, he's upstairs changing. Yes, he's awfully well. Take off your wet things; I'll send them to be dried."

"And how are you both, in spirits? He doesn't fret?"

"No—no, not at all. No, on the contrary, really. We've been wonderfully happy, incredibly. It's more than I can understand—so wonderful: the nearness, and the peace—"

"Ah! Well, that's awfully good news—"

They moved away. Pervin heard no more. But a childish sense of desolation had come over him, as he heard their brisk voices. He seemed shut out—like a child that is left out. He was aimless and excluded, he did not know what to do with himself. The helpless desolation came over him. He fumbled nervously as he dressed himself, in a state almost of childishness. He disliked the Scotch accent in Bertie's speech, and the slight response it found on Isabel's tongue. He disliked the slight purr of complacency in the Scottish speech. He disliked intensely the glib way in which Isabel spoke of their happiness and nearness. It made him recoil. He was fretful and beside himself like a child, he had almost a childish nostalgia to be included in the life circle. And at the same time he was a man, dark and powerful and infuriated by his own weakness. By some fatal flaw, he could not be by himself, he had to depend on the support of another. And this very dependence enraged him. He hated Bertie Reid, and at the same time he knew the hatred was nonsense, he knew it was the outcome of his own weakness.

He went downstairs. Isabel was alone in the dining-room. She watched him enter, head erect, his feet tentative. He looked so strong-blooded and healthy and, at the same time, cancelled. Cancelled—that was the word that flew across her mind. Perhaps it was his scar suggested it.

"You heard Bertie come, Maurice?" she said.

"Yes—isn't he here?"

"He's in his room. He looks very thin and worn."

"I suppose he works himself to death."

A woman came in with a tray—and after a few minutes Bertie came down. He was a little dark man, with a very big forehead, thin, wispy hair, and sad, large eyes. His expression was inordinately sad—almost funny. He had odd, short legs.

Isabel watched him hesitate under the door, and glance nervously at her husband. Pervin heard him and turned.

"Here you are, now," said Isabel. "Come, let us eat."

Bertie went across to Maurice.

"How are you, Pervin?" he said, as he advanced.

The blind man stuck his hand out into space, and Bertie took it.

"Very fit. Glad you've come," said Maurice.

Isabel glanced at them, and glanced away, as if she could not bear to see them.

"Come," she said. "Come to table. Aren't you both awfully hungry? I am tremendously."

"I'm afraid you waited for me," said Bertie, as they sat down.

Maurice had a curious monolithic way of sitting in a chair, erect and distant. Isabel's heart always beat when she caught sight of him thus.

"No," she replied to Bertie. "We're very little later than usual. We're having a sort of high tea, not dinner. Do you mind? It gives us such a nice long evening, uninterrupted."

"I like it," said Bertie.

Maurice was feeling, with curious little movements, almost like a cat kneading her bed, for his plate, his knife and fork, his napkin. He was getting the whole geography of his cover into his consciousness. He sat erect and inscrutable, remote-seeming. Bertie watched the static figure of the blind man, the delicate tactile discernment of the large, ruddy hands, and the curious mindless silence of the brow, above the scar. With difficulty he looked away, and without knowing what he did, picked up a little crystal bowl of violets from the table, and held them to his nose.

"They are sweet-scented," he said. "Where do they come from?"

"From the garden—under the windows," said Isabel.

"So late in the year—and so fragrant! Do you remember the violets under Aunt Bell's south wall?"

The two friends looked at each other and exchanged a smile, Isabel's eyes lighting up.

"Don't I?" she replied. "*Wasn't* she queer!"

"A curious old girl," laughed Bertie. "There's a streak of freakishness in the family, Isabel."

"Ah—but not in you and me, Bertie," said Isabel. "Give them to Maurice, will you?" she added, as Bertie was putting down the flowers. "Have you smelled the violets, dear? Do!—they are so scented."

Maurice held out his hand, and Bertie placed the tiny bowl against his large, warm-looking fingers. Maurice's hand closed over the thin white fingers of the barrister. Bertie carefully extricated himself. Then the two watched the blind man smelling the violets. He bent his head and seemed to be thinking. Isabel waited.

"Aren't they sweet, Maurice?" she said at last, anxiously.

"Very," he said. And he held out the bowl. Bertie took it. Both he and Isabel were a little afraid, and deeply disturbed.

The meal continued. Isabel and Bertie chatted spasmodically. The blind man was silent. He touched his food repeatedly, with quick, delicate touches of his knife-point, then cut irregular bits. He could not bear to be helped. Both Isabel and Bertie suffered: Isabel wondered why. She did not suffer when she was alone with Maurice. Bertie made her conscious of a strangeness.

After the meal the three drew their chairs to the fire, and sat down to talk. The decanters were put on a table near at hand. Isabel knocked the logs on the fire, and clouds of brilliant sparks went up the chimney. Bertie noticed a slight weariness in her bearing.

"You will be glad when your child comes now, Isabel?" he said.

She looked up to him with a quick wan smile.

"Yes, I shall be glad," she answered. "It begins to seem long. Yes, I shall be very glad. So will you, Maurice, won't you?" she added.

"Yes, I shall," replied her husband.

"We are both looking forward so much to have it," she said.

"Yes, of course," said Bertie.

He was a bachelor, three or four years older than Isabel. He lived in beautiful rooms overlooking the river, guarded by a faithful Scottish man-servant. And he had his friends among the fair sex—not lovers, friends. So long as he could avoid any danger of courtship or marriage, he adored a few good women with constant and unfailing homage, and he was chivalrously fond of quite a number. But if they seemed to encroach on him, he withdrew and detested them.

Isabel knew him very well, knew his beautiful constancy, and kindness, also his incurable weakness, which made him unable ever to enter into close contact of any sort. He was ashamed of himself because he could not marry, could not approach women physically. He wanted to do so. But he could not. At the center of him he was afraid, helplessly and even brutally afraid. He had given up hope, had ceased to expect any more that he could escape his own weakness. Hence he was a brilliant and successful barrister, also a *littérateur* of high repute, a rich man, and a great social success. At the center he felt himself neuter, nothing.

Isabel knew him well. She despised him even while she admired him. She looked at his sad face, his little short legs, and felt contempt of him. She looked at his dark gray eyes, with their uncanny, almost childlike, intuition, and she loved him. He understood amazingly—but she had no fear of his understanding. As a man she patronized him.

And she turned to the impassive, silent figure of her husband. He sat leaning back, with folded arms, and face a little uptilted. His knees were straight and massive. She sighed, picked up the poker, and again began to prod the fire, to rouse the clouds of soft brilliant sparks.

"Isabel tells me," Bertie began suddenly, "that you have not suffered unbearably from the loss of sight."

Maurice straightened himself to attend but kept his arms folded.

"No," he said, "not unbearably. Now and again one struggles against it, you know. But there are compensations."

"They say it is much worse to be stone deaf," said Isabel.

"I believe it is," said Bertie. "Are there compensations?" he added, to Maurice.

"Yes. You cease to bother about a great many things." Again Maurice stretched his figure, stretched the strong muscles of his back, and leaned backwards, with uplifted face.

"And that is a relief," said Bertie. "But what is there in place of the bothering? What replaces the activity?"

There was a pause. At length the blind man replied, as out of a negligent, unattentive thinking:

"Oh, I don't know. There's a good deal when you're not active."

"Is there?" said Bertie. "What, exactly? It always seems to me that when there is no thought and no action, there is nothing."

Again Maurice was slow in replying.

"There is something," he replied. "I couldn't tell you what it is."

And the talk lapsed once more, Isabel and Bertie chatting gossip and reminiscence, the blind man silent.

At length Maurice rose restlessly, a big obtrusive figure. He felt tight and hampered. He wanted to go away.

"Do you mind," he said, "if I go and speak to Wernham?"

"No—go along dear," said Isabel.

And he went out. A silence came over the two friends. At length Bertie said:

"Nevertheless, it is a great deprivation, Cissie."

"It is, Bertie. I know it is."

"Something lacking all the time," said Bertie.

"Yes, I know. And yet—and yet—Maurice is right. There is something else, something *there,* which you never knew was there, and which you can't express."

"What is there?" asked Bertie.

"I don't know—it's awfully hard to define it—but something strong and immediate. There's something strange in Maurice's presence—indefinable—but I couldn't do without it. I agree that it seems to put one's mind to sleep. But when we're alone I miss nothing; it seems awfully rich, almost splendid, you know,"

"I'm afraid I don't follow," said Bertie.

They talked desultorily. The wind blew loudly outside, rain chattered on the window-panes, making a sharp drum-sound because of the closed, mellow-golden shutters inside. The logs burned slowly, with hot, almost invisible small flames. Bertie seemed uneasy, there were dark circles round his eyes. Isabel, rich with her approaching maternity, leaned looking into the fire. Her hair curled in odd, loose strands, very pleasing to the man. But she had a curious feeling of old woe in her heart, old, timeless night-woe.

"I suppose we're all deficient somewhere," said Bertie.

"I suppose so," said Isabel wearily.

"Damned, sooner or later."

"I don't know," she said, rousing herself. "I feel quite all right, you know. The child coming seems to make me indifferent to everything, just placid. I can't feel that there's anything to trouble about, you know."

"A good thing, I should say," he replied slowly.

"Well, there it is. I suppose it's just Nature. If only I felt I needn't trouble about Maurice, I should be perfectly content—"

"But you feel you must trouble about him?"

"Well—I don't know—" She even resented this much effort.

The night passed slowly. Isabel looked at the clock. "I say," she said, "It's nearly ten o'clock. Where can Maurice be? I'm sure they're all in bed at the back. Excuse me a moment."

She went out, returning almost immediately.

"It's all shut up and in darkness," she said. "I wonder where he is. He must have gone out to the farm—"

Bertie looked at her.

"I suppose he'll come in," he said.

"I suppose so," she said. "But it's unusual for him to be out now."

"Would you like me to go out and see?"

"Well—if you wouldn't mind. I'd go, but—" She did not want to make the physical effort.

Bertie put on an old overcoat and took a lantern. He went out from the side door. He shrank from the wet and roaring night. Such weather had a nervous effect on him: too much moisture everywhere made him feel almost imbecile. Unwilling, he went through it all. A dog barked violently at him. He peered in all the buildings. At last, as he opened the upper door of a sort of intermediate barn, he heard a grinding noise, and looking in, holding up his lantern, saw Maurice, in his shirtsleeves, standing listening, holding the handle of a turnip-pulper. He had been pulping sweet roots, a pile of which lay dimly heaped in a corner behind him.

"That you, Wernham?" said Maurice, listening.

"No, it's me," said Bertie.

A large, half-wild gray cat was rubbing at Maurice's leg. The blind man stooped to rub its sides. Bertie watched the scene, then unconsciously entered and shut the door behind him. He was in a high sort of barn-place, from which, right and left, ran off the corridors in front of the stalled cattle. He watched the slow, stooping motion of the other man, as he caressed the great cat.

Maurice straightened himself.

"You come to look for me?" he said.

"Isabel was a little uneasy," said Bertie.

"I'll come in. I like messing about doing these jobs."

The cat had reared her sinister, feline length against his leg, clawing at his thigh affectionately. He lifted her claws out of his flesh.

"I hope I'm not in your way at all at the Grange here," said Bertie, rather shy and stiff.

"My way? No, not a bit. I'm glad Isabel has somebody to talk to. I'm afraid it's I who am in the way. I know I'm not very lively company. Isabel's all right, don't you think? She's not unhappy, is she?"

"I don't think so."

"What does she say?"

"She says she's very content—only a little troubled about you."

"Why me?"

"Perhaps afraid that you might brood," said Bertie, cautiously.

"She needn't be afraid of that." He continued to caress the flattened gray head of the cat with his fingers. "What I am afraid of," he resumed, "is that she'll find me a dead weight, always alone with me down here."

"I don't think you need think that," said Bertie, though this was what he feared himself.

"I don't know," said Maurice. "Sometimes I feel it isn't fair that she's saddled with me." Then he dropped his voice curiously. "I say," he asked, secretly struggling, "is my face much disfigured? Do you mind telling me?"

"There is the scar," said Bertie, wondering. "Yes, it is a disfigurement. But more pitiable than shocking."

"A pretty bad scar, though," said Maurice.

'Oh, yes."

There was a pause.

"Sometimes I feel I am horrible," said Maurice, in a low voice, talking as if to himself. And Bertie actually felt a quiver of horror.

"That's nonsense," he said.

Maurice again straightened himself, leaving the cat.

"There's no telling," he said. Then again, in an odd tone, he added: "I don't really know you, do I?"

"Probably not," said Bertie.

"Do you mind if I touch you?"

The lawyer shrank away instinctively. And yet, out of very philanthropy, he said, in a small voice: "Not at all."

But he suffered as the blind man stretched out a strong, naked hand to him. Maurice accidently knocked off Bertie's hat.

"I thought you were taller," he said, starting. Then he laid his hand on Bertie Reid's head, closing the dome of the skull in a soft, firm grasp, gathering it, as it were; then, shifting his grasp and softly closing again, with a fine, close pressure, till he had covered the skull and the face of the smaller man, tracing the brows, and touching the full, closed eyes, touching the small nose and the nostrils, the rough, short moustache, the mouth, the rather strong chin. The hand of the blind man grasped the shoulder, the arm, the hand of the other man. He seemed to take him, in the soft, traveling grasp.

"You seem young," he said quietly, at last.

The lawyer stood almost annihilated, unable to answer.

"Your head seems tender, as if you were young," Maurice repeated. "So do your hands. Touch my eyes, will you?—touch my scar."

Now Bertie quivered with revulsion. Yet he was under the power of the blind man, as if hypnotized. He lifted his hand, and laid the fingers on the scar, on the scarred eyes. Maurice suddenly covered them with his own hand, pressed the fingers of the other man upon his disfigured eye–sockets, trembling in every fiber, and rocking slightly, slowly, from side to side. He remained thus for a minute or more, whilst Bertie stood as if in a swoon, unconscious, imprisoned.

Then suddenly Maurice removed the hand of the other man from his brow, and stood holding it in his own.

"Oh, my God," he said, "we shall know each other now, shan't we? We shall know each other now."

Bertie could not answer. He gazed mute and terror-struck, overcome by his own weakness. He knew he could not answer. He had an unreasonable fear, lest the other man should suddenly destroy him. Whereas Maurice was actually filled with hot, poignant love, the passion of friendship. Perhaps it was this very passion of friendship which Bertie shrank from most.

"We're all right together now, aren't we?" said Maurice. "It's all right now, as long as we live, so far as we're concerned?"

"Yes," said Bertie, trying by any means to escape.

Maurice stood with head lifted, as if listening. The new delicate fulfillment of mortal friendship had come as a revelation and surprise to him, something exquisite and unhoped-for. He seemed to be listening to hear if it were real.

Then he turned for his coat.

"Come," he said, "we'll go to Isabel."

Bertie took the lantern and opened the door. The cat disappeared. The two men went in silence along the causeways. Isabel, as they came, thought their footsteps sounded strange. She looked up pathetically and anxiously for their entrance. There seemed a curious elation about Maurice. Bertie was haggard, with sunken eyes.

"What is it?" she asked.

"We've become friends," said Maurice, standing with his feet apart, like a strange colossus.

"Friends!" re-echoed Isabel. And she looked again at Bertie. He met her eyes with a furtive, haggard look; his eyes were as if glazed with misery.

"I'm so glad," she said, in sheer perplexity.

"Yes," said Maurice.

He was indeed so glad. Isabel took his hand with both hers, and held it fast.

"You'll be happier now, dear," she said.

But she was watching Bertie. She knew that he had one desire—to escape from this intimacy, this friendship, which had been thrust upon him. He could not bear it that he had been touched by the blind man, his insane reserve broken in. He was like a mollusc whose shell is broken.

THE ROCKING-HORSE WINNER

There was a woman who was beautiful, who started with all the advantages, yet she had no luck. She married for love, and the love turned to dust. She had bonny children, yet she felt they had been thrust upon her, and she could not love them. They looked at her coldly, as if they were finding fault with her. And hurriedly she felt she must cover up some fault in herself. Yet what it was that she must cover up she never knew. Nevertheless, when her children were present, she always felt the centre of her heart go hard. This troubled her, and in her manner she was all the more gentle and anxious for her children, as if she loved them very much. Only she herself knew that at the centre of her heart was a hard little place that could not feel love, no, not for anybody. Everybody else said of her: "She is such a good mother. She adores her children." Only she herself, and her children themselves, knew it was not so. They read it in each other's eyes.

There were a boy and two little girls. They lived in a pleasant house, with a garden, and they had discreet servants, and felt themselves superior to anyone in the neighbourhood.

Although they lived in style, they felt always an anxiety in the house. There was never enough money. The mother had a small income, and the father had a small income, but not nearly enough for the social position which they had to keep up. The father went into town to some office. But though he had good prospects, these prospects never materialized. There was always the grinding sense of the shortage of money, though the style was always kept up.

At last the mother said: "I will see if *I* can't make something." But she did not know where to begin. She racked her brains, and tried this thing and the other, but could not find anything successful. The failure made deep lines come into her face. Her children were growing up, they would have to go to school. There must be more money, there must be more money. The father, who was always very handsome and expensive in his tastes, seemed as if he never *would* be able to do anything worth doing. And the mother, who had a great belief in herself, did not succeed any better, and her tastes were just as expensive.

And so the house came to be haunted by the unspoken phrase: *There must be more money! There must be more money!* The children could hear it all the time, though nobody said it aloud. They heard it at Christmas, when the expensive and splendid toys filled the nursery. Behind the shining modern rocking-horse, behind the smart doll's house, a voice would start whispering: "There *must* be more money! There *must* be more money!" And the children would stop playing, to listen for a moment. They would look into each other's eyes, to see if they had all heard. And each one saw in the eyes of the other two that they too had heard. "There *must* be more money! There *must* be more money!"

It came whispering from the springs of the still-swaying rocking-horse, and even the horse, bending his wooden, champing head, heard it. The big doll, sitting so pink and smirking in her new pram, could hear it quite plainly, and seemed to be smirking all the more self-consciously because of it. The foolish puppy, too, that took the place of the teddybear, he was looking so extraordinarily foolish for no other reason but that he heard the secret whisper all over the house: "There *must* be more money!"

Yet nobody ever said it aloud. The whisper was everywhere, and therefore no one spoke it. Just as no one ever says: "We are breathing!" in spite of the fact that breath is coming and going all the time.

"Mother," said the boy Paul one day, "why don't we keep a car of our own? Why do we always use uncle's, or else a taxi?"

"Because we're the poor members of the family," said the mother.

"But why *are* we, mother?"

"Well—I suppose," she said slowly and bitterly, "it's because your father has no luck."

The boy was silent for some time.

"Is luck money, mother?" he asked, rather timidly.

"No, Paul. Not quite. It's what causes you to have money."

"Oh!" said Paul vaguely. "I thought when Uncle Oscar said *filthy lucker,* it meant money."

"*Filthy lucre* does mean money," said the mother. "But it's lucre, not luck."

"Oh!" said the boy. "Then what *is* luck, mother?"

"It's what causes you to have money. If you're lucky you have money. That's why it's better to be born lucky than rich. If you're rich, you may lose your money. But if you're lucky, you will always get more money."

"Oh! Will you? And is father not lucky?"

"Very unlucky, I should say," she said bitterly.

The boy watched her with unsure eyes.

"Why?" he asked.

"I don't know. Nobody ever knows why one person is lucky and another unlucky."

"Don't they? Nobody at all? Does *nobody* know?"

"Perhaps God. But He never tells."

"He ought to, then. And aren't you lucky either, mother?"

"I can't be, if I married an unlucky husband."

"But by yourself, aren't you?"

"I used to think I was, before I married. Now I think I am very unlucky indeed."

"Why?"

"Well—never mind! Perhaps I'm not really," she said.

The child looked at her to see if she meant it. But he saw, by the lines of her mouth, that she was only trying to hide something from him.

"Well, anyhow," he said stoutly, "I'm a lucky person."

"Why?" said his mother, with a sudden laugh.

He stared at her. He didn't even know why he had said it.

"God told me," he asserted, brazening it out.

"I hope He did, dear!" she said, again with a laugh, but rather bitter.

"He did, mother!"

"Excellent!" said the mother, using one of her husband's exclamations.

The boy saw she did not believe him; or rather, that she paid no attention to his assertion. This angered him somewhere, and made him want to compel her attention.

He went off by himself, vaguely, in a childish way, seeking for the clue to 'luck.' Absorbed, taking no heed of other people, he went about with a sort of stealth, seeking inwardly for luck. He wanted luck, he wanted it, he wanted it. When the two girls were playing dolls in the nursery, he would sit on his big rocking-horse, charging madly into space, with a frenzy that made the little girls peer at him uneasily. Wildly the horse careered, the waving dark hair of the boy tossed, his eyes had a strange glare in them. The little girls dared not speak to him.

When he had ridden to the end of his mad little journey, he climbed down and stood in front of his rocking-horse, staring fixedly into its lower face. Its red mouth was slightly open, its big eye was wide and glassy-bright.

"Now!" he would silently command the snorting steed. "Now, take me to where there is luck! Now take me!"

And he would slash the horse on the neck with the little whip he had asked Uncle Oscar for. He *knew* the horse could take him to where there was luck, if only he forced it. So he would mount again and start on his furious ride, hoping at last to get there. He knew he could get there.

"You'll break your horse, Paul!" said the nurse.

"He's always riding like that! I wish he'd leave off!" said his elder sister Joan.

But he only glared down on them in silence. Nurse gave him up. She could make nothing of him. Anyhow, he was growing beyond her.

One day his mother and his Uncle Oscar came in when he was on one of his furious rides. He did not speak to them.

"Hallo, you young jockey! Riding a winner?" said his uncle.

"Aren't you growing too big for a rocking–horse? You're not a very little boy any longer, you know," said his mother.

But Paul only gave a blue glare from his big, rather close-set eyes. He would speak to nobody when he was in full tilt. His mother watched him with an anxious expression on her face.

At last he suddenly stopped forcing his horse into the mechanical gallop and slid down.

"Well, I got there!" he announced fiercely, his blue eyes still flaring, and his sturdy long legs straddling apart.

"Where did you get to?" asked his mother.

"Where I wanted to go," he flared back at her.

"That's right, son!" said Uncle Oscar. "Don't you stop till you get there. What's the horse's name?"

"He doesn't have a name," said the boy.

"Gets on without all right?" asked the uncle.

"Well, he has different names. He was called Sansovino last week."

"Sansovino, eh? Won the Ascot. How did you know this name?"

"He always talks about horse-races with Bassett," said Joan.

The uncle was delighted to find that his small nephew was posted with all the racing news. Bassett, the young gardener, who had been wounded in the left foot in the war and had got his present job through Oscar Cresswell, whose batman he had been, was a perfect blade of the 'turf.' He lived in the racing events, and the small boy lived with him.

Oscar Cresswell got it all from Bassett.

"Master Paul comes and asks me, so I can't do more than tell him, sir," said Bassett, his face terribly serious, as if he were speaking of religious matters.

"And does he ever put anything on a horse he fancies?"

"Well—I don't want to give him away—he's a young sport, a fine sport, sir. Would you mind asking him himself? He sort of takes a pleasure in it, and perhaps he'd feel I was giving him away, sir, if you don't mind."

Bassett was serious as a church.

The uncle went back to his nephew and took him off for a ride in the car.

"Say, Paul, old man, do you ever put anything on a horse?" the uncle asked.

The boy watched the handsome man closely.

"Why, do you think I oughtn't to?" he parried.

"Not a bit of it! I thought perhaps you might give me a tip for the Lincoln."

The car sped on into the country, going down to Uncle Oscar's place in Hampshire.

"Honour bright?" said the nephew.

"Honour bright, son!" said the uncle.

"Well, then, Daffodil."

"Daffodil! I doubt it, sonny. What about Mirza?"

"I only know the winner," said the boy. "That's Daffodil."

"Daffodil, eh?"

There was a pause. Daffodil was an obscure horse comparatively.

"Uncle!"

"Yes, son?"

"You won't let it go any further, will you? I promised Bassett."

"Bassett be damned, old man! What's he got to do with it?"

"We're partners. We've been partners from the first. Uncle, he lent me my first five shillings, which I lost. I promised him, honour bright, it was only between me and him; only you gave me that ten-shilling note I started winning with, so I thought you were lucky. You won't let it go any further, will you?"

The boy gazed at his uncle from those big, hot, blue eyes, set rather close together. The uncle stirred and laughed uneasily.

"Right you are, son! I'll keep your tip private. Daffodil, eh? How much are you putting on him?"

"All except twenty pounds," said the boy. "I keep that in reserve."

The uncle thought it a good joke.

"You keep twenty pounds in reserve, do you, you young romancer? What are you betting then?"

"I'm betting three hundred," said the boy gravely. "But it's between you and me, Uncle Oscar! Honour bright?"

The uncle burst into a roar of laughter.

"It's between you and me all right, you young Nat Gould," he said, laughing. "But where's your three hundred?"

"Bassett keeps it for me. We're partners."

"You are, are you! And what is Bassett putting on Daffodil?"

"He won't go quite as high as I do, I expect. Perhaps he'll go a hundred and fifty."

"What, pennies?" laughed the uncle.

"Pounds," said the child, with a surprised look at his uncle. "Bassett keeps a bigger reserve than I do."

Between wonder and amusement Uncle Oscar was silent. He pursued the matter no further, but he determined to take his nephew with him to the Lincoln races.

"Now, son," he said, "I'm putting twenty on Mirza, and I'll put five on for you on any horse you fancy. What's your pick?"

"Daffodil, uncle."

"No, not the fiver on Daffodil!"

"I should if it was my own fiver," said the child.

"Good! Good! Right you are! A fiver for me and a fiver for you on Daffodil."

The child had never been to a racemeeting before, and his eyes were blue fire. He pursed his mouth tight and watched. A Frenchman just in front had put his money on Lancelot. Wild with excitement, he flayed his arms up and down, yelling "*Lancelot! Lancelot!*" in his French accent.

Daffodil came in first, Lancelot second, Mirza third. The child, flushed and with eyes blazing, was curiously serene. His uncle brought him four five-pound notes, four to one.

"What am I to do with these?" he cried, waving them before the boy's eyes.

"I suppose we'll talk to Bassett," said the boy. "I expect I have fifteen hundred now; and twenty in reserve; and this twenty."

His uncle studied him for some moments.

"Look here, son!" he said. "You're not serious about Bassett and that fifteen hundred, are you?"

"Yes, I am. But it's between you and me, uncle. Honour bright?"

"Honour bright all right, son! But I must talk to Bassett."

"If you'd like to be a partner, uncle, with Bassett and me, we could all be partners. Only, you'd have to promise, honour bright, uncle, not to let it go beyond us three. Bassett and I are lucky, and you must be lucky, because it was your ten shillings I started winning with. . . ."

Uncle Oscar took both Bassett and Paul into Richmond Park for an afternoon, and there they talked.

"It's like this, you see, sir," Bassett said. "Master Paul would get me talking about racing events, spinning yarns, you know, sir. And he was always keen on knowing if I'd made or if I'd lost. It's about a year since, now, that I put five shillings on Blush of Dawn for him: and we lost. Then the luck turned, with that ten shillings he had from you: that we put on Singhalese. And since that time, it's been pretty steady, all things considering. What do you say, Master Paul?"

"We're all right when we're sure," said Paul. "It's when we're not quite sure that we go down."

"Oh, but we're careful then," said Bassett.

"But when are you *sure?"* smiled Uncle Oscar.

"It's Master Paul, sir," said Bassett in a secret, religious voice. "It's as if he had it from heaven. Like Daffodil, now, for the Lincoln. That was as sure as eggs."

"Did you put anything on Daffodil?" asked Oscar Cresswell.

"Yes, sir. I made my bit."

"And my nephew?"

Bassett was obstinately silent, looking at Paul.

"I made twelve hundred, didn't I, Bassett? I told uncle I was putting three hundred on Daffodil."

"That's right," said Bassett, nodding.

"But where's the money?" asked the uncle.

"I keep it safe locked up, sir. Master Paul he can have it any minute he likes to ask for it."

"What, fifteen hundred pounds?"

"And twenty! And *forty,* that is, with the twenty he made on the course."

"It's amazing!" said the uncle.

"If Master Paul offers you to be partners, sir, I would, if I were you: if you'll excuse me," said Bassett.

Oscar Cresswell thought about it.

"I'll see the money," he said.

They drove home again, and, sure enough, Bassett came round to the gardenhouse with fifteen hundred pounds in notes. The twenty pounds reserve was left with Joe Glee, in the Turf Commission deposit.

"You see, it's all right, uncle, when I'm *sure!* Then we go strong, for all we're worth. Don't we, Bassett?"

"We do that, Master Paul."

"And when are you sure?" said the uncle, laughing.

"Oh, well, sometimes I'm *absolutely* sure, like about Daffodil," said the boy; "and sometimes I have an idea; and sometimes I haven't even an idea, have I, Bassett? Then we're careful, because we mostly go down."

"You do, do you! And when you're sure, like about Daffodil, what makes you sure, sonny?"

"Oh, well, I don't know," said the boy uneasily. "I'm sure, you know, uncle; that's all."

"It's as if he had it from heaven, sir," Bassett reiterated.

"I should say so!" said the uncle.

But he became a partner. And when the Leger was coming on Paul was "sure" about Lively Spark, which was a quite inconsiderable horse. The boy insisted on putting a thousand on the horse, Bassett went for five hundred, and Oscar Cresswell two hundred. Lively Spark came in first, and the betting had been ten to one against him. Paul had made ten thousand.

"You see," he said, "I was absolutely sure of him."

Even Oscar Cresswell had cleared two thousand.

"Look here, son," he said, "this sort of thing makes me nervous."

"It needn't, uncle! Perhaps I shan't be sure again for a long time."

"But what are you going to do with your money?" asked the uncle.

"Of course," said the boy, "I started it for mother. She said she had no luck, because father is unlucky, so I thought if *I* was lucky, it might stop whispering."

"What might stop whispering?"

"Our house. I *hate* our house for whispering."

"What does it whisper?"

"Why—why"—the boy fidgeted—"why, I don't know. But it's always short of money, you know, uncle."

"I know it, son, I know it."

"You know people send mother writs, don't you uncle?"

"I'm afraid I do," said the uncle.

"And then the house whispers, like people laughing at you behind your back. It's awful, that is! I thought if I was lucky——"

"You might stop it," added the uncle.

The boy watched him with big blue eyes, that had an uncanny cold fire in them, and he said never a word.

"Well, then!" said the uncle. "What are we doing?"

"I shouldn't like mother to know I was lucky," said the boy.

"Why not, son?"

"She'd stop me."

"I don't think she would."

"Oh!"—and the boy writhed in an odd way—"I *don't* want her to know, uncle."

"All right, son! We'll manage it without her knowing."

They managed it very easily. Paul, at the other's suggestion, handed over five thousand pounds to his uncle, who deposited it with the family lawyer, who was then to inform Paul's mother that a relative had put five thousand pounds into his hands, which sum was to be paid out a thousand pounds at a time, on the mother's birthday, for the next five years.

"So she'll have a birthday present of a thousand pounds for five successive years," said Uncle Oscar. "I hope it won't make it all the harder for her later."

Paul's mother had her birthday in November. The house had been 'whispering' worse than ever lately, and, even in spite of his luck, Paul could not bear up against it. He was very anxious to see the effect of the birthday letter, telling his mother about the thousand pounds.

When there were no visitors, Paul now took his meals with his parents, as he was beyond the nursery control. His mother went into town nearly every day. She had discovered that she had an odd knack of sketching furs and dress materials, so she worked secretly in the studio of a friend who was the chief 'artist' for the leading drapers. She drew the figures of ladies in furs and ladies in silk and sequins for the newspaper advertisements. This young woman artist earned several thousand pounds a year, but Paul's mother only made several hundreds, and she was again dissatisfied. She so wanted to be first in something, and she did not succeed, even in making sketches for drapery advertisements.

She was down to breakfast on the morning of her birthday. Paul watched her face as she read her letters. He knew the lawyer's letter. As his mother read it, her face hardened and became more expressionless. Then a cold, determined look came on her mouth. She hid the letter under the pile of others, and said not a word about it.

"Didn't you have anything nice in the post for your birthday, mother?" said Paul.

"Quite moderately nice," she said, her voice cold and absent.

She went away to town without saying more.

But in the afternoon Uncle Oscar appeared. He said Paul's mother had had a long interview with the lawyer, asking if the whole five thousand could not be advanced at once, as she was in debt.

"What do you think, uncle?" asked the boy.

"I leave it to you, son."

"Oh, let her have it, then! We can get some more with the other," said the boy.

"A bird in the hand is worth two in the bush, laddie!" said Uncle Oscar.

"But I'm sure to *know* for the Grand National; or the Lincolnshire; or else the Derby. I'm sure to know for *one* of them," said Paul.

So Uncle Oscar signed the agreement, and Paul's mother touched the whole five thousand. Then something very curious happened. The voices in the house suddenly went mad, like a chorus of frogs on a spring evening. There were certain new furnishings, and Paul had a tutor. He was *really* going to Eton, his father's school, in the following autumn. There were flowers in the winter, and a blossoming of the luxury Paul's mother had been used to. And yet the voices in the house, behind the sprays of mimosa and almond-blossom, and from under the piles of iridescent cushions, simply trilled and screamed in a sort of ecstasy: "There *must* be more money! Oh-h-h; there *must* be more money. Oh, now, now-w! Now-w-w—there *must* be more money!—more than ever! More than ever!"

It frightened Paul terribly. He studied away at his Latin and Greek with his tutor. But his intense hours were spent with Bassett. The Grand National had gone by: he had not 'known,' and had lost a hundred pounds. Summer was at hand. He was in agony for the Lincoln. But even for the Lincoln he didn't 'know,' and he lost fifty pounds. He became wild-eyed and strange, as if something were going to explode in him.

"Let it alone, son! Don't you bother about it!" urged Uncle Oscar. But it was as if the boy couldn't really hear what his uncle was saying.

"I've got to know for the Derby! I've got to know for the Derby!" the child reiterated, his big blue eyes with a sort of madness.

His mother noticed how overwrought he was.

"You'd better go to the seaside. Wouldn't you like to go now to the seaside, instead of waiting? I think you'd better," she said, looking down at him anxiously, her heart curiously heavy because of him.

But the child lifted his uncanny blue eyes.

"I couldn't possibly go before the Derby, mother!" he said. "I couldn't possibly!"

"Why not?" she said, her voice becoming heavy when she was opposed. "Why not? You can still go from the seaside to see the Derby with your Uncle Oscar, if that's what you wish. No need for you to wait here. Besides, I think you care too much about these races. It's a bad sign. My family has been a gambling family, and you won't know till you grow up how much damage it has done. But it has done damage. I shall have to send Bassett away, and ask Uncle Oscar not to talk racing to you, unless you promise to be reasonable about it: go away to the seaside and forget it. You're all nerves!"

"I'll do what you like, mother, so long as you don't send me away till after the Derby," the boy said.

"Send you away from where? Just from this house?"

"Yes," he said, gazing at her.

"Why, you curious child, what makes you care about this house so much, suddenly? I never knew you loved it."

He gazed at her without speaking. He had a secret within a secret, something he had not divulged, even to Bassett or to his Uncle Oscar.

But his mother, after standing undecided and a little bit sullen for some moments, said:

"Very well, then! Don't go to the seaside till after the Derby, if you don't wish it. But promise me you won't let your nerves go to pieces. Promise you won't think so much about horse-racing and *events,* as you call them!"

"Oh no," said the boy casually. "I won't think much about them, mother. You needn't worry. I wouldn't worry, mother, if I were you."

"If you were me and I were you," said his mother, "I wonder what we *should* do!"

"But you know you needn't worry, mother, don't you?" the boy repeated.

"I should be awfully glad to know it," she said wearily.

"Oh, well, you *can,* you know. I mean, you *ought* to know you needn't worry," he insisted.

"Ought I? Then I'll see about it," she said.

Paul's secret of secrets was his wooden horse, that which had no name. Since he was emancipated from a nurse and a nursery-governess, he had had his rocking-horse removed to his own bedroom at the top of the house.

"Surely you're too big for a rocking-horse!" his mother had remonstrated.

"Well, you see, mother, till I can have a *real* horse, I like to have *some* sort of animal about," had been his quaint answer.

"Do you feel he keeps you company?" she laughed.

"Oh yes! He's very good, he always keeps me company, when I'm there," said Paul.

So the horse, rather shabby, stood in an arrested prance in the boy's bedroom.

The Derby was drawing near, and the boy grew more and more tense. He hardly heard what was spoken to him, he was very frail, and his eyes were really uncanny. His mother had sudden strange seizures of uneasiness about him. Sometimes, for half an hour, she would feel a sudden anxiety about him that was almost anguish. She wanted to rush to him at once, and know he was safe.

Two nights before the Derby, she was at a big party in town, when one of her rushes of anxiety about her boy, her firstborn, gripped her heart till she could hardly speak. She fought with the feeling, might and main, for she believed in common sense. But it was too strong. She had to leave the dance and go downstairs to telephone to the country. The children's nursery-governess was terribly surprised and startled at being rung up in the night.

"Are the children all right, Miss Wilmot?"

"Oh yes, they are quite all right."

"Master Paul? Is he all right?"

"He went up to bed as right as a trivet. Shall I run up and look at him?"

"No," said Paul's mother reluctantly. "No! Don't trouble. It's all right. Don't sit up. We shall be home fairly soon." She did not want her son's privacy intruded upon.

"Very good," said the governess.

It was about one o'clock when Paul's mother and father drove up to their house. All was still. Paul's mother went to her room and slipped off her white fur cloak. She had told her maid not to wait up for her. She heard her husband downstairs, mixing a whisky and soda.

And then, because of the strange anxiety at her heart, she stole upstairs to her son's room. Noiselessly she went along the upper corridor. Was there a faint noise? What was it?

She stood, with arrested muscles, outside his door, listening. There was a strange, heavy, and yet not loud noise. Her heart stood still. It was a soundless noise, yet rushing and powerful. Something huge, in violent, hushed motion. What was it? What in God's name was it? She ought to know. She felt that she knew the noise. She knew what it was.

Yet she could not place it. She couldn't say what it was. And on and on it went, like a madness.

Softly, frozen with anxiety and fear, she turned the door-handle.

The room was dark. Yet in the space near the window, she heard and saw something plunging to and fro. She gazed in fear and amazement.

Then suddenly she switched on the light, and saw her son, in his green pyjamas, madly surging on the rocking-horse. The blaze of light suddenly lit him up, as he urged the wooden horse, and lit her up, as she stood, blonde, in her dress of pale green and crystal, in the doorway.

"Paul!" she cried. "Whatever are you doing?"

"It's Malabar!" he screamed in a powerful, strange voice. "It's Malabar!"

His eyes blazed at her for one strange and senseless second, as he ceased urging his wooden horse. Then he fell with a crash to the ground, and she, all her tormented motherhood flooding upon her, rushed to gather him up.

But he was unconscious, and unconscious he remained, with some brain-fever. He talked and tossed, and his mother sat stonily by his side.

"Malabar! It's Malabar! Bassett, Bassett, I *know!* It's Malabar!"

So the child cried, trying to get up and urge the rocking-horse that gave him his inspiration.

"What does he mean by Malabar?" asked the heart-frozen mother.

"I don't know," said the father stonily.

"What does he mean by Malabar?" she asked her brother Oscar.

"It's one of the horses running for the Derby," was the answer.

And, in spite of himself, Oscar Cresswell spoke to Bassett, and himself put a thousand on Malabar: at fourteen to one.

The third day of the illness was critical: they were waiting for a change. The boy, with his rather long, curly hair, was tossing ceaselessly on the pillow. He neither slept nor regained consciousness, and his eyes were like blue stones. His mother sat, feeling her heart had gone, turned actually into a stone.

In the evening, Oscar Cresswell did not come, but Bassett sent a message, saying could he come up for one moment, just one moment? Paul's mother was very angry at the intrusion, but on second thoughts she agreed. The boy was the same. Perhaps Bassett might bring him to consciousness.

The gardener, a shortish fellow with a little brown moustache and sharp little brown eyes, tiptoed into the room, touched his imaginary cap to Paul's mother, and stole to the bedside, staring with glittering, smallish eyes at the tossing, dying child.

"Master Paul!" he whispered. "Master Paul! Malabar came in first all right, a clean win. I did as you told me. You've made over seventy thousand pounds, you have; you've got over eighty thousand. Malabar came in all right, Master Paul."

"Malabar! Malabar! Did I say Malabar, mother? Did I say Malabar? Do you think I'm lucky, mother? I knew Malabar, didn't I? Over eighty thousand pounds! I call that lucky, don't you, mother? Over eighty thousand pounds! I knew, didn't I know I knew? Malabar came in all right. If I ride my horse till I'm sure, then I tell you, Bassett, you can go as high as you like. Did you go for all you were worth, Bassett?"

"I went a thousand on it, Master Paul."

"I never told you, mother, that if I can ride my horse, and *get there,* then I'm absolutely sure—oh, absolutely! Mother, did I ever tell you? I *am* lucky!"

"No, you never did," said his mother.

But the boy died in the night.

And even as he lay dead, his mother heard her brother's voice saying to her: "My God, Hester, you're eighty-odd thousand to the good, and a poor devil of a son to the bad. But, poor devil, poor devil, he's best gone out of a life where he rides his rocking-horse to find a winner."

William Faulkner (1897–1962)

A ROSE FOR EMILY

1

When Miss Emily Grierson died, our whole town went to her funeral: the men through a sort of respectful affection for a fallen monument, the women mostly out of curiosity to see the inside of her house, which no one save an old manservant—a combined gardener and cook—had seen in at least ten years.

It was a big, squarish frame house that had once been white, decorated with cupolas and spires and scrolled balconies in the heavily lightsome style of the seventies, set on what had once been our most select street. But garages and cotton gins had encroached and obliterated even the august names of that neighborhood; only Miss Emily's house was left, lifting its stubborn and coquettish decay above the cotton wagons and the gasoline pumps—an eyesore among eyesores. And now Miss Emily had gone to join the representatives of those august names where they lay in the cedar-bemused cemetery among the ranked and anonymous graves of Union and Confederate soldiers who fell at the battle of Jefferson.

Alive, Miss Emily had been a tradition, a duty and a care; a sort of hereditary obligation upon the town, dating from that day in 1894 when Colonel Sartoris, the mayor—he who fathered the edict that no Negro woman should appear on the streets without an apron—remitted her taxes, the dispensation dating from the death of her father on into perpetuity. Not that Miss Emily would have accepted charity. Colonel Sartoris invented an involved tale to the effect that Miss Emily's father had loaned money to the town, which the town, as a matter of business, preferred this way of repaying. Only a man of Colonel Sartoris' generation and thought could have invented it, and only a woman could have believed it.

When the next generation, with its more modern ideas, became mayors and aldermen, this arrangement created some little dissatisfaction. On the first of the year they mailed her a tax notice. February came, and there was no reply. They wrote her a formal letter, asking her to call at the sheriff's office at her convenience. A week later the mayor wrote her himself, offering to call or send his car for her and received in reply a note on paper of an archaic shape, in a thin flowing calligraphy in faded ink, to the effect that she no longer went out at all. The tax notice was also enclosed, without comment.

They called a special meeting of the Board of Aldermen. A deputation waited upon her, knocked at the door through which no visitor had passed since she ceased giving china-painting lessons eight or ten years earlier. They were admitted by the old Negro into a dim hall from which a stairway mounted into still more shadow. It smelled of dust and disuse—a close, dank smell. The Negro led them into the parlor. It was furnished in heavy, leather-covered furniture. When the Negro opened the blinds of one window, they could see that the leather was cracked; and when they sat down, a faint dust rose sluggishly about their thighs, spinning with slow motes in the single sun-ray. On a tarnished gilt easel before the fireplace stood a crayon portrait of Miss Emily's father.

They rose when she entered—a small, fat woman in black, with a thin gold chain descending to her waist and vanishing into her belt, leaning on an ebony cane with a tarnished gold head. Her skeleton was small and spare; perhaps that was why what would have been merely plumpness in another was obesity in her. She looked bloated, like a body long submerged in motionless water, and of that pallid hue. Her eyes, lost in the fatty ridges of her face, looked like two small pieces of coal pressed into a lump of dough as they moved from one face to another while the visitors stated their errand.

She did not ask them to sit. She just stood in the door and listened quietly until the spokesman came to a stumbling halt. Then they could hear the invisible watch ticking at the end of the gold chain.

Her voice was dry and cold. "I have no taxes in Jefferson. Colonel Sartoris explained it to me. Perhaps one of you can gain access to the city records and satisfy yourselves."

"But we have. We are the city authorities, Miss Emily. Didn't you get a notice from the sheriff, signed by him?"

"I received a paper, yes." Miss Emily said. "Perhaps he considers himself the sheriff . . . I have no taxes in Jefferson."

"But there is nothing on the books to show that, you see. We must go by the—"

"See Colonel Sartoris. I have no taxes in Jefferson."

"But, Miss Emily—"

"See Colonel Sartoris." (Colonel Sartoris had been dead almost ten years.) "I have no taxes in Jefferson. Tobe!" The Negro appeared. "Show these gentlemen out."

2

So she vanquished them, horse and foot, just as she had vanquished their fathers thirty years before about the smell. That was two years after her father's death and a short time after her sweetheart—the one we believed would marry her—had deserted her. After her father's death she went out very little; after her sweetheart went away, people hardly saw her at all. A few of the ladies had the temerity to call, but were not received, and the only sign of life about the place was the Negro man—a young man then—going in and out with a market basket.

"Just as if a man—any man—could keep a kitchen properly," the ladies said; so they were not surprised when the smell developed. It was another link between the gross, teeming world and the high and mighty Griersons.

A neighbor, a woman, complained to the mayor, Judge Stevens, eighty years old.

"But what will you have me do about it, madam?" he said.

"Why, send her word to stop it," the woman said. "Isn't there a law?"

"I'm sure that won't be necessary," Judge Stevens said. "It's probably just a snake or a rat that nigger of hers killed in the yard. I'll speak to him about it."

The next day he received two more complaints, one from a man who came in diffident deprecation. "We really must do something about it, Judge. I'd be the last one in the world to bother Miss Emily, but we've got to do something." That night the Board of Aldermen met—three graybeards and one younger man, a member of the rising generation.

"It's simple enough," he said. "Send her word to have her place cleaned up. Give her a certain time to do it in, and if she don't . . ."

"Dammit, sir," Judge Stevens said, "will you accuse a lady to her face of smelling bad?"

So the next night, after midnight, four men crossed Miss Emily's lawn and slunk about the house like burglars, sniffing along the base of the brickwork and at the cellar openings while one of them performed a regular sowing motion with his hand out of a sack slung from his shoulder. They broke open the cellar door and sprinkled lime there, and in all the outbuildings. As they recrossed the lawn, a window that had been dark was lighted and Miss Emily sat in it, the light behind her, and her upright torso motionless as that of an idol. They crept quietly across the lawn and into the shadow of the locusts that lined the street. After a week or two the smell went away.

That was when people had begun to feel really sorry for her. People in our town, remembering how old lady Wyatt, her great-aunt, had gone completely crazy at last, believed that the Griersons held themselves a little too high for what they really were. None of the young men were quite good enough for Miss Emily and such. We had long thought of them as a tableau. Miss Emily a slender figure in white in the background, her father a spraddled silhouette in the foreground, his back to her and clutching a horsewhip, the two of them framed by the back-flung front door. So when she got to be thirty and was still single, we were not pleased exactly, but vindicated; even with insanity in the family she wouldn't have turned down all of her chances if they had really materialized.

When her father died, it got about that the house was all that was left to her; and in a way, people were glad. At last they could pity Miss Emily. Being left alone, and a pauper, she had become humanized. Now she too would know the old thrill and the old despair of a penny more or less.

The day after his death all the ladies prepared to call at the house and offer condolence and aid, as is our custom. Miss Emily met them at the door, dressed as usual and with no trace of grief on her face. She told them that her father was not dead. She did that for three days, with the ministers calling on her, and the doctors, trying to persuade her to let them dispose of the body. Just as they were about to resort to law and force, she broke down, and they buried her father quickly.

We did not say she was crazy then. We believed she had to do that. We remembered all the young men her father had driven away, and we knew that with nothing left, she would have to cling to that which had robbed her, as people will.

3

She was sick for a long time. When we saw her again, her hair was cut short, making her look like a girl, with a vague resemblance to those angels in colored church windows—sort of tragic and serene.

The town had just let the contracts for paving the sidewalks, and in the summer after her father's death they began the work. The construction company came with niggers and mules and machinery, and a foreman named Homer Barron, a Yankee—a big, dark, ready man, with a big voice and eyes lighter than his face. The little boys would follow in groups to hear him cuss the niggers, and the niggers singing in time to the rise and fall of picks. Pretty soon he knew everybody in town. Whenever you heard a lot of laughing anywhere about the square, Homer Barron would be in the center of the group. Presently we began to see him and Miss Emily on Sunday afternoons driving in the yellow-wheeled buggy and the matched team of bays from the livery stable.

At first we were glad that Miss Emily would have an interest, because the ladies all said, "Of course a Grierson would not think seriously of a Northerner, a day laborer." But there were still others, older people, who said that even grief could not cause a real lady to forget *noblesse oblige*—without calling it *noblesse oblige*. They just said, "Poor Emily. Her kinsfolk should come to her." She had some kin in Alabama; but years ago her father had fallen out with them over the estate of old lady Wyatt, the crazy woman, and there was no communication between the two families. They had not even been represented at the funeral.

And as soon as the old people said, "Poor Emily," the whispering began. "Do you suppose it's really so?" they said to one another. "Of course it is. What else could . . ." This behind their hands; rustling of craned silk and satin behind jalousies closed upon the sun of Sunday afternoon as the thin, swift clop-clop-clop of the matched team passed: "Poor Emily."

She carried her head high enough—even when we believed that she was fallen. It was as if she demanded more than ever the recognition of her dignity as the last Grierson; as if it had wanted that touch of earthiness to reaffirm her imperviousness. Like when she bought the rat poison, the arsenic. That was over a year after they had begun to say "Poor Emily," and while the two female cousins were visiting her.

"I want some poison," she said to the druggist. She was over thirty then, still a slight woman, though thinner than usual, with cold, haughty black eyes in a face the flesh of which was strained across the temples and about the eye-sockets as you imagine a lighthouse-keeper's face ought to look. "I want some poison," she said.

"Yes, Miss Emily. What kind? For rats and such? I'd recom—"

"I want the best you have. I don't care what kind."

The druggist named several. "They'll kill anything up to an elephant. But what you want is—"

"Arsenic," Miss Emily said. "Is that a good one?"

"Is . . . arsenic? Yes, ma'am. But what you want—"

"I want arsenic."

The druggist looked down at her. She looked back at him, erect, her face like a strained flag. "Why, of course," the druggist said. "If that's what you want. But the law requires you to tell what you are going to use it for."

Miss Emily just stared at him, her head tilted back in order to look him eye for eye, until he looked away and went and got the arsenic and wrapped it up. The Negro delivery boy brought her the package; the druggist didn't come back. When she opened the package at home there was written on the box, under the skull and bones: "For rats."

4

So the next day we all said, "She will kill herself"; and we said it would be the best thing. When she had first begun to be seen with Homer Barron, we had said, "She will marry him." Then we said, "She will persuade him yet," because Homer himself had remarked—he liked men, and it was known that he drank with the younger men in the Elks' Club—that he was not a marrying man. Later we said, "Poor Emily" behind the jalousies as they passed on Sunday afternoon in the glittering buggy. Miss Emily with her head high and Homer Barron with his hat cocked and a cigar in his teeth, reins and whip in a yellow glove.

Then some of the ladies began to say that it was a disgrace to the town, and a bad example to the young people. The men did not want to interfere, but at last the ladies forced the Baptist minister—Miss Emily's people were Episcopal—to call upon her. He would never divulge what happened during that interview, but he refused to go back again. The next Sunday they again drove about the streets, and the following day the minister's wife wrote to Miss Emily's relations in Alabama.

So she had blood-kin under her roof again and we sat back to watch developments. At first nothing happened. Then we were sure they were to be married. We learned that Miss Emily had been to the jeweler's and ordered a man's toilet set in silver, with the letters H.B. on each piece. Two days later we learned that she had bought a complete outfit of men's clothing, including a nightshirt, and we said, "They are married." We were really glad. We were glad because the two female cousins were even more Grierson than Miss Emily had ever been.

So we were not surprised when Homer Barron—the streets had been finished some time since—was gone. We were a little disappointed that there was not a public blowing-off, but we believed that he had gone on to prepare for Miss Emily's coming, or to give her a chance to get rid of the cousins. (By that time it was a cabal, and we were all Miss Emily's allies to help circumvent the cousins.) Sure enough, after another week they departed. And, as we had expected all along, within three days Homer Barron was back in town. A neighbor saw the Negro man admit him at the kitchen door at dusk one evening.

And that was the last we saw of Homer Barron. And of Miss Emily for some time. The Negro man went in and out with the market basket, but the front door remained closed. Now and then we would see her at a window for a moment, as the men did that night when they sprinkled the lime, but for almost six months she did not appear on the streets. Then we knew that this was to be expected too; as if that quality of her father which had thwarted her woman's life so many times had been too virulent and too furious to die.

When we next saw Miss Emily, she had grown fat and her hair was turning gray. During the next few years it grew grayer and grayer until it attained an even pepper-and-salt iron-gray, when it ceased turning. Up to the day of her death at seventy-four it was still that vigorous iron-gray, like the hair of an active man.

From that time on her front door remained closed, save for a period of six or seven years, when she was about forty, during which she gave lessons in china-painting. She fitted up a studio in one of the downstairs rooms, where the daughters and grand-daughters of Colonel Sartoris' contemporaries were sent to her with the same regularity and in the same spirit that they were sent to church on Sundays, with a twenty-five cent piece for the collection plate. Meanwhile her taxes had been remitted.

The newer generation became the backbone and the spirit of the town, and the painting pupils grew up and fell away and did not send their children to her with boxes of color and tedious brushes and pictures cut from the ladies' magazines. The front door closed upon the last one and remained closed for good. When the town got free postal delivery, Miss Emily alone refused to let them fasten the metal numbers above her door and attach a mailbox to it. She would not listen to them.

Daily, monthly, yearly we watched the Negro grow grayer and more stooped, going in and out with the market basket. Each December we sent her a tax notice, which would be returned by the post office a week later, unclaimed. Now and then we would see her in one of the downstairs windows—she had evidently shut up the top floor of the house—like the carven torso of an idol in a niche, looking or not looking at us, we could never tell which. Thus she passed from generation to generation—dear, inescapable, impervious, tranquil, and perverse.

And so she died. Fell ill in the house filled with dust and shadows, with only a doddering Negro man to wait on her. We did not even know she was sick; we had long since given up trying to get any information from the Negro. He talked to no one, probably not even to her, for his voice had grown harsh and rusty, as if from disuse.

She died in one of the downstairs rooms, in a heavy walnut bed with a curtain, her gray head propped on a pillow yellow and moldy with age and lack of sunlight.

5

The Negro met the first of the ladies at the front door and let them in, with their hushed, sibilant voices and their quick, curious glances, and then he disappeared. He walked right through the house and out the back and was not seen again.

The two female cousins came at once. They held the funeral on the second day, with the town coming to look at Miss Emily beneath a mass of bought flowers, with the crayon face of her father musing profoundly above the bier and the ladies sibilant and macabre; and the very old men—some in their brushed Confederate uniforms—on the porch and the lawn, talking of Miss Emily as if she had been a contemporary of theirs, believing that they had danced with her and courted her perhaps, confusing time with its mathematical progression, as the old do, to whom all the past is not a diminishing road but, instead, a huge meadow which no winter ever quite touches, divided from them now by the narrow bottleneck of the most recent decade of years.

Already we knew that there was one room in that region above stairs which no one had seen in forty years, and which would have to be forced. They waited until Miss Emily was decently in the ground before they opened it.

The violence of breaking down the door seemed to fill this room with pervading dust. A thin, acrid pall as of the tomb seemed to lie everywhere upon this room decked and furnished as for a bridal: upon the valance curtains of faded rose color, upon the rose-shaded lights, upon the dressing table, upon the delicate array of crystal and the man's toilet things backed with tarnished silver, silver so tarnished that the monogram was obscured. Among them lay a collar and tie, as if they had just been removed, which, lifted, left upon the surface a pale crescent in the dust. Upon a chair hung the suit, carefully folded; beneath it the two mute shoes and the discarded socks.

The man himself lay in the bed.

For a long while we just stood there, looking down at the profound and fleshless grin. The body had apparently once lain in the attitude of an embrace, but now the long sleep that outlasts love, that conquers even the grimace of love, had cuckolded him. What was left of him, rotted beneath what was left of the nightshirt, had become inextricable from the bed in which he lay; and upon him and upon the pillow beside him lay that even coating of the patient and biding dust.

Then we noticed that in the second pillow was the indentation of a head. One of us lifted something from it, and leaning forward, that faint and invisible dust dry and acrid in the nostrils, we saw a long strand of iron-gray hair.

THAT EVENING SUN

I

Monday is no different from any other weekday in Jefferson now. The streets are paved now, and the telephone and electric companies are cutting down more and more of the shade trees—the water oaks, the maples and locusts and elms—to make room for iron poles bearing clusters of bloated and ghostly and bloodless grapes, and we have a city laundry which makes the rounds on Monday morning, gathering the bundles of clothes into bright-colored, specially-made motor cars: the soiled wearing of a whole week now flees apparitionlike behind alert and irritable electric horns, with a long diminishing noise of rubber and asphalt like tearing silk, and even the Negro women who still take in white people's washing after the old custom, fetch and deliver it in automobiles.

But fifteen years ago, on Monday morning the quiet, dusty, shady streets would be full of Negro women with, balanced on their steady, turbaned heads, bundles of clothes tied up in sheets, almost as large as cotton bales, carried so without touch of hand between the kitchen door of the white house and the blackened washpot beside a cabin door in Negro Hollow.

Nancy would set her bundle on the top of her head, then upon the bundle in turn she would set the black straw sailor hat which she wore winter and summer. She was tall, with a high, sad face sunken a little where her teeth were missing. Sometimes we would go a part of the way down the lane and across the pasture with her, to watch the balanced bundle and the hat that never bobbed nor wavered, even when she walked down into the ditch and up the other side and stooped through the fence. She would go down on her hands and knees and crawl through the gap, her head rigid, uptilted, the bundle steady as a rock or a balloon, and rise to her feet again and go on.

Sometimes the husbands of the washing women would fetch and deliver the clothes, but Jesus never did that for Nancy, even before father told him to stay away from our house, even when Dilsey was sick and Nancy would come to cook for us.

And then about half the time we'd have to go down the lane to Nancy's cabin and tell her to come on and cook breakfast. We would stop at the ditch, because father told us to not have anything to do with Jesus—he was a short black man, with a razor scar down his face—and we would throw rocks at Nancy's house until she came to the door, leaning her head around it without any clothes on.

"What yawl mean, chunking my house?" Nancy said. "What you little devils mean?"

"Father says for you to come on and get breakfast," Caddy said. "Father says it's over a half an hour now, and you've got to come this minute."

"I aint studying no breakfast," Nancy said. "I going to get my sleep out."

"I bet you're drunk," Jason said. "Father says you're drunk. Are you drunk, Nancy?"

"Who says I is?" Nancy said. "I got to get my sleep out. I aint studying no breakfast."

So after a while we quit chunking the cabin and went back home. When she finally came, it was too late for me to go to school. So we thought it was whisky until that day they arrested her again and they were taking her to jail and they passed Mr. Stovall. He was the cashier in the bank and a deacon in the Baptist church, and Nancy began to say:

"When you going to pay me, white man? When you going to pay me, white man? It's been three times now since you paid me a cent—" Mr. Stovall knocked her down, but she kept on saying, "When you going to pay me, white man? It's been three times now since—" until Mr. Stovall kicked her in the mouth with his heel and the marshal caught Mr. Stovall back, and Nancy lying in the street, laughing. She turned her head and spat out some blood and teeth and said, "It's been three times now since he paid me a cent."

That was how she lost her teeth, and all that day they told about Nancy and Mr. Stovall, and all that night the ones that passed the jail could hear Nancy singing and yelling. They could see her hands holding to the window bars, and a lot of them stopped along the fence, listening to her and to the jailer trying to make her stop. She didn't shut up until almost daylight, when the jailer began to hear a bumping and scraping upstairs and he went up there and found Nancy hanging from the window bar. He said that it was cocaine and not whisky, because no nigger would try to commit suicide unless he was full of cocaine, because a nigger full of cocaine wasn't a nigger any longer.

The jailer cut her down and revived her; then he beat her, whipped her. She had hung herself with her dress. She had fixed it all right, but when they arrested her she didn't have on anything except a dress and so she didn't have anything to tie her hands with and she couldn't make her hands let go of the window ledge. So the jailer heard the noise and ran up there and found Nancy hanging from the window, stark naked, her belly already swelling out a little, like a little balloon.

When Dilsey was sick in her cabin and Nancy was cooking for us, we could see her apron swelling out: that was before father told Jesus to stay away from the house. Jesus was in the kitchen, sitting behind the stove, with his razor scar on his black face like a piece of dirty string. He said it was a watermelon that Nancy had under her dress.

"It never come off of your vine, though," Nancy said.

"Off of what vine?" Caddy said.

"I can cut down the vine it did come off of," Jesus said.

"What makes you want to talk like that before these chillen?" Nancy said. "Whyn't you go to work? You done et. You want Mr Jason to catch you hanging around his kitchen, talking that way before these chillen?"

"Talking what way?" Caddy said. "What vine?"

"I cant hang around white man's kitchen," Jesus said. "But white man can hang around mine. White man can come in my house, but I cant stop him. When white man want to come in my house, I aint got no house. I cant stop him, but he cant kick me outen it. He cant do that."

Dilsey was still sick in her cabin. Father told Jesus to stay off our place. Dilsey was still sick. It was a long time. We were in the library after supper.

"Isn't Nancy through in the kitchen yet?" mother said. "It seems to me that she has had plenty of time to have finished the dishes."

"Let Quentin go and see," father said. "Go and see if Nancy is through, Quentin. Tell her she can go on home."

I went to the kitchen. Nancy was through. The dishes were put away and the fire was out. Nancy was sitting in a chair, close to the cold stove. She looked at me.

"Mother wants to know if you are through," I said.

"Yes," Nancy said. She looked at me. "I done finished." She looked at me.

"What is it?" I said. "What is it?"

"I aint nothing but a nigger," Nancy said. "It aint none of my fault."

She looked at me, sitting in the chair before the cold stove, the sailor hat on her head. I went back to the library. It was the cold stove and all, when you think of a kitchen being warm and busy and cheerful. And with a cold stove and the dishes all put away, and nobody wanting to eat at that hour.

"Is she through?" mother said.

"Yessum," I said.

"What is she doing?" mother said.

"She's not doing anything. She's through."

"I'll go and see," father said.

"Maybe she's waiting for Jesus to come and take her home," Caddy said.

"Jesus is gone," I said. Nancy told us how one morning she woke up and Jesus was gone.

"He quit me," Nancy said. "Done gone to Memphis, I reckon. Dodging them city *po*-lice for a while, I reckon."

"And a good riddance," father said. "I hope he stays there."

"Nancy's scaired of the dark," Jason said.

"So are you," Caddy said.

"I'm not," Jason said.

"Scairy cat," Caddy said.

"I'm not," Jason said.

"You, Candace!" mother said. Father came back.

"I am going to walk down the lane with Nancy," he said. "She says that Jesus is back."

"Has she seen him?" mother said.

"No. Some Negro sent her word that he was back in town. I wont be long."

"You'll leave me alone, to take Nancy home?" mother said. "Is her safety more precious to you than mine?"

"I wont be long," father said.

"You'll leave these children unprotected, with that Negro about?"

"I'm going too," Caddy said. "Let me go, Father."

"What would he do with them, if he were unfortunate enough to have them?" father said.

"I want to go, too," Jason said.

"Jason!" mother said. She was speaking to father. You could tell that by the way she said the name. Like she believed that all day father had been trying to think of doing the thing she wouldn't like the most, and that she knew all the time that after a while he would think of it. I stayed quiet, because father and I both knew that mother would want him to make me stay with her if she just thought of it in time. So father didn't look at me. I was the oldest. I was nine and Caddy was seven and Jason was five.

"Nonsense," father said. "We wont be long."

Nancy had her hat on. We came to the lane. "Jesus always been good to me," Nancy said. "Whenever he had two dollars, one of them was mine." We walked in the lane. "If I can just get through the lane," Nancy said, "I be all right then."

The lane was always dark. "This is where Jason got scared on Hallowe'en," Caddy said.

"I didn't," Jason said.

"Cant Aunt Rachel do anything with him?" father said. Aunt Rachel was old. She lived in a cabin beyond Nancy's, by herself. She had white hair and she smoked a pipe in the door, all day long; she didn't work any more. They said she was Jesus' mother. Sometimes she said she was and sometimes she said she wasn't any kin to Jesus.

"Yes, you did," Caddy said. "You were scairder than Frony. You were scairder than T.P. even. Scairder than niggers."

"Cant nobody do nothing with him," Nancy said. "He say I done woke up the devil in him and aint but one thing going to lay it down again."

"Well, he's gone now," father said. "There's nothing for you to be afraid of now. And if you'd just let white men alone."

"Let what white men alone?" Caddy said. "How let them alone?"

"He aint gone nowhere," Nancy said. "I can feel him. I can feel him now, in this lane. He hearing us talk, every word, hid somewhere, waiting. I aint seen him, and I aint going to see him again but once more, with that razor in his mouth. That razor on that string down his back, inside his shirt. And then I aint going to be even surprised."

"I wasn't scaired," Jason said.

"If you'd behave yourself, you'd have kept out of this," father said. "But it's all right now. He's probably in St. Louis now. Probably got another wife by now and forgot all about you."

"If he has, I better not find out about it," Nancy said. "I'd stand there right over them, and every time he wropped her, I'd cut that arm off. I'd cut his head off and I'd slit her belly and I'd shove—"

"Hush," father said.

"Slit whose belly, Nancy?" Caddy said.

"I wasn't scaired," Jason said. "I'd walk right down this lane by myself."

"Yah," Caddy said. "You wouldn't dare to put your foot down in it if we were not here too."

II

Dilsey was still sick, so we took Nancy home every night until mother said, "How much longer is this going on? I to be left alone in this big house while you take home a frightened Negro?"

We fixed a pallet in the kitchen for Nancy. One night we waked up, hearing the sound. It was not singing and it was not crying, coming up the dark stairs. There was a light in mother's room and we heard father going down the hall, down the back stairs, and Caddy and I went into the hall. The floor was cold. Our toes curled away from it while we listened to the sound. It was like singing and it wasn't like singing, like the sounds that Negroes make.

Then it stopped and we heard father going down the back stairs, and we went to the head of the stairs. Then the sound began again, in the stairway, not loud, and we could see Nancy's eyes halfway up the stairs, against the wall. They looked like cat's eyes do, like a big cat against the wall, watching us. When we came down the steps to where she was, she quit making the sound again, and we stood there until father came back up from the kitchen, with his pistol in his hand. He went back down with Nancy and they came back with Nancy's pallet.

We spread the pallet in our room. After the light in mother's room went off, we could see Nancy's eyes again. "Nancy," Caddy whispered, "are you asleep, Nancy?"

Nancy whispered something. It was oh or no, I dont know which. Like nobody had made it, like it came from nowhere and went nowhere, until it was like Nancy was not there at all; that I had looked so hard at her eyes on the stairs that they had got printed on my eyeballs, like the sun does when you have closed your eyes and there is no sun. "Jesus," Nancy whispered. "Jesus."

"Was it Jesus?" Caddy said. "Did he try to come into the kitchen?"

"Jesus," Nancy said. Like this: Jeeeeeeeeeeeeeeesus, until the sound went out, like a match or a candle does.

"It's the other Jesus she means," I said.

"Can you see us, Nancy?" Caddy whispered. "Can you see our eyes too?"

"I aint nothing but a nigger," Nancy said. "God knows. God knows."

"What did you see down there in the kitchen?" Caddy whispered. "What tried to get in?"

"God knows," Nancy said. We could see her eyes. "God knows."

Dilsey got well. She cooked dinner. "You'd better stay in bed a day or two longer," father said.

"What for?" Dilsey said. "If I had been a day later, this place would be to rack and ruin. Get on out of here now, and let me get my kitchen straight again."

Dilsey cooked supper too. And that night, just before dark, Nancy came into the kitchen.

"How do you know he's back?" Dilsey said. "You aint seen him."

"Jesus is a nigger," Jason said.

"I can feel him," Nancy said. "I can feel him laying yonder in the ditch."

"Tonight?" Dilsey said. "Is he there tonight?"

"Dilsey's a nigger too," Jason said.

"You try to eat something," Dilsey said.

"I dont want nothing," Nancy said.

"I aint a nigger," Jason said.

"Drink some coffee," Dilsey said. She poured a cup of coffee for Nancy. "Do you know he's out there tonight? How come you know it's tonight?"

"I know," Nancy said. "He's there, waiting. I know. I done lived with him too long. I know what he's fixing to do fore he know it himself."

"Drink some coffee," Dilsey said. Nancy held the cup to her mouth and blew into the cup. Her mouth pursed out like a spreading adder's, like a rubber mouth, like she had blown all the color out of her lips with blowing the coffee.

"I aint a nigger," Jason said. "Are you a nigger, Nancy?"

"I hellborn, child," Nancy said. "I wont be nothing soon. I going back where I come from soon."

III

She began to drink the coffee. While she was drinking, holding the cup in both hands, she began to make the sound again. She made the sound into the cup and the coffee sploshed out onto her hands and her dress. Her eyes looked at us and she sat there, her elbows on her knees, holding the cup in both hands, looking at us across the wet cup, making the sound. "Look at Nancy," Jason said. "Nancy cant cook for us now. Dilsey's got well now."

"You hush up," Dilsey said. Nancy held the cup in both hands, looking at us, making the sound, like there were two of them: one looking at us and the other making the sound. "Whyn't you let Mr Jason telefoam the marshal?" Dilsey said. Nancy stopped then, holding the cup in her long brown hands. She tried to drink some coffee again, but it sploshed out of the cup, onto her hands and her dress, and she put the cup down. Jason watched her.

"I cant swallow it," Nancy said. "I swallows but it wont go down me."

"You go down to the cabin," Dilsey said. "Frony will fix you a pallet and I'll be there soon."

"Wont no nigger stop him," Nancy said.

"I aint a nigger," Jason said. "Am I, Dilsey?"

"I reckon not," Dilsey said. She looked at Nancy. "I dont reckon so. What you going to do, then?"

Nancy looked at us. Her eyes went fast, like she was afraid there wasn't time to look, without hardly moving at all. She looked at us, at all three of us at one time. "You member that night I stayed in yawls' room?" she said. She told about how we waked up early the next morning, and played. We had to play quiet, on her pallet, until father woke up and it was time to get breakfast. "Go and ask your maw to let me stay here tonight," Nancy said. "I wont need no pallet. We can play some more."

Caddy asked mother. Jason went too. "I cant have Negroes sleeping in the bedrooms," mother said. Jason cried. He cried until mother said he couldn't have any dessert for three days if he didn't stop. Then Jason said he would stop if Dilsey would make a chocolate cake. Father was there.

"Why dont you do something about it?" mother said. "What do we have officers for?"

"Why is Nancy afraid of Jesus?" Caddy said. "Are you afraid of father, mother?"

"What could the officers do?" father said. "If Nancy hasn't seen him, how could the officers find him?"

"Then why is she afraid?" mother said.

"She says he is there. She says she knows he is there tonight."

"Yet we pay taxes," mother said. "I must wait here alone in this big house while you take a Negro woman home."

"You know that I am not lying outside with a razor," father said.

"I'll stop if Dilsey will make a chocolate cake," Jason said. Mother told us to go out and father said he didn't know if Jason would get a chocolate cake or not, but he knew what Jason was going to get in about a minute. We went back to the kitchen and told Nancy.

"Father said for you to go home and lock the door, and you'll be all right," Caddy said. "All right from what, Nancy? Is Jesus mad at you?" Nancy was holding the coffee cup in her hands again, her elbows on her knees and her hands holding the cup between her knees. She was looking into the cup. "What have you done that made Jesus mad?" Caddy said. Nancy let the cup go. It didn't break on the floor, but the coffee spilled out, and Nancy sat there with her hands still holding the shape of the cup. She began to make the sound again, not loud. Not singing and not unsinging. We watched her.

"Here," Dilsey said. "You quit that, now. You get aholt of yourself. You wait here. I going to get Versh to walk home with you." Dilsey went out.

We looked at Nancy. Her shoulders kept shaking, but she quit making the sound. We watched her. "What's Jesus going to do to you?" Caddy said. "He went away."

Nancy looked at us. "We had fun that night I stayed in yawls' room, didn't we?"

"I didn't," Jason said. "I didn't have any fun."

"You were asleep in mother's room," Caddy said. "You were not there."

"Let's go down to my house and have some more fun," Nancy said.

"Mother wont let us," I said. "It's too late now."

"Dont bother her," Nancy said. "We can tell her in the morning. She wont mind."

"She wouldn't let us," I said.

"Dont ask her now," Nancy said. "Dont bother her now."

"She didn't say we couldn't go," Caddy said.

"We didn't ask," I said.

"If you go, I'll tell," Jason said.

"We'll have fun," Nancy said. "They won't mind, just to my house. I been working for yawl a long time. They won't mind."

"I'm not afraid to go," Caddy said. "Jason is the one that's afraid. He'll tell."

"I'm not," Jason said.

"Yes, you are," Caddy said. "You'll tell."

"I won't tell," Jason said. "I'm not afraid."

"Jason ain't afraid to go with me," Nancy said. "Is you, Jason?"

"Jason is going to tell," Caddy said. The lane was dark. We passed the pasture gate. "I bet if something was to jump out from behind that gate, Jason would holler."

"I wouldn't," Jason said. We walked down the lane. Nancy was talking loud.

"What are you talking so loud for, Nancy?" Caddy said.

"Who, me?" Nancy said. "Listen at Quentin and Caddy and Jason saying I'm talking loud."

"You talk like there was five of us here," Caddy said. "You talk like father was here too."

"Who; me talking loud, Mr Jason?" Nancy said.

"Nancy called Jason 'Mister,'" Caddy said.

"Listen how Caddy and Quentin and Jason talk," Nancy said.

"We're not talking loud," Caddy said. "You're the one that's talking like father—"

"Hush," Nancy said; "hush, Mr Jason."

"Nancy called Jason 'Mister' aguh—"

"Hush," Nancy said. She was talking loud when we crossed the ditch and stooped through the fence where she used to stoop through with the clothes on her head. Then we came to her house. We were going fast then. She opened the door. The smell of the house was like the lamp and the smell of Nancy was like the wick, like they were waiting for one another to begin to smell. She lit the lamp and closed the door and put the bar up. Then she quit talking loud, looking at us.

"What're we going to do?" Caddy said.

"What do yawl want to do?" Nancy said.

"You said we would have some fun," Caddy said.

There was something about Nancy's house; something you could smell besides Nancy and the house. Jason smelled it, even. "I don't want to stay here," he said. "I want to go home."

"Go home, then," Caddy said.

"I don't want to go by myself," Jason said.

"We're going to have some fun," Nancy said.

"How?" Caddy said.

Nancy stood by the door. She was looking at us, only it was like she had emptied her eyes, like she had quit using them. "What do you want to do?" she said.

"Tell us a story," Caddy said. "Can you tell a story?"

"Yes," Nancy said.

"Tell it," Caddy said. We looked at Nancy. "You don't know any stories."

"Yes," Nancy said. "Yes, I do."

She came and sat in a chair before the hearth. There was a little fire there. Nancy built it up, when it was already hot inside. She built a good blaze. She told a story. She talked like her eyes looked, like her eyes watching us and her voice talking to us did not belong to her. Like she was living somewhere else, waiting somewhere else. She was outside the cabin. Her voice was inside and the shape of her, the Nancy that could stoop under a barbed wire fence with a bundle of clothes balanced on her head as though without weight, like a balloon, was there. But that was all. "And so this here queen come walking up to the ditch, where that bad man was hiding. She was walking up to the ditch, and she say, 'If I can just get past this here ditch,' was what she say . . ."

"What ditch?" Caddy said. "A ditch like that one out there? Why did a queen want to go into a ditch?"

"To get to her house," Nancy said. She looked at us. "She had to cross the ditch to get into her house quick and bar the door."

"Why did she want to go home and bar the door?" Caddy said.

IV

Nancy looked at us. She quit talking. She looked at us. Jason's legs stuck straight out of his pants where he sat on Nancy's lap. "I don't think that's a good story," he said. "I want to go home."

"Maybe we had better," Caddy said. She got up from the floor. "I bet they are looking for us right now." She went toward the door.

"No," Nancy said. "Don't open it." She got up quick and passed Caddy. She didn't touch the door, the wooden bar.

"Why not?" Caddy said.

"Come back to the lamp," Nancy said. "We'll have fun. You don't have to go."

"We ought to go," Caddy said. "Unless we have a lot of fun." She and Nancy came back to the fire, the lamp.

"I want to go home," Jason said. "I'm going to tell."

"I know another story," Nancy said. She stood close to the lamp. She looked at Caddy, like when your eyes look up at a stick balanced on your nose. She had to look down to see Caddy, but her eyes looked like that, like when you are balancing a stick.

"I won't listen to it," Jason said. "I'll bang on the floor."

"It's a good one," Nancy said. "It's better than the other one."

"What's it about?" Caddy said. Nancy was standing by the lamp. Her hand was on the lamp, against the light, long and brown.

"Your hand is on that hot globe," Caddy said. "Don't it feel hot to your hand?"

Nancy looked at her hand on the lamp chimney. She took her hand away, slow. She stood there, looking at Caddy, wringing her long hand as though it were tied to her wrist with a string.

"Let's do something else," Caddy said.

"I want to go home," Jason said.

"I got some popcorn," Nancy said. She looked at Caddy and then at Jason and then at me and then at Caddy again. "I got some popcorn."

"I don't like popcorn," Jason said. "I'd rather have candy."

Nancy looked at Jason. "You can hold the popper." She was still wringing her hand; it was long and limp and brown.

"All right," Jason said. "I'll stay a while if I can do that. Caddy can't hold it. I'll want to go home again if Caddy holds the popper."

Nancy built up the fire. "Look at Nancy putting her hands in the fire," Caddy said. "What's the matter with you, Nancy?"

"I got popcorn," Nancy said. "I got some." She took the popper from under the bed. It was broken. Jason began to cry.

"Now we can't have any popcorn," he said.

"We ought to go home, anyway," Caddy said. "Come on, Quentin."

"Wait," Nancy said; "wait. I can fix it. Don't you want to help me fix it?"

"I don't think I want any," Caddy said. "It's too late now."

"You help me, Jason," Nancy said. "Don't you want to help me?"

"No," Jason said. "I want to go home."

"Hush," Nancy said; "hush. Watch. Watch me. I can fix it so Jason can hold it and pop the corn." She got a piece of wire and fixed the popper.

"It won't hold good," Caddy said.

"Yes, it will," Nancy said. "Yawl watch. Yawl help me shell some corn."

The popcorn was under the bed too. We shelled it into the popper and Nancy helped Jason hold the popper over the fire.

"It's not popping," Jason said. "I want to go home."

"You wait," Nancy said. "It'll begin to pop. We'll have fun then." She was sitting close to the fire. The lamp was turned up so high it was beginning to smoke.

"Why don't you turn it down some?" I said.

"It's all right," Nancy said. "I'll clean it. Yawl wait. The popcorn will start in a minute."

"I don't believe it's going to start," Caddy said. "We ought to start home, anyway. They'll be worried."

"No," Nancy said. "It's going to pop. Dilsey will tell um yawl with me. I been working for yawl long time. They won't mind if yawl at my house. You wait, now. It'll start popping any minute now."

Then Jason got some smoke in his eyes and he began to cry. He dropped the popper into the fire. Nancy got a wet rag and wiped Jason's face, but he didn't stop crying.

"Hush," she said. "Hush." But he didn't hush. Caddy took the popper out of the fire.

"It's burned up," she said. "You'll have to get some more popcorn, Nancy."

"Did you put all of it in?" Nancy said.

"Yes," Caddy said. Nancy looked at Caddy. Then she took the popper and opened it and poured the cinders into her apron and began to sort the grains, her hands long and brown, and we watching her.

"Haven't you got any more?" Caddy said.

"Yes," Nancy said; "yes. Look. This here ain't burnt. All we need to do is—"

"I want to go home," Jason said. "I'm going to tell."

"Hush," Caddy said. We all listened. Nancy's head was already turned toward the barred door, her eyes filled with red lamplight. "Somebody is coming," Caddy said.

Then Nancy began to make that sound again, not loud, sitting there above the fire, her long hands dangling between her knees; all of a sudden water began to come out on her face in big drops, running down her face, carrying in each one a little turning ball of firelight like a spark until it dropped off her chin. "She's not crying," I said.

"I ain't crying," Nancy said. Her eyes were closed. "I ain't crying. Who is it?"

"I don't know," Caddy said. She went to the door and looked out. "We've got to go now," she said. "Here comes father."

"I'm going to tell," Jason said. "Yawl made me come."

The water still ran down Nancy's face. She turned in her chair. "Listen. Tell him. Tell him we going to have fun. Tell him I take good care of yawl until in the morning. Tell him to let me come home with yawl and sleep on the floor. Tell him I won't need no pallet. We'll have fun. You member last time how we had so much fun?"

"I didn't have fun," Jason said. "You hurt me. You put smoke in my eyes. I'm going to tell."

V

Father came in. He looked at us. Nancy did not get up.

"Tell him," she said.

"Caddy made us come down here," Jason said. "I didn't want to."

Father came to the fire. Nancy looked up at him. "Can't you go to Aunt Rachel's and stay?" he said. Nancy looked up at father, her hands between her knees. "He's not here," father said. "I would have seen him. There's not a soul in sight."

"He in the ditch," Nancy said. "He waiting in the ditch yonder."

"Nonsense," father said. He looked at Nancy. "Do you know he's there?"

"I got the sign," Nancy said.

"What sign?"

"I got it. It was on the table when I come in. It was a hogbone, with blood meat still on it, laying by the lamp. He's out there. When yawl walk out that door, I gone."

"Gone where, Nancy?" Caddy said.

"I'm not a tattletale," Jason said.

"Nonsense," father said.

"He out there," Nancy said. "He looking through that window this minute, waiting for yawl to go. Then I gone."

"Nonsense," father said. "Lock up your house and we'll take you on to Aunt Rachel's."

" 'Twont do no good," Nancy said. She didn't look at father now, but he looked down at her, at her long, limp, moving hands. "Putting it off wont do no good."

"Then what do you want to do?" father said.

"I don't know," Nancy said. "I can't do nothing. Just put it off. And that don't do no good. I reckon it belong to me. I reckon what I going to get ain't no more than mine."

"Get what?" Caddy said. "What's yours?"

"Nothing," father said. "You all must get to bed."

"Caddy made me come," Jason said.

"Go on to Aunt Rachel's," father said.

"It won't do no good," Nancy said. She sat before the fire, her elbows on her knees, her long hands between her knees. "When even your own kitchen wouldn't do no good. When even if I was sleeping on the floor in the room with your chillen, and the next morning there I am, and blood—"

"Hush," father said. "Lock the door and put out the lamp and go to bed."

"I scared of the dark," Nancy said. "I scared for it to happen in the dark."

"You mean you're going to sit right here with the lamp lighted?" father said. Then Nancy began to make the sound again, sitting before the fire, her long hands between her knees. "Ah, damnation," father said. "Come along, chillen. It's past bedtime."

"When yawl go home, I gone," Nancy said. She talked quieter now, and her face looked quiet, like her hands. "Anyway, I got my coffin money saved up with Mr. Lovelady." Mr. Lovelady was a short, dirty man who collected the Negro insurance, coming around to the cabins or the kitchens every Sunday morning, to collect fifteen cents. He and his wife lived at the hotel. One morning his wife committed suicide. They had a child, a little girl. He and the child went away. After a week or two he came back alone. We would see him going along the lanes and the back streets on Saturday mornings.

"Nonsense," father said. "You'll be the first thing I'll see in the kitchen tomorrow morning."

"You'll see what you'll see, I reckon," Nancy said. "But it will take the Lord to say what that will be."

VI

We left her sitting before the fire.

"Come and put the bar up," father said. But she didn't move. She didn't look at us again, sitting quietly there between the lamp and the fire. From some distance down the lane we could look back and see her through the open door.

"What, Father?" Caddy said. "What's going to happen?"

"Nothing," father said. Jason was on father's back, so Jason was the tallest of all of us. We went down into the ditch. I looked at it, quiet. I couldn't see much where the moonlight and the shadows tangled.

"If Jesus is hid here, he can see us, cant he?" Caddy said.

"He's not there," father said. "He went away a long time ago."

"You made me come," Jason said, high; against the sky it looked like father had two heads, a little one and a big one. "I didn't want to."

We went up out of the ditch. We could still see Nancy's house and the open door, but we couldn't see Nancy now, sitting before the fire with the door open, because she was tired. "I just done got tired," she said. "I just a nigger. It ain't no fault of mine."

But we could hear her, because she began just after we came up out of the ditch, the sound that was not singing and not unsinging. "Who will do our washing now, Father?" I said.

"I'm not a nigger," Jason said, high and close above father's head.

"You're worse," Caddy said, "you are a tattletale. If something was to jump out, you'd be scairder than a nigger."

"I wouldn't," Jason said.

"You'd cry," Caddy said.

"Caddy," father said.

"I wouldn't," Jason said.

"Scairy cat," Caddy said.

"Candace!" father said.

F. Scott Fitzgerald (1896–1940)
BABYLON REVISITED

I

"And where's Mr. Campbell?" Charlie asked.

"Gone to Switzerland. Mr. Campbell's a pretty sick man, Mr. Wales."

"I'm sorry to hear that. And George Hardt?" Charlie inquired.

"Back in America, gone to work."

"And where is the Snow Bird?"

"He was in here last week. Anyway, his friend, Mr. Schaeffer, is in Paris."

Two familiar names from the long list of a year and a half ago. Charlie scribbled an address in his notebook and tore out the page.

"If you see Mr. Schaeffer, give him this," he said. "It's my brother-in law's address. I haven't settled on a hotel yet."

He was not really disappointed to find Paris was so empty. But the stillness in the Ritz bar was strange and portentous. It was not an American bar any more—he felt polite in it, and not as if he owned it. It had gone back into France. He felt the stillness from the moment he got out of the taxi and saw the doorman, usually in a frenzy of activity at this hour, gossiping with a *chasseur* by the servants' entrance.

Passing through the corridor, he heard only a single, bored voice in the once-clamorous women's room. When he turned into the bar he traveled the twenty feet of green carpet with his eyes fixed straight ahead by old habit; and then, with his foot firmly on the rail, he turned and surveyed the room, encountering only a single pair of eyes that fluttered up from a newspaper in the corner. Charlie asked for the head barman, Paul, who in the latter days of the bull market had come to work in his own custom-built car—disembarking, however, with due nicety at the nearest corner. But Paul was at his country house today and Alix giving him information.

"No, no more." Charlie said, "I'm going slow these days."

Alix congratulated him: "You were going pretty strong a couple of years ago."

"I'll stick to it all right," Charlie assured him. "I've stuck to it for over a year and a half now."

"How do you find conditions in America?"

"I haven't been to America for months. I'm in business in Prague, representing a couple of concerns there. They don't know about me down there."

Alix smiled.

"Remember the night of George Hardt's bachelor dinner here?" said Charlie. "By the way, what's become of Claude Fessenden?"

Alix lowered his voice confidentially: "He's in Paris, but he doesn't come here any more. Paul doesn't allow it. He ran up a bill of thirty thousand francs, charging all his drinks and his lunches, and usually his dinner, for more than a year. And when Paul finally told him he had to pay, he gave him a bad check."

Alix shook his head sadly.

"I don't understand it, such a dandy fellow. Now he's all bloated up—" He made a plump apple of his hands.

Charlie watched a group of strident queens installing themselves in a corner.

"Nothing affects them," he thought. "Stocks rise and fall, people loaf or work, but they go on forever." The place oppressed him. He called for the dice and shook with Alix for the drink.

"Here for long, Mr. Wales?"

"I'm here for four or five days to see my little girl."

"Oh-h! You have a little girl?"

Outside, the fire-red, gas-blue, ghost-green signs shone smokily through the tranquil rain. It was late afternoon and the streets were in movement; the *bistros* gleamed. At the corner of the Boulevard des Capucines he took a taxi. The Place de la Concorde moved by in pink majesty; they crossed the logical Seine, and Charlie felt the sudden provincial quality of the left bank.

Charlie directed his taxi to the Avenue de l'Opera, which was out of his way. But he wanted to see the blue hour spread over the magnificent facade, and imagine that the cab horns, playing endlessly the first few bars of *Le Plus que Lent,* were the trumpets of the Second Empire. They were closing the iron grill in front of Brentano's Bookstore, and people were already at dinner behind the trim little bourgeois hedge of Duval's. He had never eaten at a really cheap restaurant in Paris. Five-course dinner, four francs fifty, eighteen cents, wine included. For some odd reason he wished that he had.

As they rolled on to the Left Bank and he felt its sudden provincialism, he thought, "I spoiled this city for myself. I didn't realize it, but the days came along one after another, and then two years were gone, and everything was gone, and I was gone."

He was thirty-five, and good to look at. The Irish mobility of his face was sobered by a deep wrinkle between his eyes. As he rang his brother-in-law's bell in the Rue Palatine, the wrinkle deepened till it pulled down his brows; he felt a cramping sensation in his belly. From behind the maid who opened the door darted a lovely little girl of nine who shrieked "Daddy!" and flew up, struggling like a fish, into his arms. She pulled his head around by one ear and set her cheek against his.

"My old pie," he said.

"Oh, daddy, daddy, daddy, daddy, dads, dads, dads!"

She drew him into the salon, where the family waited, a boy and a girl his daughter's age, his sister-in-law and her husband. He greeted Marion with his voice pitched carefully to avoid either feigned enthusiasm or dislike, but her response was more frankly tepid, though she minimized her expression of unalterable distrust by directing her regard toward his child. The two men clasped hands in a friendly way and Lincoln Peters rested his for a moment on Charlie's shoulder.

The room was warm and comfortably American. The three children moved intimately about, playing through the yellow oblongs that led to other rooms; the cheer of six o'clock spoke in the eager smacks of the fire and the sounds of French activity in the kitchen. But Charlie did not relax; his heart sat up rigidly in his body and he drew confidence from his daughter, who from time to time came close to him, holding in her arms the doll he had brought.

"Really extremely well," he declared in answer to Lincoln's question. "There's a lot of business there that isn't moving at all, but we're doing even better than ever. In fact, damn well. I'm bringing my sister over from America next month to keep house for me. My income last year was bigger than it was when I had money. You see, the Czechs—"

His boasting was for a specific purpose; but after a moment, seeing a faint restiveness in Lincoln's eye, he changed the subject:

"Those are fine children of yours, well brought up, good manners."

"We think Honoria's a great little girl too."

Marion Peters came back from the kitchen. She was a tall woman with worried eyes, who had once possessed a fresh American loveliness. Charlie had never been sensitive to it and was always surprised when people spoke of how pretty she had been. From the first there had been an instinctive antipathy between them.

"Well, how do you find Honoria?" she asked.

"Wonderful. I was astonished how much she's grown in ten months. All the children are looking well."

"We haven't had a doctor for a year. How do you like being back in Paris?"

"It seems very funny to see so few Americans around."

"I'm delighted," Marion said vehemently. "Now at least you can go into a store without their assuming you're a millionaire. We've suffered like everybody, but on the whole it's a good deal pleasanter."

"But it was nice while it lasted," Charlie said. "We were a sort of royalty, almost infallible, with a sort of magic around us. In the bar this afternoon"—he stumbled, seeing his mistake—"there wasn't a man I knew."

She looked at him keenly. "I should think you'd have had enough of bars."

"I only stayed a minute. I take one drink every afternoon, and no more."

"Don't you want a cocktail before dinner?" Lincoln asked.

"I take only one drink every afternoon, and I've had that."

"I hope you keep to it," said Marion.

Her dislike was evident in the coldness with which she spoke, but Charlie only smiled; he had larger plans. Her very aggressiveness gave him an advantage, and he knew enough to wait. He wanted them to initiate the discussion of what they knew had brought him to Paris.

At dinner he couldn't decide whether Honoria was most like them or her mother. Fortunate if she didn't combine the traits of both that had brought them to disaster. A great wave of protectiveness went over him. He thought he knew what to do for her. He believed in character; he wanted to jump back a whole generation and trust in character again as the eternally valuable element. Everything else wore out.

He left soon after dinner, but not to go home. He was curious to see Paris by night with clearer and more judicious eyes than those of other days. He bought a *strapontin* for the Casino and watched Josephine Baker go through her chocolate arabesques.

After an hour he left and strolled toward Montmartre, up the Rue Pigalle into the Place Blanche. The rain had stopped and there were a few people in evening clothes disembarking from taxis in front of cabarets, and *cocottes* prowling singly or in pairs, and many Negroes. He passed a lighted door from which issued music, and stopped with the sense of familiarity; it was Bricktop's, where he had parted with so many hours and so much money. A few doors farther on he found another ancient rendezvous and incautiously put his head inside. Immediately an eager orchestra burst into sound, a pair of professional dancers leaped to their feet and a maître d'hôtel swooped toward him, crying, "Crowd just arriving, sir!" But he withdrew quickly.

"You have to be damn drunk," he thought.

Zelli's was closed, the bleak and sinister cheap hotels surrounding it were dark; up in the Rue Blanche there was more light and a local, colloquial French crowd. The Poet's Cave had disappeared, but the two great mouths of the Café of Heaven and the Café of Hell still yawned—even devoured, as he watched, the meager contents of a tourist bus—a German, a Japanese, and an American couple who glanced at him with frightened eyes.

So much for the effort and ingenuity of Montmartre. All the catering to vice and waste was on an utterly childish scale, and he suddenly realized the meaning of the word "dissipate"—to dissipate into thin air; to make nothing out of something. In the little hours of the night every move from place to place was an enormous human jump, an increase of paying for the privilege of slower and slower motion.

He remembered thousand-franc notes given to an orchestra for playing a single number, hundred-franc notes tossed to a doorman for calling a cab.

But it hadn't been given for nothing.

It had been given, even the most wildly squandered sum, as an offering to destiny that he might not remember the things most worth remembering, the things that now he would always remember—his child taken from his control, his wife escaped to a grave in Vermont.

In the glare of a *brasserie* a woman spoke to him. He bought her some eggs and coffee, and then, eluding her encouraging stare, gave her a twenty-franc note and took a taxi to his hotel.

II

He woke upon a fine fall day—football weather. The depression of yesterday was gone and he liked the people on the streets. At noon he sat opposite Honoria at Le Grand Vatel, the only restaurant he could think of not reminiscent of champagne dinners and long luncheons that began at two and ended in a blurred and vague twilight.

"Now, how about vegetables? Oughtn't you to have some vegetables?"

"Well, yes."

"Here's *épinards* and *chou-fleur* and carrots and *haricots*."

"I'd like *chou-fleur*."

"Wouldn't you like to have two vegetables?"

"I usually only have one at lunch."

The waiter was pretending to be inordinately fond of children. "*Qu'elle est mignonne la petite! Elle parle exactement comme une Française.*"

"How about dessert? Shall we wait and see?"

The waiter disappeared. Honoria looked at her father expectantly. "What are we going to do?"

"First, we're going to that toy store in the Rue Saint-Honoré and buy you anything you like. And then we're going to the vaudeville at the Empire."

She hesitated. "I like it about the vaudeville, but not the toy store."

"Why not?"

"Well, you brought me this doll." She had it with her. "And I've got lots of things. And we're not rich any more, are we?"

"We never were. But today you are to have anything you want."

"All right," she agreed resignedly.

When there had been her mother and a French nurse he had been inclined to be strict; now he extended himself, reached out for a new tolerance; he must be both parents to her and not shut any of her out of communication.

"I want to get to know you," he said gravely. "First let me introduce myself. My name is Charles J. Wales, of Prague."

"Oh, daddy!" her voice cracked with laughter.

"And who are you, please?" he persisted, and she accepted a rôle immediately: "Honoria Wales, Rue Palatine, Paris."

"Married or single?"

"No, not married. Single."

He indicated the doll. "But I see you have a child, madame."

Unwilling to disinherit it, she took it to her heart and thought quickly: "Yes, I've been married, but I'm not married now. My husband is dead."

He went on quickly, "And the child's name?"

"Simone. That's after my best friend at school."

"I'm very pleased that you're doing so well at school."

"I'm third this month," she boasted. "Elsie"—that was her cousin—"is only about eighteenth, and Richard is about at the bottom."

"You like Richard and Elsie, don't you?"

"Oh, yes. I like Richard quite well and I like her all right."

Cautiously and casually he asked: "And Aunt Marion and Uncle Lincoln—which do you like best?"

"Oh, Uncle Lincoln, I guess."

He was increasingly aware of her presence. As they came in, a murmur of ". . . adorable" followed them, and now the people at the next table bent all their silences upon her, staring as if she were something no more conscious than a flower.

"Why don't I live with you?" she asked suddenly. "Because mamma's dead?"

"You must stay here and learn more French. It would have been hard for daddy to take care of you so well."

"I don't really need much taking care of any more. I do everything for myself."

Going out of the restaurant, a man and a woman unexpectedly hailed him.

"Well, the old Wales!"

"Hello there, Lorraine. . . . Dunc."

Sudden ghosts out of the past: Duncan Schaeffer, a friend from college. Lorraine Quarrles, a lovely, pale blonde of thirty; one of a crowd who had helped them make months into days in the lavish times of three years ago.

"My husband couldn't come this year," she said, in answer to his question. "We're poor as hell. So he gave me two hundred a month and told me I could do my worst on that. . . . This your little girl?"

"What about coming back and sitting down?" Duncan asked.

"Can't do it." He was glad for an excuse. As always, he felt Lorraine's passionate, provocative attraction, but his own rhythm was different now.

"Well, how about dinner?" she asked.

"I'm not free. Give me your address and let me call you."

"Charlie, I believe you're sober," she said judicially. "I honestly believe he's sober, Dunc. Pinch him and see if he's sober."

Charlie indicated Honoria with his head. They both laughed.

"What's your address?" said Duncan skeptically.

He hesitated, unwilling to give the name of his hotel.

"I'm not settled yet. I'd better call you. We're going to see the vaudeville at the Empire."

"There! That's what I want to do," Lorraine said. "I want to see some clowns and acrobats and jugglers. That's just what we'll do, Dunc."

"We've got to do an errand first," said Charlie. "Perhaps we'll see you there."

"All right, you snob. . . . Good-by, beautiful little girl."

"Good-by."

Honoria bobbed politely.

Somehow, an unwelcome encounter. They liked him because he was functioning, because he was serious, they wanted to see him, because he was stronger than they were now, because they wanted to draw a certain sustenance from his strength.

At the Empire, Honoria proudly refused to sit upon her father's folded coat. She was already an individual with a code of her own, and Charlie was more and more absorbed by the desire of putting a little of himself into her before she crystallized utterly. It was hopeless to try to know her in so short a time.

Between the acts they came upon Duncan and Lorraine in the lobby where the band was playing.

"Have a drink?"

"All right, but not up at the bar. We'll take a table."

"The perfect father."

Listening abstractedly to Lorraine, Charlie watched Honoria's eyes leave their table, and he followed them wistfully about the room, wondering what they saw. He met her glance and she smiled.

"I liked that lemonade," she said.

What had she said? What had he expected? Going home in a taxi afterward, he pulled her over until her head rested against his chest.

"Darling, do you ever think about your mother?"

"Yes, sometimes," she answered vaguely.

"I don't want you to forget her. Have you got a picture of her?"

"Yes, I think so. Anyhow, Aunt Marion has. Why don't you want me to forget her?"

"She loved you very much."

"I loved her too."

They were silent for a moment.

"Daddy, I want to come and live with you," she said suddenly.

His heart leaped; he had wanted it to come like this.

"Aren't you perfectly happy?"

"Yes, but I love you better than anybody. And you love me better than anybody, don't you, now that mummy's dead?"

"Of course I do. But you won't always like me best, honey. You'll grow up and meet somebody your own age and go marry him and forget you ever had a daddy."

"Yes, that's true," she agreed tranquilly.

He didn't go in. He was coming back at nine o'clock and he wanted to keep himself fresh and new for the thing he must say then.

"When you're safe inside, just show yourself in that window."

"All right. Good-by, dads, dads, dads, dads."

He waited in the dark street until she appeared, all warm and glowing, in the window above and kissed her fingers out into the night.

III

They were waiting. Marion sat behind the coffee service in a dignified black dinner dress that just faintly suggested mourning. Lincoln was walking up and down with the animation of one who had already been talking. They were as anxious as he was to get into the question. He opened it almost immediately:

"I suppose you know what I want to see you about—why I really came to Paris."

Marion played with the black stars on her necklace and frowned.

"I'm awfully anxious to have a home," he continued. "And I'm awfully anxious to have Honoria in it. I appreciate your taking in Honoria for her mother's sake, but things have changed now"—he hesitated and then continued more forcibly—"changed radically with me, and I want to ask you to reconsider the matter. It would be silly for me to deny that about three years ago I was acting badly—"

Marion looked up at him with hard eyes.

"—but all that's over. As I told you, I haven't had more than a drink a day for over a year, and I take that drink deliberately, so that the idea of alcohol won't get too big in my imagination. You see the idea?"

"No," said Marion succinctly.

"It's a sort of stunt I set myself. It keeps the matter in proportion."

"I get you," said Lincoln. "You don't want to admit it's got any attraction for you."

"Something like that. Sometimes I forget and don't take it. But I try to take it. Anyhow, I couldn't afford to drink in my position. The people I represent are more than satisfied with what I've done, and I'm bringing my sister over from Burlington to keep house for me, and I want awfully to have Honoria too. You know that even when her mother and I weren't getting along well we never let anything that happened touch Honoria. I know she's fond of me and I know I'm able to take care of her and—well, there you are. How do you feel about it?"

He knew that now he would have to take a beating. It would last an hour or two hours, and it would be difficult, but if he modulated his inevitable resentment to the chastened attitude of the reformed sinner, he might win his point in the end.

Keep your temper, he told himself. You don't want to be justified. You want Honoria.

Lincoln spoke first: "We've been talking it over ever since we got your letter last month. We're happy to have Honoria here. She's a dear little thing, and we're glad to be able to help her, but of course that isn't the question—"

Marion interrupted suddenly. "How long are you going to stay sober, Charlie?" she asked.

"Permanently, I hope."

"How can anybody count on that?"

"You know I never did drink heavily until I gave up business and came over here with nothing to do. Then Helen and I began to run around with—"

"Please leave Helen out of it. I can't bear to hear you talk about her like that."

He stared at her grimly; he had never been certain how fond of each other the sisters were in life.

"My drinking only lasted about a year and a half—from the time we came over until I—collapsed."

"It was time enough."

"It was time enough," he agreed.

"My duty is entirely to Helen," she said. "I try to think what she would have wanted me to do. Frankly, from the night you did that terrible thing you haven't really existed for me. I can't help that. She was my sister."

"Yes."

"When she was dying she asked me to look out for Honoria. If you hadn't been in a sanitarium then, it might have helped matters."

He had no answer.

"I'll never in my life be able to forget the morning when Helen knocked at my door, soaked to the skin and shivering, and said you'd locked her out."

Charlie gripped the sides of the chair. This was more difficult than he expected; he wanted to launch out into a long expostulation and explanation, but he only said: "The night I locked her out—" and she interrupted, "I don't feel up to going over that again."

After a moment's silence Lincoln said: "We're getting off the subject. You want Marion to set aside her legal guardianship and give you Honoria. I think the main point for her is whether she has confidence in you or not."

"I don't blame Marion," Charlie said slowly, "but I think she can have entire confidence in me. I had a good record up to three years ago. Of course, it's within human possibilities I might go wrong any time. But if we wait much longer I'll lose Honoria's childhood and my chance for a home." He shook his head. "I'll simply lose her, don't you see?"

"Yes, I see," said Lincoln.

"Why didn't you think of all this before?" Marion asked.

"I suppose I did, from time to time, but Helen and I were getting along badly. When I consented to the guardianship, I was flat on my back in a sanitarium and the market had cleaned me out. I knew I'd acted badly, and I thought if it would bring any peace to Helen, I'd agree to anything. But now it's different. I'm functioning. I'm behaving damn well, so far as—"

"Please don't swear at me," Marion said.

He looked at her, startled. With each remark the force of her dislike became more and more apparent. She had built up all her fear of life into one wall and faced it toward him. This trivial reproof was possibly the result of some trouble with the cook several hours before. Charlie became increasingly alarmed at leaving Honoria in this atmosphere of hostility against himself; sooner or later it would come out, in a word here, a shake of the head there, and some of that distrust would be irrevocably implanted in Honoria. But he pulled his temper down out of his face and shut it up inside him; he had won a point, for Lincoln realized the absurdity of Marion's remark and asked her lightly since when she had objected to the word "damn."

"Another thing," Charlie said: "I'm able to give her certain advantages now. I'm going to take a French governess to Prague with me. I've got a lease on a new apartment—"

He stopped, realizing that he was blundering. They couldn't be expected to accept with equanimity the fact that his income was again twice as large as their own.

"I suppose you can give her more luxuries than we can," said Marion. "When you were throwing away money we were living along watching every ten francs. . . . I suppose you'll start doing it again."

"Oh, no," he said. "I've learned. I worked hard for ten years, you know—until I got lucky in the market, like so many people. Terribly lucky. It didn't seem any use working any more, so I quit."

There was a long silence. All of them felt their nerves straining, and for the first time in a year Charlie wanted a drink. He was sure now that Lincoln Peters wanted him to have his child.

Marion shuddered suddenly; part of her saw that Charlie's feet were planted on the earth now, and her own maternal feeling recognized the naturalness of his desire; but she had lived for a long time with a prejudice—a prejudice founded on a curious disbelief in her sister's happiness, and which, in the shock of one terrible night, had turned to hatred for him. It had all happened at a point in her life where the discouragement of ill health and adverse circumstances made it necessary for her to believe in tangible villainy and a tangible villain.

"I can't help what I think!" she cried out suddenly. "How much you were responsible for Helen's death, I don't know. It's something you'll have to square with your own conscience."

An electric current of agony surged through him; for a moment he was almost on his feet, an unuttered sound echoing in his throat. He hung on to himself for a moment, another moment.

"Hold on there," said Lincoln uncomfortably. "I never thought you were responsible for that."

"Helen died of heart trouble," Charlie said dully.

"Yes, heart trouble." Marion spoke as if the phrase had another meaning for her.

Then, in the flatness that followed her outburst, she saw him plainly and she knew he had somehow arrived at control over the situation. Glancing at her husband, she found no help from him, and as abruptly as if it were a matter of no importance, she threw up the sponge.

"Do what you like!" she cried, springing up from her chair. "She's your child. I'm not the person to stand in your way. I think if it were my child I'd rather see her—" She managed to check herself. "You two decide it. I can't stand this. I'm sick. I'm going to bed."

She hurried from the room; after a moment Lincoln said:

"This has been a hard day for her. You know how strongly she feels—" His voice was almost apologetic: "Where a woman gets an idea in her head."

"Of course."

"It's going to be all right. I think she sees now that you—can provide for the child, and so we can't very well stand in your way or Honoria's way."

"Thank you, Lincoln."

"I'd better go along and see how she is."

"I'm going."

He was still trembling when he reached the street, but a walk down the Rue Bonaparte to the *quais* set him up, and as he crossed the Seine, fresh and new by the *quai* lamps, he felt exultant. But back in his room he couldn't sleep. The image of Helen haunted him. Helen whom he had loved so until they had senselessly begun to abuse each other's love, tear it into shreds. On that terrible February night that Marion remembered so vividly, a slow quarrel had gone on for hours. There was a scene at the Florida, and then he attempted to take her home, and then she kissed young Webb at a table; after that there was what she had hysterically said. When he arrived home alone he turned the key in the lock in wild anger. How could he know she would arrive an hour later alone, that there would be a snowstorm in which she wandered about in slippers, too confused to find a taxi? Then the aftermath, her escaping pneumonia by a miracle, and all the attendant horror. They were "reconciled," but that was the beginning of the end, and Marion, who had seen with her own eyes and who imagined it to be one of many scenes from her sister's martyrdom, never forgot.

Going over it again brought Helen nearer, and in the white, soft light that steals upon the half sleep near morning he found himself talking to her again. She said that he was perfectly right about Honoria and that she wanted Honoria to be with him. She said she was glad he was being good and doing better. She said a lot of other things—very friendly things—but she was in a swing in a white dress, and swinging faster and faster all the time, so that at the end he could not hear clearly all that she said.

IV

He woke up feeling happy. The door of the world was open again. He made plans, vistas, futures for Honoria and himself, but suddenly he grew sad, remembering all the plans he and Helen had made. She had not planned to die. The present was the thing—work to do and someone to love. But not to love too much, for he knew the injury that a father can do to a daughter or a mother to a son by attaching them too closely: afterward, out in the world, the child would seek in the marriage partner the same blind tenderness and, failing probably to find it, turn against love and life.

It was another bright, crisp day. He called Lincoln Peters at the bank where he worked and asked if he could count on taking Honoria when he left for Prague. Lincoln agreed that there was no reason for delay. One thing—the legal guardianship. Marion wanted to retain that a while longer. She was upset by the whole matter, and it would oil things if she felt that the situation was still in her control for another year. Charlie agreed, wanting only the tangible, visible child.

Then the question of a governess. Charles sat in a gloomy agency and talked to a cross Béarnaise and to a buxom Breton peasant, neither of whom he could have endured. There were others whom he would see tomorrow.

He lunched with Lincoln Peters at Griffons, trying to keep down his exultation.

"There's nothing quite like your own child," Lincoln said. "But you understand how Marion feels too."

"She's forgotten how hard I worked for seven years there," Charlie said. "She just remembers one night."

"There's another thing," Lincoln hesitated. "While you and Helen were tearing around Europe throwing money away, we were just getting along. I didn't touch any of the prosperity because I never got ahead enough to carry anything but my insurance. I think Marion felt there was some of kind of injustice in it—you not even working toward the end, and getting richer and richer."

"It went just as quick as it came," said Charlie.

"Yes, a lot of it stayed in the hands of *chasseurs* and saxophone players and maîtres d'hôtel—well, the big party's over now. I just said that to explain Marion's feeling about those crazy years. If you drop in about six o'clock tonight before Marion's too tired, we'll settle the details on the spot."

Back at his hotel, Charlie found a *pneumatique* that had been redirected from the Ritz bar where Charlie had left his address for the purpose of finding a certain man.

> Dear Charlie: You were so strange when we saw you the other day that I wondered if I did something to offend you. If so, I'm not conscious of it. In fact, I have thought about you too much for the last year, and it's always been in the back of my mind that I might see you if I came over here. We *did* have such good times that crazy spring, like the night you and I stole the butcher's

> tricycle, and the time we tried to call on the president and you had the old derby rim and the wire cane. Everybody seems so old lately, but I don't feel old a bit. Couldn't we get together some time today for old time's sake? I've got a vile hang-over for the moment, but will be feeling better this afternoon and will look for you about five in the sweat-shop at the Ritz.
>
> Always devotedly,
>
> Lorraine.

His first feeling was one of awe that he had actually, in his mature years, stolen a tricycle and pedaled Lorraine all over the Etoile between the small hours and dawn. In retrospect it was a nightmare. Locking out Helen didn't fit in with any other act of his life, but the tricycle incident did—it was one of many. How many weeks or months of dissipation to arrive at that condition of utter irresponsibility?

He tried to picture how Lorraine had appeared to him then—very attractive; Helen was unhappy about it, though she said nothing. Yesterday, in the restaurant, Lorraine had seemed trite, blurred, worn away. He emphatically did not want to see her, and he was glad Alix had not given away his hotel address. It was a relief to think, instead, of Honoria, to think of Sundays spent with her and of saying good morning to her and of knowing she was there in his house at night, drawing her breath in the darkness.

At five he took a taxi and bought presents for all the Peters—a piquant cloth doll, a box of Roman soldiers, flowers for Marion, big linen handkerchiefs for Lincoln.

He saw, when he arrived in the apartment, that Marion had accepted the inevitable. She greeted him now as though he were a recalcitrant member of the family, rather than a menacing outsider. Honoria had been told she was going; Charlie was glad to see that her tact made her conceal her excessive happiness. Only on his lap did she whisper her delight and the question "When?" before she slipped away with the other children.

He and Marion were alone for a minute in the room, and on an impulse he spoke out boldly:

"Family quarrels are bitter things. They don't go according to any rules. They're not like aches or wounds; they're more like splits in the skin that won't heal because there's not enough material. I wish you and I could be on better terms."

"Some things are hard to forget," she answered. "It's a question of confidence." There was no answer to this and presently she asked, "When do you propose to take her?"

"As soon as I can get a governess. I hoped the day after tomorrow."

"That's impossible. I've got to get her things in shape. Not before Saturday."

He yielded. Coming back into the room, Lincoln offered him a drink.

"I'll take my daily whisky," he said.

It was warm here, it was a home, people together by a fire. The children felt very safe and important; the mother and father were serious, watchful. They had things to do for the children more important than his visit here. A spoonful of medicine was, after all, more important than the strained relations between Marion and himself. They were not dull people, but they were very much in the grip of life and circumstances. He wondered if he couldn't do something to get Lincoln out of his rut at the bank.

A long peal at the door-bell; the *bonne à tout faire* passed through and went down the corridor. The door opened upon another long ring, and then voices, and the three in the salon looked up expectantly; Richard moved to bring the corridor within his range of vision, and Marion rose. Then the maid came back along the corridor, closely followed by the voices, which developed under the light into Duncan Schaeffer and Lorraine Quarrles.

They were gay, they were hilarious, they were roaring with laughter. For a moment Charlie was astounded; unable to understand how they ferreted out the Peters' address.

"Ah-h-h!" Duncan wagged his finger roguishly at Charlie. "Ah-h-h!"

They both slid down another cascade of laughter. Anxious and at a loss, Charlie shook hands with them quickly and presented them to Lincoln and Marion. Marion nodded, scarcely speaking. She had drawn back a step toward the fire; her little girl stood beside her, and Marion put an arm about her shoulder.

With growing annoyance at the intrusion, Charlie waited for them to explain themselves. After some concentration Duncan said:

"We came to invite you out to dinner. Lorraine and I insist that all this chi-chi, cagy business 'bout your address got to stop."

Charlie came closer to them, as if to force them backward down the corridor.

"Sorry, but I can't. Tell me where you'll be and I'll phone you in half an hour."

This made no impression. Lorraine sat down suddenly on the side of a chair, and focusing her eyes on Richard, cried, "Oh, what a nice little boy! Come here, little boy." Richard glanced at his mother, but did not move. With a perceptible shrug of her shoulders, Lorraine turned back to Charlie:

"Come and dine. Sure your cousins won' mine. See you so sel'om. Or solemn."

"I can't," said Charlie sharply. "You two have dinner and I'll phone you."

Her voice became suddenly unpleasant. "All right, we'll go. But I remember once you hammered on my door at four A.M. I was enough of a good sport to give you a drink. Come on, Dunc."

Still in slow motion, with blurred, angry faces, with uncertain feet, they retired along the corridor.

"Good night," Charlie said.

"Good night!" responded Lorraine emphatically.

When he went back into the salon Marion had not moved, only now her son was standing in the circle of her other arm. Lincoln was still swinging Honoria back and forth like a pendulum from side to side.

"What an outrage!" Charlie broke out. "What an absolute outrage!"

Neither of them answered. Charlie dropped into an armchair, picked up his drink, set it down again and said:

"People I haven't seen for two years having the colossal nerve—"

He broke off. Marion had made the sound "Oh!" in one swift, furious breath, turned her body from him with a jerk, and left the room.

Lincoln set down Honoria carefully.

"You children go in and start your soup," he said, and when they obeyed, he said to Charlie:

"Marion's not well and she can't stand shocks. That kind of people make her really physically sick."

"I didn't tell them to come here. They wormed your name out of somebody. They deliberately—"

"Well, it's too bad. It doesn't help matters. Excuse me a minute."

Left alone, Charlie sat tense in his chair. In the next room he could hear the children eating, talking in monosyllables, already oblivious to the scene between their elders. He heard a murmur of conversation from a farther room and then the ticking bell of a telephone receiver picked up, and in a panic he moved to the other side of the room and out of earshot.

In a minute Lincoln came back. "Look here, Charlie, I think we'd better call off dinner for tonight. Marion's in bad shape."

"Is she angry with me?"

"Sort of," he said, almost roughly. "She's not strong and—"

"You mean she's changed her mind about Honoria?"

"She's pretty bitter right now. I don't know. You phone me at the bank tomorrow."

"I wish you'd explain to her I never dreamed these people would come here. I'm just as sore as you are."

"I couldn't explain anything to her now."

Charlie got up. He took his coat and hat and started down the corridor. Then he opened the door of the dining room and said in a strange voice, "Good night, children."

Honoria rose and ran around the table to hug him.

"Good night, sweetheart," he said vaguely, and then trying to make his voice more tender, trying to conciliate something, "Good night, dear children."

V

Charlie went directly to the Ritz bar with the furious idea of finding Lorraine and Duncan, but they were not there, and he realized that in any case there was nothing he could do. He had not touched his drink at the Peters', and now he ordered a whisky-and-soda. Paul came over to say hello.

"It's a great change," he said sadly. "We do about half the business we did. So many fellows I hear about back in the States lost everything, maybe not in the first crash, but then in the second. Your friend George Hardt lost every cent, I hear. Are you back in the States?"

"No, I'm in business in Prague."

"I heard that you lost a lot in the crash."

"I did," and he added grimly, "but I lost everything I wanted in the boom."

"Selling short."

"Something like that."

Again the memory of those days swept over him like a nightmare—the people they had met travelling; then people who couldn't add a row of figures or speak a coherent sentence. The little man Helen had consented to dance with at the ship's party, who had insulted her ten feet from the table; the women and girls carried screaming with drink or drugs out of public places—,

—The men who locked their wives out in the snow, because the snow of twenty-nine wasn't real snow. If you didn't want it to be snow, you just paid some money.

He went to the phone and called the Peters' apartment; Lincoln answered.

"I called up because this thing is on my mind. Has Marion said anything definite?"

"Marion's sick," Lincoln answered shortly. "I know this thing isn't altogether your fault, but I can't have her go to pieces about it. I'm afraid we'll have to let it slide for six months; I can't take the chance of working her up to this state again."

"I see."

"I'm sorry, Charlie."

He went back to his table. His whisky glass was empty, but he shook his head when Alix looked at it questioningly. There wasn't much he could do now except send Honoria some things; he would send her a lot of things tomorrow. He thought rather angrily that this was just money—he had given so many people money. . . .

"No, no more," he said to another waiter. "What do I owe you?"

He would come back some day; they couldn't make him pay forever. But he wanted his child, and nothing was much good now, beside that fact. He wasn't young any more, with a lot of nice thoughts and dreams to have by himself. He was absolutely sure Helen wouldn't have wanted him to be so alone.

Katherine Anne Porter (1890–1980)

THE GRAVE

The grandfather, dead for more than thirty years, had been twice disturbed in his long repose by the constancy and possessiveness of his widow. She removed his bones first to Louisiana and then to Texas as if she had set out to find her own burial place, knowing well she would never return to the places she had left. In Texas she set up a small cemetery in a corner of her first farm, and as the family connection grew, and oddments of relations came over from Kentucky to settle, it contained at last about twenty graves. After the grandmother's death, part of her land was to be sold for the benefit of certain of her children, and the cemetery happened to lie in the part set aside for sale. It was necessary to take up the bodies and bury them again in the family plot in the big new public cemetery, where the grandmother had been buried. At last her husband was to lie beside her for eternity, as she had planned.

The family cemetery had been a pleasant small neglected garden of tangled rose bushes and ragged cedar trees and cypress, the simple flat stones rising out of uncropped sweet-smelling wild grass. The graves were lying open and empty one burning day when Miranda and her brother Paul, who often went together to hunt rabbits and doves, propped their twenty-two Winchester rifles carefully against the rail fence, climbed over and explored among the graves. She was nine years old and he was twelve.

They peered into the pits all shaped alike with such purposeful accuracy, and looking at each other with pleased adventurous eyes, they said in solemn tones: "These were graves!" trying by words to shape a special, suitable emotion in their minds, but they felt nothing except an agreeable thrill of wonder: they were seeing a new sight, doing something they had not done before. In them both there was also a small disappointment at the entire commonplaceness of the actual spectacle. Even if it had once contained a coffin for years upon years, when the coffin was gone a grave was just a hole in the ground. Miranda leaped into the pit that had held her grandfather's bones. Scratching around aimlessly and pleasurably as any young animal, she scooped up a lump of earth and weighed it in her palm. It had a pleasantly sweet, corrupt smell, being mixed with cedar needles and small leaves, and as the crumbs fell apart, she saw a silver dove no larger than a hazel nut, with spread wings and a neat fan-shaped tail. The breast had a deep round hollow in it. Turning it up to the fierce sunlight, she saw that the inside of the hollow was cut in little whorls. She scrambled out, over the pile of loose earth that had fallen back into one end of the grave, calling to Paul that she had found something, he must guess what . . . His head appeared smiling over the rim of another grave. He waved a closed hand at her. "I've got something too!" They ran to compare treasures, making a game of it, so many guesses each, all wrong, and a final showdown with opened palms. Paul had found a thin wide gold ring carved with intricate flowers and leaves. Miranda was smitten at the sight of the ring and wished to have it. Paul seemed more impressed by the dove. They made a trade, with some little bickering. After he had got the dove in his hand, Paul said, "Don't you know what this is? This is a screw head for a *coffin!* . . . I'll bet nobody else in the world has one like this!"

Miranda glanced at it without covetousness. She had the gold ring on her thumb; it fitted perfectly. "Maybe we ought to go now," she said, "maybe one of the niggers 'll see us and tell somebody." They knew the land had been sold, the cemetery was no longer theirs, and they felt like trespassers. They climbed back over the fence, slung their rifles loosely under their arms—they had been shooting at targets with various kinds of firearms since they were seven years old—and set out to look for the rabbits and doves or whatever small game might happen along. On these expeditions Miranda always followed at Paul's heels along the path, obeying instructions about handling her gun when going through fences; learning how to stand it up properly so it would not slip and fire unexpectedly; how to wait her time for a shot and not just bang away in the air without looking, spoiling shots for Paul, who really could hit things if given a chance. Now and then, in her excitement at seeing birds whizz up suddenly before her face, or a rabbit leap across her very toes, she lost her head, and almost without sighting she flung her rifle up and pulled the trigger. She hardly ever hit any sort of mark. She had no proper sense of hunting at all. Her brother would be often completely disgusted with her. "You don't care whether you get your bird or not," he said. "That's no way to hunt." Miranda could not understand his indignation. She had seen him smash his hat and yell with fury when he had missed his aim. "What I like about shooting," said Miranda, with exasperating inconsequence, "is pulling the trigger and hearing the noise."

"Then, by golly," said Paul, "whyn't you go back to the range and shoot at bulls-eyes?"

"I'd just as soon," said Miranda, "only like this, we walk around more."

"Well, you just stay behind and stop spoiling my shots," said Paul, who, when he made a kill, wanted to be certain he had made it. Miranda, who alone brought down a bird once in twenty rounds, always claimed as her own any game they got when they fired at the same moment. It was tiresome and unfair and her brother was sick of it.

"Now, the first dove we see, or the first rabbit, is mine," he told her. "And the next will be yours. Remember that and don't get smarty."

"What about snakes?" asked Miranda idly. "Can I have the first snake?"

Waving her thumb gently and watching her gold ring glitter, Miranda lost interest in shooting. She was wearing her summer roughing outfit: dark blue overalls, a light blue shirt, a hired-man's straw hat, and thick brown sandals. Her brother had the same outfit except his was a sober hickory-nut color. Ordinarily Miranda preferred her overalls to any other dress, though it was making rather a scandal in the countryside, for the year was 1903, and in the back country the law of female decorum had teeth in it. Her father had been criticized for letting his girls dress like boys and go careering around astride barebacked horses. Big sister Maria, the really independent and fearless one, in spite of her rather affected ways, rode at a dead run with only a rope knotted around her horse's nose. It was said the motherless family was running down, with the Grandmother no longer there to hold it together. It was known that she had discriminated against her son Harry in her will, and that he was in straits about money. Some of his old neighbors reflected with vicious satisfaction that now he would probably not be so stiffnecked, nor have any more high-stepping horses either. Miranda knew this, though she could not say how. She had met along the road old women of the kind who smoked corn-cob pipes, who had treated her grandmother with most sincere respect. They slanted their gummy old eyes side-ways at the granddaughter and said, "Ain't you ashamed of yoself, Missy? It's aginst the Scriptures to dress like that. Whut yo Pappy thinkin about?" Miranda, with her powerful social sense, which was like a fine set of antennae radiating from every pore of her skin, would feel ashamed because she knew well it was rude and ill-bred to shock anybody, even bad-tempered old crones, though she had faith in her father's judgment and was perfectly comfortable in the clothes. Her father had said, "They're just what you need, and they'll save your dresses for school . . ." This sounded quite simple and natural to her. She had been brought up in rigorous economy. Wastefulness was vulgar. It was also a sin. These were truths; she had heard them repeated many times and never once disputed.

Now the ring, shining with the serene purity of fine gold on her rather grubby thumb, turned her feelings against her overalls and sockless feet, toes sticking through the thick brown leather straps. She wanted to go back to the farmhouse, take a good cold bath, dust herself with plenty of Maria's violet talcum powder—provided Maria was not present to object, of course—put on the thinnest, most becoming dress she owned, with a big sash, and sit in a wicker chair under the trees . . . These things were not all she wanted, of course; she had vague stirrings of desire for luxury and a grand way of living which could not take precise form in her imagination but were founded on family legend of past wealth and leisure. These immediate comforts were what she could have, and she wanted them at once. She lagged rather far behind Paul, and once she thought of just turning back without a word and going home. She stopped, thinking that Paul would never do that to her, and so she would have to tell him. When a rabbit leaped, she let Paul have it without dispute. He killed it with one shot.

When she came up with him, he was already kneeling, examining the wound, the rabbit trailing from his hands. "Right through the head," he said complacently, as if he had aimed for it. He took out his sharp, competent bowie knife and started to skin the body. He did it very cleanly and quickly. Uncle Jimbilly knew how to prepare the skins so that Miranda always had fur coats for her dolls, for though she never cared much for her dolls she liked seeing them in fur coats. The children knelt facing each other over the dead animal. Miranda watched admiringly while her brother stripped the skin away as if he were taking off a glove. The flayed flesh emerged dark scarlet, sleek, firm; Miranda with thumb and finger felt the long fine muscles with the silvery flat strips binding them to the joints. Brother lifted the oddly bloated belly. "Look," he said, in a low amazed voice. "It was going to have young ones."

Very carefully he slit the thin flesh from the center ribs to the flanks, and a scarlet bag appeared. He slit again and pulled the bag open, and there lay a bundle a tiny rabbits, each wrapped in a thin scarlet veil. The brother pulled these off and there they were, dark gray, their sleek wet down laying in minute even ripples, like a baby's head just washed, their unbelievably small delicate ears folded close, their little blind faces almost featureless.

Miranda said, "Oh, I want to *see,*" under her breath. She looked and looked—excited but not frightened, for she was accustomed to the sight of animals killed in hunting—filled with pity and astonishment and a kind of shocked delight in the wonderful little creatures for their own sakes, they were so pretty. She touched one of them ever so carefully, "Ah, there's blood running over them," she said and began to tremble without knowing why. Yet she wanted most deeply to see and to know. Having seen, she felt at once as if she had known all along. The very memory of her former ignorance faded, she had always known just this. No one had ever told her anything outright, she had been rather unobservant of the animal life around her because she was so accustomed to animals. They seemed simply disorderly and unaccountably rude in their habits, but altogether natural and not very interesting. Her brother had spoken as if he had known about everything all along. He may have seen all this before. He had never said a word to her, but she knew now a part at least of what he knew. She understood a little of the secret, formless intuitions in her own mind and body, which had been clearing up, taking form, so gradually and so steadily she had not realized that she was learning what she had to know. Paul said cautiously, as if he were talking about something forbidden: "They were just about ready to be born." His voice dropped on the last word. "I know," said Miranda, "like kittens. I know, like babies." She was quietly and terribly agitated, standing again with her rifle under her arm, looking down at the bloody heap. "I don't want the skin," she said, "I won't have it." Paul buried the young rabbits again in their mother's body, wrapped the skin around her, carried her to a clump of sage bushes, and hid her away. He came out again at once and said to Miranda, with an eager friendliness, a confidential tone quite unusual in him, as if he were taking her into an important secret on equal terms: "Listen now. Now you listen to me, and don't ever forget. Don't you ever tell a living soul that you saw this. Don't tell a soul. Don't tell Dad because I'll get into trouble. He'll say I'm leading you into things you ought not to do. He's always saying that. So now don't you go and forget and blab out sometime the way you're always doing . . . Now, that's a secret. Don't you tell."

Miranda never told, she did not wish to tell anybody. She thought about the whole worrisome affair with confused unhappiness for a few days. Then it sank quietly into her mind and was heaped over by accumulated thousands of impressions, for nearly twenty years. One day she was picking her path among the puddles and crushed refuse of a market street in a strange city of a strange country, when without warning, plain and clear in its true colors as if she looked through a frame upon a scene that had not stirred nor changed since the moment it happened, the episode of that far-off day leaped from its burial place before her mind's eye. She was so reasonlessly horrified she halted suddenly staring, the scene before her eyes dimmed by the vision back of them. An Indian vendor had held up before her a tray of dyed sugar sweets, in the shapes of all kinds of small creatures: birds, baby chicks, baby rabbits, lambs, baby pigs. They were in gay colors and smelled of vanilla, maybe . . . . It was a very hot day and the smell in the market, with its piles of raw flesh and wilting flowers, was like the mingled sweetness and corruption she had smelled that other day in the empty cemetery at home: the day she had remembered always until now vaguely as the time she and her brother had found treasure in the opened graves. Instantly upon this thought the dreadful vision faded, and she saw clearly her brother, whose childhood face she had forgotten, standing again in the blazing sunshine, again twelve years old, a pleased sober smile in his eyes, turning the silver dove over and over in his hands.

Shirley Jackson (1919–1965)
THE LOTTERY

The morning of June 27th was clear and sunny, with the fresh warmth of a full-summer day; the flowers were blossoming profusely and the grass was richly green. The people of the village began to gather in the square, between the post office and the bank, around ten o'clock; in some towns there were so many people that the lottery took two days and had to be started on June 26th, but in this village, where there were only about three hundred people, the whole lottery took less than two hours, so it could begin at ten o'clock in the morning and still be through in time to allow the villagers to get home for noon dinner.

The children assembled first, of course. School was recently over for the summer, and the feeling of liberty sat uneasily on most of them; they tended to gather together quietly for a while before they broke into boisterous play, and their talk was still of the classroom and the teacher, of books and reprimands. Bobby Martin had already stuffed his pockets full of stones, and the other boys soon followed his example, selecting the smoothest and roundest stones; Bobby and Harry Jones and Dickie Delacroix—the villagers pronounced this name "Dellacroy"—eventually made a great pile of stones in one corner of the square and guarded it against the raids of the other boys. The girls stood aside, talking among themselves, looking over their shoulders at the boys, and the very small children rolled in the dust or clung to the hands of their older brothers or sisters.

Soon the men began to gather, surveying their own children, speaking of planting and rain, tractors and taxes. They stood together, away from the pile of stones in the corner, and their jokes were quiet and they smiled rather than laughed. The women, wearing faded house dresses and sweaters, came shortly after their menfolk. They greeted one another and exchanged bits of gossip as they went to join their husbands. Soon the women, standing by their husbands, began to call to their children, and the children came reluctantly, having to be called four or five times. Bobby Martin ducked under his mother's grasping hand and ran, laughing, back to the pile of stones. His father spoke up sharply, and Bobby came quickly and took his place between his father and his oldest brother.

The lottery was conducted—as were the square dances, the teen-age club, the Halloween program—by Mr. Summers, who had time and energy to devote to civic activities. He was a round-faced jovial man and he ran the coal business, and people were sorry for him, because he had no children and his wife was a scold. When he arrived in the square, carrying the black wooden box, there was a murmur of conversation among the villagers, and he waved and called, "Little late today, folks." The postmaster, Mr. Graves, followed him, carrying a three-legged stool, and the stool was put in the center of the square and Mr. Summers set the black box down on it. The villagers kept their distance, leaving a space between themselves and the stool, and when Mr. Summers said, "Some of you fellows want to give me a hand?" there was a hesitation before two men, Mr. Martin and his oldest son, Baxter, came forward to hold the box steady on the stool while Mr. Summers stirred up the papers inside it.

The original paraphernalia for the lottery had been lost long ago, and the black box now resting on the stool had been put into use even before Old Man Warner, the oldest man in town, was born. Mr. Summers spoke frequently to the villagers about making a new box, but no one liked to upset even as much tradition as was represented by the black box. There was a story that the present box had been made with some pieces of the box that had preceded it, the one that had been constructed when the first people settled down to make a village here. Every year, after the lottery, Mr. Summers began talking again about a new box, but every year the subject was allowed to fade off without anything's being done. The black box grew shabbier each year; by now it was no longer completely black but splintered badly along one side to show the original wood color, and in some places faded or stained.

Mr. Martin and his oldest son, Baxter, held the black box securely on the stool until Mr. Summers had stirred the papers thoroughly with his hand. Because so much of the ritual had been forgotten or discarded, Mr. Summers had been successful in having slips of paper substituted for the chips of wood that had been used for generations. Chips of wood, Mr. Summers had argued, had been all very well when the village was tiny, but now that the population was more than three hundred and likely to keep on growing, it was necessary to use something that would fit more easily into the black box. The night before the lottery, Mr. Summers and Mr. Graves made up the slips of paper and put them in the box, and it was then taken to the safe of Mr. Summers' coal company and locked up until Mr. Summers was ready to take it to the square next morning. The rest of the year, the box was put away, sometimes one place, sometimes another; it had spent one year in Mr. Graves's barn and another year underfoot in the post office, and sometimes it was set on a shelf in the Martin grocery and left there.

There was a great deal of fussing to be done before Mr. Summers declared the lottery open. There were the lists to make up—of heads of families, heads of households in each family, members of each household in each family. There was the proper swearing-in of Mr. Summers by the postmaster, as the official of the lottery; at one time, some people remembered, there had been a recital of some sort, performed by the official of the lottery, a perfunctory, tuneless chant that had been rattled off duly each year; some people believed that the official of the lottery used to stand just so when he said or sang it, others believed that he was supposed to walk among the people, but years and years ago this part of the ritual had been allowed to lapse. There had been, also, a ritual salute, which the official of the lottery had had to use in addressing each person who came up to draw from the box, but this also had changed with time, until now it was felt necessary only for the official to speak to each person approaching. Mr. Summers was very good at all this; in his clean white shirt and blue jeans, with one hand resting carelessly on the black box, he seemed very proper and important as he talked interminably to Mr. Graves and the Martins.

Just as Mr. Summers finally left off talking and turned to the assembled villagers, Mrs. Hutchinson came hurriedly along the path to the square, her sweater thrown over her shoulders, and slid into place in the back of the crowd. "Clean forgot what day it was," she said to Mrs. Delacroix, who stood next to her, and they both laughed softly. "Thought my old man was out back stacking wood," Mrs. Hutchinson went on, "and then I looked out the window and the kids was gone, and then I remembered it was the twenty-seventh and came a-running." She dried her hands on her apron, and Mrs. Delacroix said, "You're in time, though. They're still talking away up there."

Mrs. Hutchinson craned her neck to see through the crowd and found her husband and children standing near the front. She tapped Mrs. Delacroix on the arm as a farewell and began to make her way through the crowd. The people separated good-humoredly to let her through; two or three people said, in voices just loud enough to be heard across the crowd, "Here comes your Missus, Hutchinson," and "Bill, she made it after all." Mrs. Hutchinson reached her husband, and Mr. Summers, who had been waiting, said cheerfully, "Thought we were going to have to get on without you, Tessie." Mrs. Hutchinson said, grinning, "Wouldn't have me leave m'dishes in the sink, now, would you Joe?," and soft laughter ran through the crowd as the people stirred back into position after Mrs. Hutchinson's arrival.

"Well, now," Mr. Summers said soberly, "guess we better get started, get this over with, so's we can go back to work. Anybody ain't here?"

"Dunbar," several people said. "Dunbar, Dunbar."

Mr. Summers consulted his list. "Clyde Dunbar," he said. "That's right. He's broke his leg, hasn't he? Who's drawing for him?"

"Me, I guess," a woman said, and Mr. Summers turned to look at her. "Wife draws for her husband," Mr. Summers said. "Don't you have a grown boy to do it for you, Janey?" Although Mr. Summers and everyone else in the village knew the answer perfectly well, it was the business of the official of the lottery to ask such questions formally. Mr. Summers waited with an expression of polite interest while Mrs. Dunbar answered.

"Horace's not but sixteen yet," Mrs. Dunbar said regretfully. "Guess I gotta fill in for the old man this year."

"Right," Mr. Summers said. He made a note on the list he was holding. Then he asked, "Watson boy drawing this year?"

A tall boy in the crowd raised his hand. "Here," he said. "I'm drawing for m'mother and me." He blinked his eyes nervously and ducked his head as several voices in the crowd said things like "Good fellow, Jack," and "Glad to see your mother's got a man to do it."

"Well," Mr. Summers said, "guess that's everyone. Old Man Warner make it?"

"Here," a voice said, and Mr. Summers nodded.

A sudden hush fell on the crowd as Mr. Summers cleared his throat and looked at the list. "All ready?" he called. "Now, I'll read the names—heads of families first—and the men come up and take a paper out of the box. Keep the paper folded in your hand without looking at it until everyone has had a turn. Everything clear?"

The people had done it so many times that they only half listened to the directions; most of them were quiet, wetting their lips, not looking around. Then Mr. Summers raise one hand high and said, "Adams." A man disengaged himself from the crowd and came forward. "Hi, Steve," Mr. Summers said, and Mr. Adams said, "Hi, Joe." They grinned at one another humorously and nervously. Then

Mr. Adams reached into the black box and took out a folded paper. He held it firmly by one corner as he turned and went hastily back to his place in the crowd, where he stood a little apart from his family, not looking down at his hand.

"Allen," Mr. Summers said. "Anderson. . . . Bentham."

"Seems like there's no time at all between lotteries any more," Mrs. Delacroix said to Mrs. Graves in the back row. "Seems like we got through with the last one only last week."

"Time sure goes fast," Mrs. Graves said.

"Clark. . . . Delacroix."

"There goes my old man," Mrs. Delacroix said. She held her breath while her husband went forward.

"Dunbar," Mr. Summers said, and Mrs. Dunbar went steadily to the box while one of the women said, "Go on, Janey," and another said, "There she goes."

"We're next," Mrs. Graves said. She watched while Mr. Graves came around from the side of the box, greeted Mr. Summers gravely, and selected a slip of paper from the box. By now, all through the crowd there were men holding the small folded papers in their large hands, turning them over and over nervously. Mrs. Dunbar and her two sons stood together, Mrs. Dunbar holding the slip of paper.

"Harburt. . . . Hutchinson."

"Get up there, Bill," Mrs. Hutchinson said, and the people near her laughed.

"Jones."

"They do say," Mr. Adams said to Old Man Warner, who stood next to him, "that over in the north village they're talking of giving up the lottery."

Old Man Warner snorted. "Pack of crazy fools," he said. "Listening to the young folks, nothing's good enough for *them.* Next thing you know, they'll be wanting to go back to living in caves, nobody work any more, live *that* way for a while. Used to be a saying about 'Lottery in June, corn be heavy soon.' First thing you know, we'd all be eating stewed chickweed and acorns. There's *always* been a lottery," he added petulantly. "Bad enough to see young Joe Summers up there joking with everybody."

"Some places have already quit lotteries," Mrs. Adams said.

"Nothing but trouble in *that,*" Old Man Warner said stoutly. "Pack of young fools."

"Martin." And Bobby Martin watched his father go forward. "Overdyke. . . . Percy."

"I wish they'd hurry," Mrs. Dunbar said to her older son. "I wish they'd hurry."

"They're almost through," her son said.

"You get ready to run tell Dad," Mrs. Dunbar said.

Mr. Summers called his own name and then stepped forward precisely and selected a slip from the box. Then he called, "Warner."

"Seventy-seventh year I been in the lottery," Old Man Warner said as he went through the crowd. "Seventy-seventh time."

"Watson." The tall boy came awkwardly through the crowd. Someone said, "Don't be nervous, Jack," and Mr. Summers said, "Take your time, son."

"Zanini."

After that, there was a long pause, a breathless pause, until Mr. Summers, holding his slip of paper in the air, said, "All right, fellows." For a minute, no one moved, and then all the slips of paper were opened. Suddenly, all the women began to speak at once, saying, "Who is it?," "Who's got it?," "Is it the Dunbars?," "Is it the Watsons?" Then the voices began to say, "It's Hutchinson. It's Bill," "Bill Hutchinson's got it."

"Go tell your father," Mrs. Dunbar said to her older son.

People began to look around to see the Hutchinsons. Bill Hutchinson was standing quiet, staring down at the paper in his hand. Suddenly, Tessie Hutchinson shouted to Mr. Summers, "You didn't give him time enough to take any paper he wanted. I saw you. I wasn't fair!"

"Be a good sport, Tessie," Mr. Delacroix called, and Mrs. Graves said, "All of us took the same chance."

"Shut up, Tessie," Bill Hutchinson said.

"Well, everyone," Mr. Summers said, "that was done pretty fast, and now we've got to be hurrying a little more to get done in time." He consulted his next list. "Bill," he said, "you draw for the Hutchinson family. You got any other households in the Hutchinsons?"

"There's Don and Eva," Mrs. Hutchinson yelled. "Make *them* take their chance!"

"Daughters draw with their husbands' families, Tessie," Mr. Summers said gently. "You know that as well as anyone else."

"It wasn't *fair,*" Tessie said.

"I guess not, Joe," Bill Hutchinson said regretfully. "My daughter draws with her husband's family, that's only fair. And I've got no other family except the kids."

"Then, as far as drawing for families is concerned, it's you," Mr. Summers said in explanation, "and as far as drawing for households is concerned, that's you, too. Right?"

"Right," Bill Hutchinson said.

"How many kids, Bill?" Mr. Summers asked formally.

"Three," Bill Hutchinson said. "There's Bill, Jr., and Nancy, and little Dave. And Tessie and me."

"All right, then," Mr. Summers said. "Harry, you got their tickets back?"

Mr. Graves nodded and held up the slips of paper. "Put them in the box, then," Mr. Summers directed. "Take Bill's and put it in."

"I think we ought to start over," Mrs. Hutchinson said, as quietly as she could. "I tell you it wasn't *fair*. You didn't give him time enough to choose. Everybody saw that."

Mr. Graves had selected the five slips and put them in the box, and he dropped all the papers but those onto the ground, where the breeze caught them and lifted them off.

"Listen, everybody," Mrs. Hutchinson was saying to the people around her.

"Ready, Bill?" Mr. Summers asked, and Bill Hutchinson, with one quick glance around at his wife and the children, nodded.

"Remember," Mr. Summers said, "take the slips and keep them folded until each person has taken one. Harry, you help little Dave." Mr. Graves took the hand of the little boy, who came willingly with him up to the box. "Take a paper out of the box, Davy," Mr. Summers said. Davy put his hand into the box and laughed. "Take just *one* paper," Mr. Summers said. "Harry, you hold it for him." Mr. Graves took the child's hand and removed the folded paper from the tight fist and held it while little Dave stood next to him and looked up at him wonderingly.

"Nancy next," Mr. Summers said. Nancy was twelve, and her school friends breathed heavily as she went forward, switching her skirt, and took a slip daintily from the box. "Bill, Jr.," Mr. Summers said, and Billy, his face red and his feet over-large, nearly knocked the box over as he got a paper out. "Tessie," Mr. Summers said. She hesitated for a minute, looking around defiantly, and then set her lips and went up to the box. She snatched a paper out and held it behind her.

"Bill," Mr. Summers said, and Bill Hutchinson reached into the box and felt around, bringing his hand out at last with the slip of paper in it.

The crowd was quiet. A girl whispered, "I hope it's not Nancy," and the sound of the whisper reached the edges of the crowd.

"It's not the way it used to be," Old Man Warner said clearly. "People ain't the way they used to be."

"All right," Mr. Summers said. "Open the papers. Harry, you open little Dave's."

Mr. Graves opened the slip of paper and there was a general sigh through the crowd as he held it up and everyone could see that it was blank. Nancy and Bill, Jr., opened theirs at the same time, and both beamed and laughed, turning around to the crowd and holding their slips of paper above their heads.

"Tessie," Mr. Summers said. There was a pause, and then Mr.

Summers looked at Bill Hutchinson, and Bill unfolded his paper and showed it. It was blank.

"It's Tessie," Mr. Summers said, and his voice was hushed. "Show us her paper, Bill."

Bill Hutchinson went over to his wife and forced the slip of paper out of her hand. It had a black spot on it, the black spot Mr. Summers had made the night before with the heavy pencil in the coal-company office. Bill Hutchinson held it up, and there was a stir in the crowd.

"All right, folks," Mr. Summers said. "Let's finish quickly."

Although the villagers had forgotten the ritual and lost the original black box, they still remembered to use stones. The pile of stones the boys had made earlier was ready; there were stones on the ground with the blowing scraps of paper that had come out of the box. Mrs. Delacroix selected a stone so large she had to pick it up with both hands and turned to Mrs. Dunbar. "Come on," she said. "Hurry up."

Mrs. Dunbar had small stones in both hands, and she said, gasping for breath, "I can't run at all. You'll have to go ahead and I'll catch up with you."

The children had stones already, and someone gave little Davey Hutchinson a few pebbles.

Tessie Hutchinson was in the center of a cleared space by now, and she held her hands out desperately as the villagers moved in on her. "It isn't fair," she said. A stone hit her on the side of the head.

Old Man Warner was saying, "Come on, come on, everyone." Steve Adams was in the front of the crowd of villagers, with Mrs. Graves beside him.

"It isn't fair, it isn't right," Mrs. Hutchinson screamed, and then they were upon her.

Peter Taylor (b. 1917)

THE FANCY WOMAN

He wanted no more of her drunken palaver. Well, sure enough. Sure enough. And he had sent her from the table like she were one of his half-grown brats. *He,* who couldn't have walked straight around to her place if she *hadn't* been lady enough to leave, sent *her* from the table like either of the half-grown kids he was so mortally fond of. At least she hadn't turned over three glasses of perfectly good stuff during one meal. Talk about vulgar. She fell across the counterpane and slept.

She awoke in the dark room with his big hands busying with her clothes, and she flung her arms about his neck. "Not a stitch on y', have you?" she said. And she said, "You marvelous, fattish thing."

His hoarse voice was in her ear, "You like it?" He chuckled deep in this throat, and she whispered:

"You're an old thing-a-ma-gig, George."

Her eyes opened in the midday sunlight, and she felt the back of her neck soaking in her own sweat on the counterpane. She saw the unfamiliar cracks in the ceiling and said, "Whose room's this?" She looked at the walnut dresser and the wardrobe and said, "Oh, the kids' room"; and as she laughed, saliva bubbled up and fell back on her upper lip. She shoved herself up with her elbows and was sitting in the middle of the bed. Damn him! Her blue silk dress was twisted about her body, and a thin army blanket covered her lower half. "He didn't put that over me, I know damn well. One of those tight-mouth niggers sneaking around!" She sprang from the bed, slipped her bare feet into her white pumps and stepped toward the door. Oh, God! She beheld herself in the dresser mirror.

She stalked to the dresser with her eyes closed and felt about for a brush. There was nothing but a tray of collar buttons there. She grabbed a handful of them and screamed as she threw them to bounce off the mirror, "This ain't my room!" She ran her fingers through her hair and went out into the hall and into her room next door. She rushed to her little dressing table. There was the bottle half full. She poured out a jigger and drank it. Clearing her throat as she sat down, she said, "Oh, what's the matter with me?" She combed her hair back quite carefully, then pulled the yellow strands out of the amber comb; and when she had greased and wiped her face and had rouged her lips and the upper portions of her cheeks, she smiled at herself in the mirror. She looked flirtatiously at the bottle but shook her head and stood up and looked about the room. It was a long, narrow room with two windows at the end. A cubbyhole beside the kids' room! Yet it *was* a canopied bed with yellow ruffles that matched the ruffles on the dressing table and on the window curtains. She went over and turned back the covers and mussed the pillow. It might not have been the niggers! She poured another drink and went down to get some nice, hot lunch.

The breakfast room was one step lower than the rest of the house, and it was all windows. But the Venetian blinds were lowered all round, and she sat at a big circular table. "I can't make out about this room," she said to the negress who was refilling her coffee-cup. She lit a cigarette and questioned the servant, "What's the crazy table made out of, Amelia?"

"It makes a good table, 'spite all."

"It sure enough does make a strong table, Amelia." She kicked the toe of her shoe against the brick column which supported the table top. "But what *was* it, old dearie?" She smiled invitingly at the servant and pushed her plate away and pulled her coffee in front of her. She stared at the straight scar on Amelia's wrist as Amelia reached for the plate. What big black buck had put it there? A lot these niggers had to complain of in her when every one of them was all dosed up.

Amelia said that the base of the table was the old cistern. "He brung that top out f'om Memphis when he done the po'ch up this way for breakfast and lunch."

The woman looked about the room, thinking, "I'll get some confab out of this one yet." And she exclaimed, "Oh, and that's the old bucket to it over there, then, with the vines on it, Amelia!"

"No'm," Amelia said. Then after a few seconds she added, "They brung that out f'om town and put it there like it was it."

"Yeah . . . yeah . . . go on, Amelia. I'm odd about old-fashioned things. I've got a lot of interest in any antiques."

"That's all."

The little negro woman started away with the coffee-pot and the plate, dragging the soft soles of her carpet slippers over the brick floor. At the door she lingered, and, too cunning to leave room for a charge of impudence, she added to the hateful "That's all" a mutter, "Miss Josephine."

And when the door closed, Miss Josephine said under her breath, "If that black bitch hadn't stuck that on, there wouldn't be another chance for her to sneak around with army blankets."

George, mounted on a big sorrel and leading a small dapple-gray horse, rode onto the lawn outside the breakfast room. Josephine saw him through the slits of the blinds looking up toward her bedroom window. "Not for me," she said to herself. "He'll not get *me* on one of those animals." She swallowed the last of her coffee on her feet and then turned and stomped across the bricks to the step-up into the hallway. There she heard him calling:

"Josie! Josie! Get out-a that bed!"

Josephine ran through the long hall cursing the rugs that slipped under her feet. She ran the length of the hall looking back now and again as though the voice were a beast at her heels. In the front parlor she pulled up the glass and took a book from the bookcase nearest to the door. It was a red book, and she hurled herself into George's chair and opened to page sixty-five:

> pity, with anxiety, and with pity. Hamilcar was rubbing himself against my legs, wild with delight.

She closed the book on her thumb and listened to George's bellowing:

"I'm coming after you!"

She could hear the noise of the hoofs as George led the horses around the side of the house. George's figure moved outside the front windows. Through the heavy lace curtains she could see him tying the horses to the branch of a tree. She heard him on the veranda and then in the hall. Damn him! God damn him, he couldn't make her ride! She opened to page sixty-five again as George passed the doorway. But he saw her, and he stopped. He stared at her for a moment, and she looked at him over the book. She rested her head on the back of the chair sullenly. Her eyes were fixed on his hairy arms, on the little bulk in his rolled sleeves, then on the white shirt over his chest, on the brown jodhpurs, and finally on the blackened leather of his shoes set apart on the polished hall floor. Her eyelids were heavy, and she longed for a drink of the three-dollar whiskey that was on her dressing table.

He crossed the carpet with a smile, showing, she guessed, his delight at finding her. She smiled. He snatched the book from her hands and read the title on the red cover. His head went back, and as he laughed she watched through the open collar the tendons of his throat tighten and take on a purplish hue.

At Josephine's feet was a needlepoint footstool on which was worked a rust-colored American eagle against a background of green. George tossed the red book onto the stool and pulled Josephine from her chair. He was still laughing, and she wishing for a drink.

"Come along, come along," he said. "We've only four days left, and you'll want to tell your friend-girls you learned to ride."

She jerked one hand loose from his hold and slapped his hard cheek. She screamed, "Friend-girl? You never heard me say Friend-girl. What black nigger do you think you're talking down to?" She was looking at him now through a mist of tears and presently she broke out into furious weeping. His laughter went on as he pushed her across the room and into the hall, but he was saying:

"Boochie, Boochie. Wotsa matter? Now, old girl, old girl. Listen: You'll want to tell your girl-friends, your *girl-friends,* that you learned to ride." That was how George was! He would never try to persuade her. He would never pay any attention to what she said. He wouldn't argue with her. He wouldn't mince words! The few times she had seen him before this week there had been no chance to talk much. When they were driving down from Memphis, Saturday, she had gone through the story about how she was tricked by Jackie Briton and married Lon and how he had left her right away and the pathetic part about the baby she never even saw in the hospital. And at the end of it she realized that George had been smiling at her as he probably would at one of his half-grown kids. When she stopped the story quickly, he had reached over and patted her hand (but still smiling) and right away had started talking about the sickly-looking tomato crops along the highway. After lunch on Saturday when she'd tried to talk to him again and he had deliberately commenced to play the victrola, she said, "Why won't you take me seriously?" But he had, of course, just laughed at her and kissed her and they had already begun drinking then. She couldn't resist him (more than other men, he could just drive her wild), and he would hardly look at her, never had. He either laughed at her or cursed her or, of course, at night would pet her. He hadn't hit her.

He was shoving her along the hall, and she had to make herself stop crying.

"Please, George."

"Come on, now! That-a girl."

"Honest to God, George. I tell you to let up, stop it."

"Come on. *Up* the steps. *Up! Up!*"

She let herself become limp in his arms but held with one hand to the banister. Then he grabbed her. He swung her up into his arms and carried her up the stair which curved around the back end of the hall, over the doorway to the breakfast room. Once in his arms she didn't move a muscle, for she thought, "I'm no featherweight, and we'll both go tumbling down these steps and break our skulls." At the top he fairly slammed her to her feet and, panting for breath, he said without a trace of softness:

"Now, put on those pants, Josie, and I'll wait for you in the yard." He turned to the stair, and she heard what he said to himself: "I'll sober her. I'll sober her up."

As he pushed Josephine onto the white, jumpy beast he must have caught a whiff of her breath. She knew that he must have! He was holding the reins close to the bit while she tried to arrange herself in the flat saddle. Then he grasped her ankle and asked her, "Did you take a drink, upstairs?" She laughed, leaned forward in her saddle and whispered:

"Two. Two jiggers."

She wasn't afraid of the horse now, but she was dizzy. "George, let me down," she said faintly. She felt the horse's flesh quiver under her leg and looked over her shoulder when it stomped one rear hoof.

George said, "Confound it, I'll sober you." He handed her the reins, stepped back and slapped the horse on the flank. "Hold on!" he called, and her horse cantered across the lawn.

Josie was clutching the leather straps tightly, and her face was almost in the horse's mane. "I could kill him for this," she said, slicing out the words with a sharp breath. God damn it! The horse was galloping along a dirt road. She saw nothing but the yellow dirt. The hoofs rumbled over a three-plank wooden bridge, and she heard George's horse on the other side of her. She turned her face that way and saw George through the hair that hung over her eyes. He was smiling. "You dirty bastard," she said.

He said, "You're doin' all right. Sit up, and I'll give you some pointers." She turned her face to the other side. Now she wished to God, she hadn't taken those two jiggers. George's horse quickened his speed and hers followed. George's slowed and hers did likewise. She could feel George's grin in the back of her neck. She had no control over her horse.

They were galloping in the hot sunlight, and Josie stole glances at the flat fields of strawberries. "If you weren't drunk, you'd fall off," George shouted. Now they were passing a cotton field. ("The back of my neck'll be blistered," she thought. "Where was it I picked strawberries once? At Dyersburg when I was ten, visiting some God-forsaken relations.") The horses turned off the road into wooded bottom land. The way now was shaded by giant trees, but here and there the sun shone between the foliage. Once after riding thirty feet in shadow, watching dumbly the cool blue-green underbrush, Josie felt the sun suddenly on her neck. Her stomach churned, and the eggs and coffee from breakfast burnt her throat as it all gushed forth, splattering her pants-leg and the brown saddle and the horse's side. She looked over the horse at George.

But there was no remorse, no compassion and no humor in George's face. He gazed straight ahead and urged on his horse.

All at once the horses turned to the right. Josie howled. She saw her right foot flying through the air, and after the thud of the fall and the flashes of light and darkness she lay on her back in the dirt and watched George as he approached on foot, leading the two horses.

"Old girl—" he said.

"You get the hell away from me!"

"Are you hurt?" He kneeled beside her, so close to her that she could smell his sweaty shirt.

Josie jumped to her feet and walked in the direction from which they had ridden. In a moment George galloped past her, leading the gray horse and laughing like the son-of-a-bitch he was.

"Last night he sent me upstairs! But this is more! I'm not gonna have it." She walked through the woods, her lips moving as she talked to herself. "He wants no more of my drunken palaver!" Well, he was going to get no more of her drunken anything now. She had had her fill of him and everybody else and was going to look out for her own little sweet self from now on.

That was her trouble, she knew. She'd never made a good thing of people. "That's why things are like they are now," she said. "I've never made a good thing out of anybody." But it was real lucky that she realized it now, just exactly when she had, for it was certain that there had never been one whom more could be made out of than George. "God damn him," she said, thinking still of his riding by her like that. "Whatever it was I liked about him is gone now."

She gazed up into the foliage and branches of the trees, and the great size of the trees made her feel really small, and young. If Jackie or Lon had been different she might have learned things when she was young. "But they were both of 'em easy-goin' and just slipped out on me." They *were* sweet. She'd never forget how sweet Jackie always was. "Just plain sweet." She made a quick gesture with her right hand: "If only they didn't all get such a hold on me!"

But she was through with George. This time *she* got through first. He was no different from a floorwalker. He had more sense. "He's educated, and the money he must have!" George had more sense than a floorwalker, but he didn't have any manners. He treated her just like the floorwalker at Jobe's had that last week she was there. But George was worth getting around. She would find out what it was. She wouldn't take another drink. She'd find out what was wrong inside him, and somehow get a hold on him. Little Josephine would make a place for herself at last. She just wouldn't think about him as a man.

At the edge of the wood she turned onto the road, and across the fields she could see his house. That house was just simply as old and big as they come, and wasn't a cheap house. "I wonder if he looked after getting it fixed over and remodeled." Not likely. She kept looking at the whitewashed brick and shaking her head. "No, by Jesus," she exclaimed. "*She* did it!" George's wife.

All of her questions seemed to have been answered. The wife had left him for his meanness, and he was lonesome. There was, then, a place to be filled. She began to run along the road. "God, I feel like somebody might step in before I get there." She laughed, but then the heat seemed to strike her all at once. Her stomach drew in. She vomited in the ditch, and, by God, it was as dry as cornflakes!

She sat still in the grass under a little maple tree beside the road, resting her forehead on her drawn-up knees. All between Josie and her new life seemed to be the walk through the sun in these smelly, dirty clothes. Across the fields and in the house was a canopied bed and a glorious new life, but she daren't go into the sun. She would pass out cold. "People kick off in weather like this!"

Presently Josie heard the voices of niggers up the road. She wouldn't look up, she decided. She'd let them pass, without looking up. They drew near to her and she made out the voices of a man and a child. Then the man said, "Hursh!" and the voices ceased. There was only the sound of their feet padding along the dusty road.

The noise of the padding grew fainter. Josie looked up and saw that the two had cut across the fields toward George's house. Already she could hear the niggers mouthing it about the kitchen. That little yellow Henry would look at her over his shoulder as he went through the swinging door at dinner tonight. If she heard them grumbling once more, as she did Monday, calling her "she," Josie decided that she was going to come right out and ask Amelia about the scar. Right before George. But the niggers were the least of her worries now.

All afternoon she lay on the bed, waking now and then to look at the bottle of whiskey on the dressing table and to wonder where George had gone. She didn't know whether it had been George or the field nigger who sent Henry after her in the truck. Once she dreamed that she saw George at the head of the stair telling Amelia how he had sobered Miss Josephine up. When she awoke that time she said, "I ought to get up and get myself good and plastered before George comes back from wherever he is." But she slept again and dreamed this time that she was working at a hat sale at Jobe's and that she had to wait on Amelia who picked up a white turban and asked Josie to model it for her. And the dream ended with Amelia telling Josie how pretty she was and how much she liked her.

Josie had taken another hot bath (to ward off soreness from the horseback ride) and was in the sitting room, which everybody called the back parlor, playing the electric victrola and feeling just prime when George came in. She let him go through the hall and upstairs to dress for dinner without calling to him. She chuckled to herself and rocked to the time of the music.

George came with a real mint julep in each hand. His hair was wet and slicked down over his head; the part, low on the left side, was straight and white. His cheeks were shaven and were pink with new sunburn. He said, "I had myself the time of my life this afternoon."

Josie smiled and said that she was glad he had enjoyed himself. George raised his eyebrows and cocked his head to one side. She kept on smiling at him, and made no movement toward taking the drink that he held out to her.

George set the glass on the little candle stand near her chair and switched off the victrola.

"George, I was listening . . ."

"Ah, now," he said, "I want to tell you about the cockfight."

"Let me finish listening to that piece, George."

George dropped down into an armchair and put his feet on a stool. His pants and shirt were white, and he wore a blue polka dot tie.

"You're nice and clean," she said, as though she had forgotten the victrola.

"Immaculate!" There was a mischievous grin on his face, and he leaned over one arm of the chair and pulled the victrola plug from the floor socket. Josie reached out and took the glass from the candle stand, stirred it slightly with a shoot of mint and began to sip it. She thought, "I *have* to take it when he acts this way."

At the dinner table George said, "You're in better shape tonight. You look better. Why don't you go easy on the bottle tonight?"

She looked at him between the two candles burning in the center of the round table. "I didn't ask you for that mint julep, I don't think."

"And you ain't gettin' any more," he said, winking at her as he lifted his fork to his lips with his left hand. This, she felt, was a gesture to show his contempt for her. Perhaps he thought she didn't know the difference, which, of course, was even more contemptuous.

"Nice manners," she said. He made no answer, but at least he could be sure that she had recognized the insult. She took a drink of water, her little finger extended slightly from the glass, and over the glass she said, "You didn't finish about the niggers having a fight after the chickens did."

"Oh, yes." He arranged his knife and fork neatly on his plate. "The two nigs commenced to watch each other before their chickens had done scrapping. And when the big rooster gave his last hop and keeled over, Ira Blakemoor jumped over the two birds onto Jimmy's shoulders. Jimmy just whirled round and round till he threw Ira the way the little mare did you this morning." George looked directly into Josie's eyes between the candles, defiantly unashamed to mention that event, and he smiled with defiance and yet with weariness. "Ira got up and the two walked around looking at each other like two black games before a fight." Josie kept her eyes on George while the story, she felt, went on and on and on.

That yellow nigger Henry was paused at the swinging door, looking over his shoulder toward her. She turned her head and glared at him. He was not even hiding this action from George, who was going on and on about the niggers' fighting. This Henry was the worst hypocrite of all. He who had slashed Amelia's wrist (it was surely Henry who had done it), and probably had raped his own children, the way niggers do, was denouncing her right out like this. Her heart pounded when he kept looking, and then George's story stopped.

A bright light flashed across Henry's face and about the room which was lit by only the two candles. Josie swung her head around, and through the front window she saw the lights of automobiles that were coming through the yard. She looked at George, and his face said absolutely nothing for itself. He moistened his lips with his tongue.

"Guests," he said, raising his eyebrows. And Josie felt that in that moment she had seen the strongest floorwalker weaken. George had scorned and laughed at everybody and every situation. But now he was ashamed. He was ashamed of her. On her behavior would depend his comfort. She was cold sober and would be *up* to whatever showed itself. It was her real opportunity.

From the back of the house a horn sounded, and above other voices a woman's voice rose, calling "Whoohoo!" George stood up and bowed to her beautifully, like something she had never seen, and said, "You'll excuse me?" Then he went out through the kitchen without saying "scat" about what she should do.

She drummed on the table with her fingers and listened to George's greetings to his friends. She heard him say, "Welcome, Billy, and welcome, Mrs. Billy!" They were the only names she recognized. It was likely the Billy Colton she'd met with George one night.

Then these *were* Memphis Society people. Here for the night, at least! She looked down at her yellow linen dress and straightened the lapels at the neck. She thought of the women with their lovely profiles and soft skin and natural-colored hair. What if she had waited on one of them once at Jobe's or, worse still, in the old days at Burnstein's? But they had probably never been to one of those cheap stores. What if they stayed but refused to talk to her, or even to meet her? They could be mean bitches, all of them, for all their soft hands and shaved legs. Her hand trembled as she rang the little glass bell for coffee.

She rang it, and no one answered. She rang it again, hard, but now she could hear Henry coming through the breakfast room to the hall, bumping the guests' baggage against the doorway. Neither Amelia nor Mammy, who cooked the evening meal, would leave the kitchen during dinner, Josie knew. "I'd honestly like to go out in the kitchen and ask 'em for a cup of coffee and tell 'em just how scared I am." But too well she could imagine their contemptuous, accusing gaze. "If only I could get something on them! Even catch 'em toting food just once! That Mammy's likely killed enough niggers in her time to fill Jobe's basement."

Josie was even afraid to light a cigarette. She went over to the side window and looked out into the yard; she could see the lights of the automobile shining on the green leaves and on the white fence around the house lot.

And she was standing thus when she heard the voices and the footsteps in the long hall. She had only just turned around when George stood in the wide doorway with the men and women from Memphis. He was pronouncing her name first: "Miss Carlson, this is Mr. Roberts, Mrs. Roberts, Mr. Jackson, Mrs. Jackson and Mr. and Mrs. Colton."

Josie stared at the group, not trying to catch the names. She could think only, "They're old. The women are old and plump. George's wife is old!" She stared at them, and when the name Colton struck her ear, she said automatically and without placing his face, "I know Billy."

George said, in the same tone in which he had said, "You'll excuse me? . . . Josie, will you take the ladies upstairs to freshen up while the men and I get some drinks started? We'll settle the rooming question later." George was the great floorwalker whose wife was old and who had now shown his pride to Josie Carlson. He had shown his shame. Finally he had decided on a course and was following it, but he had given 'way his sore spots. Only God knew what he had told his friends. Josie said to herself, "It's plain he don't want 'em to know who I am."

As Josie ascended the stair, followed by those she had already privately termed the "three matrons," she watched George and the three other men go down the hall to the breakfast room. The sight of their white linen suits and brown and white shoes in the bright hall seemed to make the climb a soaring. At the top of the stair she stopped and let the three women pass ahead of her. She eyed the costume of each as they passed. One wore a tailored seersucker dress. Another wore a navy blue linen dress with white collar and cuffs, and the third wore a striped linen skirt and silk blouse. On the wrist of this last was a bracelet from which hung a tiny silver dog, a lock, a gold heart.

Josie observed their grooming: their fingernails, their lipstick, their hair in tight curls. There was gray in the hair of one, but not one, Josie decided now, was much past forty. Their figures were neatly corseted, and Josie felt that the little saggings under their chins and under the eyes of the one in the navy blue made them more charming; were, indeed, almost a part of their smartness. She wanted to think of herself as like them. They were, she realized, at least ten years older than she, but in ten years, beginning tonight, she might become one of them.

"Just go in my room there," she said. She pointed to the open door and started down the steps, thinking that this was the beginning of the new life and thinking of the men downstairs fixing the drinks. And then she thought of the bottle of whiskey on her dressing table in the room where the matrons had gone!

"Oh, hell," she swore under her breath. She had turned to go up the two steps again when she heard the men's voices below. She heard her own name being pronounced carefully: "Josie Carlson." She went down five or six steps on tiptoe and stood still to listen to the voices that came from the breakfast room.

"You said to come any time, George, and never mentioned having this thing down here."

George laughed. "Afraid of what the girls will say when you get home? I can hear them. 'In Beatrice's own lovely house,'" he mocked.

"Well, fellow, you've a shock coming, too," one of them said. "Beatrice has sent your boys down to Memphis for a month with you. They say she has a beau."

"And in the morning," one said, "your sister Kate's sending them down here. She asked us to bring them, and then decided to keep them one night herself."

"You'd better get *her* out, George."

George laughed. Josie could hear him dropping ice into glasses. "We'll take her back at dawn, if you say."

"What would the girls say to that?" He laughed at them as he laughed at Josie.

"The girls are gonna be decent to her. They agreed in the yard."

"Female curiosity?" George said.

"Your boys'll have curiosity, too. Jock's seventeen."

Even the clank of the ice stopped. "You'll every one of you please to remember," George said slowly, "that Josie's a friend of yours and that she met the girls here by appointment."

Josie tiptoed down the stair, descending, she felt, once more into her old world. "He'll slick me some way if he has to for his kids, I think." She turned into the dining-room at the foot of the stair. The candles were burning low, and she went and stood by the open window and listened to the counterpoint of the crickets and the frogs while Henry, who had looked over his shoulder at the car lights, rattled the silver and china and went about clearing the table.

Presently George had come and put his hand on her shoulder. When she turned around she saw him smiling and holding two drinks in his left hand. He leaned his face close to hers and said, "I'm looking for the tears."

Josie said, "There aren't any to find, fellow"; and she thought it odd, really odd, that he had expected her to cry. But he was probably poking fun at her again.

She took one of the drinks and clinked glasses with George. To herself she said, "I bet they don't act any better than I do after they've got a few under their belts." At least she showed her true colors! "I'll keep my eyes open for their true ones."

If only they'd play the victrola instead of the radio. She liked the victrola so much better. She could play "Louisville Lady" over and over. But, *no*. They all wanted to switch the radio about. To get Cincinnati and Los Angeles and Bennie this and Johnny that. If they liked a piece, why did they care who played it. For God's sake! They wouldn't dance at first, either, and when she first got George to dance with her, they sat smiling at each other, grinning. They had played cards, too, but poker didn't go so well after George slugged them all with that third round of his three-dollar-whiskey drinks. Right then she had begun to watch out to see who slapped whose knee.

She asked George to dance because she so liked to dance with him, and she wasn't going to care about what the others did any more, she decided. But finally when two of them had started dancing off in the corner of the room, she looked about the sitting-room for the other four and saw that Billy Colton had disappeared not with his own wife but with that guy Jackson's. And Josie threw herself down into the armchair and laughed aloud, so hard and loud that everybody begged her to tell what was funny. But she stopped suddenly and gave them as mean a look as she could manage and said, "Nothin'. Let's dance some more, George."

But George said that he must tell Henry to fix more drinks, and he went out and left her by the radio with Roberts and Mrs. Colton. She looked at Mrs. Colton and thought, "Honey, you don't seem to be grieving about Billy."

Then Roberts said to Josie, "George says you're from Vicksburg."

"I was raised there," she said, wondering why George hadn't told her whatever he'd told them.

"He says you live there now."

Mrs. Colton, who wore the navy blue and was the fattest of the three matrons, stood up and said to Billy, "Let's dance in the hall where there are fewer rugs." And she gave a kindly smile to Josie, and Josie spit out a "Thanks." The couple skipped into the hall, laughing, and Josie sat alone by the radio wishing she could play the victrola and wishing that George would come and kiss her on the back of her neck. "And I'd slap him if he did," she said. Now and again she would cut her eyes around to watch Jackson and Mrs. Roberts dancing. They were at the far end of the room and were dancing slowly. They kept rubbing against the heavy blue drapery at the window and they were talking into each other's ears.

But the next piece that came over the radio was a hot one, and Jackson led Mrs. Roberts to the center of the room and whirled her round and round, and the trinkets at her wrist tinkled like little bells. Josie lit a cigarette and watched them dance. She realized then that Jackson was showing off for her sake.

When George came with a tray of drinks he said, "Josie, move the victrola," but Josie sat still and glared at him as if to say, What on earth are you talking about? Are you nuts? He set the tray across her lap and turned and picked up the little victrola and set it on the floor.

"Oh, good God!" Josie cried in her surprise and delight. "It's a portable."

George, taking the tray from her, said, "It's not for you to port off, old girl."

The couple in the center of the room had stopped their whirling and had followed George. "We like to dance, but there are better things," Jackson was saying.

Mrs. Roberts flopped down on the broad arm of Josie's chair and took a drink from George. Josie could only watch the trinkets on the bracelet, one of which she saw was a little gold book. George was telling Jackson about the cockfight again, and Mrs. Roberts leaned over and talked to Josie. She tried to tell her how the room seemed to be whirling around. They both giggled, and Josie thought, "Maybe we'll get to be good friends, and she'll stop pretending to be so swell."

But she couldn't think of anything to say to her, partly because she just never did have anything to say to women and partly because Jackson, who was not at all a bad-looking little man, was sending glances her way.

It didn't seem like more than twenty minutes or half an hour more before George had got to that point where he ordered her around and couldn't keep on his own feet. He finally lay down on the couch in the front parlor, and as she and Mrs. Roberts went up the stair with their arms about each other's waists, he called out something that made Mrs. Roberts giggle. But Josie knew that little Josephine was at the point where she could say nothing straight, so she didn't even ask to get the portable victrola. She just cursed under her breath.

The daylight was beginning to appear at the windows of Josie's narrow little room when waking suddenly she sat up in bed and then flopped down again and jerked the sheet about her. "That little sucker come up here," she grumbled, "and cleared out, but where was the little sucker's wife?" Who was with George, by damn, all night? After a while she said, "They're none of 'em any better than the niggers. I knew they couldn't be. Nobody is. By God, nobody's better than I am. Nobody can say anything to me." Everyone would like to live as free as she did! There was no such thing as . . . There was no such thing as what the niggers and the whites liked to pretend they were. She was going to let up, and do things in secret. Try to look like an angel. It wouldn't be as hard since there was no such thing.

It was all like a scene from a color movie, like one of the musicals. It was the prettiest scene ever. And they were like two of those lovely wax models in the boys' department at Jobe's. Like two of those models, with the tan skin and blond hair, come to life! And to see them in their white shorts springing about the green grass under the blue, blue sky, hitting the little feather thing over the high net, made Josie go weak all over. She went down on her knees and rested her elbows on the window sill and watched them springing about before the people from Memphis; these were grouped under a tree, sitting in deck chairs and on the grass. George stood at the net like a floorwalker charmed by his wax models which had come to life.

It had been George's cries of "Outside, outside!" and the jeers and applause of the six spectators that awakened Josie. She ran to the window in her pajamas, and when she saw the white markings on the grass and the net that had sprung up there overnight, she thought that this might be a dream. But the voices of George and Mrs. Roberts and Phil Jackson were completely real, and the movements of the boys' bodies were too marvelous to be doubted.

She sank to her knees, conscious of the soreness which her horseback ride had left. She thought of her clumsy self in the dusty road as she gazed down at the graceful boys on the lawn and said, "Why, they're actually pretty. Too pretty." She was certain of one thing: She didn't want any of their snobbishness. She wouldn't have it from his two kids.

One boy's racket missed the feather thing. George shouted, "Game!" The group under the tree applauded, and the men pushed themselves up from their seats to come out into the sunlight and pat the naked backs of the boys.

When the boys came close together, Josie saw that one was six inches taller than the other. "Why, that one's grown!" she thought. The two of them walked toward the house, the taller one walking with the shorter's neck in the crook of his elbow. George called to them, "You boys get dressed for lunch." He ordered them about just as he did her, but they went off smiling.

Josie walked in her bare feet into the little closet-like bathroom which adjoined her room. She looked at herself in the mirror there and said, "I've never dreaded anything so much in all my life before. You can't depend on what kids'll say." But were they kids? For all their prettiness, they were too big to be called kids. And nobody's as damn smutty as a smart-alecky shaver.

Josephine bathed in the little, square, maroon bathtub. There were maroon-and-white checkered tile steps built up around the tub, so that it gave the effect of being sunken. After her bath, she stood on the steps and powdered her whole soft body. Every garment which she put on was absolutely fresh. She went to her closet and took out her new white silk dress and slipped it over her head. She put on white shoes first, but, deciding she looked too much like a trained nurse, she changed to her tan pumps. Josie knew what young shavers thought about nurses.

She combed her yellow hair till it lay close to her head, and put on rouge and lipstick. Someone knocked at the bedroom door. "Yeah," she called. No answer came, so she went to the door and opened it. In the hall stood one of the boys. It was the little one.

He didn't look at her; he looked past her. And his eyes *were* as shiny and cold as those on a wax dummy!

"Miss Carlson, my dad says to tell you that lunch is ready. And I'm Buddy."

"Thanks." She didn't know what the hell else she could say. "Tell him, all right," she said. She stepped back into her room and shut the door.

Josie paced the room for several times. "He didn't so much as look at me." She was getting hot, and she went and put her face to the window. The people from Memphis had come indoors, and the sun shone on the brownish-green grass and on the still trees. "It's a scorcher," she said. She walked the length of the room again and opened the door. Buddy was still there. Standing there in white, his shirt open at the collar, and his white pants, long pants. He was leaning against the banister.

"Ready?" he said, smiling.

As they went down the steps together, he said, "It's nice that you're here. We didn't know it till just a few minutes ago." He was a Yankee kid, lived with his mother somewhere, and rolled his r's, and spoke as though there was a lot of meaning behind what he said. She gave him a quick glance to see what he meant by that last remark. He smiled, and this time looked right into her eyes.

After lunch, which Josie felt had been awful embarrassing, they traipsed into the back parlor, and George showed off the kids again. She had had a good look at the older one during lunch and could tell by the way the corners of his mouth drooped down that he was a surly one, unless maybe he was only trying to keep from looking so pretty. And all he said to the questions which George asked him about girls and his high school was "Yeah," or "Aw, naw." When Henry brought in the first round of drinks, and he took one, his daddy looked at him hard and said, "Jock?" And the boy looked his daddy square in the eye.

Buddy only shook his head and smiled when Henry offered him a drink, but he was the one that had started all the embarrassment for her at lunch. When they came into the dining-room he pulled her chair out, and she looked back at him—knowing how kids like to jerk chairs. Everybody laughed, but she kept on looking at him. And then she knew that she blushed, for she thought how big her behind must look to him with her bent over like she was.

The other thing that was awful was the question that Mrs. Jackson, the smallest matron and the one with the gray streak in her hair, asked her, "And how do *you* feel this morning, Miss Carlson?" It was the fact that it was Jackson's wife which got her most. But then the fool woman said, "Like the rest of us?" And Josie supposed that she meant no meanness by her remark, but she had already blushed; and Jackson, across the table, looked into his plate. Had this old woman and George been messing around? She wondered. Probably Mrs. Jackson hadn't meant anything.

As they all lounged about the sitting-room after lunch, she even felt that she was beginning to catch on to these people and that she was going to start a little pretense of her own and make a good thing out of old Georgie. It was funny the way her interest in him, any real painful interest was sort of fading. "I've never had so much happen to me at one time," she said to herself. She sat on the floor beside George's chair and put her hand on the toe of his brown-and-white shoe.

Then George said, "Buddy, you've got to give us just one recitation." And Buddy's face turned as red as a traffic light. He was sitting on a footstool and looking down at his hands.

Jock reached over and touched him on the shoulder and said: "Come on, Buddy, the one about 'if love were like a rose.' " Buddy shook his head and kept his eyes on his hands.

Josie said to herself, "The kid's honestly timid." It gave her the shivers to see anybody so shy and ignorant of things. But then he began to say the poetry without looking up. It was something about a rose and a rose leaf, but nobody could hear him very good.

George said, "Louder! Louder!" The boy looked at him and said a verse about "sweet rain at noon." Next he stood up and moved his hands about as he spoke, and the blushing was all gone. He said the next one to Mrs. Roberts, and it began:

If you were life, my darling,
And I, your love, were death . . .

That verse ended with something silly about "fruitful breath." He went to Billy Colton's wife, and the verse he said to her was sad. The boy *did* have a way with him! His eyes were big and he could look sad and happy at the same time. "And I were page to joy," he said. He actually looked like one of the pages they have in stores at Christmas.

But now the kid was perfectly sure of himself, and he had acted timid at first. It was probably all a show. She could just hear him saying dirty "limricks." She realized that he was bound to say a verse to her if he knew that many, and she listened carefully to the one he said to Mrs. Jackson:

If you were April's lady,
And I were lord in May,
We'd throw with leaves for hours
And draw for days with flowers,
Till day like night were shady
And night were bright like day;
If you were April's lady,
And I were lord in May.

He turned to Josie in his grandest manner:

If you were queen of pleasure,
And I were king of pain,
We'd hunt down love together,
Pluck out his flying-feather
And teach his feet a measure,

And find his mouth a rein;
If you were queen of pleasure,
And I were king of pain.

And Josie sat up straight and gave the brat the hardest look she knew how. It was too plain. "Queen of pleasure" sounded just as bad as whore! Especially coming right after the verse about "April's lady." The boy blushed again when she glared at him. No one made a noise for a minute. Josie looked at George, and he smiled and began clapping his hands, and everybody clapped. Buddy bowed and ran from the room.

"He's good, George. He's good," Jackson said, squinting his beady little eyes. Jackson was really a puny-looking little guy in the light of day! And he hadn't thought the boy was any better than anybody else did. It was just that he wanted to be the first to say something.

"He's really very good," Mrs. Jackson said.

George laughed. "He's a regular little actor," he said. "Gets it from Beatrice, I guess." Everybody laughed.

George's wife was an actress, then! She'd probably been the worst of the whole lot. There was no telling what this child was really like.

"How old is he, Jock?" Jackson asked. How that man liked to hear his own voice!

"Fourteen and a half," Jock said. "Have you seen him draw?" He talked about his kid brother like he was his own child. Josie watched him. He was talking about Buddy's drawings, about the likenesses. She watched him, and then he saw her watching. He dropped his eyes to his hands as Buddy had done. But in a minute he looked up; and as the talking and drinking went on he kept his eyes on Josephine.

It wasn't any of George's business. It wasn't any of his or anybody's how much she drank, and she knew very well that *he* didn't really give a damn! But it *was* smarter 'n hell of him to take her upstairs, because the boys had stared at her all afternoon and all through supper. That was really why she had kept on taking the drinks when she had made up her mind to let up. She had said, "You're jealous. You're jealous, George." And he had put his hand over her mouth, saying, "Careful, Josie." But she was sort of celebrating so much's happening to her, and she felt good, and she was plain infuriated when George kissed her and went back downstairs. "He was like his real self comin' up the steps," she said. He had told her that she didn't have the gumption God gave a crabapple.

Josie went off to sleep with her lips moving and awoke in the middle of the night with them moving again. She was feeling just prime and yet rotten at the same time. She had a headache and yet she had a happy feeling. She woke up saying, "Thank God for small favors." She had been dreaming about Jock. He was all right. She had dreamed that together she and Jock had watched a giant bear devouring a bull, and Jock had laughed. He was all right. She was practically sure. His eyes were like George's, and he was as stubborn.

It would have been perfectly plain to everybody if supper hadn't been such an all-round mess. What with Jackson's smutty jokes and his showing off (trying to get her to look at him), and Mrs. Colton's flirting with her husband (holding his hand on the table!), nobody but George paid any attention to Jock. And she was glad that she had smacked Jackson when he tried to carry her up the stair, for it made Jock smile his crooked smile.

"They all must be in bed," she thought. The house was so quiet that she could hear a screech owl, or something, down in the woods.

She thought she heard a noise in her bathroom. She lay still, and she was pretty sure she had heard it again. She supposed it was a mouse, but it might be something else; she had never before thought about where that door beside the bathtub might lead. There was only one place it could go. She got up and went in her stocking feet to the bathroom. She switched on the light and watched the knob. She glanced at herself in the mirror. Her new white silk dress was twisted and wrinkled. "Damn him," she whispered to herself. "He *could* have made me take off *this* dress." Then she thought she had seen the knob move, move as though someone had released it. She stood still, but there wasn't another sound that night.

In the morning when she turned off the bathroom light, she was still wondering. She looked out of the window; the high net was down. No one was in sight.

What they all did was to slip out on her before she woke up! And in the breakfast room that morning Amelia wanted to talk, but Josephine wasn't going to give the nigger the chance. There was no telling what they had let the niggers hear at breakfast. Amelia kept coming to the breakfast room door and asking if everything was all right, if Miss Josephine wanted this or wanted that, but Josephine would only shake her head and say not a word after Amelia had once answered, "They've went back to Memphis." For all she knew, George and the kids had gone too. It would have been like him to leave her and send after her, just because he had promised her she could stay a week. (He talked like it was such a great treat for her. She hadn't given a copper about the place at first. It had been *him*.) But he'd damned well better not have left her. She'd got a taste of this sort of thing for its own sake now, and she'd stay for good!

Buddy opened the outside door of the breakfast room.

"Good morning, Miss Carlson," he said.

"Hello," Josie said. She did wonder what Jock had told Buddy, what he had guessed to tell him. Buddy wasn't at dinner last night, or she couldn't remember him there.

He was wearing khaki riding pants and a short-sleeved shirt. He sat down across the table from her. "I guess we're all that's left," he said. He picked up the sugar bowl and smiled as he examined it. The corners of his mouth turned up like in a picture kids draw on a blackboard.

"Did Jock and George go to Memphis? Did they?"

"Jock did."

"He did?"

"Yes, he did. And Henry told me he didn't much want to go. I was off riding when they all got up this morning. Daddy wanted me to go, but I wasn't here." He smiled again, and Josie supposed he meant that he'd been hiding from them.

"Where's your dad?"

"He? Oh, he went to the village to see about some hams. What are you going to do now?"

Josie shrugged her shoulders and began to drink her coffee. Jock was gone! He might have just been scorning her with those looks all the time. She should have got that door open somehow and found out what was what. "Why didn't Jock want to go?" she asked Buddy.

"Our pleasant company, I suppose," he said. "Or yours."

She looked at him and he laughed. She wondered could this brat be poking fun at her? "Queen of pleasure!" she said out loud, not meaning to at all.

"Did you like that poem?" he asked. It was certain that he wasn't timid when he was alone with somebody, not at least when alone with her.

"I don't know," she said. Then she looked at him. "I don't like the one you picked for me."

"That's not one of the best, is it?"

Neither of them spoke while Josie finished her coffee. She put in another spoonful of sugar before taking the last few swallows, and Buddy reddened when she motioned for him to give up the sugar bowl. Amelia came and removed the breakfast plate and the butter plate. She returned for Josie's coffeecup, and, finding it not quite ready, she stood behind Buddy's chair and put her hands on his shoulders. The scar was right beside his cheek. Buddy smiled and beat the back of his head against her ribs playfully. Finally Josie put her cup down and said, "That's all."

She went upstairs to her room. Jock had tried to get in through her bathroom last night, or he had been so on her mind that her ears and eyes had made up the signs of it. Maybe Buddy had caught Jock trying to open the door and had told George. At any rate George had sent

Jock away. If he sent him away, then Jock had definitely had notions. Josie smiled over that. She was sitting on the side of her little canopied bed, smoking a red-tipped cigarette. There was the noise of an automobile motor in the yard. George was back! Josie went to her dressing table and drank the last of her whiskey.

She sat on the stool before her dressing table, with her eyes on the hall door. She listened to George's footsteps on the stair, and sat with her legs crossed, twitching the left foot, which dangled. George came in and closed the door behind him.

"I've bought you a ticket on the night train, Josie. You're goin' back tonight."

So he wasn't such a stickler for his word, after all! Not in this case! He was sending her home. Well, what did he expect her to say? Did he think she would beg to stay on? She would clear out, and she wasn't the one beaten. George was beaten. One of his kids that he was so mortally fond of, one for sure had had notions. "Almost for sure." George opened the door and left Josie staring after him. In a few minutes she heard his horse gallop past the house and out onto the dirt road.

She folded her white dress carefully and laid it on the bottom of her traveling bag. She heard Buddy somewhere in the house, singing. She wrapped her white shoes in toilet paper and stuck them at the ends of the bag. Buddy seemed to be wandering through the house, singing. His voice was high like a woman's, never breaking as she sometimes thought it did in conversation. It came from one part of the house and then another. Josie stopped her packing. "There's no such thing," she said.

She went down the steps like a child, stopping both feet on each step, then stepping to the next. One hand was on her hip, the other she ran along the banister. She walked through the front parlor with its bookcases and fancy chairs with the eagles worked in the needlepoint, and through the back parlor with the rockingchairs and the silly candle stand and the victrola. She stepped down into the breakfast room where the sunlight came through the blinds and put stripes on the brick wall. She went into the kitchen for the first time. Mammy, with a white dust cap on the back of her head, had already started supper. She stood by the big range, and Amelia sat in the corner peeling potatoes. Josie wasn't interested in the face of either. She went through the dark pantry and into the dining-room. She looked through the windows there, but no one was in the yard. She went into the hall.

Buddy was near the top of the stairway which curved around the far end of the long hall, looking down at her. "Why don't you come up here?" He pronounced every word sharply and rolled his r's. But his voice was flat, and his words seemed to remain in the hall for several minutes. His question seemed to float down from the ceiling, down through the air like a feather.

"How did he get up there without me hearing him?" Josie mumbled. She took the first two steps slowly, and Buddy hopped up to the top of the stair.

The door to the kids' room was open and Josie went in. Buddy shut the white paneled door and said, "Don't you think it's time you did something nice for me?"

Josie laughed, and she watched Buddy laugh. Queen of pleasure indeed!

"I want to draw you," he said.

"Clothes and all, Bud . . . ?"

"No. That's not what I mean!"

Josie forced a smile, and she suddenly felt afraid and thought she was going to be sick again.

"That's not what I mean," she heard the kid say again, without blinking an eye, without blushing. "I didn't know you were that sort of nasty thing here. I didn't know you was a fancy woman. Go away. Go on out of here. Go on out of here!" he ordered her.

As Josie went down the steps she kept puckering her lips and nodding her head. She was trying to talk to herself about how many times she had been up and down the steps, but she could still see the smooth brown color of his face and his yellow hair, and she could also see her hand trembling on the banister. It seemed like five years since she had come up the steps with the matrons from Memphis.

In the breakfast room she tore open the frail door to George's little liquor cabinet and took a quart of Bourbon from the shelf. Then she stepped up into the hall and went into the sitting-room and took the portable victrola and that record. As she stomped back into the hall, Buddy came running down the steps. He opened the front door and ran out across the veranda and across the lawn. His yellow hair was like a ball of gold in the sunlight as he went through the gate. But Josie went upstairs.

She locked her door and threw the big key across the room. She knocked the bottle of toilet water and the amber brush off her dressing table as she made room for the victrola. When she had started "Louisville Lady" playing she sat on the stool and began to wonder. "The kid's head was like a ball of gold, but I'm not gonna think about him ever once I get back to Memphis," she told herself. "No, by damn, but I wonder just what George'll do to me." She broke the blue seal of the whiskey with her fingernail, and it didn't seem like more than twenty minutes or half an hour before George was beating and kicking on the door, and she was sitting on the stool and listening and just waiting for him to break the door, and wondering what he'd do to her.

Eudora Welty (b. 1909)
A WORN PATH

It was December—a bright frozen day in the early morning. Far out in the country there was an old Negro woman with her head tied in a red rag, coming along a path through the pinewoods. Her name was Phoenix Jackson. She was very old and small and she walked slowly in the dark pine shadows, moving a little from side to side in her steps, with the balanced heaviness and lightness of a pendulum in a grandfather clock. She carried a thin, small cane made from an umbrella, and with this she kept tapping the frozen earth in front of her. This made a grave and persistent noise in the still air, that seemed meditative like the chirping of a solitary little bird.

She wore a dark striped dress reaching down to her shoe tops, and an equally long apron of bleached sugar sacks, with a full pocket: all neat and tidy, but every time she took a step she might have fallen over her shoelaces, which dragged from her unlaced shoes. She looked straight ahead. Her eyes were blue with age. Her skin had a pattern all its own of numberless branching wrinkles and as though a whole little tree stood in the middle of her forehead, but a golden color ran underneath, and the two knobs of her cheeks were illumined by a yellow burning under the dark. Under the red rag her hair came down on her neck in the frailest of ringlets, still black, and with an odor like copper.

Now and then there was a quivering in the thicket. Old Phoenix said, "Out of my way, all you foxes, owls, beetles, jack rabbits, coons and wild animals! . . . Keep out from under these feet, little bob-whites . . . . Keep the big wild hogs out of my path. Don't let none of those come running my direction. I got a long way." Under her small black-freckled hand her cane, limber as a buggy whip, would switch at the brush as if to rouse up any hiding things.

On she went. The woods were deep and still. The sun made the pine needles almost too bright to look at, up where the wind rocked. The cones dropped as light as feathers. Down in the hollow was the mourning dove—it was not too late for him.

The path ran up a hill. "Seem like there is chains about my feet, time I get this far," she said, in the voice of argument old people keep to use with themselves. "Something always take a hold of me on this hill—pleads I should stay."

After she got to the top she turned and gave a full, severe look behind her where she had come. "Up through pines," she said at length. "Now down through oaks."

Her eyes opened their widest, and she started down gently. But before she got to the bottom of the hill a bush caught her dress.

Her fingers were busy and intent, but her skirts were full and long, so that before she could pull them free in one place they were caught in another. It was not possible to allow the dress to tear. "I in the thorny bush," she said. "Thorns, you doing your appointed work. Never want to let folks pass, no sir. Old eyes thought you was a pretty little *green* bush."

Finally, trembling all over, she stood free, and after a moment dared to stoop for her cane.

"Sun so high!" she cried, leaning back and looking, while the thick tears went over her eyes. "The time getting all gone here."

At the foot of this hill was a place where a log was laid across the creek.

"Now comes the trial," said Phoenix.

Putting her right foot out, she mounted the log and shut her eyes. Lifting her skirt, leveling her cane fiercely before her, like a festival figure in some parade, she began to march across. Then she opened her eyes and she was safe on the other side.

"I wasn't as old as I thought," she said.

But she sat down to rest. She spread her skirts on the bank around her and folded her hands over her knees. Up above her was a tree in a pearly cloud of mistletoe. She did not dare to close her eyes, and when a little boy brought her a plate with a slice of marble-cake on it she spoke to him. "That would be acceptable," she said. But when she went to take it there was just her own hand in the air.

So she left that tree, and had to go through a barbed-wire fence. There she had to creep and crawl, spreading her knees and stretching her fingers like a baby trying to climb the steps. But she talked loudly to herself: she could not let her dress be torn now, so late in the day, and she could not pay for having her arm or her leg sawed off if she got caught fast where she was.

At last she was safe through the fence and risen up out in the clearing. Big dead trees, like black men with one arm, were standing in the purple stalks of the withered cotton field. There was a buzzard.

"Who you watching?"

In the furrow she made her way along.

"Glad this not the season for bulls," she said, looking sideways, "and the good Lord made his snakes to curl up and sleep in the winter. A pleasure I don't see no two-headed snake coming around that tree, where it come once. It took a while to get by him, back in the summer."

She passed through the old cotton and went into a field of dead corn. It whispered and shook and was taller than her head. "Through the maze now," she said, for there was no path.

Then there was something tall, black, and skinny there, moving before her.

At first she took it for a man. It could have been a man dancing in the field. But she stood still and listened, and it did not make a sound. It was as silent as a ghost.

"Ghost," she said sharply, "who be you the ghost of? For I have heard of nary death close by."

But there was no answer—only the ragged dancing in the wind.

She shut her eyes, reached out her hand, and touched a sleeve. She found a coat and inside that an emptiness, cold as ice.

"You scarecrow,"she said. Her face lighted. "I ought to be shut up for good," she said with laughter. "My senses is gone. I too old. I the oldest people I ever know. Dance, old scarecrow," she said, "while I dancing with you."

She kicked her foot over the furrow, and with mouth drawn down, shook her head once or twice in a little strutting way. Some husks blew down and whirled in streamers about her skirts.

Then she went on, parting her way from side to side with the cane, through the whispering field. At last she came to the end, to a wagon track where the silver grass blew between the red ruts. The quail were walking around like pullets, seeming all dainty and unseen.

"Walk pretty," she said. "This the easy place. This the easy going."

She followed the track, swaying through the quiet bare fields, through the little strings of trees silver in their dead leaves, past cabins silver from weather, with the doors and windows boarded shut, all like old women under a spell sitting there. "I walking in their sleep," she said, nodding her head vigorously.

In a ravine she went where a spring was silently flowing through a hollow log. Old Phoenix bent and drank. "Sweet-gum makes the water sweet," she said, and drank more. "Nobody know who made this well, for it was here when I was born."

The track crossed a swampy part where the moss hung as white as lace from every limb. "Sleep on, alligators, and blow your bubbles." Then the track went into the road.

Deep, deep the road went down between the high green-colored banks. Overhead the live-oaks met, and it was as dark as a cave.

A black dog with a lolling tongue came up out of the weeds by the ditch. She was meditating, and not ready, and when he came at her she only hit him a little with her cane. Over she went in the ditch, like a little puff of milkweed.

Down there, her senses drifted away. A dream visited her, and she reached her hand up, but nothing reached down and gave her a pull. So she lay there and presently went to talking. "Old woman," she said to herself, "that black dog come up out of the weeds to stall you off, and now there he sitting on his fine tail, smiling at you."

A white man finally came along and found her—a hunter, a young man, with his dog on a chain.

"Well, Granny!" he laughed. "What are you doing there?"

"Lying on my back like a June-bug waiting to be turned over, mister," she said, reaching up her hand.

He lifted her up, gave her a swing in the air, and set her down. "Anything broken, Granny?"

"No sir, them old dead weeds is springy enough," said Phoenix, when she had got her breath. "I thank you for your trouble."

"Where do you live, Granny?" he asked, while the two dogs were growling at each other.

"Away back yonder, sir, behind the ridge. You can't even see it from here."

"On your way home?"

"No sir, I going to town."

"Why, that's too far! That's as far as I walk when I come out myself, and I get something for my trouble." He patted the stuffed bag he carried, and there hung down a little closed claw. It was one of the bob-whites, with its beak hooked bitterly to show it was dead. "Now you go on home, Granny!"

"I bound to go to town, mister," said Phoenix. "The time come around."

He gave another laugh, filling the whole landscape. "I know you old colored people! Wouldn't miss going to town to see Santa Claus!"

But something held old Phoenix very still. The deep lines in her face went into a fierce and different radiation. Without warning, she had seen with her own eyes a flashing nickel fall out of the man's pocket onto the ground.

"How old are you, Granny?" he was saying.

"There is no telling, mister," she said, "no telling."

Then she gave a little cry and clapped her hands and said, "Git on away from here, dog! Look! Look at that dog!" She laughed as if in admiration. "He ain't scared of nobody. He a big black dog." She whispered. "Sic him!"

"Watch me get rid of that cur," said the man. "Sic him, Pete! Sic him!"

Phoenix heard the dogs fighting, and heard the man running and throwing sticks. She even heard a gunshot. But she was slowly bending forward by that time, further and further forward, the lid stretched down over her eyes, as if she were doing this in her sleep. Her chin was lowered almost to her knees. The yellow palm of her hand came out from the fold of her apron. Her fingers slid down and along the ground under the piece of money with the grace and care they would have in lifting an egg from under a setting hen. Then she slowly straightened up, she stood erect, and the nickel was in her apron pocket. A bird flew by. Her lips moved. "God watching me the whole time. I come to stealing."

The man came back, and his own dog panted about them. "Well, I scared him off that time," he said, and then he laughed and lifted his gun and pointed it at Phoenix.

She stood straight and faced him.

"Doesn't the gun scare you?" he said, still pointing it.

"No, sir, I seen plenty go off closer by, in my day, and for less than what I done," she said, holding utterly still.

He smiled, and shouldered the gun. "Well, Granny," he said, " you must be a hundred years old, and scared of nothing. I'd give you a dime if I had any money with me. But you take my advice and stay home, and nothing will happen to you."

"I bound to go on my way, mister," said Phoenix. She inclined her head in the red rag. Then they went in different directions, but she could hear the gun shooting again and again over the hill.

She walked on. The shadows hung from the oak trees to the road like curtains. Then she smelled wood-smoke, and smelled the river, and she saw a steeple and the cabins on their steep steps. Dozens of little black children whirled around her. There ahead was Natchez shining. Bells were ringing. She walked on.

In the paved city it was Christmas time. There were red and green electric lights strung and crisscrossed everywhere, and all turned on in the daytime. Old Phoenix would have been lost if she had not distrusted her eyesight and depended on her feet to know where to take her.

She paused quietly on the sidewalk where people were passing by. A lady came along in the crowd, carrying an armful of red-, green- and silver-wrapped presents; she gave off perfume like the red roses in hot summer, and Phoenix stopped her.

"Please, missy, will you lace up my shoe?" She held up her foot.

"What do you want, Grandma?"

"See my shoe," said Phoenix. "Do all right for out in the country, but wouldn't look right to go in a big building."

"Stand still then, Grandma," said the lady. She put her packages down on the sidewalk beside her and laced and tied both shoes tightly.

"Can't lace 'em with a cane," said Phoenix. "Thank you, missy. I doesn't mind asking a nice lady to tie up my shoe, when I gets out on the street."

Moving slowly and from side to side, she went into the big building, and into a tower of steps, where she walked up and around and around until her feet knew to stop.

She entered a door, and there she saw nailed up on the wall the document that had been stamped with the gold seal and framed in the gold frame, which matched the dream that was hung up in her head.

"Here I be," she said. There was a fixed and ceremonial stiffness over her body.

"A charity case, I suppose," said an attendant who sat at the desk before her.

But Phoenix only looked above her head. There was sweat on her face, the wrinkles in her skin shone like a bright net.

"Speak up, Grandma," the woman said. "What's your name? We must have your history, you know. Have you been here before? What seems to be the trouble with you?"

Old Phoenix only gave a twitch to her face as if a fly were bothering her.

"Are you deaf?" cried the attendant.

But then the nurse came in.

"Oh, that's just old Aunt Phoenix," she said. "She doesn't come for herself—she has a little grandson. She makes these trips just as regular as clockwork. She lives away back off the Old Natchez Trace." She bent down. "Well, Aunt Phoenix, why don't you just take a seat? We won't keep you standing after your long trip." She pointed.

The old woman sat down, bolt upright in the chair.

"Now, how is the boy?" asked the nurse.

Old Phoenix did not speak.

"I said, how is the boy?"

But Phoenix only waited and stared straight ahead, her face very solemn and withdrawn into rigidity.

"Is his throat any better?" asked the nurse. "Aunt Phoenix, don't you hear me? Is your grandson's throat any better since the last time you came for the medicine?"

With her hands on her knees, the old woman waited, silent, erect and motionless, just as if she were in armor.

"You mustn't take up our time this way, Aunt Phoenix," the nurse said. "Tell us quickly about your grandson, and get it over. He isn't dead, is he?"

At last there came a flicker and then a flame of comprehension across her face, and she spoke.

"My grandson. It was my memory had left me. There I sat and forgot why I made my long trip."

"Forgot?" The nurse frowned. "After you came so far?"

Then Phoenix was like an old woman begging a dignified forgiveness for waking up frightened in the night. "I never did go to school, I was too old at the Surrender," she said in a soft voice. "I'm an old woman without an education. It was my memory fail me. My little grandson, he is just the same, and I forgot it in the coming."

"Throat never heals, does it?" said the nurse, speaking in a loud, sure voice to old Phoenix. By now she had a card with something written on it, a little list. "Yes. Swallowed lye. When was it?—January—two-three years ago—"

Phoenix spoke unasked now. "No, missy, he not dead, he just the same. Every little while his throat begin to close up again, and he not able to swallow. He not get his breath. He not able to help himself. So the time come around, and I go on another trip for the soothing medicine."

"All right. The doctor said as long as you came to get it, you could have it," said the nurse. "But it's an obstinate case."

"My little grandson, he sit up there in the house all wrapped up waiting by himself," Phoenix went on. "We is the only two left in the world. He suffer and it don't seem to put him back at all. He got a sweet look. He going to last. He wear a little patch quilt and peep out holding his mouth open like a little bird. I remembers so plain now. I not going to forget him again, no, the whole enduring time. I could tell him from all the others in creation."

"All right." The nurse was trying to hush her now. She brought her a bottle of medicine. "Charity," she said, making a check mark in a book.

Old Phoenix held the bottle close to her eyes, and then carefully put it into her pocket.

"I thank you," she said.

"It's Christmas time, Grandma," said the attendant. "Could I give you a few pennies out of my purse?"

"Five pennies is a nickel," said Phoenix stiffly.

"Here's a nickel," said the attendant.

Phoenix rose carefully and held out her hand. She received the nickel and then fished the other nickel out of her pocket and laid it beside the new one. She stared at her palm closely, with her head on one side.

Then she gave a tap with her cane on the floor.

"This is what come to me to do," she said. "I going to the store and buy my child a little windmill they sells, made out of paper. He going to find it hard to believe there such a thing in the world. I'll march myself back where he waiting, holding it straight up in this hand."

She lifted her free hand, gave a little nod, turned around, and walked out of the doctor's office. Then her slow step began on the stairs, going down.

PETRIFIED MAN

"Reach in my purse and git me a cigarette without no powder in it if you kin, Mrs. Fletcher, honey," said Leota to her ten o'clock shampoo-and-set customer. "I don't like no perfumed cigarettes."

Mrs. Fletcher gladly reached over to the lavender shelf under the lavender-framed mirror, shook a hair net loose from the clasp of the patent-leather bag, and slapped her hand down quickly on a powder puff which burst out when the purse was opened.

"Why, look at the peanuts, Leota!" said Mrs. Fletcher in her marvelling voice.

"Honey, them goobers has been in my purse a week if they's been in it a day. Mrs. Pike bought them peanuts."

"Who's Mrs. Pike?" asked Mrs. Fletcher, settling back. Hidden in this den of curling fluid and henna packs, separated by a lavender swing-door from the other customers, who were being gratified in other booths, she could give her curiosity its freedom. She looked expectantly at the black part in Leota's yellow curls as she bent to light the cigarette.

"Mrs. Pike is this lady from New Orleans," said Leota, puffing, and pressing into Mrs. Fletcher's scalp with strong red-nailed fingers. "A friend, not a customer. You see, like maybe I told you last time, me and Fred and Sal and Joe all had us a fuss, so Sal and Joe up and moved out, so we didn't do a thing but rent out their room. So we rented it to Mrs. Pike. And Mr. Pike." She flicked an ash into the basket of dirty towels. "Mrs. Pike is a very decided blonde. *She* bought me the peanuts."

"She must be cute," said Mrs. Fletcher.

"Honey, 'cute' ain't the word for what she is. I'm tellin' you, Mrs. Pike is attractive. She has her a good time. She's got a sharp eye out, Mrs. Pike has."

She dashed the comb through the air, and paused dramatically as a cloud of Mrs. Fletcher's hennaed hair floated out of the lavender teeth like a small storm-cloud.

"Hair fallin'."

"Aw, Leota."

"Uh-huh, commencin' to fall out," said Leota, combing again, and letting fall another cloud.

"Is it any dandruff in it?" Mrs. Fletcher was frowning, her hair-line eyebrows diving down toward her nose, and her wrinkled, beady-lashed eyelids batting with concentration.

"Nope." She combed again. "Just fallin' out."

"Bet it was that last perm'nent you gave me that did it," Mrs. Fletcher said cruelly. "Remember you cooked me fourteen minutes."

"You had fourteen minutes comin' to you," said Leota with finality.

"Bound to be somethin'," persisted Mrs. Fletcher. "Dandruff, dandruff. I couldn't of caught a thing like that from Mr. Fletcher, could I?"

"Well," Leota answered at last, "you know what I heard in here yestiddy, one of Thelma's ladies was settin' over yonder in Thelma's booth gittin' a machineless, and I don't mean to insist or insinuate or anything, Mrs. Fletcher, but Thelma's lady just happ'med to throw out—I forgotten what she was talkin' about at the time—that you was p-r-e-g., and lots of times that'll make your hair do awful funny, fall out and God knows what all. It just ain't our fault, is the way I look at it."

There was a pause. The woman stared at each other in the mirror.

"Who was it?" demanded Mrs. Fletcher.

"Honey, I really couldn't say," said Leota. "Not that you look it."

"Where's Thelma? I'll get it out of her," said Mrs. Fletcher.

"Now, honey, I wouldn't go and git mad over a little thing like that," Leota said, combing hastily, as though to hold Mrs. Fletcher down by the hair. "I'm sure it was somebody didn't mean no harm in the world. How far gone are you?"

"Just wait," said Mrs. Fletcher, and shrieked for Thelma, who came in and took a drag from Leota's cigarette.

"Thelma, honey, throw your mind back to yestiddy if you kin," said Leota, drenching Mrs. Fletcher's hair with a thick fluid and catching the overflow in a cold wet towel at her neck.

"Well, I got my lady half wound for a spiral," said Themla doubtfully.

"This won't take but a minute," said Leota. "Who is it you got in there, old Horse Face? Just cast your mind back and try to remember who your lady was yestiddy who happ'm to mention that my customer was pregnant, that's all. She's dead to know."

Thelma drooped her blood-red lips and looked over Mrs. Fletcher's head into the mirror. "Why, honey, I ain't got the faintest," she breathed. "I really don't recollect the faintest. But I'm sure she meant no harm. I declare, I forgot my hair finally got combed and thought it was a stranger behind me."

"Was it that Mrs. Hutchinson?" Mrs. Fletcher was tensely polite.

"Mrs. Hutchinson? Oh, Mrs. Hutchinson." Thelma batted her eyes. "Naw, precious, she come on Thursday and didn't ev'm mention your name. I doubt if she ev'm knows you're on the way."

"Thelma!" cried Leota staunchly.

"All I know is, whoever it is 'll be sorry some day. Why, I just barely knew it myself!" cried Mrs. Fletcher. "Just let her wait!"

"Why? What're you gonna do to her?"

It was a child's voice, and the women looked down. A little boy was making tents with aluminum wave pinchers on the floor under the sink.

"Billy Boy, hon, mustn't bother nice ladies," Leota smiled. She slapped him brightly and behind her back waved Thelma out of the booth. "Ain't Billy Boy a sight? Only three years old and already just nuts about the beauty-parlor business."

"I never saw him here before," said Mrs. Fletcher, still unmollified.

"He ain't been here before, that's how come," said Leota. "He belongs to Mrs. Pike. She got her a job but it was Fay's Millinery. He oughtn't to try on those ladies' hats, they come down over his eyes like I don't know what. They just git to look ridiculous, that's what, an' of course he's gonna put 'em on: hats. They tole Mrs. Pike they didn't appreciate him hangin' around there. Here, he couldn't hurt a thing."

"Well! I don't like children that much," said Mrs. Fletcher.

"Well!" said Leota moodily.

"Well! I'm almost tempted not to have this one," said Mrs. Fletcher. "That Mrs. Hutchinson! Just looks straight through you when she sees you on the street and then spits at you behind your back."

"Mr. Fletcher would beat you on the head if you didn't have it now," said Leota reasonably. "After going this far."

Mrs. Fletcher sat up straight. "Mr. Fletcher can't do a thing with me."

"He can't!" Leota winked at herself in the mirror.

"No, siree, he can't. If he so much as raises his voice against me, he knows good and well I'll have one of my sick headaches, and then I'm just not fit to live with. And if I really look that pregnant already—"

"Well, now, honey, I just want you to know—I habm't told any of my ladies and I ain't goin' to tell 'em—even that you're losin' your hair. You just get you one of these Stork-a-Lure dresses and stop worryin'. What people don't know don't hurt nobody, as Mrs. Pike says."

"Did you tell Mrs. Pike?" asked Mrs. Fletcher sulkily.

"Well, Mrs. Fletcher, look, you ain't ever goin' to lay eyes on Mrs. Pike or her lay eyes on you, so what diffunce does it make in the long run?"

"I knew it!" Mrs. Fletcher deliberately nodded her head so as to destroy a ringlet Leota was working on behind her ear. "Mrs. Pike!"

Leota sighed. "I reckon I might as well tell you. It wasn't any more Thelma's lady tole me you was pregnant than a bat."

"Not Mrs. Hutchinson?"

"Naw, Lord! It was Mrs. Pike."

"Mrs. Pike!" Mrs. Fletcher could only sputter and let curling fluid roll into her ear. "How could Mrs. Pike possibly know I was pregnant or otherwise, when she doesn't even know me? The nerve of some people!"

"Well, here's how it was. Remember Sunday?"

"Yes," said Mrs. Fletcher.

"Sunday, Mrs. Pike an' me was all by ourself. Mr. Pike and Fred had gone over to Eagle Lake, sayin' they was goin' to catch 'em some fish, but they didn't a course. So we was settin' in Mrs. Pike's car, it's a 1939 Dodge—"

"1939, eh," said Mrs. Fletcher.

"—An' we was gettin' us a Jax beer apiece—that's the beer that Mrs. Pike says is made right in N.O., so she won't drink no other kind. So I seen you drive up to the drugstore an' run in for just a secont, leavin' I reckon Mr. Fletcher in the car, an' come runnin' out with looked like a perscription. So I says to Mrs. Pike, just to be makin' talk, 'Right yonder's Mrs. Fletcher, and I reckon that's Mr. Fletcher—she's one of my regular customers,' I says."

"I had on a figured print," said Mrs. Fletcher tentatively.

"You sure did," agreed Leota. "So Mrs. Pike, she give you a good look—she's very observant, a good judge of character, cute as a minute, you know—and she says, 'I bet you another Jax that lady's three months on the way.'"

"What gall!" said Mrs. Fletcher. "Mrs. Pike!"

"Mrs. Pike ain't goin' to bite you,' said Leota. "Mrs. Pike is a lovely girl, you'd be crazy about her, Mrs. Fletcher. But she can't sit still a minute. We went to the travellin' freak show yestiddy after work. I got through early—nine o'clock. In the vacant store next door. What, you ain't been?"

"No, I despise freaks," declared Mrs. Fletcher.

"Aw. Well, honey, talkin' about bein' pregnant an' all, you ought to see those twins in a bottle, you really owe it to yourself."

"What twins?" asked Mrs. Fletcher out of the side of her mouth.

"Well, honey, they got these two twins in a bottle, see? Born joined plumb together—dead a course." Leota dropped her voice into a soft lyrical hum. "They was about this long—pardon—must of been full time, all right, wouldn't you say?—an' they had these two heads an' two faces an' four arms an' four legs, all kind of joined *here*. See, this face looked this-a-way, and the other face looked that-a-way, over their shoulder, see. Kinda pathetic."

"Glah!" said Mrs. Fletcher disapprovingly.

"Well, ugly? Honey, I mean to tell you—their parents was first cousins and all like that. Billy Boy, git me a fresh towel from off Teeny's stack—this 'n's wringin' wet—an' quit ticklin' my ankles with that curler. I declare! He don't miss nothin'."

"Me and Mr. Fletcher aren't one speck of kin, or he could never of had me," said Mrs. Fletcher placidly.

"Of course not!" protested Leota. "Neither is me an' Fred, not that we know of. Well, honey, what Mrs. Pike liked was the pygmies. They've got these pygmies down there, too, an' Mrs. Pike was just wild about 'em. You know, the teeniest men in the universe? Well, honey, they can just rest back on their little bohunkus an' roll around an' you can't hardly tell if they're sittin' or standin'. That'll give you some idea. They're about forty-two years old. Just suppose it was your husband!"

"Well, Mr. Fletcher is five foot nine and one half," said Mrs. Fletcher quickly.

"Fred's five foot ten," said Leota, "but I tell him he's still a shrimp, account of I'm so tall." She made a deep wave over Mrs. Fletcher's other temple with the comb. "Well, these pygmies are a kind of a dark brown, Mrs. Fletcher. Not bad-lookin' for what they are, you know."

"I wouldn't care for them," said Mrs. Fletcher. "What does that Mrs. Pike see in them?"

"Aw, I don't know," said Leota. "She's just cute, that's all. But they got this man, this petrified man, that ever'thing ever since he was nine years old, when it goes through his digestion, see, somehow Mrs. Pike says it goes to his joints and has been turning to stone."

"How awful!" said Mrs. Fletcher.

"He's forty-two too. That looks like a bad age."

"Who said so, that Mrs. Pike? I bet she's forty-two," said Mrs. Fletcher.

"Naw, said Leota, "Mrs. Pike's thirty-three, born in January, an Aquarian. He could move his head—like this. A course his head and mind ain't a joint, so to speak, and I guess his stomach ain't, either —not yet, anyways. But see—his food, he eats it, and it goes down, see, and then he digests it"—Leota rose on her toes for an instant— "and it goes out to his joints and before you can say 'Jack Robinson,' it's stone—pure stone. He's turning to stone. How'd you like to be married to a guy like that? All he can do, he can move his head just a quarter of an inch. A course he *looks* just *terrible.*"

"I should think he would," said Mrs. Fletcher frostily. "Mr. Fletcher takes bending exercises every night of the world. I make him."

"All Fred does is lay around the house like a rug. I wouldn't be surprised if he woke up some day and couldn't move. The petrified man just sat there moving his quarter of an inch though," said Leota reminiscently.

"Did Mrs. Pike like the petrified man?" asked Mrs. Fletcher.

"Not as much as she did the others," said Leota deprecatingly. "And then she likes a man to be a good dresser, and all that."

"Is Mr. Pike a good dresser?" asked Mrs. Fletcher sceptically.

"Oh, well, yeah," said Leota, "but he's twelve or fourteen years older'n her. She ast Lady Evangeline about him."

"Who's Lady Evangeline?" asked Mrs. Fletcher.

"Well, it's this mind reader they got in the freak show," said

Leota. "Was real good. Lady Evangeline is her name, and if I had another dollar I wouldn't do a thing but have my other palm read. She had what Mrs. Pike said was the 'sixth mind' but she had the worst manicure I ever saw on a living person."

"What did she tell Mrs. Pike?" asked Mrs. Fletcher.

"She told her Mr. Pike was as true to her as he could be and besides, would come into some money."

"Humph!" said Mrs. Fletcher. "What does he do?"

"I can't tell," said Leota, "because he don't work. Lady Evangeline didn't tell me enough about my nature or anything. And I would like to go back and find out some more about this boy. Used to go with this boy until he got married to this girl. Oh, shoot, that was about three and a half years ago, when you was still goin' to the Robert E. Lee Beauty Shop in Jackson. He married her for her money. Another fortune-teller tole me that at the time. So I'm not in love with him any more, anyway, besides being married to Fred, but Mrs. Pike thought, just for the hell of it, see, to ask Lady Evangeline was he happy."

"Does Mrs. Pike know everything about you already?" asked Mrs. Fletcher unbelievingly. "Mercy!"

"Oh, yeah, I tole her ever'thing about ever'thing, from now on back to I don't know when—to when I first started goin' out," said Leota. "So I ast Lady Evangeline for one of my questions, was he happily married, and she says, just like she was glad I ask her, 'Honey,' she says, 'naw, he idn't. You write down this day, March 8, 1941,' she says, 'and mock it down: three years from today him and her won't be occupyin' the same bed.' There it is, up on the wall with them other dates—see, Mrs. Fletcher? And she says, 'Child, you ought to be glad you didn't git him, because he's so mercenary.' So I'm glad I married Fred. He sure ain't mercenary, money don't mean a thing to him. But I sure would like to go back and have my other palm read."

"Did Mrs. Pike believe in what the fortuneteller said?" asked Mrs. Fletcher in a superior tone of voice.

"Lord, yes, she's from New Orleans. Ever'body in New Orleans believes ever'thing spooky. One of 'em in New Orleans before it was raided says to Mrs. Pike one summer she was goin' to go from State to State and meet some grey-headed men, and, sure enough, she says she went on a beautician convention up to Chicago . . . ."

"Oh!" said Mrs. Fletcher. "Oh, is Mrs. Pike a beautician too?"

"Sure she is," protested Leota. "She's a beautician. I'm goin' to git her in here if I can. Before she married. But it don't leave you. She says sure enough, there was three men who was a very large part of making her trip what it was, and they all three had grey in their hair and they went in six States. Got Christmas cards from 'em. Billy Boy, go see if Thelma's got any dry cotton. Look how Mrs. Fletcher's a-drippin'."

"Where did Mrs. Pike meet Mr. Pike?" asked Mrs. Fletcher primly.

"On another train," said Leota.

"I met Mr. Fletcher, or rather he met me, in a rental library," said Mrs. Fletcher with dignity, as she watched the net come down over her head.

"Honey, me an' Fred, we met in a rumble seat eight months ago and we was practically on what you might call the way to the altar inside of half an hour," said Leota in a guttural voice, and bit a bobby pin open. "Course it don't last. Mrs. Pike says nothin' like that ever lasts."

"Mr. Fletcher and myself are as much in love as the day we married," said Mrs. Fletcher belligerently as Leota stuffed cotton into her ears.

"Mrs. Pike says it don't last," repeated Leota in a louder voice. "Now go git under the dryer. You can turn yourself on, can't you? I'll be back to comb you out. Durin' lunch I promised to give Mrs. Pike a facial. You know—free. Her bein' in the business, so to speak."

"I bet she needs one," said Mrs. Fletcher, letting the swing-door fly back against Leota. "Oh, pardon me."

A week later, on time for her appointment, Mrs. Fletcher sank heavily into Leota's chair after first removing a drug-store rental book, called *Life Is Like That,* from the seat. She stared in a discouraged way into the mirror.

"You can tell it when I'm sitting down, all right," she said.

Leota seemed preoccupied and stood shaking out a lavender cloth. She began to pin it around Mrs. Fletcher's neck in silence.

"I said you sure can tell it when I'm sitting straight on and coming at you this way," Mrs. Fletcher said.

"Why, honey, naw you can't," said Leota gloomily. "Why, I'd never know. If somebody was to come up to me on the street and say, 'Mrs. Fletcher is pregnant!' I'd say, 'Heck, she don't look it to me.'"

"If a certain party hadn't found it out and spread it around, it wouldn't be too late even now," said Mrs. Fletcher frostily, but Leota was almost choking her with the cloth, pinning it so tight, and she couldn't speak clearly. She paddled her hands in the air until Leota wearily loosened her.

"Listen, honey, you're just a virgin compared to Mrs. Montjoy," Leota was going on, still absent-minded. She bent Mrs. Fletcher back in the chair and, sighing, tossed liquid from a teacup on to her head and dug both hands into her scalp. "You know Mrs. Montjoy—her husband's that premature-grey-headed fella?"

"She's in the Trojan Garden Club, is all I know," said Mrs. Fletcher.

"Well, honey," said Leota, but in a weary voice, "she come in here not the week before and not the day before she had her baby—she come in here the very selfsame day, I mean to tell you. Child, we was all plumb scared to death. These she was! Come for her shampoo an' set. Why, Mrs. Fletcher, in an hour an' twenty minutes she was layin' up there in the Babtist Hospital with a seb'm-pound son. It was that close a shave. I declare, if I hadn't been so tired I would of drank up a bottle of gin that night."

"What gall," said Mrs. Fletcher. "I never knew her at all well."

"See, her husband was waitin' outside in the car, and her bags was all packed an' in the back seat, an' she was all ready, 'cept she wanted her shampoo an' set. An' havin' one pain right after another. Her husband kep' comin' in here, scared-like, but couldn't do nothin' with her a course. She yelled bloody murder, too, but she always yelled her head off when I give her a perm'nent."

"She must of been crazy," said Mrs. Fletcher. "How did she look?"

"Shoot!" said Leota.

"Well, I can guess," said Mrs. Fletcher. "Awful."

"Just wanted to look pretty while she was havin' her baby, is all," said Leota airily. "Course, we was glad to give the lady what she was after—that's our motto—but I bet a hour later she wasn't payin' no mind to them little end curls. I bet she wasn't thinkin' about she ought to have on a net. It wouldn't of done her no good if she had."

"No, I don't suppose it would," said Mrs. Fletcher.

"Yeah man! She was a-yellin'. Just like when I give her perm-'nent."

"Her husband ought to make her behave. Don't it seem that way to you?" asked Mrs. Fletcher. "He ought to put his foot down."

"Ha," said Leota. "A lot he could do. Maybe some women is soft."

"Oh, you mistake me, I don't mean for her to get soft—far from it! Women have to stand up for themselves, or there's just no telling. But now you take me—I ask Mr. Fletcher's advice now and then, and he appreciates it, especially on something important, like is it time for a permanent—not that I've told him about the baby. He says, 'Why, dear, go ahead!' Just ask their *advice*."

"Huh! If I ever ast Fred's advice we'd be floatin' down the Yazoo River on a houseboat or somethin' by this time," said Leota. "I'm sick of Fred. I told him to go over to Vicksburg."

"Is he going?" demanded Mrs. Fletcher.

"Sure. See, the fortune-teller—I went back and had my other

palm read, since we've got to rent the room agin—said my lover was goin' to work in Vicksburg, so I don't know who she could mean, unless she meant Fred. And Fred ain't workin' here—that much is so."

"Is he going to work in Vicksburg?" asked Mrs. Fletcher. "And—"

"Sure. Lady Evangeline said so. Said the future is going to be brighter than the present. He don't want to go, but I ain't gonna put up with nothin' like that. Lays around the house an' bulls—did bull—with that good-for-nothin' Mr. Pike. He says if he goes who'll cook, but I says I never get to eat anyway—not meals. Billy Boy, take Mrs. Grover that *Screen Secrets* and leg it."

Mrs. Fletcher heard stamping feet go out the door.

"Is that that Mrs. Pike's little boy here again?" she asked, sitting up gingerly.

"Yeah, that's still him." Leota stuck out her tongue.

Mrs. Fletcher could hardly believe her eyes. "Well! How's Mrs. Pike, your attractive new friend with the sharp eyes who spreads it around town that perfect strangers are pregnant?" she asked in a sweetened tone.

"Oh, Mizziz Pike." Leota combed Mrs. Fletcher's hair with heavy strokes.

"You act like you're tired," said Mrs. Fletcher.

"Tired? Feel like it's four o'clock in the afternoon already," said Leota. "I ain't told you the awful luck we had, me and Fred? It's the worst thing you ever heard of. Maybe *you* think Mrs. Pike's got sharp eyes. Shoot, there's a limit! Well, you know, we rented out our room to this Mr. and Mrs. Pike from New Orleans when Sal an' Joe Fentress got mad at us 'cause they drank up some home-brew we had in the closet—Sal an' Joe did. So, a week ago Sat'day Mr. and Mrs. Pike moved in. Well, I kinda fixed up the room, you know—put a sofa pillow on the couch and picked some ragged robbins and put in a vase, but they never did say they appreciated it. Anyway, then I put some old magazines on the table."

"I think that was lovely," said Mrs. Fletcher.

"Wait. So, come night 'fore last, Fred and this Mr. Pike, who Fred just took up with, was back from they said they was fishin', bein' as neither one of 'em has got a job to his name, and we was all settin' around in their room. So Mrs. Pike was settin' there readin' a old *Startling G-Man Tales* that was mine, mind you, I'd bought it myself, and all of a sudden she jumps!—into the air—you'd 'a' thought she'd set on a spider—an' says, 'Canfield'—ain't that silly, that's Mr. Pike—'Canfield, my God A'mighty,' she says, 'honey,' she says, 'we're rich, and you won't have to work.' Not that he turned one hand anyway. Well, me and Fred rushes over to her, and Mr. Pike, too, and there she sets, pointin' her finger at a photo in my copy of *Startling G-Man*. 'See that man?' yells Mrs. Pike. 'Remember him, Canfield?' 'Never forget a face,' says Mr. Pike. 'It's Mr. Petrie, that we stayed with him in the apartment next to ours in Toulouse Street in N.O. for six weeks. Mr. Petrie.' 'Well,' says Mrs. Pike, like she can't hold out one secont longer, 'Mr. Petrie is wanted for five hundred dollars cash, for rapin' four women in California, and I know where he is.'"

"Mercy!" said Mrs. Fletcher. "Where was he?"

At some time Leota had washed her hair and now she yanked her up by the back locks and sat her up.

"Know where he was?"

"I certainly don't," Mrs. Fletcher said. Her scalp hurt all over.

Leota flung a towel around the top of her customer's head. "Nowhere else but in that freak show! I saw him just as plain as Mrs. Pike. *He* was the petrified man!"

"Who would ever have thought that!" cried Mrs. Fletcher sympathetically.

"So Mr. Pike says, 'Well whatta you know about that,' an' he looks real hard at the photo and whistles. And she starts dancin' and singin' about their good luck. She meant our bad luck! I made a point of tellin' that fortune-teller the next time I saw her. I said, 'Listen, that magazine was layin' around the house for a month, and there was the freak show runnin' night an' day, not two steps away from my own beauty parlor, with Mr. Petrie just settin' there waitin'. An' it had to be Mr. and Mrs. Pike, almost perfect strangers.'"

"What gall," said Mrs. Fletcher. She was only sitting there, wrapped in a turban, but she did not mind.

"Fortune-tellers don't care. And Mrs. Pike, she goes around actin' like she thinks she was Mrs. God," said Leota. "So they're goin' to leave tomorrow, Mr. and Mrs. Pike. And in the meantime I got to keep that mean, bad little ole kid here, gettin' under my feet ever' minute of the day an' talkin' back too."

"Have they gotten the five hundred dollars' reward already?" asked Mrs. Fletcher.

"Well," said Leota, "at first Mr. Pike didn't want to do anything about it. Can you feature that? Said he kinda liked that ole bird and said he was real nice to 'em, lent 'em money or somethin'. But Mrs. Pike simply tole him he could just go to hell, and I can see her point. She says, 'You ain't worked a lick in six months, and here I make five hundred dollars in two seconts, and what thanks do I get for it? You go to hell, Canfield,' she says. So," Leota went on in a despondent voice, "they called up the cops and they caught the ole bird, all right, right there in the freak show where I saw him with my own eyes, thinkin' he was petrified. He's the one. Did it under his real name—Mr. Petrie. Four women in California, all in the month of August. So Mrs. Pike gits five hundred dollars. And my magazine, and right next door to my beauty parlor. I cried all night, but Fred said it wasn't a bit of use and to go to sleep, because the whole thing was just a sort of coincidence—you know: can't do nothin' about it. He says it put him clean out of the notion of goin' to Vicksburg for a few days till we rent out the room again—no tellin' who we'll git this time."

"But can you imagine anybody knowing this old man, that's raped four women?" persisted Mrs. Fletcher, and she shuddered audibly. "Did Mrs. Pike *speak* to him when she met him in the freak show?"

Leota had begun to comb Mrs. Fletcher's hair. "I says to her, I says, 'I didn't notice you fallin' on his neck when he was the petrified man—don't tell me you didn't recognize your fine friend?' And she says, 'I didn't recognize him with that white powder all over his face. He just looked familiar.' Mrs. Pike says, 'and lots of people look familiar.' But she says that ole petrified man did put her in mind of somebody. She wondered who it was! Kep' her awake, which man she'd ever knew it reminded her of. So when she seen the photo, it all come to her. Like a flash. Mr. Petrie. The way he'd turn his head and look at her when she took him in his breakfast."

"Took him in his breakfast!" shrieked Mrs. Fletcher. "Listen—don't tell me. I'd 'a' felt something."

"Four women. I guess those women didn't have the faintest notion at the time they'd be worth a hundred an' twenty-five bucks a piece some day to Mrs. Pike. We ast her how old the fella was then, an' she says he musta had one foot in the grave, at least. Can you beat it?"

"Not really petrified at all, of course," said Mrs. Fletcher meditatively. She drew herself up. "I'd'a' felt something," she said proudly.

"Shoot! I did feel somethin'," said Leota. "I tole Fred when I got home I felt so funny. I said, 'Fred, that ole petrified man sure did leave me with a funny feelin'.' He says, 'Funny-haha or funny-peculiar?' and I says, 'Funny-peculiar.'" She pointed her comb into the air emphatically.

"I'll bet you did, said Mrs. Fletcher.

They both heard a crackling noise.

Leota screamed, "Billy Boy! What you doin' in my purse?"

"Aw, I'm just eatin' these ole stale peanuts up," said Billy Boy.

"You come here to me!" screamed Leota, recklessly flinging down the comb, which scattered a whole ashtray full of bobby pins and knocked down a row of Coca-Cola bottles. "This is the last straw!"

"I caught him! I caught him!" giggled Mrs. Fletcher. "I'll hold him on my lap. You bad, bad boy, you! I guess I better learn how to spank little old bad boys," she said.

Leota's eleven o'clock customer pushed open the swing-door upon Leota paddling him heartily with the brush, while he gave angry but belittling screams which penetrated beyond the booth and filled the whole curious beauty parlor. From everywhere ladies began to gather round to watch the paddling. Billy Boy kicked both Leota and Mrs. Fletcher as hard as he could, Mrs. Fletcher with her new fixed smile.

Billy Boy stomped through the group of wildhaired ladies and went out the door, but flung back the words, "If you're so smart, why ain't you rich?"

Bernard Malamud (b. 1914)

THE MAGIC BARREL

Not long ago there lived in uptown New York, in a small, almost meager room, though crowded with books, Leo Finkle, a rabbinical student in the Yeshivah University. Finkle, after six years of study, was to be ordained in June and had been advised by an acquaintance that he might find it easier to win himself a congregation if he were married. Since he had no present prospects of marriage, after two tormented days of turning it over in his mind, he called Pinye Salzman, a marriage broker whose two-line advertisement he had read in the *Forward*.

The matchmaker appeared one night out of the dark fourth-floor hallway of the graystone rooming house where Finkle lived, grasping a black, strapped portfolio that had been worn thin with use. Salzman, who had been long in the business, was of slight but dignified build, wearing an old hat, and an overcoat too short and tight for him. He smelled frankly of fish, which he loved to eat, and although he was missing a few teeth, his presence was not displeasing, because of an amiable manner curiously contrasted with mournful eyes. His voice, his lips, his wisp of beard, his bony fingers were animated, but give him a moment of repose and his mild blue eyes revealed a depth of sadness, a characteristic that put Leo a little at ease although the situation, for him, was inherently tense.

He at once informed Salzman why he had asked him to come, explaining that his home was in Cleveland, and that but for his parents, who had married comparatively late in life, he was alone in the world. He had for six years devoted himself almost entirely to his studies, as a result of which, understandably, he had found himself without time for a social life and the company of young women. Therefore he thought it the better part of trial and error—of embarrassing fumbling—to call in an experienced person to advise him on these matters. He remarked in passing that the function of the marriage broker was ancient and honorable, highly approved in the Jewish community, because it made practical the necessary without hindering joy. Moreover, his own parents had been brought together by a matchmaker. They had made, if not a financially profitable marriage—since neither had possessed any worldly goods to speak of—at least a successful one in the sense of their everlasting devotion to each other. Salzman listened in embarrassed surprise, sensing a sort of apology. Later, however, he experienced a glow of pride in his work, an emotion that had left him years ago, and he heartily approved of Finkle.

The two went to their business. Leo had led Salzman to the only clear place in the room, a table near a window that overlooked the lamp-lit city. He seated himself at the matchmaker's side but facing him, attempting by an act of will to suppress the unpleasant tickle in his throat. Salzman eagerly unstrapped his portfolio and removed a loose rubber band from a thin packet of much-handled cards. As he flipped through them, a gesture and sound that physically hurt Leo, the student pretended not to see and gazed steadfastly out the window. Although it was still February, winter was on its last legs, signs of which he had for the first time in years begun to notice. He now observed the round white moon, moving high in the sky through a cloud menagerie, and watched with half-open mouth as it penetrated a huge hen, and dropped out of her like an egg laying itself. Salzman, though pretending through eyeglasses he had just slipped on to be engaged in scanning the writing on the cards, stole occasional glances at the young man's distinguished face, noting with pleasure the long, severe scholar's nose, brown eyes heavy with learning, sensitive yet ascetic lips, and a certain, almost hollow quality of the dark cheeks. He gazed around at shelves upon shelves of books and let out a soft, contented sigh.

When Leo's eyes fell upon the cards, he counted six spread out in Salzman's hand.

"So few?" he asked in disappointment.

"You wouldn't believe me how much cards I got in my office," Salzman replied. "The drawers are already filled to the top, so I keep them now in a barrel, but is every girl good for a new rabbi?"

Leo blushed at this, regretting all he had revealed of himself in a curriculum vitae he had sent to Salzman. He had thought it best to acquaint him with his strict standards and specifications, but in having done so, felt he had told the marriage broker more than was absolutely necessary.

He hesitantly inquired. "Do you keep photographs of your clients on file?"

"First comes family, amount of dowry, also what kind promises," Salzman replied, unbuttoning his tight coat and settling himself in the chair. "After comes pictures, rabbi."

"Call me Mr. Finkle, I'm not yet a rabbi."

Salzman said he would, but instead called him doctor, which he changed to rabbi when Leo was not listening too attentively.

Salzman adjusted his horn-rimmed spectacles, gently cleared his throat and read in an eager voice the contents of the top card:

"Sophie P. Twenty-four years. Widow one year. No children. Educated high school and two years college. Father promises eight thousand dollars. Has wonderful wholesale business. Also real estate. On the mother's side comes teachers, also one actor. Well known on Second Avenue."

Leo gazed up in surprise. "Did you say a widow?"

"A widow don't mean spoiled, rabbi. She lived with her husband maybe four months. He was a sick boy she made a mistake to marry him."

"Marrying a widow has never entered my mind."

"This is because you have no experience. A widow, especially if she is young and healthy like this girl, is a wonderful person to marry. She will be thankful to you the rest of her life. Believe me, if I was looking now for a bride, I would marry a widow."

Leo reflected, then shook his head.

Salzman hunched his shoulders in an almost imperceptible gesture of disappointment. He placed the card down on the wooden table and began to read another:

"Lily H. High school teacher. Regular. Not a substitute. Has savings and new Dodge car. Lived in Paris one year. Father is successful dentist thirty-five years. Interested in professional man. Well Americanized family. Wonderful opportunity."

"I knew her personally," said Salzman. "I wish you could see this girl. She is a doll. Also very intelligent. All day you could talk to her about books and theater and what not. She also knows current events."

"I don't believe you mentioned her age?"

"Her age?" Salzman said, raising his brows. "Her age is thirty-two years."

Leo said after a while, "I'm afraid that seems a little too old."

Salzman let out a laugh. "So how old are you, rabbi?"

"Twenty-seven."

"So what is the difference, tell me, between twenty-seven and thirty- two? My own wife is seven years older than me. So what did I suffer?—Nothing. If Rothschild's daughter wants to marry you, would you say on account her age, no?"

"Yes," Leo said dryly.

Salzman shook off the no in the yes. "Five years don't mean a thing I give you my word that when you will live with her for one week you will forget her age. What does it mean five years—that she lived more and knows more than somebody who is younger? On this girl, God bless her, years are not wasted. Each one that it comes makes better the bargain."

"What subject does she teach in high school?"

"Languages. If you heard the way she speaks French, you will think it is music. I am in the business twenty-five years, and I recommend her with my whole heart. Believe me, I know what I'm talking, rabbi."

"What's on the next card?" Leo said abruptly.

Salzman reluctantly turned up the third card:

"Ruth K. Nineteen years. Honor student. Father offers thirteen thousand cash to the right bridegroom. He is a medical doctor. Stomach specialist with marvelous practice. Brother-in-law owns own garment business. Particular people."

Salzman looked as if he had read his trump card.

"Did you say nineteen?" Leo asked with interest.

"On the dot."

"Is she attractive?" He blushed. "Pretty?"

Salzman kissed his finger tips. "A little doll. On this I give you my word. Let me call the father tonight and you will see what means pretty."

But Leo was troubled. "You're sure she's that young?"

"This I am positive. The father will show you the birth certificate."

"Are your positive there isn't something wrong with her?" Leo insisted.

"Who says there is wrong?"

"I don't understand why an American girl her age should go to a marriage broker."

A smile spread over Salzman's face.

"So for the same reason you went, she comes."

Leo flushed. "I am pressed for time."

Salzman, realizing he had been tactless, quickly explained. "The father came, not her. He wants she should have the best, so he looks around himself. When we will locate the right boy he will introduce him and encourage. This makes a better marriage than if a young girl without experience takes for herself. I don't have to tell you this."

"But don't you think this young girl believes in love?" Leo spoke uneasily.

Salzman was about to guffaw but caught himself and said soberly, "Love comes with the right person, not before."

Leo parted dry lips but did not speak. Noticing that Salzman had snatched a glance at the next card, he cleverly asked. "How is her health?"

"Perfect," Salzman said, breathing with difficulty. "Of course, she is a little lame on her right foot from an auto accident that it happened to her when she was twelve years, but nobody notices on account she is so brilliant and also beautiful."

Leo got up heavily and went to the window. He felt curiously bitter and upbraided himself for having called in the marriage broker. Finally, he shook his head.

"Why not?" Salzman persisted, the pitch of his voice rising.

"Because I detest stomach specialists."

"So what do you care what is his business? After you marry her do you need him? Who says he must come every Friday night in your house?"

Ashamed of the way the talk was going, Leo dismissed Salzman, who went home with heavy, melancholy eyes.

Though he had felt only relief at the marriage broker's departure, Leo was in low spirits the next day. He explained it as arising from Salzman's failure to produce a suitable bride for him. He did not care for his type of clientele. But when Leo found himself hesitating whether to seek out another matchmaker, one more polished than Pinye, he wondered if it could be—his protestations to the contrary, and although he honored his father and mother—that he did not, in essence, care for the match-making institution? This thought he quickly put out of mind yet found himself still upset. All day he ran around in the woods—missed an important appointment, forgot to give out his laundry, walked out of a Broadway cafeteria without paying and had to run back with the ticket in his hand, had even not recognized his landlady in the street when she passed with a friend and courteously called out, "A good evening to you, Doctor Finkle." By nightfall, however, he had regained sufficient calm to sink his nose into a book and there found peace from his thoughts.

Almost at once there came a knock on the door. Before Leo could say enter, Salzman, commercial cupid, was standing in the room. His face was gray and meager, his expression hungry, and he looked as if he would expire on his feet. Yet the marriage broker managed, by some trick of the muscles, to display a broad smile.

"So good evening. I am invited?"

Leo nodded, disturbed to see him again, yet unwilling to ask the man to leave.

Beaming still, Salzman laid his portfolio on the table. "Rabbi, I got for you tonight good news."

"I've asked you not to call me rabbi. I'm still a student."

"Your worries are finished. I have for you a first-class bride."

"Leave me in peace concerning this subject." Leo pretended lack of interest.

"The world will dance at your wedding."

"Please, Mr. Salzman, no more."

"But first must come back my strength," Salzman said weakly. He fumbled with the portfolio straps and took out of the leather case an oily paper bag, from which he extracted a hard, seeded roll and a small, smoked white fish. With a quick motion of his hand he stripped the fish out of its skin and began ravenously to chew. "All day in a rush," he muttered.

Leo watched him eat.

"A sliced tomato you have maybe?" Salzman hesitantly inquired.

"No."

The marriage broker shut his eyes and ate. When he had finished he carefully cleaned up the crumbs and rolled up the remains of the fish, in the paper bag. His spectacled eyes roamed the room until he discovered, amid some piles of books, a one-burner gas stove. Lifting his hat he humbly asked, "A glass of tea you got, rabbi?"

Conscience-stricken, Leo rose and brewed the tea. He served it with a chunk of lemon and two cubes of lump sugar, delighting Salzman.

After he had drunk his tea, Salzman's strength and good spirits were restored.

"So tell me, rabbi," he said amiably, "you considered some more the three clients I mentioned yesterday?"

"There was no need to consider."

"Why not?"

"None of them suits me."

"What then suits you?"

Leo let it pass because he could give only a confused answer.

Without waiting for a reply, Salzman asked, "You remember this girl I talked to you—the high school teacher?"

"Age thirty-two?"

But, surprisingly, Salzman's face lit in a smile. "Age twenty-nine."

Leo shot him a look. "Reduced from thirty- two?"

"A mistake," Salzman avowed. "I talked today with the dentist. He took me to his safety deposit box and showed me the birth certificate. She was twenty-nine years last August. They made her a party in the mountains where she went for her vacation. When her father spoke to me the first time I forgot to write the age and I told you thirty-two, but now I remember this was a different client, a widow."

"The same one you told me about? I thought she was twenty-four?"

"A different. Am I responsible that the world is filled with widows?"

"No, but I'm not interested in them, nor for that matter, in school teachers."

Salzman pulled his clasped hands to his breast. Looking at the ceiling he devoutly exclaimed, "Yiddishe kinder, what can I say to somebody that is not interested in high school teachers? So what then you are interested?"

Leo flushed but controlled himself.

"In what else will you be interested," Salzman went on, "if you not interested in this fine girl that she speaks four languages and has personally in the bank ten thousand dollars? Also her father guarantees further twelve thousand. Also, she has a new car, wonderful clothes, talks on all subjects, and she will give you a first-class home and children. How near do we come in our life to paradise?"

"If she's so wonderful, why wasn't she married ten years ago?"

"Why?" said Salzman with a heavy laugh. "—Why? Because she is *partikiler.* This is why. She wants the *best."*

Leo was silent, amused at how he had entangled himself. But Salzman had aroused his interest in Lily H., and he began seriously to consider calling on her. When the marriage broker observed how intently Leo's mind was at work on the facts he had supplied, he felt certain they would soon come to an agreement. Late Saturday afternoon, conscious of Salzman, Leo Finkle walked with Lily Hirschorn along Riverside Drive. He walked briskly and erectly, wearing with distinction the black fedora he had that morning taken with trepidation out of the dusty hat box on his closet shelf, and the heavy black Saturday coat he had thoroughly whisked clean. Leo also owned a walking stick, a present from a distant relative, but quickly put temptation aside and did not use it. Lily, petite and not unpretty, had on something signifying the approach of spring. She was au courant, animatedly, with all sorts of subjects, and he weighed her words and found her surprisingly sound—score another for Salzman, whom he uneasily sensed to be somewhere around, hiding perhaps high in a tree along the street, flashing the lady signals with a pocket mirror; or perhaps a cloven-hoofed Pan, piping nuptial ditties as he danced his invisible way before them, strewing wild buds on the walk and purple grapes in their path, symbolizing fruit of a union, though there was of course still none.

Lily startled Leo by remarking, " I was thinking of Mr. Salzman, a curious figure, wouldn't you say?"

Not certain what to answer, he nodded.

She bravely went on, blushing, "I for one am grateful for his introducing us. Aren't you?"

He courteously replied, "I am."

"I mean," she said with a little laugh—and it was all in good taste, or at least gave the effect of being not in bad—"do you mind that we came together so?"

He was not displeased with her honesty, recognizing that she meant to set the relationship aright, and understanding that it took a certain amount of experience in life, and courage, to want to do it quite that way. One had to have some sort of past to make that kind of beginning.

He said that he did not mind. Salzman's function was traditional and honorable—valuable for what it might achieve, which, he pointed out, was frequently nothing.

Lily agreed with a sigh. They walked on for a while and she said after a long silence, again with a nervous laugh, "Would you mind if I asked you something a little bit personal? Frankly, I find the subject fascinating." Although Leo shrugged, she went on half embarrassedly, "How was it that you came to your calling? I mean was it a sudden passionate inspiration?"

Leo, after a time, slowly replied, "I was always interested in the Law."

"You saw revealed in it the presence of the Highest?"

He nodded and changed the subject. "I understand that you spent a little time in Paris, Miss Hirschorn?"

"Oh, did Mr. Salzman tell you, Rabbi Finkle?" Leo winced but she went on, "It was ages ago and almost forgotten. I remember I had to return for my sister's wedding."

And Lily would not be put off. "When," she asked in a trembly voice, "did you become enamored of God?"

He stared at her. Then it came to him that she was talking not about Leo Finkle, but of a total stranger, some mystical figure, perhaps even passionate prophet that Salzman had dreamed up for her—no relation to the living or dead. Leo trembled with rage and weakness. The trickster had obviously sold her a bill of goods, just as he had him, who'd expected to become acquainted with a young lady of twenty-nine, only to behold, the moment he laid eyes upon her strained and anxious face, a woman past thirty-five and aging rapidly. Only his self-control had kept him this long in her presence.

"I am not," he said gravely, "a talented religious person," and in seeking words to go on, found himself possessed by shame and fear. "I think," he said in a strained manner, "that I came to God not because I loved Him, but because I did not."

This confession he spoke harshly because its unexpectedness shook him.

Lily wilted. Leo saw a profusion of loaves of bread go flying like ducks high over his head, not unlike the winged loaves by which he had counted himself to sleep last night. Mercifully, then, it snowed, which he would not put past Salzman's machinations.

He was infuriated with the marriage broker and swore he would throw him out of the room the minute he reappeared. But Salzman did not come that night, and when Leo's anger had subsided, an unaccountable despair grew in its place. At first he thought this was caused by his disappointment in Lily, but before long it became evident that he had involved himself with Salzman without a true knowledge of his own intent. He gradually realized—with an emptiness that seized him with six hands—that he had called in the broker to find him a bride because he was incapable of doing it himself. This terrifying insight he had derived as a result of his meeting and conversation with Lily Hirschorn. Her probing questions had somehow irritated him into revealing—to himself more than her—the true nature of his relationship to God, and from that it had come upon him, with shocking force, that apart from his parents, he had never loved anyone. Or perhaps it went the other way, that he did not love God so well as he might, because he had not loved man. It seemed to Leo that his whole life stood starkly revealed and he saw himself for the first time as he truly was—unloved and loveless. This bitter but somehow not fully unexpected revelation brought him to a point of panic, controlled only by extraordinary effort. He covered his face with his hands and cried.

The week that followed was the worst of his life. He did not eat and lost weight. His beard darkened and grew ragged. He stopped attending seminars and almost never opened a book. He seriously considered leaving the Yeshivah, although he was deeply troubled at the thought of the loss of all his years of study—saw them like pages torn from a book, strewn over the city—and at the devastating effect of this decision upon his parents. But he had lived without knowledge of himself, and never in the Five Books and all the Commentaries—mea culpa—had the truth been revealed to him. He did not know where to turn, and in all this desolating loneliness there was no *to whom,* although he often thought of Lily but not once could bring himself to go downstairs and make the call. He became touchy and irritable, especially with his landlady, who asked him all manner of personal questions, on the other hand, sensing his own disagreeableness, he waylaid her on the stairs and apologized abjectly, until mortified, she ran from him. Out of this, however, he drew the consolation that he was a Jew and that a Jew suffered. But gradually, as the long and terrible week drew to a close, he regained his composure and some idea of purpose in life: to go on as planned. Although he was imperfect, the idea was not. As for his quest of a bride, the thought of continuing afflicted him with anxiety and heartburn, yet perhaps with this new knowledge of himself he would be more successful than in the past. Perhaps love would now come to him and a bride to that love. And for this sanctified seeking who needed a Salzman?

The marriage broker, a skeleton with haunted eyes, returned that very night. He looked, withal, the picture of frustrated expectancy—as if he had steadfastly waited the week at Miss Lily Hirschorn's side for a telephone call that never came.

Casually coughing, Salzman came immediately to the point: "So how did you like her?"

Leo's anger rose and he could not refrain from chiding the matchmaker: "Why did you lie to me Salzman?"

Salzman's pale face went dead white, the world had snowed on him.

"Did you not state that she was twenty-nine?" Leo insisted.

"I give you my word—"

"She was thirty-five, if a day. *At least* thirty-five."

"Of this don't be too sure. Her father told me—"

"Never mind. The worst of it was that you lied to her."

"How did I lie to her, tell me?"

"You told her things about me that weren't true. You made me out to be more, consequently less than I am. She had in mind a totally different person, a sort of semi-mystical Wonder Rabbi."

"All I said, you was a religious man."

"I can imagine."

Salzman sighed. "This is my weakness that I have," he confessed. "My wife says to me I shouldn't be a salesman, but when I have two fine people that they would be wonderful to be married, I am so happy that I talk too much." He smiled wanly. " This is why Salzman is a poor man."

Leo's anger left him. "Well, Salzman, I'm afraid that's all."

The marriage broker fastened hungry eyes on him.

"You don't want any more a bride?"

"I do," said Leo, "but I have decided to seek her in a different way. I am no longer interested in an arranged marriage. To be frank, I now admit the necessity of premarital love. That is, I want to be in love with the one I marry."

"Love?" said Salzman, astounded. After a moment he remarked, "For us, our love is our life, not for the ladies. In the ghetto they—"

"I know, I know," said Leo. "I've thought of it often. Love, I have said to myself, should be a by-product of living and worship rather than its own end. Yet for myself I find it necessary to establish the level of my need and fulfill it."

Salzman shrugged but answered. "Listen, rabbi, if you want love, this I can find for you also. I have such beautiful clients that you will love them the minute your eyes will see them."

Leo smiled unhappily. "I'm afraid you don't understand."

But Salzman hastily unstrapped his portfolio and withdrew a manila packet from it.

"Pictures," he said, quickly laying the envelope on the table.

Leo called after him to take the pictures away, but as if on the wings of the wind, Salzman had disappeared.

March came. Leo had returned to his regular routine. Although he felt not quite himself yet—lacked energy—he was making plans for a more active social life. Of course it would cost something, but he was an expert in cutting corners; and when there were no corners left he would make circles rounder. All the while Salzman's pictures had lain on the table, gathering dust. Occasionally as Leo sat studying, or enjoying a cup of tea, his eyes fell on the manila envelope, but he never opened it.

The days went by and no social life to speak of developed with a member of the opposite sex—it was difficult, given the circumstances of his situation. One morning Leo toiled up the stairs to his room and stared out the window at the city. Although the day was bright his view of it was dark. For some time he watched the people in the street below hurrying along and then turned with a heavy heart to his little room. On the table was the packet. With a sudden relentless gesture he tore it open. For a half-hour he stood by the table in a state of excitement, examining the photographs of the ladies Salzman had included. Finally, with a deep sigh he put them down. There were six, of varying degrees of attractiveness, but look at them long enough and they all become Lily Hirschorn: all past their prime, all starved behind bright smiles, not a true personality in the lot. Life, despite their frantic yoohooings, had passed them by; they were pictures in a briefcase that stank of fish. After a while, however, as Leo attempted to return the photographs into the envelope, he found in it another, a snapshot of the type taken by a machine for a quarter. He gazed at it a moment and let out a cry.

Her face deeply moved him. Why, he could at first not say. It gave him the impression of youth—spring flowers, yet age—a sense of having been used to the bone, wasted: this came from the eyes, which were hauntingly familiar, yet absolutely strange. He had a vivid impression that he had met her before, but try as he might he could not place her although he could almost recall her name, as if he had read it in her own handwriting. No, this couldn't be; he would have remembered her. It was not, he affirmed, that she had an extraordinary beauty—no, though her face was attractive enough; it was that *something* about her moved him. Feature for feature, even some of the ladies of the photographs could do better; but she leaped forth to his heart—had *lived,* or wanted to—more than just wanted, perhaps regretted how she had lived—had somehow deeply suffered: it could be seen in the depths of those reluctant eyes, and from the way the light enclosed and shone from her, and within her, opening realms of possibility: this was her own. Her he desired. His head ached and eyes narrowed with the intensity of his gazing, then as if an obscure fog had blown up in the mind, he experienced fear of her and was aware that he had received an impression, somehow, of evil. He shuddered, saying softly, it is thus with us all. Leo brewed some tea in a small pot and sat sipping it without sugar, to calm himself. But before he had finished drinking, again with excitement he examined the face and found it good: good for Leo Finkle. Only such a one could understand him and help him seek whatever he was seeking. She might, perhaps, love him. How she had happened to be among the discards in Salzman's barrel he could never guess, but he knew he must urgently go find her.

Leo rushed downstairs, grabbed up the Bronx telephone book, and searched for Salzman's home address. He was not listed nor was his office. Neither was he in the Manhattan book. But Leo remembered having written down the address on a slip of paper after he had read Salzman's advertisement in the "personals" column of the *Forward*. He ran up to his room and tore through his papers, without luck. It was exasperating. Just when he needed the matchmaker he was nowhere to be found. Fortunately Leo remembered to look in his wallet. There on a card he found his name written and a Bronx address. No phone number was listed, the reason—Leo now recalled—he had originally communicated with Salzman by letter. He got on his coat, put a hat on over his skull cap and hurried to the subway station. All the way to the far end of the Bronx he sat on the edge on his seat. He was more than once tempted to take out the picture and see if the girl's face was as he remembered it, but he refrained, allowing the snapshot to remain in his inside coat pocket, content to have her so close. When the train pulled into the station he was waiting at the door and bolted out. He quickly located the street Salzman had advertised.

The building he sought was less than a block from the subway, but it was not an office building, nor even a loft, nor a store in which one could rent office space. It was a very old tenement house. Leo found Salzman's name in pencil on a soiled tag under the bell and climbed three dark flights to his apartment. When he knocked, the door was opened by a thin, asthmatic, gray-haired woman, in felt slippers.

"Yes?" she said, expecting nothing. She listened without listening. He could have sworn he had seen her, too, before but knew it was an illusion.

"Salzman—does he live here? Pinye Salzman," he said, "the matchmaker?"

She stared at him a long minute. "Of course."

He felt embarrassed. "Is he in?"

"No." Her mouth, though left open, offered nothing more.

"The matter is urgent. Can you tell me where his office is?"

"In the air." She pointed upward.

"You mean he has no office?" Leo asked.

"In his socks."

He peered into the apartment. It was sunless and dingy, one large room divided by a half-open curtain, beyond which he could see a sagging metal bed. The near side of the room was crowded with rickety chairs, old bureaus, a three-legged table, racks of cooking utensils, and all the apparatus of a kitchen. But there was no sign of Salzman or his magic barrel, probably also a figment of the imagination. An odor of frying fish made Leo weak to the knees.

"Where is he?" he insisted. "I've got to see your husband."

At length she answered. "So who knows where his is? Every time he thinks a new thought he runs to a different place. Go home, he will find you."

"Tell him Leo Finkle."

She gave no sign she had heard.

He walked downstairs, depressed.

But Salzman, breathless, stood waiting at his door.

Leo was astounded and overjoyed. "How did you get here before me?"

"I rushed."

"Come inside."

They entered. Leo fixed tea, and a sardine sandwich for Salzman. As they were drinking he reached behind him for the packet of pictures and handed them to the marriage broker.

Salzman put down his glass and said expectantly, "You found somebody you like?"

"Not among these."

The marriage broker turned away.

"Here is the one I want." Leo held forth the snapshot.

Salzman slipped on his glasses and took the picture into his trembling hand. He turned ghastly and let out a groan.

"What's the matter?" cried Leo.

"Excuse me. Was an accident this picture. She isn't for you."

Salzman frantically shoved the manila packet into his portfolio. He thrust the snapshot into his pocket and fled down the stairs.

Leo, after momentary paralysis, gave chase and cornered the marriage broker in the vestibule. The landlady made hysterical outcries but neither of them listened. "Give me back the picture, Salzman."

"No." The pain in his eyes was terrible.

"Tell me who she is then."

"This I can't tell you. Excuse me."

He made to depart, but Leo, forgetting himself, seized the matchmaker by his tight coat and shook him frenziedly.

"Please," sighed Salzman. *"Please."*

Leo ashamedly let him go. "Tell me who she is," he begged. "It's very important for me know."

"She is not for you. She is a wild one—wild, without shame. This is not a bride for a rabbi."

"What do you mean wild?"

"Like an animal. Like a dog. For her to be poor was a sin. This is why to me she is dead now."

"In God's name, what do you mean?"

"Her I can't introduce to you," Salzman cried.

"Why are you so excited?"

"Why, he asks," Salzman said, bursting into tears. "This is my baby, my Stella, she should burn in hell."

Leo hurried up to bed and hid under the covers. Under the covers he thought his life through. Although he soon fell asleep he could not sleep her out of his mind. He woke, beating his breast. Though he prayed to be rid of her, his prayers were unanswered. Through days of torment he endlessly struggled not to love her: fearing success, he escaped it. He then concluded to convert her to goodness, himself to God. The idea alternately nauseated and exalted him.

He perhaps did not know that he had come to a final decision until he encountered Salzman in a Broadway cafeteria. He was sitting alone at a rear table, sucking the bony remains of a fish. The marriage broker appeared haggard, and transparent to the point of vanishing.

Salzman looked up at first without recognizing him. Leo had grown a pointed beard and his eyes were weighted with wisdom.

"Salzman," he said, "love has at last come to my heart."

"Who can love from a picture?" mocked the marriage broker.

"It is not impossible."

"If you can love her, then you can love anybody. Let me show you some new clients that they just sent me their photographs. One is a little doll."

"Just her I want," Leo murmured.

"Don't be a fool, doctor. Don't bother with her."

"Put me in touch with her, Salzman," Leo said humbly. "Perhaps I can be of service."

Salzman had stopped eating and Leo understood with emotion that it was now arranged.

Leaving the cafeteria, he was, however, afflicted by a tormenting suspicion that Salzman had planned it all to happen this way.

Leo was informed by letter that she would meet him on a certain corner, and she was there one spring night, waiting under a street lamp. He appeared, carrying a small bouquet of violets and rosebuds.

Stella stood by the lamp post, smoking. She wore white with red shoes, which fitted his expectations, although in a troubled moment he had imagined the dress red, and only the shoes white. She waited uneasily and shyly. From afar he saw that her eyes—clearly her father's—were filled with desperate innocence. He pictured, in her, his own redemption. Violins and lit candles revolved in the sky. Leo ran forward with flowers outthrust.

Around the corner, Salzman, leaning against a wall, chanted prayers for the dead.

Grace Paley (b. 1922)

THE LOUDEST VOICE

There is a certain place where dumb-waiters boom, doors slam, dishes crash; every window is a mother's mouth bidding the street shut up, go skate somewhere else, come home. My voice is the loudest.

There, my own mother is still as full of breathing as me and the grocer stands up to speak to her. "Mrs. Abramowitz," he says, "people should not be afraid of their children."

"Ah, Mr. Bialik," my mother replies, "if you say to her or her father 'Ssh,' they say, 'In the grave it will be quiet.'"

"From Coney Island to the cemetery," says my papa. "It's the same subway; it's the same fare."

I am right next to the pickle barrel. My pinky is making tiny whirlpools in the brine. I stop a moment to announce: "Campbell's Tomato Soup. Campbell's Vegetable Beef Soup. Campbell's S-c-otch Broth . . ."

"Be quiet," the grocer says, "the labels are coming off."

"Please, Shirley, be a little quiet," my mother begs me.

In that place the whole street groans: Be quiet! Be quiet! but steals from the happy chorus of my inside self not a tittle or a jot.

There, too, but just around the corner, is a red brick building that has been old for many years. Every morning the children stand before it in double lines which must be straight. They are not insulted. They are waiting anyway.

I am usually among them. I am, in fact, the first, since I begin with "A."

One cold morning the monitor tapped me on the shoulder. "Go to Room 409, Shirley Abramowitz," he said. I did as I was told. I went in a hurry up a down staircase to Room 409, which contained sixth-graders. I had to wait at the desk without wiggling until Mr. Hilton, their teacher, had time to speak.

After five minutes he said, "Shirley?"

"What?" I whispered.

He said, "My! My! Shirley Abramowitz! They told me you had a particularly loud, clear voice and read with lots of expression. Could that be true?"

"Oh yes," I whispered.

"In that case, don't be silly; I might very well be your teacher someday. Speak up, speak up."

"Yes," I shouted.

"More like it," he said. "Now, Shirley, can you put a ribbon in your hair or a bobby pin? It's too messy."

"Yes!" I bawled.

"Now, now, calm down." He turned to the class. "Children, not a sound. Open at page 39. Read till 52. When you finish, start again." He looked me over once more. "Now, Shirley, you know, I suppose, that Christmas is coming. We are preparing a beautiful play. Most of the parts have been given out. But I still need a child with a strong voice, lots of stamina. Do you know what stamina is? You do? Smart kid. You know, I heard you read 'The Lord is my shepherd' in Assembly yesterday. I was very impressed. Wonderful delivery. Mrs. Jordan, your teacher, speaks highly of you. Now listen to me, Shirley Abramowitz, if you want to take the part and be in the play repeat after me, 'I swear to work harder than I ever did before.'"

I looked to heaven and said at once, "Oh, I swear." I kissed my pinky and looked at God.

"That is an actor's life, my dear," he explained. "Like a soldier's, never tardy or disobedient to his general, the director. Everything," he said, "absolutely everything will depend on you."

That afternoon, all over the building, children scraped and scrubbed the turkeys and the sheaves of corn off the schoolroom windows. Goodbye Thanksgiving. The next morning a monitor brought red paper and green paper from the office. We made new shapes and hung them on the walls and glued them to the doors.

The teachers became happier and happier. Their heads were ringing like the bells of childhood. My best friend Evie was prone to evil, but she did not get a single demerit for whispering. We learned "Holy Night" without an error. "How wonderful!" said Miss Glacé, the student teacher. "To think that some of you don't even speak the language!" We learned "Deck the Halls" and "Hark! The Herald Angels". . . . They weren't ashamed and we weren't embarrassed.

Oh, but when my mother heard about it all, she said to my father: "Misha, you don't know what's going on there. Cramer is the head of the Tickets Committee."

"Who?" asked my father. "Cramer? Oh yes, an active woman."

"Active? Active has to have a reason. Listen," she said sadly, "I'm surprised to see my neighbors making tra-la-la for Christmas."

My father couldn't think of what to say to that. Then he decided: "You're in America! Clara, you wanted to come here. In Palestine the Arabs would be eating you alive. Europe you had pogroms. Argentina is full of Indians. Here you got Christmas. . . . Some joke, ha?"

"Very funny, Misha. What is becoming of you? If we came to a new country a long time ago to run away from tyrants, and instead we fall into a creeping pogrom, that our children learn a lot of lies, so what's the joke? Ach, Misha, your idealism is going away."

"So is your sense of humor."

"That I never had, but idealism you had a lot of."

"I'm the same Misha Abramovitch, I didn't change an iota. Ask anyone."

"Only ask me," says my mama, may she rest in peace, "I got the answer."

Meanwhile the neighbors had to think of what to say too.

Marty's father said: "You know, he has a very important part, my boy."

"Mine also," said Mr. Sauerfeld.

"Not my boy!" said Mrs. Klieg. "I said to him no. The answer is no. When I say no! I mean no!"

The rabbi's wife said, "It's disgusting!" But no one listened to her. Under the narrow sky of God's great wisdom she wore a strawberry-blond wig.

Every day was noisy and full of experience. I was Right-hand Man. Mr. Hilton said: "How could I get along without you, Shirley?"

He said: "Your mother and father ought to get down on their knees every night and thank God for giving them a child like you."

He also said: "You're absolutely a pleasure to work with, my dear, dear child."

Sometimes he said: "For God's sakes, what did I do with the script? Shirley! Shirley! Find it."

Then I answered quietly: "Here it is, Mr. Hilton."

Once in a while, when he was very tired, he would cry out: "Shirley, I'm just tired of screaming at those kids. Will you tell Ira Pushkov not to come in till Lester points to that star the second time?"

Then I roared: "Ira Pushkov, what's the matter with you? Dope! Mr. Hilton told you five times already, don't come in till Lester points to that star the second time."

"Ach, Clara," my father asked, "what does she do there till six o'clock she can't even put the plates on the table?"

"Christmas," said my mother coldly.

"Ho! Ho!" my father said. "Christmas. What's the harm? After all, history teaches everyone. We learn from reading this is a holiday from pagan times also, candles, lights, even Chanukah. So we learn it's not altogether Christian. So if they think it's a private holiday, they're only ignorant, not patriotic. What belongs to history, belongs to all men. You want to go back to the Middle Ages? Is it better to shave your head with a secondhand razor? Does it hurt Shirley to learn to speak up? It does not. So maybe someday she won't live between the kitchen and the shop. She's not a fool."

I thank you, Papa, for your kindness. It is true about me to this day. I am foolish but I am not a fool.

That night my father kissed me and said with great interest in my career, "Shirley, tomorrow's your big day. Congrats."

"Save it," my mother said. Then she shut all the windows in order to prevent tonsillitis.

In the morning it snowed. On the street corner a tree had been decorated for us by a kind city administration. In order to miss its chilly shadow our neighbors walked three blocks east to buy a loaf of bread. The butcher pulled down black window shades to keep the colored lights from shining on his chickens. Oh, not me. On the way to school, with both my hands I tossed it a kiss of tolerance. Poor thing, it was a stranger in Egypt.

I walked straight into the auditorium past the staring children. "Go ahead, Shirley!" said the monitors. Four boys, big for their age, had already stated work as propmen and stagehands.

Mr. Hilton was very nervous. He was not even happy. Whatever he started to say ended in a sideward look of sadness. He sat slumped in the middle of the fist row and asked me to help Miss Glacé. I did this, although she thought my voice too resonant and said, "Show-off!"

Parents began to arrive long before we were ready. They wanted to make a good impression. From among the yards of drapes I peeked out at the audience. I saw my embarrassed mother.

Ira, Lester, and Meyer were pasted to their beards by Miss Glacé. She almost forgot to thread the star on its wire, but I reminded her. I coughed a few times to clear my throat. Miss Glacé looked around and saw that everyone was in costume and on line waiting to play his part. She whispered, "All right . . ." Then:

Jackie Sauerfeld, the prettiest boy in first grade, parted the curtains with his skinny elbow and in a high voice sang out:

"Parents dear
We are here
To make a Christmas play in time.
It we give
In narrative
And illustrate with pantomime."

He disappeared.

My voice burst immediately from the wings to the great shock of Ira, Lester, and Meyer, who were waiting for it but were surprised all the same.

"I remember, I remember, the house where I was born . . ."

Miss Glacé yanked the curtain open and there it was, the house—an old hayloft, where Celia Kornbluh lay in the straw with Cindy Lou, her favorite doll. Ira, Lester, and Meyer moved slowly from the wings toward her, sometimes pointing to a moving star and sometimes ahead to Cindy Lou.

It was a long story and it was a sad story. I carefully pronounced all the words about my lonesome childhood, while little Eddie Braunstein wandered upstage and down with his shepherd's stick, looking for sheep. I brought up lonesomeness again, and not being understood at all except by some women everybody hated. Eddie was too small for that and Marty Groff took his place, wearing his father's prayer shawl. I announced twelve friends, and half the boys in the fourth grade gathered round Marty, who stood on an orange crate while my voice harangued. Sorrowful and loud, I declaimed about love and God and Man, but because of the terrible deceit of Abie Stock we came suddenly to a famous moment. Marty, whose remembering tongue I was, waited at the foot of the cross. He stared desperately at the audience. I groaned, "My God, my God why hast thou forsaken me?" The soldiers who were sheiks grabbed poor Marty to pin him up to die, but he wrenched free, turned again to the audience, and spread his arms aloft to show despair and the end. I murmured at the top of my voice, "The rest is silence, but as everyone in this room, in this city—in this world—now knows, I shall have life eternal."

That night Mrs. Kornbluh visited our kitchen for a glass of tea.

"How's the virgin?" asked my father with a look of concern.

"For a man with a daughter, you got a fresh mouth, Abramovitch."

"Here," said my father kindly, "have some lemon, it'll sweeten your disposition."

They debated a little in Yiddish, then fell in a puddle of Russian and Polish. What I understood next was my father, who said, "Still and all, it was certainly a beautiful affair, you have to admit, introducing us to the beliefs of a different culture."

"Well, yes," said Mrs. Kornbluh. "The only thing . . . you know Charlie Turner—that cute boy in Celia's class—a couple others? They got very small parts or no part at all. In very bad taste, it seemed to me. After all, it's their religion."

"Ach," explained my mother, "what could Mr. Hilton do? They got very small voices; after all, why should they holler? The English language they know from the beginning by heart. They're blond like angels. You think it's so important they should get in the play? Christmas . . . the whole piece of goods . . . they own it."

I listened and listened until I couldn't listen any more. Too sleepy, I climbed out of bed and kneeled. I made a little church of my hands and said, "Hear, O Israel . . ." Then I called out in Yiddish, "Please, good night, good night. Ssh." My father said, "Ssh yourself," and slammed the kitchen door.

I was happy. I fell asleep at once. I had prayed for everybody: my talking family, cousins far away, passersby, and all the lonesome Christians. I expected to be heard. My voice was certainly the loudest.

Flannery O'Connor (1925–1964)

A GOOD MAN IS HARD TO FIND

The grandmother didn't want to go to Florida. She wanted to visit some of her connections in east Tennessee and she was seizing at every chance to change Bailey's mind. Bailey was the son she lived with, her only boy. He was sitting on the edge of his chair at the table, bent over the orange sports section of the *Journal.* "Now look here, Bailey," she said, "see here, read this," and she stood with one hand on her thin hip and the other rattling the newspaper at his bald head. "Here this fellow that calls himself The Misfit is aloose from the Federal Pen and headed toward Florida and you read here what it says he did to these people. Just you read it. I wouldn't take my children in any direction with a criminal like that aloose in it. I couldn't answer to my conscience if I did."

Bailey didn't look up from his reading so she wheeled around then and faced the children's mother, a young woman in slacks, whose face was as broad and innocent as a cabbage and was tied round with a green head-kerchief that had two points on the top like rabbit's ears. She was sitting on the sofa, feeding the baby his apricots out of a jar. "The children have been to Florida before," the old lady said. "You all ought to take them somewhere else for a change so they would see different parts of the world and be broad. They never have been to east Tennessee."

The children's mother didn't seem to hear her but the eight-year-old boy, John Wesley, a stocky child with glasses, said, "If you don't want to go to Florida, why dontcha stay at home?" He and the little girl, June Star, were reading the funny papers on the floor.

"She wouldn't stay at home to be queen for a day," June Star said without raising her yellow head.

"Yes, and what would you do if this fellow, The Misfit, caught you?" the grandmother asked.

"I'd smack his face," John Wesley said.

"She wouldn't stay at home for a million bucks," June Star said. "Afraid she'd miss something. She has to go everywhere we go."

"All right, Miss," the grandmother said. "Just remember that the next time you want me to curl your hair."

June Star said her hair was naturally curly.

The next morning the grandmother was the first one in the car, ready to go. She had her big black valise that looked like the head of a hippopotamus in one corner, and underneath it she was hiding a basket with Pitty Sing, the cat, in it. She didn't intend for the cat to be left alone in the house for three days because he would miss her too much and she was afraid he might brush against one of the gas burners and accidentally asphyxiate himself. Her son, Bailey, didn't like to arrive at a motel with a cat.

She sat in the middle of the back seat with John Wesley and June Star on either side of her. Bailey and the children's mother and the baby sat in front and they left Atlanta at eight forty-five with the mileage on the car at 55890. The grandmother wrote this down because she thought it would be interesting to say how many miles they had been when they got back. It took them twenty minutes to reach the outskirts of the city.

The old lady settled herself comfortably, removing her white cotton gloves and putting them up with her purse on the shelf in front of the back window. The children's mother still had on slacks and still had her head tied up in a green kerchief, but the grandmother had on a navy blue straw sailor hat with a bunch of white violets on the brim and a navy blue dress with a small white dot in the print. Her collars and cuffs were white organdy trimmed with lace and at her neckline she had pinned a purple spray of cloth violets containing a sachet. In case of an accident, anyone seeing her dead on the highway would know at once that she was a lady.

She said she thought it was going to be a good day for driving, neither too hot nor too cold, and she cautioned Bailey that the speed limit was fifty-five miles an hour and that the patrolmen hid themselves behind billboards and small clumps of trees and sped out after you before you had a chance to slow down. She pointed out interesting details of the scenery: Stone Mountain; the blue granite that in some places came up to both sides of the highway; the brilliant red clay banks slightly streaked with purple; and the various crops that made rows of green lacework on the ground. The trees were full of silver-white sunlight and the meanest of them sparkled. The children were reading comic magazines and their mother had gone back to sleep.

"Let's go through Georgia fast so we won't have to look at it much," John Wesley said.

"If I were a little boy," said the grandmother, "I wouldn't talk about my native state that way. Tennessee has the mountains and Georgia has the hills."

"Tennessee is just a hillbilly dumping ground," John Wesley said, "and Georgia is a lousy state too."

"You said it," June Star said.

"In my time," said the grandmother, folding her thin veined fingers, "children were more respectful of their native states and their parents and everything else. People did right then. Oh look at the cute little pickaninny!" she said and pointed to a Negro child standing in the door of a shack. "Wouldn't that make a picture, now?" she asked and they all turned and looked at the little Negro out of the back window. He waved.

"He didn't have any britches on," June Star said.

"He probably didn't have any," the grandmother explained. "Little niggers in the country don't have things like we do. If I could paint, I'd paint that picture," she said.

The children exchanged comic books.

The grandmother offered to hold the baby and the children's mother passed him over the front seat to her. She set him on her knee and bounced him and told him about the things they were passing. She rolled her eyes and screwed up her mouth and stuck her leathery thin face into his smooth bland one. Occasionally he gave her a faraway smile. They passed a large cotton field with five or six graves fenced in the middle of it, like a small island. "Look at the graveyard!" the grandmother said, pointing it out. "That was the old family burying ground. That belonged to the plantation."

"Where's the plantation?" John Wesley asked.

"Gone With the Wind," said the grandmother. "Ha. Ha."

When the children finished all the comic books they had brought, they opened the lunch and ate it. The grandmother ate a peanut butter sandwich and an olive and would not let the children throw the box and the paper napkins out the window. When there was nothing else to do they played a game by choosing a cloud and making the other two guess what shape it suggested. John Wesley took one the shape of a cow and June Star guessed a cow and John Wesley said, no, an automobile, and June Star said he didn't play fair, and they began to slap each other over the grandmother.

The grandmother said she would tell them a story if they would keep quiet. When she told a story, she rolled her eyes and waved her head and was very dramatic. She said once when she was a maiden lady she had been courted by a Mr. Edgar Atkins Teagarden from Jasper, Georgia. She said he was a very good-looking man and a gentleman and that he brought her a watermelon every Saturday afternoon with his initials cut in it, E.A.T. Well, one Saturday, she said, Mr. Teagarden brought the watermelon and there was nobody at home and he left it on the front porch and returned in his buggy to Jasper, but she never got the watermelon, she said, because a nigger boy ate it when he saw the initials, E.A.T.! This story tickled John Wesley's funny bone and he giggled and giggled but June Star didn't think it was any good. She said she wouldn't marry a man that just brought her a watermelon on Saturday. The grandmother said she would have done well to marry Mr. Teagarden because he was a gentleman and had bought Coca-Cola stock when it first came out and that he had died only a few years ago, a very wealthy man.

They stopped at The Tower for barbecued sandwiches. The Tower was a part stucco and part wood filling station and dance hall set in a clearing outside of Timothy. A fat man named Red Sammy Butts ran it and there were signs stuck here and there on the building and for miles up and down the highway saying, TRY RED SAMMY'S FAMOUS BARBEQUE. NONE LIKE FAMOUS RED SAMMY'S! RED SAM! THE FAT BOY WITH THE HAPPY LAUGH. A VETERAN! RED SAMMY'S YOUR MAN!

Red Sammy was lying on the bare ground outside The Tower with his head under a truck while a gray monkey about a foot high, chained to a small chinaberry tree, chattered nearby. The monkey sprang back into the tree and got on the highest limb as soon as he saw the children jump out of the car and run toward him.

Inside, The Tower was a long dark room with a counter at one end and tables at the other and dancing space in the middle. They all sat down at a board table next to the nickelodeon and Red Sam's wife, a tall burnt-brown woman with hair and eyes lighter than her skin, came and took their order. The children's mother put a dime in the machine and played "The Tennessee Waltz," and the grandmother said that tune always made her want to dance. She asked Bailey if he would like to dance but he only glared at her. He didn't have a naturally sunny disposition like she did and trips made him nervous. The grandmother's brown eyes were very bright. She swayed her head from side to side and pretended she was dancing in their chair. June Star said play something she could tap to so the children's mother put in another dime and played a fast number and June Star stepped out onto the dance floor and did her tap routine.

"Ain't she cute?" Red Sam's wife said, leaning over the counter. "Would you like to come be my little girl?"

"No I certainly wouldn't," June Star said. "I wouldn't live in a broken-down place like this for a million bucks!" and she ran back to the table.

"Ain't she cute?" the woman repeated, stretching her mouth politely.

"Aren't you ashamed?" hissed the grandmother.

Red Sam came in and told his wife to quit lounging on the counter and hurry with these people's order. His khaki trousers reached just to his hip bones and his stomach hung over them like a sack of meal swaying under his shirt. He came over and sat down at a table nearby and let out a combination sigh and yodel. "You can't win," he said. "You can't win," and he wiped his sweating red face off with a gray handkerchief. "These days you don't know who to trust," he said. "Ain't that the truth?"

"People are certainly not nice like they used to be," said the grandmother.

"Two fellers come in here last week," Red Sammy said, "driving a Chrysler. It was a old beat-up car but it was a good one and these boys looked all right to me. Said they worked at the mill and you know I let them fellers charge the gas they bought? Now why did I do that?"

"Because you're a good man!" the grandmother said at once.

"Yes'm, I suppose so," Red Sam said as if he were struck with the answer.

His wife brought the orders, carrying the five plates all at once without a tray, two in each hand and one balanced on her arm. "It isn't a soul in this green world of God's that you can trust," she said. "And I don't count nobody out of that, not nobody," she repeated, looking at Red Sammy.

"Did you read about that criminal, The Misfit, that's escaped?" asked the grandmother.

"I wouldn't be a bit surprised if he didn't attack this place right here," said the woman. "If he hears about it being here, I wouldn't be none surprised to see him. If he hears it's two cent in the cash register, I wouldn't be a tall surprised if he . . ."

"That'll do," Red Sam said. "Go bring these people their Co'Colas," and the woman went off to get the rest of the order.

"A good man is hard to find," Red Sammy said. "Everything is getting terrible. I remember the day you could go off and leave your screen door unlatched. Not no more."

He and the grandmother discussed better times. The old lady said that in her opinion Europe was entirely to blame for the way things were now. She said the way Europe acted you would think we were made of money and Red Sam said it was no use talking about it, she was exactly right. The children ran outside into the white sunlight and looked at the monkey in the lacy chinaberry tree. He was busy catching fleas on himself and biting each one carefully between his teeth as if it were a delicacy.

They drove off again into the hot afternoon. The grandmother took cat naps and woke up every few minutes with her own snoring. Outside of Toombsboro she woke up and recalled an old plantation that she had visited in this neighborhood once when she was a young lady. She said the house had six white columns across the front and that there was an avenue of oaks leading up to it and two little wooden trellis arbors on either side in front where you sat down with your suitor after a stroll in the garden. She recalled exactly which road to turn off to get to it. She knew that Bailey would not be willing to lose any time looking at an old house, but the more she talked about it, the more she wanted to see it once again and find out if the little twin arbors were still standing. "There was a secret panel in this house," she said craftily, not telling the truth but wishing that she were, "and the story went that all the family silver was hidden in it when Sherman came through but it was never found . . . ."

"Hey!" John Wesley said. "Let's go see it! We'll find it! We'll poke all the woodwork and find it! Who lives there? Where do you turn off at? Hey Pop, can't we turn off there?"

"We never have seen a house with a secret panel!" June Star shrieked. "Let's go to the house with the secret panel! Hey Pop, can't we go see the house with the secret panel!"

"It's not far from here, I know," the grandmother said. "It wouldn't take over twenty minutes."

Bailey was looking straight ahead. His jaw was as rigid as a horseshoe. "No," he said.

The children began to yell and scream that they wanted to see the house with the secret panel. John Wesley kicked the back of the front seat and June Star hung over her mother's shoulder and whined desperately into her ear that they never had any fun even on their vacation, that they could never do what THEY wanted to do. The baby began to scream and John Wesley kicked the back of the seat so hard that his father could feel the blows in his kidney.

"All right!" he shouted and drew the car to a stop at the side of the rode. "Will you all shut up? Will you all just shut up for one second? If you don't shut up, we won't go anywhere."

"It would be very educational for them," the grandmother murmured.

"All right," Bailey said, "but get this: this is the only time we're going to stop for anything like this. This is the one and only time."

"The dirt road that you have to turn down is about a mile back," the grandmother directed. "I marked it when we passed."

"A dirt road," Bailey groaned.

After they had turned around and were headed toward the dirt road, the grandmother recalled other points about the house, the beautiful glass over the front doorway and the candle-lamp in the hall. John Wesley said that the secret panel was probably in the fireplace.

"You can't go inside this house," Bailey said. "You don't know who lives there."

"While you all talk to the people in front, I'll run around behind and get in a window," John Wesley suggested.

"We'll all stay in the car," his mother said.

They turned onto the dirt road and the car raced roughly along in a swirl of pink dust. The grandmother recalled the times when there were no paved roads and thirty miles was a day's journey. The dirt road was hilly and there were sudden washes in it and sharp curves on dangerous embankments. All at once they would be on a hill, looking down over the blue tops of trees for miles around, then the next minute, they would be in a red depression with the dust-coated trees looking down on them.

"This place had better turn up in a minute," Bailey said, "or I'm going to turn around."

The road looked as if no one had traveled on it in months.

"It's not much farther," the grandmother said and just as she said it, a horrible thought came to her. The thought was so embarrassing that she turned red in the face and her eyes dilated and her feet jumped up, upsetting her valise in the corner. The instant the valise moved, the newspaper top she had over the basket under it rose with a snarl and Pitty Sing, the cat, sprang onto Bailey's shoulder.

The children were thrown to the floor and their mother, clutching the baby, was thrown out the door onto the ground; the old lady was thrown into the front seat. The car turned over once and landed right-side-up in a gulch on the side of the road. Bailey remained in the driver's seat with the cat—gray-striped with a broad white face and an orange nose—clinging to his neck like a caterpillar.

As soon as the children saw they could move their arms and legs, they scrambled out of the car, shouting, "We've had an ACCIDENT!" The grandmother was curled up under the dashboard, hoping she was injured so that Bailey's wrath would not come down on her all at once. The horrible thought she had had before the accident was that the house she had remembered so vividly was not in Georgia but in Tennessee.

Bailey removed the cat from his neck with both hands and flung it out the window against the side of a pine tree. Then he got out of the car and started looking for the children's mother. She was sitting against the side of the red gutted ditch, holding the screaming baby, but she only had a cut down her face and a broken shoulder. "We've had an ACCIDENT!" the children screamed in a frenzy of delight.

"But nobody's killed," June Star said with disappointment as the grandmother limped out of the car, her hat still pinned to her head but the broken front brim standing up at a jaunty angle and the violet spray hanging off the side. They all sat down in the ditch, except the children, to recover from the shock. They were all shaking.

"Maybe a car will come along," said the children's mother hoarsely.

"I believe I have an injured organ," said the grandmother, pressing her side, but no one answered her. Bailey's teeth were clattering. He had on a yellow sport shirt with bright blue parrots designed on it and his face was as yellow as the shirt. The grandmother decided that she would not mention that the house was in Tennessee.

The road was about ten feet above and they could see only the tops of the trees on the other side of it. Behind the ditch they were sitting in there were more woods, tall and dark and deep. In a few minutes they saw a car some distance away on top of a hill, coming slowly as if the occupants were watching them. The grandmother stood up and waved both arms dramatically to attract their attention. The car continued to come on slowly, disappeared around a bend and appeared again, moving even slower, on top of the hill they had gone over. It was a big black battered hearse-like automobile. There were three men in it.

It came to a stop just over them and for some minutes, the driver looked down with a steady expressionless gaze to where they were sitting, and didn't speak. Then he turned his head and muttered something to the other two and they got out. One was a fat boy in black trousers and a red sweat shirt with a silver stallion embossed on the front of it. He moved around on the right side of them and stood staring, his mouth partly open in a kind of loose grin. The other had on khaki pants and a blue striped coat and a gray hat pulled down very low, hiding most of his face. He came around slowly on the left side. Neither spoke.

The driver got out of the car and stood by the side of it, looking down at them. He wan an older man than the other two. His hair was just beginning to gray and he wore silver-rimmed spectacles that gave him a scholarly look. He had a long creased face and didn't have on any shirt or undershirt. He had on blue jeans that were too tight for him and was holding a black hat and a gun. The two boys also had guns.

"We've had an ACCIDENT!" the children screamed.

The grandmother had the peculiar feeling that the bespectacled man was someone she knew. His face was as familiar to her as if she had known him all her life but she could not recall who he was. He moved away from the car and began to come down the embankment, placing his feet carefully so that he wouldn't slip. He had on tan and white shoes and no socks, and his ankles were red and thin. "Good afternoon," he said. "I see you all had you a little spill."

"We turned over twice!" said the grandmother.

"Oncet," he corrected. "We seen it happen. Try their car and see will it run, Hiram," he said quietly to the boy with the gray hat.

"What you got that gun for?" John Wesley asked. "Whatcha gonna do with that gun?"

"Lady," the man said to the children's mother, "would you mind calling them children to sit down by you? Children make me nervous. I want all you all to sit down right together there where you're at."

"What are you telling US what to do for?" June Star asked.

Behind them the line of woods gaped like a dark open mouth. "Come here," said their mother.

"Look here now," Bailey began suddenly, "we're in a predicament! We're in . . ."

The grandmother shrieked. She scrambled to her feet and stood staring. "You're The Misfit!" she said. "I recognized you at once!"

"Yes'm," the man said, smiling slightly as if he were pleased in spite of himself to be known, "but it would have been better for all of you, lady, if you hadn't of reckernized me."

Bailey turned his head sharply and said something to his mother that shocked even the children. The old lady began to cry and The Misfit reddened.

"Lady," he said, "don't you get upset. Sometimes a man says things he don't mean. I don't reckon he meant to talk to you thataway."

"You wouldn't shoot a lady, would you?" the grandmother said and removed a clean handkerchief from her cuff and began to slap at her eyes with it.

The Misfit pointed the toe of his shoe into the ground and made a little hole and then covered it up again. "I would hate to have to," he said.

"Listen," the grandmother almost screamed, "I know you're a good man. You don't look a bit like you have common blood. I know you must come from nice people!"

"Yes mam," he said, "finest people in the world." When he smiled he showed a row of strong white teeth. "God never made a finer woman than my mother and my daddy's heart was pure gold," he said. The boy with the red sweat shirt had come around behind them and was standing with his gun at his hip. The Misfit squatted down on the ground. "Watch them children, Bobby Lee," he said. "You know they make me nervous." He looked at the six of them huddled together in front of him and he seemed to be embarrassed as if he couldn't think of anything to say. "Ain't a cloud in the sky," he remarked, looking up at it. "Don't see no sun but don't see no cloud neither."

"Yes, it's a beautiful day," said the grandmother. "Listen," she said, "you shouldn't call yourself The Misfit because I know you're a good man at heart. I can just look at you and tell."

"Hush!" Bailey yelled. "Hush! Everybody shut up and let me handle this!" He was squatting in the position of a runner about to sprint forward but he didn't move.

"I pre-chate that, lady," The Misfit said and drew a little circle in the ground with the butt of his gun.

"It'll take a half a hour to fix this here car," Hiram called, looking over the raised hood of it.

"Well, first you and Bobby Lee get him and that little boy to step over yonder with you," The Misfit said, pointing to Bailey and John Wesley. "The boys want to ask you something," he said to Bailey. "Would you mind stepping back in them woods there with them?"

"Listen," Bailey began, "we're in a terrible predicament! Nobody realizes what this is," and his voice cracked. His eyes were as blue and intense as the parrots on his shirt and he remained perfectly still.

The grandmother reached up to adjust her hat brim as if she were going to the woods with him but it came off in her hand. She stood staring at it and after a second she let it fall on the ground. Hiram pulled Bailey up by the arm as if he were assisting an old man. John Wesley caught hold of his father's hand and Bobby Lee followed. They went off toward the woods and just as they reached the dark edge, Bailey turned and supporting himself against a gray naked pine trunk, he shouted. "I'll be back in a minute, Mamma, wait on me!"

"Come back this instant!" his mother shrilled but they all disappeared into the woods.

"Bailey Boy!" the grandmother called in a tragic voice but she found she was looking at The Misfit squatting on the ground in front of her. "I just know you're a good man," she said desperately. "You're not a bit common!"

"Nome, I ain't a good man," The Misfit said after a second as if he had considered her statement carefully, "but I ain't the worst in the world neither. My daddy said I was different breed of dog from my brothers and sisters. 'You know,' Daddy said, 'it's some that can live their whole life out without asking about it and it's others has to know why it is, and this boy is one of the latters. He's going to be into everything!'" He put on his black hat and looked up suddenly and then away deep into the woods as if he were embarrassed again. "I'm sorry I don't have on a shirt before you ladies," he said, hunching his shoulders slightly. "We buried our clothes that we had on when we escaped and we're just making do until we can get better. We borrowed these from some folks we met," he explained.

"That's perfectly all right," the grandmother said. "Maybe Bailey has an extra shirt in his suitcase."

"I'll look and see terrectly," The Misfit said.

"Where are they taking him?" the children's mother screamed.

"Daddy was a card himself," The Misfit said. "You couldn't put anything over on him. He never got in trouble with the Authorities though. Just had the knack of handling them."

"You could be honest too if you'd only try," said the grandmother. "Think how wonderful it would be to settle down and live a comfortable life and not have to think about somebody chasing you all the time."

The Misfit kept scratching in the ground with the butt of his gun as if he were thinking about it. "Yes'm, somebody is always after you," he murmured.

The grandmother noticed how thin his shoulder blades were just behind his hat because she was standing up looking down on him. "Do you ever pray?" she asked.

He shook his head. All she saw was the black hat wiggle between his shoulder blades. "Nome," he said.

There was a pistol shot from the woods, followed closely by another. Then silence. The old lady's head jerked around. She could hear the wind move through the tree tops like a long satisfied insuck of breath. "Bailey Boy!" she called.

"I was a gospel singer for a while," The Misfit said. "I been most everything. Been in the arm service, both land and sea, at home and abroad, been twict married, been an undertaker, been with the railroads, plowed Mother Earth, been in a tornado, seen a man burnt alive oncet," and he looked up at the children's mother and the little girl who were sitting close together, their faces white and their eyes glassy; "I even seen a woman flogged," he said.

"Pray, pray," the grandmother began, "pray, pray . . ."

"I never was a bad boy that I remember of," The Misfit said in an almost dreamy voice, "but somewheres along the line I done something wrong and got sent to the penitentiary. I was buried alive," and he looked up and held her attention to him by a steady stare.

"That's when you should have started to pray," she said. "What did you do to get sent to the penitentiary the first time?"

"Turn to the right, it was a wall," The Misfit said, looking up again at the cloudless sky. "Turn to the left, it was a wall. Look up it was a ceiling, look down it was a floor. I forgot what I done, lady. I set there and set there, trying to remember what it was I done and I ain't recalled it to this day. Oncet in a while, I would think it was coming to me, but it never come."

"Maybe they put you in by mistake," the old lady said vaguely.

"Nome," he said. "It wasn't no mistake. They had the papers on me."

"You must have stolen something," she said.

The Misfit sneered slightly. "Nobody had nothing I wanted," he said. "It was a head-doctor at the penitentiary said what I had done was kill my daddy but I known that for a lie. My daddy died in nineteen ought nineteen of the epidemic flu and I never had a thing to do with it. He was buried in the Mount Hopewell Baptist churchyard and you can go there and see for yourself."

"If you would pray," the old lady said, "Jesus would help you."

"That's right," The Misfit said.

"Well then, why don't you pray?" she asked trembling with delight suddenly.

"I don't want no help," he said. "I'm doing all right by myself."

Bobby Lee and Hiram came ambling back from the woods. Bobby Lee was dragging a yellow shirt with bright blue parrots in it.

"Throw me that shirt, Bobby Lee," The Misfit said. The shirt came flying at him and landed on his shoulder and he put it on. The grandmother couldn't name what the shirt reminded her of. "No, lady," The Misfit said while he was buttoning it up, "I found out the crime don't matter. You can do one thing or you can do another, kill a man or take a tire off his car, because sooner or later you're going to forget what it was you done and just be punished for it."

The children's mother had begun to make heaving noises as if she couldn't get her breath. "Lady," he asked, "would you and that little girl like to step off yonder with Bobby Lee and Hiram and join your husband?"

"Yes, thank you," the mother said faintly. Her left arm dangled helplessly and she was holding the baby, who had gone to sleep, in the other. "Hep that lady up, Hiram," The Misfit said as she struggled to climb out of the ditch, "and Bobby Lee, you hold onto that little girl's hand."

"I don't want to hold hands with him," June Star said. "He reminds me of a pig."

The fat boy blushed and laughed and caught her by the arm and pulled her off into the woods after Hiram and her mother.

Alone with The Misfit, the grandmother found that she had lost her voice. There was not a cloud in the sky nor any sun. There was nothing around her but woods. She wanted to tell him that he must pray. She opened and closed her mouth several times before anything came out. Finally she found herself saying, "Jesus, Jesus," meaning Jesus will help you, but the way she was saying it, it sounded as if she might be cursing.

"Yes'm," The Misfit said as if he agreed. "Jesus thown everything off balance. It was the same case with Him as with me except He hadn't committed any crime and they could prove I had committed one because they had the papers on me. Of course," he said, "they never shown me my papers. That's why I sign myself now. I said long ago, you get you a signature and sign everything you do and keep a copy of it. Then you'll know what you done and you can hold up the crime to the punishment and see do they match and in the end you'll have something to prove you ain't been treated right. I call myself The Misfit," he said, "because I can't make what all I done wrong fit what all I gone through in punishment."

There was a piercing scream from the woods, followed closely by a pistol report. "Does it seem right to you, lady, that one is punished a heap and another ain't punished at all?"

"Jesus!" the old lady cried. "You've got good blood! I know you wouldn't shoot a lady! I know you come from nice people! Pray!

Jesus, you ought not to shoot a lady. I'll give you all the money I've got!"

"Lady," The Misfit said, looking beyond her far into the woods, "there never was a body that give the undertaker a tip."

There were two more pistol reports and the grandmother raised her head like a parched old turkey hen crying for water and called, "Bailey Boy, Bailey Boy!" as if her heart would break.

"Jesus was the only One that ever raised the dead," The Misfit continued, "and He shouldn't have done it. He thown everything off balance. If He did what He said, then it's nothing for you to do but thow away everything and follow Him, and if He didn't, then it's nothing for you to do but enjoy the few minutes you got left the best way you can—by killing somebody or burning down his house or doing some other meanness to him. No pleasure but meanness," he said and his voice had become almost a snarl.

"Maybe He didn't raise the dead," the old lady mumbled, not knowing what she was saying and feeling so dizzy that she sank down in the ditch with her legs twisted under her.

"I wasn't there so I can't say He didn't, " The Misfit said. "I wisht I had of been there," he said, hitting the ground with his fist. "It ain't right I wasn't there because if I had of been there I would of known. Listen lady," he said in a high voice, "if I had of been there I would of known and I wouldn't be like I am now." His voice seemed about to crack and the grandmother's head cleared for an instant. She saw the man's face twisted close to her own as if he was going to cry and she murmured, "Why you're one of my babies. You're one of my own children!" She reached out and touched him on the shoulder. The Misfit sprang back as if a snake had bitten him and shot her three times through the chest. Then he put his gun down on the ground and took off his glasses and began to clean them.

Hiram and Bobby Lee returned from the woods and stood over the ditch, looking down at the grandmother who half sat and half lay in a puddle of blood and with her legs crossed under her like a child's and her face smiling up at the cloudless sky.

Without his glasses, The Misfit's eyes were red-rimmed and pale and defenseless-looking. "Take her off and throw her where you thrown the others," he said, picking up the cat that was rubbing itself against his leg.

"She was a talker, wasn't she?" Bobby Lee said, sliding down the ditch with a yodel.

"She would of been a good woman," The Misfit said, "if it had been somebody there to shoot her every minute of her life."

"Some fun!" Bobby Lee said.

"Shut up, Bobby Lee," The Misfit said. "It's no real pleasure in life."

Claude Koch (b. 1918)
GRANDFATHER

The major event of Andrew's ninth birthday was his introduction to semaphore and the Morse code. "You have to know both," his Grandfather said; "there's no point in doing anything halfway."

"Now semaphore," his Grandfather said, "is 'a system of visual signaling by two flags held one in each hand.' That definition is precise." He reared up from his chair in the garden, using his cane like a vaulter's pole: "It happens I have only one flag at the moment, but we'll make do." He held out a two-by-four inch American flag that had been on Andrew's birthday cake that afternoon. "You go down to the end of the garden."

There were obstacles to getting to the end of the garden. Grandfather's Spring enthusiasm had somewhat waned, and the zucchini he had planted where he meant to have lettuce had done very well—so that the mid-portion of the yard that was the garden was largely impassable. "Now, Andrew, watch where you walk. A garden is an extraordinary thing—and the seedlings are our charge." The zucchini seedlings were a foot high and four feet across.

"Shall I walk around the block?" Andrew asked.

"It might be wise," Grandfather said.

So Andrew left by the iron gate of Grandfather's house, its forbidding points softened by late honeysuckle and blue morning glory, where his Mother as a child had swung creaking into the path of progress (as, indeed, his father said she still could do, on occasion) and entered upon the road of her childhood, crossing ragged plots of chicory and snow-on-the-mountain to the back lane and the back gate and the lower yard and the mulch pile, that grew mountainous year after year because Grandfather never got around to using it. The tomato vines cut Grandfather off at the waist, but he was tall and dignified—like a scarecrow or Don Quixote—and he waited with arms outstretched and a pigeon circling his head.

One of Grandfather's projects was to tell Andrew about Don Quixote, and he would have related more except that he had not yet gotten in his own reading beyond chapter one of Book One. But he had pointed out at St. Philomena's Church how the elongated statue of St. Francis (feeding the birds) bore some resemblance to the noble Spaniard, and Andrew could see how they all came together in that gaunt figure whose interest in nature and peanuts had brought squirrels to his feet and pigeons to other parts of his anatomy at the top of the autumn garden beyond the tomato vines.

"Andrew!" Grandfather had a voice for ampitheatres and large rooms that had lately been reduced by a numbing cough. "The message is: 'You may fire when you are ready, Girdley!' " That was when Andrew became aware that Father had been watching the entire performance from the second-floor back window.

When Father spoke of Grandfather he had always a rasp in his throat, as though he were suppressing a roar. He had said to Mother more than once in Andrew's hearing:"It's good for 'Grand' to live where he does. If he lived with us it would curtail his independence." Hence, because of Grandfather's advanced age, Andrew's birthdays were always held at Grandfather's house, a good five miles and one wide river from Andrew's home, and yet, Andrew's father sometimes said, hardly far enough. (Then Mother would explain that it was Father's work that made him impatient. He was a medical proofreader, and he worried about his memory. "Not like Grand, of course," he would say, in a tone that Andrew did not quite understand.)

Now Father was half out the back window: "It's *Gridley,* damnit. And remember that child's *polyarthritus rheumatica.*" Then he slammed the window, and squirrels and pigeons took flight.

"Watch me," Grandfather raised his right hand, from which the American flag peeped forth, at approximately ten o'clock; his left, clutching unshelled peanuts, held firm at three. "This is *Y,* Andrew. Commit it to memory. You never know when it may come in handy."

"Got it, Grand." And Andrew heard the salvoes of the guns.

"Where are you, boy? Come out from under those vines. You're supposed to be on the flag deck."

In the crotch of the pear tree there was room for a signalman. There, while the bees (that father called *multitudinous* with the emphasis he reserved for certain words) tumbled up from the fallen pears. Andrew held on, and his eyes filled with pride as Grand snapped to an *O.* "That's an *O,* boy, an *O.* Never forget it." He didn't. He tried the signal, and there was a breathless minute when he almost pitched from the tree, while through his legs he saw Grandfather, his hands outstretched and angled up, like St. Peter crucified upside-down at St. Philomena's. *"U,"* Grandfather shouted; "*U.* Never forget it." Then Mother came to the door, and it was supper time, when there were always plenty of cucumbers because the vines had gotten away from Grandfather this year and roamed wantonly over the front porch railing.

After supper, while Mother and Father did the dishes, they were to catch a cricket in the cage that Grand had gotten for Andrew's birthday, but Grandfather thought it best to put that off to another day. "I want to show you, 'And', the uniform I wore with Dewey at Manila."

There was a familiar noise that could best be described as a growl from Father's throat, and Mother said: "Now, now, Drew." Grandfather looked archly around at them all and crooked a finger at Andrew. "Go ahead, dear," Mother said; "go up with Grand, and we'll have some of the cake that's left when you come down."

The back stairs wound to the second floor, and Grand and Andrew were halfway up when Father said *"cockamanie."*

"Go on, Grand. I'll just be a minute." Andrew came back and sat on the fourth step, just beyond the corkscrew turn in the stairs.

"What'll it do to the child when he discovers it's all *cockamanie,*" his Father was saying. Andrew puffed his lips to get them around the word. Father was doing crossword puzzles again.

When Father did crosswords the family was in for a hard time. "Damnit," Father would say, "how could that escape me?" It affected his digestion. And then, after he'd discovered the word, and used it religiously for a week or so, perhaps he'd forget its definition. So that if Andrew asked him, he'd groan and clutch his stomach. But sometimes the words were magnificent, and Andrew would try them at school. *Dizzard* had gotten him a reprimand. He still did not know what it meant; his nun's reaction to the epithet inhibited his question, and he dared not ask Father, who had long since gone on to *gowk* and *jabbernowl.* Ordinarily, Mother would simply say: "I can't imagine, dear."

"I don't want the child knocked into a cockamanie."

"I'm sure you mean 'a cocked hat,' Drew." Mother's voice was compounded of the pile of soft blankets on an autumn evening and the cupped palm of Indian Summer sun on his face. Then his Father growled again, and Andrew knew the discussion was at an end.

Just at the second floor landing, outside the door to Grandfather's room, Grand was tapping on the railing: *tap tap* pause *tap tap,* then a long pause while Andrew sat on the steps and listened. *Tap tap tap,* and again a pause. "Listen carefully," Grandfather said; "it's important." *Tap tap bang.* "There it is. If you're going to know semaphore, you might as well know Morse. That was *Y-O-U.* The first word of that memorable message: 'You may fire when you are ready, Girdley.' We'll learn the rest later—but keep that in mind." There was an old wood smell to the stairs, as though the sunlight had never reached them and time was pausing there. The presences of Grandfather's house were all about him. And Andrew could hear the inexorable statement of the railway clock in Grandfather's room, that never rang, but added second to second without emphasis, and sometimes frightened him because it seemed the beating of his heart, and he'd think of his heart swaying back and forth on a frail string and then it would thunder a warning in his ears.

"Come on up, child," Grandfather said. And Andrew came up under his arm. "That Morse, now; I could do it with the shade. Up and down, with a long pause for the dash. Not right now, though. That shade needs adjustment. I've been kind of busy—haven't gotten around to it. Just now, it doesn't come down."

There were books in all corners of the room. Over a rolltop desk (that didn't exactly work because Grandfather had misplaced the key) were the two volumes of the *Oxford English Dictionary* that Grandfather had gotten for five dollars at the Salvation Army, and that Father used when he came to Grandfather's. In fact, that was probably why he was in Grandfather's room when the matter of Gridley arose. Grandfather couldn't use the dictionary because it was fourteen volumes reduced to two, and a magnifying glass was necessary to read the print and Grandfather hadn't gotten around to getting one. Father's eyes were sharp.

"Grand," Andrew said, "tell me about all of them again . . . ," he leaned his chin on the mahogany table where daguerreotypes and yellowing photographs were displayed. "Well, yes, I will," Grandfather said, "but there's something more important. I have a surprise. Did I say I'm going to show you the uniform I wore with Dewey at Manila? On the very bridge where the signal was given: 'You may fire when you are ready'? Yes, I had the real signal flags in my hands then—the Real McCoy."

"Gosh," Andrew said.

Sometimes his friends made fun of him. There were those words Grandfather had taught him, not quite like Father's words: *gosh, the Real McCoy,* even *magic lantern*—and Grandfather had one of those in his closet. It didn't work (the lens had gotten misplaced): Grandfather said it was mice, but no one at St. Philomena's Grammar School had heard of it anyway. And no one had heard of Manila either, but Andrew had seen pictures in the huge blue dog-eared two volume history of the Spanish American War on Grandfather's table, and he had thought from certain hints that Grand had charged up San Juan Hill with Teddy Roosevelt. So it came as a surprise, but not an unpleasant one, that—all those years ago—his own Grandfather had served in the Great White Fleet, flag-draped and smoke-crowned, and ghostly as the dreams that awaited him on the edge of sleep. These were things he could not tell his friends, if only because of Grand's C.I.A. Connections.

"The Real McCoy," Andrew came over under his Grandfather's arm; "gosh."

"I've been saving this," Grandfather said. "I've been saving it until you could appreciate it." There was a cedar chest across from the foot of his four-poster, brass bound and brass locked, and the last secret place in the house that Andrew had not seen. It was a promise unfulfilled.

"Nine," Grandfather said; "that's a good time, a right time," and he sat on the bed to catch his breath.

"Does it hurt, Grand?"

"Sometimes." Grandfather's hand trembled as he pulled it from under his sweater and over the place where the Jezail bullet had entered his shoulder when he served with his friend Dr. Watson in the Second Afghan War. "But it's nothing that time won't cure."

Andrew understood. Sometimes he could feel it too, when his chest grew tight and there didn't seem to be enough air for everyone; and sometimes when his head grew hot and he had to rest, and there were dangers of fearful dreams if he let himself sleep, he knew what it must have been like in the Black Hole of Calcutta and on those dark ships to Van Dieman's Land.

"First," Grandfather used his arms again to thrust himself erect, "we want to go through it all again: semaphore and Morse—a Navy man must know them both." He sat down heavily: "You go across the room. Let's see it again. *Y . . . O . . . U . . .*" And Grandfather corrected him from his seat on the bed. "Good. This is just the beginning, you remember. Now Morse—tap it out with that slipper on the turret," and he pointed to the wooden castle that he'd started three years ago for Andrew, but that had gotten bogged down when he needed a certain type of sandpaper. *Tap tap . . . tap tap . . . tap tap tap . . . tap bang.* "Fine, fine. You've got a memory like a steel trap. You'll be on the bridge of a cruiser in no time. Perhaps we'd better skip ahead a bit. You've got to know S.O.S. Now tap this out: *dot dot dot . . . dash dash dash . . . dot dot dot . . .* We'll work on the semaphore later." He reached out a long arm and pulled himself to the bed post and then to his feet: "The *piece d'resistance,* now . . . ." But a fit of coughing sent him back on the bed again.

"Shall I get Mother, Grand?"

"Of course not. It's just a touch of that malaria I got in the Solomons, coastwatching. Open that Maiori box on the bureau."

"Maiori?"

"Native New Zealanders—it's a gift from a Chief."

Andrew pulled Grandfather's stool over to the bureau and delicately opened the box. He had seen something resembling it in the Five and Ten in Wallingford, but an imitation just wasn't the real thing. He felt the rough edge of jungle and the prick of spears. Inside was a pair of cufflinks, a shoehorn, a tiepin, two liberty-head nickles, a frayed Mass card, and a large brass key.

"The key," Grandfather said; "bring it here."

It was as large as his hand, and Andrew could believe in its secrets.

"Now what I'm going to show you is going to be yours someday." Grandfather paused and coughed a bit and was silent. Then: "This is to be kept just between us. Thieves, you know—and envious people."

"Gosh."

Grandfather lifted his hand and his long, bent forefinger toward the bay window. "That's it." The cedar chest was wedged in the bay between the three-legged table with the empty goldfish bowl (Grandfather had had other things on his mind while the water evaporated last winter), and the radiator that always in Andrew's imagination hissed and bubbled on the verge of leaping, barely restrained, like one of the hooting, brass-stacked engines on the B & O that Grand had driven in his youth.

"Can I turn the key?" Andrew held it up to the light like a monocle. "Can I?" The sun nicked its edges.

"I was about to suggest it." Grandfather settled back in a fit of coughing. "Open it carefully and wait for me."

The lid squeaked up on a brass hinge, and Andrew felt the presences about him again. There was an odd, clean, woodsy, weathered smell—heavy with the scent of Grandmother and her voluminous clothes; and he looked up, startled, into Grandfather's eyes that saw what he saw too. The room was filled with her presence, and she was no longer out there across the river where the early autumn sigh of wind tumbled leaves over the stones, and where sometimes Mother took him and stood as though there was something she had forgotten that a long look inward would reveal.

Grandfather said, very quietly: "Help me up, Andrew." He had never seemed so old to Andrew as when he knelt by the cedar chest. It was labor for him to lift out the layers of clothes.

"These were Mother's, Andrew," he said. "Handle them with care."

There was a white dress, intricately trimmed in lace.

"Did Grandma wear this?"

"This was your Grandmother's wedding dress." Grandfather spoke as though he had swallowed his voice. Then a strange, shiny black suit with velvet lapels; a very small, white First Communion gown; a pair of ballet shoes; a May crown of lace with withered flowers; a private soldier's fatigue cap from World War I; a veil spotted with tiny lavender knots . . . .

"Ah," said Grandfather.

It was magnificent. First, on top of the dark blue uniform and the red velvet sash, was the sword, and the silver scabbard, and on top of the sword the long hat, pointed fore and aft, and crowned with a sweeping white plume.

"A sword!" Andrew wondered if he could continue to breathe. On the pommel of the sword, and on the left breast of the scarlet-lined cape, in gold and red and blue and white, were the letters *K of C*, and Andrew knew that these were a part of the Navy code that Admiral Dewey had used to conquer the Spanish Fleet at Manila. He drew his finger under the *K of C* on the pommel of the sword and spelled out *St. Phil. Chapter*. "Is this part of the code, Grand?" His voice cracked with awe.

"Right," Grand said; "right. It's our secret. Now you know where to come and what is yours."

"The sword and all?"

"Yes, And. Sword and all." Grandfather slowly lowered the lid: "But we're surrounded by assassins, and we must be careful." Then, as though he had prepared for Andrew yet a fresh surprise, he gasped and fell to the floor.

Andrew slid down the last four steps, and Mother and Father were gentler than they had ever been with him as Grandfather was lifted by the strange men and taken away.

The next day they came back ("to get Grand's things," Father said). Mother had been too upset the night before, and Father had been upset because Mother was upset. They passed the hospital on the way, across the river and only two blocks from their home. Andrew strained to see Grandfather at the window there, but Mother said that he was likely to be in bed. "Maybe the shade doesn't work," Andrew said. Back home Father had said something about *"hematoma"* but Andrew knew that he was at crosswords again.

"We'll see him every day, And," Mother said.

"I'll take him the semaphore flag. Grand is teaching me semaphore and Morse."

"Yes," Father said. "Fine." He cleared his throat: "but you must not expect to see him for a while. Just now only adults can be admitted. He can't stand any excitement."

"I'm not excitement," Andrew said.

"Yes. Well, that's the way it is," and Father raced the motor and pulled out belligerently into traffic.

At Grand's, Father discovered that he had forgotten the key. So they went from window to window, trying them all. Finally, Father had to break a cellar pane, and then they got in. But the house was awfully quiet, and there was no heat in the kitchen where Grandfather depended on the stove because the President had asked him to save energy, or in the parlor where he burned mostly wood brought from India long ago in the clippers, or in his room that had one of the very first electric heaters devised by Thomas A. Edison himself.

While Mother and Father packed odds and ends into a PAN-AM flight bag, Andrew stood at the window from which Grandfather had watched a runaway slave sneak up the back street in the old days. A squirrel sat in the crown of the dogwood that tapped the window, and ate berries redder than the lining of Grandfather's cape in the cedar chest. Andrew guarded the Maiori box and the chest out of the corner of his eye. There were some things even his parents couldn't know about, but they didn't seem interested and instead worried because they couldn't find a medicare card. Then they would have forgotten Grandfather's slippers with the toe out, but Andrew brought them to Father who said: "There's no . . . ," and then stopped and said: "Thank you, Andrew; Grandfather will need these." That was the first time Andrew had heard Father call 'Grand' Grandfather.

The days without Grand were strange. There had not been a week since Grandmother's death when they had not, two or three times, crossed the river to the old house, and when Father had not groaned and done his crosswords. But two weeks passed without And seeing the old house, and then his mother said: "Grandfather is sitting up in bed."

"I have to hand it to him," Father said; "he's perdurable."

"Can I see Grand today?" Andrew had trouble with the words; there was a place so large he seemed to wander in, so empty—though he never moved except between St. Philomena's Grammar School and the tidy split-level where his parents lived—that he felt as he had once when he was spun away, alone, on one of the whirling amusements at Fairaway. "Can I see Grand, Mother?"

"We'll walk to the hospital, and you can wait across the street in the playground. I'm sorry, son, but he can only see your Mother now." Father pulled his head against his chest and was kind. But there were so many things to be done; the fire to be built in Grandfather's yard for Tedyuscum of the Lenapes, should he return; the almond cake to be placed on Grandfather's mantel for St. Nicholas; the candle for the spirits at All Souls. How could he do all this himself? Andrew sat in his room and hunched his shoulders and wondered where he could turn.

Then they went to the hospital, Andrew for the first time.

"Wait for us here," Mother said. "You can play on the slides, and it's fun to push that merry-go-round. There'll be other children here. We'll tell Grandfather where you are and that you're thinking of him. We'll be right back; Mother is only allowed to stay a moment." Then she stopped beside Andrew: "Look, that room just above the entrance is his."

The hospital windows were glinting at the edges like Grandfather's great key, and Andrew felt the lowering sun warm on his back as he peered to see Grand at that window above all others. Because it was Daylight Saving (and Grandfather's letter to the Governor had helped save Daylight for once and all) the lights did not begin to show until Andrew saw Mother and Father crossing the street, coming back toward the playground. They were almost up to him when the light went on in Grandfather's room . . . and off and on again and off . . . His Father bridled, and said something about *"cantankerous."* But Andrew strained forward like a runner, though it was his heart that was reaching at the end of its frail string: "Look, look!" And he formed the letters silently on his lips: *S . . . O . . . S, S . . . O . . . S, S . . . O . . . S . . .*

"For heaven's sake, now what? Well, Grand's their problem." His Father's voice was really not unkind, and he and Mother almost smiled as they walked away.

Then Father turned: "Mother! Will you kindly tell me what's *animating* that child?"

Andrew's right arm was at approximately ten o'clock; his left, held firm at three. And while his father pointed and sighed, the arms moved, desperately: *Y . . . O . . . U, Y . . . O . . . U, Y . . . O . . . U . . .*

Raymond Carver (1939–1988)

CATHEDRAL

This blind man, an old friend of my wife's, he was on his way to spend the night. His wife had died. So he was visiting the dead wife's relatives in Connecticut. He called my wife from his in-laws'. Arrangements were made. He would come by train, a five-hour trip, and my wife would meet him at the station. She hadn't seen him since she worked for him one summer in Seattle ten years ago. But she and the blind man had kept in touch. They made tapes and mailed them back and forth. I wasn't enthusiastic about his visit. He was no one I knew. And his being blind bothered me. My idea of blindness came from the movies. In the movies, the blind moved slowly and never laughed. Sometimes they were led by seeing-eye dogs. A blind man in my house was not something I looked forward to.

That summer in Seattle she had needed a job. She didn't have any money. The man she was going to marry at the end of the summer was in officers' training school. He didn't have any money, either. But she was in love with the guy, and he was in love with her, etc. She'd seen something in the paper: HELP WANTED—*Reading to Blind Man,* and a telephone number. She phoned and went over, was hired on the spot. She'd worked with this blind man all summer. She read stuff to him, case studies, reports, that sort of thing. She helped him organize his little office in the county social-service department. They'd become good friends, my wife and the blind man. How do I know these things? She told me. And she told me something else. On her last day in the office, the blind man asked if he could touch her face. She agreed to this. She told me he touched his fingers to every part of her face, her nose—even her neck! She never forgot it. She even tried to write a poem about it. She was always trying to write a poem. She wrote a poem or two every year, usually after something really important had happened to her.

When we first started going out together, she showed me the poem. In the poem, she recalled his fingers and the way they had moved around over her face. In the poem, she talked about what she had felt at the time, about what went through her mind when the blind man touched her nose and lips. I can remember I didn't think much of the poem. Of course, I didn't tell her that. Maybe I just don't understand poetry. I admit it's not the first thing I reach for when I pick up something to read.

Anyway, this man who'd first enjoyed her favors, the officer-to-be, he'd been her childhood sweetheart. So okay. I'm saying that at the end of the summer she let the blind man run his hands over her face, said goodbye to him, married her childhood etc., who was now a commissioned officer, and she moved away from Seattle. But they'd kept in touch, she and the blind man. She made the first contact after a year or so. She called him up one night from an Air Force base in Alabama. She wanted to talk. They talked. He asked her to send him a tape and tell him about her life. She did this. She sent the tape. On the tape, she told the blind man about her husband and about their life together in the military. She told the blind man she loved her husband but she didn't like it where they lived and she didn't like it that he was a part of the military-industrial thing. She told the blind man she'd written a poem and he was in it. She told him that she was writing a poem about what it was like to be an Air Force officer's wife. The poem wasn't finished yet. She was still writing it. The blind man made a tape. He sent her the tape. She made a tape. This went on for years. My wife's officer was posted to one base and then another. She sent tapes from Moody AFB, McGuire, McConnell, and finally Travis, near Sacramento, where one night she got to feeling lonely and cut off from people she kept losing in that moving-around life. She got to feeling she couldn't go it another step. She went in and swallowed all the pills and capsules in the medicine chest and washed them down with a bottle of gin. Then she got into a hot bath and passed out.

But instead of dying, she got sick. She threw up. Her officer—why should he have a name? he was the childhood sweetheart, and what more does he want?—came home from somewhere, found her, and called the ambulance. In time, she put it all on a tape and sent the tape to the blind man. Over the years, she put all kinds of stuff on tapes and sent the tapes off lickety-split. Next to writing a poem every year, I think it was her chief means of recreation. On one tape, she told the blind man she'd decided to live away from her officer for a time. On another tape, she told him about her divorce. She and I began going out, and of course she told her blind man about it. She told him everything, or so it seemed to me. Once she asked me if I'd like to hear the latest tape from the blind man. This was a year ago. I was on the tape, she said. So I said okay, I'd listen to it. I got us drinks and we settled down in the living room. We made ready to listen. First she inserted the tape into the player and adjusted a couple of dials. Then she pushed a lever. The tape squeaked and someone began to talk in this loud voice. She lowered the volume. After a few minutes of harmless chitchat, I heard my own name in the mouth of this stranger, this blind man I didn't even know! And then this: "From all you've said about him, I can only conclude—" But we were interrupted, a knock at the door, something, and we didn't ever get back to the tape. Maybe it was just as well. I'd heard all I wanted to.

Now this same blind man was coming to sleep in my house.

"Maybe I could take him bowling," I said to my wife. She was at the draining board doing scalloped potatoes. She put down the knife she was using and turned around.

"If you love me," she said, "you can do this for me. If you don't love me, okay. But if you had a friend, any friend, and the friend came to visit, I'd make him feel comfortable." She wiped her hands with the dish towel.

"I don't have any blind friends," I said.

"You don't have *any* friends," she said. "Period. Besides," she said, "god-damn it, his wife's just died! Don't you understand that? The man's lost his wife!"

I didn't answer. She'd told me a little about the blind man's wife. Her name was Beulah, Beulah! That's a name for a colored woman.

"Was his wife a Negro?" I asked.

"Are you crazy?" my wife said. "Have you just flipped or something?" She picked up a potato. I saw it hit the floor, then roll under the stove. "What's wrong with you?" she said. "Are you drunk?"

"I'm just asking," I said.

Right then my wife filled me in with more detail than I cared to know. I made a drink and sat at the kitchen table to listen. Pieces of the story began to fall into place.

Beulah had gone to work for the blind man the summer after my wife had stopped working for him. Pretty soon Beulah and the blind man had themselves a church wedding. It was a little wedding—who'd want to go to such a wedding in the first place?—just the two of them, plus the minister and the minister's wife. But it was a church wedding just the same. It was what Beulah had wanted, he'd said. But even then Beulah must have been carrying the cancer in her glands. After they had been inseparable for eight years—my wife's word, *inseparable*—Beulah's health went into a rapid decline. She died in a Seattle hospital room, the blind man sitting beside the bed and holding on to her hand. They'd married, lived and worked together, slept together—had sex, sure—and then the blind man had to bury her. All this without his having ever seen what the goddamned woman looked like. It was beyond my understanding. Hearing this, I felt sorry for the blind man for a little bit. And then I found myself thinking what a pitiful life this woman must have led. Imagine a woman who could never see herself as she was seen in the eyes of her loved one. A woman who could go on day after day and never receive the smallest compliment from her beloved. A woman whose husband could never read the expression on her face, be it misery or something better. Someone who could wear makeup or not—what difference to him? She could, if she wanted, wear green eyeshadow around one eye, a straight pin in her nostril, yellow slacks and purple shoes, no matter. And then to slip off into death, the blind man's hand on her hand, his blind eyes streaming tears—I'm imagining now—her last thought maybe this: that he never even knew what she looked like, and she on an express to the grave. Robert was left with a small insurance policy and half of a twenty-peso Mexican coin. The other half of the coin went into the box with her. Pathetic.

So when the time rolled around, my wife went to the depot to pick him up. With nothing to do but wait—sure, I blamed him for that—I was having a drink and watching the TV when I heard the car pull into the drive. I got up from the sofa with my drink and went to the window to have a look.

I saw my wife laughing as she parked the car. I saw her get out of the car and shut the door. She was still wearing a smile. Just amazing. She went around to the other side of the car to where the blind man was already starting to get out. This blind man, feature this, he was wearing a full beard! A beard on a blind man! Too much, I say. The blind man reached into the back seat and dragged out a suitcase. My wife took his arm, shut the car door, and, talking all the way, moved him down the drive and then up the steps to the front porch. I turned off the TV. I finished my drink, rinsed the glass, dried my hands. Then I went to the door.

My wife said, "I want you to meet Robert. Robert, this is my husband. I've told you all about him." She was beaming. She had this blind man by his coat sleeve.

The blind man let go of his suitcase and up came his hand.

I took it. He squeezed hard, held my hand, and then he let it go.

"I feel like we've already met," he boomed.

"Likewise," I said. I didn't know what else to say. Then I said, "Welcome. I've heard a lot about you." We began to move then, a little group, from the porch into the living room, my wife guiding him by the arm. The blind man was carrying his suitcase in his other hand. My wife said things like, "To your left here, Robert. That's right. Now watch it, there's a chair. That's it. Sit down right here. This is the sofa. We just bought this sofa two weeks ago."

I started to say something about the old sofa. I'd liked that old sofa. But I didn't say anything. Then I wanted to say something else, small-talk, about the scenic ride along the Hudson. How going *to* New York, you should sit on the right-hand side of the train, and coming *from* New York, the left-hand side.

"Did you have a good train ride?" I said. "Which side of the train did you sit on, by the way?"

"What a question, which side!" my wife said. "What's it matter which side?" she said.

"I just asked," I said.

"Right side," the blind man said. "I hadn't been on a train in nearly forty years. Not since I was a kid. With my folks. That's been a long time. I'd nearly forgotten the sensation. I have winter in my beard now," he said. "So I've been told, anyway. Do I look distinguished, my dear?" the blind man said to my wife.

"You look distinguished, Robert," she said. "Robert," she said. "Robert, it's just so good to see you."

My wife finally took her eyes off the blind man and looked at me. I had the feeling she didn't like what she saw. I shrugged.

I've never met, or personally known, anyone who was blind. This blind man was late forties, a heavy-set, balding man with stooped shoulders, as if he carried great weight there. He wore brown slacks, brown shoes, a light-brown shirt, a tie, a sports coat. Spiffy. He also had this full beard. But he didn't use a cane and he didn't wear dark glasses. I'd always thought dark glasses were a must for the blind. Fact was, I wished he had a pair. At first glance, his eyes looked like anyone else's eyes. But if you looked close, there was something different about them. Too much white in the iris, for one thing, and the pupils seemed to move around in the sockets without his knowing it or being able to stop it. Creepy. As I stared at his face, I saw the left pupil turn in toward his nose while the other made an effort to keep in one place. But it was only an effort, for that eye was on the roam without his knowing it or wanting it to be.

I said, "Let me get you a drink. What's your pleasure? We have a little of everything. It's one of our pastimes."

"Bub, I'm a Scotch man myself," he said fast enough in this big voice.

"Right," I said. Bub! "Sure you are. I knew it."

He let his fingers touch his suitcase, which was sitting alongside the sofa. He was taking his bearings. I didn't blame him for that.

"I'll move that up to your room," my wife said.

"No, that's fine," the blind man said loudly. "It can go up when I go up."

"A little water with the Scotch?" I said.

"Very little," he said.

"I knew it," I said.

He said, "Just a tad. The Irish actor, Barry Fitzgerald? I'm like that fellow. When I drink water, Fitzgerald said, I drink water. When I drink whiskey, I drink whiskey." My wife laughed. The blind man brought his hand up under his beard. He lifted his beard slowly and let it drop.

I did the drinks, three big glasses of Scotch with a splash of water in each. Then we made ourselves comfortable and talked about Robert's travels. First the long flight from the West Coast to Connecticut, we covered that. Then from Connecticut up here by train. We had another drink concerning that leg of the trip.

I remembered having read somewhere that the blind didn't smoke because, as speculation had it, they couldn't see the smoke they exhaled. I thought I knew that much and that much only about blind people. But this blind man smoked his cigarette down to the nubbin and then lit another one. This blind man filled his ashtray and my wife emptied it.

When we sat down at the table for dinner, we had another drink. My wife heaped Robert's plate with cube steak, scalloped potatoes, green beans. I buttered him up two slices of bread. I said, "Here's bread and butter for you." I swallowed some of my drink. "Now let us pray," I said, and the blind man lowered his head. My wife looked at me, her mouth agape. "Pray the phone won't ring and the food doesn't get cold," I said.

We dug in. We ate everything there was to eat on the table. We ate like there was no tomorrow. We didn't talk. We ate. We scarfed. We grazed that table. We were into serious eating. The blind man had right away located his foods, he knew just where everything was on his plate. I watched with admiration as he used his knife and fork on the meat. He'd cut two pieces of meat, fork the meat into his mouth, and then go all out for the scalloped potatoes, the beans next, and then he'd tear off a hunk of buttered bread and eat that. He'd follow this up with a big drink of milk. It didn't seem to bother him to use his fingers once in a while, either.

We finished everything, including half a strawberry pie. For a few moments, we sat as if stunned. Sweat beaded on our faces. Finally, we got up from the table and left the dirty plates. We didn't look back. We took ourselves into the living room and sank into our places again. Robert and my wife sat on the sofa. I took the big chair. We had us two or three more drinks while they talked about the major things that had come to pass for them in the past ten years. For the most part, I just listened. Now and then I joined in. I didn't want him to think I'd left the room, and I didn't want her to think I was feeling left out. They talked of things that had happened to them—to them!—these past ten years. I waited in vain to hear my name on my wife's sweet lips: "And then my dear husband came into my life"—something like that. But I heard nothing of the sort. More talk of Robert. Robert had done a little of everything, it seemed, a regular blind jack-of-all-trades. But most recently he and his wife had had an Amway distributorship, from which, I gathered, they'd earned their living, such as it was. The blind man was also a ham radio operator. He talked in his loud voice about conversations he'd had with fellow operators in Guam, in the Philippines, in Alaska, and even in Tahiti. He said he'd have a lot of friends there if he ever wanted to go visit those places. From time to time, he'd turn his blind face toward me, put his hand under his beard, ask me something. How long had I been in my present position? (Three years.) Did I like my work? (I didn't.) Was I going to stay with it? (What were the options?) Finally, when I thought he was beginning to run down, I got up and turned on the TV.

My wife looked at me with irritation. She was heading toward a boil. Then she looked at the blind man and said, "Robert, do you have a TV?"

The blind man said, "My dear, I have two TVs. I have a color set and a black-and-white thing, an old relic. It's funny, but if I turn the TV on, and I'm always turning it on, I turn on the color set. It's funny, don't you think?"

I didn't know what to say to that. I had absolutely nothing to say to that. No opinion. So I watched the news program and tried to listen to what the announcer was saying.

"This is a color TV," the blind man said. "Don't ask me how, but I can tell."

"We traded up a while ago," I said.

The blind man had another taste of his drink. He lifted his beard, sniffed it, and let it fall. He leaned forward on the sofa. He positioned his ashtray on the coffee table, then put the lighter to his cigarette. He leaned back on the sofa and crossed his legs at the ankles.

My wife covered her mouth, and then she yawned. She stretched. She said, "I think I'll go upstairs and put on my robe. I think I'll change into something else. Robert, you make yourself comfortable," she said.

"I'm comfortable," the blind man said.

"I want you to feel comfortable in this house," she said.

"I am comfortable," the blind man said.

After she'd left the room, he and I listened to the weather report and then to the sports roundup. By that time, she'd been gone so long I didn't know if she was going to come back. I thought she might have gone to bed. I wished she'd come back downstairs. I didn't want to be left alone with a blind man. I asked him if he wanted another drink, and he said sure. Then I asked if he wanted to smoke some dope with me. I said I'd just rolled a number. I hadn't, but I planned to do so in about two shakes.

"I'll try some with you," he said.

"Damn right," I said. "That's the stuff."

I got our drinks and sat down on the sofa with him. Then I rolled us two fat numbers. I lit one and passed it. I brought it to his fingers. He took it and inhaled.

"Hold it as long as you can," I said. I could tell he didn't know the first thing.

My wife came back downstairs wearing her pink robe and her pink slippers.

"What do I smell?" she said.

"We thought we'd have us some cannabis," I said.

My wife gave me a savage look. Then she looked at the blind man and said, "Robert, I didn't know you smoked."

He said, "I do now, my dear. There's a first time for everything. But I don't feel anything yet."

"This stuff is pretty mellow," I said. "This stuff is mild. It's dope you can reason with," I said. "It doesn't mess you up."

"Not much it doesn't, bub," he said, and laughed.

My wife sat on the sofa between the blind man and me. I passed her the number. She took it and toked and then passed it back to me. "Which way is this going?" she said. Then she said, "I shouldn't be smoking this. I can hardly keep my eyes open as it is. That dinner did me in. I shouldn't have eaten so much."

"It was the strawberry pie," the blind man said. "That's what did it," he said, and he laughed his big laugh. Then he shook his head.

"There's more strawberry pie," I said.

"Do you want some more, Robert?" my wife said.

"Maybe in a little while," he said.

We gave our attention to the TV. My wife yawned again. She said, "Your bed is made up when you feel like going to bed, Robert. I know you must have had a long day. When you're ready to go to bed, say so." She pulled his arm. "Robert?"

He came to and said, "I've had a real nice time. This beats tapes, doesn't it?"

I said, "Coming at you," and I put the number between his fingers. He inhaled, held the smoke, and then let it go. It was like he'd been doing it since he was nine years old.

"Thanks, bub," he said. "But I think this is all for me. I think I'm beginning to feel it," he said. He held the burning roach out for my wife.

"Same here," she said. "Ditto. Me, too." She took the roach and passed it to me. "I may just sit here for a while between you two guys with my eyes closed. But don't let me bother you, okay? Either one of you. If it bothers you, say so. Otherwise, I may just sit here with my eyes closed until you're ready to go to bed," she said. "Your bed's made up, Robert, when you're ready. It's right next to our room at the top of the stairs. We'll show you up when you're ready. You wake me up now, you guys, if I fall asleep." She said that and then she closed her eyes and went to sleep.

The news program ended. I got up and changed the channel. I sat back down on the sofa. I wished my wife hadn't pooped out. Her head lay across the back of the sofa, her mouth open. She'd turned so that her robe had slipped away from her legs, exposing a juicy thigh. I reached to draw her robe back over her, and it was then that I glanced at the blind man. What the hell? I flipped the robe open again.

"You say when you want some strawberry pie," I said.

"I will," he said.

I said, "Are you tired? Do you want me to take you up to your bed? Are you ready to hit the hay?"

"Not yet," he said. "No, I'll stay up with you, bub. If that's all right. I'll stay up until you're ready to turn in. We haven't had a chance to talk. Know what I mean? I feel like me and her monopolized the evening." He lifted his beard and he let it fall. He picked up his cigarettes and his lighter.

"That's all right," I said. Then I said, "I'm glad for the company."

And I guess I was. Every night I smoked dope and stayed up as long as I could before I fell asleep. My wife and I hardly ever went to bed at the same time. When I did go to sleep, I had these dreams. Sometimes I'd wake up from one of them, my heart going crazy.

Something about the church and the Middle Ages was on the TV. Not your run-of-the-mill TV fare. I wanted to watch something else. I turned to the other channels. But there was nothing on them, either. So I turned back to the first channel and apologized.

"Bub, it's all right," the blind man said. "It's fine with me. Whatever you want to watch is okay. I'm always learning something. Learning never ends. It won't hurt me to learn something tonight. I got ears," he said.

We didn't say anything for a time. He was leaning forward with his head turned at me, his right ear aimed in the direction of the set. Very disconcerting. Now and then his eyelids drooped and then they snapped open again. Now and then he put his fingers into his beard and tugged, like he was thinking about something he was hearing on the television.

On the screen, a group of men wearing cowls was being set upon and tormented by men dressed in skeleton costumes and men dressed as devils. The men dressed as devils wore devil masks, horns, and long tails. This pageant was part of a procession. The Englishman who was narrating the thing said it took place in Spain once a year. I tried to explain to the blind man what was happening.

"Skeletons," he said. "I know about skeletons," he said, and he nodded.

The TV showed this one cathedral. Then there was a long, slow look at another one. Finally, the picture switched to the famous one in Paris, with its flying buttresses and its spires reaching up to the clouds. The camera pulled away to show the whole of the cathedral rising above the skyline.

There were times when the Englishman who was telling the thing would shut up, would simply let the camera move around over the cathedrals. Or else the camera would tour the countryside, men in fields walking behind oxen. I waited as long as I could. Then I felt I had to say something. I said, "They're showing the outside of this cathedral now. Gargoyles. Little statues carved to look like monsters. Now I guess they're in Italy. Yeah, they're in Italy. There's paintings on the walls of this one church."

"Are those fresco paintings, bub?" he asked, and he sipped from his drink.

I reached for my glass. But it was empty. I tried to remember what I could remember. "You're asking me are those frescoes?" I said. "That's a good question. I don't know."

The camera moved to a cathedral outside Lisbon. The differences in the Portuguese cathedral compared with the French and Italian were not that great. But they were there. Mostly the interior stuff. Then something occurred to me, and I said, "Something has occurred to me. Do you have any idea what a cathedral is? What they look like, that is? Do you follow me? If somebody says cathedral to you, do you have any notion what they're talking about? Do you know the difference between that and a Baptist church, say?"

He let the smoke dribble from his mouth. "I know they took hundreds of workers fifty or a hundred years to build," he said. "I just heard the man say that, of course. I know generations of the same families worked on a cathedral. I heard him say that, too. The men who began their life's work on them, they never lived to see the completion of their work. In that wise, bub, they're no different from the rest of us, right?" He laughed. Then his eyelids drooped again. His head nodded. He seemed to be snoozing. Maybe he was imagining himself in Portugal. The TV was showing another cathedral now. This one was in Germany. The Englishman's voice droned on. "Cathedrals," the blind man said. He sat up and rolled his head back and forth. "If you want the truth, bub, that's about all I know.

What I just said. What I heard him say. But maybe you could describe one to me? I wish you'd do it. I'd like that. If you want to know, I really don't have a good idea."

I stared hard at the shot of the cathedral on the TV. How could I even begin to describe it? But say my life depended on it. Say my life was being threatened by an insane guy who said I had to do it or else.

I stared some more at the cathedral before the picture flipped off into the countryside. There was no use. I turned to the blind man and said, "To begin with, they're very tall." I was looking around the room for clues. "They reach way up. Up and up. Toward the sky. They're so big, some of them, they have to have these supports. To help hold them up, so to speak. These supports are called buttresses. They remind me of viaducts, for some reason. But maybe you don't know viaducts, either? Sometimes the cathedrals have devils and such carved into the front. Sometimes lords and ladies. Don't ask me why this is," I said.

He was nodding. The whole upper part of his body seemed to be moving back and forth.

"I'm not doing so good, am I?" I said.

He stopped nodding and leaned forward on the edge of the sofa. As he listened to me, he was running his fingers through his beard. I wasn't getting through to him, I could see that. But he waited for me to go on just the same. He nodded, like he was trying to encourage me. I tried to think what else to say. "They're really big," I said. "They're massive. They're built of stone. Marble, too, sometimes. In those olden days, when they built cathedrals, men wanted to be close to God. In those olden days, God was an important part of everyone's life. You could tell this from their cathedral-building. I'm sorry," I said, "but it looks like that's the best I can do for you. I'm just no good at it."

"That's all right, bub," the blind man said. "Hey, listen. I hope you don't mind my asking you: Can I ask you something? Let me ask you a simple question, yes or no. I'm just curious and there's no offense. You're my host. But let me ask if you are in any way religious? You don't mind my asking?"

I shook my head. He couldn't see that, though. A wink is the same as a nod to a blind man. "I guess I don't believe in it. In anything. Sometimes it's hard. You know what I'm saying?"

"Sure, I do," he said.

"Right," I said.

The Englishman was still holding forth. My wife sighed in her sleep. She drew a long breath and went on with her sleeping.

"You'll have to forgive me," I said. "But I can't tell you what a cathedral looks like. It just isn't in me to do it. I can't do any more than I've done."

The blind man sat very still, his head down, as he listened to me.

I said, "The truth is, cathedrals don't mean anything special to me. Nothing. Cathedrals. They're something to look at on late-night TV. That's all they are."

It was then that the blind man cleared his throat. He brought something up. He took a handkerchief from his back pocket. Then he said, "I get it, bub. It's okay. It happens. Don't worry about it," he said. "Hey, listen to me. Will you do me a favor? I got an idea. Why don't you find us some heavy paper? And a pen. We'll do something. We'll draw one together. Get us a pen and some heavy paper. Go on, bub, get the stuff," he said.

So I went upstairs. My legs felt like they didn't have any strength in them. They felt like they did after I'd done some running. In my wife's room, I looked around. I found some ballpoints in a little basket on her table. And then I tried to think where to look for the kind of paper he was talking about.

Downstairs, in the kitchen, I found a shopping bag with onion skins in the bottom of the bag. I emptied the bag and shook it. I brought it into the living room and sat down with it near his legs. I moved some things, smoothed the wrinkles from the bag, spread it out on the coffee table.

The blind man got down from the sofa and sat next to me on the carpet.

He ran his fingers over the paper. He went up and down the sides of the paper. The edges, even the edges. He fingered the corners.

"All right," he said. "All right, let's do her."

He found my hand, the hand with the pen. He closed his hand over my hand. "Go ahead, bub, draw," he said. "Draw. You'll see. I'll follow along with you. It'll be okay. Just begin now like I'm telling you. You'll see. Draw," the blind man said.

So I began. First I drew a box that looked like a house. It could have been the house I lived in. Then I put a roof on it. At either end of the roof, I drew spires. Crazy.

"Swell," he said. "Terrific. You're doing fine," he said. "Never thought anything like this could happen in your lifetime, did you, bub? Well, it's a strange life, we all know that. Go on now. Keep it up."

I put in windows with arches. I drew flying buttresses. I hung great doors. I couldn't stop. The TV station went off the air. I put down the pen and closed and opened my fingers. The blind man felt around over the paper. He moved the tips of his fingers over the paper, all over what I had drawn, and he nodded.

"Doing fine," the blind man said.

I took up the pen again, and he found my hand. I kept at it. I'm no artist. But I kept drawing just the same.

My wife opened up her eyes and gazed at us. She sat up on the sofa, her robe hanging open. She said, "What are you doing? Tell me, I want to know."

I didn't answer her.

The blind man said, "We're drawing a cathedral. Me and him are working on it. Press hard," he said to me. "That's right. That's good," he said. "Sure. You got it, bub. I can tell. You didn't think you could. But you can, can't you? You're cooking with gas now. You know what I'm saying? We're going to really have us something here in a minute. How's the old arm?" he said. "Put some people in there now. What's a cathedral without people?"

My wife said, "What's going on? Robert, what are you doing? What's going on?"

"It's all right," he said to her. "Close your eyes now," the blind man said to me.

I did it. I closed them just like he said.

"Are they closed?" he said. "Don't fudge."

"They're closed," I said.

"Keep them that way," he said. He said, "Don't stop now. Draw."

So we kept on with it. His fingers rode my fingers as my hand went over the paper. It was like nothing else in my life up to now.

Then he said, "I think that's it. I think you got it," he said. "Take a look. What do you think?"

But I had my eyes closed. I thought I'd keep them that way for a little longer. I thought it was something I ought to do.

"Well?" he said. "Are you looking?"

My eyes were still closed. I was in my house. I knew that. But I didn't feel like I was inside anything.

"It's really something," I said.

Bobbie Ann Mason (b. 1940)

A NEW-WAVE FORMAT

Edwin Creech drives a yellow bus, transporting a group of mentally retarded adults to the Cedar Hill Mental Health Center, where they attend training classes. He is away from 7:00 to 9:30 A.M. and from 2:30 to 5:00 P.M. His hours are so particular that Sabrina Jones, the girl he was been living with for several months, could easily cheat on him. Edwin devises schemes to test her. He places a long string of dental floss on her pillow (an idea he got from a mystery novel), but it remains undisturbed. She is away four nights a week, at rehearsals for *Oklahoma!* with the Western Kentucky Little Theatre, and she often goes out to eat afterward with members of the cast. Sabrina won't let him go to rehearsals, saying she wants the play to be complete when he sees it. At home, she sings and dances along with the movie sound track, and she acts out scenes for him. In the play, she's in the chorus, and she has two lines in Act I, Scene 3. Her lines are "And to yer house a dark clubman!" and "Then out of your dreams you'll go." Edwin loves the dramatic way Sabrina waves her arms on her first line. She is supposed to be a fortune teller.

One evening when Sabrina comes home, Edwin is still up, as she puts on the sound track of *Oklahoma!* and sings along with Gordon MacRae while she does splits on the living room floor. Her legs are long and slender, and she still has her summer tan. She is wearing her shorts, even though it is late fall. Edwin suddenly has an overwhelming feeling of love for her. She really seems to believe what she is singing—"Oh, What a Beautiful Mornin'." When the song ends, he tells her that.

"It's the middle of the night," he says, teasing. "And you think it's morning."

"I'm just acting."

"No, you really believe it. You believe it's morning, a beautiful morning."

Sabrina gives him a fishy look, and Edwin feels embarrassed. When the record ends, Sabrina goes into the bedroom and snaps on the radio. Rock music helps her relax before going to sleep. The new rock music she likes is monotonous and bland, but Edwin tells himself that he likes it because Sabrina likes it. As she undresses, he says to her, "I'm sorry. I wasn't accusing you of nothing."

"That's O.K." She shrugs. The T-shirt she sleeps in has a hole revealing a spot of her skin that Edwin would like to kiss, but he doesn't because it seems like a corny thing to do. So many things about Sabrina are amazing: her fennel toothpaste and herbal deodorant; her slim, snaky hips; the way she puts Vaseline on her teeth for a flashier smile, something she learned to do in a beauty contest.

When she sits on the bed, Edwin says, " If I say the wrong things, I want you to tell me. It's just that I'm so crazy about you I can't think sometimes. But if I can do anything better, I will. I promise. Just tell me."

"I don't think of you as the worrying type," she says, lying down beside him. She still has her shoes on.

"I didn't used to be."

"You're the most laid back guy I know."

"Is that some kind of actor talk from your actor friends?"

"No. You're just real laid back. Usually good-looking guys are so stuck up. But you're not." The music sends vibrations through Edwin like a cat's purr. She says, "I brag on you all the time to Jeff and Sue—Curly and Laurey."

"I know who Jeff and Sue are." Sabrina talks constantly about Jeff and Sue, the romantic leads in the play.

Sabrina says, "Here's what I wish. If we had a big pile of money, we could have a house like Sue's. Did I tell you she's got *woven* blinds on her patio that she made herself? Everything she does is so *artistic*." Sabrina shakes Edwin's shoulder. "Wake up and talk to me."

"I can't. I have to get up at six."

Sabrina whispers to him, "Sue has the hots for Jeff. And Jeff's wife is going to have a duck with a rubber tail if she finds out." Sabrina giggles. "He kept dropping hints about how his wife was going to Louisville next week. And he and Sue were eating off the same slice of pizza."

"Is that supposed to mean something?"

"You figure it out."

"Would you do me that way?"

"Don't be silly." Sabrina turns up the radio, then unties her shoes and tosses them over Edwin's head into a corner.

Edwin is forty-three and Sabrina is only twenty, but he does not want to believe age is a barrier between them. Sometimes he cannot believe his good luck, that he has a beautiful girl who finds him still attractive. Edwin has a deep dimple in his chin, which reminded his first wife, Lois Ann, of Kirk Douglas. She had read in a movie magazine that Kirk Douglas has a special attachment for shaving his dimple. But Sabrina thinks Edwin looks like John Travolta, who also has a dimple. Now and then Edwin realizes how much older he is than Sabrina, but time has passed quickly, and he still feels like the same person, unchanged, that he was twenty years ago. His two ex-wives had seemed to drift away from him, and he never tried to hold them back. But with Sabrina, he knows he must make an effort, for it is beginning to dawn on him that sooner or later women get disillusioned with him. Maybe he's too laid back. But Sabrina likes this quality. Sabrina has large round gray eyes and limp, brownish-blond hair, the color of birch paneling, which she highlights with Miss Clairol. They share a love of Fudgsicles, speedboats, and *WKRP in Cincinnati*. At the beginning, he thought that was enough to build a relationship on, because he knew so many couples who never shared such simple pleasures, but gradually he has begun to see that it is more complicated than that. Sabrina's liveliness makes him afraid that she will be fickle. He can't bear the thought of losing her, and he doesn't like the idea that his new possessiveness may be the same uneasy feeling a man would have for a daughter.

Sabrina's parents sent her to college for a year, but her father, a farmer, lost money on his hogs and couldn't afford to continue. When Edwin met her, she was working as a waitress in a steak house. She wants to go back to college, but Edwin does not have the money to send her either. In college, she learned things that make him feel ignorant around her. She said that in an anthropology course, for instance, she learned for a fact the people evolved from animals. But when he tried to argue with her, she said his doubts were too silly to discuss. Edwin doesn't want to sound like a father, so he usually avoids such topics. Sabrina believes in the ERA, although she likes to keep house. She cooks odd things for him, like eggplant, and a weird lasagna with vegetables. She says she knows how to make a Big Mac from scratch, but she never does. Her specialty is pizza. She puts sliced dill pickles on it, which Edwin doesn't dare question. She likes to do things in what she calls an arty way. Now Sabrina is going out for pizza with people in the Theatre. Sabrina talks of "the Theatre."

Until he began driving the bus, Edwin had never worked closely with people. He worked on an offshore oil rig for a time, but kept his distance from the other men. He drove a bulldozer in a logging camp out West. In Kentucky, during his marriages, he worked in an aluminum products company, an automotive machine shop, and numerous gas stations, going from job to job as casually as he did with women. He used to think of himself as an adventurer, but now he believes he has gone through life rather blindly, without much pain or sense of loss.

When he drives the bus, he feels stirred up, perhaps the way Sabrina feels about *Oklahoma!* The bus is a new luxury model with a tape deck, AM-FM, CB, and built-in first-aid kit. He took a first-aid course, so he feels prepared to handle emergencies. Edwin has to stay alert, for anything could happen. The guys who came back from Vietnam said it was like this every moment. Edwin was in the army, but he was never sent to Vietnam, and now he feels that he has bypassed some critical stage in his life: a knowledge of terror. Edwin has never had this kind of responsibility, and he has never been around mentally retarded people before. His passengers are like bizarre, overgrown children, badly behaved and unpredictable. Some of them stare off into space, others are hyperactive. A woman named Freddie Johnson kicks aimlessly at the seat in front of her, spouting her ten-word vocabulary. She can say, "Hot! Shorts," "*Popeye* on?" "*Dukes* on!" "Cook supper," and "Go bed." She talks continuously. A gangly man with a clubfoot has learned to get Hershey bars from a vending machine, and every day he brings home Hershey bars, clutching them in his hand until he squeezes them out of shape. A pretty blond woman shows Edwin the braces on her teeth every day when she gets on the bus. She gets confused if Edwin brings up another topic. The noises on the bus are chaotic and eerie—spurts, gurgles, yelps, squeals. Gradually, Edwin has learned how to keep his distance and keep order at the same time. He plays tape-recorded music to calm and entertain the passengers. In effect, he has become a disc jockey, taking requests and using the microphone, but he avoids fast talk. The supervisors at the center have told him that the developmentally disabled—they always use this term—need a world that is slowed down; they can't keep up with today's fast pace. So he plays mellow old sixties tunes by the Lovin' Spoonful, Joni Mitchell, Donovan. It seems to work. The passengers have learned to clap or hum along with the music. One man, Merle Cope, has been learning to clap his hands in a body-awareness class. Merle is forty-seven years old, and he walks two miles—in an hour—to the bus stop, down a country road. He climbs onto the bus with agonizing slowness. When he gets on, he makes an exaggerated clapping motion, as if to congratulate himself for having made it, but he never lets his hands quite touch. Merle Cope always has an eager grin on his face, and when he tries to clap his hands he looks ecstatic. He looks happier than Sabrina singing "Oh, What a Beautiful Mornin'."

On Thursday, November 14, Edwin stops at the junction of a state road and a gravel road called Ezra Combs Lane to pick up a new passenger. The country roads have shiny new green signs, with the names of the farmers who originally settled there three or four generations ago. The new passenger is Laura Combs, who he has been told is thirty-seven and has never been to school. She will take classes in Home Management and Living Skills. When she gets on the bus, the people who were with her drive off in a blue Pacer. Laura Combs, a large, angular woman with buckteeth, stomps deliberately down the aisle, then plops down beside a young black man named Ray Watson, who has been riding the bus for about three weeks. Ray has hardly spoken, except to say "Have a nice day" to Edwin when he leaves the bus. Ray, who is mildly retarded from a blow on the head in his childhood, is subject to seizures, but so far he has not had one on the bus. Edwin watches him carefully. He learned about convulsions in his first-aid course.

When Laura Combs sits down by Ray Watson, she shoves him and says, "Scoot over. And cheer up."

Her tone is not cheerful. Edwin watches in the rear-view mirror, ready to act. He glides around a curve and slows down for the next passenger. A tape has ended and Edwin hesitates before inserting another. He hears Ray Watson say, "I never seen anybody as ugly as you."

"Shut up or I'll send you to the back of the bus." Laura Combs speaks with a snappy authority that makes Edwin wonder if she is really retarded. Her hair is streaked gray and yellow, and her face is filled with acne pits.

Ray Watson says, "That's fine with me, long as I don't have to set by you."

"Want me to throw you back in the woodpile where you come from?"

"I bet you could throw me plumb out the door, you so big."

It is several minutes before it is clear to Edwin that they are teasing. He is pleased the Ray is talking, but he can't understand why it took a person like Laura Combs to motivate him. She is an imposing woman with a menacing stare. She churns gum, her mouth open.

For a few weeks, Edwin watches them joke with each other, and whenever he decides he should separate them, they break out into big grins and pull at each other's arms. The easy intimacy they develop seems strange to Edwin, but then it suddenly occurs to him what a fool he is being about a twenty-year-old girl, and that seems even stranger. He hears Ray ask Laura, "Did you get that hair at the Piggly Wiggly?" Laura's hair is in pigtails, which seem to be freshly plaited on Mondays and untouched the rest of the week. Laura says, "I don't want no birds nesting in *my* hair."

Edwin takes their requests. Laura has to hear "Mister Bojangles" every day, and Ray demands that Edwin play something from Elvis's Christmas album. They argue over tastes. Each says the other's favorite songs are terrible.

Laura tells Ray she never heard of a black person liking Elvis, and Ray says, "There's a lot about black people you don't know."

"What?"

"That's for me to know and you to find out. You belong on the moon. All white peoples belong on the moon."

"You belong in Atlanta," Laura says, doubling over with laughter.

When Edwin reports their antics one day to Sabrina, she says, "That's too depressing for words."

"They're a lot smarter than you'd think."

"I don't see how you can stand it." Sabrina shudders. She says, "Out in the woods, animals that are defective wouldn't survive. Even back in history, deformed babies were abandoned."

"Today's different," says Edwin, feeling alarmed. "Now they have rights."

"Well, I'll say one thing. If I was going to have a retarded baby, I'd get an abortion."

"That's killing."

"It's all in how you look at it," says Sabrina, changing the radio station.

They are having lunch. Sabrina has made a loaf of zucchini bread, because Sue made one for Jeff. Edwin doesn't understand her reasoning, but he takes it as a compliment. She gives him another slice, spreading it with whipped margarine. All of his women were good cooks. Maybe he didn't praise them enough. He suddenly blurts out so much praise for the zucchini bread that Sabrina looks at him oddly. Then he realizes that her attention is on the radio. The Humans are singing a song about paranoia, which begins, "Attention, all you K Mart shoppers, fill your carts, 'cause your time is almost up." It is Sabrina's favorite song.

"Most of my passengers are real poor country people," Edwin says. "Use to, they'd be kept in the attic or out in the barn. Now they're riding a bus, going to school and having a fine time."

"In the attic? I never knew that. *I'm* a poor country girl and I never knew that."

"Everybody knows that," says Edwin, feeling a little pleased. "But don't call yourself a poor country girl."

"It's true. My daddy said he'd give me a calf to raise if I came back home. Big deal! My greatest dread is that I'll end up on a farm, raising a bunch of dirty-faced younguns. Just like some of those characters on your bus."

Edwin does not know what to say. The song ends. The last line is, "They're looking in your picture window."

While Sabrina clears away the dishes, Edwin practices rolling bandages. He has been reviewing his first-aid book. "I want you to help me practice a simple splint," he says to Sabrina.

"If I broke a leg, I couldn't be in *Oklahoma!*"

"You won't break a leg." He holds out the splint. It is a fraternity paddle, a souvenir of her college days. She sits down for him and stretches out her leg.

"I can't stand this," she says.

"I'm just practicing. I have to be prepared. I might have an emergency."

Sabrina, wincing, closes her eyes while Edwin ties the fraternity paddle to her ankle.

"It's perfect," he says, tightening the knot.

Sabrina opens her eyes and wiggles her foot. "Jim says he's sure I can have a part in *Life with Father,*" she says. Jim is the director of *Oklahoma!* She adds, "Jeff is probably going to be the lead."

"I guess you're trying to make me jealous."

"No, I'm not. It's not even a love story."

"I'm glad then. Is that what you want to do?"

"I don't know. Don't you think I ought to go back to school and take a drama class? It'd be a real great experience, and I'm not going to get a job anytime soon, looks like. Nobody's hiring." She shakes her leg impatiently, and Edwin begins untying the bandage. "What do you think I ought to do?"

"I don't know. I never know how to give you advice, Sabrina. What do I know? I haven't been to college like you."

"I wish I were rich, so I could go back to school, Sabrina says sadly. The fraternity paddle falls to the floor, and she says, with her hands rushing to her face, "Oh, God, I can't stand the thought of breaking a leg."

The play opens in two weeks, during the Christmas season, and Sabrina has been making her costumes—two gingham outfits, virtually identical. She models them for Edwin and practices her dances for him. Edwin applauds, and she gives him a stage bow, as the director has taught her to do. Everything Sabrina does now seems like a performance. When she slices the zucchini bread, sawing at it because it has hardened, it is a performance. When she sat in the kitchen chair with the splint, it was as though she imagined her audience. Edwin has been involved in his own performances, on the bus. He emulates Dr. Johnny Fever on *WKRP,* because he likes to be low-key, cool. But he hesitates to tell Sabrina about his disc jockey role because she doesn't watch *WKRP in Cincinnati* with him anymore. She goes to rehearsals early.

Maybe it is out of resistance to the sappy *Oklahoma!* sound track, or maybe it is an inevitable progression, but Edwin finds himself playing a few Dylan tunes, some Janis Joplin, nothing too hectic. The passengers shake their heads in pleasure or beat things with their fists. It makes Edwin sad to think how history passes them by, but sometimes he feels the same way about his own life. As he drives along, playing these old songs, he thinks about what his life was like back then. During his first marriage, he worked in a gas station, saving for a down payment on a house. Lois Ann fed him on a TV tray while he watched the war. It was like a drama series. After Lois Ann, and then his travels out West, there was Carolyn and another down payment on another house and more of the war. Carolyn had a regular schedule—pork chops on Mondays, chicken on Tuesdays. Thursday's menu has completely escaped his memory. He feels terrible, remembering his wives by their food, and remembering the war as a TV series. His life has been a delayed reaction. He feels as if he's about Sabrina's age. He plays music he did not understand fifteen years ago, music that now seems full of possibility: the Grateful Dead, the Jefferson Airplane, groups with vision. Edwin feels that he is growing and changing for the first time in years. The passengers on his bus fill him with a compassion he has never felt before. When Freddie Johnson learns a new word—"bus"—Edwin is elated. He feels confident. He could drive his passengers all the way to California if he had to.

One day a stringbean girl with a speech impediment gives Edwin a tape cassette she wants him to play. Her name is Lou Murphy. Edwin has tried to encourage her to talk, but today he hands the tape back to her abruptly.

"I don't like the Plasmatics," he explains, enjoying his authority. "I don't play new-wave. I have a golden-oldie format. I just play sixties stuff."

The girl takes the tape cassette and sits down by Laura Combs. Ray Watson is absent today. She starts pulling at her hair, and the cassette jostles in her lap. Laura is wound up too, jiggling her knees.

The pair of them make Edwin think of those vibrating machines that mix paint by shaking the cans.

Edwin takes the microphone and says, "If you want a new-wave format, you'll have to ride another bus. Now let's crawl back in the stacks of wax for this oldie but goodie—Janis Joplin and 'A Little Bit Harder.' "

Lou Murphy nods along with the song. Laura's chewing gum pops like BBs. A while later, after picking up another passenger, Edwin glances in the rear-view mirror and sees Laura playing with the Plasmatics tape, pulling it out in a curly heap. Lou seems to be trying to shriek, but nothing comes out. Before Edwin can stop the bus, Laura has thrown the tape out the window.

"You didn't like it, Mr. Creech," Laura says when Edwin, after halting the bus on a shoulder, stalks down the aisle. "You said you didn't like it."

Edwin has never heard anyone sound so matter-of-fact, or look so reasonable. He has heard that since Laura began her classes, she has learned to set a table, make change, and dial a telephone. She even has a job at the training center, sorting seeds and rags. She is as hearty and domineering, yet as delicate and vulnerable, as Janis Joplin must have been. Edwin manages to move Lou to a front seat. She is sobbing silently, her lower jaw jerking, and Edwin realizes he is trembling too. He feels ashamed. After all, he is not driving the bus in order to make a name for himself. Yet it had felt right to insist on the format for his show. There is no appropriate way to apologize, or explain.

Edwin doesn't want to tell Sabrina about the incident. She is preoccupied with the play and often listens to him distractedly. Edwin has decided that he was foolish to suspect that she had a lover. The play is her love. Her nerves are on edge. One chilly afternoon, on the weekend before *Oklahoma!* opens, he suggests driving over to Kentucky Lake.

"You need a break," he tells her. "A little relaxation. I'm worried about you."

"This is nothing," she says "Two measly lines. I'm not exactly a star."

"What if you were? Would you get an abortion?"

"What are you talking about? I'm not pregnant."

"You said once you would. Remember?"

"Oh. I would if the baby was going to be creepy like those people on your bus."

"But how would you know if it was?"

"They can tell." Sabrina stares at him and then laughs. "Through science."

In the early winter, the lake is deserted. The beaches are washed clean, and the water is clear and gray. Now and then, as they walk by the water, they hear a gunshot from the Land Between the Lakes wilderness area. "The Surrey with the Fringe on Top" is going through Edwin's head, and he wishes he could throw the *Oklahoma!* sound track in the lake, as easily as Laura Combs threw the Plasmatics out the window of the bus. He has an idea that after the play, Sabrina is going to feel a letdown too great for him to deal with.

When Sabrina makes a comment about the "artistic intention" of Rodgers and Hammerstein, Edwin says, "Do you know what Janis Joplin said?"

"No—what?" Sabrina stubs the toe of her jogging shoe in the sand.

"Janis Joplin said, 'I don't write songs. I just make 'em up.' I thought that was clever."

"That's funny, I guess."

"She said she was going to her high school reunion in Port Arthur, Texas. She said, 'I'm going to laugh a lot. They laughed me out of class, out of town, and out of the state.' "

"You sound like you've got that memorized," Sabrina says, looking at the sky.

"I saw it on TV one night when you were gone, an old tape of a Dick Cavett show. It seemed worth remembering." Edwin rests his arm around Sabrina's waist, as thin as a post. He says, "I see a lot of things on TV, when you're not there."

Wild ducks are landing on the water, scooting in like water skiers. Sabrina seems impressed by them. They stand there until the last one lands.

Edwin says, "I bet you can't even remember Janis Joplin. You're just a young girl, Sabrina. *Oklahoma!* will seem silly to you one of these days."

Sabrina hugs his arm. "That don't matter." She breaks into laughter. "You're cute when you're being serious."

Edwin grabs her hand and jerks her toward him. "Look, Sabrina. I was never serious before in my life. I'm just now, at this point in my life—this week—getting to be serious." His words scare him, and he adds with a grin that stretches his dimple, "I'm serious about *you*."

"I know that," she says. She is leading the way along the water, through the trees, pulling him by the hand. "But you never believe how much I care about you," she says, drawing him to her. "I think we get along real good. That's why I wish you'd marry me instead of just stringing me along."

Edwin gasps like a swimmer surfacing. It is very cold on the beach. Another duck skis onto the water.

Oklahoma! has a four-night run, with one matinee. Edwin goes to the play three times, surprised that he enjoys it. Sabrina's lines come off differently each time, and each evening she discusses the impression she made. Edwin tells her that she is the prettiest woman in the cast, and that her lines are cute. He wants to marry Sabrina, although he hasn't yet said he would. He wishes he could buy her a speedboat for a wedding present. She wants him to get a better-paying job, and she has ideas about a honeymoon cottage at the lake. It feels odd that Sabrina has proposed to him. He thinks of her as a liberated woman. The play is old-fashioned and phony. The love scenes between Jeff and Sue are comically stilted, resembling none of the passion and intrigue that Sabrina has reported. She compared them to Bogart and Bacall, but Edwin can't remember if she meant Jeff and Sue's roles or their actual affair. How did Sabrina know about Bogart and Bacall?

At the cast party, at Jeff's house, Jeff and Sue are publicly affectionate, getting away with it by playing their Laurey and Curly roles, but eventually Jeff's wife, who has made ham, potato salad, chiffon cakes, eggnog, and cranberry punch for sixty people, suddenly disappears from the party. Jeff whizzes off in his Camaro to find her. Sabrina whispers to Edwin, "Look how Sue's pretending nothing's happened. She's flirting with the guy who played Jud Fry." Sabrina, so excited that she bounces around on her tiptoes, is impressed by Jeff's house, which has wicker furniture and rose plush carpets.

Edwin drinks too much cranberry punch at the party, and most of the time he sits on a wicker love seat watching Sabrina flit around the room, beaming with the joy of her success. She is out of costume, wearing a sweatshirt with a rainbow on the front and pots of gold on her breasts. He realizes how proud he is of her. Her complexion is as smooth as a white mushroom, and she has crinkled her hair by braiding and unbraiding it. He watches her join some of the cast members around the piano to sing songs from the play, as though they cannot bear it that the play has ended. Sabrina seems to belong with them, these theatre people. Edwin knows they are not really theatre people. They are only local merchants putting on a play in their spare time. But Edwin is just a bus driver. He should get a better job so that he can send Sabrina to college, but he knows that he has to take care of his passengers. Their faces have become as familiar to him as the sound track of *Oklahoma!* He can practically hear Freddie Johnson shouting out her TV shows: "*Popeye* on! *Dukes* on!" He sees Sabrina looking at him lovingly. The singers shout, "Oklahoma, O.K.!"

Sabrina brings him a plastic glass of cranberry punch and sits with him on the love seat, holding his hand. She says, "Jim definitely said I should take a drama course at Murray State next semester. He was real encouraging. He said, 'Why not be in the play *and* take a course or two?' I could drive back and forth, don't you think?"

"Why not? You can have anything you want." Edwin plays with her hand.

"Jeff took two courses at Murray and look how good he was. Didn't you think he was good? I loved that cute way he went into that dance."

Edwin is a little drunk. He finds himself telling Sabrina about how he plays disc jockey on the bus, and he confesses to her his shame about the way he sounded off about his golden-oldie format. His mind is reeling and the topic sounds trivial, compared to Sabrina's future.

"Why *don't* you play a new-wave format?" she asks him. "It's what *every*body listens to." She nods at the stereo, which is playing "You're Living in Your Own Private Idaho," by the B-52s, a song Edwin has often heard on the radio late at night when Sabrina is unwinding, moving into his arms. The music is violent and mindless, with a fast beat like a crazed parent abusing a child, thrashing it senseless.

"I don't know," Edwin says. "I shouldn't have said that to Lou Murphy. It bothers me."

"She don't know the difference," Sabrina says, patting his head. "It's ridiculous to make a big thing out of it. Words are so arbitrary, and people don't say what they mean half the time anyway."

"You should talk, Miss Oklahoma!" Edwin laughs, spurting a little punch on the love seat. "You and your two lines!"

"They're just lines," she says, smiling up at him and poking her finger into his dimple.

Some of Edwin's passengers bring him Christmas presents, badly wrapped, with tags that say his name in wobbly writing. Edwin puts the presents in a drawer, where Sabrina finds them.

"Aren't you going to open them?" she asks. "I'd be dying to know what was inside."

"I will eventually. Leave them there." Edwin knows what is in them without opening them. There is a bottle of shaving cologne, a tie (he never wears a tie), and three boxes of chocolate-covered cherries (he peeked in one, and the others are exactly the same shape). The presents are so pathetic Edwin could cry. He cannot bring himself to tell Sabrina what happened on the bus.

On the bus, the day before Christmas break, Ray Watson had a seizure. During that week, Edwin had been playing more Dylan and even some Stones. No Christmas music, except the Elvis album as usual for Ray. And then, almost unthinkingly, following Sabrina's advice, Edwin shifted formats. It seemed a logical course, as natural as Sabrina's herbal cosmetics, her mushroom complexion. It started with a revival of The Doors—Jim Morrison singing "Light My Fire," a song that was so long it carried them from the feed mill on one side of town to the rendering plant on the other. The passengers loved the way it stretched out, and some shook their heads and stomped their feet. As Edwin realized later, the whole bus was in a frenzy, and he should have known he was leading the passengers toward disaster, but the music seemed so appropriate. The Doors were a bridge from the past to the present, spanning those empty years—his marriages, the turbulence of the times—and connecting his youth solidly with the present. That day Edwin taped more songs from the radio—Adam and the Ants, Squeeze, the B-52s, the Psychedelic Furs, the Flying Lizards, Frankie and the Knockouts—and he made a point of replacing the Plasmatics tape for Lou Murphy. The new-wave format was a hit. Edwin believed the passengers understood what was happening. The frantic beat was a perfect expression of their aimlessness and frustration. Edwin had the impression that his passengers were growing, expanding, like the corn in *Oklahoma!*, like his own awareness. The new format went on for two days before Ray had his seizure. Edwin did not know exactly what happened, and it was possible Laura Combs had shoved Ray into the aisle. Edwin was in an awkward place on the highway, and he had to shoot across a bridge and over a hill before he could find a good place to stop. Everyone on the bus was making an odd noise, gasping or clapping, some imitating Ray's convulsions. Freddie Johnson was saying, "*Popeye* on! *Dukes* on!" Ray was on the floor, gagging, with his head thrown back, and twitching like someone being electrocuted. Laura Combs stood hunched in her seat, her mouth open in speechless terror, pointing her finger at Edwin. During the commotion, the Flying Lizards were chanting tonelessly, "I'm going to take my problems to the United Nations; there ain't no cure for the summertime blues."

Edwin followed all the emergency steps he had learned. He loosened Ray's clothing, slapped his cheeks, turned him on his side. Ray's skin was the color of the Hershey bars the man with the clubfoot collected. Edwin recalled grimly the first-aid book's ironic assurance that facial coloring was not important in cases of seizure. On the way to the hospital, Edwin clicked in a Donovan cassette. To steady himself, he sang along under his breath. "I'm just wild about saffron," he sang. It was a tune as carefree and lyrical as a field of daffodils. The passengers were screaming. All the way to the hospital, Edwin heard their screams, long and drawn out, orchestrated together into an accusing wail—eerie and supernatural.

Edwin's supervisors commended him for his quick thinking in handling Ray and getting him to the hospital, and everyone he has seen at the center has congratulated him. Ray's mother sent him an uncooked fruitcake made with graham cracker crumbs and marshmallows. She wrote a poignant note, thanking him for saving her son from swallowing his tongue. Edwin keeps thinking: what he did was no big deal; you can't swallow your tongue anyway; and it was Edwin's own fault that Ray had a seizure. He does not feel like a hero. He feels almost embarrassed.

Sabrina seems incapable of embarrassment. She is full of hope, like the Christmas season. *Oklahoma*! was only the beginning for her. She has a new job at McDonald's and a good part in *Life with Father.* She plans to commute to Murray State next semester to take a drama class and a course in Western Civilization that she needs to fulfill a requirement. She seems to assume that Edwin will marry her. He finds it funny that it is up to him to say yes. When she says she will keep her own name, Edwin wonders what the point is.

"My parents would just love it if we got married," Sabrina explains. "For them, it's worse for me to live in sin than to be involved with an older man."

"I didn't think I was really older," says Edwin. "But now I know it. I feel like I've had a developmental disability and it suddenly went away. Something like if Freddie Johnson learned to read. That's how I feel."

"I never thought of you as backward. Laid back is what I said." Sabrina laughs at her joke. "I'm sure you're going to impress Mom and Dad."

Tomorrow, she is going to her parents' farm, thirty miles away, for the Christmas holidays, and she has invited Edwin to go with her. He does not want to disappoint her. He does not want to go through Christmas without her. She has arranged her Christmas cards on a red string between the living room and the kitchen. She is making cookies, and Edwin has a feeling she is adding something strange to them. Her pale, fine hair is falling down in her face. Flour streaks her jeans.

"Let me show you something," Edwin says, bringing out a drugstore envelope of pictures. "One of my passengers, Merle Cope, gave me these."

"Which one is he? The one with the fits?"

"No. The one that claps all the time. He lives with a lot of sisters and brothers down in Langley's Bottom. It's a case of incest. The whole family's backward—your word. He's forty-seven and goes around with this big smile on his face, clapping." Edwin demonstrates.

He pins the pictures on Sabrina's Christmas card line with tiny red and green clothespins. "Look at these and tell me what you think."

Sabrina squints, going down the row of pictures. Her hands are covered with flour and she holds them in front of her, the way she learned from her actor friends to hold an invisible baby.

The pictures are black-and-white snapshots: fried eggs on cracked plates, an oilclothed kitchen table, a bottle of tomato ketchup, a fence post, a rusted tractor seat sitting on a stump, a corn crib, a sagging door, a toilet bowl, a cow, and finally, a horse's rear end.

"I can't look," says Sabrina. "These are disgusting."

"I think they're arty."

Sabrina laughs. She points to the pictures one by one, getting flour on some of them. Then she gets the giggles and can't stop. "Can you imagine what the developers thought when they saw that horse's ass?" she gasps. Her laughter goes on and on, then subsides with a little whimper. She goes back to the cookies. While she cuts out the cookies, Edwin takes the pictures down and puts them in the envelope. He hides the envelope in the drawer with the Christmas presents. Sabrina sets the cookie sheet in the oven and washes her hands.

Edwin asks, "How long do those cookies take?"

"Twelve minutes. Why?"

"Let me show you something else—in case you ever need to know it. The CPR technique—that's cardio-pulmonary resuscitation, in case you've forgotten."

Sabrina looks annoyed. "I'd rather do the Heimlich maneuver," she says. "Besides, you've practiced CPR on me a hundred times."

"I'm not practicing. I don't have to anymore. I'm beyond that." Edwin notices Sabrina's puzzled face. The thought of her fennel toothpaste, which makes her breath smell like licorice, fills him with something like nostalgia, as though she is already only a memory. He says, "I just want you to feel what it would be like. Come on." He leads her to the couch and sets her down. Her hands are still moist. He says, "Now just pretend. Bend over like this. Just pretend you have the biggest pain, right here, right in your chest, right there."

"Like this?" Sabrina is doubled over, her hair falling to her knees and her fists knotted between her breasts.

"Yes. Right in your heart."

Joy Williams (b. 1944)
THE SKATER

Annie and Tom and Molly are looking at boarding schools. Molly is the applicant, fourteen years old. Annie and Tom are the mom and dad. This is how they are referred to by the admissions directors. "Now if Mom and Dad would just make themselves comfortable while we steal Molly away for a moment . . ." Molly is stolen away and Tom and Annie drink coffee. There are brown donuts on a plate. Colored slides are slapped upon a screen showing children earnestly learning and growing and caring through the seasons. These things have been captured. Rather, it's clear that's what they're getting at. The children's faces blur in Tom's mind. And all those autumn leaves. All those laboratories and playing fields and bell towers.

It is winter and there is snow on the ground. They have flown in from California and rented a car. Their plan is to see seven New England boarding schools in five days. Icicles hang from the admissions building. Tom gazes at them. They are lovely and refractive. They are formed and then they vanish. Tom looks away.

Annie is sitting on the other side of the room, puzzling over a mathematics problem. There are sheets of problems all over the waiting room. The sheets are to keep parents and kids on their toes as they wait. Annie's foot is bent fiercely beneath her as though broken. The cold, algebraic problems are presented in little stories. Five times as many girls as boys are taking music lessons or trees are growing at different rates or ladies in a bridge club are lying about their age. The characters and situations are invented only to be exiled to measurement. Watching Annie search for solutions makes Tom's heart ache. He remembers a class he took once himself, almost twenty years ago, a class in myth. In mythical stories, it seems, there were two ways to disaster. One of the ways was to answer an unanswerable question. The other was to fail to answer an answerable question.

Down a corridor there are several shut doors and behind one is Molly. Molly is their living child. Tom and Annie's other child, Martha, has been dead a year. Martha was one year older than Molly. Now Molly is her age. Martha choked to death in her room on a piece of bread. It was early in the morning and she was getting ready for school. The radio was playing and two disc jockeys called the Breakfast Flakes chattered away between songs.

The weather is bad, the roads are slippery. From the back seat, Molly says, "He asked what my favorite ice cream was and I said, 'Quarterback Crunch.' The he asked who was President of the United States when the school was founded and I said, 'No one.' Wasn't that good?"

"I hate trick questions," Annie says.

"Did you like the school?" Tom asks.

"Yeah," Molly says.

"What did you like best about it?"

"I liked the way our guide, you know, Peter, just walked right across the street that goes through the campus and the cars just stopped. You and Mom were kind of hanging back, looking both ways and all, but Peter and I just trucked right across."

Molly was chewing gum that smelled like oranges.

"Peter was cute," Molly says.

Tom and Annie and Molly are at the Motel Lenore. Snow accumulates beyond the room's walls. There is a small round table in the room and they sit around it. Molly drinks cranberry juice from a box and Tom and Annie drink Scotch. They are nowhere. The brochure that the school sent them states that the school is located thirty-five miles from Boston. Nowhere! They are all exhausted and merely sit there, regarding their beverages. The television set is chained to the wall. This is indicative, Tom thinks, of considerable suspicion on the part of the management. There was also a four-dollar deposit on the room key. The management, when Tom checked in, was in the person of a child about Molly's age, a boy eating from a bag of potato chips and doing his homework.

"There's a kind of light that glows in the bottom of the water in an atomic reactor that exists nowhere else, do you know that?" the boy said to Tom.

"Is that right?" Tom said.

"Yeah," the boy said, and marked the book he was reading with his pencil. "I think that's right."

The motel room is darkly paneled and there is a picture of a moose between the two beds. The moose is knee-deep in a lake and he has raised his head to some sound, the sound of a hunter approaching, one would imagine. Water drips from his muzzle. The woods he gazes at are dark. Annie looks at the picture. The moose is preposterous and doomed. After a few moments, after she has finished her Scotch, Annie realizes she is waiting to hear the sound. She goes into the bathroom and washes her hands and face. The towel is thin. It smells as if it's been line-dried. It was her idea that Molly go away to school. She wants Molly to be free. She doesn't want her to be afraid. She fears that she is making her afraid, as she is afraid. Annie hears Molly and Tom talking in the other room and then she hears Molly laugh. She raises her fingers to the window frame and feels the cold air seeping in. She adjusts the lid to the toilet tank. It shifts slightly. She washes her hands again. She goes into the room and sits on one of the beds.

"What are you laughing about?" she says. She means to be offhand, but her words come out heavily.

"Did you see the size of that girl's radio in the dorm room we visited?" Molly says, laughing. "It was the biggest radio I'd ever seen. I told Daddy there was a real person lying in it, singing." Molly giggles. She pulls her turtleneck sweater up to just below her eyes.

Annie laughs, then she thinks she has laughed at something terrible, the idea of someone lying trapped and singing. She raises her hands to her mouth. She had not seen a radio large enough to hold anyone. She saw children in classes, in laboratories in some brightly painted basement. The children were dissecting sheep's eyes. "Every winter term in Biology you've got to dissect sheep's eyes," their guide said wearily. "The colors are really nice though." She saw sacks of laundry tumbled down a stairwell with names stenciled on them. Now she tries not to see a radio large enough to hold anyone singing.

At night, Tom drives in his dreams. He dreams of ice, of slick treachery. All night he fiercely holds the wheel and turns in the direction of the skid.

In the morning when he returns the key, the boy has been replaced by an old man with liver spots the size of quarters on his hands. Tom thinks of asking where the boy is, but then realizes he must be in school learning about eerie, deathly light. The bills the old man returns to Tom are soft as cloth.

In California, they live in a canyon. Martha's room is there, facing the canyon. It is not situated with a glimpse of the ocean like some of the other rooms. It faces a rocky ledge where owls nest. The canyon is full of small birds and bitter-smelling shrubs. There are larger animals too who come down in the night and drink from the pans of water the family puts out. Each evening they put out large white pans of clear water and in the morning the pans are muddy and empty. The canyon is cold. The sun moves quickly through it. When the rocks are touched by the sun, they steam. All of Martha's things remain in her room—the radio, the posters and mirrors and books. It is a "guest" room now, although no one ever refers to it in that way. They refer to it as "Martha's room." But it has become a guest room, even though there are never any guests.

The rental car is blue and without distinction. It is a four-door sedan with automatic transmission and a poor turning circle. Martha would have been mortified by it. Martha had a boyfriend who, with his brothers, owned a monster truck. The Super Swamper tires were as tall as Martha, and all the driver of an ordinary car would see when it passed by was its colorful undercarriage with its huge shock and suspension coils, its long orange stabilizers. For hours on a Saturday they would wallow in sloughs and rumble and pitch across stony creek beds, and then they would wash and wax the truck or, as Dwight, the boyfriend, would say, dazzle the hog. The truck's name was Bear. Tom and Annie didn't care for Dwight, and they hated and feared Bear. Martha loved Bear. She wore a red and white peaked cap with MONSTER TRUCK stenciled on it. After Martha died, Molly put the cap on once or twice. She thought it would help her feel closer to Martha but it didn't. The sweatband smelled slightly of shampoo, but it was just a cap.

Tom pulls into the frozen field that is the parking lot for the Northwall School. The admissions office is very cold. The receptionist is wearing an old worn Chesterfield coat and a scarf. Someone is playing a hesitant and plaintive melody on a piano in one of the nearby rooms. They are shown the woodlot, the cafeteria, and the arts department, where people are hammering out their own silver bracelets. They are shown the language department, where a class is doing tarot card readings in French. They pass a room and hear a man's voice say, "Matter is a sort of blindness."

While Molly is being interviewed, Tom and Annie walk to the barn. The girls are beautiful in this school. The boys look a little dull. Two boys run past them, both wearing jeans and denim jackets. Their hair is short and their ears are red. They appear to be pretending that they are in a drama, that they are being filmed. They dart and feint. One stumbles into a building while the other crouches outside, tossing his head and scowling, throwing an imaginary knife from hand to hand.

Annie tries a door to the barn but it is latched from the inside. She walks around the barn in her high heels. The hem of her coat dangles. She wears gloves on her pale hands. Tom walks beside her, his own hands in his pockets. A flock of starlings fly overhead in an oddly tight formation. A hawk flies above them. The hawk will not fall upon them, clenched like this. If one would separate from the flock, then the hawk could fall.

"I don't know about this 'matter is a sort of blindness' place," Tom says. "It's not what I had in mind."

Annie laughs but she's not paying attention. She wants to get into the huge barn. She tugs at another door. Dirt and flakes of rust smear the palms of her gloves. Then suddenly, the wanting leaves her face.

"Martha would like this school, wouldn't she," she says.

"We don't know, Annie," Tom says. "Please don't, Annie."

"I feel that I've lived my whole life in one corner of a room," Annie says. "That's the problem. It's just having always been in this one corner. And now I can't see anything. I don't even know the room, do you see what I'm saying?"

Tom nods but he doesn't see the room. The sadness in him has become his blood, his life flowing in him. There's no room for him.

In the admissions building, Molly sits in a wooden chair facing her interviewer, Miss Plum. Miss Plum teaches composition and cross-country skiing.

"You asked if I believe in *aluminum?*" Molly asks.

"Yes, dear. Uh-huh, I did," Miss Plum says.

"Well, I suppose I'd have to *believe* in it," Molly says.

Annie has a large cardboard file that holds compartmentalized information on the schools they're visiting. The rules and regulations for one school are put together in what is meant to look like an

American passport. In the car's back seat, Molly flips through the book annoyed.

"You can't do anything in this place!" she says. "The things on the walls have to be framed and you can only cover sixty percent of the wall space. You can't wear jeans." Molly gasps. "And you have to eat breakfast!" Molly tosses the small book onto the floor, on top of the ice scraper. She gazes glumly out the window at an orchard. She is sick of the cold. She is sick of discussing her "interests." White fields curve by. Her life is out there somewhere, fleeing from her while she is in the back seat of this stupid car. Her life is never going to be hers. She thinks of it raining, back home in the canyon, the rain falling upon the rain. Her legs itch and her scalp itches. She has never been so bored. She thinks that the worst thing she has done so far in her life was to lie in a hot bath one night, smoking a cigarette and saying *I hate God*. That was the very worst thing. It's pathetic. She bangs her knees irritably against the front seat.

"You want to send me far enough away," she says to her parents. "I mean, it's the other side of the dumb continent. Maybe I don't even want to do this," she says.

She looks at the thick sky holding back snow. She doesn't hate God anymore. She doesn't even think about God. Anybody who would let a kid choke on a piece of bread . . .

The next school has chapel four times a week and an indoor hockey rink. In the chapel, two fir trees are held in wooden boxes. Wires attached to the ceiling hold them upright. It is several weeks before Christmas.

"When are you going to decorate them?" Molly asks Shirley, her guide. Shirley is handsome and rather horrible. The soles of her rubber boots are a bright, horrible orange. She looks at Molly.

"We don't decorate the trees in the chapel," she says.

Molly looks at the tree stumps bolted into the wooden boxes. Beads of sap pearl golden on the bark.

"This is a very old chapel," Shirley says. "See those pillars? They look like marble, but they're just pine, painted to look like marble." She isn't being friendly, she's just saying what she knows. They walk out of the chapel, Shirley soundlessly, on her horrible orange soles.

"Do you play hockey?" she asks.

"No," Molly says.

"Why not?"

"I like my teeth," Molly says.

"You *do*," Shirley says in mock amazement. "Just kidding," she says. "I'm going to show you the hockey rink anyway. It's new. It's a big deal."

Molly sees Tom and Annie standing some distance away beneath a large tree draped with many strings of extinguished lights. Her mother's back is to her, but Tom sees her and waves.

Molly follows Shirley into the cold, odd air of the hockey rink. No one is on the ice. The air seems distant, used up. On one wall is a big painting of a boy in a hockey uniform. He is in a graceful easy posture, skating alone on bluish ice, skating toward the viewer, smiling. He isn't wearing a helmet. He has brown hair and wide golden eyes. Molly reads the plaque beneath the painting. His name is Jimmy Watkins and he had died six years before at the age of seventeen. His parents had built the rink and dedicated it to him.

Molly takes a deep breath. "My sister, Martha, knew him," she says.

"Oh yeah?" Shirley says with interest. "Did your sister go here?"

"Yes," Molly says. She frowns a little as she lies. Martha and Jimmy Watkins of course know each other. They know everything but they have secrets too.

The air is not like real air in here. Neither does the cold seem real. She looks at Jimmy Watkins, bigger than life, skating toward them on his black skates. It is not a very good painting. Molly thinks that those who love Jimmy Watkins must be disappointed in it.

"They were very good friends," Molly says.

"How come you didn't tell me before your sister went here?"

Molly shrugs. She feels happy, happier than she has in a long time. She has brought Martha back from the dead and put her in school. She has given her a room, friends, things she must do. It can go on and on. She has given her a kind of life, a place in death. She has freed her.

"Did she date him or what?" Shirley asks.

"It wasn't like that," Molly says. "It was better than that."

She doesn't want to go much further, not with this girl whom she dislikes, but she goes a little further.

"Martha knew Jimmy better than anybody," Molly says.

She thinks of Martha and Jimmy Watkins being together, telling each other secrets. They will like each other. They are seventeen and fourteen, living in the single moment that they have been gone.

Molly is with her parents in the car again on a winding road, going through the mountains. Tonight they will stay in an inn that Annie has read about and tomorrow they will visit the last school. Several large rocks, crusted with dirty ice, have slid upon the road. They are ringed with red cones and traffic moves slowly around them. The late low sun hotly strikes the windshield.

"Bear could handle those rocks," Molly says. "Bear would go right over them."

"Oh, that truck," Annie says.

"That truck is an ecological criminal," Tom says.

"Big Bad Bear," Molly says.

Annie shakes her head and sighs. Bear is innocent. Bear is only a machine, gleaming in a dark garage.

Molly can't see her parents' faces. She can't remember the way they looked when she was a baby. She can't remember what she and Martha last argued about. She wants to asks them about Martha. She wants to ask them if they are sending her so far away so that they can imagine Martha is just far away too. But she knows she will never ask such questions. There are secrets now. The dead have their secrets and the living have their secrets with the dead. This is the way it must be.

Molly has her things. And she sets them up each night in the room she's in. She lays a little scarf upon the bureau first, and then her things upon it. Painted combs for her hair, a little dish for her rings. They are the only guests at the inn. It is an old rambling structure on a lake. In a few days, the owner will be closing it down for the winter. It's too cold for such an old place in the winter, the owner says. He had planned to keep it open for skating on the lake when he first bought it and had even remodeled part of the cellar as a skate room. There is a bar down there, a wooden floor, and shelves of old skates in all sizes. Window glass runs the length of one wall just above ground level and there are spotlights that illuminate a portion of the lake. But winter isn't the season here. The pipes are too old and there are not enough guests.

"Is this the deepest lake in the state?" Annie asks. "I read that somewhere, didn't I?" She has her guidebooks which she examines each night. Everywhere she goes, she buys books.

"No," the inn's owner says. "It's not the deepest, but it's deep. You should take a look at that ice. It's beautiful ice."

He is a young man, balding, hopelessly proud of his ice. He lingers with them, having given them thick towels and new bars of soap. He offers them venison for supper, fresh bread and pie. He offers them his smooth, frozen lake.

"Do you want to skate?" Tom asks his wife and daughter. Molly shakes her head.

"No," Annie says. She takes a bottle of Scotch from her suitcase. "Are there any glasses?" she asks the man.

"I'm sorry," the man says, startled. He seems to blush. "They're all down in the skate room, on the bar." He gives a slight nod and walks away.

Tom goes down into the cellar for the glasses. The skates, their runners bright, are jumbled upon the shelves. The frozen lake glitters in the window. He pushes open the door and steps out onto the ice.

Annie, in their room, waits without taking off her coat, without looking at the bottle. Tom takes a few quick steps and then slides. He is wearing a suit and tie, his good shoes. It is a windy night and the trees clatter with the wind and the old inn's sign creaks on its chains. Tom slides across the ice, his hands pushed out, then he holds his hands behind his back, going back and forth in the space where the light is cast. There is no skill without the skates, he knows, and probably no grace without them either, but i' is enough to be here under the black sky, cold and light and moving. He wants to be out here. He wants to be out here with Annie.

From a window, Molly sees her father on the ice. After a moment, she sees her mother moving toward him, not skating, but slipping forward, making her way. She sees their heavy awkward shapes embrace.

Molly sees them, already remembering it.

Lynn Sharon Schwartz (b. 1939)

MRS. SAUNDERS WRITES TO THE WORLD

Mrs. Saunders placed her white plastic bag of garbage in one of the cans behind the row of garden apartments and looked about for a familiar face, but finding nothing except two unknown toddlers with a babysitter in the playground a short distance off, she shrugged, gazed briefly into the wan early spring sun, and climbed the stairs back to her own door. She was looking for someone because she had a passion to hear her name spoken. But once inside, as she sponged her clean kitchen counter with concentrated elliptical strokes, she had to acknowledge that hearing "Mrs. Saunders" would not be good enough anymore. She needed—she had begun to long, in fact, with a longing she found frightening in its intensity—to hear her real name.

She squeezed the sponge agonizingly over the sink, producing a few meager drops. No one called her anything but Mrs. Saunders now. Her name was Fran. Frances. She whispered it in the direction of the rubber plant on the windowsill. Fran, Franny, Frances. Anyone seeing her, she thought, might suspect she was going crazy. Yet they said it was good to talk to your plants. She could always explain that she was whispering to them for their health and growth. Fran, Franny, Frances, she breathed again. Then she added a few wordless breaths, purely for the plants' sake, and felt somewhat less odd.

There was no one left to call her Fran. Her husband had called her Franny, but he was long dead. Her children, scattered across the country, called her Ma when they came at wide intervals to visit, or when she paid her yearly visit to each of the three. Except for Walter, she reminded herself, as she was fussy over accuracy, except for Walter, whom she saw only about once every year and a half, since he lived far away in Oregon and since his wife was what they called unstable and couldn't stand visitors too often or for too long a period.

Her old friends were gone or far off, and the new ones stuck to "Mrs. Saunders." The young people who moved in and out of these garden apartments thought of themselves as free and easy, she mused, but in fact they had their strange formalities, like always calling her Mrs. Saunders, even though they might run in two or three times a week to borrow groceries or ask her to babysit or see if she needed a lift to the supermarket. She pursed her lips in annoyance, regarded her impeccable living room, then pulled out the pack of cigarettes hidden in a drawer in the end table beside her chair. Mrs. Saunders didn't like these young girls who ran in and out to see her smoking; it wasn't seemly. She lit one and inhaled deeply, feeling a small measure of relief.

It wasn't that they were cold or unfriendly. Just that they didn't seem to realize she had a name like anyone else and might wish to hear it spoken aloud once in a while by someone other than herself in her darkened bedroom at night, or at full volume in the shower, mornings. And though she knew she could say to her new neighbors, "Call me Fran," as simply as that, somehow whenever the notion came to her the words got stuck in her throat. Then she lost the drift of the conversation and worried that the young people might think her strange, asking them to repeat things they had probably said perfectly clearly the first time. And if there was one thing she definitely did not want, she thought, stubbing the cigarette out firmly, it was to be regarded as senile. She had a long way to go before that.

Suddenly the air in the neat room seemed intolerably stuffy. Cigarette smoke hung in a cloud around her. Mrs. Saunders felt weak and terribly unhappy. She rose heavily and stepped out onto her small balcony for a breath of air. Jill was lounging on the next balcony with a friend.

"Oh, hi, Mrs. Saunders. How are you? Isn't it a gorgeous day?" Tall, blond, and narrow-shouldered, Jill drew in a lungful of smoke and pushed it out with pleasure.

"Hello, Jill dear. How's everything?"

"Struggling along." Jill stretched out her long jean-clad legs till her feet rested on the railing. "Mrs. Saunders, this is my friend, Wendy. Wendy, Mrs. Saunders. Mrs. Saunders has been so terrific to us," she said to Wendy. "And she never complains about the kids screeching on the other side of the wall."

"Hi," said Wendy.

"Nice to meet you, Wendy," said Mrs. Saunders. "I don't mind the children, Jill, really I don't. After all, I had children of my own. I know what it's like."

"That's right. Three, aren't there?"

"Yes," Mrs. Saunders said. "Walter, Louise, and Edith. Walter was named after his father."

"We named Jeff after his father too," Wendy remarked.

"Mrs. Saunders sometimes babysits for Luke and Kevin," Jill explained to Wendy. "They adore her. Sometimes they even tell us to go out so she can come and stay with them. I don't know what it is you do with them, Mrs. Saunders."

She smiled, and would have liked to linger with the two young women, but suddenly she had to go in, because a furious sob rose in her throat, choking her. She threw herself down on the bed and wept uncontrollably into the plumped-up pillows. Everyone in the world had a name except her. And it would never change. Nobody here, at this stage in her life, was going to come along and start calling her Fran. Franny, surely never again. She remembered the days—they were never far from her mind—when her husband was sick and dying in the bedroom upstairs in the old house, and fifteen, maybe twenty times a day she would hear his rasping, evaporating voice calling, "Franny, Franny." She would drop everything each time to see what it was he wanted, and although she had loved him deeply, there were moments when she felt if she heard that rasping voice wailing out her name once more she would scream in exasperation; her fists would clench with the power and the passion to choke him. And yet now, wasn't life horribly cruel, she would give half her remaining days to hear her name wailed once more by him. Or by anyone else, for that matter. She gave in utterly to her despair and cried for a long time. She felt she might die gasping for breath if she didn't hear her own name.

At last she made an effort to pull herself together. She fixed the crumpled pillows so that they looked untouched, then went into the bathroom, washed her face and put on powder and lipstick, released her gray hair from its bun and brushed it out. It looked nice, she thought, long and still thick, thank God, falling down her back in a glossy, smooth sheet. Feeling young and girlish for a moment, she fancied herself going about with it loose and swinging, like Jill and Wendy and the other young girls. Jauntily she tossed her head to right and left a few times and reveled in the swing of her hair. As a matter of fact it was better hair than Jill's, she thought, thicker, with more body. Except it was gray. She gave a secretive smile to the mirror and pinned her hair up in the bun again. She would go into town and browse around Woolworth's to cheer herself up.

Mrs. Saunders got a ride in with Jill, who drove past the shopping center every noon on her way to get Luke and Kevin at nursery school. In Woolworth's she bought a new bathmat, a bottle of shampoo and some cream rinse for her hair, a butane cigarette lighter, and last, surprising herself, two boxes of colored chalk. She couldn't have explained why she bought the chalk, but since it only amounted to fifty-six cents she decided it didn't need justification. The colors looked so pretty, peeking out from the open circle in the center of the box—lime, lavender, rose, yellow, beige, and powder blue. It was spring, and they seemed to go with the spring. It occurred to her as she took them from the display case that the pale yellow was exactly the color of her kitchen cabinets; she might use it to cover a patch of white that had appeared on one drawer after she scrubbed too hard with Ajax. Or she might give Luke and Kevin each a box, and buy them slates as well, to practice their letters and numbers. They were nice little boys, and she often gave them small presents or candy when she babysat.

Feeling nonetheless as though she had done a slightly eccentric thing, Mrs. Saunders meandered through the shopping center, wondering if there might be some sensible, inexpensive thing she needed. Then she remembered that the shoes she had on were nearly worn out. Certainly she was entitled to some lightweight, comfortable new shoes for spring. With the assistance of a civil young man, she quickly was able to find just the right pair. The salesman was filling out the slip. "Name, please?" he said. And then something astonishing happened. Hearing so unexpectedly the word that had been obsessing her gave Mrs. Saunders a great jolt, and, as she would look back on it later, seemed to loosen and shake out of its accustomed place a piece of her that rebelled against the suffocation she had been feeling for more years than she cared to remember.

She knew exactly the answer that was required, so that she could find reassurance afterwards in recalling that she had been neither mad nor senile. As the clerk waited with his pencil poised, the thing that was jolted loose darted swiftly through her body, producing vast exhilaration, and rose out from her throat to her lips.

"Frances."

She expected him to look at her strangely—it was strange, she granted that—and say, "Frances what?" And then, at long last she would hear it. It would be, she imagined, something like making love years ago with Walter, when in the dark all at once her body streamed and compressed to one place and exploded with relief and wonder. She felt a tinge of that same excitement now, as she waited. And it did not concern her that the manner of her gratification would be so pathetic and contrived, falling mechanically from the lips of a stranger. All that mattered was that the name be spoken.

"Last name, please." He did not even look up.

Mrs. Saunders gave it, and gave her address, and thought she would faint with disappointment. She slunk from the store and stood weakly against a brick wall outside. Was there to be no easing of this pain? Dazed, she stared hopelessly at her surroundings, which were sleek, buzzing with shoppers, and unappealing. She slumped and turned her face to the wall.

On the brick before her, in small letters, were scratched the words "Tony" and "Annette." An arrow went through them. Mrs. Saunders gazed for a long time, aware that she would be late meeting Jill, but not caring, for once. She broke the staple on the Woolworth's bag, slipped her hand in, and drew out a piece of chalk. It turned out to be powder blue. Shielding her actions with her coat, she printed in two-inch-high letters on the brick wall outside the shoe store, FRANNY. Then she moved off briskly to the parking lot.

At home, after fixing herself a light lunch, which she ate excitedly and in haste, and washing the few dishes, she went back down to the garbage area behind the buildings. In lavender on the concrete wall just behind the row of cans, she wrote FRANNY. A few feet off she wrote again, FRANNY, and added WALTER, with an arrow through the names. But surveying her work, she took a tissue from her pocket and with some difficulty rubbed out WALTER and the arrow. Walter was dead. She was not senile yet. She was not yet one of those old people who live in a world of illusions.

Then she went to the children's playground, deserted at naptime, and wrote FRANNY in small letters on the wooden rail of the slide, on the wooden pillars of the newfangled jungle gym, and on the concrete border of the sandbox, in yellow, lavender, and blue, respectively. Choosing a quite private corner behind some benches, she crouched down and wrote the six letters of her name, using a different color for each letter. She regarded her work with a fierce, proud elation, and decided then and there that she would not, after all, give the chalk to Luke and Kevin. She was not sure, in fact, that she would ever give them anything else again.

The next week was a busy and productive one for Mrs. Saunders. She carried on her usual round of activities—shopping, cooking, cleaning her apartment daily, and writing to Walter, Louise, and Edith; evenings she babysat or watched television, and once attended a tenants' meeting on the subject of limited space for guest parking, though she possessed neither a car nor guests; she went to the bank to cash her social security check, as well as to a movie and to the dentist for some minor repair work on her bridge. But in addition to all this she went to the shopping center three times with Jill at noon, where, using caution, she managed to adorn several sidewalks and walls with her name.

She was not at all disturbed when Jill asked, "Anything special that you're coming in so often for, Mrs. Saunders? If it's anything I could do for you . . ."

"Oh, no, Jill dear." She laughed. "I'd be glad if you could do this for me, believe me. It's my bridge." She pointed to her teeth. "I've got to keep coming, he says, for a while longer, or else leave it with him for a few weeks, and then what would I do? I'd scare the children."

"Oh, no. Never that, Mrs. Saunders. Is it very painful?" Jill swerved around neatly into a parking space.

"Not at all. Just a nuisance. I hope you don't mind—"

"Don't be ridiculous, Mrs. Saunders. What are friends for?"

That day she was more busy than ever, for she had not only to add new FRANNYs but to check on the old. There had been a rainstorm over the weekend, which obliterated her name from the parking lot and the sidewalks. Also, a few small shopkeepers, specifically the butcher and the baker, evidently cleaned their outside walls weekly. She told Jill not to pick her up, for she might very likely be delayed, and as it turned out, she was. The constant problem of not being noticed was time-consuming, especially in the parking lot with its endless flow of cars in and out. Finished at last, she was amazed to find it was past two-thirty. Mrs. Saunders was filled with the happy exhaustion of one who has accomplished a decent and useful day's work. Looking about and wishing there were a comfortable place to rest for a while, she noticed that the window she was leaning against belonged to a paint store. Curious, she studied the cans and color charts. The colors were beautiful: vivid reds, blues, golds, and violets, infinitely more beautiful than her pastels. She had never cared much for pastels anyway. With a sly, physical excitement floating through her, Mrs. Saunders straightened up and entered.

She knew something about spray paint. Sukie, Walter's wife, had sprayed the kitchen chairs with royal blue down in the cellar last time Mrs. Saunders visited, nearly two years ago. She remembered it well, for Sukie, her hair, nose, and mouth covered with scarves, had called out somewhat harshly as Mrs. Saunders came down the steps, "For God's sake, stay away from it. It'll choke you. And would you mind opening some windows upstairs so when I'm done I can breathe?" Sukie was not a welcoming kind of girl. Mrs. Saunders sighed, then set her face into a smile for the paint salesman.

As she left the store contentedly with a shopping bag on her arm, she heard the insistent beep of a car horn. It was Jill. "Mrs. Saunders, hop in," she called. "I had a conference with Kevin's teacher," Jill explained, "and then the mothers' meeting to plan the party for the end of school, and after I dropped the kids at Wendy's I thought maybe I could still catch you."

Jill looked immensely pleased with her good deed, Mrs. Saunders thought, just as Louise and Edith used to look when they fixed dinner on her birthday, then sat beaming with achievement and waiting for praise, which she always gave in abundance.

"Isn't that sweet of you, Jill." But she was not as pleased as she tried to appear, for she had been looking forward to the calm bus ride and to privately planning when and where to use her new purchases. "You're awfully good to me."

"Oh, it's nothing, really. Buying paint?"

"Yes, I've decided to do the kitchen and bathroom."

"But they'll do that for you. Every two years. If you're due you just call the landlord and say so."

"But they don't use the colors I like and I thought it might be nice to try. . . ."

"It's true, they do make you pay a lot extra for colors," Jill said thoughtfully.

Mrs. Saunders studied the instructions on the cans carefully, and went over in her mind all the advice the salesman had given her. Late that evening after the family noises in the building had subsided, she took the can of red paint down to the laundry room in the basement. She also took four quarters and a small load of wash—the paint can was buried under the wash—in case she should meet anyone. She teased herself about this excessive precaution at midnight, but as it happened she did meet one of the young mothers, Nancy, pulling overalls and polo shirts out of the dryer.

"Oh, Mrs. Saunders! I was frightened for a minute. I didn't expect anyone down here so late. So you're another night owl, like me."

"Hello, Nancy. I meant to get around to this earlier, but it slipped my mind." She took the items out of her basket slowly, one by one, wishing Nancy would hurry.

"Since I took this part-time job I spend all my evenings doing housework. Sometimes I wonder if it's worth it." At last Nancy had the machine emptied. "Do you mind staying all alone? I could wait." She hesitated in the doorway, clutching her basket to her chest, pale and plainly exhausted.

"Oh no, Nancy dear. I don't mind at all, and anyhow, you look like you need some rest. Go on and get to sleep. I'll be fine."

She inserted her quarters and started the machine as Nancy disappeared. The clothes were mostly clean; she had grabbed any old thing to make a respectable-looking load. The extra washing wouldn't hurt them. With a tingling all over her skin and an irrepressible smile, she unsealed the can. Spraying was much easier than she had expected. The *F*, which she put on the wall behind the washer, took barely any time and effort. Paint dripped thickly from its upper left corner, though, indicating she had pressed too hard and too long. It was simple to adjust the pressure, and by the second *N* she felt quite confident, as if she had done this often before. She took a few steps back to look it over. It was beautiful—bold, thick, and bright against the cream-colored wall. So beautiful that she did another directly across the room. Then on the inside of the open door, rarely seen, she tried it vertically; aside from some long amateurish drips, she was delighted at the effect. She proceeded to the boiler room, where she sprayed FRANNY on the boiler and on the wall, then decided she had done enough for one night. Waiting for the laundry cycle to end, she was surrounded by the red, lustrous reverberations of her name, vibrating across the room at each other; she felt warmed and strengthened by the firm, familiar walls of her own self. While the room filled and teemed with visual echoes of FRANNY, Mrs. Saunders became supremely at peace.

She climbed the stairs slowly, adrift in this happy glow. She would collect her things from the dryer late tomorrow morning. Lots of young mothers and children would have been in and out by then. Nancy was the only one who could suspect, but surely Nancy didn't come down with a load every day; besides, she was so tired and harassed she probably wouldn't remember clearly. Mrs. Saunders entered her apartment smiling securely with her secret.

Yet new difficulties arose over the next few days. The deserted laundry room at night was child's play compared to the more public, open, and populated areas of the development. Mrs. Saunders finally bought a large tote bag in Woolworth's so she could carry the paint with her and take advantage of random moments of solitude. There were frequent lulls when the children's playground was empty, but since it was in full view of the balconies and rear windows, only once, at four-thirty on a Wednesday morning, did she feel safe, working quickly and efficiently to complete her name five times. The parking lot needed to be done in the early hours too, as well as the front walk and the wall space near the mailboxes. It was astonishing, she came to realize, how little you could rely on being unobserved in a suburban garden apartment development, unless you stayed behind your own closed door.

Nevertheless, she did manage to get her name sprayed in half a dozen places, and she took to walking around the grounds on sunny afternoons to experience the fairly delirious sensation of her identity, secretly yet miraculously out in the open, sending humming rays towards her as she moved along. Wherever she went she encountered herself. Never in all her life had she had such a potent sense of occupying and making an imprint on the world around her. The reds and blues and golds seemed even to quiver and heighten in tone as she approached, as if in recognition and tribute, but this she knew was an optical illusion. Still, if only they could speak. Then her joy and fulfillment would be complete. After her walks she sat in her apartment and smoked and saw behind her closed eyes parades of brilliantly colored FRANNYs move along in the darkness, and felt entranced as with the warmth of a soothing physical embrace. Only once did she have a moment of unease, when she met Jill on her way back in early one morning.

"Mrs. Saunders, did anything happen? What's the red stuff on your fingers?"

"Just nail polish, dear. I spilled some."

Jill glanced at her unpolished nails and opened her mouth to speak, but apparently changed her mind.

"Fixing a run in a stocking," Mrs. Saunders added as she carried her shopping bag inside. She sensed potential danger in that meeting, yet also enjoyed a thrill of defiance and a deep, faint flicker of expectation.

Then one evening Harris, Jill's husband, knocked on Mrs. Saunders' door to tell her there would be a tenants' meeting tomorrow night in the community room.

"You must have noticed," he said, "the way this place has been deteriorating lately. I mean, when we first moved in four years ago it was brand-new and they took care of it. Now look! First of all there's this graffiti business. You must've seen it, haven't you? Every kid and his brother have got their names outside—it's as bad as the city. Of course that Franny character takes the cake, but the others are running her a close second. Then the garbage isn't removed as often as it used to be, the mailboxes are getting broken, there's been a light out for weeks in the hall. . . . I could go on and on."

She was afraid he would, too, standing there leaning on her doorframe, large and comfortably settled. Harris was an elementary-school teacher; Mrs. Saunders guessed he was in the habit of making long speeches. She smiled and wondered if she ought to ask him in, but she had left a cigarette burning in the ashtray. In fact she had not noticed the signs of negligence that Harris mentioned, but now that she heard, she was grateful for them. She felt a trifle weak in the knees; the news of the meeting was a shock. If he didn't stop talking soon she would ask him in just so she could sit down, cigarette or no cigarette.

"Anyhow," Harris continued, "I won't keep you, but I hope you'll come. The more participation, the better. There's power in numbers."

"Yes, I'll be there, Harris. You're absolutely right."

"Thanks, Mrs. Saunders. Good night." She was starting to close the door when he abruptly turned back. "And by the way, thanks for the recipe for angel food cake you gave Jill. It was great."

"Oh, I'm glad, Harris. You're quite welcome. Good night, now."

Of course she would go. Her absence would be noted, for she always attended the meetings, even those on less crucial topics. Beneath her surface nervousness the next day, Mrs. Saunders was aware of an abiding calm. Buoyed up by her name glowing almost everywhere she turned, she felt strong and impregnable as she took her seat in the community room.

"Who the hell is Franny anyway?" asked a man from the neighboring unit. "She started it all. Anyone here got a kid named Franny?" One woman had a Frances, but, she said, giggling, her Frances was only nine months old. Mrs. Saunders felt a throb of alarm in her chest. But she soon relaxed: the nameplates on her door and mailbox read "Saunders" only, and her meager mail, even the letters from Walter, Louise, and Edith, she had recently noticed, was all addressed to Mrs. F. Saunders or Mrs. Walter Saunders. And of course, since these neighbors had never troubled to ask. . . . She suppressed a grin. You make your own bed, she thought, watching them, and you lie in it.

The talk shifted to the broken mailboxes, the uncollected garbage, the inadequacy of guest parking, and the poor TV reception, yet every few moments it returned to the graffiti, obviously the most chafing symptom of decay. To Mrs. Saunders the progress of the meeting was haphazard, without direction or goal. As in the past, people seemed more eager to air their grievances than to seek a practical solution. But she conceded that her experience of community action was limited; perhaps this was the way things got done. In any case, their collective obtuseness appeared a more than adequate safeguard, and she remained silent. She always remained silent at tenants' meetings—no one would expect anything different of her. She longed for a cigarette, and inhaled deeply the smoke of others' drifting around her.

At last—she didn't know how it happened for she had ceased to pay attention—a committee was formed to draft a petition to the management listing the tenants' complaints and demanding repairs and greater surveillance of the grounds. The meeting was breaking up. They could relax, she thought wryly, as she milled about with her neighbors, moving to the door. She had done enough painting for now anyway. She smiled with cunning and some contempt at their innocence of the vandal in their midst. Certainly, if it upset them so much she would stop. They did have rights, it was quite true.

She walked up with Jill. Harris was still downstairs with the other members of the small committee which he was, predictably, chairing.

"Well, it was a good meeting," Jill said. "I only hope something comes out of it."

"Yes," said Mrs. Saunders vaguely, fumbling for her key in the huge, heavy tote bag.

"By the way, Mrs. Saunders . . ." Jill hesitated at her door and nervously began brushing the wispy hair from her face. "I've been meaning to ask, what's your first name again?"

In her embarrassment Jill was blinking childishly and didn't know where to look. Mrs. Saunders felt sorry for her. In the instant before she replied—and Mrs. Saunders didn't break the rhythm of question and answer by more than a second's delay—she grasped fully that she was sealing her own isolation as surely as if she had bricked up from inside the only window in a cell.

"Faith," she said.

The longing she still woke with in the dead of night, despite all her work, would never now be eased. But when, in that instant before responding, her longing warred with the rooted habits and needs of a respectable lifetime, she found the longing no match for the life. And that brief battle and its outcome, she accepted, were also, irrevocably, who Franny was.

The profound irony of this turn of events seemed to loosen some old, stiff knot in the joints of her body. Feeling the distance and wisdom of years rising in her like sap released, she looked at Jill full in the face with a vast, unaccustomed compassion. The poor girl could not hide the relief that spread over her, like the passing of a beam of light.

"Isn't it funny, two years and I never knew," she stammered. "All that talk about names made me curious, I guess." Finally Jill turned the key in her lock and smiled over her shoulder. "Okay, good night, Mrs. Saunders. See you tomorrow night, right? The boys are looking forward to it."

Part Four

Drama and the Reader's Response

One
The Languages of Drama

What is it like to attend a play? It's a social event, both in the sense that you often go with someone else, and in the sense that while in the theater you enter into relationships with social institutions and rules. You have to buy a ticket so that the production of the play can be financed. You have to dress properly and behave politely, following the social rules for behavior at a fairly formal occasion. You applaud, you laugh at the right places. You try not to cough or sneeze. You don't kick the seat in front of you. You engage in polite conversation with your companion at the play.

Within this intricate web of social and economic and personal relations, you take in what happens on the stage. And what is happening on stage? Up there, an intricate web of social and economic and personal relations is also being created. Characters relate to one another within very specific social structures. Perhaps a daughter defies her father, or a policeman questions a suspect, or a woman laments the loss of her family home. Plays are about relationships between characters—conflicts, friendships, love, hate. The characters in the play are just like the audience in the theater, individuals within a world of social relationships. When we look at them we see ourselves.

Watching a Play

Characters in a play are enmeshed in language. When the actors, directors, designers, and the rest of the crew of a play begin, they have in front of them the written word—the **script.** There are in the script some stage directions or brief descriptions of the characters and their actions, but mainly there is **dialogue,** what the characters say. Dialogue is written language that the actors will turn into speech. Beginning with what the characters say, actors develop a sense of the characters' natures, and then devise ways to communicate those characters to us in a theatrical setting. This means that they have to turn the marks on a page into characters on a stage who speak and move and act.

This can happen because actors know how to multiply messages, speak to us in many "languages," or cultural codes. Once they get a sense from the dialogue of the identity of the character, they can imagine not only how such a character would talk but also how he would move and dress, how his body would react to events, how his face would express his emotions. Is the character aggressive? Let him walk with an aggressive stride, speak in a loud voice, glare at the other characters. Those of us who are part of this culture will know what such movements and gestures mean, because we participate in cultural systems of meaning, "languages" that communicate emotion and personality.

As the audience of a play, our job is to make sense of and react to those languages. We must be alert to the messages being sent, so that the characters can come richly to life within us. To do that we have to draw on our experience and apply our knowledge of human communications. An actor makes a gesture assuming that the audience knows what such a gesture means. In the moment of performance we can feel that communication happen; later, when we analyze the performance, we can explain how it was accomplished. And understanding *how* it happened will make us more available to future theatrical experiences. Actors, directors, set designers, and lighting experts all can send us direct and subtle messages, but only an active audience can make sense of all this information. We go to the theater to see these artists display their skills. They have taken words on a page and turned them into embodied characters who communicate through all the channels open to human beings.

Reading a Play

Of course, in *reading* a play you will *not* be the audience of a theatrical production. You will be in a position that in some ways requires more of you. You will, in fact, be in the position of those actors, directors, and designers when they begin their work—faced with words on the page. Instead of those theater people bringing the script to life, *you* will have to do it in your own imagination.

Let's take Bertolt Brecht's play *The Good Woman of Setzuan* as an example. This is a play that places extreme demands on our imaginative powers as readers. For instance, there is a young woman in the play who finds it useful at times to disguise herself as a man, supposedly her own cousin. As we read, we have to produce a mental image of the woman, Shen Te, and then imagine her in disguise—a complex imaginative act. As we read the play, we are told by other characters some facts about Shen Te's life and her appearance, but mainly what we have is her dialogue, from which we must derive a sense of her personal identity. We then produce a visual image that for us embodies that identity. As readers, *we* must do this work rather than have images presented to us by theatrical techniques. We are engaged in the production of a mental theater.

In reading drama, then, we have to move mentally from written language to the embodied languages of speech, movement, and gesture. In doing so we are producing the world of the play. Scripts do very little work for us. They don't *give* us images, they invite us to create them. We therefore take the verbal cues and build up an image of a character who moves and gestures and dresses and acts in ways that reflect his or her identity. And if we attend to our own imaginative process, we can learn something about those systems of communication and meaning that make drama possible.

Two
Action and Conflict

Twenty-five hundred years ago the Greek philosopher Aristotle argued that the essence of a play is action, and this definition continues to dominate our thinking about drama. The actors in a play do not just recite lines, they try to bring the play to life, to *act out* its story. Plays are depictions of people in action. They present us with human behavior, so that we can feel along with the characters, try to understand and judge their actions, and experience their lives along with them. As we read a play, we have to turn its language by an act of imagination into living characters whose actions affect each other's lives.

The language of the play can tell us a great deal about its characters. If we read the language actively enough, we can begin to see the world through the same framework that the characters bring to it. We can also feel their emotions along with them, as we experience the connotative power of their language. A character's language can communicate his or her emotion as well as the conceptual framework through which he or she looks at the world. As an example, in Ibsen's *A Doll House* a husband calls his wife "my little sky lark" and "my little squirrel." We don't need to hear more to feel his need to possess her, to take care of her, to treat her as a dependent. His feeling for his wife lives in his language.

Acting the Parts

When an actor attempts to bring this husband to life, he has to imagine the tone of voice that goes with that emotion, as well as the mannerisms and habits of such a man, so that the audience sees those emotions in action. As readers, we need to provide those images for ourselves. If we think and feel through the language, we can live inside the character's emotion, feel what such attitudes commit us to. If the playwright gives us rich enough language, the character's emotional life makes sense to us, takes on a powerful validity of its own. Even if we don't habitually feel as that husband does, reading his dialogue will put us at least temporarily in his shoes.

More generally, the language of a character can indicate how he or she looks at the world, and makes sense of events. In Susan Glaspell's *Trifles,* for example, one of the male characters, Hale, makes fun of the concerns of the women by using the word that gives the play its title, *trifles.* Hale along with two other men and two women have come to a house where a man has died suspiciously. In the men's minds, any details the women notice are "trifles", and the word reveals the men's habits of thought. Women, they believe, live outside of contact with the important concerns of the world, and worry only about the trivial and marginal. Of course, the "trifles" that the women notice in the play provide the keys to our solving the mystery. But we learn about the attitudes and beliefs of the men in the play through their use of this word.

One of the fascinating things about drama is that its essence is *dialogue,* not monologue. Each character in a play presents a distinct and powerful way of seeing and feeling the world. All of the characters can speak for themselves, and thus maintain their own points of view. The play is therefore made up of many competing voices. There is no narrator to tell us how to feel, or to describe the characters or tell us their deepest thoughts. There is only the language of the characters, standing alone, requiring us as readers to fill in the characters' personalities. We may judge the characters harshly, but we have still been put in their positions, asked to look at the world as they do. We can judge them, but we can't rush to judgment. We have to give all of them their due.

In Shakespeare's *King Lear,* for example, there is a bastard son, Edmund, who plots the destruction of his father and his half brother. He is cold enough to blind his own father and to plot his brother's death. He is as evil a character as you could imagine. And yet Shakespeare gives him his moment, forcing us to see the world from Edmund's point of view. He gives Edmund powerful language that expresses his outrage and jealousy:

> Thou, Nature, art my goddess, to thy law
> My services are bound. Wherefore should I
> Stand in the plague of custom, and permit
> The curiosity of nations to deprive me,

For that I am some twelve or fourteen moonshines
Lag of a brother? Why bastard? Wherefore base?
When my dimensions are as well compact,
My mind as generous and my shape as true,
As honest madam's issue? Why brand they us
With base? With baseness? Bastardy? Base, base?
Who in the lusty stealth of nature take
More composition and fierce quality
Than doth, within a dull, stale, tired bed,
Go to the creating a whole tribe of fops
Got 'tween asleep and wake? Well then,
Legitimate Edgar, I must have your land.
Our father's love is to the bastard Edmund
As to the legitimate—fine word, "legitimate"!
Well, my legitimate, if this letter speed
And my invention thrive, Edmund the base
Shall top the legitimate. I grow, I prosper.
Now, gods, stand up for bastards!

Edmund makes a very strong argument for himself here, depicting marriage as a mere "custom" that raises his legitimate brother above him unfairly. From this speech we can get a sense of Edmund's motives—his belief in his *natural* equality with his brother, and his outrage that he is not treated as an equal.

Now, I am not saying that seeing the world as the characters see it should keep us from making judgments about these characters. Of course we make judgments. My own response to this speech of Edmund's is that he claims a strong natural tie to his father and brother, but then does all he can to destroy them out of jealous revenge, denying all the "natural" ties of blood. Edmund is a self-serving hypocrite. But this speech does succeed in explaining where his evil energy comes from. It opens a window into an emotional life that we can imagine. He has not, after all, chosen to be illegitimate, and yet he suffers the consequences. His anger at this injustice, however, takes him beyond all concern with justice into a purely personal and cold revenge. We need not accept Edmund, but we do need to recognize how powerfully he believes what he believes.

Building around Conflict

In any play, a variety of points of view is presented. If each of the characters embodies a different way of looking at the world, then they all will inevitably come into conflict with one another. Thus, a play is usually built around conflict. Again an example from *King Lear.* At the beginning of the play we are presented with a father who has an emotional *need* for his daughters to prove their love to him. And we see a daughter whose integrity will not allow her on demand to make a public, artificial declaration of the love she truly feels. Those two ways of feeling cannot comfortably coexist. They can only lead to anger and bafflement. The plot of this play traces out the results of that conflict.

In general, dramatic plot can be defined in terms of such conflicts. The central character, or **protagonist,** comes into conflict with an opposing force, the **antagonist.** In the **exposition** of the plot, the opposing forces are introduced and brought into conflict. In the **complication,** the two forces continue to struggle, usually in increasingly intense fashion. These escalating conflicts lead to a **climax,** a final confrontation of the two forces, which resolves the conflict one way or another. The **denouement** of the play is the concluding section that presents the results of the conflicts. As you can see, plots are very orderly. If you begin with two characters who represent opposing attitudes toward life, certain conflicts will flow from their encounter, and out of those conflicts a logical result will follow.

The conflicts that occur within plots are a result of the dialogue and action that the play promotes. Strongly defined characters who see the world differently will glance off of one another, and if the opposition is strong enough, they will collide. Our job as readers is to read the characters' languages as signs of their personalities, to know what values they represent, and therefore to recognize their conflicts.

Sometimes those conflicts will be worked out in direct, physical action. The stage directions will tell us that a character attacks another, or that two characters kiss. But more frequently the action of the play is furthered by language, the speeches of the characters. In these cases language is symbolic action. In *The Good Woman of Setzuan,* for example, a woman *tells* a man that she will not marry him. In doing so she *does* something to him—pushes him away and punishes him for his cruel treatment of her—but verbally, not physically.

In drama, in other words, we have a direct experience of the power of language. In *King Lear,* the right words of love can win a daughter a kingdom. In *A Doll House,* a husband's condescending language can make a wife feel imprisoned. Language has the power to change the world, particularly to change people. Reading plays can alert us to how the people in our lives use language as an instrument of power. If you stick someone with a label—to use a common example, let's say *wimp*—you affect how other people will perceive that person, whose life will be changed as a result. In drama, often the only weapon characters have is their speech, and by attending to it we can participate in the conflicts of the play.

Thus, for many reasons reading plays requires close attention to language. Out of language grow characters, out of characters grow plots, and often the mode of action in the plot is language itself. As readers of drama our resources are almost completely limited to the speeches of the characters. From those we are invited to imagine a human world. The characters in the play are related to others through language. They become a social group, interacting each out of his or her own view of the world. Drama can be a way of teaching us how we relate to one another, and how those relations are defined by the power of language.

Three
Tragedy and Comedy

One of the best-known symbols in our culture is the pair of masks representing tragedy and comedy. The two masks are exact opposites—one extreme agony, the other extreme joy. The mask of tragedy suggests suffering and tears, particularly tears of grief; the mask of comedy suggests an uncontrollable, hysterical laughter. Yet somehow the masks are the same. For one thing the eyes are identical, empty and staring, as though the body and its emotions have driven out reason and restraint. Also, both masks are *extreme*—one is extreme joy, the other extreme sorrow, but both are exaggerations of normal emotions. It is as though the masks stake out the extremes of human life, and yet suggest that those extremes are somehow the same. In both states, tragedy and comedy, we are taken out of normal life, into a world of heightened drama and intensity. A world that can instruct us about human emotion and response.

Many plays openly identify themselves as either tragedies or comedies. By doing so they set up in their readers or in their audiences a set of expectations. If it's a tragedy we expect suffering and grief; if it's a comedy, amusement and laughter. When a play carries such a label, it pre-programs our emotional response to its events. As we read or see the play, we will process it differently, depending on the label. Let's take our two Shakespeare plays as examples. In *King Lear,* the tragedy, a father is cut off from his children; in *As You Like It,* the comedy, brother betrays brother, and a daughter is banished by her father. Both plays focus on the same kind of events, family conflicts. Yet our expectations as readers are different. In a tragedy, we expect that father to be destroyed; in a comedy, we expect those families to be reunited. So each rejection in *Lear* seems like another nail in Lear's coffin, whereas each betrayal in *As You Like It* seems like a complication that can be overcome. It has been said that tragedies end in death and comedies end in marriage. It's not always that simple, but our awareness of these tendencies in tragedies and comedies sets up our expectations for an appropriate emotional response.

Tragedy

The ancient philosopher Aristotle defined the emotional effect of tragedy as **purgation,** an effect we still experience today. For Aristotle, a tragedy is an emotional medicine, a purgative that rids us of excessive emotion. But it does so by heightening those same emotions. A tragedy presents us with the destruction of a hero. Because we admire and sympathize with the hero, his destruction calls for our sympathy and reminds us fearfully of our own vulnerability.

One of our tasks as readers of tragedy is therefore to open ourselves to pain. In a tragedy, *someone we like* is destroyed. This is a character in which we have invested a lot of work and emotion. We have brought that character to life by our imaginative effort as readers to transform language into a living person. We like the person we've created, and when that person blunders his or her way into destruction, we experience a frustrating loss. As Lear wanders madly on the heath, we feel his pain. By this I do not mean some kind of loose sentimentalism. Rather, I mean that we participate as active readers in the experience of that pain—which would not even make sense without our effort to embody the language of the play—we literally suffer along with him. A tragedy puts us through an emotional experience that few popular entertainments ask of us. In most popular films and TV shows, the villain is destroyed, the hero prevails. But in a tragedy the hero is destroyed, and we know that is going to be the case from the very beginning.

So why do we do it? Why go to or read a "play" (the word seems ironic here) where all we will do is suffer? I would suggest two different answers, each of which explains something about how we respond to tragedy. First of all, of course we do much more at a tragedy than suffer. But second, tragedy *does* teach us very profoundly about suffering.

If all there were to tragedy were suffering, such plays would be barbaric, sadomasochistic rituals. As Aristotle said, the purpose of tragedy is the *purgation* of emotion—after the emotions are aroused, they are supposed to be brought back into balance. How? The characters we have helped bring to life call for our sympathy. But the actions of those characters force us to recognize that in one way or another their suffering *makes sense.* It is the logical result of their actions. King Lear shattered on the heath is horrible, but his suffering comes about because of his foolish and weak need for his daughters to prove their love to him. Of course the best of them can't do it, and of course the good talkers have no real love for him—his isolation and abandonment come from his own actions. We can sympathize with him, but the logic of the play's action also helps us to *understand* his suffering.

In the history of tragedy there are two dominant explanations of that suffering. The destruction of the hero can be caused by a fate that predestines it, or by a tragic flaw in his or her character. *Oedipus Rex* is a tragedy based on fate. Oedipus has been cursed, his fate has been announced to him. No matter how strongly he believes he can take control of his life, there are powers beyond him that he can't control, and they lead him to his destruction. To a modern audience brought up with the belief that we *can* take control of our lives, Oedipus's destruction by fate is hard to accept. The play undermines our belief in human freedom, offering instead a belief in divine powers that control our lives. Our suffering then makes sense as the will of these divine powers, even if their motives are beyond our understanding. We can be consoled by believing that suffering is beyond our control, unavoidable.

King Lear is a tragedy based on a tragic flaw. Lear is a monarch coming to the end of his life and facing the diminishment of his powers who needs to be reassured of his daughters' love. When he exiles his good daughter and trusts his evil daughters, he brings about his own destruction. But Lear's suffering leads him through madness to a higher level of wisdom, from which he can see the truth about himself. Lear's suffering makes sense because it's the logical result of his acts, and because he moves beyond suffering into understanding.

In both plays, suffering is considered part of what it means to be human. Any emotion the play creates, it also makes sense of. Tragedy invites the reader to participate in an emotional ritual, allowing us to face some harsh facts about human life. Since the events are *fictional*, we can stand back from them and understand our emotions.

Comedy

As the audience of a comedy, we come to the play with very different expectations than to a tragedy. We can almost be sure, for example, that the sympathetic characters will prosper and that we will not have to face the loss of a character we like. In all probability, our heroes will find what they desire, make a connection, find a community that can sustain them. The evil characters—the hypocrites, the busybodies—will suffer a satisfying humiliation. Which is all to say, we expect to laugh.

Comedies promise us the opportunity to take joy in the moments when life works out. We go to them expecting the good characters to come together, to unite. We want to laugh along with them when they triumph. We also want to laugh at those who stand in the way of love or joy. Comedies, in other words, ask the audience to react emotionally in two very different ways. There is the laugh of joy, and there is the laugh of ridicule. One unites us as humans; the other separates us, seeks a victim. As the comedian Steve Martin says, "Comedy isn't pretty." There is an element of purgation in comedy as well as in tragedy. Comedy allows us to participate in ridicule, to act out aggression against a victim we can all agree deserves such treatment. After we have purged those separating emotions, we are able to participate in the ritual of unity that often concludes a comic plot. Comedies may end in marriages, symbols of human unity, but they have to pass through more violent human emotions first.

In order to produce these emotional reactions, comedies often focus around certain types of characters and plots. There is often a love story at the center of a comedy, so that we can identify with the lovers in their search for unity. The plot involves their efforts to overcome the obstacles that stand in their way. In *As You Like It,* the obstacles to be overcome are many; there are misunderstandings and disguises, as well as powerful enemies of love. As readers of a comedy, though, we *expect* those obstacles to be overcome. When the lovers are united we aren't surprised, but rather we get a satisfying sense of a promise fulfilled. We have seen that the lovers are destined for each other, and that expectation is rarely overturned. In this sense comedies are more reassuring, less challenging than tragedies. Comedies are easier on the emotions, relaxing rather than unsettling.

But as I have suggested, there is a darker side to comedy. For one thing, comedies often deal with very volatile human experiences—with betrayal and jealousy, hypocrisy and violence. The forces that oppose unity are often truly dangerous, such as the Duke in *As You Like It* or Moliere's Tartuffe. Tartuffe is the perfect hypocrite, condemning all humans in the name of a moral code that he doesn't hesitate to break himself. He is a moral monster who unfortunately reminds us that his vices are common—there is some Tartuffe in each of us. So we would like to destroy him, and as readers we participate in constructing the plot that undoes him. No one feels sympathy for Tartuffe. Even though we know we are like him, we laugh at his destruction, and thus become more like him in our cruelty. Now, I'm not saying that he deserves our sympathy, but I am saying we *enjoy* his destruction. Comedy needs a victim. The audience gets to act out an aggressive need, bringing that need back into balance by going through it in a ritual process.

To take a more modern example, look at *Crimes of the Heart.* In this play, the people who need to be united are three sisters. Their lives are all at crisis points, and they need each other's love in order to be able to deal with their problems. The play shows us those problems at least for the moment resolved, and the play ends in an almost magical moment of unity. All our expectations and emotional commitments are fulfilled. There is also a character who we get to see humiliated, the sisters' cousin Chick. She has opposed them at every step, and she gets hers in a triumphant scene in which the long-suffering oldest sister Lennie drives her screaming out of the house. The play performs the classical functions of comedy—it gets us to laugh at human vices and to laugh along with human joys.

Some comedies emphasize one response more than the other. We call comedies that emphasize ridicule **satires,** and those that emphasize unity are called **sentimental comedies.** Satires are attacks on characters who exhibit moral weaknesses. They have a moral point to make, and could be thought of as appeals to the audience to scorn and then to learn from these examples of human weakness. Some satires, though, present such a bleak view of human nature that they hold out no hope for improvement and allow us no possibility for real joy. Sentimental comedy, however, does not attack, it unifies. It asks the audience to join in a community of feeling. We have worked to bring the language to life, and we then watch those characters, our own creations, come to fulfill their desires. Most comedies fit somewhere between these two extremes, allowing us to purge our aggressions and still enjoy the ritual of unity.

Readers must be aware of the emotions that these two types of plays elicit. Just knowing that a play is a tragedy or a comedy doesn't tell you everything about it, but it does set you up as a knowledgeable participant in the imaginative process. There are, of course, many plays that overturn those expectations; but even so, such a play assumes you have those expectations and can therefore be surprised.

Take the case of **tragicomedy,** of which Shakespeare is the master. In Shakespeare's plays we often go from comedy to tragedy within a single scene, as in *King Lear,* where the fool is a source of ridicule and wit. We have a modern example here in Sean O'Casey's *The Plough and the Stars,* which calls itself a tragedy but is full of wildly comic scenes. Such plays obviously ask their readers for a very complex emotional response. The fool's comedy, for example, often reveals the very weaknesses that bring about Lear's destruction. The audience is asked to feel the sympathy that comedy can bring, which heightens the loss that the tragedy produces.

What tragicomedy tells us is that tragedy and comedy are not opposites but complements. Both are ways for the audience to deal with its own emotions in a literary or theatrical ritual. The events aren't real; they're fictional. Because of this our reactions don't devastate us as they would in real life. We can examine them, think about why we react as we do. Both tragedy and comedy offer us purgation, ways of coming to terms with strong emotions and needs. We need to understand suffering, we need to feel joy and to laugh out our cruelty. These plays give us that opportunity.

TRAGEDY

Sophocles (496–406 B.C.)
OEDIPUS REX

CHARACTERS

OEDIPUS, *King of Thebes, supposed son of Polybos and Meropê, King and Queen of Corinth*
IOKASTÊ, *wife of Oedipus and widow of the late King Laïos*
KREON, *brother of Iokastê, a prince of Thebes; son of Menoikeus*
TEIRESIAS, *a blind seer who serves Apollo*
PRIEST
MESSENGER, *from Corinth*
SHEPHERD, *former servant of Laïos*
SECOND MESSENGER, *from the palace*
CHORUS OF THEBAN ELDERS
CHORAGOS, *leader of the Chorus*
ANTIGONE *and* ISMENE, *young daughters of Oedipus and Iokastê. They appear in the Exodus but do not speak.*
SUPPLIANTS, GUARDS, SERVANTS

The Scene. Before the palace of OEDIPUS, *King of Thebes. A central door and two lateral doors open onto a platform which runs the length of the façade. On the platform, right and left, are altars; and three steps lead down into the orchestra, or chorus-ground. At the beginning of the action these steps are crowded by suppliants who have brought branches and chaplets of olive leaves and who sit in various attitudes of despair.* OEDIPUS *enters.*

PROLOGUE

OEDIPUS. My children, generations of the living
In the line of Kadmos, nursed at his ancient hearth:
Why have you strewn yourselves before these altars
In supplication, with your boughs and garlands?
The breath of incense rises from the city
With a sound of prayer and lamentations.
Children,
I would not have you speak through messengers,
And therefore I have come myself to hear you—
I, Oedipus, who bear the famous name.
[*To a* PRIEST] You, there, since you are eldest in the company,
Speak for them all, tell me what preys upon you,
Whether you come in dread, or crave some blessing:

Tell me, and never doubt that I will help you
In every way I can; I should be heartless
Were I not moved to find you suppliant here.

PRIEST. Great Oedipus, O powerful king of Thebes!
You see how all the ages of our people
Cling to your altar steps: here are boys
Who can barely stand alone, and here are priests
By weight of age, as I am a priest of God,
And young men chosen from those yet unmarried;
As for the others, all that multitude,
They wait with olive chaplets in the squares,
At the two shrines of Pallas, and where Apollo
Speaks in the glowing embers.
Your own eyes
Must tell you: Thebes is tossed on a murdering sea
And can not lift her head from the death surge.
A rust consumes the buds and fruits of the earth;
The herds are sick; children die unborn,
And labor is vain. The god of plague and pyre
Raids like detestable lightning through the city,
And all the house of Kadmos is laid waste,
All emptied, and all darkened: Death alone
Battens upon the misery of Thebes.

You are not one of the immortal gods, we know;
Yet we have come to you to make our prayer
As to the man surest in mortal ways
And wisest in the ways of God. You saved us
From the Sphinx, that flinty singer, and the tribute
We paid to her so long; yet you were never
Better informed than we, nor could we teach you:
A god's touch, it seems, enabled you to help us.

Therefore, O mighty power, we turn to you:
Find us our safety, find us a remedy,
Whether by counsel of the gods or of men.
A king of wisdom tested in the past
Can act in a time of troubles, and act well.
Noblest of men, restore
Life to your city! Think how all men call you
Liberator for your boldness long ago;
Ah, when your years of kingship are remembered,
Let them not say *We rose, but later fell*—
Keep the State from going down in the storm!
Once, years ago, with happy augury,

You brought us fortune; be the same again!
No man questions your power to rule the land:
But rule over men, not over a dead city!
Ships are only hulls, high walls are nothing,
When no life moves in the empty passageways.
OEDIPUS. Poor children! You may be sure I know
All that you longed for in your coming here.
I know that you are deathly sick; and yet,
Sick as you are, not one is as sick as I.
Each of you suffers in himself alone
His anguish, not another's; but my spirit
Groans for the city, for myself, for you.

I was not sleeping, you are not waking me.
No, I have been in tears for a long while
And in my restless thought walked many ways.
In all my search I found one remedy,
And I have adopted it: I have sent Kreon,
Son of Menoikeus, brother of the queen,
To Delphi, Apollo's place of revelation,
To learn there, if he can,
What act or pledge of mine may save the city.
I have counted the days, and now, this very day,
I am troubled, for he has overstayed his time.
What is he doing? He has been gone too long.
Yet whenever he comes back, I should do ill
Not to take any action the god orders.
PRIEST. It is a timely promise. At this instant
They tell me Kreon is here.
OEDIPUS. O Lord Apollo!
May his news be fair as his face is radiant!
PRIEST. Good news, I gather! he is crowned with bay,
The chaplet is thick with berries.
OEDIPUS. We shall soon know;
He is near enough to hear us now.
[*Enter* KREON.]
O Prince:
Brother: son of Menoikeus:
What answer do you bring us from the god?
KREON. A strong one, I can tell you, great afflictions
Will turn out well, if they are taken well.
OEDIPUS. What was the oracle? These vague words
Leave me still hanging between hope and fear.
KREON. Is it your pleasure to hear me with all these
Gathered around us? I am prepared to speak,
But should we not go in?

OEDIPUS. Speak to them all,
It is for them I suffer, more than for myself.
KREON. Then I will tell you what I heard at Delphi.
In plain words
The god commands us to expel from the land of Thebes
An old defilement we are sheltering.
It is a deathly thing, beyond cure;
We must not let it feed upon us longer.
OEDIPUS. What defilement? How shall we rid ourselves of it?
KREON. By exile or death, blood for blood. It was
Murder that brought the plague-wind on the city.
OEDIPUS. Murder of whom? Surely the god has named him?
KREON. My lord: Laïos once ruled this land,
Before you came to govern us.
OEDIPUS. I know;
I learned of him from others; I never saw him.
KREON. He was murdered; and Apollo commands us now
To take revenge upon whoever killed him.
OEDIPUS. Upon whom? Where are they? Where shall we find a clue
To solve that crime, after so many years?
KREON. Here in this land, he said. Search reveals
Things that escape an inattentive man.
OEDIPUS. Tell me: Was Laïos murdered in his house,
Or in the fields, or in some foreign country?
KREON. He said he planned to make a pilgrimage.
He did not come home again.
OEDIPUS. And was there no one,
No witness, no companion, to tell what happened?
KREON. They were all killed but one, and he got away
So frightened that he could remember one thing only.
OEDIPUS. What was that one thing? One may be the key
To everything, if we resolve to use it.
KREON. He said that a band of highwaymen attacked them,
Outnumbered them, and overwhelmed the king.
OEDIPUS. Strange, that a highwayman should be so daring—
Unless some faction here bribed him to do it.
KREON. We thought of that. But after Laïos' death
New troubles arose and we had no avenger.
OEDIPUS. What troubles could prevent your hunting down the killers?
KREON. The riddling Sphinx's song
Made us deaf to all mysteries but her own.
OEDIPUS. Then once more I must bring what is dark to light.
It is most fitting that Apollo shows,
As you do, this compunction for the dead.

You shall see how I sand by you, as I should,
Avenging this country and the god as well,
And not as though it were for some distant friend,
But for my own sake, to be rid of evil.
Whoever killed King Laïos might—who knows?—
Lay violent hands even on me—and soon.
I act for the murdered king in my own interest.
Come, then, my children: leave the altar steps,
Lift up your olive boughs!
One of you go
And summon the people of Kadmos to gather here.
I will do all that I can; you may tell them that.
[*Exit a* PAGE.]
So, with the help of God,
We shall be saved—or else indeed we are lost.

PRIEST. Let us rise, children. It was for this we came,
And now the king has promised it.
Phoibos has sent us an oracle; may he descend
Himself to save us and drive out the plague.

[*Exeunt* OEDIPUS *and* KREON *into the palace by the central door. The* PRIEST *and the* SUPPLIANTS *disperse right and left. After a short pause the* CHORUS *enters the orchêstra.*]

PÁRODOS

Strophe 1

CHORUS. What is God singing in his profound
Delphi of gold and shadow?
What oracle for Thebes, the sunwhipped city?
Fear unjoints me, the roots of my heart tremble.
Now I remember, O Healer, your power, and wonder:
Will you send doom like a sudden cloud, or weave it
Like nightfall of the past?
Speak to me, tell me, O
Child of golden Hope, immortal Voice.

Antistrophe 1

Let me pray to Athenê, the immortal daughter of Zeus,
And to Artemis her sister
Who keeps her famous throne in the market ring,
And to Apollo, archer from distant heaven—
O gods, descend! Like three streams leap against
The fires of our grief, the fires of darkness;
Be swift to bring us rest!
As in the old time from the brilliant house
Of air you stepped to save us, come again!

Strophe 2

Now our afflictions have no end,
Now all our stricken host lies down
And no man fights off death with his mind;
The noble plowland bears no grain,
And groaning mothers can not bear—
See, how our lives like birds take wing,
Like sparks that fly when a fire soars,
To the shore of the god of evening.

Antistrophe 2

The plague burns on, it is pitiless,
Though pallid children laden with death
Lie unwept in the stony ways,
And old gray women by every path
Flock to the strand about the altars
There to strike their breasts and cry
Worship of Phoibos in wailing prayers:
Be kind, God's golden child!

Strophe 3

There are no swords in this attack by fire,
No shields, but we are ringed with cries.
Send the besieger plunging from our homes
Into the vast sea-room of the Atlantic
Or into the waves that foam eastward of Thrace—
For the day ravages what the night spares—
Destroy our enemy, lord of the thunder!
Let him be riven by lightning from heaven!

Antistrophe 3

Phoibos Apollo, stretch the sun's bowstring,
That golden cord, until it sing for us,
Lashing arrows in heaven!
Artemis, Huntress,
Race with flaring lights upon our mountains!
O scarlet god, O golden-banded brow,
O Theban Bacchos in a storm of Maenads,
[*Enter* OEDIPUS, *center.*]
Whirl upon Death, that all the Undying hate!
Come with blinding torches, come in joy!

SCENE I

OEDIPUS. Is this your prayer? It may be answered. Come,
Listen to me, act as the crisis demands,
And you shall have relief from all these evils.

Until now I was a stranger to this tale,
As I had been a stranger to the crime.
Could I track down the murderer without a clue?
But now, friends,
As one who became a citizen after the murder,
I make this proclamation to all Thebans:
If any man knows by whose hand Laïos, son of Labdakos,
Met his death, I direct that man to tell me everything,
No matter what he fears for having so long withheld it.
Let it stand as promised that no further trouble
Will come to him, but he may leave the land in safety.
Moreover: If anyone knows the murderer to be foreign,
Let him not keep silent: he shall have his reward from me.
However, if he does conceal it; if any man
Fearing for his friend or for himself disobeys this edict,
Hear what I propose to do:

I solemnly forbid the people of this country,
Where power and throne are mine, ever to receive that man
Or speak to him, no matter who he is, or let him
Join in sacrifice, lustration, or in prayer.
I decree that he be driven from every house,
Being, as he is, corruption itself to us: the Delphic
Voice of Apollo has pronounced this revelation.
Thus I associate myself with the oracle
And take the side of the murdered king.

As for the criminal, I pray to God—
Whether it be a lurking thief, or one of a number—
I pray that that man's life be consumed in evil and
  wretchedness.
And as for me, this curse applies no less
If it should turn out that the culprit is my guest here,
Sharing my hearth.
                    You have heard the penalty.
I lay it on you now to attend to this
For my sake, for Apollo's, for the sick
Sterile city that heaven has abandoned.
Suppose the oracle had given you no command:
Should this defilement go uncleansed for ever?
You should have found the murderer: your king,
A noble king, had been destroyed!
                    Now I,
Having the power that he held before me,
Having his bed, begetting children there

Upon his wife, as he would have, had he lived—
Their son would have been my children's brother,
If Laïos had had luck in fatherhood!
(And now his bad fortune has struck him down)—
I say I take the son's part, just as though
I were his son, to press the fight for him
And see it won! I'll find the hand that brought
Death to Labdakos' and Polydoros' child,
Heir of Kadmos' and Agenor's line.
And as for those who fail me,
May the gods deny them the fruit of the earth,
Fruit of the womb, and may they rot utterly!
Let them be wretched as we are wretched, and worse!

For you, for loyal Thebans, and for all
Who find my actions right, I pray the favor
Of justice, and of all the immortal gods.

CHORAGOS. Since I am under oath, my lord, I swear
I did not do the murder, I can not name
The murderer. Phoibos ordained the search;
Why did he not say who the culprit was?

OEDIPUS. An honest question. But no man in the world
Can make the gods do more than the gods will.

CHORAGOS. There is an alternative, I think—

OEDIPUS. Tell me.
Any or all, you must not fail to tell me.

CHORAGOS. A lord clairvoyant to the lord Apollo,
As we all know, is the skilled Teiresias.
One might learn much about this from him, Oedipus.

OEDIPUS. I am not wasting time;
Kreon spoke of this, and I have sent for him—
Twice, in fact; it is strange that he is not here.

CHORAGOS. The other matter—that old report—seems useless.

OEDIPUS. What was that? I am interested in all reports.

CHORAGOS. The king was said to have been killed by
highwaymen.

OEDIPUS. I know. But we have no witnesses to that.

CHORAGOS. If the killer can feel a particle of dread,
Your curse will bring him out of hiding!

OEDIPUS. No.
The man who dared that act will fear no curse.

[*Enter the blind seer* TEIRESIAS, *led by a* PAGE.]

CHORAGOS. But there is one man who may detect the criminal.
This is Teiresias, this the holy prophet
In whom, alone of all men, truth was born.

OEDIPUS. Teiresias: seer: student of mysteries,
Of all that's taught and all that no man tells,
Secrets of Heaven and secrets of the earth:
Blind though you are, you know the city lies
Sick with plague; and from this plague, my lord,
We find that you alone can guard or save us.

Possibly you did not hear the messengers?
Apollo, when we sent to him,
Sent us back word that his great pestilence
Would lift, but only if we established clearly
The identity of those who murdered Laïos.
They must be killed or exiled.
Can you use
Birdflight or any art of divination
To purify yourself, and Thebes, and me
From this contagion? We are in your hands.
There is no fairer duty
Than that of helping others in distress.
TEIRESIAS. How dreadful knowledge of the truth can be
When there's no help in truth! I knew this well,
But did not act on it: else I should not have come.
OEDIPUS. What is troubling you? Why are your eyes so cold?
TEIRESIAS. Let me go home. Bear your own fate, and I'll
Bear mine. It is better so: trust what I say.
OEDIPUS. What you say is ungracious and unhelpful
To your native country. Do not refuse to speak.
TEIRESIAS. When it comes to speech, your own is neither temperate
Nor opportune. I wish to be more prudent.
OEDIPUS. In God's name, we all beg you—
TEIRESIAS. You are all ignorant.
No; I will never tell you what I know.
Now it is my misery; then, it would be yours.
OEDIPUS. What! You do know something, and will not tell us?
You would betray us all and wreck the State?
TEIRESIAS. I do not intend to torture myself, or you.
Why persist in asking? You will not persuade me.
OEDIPUS. What a wicked old man you are! You'd try a stone's
Patience! Out with it! Have you no feeling at all?
TEIRESIAS. You call me unfeeling. If you could only see
The nature of your own feelings . . .
OEDIPUS. Why,
Who would not feel as I do? Who could endure
Your arrogance toward the city?

TEIRESIAS. What does it matter?
Whether I speak or not, it is bound to come.
OEDIPUS. Then, if "it" is bound to come, you are bound to tell me.
TEIRESIAS. No, I will not go on. Rage as you please.
OEDIPUS. Rage? Why not!

And I'll tell you what I think:
You planned it, you had it done, you all but
Killed him with your own hands: if you had eyes,
I'd say the crime was yours, and yours alone.
TEIRESIAS. So? I charge you, then,
Abide by the proclamation you have made:
From this day forth
Never speak again to these men or to me;
You yourself are the pollution of this country.
OEDIPUS. You dare say that! Can you possibly think you have
Some way of going free, after such insolence?
TEIRESIAS. I have gone free. It is the truth sustains me.
OEDIPUS. Who taught you shamelessness? It was not your craft.
TEIRESIAS. You did. You made me speak. I did not want to.
OEDIPUS. Speak what? Let me hear it again more clearly.
TEIRESIAS. Was it not clear before? Are you tempting me?
OEDIPUS. I did not understand it. Say it again.
TEIRESIAS. I say that you are the murderer whom you seek.
OEDIPUS. Now twice you have spat out infamy. You'll pay for it!
TEIRESIAS. Would you care for more? Do you wish to be really angry?
OEDIPUS. Say what you will. Whatever you say is worthless.
TEIRESIAS. I say you live in hideous shame with those
Most dear to you. You can not see the evil.
OEDIPUS. Can you go on babbling like this for ever?
TEIRESIAS. I can, if there is power in truth.
OEDIPUS. There is:

But not for you, not for you,
You sightless, witless, senseless, mad old man!
TEIRESIAS. You are the madman. There is no one here
Who will not curse you soon, as you curse me.
OEDIPUS. You child of total night! I would not touch you;
Neither would any man who sees the sun.
TEIRESIAS. True; it is not from you my fate will come.
That lies within Apollo's competence,
As it is his concern.

OEDIPUS. Tell me, who made
These fine discoveries? Kreon? or someone else?
TEIRESIAS. Kreon is no threat. You weave your own doom.
OEDIPUS. Wealth, power, craft of statesmanship!
Kingly position, everywhere admired!
What savage envy is stored up against these,
If Kreon, whom I trusted, Kreon my friend,
For this great office which the city once
Put in my hands unsought—if for this power
Kreon desires in secret to destroy me!
He has bought this decrepit fortune-teller, this
Collector of dirty pennies, this prophet fraud—
Why, he is no more clairvoyant than I am!
Tell us:
Has your mystic mummery ever approached the truth?
When that hellcat the Sphinx was performing here,
What help were you to these people?
Her magic was not for the first man who came along:
It demanded a real exorcist. Your birds—
What good were they? or the gods, for the matter of that?
But I came by,
Oedipus, the simple man, who knows nothing—
I thought it out for myself, no birds helped me!
And this is the man you think you can destroy,
That you may be close to Kreon when he's king!
Well, you and your friend Kreon, it seems to me,
Will suffer most. If you were not an old man,
You would have paid already for your plot.
CHORAGOS. We can not see that his words or yours
Have been spoken except in anger, Oedipus,
And of anger we have no need. How to accomplish
The god's will best: that is what most concerns us.
TEIRESIAS. You are a king. But where argument's concerned
I am your man, as much a king as you.
I am not your servant, but Apollo's.
I have no need of Kreon or Kreon's name.
Listen to me. You mock my blindness, do you?
But I say that you, with both your eyes, are blind:
You can not see the wretchedness of your life,
Nor in whose house you live, no, nor with whom.
Who are your father and mother? Can you tell me?
You do not even know the blind wrongs
That you have done them, on earth and in the world below.
But the double lash of your parents' curse will whip you
Out of this land some day, with only night

Upon your precious eyes.
Your cries then—where will they not be heard?
What fastness of Kithairon will not echo them?
And that bridal-descant of yours—you'll know it then,
The song they sang when you came here to Thebes
And found your misguided berthing.
All this, and more, that you can not guess at now,
Will bring you to yourself among your children.

Be angry, then. Curse Kreon. Curse my words.
I tell you, no man that walks upon the earth
Shall be rooted out more horribly than you.

OEDIPUS. Am I to bear this from him?—Damnation
Take you! Out of this place! Out of my sight!

TEIRESIAS. I would not have come at all if you had not asked me.

OEDIPUS. Could I have told that you'd talk nonsense, that
You'd come here to make a fool of yourself, and of me?

TEIRESIAS. A fool? Your parents thought me sane enough.

OEDIPUS. My parents again!—Wait: who were my parents?

TEIRESIAS. This day will give you a father, and break your heart.

OEDIPUS. Your infantile riddles! Your damned abracadabra!

TEIRESIAS. You were a great man once at solving riddles.

OEDIPUS. Mock me with that if you like; you will find it true.

TEIRESIAS. It was true enough. It brought about your ruin.

OEDIPUS. But if it saved this town?

TEIRESIAS. [*to the* PAGE]. Boy, give me your hand.

OEDIPUS. Yes, boy; lead him away.
—While you are here
We can do nothing. Go; leave us in peace.

TEIRESIAS. I will go when I have said what I have to say.
How can you hurt me? And I tell you again:
The man you have been looking for all this time,
The damned man, the murderer of Laïos,
That man is in Thebes. To your mind he is foreign-born,
But it will soon be shown that he is a Theban,
A revelation that will fail to please.
A blind man,
Who has his eyes now; a penniless man, who is rich now;
And he will go tapping the strange earth with his staff.
To the children with whom he lives now he will be
Brother and father—the very same; to her
Who bore him, son and husband—the very same
Who came to his father's bed, wet with his father's blood.

Enough. Go think that over.
If later you find error in what I have said,
You may say that I have no skill in prophecy.
[*Exit* TEIRESIAS, *led by his* PAGE. OEDIPUS *goes into the palace.*]

ODE I

Strophe 1

CHORUS. The Delphic stone of prophecies
Remembers ancient regicide
And a still bloody hand.
That killer's hour of flight has come.
He must be stronger than riderless
Coursers of untiring wind,
For the son of Zeus armed with his father's thunder
Leaps in lightning after him;
And the Furies hold his track, the sad Furies.

Antistrophe 1

Holy Parnassos' peak of snow
Flashes and blinds that secret man,
That all shall hunt him down:
Though he may roam the forest shade
Like a bull gone wild from pasture
To rage through glooms of stone.
Doom comes down on him; flight will not avail him;
For the world's heart calls him desolate,
And the immortal voices follow, for ever follow.

Strophe 2

But now a wilder thing is heard
From the old man skilled at hearing Fate in the wing-beat of a bird.
Bewildered as a blown bird, my soul hovers and can not find
Foothold in this debate, or any reason or rest of mind.
But no man ever brought—none can bring
Proof of strife between Thebes' royal house,
Labdakos' line, and the son of Polybos;
And never until now has any man brought word
Of Laïos' dark death staining Oedipus the King.

Antistrophe 2

Divine Zeus and Apollo hold
Perfect intelligence alone of all tales ever told;

And well though this diviner works, he works in his own
night;
No man can judge that rough unknown or trust in second
sight,
For wisdom changes hands among the wise.
Shall I believe my great lord criminal
At a raging word that a blind old man let fall?
I saw him, when the carrion woman faced him of old,
Prove his heroic mind. These evil words are lies.

SCENE II

KREON. Men of Thebes:
I am told that heavy accusations
Have been brought against me by King Oedipus.

I am not the kind of man to bear this tamely.
If in these present difficulties
He holds me accountable for any harm to him
Through anything I have said or done—why, then,
I do not value life in this dishonor.
It is not as though this rumor touched upon
Some private indiscretion. The matter is grave.
The fact is that I am being called disloyal
To the State, to my fellow citizens, to my friends.
CHORAGOS. He may have spoken in anger, not from his mind.
KREON. But did you not hear him say I was the one
Who seduced the old prophet into lying?
CHORAGOS. The thing was said; I do not know how seriously.
KREON. But you were watching him! Were his eyes steady?
Did he look like a man in his right mind?
CHORAGOS. I do not know.
I can not judge the behavior of great men.
But here is the king himself.
[*Enter* OEDIPUS.]
OEDIPUS. So you dared come back.
Why? How brazen of you to come to my house,
You murderer!
Do you think I do not know
That you plotted to kill me, plotted to steal my throne?
Tell me, in God's name: am I coward, a fool,
That you should dream you could accomplish this?
A fool who could not see your slippery game?
A coward, not to fight back when I saw it?
You are the fool, Kreon, are you not? hoping

Without support or friends to get a throne?
Thrones may be won or bought: you could do neither.

KREON. Now listen to me. You have talked; let me talk, too.
You can not judge unless you know the facts.

OEDIPUS. You speak well: there is one fact; but I find it hard
To learn from the deadliest enemy I have.

KREON. That above all I must dispute with you.

OEDIPUS. That above all I will not hear you deny.

KREON. If you think there is anything good in being stubborn
Against all reason, then I say you are wrong.

OEDIPUS. If you think a man can sin against his own kind
And not be punished for it, I say you are mad.

KREON. I agree. But tell me: what have I done to you?

OEDIPUS. You advised me to send for that wizard, did you not?

KREON. I did. I should do it again.

OEDIPUS. Very well. Now tell me:
How long has it been since Laïos—

KREON. What of Laïos?

OEDIPUS Since he vanished in that onset by the road?

KREON. It was long ago, a long time.

OEDIPUS. And this prophet,
Was he practicing here then?

KREON. He was; and with honor, as now.

OEDIPUS. Did he speak of me at that time?

KREON. He never did,
At least, not when I was present.

OEDIPUS. But . . . the enquiry?
I suppose you held one?

KREON. We did, but we learned nothing.

OEDIPUS. Why did the prophet not speak against me then?

KREON. I do not know; and I am the kind of man
Who holds his tongue when he has no facts to go on.

OEDIPUS. There's one fact that you know, and you could tell it.

KREON. What fact is that? If I know it, you shall have it.

OEDIPUS. If he were not involved with you, he could not say
That it was I who murdered Laïos.

KREON. If he says that, you are the one that knows it!—
But now it is my turn to question you.

OEDIPUS. Put your questions. I am no murderer.

KREON. First, then: You married my sister?

OEDIPUS. I married your
sister.

KREON. And you rule the kingdom equally with her?

OEDIPUS. Everything that she wants she has from me.

KREON. And I am the third, equal to both of you?
OEDIPUS. That is why I call you a bad friend.
KREON. No. Reason it out, as I have done.
Think of this first: Would any sane man prefer
Power, with all a king's anxieties,
To that same power and the grace of sleep?
Certainly not I.
I have never longed for the king's power—only his rights.
Would any wise man differ from me in this?
As matters stand, I have my way in everything
With your consent, and no responsibilities.
If I were king, I should be a slave to policy.
How could I desire a scepter more
Than what is now mine—untroubled influence?
No, I have not gone mad; I need no honors,
Except those with the perquisites I have now.
I am welcome everywhere; every man salutes me,
And those who want your favor seek my ear,
Since I know how to manage what they ask.
Should I exchange this ease for that anxiety?
Besides, no sober mind is treasonable.
I hate anarchy
And never would deal with any man who likes it.
Test what I have said. Go to the priestess
At Delphi, ask if I quoted her correctly.
And as for this other thing: if I am found
Guilty of treason with Teiresias,
Then sentence me to death. You have my word
It is a sentence I should cast my vote for—
But not without evidence!
You do wrong
When you take good men for bad, bad men for good.
A true friend thrown aside—why, life itself
Is not more precious!
In time you will know this well:
For time, and time alone, will show the just man,
Though scoundrels are discovered in a day.
CHORAGOS. This is well said, and a prudent man would ponder it.
Judgments too quickly formed are dangerous.
OEDIPUS. But is he not quick in his duplicity?
And shall I not be quick to parry him?
Would you have me stand still, hold my peace, and let
This man win everything, through my inaction?

KREON. And you want—what is it, then? To banish me?
OEDIPUS. No, not exile. It is your death I want,
So that all the world may see what treason means.
KREON. You will persist, then? You will not believe me?
OEDIPUS. How can I believe you?
KREON. Then you are a fool.
OEDIPUS. To save myself?
KREON. In justice, think of me.
OEDIPUS. You are evil incarnate.
KREON. But suppose that you are wrong?
OEDIPUS. Still I must rule.
KREON. But not if you rule badly.
OEDIPUS. O city, city!
KREON. It is my city, too!
CHORAGOS. Now, my lords, be still. I see the queen,
Iokastê, coming from her palace chambers;
And it is time she came, for the sake of you both.
This dreadful quarrel can be resolved through her.
[*Enter* IOKASTÊ.]
IOKASTÊ. Poor foolish men, what wicked din is this?
With Thebes sick to death, is it not shameful
That you should rake some private quarrel up?
[*To* OEDIPUS]. Come into the house.
—And you, Kreon, go now:
Let us have no more of this tumult over nothing.
KREON. Nothing? No, sister: what your husband plans for me
Is one of two great evils: exile or death.
OEDIPUS. He is right.
Why, woman I have caught him squarely
Plotting against my life.
KREON. No! Let me die
Accurst if ever I have wished you harm!
IOKASTÊ. Ah, believe it, Oedipus!
In the name of the gods, respect this oath of his
For my sake, for the sake of these people here!

Strophe 1

CHORAGOS. Open your mind to her, my lord. Be ruled by her, I beg you!
OEDIPUS. What would you have me do?
CHORAGOS. Respect Kreon's word. He has never spoken like a fool,
And now he has sworn an oath.

OEDIPUS. You know what you ask?
CHORAGOS. I do.
OEDIPUS. Speak on, then.
CHORAGOS. A friend so sworn should not be baited so.
In blind malice, and without final proof.
OEDIPUS. You are aware, I hope, that what you say
Means death for me, or exile at the least.

Strophe 2

CHORAGOS. No, I swear by Helios, first in heaven!
May I die friendless and accurst,
The worst of deaths, if ever I meant that!
It is the withering fields
That hurt my sick heart:
Must we bear all these ills,
And now your bad blood as well?
OEDIPUS. Then let him go. And let me die, if I must,
Or be driven by him in shame from the land of Thebes.
It is your unhappiness, and not his talk,
That touches me.
As for him—
Wherever he goes, hatred will follow him.
KREON. Ugly in yielding, as you were ugly in rage!
Natures like yours chiefly torment themselves.
OEDIPUS. Can you not go? Can you not leave me?
KREON. I can.
You do not know me; but the city knows me,
And in its eyes I am just, if not in yours. [*Exit* KREON.]

Antistrophe 1

CHORAGOS. Lady Iokastê, did you not ask the King to go to his chambers?
IOKASTÊ. First tell me what has happened.
CHORAGOS. There was suspicion without evidence; yet it rankled
As even false charges will.
IOKASTÊ. On both sides?
CHORAGOS. On both.
IOKASTÊ. But what was said?
CHORAGOS. Oh let it rest, let it be done with!
Have we not suffered enough?
OEDIPUS. You see to what your decency has brought you:
You have made difficulties where my heart saw none.

Antistrophe 2

CHORAGOS. Oedipus, it is not once only I have told you—
You must know I should count myself unwise
To the point of madness, should I now forsake you—
You, under whose hand,
In the storm of another time,
Our dear land sailed out free.
But now stand fast at the helm!

IOKASTÊ. In God's name, Oedipus, inform your wife as well:
Why are you so set in this hard anger?

OEDIPUS. I will tell you, for none of these men deserves
My confidence as you do. It is Kreon's work,
His treachery, his plotting against me.

IOKASTÊ. Go on, if you can make this clear to me.

OEDIPUS. He charges me with the murder of Laïos.

IOKASTÊ. Has he some knowledge? Or does he speak from hearsay?

OEDIPUS. He would not commit himself to such a charge,
But he has brought in that damnable soothsayer
To tell his story.

IOKASTÊ. Set your mind at rest.
If it is a question of soothsayers, I tell you
That you will find no man whose craft gives knowledge
Of the unknowable.
Here is my proof:
An oracle was reported to Laïos once
(I will not say from Phoibos himself, but from
His appointed ministers, at any rate)
That his doom would be death at the hands of his own son—
His son, born of his flesh and of mine!

Now, you remember the story: Laïos was killed
By marauding strangers where three highways meet;
But his child had not been three days in this world
Before the king had pierced the baby's ankles
And left him to die on a lonely mountainside.

Thus, Apollo never caused that child
To kill his father, and it was not Laïos' fate
To die at the hands of his son, as he had feared.
This is what prophets and prophecies are worth!
Have no dread of them.
It is God himself
Who can show us what he wills, in his own way.

OEDIPUS. How strange a shadowy memory crossed my mind,
Just now while you were speaking; it chilled my heart.
IOKASTÊ. What do you mean? What memory do you speak of?
OEDIPUS. If I understand you, Laïos was killed
At a place where three roads meet.
IOKASTÊ. So it was said;
We have no later story.
OEDIPUS. Where did it happen?
IOKASTÊ. Phokis, it is called: at a place where the Theban Way
Divides into the roads toward Dephi and Daulia.
OEDIPUS. When?
IOKASTÊ. We had the news not long before you came
And proved the right to your succession here.
OEDIPUS. Ah, what net has God been weaving for me?
IOKASTÊ. Oedipus! Why does this trouble you?
OEDIPUS. Do not ask me yet.
First, tell me how Laïos looked, and tell me
How old he was.
IOKASTÊ. He was tall, his hair just touched
With white; his form was not unlike your own.
OEDIPUS. I think that I myself may be accurst
By my own ignorant edict.
IOKASTÊ. You speak strangely.
It makes me tremble to look at you, my king.
OEDIPUS. I am not sure that the blind man can not see.
But I should know better if you were to tell me—
IOKASTÊ. Anything—though I dread to hear you ask it.
OEDIPUS. Was the king lightly escorted, or did he ride
With a large company, as a ruler should?
IOKASTÊ. There were five men with him in all: one was a
herald;
And a single chariot, which he was driving.
OEDIPUS. Alas, that makes it plain enough!
But who—
Who told you how it happened?
IOKASTÊ. A household servant,
The only one to escape.
OEDIPUS. And is he still
A servant of ours?
IOKASTÊ. No; for when he came back at last
And found you enthroned in the place of the dead king,
He came to me, touched my hand with his, and begged
That I would send him away to the frontier district
Where only the shepherds go—

As far away from the city as I could send him.
I granted his prayer; for although the man was a slave,
He had earned more than this favor at my hands.
OEDIPUS. Can he be called back quickly?
IOKASTÊ. Easily.
But why?
OEDIPUS. I have taken too much upon myself
Without enquiry; therefore I wish to consult him.
IOKASTÊ. Then he shall come.
But am I not one also
To whom you might confide these fears of yours?
OEDIPUS. That is your right; it will not be denied you,
Now least of all; for I have reached a pitch
Of wild foreboding. Is there anyone
To whom I should sooner speak?

Polybos of Corinth is my father.
My mother is a Dorian: Meropê.
I grew up chief among the men of Corinth
Until a strange thing happened—
Not worth my passion, it may be, but strange.
At a feast, a drunken man maundering in his cups
Cries out that I am not my father's son!

I contained myself that night, though I felt anger
And a sinking heart. The next day I visited
My father and mother, and questioned them. They stormed,
Calling it all the slanderous rant of a fool;
And this relieved me. Yet the suspicion
Remained always aching in my mind;
I knew there was talk; I could not rest;
And finally, saying nothing to my parents,
I went to the shrine at Delphi.

The god dismissed my question without reply;
He spoke of other things.
Some were clear,
Full of wretchedness, dreadful, unbearable:
As, that I should lie with my own mother, breed
Children from whom all men would turn their eyes;
And that I should be my father's murderer.
I heard all this, and fled. And from that day
Corinth to me was only in the stars
Descending in that quarter of the sky,
As I wandered farther and farther on my way

To a land where I should never see the evil
Sung by the oracle. And I came to this country
Where, so you say, King Laïos was killed.

I will tell you all that happened there, my lady.

There were three highways
Coming together at a place I passed;
And there a herald came towards me, and a chariot
Drawn by horses, with a man such as you describe
Seated in it. The groom leading the horses
Forced me off the road at his lord's command;
But as this charioteer lurched over towards me
I struck him in my rage. The old man saw me
And brought his double goad down upon my head
As I came abreast.
He was paid back, and more!
Swinging my club in this right hand I knocked him
Out of his car, and he rolled on the ground.
I killed him.

I killed them all.
Now if that stranger and Laïos were—kin,
Where is a man more miserable than I?
More hated by the gods? Citizen and alien alike
Must never shelter me or speak to me—
I must be shunned by all.
And I myself
Pronounced this malediction upon myself!

Think of it: I have touched you with these hands,
These hands that killed your husband. What defilement!

Am I all evil, then? It must be so,
Since I must flee from Thebes, yet never again
See my own countrymen, my own country,
For fear of joining my mother in marriage
And killing Polybos, my father.
Ah,
If I was created so, born to this fate,
Who could deny the savagery of God?

O holy majesty of heavenly powers!
May I never see that day! Never!
Rather let me vanish from the race of men
Than know the abomination destined me!

CHORAGOS. We too, my lord, have felt dismay at this.
But there is hope: you have yet to hear the shepherd.
OEDIPUS. Indeed, I fear no other hope is left me.
IOKASTÊ. What do you hope from him when he comes?
OEDIPUS. This much:
If his account of the murder tallies with yours,
Then I am cleared.
IOKASTÊ. What was it that I said
Of such importance?
OEDIPUS. Why, "marauders," you said,
Killed the king, according to this man's story.
If he maintains that still, if there were several,
Clearly the guilt is not mine: I was alone.
But if he says one man, singlehanded, did it,
Then the evidence all points to me.
IOKASTÊ. You may be sure that he said there were several;
And can he call back that story now? He can not.
The whole city heard it as plainly as I.
But suppose he alters some detail of it:
He can not ever show that Laïos' death
Fulfilled the oracle: for Apollo said
My child was doomed to kill him; and my child—
Poor baby!—it was my child that died first.

No. From now on, where oracles are concerned,
I would not waste a second thought on any.
OEDIPUS. You may be right.
But come: let someone go
For the shepherd at once. This matter must be settled.
IOKASTÊ. I will send for him.
I would not wish to cross you in anything,
And surely not in this.—Let us go in.
[*Exeunt into the palace.*]

ODE II

Strophe 1

CHORUS. Let me be reverent in the ways of right,
Lowly the paths I journey on;
Let all my words and actions keep
The laws of the pure universe
From highest Heaven handed down.
For Heaven is their bright nurse,
Those generations of the realms of light;

Ah, never of mortal kind were they begot,
Nor are they slaves of memory, lost in sleep:
Their Father is greater than Time, and ages not.

Antistrophe 1

The tyrant is a child of Pride
Who drinks from his great sickening cup
Recklessness and vanity,
Until from his high crest headlong
He plummets to the dust of hope.
That strong man is not strong.
But let no fair ambition be denied;
May God protect the wrestler for the State
In government, in comely policy,
Who will fear God, and on His ordinance wait.

Strophe 2

Haughtiness and the high hand of disdain
Tempt and outrage God's holy law;
And any mortal who dares hold
No immortal Power in awe
Will be caught up in a net of pain:
The price for which his levity is sold.
Let each man take due earnings, then,
And keep his hands from holy things,
And from blasphemy stand apart—
Else the crackling blast of heaven
Blows on his head, and on his desperate heart.
Though fools will honor impious men,
In their cities no tragic poet sings.

Antistrophe 2

Shall we lose faith in Delphi's obscurities,
We who have heard the world's core
Discredited, and the sacred wood
Of Zeus at Elis praised no more?
The deeds and the strange prophecies
Must make a pattern yet to be understood.
Zeus, if indeed you are lord of all,
Throned in light over night and day,
Mirror this in your endless mind:
Our masters call the oracle
Words on the wind, and the Delphic vision blind!
Their hearts no longer know Apollo,
And reverence for the gods has died away.

SCENE III

[*Enter* IOKASTÊ.]

IOKASTÊ. Princes of Thebes, it has occurred to me
To visit the altars of the gods, bearing
These branches as a suppliant, and this incense.
Our king is not himself: his noble soul
Is overwrought with fantasies of dread,
Else he would consider
The new prophecies in the light of the old.
He will listen to any voice that speaks disaster,
And my advice goes for nothing.
[*She approaches the altar, right.*]
To you, then Apollo,
Lycéan lord, since you are nearest, I turn in prayer.
Receive these offerings, and grant us deliverance
From defilement. Our hearts are heavy with fear
When we see our leader distracted, as helpless sailors
Are terrified by the confusion of their helmsman.
[*Enter* MESSENGER.]
MESSENGER. Friends, no doubt you can direct me:
Where shall I find the house of Oedipus,
Or, better still, where is the king himself?
CHORAGOS. It is this very place, stranger; he is inside.
This is his wife and mother of his children.
MESSENGER. I wish her happiness in a happy house,
Blest in all the fulfillment of her marriage.
IOKASTÊ. I wish as much for you: your courtesy
Deserves a like good fortune. But now, tell me:
Why have you come? What have you to say to us?
MESSENGER. Good news, my lady, for your house and your husband.
IOKASTÊ. What news? Who sent you here?
MESSENGER. I am from Corinth.
The news I bring ought to mean joy for you,
Though it may be you will find some grief in it.
IOKASTÊ. What is it? How can it touch us in both ways?
MESSENGER. The word is that the people of the Isthmus
Intend to call Oedipus to be their king.
IOKASTÊ. But old King Polybos—is he not reigning still?
MESSENGER. No. Death holds him in his sepulchre.
IOKASTÊ. What are you saying? Polybos is dead?
MESSENGER. If I am not telling the truth, may I die myself.

IOKASTÊ. [*to a* MAIDSERVANT]. Go in, go quickly; tell this to your master.
O riddlers of God's will, where are you now!
This was the man whom Oedipus, long ago,
Feared so, fled so, in dread of destroying him—
But it was another fate by which he died.
[*Enter* OEDIPUS, *center.*]
OEDIPUS. Dearest Iokastê, why have you sent for me?
IOKASTÊ. Listen to what this man says, and then tell me
What has become of the solemn prophecies.
OEDIPUS. Who is this man? What is his news for me?
IOKASTÊ. He has come from Corinth to announce your father's death!
OEDIPUS. Is it true, stranger? Tell me in your own words.
MESSENGER. I can not say it more clearly: the king is dead.
OEDIPUS. Was it by treason? Or by an attack of illness?
MESSENGER. A little thing brings old men to their rest.
OEDIPUS. It was sickness, then?
MESSENGER. Yes, and his many years.
OEDIPUS. Ah!
Why should a man respect the Pythian hearth, or
Give heed to the birds that jangle above his head?
They prophesied that I should kill Polybos,
Kill my own father; but he is dead and buried,
And I am here—I never touched him, never,
Unless he died of grief for my departure,
And thus, in a sense, through me. No. Polybos
Has packed the oracles off with him underground.
They are empty words.
IOKASTÊ. Had I not told you so?
OEDIPUS. You had; it was my faint heart that betrayed me.
IOKASTÊ. From now on never think of those things again.
OEDIPUS. And yet—must I not fear my mother's bed?
IOKASTÊ. Why should anyone in this world be afraid,
Since Fate rules us and nothing can be foreseen?
A man should live only for the present day.

Have no more fear of sleeping with your mother:
How many men, in dreams, have lain with their mothers!
No reasonable man is troubled by such things.
OEDIPUS. This is true; only—
If only my mother were not still alive!
But she is alive. I can not help my dread.
IOKASTÊ. Yet this news of your father's death is wonderful.
OEDIPUS. Wonderful. But I fear the living woman.

MESSENGER. Tell me, who is this woman that you fear?
OEDIPUS. It is Meropê, man; the wife of King Polybos.
MESSENGER. Meropê? Why should you be afraid of her?
OEDIPUS. An oracle of the gods, a dreadful saying.
MESSENGER. Can you tell me about it or are you sworn to silence?
OEDIPUS. I can tell you, and I will.
Apollo said through this prophet that I was the man
Who should marry his own mother, shed his father's blood
With his own hands. And so, for all these years
I have kept clear of Corinth, and no harm has come—
Though it would have been sweet to see my parents again.
MESSENGER. And is this the fear that drove you out of Corinth?
OEDIPUS. Would you have me kill my father?
MESSENGER. As for that
You must be reassured by the news I gave you.
OEDIPUS. If you could reassure me, I would reward you.
MESSENGER. I had that in mind, I will confess: I thought
I could count on you when you returned to Corinth.
OEDIPUS. No: I will never go near my parents again.
MESSENGER. Ah, son, you still do not know what you are doing—
OEDIPUS. What do you mean? In the name of God tell me!
MESSENGER. —If these are your reasons for not going home.
OEDIPUS. I tell you, I fear the oracle may come true.
MESSENGER. And guilt may come upon you through your parents?
OEDIPUS. That is the dread that is always in my heart.
MESSENGER. Can you not see that all your fears are groundless?
OEDIPUS. Groundless? Am I not my parents' son?
MESSENGER. Polybos was not your father.
OEDIPUS. Not my father?
MESSENGER. No more your father than the man speaking to you.
OEDIPUS. But you are nothing to me!
MESSENGER. Neither was he.
OEDIPUS. Then why did he call me son?
MESSENGER. I will tell you:
Long ago he had you from my hands, as a gift.
OEDIPUS. Then how could he love me so, if I was not his?
MESSENGER. He had no children, and his heart turned to you.
OEDIPUS. What of you? Did you buy me? Did you find me by chance?
MESSENGER. I came upon you in the woody vales of Kithairon.
OEDIPUS. And what were you doing there?

MESSENGER. Tending my flocks.
OEDIPUS. A wandering shepherd?
MESSENGER. But your savior, son, that day.
OEDIPUS. From what did you save me?
MESSENGER. Your ankles should tell you that.
OEDIPUS. Ah, stranger, why do you speak of that childhood pain?
MESSENGER. I pulled the skewer that pinned your feet together.
OEDIPUS. I have had the mark as long as I can remember.
MESSENGER. That was why you were given the name you bear.
OEDIPUS. God! Was it my father or my mother who did it? Tell me!
MESSENGER. I do not know. The man who gave you to me
Can tell you better than I.
OEDIPUS. It was not you that found me, but another?
MESSENGER. It was another shepherd gave you to me.
OEDIPUS. Who was he? Can you tell me who he was?
MESSENGER. I think he was said to be one of Laïos' people.
OEDIPUS. You mean the Laïos who was king here years ago?
MESSENGER. Yes, King Laïos; and the man was one of his herdsmen.
OEDIPUS. Is he still alive? Can I see him?
MESSENGER. These men here
Know best about such things.
OEDIPUS. Does anyone here
Know this shepherd that he is talking about?
Have you seen him in the fields, or in the town?
If you have, tell me. It is time things were made plain.
CHORAGOS. I think the man he means is that same shepherd
You have already asked to see. Iokastê perhaps
Could tell you something.
OEDIPUS. Do you know anything
About him, Lady? Is he the man we have summoned?
Is that the man this shepherd means?
IOKASTÊ. Why think of him?
Forget this herdsman. Forget it all.
This talk is a waste of time.
OEDIPUS. How can you say that,
When the clues to my true birth are in my hands?
IOKASTÊ. For God's love, let us have no more questioning!
Is your life nothing to you?
My own is pain enough for me to bear.
OEDIPUS. You need not worry. Suppose my mother a slave.
And born of slaves: no baseness can touch you.

IOKASTÊ. Listen to me, I beg you: do not do this thing!
OEDIPUS. I will not listen; the truth must be made known.
IOKASTÊ. Everything that I say is for your own good!
OEDIPUS. My own good
Snaps my patience, then; I want none of it.
IOKASTÊ. You are fatally wrong! May you never learn who you are!
OEDIPUS. Go, one of you, and bring the shepherd here.
Let us leave this woman to brag of her royal name.
IOKASTÊ. Ah, miserable!
That is the only word I have for you now.
That is the only word I can ever have. [*Exit into the palace.*]
CHORAGOS. Why has she left us, Oedipus? Why has she gone
In such a passion of sorrow? I fear this silence:
Something dreadful may come of it.
OEDIPUS. Let it come!
However base my birth, I must know about it.
The Queen, like a woman, is perhaps ashamed
To think of my low origin. But I
Am a child of Luck; I can not be dishonored.
Luck is my mother; the passing months, my brothers,
Have seen me rich and poor.
If this is so,
How could I wish that I were someone else?
How could I not be glad to know my birth?

ODE III

Strophe

CHORUS. If ever the coming time were known
To my heart's pondering,
Kithairon, now by Heaven I see the torches
At the festival of the next full moon,
And see the dance, and hear the choir sing
A grace to your gentle shade:
Mountain where Oedipus was found,
O mountain guard of a noble race!
May the god who heals us lend his aid,
And let that glory come to pass
For our king's cradling-ground.

Antistrophe

Of the nymphs that flower beyond the years,
Who bore you, royal child,
To Pan of the hills or the timberline Apollo,

Cold in delight where the upland clears,
Or Hermês for whom Kyllenê's heights are piled?
Or flushed as evening cloud,
Great Dionysos, roamer of mountains,
He—was it he who found you there,
And caught you up in his own proud
Arms from the sweet god-ravisher
Who laughed by the Muses' fountains?

SCENE IV

OEDIPUS. Sirs: though I do not know the man,
I think I see him coming, this shepherd we want:
He is old, like our friend here, and the men
Bringing him seem to be servants of my house.
But you can tell, if you have ever seen him.
[*Enter* SHEPHERD *escorted by* SERVANTS.]
CHORAGOS. I know him, he was Laïos' man. You can trust him.
OEDIPUS. Tell me first, you from Corinth: is this the shepherd
We were discussing?
MESSENGER. This is the very man.
OEDIPUS. [*to* SHEPHERD]. Come here. No, look at me. You must answer
Everything I ask—You belonged to Laïos?
SHEPHERD. Yes: born his slave, brought up in his house.
OEDIPUS. Tell me: what kind of work did you do for him?
SHEPHERD. I was a shepherd of his, most of my life.
OEDIPUS. Where mainly did you go for pasturage?
SHEPHERD. Sometimes Kithairon, sometimes the hills near-by.
OEDIPUS. Do you remember ever seeing this man out there?
SHEPHERD. What would he be doing there? This man?
OEDIPUS. This man standing here. Have you ever seen him before?
SHEPHERD. No. At least, not to my recollection.
MESSENGER. And that is not strange, my lord. But I'll refresh
His memory: he must remember when we two
Spent three whole seasons together, March to September,
On Kithairon or thereabouts. He had two flocks;
I had one. Each autumn I'd drive mine home
And he would go back with his to Laïos' sheepfold.—
Is this not true, just as I have described it?
SHEPHERD. True, yes; but it was all so long ago.
MESSENGER. Well, then: do you remember, back in those days,
That you gave me a baby boy to bring up as my own?
SHEPHERD. What if I did? What are you trying to say?
MESSENGER. King Oedipus was once that little child.

SHEPHERD. Damn you, hold your tongue!
OEDIPUS. No more of that!
It is your tongue needs watching, not this man's.
SHEPHERD. My king, my master, what is it I have done wrong?
OEDIPUS. You have not answered his question about the boy.
SHEPHERD. He does not know . . . He is only making trouble . . .
OEDIPUS. Come, speak plainly, or it will go hard with you.
SHEPHERD. In God's name, do not torture an old man!
OEDIPUS. Come here, one of you; bind his arms behind him.
SHEPHERD. Unhappy king! What more do you wish to learn?
OEDIPUS. Did you give this man the child he speaks of?
SHEPHERD. I did.
And I would to God I had died that very day.
OEDIPUS. You will die now unless you speak the truth.
SHEPHERD. Yet if I speak the truth, I am worse than dead.
OEDIPUS. [*to* ATTENDANT]. He intends to draw it out, apparently—
SHEPHERD. No! I have told you already that I gave him the boy.
OEDIPUS. Where did you get him? From your house? From somewhere else?
SHEPHERD. Not from mine, no. A man gave him to me.
OEDIPUS. Is that man here? Whose house did he belong to?
SHEPHERD. For God's love, my king, do not ask me any more!
OEDIPUS. You are a dead man if I have to ask you again.
SHEPHERD. Then . . . Then the child was from the palace of Laïos.
OEDIPUS. A slave child? or a child of his own line?
SHEPHERD. Ah, I am on the brink of dreadful speech!
OEDIPUS. And I of dreadful hearing. Yet I must hear.
SHEPHERD. If you must be told, then . . .
They said it was Laïos' child;
But it is your wife who can tell you about that.
OEDIPUS. My wife—Did she give it to you?
SHEPHERD. My lord, she did.
OEDIPUS. Do you know why?
SHEPHERD. I was told to get rid of it.
OEDIPUS. Oh heartless mother!
SHEPHERD. But in dread of prophecies . . .
OEDIPUS. Tell me.
SHEPHERD. It was said that the boy would kill his own father.
OEDIPUS. Then why did you give him over to this old man?
SHEPHERD. I pitied the baby, my king,
And I thought that this man would take him far away

To his own country.
He saved him—but for what a fate!
For if you are what this man says you are,
No man living is more wretched than Oedipus.

OEDIPUS. Ah God!
It was true!
All the prophecies!
—Now,
O Light, may I look on you for the last time!
I, Oedipus,
Oedipus, damned in his birth, in his marriage damned,
Damned in the blood he shed with his own hand! [*He rushes into the palace.*]

ODE IV

Strophe 1

CHORUS. Alas for the seed of men.
What measure shall I give these generations
That breathe on the void and are void
And exist and do not exist?
Who bears more weight of joy
Than mass of sunlight shifting in images,
Or who shall make his thought stay on
That down time drifts away?
Your splendor is all fallen.
O naked brow of wrath and tears,
O change of Oedipus!
I who saw your days call no man blest—
Your great days like ghosts gone.

Antistrophe 1

That mind was a strong bow.
Deep, how deep you drew it then, hard archer,
At a dim fearful range,
And brought dear glory down!
You overcame the stranger—
The virgin with her hooking lion claws—
And though death sang, stood like a tower
To make pale Thebes take heart.
Fortress against our sorrow!
True king, giver of laws,
Majestic Oedipus!
No prince in Thebes had ever such renown,
No prince won such grace of power.

Strophe 2

And now of all men ever known
Most pitiful is this man's story:
His fortunes are most changed, his state
Fallen to a low slave's
Ground under bitter fate.
O Oedipus, most royal one!
The great door that expelled you to the light
Gave at night—ah, gave night to your glory:
As to the father, to the fathering son.
All understood too late.
How could that queen whom Laïos won,
The garden that he harrowed at his height,
Be silent when that act was done?

Antistrophe 2

But all eyes fail before time's eye,
All actions come to justice there.
Though never willed, though far down the deep past,
Your bed, your dread sirings,
Are brought to book at last.
Child by Laïos doomed to die,
Then doomed to lose that fortunate little death,
Would God you never took breath in this air
That with my wailing lips I take to cry:
For I weep the world's outcast.
I was blind, and now I can tell why:
Asleep, for you had given ease of breath
To Thebes, while the false years went by.

EXODOS

[*Enter, from the palace,* SECOND MESSENGER.]

SECOND MESSENGER. Elders of Thebes, most honored in this land,
What horrors are yours to see and hear, what weight
Of sorrow to be endured, if, true to your birth,
You venerate the line of Labdakos!
I think neither Istros nor Phasis, those great rivers,
Could purify this place of all the evil
It shelters now, or soon must bring to light—
Evil not done unconsciously, but willed.

The greatest griefs are those we cause ourselves.

CHORAGOS. Surely, friend, we have grief enough already;
What new sorrow do you mean?

SECOND MESSENGER. The queen is dead.

CHORAGOS. O miserable queen! But at whose hand?

SECOND MESSENGER. Her own.
The full horror of what happened you can not know,
For you did not see it; but I, who did, will tell you
As clearly as I can how she met her death.

When she had left us,
In passionate silence, passing through the court,
She ran to her apartment in the house,
Her hair clutched by the fingers of both hands.
She closed the doors behind her; then, by that bed
Where long ago the fatal son was conceived—
That son who should bring about his father's death—
We heard her call upon Laïos, dead so many years,
And heard her wail for the double fruit of her marriage,
A husband by her husband, children by her child.

Exactly how she died I do not know:
For Oedipus burst in moaning and would not let us
Keep vigil to the end: it was by him
As he stormed about the room that our eyes were caught.
From one to another of us he went, begging a sword,
Hunting the wife who was not his wife, the mother
Whose womb had carried his own children and himself.
I do not know: it was none of us aided him,
But surely one of the gods was in control!
For with a dreadful cry
He hurled his weight, as though wrenched out of himself,
At the twin doors: the bolts gave, and he rushed in.
And there we saw her hanging, her body swaying
From the cruel cord she had noosed about her neck.
A great sob broke from him, heartbreaking to hear,
As he loosed the rope and lowered her to the ground.

I would blot out from my mind what happened next!
For the king ripped from her gown the golden brooches
That were her ornament, and raised them, and plunged them down
Straight into his own eyeballs, crying, "No more,
No more shall you look on the misery about me,
The horrors of my own doing! Too long you have known

The faces of those whom I should never have seen,
Too long been blind to those for whom I was searching!
From this hour, go in darkness!" And as he spoke,
He struck at his eyes—not once, but many times;
And the blood spattered his beard,
Bursting from his ruined sockets like red hail.

So from the unhappiness of two this evil has sprung,
A curse on the man and woman alike. The old
Happiness of the house of Labdakos
Was happiness enough: where is it today?
It is all wailing and ruin, disgrace, death—all
The misery of mankind that has a name—
And it is wholly and for ever theirs.

CHORAGOS. Is he in agony still? Is there no rest for him?

SECOND MESSENGER. He is calling for someone to open the doors wide
So that all the children of Kadmos may look upon
His father's murderer, his mother's—no,
I can not say it!
And then he will leave Thebes,
Self-exiled, in order that the curse
Which he himself pronounced may depart from the house.
He is weak, and there is none to lead him,
So terrible is his suffering.
But you will see:
Look, the doors are opening; in a moment
You will see a thing that would crush a heart of stone.

[*The central door is opened;* OEDIPUS, *blinded, is led in.*]

CHORAGOS. Dreadful indeed for men to see.
Never have my own eyes
Looked on a sight so full of fear.

Oedipus!
What madness came upon you, what daemon
Leaped on your life with heavier
Punishment than a mortal man can bear?
No: I can not even
Look at you, poor ruined one.
And I would speak, question, ponder,
If I were able. No.
You make me shudder.

OEDIPUS. God. God.
Is there a sorrow greater?
Where shall I find harbor in this world?

My voice is hurled far on a dark wind.
What has God done to me?
CHORAGOS. Too terrible to think of, or to see.

Strophe 1

OEDIPUS. O cloud of night,
Never to be turned away: night coming on,
I can not tell how: night like a shroud!
My fair winds brought me here.
O God. Again
The pain of the spikes where I had sight,
The flooding pain
Of memory, never to be gouged out.
CHORAGOS. This is not strange.
You suffer it all twice over, remorse in pain,
Pain in remorse.
OEDIPUS. Ah dear friend
Are you faithful even yet, you alone?
Are you still standing near me, will you stay here,
Patient, to care for the blind?
The blind man!
Yet even blind I know who it is attends me,
By the voice's tone—
Though my new darkness hide the comforter.
CHORAGOS. Oh fearful act!
What god was it drove you to rake black
Night across your eyes?

Strophe 2

OEDIPUS. Apollo. Apollo. Dear
Children, the god was Apollo.
He brought my sick, sick fate upon me.
But the blinding hand was my own!
How could I bear to see
When all my sight was horror everywhere?
CHORAGOS. Everywhere; that is true.
OEDIPUS. And now what is left?
Images? Love? A greeting even,
Sweet to the senses? Is there anything?
Ah, no, friends: lead me away.
Lead me away from Thebes.
Lead the great wreck
And hell of Oedipus, whom the gods hate.
CHORAGOS. Your misery, you are not blind to that.
Would God you had never found it out!

Antistrophe 2

OEDIPUS. Death take the man who unbound
My feet on that hillside
And delivered me from death to life! What life?
If only I had died,
This weight of monstrous doom
Could not have dragged me and my darlings down.
CHORAGOS. I would have wished the same.
OEDIPUS. Oh never to have come here
With my father's blood upon me! Never
To have been the man they call his mother's husband!
Oh accurst! Oh child of evil,
To have entered that wretched bed—
The selfsame one!
More primal than sin itself, this fell to me.
CHORAGOS. I do not know what words to offer you.
You were better dead than alive and blind.
OEDIPUS. Do not counsel me any more. This punishment
That I have laid upon myself is just.
If I had eyes,
I do not know how I could bear the sight
Of my father, when I came to the house of Death,
Or my mother: for I have sinned against them both
So vilely that I could not make my peace
By strangling my own life.
Or do you think my children,
Born as they were born, would be sweet to my eyes?
Ah never, never! Nor this town with its high walls,
Nor the holy images of the gods.
For I,
Thrice miserable!—Oedipus, noblest of all the line
Of Kadmos, have condemned myself to enjoy
These things no more, by my own malediction
Expelling that man whom the gods declared
To be a defilement in the house of Laïos.
After exposing the rankness of my own guilt,
How could I look men frankly in the eyes?
No, I swear it,
If I could have stifled my hearing at its source,
I would have done it and made all this body
A tight cell of misery, blank to light and sound:
So I should have been safe in my dark mind
Beyond external evil.
Ah Kithairon!

Why did you shelter me? When I was cast upon you,
Why did I not die? Then I should never
Have shown the world my execrable birth.

Ah Polybos! Corinth, city that I believed
The ancient seat of my ancestors: how fair
I seemed, your child! And all the while this evil
Was cancerous within me!
For I am sick
In my own being, sick in my origin.
O three roads, dark ravine, woodland and way
Where three roads met: you, drinking my father's blood,
My own blood, spilled by my own hand: can you remember
The unspeakable things I did there, and the things
I went on from there to do?
O marriage, marriage!
The act that engendered me, and again the act
Performed by the son in the same bed—
Ah, the net
Of incest, mingling fathers, brothers, sons,
With brides, wives, mothers: the last evil
That can be known by men: no tongue can say
How evil!
No. For the love of God, conceal me
Somewhere far from Thebes; or kill me; or hurl me
Into the sea, away from men's eyes for ever.

Come, lead me. You need not fear to touch me.
Of all men, I alone can bear this guilt.
[*Enter* KREON.]

CHORAGOS. Kreon is here now. As to what you ask,
He may decide the course to take. He only
Is left to protect the city in your place.

OEDIPUS. Alas, how can I speak to him? What right have I
To beg his courtesy whom I have deeply wronged?

KREON. I have not come to mock you, Oedipus,
Or to reproach you, either.
[*To* ATTENDANTS]—You, standing
there:
If you have lost all respect for man's dignity,
At least respect the flame of Lord Helios:
Do not allow this pollution to show itself
Openly here, an affront to the earth
And Heaven's rain and the light of day. No, take him
Into the house as quickly as you can.

For it is proper
That only the close kindred see his grief.

OEDIPUS. I pray you in God's name, since your courtesy
Ignores my dark expectation, visiting
With mercy this man of all men most execrable:
Give me what I ask—for your good, not for mine.

KREON. And what is it that you turn to me begging for?

OEDIPUS. Drive me out of this country as quickly as may be
To a place where no human voice can ever greet me.

KREON. I should have done that before now—only,
God's will had not been wholly revealed to me.

OEDIPUS. But his command is plain: the parricide
Must be destroyed. I am that evil man.

KREON. That is the sense of it, yes; but as things are,
We had best discover clearly what is to be done.

OEDIPUS. You would learn more about a man like me?

KREON. You are ready now to listen to the god.

OEDIPUS. I will listen. But it is to you
That I must turn for help. I beg you, hear me.

The woman is there—
Give her whatever funeral you think proper:
She is your sister.
—But let me go, Kreon!
Let me purge my father's Thebes of the pollution
Of my living here, and go out to the wild hills,
To Kithairon, that has won such fame with me,
The tomb my mother and father appointed for me,
And let me die there, as they willed I should.
And yet I know
Death will not ever come to me through sickness
Or in any natural way: I have been preserved
For some unthinkable fate. But let that be.

As for my sons, you need not care for them.
They are men, they will find some way to live.
But my poor daughters, who have shared my table,
Who never before have been parted from their father—
Take care of them, Kreon; do this for me.

And will you let me touch them with my hands
A last time, and let us weep together?
Be kind, my lord.
Great prince, be kind!
Could I but touch them,

They would be mine again, as when I had my eyes.
[*Enter* ANTIGONE *and* ISMENE, *attended.*]
Ah, God!
Is it my dearest children I hear weeping?
Has Kreon pitied me and sent my daughters?
KREON. Yes, Oedipus: I knew that they were dear to you
In the old days, and know you must love them still.
OEDIPUS. May God bless you for this—and be a friendlier
Guardian to you than he has been to me!

Children, where are you?
Come quickly to my hands: they are your brother's—
Hands that have brought your father's once clear eyes
To this way of seeing—
Ah dearest ones,
I had neither sight nor knowledge then, your father
By the woman who was the source of his own life!
And I weep for you—having no strength to see you—,
I weep for you when I think of the bitterness
That men will visit upon you all your lives.
What homes, what festivals can you attend
Without being forced to depart again in tears?
And when you come to marriageable age,
Where is the man, my daughters, who would dare
Risk the bane that lies on all my children?
Is there any evil wanting? Your father killed
His father; sowed the womb of her who bore him;
Engendered you at the fount of his own existence!
That is what they will say of you.
Then, whom
Can you ever marry? There are no bridegrooms for you,
And your lives must wither away in sterile dreaming.

O Kreon, son of Menoikeus!
You are the only father my daughters have,
Since we, their parents, are both of us gone for ever.
They are your own blood: you will not let them
Fall into beggary and loneliness;
You will keep them from the miseries that are mine!
Take pity on them; see, they are only children,
Friendless except for you. Promise me this,
Great prince, and give me your hand in token of it.
[KREON *clasps his right hand.*]
Children:
I could say much, if you could understand me,

But as it is, I have only this prayer for you:
Live where you can, be as happy as you can—
Happier, please God, than God has made your father.

KREON. Enough. You have wept enough. Now go within.

OEDIPUS. I must; but it is hard.

KREON. Time eases all things.

OEDIPUS. You know my mind, then?

KREON. Say what you desire.

OEDIPUS. Send me from Thebes!

KREON. God grant that I may!

OEDIPUS. But since God hates me . . .

KREON. No, he will grant your wish.

OEDIPUS. You promise?

KREON. I can not speak beyond my knowledge.

OEDIPUS. Then lead me in.

KREON. Come now, and leave your children.

OEDIPUS. No! Do not take them from me!

KREON. Think no longer
That you are in command here, but rather think
How, when you were, you served your own destruction.

[*Exeunt into the house all but the* CHORUS; *the* CHORAGOS *chants directly to the audience.*]

CHORAGOS. Men of Thebes: look upon Oedipus.

This is the king who solved the famous riddle
And towered up, most powerful of men.
No mortal eyes but looked on him with envy,
Yet in the end ruin swept over him.

Let every man in mankind's frailty
Consider his last day; and let none
Presume on his good fortune until he find
Life, at his death, a memory without pain.

William Shakespeare (1564–1616)
KING LEAR

DRAMATIS PERSONAE

LEAR, *King of Britain*
KING OF FRANCE
DUKE OF BURGUNDY
DUKE OF CORNWALL
DUKE OF ALBANY
EARL OF KENT
EARL OF GLOUCESTER
EDGAR, *son to Gloucester*
EDMUND, *bastard son to Gloucester*
CURAN, *a courtier*
OLD MAN, *tenant to Gloucester*
DOCTOR
FOOL
OSWALD, *steward to Goneril*
A CAPTAIN *employed by Edmund*
GENTLEMAN *attendant on Cordelia*
HERALD
SERVANTS *to Cornwall*
GONERIL, REGAN, CORDELIA — *daughters to Lear*
KNIGHTS *of Lear's train,* CAPTAINS, MESSENGERS, SOLDIERS, *and* ATTENDANTS
SCENE—*Britain.*

ACT I

Scene I.° KING LEAR*'s palace.*

[*Enter* KENT, GLOUCESTER, *and* EDMUND.]

KENT. I thought the King had more affected° the Duke of Albany than Cornwall.

GLO. It did always seem so to us. But now, in the division of the kingdom, it appears not which of the Dukes he values most, for equalities are so weighed that curiosity in neither can make choice of either's moiety.°

KENT. Is not this your son, my lord?

Act I, Sc. i: As the opening words of this scene show, Lear has already decided on the division of the kingdom. There remains only the public and ceremonious announcement of his abdication. *1. more affected:* had more affection for. *5–6. equalities . . . moiety:* for their shares are so equal that a close examination *(curiosity)* cannot decide which share *(moiety)* is to be preferred.

GLO. His breeding, sir, hath been at my charge. I have so often blushed to acknowledge him that now I am brazed° to it.

KENT. I cannot conceive° you.

GLO. Sir, this young fellow's mother could. Whereupon she grew round-wombed, and had indeed, sir, a son for her cradle ere she had a husband for her bed. Do you smell a fault?

KENT. I cannot wish the fault undone, the issue° of it being so proper.°

GLO. But I have, sir, a son by order of law, some year elder than this, who yet is no dearer in my account. Though this knave came something saucily into the world before he was sent for, yet was his mother fair, there was good sport at his making, and the whoreson° must be acknowledged. Do you know this noble gentleman, Edmund?

EDM. No, my lord.

GLO. My Lord of Kent. Remember him hereafter as my honorable friend.

EDM. My services to your lordship.

KENT. I must love you, and sue to know you better.

EDM. Sir, I shall study deserving.°

GLO. He hath been out nine years, and away he shall again. The King is coming.

[*Sennet.*° *Enter one bearing a coronet,*° KING LEAR, CORNWALL, ALBANY, GONERIL, REGAN, CORDELIA, *and* ATTENDANTS.]

LEAR. Attend° the lords of France and Burgundy, Gloucester.

GLO. I shall, my liege.

[*Exeunt* GLOUCESTER *and* EDMUND.]

LEAR. Meantime we shall express our darker purpose.°
Give me the map there. Know that we have divided
In three our kingdom. And 'tis our fast intent
To shake all cares and business from our age,
Conferring them on younger strengths while we
Unburdened crawl toward death. Our son° of Cornwall,
And you, our no less loving son of Albany,
We have this hour a constant will° to publish
Our daughters' several° dowers, that future strife
May be prevented° now. The Princes, France and Burgundy,

9. brazed: become brazen; lit., brass-plated. *10. conceive:* understand. *14. issue:* result; i.e., child. *15. proper:* handsome. *19. whoreson:* rogue; lit., son of a whore. *27. I . . . deserving:* I shall do my best to deserve your favor. *29 s.d., Sennet:* trumpet call used to announce the approach of a procession. *coronet:* a small crown worn by those of lesser rank than King. *30. Attend:* wait on. *32. we . . . purpose:* we will explain what we have hitherto kept dark. Lear, speaking officially as King, uses the royal "we." *37. son:* son-in-law. *39. constant will:* firm intention. *40. several:* separate. *41. prevented:* forestalled.

Great rivals in our youngest daughter's love,
Long in our Court have made their amorous sojourn,
And here are to be answered. Tell me, my daughters,
Since now we will divest us both of rule,
Interest of territory, cares of state,
Which of you shall we say doth love us most?
That we our largest bounty may extend
Where nature doth with merit challenge.° Goneril,
Our eldest-born, speak first.

GON. Sir, I love you more than words can wield° the matter,
Dearer than eyesight, space, and liberty,
Beyond what can be valued, rich or rare,
No less than life, with grace, health, beauty, honor,
As much as child e'er loved or father found—
A love that makes breath poor and speech unable—
Beyond all manner of so much° I love you.

COR. [*Aside*] What shall Cordelia do? Love, and be silent.

LEAR. Of all these bounds, even from this line to this,
With shadowy forests and with champaigns riched,°
With plenteous rivers and wide-skirted meads,°
We make thee lady. To thine and Albany's issue
Be this perpetual. What says our second daughter,
Our dearest Regan, wife to Cornwall? Speak.

REG. I am made of that self metal° as my sister,
And prize me at her worth.° In my true heart
I find she names my very deed of love,
Only she comes too short. That I profess
Myself an enemy to all other joys
Which the most precious square of sense possesses,°
And find I am alone felicitate°
In your dear Highness' love.

COR. [*Aside*]Then poor Cordelia!
And yet not so, since I am sure my love's
More ponderous than my tongue.°

LEAR. To thee and thine hereditary ever
Remain this ample third of our fair kingdom,
No less in space, validity° and pleasure
Than that conferred on Goneril. Now, our joy,

49. Where . . . challenge: where natural affection and desert have an equal claim on my bounty. *51. wield:* declare. *57. Beyond . . . much:* i.e., beyond all these things. *60. champaigns riched:* enriched with fertile fields. *61. wide-skirted meads:* extensive pasture lands. *65. self metal:* same material. *66. prize . . . worth:* value me at the same price. *70. most . . . possesses:* feeling in the highest degree possesses. *square:* the carpenter's rule; i.e., measurement. *71. felicitate:* made happy. *74–5. love's . . . tongue:* love is heavier than my words. *78. validity:* value.

Although the last, not least, to whose young love
The vines of France and milk of Burgundy
Strive to be interessed,° what can you say to draw
A third more opulent than your sisters? Speak.
COR. Nothing, my lord.
LEAR. Nothing!
COR. Nothing.
LEAR. Nothing will come of nothing.° Speak again.
COR. Unhappy that I am, I cannot heave
My heart into my mouth. I love your Majesty
According to my bond,° nor more nor less.
LEAR. How, how, Cordelia! Mend your speech a little,
Lest it may mar your fortunes.
COR. Good my lord,
You have begot me, bred me, loved me. I
Return those duties back as are right fit,
Obey you, love you, and most honor you.
Why have my sisters husbands if they say
They love you all? Haply,° when I shall wed,
That lord whose hand must take my plight° shall carry
Half my love with him, half my care and duty.
Sure, I shall never marry like my sisters,
To love my father all.
LEAR. But goes thy heart with this?
COR. Aye, good my lord.
LEAR. So young, and so untender?
COR. So young, my lord, and true.
LEAR. Let it be so. Thy truth then be thy dower.
For, by the sacred radiance of the sun,
The mysteries of Hecate,° and the night,
By all the operation of the orbs°
From whom we do exist and cease to be,
Here I disclaim° all my paternal care,
Propinquity,° and property of blood,°
And as a stranger to my heart and me
Hold thee from this forever. The barbarous Scythian,°
Or he that makes his generation messes
To gorge his appetite° shall to my bosom

82. interessed: have a share in. *87. Nothing . . . nothing:* the old maxim *Ex nihilo nihil fit.* *90. bond:* i.e., the tie of natural affection and duty which binds daughter to father. *97. Haply:* it may happen. *98. plight:* promise made at betrothal. *107. Hecate:* goddess of witchcraft. *108. orbs:* stars. *110. disclaim:* renounce. *111. Propinquity:* relationship. *property of blood:* claim which you have as being of my blood. *113. Scythian:* inhabitant of South Russia, regarded as the worst kind of savage. *114–5. Or . . . appetite:* or he that feeds gluttonously on his own children.

Be as well neighbored, pitied, and relieved°
As thou my sometime daughter.
KENT. Good my liege—
LEAR. Peace, Kent!
Come not between the dragon° and his wrath.
I loved her most, and thought to set my rest°
On her kind nursery.° Hence, and avoid° my sight!
So be my grave my peace, as here I give
Her father's heart from her! Call France. Who stirs?
Call Burgundy. Cornwall and Albany,
With my two daughters' dowers digest° this third.
Let pride, which she calls plainness,° marry her.
I do invest you jointly with my power,
Pre-eminence,° and all the large effects
That troop with majesty.° Ourself, by monthly course,°
With reservation of a hundred knights
By you to be sustained, shall our abode
Make with you by due turns. Only we still retain
The name and all the additions° to a king.
The sway, revenue, execution of the rest,
Belovèd Sons, be yours, which to confirm,
This coronet° part betwixt you.
KENT. Royal Lear,
Whom I have ever honored as my King,
Loved as my father, as my master followed,
As my great patron thought on in my prayers—
LEAR. The bow is bent and drawn, make from the shaft.°
KENT. Let it fall rather, though the fork° invade
The region of my heart. Be Kent unmannerly
When Lear is mad. What wouldst thou do, old man?°
Think'st thou that duty shall have dread to speak
When power to flattery bows? To plainness honor's bound
When majesty stoops to folly.° Reverse thy doom,°

116. relieved: helped in distress. *119. dragon:* the Dragon of Britain was Lear's heraldic device and also a symbol of his ferocity. *120. set . . . my rest:* lit., to risk all—a term in the card game called primero. Lear uses it with the double meaning of "find rest." *121. nursery:* care. *avoid:* depart from. *125. digest:* absorb. *126. plainness:* honest plain speech. *128. Pre-eminence:* authority. *128–9. large . . . majesty:* the outward show of power that goes with rule. *129. course:* turn. *133. additions:* titles of honor. *136. coronet:* i.e., the coronet which was to have been the symbol of Cordelia's kingdom. *140. shaft:* arrow. *141. fork:* point of a forked arrow. *143. old man:* Kent, who is as quick-tempered as Lear, has lost control of his tongue. The phrase to a still ruling king is grossly insulting. *144–6. Think'st . . . folly:* This is one of many passages in *Lear* where the abstract is strikingly and effectively used for the person. It means: "Do you think that a man who keeps his sense of duty will be afraid to speak when he sees a king yielding to his flatterers? An honorable man is forced to speak plainly when a king becomes a fool." *146. doom:* sentence.

And in thy best consideration check
This hideous rashness. Answer my life my judgment,
Thy youngest daughter does not love thee least,
Nor are those empty-hearted whose low sound
Reverbs° no hollowness.

LEAR. Kent, on thy life, no more.

KENT. My life I never held but as a pawn°
To wage against thy enemies, nor fear to lose it,
Thy safety being the motive.

LEAR. Out of my sight!

KENT. See better, Lear, and let me still remain
The true blank° of thine eye.

LEAR. Now, by Apollo—

KENT. Now, by Apollo, King.
Thou swear'st thy gods in vain.

LEAR. O vassal!° Miscreant!°

[*Laying his hand on his sword.*]

ALB. & CORN. Dear sir, forbear.

KENT. Do.
Kill thy physician, and the fee bestow
Upon the foul disease. Revoke thy doom,
Or whilst I can vent clamor° from my throat
I'll tell thee thou dost evil.

LEAR. Hear me, recreant!°
On thy allegiance,° hear me!
Since thou hast sought to make us break our vow,
Which we durst never yet, and with strained° pride
To come between our sentence and our power°—
Which nor our nature nor our place can bear,
Our potency made good°—take thy reward.
Five days we do allot thee, for provision°
To shield thee from diseases of the world,
And on the sixth to turn thy hated back
Upon our kingdom. If on the tenth day following
Thy banished trunk° be found in our dominions,
The moment is thy death. Away! By Jupiter,
This shall not be revoked.

151. Reverbs: re-echoes. *152. pawn:* a pledge to be sacrificed. *156. blank:* aim; i.e., something which you look at. The blank is the center of the target. *158. vassal:* wretch. *Miscreant:* lit., misbeliever. *163. vent clamor:* utter a cry. *164. recreant:* traitor. *165. On . . . allegiance:* The most solemn form of command that can be laid upon a subject, for to disobey it is to commit high treason. *167. strained:* excessive. *168. To . . . power:* to interpose yourself between my decree and my royal will; i.e., to make me revoke an order. *170. Our . . . good:* my power being now asserted. *171. for provision:* for making your preparations. *175. trunk:* body.

KENT. Fare° thee well, King. Sith° thus thou wilt appear,
Freedom lives hence, and banishment is here.
[*To* CORDELIA] The gods to their dear shelter take thee, maid,
That justly think'st and hast most rightly said!
[*To* REGAN *and* GONERIL] And your large° speeches may your deeds approve,°
That good effects° may spring from words of love.
Thus Kent, O Princes, bids you all adieu.
He'll shape his old course in a country new.
[*Exit.*]

[*Flourish.*° *Re-enter* GLOUCESTER, *with* FRANCE, BURGUNDY, *and* ATTENDANTS.]

GLO. Here's France and Burgundy, my noble lord.
LEAR. My lord of Burgundy,
We first address toward you, who with this King
Hath rivaled for our daughter. What, in the least,
Will you require° in present° dower with her,
Or cease your quest of love?
BUR. Most royal Majesty,
I crave no more than what your Highness offered,
Nor will you tender° less.
LEAR. Right noble Burgundy,
When she was dear° to us, we did hold her so,
But now her price is fall'n. Sir, there she stands.
If aught within that little seeming substance,°
Or all of it, with our displeasure pieced°
And nothing more, may fitly like° your Grace,
She's there, and she is yours.
BUR. I know no answer.
LEAR. Will you, with those infirmities she owes,°
Unfriended, new-adopted to our hate,
Dowered with our curse and strangered with our oath,°
Take her, or leave her?
BUR. Pardon me, royal sir,
Election makes not up on such conditions.°
LEAR. Then leave her, sir. For, by the power that made me,
I tell you all her wealth. [*To* FRANCE] For you, great King,

178–85. Fare . . . new: The rhyme in this passage and elsewhere in the play is used for the particular purpose of stiffening the speech and giving it a special prophetic or moral significance *178. Sith:* since. *182. large:* fine-sounding. *approve:* i.e., be shown in deeds. *183. effects:* results. *185 s.d., Flourish:* trumpet fanfare. *190. require:* request. *present:* immediate. *193. tender:* offer. *194. dear:* in the double sense of "beloved" and "valuable." *196. little . . . substance:* creature that seems so small. Part of Lear's anger with Cordelia is that so small a body seems to hold so proud a heart. *197. pieced:* added to it. *198. fitly like:* suitably please. *200. owes:* possesses. *202. strangered . . . oath:* made a stranger to me by my oath. *204. Election . . . conditions:* i.e., one does not choose one's wife on such conditions.

I would not from your love make such a stray,°
To match you where I hate. Therefore beseech you
To avert your liking° a more worthier way
Than on a wretch whom Nature is ashamed
Almost to acknowledge hers.

FRANCE. This is most strange,
That she that even but now was your best object,
The argument° of your praise, balm of your age,
Most best, most dearest, should in this trice of time
Commit a thing so monstrous, to dismantle°
So many folds of favor. Sure, her offense
Must be of such unnatural degree
That monsters it,° or your forevouched° affection
Fall'n into taint.° Which to believe of her
Must be a faith that reason without miracle
Could never plant in me.°

COR. I yet beseech your Majesty—
If for I want that glib and oily art,
To speak and purpose not,° since what I well intend
I'll do 't before I speak—that you make known
It is no vicious blot,° murder, or foulness,
No unchaste action or dishonored step,
That hath deprived me of your grace and favor,
But even for want of that for which I am richer,
A still-soliciting° eye, and such a tongue
As I am glad I have not, though not to have it
Hath lost me in° your liking.

LEAR. Better thou
Hadst not been born than not to have pleased me better.

FRANCE. Is it but this? A tardiness in nature°
Which often leaves the history unspoke
That it intends to do? My Lord of Burgundy,
What say you to the lady? Love's not love
When it is mingled with regards that stand
Aloof from the entire point.° Will you have her?
She is herself a dowry.

207. *from . . . stray:* remove myself so far from showing love to you. 209. *avert . . . liking:* turn your affection. 213. *argument:* topic. 215. *dismantle:* lit., take off (as a cloak). 218. *monsters it:* makes it a monster. *forevouched:* previously declared. 219. *Fall'n . . . taint:* become bad. 219–21. *Which . . . me:* that is so contrary to reason that only a miracle could make me believe it. 223. *and . . . not:* and not mean it. 225. *vicious blot:* vicious act which blots my honor. 229. *still-soliciting:* always begging favors. 231. *lost me in:* deprived me of. 233. *tardiness in nature:* natural slowness. 237–8. *When . . . point:* when it is mixed with other motives (the amount of the dowry) which have nothing to do with the thing itself (love).

BUR. Royal Lear,
Give but that portion which yourself proposed,
And here I take Cordelia by the hand,
Duchess of Burgundy.
LEAR. Nothing. I have sworn, I am firm.
BUR. I am sorry then you have so lost a father
That you must lose a husband.
COR. Peace be with Burgundy!
Since that respects of fortune° are his love,
I shall not be his wife.
FRANCE. Fairest Cordelia, that art most rich being poor,
Most choice forsaken, and most loved despised,
Thee and thy virtues here I seize upon,
Be it lawful I take up what's cast away.
Gods, gods! 'Tis strange that from their cold'st neglect
My love should kindle to inflamed respect.°
Thy dowerless daughter, King, thrown to my chance,
Is Queen of us, of ours, and our fair France.
Not all the dukes of waterish° Burgundy
Can buy this unprized precious maid of me.
Bid them farewell, Cordelia, though unkind.
Thou losest here, a better where to find.
LEAR. Thou hast her, France. Let her be thine, for we
Have no such daughter, nor shall ever see
That face of hers again. Therefore be gone
Without our grace, our love, our benison.°
Come, noble Burgundy.
[*Flourish. Exeunt all but* FRANCE, GONERIL, REGAN, *and* CORDELIA.]
FRANCE. Bid farewell to your sisters.
COR. The jewels of our father,° with washed° eyes
Cordelia leaves you. I know you what you are,
And, like a sister, am most loath to call
Your faults as they are named. Use well our father.
To your professèd° bosoms I commit him.
But yet, alas, stood I within his grace,°
I would prefer° him to a better place.
So farewell to you both.
REG. Prescribe not us our duties.
GON. Let your study
Be to content your lord, who hath received you

246. respects of fortune: considerations of my dowry. *253. inflamed respect:* warmer affection. *256. waterish:* with the double meaning of "with many rivers" and "feeble." *263. benison:* blessing. *266. The . . . father:* i.e., creatures whom my father values so highly. *washed:* weeping, but also made clearsighted by tears. *270. professed:* which profess such love. *271. within . . . grace:* in his favor. *272. prefer:* promote.

At Fortune's alms.° You have obedience scanted,°
And well are worth the want that you have wanted.°

COR. Time shall unfold what plaited° cunning hides.
Who cover faults, at last shame them derides.
Well may you prosper!

FRANCE. Come, my fair Cordelia.

[*Exeunt* FRANCE *and* CORDELIA.]

GON. Sister,° it is not a little I have to say of what most nearly appertains to us both. I think our father will hence tonight.

REG. That's most certain, and with you, next month with us.

GON. You see how full of changes his age is, the observation we have made of it hath not been little. He always loved our sister most, and with what poor judgment he hath now cast her off appears too grossly.

REG. 'Tis the infirmity of his age. Yet he hath ever but slenderly known himself.

GON. The best and soundest of his time hath been but rash. Then must we look to receive from his age not alone the imperfections of long- ingrafted condition,° but therewithal the unruly waywardness that infirm and choleric years bring with them.

REG. Such unconstant starts° are we like to have from him as this of Kent's banishment.

GON. There is further compliment° of leave-taking between France and him. Pray you, let's hit° together. If our father carry authority with such dispositions° as he bears, this last surrender of his will but offend us.

REG. We shall further think on 't.

GON. We must do something, and i' the heat.°

[*Exeunt.*]

Scene II. The EARL OF GLOUCESTER'*s castle.*

[*Enter* EDMUND, *with a letter.*]

EDM. Thou, Nature,° art my goddess, to thy law

276. At . . . alms: as an act of charity from Fortune. *scanted:* neglected. *277. And . . . wanted:* and well deserve the same lack of love which you have shown. *278. plaited:* pleated, enfolded. *281–301. Sister . . . heat:* The abrupt change from rhyme to prose marks the change from the emotion of the previous episodes to the cynical frankness of the two sisters. *292. long-ingrafted condition:* temper which has long been part of his nature. *294. unconstant starts:* sudden outbursts. *296. compliment:* formality. *297. hit:* agree. *298. dispositions:* frame of mind. *301. i' the heat:* while the iron is hot.

Sc. ii: *1. Thou, Nature:* Edmund, the "natural" son of his father, appeals to Nature, whose doctrine is every man ruthlessly for himself.

My services are bound. Wherefore should I
Stand in the plague of custom, and permit
The curiosity of nations to deprive me,
For that I am some twelve or fourteen moonshines
Lag of a brother?° Why bastard? Wherefore base?
When my dimensions are as well compact,°
My mind as generous° and my shape as true,
As honest madam's issue? Why brand they us
With base? With baseness? Bastardy? Base, base?
Who in the lusty stealth of nature take
More composition and fierce quality°
Than doth, within a dull, stale, tired bed,
Go to the creating a whole tribe of fops°
Got° 'tween asleep and wake? Well then,
Legitimate Edgar, I must have your land.
Our father's love is to the bastard Edmund
As to the legitimate—fine word, "legitimate"!
Well, my legitimate, if this letter speed°
And my invention° thrive, Edmund the base
Shall top the legitimate. I grow, I prosper.
Now, gods, stand up for bastards!
[*Enter* GLOUCESTER.]

GLO. Kent banished thus! And France in choler parted!
And the King gone tonight! Subscribed° his power!
Confined to exhibition!° All this done
Upon the gad!° Edmund, how now! What news?

EDM. So please your lordship, none.
[*Putting up the letter.*]

GLO. Why so earnestly seek you to put up that letter?

EDM. I know no news, my lord.

GLO. What paper were you reading?

EDM. Nothing, my lord.°

GLO. No? What needed then that terrible dispatch° of it into your

2–6. Wherefore . . . brother: Why should I allow myself to be plagued by custom and nice distinctions *(curiosity)* which deprive me of my natural rights, because I am a year younger (*lag:* lagging behind) than my legitimate brother? *7. compact:* put together, framed. *8. generous:* noble. *12. More . . . quality:* more fiber and ferocity. *14. fops:* fools. *15. Got:* begotten. *19. speed:* prosper. *20. invention:* plan. *24. Subscribed:* signed away. *25. Confined to exhibition:* reduced to a pension. *26. gad:* prick of a goad; i.e., the spur of the moment. *31. Nothing, my lord:* Gloucester's tragedy also begins with the word "nothing." *32. terrible dispatch:* i.e., hasty thrusting.

pocket? The quality of nothing hath not such need to hide itself. Let's see. Come, if it be nothing, I shall not need spectacles.

EDM. I beseech you, sir, pardon me. It is a letter from my brother that I have not all o'erread, and for so much as I have perused, I find it not fit for your o'erlooking.°

GLO. Give me the letter, sir.

EDM. I shall offend, either to detain or give it. The contents, as in part I understand them, are to blame.

GLO. Let's see, let's see.

EDM. I hope, for my brother's justification, he wrote this but as an essay° or taste of my virtue.

GLO. [*Reads.*] "This policy and reverence of age° makes the world bitter to the best of our times,° keeps our fortunes from us till our oldness cannot relish them. I begin to find an idle and fond° bondage in the oppression of aged tyranny, who sways not as it hath power, but as it is suffered.° Come to me, that of this I may speak more. If our father would sleep till I waked him, you should enjoy half his revenue forever, and live the beloved of your brother, EDGAR."

Hum! Conspiracy!—"Sleep till I waked him, you should enjoy half his revenue!"—My son Edgar! Had he a hand to write this? A heart and brain to breed it in? When came this to you? Who brought it?

EDM. It was not brought me, my lord, there's the cunning of it. I found it thrown in at the casement° of my closet.°

GLO. You know the character° to be your brother's?

EDM. If the matter were good, my lord, I durst swear it were his, but in respect of that, I would fain think it were not.

GLO. It is his.

EDM. It is his hand, my lord, but I hope his heart is not in the contents.

GLO. Hath he never heretofore sounded you in this business?

EDM. Never, my lord. But I have heard him oft maintain it to be fit that, sons at perfect age and fathers declining, the father should be as ward to the son, and the son manage his revenue.

GLO. Oh, villain, villain! His very opinion in the letter! Abhorred villain! Unnatural, detested, brutish villain! Worse than brutish! Go, sirrah, seek him—aye, apprehend him. Abominable villain! Where is he?

EDM. I do not well know, my lord. If it shall please you to suspend

37. o'erlooking: reading. *43. essay:* trial. *44. policy . . . age:* this custom of respecting old men. *45. best . . . times:* i.e., when we are still young. *46. fond:* foolish. *48. suffered:* allowed. *56. casement:* window. *56. closet:* room. *57. character:* handwriting.

your indignation against my brother till you can derive from him better testimony of his intent, you should run a certain course.° Where, if you violently proceed against him, mistaking his purpose, it would make a great gap° in your own honor and shake in pieces the heart of his obedience.° I dare pawn down my life for him that he hath wrote this to feel° my affection to your honor and to no further pretense of danger.

GLO. Think you so?

EDM. If your honor judge it meet, I will place you where you shall hear us confer of this, and by an auricular assurance° have your satisfaction, and that without any further delay than this very evening.

GLO. He cannot be such a monster—

EDM. Nor is not, sure.

GLO. —to his father, that so tenderly and entirely loves him. Heaven and earth! Edmund, seek him out, wind me into him,° I pray you. Frame the business after your own wisdom. I would unstate myself, to be in a due resolution.°

EDM. I will seek him, sir, presently,° convey° the business as I shall find means, and acquaint you withal.

GLO. These late eclipses in the sun and moon portend no good to us. Though the wisdom of nature° can reason° it thus and thus, yet nature finds itself scourged by the sequent° effects. Love cools, friendship falls off, brothers divide. In cities, mutinies; in countries, discord; in palaces, treason; and the bond cracked 'twixt son and father. This villain of mine comes under the prediction, there's son against father. The King falls from bias of nature,° there's father against child. We have seen the best of our time. Machinations, hollowness, treachery, and all ruinous disorders follow us disquietly to our graves. Find out this villain, Edmund, it shall lose thee nothing. Do it carefully. And the noble and true-hearted Kent banished! His offense, honesty! 'Tis strange.

[*Exit.*]

EDM. This is the excellent foppery° of the world, that when we are sick in fortune—often the surfeit° of our own behavior—we

73. certain course: i.e., know where you are going. *75. gap:* hole. *75–6. shake . . . obedience:* cause him no longer to obey you loyally. *77. feel:* test. *81. auricular assurance:* proof heard with your own ears. *87. wind . . . him:* worm your way into his confidence for me. *88–9. I . . . resolution:* I would lose my earldom to learn the truth. This is one of many touches of bitter irony in this tragedy, for it is not until he has "unstated himself" that Gloucester does indeed learn the truth about his two sons. *90. presently:* at once. *convey:* manage. *93. wisdom of nature:* i.e., a rational explanation. *93. reason:* explain. *94. sequent:* subsequent. *98. bias of nature:* natural inclination. *104. foppery:* folly. *105. surfeit:* lit., eating to excess and its results.

make guilty of our disasters the sun, the moon, and the stars, as if we were villains by necessity, fools by heavenly compulsion; knaves, thieves, and treachers by spherical predominance;° drunkards, liars, and adulterers by an enforced obedience of planetary influence;° and all that we are evil in, by a divine thrusting on—an admirable evasion of whoremaster° man, to lay his goatish disposition to the charge of a star!° My father compounded with my mother under the dragon's tail, and my nativity° was under Ursa Major,° so that it follows I am rough and lecherous. Tut, I should have been that I am had the maidenliest star in the firmament twinkled on my bastardizing. Edgar—[*Enter* EDGAR.] And pat he comes like the catastrophe° of the old comedy. My cue is villainous melancholy, with a sigh like Tom o' Bedlam.° Oh, these eclipses do portend these divisions! Fa, sol, la, mi.°

EDG. How now, Brother Edmund! What serious contemplation are you in?

EDM. I am thinking, Brother, of a prediction I read this other day, what should follow these eclipses.

EDG. Do you busy yourself about that?

EDM. I promise you the effects he writes of succeed° unhappily, as of unnaturalness between the child and the parent; death, dearth, dissolutions of ancient amities;° divisions in state, menaces and maledictions against King and nobles; needless diffidences,° banishment of friends, dissipation of cohorts,° nuptial breaches, and I know not what.

EDG. How long have you been a sectary astronomical?°

EDM. Come, come, when saw you my father last?

EDG. Why, the night gone by.

EDM. Spake you with him?

EDG. Aye, two hours together.

EDM. Parted you in good terms? Found you no displeasure in him by word or countenance?

EDG. None at all.

EDM. Bethink yourself wherein you may have offended him. And at my entreaty forbear his presence till some little time hath

108. treachers . . . predominance: traitors because the stars so decreed when we were born. *109–10. enforced . . . influence:* because we were forced to be so in obeying the influence of the stars. *111. whoremaster:* lecherous. *111–2. to . . . star:* to say that some star caused him to have the morals of a goat. *113. nativity:* moment of birth. *113–4. Ursa Major:* the Great Bear. *117. catastrophe:* the final episode. *117–8. my . . . Bedlam:* I must now pretend to be a melancholic and sigh like a lunatic beggar. Tom o' Bedlam was a lunatic discharged from Bedlam (Bethlehem Hospital for lunatics). *119. Fa . . . mi:* Edmund hums to himself. *125. succeed:* follow. *127. amities:* friendships. *128. diffidences:* distrusts. *129. dissipation of cohorts:* breaking-up of established friendships (lit., of troops of soldiers). *131. sectary astronomical:* a follower of the sect of astrologers.

qualified° the heat of his displeasure, which at this instant so rageth in him that with the mischief of your person it would scarcely allay.°

EDG. Some villain hath done me wrong.

EDM. That's my fear. I pray you have a continent forbearance° till the speed of his rage goes slower, and, as I say, retire with me to my lodging, from whence I will fitly bring you to hear my lord speak. Pray ye, go, there's my key. If you do stir abroad, go armed.

EDG. Armed, Brother!

EDM. Brother, I advise you to the best—go armed. I am no honest man if there be any good meaning toward you. I have told you what I have seen and heard, but faintly, nothing like the image and horror of it. Pray you, away.

EDG. Shall I hear from you anon?

EDM. I do serve you in this business.

[*Exit* EDGAR.]

A credulous father, and a brother noble,
Whose nature is so far from doing harms
That he suspects none, on whose foolish honesty
My practices° ride easy. I see the business.
Let me, if not by birth, have lands by wit.
All with me's meet° that I can fashion fit.°

[*Exit.*]

Scene III. The DUKE OF ALBANY*'s palace.*

[*Enter* GONERIL *and* OSWALD, *her steward.*]

GON. Did my father strike my gentleman for chiding of his fool?°

OSW. Yes, madam.

GON. By day and night he wrongs me. Every hour
He flashes into one gross crime or other
That sets us all at odds. I'll not endure it.
His knights grow riotous, and himself upbraids us
On every trifle. When he returns from hunting,
I will not speak with him. Say I am sick.
If you come slack of former services,°
You shall do well, the fault of it I'll answer.

141. *qualified:* lessened. 142–3. *with . . . allay:* it would scarcely be lessened even if he did you some bodily injury. 145. *continent forbearance:* self-control which will keep you from any rash action. 159. *practices:* plots. 161. *meet:* suitable. *fashion fit:* make fit my purposes.

Sc. iii: 1. *fool:* professional jester. 9. *come . . . services:* do not wait on him as efficiently as you used to.

OSW. He's coming, madam, I hear him.

[*Horns within.*]

GON. Put on what weary negligence you please,
You and your fellows, I'd have it come to question.°
If he distaste it, let him to our sister,
Whose mind and mine, I know, in that are one,
Not to be overruled. Idle old man,
That still would manage those authorities
That he hath given away! Now, by my life,
Old fools are babes again, and must be used
With checks as flatteries when they are seen abused.°
Remember what I tell you.

OSW. Very well, madam.

GON. And let his knights have colder looks among you.
What grows of it, no matter, advise your fellows so.
I would breed from hence occasions,° and I shall,
That I may speak. I'll write straight to my sister
To hold my very course. Prepare for dinner.

[*Exeunt.*]

Scene IV. A hall in the same.

[*Enter* KENT, *disguised.*]

KENT. If but as well I other accents borrow
That can my speech defuse,° my good intent
May carry through itself to that full issue
For which I razed° my likeness. Now, banished Kent,
If thou canst serve where thou dost stand condemned,
So may it come, thy master whom thou lovest
Shall find thee full of labors.

[*Horns within. Enter* LEAR, KNIGHTS, *and* ATTENDANTS.]

LEAR. Let me not stay a jot for dinner. Go get it ready. [*Exit an* ATTENDANT.] How now! What art thou?

KENT. A man, sir.

LEAR. What dost thou profess?° What wouldst thou with us?

KENT. I do profess to be no less than I seem—to serve him truly that will put me in trust, to love him that is honest, to converse with him that is wise and says little, to fear judgment,° to fight when I cannot choose, and to eat no fish.°

13. *to question:* or in modern slang, to a showdown. 19–20. *Old . . . abused:* old men must be treated like babies, and scolded, not flattered, when they are naughty. 24. *breed . . . occasions:* find excuses for taking action.

Sc. iv: 2. *defuse:* make indistinct, disguise. 4. *razed:* lit., shaved off, disguised. 11. *What . . . profess:* what is your profession? 14. *judgment:* The Day of Judgment; i.e., I have a conscience. 15. *eat no fish:* I don't observe fast days, and am therefore no Catholic.

LEAR. What art thou?

KENT. A very honest-hearted fellow, and as poor as the King.

LEAR. If thou be as poor for a subject as he is for a king, thou art poor enough. What wouldst thou?

KENT. Service.

LEAR. Who wouldst thou serve?

KENT. You.

LEAR. Dost thou know me, fellow?

KENT. No, sir, but you have that in your countenance° which I would fain call master.

LEAR. What's that?

KENT. Authority.

LEAR. What services canst thou do?

KENT. I can keep honest counsel, ride, run, mar a curious tale in telling it,° and deliver a plain message bluntly. That which ordinary men are fit for, I am qualified in, and the best of me is diligence.

LEAR. How old art thou?

KENT. Not so young, sir, to love a woman for singing, nor so old to dote on her for anything. I have years on my back forty-eight.

LEAR. Follow me, thou shalt serve me. If I like thee no worse after dinner, I will not part from thee yet. Dinner, ho, dinner! Where's my knave? My fool? Go you, and call my fool hither. [*Exit an* ATTENDANT. *Enter* OSWALD.] You, you, sirrah, where's my daughter?

OSW. So please you—

[*Exit.*]

LEAR. What says the fellow there? Call the clotpoll° back. [*Exit a* KNIGHT.] Where's my fool, ho? I think the world's asleep. [*Re-enter* KNIGHT.] How now! Where's that mongrel?

KNIGHT. He says, my lord, your daughter is not well.

LEAR. Why came not the slave back to me when I called him?

KNIGHT. Sir, he answered me, in the roundest° manner, he would not.

LEAR. He would not!

KNIGHT. My lord, I know not what the matter is, but, to my judgment, your Highness is not entertained° with that ceremonious affection° as you were wont. There's a great abatement of kindness appears as well in the general dependents° as in the Duke himself also and your daughter.

24. countenance: bearing. *29–30. mar . . . it:* I'm not one to delight in overelaborate *(curious)* phrases when telling my tale; i.e., he will have none of the fantastic talk of the typical courtier. *41. clotpoll:* clodpole, blockhead. *46. roundest:* plainest. *50. entertained:* treated. *51. ceremonious affection:* affection which shows itself in ceremony. Manners even between children and parents were very formal. Neglect of courtesies to the ex-King shows deliberate disrespect. *52. dependents:* servants of the house.

LEAR. Ha! Sayest thou so?

KNIGHT. I beseech you pardon me, my lord, if I be mistaken, for my duty cannot be silent when I think your Highness wronged.

LEAR. Thou but rememberest° me of mine own conception. I have perceived a most faint neglect° of late, which I have rather blamed as mine own jealous curiosity° than as a very pretense° and purpose of unkindness. I will look further into 't. But where's my fool? I have not seen him this two days.

KNIGHT. Since my young lady's going into France, sir, the fool hath much pined away.

LEAR. No more of that, I have noted it well. Go you, and tell my daughter I would speak with her. [*Exit an* ATTENDANT.] Go you, call hither my fool. [*Exit an* ATTENDANT. *Re- enter* OSWALD.] Oh, you sir, you, come you hither, sir. Who am I, sir?

OSW. My lady's father.

LEAR. My lady's father! My lord's knave. You whoreson dog! You slave! You cur!

OSW. I am none of these, my lord, I beseech your pardon.

LEAR. Do you bandy° looks with me, you rascal?

[*Striking him.*]

OSW. I'll not be struck, my lord.

KENT. Nor tripped neither, you base football player.

[*Tripping up his heels.*]

LEAR. I thank thee, fellow. Thou servest me, and I'll love thee.

KENT. Come, sir, arise, away! I'll teach you differences.° Away, away! If you will measure your lubber's length again, tarry. But away! Go to, have you wisdom? So.

[*Pushes* OSWALD *out.*]

LEAR. Now, my friendly knave, I thank thee. There's earnest°of thy service.

[*Giving* KENT *money.*]

[*Enter* FOOL.]

FOOL. Let me hire him too. Here's my coxcomb.°

[*Offering* KENT *his cap.*]

LEAR. How now, my pretty knave! How dost thou?

FOOL. Sirrah, you were best take my coxcomb.

KENT. Why, fool?

FOOL. Why, for taking one's part that's out of favor. Nay, an thou canst not smile as the wind sits,° thou'lt catch cold shortly. There, take my coxcomb. Why, this fellow hath banished two on 's

57. *rememberest:* remind. 58. *faint neglect:* i.e., the "weary negligence" commanded by Goneril (I.iii.12). 59. *jealous curiosity:* excessive suspicion. *pretense:* deliberate intention. 72. *bandy:* lit., hit the ball to and fro as in tennis. 76. *differences:* of rank. 79. *earnest:* money given on account of services to be rendered. Lear thus formally engages Kent as his servant. 81. *coxcomb:* the cap shaped like a cock's comb (crest) worn by the professional fool. 85–6. *an . . . . sits:* i.e., if you can't curry favor with those in power.

daughters, and done the third a blessing against his will. If thou follow him, thou must needs wear my coxcomb. How now, Nuncle!° Would I had two coxcombs and two daughters!

LEAR. Why, my boy?

FOOL. If I gave them all my living, I'd keep my coxcomb myself. There's mine, beg another of thy daughters.

LEAR. Take heed, sirrah, the whip.°

FOOL. Truth's a dog must to kennel. He must be whipped out, when Lady the brach° may stand by the fire and stink.

LEAR. A pestilent gall to me!°

FOOL. Sirrah, I'll teach thee a speech.

LEAR. Do.

FOOL. Mark it, Nuncle:

"Have more than thou showest,
Speak less than thou knowest,
Lend less than thou owest,°
Ride more than thou goest,°
Learn more than thou trowest,°
Set less than thou throwest.°
Leave thy drink and thy whore
And keep in-a-door,
And thou shalt have more
Than two tens to a score."°

KENT. This is nothing, fool.

FOOL. Then 'tis like the breath of an unfeed lawyer. You gave me nothing for 't. Can you make no use of nothing, Nuncle?

LEAR. Why, no, boy, nothing can be made out of nothing.°

FOOL. [*To* KENT] Prithee tell him so much the rent of his land comes to. He will not believe a fool.

LEAR. A bitter fool!

FOOL. Dost thou know the difference, my boy, between a bitter fool and a sweet fool?

LEAR. No, lad, teach me.

FOOL.
"That Lord that counseled thee
To give away thy land,
Come place him here by me,
Do thou for him stand.
The sweet and bitter fool

90. Nuncle: Uncle. *94. the whip:* The fool's profession was precarious and in real life too smart a joke brought its painful reward. In March 1605 Stone, a professional fool, was whipped for commenting on the diplomatic mission about to sail for Spain that "there went sixty fools into Spain, besides my Lord Admiral and his two sons." *96. Lady . . . brach:* Lady the pet bitch. *97. A . . . me:* this pestilent fool rubs me on a sore spot. *103. owest:* possess. *104. goest:* walk. *105 trowest:* know. *106. Set . . . throwest:* don't bet a larger stake than you can afford to lose. *108–10. And . . . score:* and then your money will increase. *114. nothing . . . nothing:* Lear unconsciously repeats himself.

Will presently appear—
The one in motley° here,
The other found out there."

LEAR. Dost thou call me fool, boy?

FOOL. All thy other titles thou hast given away. That thou wast born with.

KENT. This is not altogether fool, my lord.

FOOL. No, faith, lords and great men will not let me.° If I had a monopoly° out, they would have part on 't. And ladies too, they will not let me have all the fool to myself, they'll be snatching. Give me an egg, Nuncle, and I'll give thee two crowns.

LEAR. What two crowns shall they be?

FOOL. Why, after I have cut the egg in the middle and eat up the meat, the two crowns of the egg. When thou clovest thy crown i' the middle and gavest away both parts, thou borest thine ass on thy back o'er the dirt.° Thou hadst little wit in thy bald crown when thou gavest thy golden one away. If I speak like myself° in this, let him be whipped that first finds it so. [*Singing*]

"Fools had ne'er less wit in a year,
For wise men are grown foppish,
And know not how their wits to wear,
Their manners are so apish."°

LEAR. When were you wont to be so full of songs, sirrah?

FOOL. I have used it, Nuncle, ever since thou madest thy daughters thy mother. For when thou gavest them the rod and puttest down thine own breeches, [*Singing*]

"Then they for sudden joy did weep,
And I for sorrow sung,
That such a king should play bopeep,
And go the fools among."

Prithee, Nuncle, keep a schoolmaster that can teach thy fool to lie. I would fain learn to lie.

LEAR. An° you lie, sirrah, we'll have you whipped.

FOOL. I marvel what kin thou and thy daughters are. They'll have me whipped for speaking true, thou'lt have me whipped for lying, and sometimes I am whipped for holding my peace. I had rather be any kind o' thing than a fool. And yet I would not be thee, Nuncle. Thou hast pared thy wit o' both sides and left nothing i' the middle. Here comes one o' the pairings.

127. motley: the particolored uniform worn by a fool. *133. will . . . me:* i.e., keep all my folly to myself. *134. monopoly:* a royal patent giving the holders the sole right to deal in some commodity. The granting of such monopolies to courtiers was one of the crying scandals of the time. *140–1. thine . . . dirt:* an old tale of the typical simple-minded countryman. *142. like myself:* i.e., like a fool. *144–7. Fools . . . apish:* there's no job left for fools nowadays, because the wise men are so like them. *147. apish:* like apes, who always imitate. *158. An:* if.

[*Enter* GONERIL.]

LEAR. How now, Daughter! What makes that frontlet° on? Methinks you are too much of late i' the frown.

FOOL. Thou wast a pretty fellow when thou hadst no need to care for her frowning. Now thou art an O without a figure.° I am better than thou art now. I am a fool, thou art nothing. [*To* GONERIL] Yes, forsooth, I will hold my tongue, so your face bids me, though you say nothing.

"Mum, mum.
He that keeps nor crust nor crumb,°
Weary of all, shall want some."

[*Pointing to* LEAR] That's a shealed peascod.°

GON. Not only, sir, this your all-licensed° fool,
But other of your insolent retinue
Do hourly carp° and quarrel, breaking forth
In rank and not to be endurèd riots. Sir,
I had thought, by making this well known unto you,
To have found a safe redress, but now grow fearful
By what yourself too late have spoke and done
That you protect this course and put it on°
By your allowance.° Which if you should, the fault
Would not 'scape censure, nor the redresses sleep,
Which, in the tender of a wholesome weal,
Might in their working do you that offense
Which else were shame, that then necessity
Will call discreet proceeding.°

FOOL. For, you know, Nuncle,
"The hedge sparrow fed the cuckoo so long
That it had it head bit off by it young."
So out went the candle, and we were left darkling.°

LEAR. Are you our daughter?

GON. Come, sir,
I would you would make use of that good wisdom
Whereof I know you are fraught,° and put away
These dispositions° that of late transform you
From what you rightly are.

FOOL. May not an ass know when the cart draws the horse? Whoop, Jug! I love thee.°

165. *frontlet:* frown; lit., a band worn on the forehead. 168. *an . . . figure:* a cipher. 173. *crumb:* inside of the loaf. 175. *shealed peascod:* a shelled peapod. 176. *all-licensed:* allowed to take all liberties. 178. *carp:* find fault. 183. *put it on:* encourage it. 184. *allowance:* approval. 186–9. *Which . . . proceeding:* if you continue to be a nuisance I shall be forced to keep my state peaceful by taking measures which will annoy you and would at other times be shameful toward a father, but would be justified as mere discretion. 193. *darkling:* in the dark. 197. *fraught:* stored, endowed. 198. *dispositions:* moods. 201. *Whoop . . . thee:* one of the meaningless cries made by the fool to distract attention.

LEAR. Doth any here know me? This is not Lear.
Doth Lear walk thus? Speak thus? Where are his eyes?
Either his notion° weakens, his discernings
Are lethargied°—Ha! Waking? 'Tis not so.
Who is it that can tell me who I am?
FOOL. Lear's shadow.
LEAR. I would learn that, for, by the marks of sovereignty,° knowledge, and reason, I should be false persuaded I had daughters.
FOOL. Which they will make an obedient father.
LEAR. Your name, fair gentlewoman?
GON. This admiration,° sir, is much o' the savor
Of° other your new pranks. I do beseech you
To understand my purposes aright.
As you are old and reverend, you should be wise.
Here do you keep a hundred knights and squires,
Men so disordered,° so deboshed° and bold,
That this our Court, infected with their manners,
Shows like a riotous inn. Epicurism° and lust
Make it more like a tavern or a brothel
Than a graced° palace. The shame itself doth speak
For instant remedy. Be then desired
By her that else will take the thing she begs
A little to disquantity your train,°
And the remainder that shall still depend,°
To be such men as may besort° your age,
Which know themselves and you.
LEAR. Darkness and devils!
Saddle my horses, call my train together.
Degenerate bastard! I'll not trouble thee.
Yet have I left a daughter.
GON. You strike my people, and your disordered rabble
Make servants of their betters.
[*Enter* ALBANY.]
LEAR. Woe, that too late repents.— [*To* ALBANY]
Oh, sir, are you come?
Is it your will? Speak, sir. Prepare my horses.
Ingratitude, thou marble-hearted fiend,
More hideous when thou show'st thee in a child
Than the sea monster!

204. notion: understanding. *205. lethargied:* paralyzed. *208. marks of sovereignty:* the outward signs which show that I am King. *212. admiration:* pretended astonishment. *212–3. much . . . Of:* tastes much the same as. *217. disordered:* disorderly. *deboshed:* debauched. *219. Epicurism:* self-indulgence, riotous living. *221. graced:* gracious. *224. disquantity . . . train:* diminish the number of your followers. *225. depend:* by your dependents. *226. besort:* be suitable for.

ALB. Pray, sir, be patient.
LEAR. [*To* GONERIL] Detested kite!° Thou liest.
My train are men of choice and rarest parts,°
That all particulars of duty know,
And in the most exact regard support
The worships of their name.° O most small fault,
How ugly didst thou in Cordelia show!
That, like an engine, wrenched my frame of nature
From the fixed place,° drew from my heart all love
And added to the gall.° O Lear, Lear, Lear!
Beat at this gate, that let thy folly in

[*Striking his head*]

And thy dear judgment out!° Go, go, my people.
ALB. My lord, I am guiltless, as I am ignorant
Of what hath moved you.
LEAR. It may be so, my lord.
Hear, Nature, hear,° dear goddess, hear!
Suspend thy purpose if thou didst intend
To make this creature fruitful.
Into her womb convey sterility.
Dry up in her the organs of increase,°
And from her derogate° body never spring
A babe to honor her! If she must teem,°
Create her child of spleen,° that it may live
And be a thwart disnatured° torment to her.
Let it stamp wrinkles in her brow of youth,
With cadent° tears fret channels in her cheeks,
Turn all her mother's pains and benefits
To laughter and contempt, that she may feel
How sharper than a serpent's tooth it is
To have a thankless child! Away, away!

[*Exit.*]

ALB. Now, gods that we adore, whereof comes this?
GON. Never afflict yourself to know the cause,
But let his disposition have that scope
That dotage gives it.
[*Re-enter* LEAR.]

239. kite: the lowest of the birds of prey, an eater of offal. *240. parts:* accomplishments. *242–3. in . . . name:* and in every minute detail uphold their honorable names. *245–6. like . . . place:* like a little instrument (e.g., a lever) dislodged my firm nature. *247. gall:* bitterness. *248–9. Beat . . . out:* the first signs of madness in Lear. *252. Hear . . . hear:* In making this terrible curse, Lear also calls on Nature, but as goddess of natural affection. *256. increase:* childbearing. *257. derogate:* debased. *258. teem:* conceive. *259. spleen:* malice. *260. thwart disnatured:* perverse and unnatural. *262. cadent:* falling. *fret:* wear away.

LEAR. What, fifty of my followers at a clap!°
Within a fortnight!°
ALB. What's the matter, sir?
LEAR. I'll tell thee. [*To* GONERIL] Life and death! I am ashamed
That thou hast power to shake my manhood° thus,
That these hot tears, which break from me perforce,
Should make thee worth them. Blasts and fogs upon thee!
The untented woundings° of a father's curse
Pierce every sense about thee! Old fond° eyes,
Beweep this cause again, I'll pluck ye out
And cast you with the waters that you lose
To temper° clay. Yea, is it come to this?
Let it be so. Yet have I left a daughter
Who I am sure is kind and comfortable.°
When she shall hear this of thee, with her nails
She'll flay thy wolvish visage. Thou shalt find
That I'll resume the shape which thou dost think
I have cast off forever. Thou shalt, I warrant thee.
[*Exeunt* LEAR, KENT, *and* ATTENDANTS.]
GON. Do you mark that, my lord?
ALB. I° cannot be so partial, Goneril,
To the great love I bear you—
GON. Pray you, content. What, Oswald, ho!
[*To the* FOOL] You, sir, more knave than fool, after your master.
FOOL. Nuncle Lear, Nuncle Lear, tarry, take the fool with thee.°
"A fox, when one has caught her,
And such a daughter,
Should sure to the slaughter,
If my cap would buy a halter.
So the fool follows after."
[*Exit.*]
GON. This man hath had good counsel. A hundred knights!
'Tis politic° and safe to let him keep
At point° a hundred knights. Yes, that on every dream,
Each buzz,° each fancy, each complaint, dislike,

271. at a clap: at one blow. *271–2. What . . . fortnight:* As Lear goes out he learns that Goneril has herself already begun to take steps "a little to disquantity his train" by ordering that fifty of them shall depart within a fortnight. To a man who regards his own dignity so highly, this fresh blow is devastating. *274. shake my manhood:* i.e., with sobs. *277. untented woundings:* raw wounds. A tent was a small roll of lint used to clean out a wound before it was bound up. *278. fond:* foolish. *281. temper:* mix. *283. comfortable:* full of comfort. *289–90. I . . . you:* i.e., although my love makes me partial to you, yet I must protest. *293. take . . . thee:* i.e., take your fool and your own folly. *300. politic:* good policy. *301 At point:* fully armed. *302. buzz:* rumor.

He may enguard his dotage with their powers
And hold our lives in mercy. Oswald, I say!
ALB. Well, you may fear too far.
GON. Safer than trust too far.
Let me still take away the harms I fear,
Not fear still to be taken.° I know his heart.
What he hath uttered I have writ my sister.
If she sustain him and his hundred knights
When I have showed the unfitness—
[*Re-enter* OSWALD.] How now, Oswald!
What, have you writ that letter to my sister?
OSW. Yes, madam.
GON. Take you some company, and away to horse.
Inform her full of my particular fear,
And thereto add such reasons of your own
As may compact it more.° Get you gone,
And hasten your return. [*Exit* OSWALD.] No, no, my lord,
This milky gentleness and course° of yours
Though I condemn not, yet, under pardon,
You are much more attasked° for want of wisdom
Than praised for harmful mildness.°
ALB. How far your eyes may pierce I cannot tell.
Striving to better, oft we mar what's well.
GON. Nay, then—
ALB. Well, well, the event.°

[*Exeunt.*]

Scene V. Court before the same.

[*Enter* LEAR, KENT, *and* FOOL.]

LEAR. Go you before to Gloucester with these letters. Acquaint my daughter no further with anything you know than comes from her demand out of the letter. If your diligence be not speedy, I shall be there afore you.

KENT. I will not sleep, my lord, till I have delivered your letter.

[*Exit*]

306–7. Let . . . taken: let me always remove what I fear will harm me rather than live in perpetual fear. *317. compact it more:* make my argument more convincing. *319. milky . . . course:* this milksop behavior. *321 attasked:* blamed. *322. harmful mildness:* a mildness which may prove harmful. *326. the event:* i.e., we must see what will happen.

FOOL. If a man's brains were in 's heels, were 't not in danger of kibes?°

LEAR. Aye, boy.

FOOL. Then I prithee be merry. Thy wit shall ne'er go slipshod.°

LEAR. Ha, ha, ha!

FOOL. Shalt see thy other daughter will use thee kindly,° for though she's as like this as a crab's° like an apple, yet I can tell what I can tell.

LEAR. Why, what canst thou tell, my boy?

FOOL. She will taste as like this as a crab does to a crab. Thou canst tell why one's nose stands i' the middle on 's face?

LEAR. No.

FOOL. Why, to keep one's eyes of either side 's nose, that what a man cannot smell out he may spy into.

LEAR. I did her wrong—

FOOL. Canst tell how an oyster makes his shell?

LEAR. No.

FOOL. Nor I neither, but I can tell why a snail has a house.

LEAR. Why?

FOOL. Why, to put 's head in, not to give it away to his daughters and leave his horns without a case.

LEAR. I will forget my nature.—So kind a father!—Be my horses ready?

FOOL. Thy asses are gone about 'em. The reason why the seven stars are no more than seven is a pretty reason.

LEAR. Because they are not eight?

FOOL. Yes, indeed. Thou wouldst make a good fool.

LEAR. To take 't again perforce!° Monster ingratitude!

FOOL. If thou wert my fool, Nuncle, I'd have thee beaten for being old before thy time.

LEAR. How's that?

FOOL. Thou shouldst not have been old till thou hadst been wise.

LEAR. Oh, let me not be mad, not mad, sweet Heaven!
Keep me in temper.° I would not be mad!
[*Enter* GENTLEMAN.] How now! Are the horses ready?

GENT. Ready, my lord.

LEAR. Come, boy.

FOOL. She that's a maid now and laughs at my departure
Shall not be a maid long, unless things be cut shorter.

[*Exeunt.*]

Sc. v: *7. kibes:* chilblains. *9. Thy . . . slipshod:* i.e., you don't need slippers, for you have no brains to be protected from chilblains. *11. kindly:* after her kind; i.e., nature. *12. crab:* crab apple. *33. To . . . perforce:* I will take back my kingdom by force. *39. temper:* sanity.

ACT II

Scene I. The EARL OF GLOUCESTER*'s castle.*

[*Enter* EDMUND *and* CURAN, *meeting.*]

EDM. Save thee,° Curan.

CUR. And you, sir. I have been with your father, and given him notice that the Duke of Cornwall and Regan his Duchess will be here with him this night.

EDM. How comes that?

CUR. Nay, I know not. You have heard of the news abroad—I mean the whispered ones, for they are yet but ear-kissing° arguments?

EDM. Not I. Pray you what are they?

CUR. Have you heard of no likely wars toward 'twixt the Dukes of Cornwall and Albany?

EDM. Not a word.

CUR. You may do, then, in time. Fare you well, sir.

[*Exit.*]

EDM. The Duke be here tonight? The better! Best!
This weaves itself perforce into my business.
My father hath set guard to take my brother,
And I have one thing, of a queasy question,°
Which I must act. Briefness and fortune, work!
Brother, a word, descend.° Brother, I say!
[*Enter* EDGAR.] My father watches. O sir, fly this place.
Intelligence° is given where you are hid.
You have now the good advantage of the night.
Have you not spoken 'gainst the Duke of Cornwall?
He's coming hither, now, i' the night, i' the haste,
And Regan with him. Have you nothing said
Upon his party 'gainst the Duke of Albany?
Advise yourself.

EDG. I am sure on 't, not a word.

EDM. I hear my father coming. Pardon me,
In cunning° I must draw my sword upon you.
Draw. Seem to defend yourself. Now quit you well.°
Yield. Come before my father. Light, ho, here!
Fly, Brother. Torches, torches! So farewell.

[*Exit* EDGAR.]

Act II, Sc. i: *1. Save thee:* God save thee. *7. ear-kissing:* whispered close in the ear. *16. queasy question:* which needs delicate handling; *queasy* means on the point of vomiting. *18. descend:* i.e., from the chamber where he has been hiding. *20. Intelligence:* information. *28. In cunning:* as a pretense. *29. quit . . . well:* defend yourself well. Here they clash their swords together.

Some blood drawn on me would beget opinion°
[*Wounds his arm.*]
Of my more fierce endeavor. I have seen drunkards
Do more than this sport. Father, Father!
Stop, stop! No help?
[*Enter* GLOUCESTER *and* SERVANTS *with torches.*]

GLO. Now, Edmund, where's the villain?

EDM. Here stood he in the dark, his sharp sword out,
Mumbling° of wicked charms, conjuring the moon°
To stand 's auspicious° mistress.

GLO. But where is he?

EDM. Look, sir, I bleed.

GLO. Where is the villain, Edmund?

EDM. Fled this way, sir. When by no means he could—

GLO. Pursue him, ho!—Go after.
[*Exeunt some* SERVANTS.]
"By no means" what?

EDM. Persuade me to the murder of your lordship,
But that I told him the revenging gods
'Gainst parricides did all their thunders bend,
Spoke with how manifold and strong a bond
The child was bound to the father. Sir, in fine,°
Seeing how loathly opposite I stood°
To his unnatural purpose, in fell° motion
With his preparèd° sword he charges home
My unprovided° body, lanced mine arm.
But when he saw my best alarumed spirits°
Bold in the quarrel's right, roused to the encounter,
Or whether gasted° by the noise I made,
Full suddenly he fled.

GLO. Let him fly far.
Not in this land shall he remain uncaught,
And found—dispatch.° The noble Duke my master,
My worthy arch and patron,° comes tonight.
By his authority I will proclaim it,
That he which finds him shall deserve our thanks,
Bringing the murderous caitiff° to the stake.°
He that conceals him, death.

32. beget opinion: give the impression. *38–9. Mumbling . . . mistress:* This is the kind of story which would especially appeal to Gloucester. *38. conjuring . . . moon:* calling on Hecate, goddess of witchcraft. *39. auspicious:* favorable. *47. in fine:* in short. *48. how . . . stood:* with what loathing I opposed. *49. fell:* fearful. *50. prepared:* drawn. *51. unprovided:* unguarded. *52. my . . . spirits:* my stoutest spirits called out by the alarm. *54. gasted:* terrified. *57. And . . . dispatch:* and when he's found, kill him. *58. arch . . . patron:* chief support and protector. *61. caitiff:* wretch; lit., captive. *to . . . stake:* i.e., place of execution.

EDM. When I dissuaded him from his intent
And found him pight° to do it, with curst° speech
I threatened to discover him. He replied,
"Thou unpossessing bastard! Dost thou think,
If I would stand against thee, could the reposal
Of any trust, virtue, or worth in thee
Make thy words faithed?° No. What I should deny—
As this I would, aye, though thou didst produce
My very character°—I'd turn it all°
To thy suggestion,° plot, and damnèd practice.°
And thou must make° a dullard of the world
If they not thought the profits of my death
Were very pregnant and potential spurs°
To make thee seek it."
GLO. Strong and fastened° villain!
Would he deny his letter? I never got° him.
[*Tucket° within*]
Hark, the Duke's trumpets! I know not why he comes.
All ports I'll bar,° the villain shall not 'scape,
The Duke must grant me that. Besides, his picture
I will send far and near, that all the kingdom
May have due note of him, and of my land,
Loyal and natural° boy, I'll work the means
To make thee capable.°
[*Enter* CORNWALL, REGAN, *and* ATTENDANTS.]
CORN. How now, my noble friend! Since I came hither,
Which I can call but now, I have heard strange news.
REG. If it be true, all vengeance comes too short
Which can pursue the offender. How dost, my lord?
GLO. Oh, madam, my old heart is cracked, is cracked!
REG. What, did my father's godson seek your life?
He whom my father named? Your Edgar?
GLO. Oh, lady, lady, shame would have it hid!
REG. Was he not companion with the riotous knights
That tend upon my father?
GLO. I know not, madam. 'Tis too bad, too bad.

64. *pight:* determined. *curst:* bitter. 69. *faithed:* believed. 71. *character:* handwriting. *turn it all:* make it appear to be. 72. *suggestion:* idea. *practice:* plot. 73–6. *make . . . it:* you would have to make people dull indeed before they would disbelieve that your chief motive was to benefit by my death. 75. *pregnant . . . spurs:* obvious and powerful encouragements. 76. *fastened:* confirmed. 77. *got:* begot. *s.d., Tucket:* trumpet call. 79. *ports . . . bar:* I'll have the seaports watched to prevent his escape. 83. *natural:* i.e., one who has the proper feelings of son to father. Gloucester does not as yet realize what "nature" means to Edmund. 84. *capable:* i.e., legitimate; lit., capable of succeeding as my heir.

EDM. Yes, madam, he was of that consort.°
REG. No marvel then, though he were ill affected.°
'Tis they have put him on° the old man's death,
To have the waste and spoil of his revènues.
I have this present evening from my sister
Been well informed of them, and with such cautions
That if they come to sojourn at my house,
I'll not be there.
CORN. Nor I, assure thee, Regan.
Edmund, I hear that you have shown your father
A childlike office.°
EDM. 'Twas my duty, sir.
GLO. He did bewray° his practice, and received
This hurt you see, striving to apprehend him.
CORN. Is he pursued?
GLO. Aye, my good lord.
CORN. If he be taken, he shall never more
Be feared of doing° harm. Make your own purpose,
How in my strength you please.° For you, Edmund,
Whose virtue and obedience doth this instant
So much commend itself, you shall be ours.
Natures of such deep trust we shall much need.
You we first seize on.
EDM. I shall serve you, sir,
Truly, however else.
GLO. For him I thank your Grace.
CORN. You know not why we came to visit you—
REG. Thus out of season, threading dark-eyed night.°
Occasions, noble Gloucester, of some poise,°
Wherein we must have use of your advice.
Our father he hath writ, so hath our sister,
Of differences, which I least thought it fit
To answer from° our home. The several messengers
From hence attend dispatch.° Our good old friend,
Lay comforts to your bosom, and bestow
Your needful counsel to our business,
Which craves the instant use.°
GLO. I serve you, madam.
Your Graces are right welcome.

[*Flourish. Exeunt.*]

96. consort: party. *97. though . . . affected:* if he had traitorous thoughts. *98. put . . . on:* persuaded him to cause. *105. childlike office:* filial service. *106. bewray:* reveal. *110. of doing:* because he might do. *110–1. Make . . . please:* use my authority for any action you care to take. *118. threading . . . night:* making our way through the darkness. *119. poise:* weight. *123. from:* away from. *124. attend dispatch:* are waiting to be sent back. *127. craves . . . use:* requires immediate action.

Scene II. Before GLOUCESTER*'s castle.*

[*Enter* KENT *and* OSWALD, *severally.*°]

OSW. Good dawning to thee, friend. Art of this house?

KENT. Aye.

OSW. Where may we set our horses?

KENT. I' the mire.

OSW. Prithee, if thou lovest me, tell me.

KENT. I love thee not.

OSW. Why, then I care not for thee.

KENT. If I had thee in Lipsbury pinfold,° I would make thee care for me.

OSW. Why dost thou use me thus? I know thee not.

KENT. Fellow, I know thee.

OSW. What dost thou know me for?

KENT. A° knave, a rascal, an eater of broken meats; a base, proud, shallow, beggarly, three-suited, hundred-pound, filthy, worsted-stocking knave; a lily-livered, action-taking knave; a whoreson, glass-gazing, superserviceable, finical rogue; one-trunk-inheriting slave; one that wouldst be a bawd in way of good service, and art nothing but the composition of a knave, beggar, coward, pander, and the son and heir of a mongrel bitch—one whom I will beat into clamorous whining if thou deniest the least syllable of thy addition.

OSW. Why, what a monstrous fellow art thou, thus to rail on one that is neither known of thee nor knows thee!

KENT. What a brazen-faced varlet art thou, to deny thou knowest me! Is it two days ago since I tripped up thy heels and beat thee before the King? Draw, you rogue. For though it be night, yet the moon shines. I'll make a sop o' the moonshine of you.° Draw, you whoreson cullionly° barbermonger,° draw.

[*Drawing his sword.*]

Sc.ii: *s.d., severally:* by different entrances. *8. Lipsbury pinfold:* This phrase has not been convincingly explained. A pinfold is a village pound, a small enclosure in which strayed beasts are kept until reclaimed by their owners; a pinfold was a good place for a fight whence neither side could escape. *13–21. A . . . addition:* Kent here sums up the characteristics of the more unpleasant kind of gentleman servingman of whom Oswald is a fair specimen *broken meats:* remains of food sent down from the high table. *three-suited:* allowed three suits a year. *hundred-pound:* i.e., the extent of his wealth. *worsted-stocking:* no gentleman, or he would have worn silk. *lily-livered:* cowardly. *action-taking knave:* one who goes to law instead of risking a fight. *glass-gazing:* always looking at himself in a mirror. *superserviceable:* too eager to do what his master wishes. *finical:* finicky. *one-trunk-inheriting:* whose whole inheritance from his father will go into one trunk. *bawd . . . service:* ready to serve his master's lusts if it will please him. *composition:* mixture. *pander:* pimp. *addition:* lit., title of honor added to a man's name. *27. sop . . . you:* Not satisfactorily explained, but obviously something unpleasant; probably Kent means no more than "I'll make a wet mess of you." *28. cullionly:* base. *28. barbermonger:* a man always in the barber's shop.

OSW. Away! I have nothing to do with thee.

KENT. Draw, you rascal. You come with letters against the King, and take vanity the puppet's part° against the royalty of her father. Draw, you rogue, or I'll so carbonado° your shanks. Draw, you rascal, come your ways.

OSW. Help, ho! Murder! Help!

KENT. Strike, you slave. Stand, rogue, stand, you neat slave, strike.

[*Beating him.*]

OSW. Help, ho! Murder! Murder!

[*Enter* EDMUND, *with his rapier drawn,* CORNWALL, REGAN, GLOUCESTER, *and* SERVANTS.]

EDM. How now! What's the matter?

[*Parting them.*]

KENT. With you, goodman boy,° an you please. Come, I'll flesh you,° come on, young master.

GLO. Weapons! Arms! What's the matter here?

CORN. Keep peace, upon your lives. He dies that strikes again. What is the matter?

REG. The messengers from our sister and the King.

CORN. What is your difference?° Speak.

OSW. I am scarce in breath, my lord.

KENT. No marvel, you have so bestirred your valor. You cowardly rascal, Nature disclaims in thee. A tailor made thee.°

CORN. Thou art a strange fellow—a tailor make a man?

KENT. Aye, a tailor, sir. A stonecutter or a painter could not have made him so ill, though he had been but two hours at the trade.

CORN. Speak yet, how grew your quarrel?

OSW. This ancient ruffian, sir, whose life I have spared at suit of his gray beard—

KENT. Thou whoreson zed! Thou unnecessary letter!° My lord, if you will give me leave, I will tread this unbolted° villain into mortar, and daub the walls of a jakes° with him. Spare my gray beard, you wagtail?°

CORN. Peace, sirrah!
You beastly knave, know you no reverence?°

31. vanity . . . part: Vanity appeared as an evil character in the old Morality plays of the early sixteenth century, which still survived in a degenerate form in puppet shows exhibited at fairs. *32. carbonado:* lit., a steak slashed for cooking, so "slice." *39. goodman boy:* my young man. Edmund is still a young man, but it was an insult to call him boy. *40. flesh you:* give you your first fight. *45. difference:* disagreement. *48. Nature . . . thee:* Nature refuses to own you, you are nothing but clothes—from the English proverb "The tailor makes the man." *55. zed . . . letter:* because *z* does not exist in Latin and is not necessary in the English alphabet, since *s* can usually take its place. *56. unbolted:* unsifted, coarse. *57. jakes:* privy. *58. wagtail:* a small bird which wags its tail up and down as it struts. *60. know . . . reverence;* i.e., do you have the impertinence to raise your voice in the presence of your betters?

KENT. Yes, sir, but anger hath a privilege.°
CORN. Why art thou angry?
KENT. That such a slave as this should wear a sword,
Who wears no honesty. Such smiling rogues as these,
Like rats, oft bite the holy cords a-twain
Which are too intrinse to unloose;° smooth° every passion
That in the natures of their lords rebel;
Bring oil to fire, snow to their colder moods;
Renege, affirm,° and turn their halcyon° beaks
With every gale and vary of their masters,
Knowing naught, like dogs, but following.
A plague upon your epileptic visage!
Smile you my speeches, as I were a fool?
Goose,° if I had you upon Sarum° plain,
I'd drive ye cackling home to Camelot.°
CORN. What, art thou mad, old fellow?
GLO. How fell you out? Say that.
KENT. No contraries hold more antipathy
Than I and such a knave.
CORN. Why dost thou call him knave? What is his fault?
KENT. His countenance likes me not.°
CORN. No more perchance does mine, nor his, nor hers.
KENT. Sir, 'tis my occupation to be plain.
I have seen better faces in my time
Than stands on any shoulder that I see
Before me at this instant.
CORN. This is some fellow
Who, having been praised for bluntness, doth affect
A saucy roughness,° and constrains the garb
Quite from his nature.° He cannot flatter, he—
An honest mind and plain—he must speak truth!
An they will take it, so. If not, he's plain.
These kind of knaves I know, which in this plainness
Harbor more craft and more corrupter ends
Than twenty silly ducking observants
That stretch their duties nicely.°

61. anger . . . privilege: something must be allowed to a man who has lost temper. *65–6. bite . . . unloose:* i.e., cause the bonds of holy matrimony to be broken by serving the lusts of their employers. *66. smooth:* help to gratify. *69. Renege, affirm:* deny or agree; i.e., a perfect "yes man." *halcyon:* kingfisher. A kingfisher hung up by the neck was supposed to turn its bill into the prevailing wind. *74–5. Goose . . . Camelot:* These lines cannot be explained. *Sarum:* Salisbury Plain, in the south of England. *Camelot:* the home of King Arthur and the knights of his Round Table. *81. His . . . not:* I don't like his face. *88. saucy roughness:* impudent rudeness. *88–9. constrains . . . nature:* affects a manner which is quite unnatural. *94–5. silly . . . nicely:* silly servants who are always bowing to their masters as they strain to carry out their orders.

KENT. Sir,° in good faith, in sincere verity,
Under the allowance of your great aspéct,
Whose influence, like the wreath of radiant fire
On flickering Phoebus'° front—

CORN. What mean'st by this?

KENT. To go out of my dialect, which you discommend so much. I know, sir, I am no flatterer. He that beguiled you in a plain accent was a plain knave, which, for my part, I will not be, though I should win your displeasure to entreat me to 't.°

CORN. What was the offense you gave him?

OSW. I never gave him any.
It pleased the King his master very late
To strike at me, upon his misconstruction,°
When he, conjunct,° and flattering his displeasure,
Tripped me behind; being down, insulted, railed,
And put upon him such a deal of man
That worthied him,° got praises of the King
For him attempting° who was self-subdued,°
And in the fleshment° of this dread exploit
Drew on me here again.

KENT. None of these rogues and cowards
But Ajax is their fool.°

CORN. Fetch forth the stocks!
You stubborn° ancient knave, you reverend° braggart,
We'll teach you—

KENT. Sir, I am too old to learn.
Call not your stocks for me. I serve the King,
On whose employment I was sent to you.
You shall do small respect, show too bold malice
Against the grace and person of my master,
Stocking his messenger.°

96–9. Sir . . . front: Kent now changes his tone from the honest blunt man to the affected courtier. *Phoebus:* the sun god. *101–3. He . . . to't:* the man who posed as blunt and honest and deceived you was simply a knave. I shall never be a knave, even if you ask me and are angry because I refuse. *107. upon . . . misconstruction:* because he deliberately misinterpreted my words. *108. conjunct:* i.e., joining with the King. *111. worthied him:* got him favor. *112. attempting:* attacking. *self-subdued:* make no resistance. *113. fleshment:* excitement. *114–5. None . . . fool:* This cryptic but devastating remark rouses Cornwall to fury, for he realizes from Kent's insolent tone, manner, and gesture that by "Ajax" he is himself intended. Ajax was the ridiculous braggart of the Greek army whom Shakespeare had already dramatized in *Tr & Cr.* The name Ajax had further unsavory significances for the original audience, for "Ajax" was a common synonym for a jakes—a very evil-smelling place. Kent thus implies "All these knaves and cowards are fooling this stinking braggart." *116. stubborn:* rude. *reverend:* old. *120–2. You . . . messenger:* As the King's representative, Kent is entitled to respectful treatment; to put him in the stocks is to offer an intolerable insult to the King.

CORN. Fetch forth the stocks! As I have life and honor,
There shall he sit till noon.
REG. Till noon! Till night, my lord, and all night too.
KENT. Why, madam, if I were your father's dog,
You should not use me so.
REG. Sir, being his knave, I will.
CORN. This is a fellow of the selfsame color
Our sister speaks of. Come, bring away° the stocks!
[*Stocks brought out*]
GLO. Let me beseech your Grace not to do so.
His fault is much, and the good King his master
Will check° him for 't. Your purposed low correction°
Is such as basest and contemned'st° wretches
For pilferings and most common trespasses
Are punished with. The King must take it ill
That he, so slightly valued in his messenger,
Should have him thus restrained.
CORN. I'll answer that.
REG. My sister may receive it much more worse
To have her gentleman abused, assaulted,
For following her affairs. Put in his legs.
[KENT *is put in the stocks.*]
Come, my good lord, away.
[*Exeunt all but* GLOUCESTER *and* KENT.]
GLO. I am sorry for thee, friend. 'Tis the Duke's pleasure,
Whose disposition all the world well knows
Will not be rubbed° nor stopped. I'll entreat for thee.
KENT. Pray do not, sir. I have watched and traveled hard,
Some time I shall sleep out, the rest I'll whistle.
A good man's fortune may grow out at heels.°
Give you good morrow!°
GLO. The Duke's to blame in this, 'twill be ill-taken.
[*Exit.*]
KENT. Good King, that must approve the common saw,°
Thou out of Heaven's benediction comest
To the warm sun!°
Approach, thou beacon to this underglobe,°
That by thy comfortable beams I may

129. bring away: fetch out. *132. check:* rebuke, punish. *purposed . . . correction:* the degrading punishment which you propose. *133. contemned'st:* most despised. *144. rubbed:* turned aside, a metaphor from the game of bowls. *147. A . . . heels:* even a good man may suffer a shabby fate. *148. Give . . . morrow:* a good morning to you. *150. approve . . . saw:* stress the truth of the common proverb. *151–2. Thou . . . sun:* you are coming out of the shade into the heat. *153. beacon . . . underglobe:* the rising sun.

Peruse this letter! Nothing almost sees miracles
But misery.° I know 'tis from Cordelia,
Who hath most fortunately been informed
Of my obscurèd course,° and shall find time
From this enormous state,° seeking to give
Losses their remedies. All weary and o'erwatched,
Take vantage, heavy eyes, not to behold
This shameful lodging.
Fortune, good night. Smile once more, turn thy wheel!

[*Sleeps.*]

Scene III. A wood.

[*Enter* EDGAR.]

EDG. I heard myself proclaimed,
And by the happy° hollow of a tree
Escaped the hunt. No port is free, no place,
That guard and most unusual vigilance
Does not attend my taking.° Whiles I may 'scape
I will preserve myself, and am bethought°
To take the basest and most poorest shape
That ever penury in contempt of man
Brought near to beast.° My face I'll grime with filth,
Blanket° my loins, elf° all my hair in knots,
And with presented nakedness° outface
The winds and persecutions of the sky.
The country gives me proof and precedent°
Of Bedlam beggars,° who with roaring voices
Strike in their numbed and mortified° bare arms
Pins, wooden pricks, nails, sprigs of rosemary,
And with this horrible object, from low° farms,
Poor pelting° villages, sheepcotes and mills,
Sometime with lunatic bans,° sometime with prayers,

155–6. Nothing . . . misery: only those who are wretched appreciate miracles. *158. obscured course:* i.e., my actions in disguise. *159. this . . . state:* these wicked times.

Sc. iii: *2. happy:* lucky. *5. attend my taking:* watch to take me. *6. am bethought:* have decided. *8–9. penury . . . beast:* poverty, to show that man is a contemptible creature, reduced to the level of a beast. *10. Blanket:* cover with only a blanket. *elf:* mat. Matted hair was believed to be caused by elves. *11. with . . . nakedness:* bold in my nakedness. *13. proof . . . precedent:* examples. *14. Bedlam beggars:* lunatics discharged from Bedlam (or Bethlehem) Hospital, the London madhouse. These sturdy beggars were the terror of the countryside. *15. mortified:* numbed. *17. low:* humble. *18. pelting:* paltry. *19. bans:* curses.

Enforce their charity. Poor Turlygod! Poor Tom!°
That's something yet. Edgar I nothing am.°

[*Exit.*]

Scene IV. Before GLOUCESTER*'s castle.* KENT *in the stocks.*

[*Enter* LEAR, FOOL, *and* GENTLEMAN.]

LEAR. 'Tis strange that they should so depart from home
And not send back my messenger.
GENT. As I learned,
The night before there was no purpose° in them
Of this remove.
KENT. Hail to thee, noble master!
LEAR. Ha!
Makest thou this shame thy pastime?°
KENT. No, my lord.
FOOL. Ha, ha! He wears cruel° garters. Horses are tied by the heads, dogs and bears by the neck, monkeys by the loins, and men by the legs. When a man's overlusty at legs,° then he wears wooden netherstocks.°
LEAR. What's he that hath so much thy place mistook
To set thee here?
KENT. It is both he and she,
Your son and daughter.
LEAR. No.
KENT. Yes.
LEAR. No, I say.
KENT. I say yea.
LEAR. No, no, they would not.
KENT. Yes, they have.
LEAR. By Jupiter, I swear no.
KENT. By Juno, I swear aye.
LEAR. They durst not do 't,
They could not, would not do 't. 'Tis worse than murder
To do upon respect° such violent outrage.
Resolve° me with all modest haste which way

20. Poor . . . Tom: Edgar rehearses the names which a bedlam calls himself. *21. That's . . . am:* there's still a chance for me; as Edgar I am a dead man.

Sc. iv: *3. purpose:* intention. *6. Makest . . . pastime:* are you sitting there for amusement? *7. cruel:* with a pun on "crewel"—worsted. *9. overlusty at legs:* i.e., a vagabond. *15. netherstocks:* stockings. *23. upon respect:* the respect due to me, their King and father. *24. Resolve:* inform.

Thou mightest deserve, or they impose, this usage,
Coming from us.°

KENT. My lord, when at their home
I did commend your Highness' letters to them,
Ere I was risen from the place that showed
My duty kneeling, came there a reeking post,°
Stewed in his haste, half-breathless, panting forth
From Goneril his mistress salutations,
Delivered letters, spite of intermission,°
Which presently° they read. On whose contents
They summoned up their meiny,° straight took horse,
Commanded me to follow and attend
The leisure of their answer, gave me cold looks.
And meeting here the other messenger,
Whose welcome, I perceived, had poisoned mine—
Being the very fellow that of late
Displayed so saucily° against your Highness—
Having more man than wit about me, drew.
He raised the house with loud and coward cries.
Your son and daughter found this trespass worth°
The shame which here it suffers

FOOL. Winter's not gone yet° if the wild geese fly that way.
"Fathers that wear rags
Do make their children blind,
But fathers that bear bags°
Shall see their children kind.
Fortune, that arrant whore,
Ne'er turns the key° to the poor."
But for all this, thou shalt have as many dolors° for thy daughters as thou canst tell° in a year.

LEAR. Oh,° how this mother swells up toward my heart!
Hysterica passio, down, thou climbing sorrow,
Thy element's° below! Where is this daughter?

26. Coming . . . us: Lear uses the royal "we"—"from us, the King." *29. reeking post:* sweating messenger. *32. spite of intermission:* in spite of the delay in reading my letter (which should have come first). *33. presently:* immediately. *34. meiny:* followers. *40. Displayed so saucily:* behaved so insolently. *43. worth:* deserving. *45. Winter's . . . yet:* there's more trouble to come. *48. bear bags:* have money. *51. turns . . . key:* opens the door. *52. dolors:* with a pun on "dollars." *53. tell:* count. *54–6. Oh . . . below:* The *mother,* called also *hysterica passio,* was an overwhelming feeling of physical distress and suffocation. Lear's mental suffering is now beginning to cause a physical breakdown. This sensation, and the violent throbbing of his heart until finally it ceases, can be traced in Lear's speeches. *56. element:* natural place.

KENT. With the Earl, sir, here within.

LEAR. Follow me not, stay here.

[*Exit.*]

GENT. Made you no more offense but what you speak of?

KENT. None.
How chance the King comes with so small a train?

FOOL. An thou hadst been set i' the stocks for that question, thou hadst well deserved it.

KENT. Why, fool?

FOOL. We'll° set thee to school to an ant, to teach thee there's no laboring i' the winter. All that follow their noses° are led by their eyes but blind men, and there's not a nose among twenty but can smell him that's stinking. Let go thy hold when a great wheel runs down a hill, lest it break thy neck with following it, but the great one that goes up the hill, let him draw thee after. When a wise man gives thee better counsel, give me mine again. I would have none but knaves follow it, since a fool gives it.

"That sir which serves and seeks for gain,
And follows but for form,°
Will pack° when it begins to rain,
And leave thee in the storm.

"But I will tarry, the fool will stay,
And let the wise man fly.
The knave turns fool that runs away,
The fool no knave, perdy."°

KENT. Where learned you this, fool?

FOOL. Not i' the stocks, fool.

[*Re-Enter* LEAR, *with* GLOUCESTER.]

LEAR. Deny to speak with me? They are sick? They are weary?
They have traveled all the night? Mere fetches,°
The images° of revolt and flying off.
Fetch me a better answer.

GLO. My dear lord,
You know the fiery quality° of the Duke,
How unremovable and fixed he is
In his own course.

LEAR. Vengeance! Plague! Death! Confusion!
Fiery? What quality? Why, Gloucester, Gloucester,

65–72. We'll . . . it: The fool is so much amused at Kent's discomfiture that he strings off a series of wise sayings to show his own clearer understanding of Lear's state. *66. follow . . . noses:* go straight ahead. *74. but . . . form:* merely for show. *75. pack:* clear out. *80. perdy:* by God. *84. fetches:* excuses. *85. images:* exact likenesses. *87. quality:* nature.

I'd speak with the Duke of Cornwall and his wife.
GLO. Well, my good lord, I have informed them so.
LEAR. Informed them! Dost thou understand me, man?
GLO. Aye, my good lord.
LEAR. The King would speak with Cornwall, the dear father
Would with his daughter speak, commands her service,
Are they informed of this? My breath and blood!
"Fiery"? "The fiery Duke"? Tell the hot Duke that—
No, but not yet. Maybe he is not well.
Infirmity doth still neglect all office
Whereto our health is bound.° We are not ourselves
When nature being oppressed commands the mind
To suffer with the body. I'll forbear,
And am fall'n out with my more headier will,°
To take the indisposed and sickly fit
For the sound man. [*Looking on* KENT] Death on my state!
Wherefore
Should he sit here? This act persuades me
That this remotion° of the Duke and her
Is practice° only. Give me my servant forth.°
Go tell the Duke and 's wife I'd speak with them,
Now, presently. Bid them come forth and hear me,
Or at their chamber door I'll beat the drum
Till it cry sleep to death.°
GLO. I would have all well betwixt you.
[*Exit.*]
LEAR. Oh, me, my heart, my rising heart! But down!
FOOL. Cry to it, Nuncle, as the cockney° did to the eels when she put 'em i' the paste alive. She knapped° 'em o' the coxcombs with a stick, and cried "Down, wantons, down!" 'Twas her brother that, in pure kindness to his horse, buttered his hay.
[*Re-enter* GLOUCESTER, *with* CORNWALL, REGAN, *and* SERVANTS.]
LEAR. Good morrow to you both.
CORN. Hail to your Grace! [KENT *is set at liberty.*]
REG. I am glad to see your Highness.
LEAR. Regan, I think you are, I know what reason
I have to think so. If thou shouldst not be glad,
I would divorce me from thy mother's tomb,
Sepúlchring an adultress.° [*To* KENT] Oh, are you free?
Some other time for that. Belovèd Regan,

101–2. Infirmity . . . bound: when a man is sick, he neglects his proper duty. *105. am . . . will:* regret my hastiness. *109. remotion:* removal. *110. practice:* pretense. *Give . . . forth:* release my servant at once. *114. cry . . . death:* kill sleep by its noise. *117. cockney:* Londoner. *118. knapped:* cracked. *127. divorce . . . adultress:* i.e., I would suspect that your dead mother had been false to me.

Thy sister's naught.° O Regan, she hath tied
Sharp-toothed unkindness, like a vulture, here.
[*Points to his heart.*]
I can scarce speak to thee, thou'lt not believe
With how depraved a quality—O Regan!

REG. I pray you, sir, take patience. I have hope
You less know how to value her desert
Than she to scant her duty.

LEAR. Say, how is that?

REG. I cannot think my sister in the least
Would fail her obligation. If, sir, perchance
She have restrained the riots of your followers,
'Tis on such ground and to such wholesome end
As clears her from all blame.

LEAR. My curses on her!

REG. Oh, sir, you are old,
Nature in you stands on the very verge
Of her confine.° You should be ruled and led
By some discretion that discerns your state
Better than you yourself. Therefore I pray you
That to our sister you do make return.
Say you have wronged her, sir.

LEAR. Ask her forgiveness?
Do you but mark how this becomes the house.°—
[*Kneeling*] "Dear daughter, I confess that I am old,
Age is unnecessary. On my knees I beg
That you'll vouchsafe me raiment, bed, and food."

REG. Good sir, no more, these are unsightly tricks.
Return you to my sister.

LEAR. [*Rising*] Never, Regan.
She hath abated me of half my train,
Looked black upon me, struck me with her tongue,
Most serpentlike, upon the very heart.
All the stored vengeances of Heaven fall
On her ingrateful top!° Strike her young bones,
You taking airs, with lameness.

CORN. Fie, sir, fie!

LEAR. You nimble lightnings, dart your blinding flames
Into her scornful eyes. Infect her beauty,
You fen-sucked fogs, drawn by the powerful sun
To fall° and blast her pride.

129. *naught:* wicked. 143. *confine:* boundary, edge. 148. *becomes . . . house:* i.e., suits my dignity. 159. *top:* head. 164. *fall:* fall upon.

REG. Oh, the blest gods! So will you wish on me
When the rash mood is on.
LEAR. No, Regan, thou shalt never have my curse.
Thy tender-hefted° nature shall not give
Thee o'er to harshness. Her eyes are fierce, but thine
Do comfort and not burn. 'Tis not in thee
To grudge my pleasures, to cut off my train,
To bandy hasty words, to scant my sizes,°
And in conclusion to oppose the bolt°
Against my coming in. Thou better know'st
The offices of nature, bond of childhood,
Effects of courtesy, dues of gratitude.
Thy half o' the kingdom hast thou not forgot,
Wherein I thee endowed.
REG. Good sir, to the purpose.°
LEAR. Who put my man i' the stocks?
[*Tucket within.*]
CORN. What trumpet's that?
REG. I know 't, my sister's. This approves° her letter,
That she would soon be here.
[*Enter* OSWALD.] Is your lady come?
LEAR. This is a slave whose easy-borrowed pride
Dwells in the fickle grace of her he follows.°
Out, varlet,° from my sight!
CORN. What means your Grace?
LEAR. Who stocked my servant? Regan, I have good hope
Thou didst not know on 't. Who comes here?
[*Enter* GONERIL.] O Heavens,
If you do love old men, if your sweet sway
Allow° obedience, if yourselves are old,
Make it your cause. Send down, and take my part!
[*To* GONERIL] Art not ashamed to look upon this beard?
O Regan, wilt thou take her by the hand?
GON. Why not by the hand, sir? How have I offended?
All's not offense that indiscretion finds
And dotage terms so.°
LEAR. O sides, you are too tough,
Will you yet hold? How came my man i' the stocks?
CORN. I set him there, sir. But his own disorders
Deserved much less advancement.°

168. *tender-hefted:* gently framed. 172. *scant my sizes:* reduce my allowances. 173. *oppose . . . bolt:* bar the door. 178. *Good . . . purpose:* and in good time to; or, please talk sense. 180. *approves:* confirms. 183–4. *whose . . . follows:* who soon puts on airs because his fickle mistress favors him. 184. *varlet:* knave. 189. *Allow:* approve of. 194–5. *that . . . so:* because a silly old man says so. 198. *advancement:* promotion.

LEAR. You! Did you?
REG. I pray you, Father, being weak, seem so.°
If till the expiration of your month
You will return and sojourn with my sister,
Dismissing half your train, come then to me.
I am now from home and out of that provision
Which shall be needful for your entertainment.°
LEAR. Return to her, and fifty men dismissed?
No, rather I abjure° all roofs, and choose
To wage against the enmity o' the air,
To be a comrade with the wolf and owl—
Necessity's sharp pinch! Return with her?
Why, the hot-blooded France, that dowerless took
Our youngest-born—I could as well be brought
To knee his throne and, squirelike,° pension beg
To keep base life afoot. Return with her?
Persuade me rather to be slave and sumpter°
To this detested groom. [*Pointing at* OSWALD.]
GON. At your choice, sir.
LEAR. I prithee, Daughter, do not make me mad.
I will not trouble thee, my child. Farewell.
We'll no more meet, no more see one another.
But yet thou art my flesh, my blood, my daughter,
Or rather a disease that's in my flesh
Which I must needs call mine. Thou art a boil,
A plague sore, an embossed carbuncle,°
In my corrupted blood. But I'll not chide thee.
Let shame come when it will, I do not call it.
I do not bid the thunderbearer° shoot,
Nor tell tales of thee to high-judging Jove.
Mend when thou canst, be better at thy leisure.
I can be patient, I can stay with Regan,
I and my hundred knights.
REG. Not altogether so.
I looked not for you yet, nor am provided
For your fit welcome. Give ear, sir, to my sister,
For those that mingle reason with your passion
Must be content to think you old,° and so—
But she knows what she does.
LEAR. Is this well spoken?

199. seem so: i.e., behave suitably. *204. entertainment:* maintenance. *206. abjure:* refuse with an oath. *212. squirelike:* like a servant. *214. sumpter:* pack horse, beast of burden. *222. embossed carbuncle:* swollen boil. *225. thunderbearer:* Jupiter. *232–3. those . . . old:* those who consider your passion with reason realize that you are old—and should be wise.

REG. I dare avouch° it, sir. What, fifty followers?
Is it not well? What should you need of more?
Yea, or so many, sith° that both charge and danger°
Speak 'gainst so great a number? How in one house
Should many people under two commands
Hold amity? 'Tis hard, almost impossible.
GON. Why might not you, my lord, receive attendance
From those that she calls servants or from mine?
REG. Why not, my lord? If then they chanced to slack° you,
We could control them. If you will come to me,
For now I spy a danger, I entreat you
To bring but five and twenty. To no more
Will I give place or notice.
LEAR. I gave you all—
REG. And in good time you gave it.
LEAR. Made you my guardians, my depositaries,°
But kept a reservation° to be followed
With such a number. What, must I come to you
With five and twenty, Regan? Said you so?
REG. And speak 't again, my lord, no more with me.
LEAR. Those wicked creatures yet do look well-favored,°
When others are more wicked. Not being the worst
Stands in some rank of praise.° [*To* GONERIL] I'll go with thee,
Thy fifty yet doth double five and twenty,
And thou art twice her love.
GON. Hear me, my lord.
What need you five and twenty, ten, or five,
To follow in a house where twice so many
Have a command to tend you?
REG. What need one?
LEAR. Oh,° reason not the need. Our basest beggars
Are in the poorest thing superfluous.°
Allow not nature more than nature needs,
Man's life's as cheap as beast's. Thou art a lady.
If only to go warm were gorgeous,
Why, nature needs not what thou gorgeous wear'st,
Which scarcely keeps thee warm. But for true need—
You Heavens, give me that patience, patience I need!

235. avouch: guarantee. *237. sith:* since. *charge . . . danger:* expense and risk of maintaining. *243. slack:* neglect. *249. depositaries:* trustees. *250. reservation:* condition. *254. well-favored:* handsome. *255–6. Not . . . praise:* i.e., since Goneril is not so bad as Regan, that is one thing in her favor. *262. Oh . . . need:* the needs of a beggar are very different from the needs of a king—but above all Lear needs not dignity but patience. *262–3. Our . . . superfluous:* even the few possessions of a beggar are not absolutely necessary.

You see me here, you gods, a poor old man,
As full of grief as age, wretched in both.
If it be you that stirs these daughters' hearts
Against their father, fool me not so much
To bear it tamely.° Touch me with noble anger,
And let not women's weapons, water drops,
Stain my man's cheeks! No, you unnatural hags,
I will have such revenges on you both
That all the world shall—I will do such things—
What they are, yet I know not, but they shall be
The terrors of the earth. You think I'll weep.
No, I'll not weep.
I have full cause of° weeping, but this heart
Shall break into a hundred thousand flaws°
Or ere I'll weep. O fool, I shall go mad!

[*Exeunt* LEAR, GLOUCESTER, KENT, *and* FOOL.]

CORN. Let us withdraw, 'twill be a storm.

[*Storm and tempest.*]

REG. This house is little, The old man and his people
Cannot be well bestowed.

GON. 'Tis his own blame. Hath put himself from rest,
And must needs taste his folly.

REG. For his particular,° I'll receive him gladly,
But not one follower.

GON. So am I purposed.
Where is my Lord of Gloucester?

CORN. Followed the old man forth. He is returned.

[*Re-enter* GLOUCESTER.]

GLO. The King is in high rage.

CORN. Whither is he going?

GLO. He calls to horse, but will I know not whither.

CORN. 'Tis best to give him way, he leads himself.

GON. My lord, entreat him by no means to stay.

GLO. Alack, the night comes on, and the bleak winds
Do sorely ruffle. For many miles about
There's scarce a bush.

REG. Oh, sir, to willful men
The injuries that they themselves procure
Must be their schoolmasters. Shut up your doors.
He is attended with a desperate train,
And what they may incense° him to, being apt°

273–4. fool . . . tamely: do not degrade me so much that I just tamely endure it. *283. of:* for. *282. flaws:* broken pieces. *290. his particular:* himself personally. *304. incense:* incite. *apt:* ready.

To have his ear abused,° wisdom bids fear.
CORN. Shut up your doors, my lord, 'tis a wild night.
My Regan counsels well. Come out o' the storm.
[*Exeunt.*]

ACT III

Scene I. A heath.

[*Storm still.° Enter* KENT *and a* GENTLEMAN, *meeting.*]

KENT. Who's there, besides foul weather?
GENT. One minded like the weather, most unquietly.
KENT. I know you. Where's the King?
GENT. Contending with the fretful elements.
Bids the wind blow the earth into the sea,
Or swell the curlèd waters 'bove the main,°
That things might change or cease; tears his white hair,
Which the impetuous blasts, with eyeless° rage,
Catch in their fury, and make nothing of;
Strives in his little world of man° to outscorn
The to-and-fro-conflicting wind and rain.
This night, wherein the cub-drawn bear° would couch,°
The lion and the belly-pinchèd° wolf
Keep their fur dry, unbonneted° he runs,
And bids what will take all.
KENT. But who is with him?
GENT. None but the fool, who labors to outjest
His heart-struck injuries.
KENT. Sir, I do know you,
And dare, upon the warrant of my note,°
Commend a dear° thing to you. There is division,
Although as yet the face of it be covered
With mutual cunning, 'twixt Albany and Cornwall,
Who have—as who have not that their great stars
Throned and set high?°—servants, who seem no less,
Which are to France the spies and speculations°
Intelligent of our state°—what hath been seen,

305. abused: deceived.

Act III, Sc. i: *s.d., still:* continuing. *6. main:* mainland. *8. eyeless:* blind. *10. little . . . man:* It was a common Elizabethan idea, sometimes elaborately worked out, that individual man was a little world (microcosm) and reproduced in himself the universe (macrocosm). *12. cub-drawn bear:* she-bear sucked dry, and therefore hungry. *couch:* take shelter. *13. belly-pinched:* ravenous. *14. unbonneted:* without a hat. *18. upon . . . note:* guaranteed by my observation of you. *19. dear:* precious. *22–3. that . . . high:* whom Fate has set in a great position. *24. speculations:* informers. *25. Intelligent . . . state:* report on the state of our affairs.

Either in snuffs and packings° of the Dukes,
Or the hard rein which both of them have borne
Against the old kind King, or something deeper,
Whereof perchance these are but furnishings°—
But true it is, from France there comes a power°
Into this scattered kingdom, who already,
Wise in our negligence, have secret feet
In some of our best ports and are at point°
To show their open banner. Now to you.
If on my credit° you dare build so far
To make your speed to Dover, you shall find
Some that will thank you, making just report
Of how unnatural and bemadding sorrow
The King hath cause to plain.°
I am a gentleman of blood° and breeding,
And from some knowledge and assurance° offer
This office° to you.

GENT. I will talk further with you.

KENT. No, do not.
For confirmation that I am much more
Than my outwall,° open this purse and take
What it contains. If you shall see Cordelia—
As fear not but you shall—show her this ring,
And she will tell you who your fellow° is
That yet you do not know. Fie on this storm!
I will go seek the King.

GENT. Give me your hand.
Have you no more to say?

KENT. Few words, but, to effect, more than all yet—
That when we have found the King—in which your pain°
That way, I'll this—he that first lights on him
Holloa the other.

[*Exeunt severally.*]

Scene II. Another part of the heath. Storm still.

[*Enter* LEAR *and* FOOL.]

LEAR. Blow, winds, and crack your cheeks! Rage! Blow!
You cataracts and hurricanoes,° spout

26. snuffs . . . packings: resentment and plotting against each other. *29. furnishings:* excuses. The sentence is not finished. *30. power:* army. *33. at point:* on the point of, about to. *35. credit:* trustworthiness. *39. plain:* complain. *40. blood:* noble family. *41. knowledge . . . assurance:* sure knowledge. *42. office:* undertaking. *45. outwall:* outside. *48. fellow:* companion. *53. pain:* labor.

Sc. ii: *2. hurricanoes:* waterspouts.

Till you have drenched our steeples, drowned the cocks!°
You sulphurous and thought-executing° fires,
Vaunt-couriers° to oak-cleaving thunderbolts,
Singe my white head! And thou, all-shaking thunder,
Smite flat the thick rotundity o' the world!
Crack nature's molds,° all germens° spill at once
That make ingrateful man!

FOOL. O Nuncle, Court holy water° in a dry house is better than this rain water out o' door. Good Nuncle, in, and ask thy daughters' blessing. Here's a night pities neither wise man nor fool.

LEAR. Rumble thy bellyful! Spit, fire! Spout, rain!
Nor rain, wind, thunder, fire, are my daughters.
I tax° not you, you elements, with unkindness.
I never gave you kingdom, called you children,
You owe me no subscription.° Then let fall
Your horrible pleasure. Here I stand, your slave,
A poor, infirm, weak, and despised old man.
But yet I call you servile ministers°
That have with two pernicious daughters joined
Your high-engendered battles° 'gainst a head
So old and white as this. Oh, oh! 'Tis foul!

FOOL. He that has a house to put 's head in has a good headpiece.

"The° codpiece° that will house
Before the head has any,
The head and he shall louse
So beggars marry many.
The man that makes his toe
What he his heart should make
Shall of a corn cry woe,
And turn his sleep to wake."

For there was never yet fair woman but she made mouths in a glass.°

LEAR. No, I will be the pattern of all patience,
I will say nothing.

[*Enter* KENT.]

3. *cocks:* weathercocks on top of the steeples. 4. *thought-executing:* killing as quick as thought. 5. *Vaunt-couriers:* forerunners. 8. *nature's molds:* the molds in which men are made. *germens:* seeds of life. 10. *Court . . . water:* flattery of great ones. 15. *tax:* accuse. 17. *subscription:* submission. 20. *servile ministers:* servants who slavishly obey your masters. 22. *high-engendered battles:* armies begotten on high. 25–32. *The . . . wake:* the man who goes wenching before he has a roof over his head will become a lousy beggar. The man who is kinder to his toe than to his heart will be kept awake by his corns—i.e., Lear has been kinder to his feet (his daughters) than to his heart (himself). The Fool's remarks, especially when cryptic and indecent, are not easy to paraphrase. 25. *codpiece:* lit., the opening in the hose. 33–4. *made . . . glass:* made faces in a mirror.

KENT. Who's there?
FOOL. Marry,° here's grace and a codpiece—that's a wise man and a fool.
KENT. Alas, sir, are you here? Things that love night
Love not such nights as these. The wrathful skies
Gallow° the very wanderers of the dark
And make them keep their caves. Since I was man,
Such sheets of fire, such bursts of horrid thunder,
Such groans of roaring wind and rain, I never
Remember to have heard. Man's nature cannot carry°
The affliction nor the fear.
LEAR. Let the great gods,
That keep this dreadful pother° o'er our heads,
Find out their enemies now. Tremble, thou wretch,
That hast within thee undivulgèd crimes
Unwhipped of justice. Hide thee, thou bloody hand,
Thou perjured, and thou simular man of virtue°
That art incestuous. Caitiff, to pieces shake,
That under covert and convenient seeming°
Hast practiced on man's life. Close pent-up guilts,
Rive your concealing continents° and cry
These dreadful summoners grace.° I am a man
More sinned against than sinning.
KENT. Alack, bareheaded!
Gracious my lord, hard by here is a hovel.
Some friendship will it lend you 'gainst the tempest.
Repose you there while I to this hard house—
More harder than the stones whereof 'tis raised,
Which even but now, demanding after you,
Denied me to come in—return, and force
Their scanted courtesy.
LEAR. My wits begin to turn.
Come on, my boy. How dost, my boy? Art cold?
I am cold myself. Where is this straw, my fellow?
The art of our necessities is strange,
That can make vile things precious.° Come, your hovel.
Poor fool and knave, I have one part in my heart

38. Marry: Mary, by the Virgin. *42. Gallow:* terrify. *46. carry:* endure. *48. pother:* turmoil. *52. simular . . . virtue:* a man who pretends to be virtuous. *54. under . . . seeming:* under a false appearance of propriety. *56. Rive . . . continents:* split open that which covers and conceals you. *56–7. cry . . . grace:* ask for mercy from these dreadful summoners. The summoner was the officer of the ecclesiastical court who summoned a man to appear to answer a charge of immorality. *68–9. art . . . precious:* our needs are like the art of the alchemist (who was forever experimenting to try to transmute base metal into gold).

That's sorry yet for thee.

FOOL. [*Singing*]

"He° that has and a little tiny wit—
With hey, ho, the wind and the rain—
Must make content with his fortunes fit,°
For the rain it raineth every day."

LEAR. True, my good boy. Come, bring us to this hovel.

[*Exeunt* LEAR *and* KENT.]

FOOL. This is a brave night to cool a courtesan.
I'll speak a prophecy° ere I go:
"When priests are more in word than matter,
When brewers mar their malt with water,
When nobles are their tailors' tutors,°
No heretics burned, but wenches' suitors,
When every case in law is right,
No squire in debt, nor no poor knight,
When slanders do not live in tongues,
Nor cutpurses come not to throngs,
When usurers tell their gold i' the field,
And bawds and whores do churches build—
Then shall the realm of Albion°
Come to great confusion.
Then comes the time, who lives to see 't,
That going shall be used with feet."°
This prophecy Merlin shall make, for I live before his time.°

[*Exit.*]

Scene III. GLOUCESTER*'s castle.*

[*Enter* GLOUCASTER *and* EDMUND.]

GLO. Alack, alack, Edmund, I like not this unnatural dealing. When I desired their leave that I might pity him,° they took from me the use of mine own house, charged me, on pain of their perpetual

72–5. *He . . . day:* another stanza of the song which the Fool in *Twelfth Night* sings at the end of the play. 74. *Must . . . fit:* i.e., must be content with a fortune as slim as his wit. 78–92. *prophecy . . . feet:* The fool gives a list of common events, pretending that they are never likely to happen. The prophecy is a parody of riddling prophecies popular at this time which were attributed to Merlin, the old magician of King Arthur's Court. 81. *nobles . . . tutors:* Young noblemen and gallants were very particular about the fashion and cut of their clothes. 89. *Albion:* England. 92. *going . . . feet:* feet will be used for walking. 93. *This . . . time:* A piece of mock pedantry, for—according to Holinshed's *Chronicles*—King Lear died some generations before King Arthur.

Sc iii: 2. *him:* Lear.

displeasure, neither to speak of him, entreat for him, nor any way sustain$^{\circ}$ him.

EDM. Most savage and unnatural!

GLO. Go to, say you nothing. There's division betwixt the Dukes, and a worse matter than that. I have received a letter this night, 'tis dangerous to be spoken.—I have locked the letter in my closet. These injuries the King now bears will be revenged home.$^{\circ}$ There is part of a power already footed.$^{\circ}$ We must incline to the King, I will seek him and privily$^{\circ}$ relieve him. Go you, and maintain talk with the Duke, that my charity be not of him perceived. If he ask for me, I am ill and gone to bed. Though I die for it, as no less is threatened me, the King my old master must be relieved. There is some strange thing toward, Edmund. Pray you be careful.

[*Exit.*]

EDM. This courtesy, forbid thee,$^{\circ}$ shall the Duke
Instantly know, and of that letter too.
This seems a fair deserving,$^{\circ}$ and must draw me
That which my father loses, no less than all.
The younger rises when the old doth fall.

[*Exit.*]

Scene IV. The heath. Before a hovel.

[*Enter* LEAR, KENT, *and* FOOL.]

KENT. Here is the place, my lord. Good my lord, enter.
The tyranny$^{\circ}$ of the open night's too rough
For nature to endure.

[*Storm still.*]

LEAR. Let me alone.
KENT. Good my lord, enter here.
LEAR. Wilt break my heart?
KENT. I had rather break mine own. Good my lord, enter.
LEAR. Thou think'st 'tis much that this contentious$^{\circ}$ storm
Invades us to the skin. So 'tis to thee,
But where the greater malady is fixed$^{\circ}$
The lesser is scarce felt. Thou'dst shun a bear,
But if thy flight lay toward the raging sea
Thou'dst meet the bear i' the mouth. When the mind's free$^{\circ}$

5. *sustain:* relieve. 10. *home:* to the utmost. 11. *footed:* landed. 12. *privily:* secretly. 17. *forbid thee:* forbidden to thee. 19. *This . . . deserving:* i.e., by betraying my father, I shall deserve much of (be rewarded by) the Duke.

Sc iv: 2. *tyranny:* cruelty. 6. *contentious:* striving against us. 8. *the . . . fixed:* i.e., in the mind. 11. *free;* i.e., from cares.

The body's delicate. The tempest in my mind
Doth from my senses take all feeling else
Save what beats there.° Filial ingratitude!
Is it not as this mouth should tear this hand
For lifting food to 't? But I will punish home.
No, I will weep no more. In such a night
To shut me out! Pour on, I will endure.
In such a night as this! O Regan, Goneril!
Your old kind father, whose frank heart gave all—
Oh, that way madness lies, let me shun that,
No more of that.

KENT. Good my lord, enter here.

LEAR. Prithee, go in thyself, seek thine own ease.
This tempest will not give me leave to ponder
On things would hurt me more. But I'll go in.
[*To the* FOOL] In, boy, go first. You houseless poverty°—
Nay, get thee in. I'll pray, and then I'll sleep.

[FOOL *goes in.*]

Poor naked wretches, wheresoe'er you are,
That bide° the pelting of this pitiless storm,
How shall your houseless heads and unfed sides,
Your looped and windowed° raggedness, defend you
From seasons such as these? Oh, I have ta'en
Too little care of this! Take physic, pomp.°
Expose thyself to feel what wretches feel,
That thou mayst shake the superflux° to them
And show the Heavens more just.

EDG. [*Within*] Fathom and half, fathom and half!
Poor Tom!

[*The* FOOL *runs out from the hovel.*]

FOOL. Come not in here, Nuncle, here's a spirit.
Help me, help me!

KENT. Give me thy hand. Who's there?

FOOL. A spirit, a spirit. He says his name's Poor Tom.

KENT. What art thou that dost grumble there i' the straw?
Come forth.

[*Enter* EDGAR *disguised as a madman.*]

EDG. Away! The foul fiend follows me!
"Through the sharp hawthorn blows the cold wind."
Hum! Go to thy cold bed and warm thee.

14. what . . . there: i.e., the mental anguish which is increased by the thumping of Lear's overtaxed heart. *26. houseless poverty:* poor homeless people. *29. bide:* endure. *31. looped . . . windowed:* full of holes and gaps. *33. Take . . . pomp:* i.e., cure yourselves, you great men. *35. superflux:* superfluity, what you do not need.

LEAR. Hast thou given all to thy two daughters?
And art thou come to this?°

EDG. Who gives anything to Poor Tom? Whom the foul fiend hath led through fire and through flame, through ford and whirlpool, o'er bog and quagmire, that hath laid knives under his pillow and halters in his pew,° set ratsbane° by his porridge, made him proud of heart to ride on a bay trotting horse over four-inched° bridges, to course° his own shadow for a traitor. Bless thy five wits° Tom's a-cold. Oh, do de, do de, do de. Bless thee from whirlwinds, star-blasting,° and taking!° Do Poor Tom some charity, whom the foul fiend vexes. There could I have him now, and there, and there again, and there.°

[*Storm still.*]

LEAR. What, have his daughters brought him to this pass?
Couldst thou save nothing? Didst thou give them all?

FOOL. Nay, he reserved a blanket,° else we had been all shamed.

LEAR. Now, all the plagues that in the pendulous° air
Hang fated o'er men's faults light on thy daughters!

KENT. He hath no daughters, sir.

LEAR. Death, traitor! Nothing could have subdued nature
To such a lowness but his unkind daughters.
Is it the fashion that discarded fathers
Should have thus little mercy on their flesh?
Judicious punishment! 'Twas this flesh begot
Those pelican° daughters.

EDG. "Pillicock sat on Pillicock Hill.
Halloo, halloo, loo, loo!"°

FOOL. This cold night will turn us all to fools and madmen.

EDG. Take heed o' the foul fiend. Obey thy parents, keep thy word justly, swear not, commit not with man's sworn spouse, set not thy sweet heart on proud array. Tom's a-cold.

LEAR. What hast thou been?

EDG. A servingman,° proud in heart and mind, that curled my hair, wore gloves in my cap, served the lust of my mistress's heart and did the act of darkness with her, swore as many oaths as I spake words and broke them in the sweet face of Heaven. One that slept

48–9. *Hast . . . this:* At the sight of the supposed lunatic Lear goes quite mad. Such utter destitution, he says, can only have been caused by daughters as unkind as his own. 53. *pew:* seat. *ratsbane:* rat poison. 54. *four-inched:* i.e., narrow. 55. *course:* hunt after. 56. *five wits:* i.e., common wit, imagination, fantasy, estimation, and memory. 57. *star-blasting:* evil caused by a planet. *taking:* malignant influence of fairies. 59. *There . . . there:* Poor Tom is chasing his own vermin. 62. *blanket:* i.e., his only covering. 63. *pendulous:* overhanging. 71. *pelican:* The pelican was the pattern of devoted motherhood because it fed its young on its own blood; but when the young grew strong, they turned on their parents. 72–3. *Pillicock . . . loo:* an old rhyme. 79–86. *A servingman . . . prey:* This is another description of the gentleman servingman.

in the contriving of lust and waked to do it. Wine loved I deeply, dice dearly, and in woman outparamoured° the Turk.° False of heart, light of ear, bloody of hand, hog in sloth, fox in stealth, wolf in greediness, dog in madness, lion in prey. Let not the creaking of shoes nor the rustling of silks betray thy poor heart to woman. Keep thy foot out of brothels, thy hand out of plackets,° thy pen from lenders' books,° and defy the foul fiend.

"Still through the hawthorn
blows the cold wind.
Says suum, mun, ha, no, nonny.
Dolphin my boy, my boy, sessa!
Let him trot by."

[*Storm still.*]

LEAR. Why, thou wert better in thy grave than to answer with thy uncovered body this extremity of the skies. Is man no more than this? Consider him well. Thou° owest the worm no silk, the beast no hide, the sheep no wool, the cat no perfume.° Ha! Here's three on 's are sophisticated. Thou art the thing itself. Unaccommodated man is no more but such a poor, bare, forked animal as thou art. Off, off, you lendings!° Come, unbutton here.

[*Tearing off his clothes.*]

FOOL. Prithee, Nuncle, be contented, 'tis a naughty night to swim in. Now a little fire in a wild field were like an old lecher's heart, a small spark, all the rest on 's body cold. Look, here comes a walking fire.

[*Enter* GLOUCESTER, *with a torch.*]

EDG. This is the foul fiend Flibbertigibbet. He begins at curfew° and walks till the first cock, he gives the web and the pin,° squints the eye and makes the harelip, mildews the white wheat and hurts the poor creature of earth.

"Saint° Withold footed thrice the 'old,°
He met the nightmare° and her ninefold.°

84. outparamoured: had more mistresses than. *the Turk:* The Turkish Emperor. *88. plackets:* openings in a petticoat. *89. pen . . . books:* The debtor often acknowledged the debt by signing in the lender's account book. *97–98. Thou . . . here:* There is usually an underlying sense in Lear's ravings. The bedlam, he says, has not borrowed silk from the silkworm, or furs from the beast, or wool from the sheep to cover himself. Kent, the Fool, and he himself are therefore *sophisticated*—adulterated, wearing coverings not their own. Natural man, *unaccommodated* (i.e., not provided with such conveniences), is just a naked animal. Lear will therefore strip himself naked and cease to be artificial. *98. cat . . . perfume:* a perfume taken from the civet cat, which has glands that function in the same manner as the skunk's. *101. lendings:* things borrowed. *106. curfew:* sounded at 9 P.M. *107.web . . . pin:* eye diseases, cataract. *110–4. Saint . . . thee:* a charm to keep horses from suffering from nightmare. *110. 'old:* wold, uncultivated downland. *111. nightmare:* nightmare was believed to be caused by a fiend, *ninefold:* nine young.

Bid her alight,
And her troth plight,
And aroint thee, witch, aroint° thee!"

KENT. How fares your Grace?

LEAR. What's he?

KENT. Who's there? What is 't you seek?

GLO. What are you there? Your names?

EDG. Poor Tom, that eats the swimming frog, the toad, the tadpole, the wall newt, and the water; that in the fury of his heart, when the foul fiend rages, eats cow dung for sallets;° swallows the old rat and the ditch dog;° drinks the green mantle of the standing pool; who is whipped from tithing to tithing,° and stock-punished, and imprisoned; who hath had three suits to his back, six shirts to his body, horse to ride, and weapon to wear.

"But mice and rats and such small deer
Have been Tom's food for seven long
year."

Beware my follower. Peace, Smulkin,° peace, thou fiend!

GLO. What, hath your Grace no better company?

EDG. The Prince of Darkness is a gentleman.
Modo he's called, and Mahu.

GLO. Our flesh and blood is grown so vile, my lord,
That it doth hate what gets° it.

EDG. Poor Tom's a-cold.

GLO. Go in with me. My duty cannot suffer
To obey in all your daughters' hard commands.
Though their injunction be to bar my doors
And let this tyrannous night take hold upon you,
Yet have I ventured to come seek you out
And bring you where both fire and food is ready.

LEAR. First let me talk with this philosopher.
What is the cause of the thunder?°

KENT. Good my lord, take his offer, go into the house.

LEAR. I'll talk a word with this same learnèd Theban.°
What is your study?°

EDG. How to prevent the fiend and to kill vermin.

LEAR. Let me ask you one word in private.

KENT. Impórtune him once more to go, my lord.
His wits begin to unsettle.

114. aroint: be gone. *121. sallets:* salads. *122. ditch dog:* dog drowned in a ditch. *123. tithing:* district, parish. *129–32. Smulkin . . . Mahu:* familiar spirits. *134. gets:* begets. *143. cause of thunder:* This was much disputed by philosophers of the time. *145. Theban:* i.e., Greek philosopher. *146. study:* particular interest, or in modern academic jargon, "special field."

GLO. Canst thou blame him? [*Storm still.*]
His daughters seek his death. Ah, that good Kent!
He said it would be thus, poor banished man!
Thou say'st the King grows mad. I'll tell thee, friend,
I am almost mad myself. I had a son,
Now outlawed from my blood. He sought my life
But lately, very late. I loved him, friend,
No father his son dearer. Truth to tell thee,
The grief hath crazed my wits. What a night's this!
I do beseech your Grace—
LEAR. Oh, cry you mercy, sir.
Noble philosopher, your company.
EDG. Tom's a-cold.
GLO. In, fellow, there, into the hovel. Keep thee warm.
LEAR. Come, let's in all.
KENT. This way, my lord.
LEAR. With him,
I will keep still with my philosopher.
KENT. Good my lord, soothe him, let him take the fellow.
GLO. Take him you on.
KENT. Sirrah, come on, go along with us.
LEAR. Come, good Athenian.°
GLO. No words, no words. Hush.
EDG. "Child° Rowland to the dark tower came.
His word was still 'Fie, foh, and fum,
I smell the blood of a British man.' "
[*Exeunt.*]

Scene V. GLOUCESTER'*s castle.*

[*Enter* CORNWALL *and* EDMUND.]

CORN. I will have my revenge ere I depart his house.

EDM. How, my lord, I may be censured,° that nature° thus gives way to loyalty, something fears me to think of.

CORN. I now perceive it was not altogether your brother's evil disposition made him seek his death, but a provoking merit, set a-work by a reprovable badness in himself.°

EDM. How malicious is my fortune, that I must repent to be just!° This is the letter he spoke of, which approves° him an intelligent

169. Athenian: like "Theban." *171–73. Child . . . man:* jumbled snatches of old ballads. *Child* in old ballads is used of young warriors who have not yet been knighted.

Sc. v: *2. censured:* judged. *2. nature:* i.e., natural affection toward my father yielding to loyalty to my Duke. *5–6. but . . . himself:* i.e., but a good quality in Edgar that provoked him to commit murder because of the reprehensible badness in Gloucester. *7. repent . . . just:* be sorry because I have acted rightly (in betraying my father). *8. approves:* proves.

party° to the advantages of France. Oh heavens, that this treason were not, or not I the detector!

CORN. Go with me to the Duchess.

EDM. If the matter of this paper be certain, you have mighty business in hand.

CORN. True or false, it hath made thee Earl of Gloucester. Seek out where thy father is, that he may be ready for our apprehension.°

EDM. [*Aside*] If I find him comforting the King, it will stuff his suspicion more fully.—I will persever° in my course of loyalty, though the conflict be sore between that and my blood.

CORN. I will lay trust upon thee, and thou shalt find a dearer father in my love.

[*Exeunt.*]

Scene VI.° A chamber in a farmhouse adjoining the castle.

[*Enter* GLOUCESTER, LEAR, KENT, FOOL, *and* EDGAR.]

GLO. Here is better than the open air, take it thankfully. I will piece out the comfort with what addition I can. I will not be long from you.

KENT. All the power of his wits has given way to his impatience.° The gods reward your kindness!

[*Exit* GLOUCESTER.]

EDG. Frateretto° calls me, and tells me Nero° is an angler in the lake of darkness. Pray, innocent,° and beware the foul fiend.

FOOL. Prithee, Nuncle, tell me whether a madman be a gentleman or a yeoman.°

LEAR. A king, a king!

FOOL. No, he's a yeoman that has a gentleman to his son, for he's a mad yeoman that sees his son a gentleman before him.°

LEAR. To have a thousand with red burning spits°
Come hissing in upon 'em—

9. *intelligent party:* spy, one with secret information. 15. *apprehension:* arrest. 17. *persever:* persevere.

Sc. vi: In this scene Lear is completely mad, the Fool is half-witted, and Edgar is pretending to be a lunatic. 4. *impatience:* suffering. 6. *Frateretto:* another fiend's name. *Nero:* the debauched Roman Emperor who fiddled while Rome burned. 7. *innocent:* fool. 8–9. *whether . . . yeoman:* The fool is much interested in the social status of a madman and proceeds to discuss the problem. *yeoman:* farmer, a notoriously wealthy class at this time. 11–2. *No . . . him:* Many yeomen farmers who had become wealthy by profiteering from the wars and dearths sent their sons to London to learn to become gentlemen, as fifty years ago Chicago meat packers sent their sons to Harvard and their daughters to England, to be presented at Court. This social change was much commented on, and is illustrated in Jonson's comedy *Every Man out of His Humour*. 13. *spits:* thin iron rods thrust through meat on which the meat was turned before the fire in roasting; very useful weapons in emergency.

EDG. The foul fiend bites my back.
FOOL. He's mad that trusts in the tameness of a wolf, a horse's health, a boy's love, or a whore's oath.
LEAR. It shall be done, I will arraign them straight.°
[*To* EDGAR] Come, sit thou here, most learned justicer.°
[*To the* FOOL] Thou, sapient° sir, sit here. Now, you she-foxes!
EDG. Look where he stands and glares! Wantest thou eyes at trial,° madam?
"Come o'er the bourn, Bessy, to me."
FOOL. *"Her boat hath a leak,*
And she must not speak
Why she dares not come over to thee."
EDG. The foul fiend haunts poor Tom in the voice of a nightingale. Hopdance° cries in Tom's belly for two white herring. Croak not,° black angel, I have no food for thee.
KENT. How do you, sir? Stand you not so amazed.°
Will you lie down and rest upon the cushions?
LEAR. I'll see their trial first. Bring in the evidence.
[*To* EDGAR] Thou robèd man of justice,° take thy place.
[*To the* FOOL] And thou, his yokefellow of equity,°
Bench° by his side. [*To* KENT] You are o' the commission,°
Sit you too.
EDG. Let us deal justly.
"Sleepest or wakest thou, jolly shepherd?
Thy sheep be in the corn,
And for one blast of thy minikin° mouth,
Thy sheep shall take no harm"
Purr! The cat is gray.
LEAR. Arraign her first. 'Tis Goneril. I here take my oath before this honorable assembly, she kicked the poor King her father.
FOOL. Come hither, mistress. Is your name Goneril?
LEAR. She cannot deny it.
FOOL. Cry you mercy,° I took you for a joint stool.°
LEAR. And here's another, whose warped° looks proclaim
What store° her heart is made on. Stop her there!

18. straight: straightway. *19. justicer:* judge. *20. sapient:* wise. *21. Wantest . . . trial:* can you not see who is at your trial (i.e., this fiend)? But Edgar is deliberately talking madly. *28. Hopdance:* another fiend. *28. Croak not:* don't rumble in my empty belly. The correct Elizabethan word for this embarrassing manifestation is "wamble." *30. amazed:* astonished—a strong word. *33. robed . . . justice:* another glance at Edgar's blanket. *34. yokefellow of equity:* partner in the law. *35. Bench:* sit on the judge's bench. *commission:* Persons of high rank or those accused of extraordinary crimes were not tried before the ordinary courts, but by a commission specially appointed. *40. minikin:* dainty. *47. Cry . . . mercy:* I beg your pardon. *joint stool:* wooden stool of joiner's work. *48. warped:* malignant. *49. store:* material.

Arms, arms, sword, fire! Corruption° in the place!
False justicer, why hast thou let her 'scape?
EDG. Bless thy five wits!
KENT. Oh, pity! Sir, where is the patience now,
That you so oft have boasted to retain?
EDG. [*Aside*] My tears begin to take his part so much
They'll mar my counterfeiting.°
LEAR. The little dogs and all,
Tray, Blanch, and Sweetheart, see, they bark at me.
EDG. Tom will throw his head at them. Avaunt, you curs!
Be thy mouth or black or white,
Tooth that poisons if it bite,
Mastiff, greyhound, mongrel grim,
Hound or spaniel, brach° or lym,°
Or bobtail tike or trundletail,°
Tom will make them weep and wail.
For, with throwing thus my head,
Dogs leap the hatch, and all are fled.
Do de, de, de. Sessa! Come, march to wakes° and fairs and market towns. Poor Tom, thy horn° is dry.

LEAR. Then let them anatomize° Regan, see what breeds about her heart. Is there any cause in nature that makes these hard hearts? [*To* EDGAR] You, sir, I entertain° for one of my hundred, only I do not like the fashion of your garments. You will say they are Persian attire,° but let them be changed.

KENT. Now, good my lord, lie here and rest awhile.
LEAR. Make no noise, make no noise. Draw the curtains. So, so, so.°
We'll go to supper i' the morning. So, so, so.
FOOL. And I'll go to bed at noon.°
[*Re-enter* GLOUCESTER.]
GLO. Come hither, friend. Where is the King my master?
KENT. Here, sir, but trouble him not. His wits are gone.
GLO. Good friend, I prithee take him in thy arms.
I have o'erheard a plot of death upon him.
There is a litter° ready, lay him in 't,

50. Corruption: bribery. *56. My . . . counterfeiting:* i.e., I am so sorry for the King that I can hardly keep up this pretense. *63. brach:* bitch. *lym:* bloodhound. *64. trundletail:* curly tail. *68. wakes:* merrymakings. *69. horn:* a horn bottle carried by beggars in which they stored the drink given by the charitable. *70. anatomize:* dissect. *72. entertain:* engage. *74. Persian attire:* i.e., of a magnificent and foreign fashion. There had been considerable interest in Persia for some years, especially after the return of some of the followers of Sir Anthony Shirley from his famous expedition. *76. So . . . so:* In dialogue "so, so" usually indicates action. Here Lear imagines the bed curtains are being drawn. *78. And . . . noon:* i.e., if it's suppertime in the morning, it will be bedtime at noon. The fool disappears after this scene. *83. litter:* a form of bed or stretcher enclosed by curtains used for carrying the sick or the wealthy.

And drive toward Dover, friend, where thou shalt meet
Both welcome and protection. Take up thy master.
If thou shouldst dally° half an hour, his life,
With thine and all that offer to defend him,
Stand in assurèd loss. Take up, take up,
And follow me, that will to some provision
Give thee quick conduct.

KENT. Oppressèd nature sleeps.
This rest might yet have balmed° thy broken sinews,
Which, if convenience will not allow,
Stand in hard cure.° [*To the* FOOL] Come, help to bear thy master.
Thou must not stay behind.

GLO. Come, come, away.

[*Exeunt all but* EDGAR.]

EDG. When we our betters see bearing our woes,
We scarcely think our miseries our foes.
Who alone suffers suffers most i' the mind,
Leaving free things and happy shows behind.
But then the mind much sufferance doth o'erskip
When grief hath mates, and bearing fellowship.°
How light and portable my pain seems now
When that which makes me bend makes the King bow,
He childed as I fathered! Tom, away!
Mark the high noises,° and thyself° bewray
When false opinion, whose wrong thought defiles thee,
In thy just proof repeals° and reconciles thee.
What will hap more tonight, safe 'scape the King!
Lurk,° lurk.

[*Exit.*]

Scene VII. GLOUCESTER*'s castle.*

[*Enter* CORNWALL, REGAN, GONERIL, EDMUND, *and* SERVANTS.]

CORN. Post speedily to my lord your husband.°
Show him this letter. The army of France is landed.
Seek out the traitor Gloucester.

[*Exeunt some of the* SERVANTS.]

86. daily: hesitate. *91. balmed:* soothed. *93. Stand . . . cure:* will hardly be cured. *100. When . . . fellowship:* when we see better men than ourselves suffering as we do, our sufferings seem slight. The man who suffers endures most in his mind because he contrasts his present misery with his happy past; but when he has companions in misery *(bearing fellowship)*, his mind suffers less. *104. high noises:* i.e., the "hue and cry" of the pursuers. *104–5. thyself . . . thee:* do not reveal yourself until the belief in your guilt is proved wrong and you are called back. *106. repeals:* calls back from banishment. *108. Lurk:* lie hid.

Sc. vii: *1. Post . . . husband:* These words are addressed to Goneril. *Post:* ride fast.

REG. Hang him instantly.
GON. Pluck out his eyes.
CORN. Leave him to my displeasure. Edmund, keep you our sister company. The revenges we are bound to take upon your traitorous father are not fit for your beholding. Advise the Duke, where you are going, to a most festinate° preparation. We are bound to the like. Our posts° shall be swift and intelligent° betwixt us. Farewell, dear Sister. Farewell, my Lord of Gloucester.°
[*Enter* OSWALD.] How now! Where's the King?
OSW. My Lord of Gloucester° hath conveyed him hence.
Some five or six and thirty of his knights,
Hot questrists° after him, met him at gate,
Who, with some other of the lords dependents,°
Are gone with him toward Dover, where they boast
To have well-armèd friends.
CORN. Get horses for your mistress.
GON. Farewell, sweet lord, and Sister.
CORN. Edmund, farewell.
[*Exeunt* GONERIL, EDMUND, *and* OSWALD.]
Go seek the traitor Gloucester.
Pinion him like a thief, bring him before us.
[*Exeunt other* SERVANTS.]
Though well we may not pass° upon his life
Without the form of justice, yet our power
Shall do a courtesy to our wrath,° which men
May blame but not control. Who's there? The traitor?
[*Enter* GLOUCESTER, *brought in by two or three.*]
REG. Ungrateful fox! 'Tis he.
CORN. Bind fast his corky° arms.
GLO. What mean your Graces? Good my friends, consider
You are my guests. Do me no foul play, friends.
CORN. Bind him, I say. [SERVANTS *bind him.*]
REG. Hard, hard. O filthy traitor!
GLO. Unmerciful lady as you are, I'm none.
CORN. To this chair bind him. Villain, thou shalt find—
[REGAN *plucks his beard.*]
GLO. By the kind gods, 'tis most ignobly done
To pluck me by the beard.°
REG. So white, and such a traitor!
GLO. Naughty lady,

9. festinate: hasty. *10. posts:* messengers. *10. intelligent:* full of information. *11. Lord of Gloucester:* i.e., Edmund, who has been promoted for his treachery. *13. Lord of Gloucester:* i.e., the old Earl. *15. questrists:* seekers. *16. lords dependents:* lords of his party. *22. pass:* pass judgment on. *23–4. yet . . . wrath:* yet because we are all-powerful we will give way to our wrath. *27. corky:* dry and withered. *34. pluck . . . beard:* the greatest indignity that could be offered.

These hairs which thou dost ravish° from my chin
Will quicken° and accuse thee, I am your host.
With robbers' hands my hospitable favors°
You should not ruffle thus. What will you do?
CORN. Come, sir, what letters had you late from France?
REG. Be simple answerer, for we know the truth.
CORN. And what confederacy° have you with the traitors
Late footed in the kingdom?
REG. To whose hands have you sent the lunatic King?
Speak.
GLO. I have a letter guessingly set down,
Which came from one that's of a neutral heart,
And not from one opposed.
CORN. Cunning.
REG. And false.
CORN. Where hast thou sent the King?
GLO. To Dover.
REG. Wherefore to Dover? Wast thou not charged at peril°—
CORN. Wherefore to Dover? Let him first answer that.
GLO. I am tied to the stake, and I must stand the course.°
REG. Wherefore to Dover, sir?
GLO. Because I would not see thy cruel nails
Pluck out his poor old eyes, nor thy fierce sister
In his anointed° flesh stick boarish fangs.
The sea, with such a storm as his bare head
In hell-black night endured, would have buoyed up,°
And quenched the stellèd fires.°
Yet, poor old heart, he holp° the heavens to rain.
If wolves had at thy gate howled that stern time,
Thou shouldst have said, "Good porter, turn the key,"°
All cruels else subscribed.° But I shall see
The wingèd vengeance overtake such children.
CORN. See 't shalt thou never. Fellows, hold the chair.
Upon these eyes of thine I'll set my foot.
GLO. He that will think to live till he be old,
Give me some help! Oh, cruel! Oh, you gods!
[GLOUCESTER'*s eye is put out.*]
REG. One side will mock another, the other too.
CORN. If you see vengeance—

36. ravish: seize. *37. quicken:* come to life. *38. hospitable favors:* the face of your host. *42. confederacy:* alliance, understanding. *50. at peril:* under penalty. *52. I . . . course:* like a bear in the bear pit I must endure the onslaught. *52. anointed:* i.e., anointed as a king, and therefore holy. *58. buoyed up:* swelled up. *59. stelled fires:* the light of the stars. *60. holp:* helped. *62. turn . . . key:* open the gate. *63. All . . . subscribed:* all other cruel things were on his side.

1. SERV. Hold your hand, my lord
I have served you ever since I was a child,
But better service have I never done you
Than now to bid you hold.
REG. How now, you dog!
1. SERV. If you did wear a beard upon your chin,
I'd shake it on this quarrel. What do you mean?
CORN. My villain!
[*They draw and fight.* CORNWALL *is wounded.*]
1. SERV. Nay, then, come on, and take the chance of anger.
REG. Give me thy sword. A peasant stand up thus!
[*Takes a sword and runs at him behind.*]
1. SERV. Oh, I am slain! My lord, you have one eye left
To see some mischief on him. Oh!
[*Dies.*]
CORN. Lest it see more, prevent it. Out, vile jelly!
Where is thy luster now?
[*Puts out* GLOUCESTER*'s other eye.*]
GLO. All dark and comfortless. Where's my son Edmund?
Edmund, enkindle all the sparks° of nature,
To quit° this horrid act.
REG. Out, treacherous villain!
Thou call'st on him that hates thee. It was he
That made the overture° of thy treasons to us,
Who is too good to pity thee.
GLO. Oh, my follies! Then Edgar was abused.
Kind gods, forgive me that, and prosper him!
REG. Go thrust him out at gates, and let him smell
His way to Dover.
[*Exit one with* GLOUCESTER.]
How is 't, my lord? How look you?
CORN. I have received a hurt. Follow me, lady.
Turn out that eyeless villain. Throw this slave
Upon the dunghill. Regan, I bleed apace.°
Untimely comes this hurt. Give me your arm.
[*Exit* CORNWALL, *led by* REGAN.]

2. SERV. I'll never care what wickedness I do
If this man come to good.
3. SERV. If she live long,
And in the end meet the old course of death,°
Women will all turn monsters.

84. enkindle . . . sparks: i.e., blow into flame your natural love. *85. quit:* requite. *87. overture:* revelation. *95. apace:* quickly, profusely. *99. old . . . death:* natural death in old age.

2. SERV. Let's follow the old Earl, and get the bedlam°
To lead him where he would. His roguish madness
Allows itself to anything.
3. SERV. Go thou. I'll fetch some flax and whites of eggs
To apply to his bleeding face. Now, Heaven help him!
[*Exeunt severally.*]

ACT IV

Scene I. The heath.

[*Enter* EDGAR.]

EDG. Yet better thus, and known to be contemned,°
Than still° contemned and flattered. To° be worst,
The lowest and most dejected thing of fortune,
Stands still in esperance, lives not in fear.
The lamentable change is from the best,
The worst returns to laughter. Welcome then,
Thou unsubstantial air that I embrace!
The wretch that thou hast blown unto the worst
Owes nothing to thy blasts.—But who comes here?
[*Enter* GLOUCESTER, *led by an* OLD MAN.]
My father, poorly led?° World, world, O world!
But that thy strange mutations make us hate thee,
Life would not yield to age.
OLD MAN. Oh, my good lord, I have been your tenant, and your father's tenant, these fourscore years.
GLO. Away, get thee away. Good friend, be gone.
Thy comforts can do me no good at all,
Thee they may hurt.
OLD MAN. Alack, sir, you cannot see your way.
GLO. I have no way and therefore want no eyes.
I stumbled when I saw. Full oft 'tis seen,
Our means secure us, and our mere defects
Prove our commodities.° Ah, dear Son Edgar,

101. bedlam: i.e., Poor Tom.

Act IV, Sc. i: *1. contemned:* despised; i.e., as a beggar. *2. still:* always. *2–12. To . . . age:* when a man has reached the lowest state of misfortune, he has hope *(esperance)* for the better, and no fear for the worse. The change to be lamented is when the best things turn to bad; the worst can only change to joy. After this poor consolation that nothing worse can happen to him, Edgar sees his blinded father and continues (l. 10): One would not trouble to live to old age except to spite the world. *10. poorly led:* led by one poor old man—and not accompanied by the usual party of servants. *21–2. Our . . . commodities:* when we are well off we grow careless, and then our misfortunes prove blessings.

The food° of thy abusèd father's wrath,
Might I but live to see thee in my touch,
I'd say I had eyes again!

OLD MAN. How now! Who's there?

EDG. [*Aside*] Oh gods! Who is 't can say "I am at the worst"?
I am worse than e'er I was.

OLD MAN. 'Tis poor mad Tom.

EDG. [*Aside*] And worse I may be yet. The worst is not
So long as we can say "This is the worst."°

OLD MAN. Fellow, where goest?

GLO. Is it a beggarman?

OLD MAN. Madman and beggar too.

GLO. He has some reason, else he could not beg.
I' the last night's storm I such a fellow saw,
Which made me think a man a worm. My son
Came then into my mind, and yet my mind
Was then scarce friends with him. I have heard more since.
As flies to wanton boys are we to the gods,
They kill us for their sport.

EDG. [*Aside*] How should this be?
Bad is the trade that must play fool to sorrow,
Angering itself and others.° Bless thee, master!

GLO. Is that the naked fellow?

OLD MAN. Aye, my lord.

GLO. Then, prithee get thee gone. If for my sake
Thou wilt o'ertake us hence a mile or twain
I' the way toward Dover, do it for ancient love,
And bring some covering for this naked soul,
Who I'll entreat to lead me.

OLD MAN. Alack, sir, he is mad.

GLO. 'Tis the times' plague° when madmen lead the blind.
Do as I bid thee, or rather do thy pleasure.
Above the rest, be gone.

OLD MAN. I'll bring him the best 'parel° that I have,
Come on 't what will.

[*Exit.*]

GLO. Sirrah, naked fellow—

EDG. Poor Tom's a-cold. [*Aside*] I cannot daub° it further.

GLO. Come hither, fellow.

EDG. [*Aside*] And yet I must.—Bless thy sweet eyes, they bleed.

GLO. Know'st thou the way to Dover?

23. *food:* object. 28–9. *The . . . worst:* so long as a man is alive, he may yet reach a lower depth of misery. 39–40. *Bad . . . others:* this business of pretending to be mad and fooling a man in such distress as Gloucester is now hateful. 47. *times' plague:* a sign of these diseased times. 50. *'parel:* apparel. 53. *daub:* plaster it over, pretend.

EDG. Both stile and gate, horseway and footpath. Poor Tom hath been scared out of his good wits. Bless thee, good man's son, from the foul fiend! Five fiends have been in Poor Tom at once—of lust, as Obidicut; Hobbididence, prince of dumbness; Mahu, of stealing; Modo, of murder; Flibbertigibbet,° of mopping and mowing,° who since possesses chambermaids and waiting-women. So, bless thee, master!

GLO. Here, take this purse, thou whom the Heavens' plagues
Have humbled to all strokes.° That I am wretched
Makes thee the happier. Heavens, deal so still!
Let the superfluous and lust-dieted man,
That slaves your ordinance, that will not see
Because he doth not feel, feel your power quickly.°
So distribution should undo excess°
And each man have enough. Dost thou know Dover?

EDG. Aye, master.

GLO. There is a cliff whose high and bending° head
Looks fearfully in the confinèd deep.
Bring me but to the very brim of it,
And I'll repair the misery thou dost bear
With something rich about me. From that place
I shall no leading need.

EDG. Give me thy arm.
Poor Tom shall lead thee.

[*Exeunt.*]

Scene II. Before the DUKE OF ALBANY*'s palace.*

[*Enter* GONERIL *and* EDMUND.]

GON. Welcome, my lord. I marvel our mild husband
Not met us on the way.
[*Enter* OSWALD.] Now, where's your master?

OSW. Madam, within, but never man so changed.
I told him of the army that was landed.
He smiled at it. I told him you were coming.
His answer was "The worse." Of Gloucester's treachery
And of the loyal service of his son
When I informed him, then he called me sot

60–1. *Obidicut . . . Flibbertigibbet:* these are also the names of fiends. 62. *mopping . . . mowing:* making faces and grimaces. 65. *humbled . . . strokes:* made so humble that you can endure anything. 66–9. *Heavens . . . quickly:* you gods, deal with others as you have dealt with me; let the man who has too much and pampers his own lusts, who regards your commands as contemptuously as he regards his slaves, that will not understand until he is hurt, feel your power quickly. 70. *So . . . excess:* then the man with too much would distribute his excessive wealth. 73. *bending:* overhanging.

And told me I had turned the wrong side out.
What most he should dislike seems pleasant to him,
What like, offensive.

GON. [*To* EDMUND] Then shall you go no further.
It is the cowish° terror of his spirit,
That dares not undertake.° He'll not feel wrongs
Which tie° him to an answer. Our wishes on the way
May prove effects.° Back, Edmund, to my brother.
Hasten his musters° and conduct his powers.°
I° must change arms at home and give the distaff°
Into my husband's hands. This trusty servant
Shall pass between us. Ere long you are like to hear,
If you dare venture in your own behalf,
A mistress's° command. Wear this. Spare speech.
[*Giving a favor.*]
Decline your head. This kiss, if it durst speak,
Would stretch thy spirits up into the air.
Conceive,° and fare thee well.

EDM. Yours in the ranks of death.

GON. My most dear Gloucester!

[*Exit* EDMUND.]

Oh, the difference of man and man!
To thee a woman's services are due,
My fool° usurps my body.

OSW. Madam, here comes my lord.

[*Exit.*]

[*Enter* ALBANY.]

GON. I have been worth the whistle.°

ALB. O Goneril!
You are not worth the dust which the rude wind
Blows in your face. I fear your disposition.
That° nature which contemns its origin
Cannot be bordered certain in itself.

Sc. ii: *14. cowish:* cowardly. *15. undertake:* show initiative, venture. *16. tie:* force. *16–7. Our . . . effects:* our hopes (of love) as we rode together may be fulfilled. *18. musters:* troops which have been collected. *powers:* forces. *19–20. I . . . hands:* I must become the soldier and leave my husband to do the spinning. *19. distaff:* stick used in spinning, traditionally the work of the housewife. *23. mistress's:* in the double sense of lady and lover. Edmund, having disposed of his brother and father, now looks higher; he will through Goneril become possessed of her half of the kingdom of Lear. *26. Conceive:* use your imagination. *31. My fool:* i.e., my husband is no more than a fool to me. *32. worth . . . whistle:* There is a proverb "'Tis a poor dog that is not worth the whistle." Goneril means: I was once worth being regarded as your dog. *35–9. That . . . use:* that creature which despises its father *(origin)* cannot be kept within bounds; she that cuts herself off from her family tree will perish and like a dead branch come to the burning.

She that herself will sliver° and disbranch
From her material sap,° perforce must wither
And come to deadly use.

GON. No more, the text is foolish.°

ALB. Wisdom and goodness to the vile seem vile.
Filths savor but themselves.° What have you done?
Tigers, not daughters, what have you performed?
A father, and a gracious agèd man
Whose reverence even the head-lugged bear° would lick,
Most barbarous, most degenerate, have you madded!
Could my good brother° suffer you to do it?
A man, a prince, by him so benefited!
If that the Heavens do not their visible spirits°
Send quickly down to tame these vile offenses,
It will come.
Humanity must perforce prey on itself,
Like monsters of the deep.°

GON. Milk-livered° man!
That bear'st a cheek for blows, a head for wrongs,
Who hast not in thy brows an eye discerning
Thine honor from thy suffering;° that not know'st
Fools do those villains pity who are punished
Ere they have done their mischief.° Where's thy drum?
France spreads his banners in our noiseless land,
With plumèd helm thy state begins to threat,
Whiles thou, a moral° fool, sit'st still and criest
"Alack, why does he so?"

ALB. See thyself, devil!
Proper deformity° seems not in the fiend
So horrid as in woman.

GON. O vain fool!

ALB. Thou changèd and self-covered° thing, for shame,
Bemonster not thy feature.° Were't my fitness
To let these hands obey my blood,°

37. *sliver:* slice off. 38. *material sap:* that sap which is part of herself. 40. *text is foolish:* i.e., this is a silly sermon. 42. *Filths . . . themselves:* the filthy like the taste only of filth. 45. *head-lugged bear:* a bear with its head torn by the hounds. 47. *good brother:* Cornwall. 49. *visible spirits:* avenging spirits in visible form. 52–3. *Humanity . . . deep:* A thought more than once expressed by Shakespeare—that when natural law is broken, men will degenerate into beasts and prey on each other. 53. *Milk- livered:* cowardly; the liver was regarded as the seat of courage. 55–6. *Who . . . suffering:* who cannot see when the insults which you endure are dishonorable to you. 57–8. *Fools . . . mischief:* only a fool pities a villain when he is punished to prevent his committing a crime. 61. *moral:* moralizing. 63. *Proper deformity:* deformity natural to a fiend. 65. *self-covered:* hiding your true self (i.e., devil) under the guise of a woman. 66. *Bemonster . . . feature:* do not change your shape into a fiend. 67. *blood:* anger.

They are apt enough to dislocate and tear
Thy flesh and bones. Howe'er° thou art a fiend,
A woman's shape doth shield thee.

GON. Marry, your manhood!° Mew!°

[*Enter a* MESSENGER.]

ALB. What news?

MESS. O my good lord, the Duke of Cornwall's dead,
Slain by his servant, going to put out
The other eye of Gloucester.

ALB. Gloucester's eyes!

MESS. A servant that he bred, thrilled with remorse,°
Opposed against the act, bending his sword
To his great master, who thereat enraged
Flew on him and amongst them felled him dead,
But not without that harmful stroke which since
Hath plucked him after.

ALB. This shows you are above,
You justicers, that these our nether crimes°
So speedily can venge. But, oh, poor Gloucester!
Lost he his other eye?

MESS. Both, both, my lord.
This letter, madam, craves a speedy answer.
'Tis from your sister.

GON. [*Aside*] One way I like this well,
But being widow, and my Gloucester° with her,
May all the building in my fancy pluck°
Upon my hateful life. Another way,
The news is not so tart.—I'll read, and answer.

[*Exit.*]

ALB. Where was his son when they did take his eyes?

MESS. Come with my lady hither.

ALB. He is not here.

MESS. No, my good lord, I met him back again.°

ALB. Knows he the wickedness?

MESS. Aye, my good lord, 'twas he informed against him,
And quit the house on purpose, that their punishment
Might have the freer course.

ALB. Gloucester, I live
To thank thee for the love thou show'dst the King,

69. Howe'er: although. *71. Marry . . . manhood:* you're a fine specimen of a man! *Mew:* a catcall. *76. thrilled . . . remorse:* trembling with pity. *82. nether crimes:* crimes committed on earth below. *87. my Gloucester:* i.e., Edmund. *88. May . . . pluck:* may pull down my castle in the air (i.e., her desire to marry Edmund). *93. met . . . again:* met him as he was on his way back.

And to revenge thine eyes. Come hither, friend.
Tell me what more thou know'st.
[*Exeunt.*]

Scene III. The French camp near Dover.

[*Enter* KENT *and a* GENTLEMAN.]

KENT. Why the King of France is so suddenly gone back know you the reason?

GENT. Something he left imperfect in the state which since his coming-forth is thought of, which imports to the kingdom so much fear and danger that his personal return was most required and necessary.

KENT. Who hath he left behind him general?

GENT. The Marshal of France, Monsieur La Far.

KENT. Did your letters pierce the Queen to any demonstration of grief?

GENT. Aye, sir. She took them, read them in my presence,
And now and then an ample tear trilled down
Her delicate cheek. It seemed she was a queen
Over her passion,° who most rebel-like
Sought to be king o'er her.

KENT. Oh, then it moved her.

GENT. Not to a rage. Patience and Sorrow strove
Who should express her goodliest.° You have seen
Sunshine and rain at once. Her smiles and tears
Were like a better way.° Those happy smilets°
That played on her ripe lip seemed not to know
What guests were in her eyes, which parted thence
As pearls from diamonds dropped. In brief,
Sorrow would be a rarity most beloved
If all could so become it.°

KENT. Made she no verbal question?

GENT. Faith, once or twice she heaved the name of "Father"
Pantingly forth, as if it pressed her heart,
Cried "Sisters! Sisters! Shame of ladies! Sisters!
Kent! Father! Sisters! What, i' the storm? i' the night?
Let pity not be believed!" There she shook
The holy water from her heavenly eyes,
And clamor-moistened.° Then away she started
To deal with grief alone.

Sc. iii: *14. passion:* emotion. *17. express . . . goodliest:* make her seem more beautiful. *19. like . . . way:* even more lovely. *smilets:* little smiles. *23–4. Sorrow . . . it:* if everyone looked so beautiful in sorrow, it would be a quality much sought after. *31. clamor-moistened:* wet her cries of grief with tears.

KENT. It is the stars,
The stars above us, govern our conditions,
Else one self° mate and mate could not beget
Such different issues.° You spoke not with her since?
GENT. No.
KENT. Was this before the King returned?
GENT. No, since.
KENT. Well, sir, the poor distressèd Lear's i' the town,
Who sometime in his better tune remembers
What we are come about, and by no means
Will yield to see his daughter.
GENT. Why, good sir?
KENT. A sovereign° shame so elbows° him. His own unkindness
That stripped her from his benediction, turned her
To foreign casualties,° gave her dear rights
To his doghearted daughters. These things sting
His mind so venomously that burning shame
Detains him from Cordelia.
GENT. Alack, poor gentleman!
KENT. Of Albany's and Cornwall's powers you heard not?
GENT. 'Tis so, they are afoot.
KENT. Well, sir, I'll bring you to our master Lear,
And leave you to attend him. Some dear cause°
Will in concealment wrap me up awhile.
When I am known aright, you shall not grieve
Lending° me this acquaintance. I pray you, go
Along with me.

[*Exeunt.*]

Scene IV. The same. A tent.

[*Enter, with drum and colors,*° CORDELIA, DOCTOR, *and* SOLDIERS.]

COR. Alack, 'tis he. Why, he was met even now
As mad as the vexed sea, singing aloud,
Crowned with rank fumiter and furrow weeds,
With burdocks, hemlock, nettles, cuckoo flowers,
Darnel,° and all the idle weeds that grow
In our sustaining° corn. A century° send forth.

34. *self:* same. 35. *issues:* children. 42. *sovereign:* overpowering. *elbows:* plucks him by the elbow, reminding him of the past. 49. *casualties:* chances, accidents. 51. *dear cause:* important reason. 54. *Lending:* bestowing on.

Sc. iv: *s.d., drum . . . colors:* a drummer and a soldier carrying a flag. 3–5. *fumiter . . . Darnel:* These are all English wild flowers and weeds. 6. *sustaining:* which maintains life. *century:* company of a hundred soldiers.

Search every acre in the high-grown° field,
And bring him to our eye. [*Exit an* OFFICER.] What can man's wisdom
In the restoring his bereavèd sense?
He that helps him take all my outward worth.°
DOCT. There is means, madam.
Our foster nurse° of nature is repose,
The which he lacks. That to provoke in him
Are many simples operative,° whose power
Will close the eye of anguish.
COR. All blest secrets,
All you unpublished virtues° of the earth,
Spring with my tears! Be aidant and remediate°
In the good man's distress! Seek, seek for him,
Lest his ungoverned rage dissolve the life
That wants the means to lead it.°
[*Enter a* MESSENGER.]
MESS. News, madam.
The British powers are marching hitherward.
COR. 'Tis known before, our preparation stands
In expectation of them.° O dear Father,
It is thy business that I go about,
Therefore great France
My mourning and important° tears hath pitied.
No blown° ambition doth our arms incite,
But love, dear love, and our aged father's right.
Soon may I hear and see him!
[*Exeunt.*]

Scene V. GLOUCESTER*'s castle.*

[*Enter* REGAN *and* OSWALD.]

REG. But are my brother's powers set forth?
OSW. Aye, madam.
REG. Himself in person there?
OSW. Madam, with much ado.
Your sister is the better soldier.
REG. Lord Edmund spake not with your lord at home?
OSW. No, madam.

7. *high-grown:* The season is therefore late summer. 10. *outward worth:* visible wealth. 12. *foster nurse:* the nurse who feeds. 14. *simples operative:* efficacious herbs. 16. *unpublished virtues:* secret remedies. 17. *aidant . . . remediate:* helpful and remedial. 20. *wants . . . it:* that has no sense to guide it. 22–3. *our . . . them:* our army is ready to meet them. 26. *important:* importunate, pleading. 27. *blown:* puffed up.

REG. What might import my sister's letter to him?
OSW. I know not, lady.
REG. Faith, he is posted° hence on serious matter.
It was great ignorance, Gloucester's eyes being out,
To let him live. Where he arrives he moves
All hearts against us. Edmund, I think, is gone,
In pity of his misery, to dispatch
His nighted° life, moreover to descry
The strength o' the enemy.
OSW. I must needs after him, madam, with my letter.
REG. Our troops set forth tomorrow. Stay with us,
The ways are dangerous.
OSW. I may not, madam.
My lady charged my duty° in this business.
REG. Why should she write to Edmund? Might not you
Transport her purposes by word? Belike,
Something—I know not what—I'll love thee much,
Let me unseal the letter.
OSW. Madam, I had rather—
REG. I know your lady does not love her husband,
I am sure of that. And at her late being here
She gave strange œillades° and most speaking looks
To noble Edmund. I know you are of her bosom.°
OSW. I, madam?
REG. I speak in understanding. You are, I know't.
Therefore I do advise you, take this note.°
My lord is dead, Edmund and I have talked,
And more convenient is he for my hand
Than for your lady's. You may gather more.
If you do find him, pray you give him this,
And when your mistress hears thus much from you,
I pray desire her call her wisdom to her.
So, fare you well.
If you do chance to hear of that blind traitor,
Preferment° falls on him that cuts him off.
OSW. Would I could meet him madam! I should show
What party I do follow.
REG. Fare thee well.
[*Exeunt.*]

Sc v: *8. is posted:* has ridden fast. *13. nighted:* blinded. *18. charged my duty:* entrusted it to me as a solemn duty. *25. œillades:* loving looks. *26. of . . . bosom:* in her confidence. *29. take . . . note:* observe this. *38. Preferment:* promotion.

Scene VI. Fields near Dover.

[*Enter* GLOUCESTER, *and* EDGAR *dressed like a peasant.*]

GLO. When shall we come to the top of that same hill?
EDG. You do climb up it now. Look how we labor.
GLO. Methinks the ground is even.
EDG. Horrible steep.
Hark, do you hear the sea?
GLO. No, truly.
EDG. Why then your other senses grow imperfect
By your eyes' anguish.
GLO. So may it be, indeed.
Methinks thy voice is altered, and thou speak'st
In better phrase and matter than thou didst.
EDG. You're much deceived. In nothing am I changed
But in my garments.
GLO. Methinks you're better-spoken.
EDG. Come on, sir, here's the place. Stand still. How° fearful
And dizzy 'tis to cast one's eyes so low!
The crows and choughs° that wing the midway air
Show scarce so gross as beetles. Halfway down
Hangs one that gathers samphire,° dreadful trade!
Methinks he seems no bigger than his head.
The fishermen that walk upon the beach
Appear like mice, and yond tall anchoring bark°
Diminished to her cock°—her cock, a buoy
Almost too small for sight. The murmuring surge
That on the unnumbered idle pebbles chafes
Cannot be heard so high. I'll look no more,
Lest my brain turn and the deficient sight
Topple down headlong.°
GLO. Set me where you stand.
EDG. Give me your hand. You are now within a foot
Of the extreme verge. For all beneath the moon
Would I not leap upright.
GLO. Let go my hand.
Here, friend, 's another purse, in it a jewel
Well worth a poor man's taking. Fairies and gods°

Sc. vi: *11–24. How . . . headlong:* This vivid description of the cliffs at Dover seems to have been written from direct observation. The King's Players visited Dover in September 1606. *13. choughs:* jackdaws. *15. samphire:* a strongly perfumed plant which grows on the chalk cliffs of Dover. *18. bark:* ship. *19. cock:* cockboat, the small ship's boat, usually towed behind. *23–4. deficient . . . headlong:* my sight failing, cause me to topple headlong. *29. Fairies . . . gods:* As this tale is pre-Christian, it is natural for the characters to call on the gods of the "elder world."

Prosper it with thee! Go thou further off.
Bid me farewell, and let me hear thee going.
EDG. Now fare you well, good sir.
GLO. With all my heart.
EDG. Why I do trifle thus with his despair
Is done to cure it.°
GLO. [*Kneeling*] O you mighty gods!
This world I do renounce, and in your sights
Shake patiently my great affliction off.
If° I could bear it longer and not fall
To quarrel with your great opposeless wills,
My snuff° and loathèd part of nature should
Burn itself out. If Edgar live, oh, bless him!
Now, fellow, fare thee well. [*He falls forward.*°]
EDG. Gone, sir. Farewell.
And yet I know not how conceit° may rob
The treasury of life when life itself
Yields to the theft.° Had he been where he thought,
By this had thought been past. Alive or dead?
Ho, you sir! Friend! Hear you, sir! Speak!
Thus might he pass° indeed. Yet he revives.
What are you, sir?
GLO. Away, and let me die.
EDG. Hadst thou been aught but gossamer,° feathers, air,
So many fathom down precipitating,
Thou'dst shivered like an egg. But thou dost breathe,
Hast heavy substance, bleed'st not, speak'st, art sound.
Ten masts at each° make not the altitude
Which thou hast perpendicularly fell.
Thy life's a miracle. Speak yet again.
GLO. But have I fall'n, or no?
EDG. From the dread summit of this chalky bourn.°
Look up a-height, the shrill-gorged° lark so far

33–4. Why . . . it: Edgar's purpose is to persuade his blinded father to go on living by the thought that he has been miraculously preserved after falling from a great height. When Gloucester begins to recover from the shock, Edgar has dropped his pretense of being a bedlam and speaks in a natural (but still disguised) voice. *38–41. If . . . out:* if I could endure my misery longer without quarreling with the wish of Heaven, I would wait for the rest of my hateful life to burn itself out. *40. snuff:* lit., smoking end of a burnt out candle. *42 s.d., falls forward:* To be effective this episode needs an actor who is not afraid of hurting himself, for unless Gloucester's fall is heavy it is quite unconvincing. After his fall, he lies stunned for a few moments. *43. conceit:* imagination. *45. Yields . . . theft:* i.e., is willing to die. *48. pass:* pass away, die. *50. gossamer:* the parachute-like web made by a species of small spider by which it floats through the air. *54. Ten . . . each:* ten masts, one on top of the other. *58. bourn:* boundary. *59. shrill-gorged:* shrill-throated. The lark is a small brown bird which flies to a great height and there remains fluttering and singing a shrill but beautiful song.

Cannot be seen or heard. Do but look up.
GLO. Alack, I have no eyes.
Is wretchedness deprived that benefit,
To end itself by death? 'Twas yet some comfort
When misery could beguile° the tyrant's rage
And frustrate his proud will.
EDG. Give me your arm.
Up, so. How is 't? Feel you your legs? You stand.
GLO. Too well, too well.
EDG. This is above all strangeness.
Upon the crown o' the cliff, what thing was that
Which parted from you?
GLO. A poor unfortunate beggar.
EDG. As I stood here below, methought his eyes
Were two full moons, he had a thousand noses,
Horns whelked° and waved like the enridgèd° sea.
It was some fiend, therefore, thou happy father,
Think that the clearest° gods, who make them honors
Of men's impossibilities,° have preserved thee.
GLO. I do remember now. Henceforth I'll bear
Affliction till it do cry out itself
"Enough, enough," and die. That thing you speak of,
I took it for a man. Often 'twould say
"The fiend, the fiend." He led me to that place.
EDG. Bear free° and patient thoughts. But who comes here?
[*Enter* LEAR, *fantastically dressed with wild flowers.*]
The safer sense will n'er accommodate
His master thus.°
LEAR. No,° they cannot touch me for coining, I am the King himself.
EDG. O thou side-piercing sight!
LEAR. Nature's above art in that respect. There's your press money. That fellow handles his bow like a crowkeeper,° draw me a cloth-

64. beguile: cheat (by death). *72. whelked:* with spiral twists. *enridgèd:* wavy. *74. clearest:* most glorious. *74–5. who . . . impossibilities:* who cause themselves to be honored by performing miracles impossible to men. *81. free:* innocent. *82–3. The . . . thus:* a man in his right senses would never adorn himself thus. Edgar with unconscious irony repeats Lear's "accommodated." *84–91. No . . . word:* Lear's madness has a sort of logical coherence. He begins by saying that he cannot be charged with coining, because it was his right as king to issue the coin, a natural right. From coin his mind goes to the use of coin as *press money* for soldiers (money given to a conscripted recruit as token that he has been engaged), thence to the recruits at archery practice. Then his mind is distracted by a mouse, but comes back to his quarrel with his sons-in-law. He will throw down his gauntlet as a challenge to single combat against any odds. He comes back to the archery range, and a good shot right in the bull's-eye. *87. crowkeeper:* a man hired to scare away crows from the crop.

ier's yard.° Look, look, a mouse! Peace, peace, this piece of toasted cheese will do 't. There's my gauntlet,° I'll prove it on a° giant. Bring up the brown bills.° Oh, well-flown, bird! I' the clout,° i' the clout. Hewgh!° Give the word.°

EDG. Sweet marjoram.°

LEAR. Pass.

GLO. I know that voice.

LEAR. Ha! Goneril, with a white beard! They flattered me like a dog, and told me I had white hairs in my beard ere the black ones were there. To say "aye" and "no" to everything that I said! "Aye" and "no" too was no good divinity.° When the rain came to wet me once and the wind to make me chatter, when the thunder would not peace at my bidding, there I found 'em, there I smelt 'em out. Go to, they are not men o' their words. They told me I was everything. 'Tis a lie, I am not agueproof.

GLO. The trick° of that voice I do well remember.
Is 't not the King?

LEAR. Aye, every inch a king.
When I do stare, see how the subject quakes.
I pardon that man's life. What was thy cause?
Adultery?
Thou shalt not die. Die for adultery! No.
The wren goes to 't, and the small gilded fly
Does lecher in my sight.
Let copulation thrive, for Gloucester's bastard son
Was kinder to his father than my daughters
Got 'tween the lawful sheets.
To 't, luxury,° pell-mell! For I lack soldiers.
Behold yond simpering dame,
Whose face between her forks° presages snow,
That minces virtue° and does shake the head
To hear of pleasure's name.
The fitchew,° nor the soilèd° horse, goes to 't
With a more riotous appetite.
Down from the waist they are Centaurs,°
Though women all above.
But to° the girdle do the gods inherit,
Beneath is all the fiends'.

88. clothier's yard: The expert archer drew his arrow back a full yard to the ear. *89. gauntlet:* glove, token of challenge. *89. prove . . . a:* i.e., fight even a. *90. brown bills:* i.e., the infantry. *brown:* varnished to keep from rusting. *90. clout:* the canvas target. *91. Hewgh:* imitation of the whizz of the arrow. *91. word:* password. *92. marjoram:* a savory herb. *98. no . . . divinity:* i.e., false doctrine. *103. trick:* peculiar note. *114. luxury:* lust. *116. forks:* legs. *117. minces virtue:* walks with a great air of virtue. *119. fitchew:* polecat, a creature demonstratively oversexed. *soiled:* fed on spring grass. *121. Centaurs:* creatures half man and half stallion. *123. But to:* only down to.

There's Hell, there's darkness, there's the sulphurous pit,
Burning, scalding, stench, consumption, fie, fie, fie!
Pah, pah! Give me an ounce of civet,° good apothecary, to sweeten my imagination. There's money for thee.

GLO. Oh, let me kiss that hand!

LEAR. Let me wipe it first, it smells of mortality.

GLO. O ruined piece of nature! This great world
Shall so wear out to naught.° Dost thou know me?

LEAR. I remember thine eyes well enough. Dost thou squiny° at me? No, do thy worst, blind Cupid,° I'll not love. Read thou this challenge, mark but the penning on 't.

GLO. Were all the letters suns, I could not see one.

EDG. I would not take this from report. It is,
And my heart breaks at it.

LEAR. Read.

GLO. What, with the case of eyes?

LEAR. Oh ho, are you there with me?° No eyes in your head, nor no money in your purse? Your eyes are in a heavy case, your purse in a light. Yet you see how this world goes.

GLO. I see it feelingly.

LEAR. What, art mad? A man may see how this world goes with no eyes. Look with thine ears. See how yond Justice rails upon yond simple thief. Hark, in thine ear. Change places and, handy-dandy,° which is the Justice, which is the thief? Thou hast seen a farmer's dog bark at a beggar?

GLO. Aye, sir.

LEAR. And the creature run from the cur? There thou mightst behold the great image of authority.°
A dog's obeyed in office.
Thou rascal beadle,° hold thy bloody hand!
Why dost thou lash that whore? Strip thine own back.
Thou hotly lust'st to use her in that kind°
For which thou whip'st her. The usurer hangs the cozener.°
Through tattered clothes small vices do appear,
Robes and furred gowns hide all. Plate sin with gold
And the strong lance of justice hurtless breaks.
Arm it in rags, a pigmy's straw does pierce it.
None does offend, none, I say, none, I'll able° 'em.
Take that of me, my friend, who have the power

127. *civet:* perfume. 131–2. *O . . . naught:* O ruined masterpiece of nature, the universe likewise will come to nothing. 133. *squiny:* look sideways, like a prostitute. 134. *blind Cupid:* the usual sign hung over a brothel. 141. *are . . . me:* do you agree with me? 147. *handy-dandy:* the nursery game of "Handy-pandy, sugar candy, which hand will you have?" 152. *image of authority:* figure showing the true meaning of authority. 154. *beadle:* parish officer. 156. *kind:* manner. 157. *usurer . . . cozener:* the swindler hangs the crook. 162. *able:* give power to.

To seal the accuser's lips. Get thee glass eyes°
And, like a scurvy° politician, seem
To see the things thou dost not.
Now, now, now, now. Pull off my boots. Harder, harder. So.

EDG. Oh, matter and impertinency° mixed!
Reason in madness!

LEAR. If thou wilt weep my fortunes, take my eyes.
I know thee well enough. Thy name is Gloucester.
Thou must be patient, we came crying hither.
Thou know'st the first time that we smell the air,
We wawl and cry. I will preach to thee. Mark.

GLO. Alack, alack the day!

LEAR. When we are born, we cry that we are come
To this great stage of fools. This 's a good block.°
It were a delicate stratagem to shoe
A troop of horse with felt. I'll put 't in proof,°
And when I have stol'n upon these sons-in-law,
Then, kill, kill, kill, kill, kill, kill!

[*Enter a* GENTLEMAN, *with* ATTENDANTS.]

GENT. Oh, here he is. Lay hand upon him. Sir,
Your most dear daughter—

LEAR. No rescue? What, a prisoner? I am even
The natural fool of Fortune.° Use me well,
You shall have ransom.° Let me have a surgeon,
I am cut to the brains.

GENT. You shall have anything.

LEAR. No seconds?° All myself?
Why, this would make a man a man of salt,°
To use his eyes for garden waterpots,
Aye, and laying autumn's dust.

GENT. Good sir—

LEAR. I will die bravely, like a smug bridegroom.° What!
I will be jovial. Come, come, I am a king,
My masters, know you that.

GENT. You are a royal one, and we obey you.

LEAR. Then there's life in 't. Nay, an you get it, you shall get it
by running. Sa, sa, sa, sa.°

[*Exit running.* ATTENDANTS *follow.*]

164. glass eyes: spectacles. *165. scurvy:* lit., with skin disease, "lousy." *168. matter . . . impertinency:* sense and nonsense. *177. block:* hat; lit., the block on which a felt hat is molded. From hat Lear's mind turns to *felt*. *179. put . . . proof:* try it out. *185. natural . . . Fortune:* born to be fooled by Fortune. *186. ransom:* Prisoners of good family could buy their freedom from their captors. *188. No seconds:* no one to help me. *189. man of salt:* because tears are salt. *193. like . . . bridegroom:* It was said of Lord Grey of Wilton, who was led out as if to be executed on December 9, 1603, that he "had such gaiety and cheer in his countenance that he seemed a dapper young bridegroom" *197. Sa . . . sa:* a cry used sometimes in sudden action.

GENT. A sight most pitiful in the meanest wretch,
Past speaking of in a king! Thou hast one daughter
Who redeems nature from the general curse
Which twain have brought her to.
EDG. Hail, gentle sir.
GENT. Sir, speed you. What's your will?
EDG. Do you hear aught, sir, of a battle toward?°
GENT. Most sure and vulgar.° Everyone hears that
Which can distinguish sound.
EDG. But, by your favor,
How near's the other army?
GENT. Near and on speedy foot, the main descry
Stands on the hourly thought.°
EDG. I thank you, sir. That's all.
GENT. Though that the Queen on special cause is here,
Her army is moved on.
EDG. I thank you, sir. [*Exit* GENTLEMAN.]
GLO. You ever-gentle gods, take my breath from me.
Let not my worser spirit tempt me again
To die before you please!
EDG. Well pray you, Father.
GLO. Now, good sir, what are you?
EDG. A most poor man, made tame to fortune's blows,
Who, by the art° of known and feeling sorrows,
Am pregnant to° good pity. Give me your hand.
I'll lead you to some biding.°
GLO. Hearty thanks.
The bounty and the benison° of Heaven
To boot, and boot!°
[*Enter* OSWALD.]
OSW. A proclaimed prize! Most happy!
That eyeless head of thine was first framed flesh
To raise my fortunes. Thou old unhappy traitor,
Briefly thyself remember.° The sword is out
That must destroy thee.
GLO. Now let thy friendly hand
Put strength enough to 't.
[EDGAR *interposes.*]
OSW. Wherefore, bold peasant,
Darest thou support a published° traitor? Hence,

203. toward: at hand. *204. vulgar:* common, in everyone's mouth. *207–8. the . . . thought:* the main body is expected to come into sight at any time now. *216. art:* long experience. *217. pregnant to:* able to conceive. *218. biding:* resting-place. *219 benison:* blessing. *220. To . . . boot:* in the highest degree. *223. thyself remember:* prepare for death—by confessing your sins. *226. published:* publicly proclaimed.

Lest that the infection of his fortune take
Like hold on thee! Let go his arm.

EDG. Chill° not let go, zir, without vurther 'casion.°

OSW. Let go, slave, or thou diest!

EDG. Good gentleman, go your gait,° and let poor volk pass. An chud° ha' been zwaggered out of my life, 'twould not ha' been zo long as 'tis by a vortnight. Nay, come not near th' old man, keep out, che vor ye,° or I'se try whether your costard° or my ballow° be the harder. Chill be plain with you.

OSW. Out, dunghill!

[They fight.]

EDG. Chill pick your teeth, zir. Come, no matter vor your foins.°

[OSWALD *falls.*]

OSW. Slave, thou hast slain me. Villain, take my purse.
If ever thou wilt thrive, bury my body,
And give the letters which thou find'st about me
To Edmund Earl of Gloucester. Seek him out
Upon the British party. Oh, untimely death!
Death!

[Dies.]

EDG. I know thee well—a serviceable° villain,
As duteous to the vices of thy mistress
As badness would desire.

GLO. What, is he dead?

EDG. Sit you down, Father, rest you.
Let's see these pockets. The letters that he speaks of
May be my friends. He's dead. I am only sorry
He had no other deathsman. Let us see.
Leave, gentle wax,° and, manners, blame us not.
To know our enemies' minds, we'd rip their hearts,
Their papers is more lawful. *[Reads.]*

"Let our reciprocal vows be remembered. You have many opportunities to cut him off. If your will want not,° time and place will be fruitfully offered. There is nothing done if he return the conqueror. Then am I the prisoner, and his bed my jail, from the loathed warmth whereof deliver me, and supply the place for your labor.

"Your—wife, so I would say—affectionate servant,
GONERIL."

229–35. Chill . . . you: Edgar speaks stage rustic dialect. *229. Chill:* I'll. *vurther 'casion:* further occasion, reason. *231. go . . . gait:* go your own way. *232. chud:* should. *234. che . . . ye:* I warn yer. *costard:* head; lit., apple. *ballow:* cudgel. *237. foins:* thrusts. *244. serviceable:* diligent. *251. Leave . . . wax:* Here he breaks the seal. *255. will . . . not:* desire is not lacking. *Will* means both willingness and lust.

Oh, undistinguished space° of woman's will!
A plot upon her virtuous husband's life,
And the exchange my brother! Here, in the sands,
Thee I'll rake up,° the post unsanctified°
Of murderous lechers, and in the mature time
With this ungracious paper strike the sight
Of the death-practiced° Duke. For him 'tis well
That of thy death and business I can tell.

GLO. The King is mad. How° stiff° is my vile sense,°
That I stand up, and have ingenious° feeling
Of my huge sorrows! Better I were distract.°
So should my thoughts be severed from my griefs,
And woes by wrong imaginations lose
The knowledge of themselves.

[*Drum afar off*]

EDG. Give me your hand.
Far off methinks I hear the beaten drum.
Come, Father, I'll bestow you with a friend.

[*Exeunt.*]

Scene VII. A tent in the French camp. LEAR *on a bed asleep, soft music playing,* GENTLEMAN, *and others attending.*

[*Enter* CORDELIA, KENT, *and* DOCTOR.]

COR. O thou good Kent, how shall I live and work,
To match thy goodness? My life will be too short,
And every measure fail me.

KENT. To be acknowledged, madam, is o'erpaid.
All my reports go with the modest truth,
Nor more nor clipped, but so.°

COR. Be better suited.°
These weeds° are memories of those worser hours.
I prithee put them off.

KENT. Pardon me, dear madam,
Yet to be known shortens my made intent.°
My boon° I make it that you know me not
Till time and I think meet.

261. undistinguished space: limitless, extending beyond the range of sight. *264. rake up:* hide in the dust. *post unsanctified:* unholy messenger. *267. death-practiced:* whose death is plotted. *269–71. How . . . sorrows:* i.e., if only I could go mad and forget my sorrows. *stiff:* strong. *sense:* sanity. *270. ingenious:* sensitive. *271. distract:* mad.

Sc. vii: *6. Nor . . . so:* neither exaggerated nor curtailed, but exact. *suited:* garbed. *7. weeds:* garments; i.e., his livery as Lear's servant. *9. Yet . . . intent:* my plan will be frustrated if I am revealed now. *10. boon:* request for a favor.

COR. Then be 't so, my good lord. [*To the* DOCTOR]
How does the King?
DOCT. Madam, sleeps still.
COR. O you kind gods,
Cure this great breach in his abusèd nature!
The untuned and jarring senses, oh, wind up°
Of this child-changèd° father!
DOCT. So please your Majesty
That we may wake the King. He hath slept long.
COR. Be governed by your knowledge, and proceed
I' the sway° of your own will. Is he arrayed?
GENT. Aye, madam. In the heaviness of his sleep
We put fresh garments on him.
DOCT. Be, by, good madam, when we do awake him.
I doubt not of his temperance.°
COR. Very well.
DOCT. Please you, draw near. Louder the music there!
COR. O my dear Father! Restoration hang
Thy medicine on my lips, and let this kiss
Repair those violent harms that my two sisters
Have in thy reverence made!
KENT. Kind and dear Princess!
COR. Had you not been their father, these white flakes
Had challenged pity of them. Was this a face
To be opposed against the warring winds?
To stand against the deep dread-bolted thunder?
In the most terrible and nimble stroke
Of quick, cross lightning?° To watch—poor perdu!°—
With this thin helm? Mine enemy's dog,
Though he had bit me, should have stood that night
Against my fire, and wast thou fain, poor Father,
To hovel thee with swine and rogues forlorn
In short and musty straw? Alack, alack!
'Tis wonder that thy life and wits at once
Had not concluded all. He wakes. Speak to him.
DOCT. Madam, do you, 'tis fittest.
COR. How does my royal lord? How fares your Majesty?
LEAR. You do me wrong to take me out o' the grave.
Thou art a soul in bliss,° but I am bound
Upon a wheel of fire that mine own tears
Do scald like molten lead.

17. *wind up:* i.e., as the loose string of a musical instrument is tightened. 18. *child-changed:* transformed by the treatment of his children. 21. *sway:* direction. 25. *temperance:* sanity. 36. *cross lightning:* forked lightning. *perdu:* sentry in an exposed position. 47. *bliss:* Heaven.

COR. Sir, do you know me?
LEAR. You are a spirit, I know. When did you die?
COR. Still, still far wide!
DOCT. He's scarce awake. Let him alone awhile.
LEAR. Where have I been? Where am I? Fair daylight?
I am mightily abused. I should e'en die with pity
To see another thus. I know not what to say.
I will not swear these are my hands. Let's see,
I feel this pin prick. Would I were assured
Of my condition!
COR. Oh, look upon me, sir,
And hold your hands in benediction o'er me.
No, sir, you must not kneel.
LEAR. Pray do not mock me.
I am a very foolish fond old man,
Fourscore and upward, not an hour more nor less,
And, to deal plainly,
I fear I am not in my perfect mind.
Methinks I should know you and know this man,
Yet I am doubtful, for I am mainly ignorant
What place this is, and all the skill I have
Remembers not these garments, nor I know not
Where I did lodge last night. Do not laugh at me,
For, as I am a man, I think this lady
To be my child Cordelia.
COR. And so I am, I am.
LEAR. Be your tears wet? Yes, faith. I pray weep not.
If you have poison for me, I will drink it.
I know you do not love me, for your sisters
Have, as I do remember, done me wrong.
You have some cause, they have not.
COR. No cause, no cause.
LEAR. Am I in France?
KENT. In your own kingdom, sir.
LEAR. Do not abuse me.
DOCT. Be comforted, good madam. The great rage,
You see, is killed in him. And yet it is danger
To make him even o'er° the time he has lost.
Desire him to go in, trouble him no more
Till further settling.
COR. Will 't please your Highness walk?
LEAR. You must bear with me.
Pray you now, forget and forgive. I am old and foolish.
[*Exeunt all but* KENT *and* GENTLEMAN.]

81. even o'er: go over.

GENT. Holds it true, sir, that the Duke of Cornwall was so slain?
KENT. Most certain, sir.
GENT. Who is conductor of his people?
KENT. As 'tis said, the bastard son of Gloucester.
GENT. They say Edgar, his banished son, is with the Earl of Kent in Germany.
KENT. Report is changeable.° 'Tis time to look about. The powers of the kingdom approach apace.
GENT. The arbiterment° is like to be bloody. Fare you well, sir.
[*Exit.*]
KENT. My point and period° will be throughly° wrought,
Or well or ill, as this day's battle's fought.
[*Exit.*]

ACT V

Scene I. The British camp near Dover.

[*Enter, with drum and colors,* EDMUND, REGAN, GENTLEMEN, *and* SOLDIERS.]

EDM. Know° of the Duke if his last purpose hold,
Or whether since he is advised by aught
To change the course. He's full of alteration
And self-reproving. Bring his constant° pleasure.
[*To a* GENTLEMAN, *who goes out.*]
REG. Our sister's man is certainly miscarried.
EDM. 'Tis to be doubted,° madam.
REG. Now, sweet lord,
You know the goodness I intend upon you.
Tell me, but truly, but then speak the truth,
Do you not love my sister?
EDM. In honored love.
REG. But have you never found my brother's way
To the forfended° place?
EDM. That thought abuses° you.
REG. I am doubtful that you have been conjunct
And bosomed with her, as far as we call hers.°
EDM. No, by mine honor, madam.

92. Report . . . changeable: rumors are not reliable. *94. arbiterment:* decision. *95. point . . . period:* lit., full stop; the end of my chapter. *throughly:* thoroughly.

Act V, Sc. i: *1. Know:* learn. *4. constant:* firm;i.e., final decision. *6. doubted:* feared. *11. forfended:* forbidden. *abuses:* wrongs; i.e., you should not have such a thought. *12–3. I . . . hers:* I am afraid that you have been united in intimacy with her in every way.

REG. I never shall endure her. Dear my lord,
Be not familiar with her.
EDM. Fear me not.—
She and the Duke her husband!
[*Enter, with drum and colors,* ALBANY, GONERIL, *and* SOLDIERS.]
GON. [*Aside*] I had rather lose the battle than that sister
Should loosen him and me.
ALB. Our very loving sister, well bemet.
Sir, this I hear: The King is come to his daughter,
With others whom the rigor of our state°
Forced to cry out.° Where I could not be honest,
I never yet was valiant. For this business,
It toucheth us, as France invades our land,
Not bolds the King, with others, whom I fear
Most just and heavy causes make oppose.°
EDM. Sir, you speak nobly.
REG. Why is this reasoned?°
GON. Combine together 'gainst the enemy,
For these domestic and particular broils
Are not the question here.
ALB. Let's then determine
With the ancient of war° on our proceedings.
EDM. I shall attend you presently at your tent.
REG. Sister, you'll go with us?
GON. No.
REG. 'Tis most convenient. Pray you go with us.
GON. [*Aside*] Oh ho, I know the riddle.°—I will go.
[*As they are going out, enter* EDGAR *disguised.*]
EDG. If e'er your Grace had speech with man so poor,
Hear me one word.
ALB. I'll overtake you. Speak.
[*Exeunt all but* ALBANY *and* EDGAR.]
EDG. Before you fight the battle, ope this letter.
If you have victory, let the trumpet sound
For him that brought it. Wretched though I seem,
I can produce a champion that will prove
What is avouchèd° there. If you miscarry,
Your business of the world hath so an end,
And machination ceases. Fortune love you!
ALB. Stay till I have read the letter.

22. rigor . . . state: our harsh government. *23. cry out:* protest. *24–7. For . . . oppose:* this business concerns us particularly, not because France is encouraging Lear and others who rightly oppose us, but because he is invading our country. *28. reasoned:* argued. *32. ancient of war:* experienced commanders. *37. Oh . . . riddle:* i.e., you are afraid to leave me alone with Edmund. *44. avouched:* declared.

EDG. I was forbid it.
When time shall serve, let but the herald cry
And I'll appear again.
ALB. Why, fare thee well. I will o'erlook° thy paper.
[*Exit* EDGAR.]

[*Re-enter* EDMUND.]

EDM. The enemy's in view. Draw up your powers.
Here is the guess° of their true strength and forces
By diligent discovery, but your haste
Is now urged on you.
ALB. We will greet the time.°
[*Exit.*]

EDM. To° both these sisters have I sworn my love,
Each jealous of the other, as the stung
Are of the adder. Which of them shall I take?
Both? One? Or neither? Neither can be enjoyed
If both remain alive. To take the widow
Exasperates, makes mad her sister Goneril,
And hardly shall I carry out my side,°
Her husband being alive. Now then we'll use
His countenance° for the battle, which being done,
Let her who would be rid of him devise
His speedy taking-off. As for the mercy
Which he intends to Lear and to Cordelia,
The battle done, and they within our power,
Shall never see his pardon, for my state
Stands on me to defend, not to debate.°
[*Exit.*]

Scene II. A field between the two camps.

[*Alarum within. Enter, with drum and colors,* LEAR, CORDELIA, *and* SOLDIERS, *over the stage; and exeunt. Enter* EDGAR *and* GLOUCESTER.]

EDG. Here, Father, take the shadow of this tree
For your good host. Pray that the right may thrive.
If ever I return to you again,
I'll bring you comfort.
GLO. Grace go with you, sir!
[*Exit* EDGAR.]

50. o'erlook: read. *52. guess:* estimate. *54. greet . . . time:* i.e., go to meet our enemy. *55–69. To . . . debate:* Edmund has now reached the crisis in his fortunes. Both sisters are in love with him, he can have either. Or he can aim higher and, with Lear and Cordelia out of the way, achieve the whole kingdom for himself. *61. my side:* i.e., of the bargain. *63. countenance:* authority. *68–9. for . . . debate:* my fortune is now in such a state that I must act, not argue.

[*Alarum and retreat within. Re-enter* EDGAR.]

EDG. Away, old man. Give me thy hand, away!
King Lear hath lost, he and his daughter ta'en.°
Give me thy hand, come on.

GLO. No farther, sir. A man may rot even here.

EDG. What, in ill thoughts again? Men must endure
Their going hence, even as their coming hither.
Ripeness° is all. Come on.

GLO. And that's true too.

[*Exeunt.*]

Scene III. The British camp near Dover.

[*Enter, in conquest, with drum and colors,* EDMUND, LEAR *and* CORDELIA, *as prisoners,* CAPTAIN, SOLDIERS, *etc.*]

EDM. Some officers take them away. Good guard,
Until their greater pleasures° first be known
That are to censure them.

COR. We are not the first
Who with best meaning have incurred the worst.
For thee, oppressèd King, am I cast down.
Myself could else outfrown false fortune's frown.
Shall we not see these daughters and these sisters?

LEAR. No, no, no, no! Come, let's away to prison.
We two alone will sing like birds i' the cage.
When thou dost ask me blessing, I'll kneel down
And ask of thee forgiveness. So we'll live,
And pray, and sing, and tell old tales, and laugh
At gilded butterflies,° and hear poor rogues
Talk of Court news. And we'll talk with them too,
Who loses and who wins, who's in, who's out,
And take upon 's the mystery of things°
As if we were God's spies. And we'll wear out,
In a walled prison, packs and sects of great ones
That ebb and flow by the moon.°

EDM. Take them away.

LEAR. Upon such sacrifices, my Cordelia,
The gods themselves throw incense. Have I caught thee?
He that parts us shall bring a brand° from Heaven,

Sc. ii: *6. ta'en:* taken. *11. Ripeness:* perfect readiness.

Sc. iii: *2. their . . . pleasures:* the will of my superiors. *13. gilded butterflies:* i.e., Court folk. *16. take . . . things:* pretend to understand deep secrets. *18–9. packs . . . moon:* parties at Court whose fortunes change monthly. *22. a brand:* fire.

And fire us° hence like foxes. Wipe thine eyes.
The goodyears° shall devour them, flesh and fell,°
Ere they shall make us weep. We'll see 'em starve first.
Come.

[*Exeunt* LEAR *and* CORDELIA, *guarded.*]

EDM. Come hither, Captain, hark.
Take thou this note. Go follow them to prison.
One step I have advanced thee. If thou dost
As this instructs thee, thou dost make thy way
To noble fortunes. Know thou this, that men
Are as the time is.° To be tender-minded
Does not become a sword.° Thy great employment
Will not bear question.° Either say thou'lt do 't,
Or thrive by other means.

CAPT. I'll do 't, my lord.

EDM. About it, and write happy° when thou hast done.
Mark, I say, instantly, and carry it so
As I have set it down.

CAPT. I cannot draw a cart, nor eat dried oats.
If it be man's work, I'll do 't.

[*Exit.*]

[*Flourish. Enter* ALBANY, GONERIL, REGAN, *another* CAPTAIN, *and* SOLDIERS.]

ALB. Sir, you have shown today your valiant strain,°
And fortune led you well. You have the captives
That were the opposites° of this day's strife.
We do require them of you, so to use them
As we shall find their merits and our safety
May equally determine.

EDM. Sir, I thought it fit
To send the old and miserable King
To some retention and appointed guard,°
Whose age has charms in it, whose title more,
To pluck the common bosom° on his side
And turn our impressed lances° in our eyes
Which do command them. With him I sent the Queen,
My reason all the same, and they are ready
Tomorrow or at further space to appear

23. *fire us:* drive us out by fire. 24. *goodyears:* The phrase "what the goodyear" meant "what the deuce"; hence "goodyear" means something vaguely evil. Lear is talking baby talk—"The bogeymen shall have them." *fell:* skin. 31–2. *men . . . is:* i.e., in brutal times men must be brutes. 33. *sword:* soldier. 33–4. *Thy . . . question:* the duty now laid on you is too important and brutal to be argued about. 36. *happy:* fortunate. 41. *strain:* blood courage. 43. *opposites:* opponents. 48. *retention . . . guard:* where he can be kept and properly guarded. 50. *common bosom:* the sympathies of our soldiers. 51. *impressed lances:* the soldiers we have conscripted.

Where you shall hold your session.° At this time
We sweat and bleed. The friend hath lost his friend,
And the best quarrels, in the heat, are cursed
By those that feel their sharpness.°
The question of Cordelia and her father
Requires a fitter place.

ALB. Sir, by your patience,
I hold you but a subject° of this war,
Not as a brother.

REG. That's as we list to grace him.
Methinks our pleasure might have been demanded
Ere you had spoke so far. He led our powers,
Bore the commission of my place and person,°
The which immediacy may well stand up
And call itself your brother.°

GON. Not so hot.
In his own grace he doth exalt himself
More than in your addition.°

REG. In my rights,
By me invested, he compeers° the best.

GON. That were the most, if he should husband you.

REG. Jesters do oft prove prophets.

GON. Holloa, holloa!
That eye that told you so looked but a-squint.

REG. Lady, I am not well, else I should answer
From a full-flowing stomach.° General,
Take thou my soldiers, prisoners, patrimony,
Dispose of them, of me, the walls are thine.°
Witness the world that I create thee here
My lord and master.

GON. Mean you to enjoy him?

ALB. The let-alone° lies not in your goodwill.

EDM. Nor in thine, lord.

ALB. Half-blooded fellow, yes.

REG. [*To* EDMUND] Let the drum strike, and prove my title thine.

ALB. Stay yet, hear reason. Edmund, I arrest thee
On capital treason,° and in thine attaint°

55. session: trial. *57–8. And . . . sharpness:* i.e., with the battle hardly over we are in no condition to judge this matter calmly. *61. subject:* 'i.e., not one who gives orders. *65. commission . . . person:* commission appointing him commander as my deputy. *66–7. The . . . brother:* since he is my general, he is fit to be considered your equal. *69. your addition:* the title which you have given him. *70. compeers:* equals. *75. full-flowing stomach:* in full wrath. *77. walls . . . thine:* i.e., you have won the outer defenses. *80. let-alone:* power to prevent. *84. capital treason:* treason deserving death. *and . . . attaint:* and accused with you (*attaint:* impeachment).

This gilded serpent. [*Pointing to* GONERIL] For your claim, fair Sister,
I bar it in the interest of my wife.
'Tis she is subcontracted° to this lord,
And I, her husband, contradict your bans.°
If you will marry, make your loves to me.
My lady is bespoke.°
GON. An interlude!°
ALB. Thou art armed, Gloucester. Let the trumpet sound.
If none appear to prove upon thy person
Thy heinous,° manifest, and many treasons,
There is my pledge. [*Throwing down a glove*] I'll prove it on thy heart
Ere I taste bread, thou art in nothing less
Than I have here proclaimed thee.
REG. Sick, oh, sick!
GON. [*Aside*] If not, I'll ne'er trust medicine.°
EDM. [*Throwing down a glove*] There's my exchange. What in the world he is
That names me traitor, villainlike he lies.°
Call by thy trumpet. He that dares approach,
On him, on you—who not?—I will maintain
My truth and honor firmly.
ALB. A herald, ho!
EDM. A herald, ho, a herald!
ALB. Trust to thy single° virtue, for thy soldiers,
All levied in my name, have in my name
Took their discharge.
REG. My sickness grows upon me.
ALB. She is not well. Convey her to my tent.
[*Exit* REGAN, *led.*]
[*Enter a* HERALD.] Come hither, herald.—Let the trumpet sound.—
And read out this.
CAPT. Sound, trumpet! [*A trumpet sounds.*]
HER. [*Reads.*] "If any man of quality or degree° within the lists° of the army will maintain upon Edmund, supposed Earl of Gloucester, that he is a manifold traitor, let him appear by the third sound of the trumpet. He is bold in his defense."

87. *subcontracted:* already betrothed. 88. *bans:* notice of intention to marry, read out in church for three Sundays previous to the marriage. 90. *bespoke:* already reserved. *An interlude:* i.e., this is mere play-acting. 93. *heinous:* odious. 97. *medicine:* poison. 99. *villainlike . . . lies:* he lies like a villain. This is the lie direct, which was a direct challenge to mortal combat. 104. *single:* solitary, unaided. 111. *quality or degree:* rank or high position. 111. *lists:* roll call, roster.

EDM. Sound!
[First trumpet.]
HER. Again!
[Second trumpet.]
Again!
[Third trumpet.]
[Trumpet answers within.]
[Enter EDGAR *at the third sound, armed, with a trumpet before him.]*
ALB. Ask him his purposes, why he appears
Upon this call o' the trumpet.°
HER. What are you?
Your name, your quality? And why you answer
This present summons?
EDG. Know my name is lost,
By treason's tooth bare-gnawn and canker-bit.°
Yet am I noble as the adversary
I come to cope.°
ALB. Which is that adversary?
EDG. What's he that speaks for Edmund, Earl of Gloucester?
EDM. Himself. What say'st thou to him?
EDG. Draw thy sword,
That if my speech offend a noble heart,
Thy arm may do thee justice. Here is mine.
Behold, it is the privilege of mine honors,
My oath, and my profession.° I protest,
Mauger° thy strength, youth, place, and eminence,
Despite thy victor sword and fire-new° fortune,
Thy valor and thy heart, thou art a traitor,
False to thy gods, thy brother, and thy father,
Conspirant° 'gainst this high illustrious Prince,
And from the extremest upward of thy head
To the descent and dust below thy foot
A most toad-spotted° traitor. Say thou "No,"
This sword, this arm, and my best spirits are bent
To prove upon thy heart, whereto I speak,
Thou liest.
EDM. In wisdom I should ask thy name,
But since thy outside looks so fair and warlike
And that thy tongue some say of breeding° breathes,

118–9. Ask . . . trumpet: The combat follows the normal procedure of chivalry. Edgar is wearing full armor, his face concealed by his closed helmet. *122. canker- bit:* corrupted by maggots. *124. cope:* meet, encounter. *130. profession:* i.e., as a knight. *131. Mauger:* in spite of. *132. fire-new:* brand-new—like a new coin. *135. Conspirant:* conspiring. *138. toad-spotted:* i.e., venomous as a toad. *144. say of breeding:* accent of a gentlemen.

What safe and nicely° I might well delay
By rule of knighthood I disdain and spurn.
Back do I toss these treasons to thy head,
With the hell-hated lie o'erwhelm thy heart,
Which for they yet glance by and scarcely bruise,
This sword of mine shall give them instant way
Where they shall rest forever. Trumpets, speak!
[*Alarums. They fight.* EDMUND *falls.*]

ALB. Save him, save him!

GON. This is practice,° Gloucester.
By the law of arms thou wast not bound to answer
An unknown opposite. Thou art not vanquished,
But cozened° and beguiled.

ALB. Shut your mouth, dame,
Or with this paper° shall I stop it. Hold, sir,
Thou worse than any name, read thine own evil.
No tearing, lady. I perceive you know it.

GON. Say if I do, the laws are mine, not thine.
Who can arraign me for 't?

ALB. Most monstrous!
Know'st thou this paper?

GON. Ask me not what I know.
[*Exit.*]

ALB. Go after her. She's desperate, govern° her.

EDM. What you have charged me with, that have I done,
And more, much more. The time will bring it out.
'Tis past, and so am I. But what art thou
That hast this fortune on me? If thou 'rt noble,
I do forgive thee.

EDG. Let's exchange charity.
I am no less in blood than thou art, Edmund.
If more, the more thou hast wronged me.
My name is Edgar, and thy father's son.
The gods are just, and of our pleasant vices
Make instruments to plague us.°
The dark and vicious place where thee he got°
Cost him his eyes.

EDM. Thou hast spoken right, 'tis true.
The wheel is come full circle,° I am here.

145. nicely: i.e., if I stood on niceties of procedure. *152. practice:* treachery. *155. cozened:* cheated. *156. this paper:* her love letter to Edmund, which Edgar had taken from Oswald's corpse. *162. govern:* control. *171–2. of . . . us:* This is the answer to Gloucester's lighthearted words at the opening of the play—"Do you smell a fault?" *173. got:* begot. *175. The . . . circle:* i.e., I end as I began—an outcast of fortune.

ALB. Methought thy very gait did prophesy
A royal nobleness. I must embrace thee.
Let sorrow split my heart if ever I
Did hate thee or thy father!
EDG. Worthy Prince, I know 't.
ALB. Where have you hid yourself?
How have you known the miseries of your father?
EDG. By nursing them, my lord. List a brief tale,
And when 'tis told, oh, that my heart would burst!
The bloody proclamation to escape°
That followed me so near—Oh, our lives' sweetness!
That we the pain of death would hourly die
Rather than die at once!°—taught me to shift
Into a madman's rags, to assume a semblance
That very dogs disdained. And in this habit
Met I my father with his bleeding rings,
Their precious stones new-lost, became his guide,
Led him, begged for him, saved him from despair,
Never—oh, fault!—revealed myself unto him
Until some half-hour past, when I was armed.
Not sure, though hoping, of this good success,
I asked his blessing, and from first to last
Told him my pilgrimage. But his flawed heart—
Alack, too weak the conflict to support!—
'Twixt two extremes of passion, joy and grief,
Burst smilingly.°
EDM. This speech of yours hath moved me,
And shall perchance do good. But speak you on.
You look as you had something more to say.
ALB. If there be more, more woeful, hold it in,
For I am almost ready to dissolve,
Hearing of this.
EDG. This would have seemed a period°
To such as love not sorrow, but another,
To amplify too much, would make much more,
And top extremity.°
Whilst I was big in clamor,° came there in a man
Who, having seen me in my worst estate,
Shunned my abhorred society. But then, finding

184. The . . . escape: in order to escape after the proclamation for my arrest. *185–7. Oh . . . once:* life is so sweet to us that we will endure the pains of death hourly if only we can live. *197–200. But . . . smilingly:* In the performance the significance of Edgar's speech can easily be missed. Gloucester has died from excessive emotion *(passion),* and Kent is near his end. *205. period:* end. *208. top extremity:* exceed the extreme limit of what could be endured. *209. clamor:* grief.

Who 'twas that so endured, with his strong arms
He fastened on my neck, and bellowed out
As he'd burst heaven, threw him on my father,
Told the most piteous tale of Lear and him
That ever ear received. Which in recounting
His grief grew puissant,° and the strings of life°
Began to crack. Twice then the trumpets sounded,
And there I left him tranced.°

ALB. But who was this?

EDG. Kent, sir, the banished Kent, who in disguise
Followed his enemy King,° and did him service
Improper for a slave.

[*Enter a* GENTLEMAN, *with a bloody knife.*]

GENT. Help, help, oh, help!

EDG. What kind of help?

ALB. Speak, man.

EDG. What means this bloody knife?

GENT. 'Tis hot, it smokes.
It came even from the heart of—oh, she's dead!

ALB. Who dead? Speak, man.

GENT. Your lady, sir, your lady. And her sister
By her is poisoned. She hath confessed it.

EDM. I was contracted° to them both. All three
Now marry in an instant.

EDG. Here comes Kent.

ALB. Produce the bodies, be they alive or dead.

[*Exit* GENTLEMAN.]

This judgment of the Heavens, that makes us tremble,
Touches us not with pity.
[*Enter* KENT.] Oh, is this he?
The time will not allow the compliment
Which very manners urges.

KENT. I am come
To bid my King and master aye good night.
Is he not here?

ALB. Great thing of us forgot!
Speak, Edmund, where's the King? And where's Cordelia?
See's thou this object, Kent?

[*The bodies of* GONERIL *and* REGAN *are brought in.*]

KENT. Alack, why thus?

EDM. Yet Edmund was beloved.°

217. *puissant:* powerful, overwhelming. *strings of life:* heartstrings. 219. *tranced:* in a faint. 221. *enemy King:* the King who had declared him an enemy. 229. *contracted:* betrothed. 241. *Yet . . . beloved:* The bastard's last grim triumph—two women died for his love.

The one the other poisoned for my sake,
And after slew herself.

ALB. Even so. Cover their faces.

EDM. I pant for life. Some good I mean to do,
Despite of mine own nature. Quickly send—
Be brief in it—to the castle, for my writ
Is on the life of Lear and on Cordelia.
Nay, send in time.

ALB. Run, run, oh, run!

EDG. To who, my lord? Who hath the office? Send
Thy token of reprieve.°

EDM. Well thought on. Take my sword.
Give it the Captain.

ALB. Haste thee, for thy life.

[*Exit* EDGAR.]

EDM. He hath commission from thy wife and me
To hang Cordelia in the prison and
To lay the blame upon her own despair,
That she fordid° herself.

ALB. The gods defend her! Bear him hence awhile.

[EDMUND *is borne off.*]

[*Re-enter* LEAR, *with* CORDELIA *dead in his arms,* EDGAR, CAPTAIN, *and others following.*]

LEAR. Howl, howl, howl, howl! Oh, you are men of stones.
Had I your tongues and eyes, I'd use them so
That heaven's vault should crack. She's gone forever!
I know when one is dead and when one lives.
She's dead as earth. Lend me a looking-glass.
If that her breath will mist or stain the stone,°
Why, then she lives.

KENT. Is this the promised end?°

EDG. Or image of that horror?

ALB. Fall and cease.°

LEAR. This feather stirs, she lives. If it be so,
It is a chance which does redeem all sorrows
That ever I have felt.

KENT. [*Kneeling*] Oh, my good master!

LEAR. Prithee, away.

EDG. 'Tis noble Kent, your friend.

LEAR. A plague upon you, murderers, traitors all!
I might have saved her. Now she's gone forever!
Cordelia, Cordelia! Stay a little. Ha!

251. token of reprieve: sign that they are reprieved. *257. fordid:* destroyed. *264. stone:* glass. *265. the . . . end:* i.e., Doomsday. *266. Fall . . . cease:* i.e., let Doomsday come and the world end.

What is 't thou say'st? Her voice was ever soft,
Gentle and low, an excellent thing in woman.
I killed the slave that was a-hanging thee.

CAPT. 'Tis true, my lords, he did.

LEAR. Did I not, fellow?
I have seen the day with my good biting falchion°
I would have made them skip. I am old now,
And these same crosses° spoil me. Who are you?
Mine eyes are not o' the best, I'll tell you straight.

KENT. If fortune brag of two she loved and hated,
One of them we behold.

LEAR. This is a dull sight. Are you not Kent?

KENT. The same,
Your servant Kent. Where is your servant Caius?

LEAR. He's a good fellow, I can tell you that.
He'll strike, and quickly too. He's dead and rotten.

KENT. No, my good lord, I am the very man°—

LEAR. I'll see that straight.

KENT. That from your first of difference° and decay
Have followed your sad steps.

LEAR. You are welcome hither.

KENT. Nor no man else. All's cheerless, dark, and deadly.
Your eldest daughters have fordone themselves,
And desperately are dead.

LEAR. Aye, so I think.

ALB. He knows not what he says, and vain is it
That we present us to him.

EDG. Very bootless.°

[*Enter a* CAPTAIN.]

CAPT. Edmund is dead, my lord.

ALB. That's but a trifle here.
You lords and noble friends, know our intent.
What comfort to this great decay° may come
Shall be applied. For us, we will resign,
During the life of this old Majesty,
To him our absolute power.
[*To* EDGAR *and* KENT] You, to your rights,
With boot,° and such addition as your honors
Have more than merited. All friends shall taste
The wages of their virtue, and all foes
The cup of their deservings. Oh, see, see!°

279. falchion: curved sword. *281. crosses:* troubles. *286–9. Your . . . man:* This is the first and only mention of a Caius, which was apparently the name assumed by Kent in his disguise. *291. difference:* changed state. *297. bootless:* useless. *300. decay:* i.e., Lear. *305. boot:* advantage. *308. Oh . . . see:* There is a sudden change in Lear.

LEAR. And my poor fool° is hanged! No, no, no life!
Why should a dog, a horse, a rat, have life
And thou no breath at all? Thou'lt come no more,
Never, never, never, never, never!
Pray you, undo this button.° Thank you, sir.
Do you see this? Look on her, look, her lips,
Look there, look there!
[*Dies.*]
EDG. He faints. My lord, my lord!
KENT. Break, heart, I prithee break!
EDG. Look up, my lord.
KENT. Vex not his ghost. Oh, let him pass! He hates him
That would upon the rack of this tough world
Stretch him out longer.
EDG. He is gone indeed.
KENT. The wonder is he hath endured so long.
He but usurped his life.
ALB. Bear them from hence. Our present business
Is general woe. [*To* KENT *and* EDGAR] Friends of my soul, you twain
Rule in this realm and the gored state sustain.
KENT. I have a journey, sir, shortly to go.
My master calls me,° I must not say no.
ALB. The weight of this sad time we must obey,
Speak what we feel, not what we ought to say.
The oldest hath borne most. We that are young
Shall never see so much, nor live so long.
[*Exeunt, with a dead march.*]

309. fool: Cordelia; *fool* is often used as a term of affection. *313. Pray . . . button:* For the last time Lear is oppressed by the violent beating of his heart before it is stilled forever. *326. calls me:* i.e., to follow him into the darkness.

Sean O'Casey (1880–1964)

THE PLOUGH AND THE STARS

A Tragedy in Four Acts

To the gay laugh of my mother
at the gate of the grave

CHARACTERS IN THE PLAY

JACK CLITHEROE *(a bricklayer), Commandant in the Irish Citizen Army*
NORA CLITHEROE, *his wife*
PETER FLYNN *(a labourer), Nora's uncle*
THE YOUNG COVEY *(a fitter), Clitheroe's cousin*
BESSIE BURGESS *(a street fruit-vendor)*
MRS. GOGAN *(a charwoman)*
MOLLSER, *her consumptive child*
FLUTHER GOOD *(a carpenter)*

Residents in the Tenement

LIEUT. LANGON *(a Civil Servant), of the Irish Volunteers*
CAPT. BRENNAN *(a chicken butcher), of the Irish Citizen Army*
CORPORAL STODDART, *of the Wiltshires*
SERGEANT TINLEY, *of the Wiltshires*
ROSIE REDMOND, *a daughter of "the Digs"*
A BAR-TENDER
A WOMAN
THE FIGURE IN THE WINDOW

Act I.— The living-room of the Clitheroe flat in a Dublin tenement.
Act II.—A public-house, outside of which a meeting is being held.
Act III.— The street outside the Clitheroe tenement.
Act IV.— The room of Bessie Burgess.

Time.— Acts I and II, November 1915; Acts III and IV, Easter Week, 1916. A few days elapse between Acts III and IV.

ACT I

The home of the Clitheroes. It consists of the front and back drawing-rooms in a fine old Georgian house, struggling for its life against the assaults of time, and the more savage assaults of the tenants. The room shown is the back drawing-room, wide, spacious, and lofty. At back is the entrance to the front drawing-room. The space, originally occupied by folding doors, is now draped with casement cloth of a dark purple, decorated with a design in reddish-purple and cream. One of the curtains is pulled aside, giving a glimpse of front drawing-room, at the end of which can be seen the wide, lofty windows looking out into the street. The room directly in front of the audience is furnished in a way that suggests an attempt towards a finer expression of domestic life. The large fireplace on right is of wood, painted to look like marble (the original has been taken away by the landlord). On the mantelshelf are two candlesticks of dark carved wood. Between them is a small clock. Over the clock is hanging a calendar which displays a picture of "The Sleeping Venus". In the centre of the breast of the chimney hangs a picture of Robert Emmet. On the right of the entrance to the front drawing-room is a copy of "The Gleaners", on the opposite side a copy of "The Angelus". Underneath "The Gleaners" is a chest of drawers on which stands a green bowl filled with scarlet dahlias and white chrysanthemums. Near to the fireplace is a settee which at night forms a double bed for Clitheroe and Nora. Underneath "The Angelus" are a number of shelves containing saucepans and a frying-pan. Under these is a table on which are various articles of delf ware. Near the end of the room, opposite to the fireplace is a gate-legged table, covered with a cloth. On top of the table a huge cavalry sword is lying. To the right is a door which leads to a lobby from which the staircase leads to the hall. The floor is covered with a dark green linoleum. The room is dim except where it is illuminated from the glow of the fire. Through the window of the room at back can be seen the flaring of the flame of a gasolene lamp giving light to workmen repairing the street. Occasionally can be heard the clang of crowbars striking the setts. FLUTHER GOOD *is repairing the lock of door, Right. A claw-hammer is on a chair beside him, and he has a screw-driver in his hand. He is a man of forty years of age, rarely surrendering to thoughts of anxiety, fond of his "oil" but determined to conquer the habit before he dies. He is square-jawed and harshly featured; under the left eye is a scar, and his nose is bent from a smashing blow received in a fistic battle long ago. He is bald, save for a few peeping tufts of reddish hair around his ears; and his upper lip is hidden by a scrubby red moustache, embroidered here and there with a grey hair. He is dressed in a seedy black suit, cotton shirt with a soft collar, and wears a very respectable little black bow. On his head is a faded jerry hat, which, when he is excited, he has a habit of knocking farther back on his bead, in a series of taps. In an argument he usually fills with sound and fury generally signifying a row. He is in his shirt-sleeves at present, and wears a soiled white apron, from a pocket in which sticks a carpenter's two-foot rule. He has just finished the job of putting on a new lock, and, filled with satisfaction, he is opening and shutting the door, enjoying the completion of a work well done. Sitting at the fire, airing a white shirt, is* PETER FLYNN. *He is a little, thin bit of a man, with a face shaped like a lozenge; on his cheeks and under his chin is a straggling wiry beard of a dirty-white and lemon hue. His face invariably wears a look of animated anguish, mixed with irritated defiance, as if everybody was at war with him, and he at war with everybody. He is cocking his head in a way that suggests resentment at the presence of* FLUTHER, *who pays no attention to him, apparently, but is really furtively watching him.* PETER *is clad in a singlet, white whipcord knee-breeches, and is in his stocking-feet.*

A voice is heard speaking outside of door, Left (it is that of MRS. GOGAN*).*

MRS. GOGAN [*outside*]. Who are you lookin' for, sir? Who? Mrs. Clitheroe? . . . Oh, excuse me. Oh ay, up this way. She's out, I think: I seen her goin'. Oh, you've somethin' for her; oh, excuse me. You're from Arnott's. . . . I see. . . . You've a parcel for her. . . .

Righto. . . . I'll take it. . . . I'll give it to her the minute she comes in. . . . It'll be quite safe. . . . Oh, sign that. . . . Excuse me. . . . Where? . . . Here? . . . No, there; righto. Am I to put Maggie or Mrs.? What is it? You dunno? Oh, excuse me.

[MRS. GOGAN *opens the door and comes in. She is a doleful-looking little woman of forty, insinuating manner and sallow complexion. She is fidgety and nervous, terribly talkative, has a habit of taking up things that may be near her and fiddling with them while she is speaking. Her heart is aflame with curiosity, and a fly could not come into nor go out of the house without her knowing. She has a draper's parcel in her hand, the knot of the twine tying it is untied.* PETER, *more resentful of this intrusion than of* FLUTHER*'s presence, gets up from the chair, and without looking around, his head carried at an angry cock, marches into the room at back.*]

MRS. GOGAN [*removing the paper and opening the cardboard box it contains.*] I wondher what's that now? A hat! [*She takes out a hat, black, with decorations in red and gold.*] God, she's goin' to th' divil lately for style! That hat, now, cost more than a penny. Such notions of upperosity she's gettin'. [*Putting the hat on her head*] Oh, swank, what! [*She replaces it in parcel.*]

FLUTHER. She's a pretty little Judy, all the same.

MRS. GOGAN. Ah, she is an' she isn't. There's prettiness an' prettiness in it. I'm always sayin' that her skirts are a little too short for a married woman. An' to see her, sometimes of an evenin', in her glad-neck gown would make a body's blood run cold. I do be ashamed of me life before her husband. An' th' way she thries to be polite, with her "Good mornin', Mrs. Gogan," when she's goin' down, an' her "Good evenin', Mrs. Gogan," when she's comin' up. But there's politeness an' politeness in it.

FLUTHER. They seem to get on well together, all th' same.

MRS. GOGAN. Ah, they do, an' they don't. The pair o' them used to be like two turtle doves always billin' an' cooin'. You couldn't come into th' room but you'd feel, instinctive like, that they'd just been afther kissin' an' cuddlin' each other. . . . It often made me shiver, for, afther all, there's kissin' an' cuddlin' in it. But I'm thinkin' he's beginnin' to take things more quietly; the mysthery of havin' a woman's a mysthery no longer. . . . She dhresses herself to keep him with her, but it's no use—afther a month or two, th' wondher of a woman wears off.

FLUTHER. I dunno, I dunno. Not wishin' to say anything derogatory, I think it's all a question of location: when a man finds th' wondher of one woman beginnin' to die, its usually beginnin' to live in another.

MRS. GOGAN. She's always grumblin' about havin' to live in a tenement house. "I wouldn't like to spend me last hour in one, let alone live me life in a tenement," says she. "Vaults," says she, "'that are hidin' th' dead, instead of homes that are shelterin' th' livin'."

"Many a good one," says I, "was reared in a tenement house." Oh, you know, she's a well-up little lassie, too; able to make a shillin' go where another would have to spend a pound. She's wipin' th' eyes of th' Covey an' poor oul' Pether—everybody knows that—screwin' every penny she can out o' them, in order to turn th' place into a babby-house. An' she has th' life frightened out o' them; washin' their face, combin' their hair, wipin' their feet, brushin' their clothes, thrimmin' their nails, cleanin' their teeth—God Almighty, you'd think th' poor men were undhergoin' penal servitude.

FLUTHER [*with an exclamation of disgust*]. A-a-ah, that's goin' beyond th' beyonds in a tenement house. That's a little bit too derogatory.

[PETER *enters from room, Back, head elevated and resentful fire in his eyes; he is still in his singlet and trousers, but is now wearing a pair of unlaced boots—possibly to be decent in the presence of* MRS. GOGAN. *He places the white shirt, which he has carried in on his arm, on the back of a chair near the fire, and, going over to the chest of drawers, he opens drawer after drawer, looking for something; as he fails to find it he closes each drawer with a snap; he pulls out pieces of linen neatly folded, and bundles them back again any way.*]

PETER [*in accents of anguish*]. Well, God Almighty, give me patience!

[*He returns to room, Back, giving the shirt a vicious turn as he passes.*]

MRS. GOGAN. I wondher what he is foostherin' for now?

FLUTHER. He's adornin' himself for th' meeting to-night. [*Pulling a handbill from his pocket and reading*] "Great Demonstration an' torchlight procession around places in th' city sacred to th' memory of Irish Patriots, to be concluded be a meetin', at which will be taken an oath of fealty to th' Irish Republic. Formation in Parnell Square at eight o'clock." Well, they can hold it for Fluther. I'm up th' pole; no more dhrink for Fluther. It's three days now since I touched a dhrop, an' I feel a new man already.

MRS. GOGAN. Isn't oul' Peter a funny-lookin' little man? . . . Like somethin' you'd pick off a Christmas Tree. . . . When he's dhressed up in his canonicals, you'd wondher where he'd been got. God forgive me, when I see him in them, I always think he must ha' had a Mormon for a father! He an' th' Covey can't abide each other; th' pair o' them is always at it, thryin' to best each other. There'll be blood dhrawn one o' these days.

FLUTHER. How is it that Clitheroe himself, now, doesn't have anythin' to do with th' Citizen Army? A couple o' months ago, an' you'd hardly ever see him without his gun, an' th' Red Hand o' Liberty Hall in his hat.

MRS. GOGAN. Just because he wasn't made a Captain of. He wasn't goin' to be in anything where he couldn't be conspishuous. He was so cocksure o' being made one that he bought a Sam Browne belt, an' was always puttin' it on an' standin' at th' door showing it off, till th' man came an' put out th' street lamps on him. God, I think he used to bring it to bed with him! But I'm tellin' you herself was delighted that that cock didn't crow, for she's like a clockin' hen if he leaves her sight for a minute.

[*While she is talking, she takes up book after book from the table, looks into each of them in a near-sighted way, and then leaves them back. She now lifts up the sword, and proceeds to examine it.*]

MRS. GOGAN. Be th' look of it, this must ha' been a general's sword. . . . All th' gold lace an' th' fine figaries on it. . . . Sure it's twiced too big for him.

FLUTHER. A-ah; it's a baby's rattle he ought to have, an' he as he is with thoughts tossin' in his head of what may happen to him on th' day o' judgement.

[PETER *has entered, and seeing* MRS. GOGAN *with the sword, goes over to her, pulls it resentfully out of her hands, and marches into the room, Back, without speaking.*]

MRS. GOGAN. [*as* PETER *whips the sword*]. Oh, excuse me! . . . [*To* FLUTHER] Isn't he th' surly oul' rascal!

FLUTHER. Take no notice of him. . . . You'd think he was dumb, but when you get his goat, or he has a few jars up, he's vice versa. [*He coughs.*]

MRS. GOGAN [*she has now sidled over as far as the shirt hanging on the chair*]. Oh, you've got a cold on you, Fluther.

FLUTHER [*carelessly*]. Ah, it's only a little one.

MRS. GOGAN. You'd want to be careful, all th' same. I knew a woman, a big lump of a woman, red-faced an' round-bodied, a little awkward on her feet; you'd think, to look at her, she could put out her two arms an' lift a two-storied house on th' top of her head; got a ticklin' in her throat, an' a little cough, an' th' next mornin' she had a little catchin' in her chest, an' they had just time to wet her lips with a little rum, an' off she went.

[*She begins to look at and handle the shirt.*]

FLUTHER [*a little nervously*]. It's only a little cold I have; there's nothing derogatory wrong with me.

MRS. GOGAN. I dunno; there's many a man this minute lowerin' a pint, thinkin' of a woman, or pickin' out a winner, or doin' work as you're doin', while th' hearse dhrawn be th' horses with the black plumes is dhrivin' up to his own hall door, an' a voice that he doesn't hear is muttherin' in his ear, "Earth to earth, an' ashes t' ashes, an' dust to dust."

FLUTHER [*faintly*]. A man in th' pink o' health should have a holy horror of allowin' thoughts o' death to be festherin' in his mind, for—[*with a frightened cough*] be God, I think I'm afther gettin' a little catch in me chest that time—it's a creepy thing to be thinkin' about.

MRS. GOGAN. It is, an' it isn't; it's both bad an' good. . . . It always gives meself a kind o' thresspassin' joy to feel meself movin' along in a mournin' coach, an' me thinkin' that, maybe, th' next funeral 'll be me own, an' glad, in a quiet way, that this is somebody else's.

FLUTHER. An' a curious kind of a gaspin' for breath—I hope there's nothin' derogatory wrong with me.

MRS. GOGAN [*examining the shirt*]. Frills on it, like a woman's petticoat.

FLUTHER. Suddenly gettin' hot, an' then, just as suddenly, gettin' cold.

MRS. GOGAN [*holding out the shirt towards* FLUTHER]. How would you like to be wearin' this Lord Mayor's nightdhress, Fluther?

FLUTHER [*vehemently*]. Blast you an' your nightshirt! Is a man fermentin' with fear to stick th' showin' off to him of a thing that looks like a shinin' shroud?

MRS. GOGAN. Oh, excuse me!

[PETER *has again entered, and he pulls the shirt from the hands of* MRS. GOGAN, *replacing it on the chair. He returns to room.*]

PETER [*as he goes out*]. Well, God Almighty, give me patience!

MRS. GOGAN [*to* PETER]. Oh, excuse me!

[*There is heard a cheer from the men working outside on the street, followed by the clang of tools being thrown down, then silence. The glare of the gasolene light diminishes and finally goes out.*]

MRS. GOGAN [*running into the back room to look out of the window*]. What's the men repairin' th' streets cheerin' for?

FLUTHER [*sitting down weakly on a chair*]. You can't sneeze but that oul' one wants to know th' why an' th' wherefore. . . . I feel as dizzy as bedamned! I hope I didn't give up th' beer too suddenly.

[THE COVEY *comes in by door, Right. He is about twenty-five, tall, thin, with lines on his face that form a perpetual protest against life as he conceives it to be. Heavy seams fall from each side of nose, down around his lips, as if they were suspenders keeping his mouth from falling. He speaks in a slow, wailing drawl; more rapidly when he is excited. He is dressed in dungarees, and is wearing a vividly red tie. He flings his cap with a gesture of disgust on the table, and begins to take off his overalls.*]

MRS. GOGAN [*to* THE COVEY, *as she runs back into the room*]. What's after happenin', Covey?

THE COVEY [*with contempt*]. Th' job's stopped. They've been mobilized to march in th' demonstration to-night undher th' Plough an' th' Stars. Didn't you hear them cheerin', th' mugs! They have to renew their political baptismal vows to be faithful in seculo seculorum.

FLUTHER [*forgetting his fear in his indignation*]. There's no reason to bring religion into it. I think we ought to have as great a regard for religion as we can, so as to keep it out of as many things as possible.

THE COVEY [*pausing in the taking off of his dungarees*]. Oh, you're one o' the boys that climb into religion as high as a short Mass on Sunday mornin's? I suppose you'll be singin' songs o' Sion an' songs o' Tara at th' meetin', too.

FLUTHER. We're all Irishmen, anyhow; aren't we?

THE COVEY [*with hand outstretched, and in a professional tone*]. Look here, comrade, there's no such thing as an Irishman, or an Englishman, or a German or a Turk; we're all only human bein's. Scientifically speakin', it's all a question of the accidental gatherin' together of mollycewels an' atoms.

[PETER *comes in with a collar in his hand. He goes over to mirror, Left, and proceeds to try to put it on.*]

FLUTHER. Mollycewels an' atoms! D'ye think I'm goin' to listen to you thryin' to juggle Fluther's mind with complicated cunundhrums of mollycewels an' atoms?

THE COVEY [*rather loudly*]. There's nothin' complicated in it. There's no fear o' th' Church tellin' you that mollycewels is a stickin' together of millions of atoms o' sodium, carbon, potassium o' iodide, etcetera, that accordin' to th' way they're mixed, make a flower, a fish, a star that you see shinin' in th' sky, or a man with a big brain like me, or a man with a little brain like you!

FLUTHER [*more loudly still*]. There's no necessity to be raisin' your voice; shoutin's no manifestin' forth of a growin' mind.

PETER [*struggling with his collar*]. God, give me patience with this thing. . . . She makes these collars as stiff with starch as a shinin' band o' solid steel! She does it purposely to thry an' twart me. If I can't get it on th' singlet, how, in th' Name o' God, am I goin' to get it on th' shirt?

THE COVEY [*loudly*]. There's no use o' arguin' with you; it's education you want, comrade.

FLUTHER. The Covey an' God made th' world, I suppose, wha'?

THE COVEY. When I hear some men talkin' I'm inclined to disbelieve that th' world's eight-hundhred million years old, for it's not long since th' fathers o' some o' them crawled out o' th' sheltherin' slime o' the sea.

MRS. GOGAN [*from room at back*]. There, they're afther formin' fours, an' now they're goin' to march away.

FLUTHER [*scornfully*]. Mollycewels! [*He begins to untie his apron*] What about Adam an' Eve?

THE COVEY. Well, what about them?

FLUTHER [*fiercely*]. What about them, you?

THE COVEY. Adam an' Eve! Is that as far as you've got? Are you still thinkin' there was nobody in th' world before Adam an' Eve? [*Loudly*] Did you ever hear, man, of th' skeleton of th' man o' Java?

PETER [*casting the collar from him*]. Blast it, blast it, blast it!

FLUTHER [*viciously folding his apron*]. Ah, you're not goin' to be let tap your rubbidge o' thoughts into th' mind o' Fluther.

THE COVEY. You're afraid to listen to th' thruth!

FLUTHER. Who's afraid?

THE COVEY. You are!

FLUTHER. G'way, you wurum!

THE COVEY. Who's a worum?

FLUTHER. You are, or you wouldn't talk th' way you're talkin'.

THE COVEY. Th' oul', ignorant savage leppin' up in you, when science shows you that th' head of your god is an empty one. Well, I hope you're enjoyin' th' blessin' o' havin' to live be th' sweat of your brow.

FLUTHER. You'll be kickin' an' yellin' for th' priest yet, me boyo. I'm not goin' to stand silent an' simple listenin' to a thick like you makin' a maddenin' mockery o' God Almighty. It 'ud be a nice derogatory thing on me conscience, an' me dyin', to look back in rememberin' shame of talkin' to a word-weavin' little ignorant yahoo of a red flag Socialist!

MRS. GOGAN [*she has returned to the front room, and has wandered around looking at things in general, and is now in front of the fireplace looking at the picture hanging over it*]. For God's sake, Fluther, dhrop it; there's always th' makin's of a row in th' mention of religion . . . [*Looking at picture*] God bless us, it's a naked woman!

FLUTHER [*coming over to look at it*]. What's undher it? [*Reading*] "Georgina: The Sleepin' Vennis". Oh, that's a terrible picture; oh, that's a shockin' picture! Oh, th' one that got that taken, she must have been a prime lassie!

PETER [*who also has come over to look, laughing, with his body bent at the waist, and his head slightly tilted back*]. Hee, hee, hee, hee, hee!

FLUTHER [*indignantly, to* PETER]. What are you hee, hee-in' for? That's a nice thing to be hee, hee-in' at. Where's your morality, man?

MRS. GOGAN. God forgive us, it's not right to be lookin' at it.

FLUTHER. It's nearly a derogatory thing to be in th' room where it is.

MRS. GOGAN [*giggling hysterically*]. I couldn't stop any longer in th' same room with three men, afther lookin' at it! [*She goes out.*]

[THE COVEY, *who has divested himself of his dungarees, throws them with a contemptuous motion on top of* PETER'S *white shirt.*]

PETER [*plaintively*]. Where are you throwin' them? Are you thryin' to twart an' torment me again?

THE COVEY. Who's thryin' to twart you?

PETER [*flinging the dungarees violently on the floor*]. You're not goin' to make me lose me temper, me young Covey.

THE COVEY [*flinging the white shirt on the floor*]. If you're Nora's pet, aself, you're not going' to get your way in everything.

PETER [*plaintively, with his eyes looking up at the ceiling*]. I'll say nothin'. . . . I'll leave you to th' day when th' all-pitiful, all merciful, all lovin' God 'll be handin' you to th' angels to be rievin' an' roastin' you, tearin' an' tormentin' you, burnin' an' blastin' you!

THE COVEY. Aren't you th' little malignant oul' bastard, you lemon-whiskered oul' swine!

[PETER *runs to the sword, draws it, and makes for* THE COVEY, *who dodges him around the table;* PETER *has no intention of striking, but* THE COVEY *wants to take no chances.*]

THE COVEY [*dodging*]. Fluther, hold him, there. It's a nice thing to have a lunatic like this lashin' around with a lethal weapon!

[THE COVEY *darts out of the room, Right, slamming the door in the face of* PETER.]

PETER [*battering and pulling at the door*]. Lemme out, lemme out; isn't it a poor thing for a man who wouldn't say a word against his greatest enemy to have to listen to that Covey's twartin' animosities, shovin' poor, patient people into a lashin' out of curses that darken his soul with th' shadow of th' wrath of th' last day!

FLUTHER. Why d'ye take notice of him? If he seen you didn't, he'd say nothin' derogatory.

PETER. I'll make him stop his laughin' an' leerin', jibin' an' jeerin' an' scarifyin' people with his corner-boy insinuations! . . . He's always thryin' to rouse me: if it's not a song, it's a whistle; if it isn't a whistle, it's a cough. But you can taunt an' taunt—I'm laughin' at you; he, hee, hee, hee, hee, heee!

THE COVEY [*singing through the keyhole*]:

Dear harp o' me counthry, in darkness I found thee,
The dark chain of silence had hung o'er thee long—

PETER [*frantically*]. Jasus, d'ye hear that? D'ye hear him soundin' forth his divil-souled song o' provocation?

THE COVEY [*singing as before*]:

When proudly, me own island harp, I unbound thee,
An' gave all thy chords to light, freedom an' song!

PETER [*battering at door*]. When I get out I'll do for you, I'll do for you, I'll do for you!

THE COVEY [*through the keyhole*]. Cuckoo-oo!

[NORA *enters by door, Right. She is a young woman of twenty-two, alert, swift, full of nervous energy, and a little anxious to get on in the world. The firm lines of her face are considerably opposed by a soft, amorous mouth and gentle eyes. When her firmness fails her, she persuades with her feminine charm. She is dressed in a tailor-made costume, and wears around her neck a silver fox fur.*]

NORA [*running in and pushing* PETER *away from the door*]. Oh, can I not turn me back but th' two o' yous are at it like a pair o' fightin' cocks? Uncle Peter . . . Uncle Peter . . . UNCLE PETER!

PETER [*vociferously*]. Oh, Uncle Peter, Uncle Peter be damned! D'ye think I'm goin' to give a free pass to th' young Covey to turn me whole life into a Holy Manual o' penances an' martyrdoms?

THE COVEY [*angrily rushing into the room*]. If you won't exercise some sort o' conthrol over that Uncle Peter o' yours, there'll be a funeral, an' it won't be me that'll be in th' hearse!

NORA [*between* PETER *and* THE COVEY, *to* THE COVEY]. Are yous always goin' to be tearin' down th' little bit of respectability that a body's thryin' to build up? Am I always goin' to be havin' to nurse yous into th' hardy habit o' thryin' to keep up a little bit of appearance?

THE COVEY. Why weren't you here to see th' way he run at me with th' sword?

PETER. What did you call me a lemon-whiskered oul' swine for?

NORA. If th' two o' yous don't thry to make a generous altheration in your goin's on, an' keep on thryin' t' inaugurate th' customs o' th' rest o' th' house into this place, yous can flit into other lodgin's where your bowsey battlin' 'ill meet, maybe, with an encore.

PETER [*to* NORA]. Would you like to be called a lemon-whiskered oul' swine?

NORA. If you attempt to wag that sword of yours at anybody again, it'll have to be taken off you an' put in a safe place away from babies that don't know th' danger o' them things.

PETER [*at entrance to room, Back*]. Well, I'm not goin' to let anybody call me a lemon-whiskered oul' swine.

[*He goes in.*]

FLUTHER [*trying the door*]. Openin' an' shuttin' now with a well-mannered motion, like a door of a select bar in a high-class pub.

NORA [*to* THE COVEY, *as she lays table for tea*]. An', once for all, Willie, you'll have to thry to deliver yourself from th' desire of provokin' oul' Pether into a wild forgetfulness of what's proper an' allowable in a respectable home.

THE COVEY. Well let him mind his own business, then. Yestherday, I caught him hee-hee-in' out of him an' he readin' bits out of Jenersky's *Thesis on th' Origin, Development, an' Consolidation of th' Evolutionary Idea of th' Proletariat.*

NORA. Now, let it end at that, for God's sake; Jack'll be in any minute, an' I'm not goin' to have th' quiet of his evenin' tossed about in an everlastin' uproar between you an' Uncle Pether. [*To* FLUTHER] Well, did you manage to settle th' lock, yet, Mr. Good?

FLUTHER [*opening and shutting door*]. It's betther than a new one, now, Mrs. Clitheroe; it's almost ready to open and shut of its own accord.

NORA [*giving him a coin*]. You're a whole man. How many pints will that get you?

FLUTHER [*seriously*]. Ne'er a one at all, Mrs. Clitheroe, for Fluther's on th' wather waggon now. You could stan' where you're stannin' chantin', "Have a glass o' malt, Fluther; Fluther, have a glass o' malt," till th' bells would be ringin' th' ould year out an' th' New Year in, an' you'd have as much chance o' movin' Fluther as a tune on a tin whistle would move a deaf man an' he dead.

[*As* NORA *is opening and shutting door,* MRS. BESSIE BURGESS *appears at it. She is a woman of forty, vigorously built. Her face is a dogged one, hardened by toil, and a little coarsened by drink. She looks scornfully and viciously at* NORA *for a few moments before she speaks.*]

BESSIE. Puttin' a new lock on her door . . . afraid her poor neighbours ud break through an' steal. . . . [*In a loud tone*] Maybe, now, they're a damn sight more honest than your ladyship . . . checkin' th' children playin' on th' stairs . . . gettin' on th' nerves of your ladyship. . . . Complainin' about Bessie Burgess singin' her hymns at night, when she has a few up. . . . [*She comes in half-way on the threshold, and screams*] Bessie Burgess 'll sing whenever she damn well likes!

[NORA *tries to shut door, but* BESSIE *violently shoves it in, and, gripping* NORA *by the shoulders, shakes her.*]

BESSIE. You little over-dressed throllope, you, for one pin I'd paste th' white face o' you!

NORA [*frightened*]. Fluther, Fluther!

FLUTHER [*running over and breaking the hold of* BESSIE *from* NORA]. Now, now, Bessie, Bessie, leave poor Mrs. Clitheroe alone; she'd do no one any harm, an' minds no one's business but her own.

BESSIE. Why is she always thryin' to speak proud things, an' lookin' like a mighty one in th' congregation o' th' people!

[NORA *sinks frightened on to the couch as* JACK CLITHEROE *enters. He is a tall, well-made fellow of twenty-five. His face has none of the strength of* NORA'*s. It is a face in which is the desire for authority, without the power to attain it.*]

CLITHEROE [*excitedly*]. What's up? what's afther happenin'?

FLUTHER. Nothin', Jack. Nothin'. It's all over now. Come on, Bessie, come on.

CLITHEROE [*to* NORA]. What's wrong, Nora? Did she say anything to you?

NORA. She was bargin' out of her, an' I only told her to g'up ower o' that to her own place; an' before I knew where I was, she flew at me like a tiger, an' thried to guzzle me!

CLITHEROE [*going to door and speaking to* BESSIE]. Get up to your own place, Mrs. Burgess, and don't you be interferin' with my wife, or it'll be th' worse for you. . . . Go on, go on!

BESSIE [*as* CLITHEROE *is pushing her out*]. Mind who you're pushin', now. . . . I attend me place o' worship, anyhow . . . not like some o' them that go to neither church, chapel nor meetin'-house. . . . If me son was home from th' threnches he'd see me righted.

[BESSIE *and* FLUTHER *depart, and* CLITHEROE *closes the door.*]

CLITHEROE [*going over to* NORA, *and putting his arm around her*]. There, don't mind that old bitch, Nora, darling; I'll soon put a stop to her interferin'.

NORA. Some day or another, when I'm here be meself, she'll come in an' do somethin' desperate.

CLITHEROE [*kissing her*]. Oh, sorra fear of her doin' anythin' desperate. I'll talk to her to-morrow when she's sober. A taste o' me mind that'll shock her into the sensibility of behavin' herself!

[NORA *gets up and settles the table. She sees the dungarees on the floor and stands looking at them, then she turns to* THE COVEY, *who is reading Jenersky's "Thesis" at the fire.*]

NORA. Willie, is that th' place for your dungarees?

THE COVEY [*getting up and lifting them from the floor*]. Ah, they won't do th' floor any harm, will they? [*He carries them into room, Back.*]

NORA [*calling*]. Uncle Peter, now, Uncle Peter; tea's ready.

[PETER *and* THE COVEY *come in from room, Back; they all sit down to tea.* PETER *is in full dress of the Foresters: green coat, gold braided; white breeches, top boots, frilled shirt. He carries the slouch hat, with the white ostrich plume, and the sword in his hands. They eat for a few moments in silence,* THE COVEY *furtively looking at* PETER *with scorn in his eyes.* PETER *knows it and is fidgety.*]

THE COVEY [*provokingly*]. Another cut o' bread, Uncle Peter? [PETER *maintains a dignified silence.*]

CLITHEROE. It's sure to be a great meetin' to-night. We ought to go, Nora.

NORA [*decisively*]. I won't go, Jack; you can go if you wish. [*A pause.*]

THE COVEY. D'ye want th' sugar, Uncle Peter?

PETER [*explosively*]. Now, are you goin' to start your thryin' an' your twartin' again?

NORA. Now, Uncle Peter, you musn't be so touchy; Willie has only assed you if you wanted th' sugar.

PETER. He doesn't care a damn whether I want th' sugar or no. He's only thryin' to twart me!

NORA [*angrily, to* THE COVEY]. Can't you let him alone, Willie? If he wants the sugar, let him stretch his hand out an' get it himself!

THE COVEY [*to* PETER]. Now, if you want the sugar, you can stretch out your hand and get it yourself!

CLITHEROE. To-night is th' first chance that Brennan has got of showing himself off since they made a Captain of him—why, God only knows. It'll be a treat to see him swankin' it at th' head of the Citizen Army carryin' th' flag of the Plough an' th' Stars. . . . [*Looking roguishly at* NORA] He was sweet on you, once, Nora?

NORA. He may have been. . . . I never liked him. I always thought he was a bit of a thick.

THE COVEY. They're bringin' nice disgrace on that banner now.

CLITHEROE [*remonstratively*]. How are they bringin' disgrace on it?

THE COVEY [*snappily*]. Because it's a Labour flag, an' was never meant for politics. . . . What does th' design of th' field plough, bearin' on it th' stars of th' heavenly plough, mean, if it's not Communism? It's a flag that should only be used when we're buildin' th' barricades to fight for a Workers' Republic!

PETER [*with a puff of derision*]. P-phuh.

THE COVEY [*angrily*]. What are you phuhin' out o' you for? Your mind is th' mind of a mummy. [*Rising*] I betther go an' get a good place to have a look at Ireland's warriors passin' by.

[*He goes into room, Left, and returns with his cap.*]

NORA [*to* THE COVEY]. Oh, Willie, brush your clothes before you go.

THE COVEY. Oh, they'll do well enough.

NORA. Go an' brush them; th' brush is in th' drawer there.

[THE COVEY *goes to the drawer, muttering, gets the brush, and starts to brush his clothes.*]

THE COVEY [*singing at* PETER, *as he does so*]:

Oh, where's th' slave so lowly,
Condemn'd to chains unholy,
Who, could he burst his bonds at first,
Would pine beneath them slowly?

We tread th' land that . . . bore us,
Th' green flag glitters . . . o'er us,
Th' friends we've tried are by our side,
An' th' foe we hate . . . before us!

PETER [*leaping to his feet in a whirl of rage*]. Now, I'm tellin' you, me young Covey, once for all, that I'll not stick any longer these tit-therin' taunts of yours, rovin' around to sing your slights an' slan-dhers, reddenin' th' mind of a man to th' thinkin' an' sayin' of things that sicken his soul with sin! [*Hysterically; lifting up a cup to fling at* THE COVEY] Be God, I'll—

CLITHEROE [*catching his arm*]. Now then, none o' that, none o' that!

NORA. Uncle Pether, Uncle Pether, UNCLE PETHER!

THE COVEY [*at the door, about to go out*]. Isn't that th' malignant oul' varmint! Lookin' like th' illegitimate son of an illegitimate child of a corporal in th' Mexican army!

[*He goes out.*]

PETER [*plaintively*]. He's afther leavin' me now in such a state of agi-tation that I won't be able to do meself justice when I'm marchin' to th' meetin'.

NORA [*jumping up*]. Oh, for God's sake, here, buckle your sword on, and go to your meetin', so that we'll have at least one hour of peace!

[*She proceeds to belt on the sword.*]

CLITHEROE [*irritably*]. For God's sake hurry him up ou' o' this, Nora.

PETER. Are yous all goin' to thry to start to twart me now?

NORA [*putting on his plumed hat*]. S-s-sh. Now, your hat's on, your house is thatched; off you pop!

[*She gently pushes him from her.*]

PETER [*going, and turning as he reaches the door*]. Now, if that young Covey—

NORA. Go on, go on. [*He goes.*]

[CLITHEROE *sits down in the lounge, lights a cigarette, and looks thoughtfully into the fire.* NORA *takes the things from the table, placing them on the chest of drawers. There is a pause, then she swiftly comes over to him and sits beside him.*]

NORA [*softly*]. A penny for them, Jack!

CLITHEROE. Me? Oh, I was thinkin' of nothing.

NORA. You were thinkin' of th' . . . meetin' . . . Jack. When we were courtin' an' I wanted you to go, you'd say, "Oh, to hell with meetin's," an' that you felt lonely in cheerin' crowds when I was absent. An' we weren't a month married when you began that you couldn't keep away from them.

CLITHEROE. Oh, that's enough about th' meetin'. It looks as if you wanted me to go, th' way you're talkin'. You were always at me to give up th' Citizen Army, an' I gave it up; surely that ought to satisfy you.

NORA. Ay, you gave it up—because you got th' sulks when they didn't make a Captain of you. It wasn't for my sake, Jack.

CLITHEROE. For your sake or no, you're benefitin' by it, aren't you? I didn't forget this was your birthday, did I? [*He puts his arms around her*] And you liked your new hat; didn't you, didn't you?

[*He kisses her rapidly several times.*]

NORA [*panting*]. Jack, Jack; please, Jack! I thought you were tired of that sort of thing long ago.

CLITHEROE. Well, you're finding out now that I amn't tired of it yet, anyhow. Mrs. Clitheroe doesn't want to be kissed, sure she doesn't? [*He kisses her again*] Little, little red-lipped Nora!

NORA [*coquettishly removing his arm from around her*]. Oh, yes, your little, little red-lipped Nora's a sweet little girl when th' fit seizes you; but your little, little red-lipped Nora has to clean your boots every mornin', all the same.

CLITHEROE [*with a movement of irritation*]. Oh, well, if we're goin' to be snotty! [*A pause.*]

NORA. It's lookin' like as if it was you that was goin' to be . . . snotty! Bridlin' up with bittherness, th' minute a body attempts t'open her mouth.

CLITHEROE. Is it any wondher, turnin' a tendher sayin' into a meanin' o' malice an' spite!

NORA. It's hard for a body to be always keepin' her mind bent on makin' thoughts that'll be no longer than th' length of your own satisfaction. [*A pause.*]

NORA [*standing up*]. If we're goin' to dhribble th' time away sittin' here like a pair o' cranky mummies, I'd be as well sewin' or doin' something about th' place.

[*She looks appealingly at him for a few moments; he doesn't speak. She swiftly sits down beside him, and puts her arm around his neck.*]

NORA [*imploringly*]. Ah, Jack, don't be so cross!

CLITHEROE [*doggedly*]. Cross? I'm not cross; I'm not a bit cross. It was yourself started it.

NORA [*coaxingly*]. I didn't mean to say anything out o' the way. You take a body up too quickly, Jack. [*In an ordinary tone as if nothing of an angry nature had been said*] You didn't offer me me evenin' allowance yet.

[CLITHEROE *silently takes out a cigarette for her and himself and lights both.*]

NORA [*trying to make conversation*]. How quiet th' house is now; they must be all out.

CLITHEROE [*rather shortly*]. I suppose so.

NORA [*rising from the seat*]. I'm longin' to show you me new hat, to see what you think of it. Would you like to see it?

CLITHEROE. Ah, I don't mind.

[NORA *suppresses a sharp reply, hesitates for a moment, then gets the hat, puts it on, and stands before Clitheroe.*]

NORA. Well, how does Mr. Clitheroe like me new hat?

CLITHEROE. It suits you, Nora, it does right enough.

[*He stands up, puts his hand beneath her chin, and tilts her head up. She looks at him roguishly. He bends down and kisses her.*]

NORA. Here, sit down, an' don't let me hear another cross word out of you for th' rest o' the night.

[*They sit down.*]

CLITHEROE [*with his arms around her*]. Little, little, red-lipped Nora!

NORA [*with a coaxing movement of her body towards him*]. Jack!

CLITHEROE [*tightening his arms around her*]. Well?

NORA. You haven't sung me a song since our honeymoon. Sing me one now, do . . . please, Jack!

CLITHEROE. What song? "Since Maggie Went Away"?

NORA. Ah, no, Jack, not that; it's too sad. "When You Said You Loved Me."

[*Clearing his throat,* CLITHEROE *thinks for a moment, and then begins to sing.* NORA, *putting an arm around him, nestles her head on his breast and listens delightedly.*]

CLITHEROE [*singing verses following to the air of "When You and I Were Young, Maggie"*]:

Th' violets were scenting th' woods, Nora,
Displaying their charm to th' bee,
When I first said I lov'd only you, Nora,
An' you said you lov'd only me!

Th' chestnut blooms gleam'd through th' glade, Nora,
A robin sang loud from a tree,
When I first said I lov'd only you, Nora,
An' you said you lov'd only me!

Th' golden-rob'd daffodils shone, Nora,
An' danc'd in th' breeze on th' lea,
When I first said I lov'd only you, Nora,
An' you said you lov'd only me!

Th' trees, birds, an' bees sang a song, Nora,
Of happier transports to be,
When I first said I lov'd only you, Nora,
An' you said you lov'd only me!

[NORA *kisses him.*]

[*A knock is heard at the door, Right; a pause as they listen.* NORA *clings closely to* CLITHEROE. *Another knock, more imperative than the first.*]

CLITHEROE. I wonder who can that be, now?

NORA [*a little nervous*]. Take no notice of it, Jack: they'll go away in a minute. [*Another knock, followed by a voice.*]

VOICE. Commandant Clitheroe, Commandant Clitheroe, are you there? A message from General Jim Connolly.

CLITHEROE. Damn it, it's Captain Brennan.

NORA [*anxiously*]. Don't mind him, don't mind, Jack. Don't break our happiness. . . . Pretend we're not in. Let us forget everything to-night but our two selves!

CLITHEROE [*reassuringly*]. Don't be alarmed, darling; I'll just see what he wants, an' send him about his business.

NORA [*tremulously*]. No, no. Please, Jack; don't open it. Please, for your own little Nora's sake!

CLITHEROE [*rising to open the door*]. Now don't be silly, Nora.

[CLITHEROE *opens door, and admits a young man in the full uniform of the Irish Citizen Army—green suit; slouch green hat caught up at one side by a small Red Hand badge; Sam Browne belt, with a revolver in the holster. He carries a letter in his hand. When he comes in he smartly salutes* CLITHEROE. *The young man is* CAPTAIN BRENNAN.]

CAPT. BRENNAN [*giving the letter to* CLITHEROE]. A dispatch from General Connolly.

CLITHEROE [*reading. While he is doing so,* BRENNAN*'s eyes are fixed on* NORA, *who droops as she sits on the lounge*]. "Commandant Clitheroe is to take command of the eighth battalion of the I.C.A. which will assemble to proceed to the meeting at nine o'clock. He is to see that all units are provided with full equipment; two days' rations and fifty rounds of ammunition. At two o'clock A.M. the army will leave Liberty Hall for a reconnaissance attack on Dublin Castle.—Com.-Gen. Connolly."

CLITHEROE. I don't understand this. Why does General Connolly call me Commandant?

CAPT. BRENNAN. Th' Staff appointed you Commandant, and th' General agreed with their selection.

CLITHEROE. When did this happen?

CAPT. BRENNAN. A fortnight ago.

CLITHEROE. How is it word was never sent to me?

CAPT. BRENNAN. Word was sent to you. . . . I meself brought it.

CLITHEROE. Who did you give it to, then?

CAPT. BRENNAN [*after a pause*]. I think I gave it to Mrs. Clitheroe, there.

CLITHEROE. Nora, d'ye hear that? [NORA *makes no answer.*]

CLITHEROE [*there is a note of hardness in his voice*]. Nora . . . Captain Brennan says he brought a letter to me from General Connolly, and that he gave it to you. . . . Where is it? What did you do with it?

NORA [*running over to him, and pleadingly putting her arms around him*]. Jack, please, Jack, don't go out to-night an' I'll tell you; I'll explain everything. . . . Send him away, an' stay with your own little red-lipp'd Nora.

CLITHEROE [*removing her arms from around him*]. None o' this nonsense, now; I want to know what you did with th' letter? [NORA *goes slowly to the lounge and sits down.*]

CLITHEROE [*angrily*]. Why didn't you give me th' letter? What did you do with it? . . . [*He shakes her by the shoulder*] What did you do with th' letter?

NORA [*flaming up*]. I burned it, I burned it! That's what I did with it! Is General Connolly an' th' Citizen Army goin' to be your only care? Is your home goin' to be only a place to rest in? Am I goin' to be only somethin' to provide merry-makin' at night for you? Your vanity'll be th' ruin of you an' me yet. . . . That's what's movin' you: because they've made an officer of you, you'll make a glorious cause of what you're doin', while your little red-lipp'd Nora can go on sittin' here, makin' a companion of th' loneliness of th' night!

CLITHEROE [*fiercely*]. You burned it, did you? [*He grips her arm*] Well, me good lady—

NORA. Let go—you're hurtin' me!

CLITHEROE. You deserve to be hurt. . . . Any letter that comes to me for th' future, take care that I get it. . . . D'ye hear—take care that I get it!

[*He goes to the chest of drawers and takes out a Sam Browne belt, which he puts on, and then puts a revolver in the holster. He puts on his hat, and looks towards* NORA. *While this dialogue is proceeding, and while* CLITHEROE *prepares himself,* BRENNAN *softly whistles "The Soldiers' Song".*]

CLITHEROE [*at door, about to go out*]. You needn't wait up for me; if I'm in at all, it won't be before six in th' morning.

NORA [*bitterly*]. I don't care if you never come back!

CLITHEROE [*to* CAPT. BRENNAN]. Come along, Ned.

[*They go out; there is a pause.* NORA *pulls the new hat from her head and with a bitter movement flings it to the other end of the room. There is a gentle knock at door, Right, which opens, and* MOLLSER *comes into the room. She is about fifteen, but looks to be only about ten, for the ravages of consumption have shrivelled her up. She is pitifully worn, walks feebly, and frequently coughs. She goes over to* NORA.]

MOLLSER [*to* NORA]. Mother's gone to th' meetin', an' I was feelin' terrible lonely, so I come down to see if you'd let me sit with you, thinkin' you mightn't be goin' yourself. . . . I do be terrible afraid I'll die sometime when I'm be meself. . . . I often envy you, Mrs. Clitheroe, seein' th' health you have, an' th' lovely place you have here, an' wondherin' if I'll ever be sthrong enough to be keepin' a home together for a man. Oh, this must be some more o' the Dublin Fusiliers flyin' off to the front.

[*Just before* MOLLSER *ceases to speak, there is heard in the distance the music of a brass band playing a regiment to the boat on the way to the front. The tune that is being played is "It's a Long Way to Tipperary"; as the band comes to the chorus, the regiment is swinging into the street by* NORA*'s house, and the voices of the soldiers can be heard lustily singing the chorus of the song.*]

It's a long way to Tipperary, it's a long way to go;
It's a long way to Tipperary, to th' sweetest girl I know!
Goodbye Piccadilly, farewell Leicester Square.
It's a long, long way to Tipperary, but my heart's right there!

[NORA *and* MOLLSER *remain silently listening. As the chorus ends and the music is faint in the distance again,* BESSIE BURGESS *appears at door, Right, which* MOLLSER *has left open.*]

BESSIE [*speaking in towards the room*]. There's th' men marchin' out into th' dhread dimness o' danger, while th' lice is crawlin' about feedin' on th' fatness o' the land! But yous'll not escape from th' arrow that flieth be night, or th' sickness that wasteth be day. . . . An' ladyship an' all, as some o' them may be, they'll be scattered abroad, like th' dust in th' darkness!

[BESSIE *goes away;* NORA *steals over and quietly shuts the door. She comes back to the lounge and wearily throws herself on it beside* MOLLSER.]

MOLLSER [*after a pause and a cough*]. Is there anybody goin', Mrs. Clitheroe, with a titther o' sense?

CURTAIN

ACT II

A commodious public-house at the corner of the street in which the meeting is being addressed from Platform No. 1. It is the south corner of the public-house that is visible to the audience. The counter, beginning at Back about one-fourth of the width of the space shown, comes across two-thirds of the length of the stage, and, taking a circular sweep, passes out of sight to Left. On the counter are beer-pulls, glasses, and a carafe. The other three-fourths of the Back is occupied by a tall, wide, two-paned window. Beside this window at the Right is a small, box-like, panelled snug. Next to the snug is a double swing door, the entrance to that particular end of the house. Farther on is a shelf on which customers may rest their drinks. Underneath the windows is a cushioned seat. Behind the counter at Back can be seen the shelves running the whole length of the counter. On these shelves can be seen the end (or the beginning) of rows of bottles. The BARMAN *is seen wiping the part of the counter which is in view.* ROSIE *is standing at the counter toying with what remains of a half of whisky in a wine-glass. She is a sturdy, well-shaped girl of twenty; pretty, and pert in manner. She is wearing a cream blouse, with an obviously suggestive glad neck; a grey tweed dress, brown stockings and shoes. The blouse and most of the dress are hidden by a black shawl. She has no hat, and in her hair is jauntily set a cheap, glittering, jewelled ornament. It is an hour later.*

BARMAN [*wiping counter*]. Nothin' much doin' in your line to-night, Rosie?

ROSIE. Curse o' God on th' haporth, hardly, Tom. There isn't much notice taken of a pretty petticoat of a night like this. . . . They're all in a holy mood. Th' solemn-lookin' dials on th' whole o' them an' they marchin' to th' meeting.' You'd think they were th' glorious company of th' saints, an' th' noble army of martyrs thrampin' through th' sthreets of paradise. They're all thinkin' of higher things than a girl's garthers. . . . It's a tremendous meetin'; four platforms they have—there's one o' them just outside opposite th' window.

BARMAN. Oh, ay; sure when th' speaker comes [*motioning with his hand*] to th' near end, here, you can see him plain, an' hear nearly everythin' he's spoutin' out of him.

ROSIE. It's no joke thrying' to make up fifty-five shillin's a week for your keep an' laundhry, an' then taxin' you a quid for your own room if you bring home a friend for th' night. . . . If I could only put by a couple of quid for a swankier outfit, everythin' in th' garden ud look lovely—

BARMAN. Whisht, till we hear what he's sayin'.

[*Through the window is silhouetted the figure of a tall man who is speaking to the crowd. The* BARMAN *and* ROSIE *look out of the window and listen.*]

THE VOICE OF THE MAN. It is a glorious thing to see arms in the hands of Irishmen. We must accustom ourselves to the thought of arms, we must accustom ourselves to the sight of arms, we must accustom ourselves to the use of arms. . . . Bloodshed is a cleansing and sanctifying thing, and the nation that regards it as the final horror has lost its manhood. . . . There are many things more horrible than bloodshed, and slavery is one of them!

[*The figure moves away towards the Right, and is lost to sight and hearing.*]

ROSIE. It's th' sacred thruth, mind you, what that man's afther sayin'.

BARMAN. If I was only a little younger, I'd be plungin' mad into th' middle of it!

ROSIE [*who is still looking out of the window*]. Oh, here's the two gems runnin' over again for their oil!

[PETER *and* FLUTHER *enter tumultuously. They are hot, and full and hasty with the things they have seen and heard. Emotion is bubbling up in them, so that when they drink, and when they speak, they drink and speak with the fullness of emotional passion.* PETER *leads the way to the counter.*]

PETER [*splutteringly to* BARMAN]. Two halves . . . [*To* FLUTHER] A meetin' like this always makes me feel as if I could dhrink Loch Erinn dhry!

FLUTHER. You couldn't feel any way else at a time like this when th' spirit of a man is pulsin' to be out fightin' for th' thruth with his feet thremblin' on th' way, maybe to th' gallows, an' his ears tinglin' with th' faint, far-away sound of burstin' rifle-shots that'll maybe whip th' last little shock o' life out of him that's left lingerin' in his body?

PETER. I felt a burnin' lump in me throat when I heard th' band playin' "The Soldiers' Song", rememberin' last hearin' it marchin' in military formation, with th' people starin' on both sides at us, carryin' with us th' pride an' resolution o' Dublin to th' grave of Wolfe Tone.

FLUTHER. Get th' Dublin men goin' an' they'll go on full force for anything that's thryin' to bar them away from what they're wantin', where th' slim thinkin' counthry boyo ud limp away from th' first faintest touch of compromization!

PETER [*hurriedly to the* BARMAN]. Two more, Tom! . . . [*To* FLUTHER] Th' memory of all th' things that was done, an' all th' things that was suffered be th' people, was boomin' in me brain. . . . Every nerve in me body was quiverin' to do somethin' desperate!

FLUTHER. Jammed as I was in th' crowd, I listened to th' speeches pattherin' on th' people's head, like rain fallin' on th' corn; every derogatory thought went out o' me mind, an' I said to meself, "You can die now, Fluther, for you've seen th' shadow-dhreams of th' past leppin' to life in th' bodies of livin' men that show, if we were without a titther o' courage for centuries, we're vice versa now!" Looka here. [*He stretches out his arm under* PETER*'s face and rolls up his sleeve.*] The blood was BOILIN' in me veins!

[*The silhouette of the tall figure again moves into the frame of the window speaking to the people.*]

PETER [*unaware, in his enthusiasm, of the speaker's appearance, to* FLUTHER]. I was burnin' to dhraw me sword, an' wave an' wave it over me—

FLUTHER [*overwhelming* PETER]. Will you stop your blatherin' for a minute, man, an' let us hear what he's sayin'!

VOICE OF THE MAN. Comrade soldiers of the Irish Volunteers and of the Citizen Army, we rejoice in this terrible war. The old heart of the earth needed to be warmed with the red wine of the battlefields. . . . Such august homage was never offered to God as this: the homage of millions of lives given gladly for love of country. And we must be ready to pour out the same red wine in the same glorious sacrifice, for without shedding of blood there is no redemption!

[*The figure moves out of sight and hearing.*]

FLUTHER [*gulping down the drink that remains in his glass, and rushing out*]. Come on, man; this to too good to be missed!

[PETER *finishes his drink less rapidly, and as he is going out wiping his mouth with the back of his hand he runs into* THE COVEY *coming in. He immediately erects his body like a young cock, and with his chin thrust forward, and a look of venomous dignity on his face, he marches out.*]

THE COVEY [*at counter*]. Give us a glass o' malt, for God's sake, till I stimulate meself from th' shock o' seein' th' sight that's afther goin' out!

ROSIE [*all business, coming over to the counter, and standing near* THE COVEY]. Another one for me, Tommy; [*to the* BARMAN] th' young gentleman's ordherin' it in th' corner of his eye.

[*The* BARMAN *brings the drink for* THE COVEY, *and leaves it on the counter.* ROSIE *whips it up.*]

BARMAN. Ay, houl' on there, houl' on there, Rosie!

ROSIE [*to the* BARMAN]. What are you houldin' on out o' you for? Didn't you hear th' young gentleman say that he couldn't refuse anything to a nice little bird? [*To* THE COVEY] Isn't that right, Jiggs? [THE COVEY *says nothing.*] Didn't I know, Tommy, it would be all right? It takes Rosie to size a young man up, an' tell th' thoughts that are thremblin' in his mind. Isn't that right, Jiggs?

[THE COVEY *stirs uneasily, moves a little farther away, and pulls his cap over his eyes.*]

ROSIE [*moving after him*]. Great meetin' that's gettin' held outside. Well, it's up to us all, anyway, to fight for our freedom.

THE COVEY [*to* BARMAN]. Two more, please. [*To* ROSIE] Freedom! What's th' use o' freedom, if it's not economic freedom?

ROSIE [*emphasizing with extended arm and moving finger*]. I used them very words just before you come in. "A lot o' thricksters," says I, "that wouldn't know what freedom was if they got it from their mother." . . . [*To* BARMAN] Didn't I, Tommy?

BARMAN. I disremember.

ROSIE. No, you don't disremember. Remember you said, yourself, it was all "only a flash in th' pan." Well, "flash in th' pan, or no flash in th' pan," says I, "they're not goin' to get Rosie Redmond," says I, "to fight for freedom that wouldn't be worth winnin' in a raffle!"

THE COVEY. There's only one freedom for th' workin' man: conthrol o' th' means o' production, rates of exchange, an' th' means of disthribution. [*Tapping* ROSIE *on the shoulder*] Look here, comrade, I'll leave here to-morrow night for you a copy of Jenersky's *Thesis on the Origin, Development, an' Consolidation of the Evolutionary Idea of the Proletariat*.

ROSIE [*throwing off her shawl on to the counter, and shoving an exemplified glad neck, which reveals a good deal of a white bosom*]. If y'ass Rosie, it's heart-breakin' to see a young fella thinkin' of anything, or admirin' anything, but silk thransparent stockin's showin' off the shape of a little lassie's legs!

[THE COVEY, *frightened, moves a little away.*]

ROSIE [*following on*]. Out in th' park in th' shade of a warm summery evenin', with your little darlin' bridie to be, kissin' an' cuddlin' [*she tries to put her arm around his neck*], kissin' an' cuddlin', ay?

THE COVEY [*frightened*]. Ay, what are you doin'? None o' that, now; none o' that. I've something else to do besides shinannickin' afther Judies!

[*He turns away, but* ROSIE *follows, keeping face to face with him.*]

ROSIE. Oh, little duckey, oh, shy little duckey! Never held a mot's hand, an' wouldn't know how to tittle a little Judy! [*She clips him under the chin.*] Tittle him undher th' chin, tittle him undher th' chin!

THE COVEY [*breaking away and running out*]. Ay, go on, now; I don't want to have any meddlin' with a lassie like you!

ROSIE [*enraged*]. Jasus, it's in a monasthery some of us ought to be, spendin' our holidays kneelin' on our adorers, tellin' our beads, an' knockin' hell out of our buzzums!

THE COVEY [*outside*]. Cuckoo-oo!

[PETER *and* FLUTHER *come in again, followed by* MRS. GOGAN, *carrying a baby in her arms. They go over to the counter.*]

PETER [*with plaintive anger*]. It's terrible that young Covey can't let me pass without proddin' at me! Did you hear him murmurin' "cuckoo' when we were passin'?

FLUTHER [*irritably*]. I wouldn't be everlastin' cockin' me ear to hear every little whisper that was floatin' around about me! It's my rule never to lose me temper till it would be dethrimental to keep it. There's nothin' derogatory in th' use o' th' word "cuckoo", is there?

PETER [*tearfully*]. It's not th' word; it's th' way he says it: he never says it straight out, but murmurs it with curious quiverin' ripples, like variations on a flute!

FLUTHER. Ah, what odds if he gave it with variations on a thrombone! [*To* MRS. GOGAN] What's yours goin' to be, ma'am?

MRS. GOGAN. Ah, a half o' malt, Fluther.

FLUTHER [*to* BARMAN]. Three halves, Tommy.

[*The* BARMAN *brings the drinks.*]

MRS GOGAN [*drinking*]. The foresthers' is a gorgeous dhress! I don't think I've seen nicer, mind you, in a pantomime. . . . Th' loveliest part of th' dhress, I think, is th' osthrichess plume. . . . When yous are goin' along, an' I see them wavin' an' noddin' an' waggin', I seem to be lookin' at each of yous hangin' at th' end of a rope, your eyes bulgin' an' your legs twistin' an' jerkin', gaspin' an' gaspin' for breath while yous are thryin' to die for Ireland!

FLUTHER. If any o' them is hangin' at the end of a rope, it won't be for Ireland!

PETER. Are you goin' to start th' young Covey's game o' proddin' an' twartin' a man? There's not many that's talkin' can say that for twenty-five years he never missed a pilgrimage to Bodenstown!

FLUTHER. You're always blowin' about goin' to Bodenstown. D'ye think no one but yourself ever went to Bodenstown?

PETER [*plaintively*]. I'm not blowin' about it; but there's not a year that I go there but I pluck a leaf off Tone's grave, an' this very day me prayer-book is nearly full of them.

FLUTHER [*scornfully*]. Then Fluther has a vice versa opinion of them that put ivy leaves into their prayer-books, scabbin' it on th' clergy, an' thryin' to out-do th' haloes o' th' saints be lookin' as if he was wearin' around his head a glittherin' aroree boree allis! [*Fiercely*] Sure, I don't care a damn if you slep' in Bodenstown! You can take your breakfast, dinner, an' tea on th' grave in Bodenstown, if you like, for Fluther!

MRS. GOGAN. Oh, don't start a fight, boys, for God's sake; I was only sayin' what a nice costume it is—nicer than th' kilts, for, God forgive me, I always think th' kilts is hardly decent.

FLUTHER. Ah, sure, when you'd look at him, you'd wondher whether th' man was makin' fun o' th' costume, or th' costume was makin' fun o' th' man!

BARMAN. Now, then, thry to speak asy, will yous? We don't want no shoutin' here.

[THE COVEY *followed by* BESSIE BURGESS *comes in. They go over to the opposite end of the counter, and direct their gaze on the other group.*]

THE COVEY [*to* BARMAN]. Two glasses o' malt.

PETER. There he is, now; I knew he wouldn't be long till he folleyed me in.

BESSIE [*speaking to* THE COVEY, *but really at the other party*]. I can't for th' life o' me undherstand how they can call themselves Catholics, when they won't lift a finger to help poor little Catholic Belgium.

MRS. GOGAN [*raising her voice*]. What about poor little Catholic Ireland?

BESSIE [*over to* MRS. GOGAN]. You mind your own business, ma'am, an' stupefy your foolishness be gettin' dhrunk.

PETER [*anxiously*]. Take no notice of her; pay no attention to her. She's just tormentin' herself towards havin' a row with somebody.

BESSIE. There's a storm of anger tossin' in me heart, thinkin' of all th' poor Tommies, an' with them me own son, dhrenched in water an' soaked in blood, gropin' their way to a shattherin' death, in a shower o' shells! Young men with th' sunny lust o' life beamin' in them, layin' down their white bodies, shredded into torn an' bloody pieces, on th' althar that God Himself has built for th' sacrifice of heroes!

MRS. GOGAN. Isn't it a nice thing to have to be listenin' to a lassie an' hangin' our heads in a dead silence, knowin' that some persons think more of a ball of malt than they do of th' blessed saints.

FLUTHER. Whisht; she's always dangerous an' derogatory when she's well oiled. Th' safest way to hindher her from havin' any enjoyment out of her spite, is to dip our thoughts into the fact of her bein' a female person that has moved out of th' sight of ordinary sensible people.

BESSIE. To look at some o' th' women that's knockin' about, now, is a thing to make a body sigh. . . . A woman on her own, dhrinkin' with a bevy o' men, is hardly an example to her sex. . . . A woman dhrinkin' with a woman is one thing, an' a woman dhrinkin' with herself is still a woman—flappers may be put in another category altogether—but a middle-aged married woman makin' herself th' centre of a circle of men is as a woman that is loud an' stubborn, whose feet abideth not in her own house.

THE COVEY [*to* BESSIE]. When I think of all th' problems in front o' th' workers, it makes me sick to be lookin' at oul' codgers goin' about dhressed up like green-accoutred figures gone asthray out of a toy-shop!

PETER. Gracious God, give me patience to be listenin' to that blasted young Covey proddin' at me from over at th' other end of th' shop!

MRS. GOGAN [*dipping her finger in the whisky, and moistening with it the lips of her baby*]. Cissie Gogan's a woman livin' for nigh on twenty-five years in her own room, an' beyond biddin' th' time o' day to her neighbours, never yet as much as nodded her head in th' direction of other people's business, while she knows some as are never content unless they're standin' senthry over other people's doin's!

[BESSIE *is about to reply, when the tall, dark figure is again silhouetted against the window, and the voice of the speaker is heard speaking passionately.*]

VOICE OF SPEAKER. The last sixteen months have been the most glorious in the history of Europe. Heroism has come back to the earth. War is a terrible thing, but war is not an evil thing. People in Ireland dread war because they do not know it. Ireland has not known the exhilaration of war for over a hundred years. When war comes to Ireland she must welcome it as she would welcome the Angel of God!

[*The figure passes out of sight and hearing.*]

THE COVEY [*towards all present*]. Dope, dope. There's only one war worth havin': th' war for th' economic emancipation of th' proletariat.

BESSIE. They may crow away out o' them; but it ud be fitther for some o' them to mend their ways, an' cease from havin' scouts out watchin' for th' comin' of th' Saint Vincent de Paul man, for fear they'd be nailed lowerin' a pint of beer, mockin' th' man with an angel face, shinin' with th' glamour of deceit an' lies!

MRS. GOGAN. An' a certain lassie standin' stiff behind her own door with her ears cocked listenin' to what's being said, stuffed till she's sthrained with envy of a neighbour thryin' for a few little things that may be got be hard sthrivin' to keep up to th' letther an' th' law, an' th' practices of th' Church!

PETER [*to* MRS. GOGAN]. If I was you, Mrs. Gogan, I'd parry her jabbin' remarks be a powerful silence that'll keep her tantalizin' words from penethratin' into your feelin's. It's always betther to leave these people to th' vengeance o' God!

BESSIE. Bessie Burgess doesn't put up to know much, never havin' a swaggerin' mind, thanks be to God, but goin' on packin' up knowledge accordin' to her conscience: precept upon precept, line upon line; here a little, an' there a little. But [*with a passionate swing of her shawl*], thanks be to Christ, she knows when she was got, where she was got, an' how she was got; while there's some she knows, decoratin' their finger with a well-polished weddin' ring, would be hard put to it if they were assed to show their weddin' lines!

MRS. GOGAN [*plunging out into the centre of the floor in a wild tempest of hysterical rage*]. Y' oul' rip of a blasted liar, me weddin' ring's been well earned be twenty years be th' side o' me husband, now takin' his rest in heaven, married to me be Father Dempsey, in th' Chapel o' Saint Jude's, in th' Christmas Week of eighteen hundhred an' ninety-five; an' any kid, livin' or dead, that Jinnie Gogan's had since, was got between th' bordhers of th' Ten Commandments! . . . An' that's more than some o' you can say that are kep' from th' dhread o' desthruction be a few drowsy virtues, that th' first whisper of temptation lulls into a sleep, that'll know one sin from another only on th' day of their last anointin', an' that use th' innocent light o' th' shinin' stars to dip into th' sins of a night's diversion!

BESSIE [*jumping out to face* MRS. GOGAN, *and bringing the palms of her hands together in sharp claps to emphasize her remarks*]. Liar to you, too, ma'am, y' oul' hardened thresspasser on other people's good nature, wizenin' up your soul in th' arts o' dodgeries, till every dhrop of respectability in a female is dhried up in her, lookin' at your ready-made manoeuverin' with th' menkind!

BARMAN. Here, there; here, there; speak easy there. No rowin' here, no rowin' here, now.

FLUTHER [*trying to calm* MRS. GOGAN]. Now Jinnie, Jinnie, it's a derogatory thing to be smirchin' a night like this with a row; it's rompin' with th' feelin's of hope we ought to be, instead o' bein' vice versa!

PETER [*trying to quiet* BESSIE]. I'm terrible dawny, Mrs. Burgess, an' a fight leaves me weak for a long time aftherwards. . . . Please, Mrs. Burgess, before there's damage done, thry to have a little respect for yourself.

BESSIE [*with a push of her hand that sends* PETER *tottering to the end of the shop*]. G'way, you little sermonizing, little yella-faced, little consequential, little pudgy, little bum, you!

MRS. GOGAN [*screaming*]. Fluther, leggo! I'm not goin' to keep an unresistin' silence, an' her scattherin' her festherin' words in me face, stirrin' up every dhrop of decency in a respectable female, with her restless rally o' lies that would make a saint say his prayer backwards!

BESSIE [*shouting*]. Ah, everybody knows well that th' best charity that can be shown to you is to hide th' thruth as much as our thrue worship of God Almighty will allow us!

MRS. GOGAN [*frantically*]. Here, houl' th' kid, one o' yous; houl' th' kid for a minute! There's nothin' for it but to show this lassie a lesson or two. . . . [*To* PETER] Here, houl' th' kid, you. [*Before* PETER *is aware of it, she places the infant in his arms.*]

MRS. GOGAN [*to* BESSIE, *standing before her in a fighting attitude*]. Come on, now, me loyal lassie, dyin' with grief for little Catholic Belgium! When Jinnie Gogan's done with you, you'll have a little leisure lyin' down to think an' pray for your king an' counthry!

BARMAN [*coming from behind the counter, getting between the women, and proceeding to push them towards the door*]. Here, now, since yous can't have a little friendly argument quietly, you'll get out o' this place in quick time. Go on, an' settle your differences somewhere else—I don't want to have another endorsement on me licence.

PETER [*anxiously, over to* MRS. GOGAN]. Here, take your kid back, ower this. How nicely I was picked, now, for it to be plumped into me arms!

THE COVEY. She knew who she was givin' it to, maybe.

PETER [*hotly to* THE COVEY]. Now, I'm givin' you fair warnin', me young Covey, to quit firin' your jibes an' jeers at me. . . . For one o' these days, I'll run out in front o' God Almighty an' take your sacred life!

BARMAN [*pushing* BESSIE *out after* MRS. GOGAN]. Go on, now; out you go.

BESSIE [*as she goes out*]. If you think, me lassie, that Bessie Burgess has an untidy conscience, she'll soon show you to th' differ!

PETER [*leaving the baby down on the floor*]. Ay, be Jasus, wait there, till I give her back her youngster! [*He runs to the door.*] Ay, there, ay! [*He comes back.*] There, she's afther goin' without her kid. What are we goin' to do with it, now?

THE COVEY. What are we goin' to do with it? Bring it outside an' show everybody what you're afther findin'!

PETER [*in a panic to* FLUTHER]. Pick it up, you, Fluther, an' run afther her with it, will you?

FLUTHER. What d'ye take Fluther for? You must think Fluther's a right gom. D'ye think Fluther's like yourself, destitute of a titther of undherstandin'?

BARMAN [*imperatively to* PETER]. Take it up, man, an' run out afther her with it, before she's gone too far. You're not goin' to leave th' bloody thing here, are you?

PETER [*plaintively, as he lifts up the baby*]. Well, God Almighty, give me patience with all th' scorners, tormentors, an' twarters that are always an' ever thryin' to goad me into prayin' for their blindin' an' blastin' an' burnin' in th' world to come!

[*He goes out.*]

FLUTHER. God, it's a relief to get rid o' that crowd. Women is terrible when they start to fight. There's no holdin' them back. [*To* THE COVEY] Are you goin' to have anything?

THE COVEY. Ah, I don't mind if I have another half.

FLUTHER [*to* BARMAN]. Two more, Tommy, me son.

[*The* BARMAN *gets the drinks.*]

FLUTHER. You know, there's no conthrollin' a woman when she loses her head.

[ROSIE *enters and goes over to the counter on the side nearest to* FLUTHER.]

ROSIE [*to* BARMAN]. Divil a use o' havin' a thrim little leg on a night like this; things was never worse. . . . Give us a half till to-morrow, Tom, duckey.

BARMAN [*coldly*]. No more to-night, Rosie; you owe me for three already.

ROSIE [*combatively*]. You'll be paid, won't you?

BARMAN. I hope so.

ROSIE. You hope so! Is that th' way with you, now?

FLUTHER [*to* BARMAN]. Give her one; it'll be all right.

ROSIE [*clapping* FLUTHER *on the back*]. Oul' sport!

FLUTHER. Th' meetin' should be soon over, now.

THE COVEY. Th' sooner th' betther. It's all a lot o' blasted nonsense, comrade.

FLUTHER. Oh, I wouldn't say it was all nonsense. Afther all, Fluther can remember th' time, an' him only a dawny chiselur, bein' taught at his mother's knee to be faithful to th' Shan Van Vok!

THE COVEY. That's all dope, comrade; th' sort o' thing that workers are fed on be th' Boorzwawzee.

FLUTHER [*a little sharply*]. What's all dope? Though I'm sayin' it that shouldn't: [*catching his cheek with his hand, and pulling down the flesh from the eye*] d'ye see that mark there, undher me eye? . . . A sabre slice from a dragoon in O'Connell Street! [*Thrusting his head forward towards* ROSIE] Feel that dint in th' middle o' me nut!

ROSIE [*rubbing* FLUTHER'*s head, and winking at* THE COVEY]. My God, there's a holla!

FLUTHER [*putting on his hat with quiet pride*]. A skelp from a bobby's baton at a Labour meetin' in th' Phoenix Park!

THE COVEY. He must ha' hitten you in mistake. I don't know what you ever done for th' Labour movement.

FLUTHER [*loudly*]. D'ye not? Maybe, then, I done as much, an' know as much about th' Labour movement as th' chancers that are blowin' about it!

BARMAN. Speak easy, Fluther, thry to speak easy.

THE COVEY. There's no necessity to get excited about it, comrade.

FLUTHER [*more loudly*]. Excited? Who's gettin excited? There's no one gettin' excited! It would take something more than a thing like you to flutther a feather o' Fluther. Blatherin', an', when all is said, you know as much as th' rest in th' wind up!

THE COVEY. Well, let us put it to th' test, then, an' see what you know about th' Labour movement: what's the mechanism of exchange?

FLUTHER [*roaring, because he feels he is beaten*]. How th' hell do I know what it is? There's nothin' about that in th' rules of our Thrades Union!

BARMAN. For God's sake, thry to speak easy, Fluther.

THE COVEY. What does Karl Marx say about th' Relation of Value to th' Cost o' Production?

FLUTHER [*angrily*]. What th' hell do I care what he says? I'm Irishman enough not to lose me head be follyin' foreigners!

BARMAN. Speak easy, Fluther.

THE COVEY. It's only waste o' time talkin' to you, comrade.

FLUTHER. Don't be comradin' me, mate. I'd be on me last legs if I wanted you for a comrade.

ROSIE [*to* THE COVEY]. It seems a highly rediculous thing to hear a thing that's only an inch or two away from a kid, swingin' heavy words about he doesn't know th' meanin' of, an' uppishly thryin' to down a man like Misther Fluther here, that's well flavoured in th' knowledge of th' world he's livin' in.

THE COVEY [*savagely to* ROSIE]. Nobody's askin' you to be buttin' in with your prate. . . . I have you well taped, me lassie. . . . Just you keep your opinions for your own place. . . . It'll be a long time before th' Covey takes any insthructions or reprimandin' from a prostitute!

ROSIE [*wild with humiliation*]. You louse, you louse, you! . . . You're no man. . . . You're no man . . . I'm a woman, anyhow, an' if I'm a prostitute aself, I have me feelin's. . . . Thryin' to put his arm around me a minute ago, an' givin' me th' glad eye, th' little wriglin' lump o' desolation turns on me now, because he saw there was nothin' doin'. . . . You louse, you! If I was a man, or you were a woman, I'd bate th' puss o' you!

BARMAN. Ay, Rosie, ay! You'll have to shut your mouth altogether, if you can't learn to speak easy!

FLUTHER [*to* ROSIE]. Houl' on there, Rosie; houl' on there. There's no necessity to flutther yourself when you're with Fluther. . . . Any lady that's in th' company of Fluther is goin' to get a fair hunt. . . . This is outside your province. . . . I'm not goin' to let you demean yourself be talkin' to a tittherin' chancer. . . . Leave this to Fluther—this is a man's job. [*To* THE COVEY] Now, if you've anything to say, say it to Fluther, an', let me tell you, you're not goin' to be pass-remarkable to any lady in my company.

THE COVEY. Sure I don't care if you were runnin' all night afther your Mary o' th' Curlin' Hair, but, when you start tellin' luscious lies about what you done for th' Labour movement, it's nearly time to show y'up!

FLUTHER [*fiercely*]. Is it you show Fluther up? G'way, man, I'd beat two o' you before me breakfast!

THE COVEY [*contemptuously*]. Tell us where you bury your dead, will you?

FLUTHER [*with his face stuck into the face of* THE COVEY]. Sing a little less on th' high note, or, when I'm done with you, you'll put a Christianable consthruction on things, I'm tellin' you!

THE COVEY. You're a big fella, you are.

FLUTHER [*tapping* THE COVEY *threateningly on the shoulder*]. Now, you're temptin' Providence when you're temptin' Fluther!

THE COVEY [*losing his temper, and bawling*]. Easy with them hands, there, easy with them hands! You're startin' to take a little risk when you commence to paw the Covey!

[FLUTHER *suddenly springs into the middle of the shop, flings his hat into the corner, whips off his coat, and begins to paw the air.*]

FLUTHER [*roaring at the top of his voice*]. Come on, come on, you lowser; put your mits up now, if there's a man's blood in you! Be God, in a few minutes you'll see some snots flyin' around, I'm tellin' you. . . . When Fluther's done with you, you'll have a vice versa opinion of him! Come on, now, come on!

BARMAN [*running from behind the counter and catching hold of* THE COVEY]. Here, out you go, me little bowsey. Because you got a couple o' halves you think you can act as you like. [*He pushes* THE COVEY *to the door*] Fluther's a friend o' mine, an' I'll not have him insulted.

THE COVEY [*struggling with the* BARMAN]. Ay, leggo, leggo there; fair hunt, give a man a fair hunt! One minute with him is all I ask; one minute alone with him, while you're runnin' for th' priest an' th' doctor.

FLUTHER [*to the* BARMAN]. Let him go, let him go, Tom: let him open th' door to sudden death if he wants to!

BARMAN [*to* THE COVEY]. Go on, out you go an' do th' bowsey somewhere else. [*He pushes* THE COVEY *out and comes back.*]

ROSIE [*getting* FLUTHER*'s hat as he is putting on his coat*]. Be God, you put th' fear o' God in his heart that time! I thought you'd have to be dug out of him. . . . Th' way you lepped out without any of your fancy side-steppin'! "Men like Fluther," say I to meself, "is gettin' scarce nowadays."

FLUTHER [*with proud complacency*]. I wasn't goin' to let meself be malignified by a chancer. . . . He got a little bit too derogatory for Fluther. . . . Be God, to think of a cur like that comin' to talk to a man like me!

ROSIE [*fixing on his hat*]. Did j'ever!

FLUTHER. He's lucky he got off safe. I hit a man last week, Rosie, an' he's fallin' yet!

ROSIE. Sure, you'd ha' broken him in two if you'd ha' hitten him one clatther!

FLUTHER [*amorously, putting his arm around* ROSIE]. Come on into th' snug, me little darlin', an' we'll have a few dhrinks before I see you home.

ROSIE. Oh, Fluther, I'm afraid you're a terrible man for th' women.

[*They go into the snug as* CLITHEROE, CAPTAIN BRENNAN, *and* LIEUT. LANGON *of the Irish Volunteers enter hurriedly.* CAPTAIN BRENNAN *carries the banner of The Plough and the Stars, and* LIEUT. LANGON *a green, white, and orange Tri-colour. They are in a state of emotional excitement. Their faces are flushed and their eyes sparkle; they speak rapidly, as if unaware of the meaning of what they said. They have been mesmerized by the fervency of the speeches.*]

CLITHEROE [*almost pantingly*]. Three glasses o' port!

[*The* BARMAN *brings the drinks.*]

CAPT. BRENNAN. We won't have long to wait now.

LIEUT. LANGON. Th' time is rotten ripe for revolution.

CLITHEROE. You have a mother, Langon.

LIEUT. LANGON. Ireland is greater than a mother.

CAPT. BRENNAN. You have a wife, Clitheroe.

CLITHEROE. Ireland is greater than a wife.

LIEUT. LANGON. Th' time for Ireland's battle is now—th' place for Ireland's battle is here.

[*The tall, dark figure again is silhouetted against the window. The three men pause and listen.*]

VOICE OF THE MAN. Our foes are strong, but strong as they are, they cannot undo the miracles of God, who ripens in the heart of young men the seeds sown by the young men of a former generation. They think they have pacified Ireland; think they have foreseen everything; think they have provided against everything; but the fools, the fools, the fools!—they have left us our Fenian dead, and, while Ireland holds these graves, Ireland, unfree, shall never be at peace!

CAPT. BRENNAN [*catching up The Plough and the Stars*]. Imprisonment for th' Independence of Ireland!

LIEUT. LANGON [*catching up the Tri-colour*]. Wounds for th' Independence of Ireland!

CLITHEROE. Death for th' Independence of Ireland!

THE THREE [*together*]. So help us God!

[*They drink. A bugle blows the Assembly. They hurry out. A pause.* FLUTHER *and* ROSIE *come out of the snug;* ROSIE *is linking* FLUTHER, *who is a little drunk. Both are in a merry mood.*]

ROSIE. Come on home, ower o' that, man. Are you afraid or what? Are you goin' to come home, or are you not?

FLUTHER. Of course I'm goin' home. What ud ail me that I wouldn't go?

ROSIE [*lovingly*]. Come on, then, oul' sport.

OFFICER'S VOICE [*giving command outside*]. Irish Volunteers, by th' right, quick march!

ROSIE [*putting her arm round* FLUTHER *and singing*]:

I once had a lover, a tailor, but he could do nothin' for me,
An' then I fell in with a sailor as strong an' as wild as th' sea.
We cuddled an' kissed with devotion, till th' night from th' mornin' had fled;
An' there, to our joy, a bright bouncin' boy
Was dancin' a jig in th' bed!

Dancin' a jig in th' bed, an' bawlin' for butther an' bread.
An' there, to our joy, a bright bouncin' boy
Was dancin' a jig in th' bed!

[*They go out with their arms round each other.*]

CLITHEROE'S VOICE [*in command outside*]. Dublin Battalion of the Irish Citizen Army, by th' right, quick march!

CURTAIN

ACT III

*The corner house in a street of tenements: it is the home of the Clitheroes. The house is a long, gaunt, five-story tenement; its brick front is chipped and scarred with age and neglect. The wide and heavy hall door, flanked by two pillars, has a look of having been charred by a fire in the distant past. The door lurches a little to one side, disjointed by the continual and reckless banging when it is being closed by most of the residents. The diamond-paned fanlight is destitute of a single pane, the framework alone remaining. The windows, except the two looking into the front parlour [*CLITHEROE*'s room], are grimy, and are draped with fluttering and soiled fragments of lace curtains. The front parlour windows are hung with rich,* *comparatively, casement cloth. Five stone steps lead from the door to the path on the street. Branching on each side are railings to prevent people from falling into the area. At the left corner of the house runs a narrow lane, bisecting the street, and connecting it with another of the same kind. At the corner of the lane is a street lamp.*

As the house is revealed, MRS. GOGAN *is seen helping* MOLLSER *to a chair, which stands on the path beside the railings, at the left side of the steps. She then wraps a shawl around* MOLLSER*'s shoulders. It is some months later.*

MRS. GOGAN [*arranging shawl around* MOLLSER]. Th' sun'll do you all th' good in th' world. A few more weeks o' this weather, an' there's no knowin' how well you'll be. . . . Are you comfy, now?

MOLLSER [*weakly and wearily*]. Yis, ma; I'm all right.

MRS. GOGAN. How are you feelin'?

MOLLSER. Betther, ma, betther. If th' horrible sinkin' feelin' ud go, I'd be all right.

MRS. GOGAN. Ah, I wouldn't put much pass on that. Your stomach maybe's out of ordher. . . . Is th' poor breathin' any betther, d'ye think?

MOLLSER. Yis, yis, ma; a lot betther.

MRS. GOGAN. Well, that's somethin' anyhow. . . . With th' help o' God, you'll be on th' mend from this out. . . . D'your legs feel any sthronger undher you, d'ye think?

MOLLSER [*irritably*]. I can't tell, ma. I think so. . . . A little.

MRS. GOGAN. Well, a little aself is somethin'. . . . I thought I heard you coughin' a little more than usual last night. . . . D'ye think you were?

MOLLSER. I wasn't, ma, I wasn't.

MRS. GOGAN. I thought I heard you, for I was kep' awake all night with th' shootin'. An' thinkin' o' that madman, Fluther, runnin' about through th' night lookin' for Nora Clitheroe to bring her back when he heard she'd gone to folly her husband, an' in dhread any minute he might come staggerin' in covered with bandages, splashed all over with th' red of his own blood, an' givin' us barely time to bring th' priest to hear th' last whisper of his final confession, as his soul was passin' through th' dark doorway o' death into th' way o' th' wondherin' dead. . . . You don't feel cold, do you?

MOLLSER. No, ma; I'm all right.

MRS. GOGAN. Keep your chest well covered, for that's th' delicate spot in you . . . if there's any danger, I'll whip you in again. . . . [*Looking up the street*] Oh, here's th' Covey an' oul' Pether hurryin' along. God Almighty, sthrange things is happenin' when them two is pullin' together.

[THE COVEY *and* PETER *come in, breathless and excited.*]

MRS. GOGAN [*to the two men*]. Were yous far up th' town? Did yous see any sign o' Fluther or Nora? How is things lookin'? I hear they're blazin' away out o' th' G.P.O. That th' Tommies is sthretched in heaps around Nelson's Pillar an' th' Parnell Statue, an' that th' pavin' sets in O'Connell Street is nearly covered be pools o' blood.

PETER. We seen no sign o' Nora or Fluther anywhere.

MRS. GOGAN. We should ha' held her back be main force from goin' to look for her husband. . . . God knows what's happened to her—I'm always seein' her sthretched on her back in some hospital, moanin' with th' pain of a bullet in her vitals, an' nuns thryin' to get her to take a last look at th' crucifix!

THE COVEY. We can do nothin'. You can't stick your nose into O'Connell Street, an' Tyler's is on fire.

PETER. An' we seen th' Lancers—

THE COVEY [*interrupting*]. Throttin' along, heads in th' air; spurs an' sabres jinglin', an' lances quiverin', an lookin' as if they were assin' themselves, "Where's these blighters, till we get a prod at them?" when there was a volley from th' Post Office that stretched half o' them, an' sent th' rest gallopin' away wondherin' how far they'd have to go before they'd feel safe.

PETER [*rubbing his hands*]. "Damn it," says I to meself, "this looks like business!"

THE COVEY. An' then out comes General Pearse an' his staff, an', standin' in th' middle o' th' street, he reads th' Proclamation.

MRS. GOGAN. What proclamation?

PETER. Declarin' an Irish Republic.

MRS. GOGAN. Go to God!

PETER. The gunboat *Helga's* shellin' Liberty Hall, an' I hear the people livin' on th' quays had to crawl on their bellies to Mass with th' bullets that were flyin' around from Boland's Mills.

MRS. GOGAN. God bless us, what's goin' to be th' end of it all!

BESSIE [*looking out of the top window*]. Maybe yous are satisfied now; maybe yous are satisfied now. Go on an' get guns if yous are men—Johnny get your gun, get your gun, get your gun! Yous are all nicely shanghaied now; th' boyo hasn't a sword on his thigh now! Oh, yous are all nicely shanghaied now!

MRS. GOGAN [*warningly to* PETER *and* THE COVEY]. S-s-sh, don't answer her. She's th' right oul' Orange bitch! She's been chantin' "Rule, Britannia" all th' mornin'.

PETER. I hope Fluther hasn't met with any accident, he's such a wild card.

MRS. GOGAN. God grant it; but last night I dreamt I seen gettin' carried into th' house a sthretcher with a figure lyin' on it, stiff an' still, dhressed in th' habit of Saint Francis. An, then, I heard th' murmurs of a crowd no one could see sayin' th' litany for th' dead; an' then it got so dark that nothin' was seen but th' white face of th' corpse, gleamin' like a white wather-lily floatin' on th' top of the dark lake. Then a tiny whisper thrickled into me ear, sayin', "Isn't the face very like th' face o' Fluther?" an' then, with a thremblin' flutther, th' dead lips opened, an', although I couldn't hear, I knew they were sayin', "Poor oul' Fluther, afther havin' handed in his gun at last, his shakin' soul moored in th' place where th' wicked are at rest an' th' weary cease from throublin'."

PETER [*who has put on a pair of spectacles, and has been looking down the street*]. Here they are, be God, here they are; just afther turnin' th' corner—Nora an' Fluther!

THE COVEY. She must be wounded or something—he seems to be carryin' her.

[FLUTHER *and* NORA *enter.* FLUTHER *has his arm around her and is half leading, half carrying her in. Her eyes are dim and hollow, her face pale and strained-looking; her hair is tossed, and her clothes are dusty.*]

MRS. GOGAN [*running over to them*]. God bless us, is it wounded y'are, Mrs. Clitheroe, or what?

FLUTHER. Ah, she's all right, Mrs. Gogan; only worn out from thravellin' an' want o' sleep. A night's rest, now, an' she'll be as fit as a fiddle. Bring her in, an' make her lie down.

MRS. GOGAN [*to* NORA]. Did you hear e'er a whisper o' Mr. Clitheroe?

NORA [*wearily*]. I could find him nowhere, Mrs. Gogan. None o' them would tell me where he was. They told me I shamed my husband an' th' women of Ireland be carryin' on as I was. . . . They said th' women must learn to be brave an' cease to be cowardly. . . . Me who risked more for love than they would risk for hate. . . . [*Raising her voice in hysterical protest*] My Jack will be killed, my Jack will be killed! . . . He is to be butchered as a sacrifice to th' dead!

BESSIE [*from upper window*]. Yous are all nicely shanghaied now! Sorra mend th' lasses that have been kissin' an' cuddlin' their boys into th' sheddin' of blood! . . . Fillin' their minds with fairy tales that had no beginnin', but please God, 'll have a bloody quick endin'! . . . Turnin' bitther into sweet, an' sweet into bitther. . . . Stabbin' in th' back th' men that are dyin' in th' threnches for them! It's a bad thing for any one that thries to jilt th' Ten Commandments, for judgements are prepared for scorners an' sthripes for th' back o' fools! [*Going away from window as she sings*]:

Rule, Britannia, Britannia rules th'
waves,
Britons never, never, never shall be slaves!

FLUTHER [*with a roar up at the window*]. Y'ignorant oul' throllope, you!

MRS. GOGAN [*to* NORA]. He'll come home safe enough to you, you'll find, Mrs. Clitheroe; afther all, there's a power o' women that's handed over sons an' husbands to take a runnin' risk in th' fight they're wagin'.

NORA. I can't help thinkin' every shot fired 'll be fired at Jack, an' every shot fired at Jack 'll be fired at me. What do I care for th' others? I can think only of me own self. . . . An' there's no woman gives a son or a husband to be killed—if they say it, they're lyin', lyin', against God, Nature, an' against themselves! . . . One blasted hussy at a barricade told me to go home an' not be thryin' to dishearten th' men. . . . That I wasn't worthy to bear a son to a man that was out fightin' for freedom. . . . I clawed at her, an' smashed her in th' face till we were separated. . . . I was pushed down th' street, an' I cursed them—cursed the rebel ruffians an' Volunteers that had dhragged me ravin' mad into th' sthreets to seek me husband!

PETER. You'll have to have patience, Nora. We all have to put up with twarthers an' tormentors in this world.

THE COVEY. If they were fightin' for anything worth while, I wouldn't mind.

FLUTHER [*to* NORA]. Nothin' derogatory 'll happen to Mr. Clitheroe. You'll find, now, in th' finish up it'll be vice versa.

NORA. Oh, I know that wherever he is, he's thinkin' of wantin' to be with me. I know he's longin' to be passin' his hand through me hair, to be caressin' me neck, to fondle me hand an' to feel me kisses clingin' to his mouth. . . . An' he stands wherever he is because he's brave? [*Vehemently*] No, but because he's a coward, a coward, a coward!

MRS. GOGAN. Oh, they're not cowards anyway.

NORA [*with denunciatory anger*]. I tell you they're afraid to say they're afraid! . . . Oh, I saw it, I saw it, Mrs. Gogan. . . . At th' barricade in North King Street I saw fear glowin' in all their eyes. . . . An' in th' middle o' th' sthreet was somethin' huddled up in a horrible tangled heap. . . . His face was jammed again t' stones, an' his arm was twisted round his back. . . . An' every twist of his body was a cry against th' terrible thing that had happened to him. . . . An' I saw they were afraid to look at it. . . . An' some o' them laughed at me, but th' laugh was a frightened one. . . . An' some o' them shouted at me, but th' shout had in it th' shiver o' fear. . . . I tell you they were afraid, afraid, afraid!

MRS. GOGAN [*leading her towards the house*]. Come on in, dear. If you'd been a little longer together, th' wrench asundher wouldn't have been so sharp.

NORA. Th' agony I'm in since he left me has thrust away every rough thing he done, an' every unkind word he spoke; only th' blossoms that grew out of our lives are before me now; shakin' their colours before me face, an' breathin' their sweet scent on every thought springin' up in me mind, till, sometimes, Mrs. Gogan, sometimes I think I'm goin' mad!

MRS. GOGAN. You'll be a lot betther when you have a little lie down.

NORA [*turning towards* FLUTHER *as she is going in*]. I don't know what I'd have done, only for Fluther. I'd have been lyin' in th' streets, only for him. . . . [*As she goes in*] They have dhriven away th' little happiness life had to spare for me. He has gone from me for ever, for ever. . . . Oh, Jack, Jack, Jack!

[*She is led in by* MRS. GOGAN *as* BESSIE *comes out with a shawl around her shoulders. She passes by them with her head in the air. When they have gone in, she gives a mug of milk to* MOLLSER *silently.*]

FLUTHER. Which of yous has th' tossers?

THE COVEY. I have.

BESSIE [*as she is passing them to go down the street*]. You an' your Leadhers an' their sham-battle soldiers has landed a body in a nice way, havin' to go an' ferret out a bit o' bread God knows where. . . . Why aren't yous in th' G.P.O. if yous are men? It's paler an' paler yous are gettin'. . . . A lot o' vipers, that's what th' Irish people is! [*She goes out.*]

FLUTHER. Never mind her. . . . [*To* THE COVEY] Make a start an' keep us from th' sin o' idleness. [*To* MOLLSER] Well, how are you to-day, Mollser, oul' son? What are you dhrinkin', milk?

MOLLSER. Grand, Fluther, grand, thanks. Yis, milk.

FLUTHER. You couldn't get a betther thing down you. . . . This turn-up has done one good thing, anyhow; you can't get dhrink anywhere, an' if it lasts a week, I'll be so used to it that I won't think of a pint.

THE COVEY [*who has taken from his pocket two worn coins and a thin strip of wood about four inches long*]. What's th' bettin'?

PETER. Heads, a juice.

FLUTHER. Harps, a tanner.

[THE COVEY *places the coins on the strip of wood, and flips them up into the air. As they jingle on the ground the distant boom of a big gun is heard. They stand for a moment listening.*]

FLUTHER. What th' hell's that?

THE COVEY. It's like th' boom of a big gun!

FLUTHER. Surely to God they're not goin' to use artillery on us?

THE COVEY [*scornfully*]. Not goin'! [*Vehemently*] Wouldn't they use anything on us, man?

FLUTHER. Aw, holy Christ, that's not playin' th' game!

PETER [*plaintively*]. What would happen if a shell landed here now?

THE COVEY [*ironically*]. You'd be off to heaven in a fiery chariot.

PETER. In spite of all th' warnin's that's ringin' around us, are you goin' to start your pickin' at me again?

FLUTHER. Go on, toss them again, toss them again. . . . Harps, a tanner.

PETER. Heads, a juice. [THE COVEY *tosses the coins.*]

FLUTHER [*as the coins fall*]. Let them roll, let them roll. Heads, be God!

[BESSIE *runs in excitedly. She has a new hat on her head, a fox fur round her neck over her shawl, three umbrellas under her right arm, and a box of biscuits under her left. She speaks rapidly and breathlessly.*]

BESSIE. They're breakin' into th' shops, they're breakin' into th' shops! Smashin' th' windows, battherin' in th' doors, an' whippin' away everything! An' th' Volunteers is firin' on them. I seen two men an' a lassie pushin' a piano down th' sthreet, an' th' sweat rollin' off them thryin' to get it up on th' pavement; an' an oul' wan that must ha' been seventy lookin' as if she'd dhrop every minute with th' dint o' heart beatin', thryin' to pull a big double bed out of a broken shop-window! I was goin' to wait till I dhressed meself from th' skin out.

MOLLSER [*to* BESSIE, *as she is going in*]. Help me in, Bessie; I'm feelin' curious.

[BESSIE *leaves the looted things in the house, and, rapidly returning, helps* MOLLSER *in.*]

THE COVEY. Th' selfishness of that one—she waited till she got all she could carry before she'd come to tell anyone!

FLUTHER [*running over to the door of the house and shouting in to* BESSIE]. Ay, Bessie, did you hear of e'er a pub gettin' a shake up?

BESSIE [*inside*]. I didn't hear o' none.

FLUTHER [*in a burst of enthusiasm*]. Well, you're goin' to hear of one soon!

THE COVEY. Come on, man, an' don't be wastin' time.

PETER [*to them as they are about to run off*]. Ay, ay, are you goin' to leave me here?

FLUTHER. Are you goin' to leave yourself here?

PETER [*anxiously*]. Didn't yous hear her sayin' they were firin' on them?

THE COVEY AND FLUTHER [*together*]. Well?

PETER. Supposin' I happened to be potted?

FLUTHER. We'd give you a Christian burial, anyhow.

THE COVEY [*ironically*]. Dhressed up in your regimentals.

PETER [*to* THE COVEY, *passionately*]. May th' all-lovin' God give you a hot knock one o' these days, me young Covey, tuthorin' Fluther up now to be tiltin' at me, an' crossin' me with his mockeries an' jibin'!

[*A fashionalby dressed, middle-aged, stout woman comes hurriedly in, and makes for the group. She is almost fainting with fear.*]

THE WOMAN. For Gawd's sake, will one of you kind men show any safe way for me to get to Wrathmines? . . . I was foolish enough to visit a friend, thinking the howl thing was a joke, and now I cawn't get a car or a tram to take me home—isn't it awful?

FLUTHER. I'm afraid, ma'am, one way is as safe as another.

WOMAN. And what am I gowing to do? Oh, isn't this awful? . . . I'm so different from others. . . . The mowment I hear a shot, my legs give way under me—I cawn't stir, I'm paralysed—isn't it awful?

FLUTHER [*moving away*]. It's a derogatory way to be, right enough, ma'am.

WOMAN [*catching* FLUTHER'*s coat*]. Creeping along the street there, with my head down and my eyes half shut, a bullet whizzed past within an inch of my nowse. . . . I had to lean against the wall for a long time, gasping for breath—I nearly passed away—it was awful! . . . I wonder, would you kind men come some of the way and see me safe?

FLUTHER. I have to go away, ma'am, to thry an' save a few things from th' burnin' buildin's.

THE COVEY. Come on, then, or there won't be anything left to save.

[THE COVEY *and* FLUTHER *hurry away*.]

WOMAN [*to* PETER]. Wasn't it an awful thing for me to leave my friend's house? Wasn't it an idiotic thing to do? . . . I haven't the slightest idea where I am. . . . You have a kind face, sir. Could you possibly come and pilot me in the direction of Wrathmines?

PETER [*indignantly*]. D'ye think I'm goin' to risk me life throttin' in front of you? An' maybe get a bullet that would gimme a game leg or something that would leave me a jibe an' a jeer to Fluther an' th' young Covey for th' rest o' me days!

[*With an indignant toss of his head he walks into the house.*]

THE WOMAN [*going out*]. I know I'll fall down in a dead faint if I hear another shot go off anyway near me—isn't it awful!

[MRS. GOGAN *comes out of the house pushing a pram before her. As she enters the street,* BESSIE *rushes out, follows* MRS. GOGAN, *and catches hold of the pram, stopping* MRS. GOGAN'*s progress.*]

BESSIE. Here, where are you goin' with that? How quick you were, me lady, to clap your eyes on th' pram. . . . Maybe you don't know that Mrs. Sullivan, before she went to spend Easther with her people in Dunboyne, gave me sthrict injunctions to give an accasional look to see if it was still standin' where it was left in th' corner of th' lobby.

MRS. GOGAN. That remark of yours, Mrs. Bessie Burgess, requires a little considheration, seein' that th' pram was left on our lobby, an' not on yours; a foot or two a little to th' left of th' jamb of me own room door; nor is it needful to mention th' name of th' person that gave a squint to see if it was there th' first thing in th' morning', an' th' last thing in th' stillness o' th' night; never failin' to realize that her eyes couldn't be goin' wrong, be sthretchin' out her arm an' runnin' her hand over th' pram, to make sure that th' sight was no deception! Moreover, somethin's tellin' me that th' runnin' hurry of an inthrest you're takin' in it now is a sudden ambition to use th' pram for a purpose that a loyal woman of law an' ordher would stagger away from!

[*She gives the pram a sudden push that pulls* BESSIE *forward.*]

BESSIE [*still holding the pram*]. There's not as much as one body in th' house that doesn't know that it wasn't Bessie Burgess that was always shakin' her voice complainin' about people leavin' bassinettes in th' way of them that, week in an' week out, had to pay their rent, an' always had to find a regular accommodation for her own furniture in her own room. . . . An' as for law an' ordher, puttin' aside th' harp an' shamrock, Bessie Burgess 'll have as much respect as she wants for th' lion an' unicorn!

PETER [*appearing at the door*]. I think I'll go with th' pair of yous an' see th' fun. A fella might as well chance it, anyhow.

MRS. GOGAN [*taking no notice of* PETER, *and pushing the pram on another step*]. Take your rovin' lumps o' hands from pattin' th' bassinette, if you please, ma'am; an', steppin' from th' threshold of good manners, let me tell you, Mrs. Burgess, that's it's a fat wondher to Jennie Gogan that a lady-like singer o' hymns like yourself would lower her thoughts from sky-thinkin' to sthretch out her arm in a sly-seekin' way to pinch anything dhriven asthray in th' confusion of th' battle our boys is makin' for th' freedom of their counthry!

PETER [*laughing and rubbing his hands together*]. Hee, hee, hee, hee, hee! I'll go with th' pair o' yous an' give yous a hand.

MRS. GOGAN [*with a rapid turn of her head as she shoves the pram forward*]. Get up in th' prambulator an' we'll wheel you down.

BESSIE [*to* MRS. GOGAN]. Poverty an' hardship has sent Bessie Burgess to abide with sthrange company, but she always knew them she had to live with from backside to breakfast time; an' she can tell them, always havin' had a Christian kinch on her conscience, that a passion for thievin' an' pinchin' would find her soul a foreign place to live in, an' that her present intention is quite th' lofty-hearted one of pickin' up anything shaken up an' scatthered about in th' loose confusion of a general plundher!

[*By this time they have disappeared from view.* PETER *is following, when the boom of a big gun in the distance brings him to a quick halt.*]

PETER. God Almighty, that's th' big gun again! God forbid any harm would happen to them, but sorra mind I'd mind if they met with a dhrop in their mad endeyvours to plundher an' desthroy.

[*He looks down the street for a moment, then runs to the hall door of the house, which is open, and shuts it with a vicious pull; he then goes to the chair in which* MOLLSER *had sat, sits down, takes out his pipe, lights it and begins to smoke with his head carried at a haughty angle.* THE COVEY *comes staggering in with a ten-stone sack of flour on his back. On the top of the sack is a ham. He goes over to the door, pushes it with his head, and finds he can't open it; he turns slightly in the direction of* PETER.]

THE COVEY [*to* PETER]. Who shut th' door? . . . [*He kicks at it*] Here, come on an' open it, will you? This isn't a mot's hand-bag I've got on me back.

PETER. Now, me young Covey, d'ye think I'm goin' to be your lackey?

THE COVEY [*angrily*]. Will you open th' door, y'oul'—

PETER [*shouting*]. Don't be assin' me to open any door, don't be assin' me to open any door for you. . . . Makin' a shame an' a sin o' th' cause that good men are fightin' for. . . . Oh, God forgive th' people that, instead o' burnishin' th' work th' boys is doin' to-day with quiet honesty an' patience, is revilin' their sacrifices with a riot of lootin' an' roguery!

THE COVEY. Isn't your own eyes leppin' out o' your head with envy that you haven't th' guts to ketch a few o' th' things that God is givin' to His chosen people? . . . Y'oul' hypocrite, if everyone was blind you'd steal a cross off an ass's back!

PETER [*very calmly*]. You're not going to make me lose me temper; you can go on with your proddin' as long as you like; goad an' goad an' goad away; hee, hee, heee! I'll not lose me temper.

[*Somebody opens door and* THE COVEY *goes in.*]

THE COVEY [*inside, mockingly*]. Cuckoo-oo!

PETER [*running to the door and shouting in a blaze of passion as he follows* THE COVEY *in*]. You lean, long, lanky lath of a lowsey bastard. . . . [*Following him in*] Lowsey bastard, lowsey bastard!

[BESSIE *and* MRS. GOGAN *enter, the pride of a great joy illuminating their faces.* BESSIE *is pushing the pram, which is filled with clothes and boots; on the top of the boots and clothes is a fancy table, which* MRS. GOGAN *is holding on with her left hand, while with her right hand she holds a chair on the top of her head. They are heard talking to each other before they enter.*]

MRS. GOGAN [*outside*]. I don't remember ever havin' seen such lovely pairs as them, [*they appear*] with th' pointed toes an' th' cuban heels.

BESSIE. They'll go grand with th' dhresses we're afther liftin', when we've stitched a sthray bit o' silk to lift th' bodices up a little bit higher, so as to shake th' shame out o' them, an' make them fit for women that hasn't lost themselves in th' nakedness o' th' times.

[*They fussily carry in the chair, the table, and some of the other goods. They return to bring in the rest.*]

PETER [*at door, sourly to* MRS. GOGAN]. Ay, you. Mollser looks as if she was goin' to faint, an' your youngster is roarin' in convulsions in her lap.

MRS. GOGAN [*snappily*]. She's never any other way but faintin'!

[*She goes to go in with some things in her arms, when a shot from a rifle rings out. She and* BESSIE *make a bolt for the door, which* PETER, *in a panic, tries to shut before they have got inside.*]

MRS. GOGAN. Ay, ay, ay, you cowardly oul' fool, what are you thryin' to shut th' door on us for?

[*They retreat tumultuously inside. A pause; then* CAPTAIN BRENNAN *comes in supporting* LIEUTENANT LANGON, *whose arm is around* BRENNAN*'s neck.* LANGON*'s face, which is ghastly white, is momentarily convulsed with spasms of agony. He is in a state of collapse, and* BRENNAN *is almost carrying him. After a few moments* CLITHEROE, *pale, and in a state of calm nervousness, follows, looking back in the direction from which he came, a rifle, held at the ready, in his hands.*]

CAPT. BRENNAN [*savagely to* CLITHEROE]. Why did you fire over their heads? Why didn't you fire to kill?

CLITHEROE. No, no, Bill; bad as they are they're Irish men an' women.

CAPT. BRENNAN [*savagely*]. Irish be damned! Attackin' an' mobbin' th' men that are riskin' their lives for them. If these slum lice gather at our heels again, plug one o' them, or I'll soon shock them with a shot or two meself!

LIEUT. LANGON [*moaningly*]. My God, is there ne'er an ambulance knockin' around anywhere? . . . Th' stomach is ripped out o' me; I feel it—o-o-oh, Christ!

CAPT. BRENNAN. Keep th' heart up, Jim; we'll soon get help, now.

[NORA *rushes wildly out of the house and flings her arms round the neck of* CLITHEROE *with a fierce and joyous insistence. Her hair is down, her face is haggard, but her eyes are agleam with the light of happy relief.*]

NORA. Jack, Jack, Jack; God be thanked. . . . be thanked. . . . He has been kind and merciful to His poor handmaiden. . . . My Jack, my own Jack, that I thought was lost is found, that I thought was dead is alive again! . . . Oh, God be praised for ever, evermore! . . . My poor Jack. . . . Kiss me, kiss me, Jack, kiss your own Nora!

CLITHEROE [*kissing her, and speaking brokenly*]. My Nora; my little beautiful Nora, I wish to God I'd never left you.

NORA. It doesn't matter—not now, not now, Jack. It will make us dearer than ever to each other. . . . Kiss me, kiss me again.

CLITHEROE. Now, for God's sake, Nora, don't make a scene.

NORA. I won't, I won't; I promise, I promise, Jack; honest to God. I'll be silent an' brave to bear th' joy of feelin' you safe in my arms again. . . . It's hard to force away th' tears of happiness at th' end of an awful agony.

BESSIE [*from the upper window*]. Th' Minsthrel Boys aren't feelin' very comfortable now. Th' big guns has knocked all th' harps out of their hands. General Clitheroe 'd rather be unlacin' his wife's bodice than standin' at a barricade. . . . An' th' professor of chicken-butcherin' there, finds he's up against somethin' a little tougher even than his own chickens, an' that's sayin' a lot!

CAPT. BRENNAN [*up to* BESSIE]. Shut up, y'oul' hag!

BESSIE [*down to* BRENNAN]. Choke th' chicken, choke th' chicken, choke th' chicken!

LIEUT. LANGON. For God's sake, Bill, bring me some place where me wound 'll be looked afther. . . . Am I to die before anything is done to save me?

CAPT. BRENNAN [*to* CLITHEROE]. Come on, Jack. We've got to get help for Jim, here—have you no thought for his pain an' danger?

BESSIE. Choke th' chicken, choke th' chicken, choke th' chicken!

CLITHEROE [*to* NORA]. Loosen me, darling, let me go.

NORA [*clinging to him*]. No, no, no, I'll not let you go! Come on, come up to our home, Jack, my sweetheart, my lover, my husband, an' we'll forget th' last few terrible days! . . . I look tired now, but a few hours of happy rest in your arms will bring back th' bloom of freshness again, an' you will be glad, you will be glad, glad. . . . glad!

LIEUT. LANGON. Oh, if I'd kep' down only a little longer, I mightn't ha' been hit! Everyone else escapin', an' me gettin' me belly ripped asundher! . . . I couldn't scream, couldn't even scream. . . . D'ye think I'm really badly wounded, Bill? Me clothes seem to be all soakin' wet. . . . It's blood . . . My God, it must be me own blood!

CAPT. BRENNAN [*to* CLITHEROE]. Go on, Jack, bid her goodbye with another kiss, an' be done with it! D'ye want Langon to die in me arms while you're dallyin' with your Nora?

CLITHEROE [*to* NORA]. I must go, I must go, Nora. I'm sorry we met at all. . . . It couldn't be helped—all other ways were blocked be th' British. . . . Let me go, can't you, Nora? D'ye want me to be unthrue to me comrades?

NORA. No, I won't let you go. . . . I want you to be thrue to me, Jack. . . . I'm your dearest comrade; I'm your thruest comrade. . . . They only want th' comfort of havin' you in th' same danger as themselves. . . . Oh, Jack, I can 't let you go!

CLITHEROE. You must, Nora, you must.

NORA. All last night at th' barricades I sought you, Jack. . . . I didn't think of th' danger—I could only think of you. . . . I asked for you everywhere. . . . Some o' them laughed. . . . I was pushed away, but I shoved back. . . . Some o' them even sthruck me. . . . an' I screamed an' screamed your name!

CLITHEROE [*in fear her action would give him future shame*]. What possessed you to make a show of yourself, like that? . . . What way d'ye think I'll feel when I'm told my wife was bawlin' for me at th' barricades? What are you more than any other woman?

NORA. No more, maybe; but you are more to me than any other man, Jack. . . . I didn't mean any harm, honestly, Jack. . . . I couldn't help it. . . . I shouldn't have told you. . . . My love for you made me mad with terror.

CLITHEROE [*angrily*]. They'll say now that I sent you out th' way I'd have an excuse to bring you home. . . . Are you goin' to turn all th' risks I'm takin' into a laugh?

LIEUT. LANGON. Let me lie down, let me lie down, Bill; th' pain would be easier, maybe, lyin' down. . . . Oh, God, have mercy on me!

CAPT. BRENNAN [*to* LANGON]. A few steps more, Jim, a few steps more; thry to stick it for a few steps more.

LIEUT. LANGON. Oh, I can't, I can't, I can't!

CAPT. BRENNAN [*to* CLITHEROE]. Are you comin', man, or are you goin' to make an arrangement for another honeymoon? . . . If you want to act th' renegade, say so, an' we'll be off!

BESSIE [*from above*]. Runnin' from th' Tommies—choke th' chicken. Runnin' from th' Tommies—choke th' chicken!

CLITHEROE [*savagely to* BRENNAN]. Damn you, man, who wants to act th' renegade? [*To* NORA] Here, let go your hold; let go, I say!

NORA [*clinging to* CLITHEROE, *and indicating* BRENNAN]. Look, Jack, look at th' anger in his face; look at th' fear glintin' in his eyes. . . . He himself's afraid, afraid, afraid! . . . He wants you to go th' way he'll have th' chance of death sthrikin' you an' missin' him! . . . Turn round an' look at him, Jack, look at him, look at him! . . . His very soul is cold . . . shiverin' with th' thought of what may happen to him. . . . It is his fear that is thryin' to frighten you from recognizin' th' same fear that is in your own heart!

CLITHEROE [*struggling to release himself from* NORA]. Damn you, woman, will you let me go!

CAPT. BRENNAN [*fiercely, to* CLITHEROE]. Why are you beggin' her to let you go? Are you afraid of her, or what? Break her hold on you, man, or go up, an' sit on her lap! [CLITHEROE *trying roughly to break her hold.*]

NORA [*imploringly*]. Oh, Jack. . . . Jack. . . . Jack!

LIEUT. LANGON [*agonisingly*]. Brennan, a priest; I'm dyin', I think, I'm dyin'!

CLITHEROE [*to* NORA]. If you won't do it quietly, I'll have to make you! [*To* BRENNAN] Here, hold this gun, you, for a minute. [*He hands the gun to* BRENNAN.]

NORA [*pitifully*]. Please, Jack. . . . You're hurting me, Jack. . . . Honestly. . . . Oh, you're hurting . . . me! . . . I won't, I won't, I won't! . . . Oh, Jack, I gave you everything you asked of me. . . . Don't fling me from you, now!

[*He roughly loosens her grip, and pushes her away from him.* NORA *sinks to the ground and lies there.*]

NORA [*weakly*]. Ah, Jack. . . . Jack. . . . Jack!

CLITHEROE [*taking the gun back from* BRENNAN]. Come on, come on.

[*They go out.* BESSIE *looks at* NORA *lying on the street, for a few moments, then, leaving the window, she comes out, runs over to* NORA, *lifts her up in her arms, and carries her swiftly into the house. A short pause, then down the street is heard a wild, drunken yell; it comes nearer, and* FLUTHER *enters, frenzied, wild-eyed, mad, roaring drunk. In his arms is an earthen half-gallon jar of whisky; streaming from one of the pockets of his coat is the arm of a new tunic shirt; on his head is a woman's vivid blue hat with gold lacing, all of which he has looted.*]

FLUTHER [*singing in a frenzy*]:

Fluther's a jolly good fella! . . .
Fluther's a jolly good fella!
Up th' rebels! . . . That nobody can
deny!

[*He beats on the door.*]

Get us a mug or a jug, or somethin', some o' yous, one o' yous, will yous, before I lay one o' yous out! . . . [*Looking down the street*] Bang an' fire away for all Fluther cares. . . . [*Banging at door*] Come down an' open th' door, some of yous, one o' yous, will yous, before I lay some o' yous out! . . . Th' whole city can topple home to hell, for Fluther!

[*Inside the house is heard a scream from* NORA, *followed by a moan.*]

FLUTHER [*singing furiously*]:

That nobody can deny, that nobody can
deny,
For Fluther's a jolly good fella,
Fluther's a jolly good fella,
Fluther's a jolly good fella . . . Up
th' rebels! That nobody can deny!

[*His frantic movements cause him to spill some of the whisky out of the jar.*]

Blast you, Fluther, don't be spillin' th' precious liquor! [*He kicks at the door.*] Ay, give us a mug or a jug, or somethin', one o' yous, some o' yous, will yous, before I lay one o' yous out!

[*The door suddenly opens, and* BESSIE, *coming out, grips him by the collar.*]

BESSIE [*indignantly*]. You bowsey, come in ower o' that. . . . I'll thrim your thricks o' dhrunken dancin' for you, an' none of us knowin' how soon we'll bump into a world we were never in before!

FLUTHER [*as she is pulling him in*]. Ay, th' jar, th' jar, th' jar!

[*A short pause, then again is heard a scream of pain from* NORA. *The door opens and* MRS. GOGAN *and* BESSIE *are seen standing at it.*]

BESSIE. Fluther would go, only he's too dhrunk. . . . Oh, God, isn't it a pity he's so dhrunk! We'll have to thry to get a docthor somewhere.

MRS. GOGAN. I'd be afraid to go. . . . Besides, Mollser's terrible bad. I don't think you'll get a docthor to come. It's hardly any use goin'.

BESSIE [*determinedly*]. I'll risk it. . . . Give her a little of Fluther's whisky. . . . It's th' fright that's brought it on her so soon. . . . Go on back to her, you.

[MRS. GOGAN *goes in, and* BESSIE *softly closes the door. She is moving forward, when the sound of some rifle shots, and the tok, tok, tok of a distant machine-gun bring her to a sudden halt. She hesitates for a moment, then she tightens her shawl round her, as if it were a shield, then she firmly and swiftly goes out.*]

BESSIE [*as she goes out*]. Oh, God, be Thou my help in time o' throuble. An' shelter me safely in th' shadow of Thy wings!

CURTAIN

ACT IV

The living-room of BESSIE BURGESS. *It is one of two small attic rooms [the other, used as a bedroom, is to the Left], the ceiling slopes up towards the back, giving to the apartment a look of compressed confinement. In the centre of the ceiling is a small skylight. There is an unmistakable air of poverty bordering on destitution. The paper on the walls is torn and soiled, particularly near the fire where the cooking is done, and near the washstand where the washing is done. The fireplace is to the Left. A small armchair near fire. One small window at Back. A pane of this window is starred by the entrance of a bullet. Under the window to the Right is an oak coffin standing on two kitchen chairs. Near the coffin is a home-manufactured stool, on which are two lighted candles. Beside the window is a worn-out dresser on which is a small quantity of delf. Tattered remains of cheap lace curtains drape the window. Standing near the window on Left is a brass standard-lamp with a fancy shade; hanging on the wall near the same window is a vividly crimson silk dress, both of which have been looted. A door on Left leading to the bedroom. Another opposite giving a way to the rest of the house. To the Left of this door a common washstand. A tin kettle, very black, and an old saucepan inside the fender. There is no light in the room but that given from the two candles and the fire. The dusk has well fallen, and the glare of the burning buildings in the town can be seen through the window, in the distant sky.* THE COVEY *and* FLUTHER *have been playing cards, sitting on the floor by the light of the candles on the stool near the coffin. When the curtain rises* THE COVEY *is shuffling the cards,* PETER *is sitting in a stiff, dignified way beside him, and* FLUTHER *is kneeling beside the window, cautiously looking out. It is a few days later.*

FLUTHER [*furtively peeping out of the window*]. Give them a good shuffling. . . . Th' sky's gettin' reddher an' reddher. . . . You'd think it was afire. . . . Half o' th' city must be burnin'.

THE COVEY. If I was you, Fluther, I'd keep away from that window. . . . It's dangerous, an', besides, if they see you, you'll only bring a nose on th' house.

PETER. Yes; an' he knows we had to leave our own place th' way they were riddlin' it with machine-gun fire. . . . He'll keep on pimpin' an' pimpin' there, till we have to fly out o' this place too.

FLUTHER [*ironically*]. If they make any attack here, we'll send you out in your green an' glory uniform, shakin' your sword over your head, an' they'll fly before you as th' Danes flew before Brian Boru!

THE COVEY [*placing the cards on the floor, after shuffling them*]. Come on, an' cut.

[FLUTHER *comes over, sits on floor, and cuts the cards.*]

THE COVEY [*having dealt the cards*]. Spuds up again.

[NORA *moans feebly in room on Left.*]

FLUTHER. There, she's at it again. She's been quiet for a long time, all th' same.

THE COVEY. She was quiet before, sure, an' she broke out again worse than ever. . . . What was led that time?

PETER. Thray o' Hearts, Thray o' Hearts, Thray o' Hearts.

FLUTHER. It's damned hard lines to think of her deadborn kiddie lyin' there in th' arms o' poor little Mollser. Mollser snuffed it sudden too, afther all.

THE COVEY. Sure she never got any care. How could she get it, an' th' mother out day an' night lookin' for work, an' her consumptive husband leavin' her with a baby to be born before he died!

[*Voices in a lilting chant to the Left in a distant street.*] Red Cr . . . oss, Red Cr . . . oss! Ambu . . . lance, Ambu . . . lance!

THE COVEY [*to* FLUTHER]. Your deal, Fluther.

FLUTHER [*shuffling and dealing the cards*]. It'll take a lot out o' Nora—if she'll ever be th' same.

THE COVEY. Th' docthor thinks she'll never be th' same; thinks she'll be a little touched here. [*He touches his forehead.*] She's ramblin' a lot; thinkin' she's out in th' counthry with Jack; or gettin' his dinner ready for him before he comes home; or yellin' for her kiddie. All that, though, might be th' chloroform she got. . . . I don't know what we'd have done only for oul' Bessie: up with her for th' past three nights, hand runnin'.

FLUTHER. I always knew there was never anything really derogatory wrong with poor oul' Bessie. [*To* PETER, *who is taking a trick*] Ay, houl' on, there, don't be so damn quick—that's my thrick.

PETER. What's your thrick? It's my thrick, man.

FLUTHER [*loudly*]. How is it your thrick?

PETER [*answering as loudly*]. Didn't I lead th' deuce!

FLUTHER. You must be gettin' blind, man; don't you see th' ace?

BESSIE [*appearing at door of room, Left; in a tense whisper*]. D'ye want to waken her again on me, when she's just gone asleep? If she wakes will yous come an' mind her? If I hear a whisper out o' one o' yous again, I'll . . . gut yous!

THE COVEY [*in a whisper*]. S-s-s-h. She can hear anything above a whisper.

PETER [*looking up at the ceiling*]. Th' gentle an' merciful God 'll give th' pair o' yous a scawldin' an' a scarifyin' one o' these days!

[FLUTHER *takes a bottle of whisky from his pocket, and takes a drink.*]

THE COVEY [*to* FLUTHER]. Why don't you spread that out, man, an' thry to keep a sup for to-morrow?

FLUTHER. Spread it out? Keep a sup for to-morrow? How th' hell does a fella know there'll be any to-morrow? If I'm goin' to be whipped away, let me be whipped away when it's empty, an' not when it's half full! [*To* BESSIE, *who has seated herself in an armchair at the fire*] How is she, now, Bessie?

BESSIE. I left her sleeping quietly. When I'm listenin' to her babblin', I think she'll never be much betther than she is. Her eyes have a hauntin' way of lookin' in instead of lookin' out, as if her mind had been lost alive in madly minglin' memories of th' past. . . . [*Sleepily*] Crushin' her thoughts . . . together . . . in a fierce . . . an' fanciful . . . [*she nods her head and starts wakefully*] idea that dead things are livin', an' livin' things are dead. . . . [*With a start*] Was that a scream I heard her give? [*Reassured*] Blessed God, I think I hear her screamin' every minute! An' it's only there with me that I'm able to keep awake.

THE COVEY. She'll sleep, maybe, for a long time, now. Ten there.

FLUTHER. Ten here. If she gets a long sleep, she might be all right. Peter's th' lone five.

THE COVEY. Whisht! I think I hear somebody movin' below. Whoever it is, he's comin' up.

[*A pause. Then the door opens and* CAPTAIN BRENNAN *comes into the room. He has changed his uniform for a suit of civvies. His eyes droop with the heaviness of exhaustion; his face is pallid and drawn. His clothes are dusty and stained here and there with mud. He leans heavily on the back of a chair as he stands.*]

CAPT. BRENNAN. Mrs. Clitheroe; where's Mrs. Clitheroe? I was told I'd find her here.

BESSIE. What d'ye want with Mrs. Clitheroe?

CAPT. BRENNAN. I've a message, a last message for her from her husband.

BESSIE. Killed! He's not killed, is he!

CAPT. BRENNAN [*sinking stiffly and painfully on to a chair*]. In th' Imperial Hotel; we fought till th' place was in flames. He was shot through th' arm, an' then through th' lung. . . . I could do nothin' for him—only watch his breath comin' an' goin' in quick, jerky gasps, an' a tiny sthream o' blood thricklin' out of his mouth, down over his lower lip. . . . I said a prayer for th' dyin', an' twined his Rosary beads around his fingers. . . . Then I had to leave him to save meself. . . . [*He shows some holes in his coat*] Look at th' way a machine-gun tore at me coat, as I belted out o' th' buildin' an' darted across th' sthreet for shelter. . . . An' then, I seen The Plough an' th' Stars fallin' like a shot as th' roof crashed in, an' where I'd left poor Jack was nothin' but a leppin' spout o' flame!

BESSIE [*with partly repressed vehemence*]. Ay, you left him! You twined his Rosary beads round his fingers, an' then you run like a hare to get out o' danger!

CAPT. BRENNAN. I took me chance as well as him. . . . He took it like a man. His last whisper was to "Tell Nora to be brave; that I'm ready to meet my God, an' that I'm proud to die for Ireland." An' when our General heard it he said that "Commandant Clitheroe's end was a gleam of glory." Mrs. Clitheroe's grief will be a joy when she realizes that she has had a hero for a husband.

BESSIE. If you only seen her, you'd know to th' differ.

[NORA *appears at door, Left. She is clad only in her nightdress; her hair, uncared for some days, is hanging in disorder over her shoulders. Her pale face looks paler still because of a vivid red spot on the tip of each cheek. Her eyes are glimmering with the light of incipient insanity; her hands are nervously fiddling with her nightgown. She halts at the door for a moment, looks vacantly around the room, and then comes slowly in. The rest do not notice her till she speaks.*]

NORA [*in a quiet and monotonous tone*]. No . . . Not there, Jack. . . . I can feel comfortable only in our own familiar place beneath th' bramble tree. . . . We must be walking for a long time; I feel very, very tired. . . . Have we to go farther, or have we passed it by? [*Passing her hand across her eyes*] Curious mist on my eyes. . . . Why don't you hold my hand, Jack. . . . [*Excitedly*] No, no, Jack, it's not. Can't you see it's a goldfinch. Look at th' black-satiny wings with th' gold bars, an' th' splash of crimson on its head. . . . [*Wearily*] Something ails me, something ails me. . . . Don't kiss me like that; you take my breath away, Jack. . . . Why do you frown at me? . . . You're going away, and [*frightened*] I can't follow you. Something's keeping me from moving. . . . [*Crying out*] Jack, Jack, Jack!

BESSIE [*who has gone over and caught* NORA*'s arm*]. Now, Mrs. Clitheroe, you're a terrible woman to get up out of bed. . . . You'll get cold if you stay here in them clothes.

NORA. Cold? I'm feelin' very cold; it's chilly out here in th' counthry. . . . [*Looking around frightened*] What place is this? Where am I?

BESSIE [*coaxingly*]. You're all right, Nora; you're with friends, an' in a safe place. Don't you know your uncle an' your cousin, an' poor oul' Fluther?

PETER [*about to go over to* NORA]. Nora, darlin', now—

FLUTHER [*pulling him back*]. Now, leave her to Bessie, man. A crowd 'll only make her worse.

NORA [*thoughtfully*]. There is something I want to remember, an' I can't. [*With agony*] I can't, I can't, I can't! My head, my head! [*Suddenly breaking from* BESSIE, *and running over to the men, and gripping* FLUTHER *by the shoulders*] Where is it? Where's my baby? Tell me where you've put it, where 've you hidden it? My baby, my baby; I want my baby! My head, my poor head. . . . Oh, I can't tell what is wrong with me. [*Screaming*] Give him to me, give me my husband!

BESSIE. Blessin' o' God on us, isn't this pitiful!

NORA [*struggling with* BESSIE]. I won't go away for you; I won't. Not till you give me back my husband. [*Screaming*] Murderers, that's what yous are; murderers, murderers!

BESSIE. S-s-sh. We'll bring Mr. Clitheroe back to you, if you'll only lie down an' stop quiet. . . . [*Trying to lead her in*] Come on, now, Nora, an' I'll sing something to you.

NORA. I feel as if my life was thryin' to force its way out of my body. . . . I can hardly breathe . . . I'm frightened, I'm frightened, I'm frightened! For God's sake, don't leave me, Bessie. Hold my hand, put your arms around me!

FLUTHER [*to* BRENNAN]. Now you can see th' way she is, man.

PETER. An' what way would she be if she heard Jack had gone west?

THE COVEY [*to* PETER]. Shut up, you, man!

BESSIE [*to* NORA]. We'll have to be brave, an' let patience clip away th' heaviness of th' slow-movin' hours, rememberin' that sorrow may endure for th' night, but joy cometh in th' mornin'. . . . Come on in, an' I'll sing to you, an' you'll rest quietly.

NORA [*stopping suddenly on her way to the room*]. Jack an' me are goin' out somewhere this evenin'. Where I can't tell. Isn't it curious I can't remember. . . . Maura, Maura, Jack, if th' baby's a girl; any name you like, if th' baby's a boy!. . . . He's there. [*Screaming*] He's there, an' they won't give him back to me!

BESSIE. S-ss-s-h, darlin', s-ssh. I won't sing to you, if you're not quiet.

NORA [*nervously holding* BESSIE]. Hold my hand, hold my hand, an' sing to me, sing to me!

BESSIE. Come in an' lie down, an' I'll sing to you.

NORA [*vehemently*]. Sing to me, sing to me; sing, sing!

BESSIE [*singing as she leads* NORA *into room*]:

Lead, kindly light, amid th' encircling gloom,
Lead Thou me on.
Th' night is dark an' I am far from home,
Lead Thou me on.
Keep Thou my feet, I do not ask to see
Th' distant scene—one step enough for me.

So long that Thou hast blessed me, sure Thou still
Wilt lead me on;

[*They go in.*]

BESSIE [*singing in room*]:

O'er moor an' fen, o'er crag an' torrent, till
Th' night is gone.
An' in th' morn those angel faces smile
That I have lov'd long since, an' lost
awhile!

THE COVEY [*to* BRENNAN]. Now that you've seen how bad she is, an' that we daren't tell her what has happened till she's betther, you'd best be slippin' back to where you come from.

CAPT. BRENNAN. There's no chance o' slippin' back now, for th' military are everywhere: a fly couldn't get through. I'd never have got here, only I managed to change me uniform for what I'm wearin'. . . . I'll have to take me chance, an' thry to lie low here for a while.

THE COVEY [*frightened*]. There's no place here to lie low. Th' Tommies 'll be hoppin' in here, any minute!

PETER [*aghast*]. An' then we'd all be shanghaied!

THE COVEY. Be God, there's enough afther happenin' to us!

FLUTHER [*warningly, as he listens*]. Whisht, whisht, th' whole o' yous. I think I heard th' clang of a rifle butt on th' floor of th' hall below. [*All alertness.*] Here, come on with th' cards again. I'll deal. [*He shuffles and deals the cards to all.*]

FLUTHER. Clubs up. [*to* BRENNAN] Thry to keep your hands from shakin', man. You lead, Peter. [*As* PETER *throws out a card*] Four o' Hearts led.

[*The door opens and* CORPORAL STODDART *of the Wiltshires enters in full war kit; steel helmet, rifle and bayonet, and trench tool. He looks round the room. A pause and a palpable silence.*]

FLUTHER [*breaking the silence*]. Two tens an' a five.

CORPORAL STODDART. 'Ello. [*Indicating the coffin*] This the stiff?

THE COVEY. Yis.

CORPORAL STODDART. Who's gowing with it? Ownly one allowed to gow with it, you know.

THE COVEY. I dunno.

CORPORAL STODDART. You dunnow?

THE COVEY. I dunno.

BESSIE [*coming into the room*]. She's afther slippin' off to sleep again, thanks be to God. I'm hardly able to keep my own eyes open. [*To the soldier*] Oh, are yous goin' to take away poor little Mollser?

CORPORAL STODDART. Ay; 'oo's agowing with 'er?

BESSIE. Oh, th' poor mother, o' course. God help her, it's a terrible blow to her!

FLUTHER. A terrible blow? Sure, she's in her element now, woman, mixin' earth to earth, an' ashes t'ashes an' dust to dust, an' revellin' in plumes an' hearses, last days an' judgements!

BESSIE [*falling into chair by the fire*]. God bless us! I'm jaded!

CORPORAL STODDART. Was she plugged?

THE COVEY. Ah, no; died o' consumption.

CORPORAL STODDART. Ow, is that all? Thought she moight 'ave been plugged.

THE COVEY. Is that all? Isn't it enough? D'ye know, comrade, that more die o' consumption than are killed in th' wars? An' it's all because of th' system we're livin' undher?

CORPORAL STODDART. Ow, I know. I'm a Sowcialist moiself, but I 'as to do my dooty.

THE COVEY [*ironically*]. Dooty! Th' only dooty of a Socialist is th' emancipation of th' workers.

CORPORAL STODDART. Ow, a man's a man, an 'e 'as to foight for 'is country, 'asn't 'e?

FLUTHER [*aggressively*]. You're not fightin' for your counthry here, are you?

PETER [*anxiously, to* FLUTHER]. Ay, ay, Fluther, none o' that, none o' that!

THE COVEY. Fight for your counthry! Did y'ever read, comrade, Jenersky's *Thesis on the Origin, Development, an' Consolidation of th' Evolutionary Idea of the Proletariat*?

CORPORAL STODDART. Ow, cheese it, Paddy, cheese it!

BESSIE [*sleepily*]. How is things in th' town, Tommy?

CORPORAL STODDART. Ow, I fink it's nearly hover. We've got 'em surrounded, and we're clowsing in on the bloighters. Ow, it was only a little bit of a dawgfoight.

[*The sharp ping of the sniper's rifle is heard, followed by a squeal of pain.*]

[*Voices to the Left in a chant*]. Red Cr . . . oss, Red Cr . . . oss! Ambu . . . lance, Ambu . . . lance!

CORPORAL STODDART [*excitedly*]. Christ, that's another of our men 'it by that blawsted sniper! 'E's knocking abaht 'ere, somewheres. Gawd, when we gets th' bloighter, we'll give 'im the cold steel, we will. We'll jab the belly aht of 'im, we will!

[MRS. GOGAN *comes in tearfully, and a little proud of the importance of being directly connected with death.*]

MRS. GOGAN [*to* FLUTHER]. I'll never forget what you done for me, Fluther, goin' around at th' risk of your life settlin' everything with th' undhertaker an' th' cemetery people. When all me own were afraid to put their noses out, you plunged like a good one through hummin' bullets, an' they knockin' fire out o' th' road, tinklin' through th' frightened windows, an' splashin' themselves to pieces on th' walls! An' you'll find, that Mollser, in th' happy place she's gone to, won't forget to whisper, now an' again, th' name o' Fluther.

CORPORAL STODDART. Git it aht, mother, git it aht.

BESSIE [*from the chair*]. It's excusin' me you'll be, Mrs. Gogan, for not stannin' up, seein' I'm shaky on me feet for want of a little sleep, an' not desirin' to show any disrespect to poor little Mollser.

FLUTHER. Sure, we all know, Bessie, that it's vice versa with you.

MRS. GOGAN [*to* BESSIE]. Indeed, it's meself that has well chronicled, Mrs. Burgess, all your gentle hurryin's to me little Mollser, when she was alive, bringin' her somethin' to dhrink, or somethin' t'eat, an' never passin' her without liftin' up her heart with a delicate word o' kindness.

CORPORAL STODDART [*impatiently, but kindly*]. Git it aht, git it aht, mother.

[THE COVEY, FLUTHER, BRENNAN, *and* PETER *carry out the coffin, followed by* MRS. GOGAN.]

CORPORAL STODDART [*to* BESSIE, *who is almost asleep*]. 'Ow many men is in this 'ere 'ouse? [*No answer. Loudly*] 'Ow many men is in this 'ere 'ouse?

BESSIE [*waking with a start*]. God, I was nearly asleep! . . . How many men? Didn't you see them?

CORPORAL STODDART. Are they all that are in the 'ouse?

BESSIE. Oh, there's none higher up, but there may be more lower down. Why?

CORPORAL STODDART. All men in the district 'as to be rounded up. Somebody's giving 'elp to the snipers, and we 'as to take precautions. If I 'ad my woy, I'd make 'em all join hup, and do their bit! But I suppowse they and you are all Shinners.

BESSIE [*who has been sinking into sleep, waking up to a sleepy vehemence*]. Bessie Burgess is no Shinner, an' never had no thruck with anything spotted be th' fingers o' th' Fenians; but always made it her business to harness herself for Church whenever she knew that God Save the King was goin' to be sung at t'end of th' service; whose only son went to th' front in th' first contingent of the Dublin Fusiliers, an' that's on his way home carryin' a shatthered arm that he got fightin' for his King an' counthry!

[*Her head sinks slowly forward again.* PETER *comes into the room; his body is stiffened and his face is wearing a comically indignant look. He walks to and fro at the back of the room, evidently repressing a violent desire to speak angrily. He is followed in by* FLUTHER, THE COVEY, *and* BRENNAN, *who slinks into an obscure corner of the room, nervous of notice.*]

FLUTHER [*after an embarrassing pause*]. Th' air in th' sthreet outside's shakin' with the firin' o' rifles an' machine-guns. It must be a hot shop in th' middle o' th' scrap.

CORPORAL STODDART. We're pumping lead in on 'em from every side, now; they'll soon be shoving up th' white flag.

PETER [*with a shout*]. I'm tellin' you either o' yous two lowsers 'ud make a betther hearse-man than Peter; proddin' an' pokin' at me an' I helpin' to carry out a corpse!

FLUTHER. It wasn't a very derogatory thing for th' Covey to say that you'd make a fancy hearse-man, was it?

PETER [*furiously*]. A pair o' redjesthered bowseys pondherin' from mornin' till night on how they'll get a chance to break a gap through th' quiet nature of a man that's always endeavourin' to chase out of him any sthray thought of venom against his fella-man!

THE COVEY. Oh, shut it, shut it, shut it!

PETER. As long as I'm a livin' man, responsible for me thoughts, words, an' deeds to th' Man above, I'll feel meself instituted to fight again' th' sliddherin' ways of a pair o' picaroons, whisperin', concurrin', concoctin', an' conspirin' together to rendher me unconscious of th' life I'm thryin' to live!

CORPORAL STODDART [*dumbfounded*]. What's wrong, Daddy; wot 'ave they done to you?

PETER [*savagely to the* CORPORAL]. You mind your own business! What's it got to do with you, what's wrong with me?

BESSIE [*in a sleepy murmur*]. Will yous thry to conthrol yourselves into quietness? Yous'll waken her . . . up . . . on . . . me . . . again. [*She sleeps.*]

FLUTHER. Come on, boys, to th' cards again, an' never mind him.

CORPORAL STODDART. No use of you gowing to start cawds; you'll be gowing out of 'ere, soon as Sergeant comes.

FLUTHER. Goin' out o' here? An' why're we goin' out o' here?

CORPORAL STODDART. All men in district to be rounded up, and 'eld in till the scrap is hover.

FLUTHER. An' where're we goin' to be held in?

CORPORAL STODDART. They're puttin 'em in a church.

THE COVEY. A church?

FLUTHER. What sort of a church? Is it a Protestan' Church?

CORPORAL STODDART. I dunnow, I suppowse so.

FLUTHER [*dismayed*]. Be God, it'll be a nice thing to be stuck all night in a Protestan' Church!

CORPORAL STODDART. Bring the cawds; you moight get a chance of a goime.

FLUTHER. Ah, no, that wouldn't do. . . . I wondher? [*After a moment's thought*] Ah, I don't think we'd be doin' anything derogatory be playin' cards in a Protestan' Church.

CORPORAL STODDART. If I was you I'd bring a little snack with me; you moight be glad of it before the mawning. [*Sings*]:

I do loike a snoice mince poy,
I do loike a snoice mince poy!

[*The snap of the sniper's rifle rings out again, followed simultaneously by a scream of pain.* CORPORAL STODDART *goes pale, and brings his rifle to the ready, listening.*]

[*Voices chanting to the Right*]. Red Cro . . . ss, Red Cro . . . ss! Ambu . . . lance, Ambu . . . lance!

[SERGEANT TINLEY *comes rapidly in, pale, agitated, and fiercely angry.*]

CORPORAL STODDART [*to* SERGEANT]. One of hour men 'it, Sergeant?

SERGEANT TINLEY. Private Taylor; got 'it roight through the chest, 'e did; an 'ole in front of 'im as 'ow you could put your fist through, and 'arf 'is back blown awoy! Dum-dum bullets they're using. Gang of Hassassins potting at us from behind roofs. That's not playing the goime: why down't they come into the owpen and foight fair!

FLUTHER [*unable to stand the slight*]. Fight fair! A few hundhred scrawls o' chaps with a couple o' guns an' Rosary beads, again' a hundhred thousand thrained men with horse, fut, an' artillery . . . an' he wants us to fight fair! [*To* SERGEANT] D'ye want us to come out in our skins an' throw stones?

SERGEANT TINLEY [*to* CORPORAL]. Are these four all that are 'ere?

CORPORAL STODDART. Four; that's all, Sergeant.

SERGEANT TINLEY [*vindictively*]. Come on, then; get the blighters aht. [*To the men*] 'Ere, 'op it 'aht! Aht into the streets with you, and if a snoiper sends another of our men west, you gow with 'im! [*He catches* FLUTHER *by the shoulder*] Gow on, git aht!

FLUTHER. Eh, who are you chuckin', eh?

SERGEANT TINLEY [*roughly*]. Gow on, git aht, you blighter.

FLUTHER. Who are you callin' a blighter to, eh? I'm a Dublin man, born an' bred in th' city, see?

SERGEANT TINLEY. I down't care if you were Broin Buroo; git aht, git aht.

FLUTHER [*halting as he is going out*]. Jasus, you an' your guns! Leave them down, an' I'd beat th' two o' yous without sweatin'!

[PETER, BRENNAN, THE COVEY, *and* FLUTHER, *followed by the soldiers, go out.* BESSIE *is sleeping heavily on the chair by the fire. After a pause,* NORA *appears at door, Left, in her nightdress. Remaining at door for a few moments she looks vaguely around the room. She then comes in quietly, goes over to the fire, pokes it, and puts the kettle on. She thinks for a few moments, pressing her hand to her forehead. She looks questioningly at the fire, and then at the press at back. She goes to the press, opens it, takes out a soiled cloth and spreads it on the table. She then places things for tea on the table.*]

NORA. I imagine th' room looks very odd somehow. . . . I was nearly forgetting Jack's tea. . . . Ah, I think I'll have everything done before he gets in. . . . [*She lilts gently, as she arranges the table.*]

Th' violets were scenting th' woods, Nora,
Displaying their charms to th' bee,
When I first said I lov'd only you, Nora,
An' you said you lov'd only me.

Th' chestnut blooms gleam'd through th'
glade, Nora,
A robin sang loud from a tree,
When I first said I lov'd only you, Nora,
An' you said you lov'd only me.

[*She pauses suddenly, and glances round the room.*]

NORA [*doubtfully*]. I can't help feelin' this room very strange. . . . What is it? . . . What is it? . . . I must think. . . . I must try to remember. . . .

[*Vocies chanting in a distant street.*] Ambu . . . lance, Ambu . . . lance! Red Cro . . . ss, Red Cro . . . ss!

NORA [*startled and listening for a moment, then resuming the arrangement of the table*]:

Trees, birds, an' bees sang a song, Nora,
Of happier transports to be,
When I first said I lov'd only you, Nora,
An' you said you lov'd only me.

[*A burst of rifle fire is heard in a street near by, followed by the rapid rok, tok, tok of a machine-gun.*]

NORA [*staring in front of her and screaming*]. Jack, Jack, Jack! My baby, my baby, my baby!

BESSIE [*waking with a start*]. You divil, are you afther gettin' out o' bed again!

[*She rises and runs towards* NORA, *who rushes to the window, which she frantically opens.*]

NORA [*at window, screaming*]. Jack, Jack, for God's sake, come to me!

SOLDIERS [*outside, shouting*]. Git away, git away from that window, there!

BESSIE [*seizing hold of* NORA]. Come away, come away, woman, from that window!

NORA [*struggling with* BESSIE]. Where is it; where have you hidden it? Oh, Jack, Jack, where are you?

BESSIE [*imploringly*]. Mrs. Clitheroe, for God's sake, come away!

NORA [*fiercely*]. I won't; he's below. Let . . . me . . . go! You're thryin' to keep me from me husband. I'll follow him. Jack, Jack, come to your Nora!

BESSIE. Hus-s-sh, Nora, Nora! He'll be here in a minute. I'll bring him to you, if you'll only be quiet—honest to God, I will.

[*With a great effort* BESSIE *pushes* NORA *away from the window, the force used causing her to stagger against it herself. Two rifle shots ring out in quick succession.* BESSIE *jerks her body convulsively; stands stiffly for a moment, a look of agonized astonishment on her face, then she staggers forward, leaning heavily on the table with her hands.*]

BESSIE [*with an arrested scream of fear and pain*]. Merciful God, I'm shot, I'm shot, I'm shot! . . . Th' life's pourin' out o' me! [*To* NORA] I've got this through . . . through you . . . through you, you bitch, you! . . . O God, have mercy on me! . . . [*To* NORA] You wouldn't stop quiet, no, you wouldn't, you wouldn't, blast you! Look at what I'm afther gettin', look at what I'm afther gettin' . . . I'm bleedin' to death, an' no one's here to stop th' flowin' blood! [*Calling*] Mrs. Gogan, Mrs. Gogan! Fluther, Fluther, for God's sake, somebody, a doctor, a doctor!

[*She staggers frightened towards the door, to seek for aid, but, weakening half-way across the room, she sinks to her knees, and bending forward, supports herself with her hands resting on the floor.* NORA *is standing rigidly with her back to the wall opposite, her trembling hands held out a little from the sides of her body, her lips quivering, her breast heaving, staring wildly at the figure of* BESSIE.]

NORA [*in a breathless whisper*]. Jack, I'm frightened. . . . I'm frightened, Jack. . . . Oh, Jack, where are you?

BESSIE [*moaningly*]. This is what 's afther comin' on me for nursin' you day an' night. . . . I was a fool, a fool, a fool! Get me a dhrink o' wather, you jade, will you? There's a fire burnin' in me blood! [*Pleadingly*] Nora, Nora, dear, for God's sake, run out an' get Mrs. Gogan, or Fluther, or somebody to bring a doctor, quick, quick, quick! [*As* NORA *does not stir*] Blast you, stir yourself, before I'm gone!

NORA. Oh, Jack, Jack, where are you?

BESSIE [*in a whispered moan*]. Jesus Christ, me sight's goin'! It's all dark, dark! Nora, hold me hand!

[BESSIE'*s body lists over and she sinks into a prostrate position on the floor.*]

BESSIE. I'm dyin', I'm dyin' . . . I feel it. . . . Oh God, oh God! [*She feebly sings*]

I do believe, I will believe
That Jesus died for me;
That on th' cross He shed His blood,
From sin to set me free. . . .

I do believe . . . I will believe
. . . Jesus died . . . me;
. . . th' cross He shed . . . blood,
From sin . . . free.

[*She ceases singing, and lies stretched out, still and very rigid. A pause. Then* MRS. GOGAN *runs hastily in.*]

MRS. GOGAN [*quivering with fright*]. Blessed be God, what's afther happenin'? [*To* NORA] What's wrong, child, what's wrong? [*She sees* BESSIE, *runs to her and bends over the body*] Bessie, Bessie! [*She shakes the body*] Mrs. Burgess, Mrs. Burgess! [*She feels* BESSIE'*s forehead*] My God, she's as cold as death. They're afther murdherin' th' poor inoffensive woman!

[SERGEANT TINLEY *and* CORPORAL STODDART *enter agitatedly, their rifles at the ready.*]

SERGEANT TINLEY [*excitedly*]. This is the 'ouse. That's the window!

NORA [*pressing back against the wall*]. Hide it, hide it; cover it up, cover it up!

SERGEANT TINLEY [*going over to the body*]. 'Ere, what's this? Who's this? [*Looking at* BESSIE] Oh Gawd, we've plugged one of the women of the 'ouse.

CORPORAL STODDART. Whoy the 'ell did she gow to the window? Is she dead?

SERGEANT TINLEY. Oh, dead as bedamned. Well, we could't afford to toike any chawnces.

NORA [*screaming*]. Hide it, hide it; don't let me see it! Take me away, take me away, Mrs. Gogan!

[MRS GOGAN *runs into room, Left, and runs out again with a sheet which she spreads over the body of* BESSIE.]

MRS. GOGAN [*as she spreads the sheet*]. Oh, God help her, th' poor woman, she's stiffenin' out as hard as she can! Her face has written on it th' shock o' sudden agony, an' her hands is whitenin' into th' smooth shininess of wax.

NORA [*whimperingly*]. Take me away, take me away; don't leave me here to be lookin' an' lookin' at it!

MRS. GOGAN [*going over to* NORA *and putting her arm around her*]. Come on with me, dear, an' you can doss in poor Mollser's bed, till we gather some neighbours to come an' give th' last friendly touches to Bessie in th' lonely layin' of her out. [MRS. GOGAN *and* NORA *go slowly out.*]

CORPORAL STODDART [*who has been looking around, to* SERGEANT TINLEY]. Tea, here, Sergeant. Wot abaht a cup of scald?

SERGEANT TINLEY. Pour it aht, Stoddart, pour it aht. I could scoff hanything just now.

[CORPORAL STODDART *pours out two cups of tea, and the two soldiers begin to drink. In the distance is heard a bitter burst of rifle and machine-gun fire, interspersed with the boom, boom of artillery. The glare in the sky seen through the window flares into a fuller and a deeper red.*]

SERGEANT TINLEY. There gows the general attack on the Powst Office.

[*Voices in a distant street*]. Ambu . . . lance, Ambu . . . lance! Red Cro . . . ss, Red Cro . . . ss!

[*The voices of soldiers at a barricade outside the house are heard singing*]:

They were summoned from the 'illside,
They were called in from the glen,
And the country found 'em ready
At the stirring call for men.
Let not tears add to their 'ardship,
As the soldiers pass along,
And although our 'eart is breaking,
Make it sing this cheery song.

SERGEANT TINLEY *and* CORPORAL STODDART [*joining in the chorus, as they sip the tea*]:

Keep the 'owme fires burning,
While your 'earts are yearning;
Though your lads are far away
They dream of 'owme;
There's a silver loining
Through the dark cloud shoining,
Turn the dark cloud inside out,
Till the boys come 'owme!

CURTAIN

COMEDY

William Shakespeare

AS YOU LIKE IT

DRAMATIS PERSONAE

DUKE, *living in banishment*
FREDERICK, *his brother, and usurper of his dominions*
AMIENS, JAQUES } *lords attending on the banished Duke*
LE BEAU, *a courtier attending upon Frederick*
CHARLES, *wrestler to Frederick*
OLIVER, JAQUES, ORLANDO } *sons of Sir Rowland de Boys*
ADAM, DENNIS } *servants to Oliver*
TOUCHSTONE, *a clown*
SIR OLIVER MARTEXT, *a vicar*
CORIN, SILVIUS } *shepherds*
WILLIAM, *a country fellow, in love with Audrey*
A person representing Hymen

ROSALIND, *daughter to the banished Duke*
CELIA, *daughter to Frederick*
PHEBE, *a shepherdess*
AUDREY, *a country wench*

LORDS, PAGES, *and* ATTENDANTS, *&c.*

SCENE—*Oliver's house; Duke Frederick's court; and the Forest of Arden.*

ACT I

Scene I. Orchard of OLIVER*'s house.*

[*Enter* ORLANDO *and* ADAM.]

ORL As I remember it, Adam, it was upon this fashion: Bequeathed° me by will but poor a° thousand crowns, and, as thou sayest, charged my brother, on his blessing,° to breed° me well—and there

Act I, Sc. i: *1. Bequeathed:* i.e., my father bequeathed. *2. poor a:* a poor; i.e., only. *3. on . . . blessing:* if he wished to receive his blessing. *breed:* educate.

begins my sadness. My brother Jaques he keeps at school, and report speaks goldenly of his profit; for my part, he keeps me rustically at home, or, to speak more properly, stays me° here at home unkept. For call you that keeping for a gentleman of my birth that differs not from the stalling of an ox? His horses are bred better, for besides that they are fair with their feeding, they are taught their manage,° and to that end riders dearly° hired. But I, his brother, gain nothing under him but growth, for the which his animals on his dunghills are as much bound to° him as I. Besides this nothing that he so plentifully gives me, the something that nature gave me his countenance seems to take from me.° He lets me feed with his hinds,° bars me° the place of a brother, and, as much as in him lies, mines my gentility with my education.° This is it, Adam, that grieves me, and the spirit of my father, which I think is within me, begins to mutiny against this servitude. I will no longer endure it, though yet I know no wise remedy how to avoid it.

ADAM Yonder comes my master, your brother.

ORL Go apart, Adam, and thou shalt hear how he will shake me up.°

[*Enter* OLIVER.]

OLI Now, Sir! What make you here?

ORL Nothing. I am not taught to make anything.

OLI What mar you then, sir?

ORL Marry,° sir, I am helping you to mar that which God made, a poor unworthy brother of yours, with idleness.

OLI Marry, sir, be better employed, and be naught awhile.°

ORL Shall I keep your hogs and eat husks with them? What prodigal portion° have I spent that I should come to such penury?

OLI Know you where you are, sir?

ORL Oh, sir, very well, here in your orchard.

OLI Know you before whom, sir?

ORL Aye, better than him I am before knows me. I know you are my eldest brother, and, in the gentle condition of blood, you should so know me.° The courtesy of nations° allows you my better, in that you are the firstborn. But the same tradition takes not away my blood, were there twenty brothers betwixt us. I have as much of my

6. *stays me:* forces me to stay. 10. *manage:* training. *dearly:* at great cost. 12. *bound to:* owe him as much gratitude; i.e., nothing. 13–4. *something . . . me:* even the natural claims that I have of him as my brother he denies by his unfriendly treatment. 14. *countenance:* lit., face, so kindly (or unkindly) looks. 15. *hinds:* laborers. *bars me:* prevents me from holding. 16. *mines . . . education:* undermines my gentle birth by lack of education. 21. *shake me up:* treat me violently. 25. *Marry:* Mary, by the Virgin. 27. *be . . . awhile:* make yourself scarce. 29. *prodigal portion:* i.e., I have not wasted my portion like the Prodigal Son. See Luke 15: 11–32. 34–5. *in . . . me:* if you were a true gentleman you would treat me as one. 35. *courtesy of nations:* the custom of civilized society.

father in me as you, albeit I confess your coming before me is nearer to his reverence.°

OLI What, boy!°

ORL Come, come, elder brother, you are too young in this.

OLI Wilt thou lay hands on me, villain?

ORL I am no villain. I am the youngest son of Sir Rowland de Boys; he was my father, and he is thrice a villain that says such a father begot villains. Wert thou not my brother, I would not take this hand from thy throat till this other had pulled out thy tongue for saying so. Thou hast railed on° thyself.

ADAM Sweet masters, be patient. For your father's remembrance, be at accord.

OLI Let me go, I say.

ORL I will not, till I please. You shall hear me. My father charged you in his will to give me good education. You have trained me like a peasant, obscuring and hiding from me all gentlemanlike qualities. The spirit of my father grows strong in me, and I will no longer endure it. Therefore allow me such exercises° as may become a gentleman, or give me the poor allottery° my father left me by testament. With that I will go buy my fortunes.

OLI And what wilt thou do? Beg, when that is spent? Well, sir, get you in. I will not long be troubled with you, you shall have some part of your will.° I pray you leave me.

ORL I will no further offend you than becomes me for my good.

OLI Get you with him, you old dog.

ADAM Is "old dog" my reward? Most true, I have lost my teeth in your service. God be with my old master! He would not have spoke such a word.

[*Exeunt* ORLANDO *and* ADAM.]

OLI Is it even so? Begin you to grow upon° me? I will physic your rankness,° and yet give no thousand crowns neither. Holla, Dennis!

[*Enter* DENNIS.]

DEN Calls your Worship?

OLI Was not Charles, the Duke's wrestler, here to speak with me?

DEN So please you, he is here at the door and importunes access° to you.

OLI Call him in. [*Exit* DENNIS.] 'Twill be a good way, and tomorrow the wrestling is.

[*Enter* CHARLES.]

38–39. is . . . reverence: gives you a greater claim to be highly regarded as he was. *40. What, boy:* Here Oliver strikes Orlando. *47. railed on:* abused. *55. exercises:* training. *56. allottery:* portion. *60. your will:* your legacy, and what you desire. *66. grow upon:* become troublesome to. *66–67. physic . . . rankness:* cure your excess of blood. Rankness was a medical term for a condition requiring the letting of blood. *70. importunes access:* asks for permission to see you on an urgent matter.

CHA Good morrow to your Worship.

OLI Good Monsieur Charles, what's the new news at the new Court?

CHA There's no news at the Court, sir, but the old news; that is, the old Duke is banished by his younger brother the new Duke, and three or four loving lords have put themselves into voluntary exile with him, whose lands and revenues enrich the new Duke; therefore he gives them good leave to wander.

OLI Can you tell if Rosalind, the Duke's daughter, be banished with her father?

CHA Oh no, for the Duke's daughter, her cousin, so loves her, being ever from their cradles bred together, that she would have followed her exile or have died to stay behind her. She is at the Court and no less beloved of her uncle than his own daughter, and never two ladies loved as they do.

OLI Where will the old Duke live?

CHA They say he is already in the Forest of Arden,° and a many merry men with him, and there they live like the old Robin Hood° of England. They say many young gentlemen flock to him every day, and fleet° the time carelessly,° as they did in the golden world.°

OLI What, you wrestle tomorrow before the new Duke?

CHA Marry do I, sir, and I came to acquaint you with a matter. I am given, sir, secretly to understand that your younger brother, Orlando, hath a disposition to come in disguised against me to try a fall.° Tomorrow, sir, I wrestle for my credit, and he that escapes me without some broken limb shall acquit° him well. Your brother is but young and tender, and, for your love, I would be loath to foil° him, as I must for my own honor if he come in. Therefore, out of my love to you, I came hither to acquaint you withal, that either you might stay him from his intendment or brook° such disgrace well as he shall run into, in that it is a thing of his own search, and altogether against my will.

OLI Charles, I thank thee for thy love to me, which thou shalt find I will most kindly requite. I had myself notice of my brother's purpose herein, and have by underhand means labored to dissuade him from it, but he is resolute. I'll tell thee, Charles—it is the stubbornest young fellow of France, full of ambition, an envious emulator° of every man's good parts, a secret and villainous contriver° against me his natural brother. Therefore use thy discretion. I had as lief thou didst break his neck as his finger. And thou

90. Arden: the Ardennes, in Belgium. *91. Robin Hood:* the famous English outlaw of legend and ballad. *93. fleet:* spend. *carelessly:* without a care. *93. golden world:* the mythical good old days, before men learned to be wicked. *98. fall:* i.e., in wrestling. *99. acquit:* distinguish; lit., get a favorable verdict. *101. foil:* overthrow. *103. brook:* endure. *111. envious emulator:* jealous hater. *112. contriver:* plotter.

wert best look to 't, for if thou dost him any slight disgrace, or if he do not mightily grace himself on thee,° he will practice° against thee by poison, entrap thee by some treacherous device, and never leave thee till he hath ta'en thy life by some indirect means or other. For I assure thee, and almost with tears I speak it, there is not one so young and so villainous this day living. I speak but brotherly of him, but should I anatomize° him to thee as he is, I must blush and weep, and thou must look pale and wonder.

CHA I am heartily glad I came hither to you. If he come tomorrow, I'll give him his payment. If ever he go alone° again, I'll never wrestle for prize more. And so, God keep your Worship!

OLI Farewell, good Charles. [*Exit* CHARLES.] Now will I stir this gamester. I hope I shall see an end of him, for my soul, yet I know not why, hates nothing more than he. Yet he's gentle,° never schooled, and yet learned, full of noble device,° of all sorts enchantingly beloved, and indeed so much in the heart of the world, and especially of my own people, who best know him, that I am altogether misprized.° But it shall not be so long, this wrestler shall clear all. Nothing remains but that I kindle° the boy thither, which now I'll go about.

[*Exit.*]

Scene II. Lawn before the DUKE*'s palace.*

[*Enter* ROSALIND *and* CELIA.]

CEL I pray thee, Rosalind, sweet my coz,° be merry.

ROS Dear Celia, I show more mirth than I am mistress of, and would you yet I were merrier? Unless you could teach me to forget a banished father, you must not learn° me how to remember any extraordinary pleasure.

CEL Herein I see thou lovest me not with the full weight that I love thee. If my uncle, thy banished father, had banished thy uncle, the Duke my father, so thou hadst been still with me I could have taught my love to take thy father for mine. So wouldst thou if the truth of thy love to me were so righteously tempered° as mine is to thee.

ROS Well, I will forget the condition of my estate, to rejoice in yours.

CEL You know my father hath no child but I, nor none is like to have. And truly, when he dies, thou shalt be his heir, for what he

115. *grace . . . thee:* distinguish himself at your expense. *practice:* plot. 120. *anatomize:* dissect, analyze. 123. *alone:* i.e., without support. 127. *gentle:* a natural gentleman. 128. *noble device:* noble thoughts 131. *misprized:* considered worthless, despised. 132. *kindle:* incite.

Sc. ii: 1. *coz:* cousin. 4. *learn:* teach. 10. *tempered:* compounded.

hath taken away from thy father perforce, I will render thee again in affection. By mine honor, I will, and when I break that oath, let me turn monster. Therefore, my sweet Rose, my dear Rose, be merry.

ROS From henceforth I will, Coz, and devise sports. Let me see, what think you of falling in love?

CEL Marry, I prithee do, to make sport withal. But love no man in good earnest, nor no further in sport neither than with safety of a pure blush thou mayst in honor come off again.

ROS What shall be our sport, then?

CEL Let us sit and mock the good housewife Fortune from her wheel,° that her gifts may henceforth be bestowed equally.

ROS I would we could do so, for her benefits are mightily misplaced, and the bountiful blind woman doth most mistake in her gifts to women.

CEL 'Tis true, for those that she makes fair she scarce° makes honest,° and those that she makes honest she makes very ill-favoredly.°

ROS Nay, now thou goest from Fortune's office to Nature's. Fortune reigns in gifts of the world, not in the lineaments° of Nature.

[*Enter* TOUCHSTONE.]

CEL No? When Nature hath made a fair creature, may she not by Fortune fall into the fire? Though Nature hath given us wit to flout° at Fortune, hath not Fortune sent in this fool to cut off the argument?

ROS Indeed, there is Fortune too hard for Nature, when Fortune makes Nature's natural° the cutter-off of Nature's wit.

CEL Peradventure this is not Fortune's work neither, but Nature's, who perceiveth our natural wits too dull to reason of such goddesses, and hath sent this natural for our whetstone; for always the dullness of the fool is the whetstone of the wits. How now, wit! Whither wander you?°

TOUCH Mistress, you must come away to your father.

CEL Were you made the messenger?

TOUCH No, by mine honor, but I was bid to come for you.

ROS Where learned you that oath, fool?

TOUCH Of a certain knight that swore by his honor they were good pancakes, and swore by his honor the mustard was naught.°

25–6. Fortune . . . wheel: Fortune was personified as a blind woman spinning men's fortunes at a spinning wheel. *30. scarce:* seldom *31. honest:* chaste. *32. illfavoredly:* ugly. *34. lineaments:* characteristics; i.e., features. *36. flout:* mock. *40. natural:* fool, one who is by nature an idiot. Touchstone, however, hardly comes into this category of fools; he is rather the professional jester. *44–5. wit . . . you:* a variant form of the saying "wit, whither wilt?" *51. naught:* bad.

Now I'll stand to it the pancakes were naught and the mustard was good, and yet was not the knight forsworn.°

CEL How prove you that, in the great heap of your knowledge?

ROS Aye, marry, now unmuzzle your wisdom.

TOUCH Stand you both forth now. Stroke your chins, and swear by your beards that I am a knave.

CEL By our beards, if we had them, thou art.

TOUCH By my knavery, if I had it, then I were. But if you swear by that that is not, you are not forsworn. No more was this knight swearing by his honor, for he never had any, or if he had, he had sworn it away before ever he saw those pancakes or that mustard.

CEL Prithee who is 't that thou meanest?

TOUCH One that old Frederick, your father, loves.

CEL My father's love is enough to honor him. Enough! Speak no more of him, you'll be whipped for taxation° one of these days.

TOUCH The more pity that fools may not speak wisely what wise men do foolishly.

CEL By my troth, thou sayest true, for since the little wit that fools have was silenced, the little foolery that wise men have makes a great show. Here comes Monsieur Le Beau.

ROS With his mouth full of news.

CEL Which he will put on us, as pigeons feed their young.°

ROS Then shall we be news-crammed.

CEL All the better. We shall be the more marketable. [*Enter* LE BEAU.] *Bon jour,* Monsieur Le Beau. What's the news?

LE BEAU Fair Princess, you have lost much good sport.

CEL Sport! Of what color?°

LE BEAU What color, madam! How shall I answer you?

ROS As wit and fortune will.

TOUCH Or as the Destinies decree.

CEL Well said. That was laid on with a trowel.°

TOUCH Nay, if I keep not my rank—

ROS Thou losest thy old smell.°

LE BEAU You amaze me, ladies. I would have told you of good wrestling which you have lost the sight of.

ROS Yet tell us the manner of the wrestling.

LE BEAU I will tell you the beginning, and if it please your ladyships, you may see the end; for the best is yet to do, and here where you are they are coming to perform it.

53. forsworn: false in his oath. *66. taxation:* satire. *73. pigeons . . . young:* Pigeons thrust the food into the mouths of their young. *78. Sport . . . color:* Celia pretends that Le Beau had said "spot," the two words, in Shakespeare's time, being pronounced alike. *82. laid . . . trowel:* i.e., as a bricklayer slaps down the mortar. *83–4. rank . . . smell:* position as a professional fool; but Celia pretends that it means highly scented—like a fox.

CEL Well, the beginning, that is dead and buried.°

LE BEAU There comes an old man and his three sons—

CEL I could match this beginning with an old tale.°

LE BEAU Three proper° young men, of excellent growth and presence.°

ROS With bills on their necks, "Be it known unto all men by these presents."°

LE BEAU The eldest of the three wrestled with Charles, the Duke's wrestler, which Charles in a moment threw him, and broke three of his ribs, that there is little hope of life in him. So he served the second, and so the third. Yonder they lie, the poor old man, their father, making such pitiful dole° over them that all the beholders take his part with weeping.

ROS Alas!

TOUCH But what is the sport, monsieur, that the ladies have lost?

LE BEAU Why, this that I speak of.

TOUCH Thus men may grow wiser every day. It is the first time that ever I heard breaking of ribs was sport for ladies.

CEL Or I, I promise thee.

ROS But is there any else longs to see this broken music° in his sides? Is there yet another dotes upon rib-breaking? Shall we see this wrestling, Cousin?

LE BEAU You must if you stay here, for here is the place appointed for the wrestling, and they are ready to perform it.

CEL Yonder, sure, they are coming. Let us now stay and see it.

[*Flourish.*° *Enter* DUKE FREDERICK, LORDS, ORLANDO, CHARLES, *and* ATTENDANTS.]

DUKE F Come on. Since the youth will not be entreated, his own peril° on his forwardness.

ROS Is yonder the man?

LE BEAU Even he, madam.

CEL Alas, he is too young! Yet he looks successfully.°

DUKE F How now, Daughter and Cousin!° Are you crept hither to see the wrestling?

ROS Aye, my liege, so please you give us leave.

DUKE F You will take little delight in it, I can tell you, there is such

91. the . . . buried: i.e., tell the beginning that is now past history. *93. I . . . tale:* your words sound like the beginning of an old tale. *94. proper:* handsome. *95. presence:* appearance. *96–7. With . . . presents:* Rosalind makes a far-fetched pun. Le Beau's "presence" reminds her of "presents" as it occurs in the common formula at the beginning of many legal documents: "Know all men by these presents"—*noverint universi per praesentes. bills:* advertisements. *102. dole:* lamentation. *110. broken music:* lit., music performed by different kinds of instruments. *115. s.d., Flourish:* fanfare of trumpets. *116–7. his . . . peril:* i.e., he does it at his own risk. *120. successfully:* as if he would succeed. *121. Cousin:* used of any near relation.

odds in the man.° In pity of the challenger's youth I would fain° dissuade him, but he will not be entreated. Speak to him, ladies, see if you can move him.

CEL Call him hither, good Monsieur Le Beau.

DUKE F Do so. I'll not be by.

LE BEAU Monsieur the challenger, the Princess calls for you.

ORL I attend° them with all respect and duty.

ROS Young man, have you challenged Charles the wrestler?

ORL No, fair Princess, he is the general challenger. I come but in, as others do, to try with him the strength of my youth.

CEL Young gentleman, your spirits are too bold for your years. You have seen cruel proof of this man's strength. If you saw yourself with your eyes, or knew yourself with your judgment, the fear of your adventure would counsel you to a more equal enterprise. We pray you, for your own sake, to embrace your own safety and give over this attempt.

ROS Do, young sir, your reputation shall not therefore be misprized. We will make it our suit to the Duke that the wrestling might not go forward.

ORL I beseech you punish me not with your hard thoughts, wherein I confess me much guilty, to deny so fair and excellent ladies anything. But let your fair eyes and gentle wishes go with me to my trial. Wherein if I be foiled, there is but one shamed that was never gracious; if killed, but one dead that is willing to be so. I shall do my friends no wrong, for I have none to lament me; the world no injury, for in it I have nothing. Only in the world I fill up a place which may be better supplied when I have made it empty.

ROS The little strength that I have, I would it were with you.

CEL And mine, to eke out hers.

ROS Fare you well. Pray Heaven I be deceived in you!

CEL Your heart's desires be with you!

CHA Come, where is this young gallant that is so desirous to lie with his mother earth?

ORL Ready, sir, but his will hath in it a more modest working.°

DUKE F You shall try but one fall.

CHA No, I warrant your Grace, you shall not entreat him to a second, that have so mightily persuaded him from a first.

ORL You mean to mock me after, you should not have mocked me before. But come your ways.°

ROS Now Hercules be thy speed,° young man!

124–5. such . . . man: the odds on Charles are so great. *125. fain:* gladly. *131. attend:* wait on. *158. more . . . working:* i.e., I do not intend to do anything so improper. *163. come . . . ways:* i.e., come on. *164. speed:* aid.

CEL I would I were invisible, to catch the strong fellow by the leg.

[*They wrestle.*]

ROS Oh, excellent young man!

CEL If I had a thunderbolt in mine eye, I can tell who should down.

[*Shout.* CHARLES *is thrown.*]

DUKE F No more, no more.

ORL Yes, I beseech your Grace. I am not yet well breathed.°

DUKE F How dost thou, Charles?

LE BEAU He cannot speak, my lord.

DUKE F Bear him away. What is thy name, young man?

ORL Orlando, my liege, the youngest son of Sir Rowland de Boys.

DUKE F I would thou hadst been son to some man else.
The world esteemed thy father honorable,
But I did find him still° mine enemy.
Thou shouldst have better pleased me with this deed
Hadst thou descended from another house.
But fare thee well, thou art a gallant youth.
I would thou hadst told me of another father.

[*Exeunt* DUKE FREDERICK, *train, and* LE BEAU.]

CEL Were I my father, Coz, would I do this?

ORL I am more proud to be Sir Rowland's son,
His youngest son, and would not change that calling°
To be adopted heir to Frederick.

ROS My father loved Sir Rowland as his soul,
And all the world was of my father's mind.
Had I before known this young man his son,
I should have given him tears unto° entreaties
Ere he should thus have ventured.

CEL Gentle Cousin,
Let us go thank him and encourage him.
My father's rough and envious disposition
Sticks me at heart.° Sir, you have well deserved.
If you do keep your promises in love
But justly, as you have exceeded all promise,
Your mistress shall be happy.

ROS Gentleman,
[*Giving him a chain from her neck*]
Wear this for me, one out of suits° with Fortune,
That could° give more but that her hand lacks means.
Shall we go, Coz?

170. *breathed:* exercised. 177. *still:* always. 184. *calling:* name. 189. *unto:* added to. 193. *Sticks . . . heart:* pierces me to the heart. 197. *out of suits:* not in the service of, not favored by. 198. *could:* would if she could.

CEL Aye. Fare you well, fair gentleman.
ORL Can I not say I thank you? My better parts
Are all thrown down,° and that which here stands up
Is but a quintain,° a mere lifeless block.
ROS He calls us back. My pride fell with my fortunes,
I'll ask him what he would. Did you call, sir?
Sir, you have wrestled well and overthrown
More than your enemies.°
CEL Will you go, Coz?
ROS Have with you. Fare you well.
[*Exeunt* ROSALIND *and* CELIA.]
ORL What passion hangs these weights upon my tongue?
I cannot speak to her, yet she urged conference.°
O poor Orlando, thou art overthrown!
Or Charles or something weaker masters thee.
[*Re-enter* LE BEAU.]
LE BEAU Good sir, I do in friendship counsel you
To leave this place. Albeit you have deserved
High commendation, true applause, and love,
Yet such is now the Duke's condition
That he miscónstrues all that you have done.
The Duke is humorous.° What he is, indeed,
More suits you to conceive° than I to speak of.
ORL I thank you, sir. And pray you tell me this:
Which of the two was daughter of the Duke
That here was at the wrestling?
LE BEAU Neither his daughter, if we judge by manners;
But yet indeed the lesser° is his daughter.
The other is daughter to the banished Duke,
And here detained by her usurping uncle,
To keep his daughter company, whose loves
Are dearer than the natural bond of sisters.
But I can tell you that of late this Duke
Hath ta'en displeasure 'gainst his gentle niece,
Grounded upon no other argument
But that the people praise her for her virtues
And pity her for her good father's sake.
And, on my life, his malice 'gainst the lady
Will suddenly break forth. Sir, fare you well.

201–2. *My . . . down:* i.e., I am behaving as if I had no manners. 203. *quintain:* a block, shaped like a man, used for tilting practice. 207. *More . . . enemies:* i.e., my heart. 210. *urged conference:* invited me to talk. 218. *humorous:* moody, touchy. 219. *conceive:* imagine. 224. *lesser:* the F1 reads "taller," but later Rosalind is described as the taller.

Hereafter, in a better world than this,
I shall desire more love and knowledge of you.

ORL I rest much bounden to you. Fare you well.

[*Exit* LE BEAU.]

Thus must I from the smoke into the smother,°
From tyrant Duke unto a tyrant brother.
But heavenly Rosalind!

[*Exit.*]

Scene III. A room in the palace.

[*Enter* CELIA *and* ROSALIND.]

CEL Why, Cousin! Why, Rosalind! Cupid have mercy! Not a word?

ROS Not one to throw at a dog.

CEL No, thy words are too precious to be cast away upon curs, throw some of them at me. Come, lame me with reasons.°

ROS Then there were two cousins laid up, when the one should be lamed with reasons and the other mad without any.

CEL But is all this for your father?

ROS No, some of it is for my child's father. Oh, how full of briers is this working-day world!

CEL They are but burrs, Cousin, thrown upon thee in holiday foolery. If we walk not in the trodden paths, our very petticoats will catch them.

ROS I could shake them off my coat. These burrs are in my heart.

CEL Hem° them away.

ROS I would try if I could cry hem and have him.

CEL Come, come, wrestle with thy affections.

ROS Oh, they take the part of a better wrestler than myself!

CEL Oh, a good wish upon you! You will try in time, in despite° of a fall. But, turning these jests out of service, let us talk in good earnest. Is it possible, on such a sudden, you should fall into so strong a liking with old Sir Rowland's youngest son?

ROS The Duke my father loved his father dearly.

CEL Doth it therefore ensue that you should love his son dearly? By this kind of chase,° I should hate him, for my father hated his father dearly, yet I hate not Orlando.

ROS No, faith, hate him not, for my sake.

CEL Why should I not? Doth he not deserve well?

239. smother: thick smoke—a phrase like "out of the frying pan into the fire."

Sc. iii: *4. lame . . . reasons:* make me lame by throwing arguments at me. *14. Hem:* i.e., cough them up. *18. despite:* spite. *23–4. By . . . chase:* by chasing after that kind of argument.

ROS Let me love him for that, and do you love him because I do. Look, here comes the Duke.

CEL With his eyes full of anger.

[*Enter* DUKE FREDERICK, *with* LORDS.]

DUKE F Mistress, dispatch you with your safest haste°
And get you from our Court.

ROS Me, Uncle?

DUKE F You, Cousin.
Within these ten days if that thou be'st found
So near our public Court as twenty miles,
Thou diest for it.

ROS I do beseech your Grace,
Let me the knowledge of my fault bear with me.
If with myself I hold intelligence,°
Or have acquaintance with mine own desires,
If that I do not dream, or be not frantic°—
As I do trust I am not—then, dear Uncle,
Never so much as in a thought unborn
Did I offend your Highness.

DUKE F Thus do all traitors.
If their purgation° did consist in words,
They are as innocent as grace° itself.
Let it suffice thee that I trust thee not.

ROS Yet your mistrust cannot make me a traitor.
Tell me whereon the likelihood depends.

DUKE F Thou art thy father's daughter, there's enough.

ROS So was I when your Highness took his dukedom,
So was I when your Highness banished him.
Treason is not inherited, my lord,
Or if we did derive° it from our friends,°
What's that to me? My father was no traitor.
Then, good my liege, mistake me not so much
To think my poverty is treacherous.

CEL Dear sovereign, hear me speak.

DUKE F Aye, Celia, we stayed her for your sake,
Else had she with her father ranged along.°

CEL I did not then entreat to have her stay,
It was your pleasure and your own remorse.°
I was too young that time to value her,

31. *safest haste:* i.e., the quicker you go, the safer for you. 37. *If . . . intelligence:* if I understood my own thoughts. 39. *frantic:* mad. 43. *purgation:* proof of innocence. 44. *grace:* i.e., divine grace. 52. *derive:* acquire by descent. *friends:* relations. 58. *ranged along:* wandered in his company. 60. *remorse:* pity.

But now I know her. If she be a traitor,
Why so am I. We still have slept together,
Rose at an instant, learned, played, eat together,
And wheresoe'er we went, like Juno's swans,°
Still we went coupled and inseparable.

DUKE F She is too subtle for thee, and her smoothness,
Her very silence and her patience,
Speak to the people, and they pity her.
Thou art a fool. She robs thee of thy name,
And thou wilt show more bright and seem more virtuous
When she is gone. Then open not thy lips.
Firm and irrevocable is my doom
Which I have passed upon her, she is banished.

CEL Pronounce that sentence then on me, my liege.
I cannot live out of her company.

DUKE F You are a fool. You, Niece, provide yourself.
If you outstay the time, upon mine honor,
And in the greatness of my word, you die.

[*Exeunt* DUKE FREDERICK *and* LORDS.]

CEL O my poor Rosalind, whither wilt thou go?
Wilt thou change fathers? I will give thee mine.
I charge thee, be not thou more grieved than I am.

ROS I have more cause.

CEL Thou hast not, Cousin.
Prithee, be cheerful. Know'st thou not the Duke
Hath banished me, his daughter?

ROS That he hath not.

CEL No, hath not? Rosalind lacks then the love
Which teacheth thee that thou and I am one.
Shall we be sundered? Shall we part, sweet girl?
No. Let my father seek another heir.
Therefore devise with me how we may fly,
Whither to go and what to bear with us.
And do not seek to take your change upon you,°
To bear your griefs yourself and leave me out;
For, by this Heaven, now at our sorrows pale,
Say what thou canst, I'll go along with thee.

ROS Why, whither shall we go?

CEL To seek my uncle in the forest of Arden.

ROS Alas, what danger will it be to us,
Maids as we are, to travel forth so far!
Beauty provoketh thieves sooner than gold.

65. Juno's swans: Editors have pointed out that Venus was the goddess who possessed a chariot drawn by swans. *92. take . . . you:* bear your changed fortunes alone.

CEL I'll put myself in poor and mean attire
And with a kind of umber smirch my face.°
The like do you. So shall we pass along
And never stir assailants.

ROS Were it not better,
Because that I am more than common tall,
That I did suit me° all points° like a man?
A gallant curtal ax° upon my thigh,
A boar spear in my hand, and—in my heart
Lie there what hidden woman's fear there will—
We'll have a swashing° and a martial outside,
As many other mannish cowards have
That do outface it with their semblances.°

CEL What shall I call thee when thou art a man?

ROS I'll have no worse a name than Jove's own page,
And therefore look you call me Ganymede.
But what will you be called?

CEL Something that hath a reference to my state,
No longer Celia, but Aliena.°

ROS But, Cousin, what if we assayed° to steal
The clownish fool out of your father's Court?
Would he not be a comfort to our travel?

CEL He'll go along o'er the wide world with me,
Leave me alone to woo him. Let's away
And get our jewels and our wealth together,
Devise the fittest time and safest way
To hide us from pursuit that will be made
After my flight. Now go we in content
To liberty and not to banishment.

[*Exeunt.*]

ACT II

Scene I. The Forest of Arden.

[*Enter* DUKE *Senior,* AMIENS, *and two or three* LORDS, *like foresters.*]

DUKE S Now, my comates and brothers in exile,
Hath not old custom° made this life more sweet

102. umber . . . face: Elizabethan ladies regarded an ivory complexion as beautiful. The pale complexions of the two girls would have made them conspicuous among countryfolk. *106. suit me:* dress myself. *all points:* in every detail. *107. curtal ax:* cutlass. *110. swashing:* swaggering. *112. semblances:* outward appearances. *118. Aliena:* i.e., the alien, stranger. *119. assayed:* attempted.

Act II, Sc. i: *2. old custom:* long experience.

Than that of painted° pomp? Are not these woods
More free from peril than the envious Court?
Here feel we but the penalty of Adam,°
The seasons' difference, as the icy fang
And churlish chiding of the winter's wind,
Which, when it bites and blows upon my body,
Even till I shrink with cold, I smile and say
"This is no flattery. These are councilors
That feelingly° persuade me what I am."
Sweet are the uses° of adversity,
Which, like the toad, ugly and venomous,
Wears yet a precious jewel in his head.°
And this our life exempt from public haunt°
Finds tongues in trees, books in the running brooks,
Sermons in stones, and good in everything.°
I would not change it.

AMI Happy is your Grace,
That can translate the stubbornness of fortune
Into so quiet and so sweet a style.

DUKE S Come, shall we go and kill us venison?
And yet it irks me the poor dappled fools,
Being native burghers° of this desert city,
Should in their own confines° with forkèd heads°
Have their round haunches gored.

1. LORD Indeed, my lord,
The melancholy Jaques grieves at that,
And, in that kind,° swears you do more usurp
Than doth your brother that hath banished you.
Today my Lord of Amiens and myself
Did steal behind him as he lay along°
Under an oak whose antique root peeps out
Upon the brook that brawls along this wood.
To the which place a poor sequestered° stag,
That from the hunter's aim had ta'en a hurt,
Did come to languish, and indeed, my lord,
The wretched animal heaved forth such groans
That their discharge did stretch his leathern coat
Almost to bursting, and the big round tears

3. *painted:* artificial. 5. *but . . . Adam:* only the penalty laid on man; i.e., to feel the cold. 11. *feelingly:* i.e., through my feelings. 12. *uses:* advantages. 13–4. *toad . . . head:* This was a common belief. 15. *exempt . . . haunt:* free from crowds. 16–7. *Finds . . . everything:* i.e., that there is everywhere a lesson in nature. 23. *burghers:* citizens. 24. *confines:* territories. *forked heads:* i.e., arrows. 27. *kind:* manner; i.e., hunting the deer. 30. *lay along:* stretched at full length. 33. *sequestered:* separated from the others.

Coursed one another down his innocent nose
In piteous chase. And thus the hairy fool,
Much markèd of the melancholy Jaques,
Stood on the extremest verge of the swift brook,
Augmenting it with tears.

DUKE S But what said Jaques?
Did he not moralize° this spectacle?

1. LORD Oh yes, into a thousand similes.
First, for his weeping into the needless stream,
"Poor deer," quoth he, "thou makest a testament
As worldlings do, giving thy sum of more°
To that which had too much." Then, being there alone,
Left and abandoned of his velvet° friends,
" 'Tis right," quoth he. "Thus misery doth part
The flux° of company." Anon a careless herd,
Full of the pasture, jumps along by him
And never stays to greet him. "Aye," quoth Jaques
"Sweep on, you fat and greasy citizens,
'Tis just the fashion. Wherefore do you look
Upon that poor and broken bankrupt there?"
Thus most invectively° he pierceth through
The body of the country, city, Court,
Yea, and of this our life, swearing that we
Are mere usurpers, tyrants, and what's worse,
To fright the animals and to kill them up
In their assigned and native dwelling-place.

DUKE S And did you leave him in this contemplation?

2. LORD We did, my lord, weeping and commenting
Upon the sobbing deer.

DUKE S Show me the place.
I love to cope° him in these sullen° fits,
For then he's full of matter.°

1. LORD I'll bring you to him straight.

[*Exeunt.*]

Scene II. A room in the palace.

[*Enter* DUKE FREDERICK, *with* LORDS.]

DUKE F Can it be possible that no man saw them?
It cannot be. Some villains of my Court

44. *moralize:* make moral comments on. 48. *sum of more:* i.e., adding your tears to the water. 50. *velvet:* velvet-coated, sleek. 52. *flux:* flow, crowd. 58. *invectively:* with bitter satire. 67. *cope:* encounter. *sullen:* moody. 68. *matter:* good sense.

Are of consent and sufferance° in this.
1. LORD I cannot hear of any that did see her.
The ladies, her attendants of her chamber,
Saw her abed, and in the morning early
They found the bed untreasured of their mistress.
2. LORD My lord, the roynish° clown at whom so oft
Your Grace was wont to laugh is also missing.
Hisperia, the Princess' gentlewoman,
Confesses that she secretly o'erheard
Your daughter and her cousin much commend
The parts and graces of the wrestler
That did but lately foil the sinewy Charles,
And she believes, wherever they are gone,
That youth is surely in their company.
DUKE F Send to his brother, fetch that gallant hither.
If he be absent, bring his brother to me.
I'll make him find him. Do this suddenly,
And let no search and inquisition° quail°
To bring again these foolish runaways.
[*Exeunt.*]

Scene III. Before OLIVER*'s house.*

[*Enter* ORLANDO *and* ADAM, *meeting.*]

ORL Who's there?
ADAM What, my young master? O my gentle master!
O my sweet master! O you memory
Of old Sir Rowland! Why, what make° you here?
Why are you virtuous? Why do people love you?
And wherefore are you gentle, strong, and valiant?
Why would you be so fond° to overcome
The bonny prizer° of the humorous Duke?
Your praise is come too swiftly home before you.
Know you not, master, to some kind of men
Their graces serve them but as enemies?
No more do yours. Your virtues, gentle master,
Are sanctified and holy traitors° to you.
Oh, what a world is this when what is comely
Envenoms° him that bears it!

Sc. ii: *3. of . . . sufferance:* willing accomplices. *8. roynish:* scurvy. *20. inquisition:* inquiry. *quail:* slacken.

Sc. iii: *4. make:* do. *7. fond:* foolish. *8. prizer:* prize fighter. *13. sanctified . . . traitors:* traitors who appear pious and holy. *15. Envenoms:* poisons.

ORL Why, what's the matter?
ADAM O unhappy youth!
Come not within these doors, within this roof
The enemy of all your graces lives.
Your brother—no, no brother, yet the son—
Yet not the son, I will not call him son
Of him I was about to call his father—
Hath heard your praises, and this night he means
To burn the lodging where you use to lie
And you within it. If he fail of that,
He will have other means to cut you off.
I overheard him and his practices.°
This is no place, this house is but a butchery.
Abhor it, fear it, do not enter it.
ORL Why, whither, Adam, wouldst thou have me go?
ADAM No matter whither so you come not here.
ORL What, wouldst thou have me go and beg my food?
Or with a base and boisterous° sword enforce
A thievish living on the common road?
This I must do, or know not what to do.
Yet this I will not do, do how I can.
I rather will subject me° to the malice
Of a diverted blood° and bloody brother.
ADAM But do not so. I have five hundred crowns,
The thrifty hire° I saved under your father,
Which I did store to be my foster nurse
When service should in my old limbs lie lame,
And unregarded age in corners thrown.
Take that, and He that doth the ravens feed,
Yea, providently caters for the sparrow,
Be comfort to my age! Here is the gold,
All this I give you. Let me be your servant.
Though I look old, yet I am strong and lusty,
For in my youth I never did apply
Hot and rebellious liquors in my blood,
Nor did not with unbashful forehead° woo
The means of° weakness and debility;
Therefore my age is as a lusty winter,
Frosty, but kindly. Let me go with you,
I'll do the service of a younger man
In all your business and necessities.

26. practices: plots. *32. boisterous:* threatening. *36. subject me:* submit. *37. diverted blood:* i.e., one whose natural feelings have been turned aside. *39. thrifty hire:* saved-up pay. *50. unbashful forehead:* vicious boldness. *51. means of:* i.e., pleasures that bring.

ORL O good old man, how well in thee appears
The constant° service of the antique° world,
When service sweat for duty, not for meed!°
Thou art not for the fashion of these times,
Where none will sweat but for promotion,
And having that do choke their service up
Even with the having.° It is not so with thee.
But, poor old man, thou prunest a rotten tree
That cannot so much as a blossom yield
In lieu of all thy pains and husbandry.°
But come thy ways, we'll go along together,
And ere we have thy youthful wages spent
We'll light upon some settled low content.°

ADAM Master, go on, and I will follow thee
To the last gasp, with truth and loyalty.
From seventeen years till now almost fourscore
Here livèd I, but now live here no more.
At seventeen years many their fortunes seek,
But at fourscore it is too late a week.°
Yet fortune cannot recompense me better
Than to die well and not my master's debtor.

[*Exeunt.*]

Scene IV. The FOREST *of Arden.*

[*Enter* ROSALIND *disguised as* GANYMEDE, CELIA *disguised as* ALIENA, *and* TOUCHSTONE.]

ROS Oh, Jupiter, how weary are my spirits!

TOUCH I care not for my spirits if my legs were not weary.

ROS I could find in my heart to disgrace my man's apparel and to cry like a woman. But I must comfort the weaker vessel, as doublet and hose° ought to show itself courageous to petticoat, therefore, courage, good Aliena.

CEL I pray you bear with me, I cannot go no further.

TOUCH For my part, I had rather bear with you than bear you. Yet I should bear no cross° if I did bear you, for I think you have no money in your purse.

57. *constant:* faithful. *antique:* ancient, "good old." 58. *meed:* reward. 61–2. *having . . . having:* and as soon as they have their reward cease to give good service. 65. *husbandry:* economy. 68. *settled . . . content:* humble but contented way of living. 74. *too . . . week:* a week too late.

Sc. iv: 4–5. *doublet . . . hose:* i.e., man's attire, for Rosalind is now dressed as Ganymede. 9. *bear no cross:* lit., endure no misfortune; but it also meant "have no money," as Elizabethan money had a cross on the reverse side.

ROS Well, this is the forest of Arden.

TOUCH Aye, now am I in Arden, the more fool I. When I was at home, I was in a better place. But travelers must be content.

ROS Aye, be so, good Touchstone. [*Enter* CORIN *and* SILVIUS.] Look you who comes here, a young man and an old in solemn talk.

COR That is the way to make her scorn you still.

SIL Oh, Corin, that thou knew'st how I do love her!

COR I partly guess, for I have loved ere now.

SIL No, Corin, being old, thou canst not guess,
Though in thy youth thou wast as true a lover
As ever sighed upon a midnight pillow.
But if thy love were ever like to mine—
As sure I think did never man love so—
How many actions most ridiculous
Hast thou been drawn to by thy fantasy?°

COR Into a thousand that I have forgotten.

SIL Oh, thou didst then ne'er love so heartily!
If thou remember'st not the slightest folly
That ever love did make thee run into,
Thou hast not loved.
Or if thou hast not sat as I do now,
Wearing° thy hearer in° thy mistress' praise,
Thou hast not loved.
Or if thou hast not broke from company
Abruptly, as my passion now makes me,
Thou hast not loved.
Oh, Phebe, Phebe, Phebe!

[*Exit*]

ROS Alas, poor shepherd! Searching of thy wound,°
I have by hard adventure° found mine own.

TOUCH And I mine. I remember when I was in love I broke my sword upon a stone and bid him take that for coming a-night to Jane Smile. And I remember the kissing of her batlet° and the cow's dugs that her pretty chopt° hands had milked. And I remember the wooing of a peascod° instead of her, from whom I took two cods° and, giving her them again, said with weeping tears, "Wear these for my sake." We that are truelovers run into strange capers, but as all is mortal in nature, so is all nature in love mortal in folly.°

ROS Thou speakest wiser than thou art ware of.

25. *fantasy:* fancy, love. 32. *Wearing:* wearing out. *in:* with. 38. *Searching . . . wound:* i.e., listening to you probing your wound. 39. *hard adventure:* painful chance. 42. *batlet:* bat used for beating clothes during washing. 43. *chopt:* chapped. 44. *peascod:* usually peapod, but here the whole plant. 44. *cods:* pods. 47. *mortal in folly:* deadly silly.

TOUCH Nay, I shall ne'er be ware of mine own wit till I break my shins against it.

ROS Jove, Jove! This shepherd's passion
Is much upon my fashion.

TOUCH And mine, but it grows something stale with me.

CEL I pray you, one of you question yon man
If he for gold will give us any food.
I faint almost to death.

TOUCH Holloa, you clown!°

ROS Peace, fool. He's not thy kinsman.

COR Who calls?

TOUCH Your betters, sir.

COR Else are they very wretched.

ROS Peace, I say. Good even to you, friend.

COR And to you, gentle sir, and to you all.

ROS I prithee, shepherd, if that love or gold
Can in this desert place buy entertainment,°
Bring us where we may rest ourselves and feed.
Here's a young maid with travel much oppressed
And faints for succor.

COR Fair sir, I pity her,
And wish, for her sake more than for mine own,
My fortunes were more able to relieve her.
But I am shepherd to another man
And do not shear the fleeces that I graze.°
My master is of churlish disposition
And little recks° to find the way to Heaven
By doing deeds of hospitality.
Besides, his cote,° his flocks and bounds of feed,°
Are now on sale, and at our sheepcote now,
By reason of his absence, there is nothing
That you will feed on. But what is, come see,
And in my voice most welcome shall you be.

ROS What is he that shall buy his flock and pasture?

COR That young swain° that you saw here but erewhile,
That little cares for buying anything.

ROS I pray thee, if it stand with honesty,
Buy thou the cottage, pasture, and the flock,
And thou shalt have to pay for it of us.

CEL And we will mend° thy wages. I like this place,
And willingly could waste my time in it.

57. *clown:* rustic. 63. *entertainment:* accommodation. 70. *do . . . graze:* do not sell the wool of the sheep I feed—because he is a hired shepherd and not the owner. 72. *recks:* cares. 74. *cote:* cottage. *bounds of feed:* pastures. 80. *swain:* a poetic word, usually implying a young man in love. 85. *mend:* improve.

COR Assuredly the thing is to be sold.
Go with me. If you like upon report
The soil, the profit, and this kind of life,
I will your very faithful feeder be
And buy it with your gold right suddenly.

[*Exeunt.*]

Scene V. The forest.

[*Enter* AMIENS, JAQUES, *and others.*]

AMI [*Sings.*]

Under the greenwood tree
Who loves to lie with me,
And turn° his merry note
Unto the sweet bird's throat,
Come hither, come hither, come hither.
Here shall he see
No enemy
But winter and rough weather.

JAQ More, more, I prithee, more.

AMI It will make you melancholy, Monsieur Jaques.

JAQ I thank it. More, I prithee, more. I can suck melancholy out of a song as a weasel sucks eggs. More, I prithee, more.

AMI My voice is ragged. I know I cannot please you.

JAQ I do not desire you to please me, I do desire you to sing. Come, more, another stanzo.° Call you 'em stanzos?

AMI What will you, Monsieur Jaques.

JAQ Nay, I care not for their names, they owe me nothing.° Will you sing?

AMI More at your request than to please myself.

JAQ Well then, if ever I thank any man, I'll thank you. But that they call compliment is like the encounter of two dog apes,° and when a man thanks me heartily, methinks I have given him a penny and he renders me the beggarly thanks.° Come, sing, and you that will not, hold your tongues.

AMI Well, I'll end the song. Sirs, cover° the while.° The Duke will drink under this tree. He hath been all this day to look you.

JAQ And I have been all this day to avoid him. He is too disputable° for my company. I think of as many matters as he, but I give Heaven thanks, and make no boast of them. Come, warble, come.

Sc. v: *3. turn:* harmonize. Some editors read "tune." *15. stanzo:* stanza: lit., a stand or set. *17. owe me nothing:* i.e., and so mean nothing to me. *21. dog apes:* male baboons. *23. beggarly thanks:* i.e., effusively like a beggar. *25. cover:* lay the table. *25. the while:* in the meanwhile. *27. disputable:* argumentative.

SONG. [*All together here.*]

Who doth ambition shun,
And loves to live i' the sun,
Seeking the food he eats,
And pleased with what he gets,
Come hither, come hither, come hither.
Here shall he see
No enemy
But winter and rough weather.

JAQ I'll give you a verse to this note,° that I made yesterday in despite of my invention.°

AMI And I'll sing it.

JAQ Thus it goes:

If it do come to pass
That any man turn ass,
Leaving his wealth and ease
A stubborn will to please,
Ducdame,° ducdame, ducdame.
Here shall he see
Gross fools as he,
An if he will come to me.

AMI What's that "ducdame?"

JAQ 'Tis a Greek invocation to call fools into a circle. I'll go sleep, if I can. If I cannot, I'll rail against all the firstborn of Egypt.

AMI And I'll go seek the Duke. His banquet is prepared.

[*Exeunt. severally.*°]

Scene VI. The forest.

[*Enter* ORLANDO *and* ADAM.]

ADAM Dear master, I can go no further. Oh, I die for food. Here lie I down, and measure out° my grave. Farewell, kind master.

ORL Why, how now, Adam! No greater heart in thee? Live a little, comfort a little, cheer thyself a little. If this uncouth forest yield anything savage, I will either be food for it or bring it for food to thee. Thy conceit° is nearer death than thy powers.° For my sake

38. to . . . note: to go with this tune. *38–9. despite . . . invention:* i.e., although I am no good at this sort of thing. *in despite:* in spite of. *invention:* the creative faculty. *46. Ducdame:* a three-syllable word. Many commentators have tried to trace the origin of this word. It is most probably one of the many meaningless syllables—like "hey nonny no"—so often used to fill out the line of a song. Jaques' own explanation is that it is a Greek invocation to call fools into a circle (i.e., set them gossiping). It has greatly stimulated scholars to make learned guesses. *53. s.d., severally:* by different exits.

Sc. vi: *2. measure out:* i.e., the length of. *6. conceit:* imagination. *powers:* strength.

be comfortable,° hold death awhile at the arm's end. I will here be with thee presently,° and if I bring thee not something to eat, I will give thee leave to die. But if thou diest before I come, thou art a mocker of my labor. Well said! Thou lookest cheerly, and I'll be with thee quickly. Yet thou liest in the bleak air. Come, I will bear thee to some shelter, and thou shalt not die for lack of a dinner if there live anything in this desert. Cheerly, good Adam!

[*Exeunt.*]

Scene VII. The forest.

[*A table set out. Enter* DUKE *Senior,* AMIENS, *and* LORDS *like outlaws.*]

DUKE S I think he be transformed into a beast,
For I can nowhere find him like a° man.
I. LORD My lord, he is but even now gone hence.
Here was he merry, hearing of a song.
DUKE S If he, compact of jars,° grow musical,
We shall have shortly discord in the spheres.
Go, seek him. Tell him I would speak with him.
[*Enter* JAQUES.]
I. LORD He saves my labor by his own approach.
DUKE S Why, how now, monsieur! What a life is this
That your poor friends must woo your company?
What, you look merrily!
JAQ A fool, a fool! I met a fool i' the forest,
A motley fool,° a miserable world!
As I do live by food, I met a fool,
Who laid him down and basked him in the sun,
And railed on Lady Fortune in good terms,
In good set terms,° and yet a motley fool.
"Good morrow, fool," quoth I. "No, sir," quoth he.
"Call me not fool till Heaven hath sent me fortune."
And then he drew a dial° from his poke,°
And looking on it with lackluster eye,
Says very wisely, "It is ten o'clock.
Thus we may see," quoth he, "how the world wags.
'Tis but an hour ago since it was nine,
And after one hour more 'twill be eleven,
And so, from hour to hour, we ripe and ripe,

7. *comfortable:* comforted. 8. *presently:* immediately.

Sc. vii: 2. *like a:* in the shape of. 5. *compact of jars:* made of discords. . . . 13. *motley fool:* i.e., a professional fool. *Motley* was the particolored dress worn by court jesters. 17. *set terms:* phrases carefully composed. 20. *dial:* watch. *poke:* pocket.

And then, from hour to hour, we rot and rot,
And thereby hangs a tale." When I did hear
The motley fool thus moral on the time,
My lungs began to crow like chanticleer,°
That fools should be so deep-contemplative,°
And I did laugh sans° intermission
An hour by his dial. Oh, noble fool!
A worthy fool! Motley's the only wear.

DUKE S What fool is this?

JAQ Oh, worthy fool! One that hath been a courtier,
And says if ladies be but young and fair,
They have the gift to know it. And in his brain,
Which is as dry as the remainder° biscuit
After a voyage, he hath strange places crammed
With observation, the which he vents°
In mangled forms.° Oh, that I were a fool!
I am ambitious for a motley coat.

DUKE S Thou shalt have one.

JAQ It is my only suit,°
Provided that you weed your better judgments
Of all opinion that grows rank° in them
That I am wise. I must have liberty
Withal, as large a charter° as the wind
To blow on° whom I please. For so fools have,
And they that are most gallèd° with my folly,
They most must laugh. And why, sir, must they so?
The "why" is plain as way to parish church.
He that a fool doth very wisely hit
Doth very foolishly, although he smart,
Not to seem senseless of the bob.° If not,
The wise man's folly is anatomized°
Even by the squandering° glances of the fool.
Invest° me in my motley, give me leave
To speak my mind, and I will through and through
Cleanse the foul body of the infected world,
If they will patiently receive my medicine.

DUKE S Fie on thee! I can tell what thou wouldst do.

JAQ What, for a counter,° would I do but good?

30. *chanticleer:* the cock. 31. *deep-contemplative:* profoundly thoughtful. 32. *sans:* without. 39. *remainder:* leftover. 41. *vents:* utters. 42. *mangled forms:* quaint phrases. 44. *suit:* with a pun on suit, meaning petition and suit of clothes. 46. *rank:* abundantly, like weeds in a garden. 48. *large a charter:* as free a privilege. 49. *blow on:* censure. 50. *galled:* rubbed sore. 55. *Not . . . bob:* not to pretend that he has not been hurt. *bob:* blow. 56. *anatomized:* dissected. 57. *squandering:* scattered far and wide. 58. *Invest:* robe. 63. *counter:* a valueless token.

DUKE S Most mischievous foul sin, in chiding sin.
For thou thyself hast been a libertine
As sensual as the brutish sting° itself,
And all the embossèd sores and headed evils
That thou with license of free foot° hast caught
Wouldst thou disgorge into the general world.
JAQ Why, who cries out on pride
That can therein tax any private party?°
Doth it not flow as hugely as the sea
Till that the weary very means do ebb?°
What woman in the city do I name
When that I say the city woman bears
The cost of princes on unworthy shoulders?
Who can come in and say that I mean her
When such a one as she such is her neighbor?
Or what is he of basest function°
That says his bravery is not on my cost,°
Thinking that I mean him, but therein suits°
His folly to the mettle° of my speech?
There then, how then? What then? Let me see wherein
My tongue hath wronged him. If it do him right,°
Then he hath wronged himself. If he be free,°
Why then my taxing like a wild goose flies,
Unclaimed of any man. But who comes here?
[*Enter* ORLANDO, *with his sword drawn.*]
ORL Forbear, and eat no more.
JAQ Why, I have eat none yet.
ORL Nor shalt not, till necessity° be served.
JAQ Of what kind should this cock come of?
DUKE S Art thou thus boldened, man, by thy distress?
Or else a rude despiser of good manners,
That in civility° thou seem'st so empty?
ORL You touched my vein at first.° The thorny point°
Of bare distress hath ta'en from me the show
Of smooth civility. Yet am I inland-bred°

66. brutish sting: i.e., lust. *67–8. embossed . . . foot:* carbuncles and boils that result from licentious living. *70–1. who . . . party:* who is attacking any particular person when he denounces pride? Satirists of the time when rebuked for attacking individuals, usually replied that they were denouncing the sin and not individual sinners. *73. weary . . . ebb:* i.e., until the means of pride (i.e., wealth) grow tired and ebb away. *79. basest function:* most degraded kind of employment. *80. bravery . . . cost:* his fine clothes have not cost me anything. *81. suits:* fits. *82. mettle:* material; i.e., his protest shows that my words have fitted him. *84. do . . . right:* if my charges are just. *85. free:* guiltless. *89. necessity:* i.e., those who must have food. *93. civility:* civilized behavior. *94. touched . . . first:* i.e., your first guess is right; I am indeed desperate. *vein:* disposition. *thorny point:* acuteness. *96. inland-bred:* one who knows civilization.

And know some nurture. But forbear, I say.
He dies that touches any of this fruit
Till I and my affairs are answered.

JAQ An° you will not be answered with reason, I must die.

DUKE S What would you have? Your gentleness shall force
More than your force move us to gentleness.

ORL I almost die for food, and let me have it.

DUKE S Sit down and feed, and welcome to our table.

ORL Speak you so gently? Pardon me, I pray you.
I thought that all things had been savage here,
And therefore put I on the countenance
Of stern commandment. But whate'er you are
That in this desert inaccessible,
Under the shade of melancholy boughs,
Lose and neglect the creeping hours of time,
If ever you have looked on better days,
If ever been where bells have knolled° to church,
If ever sat at any good man's feast,
If ever from your eyelids wiped a tear
And know what 'tis to pity and be pitied,
Let gentleness my strong enforcement° be.
In the which hope I blush, and hide my sword.

DUKE S True is it that we have seen better days,
And have with holy bell been knolled to church,
And sat at good men's feasts, and wiped our eyes
Of drops that sacred pity hath engendered.
And therefore sit you down in gentleness
And take upon command° what help we have
That to your wanting may be ministered.

ORL Then but forbear your food a little while
Whiles, like a doe, I go to find my fawn
And give it food. There is an old poor man
Who after me hath many a weary step
Limped in pure love. Till he be first sufficed,°
Oppressed with two weak evils, age and hunger,
I will not touch a bit.

DUKE S Go find him out,
And we will nothing waste till you return.

ORL I thank ye, and be blest for your good comfort!

[*Exit*]

DUKE S Thou seest we are not all alone unhappy.
This wide and universal theater

100. An: if. *113. knolled:* tolled. *117. enforcement:* means of forcing. *124. upon command:* as you may choose to order. *130. sufficed:* satisfied.

Presents more woeful pageants than the scene
Wherein we play in.

JAQ All the world's a stage,
And all the men and women merely players.
They have their exits and their entrances,
And one man in his time plays many parts,
His acts being seven ages. At first the infant,
Mewling° and puking in the nurse's arms.
Then the whining schoolboy, with his satchel
And shining morning face, creeping like snail
Unwillingly to school. And then the lover,
Sighing like furnace, with a woeful ballad°
Made to his mistress' eyebrow. Then a soldier,
Full of strange oaths and bearded like the pard,°
Jealous in honor,° sudden and quick in quarrel,
Seeking the bubble reputation°
Even in the cannon's mouth. And then the justice,
In fair round belly with good capon lined,°
With eyes severe and beard of formal cut,°
Full of wise saws° and modern instances,°
And so he plays his part. The sixth age shifts
Into the lean and slippered Pantaloon°
With spectacles on nose and pouch on side,
His youthful hose, well saved, a world too wide
For his shrunk shank, and his big manly voice,
Turning again toward childish treble, pipes
And whistles in his sound. Last scene of all,
That ends this strange eventful history,
In second childishness and mere oblivion,
Sans teeth, sans eyes, sans taste, sans everything.

[*Re-enter* ORLANDO, *with* ADAM.]

DUKE S Welcome. Set down your venerable burthen,
And let him feed.

ORL I thank you most for him.

ADAM So had you need.
I scarce can speak to thank you for myself.

DUKE S Welcome. Fall to. I will not trouble you

143. *Mewling:* whimpering. 147. *ballad:* poem. 149. *pard:* leopard. 150. *Jealous in honor:* sensitive about his honor. 151. *bubble reputation:* fame as quickly burst as a bubble. 153. *good . . . lined:* bribed with the present of a fat chicken. It was a common complaint that those who wished for justice from country magistrates had to bring presents with them. Such magistrates were known as "basket justices." 154. *formal cut:* of severe pattern, trim. 155. *saws:* sayings. *modern instances:* commonplace illustrations. 157. *Pantaloon:* the foolish old man of Italian comedy.

As yet, to question you about your fortunes.
Give us some music, and, good Cousin, sing.

AMI [*Sings.*]

Blow, blow, thou winter wind.
Thou art not so unkind
As man's ingratitude.
Thy tooth is not so keen,
Because thou art not seen,
Although thy breath be rude.
Heigh-ho! Sing, heigh-ho! unto the green holly.
Most friendship is feigning, most loving mere folly.
Then, heigh-ho, the holly!
This life is most jolly.

Freeze, freeze, thou bitter sky,
That dost not bite so nigh
As benefits forgot.
Though thou the waters warp,°
Thy sting is not so sharp
As friend remembered not.
Heigh-ho! Sing, heigh-ho! unto the green holly.
Most friendship is feigning, most loving mere folly.
Then, heigh-ho, the holly!
This life is most jolly.

DUKE S If that you were the good Sir Rowland's son,
As you have whispered faithfully you were,
And as mine eye doth his effigies° witness
Most truly limned° and living in your face,
Be truly welcome hither. I am the Duke
That loved your father. The residue of your fortune,°
Go to my cave and tell me. Good old man,
Thou art right welcome, as thy master is.
Support him by the arm. Give me your hand,
And let me all your fortunes understand.

[*Exeunt.*]

186. warp: freeze. *195. effigies:* image. *196. limned:* painted. *198. residue . . . fortune:* the rest of the story of your life.

ACT III

Scene I. A room in the palace.

[*Enter* DUKE FREDERICK, LORDS, *and* OLIVER.]

DUKE F Not see him since? Sir, sir, that cannot be.
But were I not the better part made mercy,
I should not seek an absent argument
Of my revenge, thou present.° But look to it.
Find out thy brother, wheresoe'er he is.
Seek him with candle, bring him dead or living
Within this twelvemonth, or turn thou no more
To seek a living in our territory.
Thy lands and all things that thou dost call thine
Worth seizure do we seize into our hands
Till thou canst quit° thee by thy brother's mouth
Of what we think against thee.
OLI Oh, that your Highness knew my heart in this!
I never loved my brother in my life.
DUKE F More villain thou. Well, push him out of doors,
And let my officers of such a nature
Make an extent upon° his house and lands.
Do this expediently° and turn him going.

[*Exeunt.*]

Scene II. The forest.

[*Enter* ORLANDO, *with a paper.*]

ORL "Hang there, my verse, in witness of my love.
And thou, thrice-crownèd queen° of night, survey
With thy chaste eye, from thy pale sphere° above,
Thy huntress' name that my full life doth sway.
O Rosalind! These trees shall be my books
And in their barks my thoughts I'll character,°
That every eye which in this forest looks
Shall see thy virtue witnessed° everywhere.

Act III, Sc. i: *3–4. I . . . present:* I should not look for your brother, but take vengeance on you. *11. quit:* acquit. *17. Make . . . upon:* seize upon. *18. expediently:* expeditiously.

Sc. ii: *2. thrice-crowned queen:* the goddess Diana, so called on earth; in Heaven she was Luna, the Moon, and in the underworld, Persephone. *3. pale sphere:* i.e., the moon. *6. character:* inscribe. *8. witnessed:* borne witness to.

Run, run, Orlando, carve on every tree
The fair, the chaste, and unexpressive° she."

[*Exit.*]

[*Enter* CORIN *and* TOUCHSTONE.]

COR And how like you this shepherd's life, Master Touchstone?

TOUCH Truly, shepherd, in respect of itself, it is a good life; but in respect that it is a shepherd's life, it is naught.° In respect that it is solitary, I like it very well; but in respect that it is private,° it is a very vile life. Now, in respect it is in the fields, it pleaseth me well; but in respect it is not in the Court, it is tedious. As it is a spare° life, look you, it fits my humor well; but as there is no more plenty in it, it goes much against my stomach. Hast any philosophy in thee, shepherd?

COR No° more but that I know the more one sickens, the worse at ease he is; and that he that wants money, means, and content is without three good friends; that the property of rain is to wet and fire to burn; that good pasture makes fat sheep, and that a great cause of the night is lack of the sun; that he that hath learned no wit by nature nor art may complain of good breeding or comes of a very dull kindred.

TOUCH Such a one is a natural° philosopher. Wast ever in Court, shepherd?

COR No, truly.

TOUCH Then thou art damned.

COR Nay, I hope.

TOUCH Truly, thou art damned, like an ill-roasted egg all on one side.

COR For not being at Court? Your reason.

TOUCH Why, if thou never wast at Court, thou never sawest good manners.° If thou never sawest good manners, then thy manners must be wicked, and wickedness is sin, and sin is damnation. Thou art in a parlous° state, shepherd.

COR Not a whit, Touchstone. Those that are good manners at the Court are as ridiculous in the country as the behavior of the country is most mockable at the Court. You told me you salute not at the Court, but you kiss your hands. That courtesy would be uncleanly if courtiers were shepherds.

TOUCH Instance,° briefly, come, instance.

10. *unexpressive:* inexpressible, beyond description. 13. *naught:* worthless. 14. *private:* solitary. Touchstone as a frequenter of the court prefers a public kind of life. 17. *spare:* frugal. 20–6. *No . . . kindred:* Corin answers Touchstone's Court wit with a selection of rustic wisdom. 27. *natural:* with a pun on *natural,* meaning fool. 36. *good manners:* with double meaning—polite behavior and a moral life. 38. *parlous:* perilous. 44. *Instance:* give an example.

COR Why, we are still handling our ewes, and their fells,° you know, are greasy.

TOUCH Why, do not your courtier's hands sweat? And is not the grease of a mutton as wholesome as the sweat of a man? Shallow, shallow. A better instance, I say, come.

COR Besides, our hands are hard.

TOUCH Your lips will feel them the sooner. Shallow again. A more sounder instance, come.

COR And they are often tarred over with the surgery of our sheep, and would you have us kiss tar? The courtier's hands are perfumed with civet.°

TOUCH Most shallow man! Thou wormsmeat in respect of a good piece of flesh indeed! Learn of the wise, and perpend.° Civet is of a baser birth than tar, the very uncleanly flux of a cat. Mend the instance, shepherd.

COR You have too Courtly a wit for me. I'll rest.

TOUCH Wilt thou rest damned? God help thee, shallow man! God make incision° in thee! Thou art raw.°

COR Sir, I am a true laborer. I earn that I eat, get that I wear, owe no man hate, envy no man's happiness, glad of other men's good, content with my harm,° and the greatest of my pride is to see my ewes graze and my lambs suck.

TOUCH That is another simple sin in you, to bring the ewes and the rams together and to offer to get your living by the copulation of cattle; to be bawd° to a bellwether, and to betray a she-lamb of a twelvemonth to a crooked-pated, old, cuckoldy° ram, out of all reasonable match.° If thou beest not damned for this, the Devil himself will have no shepherds. I cannot see else how thou shouldst 'scape.

COR Here comes young Master Ganymede, my new mistress's brother.

[*Enter* ROSALIND, *with a paper reading.*]

ROS *"From the east to western Ind,°*
No jewel is like Rosalind.
Her worth, being mounted on the wind,°
Through all the world bears Rosalind.
All the pictures fairest lined°
Are but black to Rosalind.
Let no face be kept in mind
But the fair of Rosalind."

45. fells: fleeces. *55. civet:* perfume obtained from glandular secretions of the civet cat. *57. perpend:* consider. *62. make incision:* cut to let blood—a common treatment for many complaints. *62. raw:* unripe, "green." *65. content . . . harm:* content to bear my own troubles. *69. bawd:* go-between. *70. cuckoldy:* lecherous. *71. match:* mating. *76. Ind:* India. *78. mounted . . . wind:* blown about by the wind. *80. lined:* drawn.

TOUCH I'll rhyme you so eight years together, dinners and suppers and sleeping hours excepted. It is the right butterwomen's rank to market.°

ROS Out, fool!

TOUCH For a taste:

If a hart do lack a hind,°
Let him seek out Rosalind.
If the cat will after kind,
So be sure will Rosalind.
Winter garments must be lined,
So must slender Rosalind.
That that reap must sheaf and bind,
Then to cart with Rosalind.
Sweetest nut hath sourest rind,
Such a nut is Rosalind.
He that sweetest rose will find
Must find love's prick and Rosalind.

This is the very false gallop° of verses. Why do you infect yourself with them?

ROS Peace, you dull fool! I found them on a tree.

TOUCH Truly, the tree yields bad fruit.

ROS I'll graff° it with you, and then I shall graff it with a medlar.° Then it will be the earliest fruit i' the country, for you'll be rotten ere you be half ripe, and that's the right virtue of the medlar.

TOUCH You have said, but whether wisely or no, let the forest judge.

[*Enter* CELIA, *with a writing.*]

ROS Peace! Here comes my sister, reading. Stand aside.

CEL [*Reads.*]

"Why should this a desert be?
For it is unpeopled? No,
Tongues I'll hang on every tree,
That shall civil° sayings show
Some, how brief the life of man
Runs his erring° pilgrimage,
That the stretching of a span°
Buckles in his sum of age;
Some, of violated vows
'Twixt the souls of friend and friend.
But upon the fairest boughs,
Or at every sentence end,

85–6. right . . . market: i.e., like a lot of old countrywomen ambling along to market. *89. hart . . . hind:* male and female deer. *101. false gallop:* canter. The rolling motion of a canter is like the even stress of Orlando's bad verses. *105. graff:* graft. *105. medlar:* a fruit resembling a small brown apple, but not eaten until it has grown soft. *113. civil:* civilized. *115. erring:* wandering. *116. span:* the distance between the thumb and forefinger of the stretched hand; about 9 inches.

Will I Rosalinda write,
Teaching all that read to know
The quintessence° of every sprite
Heaven would in little show.
Therefore Heaven Nature charged
That one body should be filled
With all graces wide-enlarged.
Nature presently distilled
Helen's cheek, but not her heart,
Cleopatra's majesty,
Atalanta's better part,
Sad Lucretia's modesty.°
Thus Rosalind of many parts
By heavenly synod° was devised,
Of many faces, eyes, and hearts,
To have the touches dearest prized.
Heaven would that she these gifts should have,
And I to live and die her slave."

ROS O most gentle pulpiter! What tedious homily° of love have you wearied your parishioners withal, and never cried "Have patience, good people!"

CEL How now! Back, friends! Shepherd, go off a little. Go with him, sirrah.

TOUCH Come, shepherd, let us make an honorable retreat, though not with bag and baggage, yet with scrip° and scrippage.°

[*Exeunt* CORIN *and* TOUCHSTONE.]

CEL Didst thou hear these verses?

ROS Oh, yes, I heard them all, and more too, for some of them had in them more feet than the verses would bear.

CEL That's no matter. The feet might bear the verses.

ROS Aye, but the feet were lame and could not bear themselves without the verse and therefore stood lamely in the verse.

CEL But didst thou hear without wondering how thy name should be hanged and carved upon these trees?

ROS I was seven of the nine days° out of the wonder before you came; for look here what I found on a palm tree. I was never so

124. quintessence: fifth essence, that which remains when the four elements have been taken away. *130–3. Helen's . . . modesty:* Rosalind has the good parts of four famous women of story. Helen was divinely fair but unfaithful, Cleopatra, a Queen most royal but unchaste, Atalanta, a swift runner but led aside by cupidity, Lucretia, a model wife but betrayed. *135. synod:* assembly. *140. homily:* sermon. *146. scrip:* the shepherd's wallet. *scrippage:* a word invented by Touchstone to balance baggage. *155. seven . . . days:* i.e., I have endured almost a nine days' wonder.

berhymed° since Pythagoras'° time, that I was an Irish rat, which I can hardly remember.

CEL Trow° you who hath done this?

ROS Is it a man?

CEL And a chain that you once wore about his neck. Change you color?

ROS I prithee—who?

CEL Oh Lord, Lord! It is a hard matter for friends to meet, but mountains may be removed with earthquakes and so encounter.

ROS Nay, but who is it?

CEL Is it possible?

ROS Nay, I prithee now with most petitionary vehemence,° tell me who it is.

CEL Oh, wonderful, wonderful, and most wonderful wonderful! And yet again wonderful, and after that, out of all whooping!°

ROS Good my complexion! Dost thou think though I am caparisoned° like a man, I have a doublet and hose in my disposition?° One inch of delay more is a South Sea of discovery.° I prithee tell me who is it quickly, and speak apace. I would thou couldst stammer, that thou mightst pour this concealed man out of thy mouth as wine comes out of a narrow-mouthed bottle, either too much at once or none at all. I prithee take the cork out of thy mouth that I may drink thy tidings.

CEL So you may put a man in your belly.

ROS Is he of God's making? What manner of man? Is his head worth a hat? Or his chin worth a beard?

CEL Nay, he hath but a little beard.

ROS Why, God will send more, if the man will be thankful. Let me stay the growth of his beard if thou delay me not the knowledge of his chin.°

CEL It is young Orlando, that tripped up the wrestler's heels and your heart both in an instant.

ROS Nay, but the devil take mocking. Speak, sad brow° and true maid.

CEL I' faith, Coz, 'tis he.

ROS Orlando?

CEL Orlando.

157. *berhymed:* rhymed to death. It was believed that in Ireland rats could be destroyed by incantations in rhyme. 157. *Pythagoras:* He taught the doctrine of the transmigration of souls—that the human soul after death passed into the body of an animal. 159. *Trow:* know. 168. *petitionary vehemence:* pleading emphasis. 171. *out . . . whooping:* beyond any cry of wonder. 173. *caparisoned:* decked out. 174. *disposition:* nature. 174. *One . . . discovery:* i.e., the slightest delay in telling me makes your story seem as endless as the South Sea to a voyager. 184–6. *let . . . chin:* I can wait for his beard to grow, so long as you tell me whose chin it is. 189. *sad brow:* in sober earnest.

ROS Alas the day! What shall I do with my doublet and hose? What did he when thou sawest him? What said he? How looked he? Wherein went he? What makes he here? Did he ask for me? Where remains he? How parted he with thee? And when shalt thou see him again? Answer me in one word.

CEL You must borrow me Gargantua's° mouth first. 'Tis a word too great for any mouth of this age's size. To say aye and no to these particulars is more than to answer in a catechism.

ROS But doth he know that I am in this forest and in man's apparel? Looks he as freshly as he did the day he wrestled?

CEL It is as easy to count atomies° as to resolve the propositions of a lover,° but take a taste of my finding him,° and relish it with good observance. I found him under a tree, like a dropped acorn.

ROS It may well be called Jove's tree when it drops forth such fruit.

CEL Give me audience, good madam.

ROS Proceed.

CEL There lay he, stretched along° like a wounded knight.

ROS Though it be pity to see such a sight, it well becomes the ground.

CEL Cry "holloa"° to thy tongue, I prithee, it curvets° unseasonably. He was furnished° like a hunter.

ROS Oh, ominous! He comes to kill my heart.

CEL I would sing my song without a burden.° Thou bringest me out of tune.

ROS Do you not know I am a woman? When I think, I must speak. Sweet, say on.

CEL You bring me out. Soft! Comes he not here?

[*Enter* ORLANDO *and* JAQUES.]

ROS 'Tis he. Slink by, and note him.

JAQ I thank you for your company, but, good faith, I had as lief have been myself alone.

ORL And so had I, but yet, for fashion sake, I thank you too for your society.

JAQ God buy you.° Let's meet as little as we can.

ORL I do desire we may be better strangers.

JAQ I pray you mar no more trees with writing love songs in their barks.

ORL I pray you mar no moe° of my verses with reading them ill-favoredly.°

199. Gargantua: the enormous giant of Rabelais' satirical tale. *204. atomies:* motes in a sunbeam. *204–5. resolve . . . lover:* solve a lover's problems. *205. taste . . . him:* i.e., to whet your appetite for my tale. *210. along:* at full length. *213. holloa:* hold up! whoa! *213. curvets:* prances. *214. furnished:* equipped. *216. burden:* refrain. *226. God . . . you:* God be with you. *230. moe:* more. *231. ill-favoredly:* with a wry face.

JAQ Rosalind is your love's name?

ORL Yes, just.°

JAQ I do not like her name.

ORL There was no thought of pleasing you when she was christened.

JAQ What stature is she of?

ORL Just as high as my heart.

JAQ You are full of pretty answers. Have you not been acquainted with goldsmiths' wives, and conned them out of rings?°

ORL Not so, but I answer you right painted cloth,° from whence you have studied your questions.

JAQ You have a nimble wit. I think 'twas made of Atalanta's heels. Will you sit down with me? And we two will rail against our mistress the world, and all our misery.

ORL I will chide no breather° in the world but myself, against whom I know most faults.

JAQ The worst fault you have is to be in love.

ORL 'Tis a fault I will not change for your best virtue. I am weary of you.

JAQ By my troth, I was seeking for a fool when I found you.

ORL He is drowned in the brook. Look but in and you shall see him.

JAQ There I shall see mine own figure.

ORL Which I take to be either a fool or a cipher.

JAQ I'll tarry no longer with you. Farewell, good Signior Love.

ORL I am glad of your departure. Adieu, good Monsieur Melancholy.

[*Exit* JAQUES.]

ROS [*Aside to* CELIA] I will speak to him like a saucy lackey,° and under that habit play the knave with him. Do you hear, forester?

ORL Very well. What would you?

ROS I pray you, what is 't o'clock?

ORL You should ask me what time o' day. There's no clock in the forest.

ROS Then there is no truelover in the forest, else sighing every minute and groaning every hour would detect the lazy foot of Time as well as a clock.°

ORL And why not the swift foot of Time? Had not that been as proper?

233. just: exactly. *240. out of rings:* Rings were often inscribed with "posies"—pretty little sentences or mottoes. *241. painted cloth:* In taverns and other rooms for which genuine tapestry was too costly, coarse cloths painted with Scriptural or classical scenes were used to cover the walls. The figures were sometimes painted with texts or labels issuing from their mouths with suitable remarks. *246. breather:* living creature. *258. lackey:* servant. *264–6. else . . . clock:* by giving a sigh at each minute and a groan at each hour you would discover the slow passage of Time as clearly as if you had a clock.

ROS By no means, sir. Time travels in divers° paces with divers persons. I'll tell you who Time ambles withal, who Time trots withal, who Time gallops withal, and who he stands still withal.

ORL I prithee who doth he trot withal?

ROS Marry, he trots hard with a young maid between the contract° of her marriage and the day it is solemnized. If the interim be but a sennight,° Time's pace is so hard that it seems the length of seven year.

ORL Who ambles Time withal?

ROS With a priest that lacks Latin and a rich man that hath not the gout; for the one sleeps easily because he cannot study, and the other lives merrily because he feels no pain, the one lacking the burden of lean and wasteful learning, the other knowing no burden of heavy tedious penury. These Time ambles withal.

ORL Who doth he gallop withal?

ROS With a thief to the gallows, for though he go as softly as foot can fall, he thinks himself too soon there.

ORL Who stays it still withal?

ROS With lawyers in the vacation, for they sleep between term and term and then they perceive not how Time moves.

ORL Where dwell you, pretty youth?

ROS With this shepherdess, my sister. Here in the skirts° of the forest, like fringe upon a petticoat.

ORL Are you native of this place?

ROS As the cony° that you see dwell where she is kindled.°

ORL Your accent is something finer than you could purchase in so removed° a dwelling.

ROS I have been told so of many. But indeed an old religious° uncle of mine taught me to speak, who was in his youth an inland man,° one that knew courtship too well, for there he fell in love. I have heard him read many lectures against it, and I thank God I am not a woman, to be touched with so many giddy offenses as he hath generally taxed their whole sex withal.

ORL Can you remember any of the principal evils that he laid to the charge of women?

ROS There were none principal, they were all like one another as halfpence are, every one fault seeming monstrous till his fellow fault came to match it.

ORL I prithee recount some of them.

ROS No, I will not cast away my physic but on those that are sick. There is a man haunts the forest that abuses our young plants with

269. divers: different. *273. contract:* formal betrothal. *275. sennight:* week. *290. skirts:* outskirts. *293. cony:* rabbit. *293. kindled:* brought forth. *295. removed:* remote. *296. religious:* i.e., a hermit. *297. inland man:* city dweller.

carving "Rosalind" on their barks, hangs odes upon hawthorns and elegies on brambles—all, forsooth, deifying the name of Rosalind. If I could meet that fancymonger,° I would give him some good counsel, for he seems to have the quotidian° of love upon him.

ORL I am he that is so love-shaked. I pray you tell me your remedy.

ROS There is none of my uncle's marks upon you. He taught me how to know a man in love, in which cage of rushes° I am sure you are not prisoner.

ORL What were his marks?

ROS A lean cheek, which you have not; a blue eye° and sunken, which you have not; an unquestionable° spirit, which you have not; a beard neglected, which you have not—but I pardon you for that, for simply your having in beard is a younger brother's revenue.° Then your hose should be ungartered, your bonnet° unbanded,° your sleeve unbuttoned, your shoe untied, and everything about you demonstrating a careless desolation. But you are no such man, you are rather point-device° in your accouterments,° as loving yourself than seeming the lover of any other.

ORL Fair youth, I would I could make thee believe I love.

ROS Me believe it! You may as soon make her that you love believe it, which, I warrant, she is apter to do than to confess she does. That is one of the points in the which women still give the lie to their consciences. But, in good sooth, are you he that hangs the verses on the trees wherein Rosalind is so admired?

ORL I swear to thee, youth, by the white hand of Rosalind, I am that he, that unfortunate he.

ROS But are you so much in love as your rhymes speak?

ORL Neither rhyme nor reason can express how much.

ROS Love is merely a madness, and I tell you deserves as well a dark house and a whip as madmen do.° And the reason why they are not so punished and cured is that the lunacy is so ordinary that the whippers are in love too. Yet I profess curing it by counsel.

ORL Did you ever cure any so?

ROS Yes, one, and in this manner. He was to imagine me his love, his mistress, and I set him every day to woo me. At which time would I, being but a moonish° youth, grieve, be effeminate, changeable, longing and liking, proud, fantastical, apish, shallow,

312. *fancymonger:* trader in love. 313. *quotidian:* fever which recurs daily. 316. *cage of rushes:* cage of reed made for little birds. 319. *blue eye:* with dark rings under the eye. 320. *unquestionable:* glum. 322–3. *having . . . revenue:* your beard anyhow is a poor thing like the income of a younger brother. 323. *bonnet:* hat. 324. *unbanded:* without a band. 326. *point-device:* very neat. 327. *accouterments:* equipment. 339–40. *dark . . . do:* This was the common treatment given to lunatics. 346. *moonish:* fickle, changeable as the moon.

inconstant, full of tears, full of smiles, for every passion something and for no passion truly anything, as boys and women are for the most part cattle of this color. Would now like him, now loathe him; then entertain him, then forswear° him; now weep for him, then spit at him; that I drave my suitor from his mad humor° of love to a living humor of madness, which was to forswear the full stream of the world° and to live in a nook merely monastic.° And thus I cured him, and this way will I take upon me to wash your liver° as clean as a sound sheep's heart, that there shall not be one spot of love in 't.

ORL I would not be cured, youth.

ROS I would cure you if you would but call me Rosalind and come every day to my cote and woo me.

ORL Now, by the faith of my love, I will. Tell me where it is.

ROS Go with me to it and I'll show it you. And by the way you shall tell me where in the forest you live. Will you go?

ORL With all my heart, good youth.

ROS Nay, you must call me Rosalind. Come, Sister, will you go?

[*Exeunt.*]

Scene III. The forest.

[*Enter* TOUCHSTONE *and* AUDREY; JAQUES *behind.*]

TOUCH Come apace,° good Audrey. I will fetch up your goats, Audrey. And how, Audrey? Am I the man yet? Doth my simple feature content you?

AUD Your features! Lord warrant us! What features?

TOUCH I am here with thee and thy goats, as the most capricious° poet, honest Ovid, was among the Goths.°

JAQ [*Aside*] Oh, knowledge ill-inhabited, worse than Jove in a thatched house!°

TOUCH When° a man's verses cannot be understood, nor a man's good wit seconded° with the forward child understanding, it strikes a man more dead than a great reckoning in a little room.° Truly, I would the gods had made thee poetical.

351. forswear: deny with an oath. *352. humor:* mood. *353–4. full . . . world:* i.e., a full life. *354. merely monastic:* an absolute monk. *355. liver:* the seat of the passions.

Sc. iii: *1. apace:* quickly. *5. capricious:* with a pun on *caper;* a goat, a most lascivious beast. *6. Ovid . . . Goths:* Ovid was banished from Rome for an intrigue with the daughter of the Emperor Augustus and forced to live with the Getae *(Goths)*. There is a second pun on Goths and goats. *7–8. Jove . . . house:* i.e., a god living in a cottage. *9–11. When . . . room:* This cryptic remark is probably topical, but the allusion is lost. *10. seconded:* supported. *11. great . . . room:* i.e., a huge bill for a private dinner party.

AUD I do not know what "poetical" is. Is it honest in deed and word? Is it a true thing?

TOUCH No, truly, for the truest poetry is the most feigning, and lovers are given to poetry, and what they swear in poetry may be said as lovers they do feign.

AUD Do you wish, then, that the gods had made me poetical?

TOUCH I do, truly, for thou swearest to me thou art honest.° Now if thou wert a poet, I might have some hope thou didst feign.

AUD Would you not have me honest?

TOUCH No, truly, unless thou were hard-favored,° for honesty coupled to beauty is to have honey a sauce to sugar.

JAQ [*Aside*] A material° fool!

AUD Well, I am not fair, and therefore I pray the gods make me honest.

TOUCH Truly, and to cast away honesty upon a foul slut were to put good meat into an unclean dish.

AUD I am not a slut, though I thank the gods I am foul.

TOUCH Well, praised be the gods for thy foulness! Sluttishness may come hereafter. But be it as it may be, I will marry thee, and to that end I have been with Sir Oliver Martext,° the vicar of the next village, who hath promised to meet me in this place of the forest and to couple us.

JAQ [*Aside*] I would fain see this meeting.

AUD Well, the gods give us joy!

TOUCH Amen. A man may, if he were of a fearful heart, stagger° in this attempt; for here we have no temple but the wood, no assembly but horn beasts. But what though? Courage! As horns° are odious, they are necessary. It is said, "Many a man knows no end of his goods." Right, many a man has good horns and knows no end of them. Well, that is the dowry of his wife, 'tis none of his own getting. Horns?—Even so.—Poor men alone? No, no, the noblest deer hath them as huge as the rascal.° Is the single man therefore blessed? No. As a walled town is more worthier than a village, so is the forehead of a married man more honorable than the bare brow of a bachelor; and by how much defense is better than no skill, by so much is a horn° more precious than to want. Here comes Sir Oliver. [*Enter* SIR OLIVER MARTEXT.] Sir Oliver Martext, you are well

19. honest: chaste. *22. hard- favored:* plain-faced, homely. *24. material:* full of matter. *32. Sir . . . Martext:* A minister of the church was often a Bachelor of Arts, and so entitled "dominus," which was translated "sir." Oliver, however, is not a properly ordained minister but a local preacher who mars texts by his misinterpretations. *37. stagger:* tremble. *39. horns:* the inevitable joke about the cuckold's horn. *44. rascal:* a young lean deer in poor condition. *48. horn:* with a pun on the cornucopia or horn of plenty.

met. Will you dispatch us here under this tree, or shall we go with you to your chapel?

SIR OLI Is there none here to give the woman?

TOUCH I will not take her on gift of any man.

SIR OLI Truly, she must be given° or the marriage is not lawful.

JAQ Proceed, proceed. I'll give her.

TOUCH Good even, good Master What-ye-call't. How do you, sir? You are very well met. God 'ild° you for your last company. I am very glad to see you. Even a toy° in hand here, sir. Nay, pray be covered.°

JAQ Will you be married, Motley?

TOUCH As the ox hath his bow,° sir, the horse his curb, and the falcon her bells, so man hath his desires; and as pigeons bill, so wedlock would be nibbling.°

JAQ And will you, being a man of your breeding, be married under a bush like a beggar? Get you to church, and have a good priest that can tell you what marriage is. This fellow will but join you together as they join wainscot;° then one of you will prove a shrunk panel, and like green timber warp, warp.

TOUCH [*Aside*] I am not in the mind, but I were better to be married of him than of another. For he is not like to marry me well, and not being well married, it will be a good excuse for me hereafter to leave my wife.

JAQ Go thou with me, and let me counsel thee.

TOUCH Come, sweet Audrey.
We must be married or we must live in bawdry.
Farewell, good Master Oliver; not—
"O sweet Oliver,
O brave Oliver,
Leave me not behind thee—"
but—
"Wind° away,
Begone, I say,
I will not to wedding with thee."

[*Exeunt* JAQUES, TOUCHSTONE *and* AUDREY.]

SIR OLI 'Tis no matter. Ne'er a fantastical knave of them all shall flout° me out of my calling.

[*Exit.*]

54. given: a woman was, in theory, the possession of her father until marriage, when he gave her away to her husband. This notion is still symbolized in the marriage service of the Church of England. *57. God 'ild:* God reward. *58. toy:* trifle. *59. be covered:* put your hat on. *61. bow:* yoke. *63. nibbling:* i.e., getting at a man. *67. wainscot:* wooden paneling. *80. Wind:* turn. *84. flout:* mock.

Scene IV. The Forest

[*Enter* ROSALIND *and* CELIA.]

ROS Never talk to me, I will weep.

CEL Do, I prithee, but yet have the grace to consider that tears do not become a man.

ROS But have I not cause to weep?

CEL As good cause as one would desire, therefore weep.

ROS His very hair is of the dissembling° color.

CEL Something browner than Judas's.° Marry, his kisses are Judas's own children.

ROS I'faith, his hair is of a good color.

CEL An excellent color. Your chestnut was ever the only color.

ROS And his kissing is as full of sanctity as the touch of holy bread.

CEL He hath bought a pair of cast° lips of Diana.° A nun of winter's sisterhood kisses not more religiously, the very ice of chastity is in them.

ROS But why did he swear he would come this morning and comes not?

CEL Nay, certainly there is no truth in him.

ROS Do you think so?

CEL Yes, I think he is not a pickpurse nor a horsestealer; but for his verity in love, I do think him as concave as a covered goblet° or a worm-eaten nut.

ROS Not true in love?

CEL Yes, when he is in, but I think he is not in.

ROS You have heard him swear downright he was.

CEL "Was" is not "is." Besides, the oath of a lover is no stronger than the word of a tapster;° they are both the confirmer of false reckonings. He attends here in the forest on the Duke your father.

ROS I met the Duke yesterday and had much question° with him. He asked me of what parentage I was. I told him of as good as he, so he laughed and let me go. But what talk we of fathers when there is such a man as Orlando?

CEL Oh, that's a brave man! He writes brave verses, speaks brave words, swears brave oaths and breaks them bravely, quite traverse, athwart° the heart of his lover—as a puisny° tilter that spurs his

Sc. iv: *6. dissembling:* cheating. *7. browner . . . Judas's:* Judas Iscariot, the traitor, was portrayed with red hair. *12. cast:* cast off. Some editors read "chaste." *12. Diana:* the goddess of chastity. *20. concave . . . goblet:* as hollow as a drinking cup with a cover. *26. tapster:* the potboy in a tavern who brings the drinks. *28. question:* conversation. *33–4. quite . . . athwart:* i.e., the glancing blow of one who is afraid to ride "full tilt" at his opponent. *34. puisny:* inexperienced, paltry.

horse but on one side breaks his staff like a noble goose. But all's brave that youth mounts and folly guides. Who comes here?

[*Enter* CORIN.]

COR Mistress and master, you have oft inquired
After the shepherd that complained of love
Who you saw sitting by me on the turf
Praising the proud disdainful shepherdess
That was his mistress.

CEL Well, and what of him?

COR If you will see a pageant° truly played
Between the pale complexion of true love
And the red glow of scorn and proud disdain,
Go hence a little and I shall conduct you,
If you will mark it.

ROS Oh, come, let us remove.
The sight of lovers feedeth those in love.
Bring us to this sight and you shall say
I'll prove a busy actor in their play.

[*Exeunt.*]

Scene V. Another part of the forest.

[*Enter* SILVIUS *and* PHEBE.]

SIL Sweet Phebe, do not scorn me, do not, Phebe.
Say that you love me not, but say not so
In bitterness. The common executioner,
Whose heart the accustomed sight of death makes hard,
Falls° not the ax upon the humbled neck
But first begs pardon. Will you sterner be
Than he that dies and lives by bloody drops?

[*Enter* ROSALIND, CELIA, *and* CORIN, *behind.*]

PHE I would not be thy executioner.
I fly thee, for I would not injure thee.
Thou tell'st me there is murder in mine eye.
'Tis pretty,° sure, and very probable,
That eyes, that are the frail'st and softest things,
Who shut their coward gates on atomies,°
Should be called tyrants, butchers, murderers!
Now I do frown on these with all my heart,
And if mine eyes can wound, now let them kill thee.

42. *pageant:* play.

Sc. v: 5. *Falls:* lets fall. 11. *pretty:* a pretty notion. 13. *atomies:* the smallest particles.

Now counterfeit° to swoon, why, now fall down.
Or if thou canst not, oh, for shame, for shame,
Lie not, to say mine eyes are murderers!
Now show the wound mine eye hath made in thee.
Scratch thee but with a pin and there remains
Some scar of it. Lean but upon a rush,
The cicatrice° and capable impressure°
Thy palm some moment keeps. But now mine eyes,
Which I have darted at thee, hurt thee not,
Nor, I am sure, there is no force in eyes
That can do hurt.

SIL O dear Phebe,
If ever—as that ever may be near—
You meet in some fresh cheek the power of fancy,°
Then shall you know the wounds invisible
That love's keen arrows make.

PHE But till that time
Come not thou near me. And when that time comes,
Afflict me with thy mocks, pity me not,
As till that time I shall not pity thee.

ROS And why, I pray you? Who might be your mother
That you insult, exult, and all at once
Over the wretched? What though you have no beauty—
As, by my faith, I see no more in you
Than without candle may go dark to bed°—
Must you be therefore proud and pitiless?
Why, what means this? Why do you look on me?
I see no more in you than in the ordinary
Of nature's salework.° 'Od's my little life,°
I think she means to tangle my eyes too!
No, faith, proud mistress, hope not after it.
'Tis not your inky brows, your black silk hair,°
Your bugle° eyeballs, nor your cheek of cream,
That can entame my spirits to your worship.
You foolish shepherd, wherefore do you follow her
Like foggy south,° puffing with wind and rain?
You are a thousand times a properer° man
Than she a woman. 'Tis such fools as you
That makes the world full of ill-favored children.

17. *counterfeit:* pretend. 23. *cicatrice:* scar. *capable impressure:* imprint retained. 29. *fancy:* love. 39. *without . . . bed:* i.e., you're not so brilliant that you can go to bed by your own light. 42–3. *ordinary . . . salework:* no extraordinary piece of goods. 45. *'Od's . . . life:* a mild oath, "bless us." 46. *black . . . hair:* Black was not considered beautiful. 47. *bugle:* beady. 50. *foggy south:* The south wind brought fogs and illness. 51. *properer:* more handsome.

'Tis not her glass, but you, that flatters her,
And out of you she sees herself more proper
Than any of her lineaments° can show her.
But, mistress, know yourself. Down on your knees
And thank Heaven, fasting, for a good man's love.
For I must tell you friendly in your ear,
Sell when you can. You are not for all markets.
Cry the man mercy,° love him, take his offer.
Foul is most foul, being foul to be a scoffer.°
So take her to thee, shepherd. Fare you well.

PHE Sweet youth, I pray you, chide a year together.
I had rather hear you chide than this man woo.

ROS He's fallen in love with your foulness and she'll fall in love with my anger. If it be so, as fast as she answers thee with frowning looks, I'll sauce her with bitter words. Why look you so upon me?

PHE For no ill will I bear you.

ROS I pray you do not fall in love with me,
For I am falser than vows made in wine.
Besides, I like you not. If you will know my house,
'Tis at the tuft° of olives here hard by.
Will you go, Sister? Shepherd, ply° her hard.
Come, Sister. Shepherdess, look on him better,
And be not proud. Though all the world could see,
None could be so abused in sight as he.
Come, to our flock.

[*Exeunt* ROSALIND, CELIA *and* CORIN.]

PHE Dead shepherd, now I find thy saw of might—
"Who ever loved that loved not at first sight?"

SIL Sweet Phebe—

PHE Ha, what say'st thou, Silvius?

SIL Sweet Phebe, pity me.

PHE Why, I am sorry for thee, gentle Silvius.

SIL Wherever sorrow is, relief would be.
If you do sorrow at my grief in love,
By giving love your sorrow and my grief
Were both extermined.

PHE Thou hast my love. Is not that neighborly?

SIL I would have you.

PHE Why, that were covetousness.
Silvius, the time was that I hated thee,
And yet it is not that I bear thee love.
But since that thou canst talk of love so well,

56. lineaments: features. *61. Cry . . . mercy:* ask his pardon. *62. Foul . . . scoffer:* i.e., you are ugly anyway, and uglier when you are disdainful. *73. tuft:* clump. *74. ply:* press, work at.

Thy company, which erst° was irksome to me,
I will endure, and I'll employ thee too.
But do not look for further recompense
Than thine own gladness that thou art employed.

SIL So holy and so perfect is my love,
And I in such a poverty of grace,°
That I shall think it a most plenteous crop
To glean the broken ears after the man
That the main harvest reaps. Loose now and then
A scattered smile, and that I'll live upon.

PHE Know'st thou the youth that spoke to me erewhile?°

SIL Not very well, but I have met him oft,
And he hath bought the cottage and the bounds
That the old carlot° once was master of.

PHE Think not I love him, though I ask for him.
'Tis but a peevish° boy, yet he talks well.
But what care I for words? Yet words do well
When he that speaks them pleases those that hear.
It is a pretty youth—not very pretty—
But, sure, he's proud, and yet his pride becomes him.
He'll make a proper man. The best thing in him
Is his complexion, and faster than his tongue
Did make offense his eye did heal it up.
He is not very tall, yet for his years he's tall.
His leg is but soso, and yet 'tis well.
There was a pretty redness in his lip,
A little riper and more lusty red
Than that mixed in his cheek, 'twas just the difference
Betwixt the constant red and mingled damask.°
There be some women, Silvius, had they marked him
In parcels° as I did, would have gone near
To fall in love with him. But for my part,
I love him not nor hate him not, and yet
I have more cause to hate him than to love him.
For what had he to do to chide at me?
He said mine eyes were black and my hair black,
And, now I am remembered, scorned at me.
I marvel why I answered not again.
But that's all one, omittance is no quittance.°

93. erst: erstwhile, formerly. *98. poverty of grace:* poor favor. *103. erewhile:* just now. *106. carlot:* carl, peasant. *108. peevish:* perverse, silly. *121. mingled damask:* blended pink (the color of damask roses). *123. In parcels:* in parts, each part separately. *131. omittance . . . quittance:* i.e., because I let him off now, that does not mean that he will get off altogether.

I'll write to him a very taunting letter,
And thou shalt bear it. Wilt thou, Silvius?
SIL Phebe, with all my heart.
PHE I'll write it straight,
The matter's in my head and in my heart.
I will be bitter with him and passing° short.
Go with me, Silvius.
[*Exeunt.*]

ACT IV

Scene I. The forest.

[*Enter* ROSALIND, CELIA, *and* JAQUES.]

JAQ I prithee, pretty youth, let me be better acquainted with thee.

ROS They say you are a melancholy fellow.

JAQ I am so, I do love it better than laughing.

ROS Those that are in extremity of either are abominable fellows, and betray themselves to every modern censure° worse than drunkards.

JAQ Why, 'tis good to be sad and say nothing.

ROS Why, then 'tis good to be a post.

JAQ I have neither the scholar's melancholy, which is emulation;° nor the musician's, which is fantastical; nor the courtier's, which is proud; nor the soldier's, which is ambitious; nor the lawyer's, which is politic;° nor the lady's, which is nice; nor the lover's, which is all these. But it is a melancholy of mine own, compounded of many simples,° extracted from many objects, and indeed the sundry comtemplation of my travels, in which my often rumination wraps me in a most humorous sadness.°

ROS A traveler!° By my faith, you have great reason to be sad. I fear you have sold your own lands to see other men's; then, to have seen much and to have nothing is to have rich eyes and poor hands.

JAQ Yes, I have gained my experience.

ROS And your experience makes you sad. I had rather have a fool to make me merry than experience to make me sad—and to travel for it too!

136. passing: exceedingly.

Act IV, Sc. i: *5. modern censure:* trifling criticism. *9. emulation:* jealous rivalry. *12. politic:* put on or crafty ends. *14. simples:* drugs, ingredients. *15–6. my . . . sadness:* by often ruminating on my experiences I am filled with moody sadness. *17. A traveler:* Jibes at Englishmen who had traveled were common.

[*Enter* ORLANDO.]

ORL Good day and happiness, dear Rosalind!

JAQ Nay, then, God buy you° an you talk in blank verse.

[*Exit.*]

ROS Farewell, Monsieur Traveler. Look you lisp° and wear strange suits. Disable° all the benefits of your own country, be out of love with your nativity° and almost chide God for making you that countenance° you are, or I will scarce think you have swam in a gondola.° Why, how now, Orlando! Where have you been all this while? You a lover! An you serve me such another trick, never come in my sight more.

ORL My fair Rosalind, I come within an hour of my promise.

ROS Break an hour's promise in love! He that will divide a minute into a thousand parts and break but a part of the thousandth part of a minute in the affairs of love, it may be said of him that Cupid hath clapped him o' the shoulder,° but I'll warrant him heart-whole.

ORL Pardon me, dear Rosalind.

ROS Nay, an you be so tardy, come no more in my sight. I had as lief be wooed of a snail.

ORL Of a snail?

ROS Aye, of a snail, for though he comes slowly, he carries his house on his head—a better jointure,° I think, than you make a woman. Besides, he brings his destiny with him.

ORL What's that?

ROS Why, horns, which such as you are fain to be beholding to your wives for. But he comes armed in his fortune and prevents the slander of his wife.°

ORL Virtue is no hornmaker, and my Rosalind is virtuous.

ROS And I am your Rosalind.

CEL It pleases him to call you so, but he hath a Rosalind of a better leer° than you.

ROS Come, woo me, woo me, for now I am in a holiday° humor and like enough to consent. What would you say to me now an I were your very very Rosalind?

ORL I would kiss before I spoke.

ROS Nay, you were better speak first, and when you were graveled° for lack of matter, you might take occasion to kiss. Very good

25. God . . . you: God be with you. *26. lisp:* affect a foreign accent. *27. Disable:* make slighting remarks about. *28. nativity:* place and moment of birth. *29. countenance:* natural face. *29–30. swam . . . gondola:* i.e., visited Venice, which (like Paris for the modern American) was the goal of all travelers. *37. clapped . . . shoulder:* arrested him, made him prisoner. *43. jointure:* marriage portion. *47–8. he . . . wife:* i.e., the snail has his horns before marriage and so forestalls *(prevents)* the slanders which his wife will bring him. *52. leer:* look. *53. holiday:* i.e., gay. *57. graveled:* run aground.

orators, when they are out, they will spit, and for lovers lacking—God warn° us!—matter, the cleanliest shift° is to kiss.

ORL How if the kiss be denied?

ROS Then she puts you to entreaty and there begins new matter.

ORL Who could be out, being before his beloved mistress?

ROS Marry, that should you if I were your mistress, or I should think my honesty ranker° than my wit.

ORL What, of my suit?

ROS Not out of your apparel, and yet out of your suit.° Am not I your Rosalind?

ORL I take some joy to say you are, because I would be talking of her.

ROS Well, in her person° I say I will not have you.

ORL Then in mine own person I die.

ROS No, faith, die by attorney.° The poor world is almost six thousand years old, and in all this time there was not any man died in his own person, videlicet,° in a love cause. Troilus had his brains dashed out with a Grecian club, yet he did what he could to die before, and he is one of the patterns of love. Leander, he would have lived many a fair year, though Hero had turned nun, if it had not been for a hot midsummer night; for, good youth, he went but forth to wash him in the Hellespont and being taken with the cramp was drowned. And the foolish chroniclers of that age found it was "Hero of Sestos."° But these are all lies. Men have died from time to time and worms have eaten them, but not for love.

ORL I would not have my right Rosalind of this mind, for I protest her frown might kill me.

ROS By this hand, it will not kill a fly. But come, now I will be your Rosalind in a more coming-on° disposition, and ask me what you will, I will grant it.

ORL Then love me, Rosalind.

ROS Yes, faith, will I, Fridays and Saturdays and all.

ORL And wilt thou have me?

ROS Aye, and twenty such.

ORL What sayest thou?

ROS Are you not good?

ORL I hope so.

ROS Why then, can one desire too much of a good thing? Come,

60. warn: collioquial for "warrant." *cleanliest shift:* the cleanest way of getting round the difficulty. *65. ranker:* fouler. *67. suit:* the same pun as in II.vii.44. *70. in . . . person:* as her representative. *72. by attorney:* by proxy. *74. videlicet:* namely, "viz." *74–81. Trolius . . . Sestos:* No one, says Rosalind, has really died for love, not even the great lovers of legend, such as Troilus, who was madly in love with Cressida, or Leander who used to swim over the Hellespont to visit Hero of Sestos and was drowned; historians in those days said that his death was caused by Hero, but in truth it was the cramp. *86. coming-on:* encouraging.

Sister, you shall be the priest and marry us. Give me your hand, Orlando. What do you say, Sister?

ORL Pray thee, marry us.

CEL I cannot say the words.

ROS You must begin, "Will you, Orlando—"

CEL Go to. Will you, Orlando, have to wife this Rosalind?

ORL I will.

ROS Aye, but when?

ORL Why now, as fast as she can marry us.

ROS Then you must say "I take thee, Rosalind, for wife."

ORL I take thee, Rosalind, for wife.

ROS I might ask you for your commission,° but I do take thee, Orlando, for my husband. There's a girl goes before the priest,° and certainly a woman's thought runs before her actions.

ORL So do all thoughts, they are winged.

ROS Now tell me how long you would have her after you have possessed her.

ORL Forever and a day.

ROS Say "a day," without the "ever." No, no, Orlando. Men are April when they woo, December when they wed. Maids are May when they are maids, but the sky changes when they are wives. I will be more jealous of thee than a Barbary cock pigeon over his hen, more clamorous than a parrot against° rain, more newfangled° than an ape, more giddy in my desires than a monkey. I will weep for nothing, like Diana in the fountain,° and I will do that when you are disposed to be merry. I will laugh like a hyen,° and that when thou art inclined to sleep.

ORL But will my Rosalind do so?

ROS By my life, she will do as I do.

ORL Oh, but she is wise.

ROS Or else she could not have the wit to do this. The wiser, the waywarder.° Make° the doors upon a woman's wit and it will out at the casement.° Shut that and 'twill out at the keyhole. Stop that, 'twill fly with the smoke out at the chimney.

ORL A man that had a wife with such a wit, he might say "Wit, whither wilt?"°

ROS Nay, you might keep that check° for it till you met your wife's wit going to your neighbor's bed.

ORL And what wit could wit have to excuse that?

107. commission: i.e., authority. *108. girl . . . priest:* i.e., anticipates the priest's words, because she is so eager. *118. against:* in anticipation of. *119. newfangled:* eager for novelties. *120. Diana . . . fountain:* i.e., like a fountain with the figure of Diana, always dripping. *121. hyen:* hyena. *127. waywarder:* more capricious. *Make:* shut. *128. casement:* window that opens on hinges. *130–1. Wit . . . wilt:* a proverb—"Wit *[intelligence]*, where are you going?" *132. check:* rebuke.

ROS Marry, to say she came to seek you there. You shall never take her without her answer, unless you take her without her tongue. Oh, that woman that cannot make her fault her husband's occasion,° let her never nurse her child herself, for she will breed it like a fool!

ORL For these two hours, Rosalind, I will leave thee.

ROS Alas, dear love, I cannot lack thee two hours!

ORL I must attend the Duke at dinner. By two o'clock I will be with thee again.

ROS Aye, go your ways, go your ways, I knew what you would prove. My friends told me as much, and I thought no less. That flattering tongue of yours won me. 'Tis but one cast away,° and so come, death! Two o'clock is your hour?

ORL Aye, sweet Rosalind.

ROS By my troth,° and in good earnest, and so God mend me, and by all pretty oaths that are not dangerous, if you break one jot of your promise or come one minute behind your hour, I will think you the most pathetical break-promise, and the most hollow lover, and the most unworthy of her you call Rosalind, that may be chosen out of the gross band° of the unfaithful. Therefore beware my censure and keep your promise.

ORL With no less religion than if thou wert indeed my Rosalind. So adieu.

ROS Well, Time is the old justice that examines all such offenders, and let Time try. Adieu.

[*Exit* ORLANDO.]

CEL You have simply misused our sex in your love prate. We must have your doublet and hose plucked over your head, and show the world what the bird hath done to her own nest.°

ROS O Coz, Coz, Coz, my pretty little coz, that thou didst know how many fathom deep I am in love! But it cannot be sounded. My affection hath an unknown bottom,° like the bay of Portugal.

CEL Or rather, bottomless, that as fast as you pour affection in, it runs out.

ROS No, that same wicked bastard of Venus° that was begot of thought, conceived of spleen, and born of madness, that blind rascally boy that abuses everyone's eyes because his own are out, let him be judge how deep I am in love. I'll tell thee, Aliena, I cannot be out of the sight of Orlando. I'll go find a shadow and sigh till he come.

CEL And I'll sleep.

[*Exeunt.*]

137–8. that . . . occasion: that cannot blame her husband as the cause of her own faults. *occasion:* that which causes. *146. cast away:* abandoned. *149. troth:* truth. *154. gross band:* vile company. *162. done . . . nest:* i.e., fouled it. *165. unknown bottom:* i.e., too deep to be measured. *168. bastard of Venus:* i.e., Cupid.

Scene II. The forest.

[*Enter* JAQUES, LORDS, *and* FORESTERS.]

JAQ Which is he that killed the deer?

A LORD Sir, it was I.

JAQ Let's present him to the Duke, like a Roman conqueror, and it would do well to set the deer's horns upon his head for a branch of victory. Have you no song, forester, for this purpose?

FOR Yes, sir.

JAQ Sing it. 'Tis no matter how it be in tune so it make noise enough.

FOR [*Sings.*]

What shall he have that killed the deer?
His leather skin and horns to wear.
Then sing him home.

[*The rest shall bear this burden.*]

Take thou no scorn to wear the horn,
It was a crest ere thou wast born.
Thy father's father wore it,
And thy father bore it.
The horn, the horn, the lusty horn
Is not a thing to laugh to scorn.

[*Exeunt.*]

Scene III. The forest.

[*Enter* ROSALIND *and* CELIA.]

ROS How say you now? Is it not past two o'clock? And here much° Orlando!

CEL I warrant you with pure love and troubled brain he hath ta'en his bow and arrows and is gone forth to sleep. Look who comes here.

[*Enter* SILVIUS.]

SIL My errand is to you, fair youth,
My gentle Phebe bid me give you this.
I know not the contents, but as I guess
By the stern brow and waspish action
Which she did use as she was writing of it,
It bears an angry tenor.° Pardon me,
I am but as a guiltless messenger.

ROS Patience herself would startle at this letter
And play the swaggerer—bear this, bear all.°
She says I am not fair, that I lack manners,

Sc. iii: *1. here much:* i.e., a fine lot of. *11. tenor:* intention. *14. bear . . . all:* a person who could endure this would bear anything.

She calls me proud, and that she could not love me
Were man as rare as phoenix. 'Od's my will!
Her love is not the hare that I do hunt.
Why writes she so to me? Well, shepherd, well,
This is a letter of your own device.
SIL No, I protest I know not the contents.
Phebe did write it.
ROS Come, come, you are a fool,
And turned into the extremity of love.
I saw her hand. She has a leathern° hand,
A freestone-colored° hand. I verily did think
That her old gloves were on, but 'twas her hands.
She has a huswife's hand, but that's no matter.
I say she never did invent this letter.
This is a man's invention and his hand.
SIL Sure, it is hers.
ROS Why, 'tis a boisterous° and a cruel style,
A style for challengers. Why, she defies me,
Like Turk to Christian. Women's gentle brain
Could not drop forth such giant-rude invention,
Such Ethiope° words, blacker in their effect°
Than in their countenance.° Will you hear the letter?
SIL So please you, for I never heard it yet,
Yet heard too much of Phebe's cruelty.
ROS She Phebes me. Mark how the tyrant writes.
[*Reads.*] *"Art thou god to shepherd turned*
That a maiden's heart hath burned?"
Can a woman rail thus?
SIL Call you this railing?
ROS [*Reads.*] *"Why, thy godhead laid apart,°*
Warr'st thou with a woman's heart?"
Did you ever hear such railing?
"Whiles the eye of man did woo me,
That could do no vengeance to me."
Meaning me a beast.
"If the scorn of your bright eyne°
Have power to raise such love in mine,
Alack, in me what strange effect
Would they work in mild aspéct!°
Whiles you chid me, I did love,

24. *leathern:* i.e., the hand of a workingwoman, not of a lady. 25. *freestone-colored:* of the color of Bath brick; i.e., yellow-brown. 31. *boisterous:* violent. 35. *Ethiope:* i.e., black. *effect:* intention. 36. *countenance:* appearance. 44. *thy . . . apart:* why do you, a god, become man? 50. *eyne:* eyes. 53. *mild aspect:* gentle looks.

How then might your prayers move!
He that brings this love to thee
Little knows this love in me.
And by him seal up thy mind,°
Whether that thy youth and kind°
Will the faithful offer take
Of me and all that I can make,
Or else by him my love deny,
And then I'll study how to die."

SIL Call you this chiding?
CEL Alas, poor shepherd!
ROS Do you pity him? No, he deserves no pity. Wilt thou love such a woman? What, to make thee an instrument and play false strains upon thee! Not to be endured! Well, go your way to her, for I see love hath made thee a tame snake, and say this to her: That if she loves me, I charge her to love thee. If she will not, I will never have her unless thou entreat for her. If you be a truelover, hence, and not a word, for here comes more company.

[*Exit* SILVIUS.]

[*Enter* OLIVER.]

OLI Good morrow, fair ones. Pray you, if you know,
Where in the purlieus° of this forest stands
A sheepcote fenced about with olive trees?
CEL West of this place, down in the neighbor bottom.
The rank° of osiers° by the murmuring stream
Left on your right hand brings you to the place.
But at this hour the house doth keep itself,
There's none within.
OLI If that an eye may profit by a tongue,
Then should I know you by description,
Such garments and such years. "The boy is fair,
Of female favor,° and bestows himself°
Like a ripe sister,° and woman low,
And browner than her brother." Are not you
The owner of the house I did inquire for?
CEL It is no boast, being asked, to say we are.
OLI Orlando doth commend him to you both,
And to that youth he calls his Rosalind
He sends this bloody napkin. Are you he?
ROS I am. What must we understand by this?
OLI Some of my shame, if you will know of me

58. seal . . . mind: write your answer and send it by him. *59. kind:* nature. *74. purlieus:* boundaries. *77. rank:* row. *osiers:* willows, of the kind used for making baskets. *84. female favor:* girlish face. *bestows himself:* behaves. *85. Like . . . sister:* like an elder sister.

What man I am, and how, and why, and where
This handkercher was stained.
CEL I pray you tell it.
OLI When last the young Orlando parted from you
He left a promise to return again
Within an hour, and pacing through the forest,
Chewing the food of sweet and bitter fancy,°
Lo, what befell! He threw his eye aside,
And mark what object did present itself.
Under an oak whose boughs were mossed with age
And high top bald with dry antiquity,
A wretched ragged man, o'ergrown with hair,
Lay sleeping on his back. About his neck
A green and gilded snake had wreathed itself,
Who with her head nimble in threats approached
The opening of his mouth. But suddenly,
Seeing Orlando, it unlinked itself
And with indented glides° did slip away
Into a bush, under which bush's shade
A lioness, with udders all drawn dry,°
Lay couching, head on ground, with catlike watch,
When that the sleeping man should stir. For 'tis
The royal disposition of that beast
To prey on nothing that doth seem as dead.
This seen, Orlando did approach the man
And found it was his brother, his elder brother.
CEL Oh, I have heard him speak of that same brother,
And he did render° him the most unnatural
That lived amongst men.
OLI And well he might so do,
For well I know he was unnatural.
ROS But to Orlando. Did he leave him there,
Food to the sucked and hungry lioness?
OLI Twice did he turn his back and purposed so.
But kindness,° nobler ever than revenge,
And nature, stronger than his just occasion,°
Made him give battle to the lioness,
Who quickly fell before him. In which hurtling°
From miserable slumber I awaked.
CEL Are you his brother?
ROS Was 't you he rescued?

98. *fancy:* love. 110. *indented glides:* wavy motion. 112. *udders . . . dry:* i.e., hungry and fierce. 120. *render:* describe. 126. *kindness:* natural affection. 127. *just occasion:* i.e., his opportunity for getting even with his wicked brother. 129. *hurtling:* noise of battle.

CEL Was't you that did so oft contrive to kill him?
OLI 'Twas I, but 'tis not I. I do not shame
To tell you what I was, since my conversion
So sweetly tastes, being the thing I am.
ROS But—for the bloody napkin?
OLI By and by.
When from the first to last betwixt us two
Tears our recountments° had most kindly bathed,
As how I came into that desert place,
In brief, he led me to the gentle Duke,
Who gave me fresh array and entertainment,°
Committing me unto my brother's love.
Who led me instantly unto his cave,
There stripped himself, and here upon his arm
The lioness had torn some flesh away,
Which all this while had bled, and now he fainted
And cried, in fainting, upon Rosalind.
Brief, I recovered him, bound up his wound,
And after some small space, being strong at heart,
He sent me hither, stranger as I am,
To tell this story, that you might excuse
His broken promise, and to give this napkin,
Dyed in his blood, unto the shepherd youth
That he in sport doth call his Rosalind.

[ROSALIND *swoons.*]

CEL Why, how now, Ganymede! Sweet Ganymede!
OLI Many will swoon when they do look on blood.
CEL There is more in it. Cousin Ganymede!
OLI Look, he recovers.
ROS I would I were at home.
CEL We'll lead you thither. I pray you, will you take him by the arm?
OLI Be of good cheer, youth. You a man! You lack a man's heart.

ROS I do so, I confess it. Ah, sirrah, a body would think this was well counterfeited!° I pray you tell your brother how well I counterfeited. Heigh-ho!

OLI This was not counterfeit. There is too great testimony in your complexion that it was a passion of ernest.°

ROS Counterfeit, I assure you.

OLI Well then, take a good heart and counterfeit to be a man.

ROS So I do. But, i' faith, I should have been a woman by right.

138. recountments: accounts of our adventures. *141. entertainment:* good treatment. *163. counterfeited:* imitated, pretended. *166. passion of earnest:* genuine emotion.

CEL Come, you look paler and paler. Pray you draw homeward. Good sir, go with us.

OLI That will I, for I must bear answer back. How you excuse my brother, Rosalind.

ROS I shall devise something. But I pray you commend my counterfeiting to him. Will you go?

[*Exeunt.*]

ACT V

Scene I. The forest.

[*Enter* TOUCHSTONE *and* AUDREY.]

TOUCH We shall find a time, Audrey. Patience, gentle Audrey.

AUD Faith, the priest was good enough, for all the old gentleman's saying.

TOUCH A most wicked Sir Oliver, Audrey, a most vile Martext. But, Audrey, there is a youth here in the forest lays claim to you.

AUD Aye, I know who 'tis. He hath no interest in me in the world. Here comes the man you mean.

TOUCH It is meat and drink to me to see a clown. By my troth, we that have good wits have much to answer for—we shall be flouting,° we cannot hold.

[*Enter* WILLIAM.]

WILL Good even, Audrey.

AUD God ye good even, William.

WILL And good even to you, sir.

TOUCH Good even, gentle friend. Cover thy head, cover thy head, nay, prithee be covered. How old are you, friend?

WILL Five and twenty, sir.

TOUCH A ripe age. Is thy name William?

WILL William, sir.

TOUCH A fair name. Wast born i' the forest here?

WILL Aye, sir, I thank God.

TOUCH "Thank God," a good answer. Art rich?

WILL Faith, sir, soso.

TOUCH "Soso" is good, very good, very excellent good. And yet it is not, it is but soso. Art thou wise?

WILL Aye, sir, I have a pretty wit.

TOUCH Why, thou sayest well. I do now remember a saying, "The fool doth think he is wise, but the wise man knows himself to be a fool." The heathen philosopher, when he had a desire to eat a grape,

Act V, Sc. i: *11. flouting:* jesting.

would open his lips when he put it into his mouth, meaning thereby that grapes were made to eat and lips to open. You do love this maid?

WILL I do, sir.

TOUCH Give me your hand. Art thou learned?

WILL No, sir.

TOUCH Then learn this of me: To have is to have; for it is a figure in rhetoric that drink, being poured out of a cup into a glass, by filling the one doth empty the other, for all your writers do consent that *ipse*° is he. Now you are not *ipse,* for I am he.

WILL Which he, sir?

TOUCH He, sir, that must marry this woman. Therefore, you clown, abandon—which is in the vulgar° leave,—the society—which in the boorish is company—of this female—which in the common is woman. Which together is, abandon the society of this female, or, clown, thou perishest; or, to thy better understanding, diest; or, to wit, I kill thee, make thee away, translate thy life into death, thy liberty into bondage. I will deal in poison with thee, or in bastinado,° or in steel, I will bandy with thee in faction,° I will o'errun thee with policy,° I will kill thee a hundred and fifty ways. Therefore tremble, and depart.

AUD Do, good William.

WILL God rest you merry sir.

[*Exit.*]

[*Enter* CORIN.]

COR Our master and mistress seek you. Come, away, away!

TOUCH Trip, Audrey! Trip, Audrey! I attend, I attend.

[*Exeunt.*]

Scene II. The forest.

[*Enter* ORLANDO *and* OLIVER.]

ORL Is 't possible that on so little acquaintance you should like her? That but seeing you should love her? And, loving, woo? And, wooing, she should grant? And will you persever to enjoy her?

OLI Neither call the giddiness° of it in question, the poverty of her, the small acquaintance, my sudden wooing, nor her sudden consenting; but say with me, I love Aliena, say with her that she loves me, consent with both that we may enjoy each other. It shall be to your good, for my father's house and all the revenue that was

39. ipse: himself. *42. vulgar:* common tongue. *48. bastinado:* a thrashing. *48. bandy . . . faction:* strive with you by intrigue. *49. o'errun . . . policy:* overcome you by some crafty device.

Sc. ii: *4. giddiness:* rashness.

old Sir Rowland's will I estate° upon you, and here live and die a shepherd.

ORL You have my consent. Let your wedding be tomorrow. Thither will I invite the Duke and all's contented followers. Go you and prepare Aliena, for look you, here comes my Rosalind.

[*Enter* ROSALIND.]

ROS God save you, Brother.

OLI And you, fair Sister.

ROS O my dear Orlando, how it grieves me to see thee wear thy heart in a scarf!

ORL It is my arm.

ROS I thought thy heart had been wounded with the claws of a lion.

ORL Wounded it is, but with the eyes of a lady.

ROS Did your brother tell you how I counterfeited to swoon when he showed me your handkercher?

ORL Aye, and greater wonders than that.

ROS Oh, I know where you are. Nay, 'tis true. There was never anything so sudden but the fight of two rams, and Caesar's thrasonical° brag of "I came, saw, and overcame."° For your brother and my sister no sooner met but they looked, no sooner looked but they loved, no sooner loved but they sighed, no sooner sighed but they asked one another the reason, no sooner knew the reason but they sought the remedy. And in these degrees have they made a pair of stairs to marriage which they will climb incontinent, or else be incontinent before marriage. They are in the very wrath° of love and they will together, clubs cannot part them.°

ORL They shall be married tomorrow, and I will bid the Duke to the nuptial. But oh, how bitter a thing it is to look into happiness through another man's eyes! By so much the more shall I tomorrow be at the height of heart-heaviness, by how much I shall think my brother happy in having what he wishes for.

ROS Why then, tomorrow I cannot serve your turn for Rosalind?

ORL I can live no longer by thinking.°

ROS I will weary you then no longer with idle talking. Know of me then, for now I speak to some purpose, that I know you are a gentleman of good conceit.° I speak not this that you should bear a good opinion of my knowledge, insomuch I say I know you are. Neither do I labor for a greater esteem than may in some little measure draw a belief from you to do yourself good and not to

9. *estate:* settle. 26. *thrasonical:* boastful. 26. *I . . . overcame:* Julius Caesar after his victory over the King of Pontus reported to the Senate in three words: *Veni, vidi, vici.* 33. *wrath:* passion. 33. *clubs . . . them:* When a brawl was started in London streets, there was a cry of "Clubs." Thereupon the apprentices in the shops seized their clubs and swarmed out to separate the parties. 40. *thinking:* i.e., pretense. 43. *conceit:* intelligence.

grace me. Believe then, if you please, that I can do strange things. I have, since I was three year old, conversed with a magician most profound in his art and yet not damnable.° If you do love Rosalind so near the heart as your gesture cries it out, when your brother marries Aliena, shall you marry her. I know into what straits of fortune° she is driven, and it is not impossible to me, if it appear not inconvenient to you, to set her before your eyes tomorrow human as she is and without any danger.

ORL Speakest thou in sober meanings?

ROS By my life, I do, which I tender° dearly, though I say I am a magician. Therefore put you in your best array, bid your friends, for if you will be married tomorrow, you shall, and to Rosalind if you will. [*Enter* SILVIUS *and* PHEBE.] Look, here comes a lover of mine and a lover of hers.

PHE Youth, you have done me much ungentleness°
To show the letter that I writ to you.

ROS I care not if I have. It is my study°
To seem despiteful and ungentle to you.
You are there followed by a faithful shepherd.
Look upon him, love him, he worships you.

PHE Good shepherd, tell this youth what 'tis to love.

SIL It is to be all made of sighs and tears,
And so am I for Phebe.

PHE And I for Ganymede.

ORL And I for Rosalind.

ROS And I for no woman.

SIL It is to be all made of faith and service,
And so am I for Phebe.

PHE And I for Ganymede.

ORL And I for Rosalind.

ROS And I for no woman.

SIL It is to be all made of fantasy,°
All made of passion, and all made of wishes,
All adoration, duty, and observance,
All humbleness, all patience and impatience,
All purity, all trial,° all observance,°
And so am I for Phebe.

PHE And so am I for Ganymede.

ORL And so am I for Rosalind.

ROS And so am I for no woman.

PHE If this be so, why blame you me to love you?

49. *not damnable:* i.e., his magic was used to good and not wicked ends. 51–2. *straits of fortune:* difficult situation. 56. *tender:* regard. 61. *done . . . ungentleness:* you have not behaved like a gentleman toward me. 63. *study:* deliberate purpose. 78. *fantasy:* imagination. 82. *all trial:* enduring any trial. *observance:* devotion.

SIL If this be so, why blame you me to love you?
ORL If this be so, why blame you me to love you?
ROS Why do you speak too, "Why blame you me to love you?"
ORL To her that is not here, nor doth not hear.
ROS Pray you, no more of this, 'tis like the howling of Irish wolves against the moon. [*To* SILVIUS] I will help you if I can. [*To* PHEBE] I would love you if I could. Tomorrow meet me all together. [*To* PHEBE] I will marry you if ever I marry woman, and I'll be married tomorrow. [*To* ORLANDO] I will satisfy you if ever I satisfied man, and you shall be married tomorrow. [*To* SILVIUS] I will content you if what pleases you contents you, and you shall be married tomorrow. [*To* ORLANDO] As you love Rosalind, meet. [*To* SILVIUS] As you love Phebe, meet. And as I love no woman, I'll meet. So, fare you well. I have left you commands.
SIL I'll not fail, if I live.
PHE Nor I.
ORL Nor I.

[*Exeunt.*]

Scene III. The forest.

[*Enter* TOUCHSTONE *and* AUDREY.]

TOUCH Tomorrow is the joyful day, Audrey, tomorrow will we be married.
AUD I do desire it with all my heart, and I hope it is no dishonest° desire to desire to be a woman of the world. Here come two of the banished Duke's pages.
[*Enter two* PAGES.]
1. PAGE Well met, honest gentleman.
TOUCH By my troth, well met. Come, sit, sit, and a song.
2. PAGE We are for you. Sit i' the middle.
1. PAGE Shall we clap into 't° roundly, without hawking° or spitting or saying we are hoarse, which are the only prologues° to a bad voice?
2. PAGE I' faith, i' faith, and both in a tune, like two gypsies on a horse.

SONG

It was a lover and his lass,
With a hey, and a ho, and a hey nonino,
That o'er the green cornfield did pass
In the springtime, the only pretty ringtime,°
When birds do sing, hey ding a ding, ding.
Sweet lovers love the spring.

Sc. iii: *3. dishonest:* unchaste. *9. clap into 't:* get down to it. *9. hawking:* clearing the throat. *10. only prologues:* usual apologies. *18. ringtime:* i.e., the time for wedding bells.

Between the acres of the rye,
With a hey, and a ho, and a hey nonino,
These pretty country folks would lie,
In the springtime, the only pretty ringtime,
When birds do sing, hey ding a ding, ding.
Sweet lovers love the spring.

This carol they began that hour,
With a hey, and a ho, and a hey nonino,
How that a life was but a flower
In the springtime, the only pretty ringtime,
When birds do sing, hey ding a ding, ding.
Sweet lovers love the spring.

And therefore take the present time,
With a hey, and a ho, and a hey nonino,
For love is crownèd with the prime°
In the springtime, the only pretty ringtime,
When birds do sing, hey ding a ding, ding.
Sweet lovers love the spring.

TOUCH Truly, young gentlemen, though there was no great matter in the ditty, yet the note was very untunable.

1. PAGE You are deceived, sir. We kept time, we lost not our time.

TOUCH By my troth, yes. I count it but time lost to hear such a foolish song. God buy you, and God mend your voices! Come, Audrey.

[*Exeunt.*]

Scene IV. The forest.

[*Enter* DUKE *Senior,* AMIENS, JAQUES, ORLANDO, OLIVER, *and* CELIA.]

DUKE S Dost thou believe, Orlando, that the boy
Can do all this that he hath promised?

ORL I sometimes do believe, and sometimes do not,
As those that fear they hope and know they fear.

[*Enter* ROSALIND, SILVIUS, *and* PHEBE.]

ROS Patience once more, whiles our compact is urged.°
You say if I bring in your Rosalind,
You will bestow her on Orlando here?

DUKE S That would I had I kingdoms to give with her.

ROS And you say you will have her when I bring her?

ORL That would I were I of all kingdoms king.

35. *prime:* perfection.

Sc. iv: 5. *compact is urged:* agreement is repeated.

ROS You say you'll marry me if I be willing?
PHE That will I, should I die the hour after.
ROS But if you do refuse to marry me,
You'll give yourself to this most faithful shepherd?
PHE So is the bargain.
ROS You say that you'll have Phebe if she will?
SIL Though to have her and death were both one thing.
ROS I have promised to make all this matter even.°
Keep you your word, O Duke, to give your daughter,
You yours, Orlando, to receive his daughter.
Keep your word, Phebe, that you'll marry me
Or else, refusing me, to wed this shepherd.
Keep your word, Silvius, that you'll marry her
If she refuse me. And from hence I go
To make these doubts all even.

[*Exeunt* ROSALIND *and* CELIA.]

DUKE S I do remember in this shepherd boy
Some lively touches of my daughter's favor.°
ORL My lord, the first time that I ever saw him
Methought he was a brother to your daughter.
But, my good lord, this boy is forest-born,
And hath been tutored in the rudiments
Of many desperate studies by his uncle,
Whom he reports to be a great magician
Obscurèd° in the circle of this forest.

[*Enter* TOUCHSTONE *and* AUDREY.]

JAQ There is, sure, another flood toward, and these couples are coming to the ark. Here comes a pair of very strange beasts, which in all tongues are called fools.

TOUCH Salutation and greeting to you all!

JAQ Good my lord, bid him welcome. This is the motley-minded gentleman that I have so often met in the forest. He hath been a courtier, he swears.

TOUCH If any man doubt that, let him put me to my purgation.° I have trod a measure.° I have flattered a lady. I have been politic° with my friend, smooth with mine enemy. I have undone three tailors.° I have had four quarrels, and like to have fought one.

JAQ And how was that ta'en up?

TOUCH Faith, we met, and found the quarrel was upon the seventh cause.

JAQ How seventh cause? Good my lord, like this fellow.

DUKE S I like him very well.

18. make . . . even: straighten out. *27. favor:* face. *34. Obscured:* living obscurely. *42. purgation:* proving the truth of my claim. *43. trod a measure:* danced a formal dance, a necessary accomplishment of a courtier. *43. politic:* crafty. *44–5. undone . . . tailors:* i.e., by not paying their bills.

TOUCH God 'ild° you, sir, I desire you of the like. I press in here, sir, amongst the rest of the country copulatives,° to swear and to forswear, according as marriage binds and blood breaks. A poor virgin, sir, an ill-favored thing, sir, but mine own. A poor humor of mine, sir, to take that that no man else will. Rich honesty dwells like a miser, sir, in a poor house, as your pearl in your foul oyster.

DUKE S By my faith, he is very swift and sententious.°

TOUCH According to the fool's bolt,° sir, and such dulcet diseases.°

JAQ But for the seventh cause, how did you find the quarrel on the seventh cause?

TOUCH Upon a lie seven times removed—Bear your body more seeming, Audrey—as thus, sir. I did dislike the cut of a certain courtier's beard. He sent me word if I said his beard was not cut well, he was in the mind it was. This is called the Retort Courteous. If I sent him word again "it was not well cut," he would send me word he cut it to please himself. This is called the Quip Modest. If again "it was not well cut," he disabled my judgment.° This is called the Reply Churlish. If again "it was not well cut," he would answer I spake not true. This is called the Reproof Valiant. If again "it was not well cut," he would say I lie. This is called the Countercheck Quarrelsome. And so to the Lie Circumstantial° and the Lie Direct.°

JAQ And how oft did you say his beard was not well cut?

TOUCH I durst go no further than the Lie Circumstantial, nor he durst not give me the Lie Direct, and so we measured swords and parted.

JAQ Can you nominate in order now the degrees of the lie?

TOUCH Oh, sir, we quarrel in print,° by the book, as you have books for good manners. I will name you the degrees. The first, the Retort Courteous; the second, the Quip Modest; the third, the Reply Churlish; the fourth, the Reproof Valiant; the fifth, the Countercheck Quarrelsome; the sixth, the Lie with Circumstance; the seventh, the Lie Direct. All these you may avoid but the Lie Direct, and you may avoid that too, with an "If." I knew when seven justices could not take up° a quarrel, but when the parties were met themselves, one of them thought but of an "If," as, "If you said so, then I said so," and they shook hands and swore brothers. Your "If" is the only peacemaker, much virtue in "If."

51. God 'ild: God yield, a form of returning thanks. *52. copulatives:* folk desirous of being mated. *57. sententious:* full of pithy sayings. *58. According . . . bolt:* i.e., ready to let fly at anything, for according to the proverb "A fool's bolt [arrow] is soon shot." *58. dulcet diseases:* pleasant failings. *67. disabled my judgment:* said my judgment was weak. *71. Circumstantial:* indirect. *72. Lie Direct:* i.e., the direct accusation that the speaker is a liar. Any man who then refused to fight to redeem his honor showed himself a coward. *78. quarrel . . . print:* Processes quite as fantastic are printed in some of the manuals of dueling. *85. take up:* make up.

JAQ Is not this a rare fellow, my lord? He's as good at anything and yet a fool.

DUKE S He uses his folly like a stalking-horse,° and under the presentation of that he shoots his wit.

[*Enter* HYMEN,° ROSALIND, *and* CELIA. *Still*° *music.*]

HYM Then is there mirth in Heaven
When earthly things made even
Atone° together.
Good Duke, receive thy daughter.
Hymen from Heaven brought her,
Yea, brought her hither,
That thou mightst join her hand with his
Whose heart within his bosom is.

ROS [*To* DUKE S.] To you I give myself, for I am yours.
[*To* ORLANDO] To you I give myself, for I am yours.

DUKE S If there be truth in sight, you are my daughter.

ORL If there be truth in sight, you are my Rosalind.

PHE If sight and shape be true,
Why then, my love adieu!

ROS I'll have no father, if you be not he.
I'll have no husband, if you be not he.
Nor ne'er wed woman, if you be not she.

HYM Peace, ho! I bar confusion.
'Tis I must make conclusion
Of these most strange events.
Here's eight that must take hands
To join in Hymen's bands
If truth holds true contents.
You and you no cross° shall part.
You and you are heart in heart.
You to his love must accord
Or have a woman to your lord.
You and you are sure together,
As the winter to foul weather.
Whiles a wedlock hymn we sing
Feed yourselves with questioning,
That reason wonder may diminish,
How thus we met, and these things finish.

SONG

Wedding is great Juno's crown.
Oh, blessed bond of board and bed!
'Tis Hymen peoples every town.

91. stalking-horse: a real or imitation horse used as cover to approach the game for a shot.
92. s.d., Hymen: god of marriage. *Still:* soft. *95. Atone:* agree. *116. cross:* trouble.

High wedlock then be honorèd.
Honor, high honor and renown,
To Hymen, god of every town!

DUKE S O my dear niece, welcome thou art to me!
Even Daughter, welcome, in no less degree.

PHE I will not eat my word now thou art mine,
Thy faith my fancy to thee doth combine.

[*Enter* JAQUES DE BOYS.]

JAQ. DE B Let me have audience for a word or two.
I am the second son of old Sir Rowland
That bring these tidings to this fair assembly.
Duke Frederick, hearing how that every day
Men of great worth resorted to this forest,
Addressed° a mighty power,° which were on foot,
In his own conduct,° purposely to take
His brother here and put him to the sword.
And to the skirts of this wild wood he came,
Where meeting with an old religious man,°
After some question with him, was converted
Both from his enterprise and from the world,
His crown bequeathing to his banished brother,
And all their lands restored to them again
That were with him exiled. This to be true
I do engage° my life.

DUKE S Welcome, young man,
Thou offer'st° fairly to thy brothers' wedding.
To one his lands withheld, and to the other
A land itself at large, a potent dukedom.
First, in this forest let us do those ends
That here were well begun and well begot.
And after, every of this happy number
That have endured shrewd° days and nights with us
Shall share the good of our returnèd fortune
According to the measure of their states.
Meantime, forget this new-fallen dignity,
And fall into our rustic revelry.
Play, music! And you, brides and bridegrooms all,
With measure heaped in joy, to the measures° fall.

JAQ Sir, by your patience. If I heard you rightly,
The Duke hath put on a religious life
And thrown into neglect the pompous Court?

141. *Addressed:* prepared. *power:* army. 142. *In . . . conduct:* under his own command. 145. *religious man:* hermit. 151. *engage:* pledge. 152. *Thou offer'st:* you make a good present. 158. *shrewd:* bitter. 164. *measures:* dances.

JAQ. DE B He hath.
JAQ To him will I. Out of these convertites°
There is much matter to be heard and learned.
[*To* DUKE] You to your former honor I bequeath,
Your patience and your virtue well deserves it.
[*To* ORLANDO] You to a love that your true faith doth merit.
[*To* OLIVER] You to your land, and love, and great allies.
[*To* SILVIUS] You to a long and well-deservèd bed.
[*To* TOUCHSTONE] And you to wrangling, for thy loving voyage
Is but for two months victualed.° So, to your pleasures.
I am for other than for dancing measures.
DUKE S Stay, Jaques, stay.
JAQ To see no pastime I. What you would have I'll stay to know at your abandoned cave.

[*Exit.*]

DUKE S Proceed, proceed. We will begin these rites,
As we do trust they'll end, in true delights.

[*A dance.*]

EPILOGUE

ROS It is not the fashion to see the lady the epilogue, but it is no more unhandsome than to see the lord the prologue. If it be true that good wine needs no bush,° 'tis true that a good play needs no epilogue. Yet to good wine they do use good bushes, and good plays prove the better by the help of good epilogues. What a case am I in then, that am neither a good epilogue nor cannot insinuate° with you in the behalf of a good play! I am not furnished° like a beggar, therefore to beg will not become me. My way is to conjure° you, and I'll begin with the women. I charge you, O women, for the love you bear to men, to like as much of this play as please you. And I charge you, O men, for the love you bear to women—as I perceive by your simpering none of you hates them—that between you and the women the play may please. If I were a woman° I would kiss as many of you as had beards that pleased me, complexions that liked° me, and breaths that I defied not. And I am sure as many as have good beards or good faces or sweet breaths will, for my kind offer, when I make curtsy bid me farewell.

[*Exeunt.*]

169. convertites: converts to the religious life. *177. victualed:* provisioned.

Epilogue: *2–3. good . . . bush:* good wine needs no advertisement, an old proverb arising from the custom of vintners of hanging up a bush as a sign of their trade. *6. insinuate:* ingratiate myself. *7. furnished:* dressed. *8. conjure:* win you over by magic. *13. If . . . woman:* In the play the part of Rosalind was acted by a boy. *15. liked:* pleased.

Molière (1622–1673)
TARTUFFE

CHARACTERS

MME PERNELLE, *Orgon's mother*
ORGON, *Elmire's husband*
ELMIRE, *Orgon's wife*
DAMIS, *Orgon's son, Elmire's stepson*
MARIANE, *Orgon's daughter, Elmire's stepdaughter, in love with Valère*
VALÈRE, *in love with Mariane*
CLÉANTE, *Orgon's brother-in-law*
TARTUFFE, *a hypocrite*
DORINE, *Mariane's lady's-maid*
M. LOYAL, *a bailiff*
A POLICE OFFICER
FLIPOTE, *Mme Pernelle's maid*

THE SCENE THROUGHOUT: ORGON'S HOUSE IN PARIS.

ACT I

Scene I

MADAME PERNELLE *and* FLIPOTE, *her maid,* ELMIRE, MARIANE, DORINE, DAMIS, CLÉANTE.

MADAME PERNELLE Come, come, Flipote; it's time I left this place.
ELMIRE I can't keep up, you walk at such a pace.
MADAME PERNELLE Don't trouble, child; no need to show me out.
It's not your manners I'm concerned about.
ELMIRE We merely pay you the respect we owe.
But, Mother, why this hurry? Must you go?
MADAME PERNELLE I must. This house appalls me. No one in it
Will pay attention for a single minute.
Children, I take my leave much vexed in spirit.
I offer good advice, but you won't hear it.
You all break in and chatter on and on.
It's like a madhouse with the keeper gone.
DORINE If . . .
MADAME PERNELLE Girl, you talk too much, and I'm afraid
You're far too saucy for a lady's-maid.
You push in everywhere and have your say.
DAMIS But . . .
MADAME PERNELLE You, boy, grow more foolish every day.
To think my grandson should be such a dunce!
I've said a hundred times, if I've said it once,

That if you keep the course on which you've started,
You'll leave your worthy father broken-hearted.

MARIANE I think . . .

MADAME PERNELLE And you, his sister, seem so pure,
So shy, so innocent, and so demure.
But you know what they say about still waters.
I pity parents with secretive daughters.

ELMIRE Now, Mother . . .

MADAME PERNELLE And as for you, child, let me add
That your behavior is extremely bad,
And a poor example for these children, too.
Their dear, dead mother did far better than you.
You're much too free with money, and I'm distressed
To see you so elaborately dressed.
When it's one's husband that one aims to please,
One has no need of costly fripperies.

CLÉANTE Oh, Madam, really . . .

MADAME PERNELLE You are her brother, Sir,
And I respect and love you; yet if I were
My son, this lady's good and pious spouse,
I wouldn't make you welcome in my house.
You're full of worldly counsels which, I fear,
Aren't suitable for decent folk to hear.
I've spoken bluntly, Sir; but it behooves us
Not to mince words when righteous fervor moves us.

DAMIS Your man Tartuffe is full of holy speeches . . .

MADAME PERNELLE And practices precisely what he preaches.
He's a fine man, and should be listened to.
I will not hear him mocked by fools like you.

DAMIS Good God! Do you expect me to submit
To the tyranny of that carping hypocrite?
Must we forgo all joys and satisfactions
Because that bigot censures all our actions?

DORINE To hear him talk—and he talks all the time—
There's nothing one can do that's not a crime.
He rails at everything, your dear Tartuffe.

MADAME PERNELLE Whatever he reproves deserves reproof.
He's out to save your souls, and all of you
Must love him, as my son would have you do.

DAMIS Ah no, Grandmother, I could never take
To such a rascal, even for my father's sake.
That's how I feel, and I shall not dissemble.
His every action makes me seethe and tremble
With helpless anger, and I have no doubt
That he and I will shortly have it out.

DORINE Surely it is a shame and a disgrace
To see this man usurp the master's place—
To see this beggar who, when first he came,
Had not a shoe or shoestring to his name
So far forget himself that he behaves
As if the house were his, and we his slaves.
MADAME PERNELLE Well, mark my words, your souls would fare far better
If you obeyed his precepts to the letter.
DORINE You see him as a saint. I'm far less awed;
In fact, I see right through him. He's a fraud.
MADAM PERNELLE Nonsense!
DORINE His man Laurent's the same, or worse;
I'd not trust either with a penny purse.
MADAME PERNELLE I can't say what his servant's morals may be;
His own great goodness I can guarantee.
You all regard him with distaste and fear
Because he tells you what you're loath to hear,
Condemns your sins, points out your moral flaws,
And humbly strives to further Heaven's cause.
DORINE If sin is all that bothers him, why is it
He's so upset when folk drop in to visit?
Is Heaven so outraged by a social call
That he must prophesy against us all?
I'll tell you what I think: if you ask me,
He's jealous of my mistress' company.
MADAME PERNELLE
Rubbish! [*To* ELMIRE.] He's not alone, child, in complaining
Of all your promiscuous entertaining.
Why, the whole neighborhood's upset, I know,
By all these carriages that come and go,
With crowds of guests parading in and out
And noisy servants loitering about.
In all of this, I'm sure there's nothing vicious;
But why give people cause to be suspicious?
CLÉANTE They need no cause; they'll talk in any case.
Madam, this world would be a joyless place
If, fearing what malicious tongues might say,
We locked our doors and turned our friends away.
And even if one did so dreary a thing,
D'you think those tongues would cease their chattering?
One can't fight slander; it's a losing battle;
Let us instead ignore their tittle-tattle.
Let's strive to live by conscience' clear decrees,
And let the gossips gossip as they please.

DORINE If there is talk against us, I know the source:
It's Daphne and her little husband, of course.
Those who have greatest cause for guilt and shame
Are quickest to besmirch a neighbor's name.
When there's a chance for libel, they never miss it;
When something can be made to seem illicit
They're off at once to spread the joyous news,
Adding to fact what fantasies they choose.
By talking up their neighbor's indiscretions
They seek to camouflage their own transgressions,
Hoping that others' innocent affairs
Will lend a hue of innocence to theirs,
Or that their own black guilt will come to seem
Part of a general shady color-scheme.

MADAME PERNELLE All that is quite irrelevant. I doubt
That anyone's more virtuous and devout
Than dear Orante; and I'm informed that she
Condemns your mode of life most vehemently.

DORINE Oh, yes, she's strict, devout, and has no taint
Of worldliness; in short, she seems a saint.
But it was time which taught her that disguise;
She's thus because she can't be otherwise.
So long as her attractions could enthrall,
She flounced and flirted and enjoyed it all,
But now that they're no longer what they were
She quits a world which fast is quitting her,
And wears a veil of virtue to conceal
Her bankrupt beauty and her lost appeal.
That's what becomes of old coquettes today:
Distressed when all their lovers fall away,
They see no recourse but to play the prude,
And so confer a style on solitude.
Thereafter, they're severe with everyone,
Condemning all our actions, pardoning none,
And claiming to be pure, austere, and zealous
When, if the truth were known, they're merely jealous,
And cannot bear to see another know
The pleasures time has forced them to forgo.

MADAME PERNELLE [*Initially to* ELMIRE]
That sort of talk is what you like to hear;
Therefore you'd have us all keep still, my dear,
While Madam rattles on the livelong day.
Nevertheless, I mean to have my say.
I tell you that you're blest to have Tartuffe
Dwelling, as my son's guest, beneath this roof;

That Heaven has sent him to forestall its wrath
By leading you, once more, to the true path;
That all he reprehends its reprehensible,
And that you'd better heed him, and be sensible.
These visits, balls, and parties in which you revel
Are nothing but inventions of the Devil.
One never hears a word that's edifying:
Nothing but chaff and foolishness and lying.
As well as vicious gossip in which one's neighbor
Is cut to bits with epee, foil, and saber.
People of sense are driven half-insane
At such affairs, where noise and folly reign
And reputations perish thick and fast.
As a wise preacher said on Sunday last,
Parties are Towers of Babylon, because
The guests all babble on with never a pause;
And then he told a story which, I think . . .
[*To* CLÉANTE.]
I heard that laugh, Sir, and I saw that wink!
Go find your silly friends and laugh some more!
Enough; I'm going; don't show me to the door.
I leave this household much dismayed and vexed;
I cannot say when I shall see you next.
[*Slapping* FLIPOTE.]
Wake up, don't stand there gaping into space!
I'll slap some sense into that stupid face.
Move, move, you slut.

Scene II.

CLÉANTE, DORINE.

CLÉANTE I think I'll stay behind:
I want no further pieces of her mind.
How that old lady . . .
DORINE Oh, what wouldn't she say
If she could hear you speak of her that way!
She'd thank you for the *lady*, but I'm sure
She'd find the *old* a little premature.
CLÉANTE My, what a scene she made, and what a din!
And how this man Tartuffe has taken her in!
DORINE Yes, but her son is even worse deceived;
His folly must be seen to be believed.
In the late troubles, he played an able part
And served his king with wise and loyal heart,
But he's quite lost his senses since he fell

Beneath Tartuffe's infatuating spell.
He calls him brother, and loves him as his life,
Preferring him to mother, child, or wife.
In him and him alone will he confide;
He's made him his confessor and his guide;
He pets and pampers him with love more tender
Than any pretty mistress could engender,
Gives him the place of honor when they dine,
Delights to see him gorging like a swine,
Stuffs him with dainties till his guts distend,
And when he belches, cries "God bless you, friend!"
In short, he's mad; he worships him; he dotes;
His deeds he marvels at, his words he quotes,
Thinking each act a miracle, each word
Oracular as those that Moses heard.
Tartuffe, much pleased to find so easy a victim,
Has in a hundred ways beguiled and tricked him,
Milked him of money, and with his permission
Established here a sort of Inquisition.
Even Laurent, his lackey, dares to give
Us arrogant advice on how to live;
He sermonizes us in thundering tones
And confiscates our ribbons and colognes.
Last week he tore a kerchief into pieces
Because he found it pressed in a *Life of Jesus:*
He said it was a sin to juxtapose
Unholy vanities and holy prose.

Scene III

ELMIRE, MARIANE, DAMIS, CLÉANTE, DORINE.

ELMIRE [*To* CLÉANTE]
You did well not to follow; she stood in the door
And said *verbatim* all she'd said before.
I saw my husband coming. I think I'd best
Go upstairs now, and take a little rest.

CLÉANTE I'll wait and greet him here; then I must go.
I've really only time to say hello.

DAMIS Sound him about my sister's wedding, please.
I think Tartuffe's against it, and that he's
Been urging Father to withdraw his blessing.
As you well know, I'd find that most distressing.
Unless my sister and Valère can marry,
My hopes to wed *his* sister will miscarry,
And I'm determined . . .

DORINE He's coming.

Scene IV

ORGON, CLÉANTE, DORINE.

ORGON Ah, Brother, good-day.
CLÉANTE Well, welcome back. I'm sorry I can't stay.
How was the country? Blooming, I trust, and green?
ORGON Excuse me, Brother; just one moment.
[*To* DORINE.] Dorine . . .
[*To* CLÉANTE.]
To put my mind at rest, I always learn
The household news the moment I return.
[*To* DORINE.]
Has all been well, these two days I've been gone?
How are the family? What's been going on?
DORINE Your wife, two days ago, had a bad fever,
And a fierce headache which refused to leave her.
ORGON Ah. And Tartuffe?
DORINE Tartuffe? Why, he's round and red,
Bursting with health, and excellently fed.
ORGON Poor fellow!
DORINE That night, the mistress was unable
To take a single bite at the dinner-table.
Her headache-pains, she said, were simply hellish.
ORGON Ah. And Tartuffe?
DORINE He ate his meal with relish,
And zealously devoured in her presence
A leg of mutton and a brace of pheasants.
ORGON Poor fellow!
DORINE Well, the pains continued strong,
And so she tossed and tossed the whole night long,
Now icy-cold, now burning like a flame.
We sat beside her bed till morning came.
ORGON Ah. And Tartuffe?
DORINE Why, having eaten, he rose
And sought his room, already in a doze,
Got into his warm bed, and snored away
In perfect peace until the break of day.
ORGON Poor fellow!
DORINE After much ado, we talked her
Into dispatching someone for the doctor.
He bled her, and the fever quickly fell.
ORGON Ah. And Tartuffe?
DORINE He bore it very well.
To keep his cheerfulness at any cost,
And make up for the blood *Madame* had lost,
He drank, at lunch, four beakers full of port.

ORGON Poor fellow!
DORINE Both are doing well, in short.
I'll go and tell *Madame* that you've expressed
Keen sympathy and anxious interest.

Scene V

ORGON, CLÉANTE.

CLÉANTE That girl was laughing in your face, and though
I've no wish to offend you, even so
I'm bound to say that she had some excuse.
How can you possibly be such a goose?
Are you so dazed by this man's hocus-pocus
That all the world, save him, is out of focus?
You've given him clothing, shelter, food, and care;
Why must you also . . .
ORGON Brother, stop right there.
You do not know the man of whom you speak.
CLÉANTE I grant you that. But my judgment's not so weak
That I can't tell, by his effect on others . . .
ORGON Ah, when you meet him, you two will be like brothers!
There's been no loftier soul since time began.
He is a man who . . . a man who . . . an excellent man.
To keep his precepts is to be reborn,
And view this dunghill of a world with scorn.
Yes, thanks to him I'm a changed man indeed.
Under his tutelage my soul's been freed
From earthly loves, and every human tie:
My mother, children, brother, and wife could die,
And I'd not feel a single moment's pain.
CLÉANTE That's a fine sentiment, Brother; most humane.
ORGON Oh, had you seen Tartuffe as I first knew him,
Your heart, like mine, would have surrendered to him.
He used to come into our church each day
And humbly kneel nearby, and start to pray.
He'd draw the eyes of everybody there
By the deep fervor of his heartfelt prayer;
He'd sigh and weep, and sometimes with a sound
Of rapture he would bend and kiss the ground;
And when I rose to go, he'd run before
To offer me holy-water at the door.
His serving-man, no less devout than he,
Informed me of his master's poverty;
I gave him gifts, but in his humbleness
He'd beg me every time to give him less.

"Oh, that's too much," he'd cry, "too much by twice!
I don't deserve it. The half, Sir, would suffice."
And when I wouldn't take it back, he'd share
Half of it with the poor, right then and there.
At length, Heaven prompted me to take him in
To dwell with us, and free our souls from sin.
He guides our lives, and to protect my honor
Stays by my wife, and keeps an eye upon her;
He tells me whom she sees, and all she does,
And seems more jealous than I ever was!
And how austere he is! Why, he can detect
A mortal sin where you would least suspect;
In smallest trifles, he's extremely strict.
Last week, his conscience was severely pricked
Because, while praying, he had caught a flea
And killed it, so he felt, too wrathfully.

CLÉANTE Good God, man! Have you lost your common sense—
Or is this all some joke at my expense?
How can you stand there and in all sobriety . . .

ORGON Brother, your language savors of impiety.
Too much free-thinking's made your faith unsteady,
And as I've warned you many times already,
'Twill get you into trouble before you're through.

CLÉANTE So I've been told before by dupes like you:
Being blind, you'd have all others blind as well;
The clear-eyed man you call an infidel,
And he who sees through humbug and pretense
Is charged, by you, with want of reverence.
Spare me your warnings, Brother; I have no fear
Of speaking out, for you and Heaven to hear,
Against affected zeal and pious knavery.
There's true and false in piety, as in bravery,
And just as those whose courage shines the most
In battle, are the least inclined to boast,
So those whose hearts are truly pure and lowly
Don't make a flashy show of being holy.
There's a vast difference, so it seems to me,
Between true piety and hypocrisy:
How do you fail to see it, may I ask?
Is not a face quite different from a mask?
Cannot sincerity and cunning art,
Reality and semblance, be told apart?
Are scarecrows just like men, and do you hold
That a false coin is just as good as gold?
Ah, Brother, man's a strangely fashioned creature

Who seldom is content to follow Nature,
But recklessly pursues his inclination
Beyond the narrow bounds of moderation,
And often, by transgressing Reason's laws,
Perverts a lofty aim or noble cause.
A passing observation, but it applies.

ORGON I see, dear Brother, that you're profoundly wise;
You harbor all the insight of the age.
You are our one clear mind, our only sage,
The era's oracle, its Cato too,
And all mankind are fools compared to you.

CLÉANTE Brother, I don't pretend to be a sage,
Nor have I all the wisdom of the age.
There's just one insight I would dare to claim:
I know that true and false are not the same;
And just as there is nothing I more revere
Than a soul whose faith is steadfast and sincere,
Nothing that I more cherish and admire
Than honest zeal and true religious fire,
So there is nothing that I find more base
Than specious piety's dishonest face—
Than these bold mountebanks, these histrios
Whose impious mummeries and hollow shows
Exploit our love of Heaven, and make a jest
Of all that men think holiest and best;
These calculating souls who offer prayers
Not to their Maker, but as public wares,
And seek to buy respect and reputation
With lifted eyes and sighs of exaltation;
These charlatans, I say, whose pilgrim souls
Proceed, by way of Heaven, toward earthly goals,
Who weep and pray and swindle and extort,
Who preach the monkish life, but haunt the court,
Who make their zeal the partner of their vice—
Such men are vengeful, sly, and cold as ice,
And when there is an enemy to defame
They cloak their spite in fair religion's name,
Their private spleen and malice being made
To seem a high and virtuous crusade,
Until, to mankind's reverent applause,
They crucify their foe in Heaven's cause.
Such knaves are all too common; yet, for the wise,
True piety isn't hard to recognize,
And, happily, these present times provide us
With bright examples to instruct and guide us.

Consider Ariston and Périandre;
Look at Oronte, Alcidamas, Clitandre;
Their virtue is acknowledged; who could doubt it?
But you won't hear them beat the drum about it.
They're never ostentatious, never vain,
And their religion's moderate and humane;
It's not their way to criticize and chide:
They think censoriousness a mark of pride,
And therefore, letting others preach and rave,
They show, by deeds, how Christians should behave.
They think no evil of their fellow man,
But judge of him as kindly as they can.
They don't intrigue and wangle and conspire;
To lead a good life is their one desire;
The sinner wakes no rancorous hate in them;
It is the sin alone which they condemn;
Nor do they try to show a fiercer zeal
For Heaven's cause than Heaven itself could feel.
These men I honor, these men I advocate
As models for us all to emulate.
Your man is not their sort at all, I fear:
And, while your praise of him is quite sincere,
I think that you've been dreadfully deluded.

ORGON Now then, dear Brother, is your speech concluded?
CLÉANTE Why, yes.
ORGON Your servant, Sir. [*He turns to go.*]
CLÉANTE No, Brother; wait.
There's one more matter. You agreed of late
That young Valère might have your daughter's hand.
ORGON I did.
CLÉANTE And set the date, I understand.
ORGON Quite so.
CLÉANTE You've now postponed it; is that true?
ORGON No doubt.
CLÉANTE The match no longer pleases you?
ORGON Who knows?
CLÉANTE D'you mean to go back on your word?
ORGON I won't say that.
CLÉANTE Has anything occurred
Which might entitle you to break your pledge?
ORGON Perhaps.
CLÉANTE Why must you hem, and haw, and hedge?
The boy asked me to sound you in this affair . . .
ORGON It's been a pleasure.
CLÉANTE But what shall I tell Valère?

ORGON Whatever you like.

CLÉANTE But what have you decided?
What are your plans?

ORGON I plan, Sir, to be guided
By Heaven's will.

CLÉANTE Come, Brother, don't talk rot.
You've given Valère your word; will you keep it, or not?

ORGON Good day.

CLÉANTE This looks like poor Valère's undoing;
I'll go and warn him that there's trouble brewing.

ACT II

Scene I

ORGON, MARIANE.

ORGON Mariane.

MARIANE Yes, Father?

ORGON A word with you; come here.

MARIANE What are you looking for?

ORGON [*Peering into a small closet.*] Eavesdroppers, dear.
I'm making sure we shan't be overheard.
Someone in there could catch our every word.
Ah, good, we're safe. Now, Mariane, my child,
You're a sweet girl who's tractable and mild,
Whom I hold dear, and think most highly of.

MARIANE I'm deeply grateful, Father, for your love.

ORGON That's well said, Daughter; and you can repay me
If, in all things, you'll cheerfully obey me.

MARIANE To please you, Sir, is what delights me best.

ORGON Good, good. Now, what d'you think of Tartuffe, our guest?

MARIANE I, Sir?

ORGON Yes. Weigh your answer; think it through.

MARIANE Oh, dear. I'll say whatever you wish me to.

ORGON That's wisely said, my Daughter. Say of him, then,
That he's the very worthiest of men,
And that you're fond of him, and would rejoice
In being his wife, if that should be my choice.
Well?

MARIANE What?

ORGON What's that?

MARIANE I . . .

ORGON Well?

MARIANE Forgive me, pray.

ORGON Did you not hear me?

MARIANE Of *whom,* Sir, must I say
That I am fond of him, and would rejoice
In being his wife, if that should be your choice?

ORGON Why, of Tartuffe.

MARIANE But, Father, that's false, you know.
Why would you have me say what isn't so?

ORGON Because I am resolved it shall be true.
That it's my wish should be enough for you.

MARIANE You can't mean, Father . . .

ORGON Yes, Tartuffe shall be
Allied by marriage to this family,
And he's to be your husband, is that clear?
It's a father's privilege . . .

Scene II

DORINE, ORGON, MARIANE.

ORGON [*To* DORINE] What are you doing in here?
Is curiosity so fierce a passion
With you, that you must eavesdrop in this fashion?

DORINE There's lately been a rumor going about—
Based on some hunch or chance remark, no doubt—
That you mean Mariane to wed Tartuffe.
I've laughed it off, of course, as just a spoof.

ORGON You find it so incredible?

DORINE Yes, I do.
I won't accept that story, even from you.

ORGON Well, you'll believe it when the thing is done.

DORINE Yes, yes, of course. Go on and have your fun.

ORGON I've never been more serious in my life.

DORINE Ha!

ORGON Daughter, I mean it; you're to be his wife.

DORINE No, don't believe your father; it's all a hoax.

ORGON See here, young woman . . .

DORINE Come, Sir, no more jokes;
You can't fool us.

ORGON How dare you talk that way?

DORINE All right, then: we believe you, sad to say.
But how a man like you, who looks so wise
And wears a mustache of such splendid size,
Can be so foolish as to . . .

ORGON Silence, please!
My girl, you take too many liberties.
I'm master here, as you must not forget.

DORINE Do let's discuss this calmly; don't be upset.
You can't be serious, Sir, about this plan.
What should that bigot want with Mariane?
Praying and fasting ought to keep him busy.
And then, in terms of wealth and rank, what is he?
Why should a man of property like you
Pick out a beggar son-in-law?
ORGON That will do.
Speak of his poverty with reverence.
His is a pure and saintly indigence
Which far transcends all worldly pride and pelf.
He lost his fortune, as he says himself,
Because he cared for Heaven alone, and so
Was careless of his interests here below.
I mean to get him out of his present straits
And help him to recover his estates—
Which, in his part of the world, have no small fame.
Poor though he is, he's a gentleman just the same.
DORINE Yes, so he tells us; and, Sir, it seems to me
Such pride goes very ill with piety.
A man whose spirit spurns this dungy earth
Ought not to brag of lands and noble birth;
Such worldly arrogance will hardly square
With meek devotion and the life of prayer.
. . . But this approach, I see, has drawn a blank;
Let's speak, then, of his person, not his rank.
Doesn't it seem to you a trifle grim
To give a girl like her to a man like him?
When two are so ill-suited, can't you see
What the sad consequence is bound to be?
A young girl's virtue is imperilled, Sir,
When such a marriage is imposed on her;
For if one's bridegroom isn't to one's taste,
It's hardly an inducement to be chaste,
And many a man with horns upon his brow
Has made his wife the thing that she is now.
It's hard to be a faithful wife, in short,
To certain husbands of a certain sort,
And he who gives his daughter to a man she hates
Must answer for her sins at Heaven's gates.
Think, Sir, before you play so risky a role.
ORGON This servant-girl presumes to save my soul!
DORINE You would do well to ponder what I've said.
ORGON Daughter, we'll disregard this dunderhead.

Just trust your father's judgment. Oh, I'm aware
That I once promised you to young Valère;
But now I hear he gambles, which greatly shocks me;
What's more, I've doubts about his orthodoxy.
His visits to church, I note, are very few.

DORINE Would you have him go at the same hours as you,
And kneel nearby, to be sure of being seen?

ORGON I can dispense with such remarks, Dorine.
[*To* MARIANE.]
Tartuffe, however, is sure of Heaven's blessing,
And that's the only treasure worth possessing.
This match will bring you joys beyond all measure;
Your cup will overflow with every pleasure;
You two will interchange your faithful loves
Like two sweet cherubs, or two turtle-doves.
No harsh word shall be heard, no frown be seen,
And he shall make you happy as a queen.

DORINE And she'll make him a cuckold, just wait and see.

ORGON What language!

DORINE Oh, he's a man of destiny;
He's *made* for horns, and what the stars demand
Your daughter's virtue surely can't withstand.

ORGON Don't interrupt me further. Why can't you learn
That certain things are none of your concern?

DORINE It's for your own sake that I interfere.
[*She repeatedly interrupts* ORGON *just as he is turning to speak to his daughter.*]

ORGON Most kind of you. Now, hold your tongue, d'you hear?

DORINE If I didn't love you . . .

ORGON Spare me your affection.

DORINE I'll love you, Sir, in spite of your objection.

ORGON Blast!

DORINE I can't bear, Sir, for your honor's sake,
To let you make this ludicrous mistake.

ORGON You mean to go on talking?

DORINE If I didn't protest
This sinful marriage, my conscience couldn't rest.

ORGON If you don't hold your tongue, you little shrew . . .

DORINE What, lost your temper? A pious man like you?

ORGON Yes! Yes! You talk and talk. I'm maddened by it.
Once and for all, I tell you to be quiet.

DORINE Well, I'll be quiet. But I'll be thinking hard.

ORGON Think all you like, but you had better guard
That saucy tongue of yours, or I'll . . .
[*Turning back to* MARIANE.]

Now, child,
I've weighed this matter fully.
DORINE [*Aside*] It drives me wild.
That I can't speak.
[ORGON *turns his head, and she is silent.*]
Tartuffe is no young dandy,
But, still, his person . . .
DORINE [*Aside*] Is as sweet as candy.
ORGON Is such that, even if you shouldn't care
For his other merits . . .
[*He turns and stands facing* DORINE, *arms crossed.*]
DORINE [*Aside*]
They'll make a lovely pair.
If I were she, no man would marry me
Against my inclination, and go scot-free;
He'd learn, before the wedding-day was over,
How readily a wife can find a lover.
ORGON [*To* DORINE] It seems you treat my orders as a joke.
DORINE Why, what's the matter? 'Twas not to you I spoke.
ORGON What *were* you doing?
DORINE Talking to myself, that's all.
ORGON Ah! [*Aside.*] One more bit of impudence and gall,
And I shall give her a good slap in the face.
[*He puts himself in position to slap her;* DORINE, *whenever he glances at her, stands immobile and silent.*]
Daughter, you shall accept, and with good grace,
The husband I've selected . . . Your wedding-day . . .
[*To* DORINE.]
Why don't you talk to yourself?
DORINE I've nothing to say.
ORGON Come, just one word.
DORINE No thank you, Sir. I pass.
ORGON Come, speak; I'm waiting.
DORINE I'd not be such an ass.
ORGON [*Turning to* MARIANE]
In short, dear Daughter, I mean to be obeyed,
And you must bow to the sound choice I've made.
DORINE [*Moving away*] I'd not wed such a monster, even in jest.
[ORGON *attempts to slap her, but misses.*]
ORGON Daughter, that maid of yours is a thorough pest;
She makes me sinfully annoyed and nettled.
I can't speak further; my nerves are too unsettled.
She's so upset me by her insolent talk,
I'll calm myself by going for a walk.

Scene III

DORINE, MARIANE.

DORINE [*Returning*] Well, have you lost your tongue, girl? Must I play
Your part, and say the lines you ought to say?
Faced with a fate so hideous and absurd,
Can you not utter one dissenting word?

MARIANE What good would it do? A father's power is great.

DORINE Resist him now, or it will be too late.

MARIANE But . . .

DORINE Tell him one cannot love at a father's whim;
That you shall marry for yourself, not him;
That since it's you who are to be the bride,
It's you, not he, who must be satisfied;
And that if his Tartuffe is so sublime,
He's free to marry him at any time.

MARIANE I've bowed so long to Father's strict control,
I couldn't oppose him now, to save my soul.

DORINE Come, come, Mariane. Do listen to reason, won't you?
Valère has asked your hand. Do you love him, or don't you?

MARIANE Oh, how unjust of you! What can you mean
By asking such a question, dear Dorine?
You know the depth of my affection for him;
I've told you a hundred times how I adore him.

DORINE I don't believe in everything I hear;
Who knows if your professions were sincere?

MARIANE They were, Dorine, and you do me wrong to doubt it;
Heaven knows that I've been all too frank about it.

DORINE You love him, then?

MARIANE Oh, more than I can express.

DORINE And he, I take it, cares for you no less?

MARIANE I think so.

DORINE And you both, with equal fire,
Burn to be married?

MARIANE That is our one desire.

DORINE What of Tartuffe, then? What of your father's plan?

MARIANE I'll kill myself, if I'm forced to wed that man.

DORINE I hadn't thought of that recourse. How splendid!
Just die, and all your troubles will be ended!
A fine solution. Oh, it maddens me
To hear you talk in that self-pitying key.

MARIANE Dorine, how harsh you are! It's most unfair.
You have no sympathy for my despair.

DORINE I've none at all for people who talk drivel
And, faced with difficulties, whine and snivel.
MARIANE No doubt I'm timid, but it would be wrong . . .
DORINE True love requires a heart that's firm and strong.
MARIANE I'm strong in my affection for Valère,
But coping with my father is his affair.
DORINE But if your father's brain has grown so cracked
Over his dear Tartuffe that he can retract
His blessing, though your wedding-day was named,
It's surely not Valère who's to be blamed.
MARIANE If I defied my father, as you suggest,
Would it not seem unmaidenly, at best?
Shall I defend my love at the expense
Of brazenness and disobedience?
Shall I parade my heart's desires, and flaunt . . .
DORINE No, I ask nothing of you. Clearly you want
To be Madame Tartuffe, and I feel bound
Not to oppose a wish so very sound.
What right have I to criticize the match?
Indeed, my dear, the man's a brilliant catch.
Monsieur Tartuffe! Now, there's a man of weight!
Yes, yes, Monsieur Tartuffe, I'm bound to state,
Is quite a person; that's not to be denied;
'Twill be no little thing to be his bride.
The world already rings with his renown;
He's a great noble—in his native town;
His ears are red, he has a pink complexion,
And all in all, he'll suit you to perfection.
MARIANE Dear God!
DORINE Oh, how triumphant you will feel
At having caught a husband so ideal!
MARIANE Oh, do stop teasing, and use your cleverness
To get me out of this appalling mess.
Advise me, and I'll do whatever you say.
DORINE Ah no, a dutiful daughter must obey
Her father, even if he weds her to an ape.
You've a bright future; why struggle to escape?
Tartuffe will take you back where his family lives,
To a small town aswarm with relatives—
Uncles and cousins whom you'll be charmed to meet.
You'll be received at once by the elite,
Calling upon the bailiff's wife, no less—
Even, perhaps, upon the mayoress,
Who'll sit you down in the *best* kitchen chair.
Then, once a year, you'll dance at the village fair

To the drone of bagpipes—two of them, in fact—
And see a puppet-show, or an animal act.
Your husband . . .

MARIANE Oh, you turn my blood to ice!
Stop torturing me, and give me your advice.

DORINE [*Threatening to go*]
Your servant, Madam.

MARIANE Dorine, I beg of you . . .

DORINE No, you deserve it; this marriage must go through.

MARIANE Dorine!

DORINE No.

MARIANE Not Tartuffe! You know I think him . . .

DORINE Tartuffe's your cup of tea, and you shall drink him.

MARIANE I've always told you everything, and relied . . .

DORINE No. You deserve to be tartuffified.

MARIANE Well, since you mock me and refuse to care,
I'll henceforth seek my solace in despair:
Despair shall be my counsellor and friend,
And help me bring my sorrows to an end.
[*She starts to leave.*]

DORINE There now, come back; my anger has subsided.
You do deserve some pity, I've decided.

MARIANE Dorine, if Father makes me undergo
This dreadful martyrdom, I'll die, I know.

DORINE Don't fret; it won't be difficult to discover
Some plan of action . . . But here's Valère, your lover.

Scene IV

VALÈRE, MARIANE, DORINE.

VALÈRE Madam, I've just received some wondrous news
Regarding which I'd like to hear your views.

MARIANE What news?

VALÈRE You're marrying Tartuffe.

MARIANE I find
That Father does have such a match in mind.

VALÈRE Your father, Madam . . .

MARIANE . . . has just this minute said
That it's Tartuffe he wishes me to wed.

VALÈRE Can he be serious?

MARIANE Oh, indeed he can;
He's clearly set his heart upon the plan.

VALÈRE And what position do you propose to take,
Madam?

MARIANE Why—I don't know.

VALÈRE For heaven's sake—
You don't know?

MARIANE No.

VALÈRE Well, well!

MARIANE Advise me, do.

VALÈRE Marry the man. That's my advice to you.

MARIANE That's your advice?

VALÈRE Yes.

MARIANE Truly?

VALÈRE Oh, absolutely.
You couldn't choose more wisely, more astutely.

MARIANE Thanks for this counsel; I'll follow it, of course.

VALÈRE Do, do; I'm sure 'twill cost you no remorse.

MARIANE To give it didn't cause your heart to break.

VALÈRE I gave it, Madam, only for your sake.

MARIANE And it's for your sake that I take it, Sir.

DORINE [*Withdrawing to the rear of the stage*] Let's see which fool will prove the stubborner.

VALÈRE So! I am nothing to you, and it was flat
Deception when you . . .

MARIANE Please, enough of that.
You've told me plainly that I should agree
To wed the man my father's chosen for me,
And since you've deigned to counsel me so wisely,
I promise, Sir, to do as you advise me.

VALÈRE Ah, no, 'twas not by me that you were swayed.
No, your decision was already made;
Though now, to save appearances, you protest
That you're betraying me at my behest.

MARIANE Just as you say.

VALÈRE Quite so. And I now see
That you were never truly in love with me.

MARIANE Alas, you're free to think so if you choose.

VALÈRE I choose to think so, and here's a bit of news:
You've spurned my hand, but I know where to turn
For kinder treatment, as you shall quickly learn.

MARIANE I'm sure you do. Your noble qualities
Inspire affection . . .

VALÈRE Forget my qualities, please.
They don't inspire you overmuch, I find.
But there's another lady I have in mind
Whose sweet and generous nature will not scorn
To compensate me for the loss I've borne.

MARIANE I'm no great loss, and I'm sure that you'll transfer
Your heart quite painlessly from me to her.

VALÈRE I'll do my best to take it in my stride.
The pain I feel at being cast aside
Time and forgetfulness may put an end to.
Or if I can't forget, I shall pretend to.
No self-respecting person is expected
To go on loving once he's been rejected.
MARIANE Now, that's a fine, high-minded sentiment.
VALÈRE One to which any sane man would assent.
Would you prefer it if I pined away
In hopeless passion till my dying day?
Am I to yield you to a rival's arms
And not console myself with other charms?
MARIANE Go then: console yourself; don't hesitate.
I wish you to; indeed, I cannot wait.
VALÈRE You wish me to?
MARIANE Yes.
VALÈRE That's the final straw.
Madam, farewell. Your wish shall be my law.
[*He starts to leave, and then returns: this repeatedly.*]
MARIANE Splendid.
VALÈRE [*Coming back again*] This breach, remember, is of your making;
It's you who've driven me to the step I'm taking.
MARIANE Of course.
VALÈRE [*Coming back again*] Remember, too, that I am merely
Following your example.
MARIANE I see that clearly.
VALÈRE Enough. I'll go and do your bidding, then.
MARIANE Good.
VALÈRE [*Coming back again*] You shall never see my face again.
MARIANE Excellent.
VALÈRE [*Walking to the door, then turning about*]
Yes?
MARIANE What?
VALÈRE What's that? What did you say?
MARIANE Nothing. You're dreaming.
VALÈRE Ah. Well, I'm on my way.
Farewell, *Madame*.
[*He moves slowly away.*]
MARIANE Farewell.
DORINE [*To* MARIANE] If you ask me,
Both of you are as mad as mad can be.
Do stop this nonsense, now. I've only let you
Squabble so long to see where it would get you.
Whoa there, Monsieure Valère!

[*She goes and seizes* VALÈRE *by the arm; he makes a great show of resistance.*]

VALÈRE What's this, Dorine?

DORINE Come here.

VALÈRE No, no, my heart's too full of spleen.
Don't hold me back; her wish must be obeyed.

DORINE Stop!

VALÈRE It's too late now; my decision's made.

DORINE Oh, pooh!

MARIANE [*Aside*] He hates the sight of me, that's plain.
I'll go, and so deliver him from pain.

DORINE [*Leaving* VALÈRE, *running after* MARIANE]
And now you run away! Come back.

MARIANE No, no.
Nothing you say will keep me here. Let go!

VALÈRE [*Aside*] She cannot bear my presence, I perceive.
To spare her further torment, I shall leave.

DORINE [*Leaving* MARIANE, *running after* VALÈRE]
Again! You'll not escape, Sir; don't you try it.
Come here, you two. Stop fussing, and be quiet.
[*She takes* VALÈRE *by the hand, then* MARIANE, *and draws them together.*]

VALÈRE [*To* DORINE] What do you want of me?

MARIANE [*To* DORINE] What is the point of this?

DORINE We're going to have a little armistice.
[*To* VALÈRE.]
Now, weren't you silly to get so overheated?

VALÈRE Didn't you see how badly I was treated?

DORINE [*To* MARIANE] Aren't you a simpleton, to have lost your head?

MARIANE Didn't you hear the hateful things he said?

DORINE [*To* VALÈRE] You're both great fools. Her sole desire, Valère,
Is to be yours in marriage. To that I'll swear.
[*To* MARIANE.]
He loves you only, and he wants no wife
But you, Mariane. On that I'll stake my life.

MARIANE [*To* VALÈRE] Then why you advised me so, I cannot see.

VALÈRE [*To* MARIANE] On such a question, why ask advice of *me?*

DORINE Oh, you're impossible. Give me your hands, you two.
[*To* VALÈRE.]
Yours first.

VALÈRE [*Giving* DORINE *his hand*] But why?

DORINE [*To* MARIANE] And now a hand from you.

MARIANE [*Also giving* DORINE *her hand*]
What are you doing?

DORINE There: a perfect fit.
You suit each other better than you'll admit.
[VALÈRE *and* MARIANE *hold hands for some time without looking at each other.*]
VALÈRE [*Turning toward* MARIANE]
Ah, come, don't be so haughty. Give a man
A look of kindness, won't you, Mariane?
[MARIANE *turns toward* VALÈRE *and smiles.*]
DORINE I tell you, lovers are completely mad!
VALÈRE [*To* MARIANE] Now come, confess that you were very bad
To hurt my feelings as you did just now.
I have a just complaint, you must allow.
MARIANE *You* must allow that you were most unpleasant . . .
DORINE Let's table that discussion for the present;
Your father has a plan which must be stopped.
MARIANE Advise us, then; what means must we adopt?
DORINE We'll use all manner of means, and all at once.
[*To* MARIANE.]
Your father's addled; he's acting like a dunce.
Therefore you'd better humor the old fossil.
Pretend to yield to him, be sweet and docile,
And then postpone, as often as necessary,
The day on which you have agreed to marry.
You'll thus gain time, and time will turn the trick.
Sometimes, for instance, you'll be taken sick,
And that will seem good reason for delay;
Or some bad omen will make you change the day—
You'll dream of muddy water, or you'll pass
A dead man's hearse, or break a looking-glass.
If all else fails, no man can marry you
Unless you take his ring and say "I do."
But now, let's separate. If they should find
Us talking here, our plot might be divined.
[*To* VALÈRE.]
Go to your friends, and tell them what's occurred,
And have them urge her father to keep his word.
Meanwhile, we'll stir her brother into action,
And get Elmire, as well, to join our faction.
Good-bye.
VALÈRE [*To* MARIANE] Though each of us will do his best,
It's your true heart on which my hopes shall rest.
MARIANE [*To* VALÈRE] Regardless of what Father may decide,
None but Valère shall claim me as his bride.
VALÈRE Oh, how those words content me! Come what will . . .
DORINE Oh, lovers, lovers! Their tongues are never still.
Be off, now.

VALÈRE [*Turning to go, then turning back*]
One last word . . .
DORINE No time to chat:
You leave by this door, and *you* leave by that.
[DORINE *pushes them, by the shoulders, toward opposing doors.*]

ACT III

Scene I

DAMIS, DORINE.

DAMIS May lightning strike me even as I speak,
May all men call me cowardly and weak,
If any fear or scruple holds me back
From settling things, at once, with that great quack!
DORINE Now, don't give way to violent emotion.
Your father's merely talked about this notion,
And words and deeds are far from being one.
Much that is talked about is left undone.
DAMIS No, I must stop that scoundrel's machinations;
I'll go and tell him off; I'm out of patience.
DORINE Do calm down and be practical. I had rather
My mistress dealt with him—and with your father.
She has some influence with Tartuffe, I've noted.
He hangs upon her words, seems most devoted,
And may, indeed, be smitten by her charm.
Pray Heaven it's true! 'Twould do our cause no harm.
She sent for him, just now, to sound him out
On this affair you're so incensed about;
She'll find out where he stands, and tell him, too,
What dreadful strife and trouble will ensue
If he lends countenance to your father's plan.
I couldn't get in to see him, but his man
Says that he's almost finished with his prayers.
Go, now. I'll catch him when he comes downstairs.
DAMIS I want to hear this conference, and I will.
DORINE No, they must be alone.
DAMIS Oh, I'll keep still.
DORINE Not you. I know your temper. You'd start a brawl,
And shout and stamp your foot and spoil it all.
Go on.
DAMIS I won't; I have a perfect right . . .
DORINE Lord, you're a nuisance! He's coming; get out of sight.
[DAMIS *conceals himself in a closet at the rear of the stage.*]

Scene II

TARTUFFE, DORINE.

TARTUFFE [*Observing* DORINE, *and calling to his manservant offstage*]
Hang up my hair-shirt, put my scourge in place,
And pray, Laurent, for Heaven's perpetual grace.
I'm going to the prison now, to share
My last few coins with the poor wretches there.
DORINE [*Aside*] Dear God, what affectation! What a fake!
TARTUFFE You wished to see me?
DORINE Yes . . .
TARTUFFE [*Taking a handkerchief from his pocket*]
For mercy's sake,
Please take this handkerchief, before you speak.
DORINE What?
TARTUFFE Cover that bosom, girl. The flesh is weak,
And unclean thoughts are difficult to control.
Such sights as that can undermine the soul.
DORINE Your soul, it seems, has very poor defenses,
And flesh makes quite an impact on your senses.
It's strange that you're so easily excited;
My own desires are not so soon ignited,
And if I saw you naked as a beast,
Not all your hide would tempt me in the least.
TARTUFFE Girl, speak more modestly; unless you do,
I shall be forced to take my leave of you.
DORINE Oh, no, it's I who must be on my way;
I've just one little message to convey.
Madame is coming down, and begs you, Sir,
To wait and have a word or two with her.
TARTUFFE Gladly.
DORINE [*Aside*] *That* had a softening effect!
I think my guess about him was correct.
TARTUFFE Will she be long?
DORINE No: that's her step I hear.
Ah, here she is, and I shall disappear.

Scene III

ELMIRE, TARTUFFE.

TARTUFFE May Heaven, whose infinite goodness we adore,
Preserve your body and soul forevermore,
And bless your days, and answer thus the plea
Of one who is its humblest votary.

ELMIRE I thank you for that pious wish. But please,
Do take a chair and let's be more at ease.
[*They sit down.*]
TARTUFFE I trust that you are once more well and strong?
ELMIRE Oh, yes: the fever didn't last for long.
TARTUFFE My prayers are too unworthy, I am sure,
To have gained from Heaven this most gracious cure;
But lately, Madam, my every supplication
Has had for object your recuperation.
ELMIRE You shouldn't have troubled so. I don't deserve it.
TARTUFFE Your health is priceless, Madam, and to preserve it
I'd gladly give my own, in all sincerity.
ELMIRE Sir, you outdo us all in Christian charity.
You've been most kind. I count myself your debtor.
TARTUFFE 'Twas nothing, Madam. I long to serve you better.
ELMIRE There's a private matter I'm anxious to discuss.
I'm glad there's no one here to hinder us.
TARTUFFE I too am glad; it floods my heart with bliss
To find myself alone with you like this.
For just this chance I've prayed with all my power—
But prayed in vain, until this happy hour.
ELMIRE This won't take long, Sir, and I hope you'll be
Entirely frank and unconstrained with me.
TARTUFFE Indeed, there's nothing I had rather do
Than bare my inmost heart and soul to you.
First, let me say what remarks I've made
About the constant visits you are paid
Were prompted not by any mean emotion,
But rather by a pure and deep devotion,
A fervent zeal . . .
ELMIRE No need for explanation.
Your sole concern, I'm sure, was my salvation.
TARTUFFE [*Taking* ELMIRE*'s hand and pressing her fingertips.*]
Quite so; and such great fervor do I feel . . .
ELMIRE Ooh! Please! You're pinching!
TARTUFFE 'Twas from excess of zeal.
I never meant to cause you pain, I swear.
I'd rather . . .
[*He places his hand on* ELMIRE*'s knee.*]
ELMIRE What can your hand be doing there?
TARTUFFE Feeling your gown; what soft, fine-woven stuff!
ELMIRE Please, I'm extremely ticklish. That's enough.
[*She draws her chair away;* TARTUFFE *pulls his after her.*]
TARTUFFE [*Fondling the lace collar of her gown*]
My, my, what lovely lacework on your dress!

The workmanship's miraculous, no less.
I've not seen anything to equal it.
ELMIRE Yes, quite. But let's talk business for a bit.
They say my husband means to break his word
And give his daughter to you, Sir. Had you heard?
TARTUFFE He did once mention it. But I confess
I dream of quite a different happiness.
It's elsewhere, Madam, that my eyes discern
The promise of that bliss for which I yearn.
ELMIRE I see: you care for nothing here below.
TARTUFFE Ah, well—my heart's not made of stone, you know.
ELMIRE All your desires mount heavenward, I'm sure,
In scorn of all that's earthly and impure.
TARTUFFE A love of heavenly beauty does not preclude
A proper love for earthly pulchritude;
Our senses are quite rightly captivated
By perfect works our Maker has created.
Some glory clings to all that Heaven has made;
In you, all Heaven's marvels are displayed.
On that fair face, such beauties have been lavished,
The eyes are dazzled and the heart is ravished;
How could I look on you, O flawless creature,
And not adore the Author of all Nature,
Feeling a love both passionate and pure
For you, his triumph of self-portraiture?
At first, I trembled lest that love should be
A subtle snare that Hell had laid for me;
I vowed to flee the sight of you, eschewing
A rapture that might prove my soul's undoing;
But soon, fair being, I became aware
That my deep passion could be made to square
With rectitude, and with my bounden duty.
I thereupon surrendered to your beauty.
It is, I know, presumptuous on my part
To bring you this poor offering of my heart,
And it is not my merit, Heaven knows,
But your compassion on which my hopes repose.
You are my peace, my solace, my salvation;
On you depends my bliss—or desolation;
I bide your judgment and, as you think best,
I shall be either miserable or blest.
ELMIRE Your declaration is most gallant, Sir,
But don't you think it's out of character?
You'd have done better to restrain your passion
And think before you spoke in such a fashion.

It ill becomes a pious man like you . . .

TARTUFFE I may be pious, but I'm human too:
With your celestial charms before his eyes,
A man has not the power to be wise.
I know such words sound strangely, coming from me,
But I'm no angel, nor was meant to be,
And if you blame my passion, you must needs
Reproach as well the charms on which it feeds.
Your loveliness I had no sooner seen
Than you became my soul's unrivalled queen;
Before your seraph glance, divinely sweet,
My heart's defenses crumbled in defeat,
And nothing fasting, prayer, or tears might do
Could stay my spirit from adoring you.
My eyes, my sighs have told you in the past
What now my lips make bold to say at last,
And if, in your great goodness, you will deign
To look upon your slave, and ease his pain,—
If, in compassion for my soul's distress,
You'll stoop to comfort my unworthiness,
I'll raise to you, in thanks for that sweet manna,
An endless hymn, an infinite hosanna.
With me, of course, there need be no anxiety,
No fear of scandal or of notoriety.
These young court gallants, whom all the ladies fancy,
Are vain in speech, in action rash and chancy;
When they succeed in love, the world soon knows it;
No favor's granted them but they disclose it
And by the looseness of their tongues profane
The very altar where their hearts have lain.
Men of my sort, however, love discreetly,
And one may trust our reticence completely.
My keen concern for my good name insures
The absolute security of yours;
In short, I offer you, my dear Elmire,
Love without scandal, pleasure without fear.

ELMIRE I've heard your well-turned speeches to the end,
And what you urge I clearly apprehend.
Aren't you afraid that I may take a notion
To tell my husband of your warm devotion,
And that, supposing he were duly told,
His feelings toward you might grow rather cold?

TARTUFFE I know, dear lady, that your exceeding charity
Will lead your heart to pardon my temerity;
That you'll excuse my violent affection

As human weakness, human imperfection;
And that—O fairest!—you will bear in mind
That I'm but flesh and blood, and am not blind.

ELMIRE Some women might do otherwise, perhaps,
But I shall be discreet about your lapse;
I'll tell my husband nothing of what's occurred
If, in return, you'll give your solemn word
To advocate as forcefully as you can
The marriage of Valère and Mariane,
Renouncing all desire to dispossess
Another of his rightful happiness,
And . . .

Scene IV

DAMIS, ELMIRE, TARTUFFE.

DAMIS [*Emerging from the closet where he has been hiding*].
No! We'll not hush up this vile affair;
I heard it all inside that closet there,
Where Heaven, in order to confound the pride
Of this great rascal, prompted me to hide.
Ah, now I have my long-awaited chance
To punish his deceit and arrogance,
And give my father clear and shocking proof
Of the black character of his dear Tartuffe.

ELMIRE Ah no, Damis; I'll be content if he
Will study to deserve my leniency.
I've promised silence—don't make me break my word;
To make a scandal would be too absurd.
Good wives laugh off such trifles, and forget them;
Why should they tell their husbands, and upset them?

DAMIS You have your reasons for taking such a course,
And I have reasons, too, of equal force.
To spare him now would be insanely wrong.
I've swallowed my just wrath for far too long
And watched this insolent bigot bringing strife
And bitterness into our family life.
Too long he's meddled in my father's affairs,
Thwarting my marriage-hopes, and poor Valère's.
It's high time that my father was undeceived,
And now I've proof that can't be disbelieved—
Proof that was furnished me by Heaven above.
It's too good not to take advantage of.
This is my chance, and I deserve to lose it
If, for one moment, I hesitate to use it.

ELMIRE Damis . . .
DAMIS No, I must do what I think right.
Madam, my heart is bursting with delight,
And, say whatever you will, I'll not consent
To lose the sweet revenge on which I'm bent.
I'll settle matters without more ado;
And here, most opportunely, is my cue.

Scene V

ORGON, DAMIS, TARTUFFE, ELMIRE.

DAMIS Father, I'm glad you've joined us. Let us advise you
Of some fresh news which doubtless will surprise you.
You've just now been repaid with interest
For all your loving-kindness to our guest.
He's proved his warm and grateful feelings toward you;
It's with a pair of horns he would reward you.
Yes, I surprised him with your wife, and heard
His whole adulterous offer, every word.
She, with her all too gentle disposition,
Would not have told you of his proposition;
But I shall not make terms with brazen lechery,
And feel that not to tell you would be treachery.
ELMIRE And I hold that one's husband's peace of mind
Should not be spoilt by tattle of this kind.
One's honor doesn't require it: to be proficient
In keeping men at bay is quite sufficient.
These are my sentiments, and I wish, Damis,
That you had heeded me and held your peace.

Scene VI

ORGON, DAMIS, TARTUFFE.

ORGON Can it be true, this dreadful thing I hear?
TARTUFFE Yes, Brother, I'm a wicked man, I fear:
A wretched sinner, all depraved and twisted,
The greatest villain that has ever existed.
My life's one heap of crimes, which grows each minute;
There's naught but foulness and corruption in it;
And I perceive that Heaven, outraged by me,
Has chosen this occasion to mortify me.
Charge me with any deed you wish to name;
I'll not defend myself, but take the blame.

Believe what you are told, and drive Tartuffe
Like some base criminal from beneath your roof;
Yes, drive me hence, and with a parting curse:
I shan't protest, for I deserve far worse.

ORGON [*To* DAMIS] Ah, you deceitful boy, how dare you try
To stain his purity with so foul a lie?

DAMIS What! Are you taken in by such a bluff?
Did you not hear . . . ?

ORGON Enough, you rogue, enough!

TARTUFFE Ah, Brother, let him speak: you're being unjust.
Believe his story; the boy deserves your trust.
Why, after all, should you have faith in me?
How can you know what I might do, or be?
Is it on my good actions that you base
Your favor? Do you trust my pious face?
Ah, no, don't be deceived by hollow shows;
I'm far, alas, from being what men suppose;
Though the world takes me for a man of worth,
I'm truly the most worthless man on earth.
[*To* DAMIS.]
Yes, my dear son, speak out now: call me the chief
Of sinners, a wretch, a murderer, a thief;
Load me with all the names men most abhor;
I'll not complain; I've earned them all, and more;
I'll kneel here while you pour them on my head
As a just punishment for the life I've led.

ORGON [*To* TARTUFFE]
This is too much, dear Brother.
[*To* DAMIS.]
Have you no heart?

DAMIS Are you so hoodwinked by this rascal's art . . . ?

ORGON Be still, you monster.
[*To* TARTUFFE.]
Brother, I pray you, rise.
[*To* DAMIS.]
Villain!

DAMIS But . . .

ORGON Silence!

DAMIS Can't you realize . . . ?

ORGON Just one word more, and I'll tear you limb from limb.

TARTUFFE In God's name, Brother, don't be harsh with him.
I'd rather far be tortured at the stake
Than see him bear one scratch for my poor sake.

ORGON [*To* DAMIS] Ingrate!

TARTUFFE If I must beg you, on bended knee,
To pardon him . . .
ORGON [*Falling to his knees, addressing* TARTUFFE]
Such goodness cannot be!
[*To* DAMIS.]
Now, *there's* true charity!
DAMIS What, you . . . ?
ORGON Villain, be still!
I know your motives; I know you wish him ill:
Yes, all of you—wife, children, servants, all—
Conspire against him and desire his fall,
Employing every shameful trick you can
To alienate me from this saintly man.
Ah, but the more you seek to drive him away,
The more I'll do to keep him. Without delay,
I'll spite this household and confound its pride
By giving him my daughter as his bride.
DAMIS You're going to force her to accept his hand?
ORGON Yes, and this very night, d'you understand?
I shall defy you all, and make it clear
That I'm the one who gives the orders here.
Come, wretch, kneel down and clasp his blessed feet,
And ask his pardon for your black deceit.
DAMIS I ask that swindler's pardon? Why, I'd rather . . .
ORGON So! You insult him, and defy your father!
A stick! A stick! [*To* TARTUFFE.] No, no—release me, do.
[*To* DAMIS.]
Out of my house this minute! Be off with you,
And never dare set foot in it again.
DAMIS Well, I shall go, but . . .
ORGON Well, go quickly, then.
I disinherit you; an empty purse
Is all you'll get from me—except my curse!

Scene VII

ORGON, TARTUFFE.

ORGON How he blasphemed your goodness! What a son!
TARTUFFE Forgive him, Lord, as I've already done.
[*To* ORGON.]
You can't know how it hurts when someone tries
To blacken me in my dear Brother's eyes.
ORGON Ahh!
TARTUFFE The mere thought of such ingratitude
Plunges my soul into so dark a mood . . .

Such horror grips my heart . . . I gasp for breath,
And cannot speak, and feel myself near death.

ORGON
[*He runs, in tears, to the door through which he has just driven his son.*]
You blackguard! Why did I spare you? Why did I not
Break you in little pieces on the spot?
Compose yourself, and don't be hurt, dear friend.

TARTUFFE These scenes, these dreadful quarrels, have got to end.
I've much upset your household, and I perceive
That the best thing will be for me to leave.

ORGON What are you saying!

TARTUFFE They're all against me here;
They'd have you think me false and insincere.

ORGON Ah, what of that? Have I ceased believing in you?

TARTUFFE Their adverse talk will certainly continue,
And charges which you now repudiate
You may find credible at a later date.

ORGON No, Brother, never.

TARTUFFE Brother, a wife can sway
Her husband's mind in many a subtle way.

ORGON No, no.

TARTUFFE To leave at once is the solution;
Thus only can I end their persecution.

ORGON No, no, I'll not allow it; you shall remain.

TARTUFFE Ah, well; 'twill mean much martyrdom and pain,
But if you wish it . . .

ORGON Ah!

TARTUFFE Enough; so be it.
But one thing must be settled, as I see it.
For your dear honor, and for our friendship's sake,
There's one precaution I feel bound to take.
I shall avoid your wife, and keep away . . .

ORGON No, you shall not, whatever they may say.
It pleases me to vex them, and for spite
I'd have them see you with her day and night.
What's more, I'm going to drive them to despair
By making you my only son and heir;
This very day, I'll give to you alone
Clear deed and title to everything I own.
A dear, good friend and son-in-law-to-be
Is more than wife, or child, or kin to me.
Will you accept my offer, dearest son?

TARTUFFE In all things, let the will of Heaven be done.

ORGON Poor fellow! Come, we'll go draw up the deed.
Then let them burst with disappointed greed!

ACT IV

Scene I

CLÉANTE, TARTUFFE.

CLÉANTE Yes, all the town's discussing it, and truly,
Their comments do not flatter you unduly.
I'm glad we've met, Sir, and I'll give my view
Of this sad matter in a word or two.
As for who's guilty, that I shan't discuss:
Let's say it was Damis who caused the fuss;
Assuming, then, that you have been ill-used
By young Damis, and groundlessly accused.
Ought not a Christian to forgive, and ought
He not to stifle every vengeful thought?
Should you stand by and watch a father make
His only son an exile for your sake?
Again I tell you frankly, be advised:
The whole town, high and low, is scandalized;
This quarrel must be mended, and my advice is
Not to push matters to a further crisis.
No, sacrifice your wrath to God above.
And help Damis regain his father's love.

TARTUFFE Alas, for my part I should take great joy
In doing so. I've nothing against the boy.
I pardon all, I harbor no resentment;
To serve him would afford me much contentment.
But Heaven's interest will not have it so:
If he comes back, then I shall have to go.
After his conduct—so extreme, so vicious—
Our further intercourse would look suspicious.
God knows what people would think! Why, they'd describe
My goodness to him as a sort of bribe;
They'd say that out of guilt I made pretense
Of loving-kindness and benevolence—
That, fearing my accuser's tongue, I strove
To buy his silence with a show of love.

CLÉANTE Your reasoning is badly warped and stretched,
And these excuses, Sir, are most far-fetched.
Why put yourself in charge of Heaven's cause?
Does Heaven need our help to enforce its laws?
Leave vengeance to the Lord, Sir; while we live,
Our duty's not to punish, but forgive;
And what the Lord commands, we should obey
Without regard to what the world may say.

What! Shall the fear of being misunderstood
Prevent our doing what is right and good?
No, no; let's simply do what Heaven ordains,
And let no other thoughts perplex our brains.

TARTUFFE Again, Sir, let me say that I've forgiven
Damis, and thus obeyed the laws of Heaven;
But I am not commanded by the Bible
To live with one who smears my name with libel.

CLÉANTE Were you commanded, Sir, to indulge the whim
Of poor Orgon, and to encourage him
In suddenly transferring to your name
A large estate to which you have no claim?

TARTUFFE 'Twould never occur to those who know me best
To think I acted from self-interest.
The treasures of this world I quite despise;
Their specious glitter does not charm my eyes;
And if I have resigned myself to taking
The gift which my dear Brother insists on making,
I do so only, as he well understands,
Lest those of whom it might descend in time
Turn it to purposes of sin and crime,
And not, as I shall do, make use of it
For Heaven's glory and mankind's benefit.

CLÉANTE Forget these trumped-up fears. Your argument
Is one the rightful heir might well resent;
It *is* a moral burden to inherit
Such wealth, but give Damis a chance to bear it.
And would it not be worse to be accused
Of swindling, than to see that wealth misused?
I'm shocked that you allowed Orgon to broach
This matter, and that you feel no self-reproach;
Does true religion teach that lawful heirs
May freely be deprived of what is theirs?
And if the Lord has told you in your heart
That you and young Damis must dwell apart,
Would it not be the decent thing to beat
A generous and honorable retreat,
Rather than let the son of the house be sent,
For your convenience, into banishment?
Sir, if you wish to prove the honesty
Of your intentions . . .

TARTUFFE Sir, it is half-past three.
I've certain pious duties to attend to,
And hope my prompt departure won't offend you.

CLÉANTE [*Alone*] Damn.

Scene II

ELMIRE, MARIANE, CLÉANTE, DORINE.

DORINE Stay, Sir, and help Mariane, for Heaven's sake!
She's suffering so, I fear her heart will break.
Her father's plan to marry her off tonight
Has put the poor child in a desperate plight.
I hear him coming. Let's stand together, now,
And see if we can't change his mind, somehow,
About this match we all deplore and fear.

Scene III

ORGON, ELMIRE, MARIANE, CLÉANTE, DORINE.

ORGON Hah! Glad to find you all assembled here.
[*To* MARIANE]]
This contract, child, contains your happiness,
And what it says I think your heart can guess.
MARIANE [*Falling to her knees*]
Sir, by that Heaven which sees me here distressed,
And by whatever else can move your breast,
Do not employ a father's power, I pray you,
To crush my heart and force it to obey you,
Nor by your harsh commands oppress me so
That I'll begrudge the duty which I owe—
And do not so embitter and enslave me
That I shall hate the very life you gave me.
If my sweet hopes must perish, if you refuse
To give me to the one I've dared to choose,
Spare me at least—I beg you, I implore—
The pain of wedding one whom I abhor;
And do not, by a heartless use of force,
Drive me to contemplate some desperate course.
ORGON [*Feeling himself touched by her*]
Be firm, my soul. No human weakness, now.
MARIANE I don't resent your love for him. Allow
Your heart free rein, Sir; give him your property,
And if that's not enough, take mine from me;
He's welcome to my money; take it, do,
But don't, I pray, include my person too.
Spare me, I beg you; and let me end the tale
Of my sad days behind a convent veil.
ORGON A convent! Hah! When crossed in their amours,
All lovesick girls have the same thought as yours.
Get up! The more you loathe the man, and dread him,

The more ennobling it will be to wed him.
Marry Tartuffe, and mortify your flesh!
Enough; don't start that whimpering afresh.

DORINE But why . . . ?

ORGON Be still, there. Speak when you're spoken to.
Not one more bit of impudence out of you.

CLÉANTE If I may offer a word of counsel here . . .

ORGON Brother, in counseling you have no peer;
All your advice is forceful, sound, and clever;
I don't propose to follow it, however.

ELMIRE [*To* ORGON] I am amazed, and don't know what to say;
Your blindness simply takes my breath away.
You are indeed bewitched, to take no warning
From our account of what occurred this morning.

ORGON Madam, I know a few plain facts, and one
Is that you're partial to my rascal son;
Hence, when he sought to make Tartuffe the victim
Of a base lie, you dared not contradict him.
Ah, but you underplayed your part, my pet;
You should have looked more angry, more upset.

ELMIRE When men make overtures, must we reply
With righteous anger and a battle-cry?
Must we turn back their amorous advances
With sharp reproaches and with fiery glances?
Myself, I find such offers merely amusing,
And make no scenes and fusses in refusing;
My taste is for good-natured rectitude,
And I dislike the savage sort of prude
Who guards her virtue with her teeth and claws,
And tears men's eyes out for the slightest cause:
The Lord preserve me from such honor as that,
Which bites and scratches like an alley-cat!
I've found that a polite and cool rebuff
Discourages a lover quite enough.

ORGON I know the facts, and I shall not be shaken.

ELMIRE I marvel at your power to be mistaken.
Would it, I wonder, carry weight with you
If I could *show* you that our tale was true?

ORGON Show me?

ELMIRE Yes.

ORGON Rot.

ELMIRE Come, what if I found a way
To make you see the facts as plain as day?

ORGON Nonsense.

ELMIRE Do answer me; don't be absurd.
I'm not now asking you to trust our word.
Suppose that from some hiding-place in here
You learned the whole sad truth by eye and ear—
What would you say of your good friend, after that?

ORGON Why, I'd say . . . nothing, by Jehoshaphat!
It can't be true.

ELMIRE You've been too long deceived,
And I'm quite tired of being disbelieved.
Come now: let's put my statements to the test,
And you shall see the truth made manifest.

ORGON I'll take that challenge. Now do your uttermost.
We'll see how you make good your empty boast.

ELMIRE [*To* DORINE] Send him to me.

DORINE He's crafty; it may be hard
To catch the cunning scoundrel off his guard.

ELMIRE No, amorous men are gullible. Their conceit
So blinds them that they're never hard to cheat.
Have him come down. [*To* CLÉANTE *and* MARIANE.] Please leave us, for a bit.

Scene IV

ELMIRE, ORGON.

ELMIRE Pull up this table, and get under it.

ORGON What?

ELMIRE It's essential that you be well-hidden.

ORGON Why there?

ELMIRE Oh, Heavens! Just do as you are bidden.
I have my plans; we'll soon see how they fare.
Under the table, now; and once you're there,
Take care that you are neither seen nor heard.

ORGON Well, I'll indulge you, since I gave my word
To see you through this infantile charade.

ELMIRE Once it is over, you'll be glad we played.
[*To her husband, who is now under the table.*]
I'm going to act quite strangely, now, and you
Must not be shocked at anything I do.
Whatever I may say, you must excuse
As part of that deceit I'm forced to use.
I shall employ sweet speeches in the task
Of making that imposter drop his mask;
I'll give encouragement to his bold desires,
And furnish fuel to his amorous fires.
Since it's for your sake, and for his destruction,

That I shall seem to yield to his seduction,
I'll gladly stop whenever you decide
That all your doubts are fully satisfied.
I'll count on you, as soon as you have seen
What sort of man he is, to intervene,
And not expose me to his odious lust
One moment longer than you feel you must.
Remember: you're to save me from my plight
Whenever . . . He's coming! Hush! Keep out of sight!

Scene V

TARTUFFE, ELMIRE, ORGON.

TARTUFFE You wish to have a word with me, I'm told.

ELMIRE Yes. I've a little secret to unfold.
Before I speak, however, it would be wise
To close that door, and look about for spies.
[TARTUFFE *goes to the door, closes it, and returns.*]
The very last thing that must happen now
Is a repetition of this morning's row.
I've never been so badly caught off guard.
Oh, how I feared for you! You saw how hard
I tried to make that troublesome Damis
Control his dreadful temper, and hold his peace.
In my confusion, I didn't have the sense
Simply to contradict his evidence;
But as it happened, that was for the best,
And all has worked out in our interest.
This storm has only bettered your position;
My husband doesn't have the least suspicion,
And now, in mockery of those who do,
He bids me be continually with you.
And that is why, quite fearless of reproof,
I now can be alone with my Tartuffe,
And why my heart—perhaps too quick to yield—
Feels free to let its passion be revealed.

TARTUFFE Madam, your words confuse me. Not long ago,
You spoke in quite a different style, you know.

ELMIRE Ah, sir, if that refusal made you smart,
It's little that you know of woman's heart,
Or what that heart is trying to convey
When it resists in such a feeble way!
Always, at first, our modesty prevents
The frank avowal of tender sentiments;
However high the passion which inflames us,

Still, to confess its power somehow shames us.
Thus we reluct, at first, yet in a tone
Which tells you that our heart is overthrown,
That what our lips deny, our pulse confesses,
And that, in time, all noes will turn to yesses.
I fear my words are all too frank and free,
And a poor proof of woman's modesty;
But since I'm started, tell me, if you will—
Would I have tried to make Damis be still,
Would I have listened, calm and unoffended,
Until your lengthy offer of love was ended,
And been so very mild in my reaction,
Had your sweet words not given me satisfaction?
And when I tried to force you to undo
The marriage-plans my husband has in view,
What did my urgent pleading signify
If not that I admired you, and that I
Deplored the thought that someone else might own
Part of a heart I wished for mine alone?

TARTUFFE Madam, no happiness is so complete
As when, from lips we love, come words so sweet;
Their nectar floods my every sense, and drains
In honeyed rivulets through all my veins.
To please you is my joy, my only goal;
Your love is the restorer of my soul;
And yet I must beg leave, now, to confess
Some lingering doubts as to my happiness.
Might this not be a trick? Might not the catch
Be that you wish me to break off the match
With Mariane, and so have feigned to love me?
I shan't quite trust your fond opinion of me
Until the feelings you've expressed so sweetly
Are demonstrated somewhat more concretely,
And you have shown, by certain kind concessions,
That I may put my faith in your professions.

ELMIRE [*She coughs, to warn her husband*]
Why be in such a hurry? Must my heart
Exhaust its bounty at the very start?
To make that sweet admission cost me dear,
But you'll not be content, it would appear,
Unless my store of favors is disbursed
To the last farthing, and at the very first.

TARTUFFE The less we merit, the less we dare to hope,
And with our doubts, mere words can never cope.
We trust no promised bliss till we receive it;

Not till a joy is ours can we believe it.
I, who so little merit your esteem,
Can't credit this fulfillment of my dream,
And shan't believe it, Madam, until I savor
Some palpable assurance of your favor.

ELMIRE My, how tyrannical your love can be,
And how it flusters and perplexes me!
How furiously you take one's heart in hand,
And make your every wish a fierce command!
Come, must you hound and harry me to death?
Will you not give me time to catch my breath?
Can it be right to press me with such force,
Give me no quarter, show me no remorse,
And take advantage, by your stern insistence,
Of the fond feelings which weaken my resistance?

TARTUFFE Well, if you look with favor upon my love,
Why, then, begrudge me some clear proof thereof?

ELMIRE But how can I consent without offense
To Heaven, toward which you feel such reverence?

TARTUFFE If Heaven is all that holds you back, don't worry.
I can remove that hindrance in a hurry.
Nothing of that sort need obstruct our path.

ELMIRE Must one not be afraid of Heaven's wrath?

TARTUFFE Madam, forget such fears, and be my pupil,
And I shall teach you how to conquer scruple.
Some joys, it's true, are wrong in Heaven's eyes;
Yet Heaven is not averse to compromise;
There is a science, lately formulated,
Whereby one's conscience may be liberated,
And any wrongful act you care to mention
May be redeemed by purity of intention.
I'll teach you, Madam, the secret of that science;
Meanwhile, just place on me your full reliance.
Assuage my keen desires, and feel no dread:
The sin, if any, shall be on my head.
[ELMIRE *coughs, this time more loudly.*]
You've a bad cough.

ELMIRE Yes, yes. It's bad indeed.

TARTUFFE [*Producing a little paper bag*]
A bit of licorice may be what you need.

ELMIRE No, I've a stubborn cold, it seems. I'm sure it
Will take much more than licorice to cure it.

TARTUFFE How aggravating.

ELMIRE Oh, more than I can say.

TARTUFFE If you're still troubled, think of things this way:

No one shall know our joys, save us alone,
And there's no evil till the act is known;
It's scandal, Madam, which makes it an offense,
And it's no sin to sin in confidence.

ELMIRE [*Having coughed once more*]
Well, clearly I must do as you require,
And yield to your importunate desire.
It is apparent, now, that nothing less
Will satisfy you, and so I acquiesce.
To go so far is much against my will;
I'm vexed that it should come to this; but still,
Since you are so determined on it, since you
Will not allow mere language to convince you,
And since you ask for concrete evidence, I
See nothing for it, now, but to comply.
If this is sinful, if I'm wrong to do it,
So much the worse for him who drove me to it.
The fault can surely not be charged to me.

TARTUFFE Madam, the fault is mine, if fault there be,
And . . .

ELMIRE Open the door a little, and peek out,
I wouldn't want my husband poking about.

TARTUFFE Why worry about the man? Each day he grows
More gullible; one can lead him by the nose.
To find us here would fill him with delight,
And if he saw the worst, he'd doubt his sight.

ELMIRE Nevertheless, do step out for a minute
Into the hall, and see that no one's in it.

Scene VI

ORGON, ELMIRE.

ORGON [*Coming out from under the table*]
That man's a perfect monster, I must admit!
I'm simply stunned. I can't get over it.

ELMIRE What, coming out so soon? How premature!
Get back in hiding, and wait until you're sure.
Stay till the end, and be convinced completely:
We mustn't stop till things are proved concretely.

ORGON Hell never harbored anything so vicious!

ELMIRE Tut, don't be hasty. Try to be judicious.
Wait, and be certain that there's no mistake.
No jumping to conclusions, for Heaven's sake!
[*She places* ORGON *behind her, as* TARTUFFE *re-enters.*]

Scene VII

TARTUFFE, ELMIRE, ORGON.

TARTUFFE [*Not seeing* ORGON]
Madam, all things have worked out to perfection;
I've given the neighboring rooms a full inspection:
No one's about; and now I may at last . . .
ORGON [*Intercepting him.*] Hold on, my passionate fellow, not so fast!
I should advise a little more restraint.
Well, so you thought you'd fool me, my dear saint!
How soon you wearied of the saintly life—
Wedding my daughter, and coveting my wife!
I've long suspected you, and had a feeling
That soon I'd catch you at your double-dealing.
Just now, you've given me evidence galore;
It's quite enough; I have no wish for more.
ELMIRE [*To* TARTUFFE] I'm sorry to have treated you so slyly,
But circumstances forced me to be wily.
TARTUFFE Brother, you can't think . . .
ORGON No more talk from you;
Just leave this household, without more ado.
TARTUFFE What I intended . . .
ORGON That seems fairly clear.
Spare me your falsehoods and get out of here.
TARTUFFE No, I'm the master, and you're the one to go!
This house belongs to me, I'll have you know,
And I shall show you that you can't hurt *me*
By this contemptible conspiracy,
That those who cross me know not what they do,
And that I've means to expose and punish you,
Avenge offended Heaven, and make you grieve
That ever you dared order me to leave.

Scene VIII

ELMIRE, ORGON.

ELMIRE What was the point of all that angry chatter?
ORGON Dear God, I'm worried. This is no laughing matter.
ELMIRE How so?
ORGON I fear I understood his drift.
I'm much disturbed about that deed of gift.
ELMIRE You gave him . . . ?
ORGON Yes, it's all been drawn and signed.
But one thing more is weighing on my mind.

ELMIRE What's that?
ORGON I'll tell you; but first let's see if there's
A certain strong-box in his room upstairs.

ACT V

Scene I

ORGON, CLÉANTE.

CLÉANTE Where are you going so fast?
ORGON God knows!
CLÉANTE Then wait;
Let's have a conference, and deliberate
On how this situation's to be met.
ORGON That strong-box has me utterly upset;
This is the worst of many, many shocks.
CLÉANTE Is there some fearful mystery in that box?
ORGON My poor friend Argas brought that box to me
With his own hands, in utmost secrecy;
'Twas on the very morning of his flight.
It's full of papers which, if they came to light,
Would ruin him—or such is my impression.
CLÉANTE Then why did you let it out of your possession?
ORGON Those papers vexed my conscience, and it seemed best
To ask the counsel of my pious guest.
The cunning scoundrel got me to agree
To leave the strong- box in his custody,
So that, in case of an investigation,
I could employ a slight equivocation
And swear I didn't have it, and thereby,
At no expense of conscience, tell a lie.
CLÉANTE It looks to me as if you're out on a limb.
Trusting him with that box, and offering him
That deed of gift, were actions of a kind
Which scarcely indicate a prudent mind.
With two such weapons, he has the upper hand,
And since you're vulnerable, as matters stand,
You erred once more in bringing him to bay.
You should have acted in some subtler way.
ORGON Just think of it: behind that fervent face,
A heart so wicked, and a soul so base!
I took him in, a hungry beggar, and then . . .
Enough, by God! I'm through with pious men:
Henceforth I'll hate the whole false brotherhood,
And persecute them worse than Satan could.
CLÉANTE Ah, there you go—extravagant as ever!

Why can you not be rational? You never
Manage to take the middle course, it seems,
But jump, instead, between absurd extremes.
You've recognized your recent grave mistake
In falling victim to a pious fake;
Now, to correct that error, must you embrace
An even greater error in its place,
And judge our worthy neighbors as a whole
By what you've learned of one corrupted soul?
Come, just because one rascal made you swallow
A show of zeal which turned out to be hollow,
Shall you conclude that all men are deceivers,
And that, today, there are no true believers?
Let atheists make that foolish inference;
Learn to distinguish virtue from pretense,
Be cautious in bestowing admiration,
And cultivate a sober moderation.
Don't humor fraud, but also don't asperse
True piety; the latter fault is worse,
And it is best to err, if err one must,
As you have done, upon the side of trust.

Scene II

DAMIS, ORGON, CLÉANTE.

DAMIS Father, I hear that scoundrel's uttered threats
Against you; that he pridefully forgets
How, in his need, he was befriended by you,
And means to use your gifts to crucify you.
ORGON It's true, my boy. I'm too distressed for tears.
DAMIS Leave it to me, Sir; let me trim his ears.
Faced with such insolence, we must not waver.
I shall rejoice in doing you the favor
Of cutting short his life, and your distress.
CLÉANTE What a display of young hotheadedness!
Do learn to moderate your fits of rage,
In this just kingdom, this enlightened age,
One does not settle things by violence.

Scene III

MADAME PERNELLE, MARIANE, ELMIRE, DORINE, DAMIS, ORGON, CLÉANTE.

MADAME PERNELLE I hear strange tales of very strange events.
ORGON Yes, strange events which these two eyes beheld.
The man's ingratitude is unparalleled.

I save a wretched pauper from starvation,
House him, and treat him like a blood relation,
Shower him every day with my largesse,
Give him my daughter, and all that I possess;
And meanwhile the unconscionable knave
Tries to induce my wife to misbehave;
And not content with such extreme rascality,
Now threatens me with my own liberality,
And aims, by taking base advantage of
The gifts I gave him out of Christian love,
To drive me from my house, a ruined man,
And make me end a pauper, as he began.

DORINE Poor fellow!

MADAME PERNELLE No, my son, I'll never bring
Myself to think him guilty of such a thing.

ORGON How's that?

MADAME PERNELLE The righteous always were maligned.

ORGON Speak clearly, Mother. Say what's on your mind.

MADAME PERNELLE I mean that I can smell a rat, my dear.
You know how everybody hates him, here.

ORGON That has no bearing on the case at all.

MADAME PERNELLE I told you a hundred times, when you were small,
That virtue in this world is hated ever;
Malicious men may die, but malice never.

ORGON No doubt that's true, but how does it apply?

MADAME PERNELLE They've turned you against him by a clever lie.

ORGON I've told you, I was there and saw it done.

MADAME PERNELLE Ah, slanderers will stop at nothing, Son.

ORGON Mother, I'll lose my temper . . . For the last time,
I tell you I was witness to the crime.

MADAME PERNELLE The tongues of spite are busy night and noon,
And to their venom no man is immune.

ORGON You're talking nonsense. Can't you realize
I saw it; saw it; saw it with my eyes?
Saw, do you understand me? Must I shout it
Into your ears before you'll cease to doubt it?

MADAME PERNELLE Appearances can deceive, my son. Dear me,
We cannot always judge by what we see.

ORGON Drat! Drat!

MADAME PERNELLE One often interprets things awry;
Good can seem evil to a suspicious eye.

ORGON Was I to see his pawing at Elmire
As an act of charity?

MADAME PERNELLE Till his guilt is clear,

A man deserves the benefit of the doubt.
You should have waited, to see how things turned out.
ORGON Great God in Heaven, what more proof did I need?
Was I to sit there, watching, until he'd . . .
You drive me to the brink of impropriety.
MADAME PERNELLE No, no, a man of such surpassing piety
Could not do such a thing. You cannot shake me.
I don't believe it, and you shall not make me.
ORGON You vex me so that, if you weren't my mother,
I'd say to you . . . some dreadful thing or other.
DORINE It's your turn now, Sir, not to be listened to;
You'd not trust us, and now she won't trust you.
CLÉANTE My friends, we're wasting time which should be spent
In facing up to our predicament.
I fear that scoundrel's threats weren't made in sport.
DAMIS Do you think he'd have the nerve to go to court?
ELMIRE I'm sure he won't; they'd find it all too crude
A case of swindling and ingratitude.
CLÉANTE Don't be too sure. He won't be at a loss
To give his claims a high and righteous gloss;
And clever rogues with far less valid cause
Have trapped their victims in a web of laws.
I say again that to antagonize
A man so strongly armed was most unwise.
ORGON I know it; but the man's appalling cheek
Outraged me so, I couldn't control my pique.
CLÉANTE I wish to Heaven that we could devise
Some truce between you, or some compromise.
ELMIRE If I had known what cards he held, I'd not
Have roused his anger by my little plot.
ORGON [*To* DORINE, *as* M. LOYAL *enters*]
What is that fellow looking for? Who is he?
Go talk to him—and tell him that I'm busy.

Scene IV

MONSIEUR LOYAL, MADAME PERNELLE, ORGON, DAMIS, MARIANE, DORINE, ELMIRE, CLÉANTE.

MONSIEUR LOYAL Good day, dear sister. Kindly let me see
Your master.
DORINE He's involved with company,
And cannot be disturbed just now, I fear.
MONSIEUR LOYAL I hate to intrude; but what has brought me here
Will not disturb your master, in any event.
Indeed, my news will make him most content.

DORINE Your name?
MONSIEUR LOYAL Just say that I bring greetings from
Monsieur Tartuffe, on whose behalf I've come.
DORINE [*To* ORGON] Sir, he's a very gracious man, and bears
A message from Tartuffe, which, he declares,
Will make you most content.
CLÉANTE Upon my word,
I think this man had best be seen, and heard.
ORGON Perhaps he has some settlement to suggest.
How shall I treat him? What manner would be best?
CLÉANTE Control your anger, and if he should mention
Some fair adjustment, give him your full attention.
MONSIEUR LOYAL Good health to you, good Sir. May Heaven confound
Your enemies, and may your joys abound.
ORGON [*Aside, to* CLÉANTE] A gentle salutation: it confirms
My guess that he is here to offer terms.
MONSIEUR LOYAL I've always held your family most dear;
I served your father, Sir, for many a year.
ORGON Sir, I must ask your pardon; to my shame,
I cannot now recall your face or name.
MONSIEUR LOYAL Loyal's my name; I come from Normandy,
And I'm a bailiff, in all modesty.
For forty years, praise God, it's been my boast
To serve with honor in that vital post,
And I am here, Sir, if you will permit
The liberty, to serve you with this writ . . .
ORGON To—*what?*
MONSIEUR LOYAL Now, please, Sir, let us have no friction:
It's nothing but an order of eviction.
You are to move your goods and family out
And make way for new occupants, without
Deferment or delay, and give the keys . . .
ORGON I? Leave this house?
MONSIEUR LOYAL Why yes, Sir, if you please.
This house, Sir, from the cellar to the roof,
Belongs now to the good Monsieur Tartuffe,
And he is lord and master of your estate
By virtue of a deed of present date,
Drawn in due form, with clearest legal phrasing . . .
DAMIS Your insolence is utterly amazing!
MONSIEUR LOYAL Young man, my business here is not with you,
But with your wise and temperate father, who,
Like every worthy citizen, stands in awe
Of justice, and would never obstruct the law.

ORGON But . . .
MONSIEUR LOYAL Not for a million, Sir, would you rebel
Against authority; I know that well.
You'll not make trouble, Sir, or interfere
With the execution of my duties here.
DAMIS Someone may execute a smart tattoo
On that black jacket of yours, before you're through.
MONSIEUR LOYAL Sir, bid your son be silent. I'd much regret
Having to mention such a nasty threat
Of violence, in writing my report.
DORINE [*Aside*] This man Loyal's a most disloyal sort!
MONSIEUR LOYAL I love all men of upright character,
And when I agreed to serve these papers, Sir,
It was your feelings that I had in mind.
I couldn't bear to see the case assigned
To someone else, who might esteem you less
And so subject you to unpleasantness.
ORGON What's more unpleasant than telling a man to leave
His house and home?
MONSIEUR LOYAL You'd like a short reprieve?
If you desire it, Sir, I shall not press you,
But wait until tomorrow to dispossess you.
Splendid. I'll come and spend the night here, then,
Most quietly, with half a score of men.
For form's sake, you might bring me, just before
You go to bed, the keys to the front door.
My men, I promise, will be on their best
Behavior, and will not disturb your rest.
But bright and early, Sir, you must be quick
And move out all your furniture, every stick:
The men I've chosen are both young and strong,
And with their help it shouldn't take you long.
In short, I'll make things pleasant and convenient,
And since I'm being so extremely lenient,
Please show me, Sir, a like consideration,
And give me your entire cooperation.
ORGON [*Aside*] I may be all but bankrupt, but I vow
I'd give a hundred louis, here and now,
Just for the pleasure of landing one good clout
Right on the end of that complacent snout.
CLÉANTE Careful; don't make things worse.
DAMIS My bootsole itches
To give that beggar a good kick in the breeches.
DORINE Monsieur Loyal, I'd love to hear the whack
Of a stout stick across your fine broad back.

MONSIEUR LOYAL Take care: a woman too may go to jail if
She uses threatening language to a bailiff.
CLÉANTE Enough, enough, Sir. This must not go on.
Give me that paper, please, and then begone.
MONSIEUR LOYAL Well, *au revoir.* God give you all good cheer!
ORGON May God confound you, and him who sent you here!

Scene V

ORGON, CLÉANTE, MARIANE, ELMIRE, MADAME PERNELLE, DORINE, DAMIS.

ORGON Now, Mother, was I right or not? This writ
Should change your notion of Tartuffe a bit.
Do you perceive his villainy at last?
MADAME PERNELLE I'm thunderstruck. I'm utterly aghast.
DORINE Oh, come, be fair. You mustn't take offense
At this new proof of his benevolence.
He's acting out of selfless love, I know.
Material things enslave the soul, and so
He kindly has arranged your liberation
From all that might endanger your salvation.
ORGON Will you not ever hold your tongue, you dunce?
CLÉANTE Come, you must take some action, and at once.
ELMIRE Go tell the world of the low trick he's tried.
The deed of gift is surely nullified
By such behavior, and public rage will not
Permit the wretch to carry out his plot.

Scene VI

VALÈRE, ORGON, CLÉANTE, ELMIRE, MARIANE, MADAME PERNELLE, DAMIS, DORINE.

VALÈRE Sir, though I hate to bring you more bad news,
Such is the danger that I cannot choose.
A friend who is extremely close to me
And knows my interest in your family
Has, for my sake, presumed to violate
The secrecy that's due to things of state,
And sends me word that you are in a plight
From which your one salvation lies in flight.
That scoundrel who's imposed upon you so
Denounced you to the King an hour ago
And, as supporting evidence, displayed
The strong-box of a certain renegade
Whose secret papers, so he testified,

You had disloyally agreed to hide.
I don't know just what charges may be pressed,
But there's a warrant out for your arrest;
Tartuffe has been instructed, furthermore,
To guide the arresting officer to your door.
CLÉANTE He's clearly done this to facilitate
His seizure of your house and your estate.
ORGON That man, I must say, is a vicious beast!
VALÈRE Quick, Sir; you mustn't tarry in the least.
My carriage is outside, to take you hence;
This thousand louis should cover all expense.
Let's lose no time, or you shall be undone;
The sole defense, in this case, is to run.
I shall go with you all the way, and place you
In a safe refuge to which they'll never trace you.
ORGON Alas, dear boy, I wish that I could show you
My gratitude for everything I owe you.
But now is not the time; I pray the Lord
That I may live to give you your reward.
Farewell, my dears; be careful . . .
CLÉANTE Brother, hurry.
We shall take care of things, you needn't worry.

Scene VII

THE OFFICER, TARTUFFE, VALÈRE, ORGON, ELMIRE, MARIANE, MADAME PERNELLE, DORINE, CLÉANTE, DAMIS.

TARTUFFE Gently, Sir, gently; stay right where you are.
No need for haste; your lodging isn't far.
You're off to prison, by order of the Prince.
ORGON This is the crowning blow, you wretch; and since
It means my total ruin and defeat,
Your villainy is now at last complete.
TARTUFFE You needn't try to provoke me; it's no use.
Those who serve Heaven must expect abuse.
CLÉANTE You are indeed most patient, sweet, and blameless.
DAMIS How he exploits the name of Heaven! It's shameless.
TARTUFFE Your taunts and mockeries are all for naught;
To do my duty is my only thought.
MARIANE Your love of duty is most meritorious,
And what you've done is little short of glorious.
TARTUFFE All deeds are glorious, Madam, which obey
The sovereign prince who sent me here today.
ORGON I rescued you when you were destitute;
Have you forgotten that, you thankless brute?
TARTUFFE No, no, I well remember everything;

But my first duty is to serve my King.
That obligation is so paramount
That other claims, beside it, do not count;
And for it I would sacrifice my wife,
My family, my friend, or my own life.

ELMIRE Hypocrite!

DORINE All that we most revere, he uses
To cloak his plots and camouflage his ruses.

CLÉANTE If it is true that you are animated
By pure and loyal zeal, as you have stated,
Why was this zeal not roused until you'd sought
To make Orgon a cuckold, and been caught?
Why weren't you moved to give your evidence
Until your outraged host had driven you hence?
I shan't say that the gift of all his treasure
Ought to have damped your zeal in any measure;
But if he is a traitor, as you declare,
How could you condescend to be his heir?

TARTUFFE [*To the* OFFICER]
Sir, spare me all this clamor; it's growing shrill.
Please carry out your orders, if you will.

OFFICER Yes, I've delayed too long, Sir. Thank you kindly.
You're just the proper person to remind me.
Come, you are off to join the other boarders
In the King's prison, according to his orders.

TARTUFFE Who? I, Sir?

OFFICER Yes.

TARTUFFE To prison? This can't be true!

OFFICER I owe an explanation, but not to you.
[*To* ORGON.]
Sir, all is well; rest easy, and be grateful.
We serve a Prince to whom all sham is hateful,
A Prince who sees into our inmost hearts,
And can't be fooled by any trickster's arts.
His royal soul, though generous and human,
Views all things with discernment and acumen;
His sovereign reason is not lightly swayed,
And all his judgments are discreetly weighed.
He honors righteous men of every kind,
And yet his zeal for virtue is not blind,
Nor does his love of piety numb his wits
And make him tolerant of hypocrites.
'Twas hardly likely that this man could cozen
A King who's foiled such liars by the dozen.
With one keen glance, the King perceived the whole
Perverseness and corruption of his soul,

And thus high Heaven's injustice was displayed:
Betraying you, the rogue stood self-betrayed.
The King soon recognized Tartuffe as one
Notorious by another name, who'd done
So many vicious crimes that one could fill
Ten volumes with them, and be writing still.
But to be brief: our sovereign was appalled
By this man's treachery toward you, which he called
The last, worst villainy of a vile career,
And bade me follow the impostor here
To see how gross his impudence could be,
And force him to restore your property.
Your private papers, by the King's command,
I hereby seize and give into your hand.
The King, by royal order, invalidates
The deed which gave this rascal your estates,
And pardons, furthermore, your grave offense
In harboring an exile's documents.
By these decrees, our Prince rewards you for
Your loyal deeds in the late civil war,
And shows how heartfelt is his satisfaction
In recompensing any worthy action,
How much he prizes merit, and how he makes
More of men's virtues than of their mistakes.

DORINE Heaven be praised!

MADAME PERNELLE I breathe again, at last.

ELMIRE We're safe.

MARIANE I can't believe the danger's past.

ORGON [*To* TARTUFFE]
Well, traitor, now you see . . .

CLÉANTE Ah, Brother, please,
Let's not descend to such indignities.
Leave the poor wretch to his unhappy fate,
And don't say anything to aggravate
His present woes; but rather hope that he
Will soon embrace an honest piety,
And mend his ways, and by a true repentance
Move our just King to moderate his sentence.
Meanwhile, go kneel before your sovereign's throne
And thank him for the mercies he has shown.

ORGON Well said: let's go at once and, gladly kneeling,
Express the gratitude which all are feeling.
Then, when that first great duty has been done,
We'll turn with pleasure to a second one,
And give Valère, whose love has proven so true,
The wedded happiness which is his due.

Beth Henley (b. 1952)
CRIMES OF THE HEART

"For Len, C.C., and Kayo."

THE CAST

LENNY MAGRATH, *30, the oldest sister*
CHICK BOYLE, *29, the sisters' first cousin*
DOC PORTER, *30, Meg's old boyfriend*
MEG MAGRATH, *27, the middle sister*
BABE BOTRELLE, *24, the youngest sister*
BARNETTE LLOYD, *26, Babe's lawyer*

THE SETTING

The setting of the entire play is the kitchen in the Magrath sisters' house in Hazlehurst, Mississippi, a small southern town. The old-fashioned kitchen is unusually spacious, but there is a lived-in, cluttered look about it. There are four different entrances and exits to the kitchen: the back door; the door leading to the dining room and the front of the house; a door leading to the downstairs bedroom; and a staircase leading to the upstairs room. There is a table near the center of the room, and a cot has been set up in one of the corners.

THE TIME

In the fall; five years after Hurricane Camille

ACT I

[*The lights go up on the empty kitchen. It is late afternoon.* LENNY MAGRATH, *a thirty-year-old woman with a round figure and face, enters from the back door carrying a white suitcase, a saxophone case, and a brown paper sack. She sets the suitcase and the sax case down and takes the brown sack to the kitchen table. After glancing quickly at the door, she gets the cookie jar from the kitchen counter, a box of matches from the stove and then brings both objects back down to the kitchen table. Excitedly, she reaches into the brown sack and pulls out a package of birthday candles. She quickly opens the package and removes a candle. She tries to stick the candle into a cookie—it falls off. She sticks the candle in again but the cookie is too hard and it crumbles. Frantically, she gets a second cookie from the jar. She strikes a match, lights the candle and begins dripping wax onto the cookie. Just as she is beginning to smile we hear* CHICK'S *voice from Offstage.*]

CHICK'S VOICE Lenny! Oh, Lenny! [LENNY *quickly blows out the candle and stuffs the cookie and candle into her dress pocket.* CHICK, *29, enters from the back door. She is a brightly dressed matron with yellow hair and shiny, red lips.*]

CHICK Hi! I saw your car pull up.

LENNY Hi.

CHICK Well, did you see today's paper? [LENNY *nods.*] It's just too awful! It's just way too awful! How I'm gonna continue holding my head up high in this community, I do not know. Did you remember to pick up those pantyhose for me?

LENNY They're in the sack.

CHICK Well, thank goodness, at least I'm not gonna have to go into town wearing holes in my stockings. [CHICK *gets the package, tears it open and proceeds to take off one pair of stockings and put on another, throughout the following scene. There should be something slightly grotesque about this woman changing her stockings in the kitchen.*]

LENNY Did Uncle Watson call?

CHICK Yes. Daddy has called me twice already. He said Babe's ready to come home. We've got to get right over and pick her up before they change their simple minds.

LENNY [*hesitantly*] Oh, I know, of course, it's just—

CHICK What?

LENNY Well, I was hoping Meg would call.

CHICK Meg?

LENNY Yes, I sent her a telegram: about Babe, and—

CHICK A telegram?! Couldn't you just phone her up?

LENNY Well, no, 'cause her phone's . . . out of order.

CHICK Out of order?

LENNY Disconnected. I don't know what.

CHICK Well, that sounds like Meg. My, these are snug. Are you sure you bought my right size?

LENNY [*looking at the box*] Size extra petite.

CHICK Well, they're skimping on the nylon material. [*Struggling to pull up the stockings.*] That's all there is to it. Skimping on the nylon. [*She finishes on one leg and starts on the other.*] Now, just what all did you say in this "telegram" to Meg?

LENNY I don't recall exactly. I, well, I just told her to come on home.

CHICK To come on home! Why, Lenora Josephine, have you lost your only brain, or what?

LENNY [*nervously, as she begins to pick up the mess of dirty stockings and plastic wrappings*] But Babe wants Meg home. She asked me to call her.

CHICK I'm not talking about what Babe wants.

LENNY Well, what then?

CHICK Listen, Lenora, I think it's pretty accurate to assume that after this morning's paper, Babe's gonna be incurring some mighty negative publicity around this town. And Meg's appearance isn't gonna help out a bit.

LENNY What's wrong with Meg?

CHICK She had a loose reputation in high school.

LENNY [*weakly*] She was popular.

CHICK She was known all over Copiah County as cheap Christmas trash, and that was the least of it. There was that whole sordid affair with Doc Porter, leaving him a cripple.

LENNY A cripple—he's got a limp. Just, kind of, barely a limp.

CHICK Well, his mother was going to keep *me* out of the Ladies' Social League because of it.

LENNY What?

CHICK That's right. I never told you, but I had to go plead with that mean, old woman and convince her that I was just as appalled and upset with what Meg had done as she was, and that I was only a first cousin anyway and I could hardly be blamed for all the skeletons in the Magraths' closet. It was humiliating. I tell you, she even brought up your mother's death. And that poor cat.

LENNY Oh! Oh! Oh, please, Chick! I'm sorry. But you're in the Ladies' League now.

CHICK Yes. That's true, I am. But frankly, if Mrs. Porter hadn't developed that tumor in her bladder, I wouldn't be in the club today, much less a committee head. [*As she brushes her hair.*] Anyway, you be a sweet potato and wait right here for Meg to call, so's you can convince her not to come back home. It would make things a whole lot easier on everybody. Don't you think it really would?

LENNY Probably.

CHICK Good, then suit yourself. How's my hair?

LENNY Fine.

CHICK Not pooching out in the back, is it?

LENNY No.

CHICK [*cleaning the hair from her brush*] All right then, I'm on my way. I've got Annie May over there keeping an eye on Peekay and Buck Jr., but I don't trust her with them for long periods of time. [*Dropping the ball of hair onto the floor.*] Her mind is like a loose sieve. Honestly it is. [*She puts the brush back into her purse.*] Oh! Oh! Oh! I almost forgot. Here's a present for you. Happy Birthday to Lenny, from the Buck Boyles! [CHICK *takes a wrapped package from her bag and hands it to* LENNY.]

LENNY Why, thank you, Chick. It's so nice to have you remember my birthday every year like you do.

CHICK [*modestly*] Oh well, now, that's just the way I am, I suppose. That's just the way I was brought up to be. Well, why don't you go on and open up the present?

LENNY All right. [*She starts to unwrap the gift.*]

CHICK It's a box of candy—assorted cremes.

LENNY Candy—that's always a nice gift.

CHICK And you have a sweet tooth, don't you?

LENNY I guess.

CHICK Well, I'm glad you like it.

LENNY I do.

CHICK Oh, speaking of which, remember that little polka dot dress you got Peekay for her fifth birthday last month?

LENNY The red and white one?

CHICK Yes; well, the first time I put it in the washing machine, I mean the very first time, it fell all to pieces. Those little polka dots just dropped right off in the water.

LENNY [*crushed*] Oh, no. Well, I'll get something else for her then—a little toy.

CHICK Oh, no, no, no, no, no! We wouldn't hear of it! I just wanted to let you know so you wouldn't go and waste any more of your hard-earned money on that make of dress. Those inexpensive brands just don't hold up. I'm sorry but not in these modern washing machines.

DOC PORTER'S VOICE Hello! Hello, Lenny!

CHICK [*taking over*] Oh, look, it's Doc Porter! Come on in, Doc! Please come right on in! [DOC PORTER *enters through the back door. He is carrying a large sack of pecans.* DOC *is an attractively worn man with a slight limp that adds rather than detracts from his quiet seductive quality. He is 30 years old, but appears slightly older.*] Well, how are you doing? How in the world are you doing?

DOC Just fine, Chick.

CHICK And how are you liking it now that you're back in Hazlehurst?

DOC Oh, I'm finding it somewhat enjoyable.

CHICK Somewhat! Only somewhat! Will you listen to him! What a silly, silly, silly man! Well, I'm on my way. I've got some people waiting on me. [*Whispering to* DOC]. It's Babe. I'm on my way to pick her up.

DOC Oh.

CHICK Well, goodbye! Farewell and goodbye!

LENNY Bye. [CHICK *exits.*]

DOC Hello.

LENNY Hi. I guess you heard about the thing with Babe.

DOC Yeah.

LENNY It was in the newspaper.

DOC Uh huh.

LENNY What a mess.

DOC Yeah.

LENNY Well, come on and sit down. I'll heat us up some coffee.

DOC That's okay. I can only stay a minute. I have to pick up Scott; he's at the dentist's.

LENNY Oh; well, I'll heat some up for myself. I'm kinda thirsty for a cup of hot coffee. [LENNY *puts the coffeepot on the burner.*]

DOC Lenny—

LENNY What?

DOC [*not able to go on*] Ah . . .

LENNY Yes?

DOC Here, some pecans for you. [*He hands her the the sack.*]

LENNY Why, thank you, Doc. I love pecans.

DOC My wife and Scott picked them up around the yard.

LENNY Well, I can use them to make a pie. A pecan pie.

DOC Yeah. Look, Lenny, I've got some bad news for you.

LENNY What?

DOC Well, you know, you've been keeping Billy Boy out on our farm; he's been grazing out there.

LENNY Yes—

DOC Well, last night, Billy Boy died.

LENNY He died?

DOC Yeah. I'm sorry to tell you when you've got all this on you; but I thought you'd want to know.

LENNY Well, yeah. I do. He died?

DOC Uh huh. He was struck by lightning.

LENNY Struck by lightning? In that storm yesterday?

DOC That's what we think.

LENNY Gosh, struck by lightning. I've had Billy Boy so long. You know. Ever since I was ten years old.

DOC Yeah. He was a mighty old horse.

LENNY [*stung*] Mighty old.

DOC Almost twenty years old.

LENNY That's right, twenty years. 'Cause; ah; I'm thirty years old today. Did you know that?

DOC No, Lenny, I didn't know. Happy Birthday.

LENNY Thanks. [*She begins to cry.*]

DOC Oh, come on now, Lenny. Come on. Hey, hey, now. You know I can't stand it when you Magrath women start to cry. You know it just gets me.

LENNY Oh-ho! Sure! You mean when Meg cries! Meg's the one you could never stand to watch cry! Not me! I could fill up a pig's trough!

DOC Now, Lenny . . . stop it. Come on. Jesus!

LENNY Okay! Okay! I don't know what's wrong with me. I don't mean to make a scene. I've been on this crying jag. [*She blows her nose.*] All this stuff with Babe and old Granddaddy's gotten worse in the hospital and I can't get in touch with Meg.

DOC You tried calling Meggy?

LENNY Yes.

DOC Is she coming home?

LENNY Who knows. She hasn't called me. That's what I'm waiting here for—hoping she'll call.

DOC She still living in California?

LENNY Yes; in Hollywood.

DOC Well, give me a call if she gets in. I'd like to see her.

LENNY Oh, you would, huh?

DOC Yeah, Lenny, sad to say, but I would.

LENNY It is sad. It's very sad indeed. [*They stare at each other, then look away. There is a moment of tense silence.*]

DOC Hey, Jello Face, your coffee's boiling.

LENNY [*going to check*] Oh, it is? Thanks. [*After she checks the pot.*] Look, you'd better go on and pick Scott up. You don't want him to have to wait for you.

DOC Yeah, you're right. Poor kid. It's his first time at the dentist.

LENNY Poor thing.

DOC Well, 'bye. I'm sorry to have to tell you about your horse.

LENNY Oh, I know. Tell Joan thanks for picking up the pecans.

DOC I will. [*He starts to leave.*]

LENNY Oh, how's the baby?

DOC She's fine. Real pretty. She, ah, holds your finger in her hand; like this.

LENNY Oh, that's cute.

DOC Yeah. 'Bye, Lenny.

LENNY 'Bye. [DOC *exits.* LENNY *stares after him for a moment, then goes and sits back down at the kitchen table. She reaches into her pocket and pulls out a somewhat crumbled cookie and a wax candle. She lights the candle again, lets the wax drip onto the cookie, then sticks the candle on top of the cookie. She begins to sing the "Happy Birthday Song" to herself. At the end of the song she pauses, silently makes a wish, and blows out the candle. She waits a moment, then re-lights the candle, and repeats her actions, only this time making a different wish at the end of the song. She starts to repeat the procedure for the third time, as the phone begins to ring. She goes to answer it.*] Hello . . . oh, hello, Lucille, how's Zackery? . . . Oh, no! . . . Oh, I'm so sorry. Of course, it must be grueling for you . . . Yes, I understand. Your only brother . . . no, she's not here yet. Chick just went to pick her up . . . oh, now, Lucille, she's still his wife, I'm sure she'll be interested . . . Well, you can just tell me the information and I'll relate it all to her . . . Uh-hum, his liver's saved. Oh, that's good news! . . . Well, of course, when you look at it like that . . . Breathing stabilized . . .

Damage to the spinal column, not yet determined . . . Okay . . . Yes, Lucille, I've got it all down . . . Uh-huh, I'll give her that message. 'Bye, 'bye. [LENNY *drops the pencil and paper down. She sighs deeply, wipes her cheeks with the back of her hand, and goes to the stove to pour herself a cup of coffee. After a few moments, the front door is heard slamming.* LENNY *starts. A whistle is heard, then* MEG'S *voice.*]

MEG'S VOICE I'm home! [*She whistles the family whistle.*] Anybody home?!!

LENNY Meg? Meg! [MEG, *27, enters from the dining room. She has sad, magic eyes and wears a hat. She carries a worn-out suitcase.*]

MEG [*dropping her suitcase, running to hug* LENNY] Lenny—

LENNY Well, Meg! Why, Meg! Oh, Meggy! Why didn't you call? Did you fly in? You didn't take a cab, did you? Why didn't you give us a call?

MEG [*overlapping*] Oh, Lenny! Why, Lenny! Dear, Lenny! [*Then she looks at* LENNY'S *face.*] My God, we're getting so old! Oh, I called for heaven's sake. Of course, I called!

LENNY Well, I never talked to you—

MEG Well, I know! I let the phone ring right off the hook!

LENNY Well, as a matter of fact, I was out most of the morning seeing to Babe—!

MEG Now just what's all this business about Babe? How could you send me such a telegram about Babe? And Zackery! You say somebody's shot Zackery?!

LENNY Yes; they have.

MEG Well, good Lord! Is he dead?

LENNY No. But he's in the hospital. He was shot in his stomach.

MEG In his stomach! How awful! Do they know who shot him? [LENNY *nods.*] Well, who? Who was it? Who? Who?

LENNY Babe! They're all saying Babe shot him! They took her to jail! And they're saying she shot him! They're all saying it! It's horrible! It's awful!

MEG [*overlapping*] Jail! Good Lord, jail! Well, who? Who's saying it? Who?!!

LENNY Everyone!! The policemen, the sheriff, Zackery, even Babe's saying it! Even Babe herself!!

MEG Well, for God's sake. For God's sake.

LENNY [*overlapping as she falls apart*] It's horrible! It's horrible! It's just horrible!!!

MEG Now calm down, Lenny. Just calm down. Would you like a Coke? Here, I'll get you some Coke. [MEG *gets a Coke from the refrigerator. She opens it and downs a large swig.*] Why? Why would she shoot him? Why? [MEG *hands the Coke bottle to* LENNY.]

LENNY I talked to her this morning and I asked her that very question. I said, "Babe, why would you shoot Zackery? He was your own husband. Why would you shoot him?" And do you know what she said? [MEG *shakes her head.*] She said, " 'Cause I didn't like his looks. I just didn't like his looks."

MEG [*after a pause*] Well, I don't like his looks.

LENNY But you didn't shoot him! You wouldn't shoot a person 'cause you didn't like their looks! You wouldn't do that! Oh, I hate to say this—I do hate to say this—but I believe Babe is ill. I mean in-her-head-ill.

MEG Oh, now, Lenny, don't you say that! There're plenty of good sane reasons to shoot another person and I'm sure that Babe had one. Now what we've got to do is get her the best lawyer in town. Do you have any ideas on who's the best lawyer in town?

LENNY Well, Zackery is, of course; but he's been shot!

MEG Well, count him out! Just count him and his whole firm out!

LENNY Anyway, you don't have to worry, she's already got her lawyer.

MEG She does? Who?

LENNY Barnette Lloyd. Annie Lloyd's boy. He just opened his office here in town. And Uncle Watson said we'd be doing Annie a favor by hiring him up.

MEG Doing Annie a favor? Doing Annie a favor?! Well, what about Babe? Have you thought about Babe? Do we want to do her a favor of thirty or forty years in jail?! Have you thought about that?

LENNY Now, don't snap at me! Just don't snap at me! I try to do what's right! All this responsibility keeps falling on my shoulders, and I try to do what's right!

MEG Well, boo hoo, hoo, hoo! And how in the hell could you send me such a telegram about Babe!

LENNY Well, if you had a phone, or if you didn't live way out there in Hollywood and not even come home for Christmas maybe I wouldn't have to pay all that money to send you a telegram!!!

MEG [*overlapping*] 'Babe's in terrible trouble—Stop! Zackery's been shot—Stop! Come home immediately—Stop! Stop! Stop!'

LENNY And what was that you said about how old we're getting? When you looked at my face, you said, "My God, we're getting so old!" But you didn't mean we—you meant me! Didn't you? I'm thirty years old today and my face is getting all pinched up and my hair is falling out in the comb.

MEG Why, Lenny! It's your birthday, October 23rd. How could I forget. Happy Birthday!

LENNY Well, it's not. I'm thirty years old and Billy Boy died last night. He was struck by lightning. He was struck dead.

MEG [*reaching for a cigarette*] Struck dead. Oh, what a mess. What a mess. Are you really thirty? Then I must be twenty-seven and Babe is twenty-four. My God, we're getting so old. [*They are silent for several moments as* MEG *drags off her cigarette and* LENNY *drinks her Coke.*] What's the cot doing in the kitchen?

LENNY Well, I rolled it out when Old Granddaddy got sick. So I could be close and hear him at night if he needed something.

MEG [*glancing toward the door leading to the downstairs bedroom*] Is Old Granddaddy here?

LENNY Why, no. Old Granddaddy's at the hospital.

MEG Again?

LENNY Meg!

MEG What?

LENNY I wrote you all about it. He's been in the hospital over three months straight.

MEG He has?

LENNY Don't you remember? I wrote you about all those blood vessels popping in his brain?

MEG Popping—

LENNY And how he was so anxious to hear from you and to find out about your singing career. I wrote it all to you. How they have to feed him through those tubes now. Didn't you get my letters?

MEG Oh, I don't know, Lenny. I guess I did. To tell you the truth, sometimes I kinda don't read your letters.

LENNY What?

MEG I'm sorry. I used to read them. It's just since Christmas reading them gives me these slicing pains right here in my chest.

LENNY I see. I see. Is that why you didn't use that money Old Granddaddy sent you to come home Christmas; because you hate us so much? We never did all that much to make you hate us. We didn't!

MEG Oh, Lenny! Do you think I'd be getting slicing pains in my chest, if I didn't care about you? If I hated you? Honestly, now, do you think I would?

LENNY No.

MEG Okay, then. Let's drop it. I'm sorry I didn't read your letters. Okay?

LENNY Okay.

MEG Anyway, we've got this whole thing with Babe to deal with. The first thing is to get her a good lawyer and get her out of jail.

LENNY Well, she's out of jail.

MEG She is?

LENNY That young lawyer, he's gotten her out.

MEG Oh, he has?

LENNY Yes, on bail. Uncle Watson's put it up. Chick's bringing her back right now—she's driving her home.

MEG Oh; well, that's a relief.

LENNY Yes, and they're due home any minute now; so we can just wait right here for 'em.

MEG Well, good. That's good. [*As she leans against the counter.*] So, Babe shot Zackery Botrelle, the richest and most powerful man in all of Hazlehurst, slap in the gut. It's hard to believe.

LENNY It certainly is. Little Babe—shooting off a gun.

MEG Little Babe.

LENNY She was always the prettiest and most perfect of the three of us. Old Granddaddy used to call her his Dancing Sugar Plum. Why, remember how proud and happy he was the day she married Zackery.

MEG Yes, I remember. It was his finest hour.

LENNY He remarked how Babe was gonna skyrocket right to the heights of Hazlehurst society. And how Zackery was just the right man for her whether she knew it now or not.

MEG Oh, Lordy, Lordy. And what does Old Granddaddy say now?

LENNY Well, I haven't had the courage to tell him all about this as yet. I thought maybe tonight we could go to visit him at the hospital and you could talk to him and . . .

MEG Yeah, well, we'll see. We'll see. Do we have anything to drink around here—to the tune of straight bourbon?

LENNY No. There's no liquor.

MEG Hell. [MEG *gets a Coke from the refrigerator and opens it.*]

LENNY Then you will go with me to see Old Granddaddy at the hospital tonight?

MEG Of course. [MEG *goes to her purse and gets out a bottle of Empirin Compound. She takes out a tablet and puts it on her tongue.*] Brother, I know he's gonna go on about my singing career. Just like he always does.

LENNY Well, how is your career going?

MEG It's not.

LENNY Why, aren't you still singing at the club down on Malibu beach?

MEG No. Not since Christmas.

LENNY Well, then, are you singing some place new?

MEG No, I'm not singing. I'm not singing at all.

LENNY Oh. Well, what do you do then?

MEG What I do is I pay cold storage bills for a dog food company. That's what I do.

LENNY [*trying to be helpful*] Gosh, don't you think it'd be a good idea to stay in the show business field?

MEG Oh, maybe.

LENNY Like Old Granddaddy says, "With your talent all you need is exposure. Then you can make your own breaks!" Did you hear his suggestion about getting your foot put in one of those blocks of cement they've got out there? He thinks that's real important.

MEG Yeh. I think I've heard that. And I'll probably hear it again when I go to visit him at the hospital tonight; so let's just drop it. Okay? [*She noticed the sack of pecans.*] What's this? Pecans? Great, I love pecans! [MEG *takes out two pecans and tries to open them by cracking them together.*] Come on . . . Crack, you demons! Crack!

LENNY We have a nutcracker!

MEG [*trying with her teeth*] Ah, where's the sport in a nutcracker? Where's the challenge?

LENNY [*getting up to get the nutcracker*] It's over here in the utensil drawer. [*As* LENNY *gets the nutcracker,* MEG *opens the pecan by stepping on it with her shoe.*]

MEG There! Open! [MEG *picks up the crumbled pecan and eats it.*] Mmmm, delicious. Delicious. Where'd you get the fresh pecans?

LENNY Oh . . . I don't know.

MEG They sure are tasty.

LENNY Doc Porter brought them over.

MEG Doc. What's Doc doing here in town?

LENNY Well, his father died a couple of months ago. Now he's back home seeing to his property.

MEG Gosh, the last I heard of Doc, he was up in the East painting the walls of houses to earn a living. [*Amused.*] Heard he was living with some Yankee woman who made clay pots.

LENNY Joan.

MEG What?

LENNY Her name's Joan. She came down here with him. That's one of her pots. Doc's married to her.

MEG Married—

LENNY Uh huh.

MEG Doc married a Yankee?

LENNY That's right; and they've got two kids.

MEG Kids—

LENNY A boy and a girl.

MEG God. Then his kids must be half-Yankee.

LENNY I suppose.

MEG God. That really gets me. I don't know why, but somehow that really gets me.

LENNY I don't know why it should.

MEG And what a stupid-looking pot! Who'd buy it anyway?

LENNY Wait—I think that's them. Yeah, that's Chick's car! Oh, there's Babe! Hello, Babe! They're home, Meg! They're home. [MEG *hides.*]

BABE'S VOICE Lenny! I'm home! I'm free! [BABE, *24, enters exuberantly. She has an angelic face and fierce, volatile eyes. She carries a pink pocketbook.*] I'm home! [MEG *jumps out of hiding.*] Oh, Meg—Look it's Meg! [*Running to hug her.*] Meg! When did you get home?

MEG Just now!

BABE Well, it's so good to see you! I'm so glad you're home! I'm so relieved. [CHICK *enters.*]

MEG Why, Chick; hello.

CHICK Hello, Cousin Margaret. What brings you back to Hazlehurst?

MEG Oh, I came on home . . . [*turning to* BABE] I came on home to see about Babe.

BABE [*running to hug* MEG] Oh, Meg—

MEG How are things with you, Babe?

CHICK Well, they are dismal, if you want my opinion. She is refusing to cooperate with her lawyer, that nice-looking young Lloyd boy. She won't tell any of us why she committed this heinous crime, except to say that she didn't like Zackery's looks—

BABE Oh, look, Lenny brought my suitcase from home! And my saxophone! Thank you! [BABE *runs over to the cot and gets out her saxophone.*]

CHICK Now that young lawyer is coming over here this afternoon, and when he gets here he expects to get some concrete answers! That's what he expects! No more of this nonsense and stubbornness from you Rebecca Magrath, or they'll put you in jail and throw away the key!

BABE Meg, come look at my new saxophone. I went to Jackson and bought it used. Feel it. It's so heavy.

MEG It's beautiful. [*The room goes silent.*]

CHICK Isn't that right, won't they throw away the key?

LENNY Well, honestly, I don't know about that—

CHICK They will! And leave you there to rot. So, Rebecca, what are you going to tell Mr. Lloyd about shooting Zackery when he gets here? What are your reasons going to be?

BABE [*glaring*] That I didn't like his looks! I just didn't like his stinking looks! And I don't like yours much either, Chick-the-Stick! So, just leave me alone! I mean it! Leave me alone! Oooh! [BABE *exits up the stairs. There is a long moment of silence.*]

CHICK Well, I was only trying to warn her that she's going to have to help herself. It's just that she doesn't understand how serious the situation is. Does she? She doesn't have the vaguest idea. Does she now?

LENNY Well, it's true, she does seem a little confused.

CHICK And that's putting it mildly. Lenny honey. That's putting it mighty mild. So, Margaret, how's your singing career going? We keep looking for your picture in the movie magazines. [MEG *moves to light a cigarette.*] You know, you shouldn't smoke. It causes cancer. Cancer of the lungs. They say each cigarette is just a little stick of cancer. A little death stick.

MEG That's what I like about it, Chick—taking a drag off of death

[MEG *takes a long, deep drag.*] Mmm! Gives me a sense of controlling my own destiny. What power! What exhilaration! Want a drag?

LENNY [*trying to break the tension*] Ah, Zackery's liver's been saved! His sister called up and said his liver was saved. Isn't that good news?

MEG Well, yes, that's fine news. Mighty fine news. Why I've been told that the liver's a powerful important bodily organ. I believe it's used to absorb all our excess bile.

LENNY Yes—well—it's been saved. [*The phone rings.* LENNY *gets it.*]

MEG So! Did you hear all that good news about the liver, Little Chicken?

CHICK I heard it. And don't you call me Chicken. [MEG *clucks like a chicken.*] I've told you a hundred times if I've told you once not to call me Chicken. You cannot call me Chicken.

LENNY . . . Oh, no! . . . Of course, we'll be right over! Bye! [*She hangs up the phone.*] That was Annie May—Peekay and Buck Jr. have eaten paints!

CHICK Oh, no! Are they all right? They're not sick? They're not sick, are they?

LENNY I don't know. I don't know. Come on. We've got to run on next door.

CHICK [*overlapping.*] Oh, God! Oh, please! Please let them be all right! Don't let them die!! Please, don't let them die!!

[CHICK *runs Off howling with* LENNY *following after.* MEG *sits alone, finishing her cigarette. After a moment,* BABE'S *voice is heard.*]

BABE'S VOICE Pst—Psst!

[MEG *looks around.* BABE *comes tiptoeing down the stairs.*]

BABE Has she gone?

MEG She's gone. Peekay and Buck Jr. just ate their paints.

BABE What idiots.

MEG Yeah.

BABE You know, Chick's hated us ever since we had to move here from Vicksburg to live with Old Grandmama and Old Granddaddy.

MEG She's an idiot.

BABE Yeah. Do you know what she told me this morning while I was still behind bars and couldn't get away?

MEG What?

BABE She told me how embarrassing it was for her all those years ago, you know, when mama—

MEG Yeah, down in the cellar.

BABE She said our mama had shamed the entire family, and we were known notoriously all through Hazlehurst. [*About to cry.*] Then she went on to say how I would now be getting just as much bad publicity and humiliating her and the family all over again.

MEG Ah, forget it, Babe. Just forget it.

BABE I told her, "Mama got national coverage! National!" And if Zackery wasn't a senator from Copiah County, I probably wouldn't even be getting state-wide.

MEG Of course you wouldn't.

BABE [*after a pause.*] Gosh, sometimes I wonder . . .

MEG What?

BABE Why she did it. Why mama hung herself.

MEG I don't know. She had a bad day. A real bad day. You know how it feels on a real bad day.

BABE And that old yellow cat. It was sad about that old cat.

MEG Yeah.

BABE I bet if Daddy hadn't of left us, they'd still be alive.

MEG Oh, I don't know.

BABE 'Cause it was after he left that she started spending whole days just sitting there and smoking on the back porch steps. She'd sling her ashes down onto the different bugs and ants that'd be passing by.

MEG Yeah. Well, I'm glad he left.

BABE That old yellow cat'd stay back there with her.

MEG God, he was a bastard.

BABE I thought if she felt something for anyone it would a been that old cat. Guess I musta been mistaken.

MEG Really, with his white teeth, Daddy was such a bastard.

BABE Was he? I don't remember. [MEG *blows out a mouthful of smoke. After a moment, uneasily.*] I think I'm gonna make some lemonade. You want some?

MEG Sure. [BABE *cuts lemons, dumps sugar, stirs ice cubes, etc. throughout the following exchange.*] Babe, Why won't you talk? Why won't you tell anyone about shooting Zackery?

BABE Oooh—

MEG Why not? You must have had a good reason. Didn't you?

BABE I guess I did.

MEG Well, what was it?

BABE I . . . I can't say.

MEG Why not? [*Pause.*] Babe, why not? You can tell me.

BABE 'Cause . . . I'm sort of . . . protecting someone.

MEG Protecting someone? Oh, Babe, then you really didn't shoot him?! I knew you couldn't have done it!! I knew it!!!

BABE No, I shot him. I shot him all right. I meant to kill him. I was aiming for his heart, but I guess my hands were shaking and I—just got him in the stomach.

MEG [*collapsing*] I see.

BABE [*stirring the lemonade*] So I'm guilty. And I'm just gonna have to take my punishment and go on to jail.

MEG Oh, Babe—

BABE Don't worry, Meg, jail's gonna be a relief to me. I can learn to play my new saxophone. I won't have to live with Zackery anymore. And I won't have his snoopy old sister, Lucille, coming over and pushing me around. Jail will be a relief. Here's your lemonade.

MEG Thanks.

BABE It taste okay?

MEG Perfect.

BABE I like a lot of sugar in mine. I'm gonna add some more sugar.

[BABE *goes to add more sugar to her lemonade, as* LENNY *bursts through the back door in a state of excitement and confusion.*]

LENNY Well, it looks like the paint is primarily on their arms and faces; but Chick wants me to drive them all over to Doctor Winn's just to make sure. [LENNY *grabs her car keys off of the counter and as she does so, she notices the mess of lemons and sugar.*] Oh, now, Babe, try not to make a mess here; and be careful with this sharp knife. Honestly, all that sugar's gonna get you sick. Well, 'bye, 'bye. I'll be back as soon as I can.

MEG Bye, Lenny.

BABE 'Bye, [LENNY *exits.*] Boy, I don't know what's happening to Lenny.

MEG What do you mean?

BABE "Don't make a mess; don't make yourself sick; don't cut yourself with that sharp knife." She's turning into Old Grandmama.

MEG You think so?

BABE More and more. Do you know she's taken to wearing Old Grandmama's torn sunhat and her green garden gloves?

MEG Those old lime green ones?

BABE Yeah; she works out in the garden wearing the lime green gloves of a dead woman. Imagine wearing those gloves on your hands.

MEG Poor Lenny. She needs some love in her life. All she does is work out at that brick yard and take care of Old Granddaddy.

BABE Yeah. But she's so shy with men.

MEG [*biting into an apple*] Probably because of that *shrunken* ovary she has.

BABE [*slinging ice cubes*] Yeah, that *deformed* ovary.

MEG Old Granddaddy's the one who's made her feel self-conscious about it. It's his fault. The old fool.

BABE It's so sad.

MEG God—you know what?

BABE What?

MEG I bet Lenny's never even slept with a man. Just think, thirty years old and never even had it once.

BABE [*slyly*] Oh; I don't know. Maybe she's . . . had it once?

MEG She has?

BABE Maybe. I think so.

MEG When? When?

BABE Well . . . maybe I shouldn't say—

MEG Babe!

BABE [*rapidly telling the story*] All right then; it was after Old Granddaddy went back to the hospital this second time. Lenny was really in a state of deep depression. I could tell that she was. Then one day she calls me up and asks me to come over and to bring along my polaroid camera. Well, when I arrive she's waiting for me out there in the sun parlour wearing her powder blue Sunday dress and this old curled up wig. She confided that she was gonna try sending in her picture to one of those lonely hearts clubs.

MEG Oh, my God.

BABE Lonely Hearts of the South. She'd seen their ad in a magazine.

MEG Jesus.

BABE Anyway, I take some snapshots and she sends them on in to the club, and about two weeks later she receives in the mail this whole load of pictures of available men, most of 'em fairly odd looking. But of course she doesn't call any of 'em up cause she's real shy. But one of 'em, this Charlie Hill from Memphis, Tennessee, he calls her.

MEG He does?

BABE Yeah. And time goes on and she says he's real funny on the phone: so they decide to get together to meet.

MEG Yeah?!

BABE Well, he drives down here to Hazlehurst 'bout three or four different times and has supper with her, then one weekend she goes up to Memphis to visit him; and I think that is where it happened.

MEG What makes you think so?

BABE Well, when I went to pick her up from the bus depot, she ran off the bus and threw her arms around me and started crying and sobbing as though she'd like to never stop. I asked her, I said, "Lenny, what's the matter?" And she said, "I've done it, Babe! Honey, I've done it!"

MEG [*whispering*] And you think she meant that she'd done *it*?

BABE [*whispering back, slyly*] I think so.

MEG Well, goddamn! [*They laugh with glee.*]

BABE But she didn't say anything else about it. She just went on to tell me about the boot factory where Charlie worked and what a nice city Memphis was.

MEG So, what happened to this Charlie?

BABE Well, he came to Hazlehurst just one more time. Lenny took him over to meet Old Granddaddy at the hospital and after that they broke it off.

MEG 'Cause of Old Granddaddy?

BABE Well, she said it was on account of her missing ovary. That Charlie didn't want to marry her on account of it.

MEG Ah, how mean. How hateful.

BABE Oh, it was. He seemed like such a nice man, too—kinda chubby with red hair and freckles, always telling these funny jokes.

MEG Hmmm, that just doesn't seem right. Something about that doesn't seem exactly right. [MEG *paces about the kitchen and comes across the box of candy* LENNY *got for her birthday.*] Oh, God. "Happy Birthday to Lenny from the Buck Boyles."

BABE Oh, no! Today's Lenny's birthday!

MEG That's right.

BABE I forgot all about it!

MEG I know, I did too.

BABE Gosh, we'll have to order up a big cake for her. She always loves to make those wishes on her birthday cake.

MEG Yeah, let's get her a big cake! A huge one! [*Suddenly noticing the plastic wrapper on the candy box.*] Oh, God, that Chick's so cheap!

BABE What do you mean?

MEG This plastic has poinsettias on it!

BABE [*running to see*] Oh, let me see—[*She looks at the package with disgust.*] Boy, oh, boy! I'm calling that bakery and ordering the very largest size cake they have! That Jumbo Deluxe!

MEG Good!

BABE Why, I imagine they can make one up to be about—*this* big. [*She demonstrates.*]

MEG Oh, at least; at least that big. Why, maybe, it'll even be *this* big. [*She makes a very, very, very, large size cake.*]

BABE You think it could be *that* big?

MEG Sure!

BABE [*after a moment, getting the idea*] Or, or what if it were *this* big? *She maps out a cake that covers the room.*] What if we get the cake and it's *this* big?!! [*She gulps down a fistful of cake.*] Gulp! Gulp! Gulp! Tasty treat!

MEG Hmmm—I'll have me some more! Give me some more of that birthday cake!

[*Suddenly there is a loud knock at the door.*]

BARNETTE'S VOICE Hello . . . hello! May I come in?

BABE [*to Meg, in a whisper, as she takes cover*] Who's that?

MEG I don't know.

BARNETTE'S VOICE [*still knocking*] Hello! Hello, Mrs. Botrelle!

BABE Oh, shoot! It's that lawyer. I don't want to see him.

MEG Oh, Babe, come on. You've got to see him sometime.

BABE No, I don't! [*She starts up the stairs.*] Just tell him I died—I'm going upstairs.

MEG Oh, Babe! Will you come back here!

BABE [*as she exits*] You talk to him, please, Meg. Please! I just don't want to see him—

MEG Babe—Babe! Oh, shit . . . ah, come on in! Door's open!

[BARNETTE LLOYD, *26, enters carrying a briefcase. He is a slender, intelligent young man with an almost fanatical intensity that he subdues by sheer will.*]

BARNETTE How do you do? I'm Barnette Lloyd.

MEG Pleased to meet you. I'm Meg Magrath, Babe's older sister.

BARNETTE Yes, I know. You're the singer.

MEG Well, yes . . .

BARNETTE I came to hear you five different times when you were singing at the club in Biloxi. Greeny's I believe was the name of it.

MEG Yes, Greeny's.

BARNETTE You were very good. There was something sad and moving about how you sang those songs. It was like you had some sort of vision. Some special sort of vision.

MEG Well, thank you. You're very kind. Now . . . about Babe's case—

BARNETTE Yes?

MEG We've just got to win it.

BARNETTE I intend to.

MEG Of course. But, ah . . . [*She looks at him.*] Ah, you know, you're very young.

BARNETTE Yes, I am. I'm young.

MEG It's just. I'm concerned, Mr. Lloyd—

BARNETTE Barnette. Please.

MEG Barnette; that, ah, just maybe we need someone with, well, with more experience. Someone totally familiar with all the ins and outs and the this and thats of the legal dealings and such. As that.

BARNETTE Ah, you have reservations.

MEG [*relieved*] Reservations. Yes, I have . . . reservations.

BARNETTE Well, possibly it would help you to know that I graduated first in my class from Ole Miss Law School. I also spent three different summers taking advanced courses in criminal law at Harvard Law School. I made A's in all the given courses. I was fascinated!

MEG I'm sure.

BARNETTE And even now, I've just completed one year working with Jackson's top criminal law firm, Manchester and Wayne. I was invaluable to them. Indispensable. They offered to double my percentage, if I'd stay on; but I refused. I wanted to return to Hazlehurst and open my own office. The reason being, and this is a key point, that I have a personal vendetta to settle with one Zackery F. Botrelle.

MEG A personal vendetta?

BARNETTE Yes, ma'am. You are correct. Indeed, I do.

MEG Hmmm. A personal vendetta . . . I think I like that. So you have some sort of a personal vendetta to settle with Zackery?

BARNETTE Precisely. Just between the two of us. I not only intend to keep that sorry S.O.B. from ever being re-elected to the state senate by exposing his shady, criminal dealings; but I also intend to decimate his personal credibility by exposing him as a bully, a brute, and a red-neck thug!

MEG Well; I can see that you're—fanatical about this.

BARNETTE Yes; I am. I'm sorry, if I seem outspoken. But, for some reason, I feel I can talk to you . . . those songs you sang. Excuse me; I feel like a jackass.

MEG It's all right. Relax. Relax, Barnette. Let me think this out a minute. [*She takes out a cigarette. He lights it for her.*] Now just exactly how do you intend to get Babe off? You know, keep her out of jail.

BARNETTE It seems to me that we can get her off with a plea of self-defense, or possibly we could go with innocent by reason of temporary insanity. But basically, I intend to prove that Zackery Botrelle brutalized and tormented this poor woman to such an extent that she had no recourse but to defend herself in the only way she knew how!

MEG I like that!

BARNETTE Then, of course, I'm hoping this will break the ice and we'll be able to go on to prove that the man's a total criminal, as well as an abusive bully and contemptible slob!

MEG That sounds good! To me that sounds very good!

BARNETTE It's just our basic game plan.

MEG But, now, how are you going to prove all this about Babe being brutalized? We don't want anyone perjured. I mean to commit perjury.

BARNETTE Perjury? According to my sources, the'll be no need for perjury.

MEG You mean it's the truth?

BARNETTE This is a small town, Miss Magrath. The word gets out.

MEG It's really the truth?

BARNETTE [*opening his briefcase*] Just look at this. It's a photostatic copy of Mrs. Botrelle's medical chart over the past four years. Take a good look at it, if you want your blood to boil!

MEG [*looking over the chart*] What! What! This is maddening. This is madness! Did he do this to her? I'll kill him; I will—I'll fry his blood!! Did he do this?

BARNETTE [*alarmed*] To tell you the truth, I can't say for certain what was accidental and what was not. That's why I need to talk with Mrs. Botrelle. That's why it's very important that I see her!

MEG [*her eyes are wild, as she shoves him toward the door*] Well, look, I've got to see her first. I've got to talk to her first. What I'll do is I'll give you a call. Maybe you can come back over later on—

BARNETTE Well, then, here's my card—

MEG Okay. Goodbye.

BARNETTE 'Bye!

MEG Oh, wait! Wait! There's one problem with you.

BARNETTE What?

MEG What if you get so fanatically obsessed with this vendetta thing that you forget about Babe? You forget about her and sell her down the river just to get at Zackery. What about that?

BARNETTE I—wouldn't do that.

MEG You wouldn't?

BARNETTE No.

MEG Why not?

BARNETTE Because. I'm—I'm fond of her.

MEG What do you mean you're fond of her?

BARNETTE Well, she . . . she sold me a pound cake at a bazaar once. And I'm fond of her.

MEG All right; I believe you. Goodbye.

BARNETTE Goodbye. [BARNETTE *exits.*]

MEG Babe! Babe, come down here! Babe!

[BABE *comes hurrying down the stairs.*]

BABE What? What is it? I called about the cake—

MEG What did Zackery do to you?

BABE They can't have it for today.

MEG Did he hurt you? Did he? Did he do that?

BABE Oh, Meg, please—

MEG Did he? Goddamnit, Babe—

BABE Yes, he did.

MEG Why? Why?

BABE I don't know! He started hating me, 'cause I couldn't laugh at his jokes. I just started finding it impossible to laugh at his jokes the way I used to. And then the sound of his voice got to where it tired me out awful bad to hear it. I'd fall asleep just listening to him at the dinner table. He'd say, "Hand me some of that gravy!" Or, "This roast beef is too damn bloody." And suddenly I'd be out cold like a light.

MEG Oh, Babe. Babe, this is very important. I want you to sit down here and tell me what all happened right before you shot Zackery. That's right, just sit down and tell me.

BABE [*after a pause*] I told you I can't tell you on account of I'm protecting someone.

MEG But Babe, you've just got to talk to someone about all this. You just do.

BABE Why?

MEG Because it's a human need. To talk about our lives. It's an important human need.

BABE Oh. Well, I do feel like I want to talk to someone. I do.

MEG Then talk to me; please.

BABE [*a decision*] All right. [*After thinking a minute.*] I don't know where to start.

MEG Just start at the beginning. Just there at the beginning.

BABE [*after a moment*] Well, do you remember Willie Jay? [MEG *shakes her head.*] Cora's youngest boy?

MEG Oh, yeah, that little kid we used to pay a nickel to, to run down to the drugstore and bring us back a cherry Coke.

BABE Right. Well, Cora irons at my place on Wednesdays now, and she just happened to mention that Willie Jay'd picked up this old stray dog and that he'd gotten real fond of him. But now they couldn't afford to feed him anymore, so she was gonna have to tell Willie Jay to set him loose in the woods.

MEG [*trying to be patient*] Uh huh.

BABE Well, I said I liked dogs and if he wanted to bring the dog over here, I'd take care of him. You see, I was alone by myself most of the time 'cause the senate was in session, and Zackery was up in Jackson.

MEG Uh huh. [MEG *reaches for* LENNY'S *box of birthday candy. She takes little nibbles out of each piece, throughout the rest of the scene.*]

BABE So the next day, Willie Jay brings over this skinny, old dog with these little crossed-eyes. Well, I asked Willie Jay what his name was, and he said they called him Dog. Well, I liked the name; so I thought I'd keep it.

MEG [*getting up*] Uh huh. I'm listening. I'm just gonna get me a glass of cold water; do you want one?

BABE Okay.

MEG So you kept the name—Dog.

BABE Yeah. Anyway, when Willie Jay was leaving he gave Dog a hug and said, "Goodbye, Dog. You're a fine ole dog." Well, I felt something for him, so I told Willie Jay he could come back and visit with Dog any time he wanted, and his face just kinda lit right up.

MEG [*offering the candy*] Candy—

BABE No thanks. Anyhow, time goes on and Willie Jay keeps coming over and over. And we talk about Dog and how fat he's getting and then, well, you know, things start up.

MEG No, I don't know. What things start up?

BABE Well, things start up. Like sex. Like that.

MEG Babe, wait a minute—Willie Jay's a boy. A small boy, about this tall. He's about this tall!

BABE No! Oh, no! He's taller now! He's fifteen now. When you knew him he was only about seven or eight.

MEG But, even so—fifteen. And he's a black boy; a colored boy; a Negro.

BABE [*flustered*] Well, I realize that, Meg. Why do you think I'm so worried about his getting public exposure? I don't want to ruin his reputation!

MEG I'm amazed, Babe. I'm really, completely amazed. I didn't even know you were a liberal.

BABE Well, I'm not! I'm not a liberal! I'm a democratic! I was just lonely! I was so lonely. And he was good. Oh, he was so, so good. I'd never had it that good. We'd always go out into the garage and—

MEG It's okay. I've got the picture; I've got the picture! Now, let's just get back to the story. To yesterday, when you shot Zackery.

BABE All right, then. Let's see . . . Willie Jay was over. And it was after we'd—

MEG Yeah! Yeah.

BABE And we were just standing around on the back porch playing with Dog. Well, suddenly, Zackery comes from around the side of the house. And he startled me 'cause he's supposed to be away at the office, and there he is coming from 'round the side of the house. Anyway, he says to Willie Jay, "Hey, boy, what are you doing back here?" And I said, "He's not doing anything. You just go on home, Willie Jay! You just run right on home." Well, before he can move, Zackery comes up and knocks him once right across the face and then shoves him down the porch steps, causing him to skin up his elbow real bad on that hard concrete. Then he says, "Don't you ever come around here again, or I'll have them cut out your gizzard!" Well, Willie Jay starts crying, these tears come streaming down his face, then he gets up real quick and runs away with Dog following off after him. After that, I don't remember much too clearly; let's see . . . I went on into the living room, and I went right up to the davenport and opened the drawer where we keep the burglar gun . . . I took it out. Then I—I brought it up to my ear. That's right. I put it right inside my ear. Why, I was gonna shoot off my own head! That's what I was gonna do. Then I heard the back door slamming and suddenly, for some reason, I thought about mama . . . how she'd hung herself. And here I was about ready to shoot myself. Then I realized—that's right I realized how I didn't want to kill myself! And she—she probably didn't want to kill herself. She wanted to kill him, and I wanted to kill him, too. I wanted to kill Zackery, not myself 'cause I—I wanted to live! So I waited for him to come on into the living room. Then I held out the gun, and I pulled the trigger, aiming for his heart, but getting him in the stomach. [*After a pause.*] It's funny that I really did that.

MEG It's a good thing that you did. It's a damn good thing that you did.

BABE It was.

MEG Please, Babe, talk to Barnette Lloyd. Just talk to him and see if he can help.

BABE But how about Willie Jay?

MEG *[starting towards the phone]* Oh, he'll be all right. You just talk to that lawyer like you did to me. *[Looking at the number on the card, she begins dialing.]* See, 'cause he's gonna be on your side.

BABE No! Stop, Meg, stop! Don't call him up! Please don't call him up! You can't! It's too awful. *[She runs over and jerks the bottom half of the phone away from* MEG. MEG *stands, holding the receiver.]*

MEG Babe! *[*BABE *slams her half of the phone into the refrigerator.]*

BABE I just can't tell some stranger all about my personal life. I just can't.

MEG Well, hell, Babe; you're the one who said you wanted to live.

BABE That's right. I did. *[She takes the phone out of the refrigerator and hands it to* MEG.*]* Here's the other part of the phone. *[*BABE *moves to sit at the kitchen table.* MEG *takes the phone back to the counter. Babe, as she fishes a lemon out of her glass and begins sucking on it.]* Meg.

MEG What?

BABE I called the bakery. They're gonna have Lenny's cake ready first thing tomorrow morning. That's the earliest they can get it.

MEG All right.

BABE I told them to write on it, "Happy Birthday Lenny—A Day Late." That sound okay?

MEG *[at the phone]* It sounds nice.

BABE I ordered up the very largest size cake they have. I told them chocolate cake with white icing and red trim. Think she'll like that?

MEG *[dialing on the phone]* Yeah, I'm sure she will. She'll like it.

BABE I'm hoping.

Blackout
End of Act I

ACT II

[The lights go up on the kitchen. It is later that evening on the same day. MEG*'s suitcase has been moved upstairs.* BABE*'s saxophone has been taken out of the case and put together.* BABE *and* BARNETTE *are sitting at the kitchen table.* BARNETTE *is writing and re-checking notes with explosive intensity.* BABE, *who has changed into a casual shift, sits eating a bowl of oatmeal, slowly.]*

BARNETTE *[to himself]* Mmm-huh! Yes! I see. I see! Well, we can work on that! And of course, this is mere conjecture! Difficult, if not impossible, to prove. Ha! Yes. Yes, indeed. Indeed—

BABE Sure you don't want any oatmeal?

BARNETTE What? Oh, no. No, thank you. Let's see, ah, where were we?

BABE I just shot Zackery.

BARNETTE [*looking at his notes*] Right. Correct. You've just pulled the trigger.

BABE Tell me, do you think Willie Jay can stay out of all this?

BARNETTE Believe me, it is in our interest to keep him as far out of this as possible.

BABE Good.

BARNETTE [*throughout the following,* BARNETTE *stays glued to* BABE'S *every word*] All right, you've just shot one Zackery Botrelle, as a result of his continual physical and mental abuse—what happens now?

BABE Well, after I shot him, I put the gun down on the piano bench and then I went out into the kitchen and made up a pitcher of lemonade.

BARNETTE Lemonade?

BABE Yes, I was dying of thirst. My mouth was just as dry as a bone.

BARNETTE So in order to quench this raging thirst that was choking you dry and preventing any possibility of you uttering intelligible sounds or phrases, you went out to the kitchen and made up a pitcher of lemonade?

BABE Right. I made it just the way I like it with lots of sugar and lots of lemon—about ten lemons in all. Then I added two trays of ice and stirred it up with my wooden stirring spoon.

BARNETTE Then what?

BABE Then I drank three glasses, one right after the other. They were large glasses, about this tall. Then suddenly, my stomach kind of swoll all up. I guess what caused it was all that sour lemon.

BARNETTE Could be.

BABE Then what I did was . . . I wiped my mouth off with the back of my hand, like this . . . [*She demonstrates.*]

BARNETTE Hmmm.

BABE I did it to clear off all those little beads of water that had settled there.

BARNETTE I see.

BABE Then I called out to Zackery. I said, "Zackery, I've made some lemonade. Can you use a glass?"

BARNETTE Did he answer? Did you hear an answer?

BABE No. He didn't answer.

BARNETTE So, what'd you do?

BABE I poured him a glass anyway and took it out to him.

BARNETTE You took it out to the living room?

BABE I did. And there he was; lying on the rug. He was looking up at me trying to speak words. I said, "What? . . . Lemonade? . . . You don't want it? Would you like a Coke instead?" Then I got the idea, he was telling me to call on the phone for medical help. So I got on the phone and called up the hospital. I gave my name and address and I told them my husband was shot and he was lying on the rug and there was plenty of blood. [BABE *pauses a minute, as* BARNETTE *works frantically on his notes.*] I guess that's gonna look kinda bad.

BARNETTE What?

BABE Me fixing that lemonade, before I called the hospital.

BARNETTE Well, not . . . necessarily.

BABE I tell you, I think the reason I made up the lemonade, I mean besides the fact that my mouth was bone dry, was that I was afraid to call the authorities. I was afraid. I—I really think I was afraid they would see that I had tried to shoot Zackery, in fact, that I had shot him, and they would accuse me of possible murder and send me away to jail.

BARNETTE Well, that's understandable.

BABE I think so. I mean, in fact, that's what did happen. That's what is happening—'cause here I am just about ready to go right off to the Parchment Prison Farm. Yes, here I am just practically on the brink of utter doom. Why, I feel so all alone.

BARNETTE Now, now, look—Why, there's no reason for you to get yourself so all upset and worried. Please, don't. Please. [*They look at each other for a moment.*] You just keep filling in as much detailed information as you can about those incidents on the medical reports. That's all you need to think about. Don't you worry, Mrs. Botrelle, we're going to have a solid defense.

BABE Please, don't call me Mrs. Botrelle.

BARNETTE All right.

BABE My name's Becky. People in the family call me Babe; but my real name's Becky.

BARNETTE All right, Becky. [BARNETTE *and* BABE *stare at each other for a long moment.*]

BABE Are you sure you didn't go to Hazlehurst High?

BARNETTE No, I went away to a boarding school.

BABE Gosh, you sure do look familiar. You sure do.

BARNETTE Well, I—I doubt you'll remember, but I did meet you once.

BABE You did? When?

BARNETTE At the Christmas bazaar, year before last. You were selling cakes and cookies and . . . candy.

BABE Oh, yes! You bought the orange pound cake!

BARNETTE Right.

BABE Of course, and then we talked for a while. We talked about the Christmas angel.

BARNETTE You do remember.

BABE I remember it very well. You were even thinner then than you are now.

BARNETTE Well, I'm surprised. I'm certainly . . . surprised. [*The phone begins to ring.*]

BABE [*as she goes to answer the phone*] This is quite a coincidence! Don't you think it is! Why, it's almost a fluke. [*She answers the phone.*] Hello . . . Oh, hello, Lucille . . . Oh, he is? . . . Oh, he does? . . . Okay. Oh, Lucille, wait! Has Dog come back to the house? . . . Oh, I see . . . Okay. Okay. [*After a brief pause.*] Hello, Zackery? How are you doing? . . . Uh huh . . . uh huh . . . oh, I'm sorry . . . Please, don't scream . . . uh huh . . . uh huh . . . You want what? . . . No, I can't come up there now . . . Well, for one thing, I don't even have the car. Lenny and Meg are up at the hospital right now, visiting with Old Granddaddy . . . What? . . . Oh, really? . . . Oh, really? . . . Well, I've got me a lawyer that's over here right now, and he's building me up a solid defense! . . . Wait just a minute, I'll see. [*to* BARNETTE.] He wants to talk to you. He says he's got some blackening evidence that's gonna convict me of attempting to murder him on the first degree!

BARNETTE [*disgustedly*] Oh, bluff! He's bluffing! Here, hand me the phone. [*He takes the phone and becomes suddenly cool and suave.*] Hello, this is Mr. Barnette Lloyd speaking. I'm Mrs. . . . ah Becky's attorney . . . Why, certainly, Mr. Botrelle, I'd be more than glad to check out any pertinent information that you may have . . . Fine, then I'll be right over. Goodbye. [*He hangs up the phone.*]

BABE What did he say?

BARNETTE He wants me to come to see him at the hospital this evening. Says he's got some sort of evidence. Sounds highly suspect to me.

BABE Oooh! Didn't you just hate his voice? Doesn't he have the most awful voice! I just hate it! I can't bear to hear it!

BARNETTE Well, now—now, wait. Wait just a minute.

BABE What?

BARNETTE I have a solution. From now on I'll handle all communications between you two. You can simply refuse to speak with him.

BABE All right—I will. I'll do that.

BARNETTE [*starting to pack his briefcase*] Well, I'd better get over there and see just what he's got up his sleeve.

BABE [*after a pause*] Barnette.

BARNETTE Yes?

BABE What's the personal vendetta about? You know, the one you have to settle with Zackery.

BARNETTE Oh, it's—it's complicated. It's a very complicated matter.

BABE I see.

BARNETTE The major thing he did was to ruin my father's life. He took away his job, his home, his health, his respectability. I don't like to talk about it.

BABE I'm sorry. I just wanted to say—I hope you win it. I hope you win your vendetta.

BARNETTE Thank you.

BABE I think it's an important thing that a person could win a life long vendetta.

BARNETTE Yes. Well, I'd better be going.

BABE All right. Let me know what happens.

BARNETTE I will. I'll get back to you right away.

BABE Thanks.

BARNETTE Goodbye, Becky.

BABE Goodbye, Barnette. [BARNETTE *exits.* BABE *looks around the room for a moment, then goes over to her white suitcase and opens it up. She takes out her pink hair curlers and a brush. She begins brushing her hair.*] Goodbye, Becky. Goodbye, Barnette. Goodbye Becky. Oooh. [LENNY *enters. She is fuming.* BABE *is rolling her hair throughout most of the following scene.*] Lenny, hi!

LENNY Hi.

BABE Where's Meg?

LENNY Oh, she had to go by the store and pick some things up. I don't know what.

BABE Well, how's Old Granddaddy?

LENNY [*as she picks up Babe's bowl of oatmeal*] He's fine. Wonderful! Never been better!

BABE Lenny, what's wrong? What's the matter?

LENNY It's Meg! I could just wring her neck! I could just wring it!

BABE Why? Wha'd she do?

LENNY She lied! She sat in that hospital room and shamelessly lied to Old Granddaddy. She went on and on telling such untrue stories and lies.

BABE Well, what? What did she say?

LENNY Well, for one thing she said she was gonna have a RCA record coming out with her picture on the cover, eating pineapples under a palm tree.

BABE Well, gosh, Lenny, maybe she is! Don't you think she really is?

LENNY Babe, she sat here this very afternoon and told me how all that she's done this whole year is work as a clerk for a dog food company.

BABE Oh, shoot. I'm disappointed.

LENNY And then she goes on to say that she'll be appearing on the "Johnny Carson Show" in two weeks' time. Two weeks' time! Why, Old Granddaddy's got a TV set right in his room. Imagine what a letdown it's gonna be.

BABE Why, mercy me.

LENNY [*slamming the coffeepot on*] Oh, and she told him the reason she didn't use the money he sent her to come home Christmas was that she was right in the middle of making a huge multi-million-dollar motion picture and was just under too much pressure.

BABE My word!

LENNY The movie's coming out this spring. It's called, "Singing in a Shoe Factory." But she only has a small leading role—not a large leading role.

BABE [*laughing*] For heaven's sake—

LENNY I'm sizzling. Oh, I just can't help it! I'm sizzling!

BABE Sometimes Meg does such strange things.

LENNY [*slowly, as she picks up the opened box of birthday candy*] Who ate this candy?

BABE [*hesitantly*] Meg.

LENNY My one birthday present, and look what she does! Why, she's taken one little bite out of each piece and then just put it back in! Ooh! That's just like her! That is just like her!

BABE Lenny, please—

LENNY I can't help it! It gets me mad! It gets me upset! Why, Meg's always run wild—she started smoking and drinking when she was fourteen years old, she never made good grades—never made her own bed! But somehow she always seemed to get what she wanted. She's the one who got singing and dancing lessons; and a store-bought dress to wear to her senior prom. Why do you remember how Meg always got to wear twelve jingle bells on her petticoats, while we were only allowed to wear three apiece? Why?! Why should Old Grandmama let her sew twelve golden jingle bells on her petticoats and us only three!!!

BABE [*who has heard all this before*] I don't know!! Maybe she didn't jingle them as much!

LENNY I can't help it! It gets me mad! I resent it. I do.

BABE Oh, don't resent Meg. Things have been hard for Meg. After all, she was the one who found Mama.

LENNY Oh, I know; she's the one who found Mama. But that's always been the excuse.

BABE But, I tell you, Lenny, after it happened, Meg started doing all sorts of these strange things.

LENNY She did? Like what?

BABE Like things I never wanted to tell you about.

LENNY What sort of things?

BABE Well, for instance, back when we used to go over to the library, Meg would spend all her time reading and looking through this old, black book called *Diseases of the Skin*. It was full of the most sickening pictures you'd ever seen. Things like rotting-away noses and eyeballs drooping off down the sides of people's faces and scabs and sores and eaten-away places all over *all* parts of people's bodies.

LENNY [*trying to pour her coffee*] Babe, please! That's enough.

BABE Anyway, she'd spend hours and hours just forcing herself to look through this book. Why, it was the same way she'd force herself to look at the poster of crippled children stuck up in the window at Dixieland Drugs. You know, that one where they want you to give a dime. Meg would stand there and stare at their eyes and look at the braces on their little crippled-up legs—then she'd purposely go and spend her dime on a double scoop ice cream cone and eat it all down. She'd say to me. "See, I can stand it. I can stand it. Just look how I'm gonna be able to stand it."

LENNY That's awful.

BABE She said she was afraid of being a weak person. I guess 'cause she cried in bed every night for such a long time.

LENNY Goodness mercy. [*After a pause.*] Well, I suppose you'd have to be a pretty hard person to be able to do what she did to Doc Porter.

BABE [*exasperated*] Oh, shoot! It wasn't Meg's fault that hurricane wiped Biloxi away. I never understood why people were blaming all that on Meg—just because that roof fell in and crunched Doc's leg. It wasn't her fault.

LENNY Well, it was Meg who refused to evacuate. Jim Craig and some of Doc's other friends were all down there and they kept trying to get everyone to evacuate. But Meg refused. She wanted to stay on because she thought a hurricane would be—oh, I don't know—a lot of fun. Then everyone says she baited Doc into staying with her. She said she'd marry him if he'd stay.

BABE [*taken aback by this new information*] Well, he has a mind of his own. He could have gone.

LENNY But he didn't. 'Cause . . . 'cause he loved her. And then after the roof caved, and they got Doc to the high school gym, Meg just left. She just left him there to leave for California—'cause of her career, she says. I think it was a shameful thing to do. It took almost a year for his leg to heal and after that he gave up his medical career altogether. He said he was tired of hospitals. It's such a sad thing. Everyone always knew he was gonna be a doctor. We've called him Doc for years.

BABE I don't know. I guess, I don't have any room to talk; 'cause I just don't know. [*Pause.*] Gosh, you look so tired.

LENNY I feel tired.

BABE They say women need a lot of iron . . . so they won't feel tired.

LENNY What's got iron in it? Liver?

BABE Yeah, liver's got it. And vitamin pills.

[*After a moment,* MEG *enters. She carries a bottle of bourbon that is already minus a few slugs and a newspaper. She is wearing black boots, a dark dress, and a hat. The room goes silent.*]

MEG Hello.

BABE [*fooling with her hair*] Hi, Meg. [LENNY *quietly sips her coffee.*]

MEG [*handing the newspaper to* BABE] Here's your paper.

BABE Thanks. [*She opens it.*] Oh, here it is, right on the front page. [MEG *lights a cigarette.*] Where's the scissors, Lenny?

LENNY Look in there in the ribbon drawer.

BABE Okay. [BABE *gets the scissors and glue out of the drawer and slowly begins cutting out the newspaper article.*]

MEG [*after a few moments, filled only with the snipping of scissors*] All right!—I lied! I lied! I couldn't help it . . . these stories just came pouring out of my mouth! When I saw how tired and sick Old Granddaddy'd gotten—they just flew out! All I wanted was to see him smiling and happy. I just wasn't going to sit there and look at him all miserable and sick and sad! I just wasn't!

BABE Oh, Meg, he is sick, isn't he—

MEG Why, he's gotten all white and milky—he's almost evaporated!

LENNY [*gasping and turning to* MEG] But still you shouldn't have lied! It just was wrong for you to tell such lies—

MEG Well, I know that! Don't you think I know that? I hate myself when I lie for that old man. I do. I feel so weak. And then I have to go and do at least three or four things that I know he'd despise just to get even with that miserable, old, bossy man!

LENNY Oh, Meg, please, don't talk so about Old Granddaddy! It sounds so ungrateful. Why, he went out of his way to make a home for us; to treat us like we were his very own children. All he ever wanted was the best for us. That's all he ever wanted.

MEG Well, I guess it was; but sometimes I wonder what we wanted.

BABE [*taking the newspaper article and glue over to her suitcase*] Well, one thing I wanted was a team of white horses to ride Mama's coffin to her grave. That's one thing I wanted. [LENNY *and* MEG *exchange looks.*] Lenny, did you remember to pack my photo album?

LENNY It's down there at the bottom, under all that night stuff.

BABE Oh, I found it.

LENNY Really, Babe, I don't understand why you have to put in the articles that are about the unhappy things in your life. Why would you want to remember them?

BABE [*pasting the article in*] I don't know. I just like to keep an accurate record, I suppose. There. [*She begins flipping through the book.*] Look, here's a picture of me when I got married.

MEG Let's see.

[BABE *brings the photo album over to the table. They all look at it.*]

LENNY My word, you look about twelve years old.

BABE I was just eighteen.

MEG You're smiling, Babe. Were you happy then?

BABE [*laughing*] Well, I was drunk on champagne punch. I remember that! [*They turn the page.*]

LENNY Oh, there's Meg singing at Greeny's!

BABE Oooh, I wish you were still singing at Greeny's! I wish you were!

LENNY You're so beautiful!

BABE Yes, you are. You're beautiful.

MEG Oh, stop! I'm not—

LENNY Look. Meg's starting to cry.

BABE Oh, Meg—

MEG I'm not—

BABE Quick, better turn the page: we don't want Meg crying—[*She flips the pages.*]

LENNY Why, it's Daddy.

MEG Where'd you get that picture, Babe? I thought she burned them all.

BABE Ah, I just found it around.

LENNY What does it say here? What's that inscription?

BABE It says "Jimmy—clowning at the beach—1952."

LENNY Well, will you look at that smile.

MEG Jesus, those white teeth—turn the page, will you; we can't do any worse than this! [*They turn the page. The room goes silent.*]

BABE It's Mama and the cat.

LENNY Oh, turn the page—

BABE That old yellow cat. You know, I bet if she hadn't of hung that old cat along with her, she wouldn't have gotten all that national coverage.

MEG [*after a moment, hopelessly*] Why are we talking about this?

LENNY Meg's right. It was so sad. It was awfully sad. I remember how we all three just sat up on that bed the day of the service all dressed up in our black velveteen suits crying the whole morning long.

BABE We used up one whole big box of Kleenexes.

MEG And then Old Granddaddy came in and said he was gonna take us out to breakfast. Remember, he told us not to cry anymore 'cause he was gonna take us out to get banana splits for breakfast.

BABE That's right—banana splits for breakfast!

MEG Why, Lenny was fourteen years old and he thought that would make it all better—

BABE Oh, I remember he said for us to eat all we wanted. I think I ate about five! He kept shoving them down us!

MEG God, we were so sick!

LENNY Oh, we were!

MEG [*laughing*] Lenny's face turned green—

LENNY I was just as sick as a dog!

BABE Old Grandmama was furious!

LENNY Oh, she was!

MEG The thing about Old Granddaddy is he keeps trying to make us happy and we end up getting stomach aches and turning green and throwing up in the flower arrangements.

BABE Oh, that was me! I threw up in the flowers! Oh, no! How embarrassing!

LENNY [*laughing*] Oh, Babe—

BABE [*hugging her sisters*] Oh, Lenny! Oh, Meg!

MEG Oh, Babe! Oh, Lenny! It's so good to be home!

LENNY Hey, I have an idea—

BABE What?

LENNY Let's play cards!!

BABE Oh, let's do!

MEG All right!

LENNY Oh, good! It'll be just like when we used to sit around the table playing hearts all night long.

BABE I know! [*getting up*] I'll fix us up some popcorn and hot chocolate—

MEG [*getting up*] Here, let me get out that old black popcorn pot.

LENNY [*getting up*] Oh, yes! Now, let's see, I think I have a deck of cards around here somewhere.

BABE Gosh, I hope I remember all the rules—Are hearts good or bad?

MEG Bad, I think. Aren't they, Lenny?

LENNY That's right. Hearts are bad, but the Black Sister is the worst of all—

MEG Oh, that's right! And the Black Sister is the Queen of Spades.

BABE [*figuring it out*] And spades are the black cards that aren't the puppy dog feet?

MEG [*thinking a moment*] Right. And she counts a lot of points.

BABE And points are bad?

MEG Right. Here, I'll get some paper so we can keep score.

[*The phone begins to ring.*]

LENNY Oh, here they are!

MEG I'll get it—

LENNY Why, look at these cards! They're years old!

BABE Oh, let me see!

MEG Hello . . . No, this is Meg Magrath . . . Doc. How are you? . . . Well, good . . . You're where? . . . Well, sure. Come on over . . . Sure, I'm sure. Yeah, come right on over . . . All right. Bye. [*She hangs up.*] That was Doc Porter. He's down the street at Al's Grill. He's gonna come on over.

LENNY He is?

MEG He said he wanted to see me.

LENNY Oh. [*after a pause*] Well, do you still want to play?

MEG No, I don't think so.

LENNY All right. [LENNY *starts to shuffle the cards, as* MEG *brushes her hair.*] You know, it's really not much fun playing Hearts with only two people.

MEG I'm sorry; maybe after Doc leaves, I'll join you.

LENNY I know; maybe Doc'll want to play, then we can have a game of bridge.

MEG I don't think so. Doc never liked cards. Maybe we'll just go out somewhere.

LENNY [*putting down the cards;* BABE *picks them up*] Meg—

MEG What?

LENNY Well, Doc's married now.

MEG I know. You told me.

LENNY Oh. Well, as long as you know that. [*Pause*] As long as you know that.

MEG [*still primping*] Yes, I know. She made the pot.

BABE How many cards do I deal out?

LENNY [*leaving the table*] Excuse me.

BABE All of 'em, or what?

LENNY Ah, Meg? Could I—could I ask you something? [BABE *proceeds to deal out all the cards.*]

MEG What?

LENNY I just wanted to ask you—

MEG What?

[*Unable to go on with what she really wants to say,* LENNY *runs up and picks up the box of candy.*]

LENNY Well, just why did you take one little bite out of each piece of candy in this box and then just put it back in?

MEG Oh. Well, I was looking for the ones with nuts.

LENNY The ones with nuts.

MEG Yeah.

LENNY But there are none with nuts. It's a box of assorted cremes—all it has in it are cremes!

MEG Oh.

LENNY Why couldn't you just read the box? It says right here. "Assorted Cremes," not nuts! Besides this was a birthday present to me! My one and only birthday present; my only one!

MEG I'm sorry. I'll get you another box.

LENNY I don't want another box. That's not the point!

MEG What is the point?

LENNY I don't know; it's—it's—You have no respect for other people's property! You just take whatever you want. You just take it!

Why, remember how you had layers and layers of jingle bells sewed onto your petticoats while Babe and I only had three apiece?!

MEG Oh, God! She's starting up about those stupid jingle bells!

LENNY Well, it's an example! A specific example of how you always got what you wanted!

MEG Oh, come on, Lenny, you're just upset because Doc called.

LENNY Who said anything about Doc? Do you think I'm upset about Doc? Why, I've long since given up worrying about you and all your men.

MEG [*turning in anger*] Look, I know I've had too many men. Believe me, I've had way too many men. But it's not my fault you haven't had any—or maybe just that one from Memphis.

LENNY [*stopping*] What one from Memphis?

MEG [*slowly*] The one Babe told me about. From the—club.

LENNY Babe!!!

BABE Meg!!!

LENNY How could you?!! I asked you not to tell anyone! I'm so ashamed! How could you?! Who else have you told? Did you tell anyone else?

BABE [*overlapping, to* MEG] Why'd you have to open your big mouth?!

MEG [*overlapping*] How am I supposed to know? You never said not to tell!

BABE Can't you use your head just for once?!! [*Then to* LENNY.] No, I never told anyone else. Somehow it just slipped out to Meg. Really, it just flew out of my mouth—

LENNY What do you two have—wings on your tongues?

BABE I'm sorry, Lenny. Really sorry.

LENNY I'll just never, never, never be able to trust you again—

MEG [*furiously, coming to* BABE*'s defense*] Oh, for heaven's sake, Lenny, we were just worried about you! We wanted to find a way to make you happy!

LENNY Happy! Happy! I'll never be happy!

MEG Well, not if you keep living your life as Old Granddaddy's nursemaid—

BABE Meg, shut up!

MEG I can't help it! I just know that the reason you stopped seeing this man from Memphis was because of Old Granddaddy.

LENNY What—Babe didn't tell you the rest of the story—

MEG Oh, she said it was something about your shrunken ovary.

BABE Meg!!

LENNY Babe!!

BABE I just mentioned it!

MEG But I don't believe a word of that story!

LENNY Oh, I don't care what you believe! It's so easy for you—you always have men falling in love with you! But I have this underdeveloped ovary and I can't have children and my hair is falling out in the comb—so what man can love me?! What man's gonna love me?

MEG A lot of men!

BABE Yeah, a lot! A whole lot!

MEG Old Granddaddy's the only one who seems to think otherwise.

LENNY 'Cause he doesn't want to see me hurt! He doesn't want to see me rejected and humiliated.

MEG Oh, come on now, Lenny, don't be so pathetic! God, you make me angry when you just stand there looking so pathetic! Just tell me, did you really ask the man from Memphis? Did you actually ask that man from Memphis all about it?

LENNY [*breaking apart*] No; I didn't. I didn't. Because I just didn't want him not to want me—

MEG Lenny—

LENNY [*furious*] Don't talk to me anymore! Don't talk to me! I think I'm gonna vomit—I just hope all this doesn't cause me to vomit! [LENNY *exits up the stairs sobbing.*]

MEG See! See! She didn't even ask him about her stupid ovary! She just broke it all off 'cause of Old Granddaddy! What a jackass fool!

BABE Oh, Meg, shut up! Why do you have to make Lenny cry? I just hate it when you make Lenny cry! [BABE *runs up the stairs.*] Lenny! Oh, Lenny—[MEG *takes a long sigh and goes to get a cigarette and a drink.*]

MEG I feel like hell. [MEG *sits in despair—smoking and drinking bourbon. There is a knock at the back door.* MEG *starts. She brushes her hair out of her face and goes to answer the door. It is* DOC.]

DOC Hello, Meggy.

MEG Well, Doc. Well, it's Doc.

DOC [*after a pause*] You're home, Meggy.

MEG Yeah; I've come home. I've come on home to see about Babe.

DOC And how's Babe?

MEG Oh, fine. Well, fair. She's fair. [DOC *nods.*] Hey, do you want a drink?

DOC Whatcha got?

MEG Bourbon.

DOC Oh, don't tell me Lenny's stocking bourbon.

MEG Well, no. I've been to the store. [MEG *gets him a glass and pours them each a drink. They click glasses.*] So, how's your wife?

DOC She's fine.

MEG I hear ya got two kids.

DOC Yeah. Yeah, I got two kids.

MEG A boy and a girl.

DOC That's right, Meggy, a boy and a girl.

MEG That's what you always said you wanted, wasn't it? A boy and a girl.

DOC Is that what I said?

MEG I don't know. I thought it's what you said. [*They finish their drinks in silence.*]

DOC Whose cot?

MEG Lenny's. She's taken to sleeping in the kitchen.

DOC Ah. Where is Lenny?

MEG She's in the upstairs room. I made her cry. Babe's up there seeing to her.

DOC How'd you make her cry?

MEG I don't know. Eating her birthday candy; talking on about her boyfriend from Memphis. I don't know. I'm upset about it. She's got a lot on her. Why can't I keep my mouth shut?

DOC I don't know, Meggy. Maybe it's because you don't want to.

MEG Maybe. [*They smile at each other.* MEG *pours each of them another drink.*]

DOC Well, it's been a long time.

MEG It has been a long time.

DOC Let's see—when was the last time we saw each other?

MEG I can't quite recall.

DOC Wasn't it in Biloxi?

MEG Ah, Biloxi. I believe so.

DOC And wasn't there a—a hurricane going on at the time?

MEG Was there?

DOC Yes, there was, one hell of a hurricane. Camille, I believe they called it Hurricane Camille.

MEG Yes, now I remember. It was a beautiful hurricane.

DOC We had a time down there. We had quite a time. Drinking vodka, eating oysters on the half shell, dancing all night long. And the wind was blowing.

MEG Oh, God, was it blowing.

DOC Goddamn, was it blowing.

MEG There never has been such a wind blowing.

DOC Oh, God, Meggy. Oh, God.

MEG I know, Doc. It was my fault to leave you. I was crazy. I thought I was choking. I felt choked!

DOC I felt like a fool.

MEG No.

DOC I just kept on wondering why.

MEG I don't know why . . . 'Cause I didn't want to care. I don't know. I did care though. I did.

DOC [*after a pause*] Ah, hell—[*He pours them both another drink.*] Are you still singing those sad songs?

MEG No.

DOC Why not?

MEG I don't know, Doc. Things got worse for me. After a while, I just couldn't sing anymore. I tell you, I had one hell of a time over Christmas.

DOC What do you mean?

MEG I went nuts. I went insane. Ended up in L.A. County Hospital. Psychiatric ward.

DOC Hell. Ah, hell, Meggy. What happened?

MEG I don't really know. I couldn't sing anymore; so I lost my job. And I had a bad toothache. I had this incredibly painful toothache. For days I had it, but I wouldn't do anything about it. I just stayed inside my apartment. All I could do was sit around in chairs, chewing on my fingers. Then one afternoon I ran screaming out of the apartment with all my money and jewelry and valuables and tried to stuff it all into one of those March of Dimes collection boxes. That was when they nabbed me. Sad story. Meg goes mad. [DOC *stares at her for a long moment. He pours them both another drink.*]

DOC [*after quite a pause*] There's a moon out.

MEG Is there?

DOC Wanna go take a ride in my truck and look out at the moon?

MEG I don't know, Doc. I don't wanna start up. It'll be too hard, if we start up.

DOC Who says we're gonna start up? We're just gonna look at the moon. For one night just you and me are gonna go for a ride in the country and look out at the moon.

MEG One night?

DOC Right.

MEG Look out at the moon?

DOC You got it.

MEG Well . . . all right. [*She gets up.*]

DOC Better take your coat. [*He helps her into her coat.*] And the bottle—[*He takes the bottle.* MEG *picks up the glasses.*] Forget the glasses—

MEG [*laughing*] Yeah—forget the glasses. Forget the goddamn glasses.

[MEG *shuts off the kitchen lights, leaving the kitchen lit by only a dim light over the kitchen sink.* MEG *and* DOC *leave. After a moment,* BABE *comes down the stairs in her slip.*]

BABE Meg—Meg?

[*She stands for a moment in the moonlight wearing only a slip. She sees her saxophone then moves to pick it up. She plays a few shrieking notes. There is a loud knock on the back door.*]

BARNETTE'S VOICE Becky! Becky, is that you? [BABE *puts down the saxophone.*]

BABE Just a minute. I'm coming. [*She puts a raincoat on over her slip and goes to answer the door. It is* BARNETTE.] Hello, Barnette. Come on in. [BARNETTE *comes in. He is troubled but is making a great effort to hide the fact.*]

BARNETTE Thank you.

BABE What is it?

BARNETTE I've, ah, I've just come from seeing Zackery at the hospital.

BABE Oh?

BARNETTE It seems . . . Well, it seems his sister, Lucille, was somewhat suspicious.

BABE Suspicious?

BARNETTE About you?

BABE Me?

BARNETTE She hired a private detective, he took these pictures. [*He hands* BABE *a small envelope containing several photographs.* BABE *opens the envelope and begins looking at the pictures in stunned silence.*] They were taken about two weeks ago. It seems, she wasn't going to show them to Botrelle straight away. She, ah, wanted to wait till the time was right. [*The phone rings one and a half times.* BARNETTE *glances uneasily towards the phone.*] Becky? [*The phone stops ringing.*]

BABE [*looking up at* BARNETTE, *slowly*] These are pictures of Willie Jay and me . . . out in the garage.

BARNETTE [*looking away*] I know.

BABE You looked at these pictures?

BARNETTE Yes—I—well . . . professionally, I looked at them.

BABE Oh, mercy. Oh, mercy! We can burn them, can't we? Quick, we can burn them—

BARNETTE It won't do any good. They have the negatives.

BABE [*holding the pictures, as she bangs herself hopelessly into the stove, table, cabinets, etc.*] Oh, no; oh, no; oh, no! Oh, no—

BARNETTE There—there, now—there—

LENNY'S VOICE Babe? Are you all right? Babe—

BABE [*hiding the pictures*] What? I'm all right. Go on back to bed. [LENNY *comes down the stairs. She is wearing a coat and wiping white night cream off of her face with a wash rag.*]

LENNY What's the matter? What's going on down here?

BABE Nothin! [*Then as she begins dancing ballet style around the room.*] We're—we're just dancing. We were just dancing around down here. [*Signaling to* BARNETTE *to dance.*]

LENNY Well, you'd better get your shoes on, 'cause we've got—

BABE All right, I will! That's a good idea! [*As she goes to get her shoes, she hides the pictures.*] Now, you go on back to bed. It's pretty late and—

LENNY Babe, will you listen a minute—

BABE [*holding up her shoes*] I'm putting 'em on—

LENNY That was the hospital that just called. We've got to get over there. Old Granddaddy had himself another stroke.

BABE Oh. All right. My shoes are on. [*She stands. They all look at each other as the lights blackout.*]

End of Act II

ACT III

[*The lights go up on the empty kitchen. It is the following morning. After a few moments,* BABE *enters from the back door. She is carrying her hair curlers in her hands. She goes and lies down on the cot. A few moments later,* LENNY *enters. She is tired and weary.* CHICK'S *voice is heard.*]

CHICK'S VOICE Lenny! Oh, Lenny! [LENNY *turns to the door.* CHICK *enters energetically.*] Well . . . how is he?

LENNY He's stabilized; they say for now his functions are all stabilized.

CHICK Well, is he still in the coma?

LENNY Uh huh.

CHICK Hmmm. So do they think he's gonna be . . . passing on?

LENNY He may be. He doesn't look so good. They said they'd phone us if there were any sudden changes.

CHICK Well, it seems to me we'd better get busy phoning on the phone ourselves. [*Removing a list from her pocket.*] Now I've made out this list of all the people we need to notify about Old Granddaddy's predicament. I'll phone half if you'll phone half.

LENNY But—what would we say?

CHICK Just tell them the facts; that Old Granddaddy's got himself in a coma, and it could be, he doesn't have long for this world.

LENNY I—I don't know. I don't feel like phoning.

CHICK Why, Lenora, I'm surprised, how can you be this way? I went to all the trouble of making up the list. And I offered to phone half of the people on it, even though I'm only one-fourth of the granddaughters. I mean, I just get tired of doing more than my fair share, when people like Meg can suddenly just disappear to where they can't even be reached in case of emergency!

LENNY All right; give me the list. I'll phone half.

CHICK Well, don't do it just to suit me.

LENNY [*she wearily tears the list into two halves*] I'll phone these here.

CHICK [*taking her half of the list*] Fine then. Suit yourself. Oh, wait—let me call Sally Bell. I need to talk to her anyway.

LENNY All right.

CHICK So you add Great Uncle Spark Dude to your list.

LENNY Okay.

CHICK Fine. Well, I've got to get on back home and see to the kids.

It is gonna be an uphill struggle till I can find someone to replace that good-for-nothing Annie May Jenkins. Well, you let me know if you hear anymore.

LENNY All right.

CHICK Goodbye, Rebecca. I said goodbye. [BABE *blows her sax.* CHICK *starts to exit in a flurry then pauses to add:*] And you really ought to try to get that phoning done before twelve noon. [CHICK *exits.*]

LENNY [*after a long pause*] Babe, I feel bad. I feel real bad.

BABE Why, Lenny?

LENNY Because yesterday I—I wished it.

BABE You wished what?

LENNY I wished that Old Granddaddy would be put out of his pain. I wished on one of my birthday candles. I did. And now he's in this coma, and they say he's feeling no pain.

BABE Well, when did you have a cake yesterday? I don't remember you having any cake.

LENNY Well, I didn't . . . have a cake. But I just blew out the candles anyway.

BABE Oh. Well, those birthday wishes don't count unless you have a cake.

LENNY They don't?

BABE No. A lot of times they don't even count when you do have a cake. It just depends.

LENNY Depends on what?

BABE On how deep your wish is, I suppose.

LENNY Still, I just wish I hadn't of wished it. Gosh, I wonder when Meg's coming home.

BABE Should be soon.

LENNY I just wish we wouldn't fight all the time. I don't like it when we do.

BABE Me, neither.

LENNY I guess it hurts my feelings, a little, the way Old Granddaddy's always put so much stock in Meg and all her singing talent. I think I've been, well, envious of her 'cause I can't seem to do too much.

BABE Why, sure you can.

LENNY I can?

BABE Sure. You just have to put your mind to it; that's all. It's like how I went out and bought that saxophone, just hoping I'd be able to attend music school and start up my own career. I just went out and did it. Just on hope. Of course, now it looks like . . . Well, it just doesn't look like things are gonna work out for me. But I know they would for you.

LENNY Well, they'll work out for you, too.

BABE I doubt it.

LENNY Listen, I heard up at the hospital that Zackery's already in fair condition. They say soon he'll probably be able to walk and everything.

BABE Yeah. And life sure can be miserable.

LENNY Well, I know, 'cause—day before yesterday, Billy Boy was struck down by lightning.

BABE He was?

LENNY [*nearing sobs*] Yeah. He was struck dead.

BABE [*crushed*] Life sure can be miserable.

[*They sit together for several moments in morbid silence.* MEG *is heard singing a loud happy song. She suddenly enters through the dining room door. She is exuberant! Her hair is a mess and the heel of one shoe has broken off. She is laughing radiantly and limping as she sings into the broken heel.*]

MEG [*spotting her sisters*] Good morning! Good morning! Oh, it's a wonderful morning! I tell you, I am surprised I feel this good. I should feel like hell. By all accounts. I should feel like utter hell! [*She is looking for the glue.*] Where's that glue? This damn heel has broken off my shoe. La, la, la, la, la! Ah, here it is! Now let me just get these shoes off. Zip, zip, zip, zip, zip! Well, what's wrong with you two? My God, you look like doom! [BABE *and* LENNY *stare helplessly at* MEG.] Oh. I know, you're mad at me 'cause I stayed out all night long. Well: I did.

LENNY No, we're—we're not mad at you. We're just . . . depressed. [*She starts to sob.*]

MEG Oh, Lenny, listen to me, now, everything's all right with Doc. I mean nothing happened. Well, actually a lot did happen, but it didn't come to anything. Not because of me, I'm afraid. [*Smearing glue on her heel.*] I mean, I was out there thinking. "What will I say when he begs me to run away with him? Will I have pity on his wife and those two half-Yankee children? I mean, can I sacrifice their happiness for mine? Yes! Oh, yes! Yes, I can!" But . . . he didn't ask me. He didn't even want to ask me. I could tell by this certain look in his eyes that he didn't even want to ask me. Why aren't I miserable! Why aren't I morbid! I should be humiliated! Devastated! Maybe these feelings are coming—I don't know. But for now it was . . . just such fun. I'm happy. I realized I could care about someone. I could want someone. And I sang! I sang all night long! I sang right up into the trees! But not for Old Granddaddy. None of it was to please Old Granddaddy! [LENNY *and* BABE *look at each other.*]

BABE Ah, Meg—

MEG What—

BABE Well, it's just—It's . . .

LENNY It's about Old Granddaddy—

MEG Oh, I know; I know. I told him all those stupid lies. Well, I'm gonna go right over there this morning and tell him the truth. I mean every horrible thing. I don't care if he wants to hear it or not.

He's just gonna have to take me like I am. And if he can't take it, if it sends him into a coma, that's just too damn bad!

[BABE *and* LENNY *look at each other;* BABE *cracks a smile.* LENNY *cracks a smile.*]

BABE You're too late—Ha, ha ha! [*They both break up laughing.*]

LENNY Oh, stop! Please! Ha, ha, ha!

MEG What is it! What's so funny?

BABE [*still laughing*] It's not—It's not funny!

LENNY [*still laughing*] No, it's not! It's not a bit funny!

MEG Well, what is it then? What?

BABE [*trying to calm down*] Well, it's just—it's just—

MEG What?

BABE Well, Old Granddaddy—he—he's in a coma! [BABE *and* LENNY *break up laughing.*]

MEG He's what?

BABE [*shrieking*] In a coma!

MEG My God! That's not funny!

BABE [*calming down*] I know. I know. For some reason it just struck us as funny.

LENNY I'm sorry. It's—it's not funny. It's sad. It's very sad. We've been up all night long.

BABE We're really tired.

MEG Well, my God. How is he? Is he gonna live?

[BABE *and* LENNY *look at each other.*]

BABE They don't think so! [*They both break up again*]

LENNY Oh, I don't know why we're laughing like this. We're just sick! We're just awful!

BABE We are—we're awful!

LENNY [*as she collects herself*] Oh, good; now I feel bad. Now, I feel like crying. I do; I feel like crying.

BABE Me, too. Me, too.

MEG Well, you've gotten me depressed!

LENNY I'm sorry. I'm sorry. It, ah, happened last night. He had another stroke. [*They laugh again.*]

MEG I see.

LENNY But he's stabilized now. [*She chokes up once more.*]

MEG That's good. You two okay? [BABE *and* LENNY *nod.*] You look like you need some rest. [BABE *and* LENNY *nod again.* MEG *goes on, about her heel.*] I hope that'll stay. [MEG *puts the top on the glue. A realization*—] Oh, of course, now I won't be able to tell him the truth about all those lies I told. I mean, finally, I get my wits about me, and he conks out. It's just like him. Babe, can I wear your slippers till this glue dries?

BABE Sure.

LENNY [*after a pause*] Things sure are gonna be different around here . . . when Old Granddaddy dies. Well, not for you two really, but for me.

BABE [*depressed*] Yeah. It'll work out.

LENNY I hope so. I'm afraid of being here all by myself. All alone.

MEG Well, you don't have to be alone. Maybe Babe'll move back in here.

[LENNY *looks at* BABE *hopefully.*]

BABE No; I don't think I'll be living here.

MEG [*realizing her mistake*] Well, anyway, you're your own woman. Invite some people over. Have some parties. Go out with strange men.

LENNY I don't know any strange men.

MEG Well you know that Charlie.

LENNY [*shaking her head*] Not anymore.

MEG Why not?

LENNY [*breaking down*] I told him we should never see each other again.

MEG Well; if you told him, you can just untell him.

LENNY Oh, no I couldn't. I'd feel like a fool.

MEG Oh, that's not a good enough reason! All people in love feel like fools. Don't they, Babe?

BABE Sure.

MEG Look, why don't you give him a call right now? See how things stand?

LENNY Oh, no! I'd be too scared—

MEG But what harm could it possibly do? I mean, it's not gonna make things any worse than this never seeing him again, at all, forever.

LENNY I suppose that's true.

MEG Of course it is; so call him up! Take a chance, will you? Just take some sort of chance!

LENNY You think I should?

MEG Of course! You've got to try—You do! [LENNY *looks over at* BABE.]

BABE You do, Lenny—I think you do.

LENNY Really? Really, really?

MEG Yes! Yes!

BABE You should!

LENNY All right. I will! I will!

MEG Oh, good!

BABE Good!

LENNY I'll call him right now, while I've got my confidence up!

MEG Have you got the number?

LENNY Uh huh. But, ah, I think I wanna call him upstairs. It'll be more private.

MEG Ah, good idea.

LENNY I'm just gonna go on, and call him up; and see what happens—[*She has started up the stairs.*] Wish me good luck!

MEG Good luck!

BABE Good luck, Lenny!

LENNY Thanks.

[LENNY *gets almost out of sight, when the phone begins to ring. She stops,* MEG *picks up the phone.*]

MEG Hello? [*Then in a whisper.*] Oh, thank you very much . . . Yes, I will. 'Bye, 'bye.

LENNY Who was it?

MEG Wrong number. They wanted Weed's Body Shop.

LENNY Oh. Well, I'll be right back down in a minute. [LENNY *exits.*]

MEG [*after a moment, whispering to* BABE] That was the bakery; Lenny's cake is ready!

BABE [*who has become increasingly depressed*] Oh.

MEG I think I'll sneak on down to the corner and pick it up. [*She starts to leave.*]

BABE Meg—

MEG What?

BABE Nothing.

MEG You okay? [BABE *shakes her head.*] What is it?

BABE It's just—

MEG What?

[BABE *gets up and goes to her suitcase. She opens it and removes the envelope containing the photographs.*]

BABE Here. Take a look.

MEG [*taking the envelope*] What is it?

BABE It's some evidence Zackery's collected against me. Looks like my goose is cooked. [MEG *opens the envelope and looks at the photographs.*]

MEG My God. it's—it's you and . . . is *that* Willie Jay?

BABE Yeh.

MEG Well, he certainly *has* grown. You were right about that. My, oh, my.

BABE Please don't tell Lenny. She'd hate me.

MEG I won't. I won't tell Lenny. [*Putting the pictures back into the envelope.*] What are you gonna do?

BABE What can I do? [*There is a knock on the door.* BABE *grabs the envelope and hides it.*]

MEG Who is it?

BARNETTE'S VOICE It's Barnette Lloyd.

MEG Oh. Come on in, Barnette.

[BARNETTE *enters. His eyes are ablaze with excitement.*]

BARNETTE [*as he paces around the room*] Well; good morning! [*Shaking* MEG'S *hand.*] Good morning, Miss Magrath. [*Touching* BABE *on the shoulder.*] Becky. [*Moving away.*] What I meant to say is . . . how are you doing this morning?

MEG Ah—fine. Fine.

BARNETTE Good. Good. I—I just had time to drop by for a minute.

MEG Oh.

BARNETTE So, ah, how's your Granddad doing?

MEG Well, not very, ah—ah, he's in this coma. [*She breaks up laughing.*]

BARNETTE I see . . . I see. [*To* BABE.] Actually, the primary reason I came by was to pick up that—envelope. I left it here last night in all the confusion. [*Pause.*] You, ah, still do have it? [BABE *hands him the envelope.*] Yes. [*Taking the envelope.*] That's the one. I'm sure it'll be much better off in my office safe. [*He puts the envelope into his coat pocket.*]

MEG I'm sure it will.

BARNETTE Beg your pardon?

BABE It's all right. I showed her the pictures.

BARNETTE Ah; I see.

MEG So what's going to happen now, Barnette? What are those pictures gonna mean?

BARNETTE [*after pacing a moment*] Hmmm. May I speak frankly and openly?

BABE Uh huh.

MEG Please do—

BARNETTE Well, I tell you now, at first glance, I admit those pictures had me considerably perturbed and upset. Perturbed to the point that I spent most of last night going over certain suspect papers and reports that had fallen into my hands—rather recklessly.

BABE What papers do you mean?

BARNETTE Papers that pending word from three varied and unbiased experts, could prove graft, fraud, forgery, as well as a history of unethical behavior.

MEG You mean about Zackery?

BARNETTE Exactly. You see, I now intend to make this matter just as sticky and gritty for one Z. Botrelle as it is for us. Why, with the amount of scandal I'll dig up, Botrelle will be forced to settle this affair on our own terms!

MEG Oh, Babe! Did you hear that?!

BABE Yes! Oh, yes! so you've won it! You've won your lifelong vendetta!

BARNETTE Well . . . well, now of course it's problematic in that, well, in that we won't be able to expose him openly in the courts. That was the original game plan.

BABE But why not? Why?

BARNETTE Well, it's only that if, well, if a jury were to—to get, say, a glance at these, ah, photographs, well . . . well possibly . . .

BABE We could be sunk.

BARNETTE In a sense. But! On the other hand, if a newspaper were to get a hold of our little item, Mr. Zackery Botrelle could find himself boiling in some awfully hot water. So what I'm looking for very simply, is—a deal.

BABE A deal?

MEG Thank you, Barnette. It's a sunny day, Babe. [*Realizing she is in the way.*] Ooh, where's that broken shoe? [*She grabs her boots and runs upstairs.*]

BABE So, you're having to give up your vendetta?

BARNETTE Well, in a way. For the time. It, ah, seems to me you shouldn't always let your life be ruled by such things as, ah, personal vendettas. [*Looking at* BABE *with meaning.*] Other things can be important.

BABE I don't know. I don't exactly know. How 'bout Willie Jay? Will he be all right?

BARNETTE Yes, it's all been taken care of. He'll be leaving incognito on the midnight bus—heading north.

BABE North.

BARNETTE I'm sorry, it seemed the only . . . way. [BARNETTE *moves to her—She moves away.*]

BABE Look, you'd better be getting on back to your work.

BARNETTE [*awkwardly*] Right—'cause I—I've got those important calls out. [*Full of hope for her.*] They'll be pouring in directly. [*He starts to leave, then says to her with love.*] We'll talk.

MEG [*reappearing in her boots*] Oh, Barnette—

BARNETTE Yes?

MEG Could you give me a ride just down to the corner? I need to stop at Helen's Bakery.

BARNETTE Be glad to.

MEG Thanks. Listen, Babe, I'll be right back with the cake. We're gonna have the best celebration! Now, ah, if Lenny asks where I've gone, just say I'm . . . just say, I've gone out back to, ah, pick up some paw paws! Okay?

BABE Okay.

MEG Fine; I'll be back in a bit. Goodbye.

BABE 'Bye.

BARNETTE Goodbye, Becky.

BABE Goodbye, Barnette. Take care. [MEG *and* BARNETTE *exit.* BABE *sits staring ahead, in a state of deep despair.*] Goodbye, Becky. Goodbye, Barnette. Goodbye, Becky. [*She stops when* LENNY *comes down the stairs in a fluster.*]

LENNY Oh! Oh! Oh! I'm so ashamed! I'm such a coward! I'm such a yellow-bellied chicken! I'm so ashamed! Where's Meg?

BABE [*suddenly bright*] She's, ah—gone out back—to pick up some paw paws.

LENNY Oh. Well, at least I don't have to face her! I just couldn't do it! I couldn't make the call!! My heart was pounding like a hammer. Pound! Pound! Pound! Why, I looked down and I could actually see my blouse moving back and forth! Oh, Babe, you look so disappointed. Are you?

BABE [*despondently*] Uh huh.

LENNY Oh, no! I've disappointed Babe! I can't stand it! I've gone and disappointed my little sister, Babe! Oh, no! I feel like howling like a dog!

CHICK'S VOICE Oooh, Lenny! [CHICK *enters dramatically; dripping with sympathy.*] Well, I just don't know what to say! I'm so sorry! I am so sorry for you! And for Little Babe, here, too. I mean to have such a sister as that!

LENNY What do you mean?

CHICK Oh, you don't need to pretend with me. I saw it all from over there in my own backyard; I saw Meg stumbling out of Doc Porter's pickup truck, not 15 minutes ago. And her looking such a disgusting mess. You must be so ashamed! You must just want to die! Why, I always said that girl was nothing but cheap Christmas trash!

LENNY Don't talk that way about Meg.

CHICK Oh, come on now, Lenny, honey. I know exactly how you feel about Meg. Why, Meg's a low-class tramp and you need not have one more blessed thing to do with her and her disgusting behavior.

LENNY I said don't you ever talk that way about my sister Meg again.

CHICK Well, my goodness gracious, Lenora, don't be such a noodle—it's the truth!

LENNY I don't care if it's the Ten Commandments. I don't want to hear it in my home. Not ever again.

CHICK In your home?! Why, I never in all my life—This is my Grandfather's home! And you're just living here on his charity; so don't you get high-falutin' with me, Miss Lenora Josephine Magrath!

LENNY Get out of here—

CHICK Don't you tell me to get out! What makes you think you can order me around? Why, I've had just about my fill of you trashy Magraths and your trashy ways; hanging your selves in cellars; carrying on with married men; shooting your own husbands!

LENNY Get out!

CHICK [*to* BABE] And don't think she's not gonna end up at the state prison farm or in some—mental institution. Why it's a clear-cut case of manslaughter with intent to kill.

LENNY Out! Get out!

CHICK [*running on*] That's what everyone's saying, deliberate intent to kill! And you'll pay for that! Do you hear me? You'll pay!

LENNY [*she picks up a broom and threatens* CHICK *with it*] And I'm telling you to get out!

CHICK You—you put that down this minute—are you a raving lunatic?

LENNY [*beating* CHICK *with the broom*] I said for you to get out! That means out! And never, never, never come back!

CHICK [*overlapping, as she runs around the room*] Oh! Oh! Oh! You're crazy! You're crazy!

LENNY [*chasing* CHICK *out the door*] Do you hear me, Chick the Stick! This is my home! This is my house! Get out! Out!

CHICK [*overlapping*] Oh! Oh! Police! Police! You're crazy! Help! Help! [LENNY *chases* CHICK *out of the house. They are both screaming. The phone rings.* BABE *goes and picks it up.*]

BABE Hello? . . . Oh, hello, Zackery! . . . Yes, he showed them to me! You're what! . . . What do you mean? . . . What! . . . You can't put me out to Whitfield . . . 'Cause I'm not crazy . . . I'm not! I'm not! . . . She wasn't crazy either . . . Don't you call my mother crazy! . . . No, you're not! You're not gonna. You're not! [*She slams the phone down and stares wildly ahead.*] He's not. He's not. [*As she walks over to the ribbon drawer.*] I'll do it. I will. And he won't . . . [*She opens the drawer; pulls out the rope; becomes terrified; throws the rope back in the drawer and slams it shut.* LENNY *enters from the back door swinging the broom and laughing.*]

LENNY Oh, my! Oh, my! You should have seen us! Why, I chased Chick the Stick right up the mimosa tree. I did! I left her right up there screaming in the tree!

BABE [*laughing; she is insanely delighted*] Oh, you did!

LENNY Yes, I did! And I feel so good! I do! I feel good! I feel good!

BABE [*overlapping*] Good! Good, Lenny! Good for you! [*They dance around the kitchen.*]

LENNY [*stopping*] You know what—

BABE What?

LENNY I'm gonna call Charlie!!! I'm gonna call him right now!

BABE You are?

LENNY Yeah, I feel like I can really do it!

BABE You do?

LENNY My courage is up; my heart's in it; the time is right! No more beating around the bush! Let's strike while the iron is hot!

BABE Right! Right! No more beating around the bush! Strike while the iron is hot! [LENNY *goes to the phone.* BABE *rushes over to the ribbon drawer. She begins tearing through it.*]

LENNY [*with the receiver in her hand*] I'm calling him up, Babe—I'm really gonna do it!

BABE [*still tearing through the drawer*] Good! Do it! Good!

LENNY [*as she dials*] Look. My hands aren't even shaking.

BABE [*pulling out a red cord of rope*] Don't we have any stronger rope than this?

LENNY I guess not. All the rope we've got's in that drawer. [*About her hands.*] Now they're shaking a little. [BABE *takes the rope and goes up the stairs.* LENNY *finishes dialing the number. She waits for an answer.*] Hello? . . . Hello, Charlie. This is Lenny Magrath . . . Well, I'm fine. I'm just fine. [*An awkward pause.*] I was, ah, just calling to see—how you're getting on. . . Well, good. Good . . . Yes, I know I said that. Now I wish I didn't say it . . . Well, the reason I said that before, about not seeing each other again, was 'cause of me, not you . . . Well, it's just I—can't have any children. I—have this ovary problem . . . Why, Charlie, what a thing to say! . . . Well, they're not all little snot-nosed pigs! . . . You think they are! . . . Oh, Charlie, stop, stop! You're making me laugh . . . Yes, I guess I was. I can see now that I was . . . You are? . . . Well, I'm dying to see you, too . . . Well, I don't know when, Charlie . . . soon. How about, well, how about tonight? . . . You will? . . . Oh, you will! . . . All right, I'll be here. I'll be right here . . . Goodbye, then, Charlie. Goodbye for now. [*She hangs up the phone in a daze.*] Babe. Oh, Babe! He's coming. He's coming! Babe! Oh, Babe, where are you? Meg! Oh . . . out back—picking up paw paws. [*As she exits through the back door.*] And those paw paws are just ripe for picking up!

[*There is a moment of silence, then a loud, horrible thud is heard coming from upstairs. The telephone begins ringing immediately. It rings five times before* BABE *comes hurrying down the stairs with a broken piece of rope hanging around her neck. The phone continues to ring.*]

BABE [*to the phone*] Will you shut up! [*She is jerking the rope from around her neck. She grabs a knife to cut it off.*] Cheap! Miserable! I hate you! I hate you! [*She throws the rope violently around the room. The phone stops ringing.*] Thank God. [*She looks at the stove, goes over to it, and turns the gas on. The sound of gas escaping is heard.* BABE *sniffs at it.*] Come on. Come on . . . Hurry up . . . I beg of you—hurry up! [*Finally,* BABE *feels the oven is ready; she takes a deep breath and opens the oven door to stick her head into it. She spots the rack and furiously jerks it out. Taking another breath, she sticks her head into the oven. She stands for several moments tapping her fingers furiously on top of the stove. She speaks from inside the oven . . .*] Oh, please. Please. [*After a few moments, she reaches for the box of matches with her head still in the oven. She tries to strike a match. It doesn't catch.*] Oh, Mama, please! [*She throws the match away and is getting a second one.*] Mama . . . Mama . . . So that's why you done it!

[*In her excitement she starts to get up, bangs her head and falls back in the stove.* MEG *enters from the back door, carrying a birthday cake in a pink box.*]

MEG Babe! [MEG *throws the box down and runs to pull* BABE'S *head out of the oven.*] Oh, my God! What are you doing? What the hell are you doing?

BABE [*dizzily*] Nothing. I don't know. Nothing. [MEG *turns off the gas and moves* BABE *to a chair near the open door.*]

MEG Sit down. Sit down! Will you sit down!

BABE I'm okay. I'm okay.

MEG Put your head between your knees and breathe deep!

BABE Meg—

MEG Just do it! I'll get you some water [MEG *gets some water for* BABE.] Here.

BABE Thanks.

MEG Are you okay?

BABE Uh-huh.

MEG Are you sure?

BABE Yeah, I'm sure. I'm okay.

MEG [*getting a damp rag and putting it over her own face.*] Well good. That's good.

BABE Meg—

MEG Yes?

BABE I know why she did it.

MEG What? Why who did what?

BABE [*with joy*] Mama. I know why she hung that cat along with her.

MEG You do?

BABE [*with enlightenment*] It's 'cause she was afraid of dying all alone.

MEG Was she?

BABE She felt so unsure, you know, as to what was coming. It seems the best thing coming up would be a lot of angels and all of them singing. But I imagine they have high, scary voices and little gold pointed fingers that are as sharp as blades and you don't want to meet 'em all alone. You'd be afraid to meet 'em all alone. So it wasn't like what people were saying about her hating that cat. Fact is, she loved that cat. She needed him with her 'cause she felt so all alone.

MEG Oh, Babe . . . Babe. Why, Babe? Why?

BABE Why what?

MEG Why did you stick you head into the oven?!

BABE I don't know, Meg. I'm having a bad day. It's been a real bad day; those pictures; and Barnette giving up his vendetta; then Willie Jay, heading north; and—Zackery called me up. [*Trembling with terror.*] He says he's gonna have me classified insane and send me on out to the Whitfield asylum.

MEG What! Why, he could never do that!

BABE Why not?

MEG 'Cause you're not insame.

BABE I'm not?

MEG No! He's trying to bluff you. Don't you see it? Barnette's got him running scared.

BABE Really?

MEG Sure. He's scared to death—calling you insane. Ha! Why, you're just as perfectly sane as anyone walking the streets of Hazlehurst, Mississippi.

BABE I am?

MEG More so! A lot more so!

BABE Good!

MEG But, Babe, we've just got to learn how to get through these real bad days here. I mean, it's getting to be a thing in our family. [*Slight pause as she looks at* BABE.] Come on now. Look, we've got Lenny's cake right here. I mean don't you wanna be around to give her her cake; watch her blow out the candles?

BABE [*realizing how much she wants to be here*] Yeah, I do, I do. Cause she always loves to make her birthday wishes on those candles.

MEG Well, then we'll give her her cake and maybe you won't be so miserable.

BABE Okay.

MEG Good. Go on and take it out of the box.

BABE Okay. [*She takes the cake out of the box. It is a magical moment.*] Gosh, it's a pretty cake.

MEG [*handing her some matches*] Here now. You can go on and light up the candles.

BABE All right. [*She starts to light the candles.*] I love to light up candles. And there are so many here. Thirty pink ones in all plus one green one to grow on.

MEG [*watching her light the candles*] They're pretty.

BABE They are. [*She stops lighting the candles.*] And I'm not like Mama. I'm not so all alone.

MEG You're not.

BABE [*as she goes back to lighting candles*] Well, you'd better keep an eye out for Lenny. She's supposed to be surprised.

MEG All right. Do you know where she's gone?

BABE Well, she's not here inside—so she must have gone on outside.

MEG Oh, well, then I'd better run and find her.

BABE Okay 'cause these candles are gonna melt down. [MEG *starts out the door.*]

MEG Wait—there she is coming. Lenny! Oh, Lenny! Come on! Hurry up!

BABE [*overlapping and improvising as she finishes lighting candles*] Oh, no! No! Well, yes—yes! No, wait! Wait! Okay! [LENNY *enters.* MEG *covers* LENNY'*s eyes with her hands.*]

LENNY [*terrified*] What?! What is it?!! What?!!

MEG & BABE Surprise! Happy Birthday! Happy Birthday to Lenny!!

LENNY Oh, no! Oh me!!! What a surprise! I could just cry! Oh, look, "Happy Birthday to Lenny—A Day Late!" How cute! My! Will you look at all those candles—it's absolutely frightening.

BABE [*spontaneous thought*] Oh, no, Lenny, it's good! 'Cause—'cause the more candles you have on your cake, the stronger your wish is.

LENNY Really?

BABE Sure!

LENNY Mercy. [*They start the song.* LENNY, *interrupting the song.*] Oh, but wait! I—I can't think of my wish! My body's gone all nervous inside.

MEG For God's sake, Lenny—come on!

BABE The wax is all melting!

LENNY My mind is just a blank, a total blank!

MEG Will you please just—

BABE [*overlapping*] Lenny, hurry! Come on!

LENNY Okay! Okay! Just go!! [MEG *and* BABE *burst into the "Happy Birthday Song." As it ends* LENNY *blows out all of the candles on the cake.* MEG *and* BABE *applaud loudly.*]

MEG Oh, you made it!

BABE Hurray!

LENNY Oh, me! Oh, me! I hope that wish comes true! I hope it does!

BABE Why? What did you wish for?

LENNY [*as she removes the candles from the cake*] Why. I can't tell you that.

BABE Oh, sure you can—

LENNY Oh, no! Then it won't come true.

BABE Why, that's just superstition! Of course it will, if you made it deep enough.

MEG Really? I didn't know that.

LENNY Well, Babe's the regular expert on birthday wishes.

BABE It's just I get these feelings. Now come on and tell us. What was it you wished for?

MEG Yes, tell us. What was it?

LENNY Well, I guess, it wasn't really a specific wish. This—this vision just sort of came into my mind.

BABE A vision? What was it of?

LENNY I don't know exactly. It was something about the three of us smiling and laughing together.

BABE Well, when was it? Was it far away or near?

LENNY I'm not sure, but it wasn't forever; it wasn't for every minute. Just this one moment and we were all laughing.

BABE What were we laughing about?

LENNY I don't know. Just nothing I guess.

MEG Well, that's a nice wish to make. [LENNY *and* MEG *look at each other a moment.*] Here, now, I'll get a knife so we can go ahead and cut the cake in celebration of Lenny being born!

BABE Oh, yes! And give each one of us a rose. A whole rose apiece!

LENNY [*cutting the cake nervously*] Well, I'll try—I'll try!

MEG [*licking the icing off a candle*] Mmmm—this icing is delicious! Here, try some!

BABE Mmmm! It's wonderful! Here, Lenny!

LENNY [*laughing joyously as she licks icing from her fingers and cuts huge pieces of cake that her sisters bite into ravenously*] Oh, how I do love having birthday cake for breakfast! How I do! [*The sisters freeze for a moment laughing and eating cake; the lights change and frame them in a magical, golden, sparkling glimmer; saxophone music is heard. The lights dim to blackout, and the saxophone continues to play.*]

End of Play

Four

Realism and the Theater of Spectacle

Plays can differ in terms of their relationship to the real world. Some plays ask readers and audiences to believe for the moment in the illusion that the play *is* reality. They ask us to forget that each is a *play,* a fiction. Other plays flaunt the fact that they are plays, don't claim at all to represent the real world. They ask us to enjoy the theater and be open to what the experience can teach us about our mental and imaginative lives. Whether we are in the theater audience or we are reading and creating our own mental theater, we know—it's one of the basic assumptions—that what we are seeing is not "real." It is a theatrical show. A play that asks us to forget this basic fact can be called **realistic;** a play that asks us to remember it can be called **spectacular,** in the sense that this type of play is a *spectacle,* something to look at.

Dramatizing on Stage

We can begin thinking about these kinds of drama by considering the ways they use language. In a realistic play, the characters speak to each other. The actors never acknowledge the audience's presence, so all their talking is to each other within the context of their dramatic situation. In spectacular theater, the actors can acknowledge the audience, can speak directly to us. There are in Shakespeare's plays, for example, famous **soliloquies,** in which a character addresses us directly in order to share his thoughts. When a character speaks directly to us, it is not possible to maintain the illusion that we are viewing real life. This technique reminds us that we are at a theater, and that the action we are viewing is fictional. Some plays go out of their way to emphasize that they're plays (such as *The Sandbox);* others maintain a strict realism, trying to spin a web of perfect illusion around us *(A Doll House).*

In realistic plays, the language has a practical function. It provides the building blocks out of which the actors or the reader will create embodied, imagined characters. The language may be enjoyable or beautiful, but it is still primarily a way of revealing character. To think about it from the author's perspective, the language of a realistic play must be appropriate to the character. It must have the right accent or dialect, the right choice of words, the right style for the character the author has in mind. In the theater of spectacle, the language often draws attention to itself. It might be richly poetic, so that an actor could deliver the lines very dramatically. The language might even be sung, as it is in musical plays, which are perfect examples of spectacles that you cannot mistake for reality, unless you hang around with people who burst spontaneously into song. Such language may still reveal character—it certainly does in Shakespeare—but as readers we must attend to it closely for itself. As in reading a poem, we have to work hard on the language, invest energy in helping to produce its meaning. The language of realistic theater tends to disappear, whereas the language of spectacular theater calls vigorous attention to itself.

The difference between realistic and spectacular theater can also be seen in acting styles. In realistic theater, the actor strives to disappear, leaving only the character. It's not the actor's personality that counts, but the personality of the character. Some actors go to extremes in this effort, trying to *become* the character in looks, studying the movements, working carefully on perfecting an accent. The actor in spectacular theater does not disappear. His or her movements might be beautiful in themselves, almost like dance or mime, and we are meant to notice. The actor can show off his or her theatrical abilities, do everything bigger than life, for the sake of the theatrical performance. Such an actor is saying in effect, "I am performing. Enjoy the show." In America we are used to realistic actors, such as Robert de Niro, say, who gained fifty pounds to play Jake La Motta in the film *Raging Bull.* But think also of the fun of seeing Eddie Murphy smirk at the camera, wink at us, letting us see that he's *playing* with his part. He asks us to appreciate his timing, his *style.*

The differences between realistic and spectacular theater extend to different designs for sets and stages. In realistic theater, there is often a carefully detailed set. The purpose of the set is to convince the audience that it is the real scene for the real events that will happen within it. The set for a realistic play can tell us a lot about the characters. If it's a room in a home, say, it can suggest the kind of environment the characters inhabit. The set surrounds the characters with objects and designs that communicate messages about them. For example, in *The Plough and the Stars,* Sean O'Casey provides very specific stage directions that show the effects he wants the set to have:

> *The home of the Clitheroes. It consists of the front and back drawing-rooms in a fine old Georgian house, struggling for its life against the assaults of time, and the more savage assaults of the tenants. The room shown is the back drawing-room, wide, spacious, and lofty. At back is the entrance to the front drawing-room. The space, originally occupied by folding doors, is now draped with casement cloth of a dark purple, decorated with a design in reddish-purple and cream. One of the curtains is pulled aside, giving a glimpse of front drawing-room, at the end of which can be seen the wide, lofty windows looking out into the street. The room directly in front of the audience is furnished in a way that suggests an attempt towards a finer expression of domestic life. The large fireplace on right is of wood, painted to look like marble (the original has been taken away by the landlord). On the mantelshelf are two candlesticks of dark carved wood. Between them is a small clock. Over the clock is hanging a calendar which displays a picture of "The Sleeping Venus." In the centre of the breast of the chimney hangs a picture of Robert Emmet. On the right of the entrance to the front drawing-room is a copy of "The Gleaners," on the opposite side a copy of "The Angelus." Underneath "The Gleaners" is a chest of drawers on which stands a green bowl filled with scarlet dahlias and white chrysanthemums. Near to the fireplace is a settee which at night forms a double bed for Clitheroe and Nora.*

We learn a lot here about the social class, the politics, and the aspirations of these characters. The atmosphere of the room, O'Casey says, should show "a finer expression of domestic life," and all the details of the set that O'Casey mentions contribute to creating that impression. The set is a run-down, formerly aristocratic house that the Clitheroes are trying—vainly—to improve with their paintings and other decorations. To see these characters inside this house is to understand what they want—a genteel life. But the set also connects the characters to the conflict in the play—the cause of Irish nationalism. One of the paintings is of Robert Emmet, a revered Irish patriot. This realistic set, then, is full of information about the characters, and it connects them visually to the main action of the story, the uprising.

In spectacular theater, the function of the stage design is not to create a sense of reality but to draw attention to its own beauty or significance. It may be elaborate and glitzy, like the set for a Broadway musical, out to get applause all on its own. Or it may be symbolic or emotionally suggestive, as in Edward Albee's *The Sandbox:*

> *The Scene: A bare stage, with only the following: Near the footlights, far stage-right, two simple chairs set side by side, facing the audience; near the footlights, far stage-left, a chair facing stage-right with a music stand before it; farther back, and stage-center, slightly elevated and raked, a large child's sandbox with a toy pail and shovel; the background is the sky, which alters from brightest day to deepest night.*

This kind of set draws attention to itself *as* a set. It doesn't pretend to be a real place, but rather it reminds you that you are in a theater. The objects in the set seem to be abstracted out of their usual context. The "world" that this set creates is not the world of real experience. A *play* will happen there, not real actions.

Realistic plays are usually produced in traditional theaters that have what is called a **proscenium arch** stage. In this kind of theater the stage is a space separate from the space of the audience. The opening into the stage space is sometimes called "the fourth wall," as though the stage were a room (say in *A Doll House*) into which we are allowed to look. This arrangement of the space within the theater fosters the illusion that we are looking at reality, at an action that we just happen to witness. In spectacular theater, the stage is often designed to reduce the distance between the audience and the play. In **theater-in-the-round,** for example, the audience surrounds the actors, so that when you look at the play you always also see the audience. You aren't allowed to forget—every glance reminds you—that you are at a play. You are in the same space as the actors.

Dramatizing in the Mind

In the previous paragraphs we have been talking about plays in the theater. What about plays in the minds of readers? How does the difference between realistic and spectacular drama affect them? Obviously it is necessary for readers to produce visual and aural images of the characters, the actions, and the settings of all the plays they read. Otherwise the plays remain inert—the language never comes to life. In realistic theater, the stage directions often help to produce a very clear image of the setting for the play. Readers must have a feel for the setting to get the right message from the objects in the space and from the space itself. And they must think about what the setting tells them about the characters and their actions. This process happens very quickly and without much reflection in a theater when we see the set, but as readers we have to make a real effort to produce an imaginative world that makes sense for the play.

In spectacular drama, the effort is even more difficult. Often the stage directions describe a world that could not exist in reality, so that we are under some mental strain to imagine it for ourselves. We do not inhabit the spatial world of *The Sandbox,* but perhaps we can imagine it by working out from our own responses to the strange events of the play. We have to imagine a space in which such actions could occur.

More generally, realistic and spectacular drama place different demands on the reader. In a realistic play, we are asked to react to the characters as if they were real people in real situations. All the rules of human behavior and relationships that we usually apply in our lives we can also apply in the play. When Nora leaves her family at the end of *A Doll House,* we are asked to judge her as we would a woman we knew who did the same thing. The play does all it can to help us see her marriage as Nora sees it, and therefore to understand her decision, but it's still up to the reader to react honestly. If you don't approve of what she does, that doesn't mean that you have to reject the play. It means that you aren't convinced by its argument, though you can still admire the craft that went into it. The play has engaged you as a reader, whether or not you agree with its point of view. It has given you language that you transformed into an imagined world, and it asked you to imagine that world so fully that it seemed real to you.

Often, realistic plays want to make a point about the social and political realities of their time. They attempt to place us in the social world that the characters have to face—for example in the slums of *The Plough and the Stars*—so that we can feel for ourselves how that world shapes behavior. In Susan Glaspell's *Trifles,* we are placed within a society with a very narrow and scornful view of women's interests, and we see how the two women operate within and around the constraints that their society imposes. The goal of such plays is to present us with a heightened depiction of reality from which we can take away lessons to apply to our own social world.

In spectacular drama, the reader's role is more complex. The theater of spectacle admits that it does not depict reality. Such a play is only a play. We aren't asked to accept it as reality but only to try it on, so to speak, to see how an alternate view of the world might look. Furthermore, spectacular theater wants us as readers to attend to the languages of culture. It makes them difficult for us—often the speeches in a play don't make immediate sense, or characters will send out nonverbal messages that seem to have no meaning. As a result, the languages in which we live our normal lives are at issue. We have to pay close attention to these languages because our usual understandings have been challenged.

Spectacular theater therefore reminds us that we view the world through our cultural system. That system has great power, defining for us how we each fit into the world. Spectacular theater challenges that system and makes us more aware of it—which is to say that spectacular plays often have a political and social concern. Bertolt Brecht is the great dramatist of this approach. His *The Good Woman of Setzuan* always reminds us that it is a play. It is a fable that a storyteller is telling us in order to illustrate a point about human life. The characters speak directly to us, acknowledging that they are in a play, not in reality. Yet the play has much to say about social and economic life. The play forces us to look at the world of work and money in a new way, challenging our preconceptions.

Although a spectacular play doesn't claim to depict reality, it affects how we perceive our own reality. That is, it makes us more aware that we are participants in a group effort to make sense of reality. We are engaged in a social dialogue, constantly using language to communicate with others. Just as the characters in the play engage in a powerful dialogue, each representing a different view of the world, we live within a social dialogue, a web of relationships that defines who we are. It's the purpose of all drama to present us with such relationships—up on the stage, or in the theater of our imagination—so that we have images of ourselves, images that can reveal us to ourselves in a new light.

REALISM

Henrik Ibsen (1828–1906)

A DOLL HOUSE

Translated by Rolf Fjelde

CHARACTERS

TORVALD HELMER, *a lawyer*
NORA, *his wife*
DR. RANK
MRS. LINDE
NILS KROGSTAD, *a bank clerk*
THE HELMERS' THREE SMALL CHILDREN
ANNE-MARIE, *their nurse*
HELENE, *a maid*
A DELIVERY BOY

The action takes place in HELMER'S *residence.*

ACT I

A comfortable room, tastefully but not expensively furnished. A door to the right in the back wall leads to the entryway; another to the left leads to HELMER'S *study. Between these doors, a piano. Midway in the left-hand wall a door, and further back a window. Near the window a round table with an armchair and a small sofa. In the right-hand wall, toward the rear, a door, and nearer the foreground a porcelain stove with two armchairs and a rocking chair beside it. Between the stove and the side door, a small table. Engravings on the walls. An étagère with china figures and other small art objects; a small bookcase with richly bound books; the floor carpeted; a fire burning in the stove. It is a winter day.*

[*A bell rings in the entryway; shortly after we hear the door being unlocked.* NORA *comes into the room, humming happily to herself; she is wearing street clothes and carries an armload of packages, which she puts down on the table to the right. She has left the hall door open; and through it a* DELIVERY BOY *is seen, holding a Christmas tree and a basket, which he gives to* THE MAID *who let them in.*]

NORA Hide the tree well, Helene. The children mustn't get a glimpse of it till this evening, after it's trimmed. [*To the* DELIVERY BOY, *taking out her purse.*] How much?

DELIVERY BOY Fifty, ma'am.

NORA There's a crown. No, keep the change. [*The* BOY *thanks her and leaves.* NORA *shuts the door. She laughs softly to herself while taking off her street things. Drawing a bag of macaroons from her pocket, she eats a couple, then steals over and listens at her husband's study door.*] Yes, he's home. [*Hums again as she moves to the table right.*]

HELMER [*from the study*] Is that my little lark twittering out there?

NORA [*busy opening some packages*] Yes, it is.

HELMER Is that my squirrel rummaging around?

NORA Yes!

HELMER When did my squirrel get in?

NORA Just now. [*Putting the macaroon bag in her pocket and wiping her mouth.*] Do come in, Torvald, and see what I've bought.

HELMER Can't be disturbed. [*After a moment he opens the door and peers in, pen in hand.*] Bought, you say? All that there? Has the little spendthrift been out throwing money around again?

NORA Oh, but Torvald, this year we really should let ourselves go a bit. It's the first Christmas we haven't had to economize.

HELMER But you know we can't go squandering.

NORA Oh yes, Torvald, we can squander a little now. Can't we? Just a tiny, wee bit. Now that you've got a big salary and are going to make piles and piles of money.

HELMER Yes—starting New Year's. But then it's a full three months till the raise comes through.

NORA Pooh! We can borrow that long.

HELMER Nora! [*Goes over and playfully takes her by the ear.*] Are your scatterbrains off again? What if today I borrowed a thousand crowns, and you squandered them over Christmas week, and then on New Year's Eve a roof tile fell on my head, and I lay there—

NORA [*putting her hand on his mouth*] Oh! Don't say such things!

HELMER Yes, but what if it happened—then what?

NORA If anything so awful happened, then it just wouldn't matter if I had debts or not.

HELMER Well, but the people I'd borrowed from?

NORA Them? Who cares about them! They're strangers.

HELMER Nora, Nora, how like a woman! No, but seriously, Nora, you know what I think about that. No debts! Never borrow! Something of freedom's lost—and something of beauty, too—from a home that's founded on borrowing and debt. We've made a brave stand up to now, the two of us; and we'll go right on like that the little while we have to.

NORA [*going toward the stove*] Yes, whatever you say, Torvald.

HELMER [*following her*] Now, now, the little lark's wings mustn't droop. Come on, don't be a sulky squirrel. [*Taking out his wallet.*] Nora, guess what I have here.

NORA [*turning quickly*] Money!

HELMER There, see. [*Hands her some notes.*] Good grief, I know how costs go up in a house at Christmastime.

NORA Ten—twenty—thirty—forty. Oh, thank you, Torvald; I can manage no end on this.

HELMER You really will have to.

NORA Oh yes, I promise I will! But come here so I can show you everything I bought. And so cheap! Look, new clothes for Ivar here—and a sword. Here a horse and a trumpet for Bob. And a doll and a doll's bed here for Emmy; they're nothing much, but she'll tear them to bits in no time anyway. And here I have dress material and handkerchiefs for the maids. Old Anne-Marie really deserves something more.

HELMER And what's in that package there?

NORA [*with a cry*] Torvald, no! You can't see that till tonight!

HELMER I see. But tell me now, you little prodigal, what have you thought of for yourself?

NORA For myself? Oh, I don't want anything at all.

HELMER Of course you do. Tell me just what—within reason—you'd most like to have.

NORA I honestly don't know. Oh, listen, Torvald—

HELMER Well?

NORA [*fumbling at his coat buttons, without looking at him*] If you want to give me something, then maybe you could—you could—

HELMER Come on, out with it.

NORA [*hurriedly*] You could give me money, Torvald. No more than you think you can spare; then one of these days I'll buy something with it.

HELMER But Nora—

NORA Oh, please, Torvald darling, do that! I beg you, please. Then I could hang the bills in pretty gilt paper on the Christmas tree. Wouldn't that be fun?

HELMER What are those little birds called that always fly through their fortunes?

NORA Oh yes, spendthrifts; I know all that. But let's do as I say, Torvald; then I'll have time to decide what I really need most. That's very sensible, isn't it?

HELMER [*smiling*] Yes, very—that is, if you actually hung onto the money I give you, and you actually used it to buy yourself something. But it goes for the house and for all sorts of foolish things, and then I only have to lay out some more.

NORA Oh, but Torvald—

HELMER Don't deny it, my dear little Nora. [*Putting his arm around her waist.*] Spendthrifts are sweet, but they use up a frightful amount of money. It's incredible what it costs a man to feed such birds.

NORA Oh, how can you say that! Really, I save everything I can.

HELMER [*laughing*] Yes, that's the truth. Everything you can. But that's nothing at all.

NORA [*humming, with a smile of quiet satisfaction*] Hm, if you only knew what expenses we larks and squirrels have, Torvald.

HELMER You're an odd little one. Exactly the way your father was. You're never at a loss for scaring up money; but the moment you have it, it runs right out through your fingers; you never know what you've done with it. Well, one takes you as you are. It's deep in your blood. Yes, these things are hereditary, Nora.

NORA Ah, I could wish I'd inherited many of Papa's qualities.

HELMER And I couldn't wish you anything but just what you are, my sweet little lark. But wait; it seems to me you have a very—what should I call it?—a very suspicious look today—

NORA I do?

HELMER You certainly do. Look me straight in the eye.

NORA [*looking at him*] Well?

HELMER [*shaking an admonitory finger*] Surely my sweet tooth hasn't been running riot in town today, has she?

NORA No. Why do you imagine that?

HELMER My sweet tooth really didn't make a little detour through the confectioner's?

NORA No, I assure you, Torvald—

HELMER Hasn't nibbled some pastry?

NORA No, not at all.

HELMER Nor even munched a macaroon or two?

NORA No, Torvald, I assure you, really—

HELMER There, there now. Of course I'm only joking.

NORA [*going to the table, right*] You know I could never think of going against you.

HELMER No, I understand that; and you *have* given me your word. [*Going over to her.*] Well, you keep your little Christmas secrets to yourself, Nora darling. I expect they'll come to light this evening, when the tree is lit.

NORA Did you remember to ask Dr. Rank?

HELMER No. But there's no need for that; it's assumed he'll be dining with us. All the same, I'll ask him when he stops by here this morning. I've ordered some fine wine. Nora, you can't imagine how I'm looking forward to this evening.

NORA So am I. And what fun for the children, Torvald!

HELMER Ah, it's so gratifying to know that one's gotten a safe, secure job, and with a comfortable salary. It's a great satisfaction, isn't it?

NORA Oh, it's wonderful!

HELMER Remember last Christmas? Three whole weeks before, you shut yourself in every evening till long after midnight, making flowers for the Christmas tree, and all the other decorations to surprise us. Ugh, that was the dullest time I've ever lived through.

NORA It wasn't at all dull for me.

HELMER [*smiling*] But the outcome *was* pretty sorry, Nora.

NORA Oh, don't tease me with that again. How could I help it that the cat came in and tore everything to shreds.

HELMER No, poor thing, you certainly couldn't. You wanted so much to please us all, and that's what counts. But it's just as well that the hard times are past.

NORA Yes, it's really wonderful.

HELMER Now I don't have to sit here alone, boring myself, and you don't have to tire your precious eyes and your fair little delicate hands—

NORA [*clapping her hands*] No, is it really true, Torvald, I don't have to? Oh, how wonderfully lovely to hear! [*Taking his arm.*] Now I'll tell you just how I've thought we should plan things. Right after Christmas—[*The doorbell rings.*] Oh, the bell. [*Straightening the room up a bit.*] Somebody would have to come. What a bore!

HELMER I'm not at home to visitors, don't forget.

MAID [*from the hall doorway*] Ma'am, a lady to see you—

NORA All right, let her come in.

MAID [*to* HELMER] And the doctor's just come too.

HELMER Did he go right to my study?

MAID Yes, he did.

[HELMER *goes into his room.* THE MAID *shows in* MRS. LINDE, *dressed in traveling clothes, and shuts the door after her.*]

MRS. LINDE [*in a dispirited and somewhat hesitant voice*] Hello, Nora.

NORA [*uncertain*] Hello—

MRS LINDE You don't recognize me.

NORA No, I don't know—but wait, I think— [*Exclaiming.*] What! Kristine! Is it really you?

MRS. LINDE Yes, it's me.

NORA Kristine! To think I didn't recognize you. But then, how could I? [*More quietly.*] How you've changed, Kristine!

MRS. LINDE Yes, no doubt I have. In nine—ten long years.

NORA Is it so long since we met! Yes, it's all of that. Oh, these last eight years have been a happy time, believe me. And so now you've come in to town, too. Made the long trip in the winter. That took courage.

MRS. LINDE I just got here by ship this morning.

NORA To enjoy yourself over Christmas, of course. Oh, how lovely! Yes, enjoy ourselves, we'll do that. But take your coat off. You're not still cold? [*Helping her.*] There now, let's get cozy here by the stove. No, the easy chair there! I'll take the rocker here. [*Seizing her hands.*] Yes, now you have your old look again; it was only in that first moment. You're a bit more pale, Kristine—and maybe a bit thinner.

MRS. LINDE And much, much older, Nora.

NORA Yes, perhaps a bit older; a tiny, tiny bit; not much at all. [*Stopping short; suddenly serious.*] Oh, but thoughtless me, to sit here, chattering away. Sweet, good Kristine, can you forgive me?

MRS LINDE What do you mean, Nora?

NORA [*softly*] Poor Kristine, you've become a widow.

MRS. LINDE Yes, three years ago.

NORA Oh, I knew it, of course: I read it in the papers. Oh, Kristine, you must believe me; I often thought of writing you then, but I kept postponing it, and something always interfered.

MRS. LINDE Nora dear, I understand completely.

NORA No, it was awful of me, Kristine. You poor thing, how much you must have gone through. And he left you nothing?

MRS. LINDE No.

NORA And no children?

MRS. LINDE No.

NORA Nothing at all, then?

MRS. LINDE Not even a sense of loss to feed on.

NORA [*looking incredulously at her*] But Kristine, how could that be?

MRS. LINDE [*smiling wearily and smoothing her hair*] Oh, sometimes it happens, Nora.

NORA So completely alone. How terribly hard that must be for you. I have three lovely children. You can't see them now; they're out with the maid. But now you must tell me everything—

MRS. LINDE No, no, no, tell me about yourself.

NORA No, you begin. Today I don't want to be selfish. I want to think only of you today. But there *is* something I must tell you. Did you hear of the wonderful luck we had recently?

MRS. LINDE No, what's that?

NORA My husband's been made manager in the bank, just think!

MRS. LINDE Your husband? How marvelous!

NORA Isn't it? Being a lawyer is such an uncertain living, you know, especially if one won't touch any cases that aren't clean and decent. And of course Torvald would never do that, and I'm with him completely there. Oh, we're simply delighted, believe me! He'll join the bank right after New Year's and start getting a huge salary and lots of commissions. From now on we can live quite differently—just as we want. Oh, Kristine, I feel so light and happy! Won't it be lovely to have stacks of money and not a care in the world?

MRS. LINDE Well, anyway, it would be lovely to have enough for necessities.

NORA No, not just for necessities, but stacks and stacks of money!

MRS. LINDE [*smiling*] Nora, Nora, aren't you sensible yet? Back in school you were such a free spender.

NORA [*with a quiet laugh*] Yes, that's what Torvald still says. [*Shaking her finger.*] But "Nora, Nora" isn't as silly as you all think. Really, we've been in no position for me to go squandering. We've had to work, both of us.

MRS. LINDE You too?

NORA Yes, at odd jobs—needlework, crocheting, embroidery, and such— [*casually*] and other things too. You remember that Torvald left the department when we were married? There was no chance of promotion in his office, and of course he needed to earn more money. But that first year he drove himself terribly. He took on all kinds of extra work that kept him going morning and night. It wore him down, and then he fell deathly ill. The doctors said it was essential for him to travel south.

MRS. LINDE Yes, didn't you spend a whole year in Italy?

NORA That's right. It wasn't easy to get away, you know. Ivar had just been born. But of course we had to go. Oh, that was a beautiful trip, and it saved Torvald's life. But it cost a frightful sum, Kristine.

MRS. LINDE I can well imagine.

NORA Four thousand, eight hundred crowns it cost. That's really a lot of money.

MRS. LINDE But it's lucky you had it when you needed it.

NORA Well, as it was, we got it from Papa.

MRS. LINDE I see. It was just about the time your father died.

NORA Yes, just about then. And, you know, I couldn't make that trip out to nurse him. I had to stay here, expecting Ivar any moment, and with my poor sick Torvald to care for. Dearest Papa, I never saw him again, Kristine. Oh, that was the worst time I've known in all my marriage.

MRS. LINDE I know how you loved him. And then you went off to Italy?

NORA Yes. We had the means now, and the doctors urged us. So we left a month after.

MRS. LINDE And your husband came back completely cured?

NORA Sound as a drum!

MRS. LINDE But—the doctor?

NORA Who?

MRS. LINDE I thought the maid said he was a doctor, the man who came in with me.

NORA Yes, that was Dr. Rank—but he's not making a sick call. He's our closest friend, and he stops by at least once a day. No, Torvald hasn't had a sick moment since, and the children are fit and strong, and I am, too. [*Jumping up and clapping her hands.*] Oh, dear God, Kristine, what a lovely thing to live and be happy! But how disgusting of me—I'm talking of nothing but my own affairs. [*Sits on a stool close by* KRISTINE, *arms resting across her knees.*] Oh, don't be angry with me! Tell me, is it really true that you weren't in love with your husband? Why did you marry him, then?

MRS. LINDE My mother was still alive, but bedridden and helpless—and I had my two younger brothers to look after. In all conscience, I didn't think I could turn him down.

NORA No, you were right there. But was he rich at the time?

MRS. LINDE He was very well off, I'd say. But the business was shaky, Nora. When he died, it all fell apart, and nothing was left.

NORA And then—?

MRS. LINDE Yes, so I had to scrape up a living with a little shop and a little teaching and whatever else I could find. The last three years have been like one endless workday without a rest for me. Now it's over, Nora. My poor mother doesn't need me, for she's passed on. Nor the boys, either; they're working now and can take care of themselves.

NORA How free you must feel—

MRS. LINDE No—only unspeakably empty. Nothing to live for now. [*Standing up anxiously.*] That's why I couldn't take it any longer out in that desolate hole. Maybe here it'll be easier to find something to do and keep my mind occupied. If I could only be lucky enough to get a steady job, some office work—

NORA Oh, but Kristine, that's so dreadfully tiring, and you already look so tired. It would be much better for you if you could go off to a bathing resort.

MRS. LINDE [*going toward the window*] I have no father to give me travel money, Nora.

NORA [*rising*] Oh, don't be angry with me.

MRS. LINDE [*going to her*] Nora dear, don't you be angry with me. The worst of my kind of situation is all the bitterness that's stored away. No one to work for, and yet you're always having to snap up your opportunities. You have to live; and so you grow selfish. When you told me the happy change in your lot, do you know I was delighted less for your sakes than for mine?

NORA How so? Oh, I see. You think maybe Torvald could do something for you.

MRS. LINDE Yes, that's what I thought.

NORA And he will, Kristine! Just leave it to me; I'll bring it up so delicately—find something attractive to humor him with. Oh, I'm so eager to help you.

MRS. LINDE How very kind of you, Nora, to be so concerned over me—doubly kind, considering you really know so little of life's burdens yourself.

NORA I—? I know so little—?

MRS. LINDE [*smiling*] Well, my heavens—a little needlework and such—Nora, you're just a child.

NORA [*tossing her head and pacing the floor*] You don't have to act so superior.

MRS. LINDE Oh?

NORA You're just like the others. You all think I'm incapable of anything serious—

MRS. LINDE Come now—

NORA That I've never had to face the raw world.

MRS. LINDE Nora dear, you've just been telling me all your troubles.

NORA Hm! Trivia! [*Quietly.*] I haven't told you the big thing.

MRS. LINDE Big thing? What do you mean?

NORA You look down on me so, Kristine, but you shouldn't. You're proud that you worked so long and hard for your mother.

MRS. LINDE I don't look down on a soul. But it *is* true: I'm proud—and happy, too—to think it was given to me to make my mother's last days almost free of care.

NORA And you're also proud thinking of what you've done for your brothers.

MRS. LINDE I feel I've a right to be.

NORA I agree. But listen to this, Kristine—I've also got something to be proud and happy for.

MRS. LINDE I don't doubt it. But whatever do you mean?

NORA Not so loud. What if Torvald heard! He mustn't, not for anything in the world. Nobody must know, Kristine. No one but you.

MRS. LINDE But what is it, then?

NORA Come here. [*Drawing her down beside her on the sofa.*] It's true—I've also got something to be proud and happy for. I'm the one who saved Torvald's life.

MRS. LINDE Saved—? Saved how?

NORA I told you about the trip to Italy. Torvald never would have lived if he hadn't gone south—

MRS. LINDE Of course; your father gave you the means—

NORA [*smiling*] That's what Torvald and all the rest think, but—

MRS. LINDE But—?

NORA Papa didn't give us a pin. I was the one who raised the money.

MRS. LINDE You? That whole amount?

NORA Four thousand, eight hundred crowns. What do you say to that?

MRS. LINDE But Nora, how was it possible? Did you win the lottery?

NORA [*disdainfully*] The lottery? Pooh! No art to that.

MRS. LINDE But where did you get it from then?

NORA [*humming, with a mysterious smile*] Hmm, tra-la-la-la.

MRS. LINDE Because you couldn't have borrowed it.

NORA No? Why not?

MRS. LINDE A wife can't borrow without her husband's consent.

NORA [*tossing her head*] Oh, but a wife with a little business sense, a wife who knows how to manage—

MRS. LINDE Nora, I simply don't understand—

NORA You don't have to. Whoever said I *borrowed* the money? I could have gotten it other ways. [*Throwing herself back on the sofa.*] I could have gotten it from some admirer or other. After all, a girl with my ravishing appeal—

MRS. LINDE You lunatic.

NORA I'll bet you're eaten up with curiosity, Kristine.

MRS. LINDE Now listen here, Nora—you haven't done something indiscreet?

NORA [*sitting up again*] Is it indiscreet to save your husband's life?

MRS. LINDE I think it's indiscreet that without his knowledge you—

NORA But that's the point: he mustn't know! My Lord, can't you understand? He mustn't ever know the close call he had. It was to *me* the doctors came to say his life was in danger—that nothing could save him but a stay in the south. Didn't I try strategy then! I began talking about how lovely it would be for me to travel abroad like other young wives; I begged and I cried; I told him please to remember my condition, to be kind and indulge me; and then I dropped a hint that he could easily take out a loan. But at that, Kristine, he nearly exploded. He said I was frivolous, and it was his duty as man of the house not to indulge me in whims and fancies—as I think he called them. Aha, I thought, now you'll just have to be saved—and that's when I saw my chance.

MRS. LINDE And your father never told Torvald the money wasn't from him?

NORA No, never. Papa died right about then. I'd considered bringing him into my secret and begging him never to tell. But he was too sick at the time—and then, sadly, it didn't matter.

MRS. LINDE And you've never confided in your husband since?

NORA For heaven's sake, no! Are you serious? He's so strict on that subject. Besides—Torvald, with all his masculine pride—how painfully humiliating for him if he ever found out he was in debt to me. That would just ruin our relationship. Our beautiful, happy home would never be the same.

MRS. LINDE Won't you ever tell him?

NORA [*thoughtfully, half smiling*] Yes—maybe sometime, years from now, when I'm no longer so attractive. Don't laugh! I only mean when Torvald loves me less than now, when he stops enjoying my dancing and dressing up and reciting for him. Then it might be wise to have something in reserve—[*Breaking off.*] How ridiculous! That'll never happen—Well, Kristine, what do you think of my big secret? I'm capable of something too, hm? You can imagine, of course, how this thing hangs over me. It really hasn't been easy meeting the payments on time. In the business world there's what they call quarterly interest and what they call amortization, and these are always so terribly hard to manage. I've had to skimp a little here and there, wherever I could, you know. I could hardly spare anything from my house allowance, because Torvald has to live well. I couldn't let the children go poorly dressed; whatever I got for them, I felt I had to use up completely—the darlings!

MRS. LINDE Poor Nora, so it had to come out of your own budget, then?

NORA Yes, of course. But I was the one most responsible, too. Every time Torvald gave me money for new clothes and such, I never used more than half; always bought the simplest, cheapest outfits. It was a godsend that everything looks so well on me that Torvald never noticed. But it did weigh me down at times, Kristine. It *is* such a joy to wear fine things. You understand.

MRS. LINDE Oh, of course.

NORA And then I found other ways of making money. Last winter I was lucky enough to get a lot of copying to do. I locked myself in and sat writing every evening till late in the night. Ah, I was tired so often, dead tired. But still it was wonderful fun, sitting and working like that, earning money. It was almost like being a man.

MRS. LINDE But how much have you paid off this way so far?

NORA That's hard to say, exactly. These accounts, you know, aren't easy to figure. I only know that I've paid out all I could scrape together. Time and again I haven't known where to turn. [*Smiling.*] Then I'd sit here dreaming of a rich old gentleman who had fallen in love with me—

MRS. LINDE What! Who is he?

NORA Oh, really! And that he'd died, and when his will was opened, there in big letters it said, "All my fortune shall be paid over in cash, immediately, to that enchanting Mrs. Nora Helmer."

MRS. LINDE But Nora dear—who *was* this gentleman?

NORA Good grief, can't you understand? The old man never existed; that was only something I'd dream up time and again whenever I was at my wits' end for money. But it makes no difference now; the old fossil can go where he pleases for all I care; I don't need him or his will—because now I'm free. [*jumping up.*] Oh, how lovely to think of that, Kristine! Carefree! To know you're carefree, utterly carefree; to be able to romp and play with the children, and to keep up a beautiful, charming home—everything just the way Torvald likes it! And think, spring is coming, with big blue skies. Maybe we can travel a little then. Maybe I'll see the ocean again. Oh yes, it *is* so marvelous to live and be happy!

[*The front doorbell rings.*]

MRS. LINDE [*rising*] There's the bell. It's probably best that I go.

NORA No, stay. No one's expected. It must be for Torvald.

MAID [*from the hall doorway*] Excuse me, ma'am—there's a gentleman here to see Mr. Helmer, but I didn't know—since the doctor's with him—

NORA Who is the gentleman?

KROGSTAD [*from the doorway*] It's me, Mrs. Helmer.

[*Mrs. Linde starts and turns away toward the window.*]

NORA [*stepping toward him, tense, her voice a whisper*] You? What is it? Why do you want to speak to my husband?

KROGSTAD Bank business—after a fashion. I have a small job in the investment bank, and I hear now your husband is going to be our chief—

NORA In other words, it's—

KROGSTAD Just dry business, Mrs. Helmer. Nothing but that.

NORA Yes, then please be good enough to step into the study. [*She nods indifferently as she sees him out by the hall door, then returns and begins stirring up the stove.*]

MRS. LINDE Nora—who was that man?

NORA That was a Mr. Krogstad—a lawyer.

MRS. LINDE Then it really was him.

NORA Do you know that person?

MRS. LINDE I did once—many years ago. For a time he was a law clerk in our town.

NORA Yes, he's been that.

MRS. LINDE How he's changed.

NORA I understand he had a very unhappy marriage.

MRS. LINDE He's a widower now.

NORA With a number of children. There now, it's burning. [*She closes the stove door and moves the rocker a bit to one side.*]

MRS. LINDE They say he has a hand in all kinds of business.

NORA Oh? That may be true: I wouldn't know. But let's not think about business. It's so dull.

[DR. RANK *enters from* HELMER'S *study.*]

RANK [*still in the doorway*] No, no, really—I don't want to intrude, I'd just as soon talk a little while with your wife. [*Shuts the door, then notices* MRS. LINDE.] Oh, beg pardon. I'm intruding here too.

NORA No, not at all. [*Introducing him.*] Dr. Rank, Mrs. Linde.

RANK Well now, that's a name much heard in this house. I believe I passed the lady on the stairs as I came.

MRS. LINDE Yes, I take the stairs very slowly. They're rather hard on me.

RANK Uh-hm, some touch of internal weakness?

MRS. LINDE More overexertion, I'd say.

RANK Nothing else? Then you're probably here in town to rest up in a round of parties?

MRS. LINDE I'm here to look for work.

RANK Is that the best cure for overexertion?

MRS. LINDE One has to live, Doctor.

RANK Yes, there's a common prejudice to that effect.

NORA Oh, come on, Dr. Rank—you really do want to live yourself.

RANK Yes, I really do. Wretched as I am, I'll gladly prolong my torment indefinitely. All my patients feel like that. And it's quite the same, too, with the morally sick. Right at this moment there's one of those moral invalids in there with Helmer—

MRS. LINDE [*softly*] Ah!

NORA Who do you mean?

RANK Oh, it's a lawyer, Krogstad, a type you wouldn't know. His character is rotten to the root—but even he began chattering all-importantly about how he had to *live.*

NORA Oh? What did he want to talk to Torvald about?

RANK I really don't know. I only heard something about the bank.

NORA I didn't know that Krog—that this man Krogstad had anything to do with the bank.

RANK Yes, he's gotten some kind of berth down there. [*To* MRS. LINDE.] I don't know if you also have, in your neck of the woods, a type of person who scuttles about breathlessly, sniffing out hints of moral corruption, and then maneuvers his victim into some sort of key position where he can keep an eye on him. It's the healthy these days that are out in the cold.

MRS. LINDE All the same, it's the sick who most need to be taken in.

RANK [*with a shrug*] Yes, there we have it. That's the concept that's turning society into a sanatorium.

[NORA, *lost in her thoughts, breaks out into quiet laughter and claps her hands.*]

RANK Why do you laugh at that? Do you have any real idea of what society is?

NORA What do I care about dreary old society? I was laughing at something quite different—something terribly funny. Tell me, Doctor—is everyone who works in the bank dependent now on Torvald?

RANK Is that what you find so terribly funny?

NORA [*smiling and humming*] Never mind, never mind! [*Pacing the floor.*] Yes, that's really immensely amusing: that we—that Torvald has so much power now over all those people. [*Taking the bag out of her pocket.*] Dr. Rank, a little macaroon on that?

RANK See here, macaroons! I thought they were contraband here.

NORA Yes, but these are some that Kristine gave me.

MRS. LINDE What? I—?

NORA Now, now, don't be afraid. You couldn't possibly know that Torvald had forbidden them. You see, he's worried they'll ruin my teeth. But hmp! Just this once! Isn't that so, Dr. Rank? Help yourself! [*Puts a macaroon in his mouth.*] And you too, Kristine. And I'll also have one, only a little one—or two, at the most. [*Walking about again.*] Now I'm really tremendously happy. Now there's just one last thing in the world that I have an enormous desire to do.

RANK Well! And what's that?

NORA It's something I have such a consuming desire to say so Torvald could hear.

RANK And why can't you say it?

NORA I don't dare. It's quite shocking.

MRS. LINDE Shocking?

RANK Well, then it isn't advisable. But in front of us you certainly can. What do you have such a desire to say so Torvald could hear?

NORA I have such a huge desire to say—to hell and be damned!

RANK Are you crazy?

MRS. LINDE My goodness, Nora!

RANK Go on, say it. Here he is.

NORA [*hiding the macaroon bag*] Shh, shh, shh!

[HELMER *comes in from his study, hat in hand, overcoat over his arm.*]

NORA [*going toward him*] Well, Torvald dear, are you through with him?

HELMER Yes, he just left.

NORA Let me introduce you—this is Kristine, who's arrived here in town.

HELMER Kristine—? I'm sorry, but I don't know—

NORA Mrs. Linde, Torvald dear. Mrs. Kristine Linde.

HELMER Of course. A childhood friend of my wife's, no doubt?

MRS LINDE Yes, we knew each other in those days.

NORA And just think, she made the long trip down here in order to talk with you.

HELMER What's this?

MRS. LINDE Well, not exactly—

NORA You see, Kristine is remarkably clever in office work, and so she's terribly eager to come under a capable man's supervision and add more to what she already knows—

HELMER Very wise, Mrs. Linde.

NORA And then when she heard that you'd become a bank manager—the story was wired out to the papers—then she came in as fast as she could and—Really, Torvald, for my sake you can do a little something for Kristine, can't you?

HELMER Yes, it's not at all impossible. Mrs. Linde, I suppose you're a widow?

MRS. LINDE Yes.

HELMER Any experience in office work?

MRS. LINDE Yes, a good deal.

HELMER Well, it's quite likely that I can make an opening for you—

NORA [*clapping her hands*] You see, you see!

HELMER You've come at a lucky moment, Mrs. Linde.

MRS. LINDE Oh, how can I thank you?

HELMER Not necessary. [*Putting his overcoat on.*] But today you'll have to excuse me—

RANK Wait, I'll go with you. [*He fetches his coat from the hall and warms it at the stove.*]

NORA Don't stay out long, dear.

HELMER An hour; no more.

NORA Are you going too, Kristine?

MRS. LINDE [*putting on her winter garments*] Yes, I have to see about a room now.

HELMER Then perhaps we can all walk together.

NORA [*helping her*] What a shame we're so cramped here, but it's quite impossible for us to—

MRS. LINDE Oh, don't even think of it! Good-bye, Nora dear, and thanks for everything.

NORA Good-bye for now. Of course you'll be back this evening. And you too, Dr. Rank. What? If you're well enough? Oh, you've got to be! Wrap up tight now.

[*In a ripple of small talk the company moves out into the hall; children's voices are heard outside on the steps.*]

NORA There they are! There they are! [*She runs to open the door. The children come in with their nurse,* ANNE-MARIE.] Come in, come in! [*Bends down and kisses them.*] Oh, you darlings—! Look at them, Kristine. Aren't they lovely!

RANK No loitering in the draft here.

HELMER Come, Mrs. Linde—this place is unbearable now for anyone but mothers.

[DR. RANK, HELMER, *and* MRS. LINDE *go down the stairs.* ANNE-MARIE *goes into the living room with the children.* NORA *follows, after closing the hall door.*]

NORA How fresh and strong you look. Oh, such red cheeks you have! Like apples and roses. [*The children interrupt her throughout the following.*] And it was so much fun? That's wonderful. Really? You pulled both Emmy and Bob on the sled? Imagine, all together! Yes, you're a clever boy, Ivar. Oh, let me hold her a bit, Anne-Marie. My sweet little doll baby! [*Takes the smallest from the nurse and dances with her.*] Yes, yes, Mama will dance with Bob as well. What? Did you throw snowballs? Oh, if I'd only been there! No, don't bother, Anne-Marie—I'll undress them myself. Oh yes, let me. It's such fun. Go in and rest; you look half frozen. There's hot coffee waiting for you on the stove. [*The nurse goes into the room to the left.* NORA *takes the children's winter things off, throwing them about, while the children talk to her all at once.*] Is that so? A big dog chased you? But it didn't bite? No, dogs never bite little, lovely doll babies. Don't peek in the packages, Ivar! What is it? Yes, wouldn't you like to know. No, no, it's an ugly something. Well? Shall we play? What shall we play? Hide-and-seek? Yes, let's play hide-and-seek. Bob must hide first. I must? Yes, let me hide first. [*Laughing and shouting, she and the children play in and out of the living room and the adjoining room to the right. At last* NORA *hides under the table. The children come storming in, search, but cannot find her, then hear her muffled laughter, dash over to the table, lift the cloth up and find her. Wild shouting. She creeps forward as if to scare them. More shouts. Meanwhile, a knock at the hall door; no one has noticed it. Now the door half opens, and* KROGSTAD *appears. He waits a moment; the game goes on.*]

KROGSTAD Beg pardon, Mrs. Helmer—

NORA [*with a strangled cry, turning and scrambling to her knees*] Oh! What do you want?

KROGSTAD Excuse me. The outer door was ajar; it must be someone forgot to shut it—

NORA [*rising*] My husband isn't home, Mr. Krogstad.

KROGSTAD I know that.

NORA Yes—then what do you want here?

KROGSTAD A word with you.

NORA With—? [*To the children, quietly.*] Go in to Anne-Marie. What? No, the strange man won't hurt Mama. When he's gone, we'll play some more. [*She leads the children into the room to the left and shuts the door after them. Then, tense and nervous*] You want to speak to me?

KROGSTAD Yes, I want to.

NORA Today? But it's not yet the first of the month—

KROGSTAD No, it's Christmas Eve. It's going to be up to you how merry a Christmas you have.

NORA What is it you want? Today I absolutely can't—

KROGSTAD We won't talk about that till later. This is something else. You do have a moment to spare, I suppose?

NORA Oh yes, of course—I do, except—

KROGSTAD Good. I was sitting over at Olsen's Restaurant when I saw your husband go down the street—

NORA Yes?

KROGSTAD With a lady.

NORA Yes. So?

KROGSTAD If you'll pardon my asking: wasn't that lady a Mrs. Linde?

NORA Yes.

KROGSTAD Just now come into town?

NORA Yes, today.

KROGSTAD She's a good friend of yours?

NORA Yes, she is. But I don't see—

KROGSTAD I also knew her once.

NORA I'm aware of that.

KROGSTAD Oh? You know all about it. I thought so. Well, then let me ask you short and sweet: is Mrs. Linde getting a job in the bank?

NORA What makes you think you can cross-examine me, Mr. Krogstad—you, one of my husband's employees? But since you ask, you might as well know—yes, Mrs. Linde's going to be taken on at the bank. And I'm the one who spoke for her, Mr. Krogstad. Now you know.

KROGSTAD So I guessed right.

NORA [*pacing up and down*] Oh, one does have a tiny bit of influence, I should hope. Just because I am a woman, don't think it means that— When one has a subordinate position, Mr. Krogstad, one really ought to be careful about pushing somebody who—hm—

KROGSTAD Who has influence?

NORA That's right.

KROGSTAD [*in a different tone*] Mrs. Helmer, would you be good enough to use your influence on my behalf?

NORA What? What do you mean?

KROGSTAD Would you please make sure that I keep my subordinate position in the bank?

NORA What does that mean? Who's thinking of taking away your position?

KROGSTAD Oh, don't play the innocent with me. I'm quite aware that your friend would hardly relish the chance of running into me again; and I'm also aware now whom I can thank for being turned out.

NORA But I promise you—

KROGSTAD Yes, yes, yes, to the point: there's still time, and I'm advising you to use your influence to prevent it.

NORA But Mr. Krogstad, I have absolutely no influence.

KROGSTAD You haven't? I thought you were just saying—

NORA You shouldn't take me so literally. I! How can you believe that I have any such influence over my husband?

KROGSTAD Oh, I've known your husband from our student days. I don't think the great bank manager's more steadfast than any other married man.

NORA You speak insolently about my husband, and I'll show you the door.

KROGSTAD The lady has spirit.

NORA I'm not afraid of you any longer. After New Year's, I'll soon be done with the whole business.

KROGSTAD [*restraining himself*] Now listen to me, Mrs. Helmer. If necessary, I'll fight for my little job in the bank as if it were life itself.

NORA Yes, so it seems.

KROGSTAD It's not just a matter of income; that's the least of it. It's something else— All right, out with it! Look, this is the thing. You know, just like all the others, of course, that once, a good many years ago, I did something rather rash.

NORA I've heard rumors to that effect.

KROGSTAD The case never got into court; but all the same, every door was closed in my face from then on. So I took up those various activities you know about. I had to grab hold somewhere; and I dare say I haven't been among the worst. But now I want to drop all that. My boys are growing up. For their sakes, I'll have to win back as much respect as possible here in town. That job in the bank was like the first rung in my ladder. And now your husband wants to kick me right back down in the mud again.

NORA But for heaven's sake, Mr. Krogstad, it's simply not in my power to help you.

KROGSTAD That's because you haven't the will to—but I have the means to make you.

NORA You certainly won't tell my husband that I owe you money?

KROGSTAD Hm—what if I told him that?

NORA That would be shameful of you. [*Nearly in tears.*] This secret—my joy and my pride—that he should learn it in such a crude and disgusting way—learn it from you. You'd expose me to the most horrible unpleasantness—

KROGSTAD Only unpleasantness?

NORA [*vehemently*] But go on and try. It'll turn out the worse for you, because then my husband will really see what a crook you are, and then you'll *never* be able to hold your job.

KROGSTAD I asked if it was just domestic unpleasantness you were afraid of?

NORA If my husband finds out, then of course he'll pay what I owe at once, and then we'd be through with you for good.

KROGSTAD [*a step closer*] Listen, Mrs. Helmer—you've either got a very bad memory, or else no head at all for business. I'd better put you a little more in touch with the facts.

NORA What do you mean?

KROGSTAD When your husband was sick, you came to me for a loan of four thousand, eight hundred crowns.

NORA Where else could I go?

KROGSTAD I promised to get you that sum—

NORA And you got it.

KROGSTAD I promised to get you that sum, on certain conditions. You were so involved in your husband's illness, and so eager to finance your trip, that I guess you didn't think out all the details. It might just be a good idea to remind you. I promised you the money on the strength of a note I drew up.

NORA Yes, and that I signed.

KROGSTAD Right. But at the bottom I added some lines for your father to guarantee the loan. He was supposed to sign down there.

NORA Supposed to? He did sign.

KROGSTAD I left the date blank. In other words, your father would have dated his signature himself. Do you remember that?

NORA Yes, I think—

KROGSTAD Then I gave you the note for you to mail to your father. Isn't that so?

NORA Yes.

KROGSTAD And naturally you sent it at once—because only some five, six days later you brought me the note, properly signed. And with that, the money was yours.

NORA Well, then; I've made my payments regularly, haven't I?

KROGSTAD More or less. But—getting back to the point—those were hard times for you then, Mrs. Helmer.

NORA Yes, they were.

KROGSTAD Your father was very ill, I believe.

NORA He was near the end.

KROGSTAD He died soon after?

NORA Yes.

KROGSTAD Tell me, Mrs. Helmer, do you happen to recall the date of your father's death? The day of the month, I mean.

NORA Papa died the twenty-ninth of September.

KROGSTAD That's quite correct; I've already looked into that. And now we come to a curious thing—[*taking out a paper*] which I simply cannot comprehend.

NORA Curious thing? I don't know—

KROGSTAD This is the curious thing: that your father co-signed the note for your loan three days after his death.

NORA How—? I don't understand.

KROGSTAD Your father died the twenty-ninth of September. But look. Here your father dated his signature October second. Isn't that curious, Mrs. Helmer? [NORA *is silent.*] Can you explain it to me? [NORA *remains silent.*] It's also remarkable that the words "October second" and the year aren't written in your father's hand, but rather in one that I think I know. Well, it's easy to understand. Your father forgot perhaps to date his signature, and then someone or other added it, a bit sloppily, before anyone knew of his death. There's nothing wrong in that. It all comes down to the signature. And there's no question about *that,* Mrs. Helmer. It really *was* your father who signed his own name here, wasn't it?

NORA [*after a short silence, throwing her head back and looking squarely at him*] No, it wasn't. *I* signed Papa's name.

KROGSTAD Wait, now—are you fully aware that this is a dangerous confession?

NORA Why? You'll soon get your money.

KROGSTAD Let me ask you a question—why didn't you send the paper to your father?

NORA That was impossible. Papa was so sick. If I'd asked him for his signature, I also would have had to tell him what the money was for. But I couldn't tell him, sick as he was, that my husband's life was in danger. That was just impossible.

KROGSTAD Then it would have been better if you'd given up the trip abroad.

NORA I couldn't possibly. The trip was to save my husband's life. I couldn't give that up.

KROGSTAD But didn't you ever consider that this was a fraud against me?

NORA I couldn't let myself be bothered by that. You weren't any concern of mine. I couldn't stand you, with all those cold complications you made, even though you knew how badly off my husband was.

KROGSTAD Mrs. Helmer, obviously you haven't the vaguest idea of what you've involved yourself in. But I can tell you this: it was nothing more and nothing worse than I once did—and it wrecked my whole reputation.

NORA You? Do you expect me to believe that you ever acted bravely to save your wife's life?

KROGSTAD Laws don't inquire into motives.

NORA Then they must be very poor laws.

KROGSTAD Poor or not—if I introduce this paper in court, you'll be judged according to law.

NORA This I refuse to believe. A daughter hasn't a right to protect her dying father from anxiety and care? A wife hasn't a right to save her husband's life? I don't know much about laws, but I'm sure that somewhere in the books these things are allowed. And you don't know anything about it—you who practice the law? You must be an awful lawyer, Mr. Krogstad.

KROGSTAD Could be. But business—the kind of business we two are mixed up in—don't you think I know about that? All right. Do what you want now. But I'm telling you *this:* if I get shoved down a second time, you're going to keep me company. [*He bows and goes out through the hall.*]

NORA [*pensive for a moment, then tossing her head*] Oh, really! Trying to frighten me. I'm not so silly as all that. [*Begins gathering up the children's clothes, but soon stops.*] But—? No, but that's impossible! I did it out of love.

THE CHILDREN [*in the doorway, left*] Mama, that strange man's gone out the door.

NORA Yes, yes, I know it. But don't tell anyone about the strange man. Do you hear? Not even Papa!

THE CHILDREN No, Mama. But now will you play again?

NORA No, not now.

THE CHILDREN Oh, but Mama, you promised.

NORA Yes, but I can't now. Go inside; I have too much to do. Go in, go in, my sweet darlings. [*She herds them gently back in the room and shuts the door after them. Settling on the sofa, she takes up a piece of embroidery and makes some stitches, but soon stops abruptly.*] No! [*Throws the work aside, rises, goes to the hall door and calls out.*] Helene! Let me have the tree in here. [*Goes to the table, left, opens the table drawer and stops again.*] No, but that's utterly impossible!

MAID [*with the Christmas tree*] Where should I put it, ma'am?

NORA There. The middle of the floor.

MAID Should I bring anything else?

NORA No, thanks. I have what I need.

[THE MAID, *who has set the tree down, goes out.*]

NORA [*absorbed in trimming the tree*] Candles here—and flowers here. That terrible creature! Talk, talk, talk! There's nothing to it at all. The tree's going to be lovely. I'll do anything to please you, Torvald. I'll sing for you, dance for you—

[HELMER *comes in from the hall, with a sheaf of papers under his arm.*]

NORA Oh! You're back so soon?

HELMER Yes. Has anyone been here?

NORA Here? No.

HELMER That's odd. I saw Krogstad leaving the front door.

NORA So? Oh yes, that's true. Krogstad was here a moment.

HELMER Nora, I can see by your face that he's been here, begging you to put in a good word for him.

NORA Yes.

HELMER And it was supposed to seem like your own idea? You were to hide it from me that he'd been here. He asked you that, too, didn't he?

NORA Yes, Torvald, but—

HELMER Nora, Nora, and you could fall for that? Talk with that sort of person and promise him anything? And then in the bargain, tell me an untruth.

NORA An untruth—?

HELMER Didn't you say that no one had been here? [*Wagging his finger.*] My little songbird must never do that again. A songbird needs a clean beak to warble with. No false notes. [*Putting his arm about her waist.*] That's the way it should be, isn't it? Yes, I'm sure of it. [*Releasing her.*] And so, enough of that. [*Sitting by the stove.*] Ah, how snug and cozy it is here. [*Leafing among his papers.*]

NORA [*busy with the tree, after a short pause*] Torvald!

HELMER Yes.

NORA I'm so much looking forward to the Stenborgs' costume party, day after tomorrow.

HELMER And I can't wait to see what you'll surprise me with.

NORA Oh, that stupid business!

HELMER What?

NORA I can't find anything that's right. Everything seems so ridiculous, so inane.

HELMER So my little Nora's come to *that* recognition?

NORA [*going behind his chair, her arms resting on its back*] Are you very busy, Torvald?

HELMER Oh—

NORA What papers are those?

HELMER Bank matters.

NORA Already?

HELMER I've gotten full authority from the retiring management to make all necessary changes in personnel and procedure. I'll need Christmas week for that. I want to have everything in order by New Year's.

NORA So that was the reason this poor Krogstad—

HELMER Hm.

NORA [*still leaning on the chair and slowly stroking the nape of his neck*] If you weren't so very busy, I would have asked you an enormous favor, Torvald.

HELMER Let's hear. What is it?

NORA You know, there isn't anyone who has your good taste—and I want so much to look well at the costume party. Torvald, couldn't you take over and decide what I should be and plan my costume?

HELMER Ah, is my stubborn little creature calling for a lifeguard?

NORA Yes, Torvald, I can't get anywhere without your help.

HELMER All right—I'll think it over. We'll hit on something.

NORA Oh, how sweet of you. [*Goes to the tree again. Pause.*] Aren't the red flowers pretty—? But tell me, was it really such a crime that this Krogstad committed?

HELMER Forgery. Do you have any idea what that means?

NORA Couldn't he have done it out of need?

HELMER Yes, or thoughtlessness, like so many others. I'm not so heartless that I'd condemn a man categorically for just one mistake.

NORA No, of course not, Torvald!

HELMER Plenty of men have redeemed themselves by openly confessing their crimes and taking their punishment.

NORA Punishment—?

HELMER But now Krogstad didn't go that way. He got himself out by sharp practices, and that's the real cause of his moral breakdown.

NORA Do you really think that would—?

HELMER Just imagine how a man with that sort of guilt in him has to lie and cheat and deceive on all sides, has to wear a mask even with the nearest and dearest he has, even with his own wife and children. And with the children, Nora—that's where it's most horrible.

NORA Why?

HELMER Because that kind of atmosphere of lies infects the whole life of a home. Every breath the children take in is filled with the germs of something degenerate.

NORA [*coming closer behind him*] Are you sure of that?

HELMER Oh, I've seen it often enough as a lawyer. Almost everyone who goes bad early in life has a mother who's a chronic liar.

NORA Why just—the mother?

HELMER It's usually the mother's influence that's dominant, but the father's works in the same way, of course. Every lawyer is quite familiar with it. And still this Krogstad's been going home year in, year out, poisoning his own children with lies and pretense; that's why I call him morally lost. [*Reaching his hands out toward her.*] So my sweet little Nora must promise me never to plead his cause. Your hand on it. Come, come, what's this? Give me your hand. There, now. All settled. I can tell you it'd be impossible for me to work alongside of him. I literally feel physically revolted when I'm anywhere near such a person.

NORA [*withdraws her hand and goes to the other side of the Christmas tree*] How hot it is here! And I've got so much to do.

HELMER [*getting up and gathering his papers*] Yes, and I have to think about getting some of these read through before dinner. I'll think about your costume, too. And something to hang on the tree in gilt paper, I may even see about that. [*Putting his hand on her head.*] Oh you, my darling little songbird. [*He goes into his study and closes the door after him.*]

NORA [*softly, after a silence*] Oh, really! It isn't so. It's impossible. It must be impossible.

ANNE-MARIE [*in the doorway, left*] The children are begging so hard to come in to Mama.

NORA No, no, no, don't let them in to me! You stay with them, Anne-Marie.

ANNE-MARIE Of course, ma'am. [*Closes the door.*]

NORA [*pale with terror*] Hurt my children—! Poison my home? [*A moment's pause; then she tosses her head.*] That's not true. Never. Never in all the world.

ACT II

[*Same room. Beside the piano the Christmas tree now stands stripped of ornaments, burned-down candle stubs on its ragged branches.* NORA'S *street clothes lie on the sofa.* NORA, *alone in the room, moves restlessly about; at last she stops at the sofa and picks up her coat.*]

NORA [*dropping the coat again*] Someone's coming! [*Goes toward the door, listens.*] No—there's no one. Of course—nobody's coming today, Christmas Day—or tomorrow, either. But maybe—[*Opens the door and looks out.*] No, nothing in the mailbox. Quite empty. [*Coming forward.*] What nonsense! He won't do anything serious. Nothing terrible could happen. It's impossible. Why, I have three small children.

[ANNE-MARIE, *with a large carton, comes in from the room to the left.*]

ANNE-MARIE Well, at last I found the box with the masquerade clothes.

NORA Thanks. Put it on the table.

ANNE-MARIE [*does so*] But they're all pretty much of a mess.

NORA Ahh! I'd love to rip them in a million pieces!

ANNE-MARIE Oh, mercy, they can be fixed right up. Just a little patience.

NORA Yes, I'll go get Mrs. Linde to help me.

ANNE-MARIE Out again now? In this nasty weather? Miss Nora will catch cold—get sick.

NORA Oh, worse things could happen—How are the children?

ANNE-MARIE The poor mites are playing with their Christmas presents, but—

NORA Do they ask for me much?

ANNE-MARIE They're so used to having Mama around, you know.

NORA Yes. But Anne-Marie, I *can't* be together with them as much as I was.

ANNE-MARIE Well, small children get used to anything.

NORA You think so? Do you think they'd forget their mother if she was gone for good?

ANNE-MARIE Oh, mercy—gone for good!

NORA Wait, tell me, Anne-Marie—I've wondered so often—how could you ever have the heart to give your child over to strangers?

ANNE-MARIE But I had to, you know, to become little Nora's nurse.

NORA Yes, but how could you *do* it?

ANNE-MARIE When I could get such a good place? A girl who's poor and who's gotten in trouble is glad enough for that. Because that slippery fish, he didn't do a thing for me, you know.

NORA But your daughter's surely forgotten you.

ANNE-MARIE Oh, she certainly has not. She's written to me, both when she was confirmed and when she was married.

NORA [*clasping her about the neck*] You old Anne-Marie, you were a good mother for me when I was little.

ANNE-MARIE Poor little Nora, with no other mother but me.

NORA And if the babies didn't have one, then I know that you'd—What silly talk! [*Opening the carton.*] Go in to them. Now I'll have to—Tomorrow you can see how lovely I'll look.

ANNE-MARIE Oh, there won't be anyone at the party as lovely as Miss Nora. [*She goes off into the room, left.*]

NORA [*begins unpacking the box, but soon throws it aside*] Oh, if I dared to go out. If only nobody would come. If only nothing would happen here while I'm out. What craziness—nobody's coming. Just don't think. This muff—needs a brushing. Beautiful gloves, beautiful gloves. Let it go. Let it go! One, two, three, four, five, six—[*With a cry.*] Oh, there they are! [*Poises to move toward the door, but remains irresolutely standing.* MRS. LINDE *enters from the hall, where she has removed her street clothes.*]

NORA Oh, it's you, Kristine. There's no one else out there? How good that you've come.

MRS. LINDE I hear you were up asking for me.

NORA Yes, I just stopped by. There's something you really can help me with. Let's get settled on the sofa. Look, there's going to be a costume party tomorrow evening at the Stenborgs' right above us, and now Torvald wants me to go as a Neapolitan peasant girl and dance the tarantella that I learned in Capri.

MRS. LINDE Really, are you giving a whole performance?

NORA Torvald says yes, I should. See, here's the dress. Torvald had it made for me down there; but now it's all so tattered that I just don't know—

MRS. LINDE Oh, we'll fix that up in no time. It's nothing more than the trimmings—they're a bit loose here and there. Needle and thread? Good, now we have what we need.

NORA Oh, how sweet of you!

MRS. LINDE [*sewing*] So you'll be in disguise tomorrow, Nora. You know what? I'll stop by then for a moment and have a look at you all dressed up. But listen, I've absolutely forgotten to thank you for that pleasant evening yesterday.

NORA [*getting up and walking about*] I don't think it was as pleasant as usual yesterday. You should have come to town a bit sooner, Kristine— Yes, Torvald really knows how to give a home elegance and charm.

MRS. LINDE And you do, too, if you ask me. You're not your father's daughter for nothing. But tell me, is Dr. Rank always so down in the mouth as yesterday?

NORA No, that was quite an exception. But he goes around critically ill all the time—tuberculosis of the spine, poor man. You know, his father was a disgusting thing who kept mistresses and so on—and that's why the son's been sickly from birth.

MRS. LINDE [*lets her sewing fall to her lap*] But my dearest Nora, how do you know about such things?

NORA [*walking more jauntily*] Hmp! When you've had three children, then you've had a few visits from—from women who know something of medicine, and they tell you this and that.

MRS. LINDE [*resumes sewing; a short pause*] Does Dr. Rank come here every day?

NORA Every blessed day. He's Torvald's best friend from childhood, and *my* good friend, too. Dr. Rank almost belongs to this house.

MRS. LINDE But tell me—is he quite sincere? I mean, doesn't he rather enjoy flattering people?

NORA Just the opposite. Why do you think that?

MRS. LINDE When you introduced us yesterday, he was proclaiming that he's often heard my name in this house; but later I noticed that your husband hadn't the slightest idea who I really was. So how could Dr. Rank—?

NORA But it's all true, Kristine. You see, Torvald loves me beyond words, and, as he puts it, he'd like to keep me all to himself. For a long time he'd almost be jealous if I even mentioned any of my old friends back home. So of course I dropped that. But with Dr. Rank I talk a lot about such things, because he likes hearing about them.

MRS. LINDE Now listen, Nora; in many ways you're still like a child. I'm a good deal older than you, with a little more experience. I'll tell you something: you ought to put an end to all this with Dr. Rank.

NORA What should I put an end to?

MRS. LINDE Both parts of it, I think. Yesterday you said something about a rich admirer who'd provide you with money—

NORA Yes, one who doesn't exist—worse luck. So?

MRS. LINDE Is Dr. Rank well off?

NORA Yes, he is.

MRS. LINDE With no dependents?

NORA No, no one, But—

MRS. LINDE And he's over here every day?

NORA Yes, I told you that.

MRS. LINDE How can a man of such refinement be so grasping?

NORA I don't follow you at all.

MRS. LINDE Now don't try to hide it, Nora. You think I can't guess who loaned you the forty-eight hundred crowns?

NORA Are you out of your mind? How could you think such a thing! A friend of ours, who comes here every single day. What an intolerable situation that would have been!

MRS. LINDE Then it really wasn't him.

NORA No, absolutely not. It never even crossed my mind for a moment—And he had nothing to lend in those days; his inheritance came later.

MRS. LINDE Well, I think that was a stroke of luck for you, Nora dear.

NORA No, it never would have occurred to me to ask Dr. Rank—Still, I'm quite sure that if I had asked him—

MRS. LINDE Which you won't, of course.

NORA No, of course not. I can't see that I'd ever need to. But I'm quite positive that if I talked to Dr. Rank—

MRS. LINDE Behind your husband's back?

NORA I've got to clear up this other thing; *that's* also behind his back. I've *got* to clear it all up.

MRS. LINDE Yes, I was saying that yesterday, but—

NORA [*pacing up and down*] A man handles these problems so much better than a woman—

MRS. LINDE One's husband does, yes.

NORA Nonsense. [*Stopping.*] When you pay everything you owe, then you get your note back, right?

MRS. LINDE Yes, naturally.

NORA And can rip it into a million pieces and burn it up—that filthy scrap of paper!

MRS LINDE [*looking hard at her, laying her sewing aside, and rising slowly*] Nora, you're hiding something from me.

NORA You can see it in my face?

MRS. LINDE Something's happened to you since yesterday morning. Nora, what is it?

NORA [*hurrying toward her*] Kristine! [*Listening.*] Shh! Torvald's home. Look, go in with the children a while. Torvald can't bear all this snipping and stitching. Let Anne-Marie help you.

MRS. LINDE [*gathering up some of the things*] All right, but I'm not leaving here until we've talked this out. [*She disappears into the room, left, as Torvald enters from the hall.*]

NORA Oh, how I've been waiting for you, Torvald dear.

HELMER Was that the dressmaker?

NORA No, that was Kristine. She's helping me fix up my costume. You know, it's going to be quite attractive.

HELMER Yes, wasn't that a bright idea I had?

NORA Brilliant! But then wasn't I good as well to give in to you?

HELMER Good—because you give in to your husband's judgment? All right, you little goose, I know you didn't mean it like that. But I won't disturb you. You'll want to have a fitting, I suppose.

NORA And you'll be working?

HELMER Yes. [*Indicating a bundle of papers.*] See. I've been down to the bank. [*Starts toward his study.*]

NORA Torvald.

HELMER [*stops*] Yes.

NORA If your little squirrel begged you, with all her heart and soul, for something—?

HELMER What's that?

NORA Then would you do it?

HELMER First, naturally, I'd have to know what it was.

NORA Your squirrel would scamper about and do tricks, if you'd only be sweet and give in.

HELMER Out with it.

NORA Your lark would be singing high and low in every room—

HELMER Come on, she does that anyway.

NORA I'd be a wood nymph and dance for you in the moonlight.

HELMER Nora—don't tell me it's that same business from this morning?

NORA [*coming closer*] Yes, Torvald, I beg you, please!

HELMER And you actually have the nerve to drag that up again?

NORA Yes, yes, you've got to give in to me; you *have* to let Krogstad keep his job in the bank.

HELMER My dear Nora, I've slated his job for Mrs. Linde.

NORA That's awfully kind of you. But you could just fire another clerk instead of Krogstad.

HELMER This is the most incredible stubbornness! Because you go and give an impulsive promise to speak up for him, I'm expected to—

NORA That's not the reason, Torvald. It's for your own sake. That man does writing for the worst papers; you said it yourself. He could do you any amount of harm. I'm scared to death of him—

HELMER Ah, I understand. It's the old memories haunting you.

NORA What do you mean by that?

HELMER Of course, you're thinking about your father.

NORA Yes, all right. Just remember how those nasty gossips wrote in the papers about Papa and slandered him so cruelly. I think they'd have had him dismissed if the department hadn't sent you up to investigate, and if you hadn't been so kind and open-minded toward him.

HELMER My dear Nora, there's a notable difference between your father and me. Your father's official career was hardly above reproach. But mine is; and I hope it'll stay that way as long as I hold my position.

NORA Oh, who can ever tell what vicious minds can invent? We could be so snug and happy now in our quiet, carefree home—you and I and the children, Torvald! That's why I'm pleading with you so—

HELMER And just by pleading for him you make it impossible for me to keep him on. It's already known at the bank that I'm firing Krogstad. What if it's rumored around now that the new bank manager was vetoed by his wife—

NORA Yes, what then—?

HELMER Oh yes—as long as our little bundle of stubbornness gets her way—! I should go and make myself ridiculous in front of the whole office—give people the idea I can be swayed by all kinds of outside pressure. Oh, you can bet I'd feel the effects of that soon enough! Besides—there's something that rules Krogstad right out at the bank as long as I'm the manager.

NORA What's that?

HELMER His moral failings I could maybe overlook if I had to—

NORA Yes, Torvald, why not?

HELMER And I hear he's quite efficient on the job. But he was a crony of mine back in my teens—one of those rash friendships that crop up again and again to embarrass you later in life. Well, I might as well say it straight out: we're on a first-name basis. And that tactless fool makes no effort at all to hide it in front of others. Quite the contrary—he thinks that entitles him to take a familiar air around me, and so every other second he comes booming out with his "Yes, Torvald!" and "Sure thing, Torvald!" I tell you, it's been excruciating for me. He's out to make my place in the bank unbearable.

NORA Torvald, you can't be serious about all this.

HELMER Oh no? Why not?

NORA Because these are such petty considerations.

HELMER What are you saying? Petty? You think I'm petty!

NORA No, just the opposite, Torvald dear. That's exactly why—

HELMER Never mind. You call my motives petty; then I might as well be just that. Petty! All right! We'll put a stop to this for good. [*Goes to the hall door and calls.*] Helene!

NORA What do you want?

HELMER [*searching among his papers*] A decision. [THE MAID *comes in.*] Look here; take this letter; go out with it at once. Get hold of a messenger and have him deliver it. Quick now. It's already addressed. Wait, here's some money.

MAID Yes, sir. [*She leaves with the letter.*]

HELMER [*straightening his papers*] There, now, little Miss Willful.

NORA [*breathlessly*] Torvald, what was that letter?

HELMER Krogstad's notice.

NORA Call it back, Torvald! There's still time. Oh, Torvald, call it back! Do it for my sake—for your sake, for the children's sake! Do you hear, Torvald; do it! You don't know how this can harm us.

HELMER Too late.

NORA Yes, too late.

HELMER Nora dear, I can forgive you this panic, even though basically you're insulting me. Yes, you are! Or isn't it an insult to think that *I* should be afraid of a courtroom hack's revenge? But I forgive you anyway, because this shows so beautifully how much you love me. [*Takes her in his arms.*] This is the way it should be, my darling Nora. Whatever comes, you'll see: when it really counts, I have strength and courage enough as a man to take on the whole weight myself.

NORA [*terrified*] What do you mean by that?

HELMER The whole weight, I said.

NORA [*resolutely*] No, never in all the world.

HELMER Good. So we'll share it, Nora, as man and wife. That's as it should be. [*Fondling her.*] Are you happy now? There, there, there—not these frightened dove's eyes. It's nothing at all but empty fantasies—Now you should run through your tarantella and practice your tambourine. I'll go to the inner office and shut both doors, so I won't hear a thing; you can make all the noise you like.

[*Turning in the doorway.*] And when Rank comes, just tell him where he can find me. [*He nods to her and goes with his papers into the study, closing the door.*]

NORA [*standing as though rooted, dazed with fright, in a whisper*] He really could do it. He will do it. He'll do it in spite of everything. No, not that, never, never! Anything but that! Escape! A way out—[*The doorbell rings*]. Dr. Rank! Anything but that! *Anything,* whatever it is! [*Her hands pass over her face, smoothing it; she pulls herself together, goes over and opens the hall door.* DR. RANK *stands outside, hanging his fur coat up. During the following scene, it begins getting dark.*]

NORA Hello, Dr. Rank. I recognized your ring. But you mustn't go in to Torvald yet; I believe he's working.

RANK And you?

NORA For you, I always have an hour to spare—you know that. [*He has entered, and she shuts the door after him.*]

RANK Many thanks. I'll make use of these hours while I can.

NORA What do you mean by that? While you can?

RANK Does that disturb you?

NORA Well, it's such an odd phrase. Is anything going to happen?

RANK What's going to happen is what I've been expecting so long—but I honestly didn't think it would come so soon.

NORA [*gripping his arm*] What is it you've found out? Dr. Rank, you have to tell me!

RANK [*sitting by the stove*] It's all over with me. There's nothing to be done about it.

NORA [*breathing easier*] Is it you—then—?

RANK Who else? There's no point in lying to one's self. I'm the most miserable of all my patients, Mrs. Helmer. These past few days I've been auditing my internal accounts. Bankrupt! Within a month I'll probably be laid out and rotting in the churchyard.

NORA Oh, what a horrible thing to say.

RANK The thing itself is horrible. But the worst of it is all the other horror before it's over. There's only one final examination left; when I'm finished with that, I'll know about when my disintegration will begin. There's something I want to say. Helmer with his sensitivity has such a sharp distaste for anything ugly. I don't want him near my sickroom.

NORA Oh, but Dr. Rank—

RANK I won't have him in there. Under no condition. I'll lock my door to him—As soon as I'm completely sure of the worst, I'll send you my calling card marked with a black cross, and you'll know then the wreck has started to come apart.

NORA No, today you're completely unreasonable. And I wanted you so much to be in a really good humor.

RANK With death up my sleeve? And then to suffer this way for somebody else's sins. Is there any justice in that? And in every single family, in some way or another, this inevitable retribution of nature goes on—

NORA [*her hands pressed over her ears*] Oh, stuff! Cheer up! Please—be gay!

RANK Yes, I'd just as soon laugh at it all. My poor, innocent spine, serving time for my father's gay army days.

NORA [*by the table, left*] He was so infatuated with asparagus tips and *pâté de foie gras,* wasn't that it?

RANK Yes—and with truffles.

NORA Truffles, yes. And then with oysters, I suppose?

RANK Yes, tons of oysters, naturally.

NORA And then the port and champagne to go with it. It's so sad that all these delectable things have to strike at our bones.

RANK Especially when they strike at the unhappy bones that never shared in the fun.

NORA Ah, that's the saddest of all.

RANK [*looks searchingly at her*] Hm.

NORA [*after a moment*] Why did you smile?

RANK No, it was you who laughed.

NORA No, it was you who smiled, Dr. Rank!

RANK [*getting up*] You're even a bigger tease than I'd thought.

NORA I'm full of wild ideas today.

RANK That's obvious.

NORA [*putting both hands on his shoulders*] Dear, dear Dr. Rank, you'll never die for Torvald and me.

RANK Oh, that loss you'll easily get over. Those who go away are soon forgotten.

NORA [*looks fearfully at him*] You believe that?

RANK One makes new connections, and then—

NORA Who makes new connections?

RANK Both you and Torvald will when I'm gone. I'd say you're well under way already. What was that Mrs. Linde doing here last evening?

NORA Oh, come—you can't be jealous of poor Kristine?

RANK Oh yes, I am. She'll be my successor here in the house. When I'm down under, that woman will probably—

NORA Shh! Not so loud. She's right in there.

RANK Today as well. So you see.

NORA Only to sew on my dress. Good gracious, how unreasonable you are. [*Sitting on the sofa.*] Be nice now, Dr. Rank. Tomorrow you'll see how beautifully I'll dance; and you can imagine then that I'm dancing only for you—yes, and of course for Torvald, too—that's understood. [*Takes various items out of the carton.*] Dr. Rank, sit over here and I'll show you something.

RANK [*sitting*] What's that?

NORA Look here. Look.

RANK Silk stockings.

NORA Flesh-colored. Aren't they lovely? Now it's so dark here, but tomorrow—No, no, no, just look at the feet. Oh well, you might as well look at the rest.

RANK Hm—

NORA Why do you look so critical? Don't you believe they'll fit?

RANK I've never had any chance to form an opinion on that.

NORA [*glancing at him a moment*] Shame on you. [*Hits him lightly on the ear with the stockings.*] That's for you. [*Puts them away again.*]

RANK And what other splendors am I going to see now?

NORA Not the least bit more, because you've been naughty. [*She hums a little and rummages among her things.*]

RANK [*after a short silence*] When I sit here together with you like this, completely easy and open, then I don't know—I simply can't imagine—whatever would have become of me if I'd never come into this house.

NORA [*smiling*] Yes, I really think you feel completely at ease with us.

RANK [*more quietly, staring straight ahead*] And then to have to go away from it all—

NORA Nonsense, you're not going away.

RANK [*his voice unchanged*] —and not even be able to leave some poor show of gratitude behind, scarcely a fleeting regret—no more than a vacant place that anyone can fill.

NORA And if I asked you now for—? No—

RANK For what?

NORA For a great proof of your friendship—

RANK Yes, yes?

NORA No, I mean—for an exceptionally big favor—

RANK Would you really, for once, make me so happy?

NORA Oh, you haven't the vaguest idea what it is.

RANK All right, then tell me.

NORA No, but I can't, Dr. Rank—it's all out of reason. It's advice and help, too—and a favor—

RANK So much the better. I can't fathom what you're hinting at. Just speak out. Don't you trust me?

NORA Of course. More than anyone else. You're my best and truest friend, I'm sure. That's why I want to talk to you. All right, then, Dr. Rank: there's something you can help me prevent. You know how deeply, how inexpressibly dearly Torvald loves me; he'd never hesitate a second to give up his life for me.

RANK [*leaning close to her*] Nora—do you think he's the only one—

NORA [*with a slight start*] Who—?

RANK Who'd gladly give up his life for you.

NORA [*heavily*] I see.

RANK I swore to myself you should know this before I'm gone. I'll never find a better chance. Yes, Nora, now you know. And also you know now that you can trust me beyond anyone else.

NORA [*rising, natural and calm*] Let me by.

RANK [*making room for her, but still sitting*] Nora—

NORA [*in the hall doorway*] Helene, bring the lamp in. [*Goes over to the stove.*] Ah, dear Dr. Rank, that was really mean of you.

RANK [*getting up*] That I've loved you just as deeply as somebody else? Was *that* mean?

NORA No, but that you came out and told me. That was quite unnecessary—

RANK What do you mean? Have you known—?

[THE MAID *comes in with the lamp, sets it on the table, and goes out again.*]

RANK Nora—Mrs. Helmer—I'm asking you: have you known about it?

NORA Oh, how can I tell what I know or don't know? Really, I don't know what to say—Why did you have to be so clumsy, Dr. Rank! Everything was so good.

RANK Well, in any case, you now have the knowledge that my body and soul are at your command. So won't you speak out?

NORA [*looking at him*] After that?

RANK Please, just let me know what it is.

NORA You can't know anything now.

RANK I have to. You mustn't punish me like this. Give me the chance to do whatever is humanly possible for you.

NORA Now there's nothing you can do for me. Besides, actually, I don't need any help. You'll see—it's only my fantasies. That's what it is. Of course! [*Sits in the rocker, looks at him, and smiles.*] What a nice one you are, Dr. Rank. Aren't you a little bit ashamed, now that the lamp is here?

RANK No, not exactly. But perhaps I'd better go—for good?

NORA No, you certainly can't do that. You must come here just as you always have. You know Torvald can't do without you.

RANK Yes, but *you?*

NORA You know how much I enjoy it when you're here.

RANK That's precisely what threw me off. You're a mystery to me. So many times I've felt you'd almost rather be with me than with Helmer.

NORA Yes—you see, there are some people that one loves most and other people that one would almost prefer being with.

RANK Yes, there's something to that.

NORA When I was back home, of course I loved Papa most. But I always thought it was so much fun when I could sneak down to the maids' quarters, because they never tried to improve me, and it was always so amusing, the way they talked to each other.

RANK Aha, so it's *their* place that I've filled.

NORA [*jumping up and going to him*] Oh, dear, sweet Dr. Rank, that's not what I mean at all. But you can understand that with Torvald it's just the same as with Papa—

[THE MAID *enters from the hall.*]

MAID Ma'am—please! [*She whispers to* NORA *and hands her a calling card.*]

NORA [*glancing at the card*] Ah! [*slips it into her pocket.*]

RANK Anything wrong?

NORA No, no, not at all. It's only some—it's my new dress—

RANK Really? But—there's your dress.

NORA Oh, that. But this is another one—I ordered it—Torvald mustn't know—

RANK Ah, now we have the big secret.

NORA That's right. Just go in with him—he's back in the inner study. Keep him there as long as—

RANK Don't worry. He won't get away. [*Goes into the study.*]

NORA [*to the Maid*] And he's standing waiting in the kitchen?

MAID Yes, he came up by the back stairs.

NORA But didn't you tell him somebody was here?

MAID Yes, but that didn't do any good.

NORA He won't leave?

MAID No, he won't go till he's talked with you, ma'am.

NORA Let him come in, then—but quietly. Helene, don't breathe a word about this. It's a surprise for my husband.

MAID Yes, yes, I understand—[*Goes out.*]

NORA This horror—it's going to happen. No, no, no, it can't happen, it mustn't. [*She goes and bolts Helmer's door.* THE MAID *opens the hall door for* KROGSTAD *and shuts it behind him. He is dressed for travel in a fur coat, boots, and a fur cap.*]

NORA [*going toward him*] Talk softly. My husband's home.

KROGSTAD Well, good for him.

NORA What do you want?

KROGSTAD Some information.

NORA Hurry up, then. What is it?

KROGSTAD You know, of course, that I got my notice.

NORA I couldn't prevent it, Mr. Krogstad. I fought for you to the bitter end, but nothing worked.

KROGSTAD Does your husband's love for you run so thin? He knows everything I can expose you to, and all the same he dares to—

NORA How can you imagine he knows anything about this?

KROGSTAD Ah, no—I can't imagine it either, now. It's not at all like my fine Torvald Helmer to have so much guts—

NORA Mr. Krogstad, I demand respect for my husband!

KROGSTAD Why, of course—all due respect. But since the lady's keeping it so carefully hidden, may I presume to ask if you're also a bit better informed than yesterday about what you've actually done?

NORA More than you ever could teach me.

KROGSTAD Yes, I *am* such an awful lawyer.

NORA What is it you want from me?

KROGSTAD Just a glimpse of how you are, Mrs. Helmer. I've been thinking about you all day long. A cashier, a night-court scribbler, a—well, a type like me also has a little of what they call a heart, you know.

NORA Then show it. Think of my children.

KROGSTAD Did you or your husband ever think of mine? But never mind. I simply wanted to tell you that you don't need to take this thing too seriously. For the present, I'm not proceeding with any action.

NORA Oh no, really! Well—I knew that.

KROGSTAD Everything can be settled in a friendly spirit. It doesn't have to get around town at all; it can stay just among us three.

NORA My husband must never know anything of this.

KROGSTAD How can you manage that? Perhaps you can pay me the balance?

NORA No, not right now.

KROGSTAD Or you know some way of raising the money in a day or two?

NORA No way that I'm willing to use.

KROGSTAD Well, it wouldn't have done you any good, anyway. If you stood in front of me with a fistful of bills, you still couldn't buy your signature back.

NORA Then tell me what you're going to do with it.

KROGSTAD I'll just hold onto it—keep it on file. There's no outsider who'll even get wind of it. So if you've been thinking of taking some desperate step—

NORA I have.

KROGSTAD Been thinking of running away from home—

NORA I have!

KROGSTAD Or even of something worse—

NORA How could you guess that?

KROGSTAD You can drop those thoughts.

NORA How could you guess I was thinking of *that?*

KROGSTAD Most of us think about *that* at first. I thought about it too, but I discovered I hadn't the courage—

NORA [*lifelessly*] I don't either.

KROGSTAD [*relieved*] That's true, you haven't the courage? You too?

NORA I don't have it—I don't have it.

KROGSTAD It would be terribly stupid, anyway. After that first storm at home blows out, why, then—I have here in my pocket a letter for your husband—

NORA Telling everything?

KROGSTAD As charitably as possible.

NORA [*quickly*] He mustn't ever get that letter. Tear it up. I'll find some way to get money.

KROGSTAD Beg pardon, Mrs. Helmer, but I think I just told you—

NORA Oh, I don't mean the money I owe you. Let me know how much you want from my husband, and I'll manage it.

KROGSTAD I don't want any money from your husband.

NORA What do you want, then?

KROGSTAD I'll tell you what. I want to recoup, Mrs. Helmer; I want to get on in the world—and there's where your husband can help me. For a year and a half I've kept myself clean of anything disreputable—all that time struggling with the worst conditions; but I was satisfied, working my way up step by step. Now I've been written right off, and I'm just not in the mood to come crawling back. I tell you, I want to move on. I want to get back in the bank—in a better position. Your husband can set up a job for me—

NORA He'll never do that!

KROGSTAD He'll do it. I know him. He won't dare breathe a word of protest. And once I'm in there together with him, you just wait and see! Inside of a year, I'll be the manager's right-hand man. It'll be Nils Krogstad, not Torvald Helmer, who runs the bank.

NORA You'll never see the day!

KROGSTAD Maybe you think you can—

NORA I have the courage now—for *that.*

KROGSTAD Oh, you don't scare me. A smart, spoiled lady like you—

NORA You'll see; you'll see!

KROGSTAD Under the ice, maybe? Down in the freezing, coal-black water? There, till you float up in the spring, ugly, unrecognizable, with your hair falling out—

NORA You don't frighten me.

KROGSTAD Nor do you frighten me. One doesn't do these things, Mrs. Helmer. Besides, what good would it be? I'd still have him safe in my pocket.

NORA Afterwards? When I'm no longer—?

KROGSTAD Are you forgetting that *I'll* be in control then over your final reputation? [NORA *stands speechless, staring at him.*] Good; now I've warned you. Don't do anything stupid. When Helmer's read my letter, I'll be waiting for his reply. And bear in mind that it's your husband himself who's forced me back to my old ways. I'll never forgive him for that. Good-bye, Mrs. Helmer. [*He goes out through the hall.*]

NORA [*goes to the hall door, opens it a crack, and listens*] He's gone. Didn't leave the letter. Oh no, no, that's impossible too! [*Opening the door more and more.*] What's that? He's standing outside—not going downstairs. He's thinking it over? Maybe he'll—? [*A letter falls in the mailbox; then Krogstad's footsteps are heard, dying away down a flight of stairs. Nora gives a muffled cry and runs over toward the sofa table. A short pause.*] In the mailbox. [*Slips warily over to the hall door.*] It's lying there. Torvald, Torvald—now we're lost!

MRS. LINDE [*entering with the costume from the room, left*] There now, I can't see anything else to mend. Perhaps you'd like to try—

NORA [*in a hoarse whisper*] Kristine, come here.

MRS. LINDE [*tossing the dress on the sofa*] What's wrong? You look upset.

NORA Come here. See that letter? *There!* Look—through the glass in the mailbox.

MRS. LINDE Yes, yes, I see it.

NORA That letter's from Krogstad—

MRS. LINDE Nora—it's Krogstad who loaned you the money!

NORA Yes, and now Torvald will find out everything.

MRS. LINDE Believe me, Nora, it's best for both of you.

NORA There's more you don't know. I forged a name.

MRS. LINDE But for heaven's sake—?

NORA I only want to tell you that, Kristine, so that you can be my witness.

MRS. LINDE Witness? Why should I—?

NORA If I should go out of my mind—it could easily happen—

MRS. LINDE Nora!

NORA Or anything else occurred—so I couldn't be present here—

MRS. LINDE Nora, Nora, you aren't yourself at all!

NORA And someone should try to take on the whole weight, all of the guilt, you follow me—

MRS. LINDE Yes, of course, but why do you think—?

NORA Then you're the witness that it isn't true, Kristine. I'm very much myself; my mind right now is perfectly clear; and I'm telling you: nobody else has known about this; I alone did everything. Remember that.

MRS. LINDE I will. But I don't understand all this.

NORA Oh, how could you ever understand it? It's the miracle now that's going to take place.

MRS. LINDE The miracle?

NORA Yes, the miracle. But it's so awful, Kristine. It mustn't take place, not for anything in the world.

MRS. LINDE I'm going right over and talk with Krogstad.

NORA Don't go near him; he'll do you some terrible harm!

MRS. LINDE There was a time once when he'd gladly have done anything for me.

NORA He?

MRS. LINDE Where does he live?

NORA Oh, how do I know? Yes. [*Searches in her pocket.*] Here's his card. But the letter, the letter—!

HELMER [*from the study, knocking on the door*] Nora!

NORA [*with a cry of fear*] Oh! What is it? What do you want?

HELMER Now, now, don't be so frightened. We're not coming in. You locked the door—are you trying on the dress?

NORA Yes. I'm trying it. I'll look just beautiful, Torvald.

MRS. LINDE [*who has read the card*] He's living right around the corner.

NORA Yes, but what's the use? We're lost. The letter's in the box.

MRS. LINDE And your husband has the key?

NORA Yes, always.

MRS. LINDE Krogstad can ask for his letter back unread; he can find some excuse—

NORA But it's just this time that Torvald usually—

MRS. LINDE Stall him. Keep him in there. I'll be back as quick as I can. [*She hurries out through the hall entrance.*]

NORA [*goes to* HELMER'S *door, opens it, and peers in*] Torvald!

HELMER [*from the inner study*] Well—does one dare set foot in one's own living room at last? Come on, Rank, now we'll get a look—[*In the doorway.*] But what's this?

NORA What, Torvald dear?

HELMER Rank had me expecting some grand masquerade.

RANK [*in the doorway*] That was my impression, but I must have been wrong.

NORA No one can admire me in my splendor—not till tomorrow.

HELMER But Nora dear, you look so exhausted. Have you practiced too hard?

NORA No, I haven't practiced at all yet.

HELMER You know, it's necessary—

NORA Oh, it's absolutely necessary, Torvald. But I can't get anywhere without your help. I've forgotten the whole thing completely.

HELMER Ah, we'll soon take care of that.

NORA Yes, take care of me, Torvald, please! Promise me that? Oh, I'm so nervous. That big party—You must give up everything this evening for me. No business—don't even touch your pen. Yes? Dear Torvald, promise?

HELMER It's a promise. Tonight I'm totally at your service—you little helpless thing. Hm—but first there's one thing I want to—[*Goes toward the hall door.*]

NORA What are you looking for?

HELMER Just to see if there's any mail.

NORA No, no, don't do that, Torvald!

HELMER Now what?

NORA Torvald, please. There isn't any.

HELMER Let me look, though. [*Starts out.* NORA, *at the piano, strikes the first notes of the tarantella.* HELMER, *at the door, stops.*] Aha!

NORA I can't dance tomorrow if I don't practice with you.

HELMER [*going over to her*] Nora dear, are you really so frightened?

NORA Yes, so terribly frightened. Let me practice right now; there's still time before dinner. Oh, sit down and play for me, Torvald. Direct me. Teach me, the way you always have.

HELMER Gladly, if it's what you want. [*Sits at the piano.*]

NORA [*snatches the tambourine up from the box, then a long, varicolored shawl, which she throws around herself, whereupon she springs forward and cries out*] Play for me now! Now I'll dance!

[HELMER *plays and* NORA *dances.* RANK *stands behind* HELMER *at the piano and looks on.*]

HELMER [*as he plays*] Slower. Slow down.

NORA Can't change it.

HELMER Not so violent, Nora!

NORA Has to be just like this.

HELMER [*stopping*] No, no, that won't do at all.

NORA [*laughing and swinging her tambourine*] Isn't that what I told you?

RANK Let me play for her.

HELMER [*getting up*] Yes, go on. I can teach her more easily then.

[RANK *sits at the piano and plays;* NORA *dances more and more wildly.* HELMER *has stationed himself by the stove and repeatedly gives her directions; she seems not to hear them; her hair loosens and falls over her shoulders; she does not notice, but goes on dancing.* MRS. LINDE *enters.*]

MRS. LINDE [*standing dumbfounded at the door*] Ah—

NORA [*still dancing*] See what fun, Kristine!

HELMER But Nora darling, you dance as if your life were at stake.

NORA And it is.

HELMER Rank, stop! This is pure madness. Stop it, I say!

[RANK *breaks off playing, and* NORA *halts abruptly.*]

HELMER [*going over to her*] I never would have believed it. You've forgotten everything I taught you.

NORA [*throwing away the tambourine*] You see for yourself.

HELMER Well, there's certainly room for instruction here.

NORA Yes, you see how important it is. You've got to teach me to the very last minute. Promise me that, Torvald?

HELMER You can bet on it.

NORA You mustn't, either today or tomorrow, think about anything else but me; you mustn't open any letters—or the mailbox—

HELMER Ah, it's still the fear of that man—

NORA Oh yes, yes, that too.

HELMER Nora, it's written all over you—there's already a letter from him out there.

NORA I don't know. I guess so. But you mustn't read such things now; there mustn't be anything ugly between us before it's all over.

RANK [*quietly to* HELMER] You shouldn't deny her.

HELMER [*putting his arm around her*] The child can have her way. But tomorrow night, after you've danced—

NORA Then you'll be free.

MAID [*in the doorway, right*] Ma'am, dinner is served.

NORA We'll be wanting champagne, Helene.

MAID Very good, ma'am. [*Goes out.*]

HELMER So—a regular banquet, hm?

NORA Yes, a banquet—champagne till daybreak! [*Calling out.*] And some macaroons, Helene. Heaps of them—just this once.

HELMER [*taking her hands*] Now, now, now—no hysterics. Be my own little lark again.

NORA Oh, I will soon enough. But go on in—and you, Dr. Rank. Kristine, help me put up my hair.

RANK [*whispering, as they go*] There's nothing wrong—really wrong, is there?

HELMER Oh, of course not. It's nothing more than this childish anxiety I was telling you about. [*They go out, right.*]

NORA Well?

MRS. LINDE Left town.

NORA I could see by your face.

MRS. LINDE He'll be home tomorrow evening. I wrote him a note.

NORA You shouldn't have. Don't try to stop anything now. After all, it's a wonderful joy, this waiting here for the miracle.

MRS. LINDE What is it you're waiting for?

NORA Oh, you can't understand that. Go in to them: I'll be along in a moment.

[MRS. LINDE *goes into the dining room. Nora stands a short while as if composing herself; then she looks at her watch.*]

NORA Five. Seven hours to midnight. Twenty-four hours to the midnight after, and then the tarantella's done. Seven and twenty-four? Thirty-one hours to live.

HELMER [*in the doorway, right*] What's become of the little lark?

NORA [*going toward him with open arms*] Here's your lark!

ACT III

[*Same scene. The table, with chairs around it, has been moved to the center of the room. A lamp on the table is lit. The hall door stands open. Dance music drifts down from the floor above.* MRS. LINDE *sits at the table, absently paging through a book, trying to read, but apparently unable to focus her thoughts. Once or twice she pauses, tensely listening for a sound at the outer entrance.*]

MRS. LINDE [*glancing at her watch*] Not yet—and there's hardly any time left. If only he's not—[*Listening again.*] Ah, there he is. [*She goes out in the hall and cautiously opens the outer door. Quiet footsteps are heard on the stairs. She whispers:*] Come in. Nobody's here.

KROGSTAD [*in the doorway*] I found a note from you at home. What's back of all this?

MRS. LINDE I just *had* to talk to you.

KROGSTAD Oh? And it just *had* to be here in this house?

MRS. LINDE At my place it was impossible; my room hasn't a private entrance. Come in; we're all alone. The maid's asleep, and the Helmers are at the dance upstairs.

KROGSTAD [*entering the room*] Well, well, the Helmers are dancing tonight? Really?

MRS. LINDE Yes, why not?

KROGSTAD How true—why not?

MRS. LINDE All right, Krogstad, let's talk.

KROGSTAD Do we two have anything more to talk about?

MRS. LINDE We have a great deal to talk about.

KROGSTAD I wouldn't have thought so.

MRS. LINDE No, because you've never understood me, really.

KROGSTAD Was there anything more to understand—except what's all too common in life? A calculating woman throws over a man the moment a better catch comes by.

MRS. LINDE You think I'm so thoroughly calculating? You think I broke it off lightly?

KROGSTAD Didn't you?

MRS. LINDE Nils—is that what you really thought?

KROGSTAD If you cared, then why did you write me the way you did?

MRS. LINDE What else could I do? If I had to break off with you, then it was my job as well to root out everything you felt for me.

KROGSTAD [*wringing his hands*] So that was it. And this—all this, simply for money!

MRS. LINDE Don't forget I had a helpless mother and two small brothers. We couldn't wait for you, Nils; you had such a long road ahead of you then.

KROGSTAD That may be; but you still hadn't the right to abandon me for somebody else's sake.

MRS. LINDE Yes—I don't know. So many, many times I've asked myself if I did have that right.

KROGSTAD [*more softly*] When I lost you, it was as if all the solid ground dissolved from under my feet. Look at me; I'm a half-drowned man now, hanging onto a wreck.

MRS. LINDE Help may be near.

KROGSTAD It was near—but then you came and blocked it off.

MRS. LINDE Without my knowing it, Nils. Today for the first time I learned that it's you I'm replacing at the bank.

KROGSTAD All right—I believe you. But now that you know, will you step aside?

MRS. LINDE No, because that wouldn't benefit you in the slightest.

KROGSTAD Not "benefit" me, hm! I'd step aside anyway.

MRS. LINDE I've learned to be realistic. Life and hard, bitter necessity have taught me that.

KROGSTAD And life's taught me never to trust fine phrases.

MRS. LINDE Then life's taught you a very sound thing. But you do have to trust in actions, don't you?

KROGSTAD What does that mean?

MRS. LINDE You said you were hanging on like a half-drowned man to a wreck.

KROGSTAD I've good reason to say that.

MRS. LINDE I'm also like a half-drowned woman on a wreck. No one to suffer with; no one to care for.

KROGSTAD You made your choice.

MRS. LINDE There wasn't any choice then.

KROGSTAD So—what of it?

MRS. LINDE Nils, if only we two shipwrecked people could reach across to each other.

KROGSTAD What are you saying?

MRS. LINDE Two on one wreck are at least better off than each on his own.

KROGSTAD Kristine!

MRS. LINDE Why do you think I came into town?

KROGSTAD Did you really have some thought of me?

MRS. LINDE I have to work to go on living. All my born days, as long as I can remember, I've worked, and it's been my best and my only joy. But now I'm completely alone in the world; it frightens me to be so empty and lost. To work for yourself—there's no joy in that. Nils, give me something—someone to work for.

KROGSTAD I don't believe all this. It's just some hysterical feminine urge to go out and make a noble sacrifice.

MRS. LINDE Have you ever found me to be hysterical?

KROGSTAD Can you honestly mean this? Tell me—do you know everything about my past?

MRS. LINDE Yes.

KROGSTAD And you know what they think I'm worth around here.

MRS. LINDE From what you were saying before, it would seem that with me you could have been another person.

KROGSTAD I'm positive of that.

MRS. LINDE Couldn't it happen still?

KROGSTAD Kristine—you're saying this in all seriousness? Yes, you are! I can see it in you. And do you really have the courage, then—?

MRS. LINDE I need to have someone to care for; and your children need a mother. We both need each other. Nils, I have faith that you're good at heart—I'll risk everything together with you.

KROGSTAD [*gripping her hands*] Kristine, thank you, thank you—Now I know I can win back a place in their eyes. Yes—but I forgot—

MRS. LINDE [*listening*] Shh! The tarantella. Go now! Go on!

KROGSTAD Why? What is it?

MRS. LINDE Hear the dance up there? When that's over, they'll be coming down.

KROGSTAD Oh, then I'll go. But—it's all pointless. Of course, you don't know the move I made against the Helmers.

MRS. LINDE Yes, Nils, I know.

KROGSTAD And all the same, you have the courage to—?

MRS. LINDE I know how far despair can drive a man like you.

KROGSTAD Oh, if I only could take it all back.

MRS. LINDE You easily could—your letter's still lying in the mailbox.

KROGSTAD Are you sure of that?

MRS. LINDE Positive. But—

KROGSTAD [*looks at her searchingly*] Is that the meaning of it, then? You'll save your friend at any price. Tell me straight out. Is that it?

MRS. LINDE Nils—anyone who's sold herself for somebody else once isn't going to do it again.

KROGSTAD I'll demand my letter back.

MRS. LINDE No, no.

KROGSTAD Yes, of course. I'll stay here till Helmer comes down; I'll tell him to give me my letter again—that it only involves my dismissal—that he shouldn't read it—

MRS. LINDE No, Nils, don't call the letter back.

KROGSTAD But wasn't that exactly why you wrote me to come here?

MRS. LINDE Yes, in that first panic. But it's been a whole day and night since then, and in that time I've seen such incredible things in this house. Helmer's got to learn everything; this dreadful secret has to be aired; those two have to come to a full understanding; all these lies and evasions can't go on.

KROGSTAD Well, then, if you want to chance it. But at least there's one thing I can do, and do right away—

MRS. LINDE [*listening*] Go now, go, quick! The dance is over. We're not safe another second.

KROGSTAD I'll wait for you downstairs.

MRS. LINDE Yes, please do; take me home.

KROGSTAD I can't believe it; I've never been so happy. [*He leaves by way of the outer door; the door between the room and the hall stays open.*]

MRS. LINDE [*straightening up a bit and getting together her street clothes*] How different now! How different! Someone to work for, to live for—a home to build. Well, it is worth the try! Oh, if they'd only come! [*Listening.*] Ah, there they are. Bundle up. [*She picks up her hat and coat.* NORA'S *and* HELMER'S *voices can be heard outside; a key turns in the lock, and* HELMER *brings* NORA *into the hall almost by force. She is wearing the Italian costume with a large black shawl about her; he has on evening dress, with a black domino open over it.*]

NORA [*struggling in the doorway*] No, no, no, not inside! I'm going up again. I don't want to leave so soon.

HELMER But Nora dear—

NORA Oh, I beg you, please, Torvald. From the bottom of my heart, *please*—only an hour more!

HELMER Not a single minute, Nora darling. You know our agreement. Come on, in we go; you'll catch cold out here. [*In spite of her resistance, he gently draws her into the room.*]

MRS. LINDE Good evening.

NORA Kristine!

HELMER Why, Mrs. Linde—are you here so late?

MRS. LINDE Yes, I'm sorry, but I did want to see Nora in costume.

NORA Have you been sitting here, waiting for me?

MRS. LINDE Yes. I didn't come early enough; you were all upstairs; and then I thought I really couldn't leave without seeing you.

HELMER [*removing* NORA'S *shawl*] Yes, take a good look. She's worth looking at, I can tell you that, Mrs. Linde. Isn't she lovely?

MRS. LINDE Yes, I should say—

HELMER A dream of loveliness, isn't she? That's what everyone thought at the party, too. But she's horribly stubborn—this sweet little thing. What's to be done with her? Can you imagine, I almost had to use force to pry her away.

NORA Oh, Torvald, you're going to regret you didn't indulge me, even for just a half hour more.

HELMER There, you see. She danced her tarantella and got a tumultuous hand—which was well earned, although the performance may have been a bit too naturalistic—I mean it rather overstepped the proprieties of art. But never mind—what's important is, she made a success, an overwhelming success. You think I could let her stay on after that and spoil the effect? Oh no; I took my lovely little Capri girl—my capricious little Capri girl, I should say—took her under my arm; one quick tour of the ballroom, a curtsy to every side, and then—as they say in novels—the beautiful vision disappeared. An exit should always be effective, Mrs. Linde, but that's what I can't get Nora to grasp. Phew, it's hot in here. [*Flings the domino on a chair and opens the door to his room*] Why's it dark in here? Oh yes, of course. Excuse me. [*He goes in and lights a couple of candles*].

NORA [*in a sharp, breathless whisper*] So?

MRS. LINDE [*quietly*] I talked with him.

NORA And—?

MRS. LINDE Nora—you must tell your husband everything.

NORA [*dully*] I knew it.

MRS. LINDE You've got nothing to fear from Krogstad, but you have to speak out.

NORA I won't tell.

MRS. LINDE Then the letter will.

NORA Thanks, Kristine. I know now what's to be done. Shh!

HELMER [*reentering*] Well, then, Mrs. Linde—have you admired her?

MRS. LINDE Yes, and now I'll say good night.

HELMER Oh, come, so soon? Is this yours, this knitting?

MRS. LINDE Yes, thanks. I nearly forgot it.

HELMER Do you knit, then?

MRS. LINDE Oh yes.

HELMER You know what? You should embroider instead.

MRS. LINDE Really? Why?

HELMER Yes, because it's a lot prettier. See here, one holds the embroidery so, in the left hand, and then one guides the needle with the right—so—in an easy, sweeping curve—right?

MRS. LINDE Yes, I guess that's—

HELMER But, on the other hand, knitting—it can never be anything but ugly. Look, see here, the arms tucked in, the knitting needles going up and down—there's something Chinese about it. Ah, that was really a glorious champagne they served.

MRS. LINDE Yes, good night, Nora, and don't be stubborn any more.

HELMER Well put, Mrs. Linde!

MRS. LINDE Good night, Mr. Helmer.

HELMER [*accompanying her to the door*] Good night, good night. I hope you get home all right. I'd be very happy to—but you don't have far to go. Good night, good night. [*She leaves. He shuts the door after her and returns.*] There, now, at last we got her out the door. She's a deadly bore, that creature.

NORA Aren't you pretty tired, Torvald?

HELMER No, not a bit.

NORA You're not sleepy?

HELMER Not at all. On the contrary, I'm feeling quite exhilarated. But you? Yes, you really look tired and sleepy.

NORA Yes, I'm very tired. Soon now I'll sleep.

HELMER See! You see! I was right all along that we shouldn't stay longer.

NORA Whatever you do is always right.

HELMER [*kissing her brow*] Now my little lark talks sense. Say, did you notice what a time Rank was having tonight?

NORA Oh, was he? I didn't get to speak with him.

HELMER I scarcely did either, but it's a long time since I've seen him in such high spirits. [*Gazes at her a moment, then comes nearer her.*] Hm—it's marvelous, though, to be back home again—to be completely alone with you. Oh, you bewitchingly lovely young woman!

NORA Torvald, don't look at me like that!

HELMER Can't I look at my richest treasure? At all that beauty that's mine, mine alone—completely and utterly.

NORA [*moving around to the other side of the table*] You mustn't talk to me that way tonight.

HELMER [*following her*] The tarantella is still in your blood, I can see—and it makes you even more enticing. Listen. The guests are beginning to go. [*Dropping his voice.*] Nora—it'll soon be quiet through this whole house.

NORA Yes, I hope so.

HELMER You do, don't you, my love? Do you realize—when I'm out at a party like this with you—do you know why I talk to you so little, and keep such a distance away; just send you a stolen look now and then—you know why I do it? It's because I'm imagining then that you're my secret darling, my secret young bride-to-be, and that no one suspects there's anything between us.

NORA Yes, yes; oh, yes, I know you're always thinking of me.

HELMER And then when we leave and I place the shawl over those fine young rounded shoulders—over that wonderful curving neck—then I pretend that you're my young bride, that we're just coming from the wedding, that for the first time I'm bringing you into my house—that for the first time I'm alone with you—completely alone with you, your trembling young beauty! All this evening I've longed for nothing but you. When I saw you turn and sway in the tarantella—my blood was pounding till I couldn't stand it—that's why I brought you down here so early—

NORA Go away, Torvald! Leave me alone. I don't want all this.

HELMER What do you mean? Nora, you're teasing me. You will, won't you? Aren't I your husband—?

[*A knock at the outside door.*]

NORA [*startled*] What's that?

HELMER [*going toward the hall*] Who is it?

RANK [*outside*] It's me. May I come in a moment?

HELMER [*with quiet irritation*] Oh, what does he want now? [*Aloud.*] Hold on. [*Goes and opens the door.*] Oh, how nice that you didn't just pass us by!

RANK I thought I heard your voice, and then I wanted so badly to have a look in. [*Lightly glancing about.*] Ah, me, these old familiar haunts. You have it snug and cozy in here, you two.

HELMER You seemed to be having it pretty cozy upstairs, too.

RANK Absolutely. Why shouldn't I? Why not take in everything in life? As much as you can, anyway, and as long as you can. The wine was superb—

HELMER The champagne especially.

RANK You noticed that too? It's amazing how much I could guzzle down.

NORA Torvald also drank a lot of champagne this evening.

RANK Oh?

NORA Yes, and that always makes him so entertaining.

RANK Well, why shouldn't one have a pleasant evening after a well-spent day?

HELMER Well spent? I'm afraid I can't claim that.

RANK [*slapping him on the back*] But I can, you see!

NORA Dr. Rank, you must have done some scientific research today.

RANK Quite so.

HELMER Come now—little Nora talking about scientific research!

NORA And can I congratulate you on the results?

RANK Indeed you may.

NORA Then they were good?

RANK The best possible for both doctor and patient—certainty.

NORA [*quickly and searchingly*] Certainty?

RANK Complete certainty. So don't I owe myself a gay evening afterwards?

NORA Yes, you're right, Dr. Rank.

HELMER I'm with you—just so long as you don't have to suffer for it in the morning.

RANK Well, one never gets something for nothing in life.

NORA Dr. Rank—are you very fond of masquerade parties?

RANK Yes, if there's a good array of odd disguises—

NORA Tell me, what should we two go as at the next masquerade?

HELMER You little featherhead—already thinking of the next!

RANK We two? I'll tell you what: you must go as Charmed Life—

HELMER Yes, but find a costume for *that!*

RANK Your wife can appear just as she looks every day.

HELMER That was nicely put. But don't you know what you're going to be?

RANK Yes, Helmer, I've made up my mind.

HELMER Well?

RANK At the next masquerade I'm going to be invisible.

HELMER That's a funny idea.

RANK They say there's a hat—black, huge—have you never heard of the hat that makes you invisible? You put it on, and then no one on earth can see you.

HELMER [*suppressing a smile*] Ah, of course.

RANK But I'm quite forgetting what I came for. Helmer, give me a cigar, one of the dark Havanas.

HELMER With the greatest pleasure. [*Holds out his case.*]

RANK Thanks. [*Takes one and cuts off the tip.*]

NORA [*striking a match*] Let me give you a light.

RANK Thank you. [*She holds the match for him; he lights the cigar.*] And now good-bye.

HELMER Good-bye, good-bye, old friend.

NORA Sleep well, Doctor.

RANK Thanks for that wish.

NORA Wish me the same.

RANK You? All right, if you like—Sleep well. And thanks for the light. [*He nods to them both and leaves.*]

HELMER [*his voice subdued*] He's been drinking heavily.

NORA [*absently*] Could be. [HELMER *takes his keys from his pocket and goes out in the hall.*] Torvald—what are you after?

HELMER Got to empty the mailbox; it's nearly full. There won't be room for the morning papers.

NORA Are you working tonight?

HELMER You know I'm not. Why—what's this? Someone's been at the lock.

NORA At the lock—?

HELMER Yes, I'm positive. What do you suppose—? I can't imagine one of the maids—? Here's a broken hairpin. Nora, it's yours—

NORA [*quickly*] Then it must be the children—

HELMER You'd better break them of that. Hm, hm—well, opened it after all. [*Takes the contents out and calls into the kitchen.*] Helene! Helene, would you put out the lamp in the hall. [*He returns to the room, shutting the hall door, then displays the handful of mail.*] Look how it's piled up. [*Sorting through them.*] Now what's this?

NORA [*at the window*] The letter! Oh, Torvald, no!

HELMER Two calling cards—from Rank.

NORA From Dr. Rank?

HELMER [*examining them*] "Dr. Rank, Consulting Physician." They were on top. He must have dropped them in as he left.

NORA Is there anything on them?

HELMER There's a black cross over the name. See? That's a gruesome notion. He could almost be announcing his own death.

NORA That's just what he's doing.

HELMER What! You've heard something? Something he's told you?

NORA Yes. That when those cards came, he'd be taking his leave of us. He'll shut himself in now and die.

HELMER Ah, my poor friend! Of course I knew he wouldn't be here much longer. But so soon—And then to hide himself away like a wounded animal.

NORA If it has to happen, then it's best it happens in silence—don't you think so, Torvald?

HELMER [*pacing up and down*] He'd grown right into our lives. I simply can't imagine him gone. He with his suffering and loneliness—like a dark cloud setting off our sunlit happiness. Well, maybe it's best this way. For him, at least. [*Standing still.*] And maybe for us too, Nora. Now we're thrown back on each other, completely. [*Embracing her.*] Oh you, my darling wife, how can I hold you close enough? You know what, Nora—time and again I've wished you were in some terrible danger, just so I could stake my life and soul and everything, for your sake.

NORA [*tearing herself away, her voice firm and decisive*] Now you must read your mail, Torvald.

HELMER No, no, not tonight. I want to stay with you, dearest.

NORA With a dying friend on your mind?

HELMER You're right. We've both had a shock. There's ugliness between us—these thoughts of death and corruption. We'll have to get free of them first. Until then—we'll stay apart.

NORA [*clinging about his neck*] Torvald—good night! Good night!

HELMER [*kissing her on the cheek*] Good night, little songbird. Sleep well, Nora. I'll be reading my mail now. [*He takes the letters into his room and shuts the door after him.*]

NORA [*with bewildered glances, groping about, seizing* HELMER's *domino, throwing it around her, and speaking in short, hoarse, broken whispers*] Never see him again. Never, never. [*Putting her shawl over her head.*] Never see the children either—them, too. Never, never. Oh, the freezing black water! The depths—down—Oh, I wish it were over—He has it now; he's reading it—now. Oh no, no, not yet. Torvald, goodbye, you and the children—[*She starts for the hall; as she does,* HELMER *throws open his door and stands with an open letter in his hand.*]

HELMER Nora!

NORA [*screams*] Oh—!

HELMER What is this? You know what's in this letter?

NORA Yes, I know. Let me go! Let me out!

HELMER [*holding her back*] Where are you going?

NORA [*struggling to break loose*] You can't save me, Torvald!

HELMER [*slumping back*] True! Then it's true what he writes? How horrible! No, no, it's impossible—it can't be true.

NORA It *is* true. I've loved you more than all this world.

HELMER Ah, none of your slippery tricks.

NORA [*taking one step toward him*] Torvald—!

HELMER What *is* this you've blundered into!

NORA Just let me loose. You're not going to suffer for my sake. You're not going to take on my guilt.

HELMER No more playacting. [*Locks the hall door.*] You stay right here and give me a reckoning. You understand what you've done? Answer! You understand?

NORA [*looking squarely at him, her face hardening*] Yes. I'm beginning to understand everything now.

HELMER [*striding about*] Oh, what an awful awakening! In all these eight years—she who was my pride and joy—a hypocrite, a liar—worse, worse—a criminal! How infinitely disgusting it all is! The shame! [*Nora says nothing and goes on looking straight at him. He stops in front of her.*] I should have suspected something of the kind. I should have known. All your father's flimsy values—Be still! All your father's flimsy values have come out in you. No religion, no morals, no sense of duty—Oh, how I'm punished for letting him off! I did it for your sake, and you repay me like this.

NORA Yes, like this.

HELMER Now you've wrecked all my happiness—ruined my whole future. Oh, it's awful to think of. I'm in a cheap little grafter's hands; he can do anything he wants with me, ask for anything, play with me like a puppet—and I can't breathe a word. I'll be swept down miserably into the depths on account of a featherbrained woman.

NORA When I'm gone from this world, you'll be free.

HELMER Oh, quit posing. Your father had a mess of those speeches too. What good would that ever do me if you were gone from this world, as you say? Not the slightest. He can still make the whole thing known; and if he does, I could be falsely suspected as your accomplice. They might even think that I was behind it—that I put you up to it. And all that I can thank you for—you that I've coddled the whole of our marriage. Can you see now what you've done to me?

NORA [*icily calm*] Yes.

HELMER It's so incredible, I just can't grasp it. But we'll have to patch up whatever we can. Take off the shawl. I said, take it off! I've got to appease him somehow or other. The thing has to be hushed up at any cost. And as for you and me, it's got to seem like everything between us is just as it was—to the outside world, that is. You'll go right on living in this house, of course. But you can't be allowed to bring up the children; I don't dare trust you with them—Oh, to have to say this to someone I've loved so much? Well, that's done with. From now on happiness doesn't matter; all that matters is saving the bits and pieces, the appearance—[*The doorbell rings.* HELMER *starts.*] What's that? And so late. Maybe the worst—? You think he'd—? Hide, Nora! Say you're sick. [NORA *remains standing motionless.* HELMER *goes and opens the door.*]

MAID [*half dressed, in the hall*] A letter for Mrs. Helmer.

HELMER I'll take it. [*Snatches the letter and shuts the door.*] Yes, it's from him. You don't get it; I'm reading it myself.

NORA Then read it.

HELMER [*by the lamp*] I hardly dare. We may be ruined, you and I. But—I've got to know. [*Rips open the letter, skims through a few lines, glances at an enclosure, then cries out joyfully.*] Nora! [NORA *looks inquiringly at him.*] Nora! Wait—better check it again—Yes, yes, it's true. I'm saved. Nora, I'm saved!

NORA And I?

HELMER You too, of course. We're both saved, both of us. Look. He's sent back your note. He says he's sorry and ashamed—that a happy development in his life—oh, who cares what he says! Nora, we're saved! No one can hurt you. Oh, Nora, Nora—but first, this ugliness all has to go. Let me see—[*Takes a look at the note.*] No, I don't want to see it; I want the whole thing to fade like a dream. [*Tears the note and both letters to pieces, throws them into the stove and watches them burn.*] There—now there's nothing left—He wrote that since Christmas Eve you—Oh, they must have been three terrible days for you, Nora.

NORA I fought a hard fight

HELMER And suffered pain and saw no escape but—No, we're not going to dwell on anything unpleasant. We'll just be grateful and keep on repeating: it's over now, it's over! You hear me, Nora? You don't seem to realize—it's over. What's it mean—that frozen look? Oh, poor little Nora, I understand. You can't believe I've forgiven you. But I have, Nora; I swear I have. I know that what you did, you did out of love for me.

NORA That's true.

HELMER You loved me the way a wife ought to love her husband. It's simply the means that you couldn't judge. But you think I love you any the less for not knowing how to handle your affairs? No, no—just lean on me; I'll guide you and teach you. I wouldn't be a man if this feminine helplessness didn't make you twice as attractive to me. You mustn't mind those sharp words I said—that was all in the first confusion of thinking my world had collapsed. I've forgiven you, Nora; I swear I've forgiven you.

NORA My thanks for your forgiveness. [*She goes out through the door, right.*]

HELMER No, wait—[*Peers in.*] What are you doing in there?

NORA [*inside*] Getting out of my costume.

HELMER [*by the open door*] Yes, do that. Try to calm yourself and collect your thoughts again, my frightened little songbird. You can rest easy now; I've got wide wings to shelter you with. [*Walking about close by the door.*] How snug and nice our home is, Nora. You're safe here; I'll keep you like a hunted dove I've rescued out of a hawk's claws. I'll bring peace to your poor, shuddering heart. Gradually it'll happen, Nora; you'll see. Tomorrow all this will look different to you; then everything will be as it was. I won't have to go on repeating I forgive you; you'll feel it for yourself. How can you imagine I'd ever conceivably want to disown you—or even blame you in any way? Ah, you don't know a man's heart, Nora. For a man there's something indescribably sweet and satisfying in knowing he's forgiven his wife—and forgiven her out of a full and open heart. It's as if she belongs to him in two ways now: in a sense he's given her fresh into the world again, and she's become his wife and his child as well. From now on that's what you'll be to me—you little, bewildered, helpless thing. Don't be afraid of anything, Nora; just open your heart to me, and I'll be conscience and will to you both—[NORA *enters in her regular clothes.*] What's this? Not in bed? You've changed your dress?

NORA Yes, Torvald, I've changed my dress.

HELMER But why now, so late?

NORA Tonight I'm not sleeping.

HELMER But Nora dear—

NORA [*looking at her watch*] It's still not so very late. Sit down, Torvald; we have a lot to talk over. [*She sits at one side of the table.*]

HELMER Nora—what is this? That hard expression—

NORA Sit down. This'll take some time. I have a lot to say.

HELMER [*sitting at the table directly opposite her*] You worry me, Nora. And I don't understand you.

NORA No, that's exactly it. You don't understand me. And I've never understood you either—until tonight. No, don't interrupt. You can just listen to what I say. We're closing out accounts, Torvald.

HELMER How do you mean that?

NORA [*after a short pause*] Doesn't anything strike you about our sitting here like this?

HELMER What's that?

NORA We've been married now eight years. Doesn't it occur to you that this is the first time we two, you and I, man and wife, have ever talked seriously together?

HELMER What do you mean—seriously?

NORA In eight whole years—longer even—right from our first acquaintance, we've never exchanged a serious word on any serious thing.

HELMER You mean I should constantly go and involve you in problems you couldn't possibly help me with?

NORA I'm not talking of problems. I'm saying that we've never sat down seriously together and tried to get to the bottom of anything.

HELMER But dearest, what good would that ever do you?

NORA That's the point right there: you've never understood me. I've been wronged greatly, Torvald—first by Papa, and then by you.

HELMER What! By us—the two people who've loved you more than anyone else?

NORA [*shaking her head*] You never loved me. You've thought it fun to be in love with me, that's all.

HELMER Nora, what a thing to say!

NORA Yes, it's true now, Torvald. When I lived at home with Papa, he told me all his opinions, so I had the same ones too; or if they were different I hid them, since he wouldn't have cared for that. He used to call me his doll-child, and he played with me the way I played with my dolls. Then I came into your house—

HELMER How can you speak of our marriage like that?

NORA [*unperturbed*] I mean, then I went from Papa's hands into yours. You arranged everything to your own taste, and so I got the same taste as you—or I pretended to; I can't remember. I guess a little of both, first one, then the other. Now when I look back, it seems as if I'd lived here like a beggar—just from hand to mouth. I've lived by doing tricks for you, Torvald. But that's the way you wanted it. It's a great sin what you and Papa did to me. You're to blame that nothing's become of me.

HELMER Nora, how unfair and ungrateful you are! Haven't you been happy here?

NORA No, never. I thought so—but I never have.

HELMER Not—not happy!

NORA No, only lighthearted. And you've always been so kind to me. But our home's been nothing but a playpen. I've been your doll-wife here, just as at home I was Papa's doll-child. And in turn the children have been my dolls. I thought it was fun when you played with me, just as they thought it fun when I played with them. That's been our marriage, Torvald.

HELMER There's some truth in what you're saying—under all the raving exaggeration. But it'll all be different after this. Playtime's over; now for the schooling.

NORA Whose schooling—mine or the children's?

HELMER Both yours and the children's, dearest.

NORA Oh, Torvald, you're not the man to teach me to be a good wife to you.

HELMER And you can say that?

NORA And I—how am I equipped to bring up children?

HELMER Nora!

NORA Didn't you say a moment ago that that was no job to trust me with?

HELMER In a flare of temper! Why fasten on that?

NORA Yes, but you were so very right. I'm not up to the job. There's another job I have to do first. I have to try to educate myself. You can't help me with that. I've got to do it alone. And that's why I'm leaving you now.

HELMER [*jumping up*] What's that?

NORA I have to stand completely alone, if I'm ever going to discover myself and the world out there. So I can't go on living with you.

HELMER Nora, Nora!

NORA I want to leave right away. Kristine should put me up for the night—

HELMER You're insane! You've no right! I forbid you!

NORA From here on, there's no use forbidding me anything. I'll take with me whatever is mine. I don't want a thing from you, either now or later.

HELMER What kind of madness is this!

NORA Tomorrow I'm going home—I mean, home where I came from. It'll be easier up there to find something to do.

HELMER Oh, you blind, incompetent child!

NORA I must learn to be competent, Torvald.

HELMER Abandon your home, your husband, your children! And you're not even thinking what people will say.

NORA I can't be concerned about that. I only know how essential this is.

HELMER Oh, it's outrageous. So you'll run out like this on your most sacred vows.

NORA What do you think are my most sacred vows?

HELMER And I have to tell you that! Aren't they your duties to your husband and children?

NORA I have other duties equally sacred.

HELMER That isn't true. What duties are they?

NORA Duties to myself.

HELMER Before all else, you're a wife and a mother.

NORA I don't believe in that any more. I believe that, before all else, I'm a human being, no less than you—or anyway, I ought to try to become one. I know the majority thinks you're right, Torvald, and plenty of books agree with you, too. But I can't go on believing what the majority says, or what's written in books. I have to think over these things myself and try to understand them.

HELMER Why can't you understand your place in your own home? On a point like that, isn't there one everlasting guide you can turn to? Where's your religion?

NORA Oh, Torvald, I'm really not sure what religion is.

HELMER What—?

NORA I only know what the minister said when I was confirmed. He told me religion was this thing and that. When I get clear and away by myself, I'll go into that problem too. I'll see if what the minister said was right, or, in any case, if it's right for me.

HELMER A young woman your age shouldn't talk like that. If religion can't move you, I can try to rouse your conscience. You do have some moral feeling? Or, tell me—has that gone too?

NORA It's not easy to answer that, Torvald. I simply don't know. I'm all confused about these things. I just know I see them so differently from you. I find out, for one thing, that the law's not at all what I'd thought—but I can't get it through my head that the law is fair. A woman hasn't a right to protect her dying father or save her husband's life! I can't believe that.

HELMER You talk like a child. You don't know anything of the world you live in.

NORA No, I don't. But now I'll begin to learn for myself. I'll try to discover who's right, the world or I.

HELMER Nora, you're sick; you've got a fever. I almost think you're out of your head.

NORA I've never felt more clearheaded and sure in my life.

HELMER And—clearheaded and sure—you're leaving your husband and children?

NORA Yes.

HELMER Then there's only one possible reason.

NORA What?

HELMER You no longer love me.

NORA No. That's exactly it.

HELMER Nora! You can't be serious!

NORA Oh, this is so hard, Torvald—you've been so kind to me always. But I can't help it. I don't love you any more.

HELMER [*struggling for composure*] Are you also clearheaded and sure about that?

NORA Yes, completely. That's why I can't go on staying here.

HELMER Can you tell me what I did to lose your love?

NORA Yes, I can tell you. It was this evening when the miraculous thing didn't come—then I knew you weren't the man I'd imagined.

HELMER Be more explicit; I don't follow you.

NORA I've waited now so patiently eight long years—for, my Lord, I know miracles don't come every day. Then this crisis broke over me, and such a certainty filled me: *now* the miraculous event would occur. While Krogstad's letter was lying out there, I never for an instant dreamed that you could give in to his terms. I was so utterly sure you'd say to him: go on, tell your tale to the whole wide world. And when he'd done that—

HELMER Yes, what then? When I'd delivered my own wife into shame and disgrace—!

NORA When he'd done that, I was so utterly sure that you'd step forward, take the blame on yourself and say: I am the guilty one.

HELMER Nora—!

NORA You're thinking I'd never accept such a sacrifice from you? No, of course not. But what good would my protests be against you? That was the miracle I was waiting for, in terror and hope. And to stave that off, I would have taken my life.

HELMER I'd gladly work for you day and night, Nora—and take on pain and deprivation. But there's no one who gives up honor for love.

NORA Millions of women have done just that.

HELMER Oh, you think and talk like a silly child.

NORA Perhaps. But you neither think nor talk like the man I could join myself to. When your big fright was over—and it wasn't from any threat against me, only for what might damage you—when all the danger was past, for you it was just as if nothing had happened. I was exactly the same, your little lark, your doll, that you'd have to handle with double care now that I'd turned out so brittle and frail. [*Gets up.*] Torvald—in that instant it dawned on me that for eight years I've been living here with a stranger, and that I'd even conceived three children—oh, I can't stand the thought of it! I could tear myself to bits.

HELMER [*heavily*] I see. There's a gulf that's opened between us —that's clear. Oh, but Nora, can't we bridge it somehow?

NORA The way I am now, I'm no wife for you.

HELMER I have the strength to make myself over.

NORA Maybe—if your doll gets taken away.

HELMER But to part! To part from you! No, Nora, no—I can't imagine it.

NORA [*going out, right*] All the more reason why it has to be. [*She reenters with her coat and a small overnight bag, which she puts on a chair by the table.*]

HELMER Nora, Nora, not now! Wait till tomorrow.

NORA I can't spend the night in a strange man's room.

HELMER But couldn't we live here like brother and sister—

NORA You know very well how long that would last. [*Throws her shawl about her.*] Good-bye, Torvald. I won't look in on the children. I know they're in better hands than mine. The way I am now, I'm no use to them.

HELMER But someday, Nora—someday—?

NORA How can I tell? I haven't the least idea what'll become of me.

HELMER But you're my wife, now and wherever you go.

NORA Listen, Torvald—I've heard that when a wife deserts her husband's house just as I'm doing, then the law frees him from all responsibility. In any case, I'm freeing you from being responsible. Don't feel yourself bound, any more than I will. There has to be absolute freedom for us both. Here, take your ring back. Give me mine.

HELMER That too?

NORA That too.

HELMER There it is.

NORA Good. Well, now it's all over. I'm putting the keys here. The maids know all about keeping up the house—better than I do. Tomorrow, after I've left town, Kristine will stop by to pack up everything that's mine from home. I'd like those things shipped up to me.

HELMER Over! All over! Nora, won't you ever think about me?

NORA I'm sure I'll think of you often, and about the children and the house here.

HELMER May I write you?

NORA No—never. You're not to do that.

HELMER Oh, but let me send you—

NORA Nothing. Nothing.

HELMER Or help you if you need it.

NORA No. I accept nothing from strangers.

HELMER Nora—can I never be more than a stranger to you?

NORA [*picking up the overnight bag*] Ah, Torvald—it would take the greatest miracle of all—

HELMER Tell me the greatest miracle!

NORA You and I both would have to transform ourselves to the point that—Oh, Torvald, I've stopped believing in miracles.

HELMER But I'll believe. Tell me! Transform ourselves to the point that—?

NORA That our living together could be a true marriage. [*She goes out down the hall.*]

HELMER [*sinks down on a chair by the door, face buried in his hands*] Nora! Nora! [*Looking about and rising.*] Empty. She's gone. [*A sudden hope leaps in him.*] The greatest miracle—?

[*From below, the sound of a door slamming shut.*]

Susan Glaspell (1882–1948)

TRIFLES

Scene: The kitchen in the now abandoned farmhouse of JOHN WRIGHT, *a gloomy kitchen, and left without having been put in order—unwashed pans under the sink, a loaf of bread outside the breadbox, a dish towel on the table—other signs of incompleted work. At the rear the outer door opens, and the* SHERIFF *comes in, followed by the* COUNTY ATTORNEY *and* HALE. *The* SHERIFF *and* HALE *are men in middle life, the* COUNTY ATTORNEY *is a young man; all are much bundled up and go at once to the stove. They are followed by the two women—the* SHERIFF'S WIFE *first; she is a slight wiry woman, a thin nervous face.* MRS. HALE *is larger and would ordinarily be called more comfortable looking, but she is disturbed now and looks fearfully about as she enters. The women have come in slowly and stand close together near the door.*

COUNTY ATTORNEY [*rubbing his hands*]. This feels good. Come up to the fire, ladies.

MRS. PETERS [*after taking a step forward*]. I'm not—cold.

SHERIFF [*unbuttoning his overcoat and stepping away from the stove as if to mark the beginning of official business*]. Now, Mr. Hale, before we move things about, you explain to Mr. Henderson just what you saw when you came here yesterday morning.

COUNTY ATTORNEY. By the way, has anything been moved? Are things just as you left them yesterday?

SHERIFF [*looking about*]. It's just the same. When it dropped below zero last night, I thought I'd better send Frank out this morning to make a fire for us—no use getting pneumonia with a big case on; but I told him not to touch anything except the stove—and you know Frank.

COUNTY ATTORNEY. Somebody should have been left here yesterday.

SHERIFF. Oh—yesterday. When I had to send Frank to Morris Center for that man who went crazy—I want you to know I had my hands full yesterday. I knew you could get back from Omaha by today, and as long as I went over everything here myself—

COUNTY ATTORNEY. Well, Mr. Hale, tell just what happened when you came here yesterday morning.

HALE. Harry and I had started to town with a load of potatoes. We came along the road from my place; and as I got here, I said, "I'm going to see if I can't get John Wright to go in with me on a party telephone." I spoke to Wright about it once before, and he put me off, saying folks talked too much anyway, and all he asked was peace and quiet—I guess you know about how much he talked himself; but I thought maybe if I went to the house and talked about it before his wife, though I said to Harry that I didn't know as what his wife wanted made much difference to John—

COUNTY ATTORNEY. Let's talk about that later, Mr. Hale. I do want to talk about that, but tell now just what happened when you got to the house.

HALE. I didn't hear or see anything; I knocked at the door, and still it was all quiet inside. I knew they must be up, it was past eight o'clock. So I knocked again, and I thought I heard somebody say,

"Come in." I wasn't sure, I'm not sure yet, but I opened the door—this door [*indicating the door by which the two women are still standing*], and there in that rocker—[*pointing to it*] sat Mrs. Wright. [*They all look at the rocker.*]

COUNTY ATTORNEY. What—was she doing?

HALE. She was rockin' back and forth. She had her apron in her hand and was kind of—pleating it.

COUNTY ATTORNEY. And how did she—look?

HALE. Well, she looked queer.

COUNTY ATTORNEY. How do you mean—queer?

HALE. Well, as if she didn't know what she was going to do next. And kind of done up.

COUNTY ATTORNEY. How did she seem to feel about your coming?

HALE. Why, I don't think she minded—one way or other. She didn't pay much attention. I said, "How do, Mrs. Wright, it's cold, ain't it?" And she said, "Is it?"—and went on kind of pleating at her apron. Well, I was surprised; she didn't ask me to come up to the stove, or to set down, but just sat there, not even looking at me, so I said, "I want to see John." And then she—laughed. I guess you would call it a laugh. I thought of Harry and the team outside, so I said a little sharp: "Can't I see John?" "No," she says, kind o' dull like. "Ain't he home?" says I. "Yes," says she, "he's home." "Then why can't I see him?" I asked her, out of patience. " 'Cause he's dead," says she. "*Dead?*" says I. She just nodded her head, not getting a bit excited, but rockin' back and forth. "Why—where is he?" says I, not knowing what to say. She just pointed upstairs—like that [*himself pointing to the room above*]. I got up, with the idea of going up there. I walked from there to here—then I says, "Why, what did he die of?" "He died of a rope around his neck," says she, and just went on pleatin' at her apron. Well, I went out and called Harry. I thought I might—need help. We went upstairs, and there he was lyin'—

COUNTY ATTORNEY. I think I'd rather have you go into that upstairs, where you can point it all out. Just go on now with the rest of the story.

HALE. Well, my first thought was to get that rope off. I looked . . . [*Stops, his face twitches.*] . . . but Harry, he went up to him, and he said, "No, he's dead all right, and we'd better not touch anything." So we went back downstairs. She was still sitting that same way. "Has anybody been notified?" I asked. "No," says she, unconcerned. "Who did this, Mrs. Wright?" said Harry. He said it businesslike—and she stopped pleatin' of her apron. "I don't know," she says. "You don't *know*?" says Harry. "No," says she. "Weren't you sleepin' in the bed with him?" says Harry. "Yes," says she, "but I was on the inside." "Somebody slipped a rope round his neck and strangled him, and you didn't wake up?" says Harry. "I didn't wake up," she said after him. We must 'a looked as if we didn't see how that could be, for after a minute she said, "I sleep sound." Harry was going to ask her more questions, but I said maybe we ought to let her tell her story first to the coroner, or the sheriff, so Harry went fast as he could to Rivers' place, where there's a telephone.

COUNTY ATTORNEY. And what did Mrs. Wright do when she knew that you had gone for the coroner?

HALE. She moved from that chair to this over here . . . [*Pointing to a small chair in the corner.*] . . . and just sat there with her hands held together and looking down. I got a feeling that I ought to make some conversation, so I said I had come in to see if John wanted to put in a telephone, and at that she started to laugh, and then she stopped and looked at me—scared. [*The* COUNTY ATTORNEY, *who has had his notebook out, makes a note.*] I dunno, maybe it wasn't scared. I wouldn't like to say it was. Soon Harry got back, and then Dr. Lloyd came, and you, Mr. Peters, and so I guess that's all I know that you don't.

COUNTY ATTORNEY [*looking around*]. I guess we'll go upstairs first—and then out to the barn and around there. [*To the* SHERIFF]. You're convinced that there was nothing important here—nothing that would point to any motive?

SHERIFF. Nothing here but kitchen things.

[*The* COUNTY ATTORNEY, *after again looking around the kitchen, opens the door of a cupboard closet. He gets up on a chair and looks on a shelf. Pulls his hand away, sticky.*]

COUNTY ATTORNEY. Here's a nice mess.

[*The women draw nearer.*]

MRS. PETERS [*to the other woman*]. Oh, her fruit; it did freeze. [*To the* LAWYER.] She worried about that when it turned so cold. She said the fir'd go out and her jars would break.

SHERIFF. Well, can you beat the women! Held for murder and worryin' about her preserves.

COUNTY ATTORNEY. I guess before we're through she may have something more serious than preserves to worry about.

HALE. Well, women are used to worrying over trifles.

[*The two women move a little closer together.*]

COUNTY ATTORNEY [*with the gallantry of a young politician*]. And yet, for all their worries, what would we do without the ladies? [*The women do not unbend. He goes to the sink, takes a dipperful of water from the pail and, pouring it into a basin, washes his hands. Starts to wipe them on the roller towel, turns it for a cleaner place.*] Dirty towels! [*Kicks his foot against the pans under the sink.*] Not much of a housekeeper, would you say, ladies?

MRS. HALE [*stiffly*]. There's a great deal of work to be done on a farm.

COUNTY ATTORNEY. To be sure, and yet . . . [*With a little bow to her.*] . . . I know there are some Dickson county farmhouses which do not have such roller towels. [*He gives it a pull to expose its full length again.*]

MRS. HALE. Those towels get dirty awful quick. Men's hands aren't always as clean as they might be.

COUNTY ATTORNEY. Ah, loyal to your sex, I see. But you and Mrs. Wright were neighbors. I suppose you were friends, too.

MRS. HALE [*shaking her head*]. I've not seen much of her of late years. I've not been in this house—it's more than a year.

COUNTY ATTORNEY. And why was that? You didn't like her?

MRS. HALE. I liked her all well enough. Farmers' wives have their hands full, Mr. Henderson. And then—

COUNTY ATTORNEY. Yes—?

MRS. HALE [*looking about*]. It never seemed a very cheerful place.

COUNTY ATTORNEY. No—it's not cheerful. I shouldn't say she had the homemaking instinct.

MRS. HALE. Well, I don't know as Wright had, either.

COUNTY ATTORNEY. You mean that they didn't get on very well?

MRS. HALE. No, I don't mean anything. But I don't think a place'd be any cheerfuler for John Wright's being in it.

COUNTY ATTORNEY. I'd like to talk more of that a little later. I want to get the lay of things upstairs now. [*He goes to the left, where three steps lead to a stair door.*]

SHERIFF. I suppose anything Mrs. Peters does'll be all right. She was to take in some clothes for her, you know, and a few little things. We left in such a hurry yesterday.

COUNTY ATTORNEY. Yes, but I would like to see what you take, Mrs. Peters, and keep an eye out for anything that might be of use to us.

MRS. PETERS. Yes, Mr. Henderson.

[*The women listen to the men's steps on the stairs, then look about the kitchen.*]

MRS. HALE. I'd hate to have men coming into my kitchen, snooping around and criticizing. [*She arranges the pans under the sink which the* LAWYER *had shoved out of place.*]

MRS. PETERS. Of course it's no more than their duty.

MRS. HALE. Duty's all right, but I guess that deputy sheriff that came out to make the fire might have got a little of this on. [*Gives the roller towel a pull.*] Wish I'd thought of that sooner. Seems mean to talk about her for not having things slicked up when she had to come away in such a hurry.

MRS. PETERS [*Who has gone to a small table in the left rear corner of the room, and lifted one end of a towel that covers a pan*]. She had bread set. [*Stands still.*]

MRS. HALE [*eyes fixed on a loaf of bread beside the breadbox, which is on a low shelf at the other side of the room. Moves slowly toward it*]. She was going to put this in there. [*Picks up loaf, then abruptly drops it. In a manner of returning to familiar things.*] It's a shame about her fruit. I wonder if it's all gone. [*Gets up on the chair and looks.*] I think there's some here that's all right, Mrs. Peters. Yes—here; [*Holding it toward the window.*] this is cherries, too. [*Looking again.*] I declare I believe that's the only one. [*Gets down, bottle in her hand. Goes to the sink and wipes it off on the outside.*] She'll feel awful bad after all her hard work in the hot weather. I remember the afternoon I put up my cherries last summer. [*She puts the bottle on the big kitchen table, center of the room, front table. With a sigh, is about to sit down in the rocking chair. Before she is seated realizes what chair it is; with a slow look at it, steps back. The chair, which she has touched, rocks back and forth.*]

MRS. PETERS. Well, I must get those things from the front-room closet. [*She goes to the door at the right, but after looking into the other room steps back.*] You coming with me, Mrs. Hale? You could help me carry them.

[*They go into the other room; reappear,* MRS. PETERS *carrying a dress and skirt,* MRS. HALE *following with a pair of shoes.*]

MRS. PETERS. My, it's cold in there. [*She puts the cloth on the big table, and hurries to the stove.*]

MRS. HALE [*examining the skirt*]. Wright was close. I think maybe that's why she kept so much to herself. She didn't even belong to the Ladies' Aid. I suppose she felt she couldn't do her part, and then you don't enjoy things when you feel shabby. She used to wear pretty clothes and be lively, when she was Minnie Foster, one of the town girls singing in the choir. But that—oh, that was thirty years ago. This all you was to take in?

MRS. PETERS. She said she wanted an apron. Funny thing to want, for there isn't much to get you dirty in jail, goodness knows. But I suppose just to make her feel more natural. She said they was in the top drawer in this cupboard. Yes, here. And then her little shawl that always hung behind the door. [*Opens stair door and looks.*] Yes, here it is. [*Quickly shuts door leading upstairs.*]

MRS. HALE [*abruptly moving toward her*]. Mrs. Peters?

MRS. PETERS. Yes, Mrs. Hale?

MRS. HALE. Do you think she did it?

MRS. PETERS [*in a frightened voice*]. Oh, I don't know.

MRS. HALE. Well, I don't think she did. Asking for an apron and her little shawl. Worrying about her fruit.

MRS. PETERS [*starts to speak, glances up, where footsteps are heard in the room above. In a low voice*]. Mr. Peters says it looks bad for her. Mr. Henderson is awful sarcastic in a speech, and he'll make fun of her sayin' she didn't wake up.

MRS. HALE. Well, I guess John Wright didn't wake when they was slipping that rope under his neck.

MRS. PETERS. No, it's strange. It must have been done awful crafty and still. They say it was such a—funny way to kill a man, rigging it all up like that.

MRS. HALE. That's just what Mr. Hale said. There was a gun in the house. He says that's what he can't understand.

MRS. PETERS. Mr. Henderson said coming out that what was needed for the case was a motive; something to show anger, or—sudden feeling.

MRS. HALE [*who is standing by the table*]. Well, I don't see any signs of anger around here. [*She puts her hand on the dish towel which lies on the table, stands looking down at the table, one half of which is clean, the other half messy.*] It's wiped here. [*Makes a move as if to finish work, then turns and looks at loaf of bread outside the breadbox. Drops towel. In that voice of coming back to familiar things.*] Wonder how they are finding things upstairs? I hope she had it a little more red-up there. You know, it seems kind of *sneaking*. Locking her up in town and then coming out here and trying to get her own house to turn against her!

MRS. PETERS. But, Mrs. Hale, the law is the law.

MRS. HALE. I s'pose 'tis. [*Unbuttoning her coat.*] Better loosen up your things, Mrs. Peters. You won't feel them when you go out.

[MRS. PETERS *takes off her fur tippet, goes to hang it on hook at back of room, stands looking at the under part of the small corner table.*]

MRS. PETERS. She was piecing a quilt. [*She brings the large sewing basket, and they look at the bright pieces.*]

MRS. HALE. It's log cabin pattern. Pretty, isn't it? I wonder if she was goin' to quilt or just knot it?

[*Footsteps have been heard coming down the stairs. The* SHERIFF *enters, followed by* HALE *and the* COUNTY ATTORNEY.]

SHERIFF. They wonder if she was going to quilt it or just knot it. [*The men laugh, the women look abashed.*]

COUNTY ATTORNEY [*rubbing his hands over the stove*]. Frank's fire didn't do much up there, did it? Well, let's go out to the barn and get that cleared up.

[*The men go outside.*]

MRS. HALE [*resentfully*]. I don't know as there's anything so strange, our takin' up our time with little things while we're waiting for them to get the evidence. [*She sits down at the big table, smoothing out a block with decision.*] I don't see as it's anything to laugh about.

MRS. PETERS [*apologetically*]. Of course they've got awful important things on their minds. [*Pulls up a chair and joins* MRS. HALE *at the table.*]

MRS. HALE [*examining another block*]. Mrs. Peters, look at this one. Here, this is the one she was working on, and look at the sewing! All the rest of it has been so nice and even. And look at this! It's all over the place! Why, it looks as if she didn't know what she was about! [*After she has said this, they look at each other, then start to glance back at the door. After an instant* MRS. HALE *has pulled at a knot and ripped the sewing.*]

MRS. PETERS. Oh, what are you doing, Mrs. Hale?

MRS. HALE [*mildly*]. Just pulling out a stitch or two that's not sewed very good. [*Threading a needle.*] Bad sewing always made me fidgety.

MRS. PETERS [*nervously*]. I don't think we ought to touch things.

MRS. HALE. I'll just finish up this end. [*Suddenly stopping and leaning forward.*] Mrs. Peters?

MRS. PETERS. Yes, Mrs. Hale?

MRS. HALE. What do you suppose she was so nervous about?

MRS. PETERS. Oh—I don't know. I don't know as she was nervous. I sometimes sew awful queer when I'm just tired. [MRS. HALE *starts to say something, looks at* MRS. PETERS, *then goes on sewing.*] Well, I must get these things wrapped up. They may be through sooner than we think. [*Putting apron and other things together.*] I wonder where I can find a piece of paper, and string.

MRS. HALE. In that cupboard, maybe.

MRS. PETERS [*looking in cupboard*]. Why, here's a birdcage. [*Holds it up.*] Did she have a bird, Mrs. Hale?

MRS. HALE. Why, I don't know whether she did or not—I've not been here for so long. There was a man around last year selling canaries cheap, but I don't know as she took one; maybe she did. She used to sing real pretty herself.

MRS. PETERS [*glancing around*]. Seems funny to think of a bird here. But she must have had one or why should she have a cage? I wonder what happened to it?

MRS. HALE. I s'pose maybe the cat got it.

MRS. PETERS. No, she didn't have a cat. She's got that feeling some people have about cats—being afraid of them. My cat got in her room, and she was real upset and asked me to take it out.

MRS. HALE. My sister Bessie was like that. Queer, ain't it?

MRS. PETERS [*examining the cage*]. Why, look at this door. It's broke. One hinge is pulled apart.

MRS. HALE [*looking, too*]. Looks as if someone must have been rough with it.

MRS. PETERS. Why, yes. [*She brings the cage forward and puts it on the table.*]

MRS. HALE. I wish if they're going to find any evidence they'd be about it. I don't like this place.

MRS. PETERS. But I'm awful glad you came with me, Mrs. Hale. It would be lonesome for me sitting here alone.

MRS. HALE. It would, wouldn't it? [*Dropping her sewing.*] But I tell you what I do wish, Mrs. Peters. I wish I had come over sometimes when *she* was here. I—[*Looking around the room.*]—wish I had.

MRS. PETERS. But of course you were awful busy, Mrs. Hale—your house and your children.

MRS. HALE. I could've come. I stayed away because it weren't cheerful—and that's why I ought to have come. I—I've never liked this place. Maybe because it's down in a hollow, and you don't see the road. I dunno what it is, but it's a lonesome place and always was. I wish I had come over to see Minnie Foster sometimes. I can see now—[*Shakes her head.*]

MRS. PETERS. Well, you mustn't reproach yourself, Mrs. Hale. Somehow we just don't see how it is with other folks until—something comes up.

MRS. HALE. Not having children makes less work—but it makes a quiet house, and Wright out to work all day, and no company when he did come in. Did you know John Wright, Mrs. Peters?

MRS. PETERS. Not to know him; I've seen him in town. They say he was a good man.

MRS. HALE. Yes—good; he didn't drink, and kept his word as well as most, I guess, and paid his debts. But he was a hard man, Mrs. Peters. Just to pass the time of day with him. [*Shivers.*] Like a raw wind that gets to the bone. [*Pauses, her eye falling on the cage.*] I should think she would 'a wanted a bird. But what do you suppose went with it?

MRS. PETERS. I don't know, unless it got sick and died. [*She reaches over and swings the broken door, swings it again; both women watch it.*]

MRS. HALE. You weren't raised round here, were you? [MRS. PETERS *shakes her head.*] You didn't know—her?

MRS. PETERS. Not till they brought her yesterday.

MRS. HALE. She—come to think of it, she was kind of like a bird herself—real sweet and pretty, but kind of timid and—fluttery. How—she—did—change. [*Silence; then as if struck by a happy thought and relieved to get back to everyday things.*] Tell you what, Mrs. Peters, why don't you take the quilt in with you? It might take up her mind.

MRS. PETERS. Why, I think that's a real nice idea, Mrs. Hale. There couldn't possibly be any objection to it, could there? Now, just what would I take? I wonder if her patches are in here—and her things. [*They look in the sewing basket.*]

MRS. HALE. Here's some red. I expect this has got sewing things in it. [*Brings out a fancy box.*] What a pretty box. Looks like something somebody would give you. Maybe her scissors are in here. [*Opens box. Suddenly puts her hand to her nose.*] Why—[MRS. PETERS *bends nearer, then turns her face away.*] There's something wrapped up in this piece of silk.

MRS. PETERS. Why, this isn't her scissors.

MRS. HALE [*lifting the silk*]. Oh, Mrs. Peters—it's—[MRS. PETERS *bends closer.*]

MRS. PETERS. It's the bird.

MRS. HALE [*jumping up*]. But, Mrs. Peters—look at it. Its neck! Look at its neck! Its all—other side *to.*

MRS. PETERS. Somebody—wrung—its neck.

[*Their eyes meet. A look of growing comprehension of horror. Steps are heard outside.* MRS. HALE *slips box under quilt pieces, and sinks into her chair. Enter* SHERIFF *and* COUNTY ATTORNEY. MRS. PETERS *rises.*]

COUNTY ATTORNEY [*as one turning from serious things to little pleasantries*].

Well, ladies, have you decided whether she was going to quilt it or knot it?

MRS. PETERS. We think she was going to—knot it.

COUNTY ATTORNEY. Well, that's interesting, I'm sure. [*Seeing the birdcage.*] Has the bird flown?

MRS. HALE [*putting more quilt pieces over the box*]. We think the—cat got it.

COUNTY ATTORNEY [*preoccupied*]. Is there a cat?

[MRS. HALE *glances in a quick covert way at* MRS. PETERS.]

MRS. PETERS. Well, not now. They're superstitious, you know. They leave.

COUNTY ATTORNEY [*to* SHERIFF PETERS, *continuing an interrupted conversation*]. No sign at all of anyone having come from the outside. Their own rope. Now let's go up again and go over it piece by piece. [*They start upstairs.*] It would have to have been someone who knew just the—

[MRS. PETERS *sits down. The two women sit there not looking at one another, but as if peering into something and at the same time holding back. When they talk now, it is in the manner of feeling their way over strange ground, as if afraid of what they are saying, but as if they cannot help saying it.*]

MRS. HALE. She liked the bird. She was going to bury it in that pretty box.

MRS. PETERS [*in a whisper*]. When I was a girl—my kitten—there was a boy took a hatchet, and before my eyes—and before I could get there—[*Covers her face an instant.*] If they hadn't held me back, I would have—[*Catches herself, looks upstairs where steps are heard, falters weakly.*]—hurt him.

MRS. HALE [*with a slow look around her*]. I wonder how it would seem never to have had any children around. [*Pause.*] No, Wright wouldn't like the bird—a thing that sang. She used to sing. He killed that, too.

MRS. PETERS [*moving uneasily*]. We don't know who killed the bird.

MRS. HALE. I knew John Wright.

MRS. PETERS. It was an awful thing was done in this house that night, Mrs. Hale. Killing a man while he slept, slipping a rope around his neck that choked the life out of him.

MRS. HALE. His neck. Choked the life out of him.

[*Her hand goes out and rests on the birdcage.*]

MRS. PETERS [*with rising voice*]. We don't know who killed him. We don't *know*.

MRS. HALE [*her own feeling not interrupted*]. If there'd been years and years of nothing, then a bird to sing to you, it would be awful—still, after the bird was still.

MRS. PETERS [*something within her speaking*]. I know what stillness is. When we homesteaded in Dakota, and my first baby died—after he was two years old, and me with no other then—

MRS. HALE [*moving*]. How soon do you suppose they'll be through, looking for evidence?

MRS. PETERS. I know what stillness is. [*Pulling herself back.*] The law has got to punish crime, Mrs. Hale.

MRS. HALE [*not as if answering that*]. I wish you'd seen Minnie Foster when she wore a white dress with blue ribbons and stood up there in the choir and sang. [*A look around the room.*] Oh, I *wish* I'd come over here once in a while! That was a crime! That was a crime! Who's going to punish that?

MRS. PETERS [*looking upstairs*]. We mustn't—take on.

MRS. HALE. I might have known she needed help! I know how things can be—for women. I tell you, it's queer, Mrs. Peters. We live close together, and we live far apart. We all go through the same things—it's all just a different kind of the same thing. [*Brushes her eyes, noticing the bottle of fruit, reaches out for it.*] If I was you, I wouldn't tell her her fruit was gone. Tell her it *ain't*. Tell her it's all right. Take this in to prove it to her. She—she may never know whether it was broke or not.

MRS. PETERS [*takes the bottle, looks about for something to wrap it in; takes petticoat from the clothes brought from the other room, very nervously begins winding this around the bottle. In a false voice*]. My, it's a good thing the men couldn't hear us. Wouldn't they just laugh! Getting all stirred up over a little thing like a—dead canary. As if that could have anything to do with—with—wouldn't they *laugh!*

[*The men are heard coming downstairs.*]

MRS. HALE [*under her breath*]. Maybe they would—maybe they wouldn't.

COUNTY ATTORNEY. No, Peters, it's all perfectly clear except a reason for doing it. But you know juries when it comes to women. If there was some definite thing. Something to show—something to make a story about—a thing that would connect up with this strange way of doing it.

[*The women's eyes meet for an instant. Enter* HALE *from outer door.*]

HALE. Well, I've got the team around. Pretty cold out there.

COUNTY ATTORNEY. I'm going to stay here awhile by myself. [*To the* SHERIFF.] You can send Frank out for me, can't you? I want to go over everything. I'm not satisfied that we can't do better.

SHERIFF. Do you want to see what Mrs. Peters is going to take in?

[*The* LAWYER *goes to the table, picks up the apron, laughs.*]

COUNTY ATTORNEY. Oh, I guess they're not very dangerous things the ladies have picked up. [*Moves a few things about, disturbing the quilt pieces which cover the box. Steps back.*] No, Mrs. Peters doesn't need supervising. For that matter, a sheriff's wife is married to the law. Ever think of it that way, Mrs. Peters?

MRS. PETERS. Not—just that way.

SHERIFF [*chuckling*]. Married to the law. [*Moves toward the other room.*] I just want you to come in here a minute, George. We ought to take a look at these windows.

COUNTY ATTORNEY [*scoffingly*]. Oh, windows!

SHERIFF. We'll be right out, Mr. Hale.

[HALE *goes outside. The* SHERIFF *follows the* COUNTY ATTORNEY *into the other room. Then* MRS. HALE *rises, hands tight together, looking intensely at* MRS. PETERS, *whose eyes take a slow turn, finally meeting* MRS. HALE'*s. A moment* MRS. HALE *holds her, then her own eyes point the way to where the box is concealed. Suddenly* MRS. PETERS *throws back quilt pieces and tries to put the box in the bag she is wearing. It is too big. She opens box, starts to take bird out, cannot touch it, goes to pieces, stands there helpless. Sound of a knob turning in the other room.* MRS. HALE *snatches the box and puts it in the pocket of her big coat. Enter* COUNTY ATTORNEY *and* SHERIFF.]

COUNTY ATTORNEY [*facetiously*]. Well, Henry, at least we found out that she was not going to quilt it. She was going to—what is it you call it, ladies?

MRS. HALE [*her hand against her pocket*]. We call it—knot it, Mr. Henderson.

CURTAIN

THEATER OF SPECTACLE

Bertolt Brecht (1898–1956)
THE GOOD WOMAN OF SETZUAN

CHARACTERS

WONG, *a water seller*
THREE GODS
SHEN TE, *a prostitute, later a shopkeeper*
MRS. SHIN, *former owner of Shen Te's shop*
A FAMILY OF EIGHT *(husband, wife, brother, sister-in-law, grandfather, nephew, niece, boy)*
AN UNEMPLOYED MAN
A CARPENTER
MRS. MI TZU, *Shen Te's landlady*
YANG SUN, *an unemployed pilot, later a factory manager*
AN OLD WHORE
A POLICEMAN
AN OLD MAN
AN OLD WOMAN, *his wife*
MR. SHU FU, *a barber*
MRS. YANG, *mother of Yang Sun*
GENTLEMEN, VOICES, CHILDREN *(three), etc.*

PROLOGUE

At the gates of the half-Westernized city of Setzuan. Evening. WONG *the water seller introduces himself to the audience.*

WONG. I sell water here in the city of Setzuan. It isn't easy. When water is scarce, I have long distances to go in search of it, and when it is plentiful, I have no income. But in our part of the world there is nothing unusual about poverty. Many people think only the gods can save the situation. And I hear from a cattle merchant—who travels a lot—that some of the highest gods are on their way here at this very moment. Informed sources have it that heaven is quite disturbed at all the complaining. I've been coming out here to the city gates for three days now to bid these gods welcome. I want to be the first to greet them. What about those fellows over there? No, no, they *work*. And that one there has ink on his fingers, he's no god, he must be a clerk from the cement factory. *Those* two are another story. They look as though they'd like to beat you. But gods don't need to beat you, do they?

[THREE GODS *appear.*]

What about those three? Old-fashioned clothes—dust on their feet—they *must* be gods! [*He throws himself at their feet.*] Do with me what you will, illustrious ones!

FIRST GOD [*with an ear trumpet*]. Ah! [*He is pleased.*] So we were expected?

WONG [*giving them water*]. Oh, yes. And I *knew* you'd come.

FIRST GOD. We need somewhere to stay the night. You know of a place?

WONG. The whole town is at your service, illustrious ones! What sort of a place would you like?

[*The* GODS *eye each other.*]

FIRST GOD. Just try the first house you come to, my son.

WONG. That would be Mr. Fo's place.

FIRST GOD. Mr. Fo.

WONG. One moment! [*He knocks at the first house.*]

VOICE FROM MR. FO'*s*. No!

[WONG *returns a little nervously.*]

WONG. It's too bad. Mr. Fo isn't in. And his servants don't dare do a thing without his consent. He'll have a fit when he finds out who they turned away, won't he?

FIRST GOD [*smiling*]. He will, won't he?

WONG. One moment! The next house is Mr. Cheng's. Won't he be thrilled!

FIRST GOD. Mr. Cheng.

[WONG *knocks.*]

VOICE FROM MR. CHENG'*s*. Keep your gods. We have our own troubles!

WONG [*back with the* GODS]. Mr. Cheng is very sorry, but he has a houseful of relations. I think some of them are a bad lot, and naturally, he wouldn't like you to see them.

THIRD GOD. Are we so terrible?

WONG. Well, only with bad people, of course. Everyone knows the province of Kwan is always having floods.

SECOND GOD. Really? How's that?

WONG. Why, because they're so irreligious.

SECOND GOD. Rubbish. It's because they neglected the dam.

FIRST GOD [*to* SECOND]. Sh! [*To* WONG.] You're still in hopes, aren't you, my son?

WONG. Certainly. All Setzuan is competing for the honor! What happened up to now is pure coincidence. I'll be back. [*He walks away, but then stands undecided.*]

SECOND GOD. What did I tell you?

THIRD GOD. It *could* be pure coincidence.

SECOND GOD. The same coincidence in Shun, Kwan, and Setzuan? People just aren't religious any more, let's face the fact. Our mission has failed!

FIRST GOD. Oh come, we might run into a good person any minute.

THIRD GOD. How did the resolution read? [*Unrolling a scroll and reading from it:*] "The world can stay as it is if enough people are found [*at the word "found" he unrolls it a little more*] living lives worthy of human beings." Good people, that is. Well, what about this water seller himself? *He's* good, or I'm very much mistaken.

SECOND GOD. You're very much mistaken. When he gave us a drink, I had the impression there was something odd about the cup. Well, look! [*He shows the cup to the* FIRST GOD.]

FIRST GOD. A false bottom!

SECOND GOD. The man is a swindler.

FIRST GOD. Very well, count *him* out. That's one man among millions. And as a matter of fact, we only need one on *our* side. These atheists are saying, "The world must be changed because no one can *be* good and *stay* good." No one, eh? I say: let us find one—just one—and we have those fellows where we want them!

THIRD GOD [*to* WONG]. Water seller, is it so hard to find a place to stay?

WONG. Nothing could be easier. It's just me. I don't go about it right.

THIRD GOD. Really?

[*He returns to the others. A* GENTLEMAN *passes by.*]

WONG. Oh dear, they're catching on. [*He accosts the* GENTLEMAN.] Excuse the intrusion, dear sir, but three gods have just turned up. Three of the very highest. They need a place for the night. Seize this rare opportunity—to have real gods as your guests!

GENTLEMAN [*laughing*]. A new way of finding free rooms for a gang of crooks. [*Exit* GENTLEMAN.]

WONG [*shouting at him*]. Godless rascal! Have you no religion, gentleman of Setzuan? [*Pause.*] Patience, illustrious ones! [*Pause.*] There's only one person left. Shen Te, the prostitute. She *can't* say no. [*Calls up to a window:*] Shen Te!

[SHEN TE *opens the shutters and looks out.*]

WONG. Shen Te, it's Wong. *They're* here, and nobody wants them. Will you take them?

SHEN TE. Oh, no, Wong, I'm expecting a gentleman.

WONG. Can't you forget about him for tonight?

SHEN TE. The rent has to be paid by tomorrow or I'll be out on the street.

WONG. This is no time for calculation, Shen Te.

SHEN TE. Stomachs rumble even on the Emperor's birthday, Wong.

WONG. Setzuan is one big dung hill!

SHEN TE. Oh, very well! I'll hide till my gentleman has come and gone. Then I'll take them. [*She disappears.*]

WONG. They mustn't see her gentleman or they'll know what she is.

FIRST GOD [*who hasn't heard any of this*]. I think it's hopeless.

[*They approach* WONG.]

WONG [*jumping, as he finds them behind him*]. A room has been found, illustrious ones! [*He wipes sweat off his brow.*]

SECOND GOD. Oh, good.

THIRD GOD. Let's see it.

WONG [*nervously*]. Just a minute. It has to be tidied up a bit.

THIRD GOD. Then we'll sit down here and wait.

WONG [*still more nervous*]. No, no! [*Holding himself back.*] Too much traffic, you know.

THIRD GOD [*with a smile*]. Of course, if you *want* us to move.

[*They retire a little. They sit on a doorstep.* WONG *sits on the ground.*]

WONG [*after a deep breath*]. You'll be staying with a single girl—the finest human being in Setzuan!

THIRD GOD. That's nice.

WONG [*to the audience*]. They gave me such a look when I picked up my cup just now.

THIRD GOD. You're worn out, Wong.

WONG. A little, maybe.

FIRST GOD. Do people here have a hard time of it?

WONG. The good ones do.

FIRST GOD. What about yourself?

WONG. You mean I'm not good. That's true. And I don't have an easy time either!

[*During this dialogue, a* GENTLEMAN *has turned up in front of Shen Te's house, and has whistled several times. Each time* WONG *has given a start.*]

THIRD GOD [*to* WONG, *softly*]. Psst! I think he's gone now.

WONG [*confused and surprised*]. Ye-e- es.

[*The* GENTLEMAN *has left now, and* SHEN TE *has come down to the street.*]

SHEN TE [*softly*]. Wong!

[*Getting no answer, she goes off down the street.* WONG *arrives just too late, forgetting his carrying pole.*]

WONG [*softly*]. Shen Te! Shen Te! [*To himself:*] So she's gone off to earn the rent. Oh dear, I can't go to the gods *again* with no room to offer them. Having failed in the service of the gods, I shall run to my den in the sewer pipe down by the river and hide from their sight!

[*He rushes off.* SHEN TE *returns, looking for him, but find the* GODS. *She stops in confusion.*]

SHEN TE. You are the illustrious ones? My name is Shen Te. It would please me very much if my simple room could be of use to you.

THIRD GOD. Where is the water seller, Miss . . . Shen Te?

SHEN TE. I missed him, somehow.

FIRST GOD. Oh, he probably thought you weren't coming, and was afraid of telling us.

THIRD GOD [*picking up the carrying pole*]. We'll leave this with you. He'll be needing it.

[*Led by* SHEN TE, *they go into the house. It grows dark, then light. Dawn. Again escorted by* SHEN TE, *who leads them through the half-light with a little lamp, the* GODS *take their leave.*]

FIRST GOD. Thank you, thank you, dear Shen Te, for your elegant hospitality! We shall not forget! And give our thinks to the water seller—he showed us a good human being.

SHEN TE. Oh, *I'm* not good. Let me tell you something: when Wong asked me to put you up, I hesitated.

FIRST GOD. It's all right to hesitate if you then go ahead! And in giving us that room you did much more than you knew. You proved that good people still exist, a point that has been disputed of late—even in heaven. Farewell!

SECOND GOD. Farewell!

THIRD GOD. Farewell!

SHEN TE. Stop, illustrious ones! I'm not sure you're right. I'd like to be good, it's true, but there's the rent to pay. And that's not all: I sell myself for a living. Even so I can't make ends meet, there's too much competition. I'd like to honor my father and mother and speak nothing but the truth and not covet my neighbor's house. I should love to stay with one man. But how? How is it done? Even breaking a few of your commandments, I can hardly manage.

FIRST GOD [*clearing his throat*]. These thoughts are but, um, the misgivings of an unusually good woman!

THIRD GOD. Good-bye, Shen Te! Give our regards to the water seller!

SECOND GOD. And above all: be good! Farewell!

FIRST GOD. Farewell!

THIRD GOD. Farewell!

[*They start to wave good-bye.*]

SHEN TE. But everything is so expensive, I don't feel sure I can do it!

SECOND GOD. That's not in our sphere. We never meddle with economics.

THIRD GOD. One moment. [*They stop.*] Isn't it true she might do better if she had more money?

SECOND GOD. Come, come! How could we ever account for it Up Above?

FIRST GOD. Oh, there are ways. [*They put their heads together and confer in dumb show. To* SHEN TE, *with embarrassment:*] As you say you can't pay your rent, well, um, we're not paupers, so of course we *insist* on paying for our room. [*Awkwardly thrusting money into her hand.*] There! [*Quickly.*] But don't tell anyone! The incident is open to misinterpretation.

SECOND GOD. It certainly is!

FIRST GOD [*defensively*]. But there's no law against it! It was never decreed that a god mustn't pay hotel bills!

[*The* GODS *leave.*]

1

A small tobacco shop. The shop is not as yet completely furnished and hasn't started doing business.

SHEN TE [*to the audience*]. It's three days now since the gods left. When they said they wanted to pay for the room, I looked down at my hand, and there was more than a thousand silver dollars! I bought a tobacco shop with the money, and moved in yesterday. I don't own the building, of course, but I can pay the rent, and I hope to do a lot of good here. Beginning with Mrs. Shin, who's just coming across the square with her pot. She had the shop before me, and yesterday she dropped in to ask for rice for her children. [*Enter* MRS. SHIN. *Both women bow.*] How do you do, Mrs. Shin.

MRS. SHIN. How do you do, Miss Shen Te. You like your new home?

SHEN TE. Indeed, yes. Did your children have a good night?

MRS. SHIN. In that hovel? The youngest is coughing already.

SHEN TE. Oh, dear!

MRS. SHIN. You're going to learn a thing or two in these slums.

SHEN TE. Slums? That's not what you said when you sold me the shop!

MRS. SHIN. Now don't start nagging! Robbing me and my innocent children of their home and then calling it a slum! That's the limit! [*She weeps.*]

SHEN TE [*tactfully*]. I'll get your rice.

MRS. SHIN. And a little cash while you're at it.

SHEN TE. I'm afraid I haven't sold anything yet.

MRS. SHIN [*screeching*]. I've got to have it. Strip the clothes from my back and then cut my throat, will you? I know what I'll do: I'll dump my children on your doorstep! [*She snatches the pot out of* SHEN TE*'s hands.*

SHEN TE. Please don't be angry. You'll spill the rice.

[*Enter an elderly* HUSBAND *and* WIFE *with their shabbily dressed* NEPHEW.]

WIFE. Shen Te, dear! You've come into money, they tell me. And we haven't a roof over our heads! A tobacco shop. We had one too. But it's gone. Could we spend the night here, do you think?

NEPHEW [*appraising the shop*]. Not bad!

WIFE. He's our nephew. We're inseparable!

MRS. SHIN. And who are these . . . ladies and gentlemen?

SHEN TE. They put me up when I first came in from the country. [*To the audience.*] Of course, when my small purse was empty, they put me out on the street, and they may be afraid I'll do the same to them. [*To the newcomers, kindly:*] Come in, and welcome, though I've only one little room for you—it's behind the shop.

HUSBAND. That'll do. Don't worry.

WIFE [*bringing* SHEN TE *some tea*]. We'll stay over here, so we won't be in your way. Did you make it a tobacco shop in memory of your first real home? We can certainly give you a hint or two! That's one reason we came.

MRS. SHIN [*to* SHEN TE]. Very nice! As long as you have a few customers too!

HUSBAND. Sh! A customer!

[*Enter an* UNEMPLOYED MAN, *in rags.*]

UNEMPLOYED MAN. Excuse me. I'm unemployed.

[MRS. SHIN *laughs.*]

SHEN TE. Can I help you?

UNEMPLOYED MAN. Have you any damaged cigarettes? I thought there might be some damage when you're unpacking.

WIFE. What nerve, begging for tobacco! [*Rhetorically.*] Why don't they ask for bread?

UNEMPLOYED MAN. Bread is expensive. One cigarette butt and I'll be a new man.

SHEN TE [*giving him cigarettes*]. That's very important—to be a new man. You'll be my first customer and bring me luck.

[*The* UNEMPLOYED MAN *quickly lights a cigarette, inhales, and goes off, coughing.*]

WIFE. Was that right, Shen Te, dear?

MRS. SHIN. If this is the opening of a shop, you can hold the closing at the end of the week.

HUSBAND. I bet he had money on him.

SHEN TE. Oh, no, he said he hadn't!

NEPHEW. How d'you know he wasn't lying?

SHEN TE [*angrily*]. How do you know he was?

WIFE [*wagging her head*]. You're too good, Shen Te, dear. If you're going to keep this shop, you'll have to learn to say no.

HUSBAND. Tell them the place isn't yours to dispose of. Belongs to . . . some relative who insists on all accounts being strictly in order . . .

MRS. SHIN. That's right! What do you think you are—a philanthropist?

SHEN TE [*laughing*]. Very well, suppose I ask you for my rice back, Mrs. Shin?

WIFE [*combatively, at* MRS. SHIN]. So that's *her* rice?

[*Enter the* CARPENTER, *a small man.*]

MRS. SHIN [*who, at the sight of him, starts to hurry away*]. See you tomorrow, Miss Shen Te! [*Exit* MRS. SHIN.]

CARPENTER. Mrs. Shin, it's you I want!

WIFE [*to* SHEN TE]. Has she some claim on you?

SHEN TE. She's hungry. That's a claim.

CARPENTER. Are you the new tenant? And filling up the shelves already? Well, they're not yours till they're paid for, ma'am. I'm the carpenter, so I should know.

SHEN TE. I took the shop "furnishings included."

CARPENTER. You're in league with that Mrs. Shin, of course. All right. I demand my hundred silver dollars.

SHEN TE. I'm afraid I haven't got a hundred silver dollars.

CARPENTER. Then you'll find it. Or I'll have you arrested.

WIFE [*whispering to* SHEN TE]. That relative: make it a cousin.

SHEN TE. Can't it wait till next month?

CARPENTER. No!

SHEN TE. Be a little patient, Mr. Carpenter, I can't settle all claims at once.

CARPENTER. Who's patient with me? [*He grabs a shelf from the wall.*] Pay up—or I take the shelves back!

WIFE. Shen Te! Dear! Why don't you let your . . . cousin settle this affair? [*To* CARPENTER:] Put your claim in writing. Shen Te's cousin will see you get paid.

CARPENTER [*derisively*]. Cousin, eh?

HUSBAND. Cousin, yes.

CARPENTER. I know these cousins!

NEPHEW. Don't be silly. He's a personal friend of mine.

HUSBAND. What a man! Sharp as a razor!

CARPENTER. All right. I'll put my claim in writing. [*Puts shelf on floor, sits on it, writes out bill.*]

WIFE [*to* SHEN TE]. He'd tear the dress off your back to get his shelves. Never recognize a claim. That's my motto.

SHEN TE. He's done a job, and wants something in return. It's shameful that I can't give it to him. What will the gods say?

HUSBAND. You did your bit when you took *us* in.

[*Enter the* BROTHER, *limping, and the* SISTER-IN-LAW, *pregnant.*]

BROTHER [*to* HUSBAND *and* WIFE]. So this is where you're hiding out! There's family feeling for you! Leaving us on the corner!

WIFE [*embarrassed, to* SHEN TE]. It's my brother and his wife. [*To them:*] Now stop grumbling, and sit quietly in that corner. [*To* SHEN TE:] It can't be helped. She's in her fifth month.

SHEN TE. Oh yes. Welcome!

WIFE [*to the couple*]. Say thank you. [*They mutter something.*] The cups are there. [*To* SHEN TE:] Lucky you bought this shop when you did!

SHEN TE [*laughing and bringing tea*]. Lucky indeed!

[*Enter* MRS. MI TZU, *the landlady.*]

MRS. MI TZU. Miss Shen Te? I am Mrs. Mi Tzu, your landlady. I hope our relationship will be a happy one. I like to think I give my tenants modern, personalized service. Here is your lease. [*To the others, as* SHEN TE *reads the lease:*] There's nothing like the opening of a little shop, is there? A moment of true beauty! [*She is looking around.*] Not very much on the shelves, of course. But everything in the gods' good time! Where are your references, Miss Shen Te?

SHEN TE. Do I *have* to have references?

MRS. MI TZU. After all, I haven't a notion who you are!

HUSBAND. Oh, *we'd* be glad to vouch for Miss Shen Te! We'd go through fire for her!

MRS. MI TZU. And who may *you* be?

HUSBAND [*stammering*]. Ma Fu, tobacco dealer.

MRS. MI TZU. Where is your shop, Mr. . . . Ma Fu?

HUSBAND. Well, um, I haven't got a shop—I've just sold it.

MRS. MI TZU. I see. [*To* SHEN TE:] Is there no one else that knows you?

WIFE [*whispering to* SHEN TO]. Your cousin! Your cousin!

MRS. MI TZU. This is a respectable house, Miss Shen Te. I never sign a lease without certain assurances.

SHEN TE [*slowly, her eyes downcast*]. I have . . . a cousin.

MRS. MI TZU. On the square? Let's go over and see him. What does he do?

SHEN TE [*as before*]. He lives . . . in another city.

WIFE [*prompting*]. Didn't you say he was in Shung?

SHEN TE. That's right. Shung.

HUSBAND [*prompting*]. I had his name on the tip of my tongue. Mr. . . .

SHEN TE [*with an effort*]. Mr. . . . Shui . . . Ta.

HUSBAND. That's it! Tall, skinny fellow!

SHEN TE. Shui Ta!

NEPHEW [*to* CARPENTER]. *You* were in touch with him, weren't you? About the shelves?

CARPENTER [*surlily*]. Give him this bill. [*He hands it over.*] I'll be back in the morning. [*Exit* CARPENTER.]

NEPHEW [*calling after him, but with his eyes on* MRS. MI TZU]. Don't worry! Mr. Shui Ta pays on the nail!

MRS. MI TZU [*looking closely at* SHEN TE]. I'll be happy to make his acquaintance, Miss Shen Te. [*Exit* MRS. MI TZU.]

[*Pause.*]

WIFE. By tomorrow morning she'll know more about you than you do yourself.

SISTER-IN-LAW [*to* NEPHEW]. This thing isn't built to last.

[*Enter* GRANDFATHER.]

WIFE. It's Grandfather! [*To* SHEN TE]. Such a good old soul!

[*The* BOY *enters.*]

BOY [*over his shoulder*]. Here they are!

WIFE. And the boy, how he's grown! But he always could eat enough for ten.

[*Enter the* NIECE.]

WIFE [*to* SHEN TE]. Our little niece from the country. There are more of us now than in your time. The less we had, the more there were of us; the more there were of us, the less we had. Give me the key. We must protect ourselves from unwanted guests. [*She takes the key and locks the door.*] Just make yourself at home. I'll light the little lamp.

NEPHEW [*a big joke*]. I hope her cousin doesn't drop in tonight! The strict Mr. Shui Ta!

[SISTER-IN-LAW *laughs.*]

BROTHER [*reaching for a cigarette*]. One cigarette more or less . . .

HUSBAND. One cigarette more or less.

[*They pile into the cigarettes. The* BROTHER *hands a jug of wine round.*]

NEPHEW. Mr. Shui Ta'll pay for it!

GRANDFATHER [*gravely, to* SHEN TE]. How do you do?

[SHEN TE, *a little taken aback by the belatedness of the greeting, bows. She has the carpenter's bill in one hand, the landlady's lease in the other.*]

WIFE. How about a bit of a song? To keep Shen Te's spirits up?

NEPHEW. Good idea. Grandfather: you start!

Song of the Smoke

GRANDFATHER.

I used to think (before old age beset me)
That brains could fill the pantry of the poor.
But where did all my cerebration get me?
I'm just as hungry as I was before.
So what's the use?
See the smoke float free
Into ever colder coldness!
It's the same with me.

HUSBAND.

The straight and narrow path leads to disaster
And so the crooked path I tried to tread.
That got me to disaster even faster.
(They say we shall be happy when we're dead.)
So what's the use?
See the smoke float free
Into ever colder coldness!
It's the same with me.

NIECE.

You older people, full of expectation,
At any moment now you'll walk the plank!
The future's for the younger generation!
Yes, even if that future is a blank.
So what's the use?
See the smoke float free
Into ever colder coldness!
It's the same with me.

NEPHEW [*to the* BROTHER]. Where'd you get that wine?

SISTER-IN-LAW [*answering for the* BROTHER]. He pawned the sack of tobacco.

HUSBAND [*stepping in*]. What? That tobacco was all we had to fall back on! You pig!

BROTHER. *You'd* call a man a pig because your wife was frigid! Did you refuse to drink it?

[*They fight. The shelves fall over.*]

SHEN TE [*imploringly*]. Oh don't! Don't break everything! Take it, take it, take it all, but don't destroy a gift from the gods!

WIFE [*disparagingly*]. This shop isn't big enough. I should never have mentioned it to Uncle and the others. When *they* arrive, it's going to be disgustingly overcrowded.

SISTER- IN-LAW. And did you hear our gracious hostess? She cools off quick!

[*Voices outside. Knocking at the door.*]

UNCLE'*s* VOICE. Open the door!

WIFE. Uncle! Is that you, Uncle?

UNCLE'*s* VOICE. Certainly, it's me. Auntie says to tell you she'll have the children here in ten minutes.

WIFE [*to* SHEN TE]. I'll have to let him in.

SHEN TE [*who scarcely hears her*]:

The little lifeboat is swiftly sent down
Too many men too greedily
Hold on to it as they drown.

1A

Wong's den in a sewer pipe.

WONG [*crouching there*]. All quiet! It's four days now since I left the city. The gods passed this way on the second day. I heard their steps on the bridge over there. They must be a long way off by this time, so I'm safe. [*Breathing a sigh of relief, he curls up and goes to sleep. In his dream the pipe becomes transparent, and the* GODS *appear. Raising an arm, as if in self-defense:*] I know, I know, illustrious ones! I found no one to give you a room—not in all Setzuan! There, it's out. Please continue on your way!

FIRST GOD [*mildly*]. But you did find someone. Someone who took us in for the night, watched over us in our sleep, and in the early morning lighted us down to the street with a lamp.

WONG. It was . . . Shen Te that took you in?

THIRD GOD. Who else?

WONG. And I ran away! "She isn't coming," I thought, "she just can't afford it."

GODS [*singing*].

O you feeble, well-intentioned, and yet feeble chap
Where there's need the fellow thinks there is no goodness!
When there's danger he thinks courage starts to ebb away!
Some people only see the seamy side!
What hasty judgment! What premature desperation!

WONG. I'm *very* ashamed, illustrious ones.

FIRST GOD. Do us a favor, water seller. Go back to Setzuan. Find Shen Te, and give us a report on her. We hear that she's come into a little money. Show interest in her goodness—for no one can be good for long if goodness is not in demand. Meanwhile we shall continue the search, and find other good people. After which, the idle chatter about the impossibility of goodness will stop!

[*The* GODS *vanish.*]

2

[*A knocking.*]

WIFE. Shen Te! Someone at the door. Where is she anyway?

NEPHEW. She must be getting the breakfast. Mr. Shui Ta will pay for it.

[*The* WIFE *laughs and shuffles to the door. Enter* MR. SHUI TA *and the* CARPENTER.]

WIFE. Who is it?

SHUI TA. I am Miss Shen Te's cousin.

WIFE. What?

SHUI TA. My name is Shui Ta.

WIFE. Her cousin?

NEPHEW. Her cousin?

NIECE. But that was a joke. She hasn't got a cousin.

HUSBAND. So early in the morning?

BROTHER. What's all the noise?

SISTER-IN-LAW. This fellow says he's her cousin.

BROTHER. Tell him to prove it.

NEPHEW. Right. If you're Shen Te's cousin, prove it by getting the breakfast.

SHUI TA [*whose regime begins as he puts out the lamp to save oil; loudly, to all present, asleep or awake*]. Would you all please get dressed! Customers will be coming! I wish to open my shop!

HUSBAND. *Your* shop? Doesn't it belong to our good friend Shen Te?

[SHUI TA *shakes his head.*]

SISTER-IN-LAW. So we've been cheated. Where *is* the little liar?

SHUI TA. Miss Shen Te has been delayed. She wishes me to tell you there will be nothing she can do—now I am here.

WIFE [*bowled over*]. I thought she was good!

NEPHEW. Do you have to believe *him?*

HUSBAND. I don't.

NEPHEW. Then do something.

HUSBAND. Certainly! I'll send out a search party at once. You, you, you, and you, go out and look for Shen Te. [*As the* GRANDFATHER *rises and makes for the door.*] Not you, Grandfather, you and I will hold the fort.

SHUI TA. You won't find Miss Shen Te. She has suspended her hospitable activity for an unlimited period. There are too many of you. She asked me to say: this is a tobacco shop, not a gold mine.

HUSBAND. Shen Te never said a thing like that. Boy, food! There's a bakery on the corner. Stuff your shirt full when they're not looking!

SISTER-IN-LAW. Don't overlook the raspberry tarts.

HUSBAND. And don't let the policeman see you.

[*The* BOY *leaves.*]

SHUI TA. Don't you depend on this shop now? Then why give it a bad name by stealing from the bakery?

NEPHEW. Don't listen to him. Let's find Shen Te. She'll give him a piece of her mind.

SISTER-IN-LAW. Don't forget to leave us some breakfast.

[BROTHER, SISTER-IN-LAW, *and* NEPHEW *leave.*]

SHUI TA [*to the* CARPENTER]. You see, Mr. Carpenter, nothing has changed since the poet, eleven hundred years ago, penned these lines:

A governor was asked what was needed
To save the freezing people in the city.
He replied:
"A blanket ten thousand feet long
to cover the city and all its suburbs."

[*He starts to tidy up the shop.*]

CARPENTER. Your cousin owes me money. I've got witnesses. For the shelves.

SHUI TA. Yes, I have your bill. [*He takes it out of his pocket.*] Isn't a hundred silver dollars rather a lot?

CARPENTER. No deductions! I have a wife and children.

SHUI TA. How many children?

CARPENTER. Three.

SHUI TA. I'll make you an offer. Twenty silver dollars.

[*The* HUSBAND *laughs.*]

CARPENTER. You're crazy. Those shelves are real walnut.

SHUI TA. Very well. Take them away.

CARPENTER. What?

SHUI TA. They cost too much. Please take them away.

WIFE. Not bad! [*And she, too, is laughing.*]

CARPENTER [*a little bewildered*]. Call Shen Te, someone! [*To* SHUI TA.] She's *good!*

SHUI TA. Certainly. She's ruined.

CARPENTER [*provoked into taking some of the shelves*]. All right, you can keep your tobacco on the floor.

SHUI TA [*to the* HUSBAND]. Help him with the shelves.

HUSBAND [*grins and carries one shelf over to the door where the* CARPENTER *now is*]. Good-bye, shelves!

CARPENTER [*to the* HUSBAND]. You dog! You want my family to starve?

SHUI TA. I repeat my offer. I have no desire to keep my tobacco on the floor. Twenty silver dollars.

CARPENTER [*with desperate aggressiveness*]. One hundred!

[SHUI TA *shows indifference, looks through the window. The* HUSBAND *picks up several shelves.*]

CARPENTER [*to* HUSBAND]. You needn't smash them against the door-post, you idiot! [*To* SHUI TA:] These shelves were made to measure. They're no use anywhere else!

SHUI TA. Precisely.

[*The* WIFE *squeals with pleasure.*]

CARPENTER [*giving up, sullenly*]. Take the shelves. Pay what you want to pay.

SHUI TA [*smoothly*]. Twenty silver dollars.

[*He places two large coins on the table. The* CARPENTER *picks them up.*]

HUSBAND [*brings the shelves back in*]. And quite enough too!

CARPENTER [*slinking off*]. Quite enough to get drunk on.

HUSBAND [*happily*]. Well, we got rid of *him*!

WIFE [*weeping with fun, gives a rendition of the dialogue just spoken*]. "Real walnut," says he. "Very well, take them away," says his lordship. "I have three children," says he. "Twenty silver dollars," says his lordship. "They're no use anywhere else," says he. "Pre-cisely," said his lordship! [*She dissolves into shrieks of merriment.*]

SHUI TA. And now: go!

HUSBAND. What's that?

SHUI TA. You're thieves, parasites. I'm giving you this chance. Go!

HUSBAND [*summoning all his ancestral dignity*]. That sort deserves no answer. Besides, one should never shout on an empty stomach.

WIFE. Where's that boy?

SHUI TA. Exactly. The boy. I want no stolen goods in this shop. [*Very loudly.*] I strongly advise you to leave! [*But they remain seated, noses in the air. Quietly.*] As you wish. [SHUI TA *goes to the door. A* POLICEMAN *appears.* SHUI TA *bows.*] I am addressing the officer in charge of this precinct?

POLICEMAN. That's right, Mr., um, what was the name, sir?

SHUI TA. Mr. Shui Ta.

POLICEMAN. Yes, of course, sir.

[*They exchange a smile.*]

SHUI TA. Nice weather we're having.

POLICEMAN. A little on the warm side, sir.

SHUI TA. Oh, a little on the warm side.

HUSBAND [*whispering to the* WIFE]. If he keeps it up till the boy's back, we're done for. [*Tries to signal* SHUI TA.]

SHUI TA [*ignoring the signal*]. Weather, of course, is one thing indoors, another out on the dusty street!

POLICEMAN. Oh, quite another, sir!

WIFE [*to the* HUSBAND]. It's all right as long as he's standing in the doorway—the boy will see him.

SHUI TA. Step inside for a moment! It's quite cool indoors. My cousin and I have just opened the place. And we attach the greatest importance to being on good terms with the, um, authorities.

POLICEMAN [*entering*]. Thank you, Mr. Shui Ta. It *is* cool!

HUSBAND [*whispering to the* WIFE]. And now the boy *won't* see him.

SHUI TA [*showing* HUSBAND *and* WIFE *to the* POLICEMAN]. Visitors, I think my cousin knows them. They were just leaving.

HUSBAND [*defeated*]. Ye-e-es, we were . . . just leaving.

SHUI TA. I'll tell my cousin you couldn't wait.

[*Noise from the street. Shouts of* "Stop, Thief!]

POLICEMAN. What's that?

[*The* BOY *is in the doorway with cakes and buns and rolls spilling out of his shirt. The* WIFE *signals desperately to him to leave. He gets the idea.*]

POLICEMAN. No, you don't! [*He grabs the* BOY *by the collar.*] Where's all this from?

BOY [*vaguely pointing*]. Down the street.

POLICEMAN [*grimly*]. So that's it. [*Prepares to arrest the* BOY.]

WIFE [*stepping in*]. And *we* knew nothing about it. [*To the* BOY:] Nasty little thief!

POLICEMAN [*dryly*]. Can you clarify the situation, Mr. Shui Ta?

[SHUI TA *is silent.*]

POLICEMAN [*who understands silence*]. Aha. You're all coming with me—to the station.

SHUI TA. I can hardly say how sorry I am that my establishment . . .

WIFE. Oh, he saw the boy leave not ten minutes ago!

SHUI TA. And to conceal the theft asked a policeman in?

POLICEMAN. Don't listen to her, Mr. Shui Ta, I'll be happy to relieve you of their presence one and all! [*To all three:*] Out! [*He drives them before him.*]

GRANDFATHER [*leaving last, gravely*]. Good morning!

POLICEMAN. Good morning!

[SHUI TA, *left alone, continues to tidy up.* MRS. MI TZU *breezes in.*]

MRS. MI TZU. You're her cousin, are you? Then have the goodness to explain what all this means—police dragging people from a respectable house! By what right does your Miss Shen Te turn my property into a house of assignation?—Well, as you see, I know all!

SHUI TA. Yes. My cousin has the worst possible reputation: that of being poor.

MRS. MI TZU. No sentimental rubbish, Mr. Shui Ta. Your cousin was a common . . .

SHUI TA. Pauper. Let's use the uglier word.

MRS. MI TZU. I'm speaking of her conduct, not her earnings. But there must have *been* earnings, or how did she buy all this? Several elderly gentlemen took care of it, I suppose. I repeat: this is a respectable house! I have tenants who prefer not to live under the same roof with such a person.

SHUI TA [*quietly*]. How much do you want?

MRS. MI TZU [*he is ahead of her now*]. I beg your pardon.

SHUI TA. To reassure yourself. To reassure your tenants. How much will it cost?

MRS. MI TZU. You're a cool customer.

SHUI TA [*picking up the lease*]. The rent is high. [*He reads on.*] I assume it's payable by the month?

MRS. MI TZU. Not in her case.

SHUI TA [*looking up*]. What?

MRS. MI TZU. Six months' rent payable in advance. Two hundred silver dollars.

SHUI TA. Six . . . ! Sheer usury! And where am I to find it?

MRS. MI TZU. You should have thought of that before.

SHUI TA. Have you no heart, Mrs. Mi Tzu? It's true Shen Te acted foolishly, being kind to all those people, but she'll improve with time. I'll see to it she does. She'll work her fingers to the bone to pay her rent, and all the time be as quiet as a mouse, as humble as a fly.

MRS. MI TZU. Her social background . . .

SHUI TA. Out of the depths! She came out of the depths! And before she'll go back there, she'll work, sacrifice, shrink from nothing. . . . Such a tenant is worth her weight in gold, Mrs. Mi Tzu.

MRS. MI TZU. It's silver we were talking about, Mr. Shui Ta. Two hundred silver dollars or . . .

[*Enter the* POLICEMAN.]

POLICEMAN. Am I intruding, Mr. Shui Ta?

MRS. MI TZU. This tobacco shop is well known to the police, I see.

POLICEMAN. Mr. Shui Ta has done us a service, Mrs. Mi Tzu. I am here to present our official felicitations!

MRS. MI TZU. That means less than nothing to me, sir. Mr. Shui Ta, all I can say is: I hope your cousin will find my terms acceptable. Good day, gentlemen. [*Exit.*]

SHUI TA. Good day, ma'am.

[*Pause.*]

POLICEMAN. Mrs. Mi Tzu a bit of a stumbling block, sir?

SHUI TA. She wants six months' rent in advance.

POLICEMAN. And you haven't got it, eh? [SHUI TA *is silent.*] But surely you can get it, sir? A man like you?

SHUI TA. What about a woman like Shen Te?

POLICEMAN. You're not staying, sir?

SHUI TA. No, and I won't be back. Do you smoke?

POLICEMAN [*taking two cigars, and placing them both in his pocket*]. Thank you, sir—I see your point. Miss Te—let's mince no words—Miss Shen Te lived by selling herself. "What else could she have done?" you ask. "How else was she to pay the rent?" True. But the fact remains, Mr. Shui Ta, it is not respectable. Why not? A very deep question. But, in the first place, love—love isn't bought and sold like cigars, Mr. Shui Ta. In the second place, it isn't respectable to go waltzing off with someone that's paying his way, so to speak—it must be for love! Thirdly and lastly, as the proverb has it: not for a handful of rice but for love! [*Pause. He is thinking hard.*] "Well," you may say, "and what good is all this wisdom if the milk's already spilt?" Miss Shen Te is what she is. Is *where* she is. We have to face the fact that if she doesn't get hold of six months' rent pronto, she'll be back on the streets. The question then as I see it—everything in this world is a matter of opinion—the question as I see it is: *how* is she to get hold of this rent? How? Mr. Shui Ta: I don't know. [*Pause.*] I take that back, sir. It's just come to me. A husband. We must find her a husband!

[*Enter a little* OLD WOMAN.]

OLD WOMAN. A good cheap cigar for my husband, we'll have been married forty years tomorrow and we're having a little celebration.

SHUI TA. Forty years? And you still want to celebrate?

OLD WOMAN. As much as we can afford to. We have the carpet shop across the square. We'll be good neighbors, I hope?

SHUI TA. I hope so too.

POLICEMAN [*who keeps making discoveries*]. Mr. Shui Ta, you know what we need? We need capital. And how do we acquire capital? We get married.

SHUI TA [*to* OLD WOMAN]. I'm afraid I've been pestering this gentleman with my personal worries.

POLICEMAN [*lyrically*]. We can't pay six months' rent, so what do we do? We marry money.

SHUI TA. That might not be easy.

POLICEMAN. Oh, I don't know. She's a good match. Has a nice, growing business. [*To the* OLD WOMAN:] What do you think?

OLD WOMAN [*undecided*]. Well—

POLICEMAN. Should she put an ad in the paper?

OLD WOMAN [*not eager to commit herself*]. Well, if *she* agrees—

POLICEMAN. I'll write it for her. *You* lend us a hand, and *we* write an ad for you! [*He chuckles away to himself, takes out his notebook, wets the stump of a pencil between his lips, and writes away.*

SHUI TA [*slowly*]. Not a bad idea.

POLICEMAN. "What . . . *respectable* . . . man . . . with small capital . . . widower . . . not excluded . . . desires . . . marriage . . . into flourishing . . . tobacco shop?" And now let's add: "Am . . . pretty . . . " No! . . . "Prepossessing appearance."

SHUI TA. If you don't think that's an exaggeration?

OLD WOMAN. Oh, not a bit. I've seen her.

[*The* POLICEMAN *tears the page out of his notebook, and hands it over to* SHUI TA.]

SHUI TA [*with horror in his voice*]. How much luck we need to keep our heads above water! How many ideas! How many friends! [*To the* POLICEMAN:] Thank you, sir, I think I see my way clear.

3

Evening in the municipal park. Noise of a plane overhead. YANG SUN, *a young man in rags, is following the plane with his eyes: one can tell that the machine is describing a curve above the park.* YANG SUN *then takes a rope out of his pocket, looking anxiously about him as he does so. He moves toward a large willow. Enter two prostitutes, one the* OLD WHORE, *the other the* NIECE *whom we have already met.*

NIECE. Hello. Coming with me?

YANG SUN [*taken aback*]. If you'd like to buy me a dinner.

OLD WHORE. Buy you a dinner! [*To the* NIECE:] Oh, we know him—it's the unemployed pilot. Waste no time on him!

NIECE. But he's the only man left in the park. And it's going to rain.

OLD WHORE. Oh, how do you know?

[*And they pass by.* YANG SUN *again looks about him, again takes his rope, and this time throws it round a branch of the willow tree. Again he is interrupted. It is the two prostitutes returning—and in such a hurry they don't notice him.*]

NIECE. It's going to pour!

[*Enter* SHEN TE.]

OLD WHORE. There's that *gorgon* Shen Te! That *drove* your family out into the cold!

NIECE. It wasn't her. It was that cousin of hers. She offered to pay for the cakes. I've nothing against her.

OLD WHORE. I have, though. [*So that* SHEN TE *can hear.*] Now where could the little lady be off to? She may be rich now but that won't stop her snatching our young men, will it?

SHEN TE. I'm going to the tearoom by the pond.

NIECE. Is it true what they say? You're marrying a widower—with three children?

SHEN TE. Yes. I'm just going to see him.

YANG SUN [*his patience at breaking point*]. Move on there! This is a park, not a whorehouse!

OLD WHORE. Shut your mouth!

[*But the two prostitutes leave.*]

YANG SUN. Even in the farthest corner of the park, even when it's raining, you can't get rid of them! [*He spits.*]

SHEN TE [*overhearing this*]. And what right have you to scold them? [*But at this point she sees the rope.*] Oh!

YANG SUN. Well, what are you staring at?

SHEN TE. That rope. What is it for?

YANG SUN. Think! Think! I haven't a penny. Even if I had, I wouldn't spend it on you. I'd buy a drink of water.

[*The rain starts.*]

SHEN TE [*still looking at the rope*]. What is the rope for? You mustn't!

YANG SUN. What's it to you? Clear out!

SHEN TE [*irrelevantly*]. It's raining.

YANG SUN. Well, don't try to come under this tree.

SHEN TE. Oh, no. [*She stays in the rain.*]

YANG SUN. Now go away. [*Pause.*] For one thing, I don't like your looks, you're bowlegged.

SHEN TE [*indignantly*]. That's not true!

YANG SUN. Well, don't show 'em to me. Look, it's raining. You better come under this tree.

[*Slowly, she takes shelter under the tree.*]

SHEN TE. Why did you want to do it?

YANG SUN. You really want to know? [*Pause.*] To get rid of you! [*Pause.*] You know what a flyer is?

SHEN TE. Oh yes, I've met a lot of pilots. At the tearoom.

YANG SUN. You call *them* flyers? Think they know what a machine is? Just 'cause they have leather helmets? They gave the airfield director a bribe, that's the way *those* fellows got up in the air! Try one of them out sometime. "Go up to two thousand feet," tell them, "then let it fall, then pick it up again with a flick of the wrist at the last moment." Know what he'll say to that? "It's not in my contract." Then again, there's the landing problem. It's like landing on your own backside. It's no different, planes are human. Those fools don't understand. [*Pause.*] And I'm the biggest fool for reading the book on flying in the Peking school and skipping the page where it says:

"We've got enough flyers and we don't need you." I'm a mail pilot with no mail. You understand that?

SHEN TE [*shyly*]. Yes. I do.

YANG SUN. No, you don't. You'd never understand that.

SHEN TE. When we were little we had a crane with a broken wing. He made friends with us and was very good-natured about our jokes. He would strut along behind us and call out to stop us going too fast for him. But every spring and autumn when the cranes flew over the villages in great swarms, he got quite restless. [*Pause.*] I understand that. [*She bursts out crying.*]

YANG SUN. Don't!

SHEN TE [*quieting down*]. No.

YANG SUN. It's bad for the complexion.

SHEN TE [*sniffing*]. I've stopped.

[*She dries her tears on her big sleeve. Leaning against the tree, but not looking at her, he reaches for her face.*]

YANG SUN. You can't even wipe your own face. [*He is wiping it for her with his handkerchief. Pause.*]

SHEN TE [*still sobbing*]. I don't know *anything!*

YANG SUN. You interrupted me! What for?

SHEN TE. It's such a rainy day. You only wanted to do . . . *that* because it's such a rainy day. [*To the audience:*]

In our country
The evenings should never be somber
High bridges over rivers
The gray hour between night and morning
And the long, long winter:
Such things are dangerous
For, with all the misery,
A very little is enough
And men throw away an unbearable life.

[*Pause.*]

YANG SUN. Talk about yourself for a change.

SHEN TE. What about me? I have a shop.

YANG SUN [*incredulous*]. You have a shop, have you? Never thought of walking the streets?

SHEN TEN. I did walk the streets. Now I have a shop.

YANG SUN [*ironically*]. A gift of the gods, I suppose!

SHEN TE. How did you know?

YANG SUN [*even more ironical*]. One fine evening the gods turned up saying: here's some money!

SHEN TE [*quickly*]. One fine morning.

YANG SUN [*fed up*]. This isn't much of an entertainment.

[*Pause.*]

SHEN TE. I can play the zither a little. [*Pause.*] And I can mimic men. [*Pause.*] I got the shop, so the first thing I did was to give my zither away. I can be as stupid as a fish now, I said to myself, and it won't matter.

I'm rich now, I said
I walk alone, I sleep alone
For a whole year, I said
I'll have nothing to do with a man.

YANG SUN. And now you're marrying one! The one at the tearoom by the pond?

[SHEN TE *is silent.*]

YANG SUN. What do you know about love?

SHEN TE. Everything.

YANG SUN. Nothing. [*Pause.*] Or d'you just mean you enjoyed it?

SHEN TE. No.

YANG SUN [*again without turning to look at her, he strokes her cheek with his hand*]. You like that?

SHEN TE. Yes.

YANG SUN [*breaking off*]. You're easily satisfied, I must say. [*Pause.*] What a town!

SHEN TE. You have no friends?

YANG SUN [*defensively*]. Yes, I have! [*Change of tone.*] But they don't want to hear I'm still unemployed. "What?" they ask. "Is there still water in the sea?" You have friends?

SHEN TE [*hesitating*]. Just a . . . cousin.

YANG SUN. Watch him carefully.

SHEN TE. He only came once. Then he went away. He won't be back. [YANG SUN *is looking away.*] But to be without hope, they say, is to be without goodness!

[*Pause.*]

YANG SUN. Go on talking. A voice is a voice.

SHEN TE. Once, when I was a little girl, I fell, with a load of brushwood. An old man picked me up. He gave me a penny too. Isn't it funny how people who don't have very much like to give some of it away? They must like to show what they can do, and how could they show it better than by being kind? Being wicked is just like being clumsy. When we sing a song, or build a machine, or plant some rice, we're being kind. You're kind.

YANG SUN. You make it sound easy.

SHEN TE. Oh, no. [*Little pause.*] Oh! A drop of rain!

YANG SUN. Where'd you feel it?

SHEN TE. Between the eyes.

YANG SUN. Near the right eye? Or the left?

SHEN TE. Near the left eye.

YANG SUN. Oh, good. [*He is getting sleepy.*] So you're through with men, eh?

SHEN TE [*with a smile*]. But I'm not bowlegged.

YANG SUN. Perhaps not.

SHEN TE. Definitely not.

[*Pause.*]

YANG SUN [*leaning wearily against the willow*]. I haven't had a drop to drink all day, I haven't eaten anything for *two* days. I couldn't love you if I tried.

[*Pause.*]

SHEN TE. I like it in the rain.

[*Enter* WONG *the water seller, singing.*]

The Song of the Water Seller in the Rain

"Buy my water," I am yelling
And my fury restraining
For no water I'm selling
'Cause it's raining, 'cause it's raining!
I keep yelling: "Buy my water!"
But no one's buying
Athirst and dying
And drinking and paying!
Buy water!
Buy water, you dogs!

Nice to dream of lovely weather!
Thnk of all consternation
Were there no precipitation
Half a dozen years together!
Can't you hear them shrieking: "Water!"
Pretending they adore me?
They all would go down on their knees
before me!
Down on your knees!
Go down on your knees, you dogs!

What are lawns and hedges thinking?
What are fields and forests saying?
"At the cloud's breast we are drinking!
And we've no idea who's paying!"
I keep yelling: "Buy my water!"
But no one's buying
Athirst and dying
And drinking and paying!
Buy water!
Buy water, you dogs!

[*The rain has stopped now.* SHEN TE *sees* WONG *and runs toward him.*]

SHEN TE. Wong! You're back! Your carrying pole's at the shop.

WONG. Oh, thank you, Shen Te. And how is life treating *you?*

SHEN TE. I've just met a brave and clever man. And I want to buy him a cup of your water.

WONG [*bitterly*]. Throw back your head and open your mouth and you'll have all the water you need—

SHEN TE [*tenderly*].

I want your *water, Wong*
The water that has tired you so
The water that you carried all this way
The water that is hard to sell because
it's been raining.

I need it for the young man over there—he's a flyer!

A flyer is a bold man:
Braving the storms
In company with the clouds
He crosses the heavens
And brings to friends in faraway lands
The friendly mail!

[*She pays* WONG, *and runs over to* YANG SUN *with the cup. But* YANG SUN *is fast asleep.*]

SHEN TE [*calling to* WONG, *with a laugh*]. He's fallen asleep! Despair and rain and I have worn him out!

3A

Wong's den. The sewer pipe is transparent, and the GODS *again appear to* WONG *in a dream.*

WONG [*radiant*]. I've seen her, illustrious ones! And she hasn't changed!

FIRST GOD. That's good to hear.

WONG. She loves someone.

FIRST GOD. Let's hope the experience gives her the strength to stay good!

WONG. It does. She's doing good deeds all the time.

FIRST GOD. Ah? What sort? What sort of good deeds, Wong?

WONG. Well, she has a kind word for everybody.

FIRST GOD [*eagerly*]. And then?

WONG. Hardly anyone leaves her shop without tobacco in his pocket—even if he can't pay for it.

FIRST GOD. Not bad at all. Next?

WONG. She's putting up a family of eight.

FIRST GOD [*gleefully, to the* SECOND GOD]. Eight! [*To* WONG:] And that's not all, of course!

WONG. She bought a cup of water from me even though it was raining.

FIRST GOD. Yes, yes, yes, all these smaller good deeds!

WONG. Even they run into money. A little tobacco shop doesn't make so much.

FIRST GOD [*sententiously*]. A prudent gardener works miracles on the smallest plot.

WONG. She hands out rice every morning. That eats up half her earnings.

FIRST GOD [*a little disappointed*]. Well, as a beginning . . .

WONG. They call her the Angel of the Slums—whatever the carpenter may say!

FIRST GOD. What's this? A carpenter speaks ill of her?

WONG. Oh, he only says her shelves weren't paid for in full.

SECOND GOD [*who has a bad cold and can't pronounce his n's and m's*]. What's this? Not paying a carpenter? Why was that?

WONG. I suppose she didn't have the money.

SECOND GOD [*severely*]. One pays what one owes, that's in our book of rules! First the letter of the law, then the spirit.

WONG. But it wasn't Shen Te, illustrious ones, it was her cousin. She called *him* in to help.

SECOND GOD. Then her cousin must never darken her threshold again!

WONG. Very well, illustrious ones! But in fairness to Shen Te, let me say that her cousin is a businessman.

FIRST GOD. Perhaps we should inquire what is customary? I find business quite unintelligible. But everybody's doing it. Business! Did the Seven Good Kings do business? Did Kung the Just sell fish?

SECOND GOD. In any case, such a thing must not occur again!

[*The* GODS *start to leave.*]

THIRD GOD. Forgive us for taking this tone with you, Wong, we haven't been getting enough sleep. The rich recommend us to the poor, and the poor tell us they haven't enough room.

SECOND GOD. Feeble, feeble, the best of them!

FIRST GOD. No great deeds! No heroic daring!

THIRD GOD. On such a *small* scale!

SECOND GOD. Sincere, yes, but what is actually *achieved?*

[*One can no longer hear them.*]

WONG [*calling after them*]. I've thought of something, illustrious ones: Perhaps you shouldn't ask—too—much—all—at—once!

4

The square in front of Shen Te's tobacco shop. Besides Shen Te's place, two other shops are seen: the carpet shop and a barber's. Morning. Outside Shen Te's the GRANDFATHER, *the* SISTER-IN-LAW, *the* UNEMPLOYED MAN, *and* MRS. SHIN *stand waiting.*

SISTER-IN-LAW. She's been out all night again.

MRS. SHIN. No sooner did we get rid of that crazy cousin of hers than Shen Te herself starts carrying on! Maybe she does give us an ounce of rice now and then, but can you depend on her? Can you depend on her?

[*Loud voices from the barber's.*]

VOICE OF SHU FU. What are you doing in my shop? Get out—at once!

VOICE OF WONG. But sir. They all let me sell . . .

[WONG *comes staggering out of the barber's shop pursued by* MR. SHU FU, *the barber, a fat man carrying a heavy curling iron.*]

SHU FU. Get out, I said! Pestering my customers with your slimy old water! Get out! Take your cup!

[*He holds out the cup.* WONG *reaches out for it.* MR. SHU FU *strikes his hand with the curling iron, which is hot.* WONG *howls.*]

SHU FU. You had it coming, my man!

[*Puffing, he returns to his shop. The* UNEMPLOYED MAN *picks up the cup and gives it to* WONG.]

UNEMPLOYED MAN. You can report that to the police.

WONG. My hand! It's smashed up!

UNEMPLOYED MAN. Any bones broken?

WONG. I can't move my fingers.

UNEMPLOYED MAN. Sit down. I'll put some water on it.

[WONG *sits.*]

MRS. SHIN. The water won't cost you anything.

SISTER-IN-LAW. You might have got a bandage from Miss Shen Te till she took to staying out all night. It's a scandal.

MRS. SHIN [*despondently*]. If you ask me, she's forgotten we ever existed!

[*Enter* SHEN TE *down the street, with a dish of rice.*]

SHEN TE [*to the audience*]. How wonderful to see Setzuan in the early morning! I always used to stay in bed with my dirty blanket over my head afraid to wake up. This morning I saw the newspaper being delivered by little boys, the streets being washed by strong men, and fresh vegetables coming in from the country on ox carts. It's a long walk from where Yang Sun lives, but I feel lighter at every step. They say you walk on air when you're in love, but it's even better walking on the rough earth, on the hard cement. In the early morning, the old city looks like a great heap of rubbish! Nice, though, with all its little lights. And the sky, so pink, so transparent, before the dust comes and muddies it! What a lot you miss if you never see your city rising from its slumbers like an honest old craftsman pumping his lungs full of air and reaching for his tools, as the poet says! [*Cheerfully, to her waiting guests:*] Good morning, everyone, here's your rice! [*Distributing the rice, she comes upon* WONG.] Good morning, Wong, I'm quite lightheaded today. On my way over, I looked at myself in all the shop windows. I'd love to be beautiful.

[*She slips into the carpet shop.* MR. SHU FU *has just emerged from his shop.*]

SHU FU [*to the audience*]. It surprises me how beautiful Miss Shen Te is looking today! I never gave her a passing thought before. But now I've been gazing upon her comely form for exactly three minutes! I begin to suspect I am in love with her. She is overpoweringly attractive! [*Crossly, to* WONG:] Be off with you, rascal!

[*He returns to his shop.* SHEN TE *comes back out of the carpet shop with the* OLD MAN, *its proprietor, and his wife—whom we have already met—the* OLD WOMAN. SHEN TE *is wearing a shawl. The* OLD MAN *is holding up a looking glass for her.*]

OLD WOMAN. Isn't it lovely? We'll give you a reduction because there's a little hole in it.

SHEN TE [*looking at another shawl on the* OLD WOMAN'*s arm*]. The other one's nice too.

OLD WOMAN [*smiling*]. Too bad there's no hole in that!

SHEN TE. That's right. My shop doesn't make very much.

OLD WOMAN. And your good deeds eat it all up! Be more careful, my dear. . . .

SHEN TE [*trying on the shawl with the hole*]. Just now, I'm lightheaded! Does the color suit me?

OLD WOMAN. You'd better ask a man.

SHEN TE [*to the* OLD MAN]. Does the color suit me?

OLD MAN. You'd better ask your young friend.

SHEN TE. I'd like to have your opinion.

OLD MAN. It suits you very well. But wear it this way: the dull side out.

[SHEN TE *pays up.*]

OLD WOMAN. If you decide you don't like it, you can exchange it. [*She pulls* SHEN TE *to one side.*] Has he got money?

SHEN TE [*with a laugh*]. Yang Sun? Oh, no.

OLD WOMAN. Then how're you going to pay your rent?

SHEN TE. I'd forgotten about that.

OLD WOMAN. And next Monday is the first of the month! Miss Shen Te, I've got something to say to you. After we [*indicating her husband*] got to know you, we had our doubts about that marriage ad. We thought it would be better if you'd let *us* help you. Out of our savings. We reckon we could lend you two hundred silver dollars. We don't need anything in writing—you could pledge us your tobacco stock.

SHEN TE. You're prepared to lend money to a person like me?

OLD WOMAN. It's folks like you that need it. We'd think twice about lending anything to your cousin.

OLD MAN [*coming up*]. All settled, my dear?

SHEN TE. I wish the gods could have heard what your wife was just saying, Mr. Ma. They're looking for good people who're happy—and helping me makes you happy because you know it was love that got me into difficulties!

[*The* OLD COUPLE *smile knowingly at each other.*]

OLD MAN. And here's the money, Miss Shen Te.

[*He hands her an envelope.* SHEN TE *takes it. She bows. They bow back. They return to their shop.*]

SHEN TE [*holding up her envelope*]. Look, Wong, here's six months' rent! Don't you believe in miracles now? And how do you like my new shawl?

WONG. For the young fellow I saw you with in the park?

[SHEN TE *nods.*]

MRS. SHIN. Never mind all that. It's time you took a look at his hand!

SHEN TE. Have you hurt your hand?

MRS. SHIN. That barber smashed it with his hot curling iron. Right in front of our eyes.

SHEN TE [*shocked at herself*]. And I never noticed! We must get you to a doctor this minute or who knows what will happen?

UNEMPLOYED MAN. It's not a doctor he should see, it's a judge. He can ask for compensation. The barber's filthy rich.

WONG. You think I have a chance?

MRS. SHIN [*with relish*]. If it's really good and smashed. But is it?

WONG. I think so. It's very swollen. Could I get a pension?

MRS. SHIN. You'd need a witness.

WONG. Well, you all saw it. You could all testify.

[*He looks round. The* UNEMPLOYED MAN, *the* GRANDFATHER, *and the* SISTER-IN-LAW *are all sitting against the wall of the shop eating rice. Their concentration on eating is complete.*]

SHEN TE [*to* MRS. SHIN]. You saw it yourself.

MRS. SHIN. I want nothing to do with the police. It's against my principles.

SHEN TE [*to* SISTER-IN-LAW]. What about you?

SISTER-IN-LAW. Me? I wasn't looking.

SHEN TE [*to the* GRANDFATHER, *coaxingly*]. Grandfather, *you'll* testify, won't you?

SISTER-IN-LAW. And a lot of good that will do. He's simple-minded.

SHEN TE [*to the* UNEMPLOYED MAN]. You seem to be the only witness left.

UNEMPLOYED MAN. My testimony would only hurt him. I've been picked up twice for begging.

SHEN TE.

Your brother is assaulted, and you shut your eyes?
He is hit, cries out in pain, and you are silent?
The beast prowls, chooses and seizes his victim, and you say:
"Because we showed no displeasure, he has spared us."

If no one present will be a witness, I will. I'll say *I* saw it.

MRS. SHIN [*solemnly*]. The name of that is perjury.

WONG. I don't know if I can accept that. Though maybe I'll have to. [*Looking at his hand.*] Is it swollen enough, do you think? The swelling's not going down?

UNEMPLOYED MAN. No, no, the swelling's holding up well.

WONG. Yes. It's *more* swollen if anything. Maybe my wrist is broken after all. I'd better see a judge at once.

[*Holding his hand very carefully, and fixing his eyes on it, he runs off.* MRS. SHIN *goes quickly into the barber's shop.*]

UNEMPLOYED MAN [*seeing her*]. She is getting on the right side of Mr. Shu Fu.

SISTER-IN-LAW. You and I can't change the world, Shen Te.

SHEN TE. Go away! Go away all of you!

[*The* UNEMPLOYED MAN, *the* SISTER-IN-LAW, *and the* GRANDFATHER *stalk off, eating and sulking.*]

[*To the audience:*]

They've stopped answering
They stay put
They do as they're told
They don't care
Nothing can make them look up
But the smell of food.

[*Enter* MRS. YANG, *Yang Sun's mother, out of breath.*]

MRS. YANG. Miss Shen Te. My son has told me everything. I am Mrs. Yang, Sun's mother. Just think. He's got an offer. Of a job as a pilot. A letter has just come. From the director of the airfield in Peking!

SHEN TE. So he can fly again? Isn't that wonderful!

MRS. YANG [*less breathlessly all the time*]. They won't give him the job for nothing. They want five hundred silver dollars.

SHEN TE. We can't let money stand in his way, Mrs. Yang!

MRS. YANG. If only you could help him out!

SHEN TE. I have the shop. I can try! [*She embraces* MRS. YANG.] I happen to have two hundred with me now. Take it. [*She gives her the old couple's money.*] It was a loan but they said I could repay it with my tobacco stock.

MRS. YANG. And they are calling Sun the Dead Pilot of Setzuan! A friend in need!

SHEN TE. We must find another three hundred.

MRS. YANG. How?

SHEN TE. Let me think. [*Slowly.*] I know someone who can help. I didn't want to call on his services again, he's hard and cunning. But a flyer must fly. And I'll make this the last time.

[*Distant sound of a plane.*]

MRS. YANG. If the man you mentioned can do it. . . . Oh, look, there's the morning mail plane, heading for Peking!

SHEN TE. The pilot can see us, let's wave!

[*They wave. The noise of the engine is louder.*]

MRS. YANG. You know that pilot up there?

SHEN TE. Wave, Mrs. Yang! I know the pilot who will be up there. He gave up hope. But he'll do it now. One man to raise himself above the misery, above us all. [*To the audience:*]

Yang Sun, my lover:
Braving the storms
In company with the clouds
Crossing the heavens
And bringing to friends in faraway lands
The friendly mail!

4A

In front of the inner curtain. Enter SHEN TE, *carrying Shui Ta's mask. She sings.*

The Song of Defenselessness

In our country
A useful man needs luck
Only if he finds strong backers
Can he prove himself useful.
The good can't defend themselves and
Even the gods are defenseless.

Oh, why don't the gods have their own ammunition
And launch against badness their own expedition
Enthroning the good and preventing sedition
And bringing the world to a peaceful condition?

Oh, why don't the gods do the buying and selling
Injustice forbidding, starvation dispelling
Give bread to each city and joy to each dwelling?
Oh, why don't the gods do the buying and selling?

[*She puts on* SHUI TA'S *mask and sings in his voice.*]

You can only help one of your luckless brothers
By trampling down a dozen others.

Why is it the gods do not feel indignation
And come down in fury to end exploitation
Defeat all defeat and forbid desperation
Refusing to tolerate such toleration?

Why is it?

5

Shen Te's tobacco shop. Behind the counter, MR. SHUI TA, *reading the paper.* MRS. SHIN *is cleaning up. She talks and he takes no notice.*

MRS. SHIN. And when certain rumors get about, what *happens* to a little place like this? It goes to pot. *I* know. So, if you want my advice, Mr. Shui Ta, find out just what has been going on between Miss Shen Te and that Yang Sun from Yellow Street. And remember: a certain interest in Miss Shen Te has been expressed by the barber next door; a man with twelve houses and only one wife, who, for that matter, is likely to drop off at any time. A certain interest has been expressed. He was even inquiring about her means and, if *that* doesn't prove a man is getting serious, what would? [*Still getting no response, she leaves with her bucket.*]

YANG SUN'S VOICE. Is that Miss Shen Te's tobacco shop?

MRS. SHIN'S VOICE. Yes, it is, but it's Mr. Shui Ta who's here today.

[SHUI TA *runs to the mirror with the short, light steps of* SHEN TE, *and is just about to start primping, when he realizes his mistake, and turns away, with a short laugh. Enter* YANG SUN. MRS. SHIN *enters behind him and slips into the back room to eavesdrop.*]

YANG SUN. I am Yang Sun. [SHUI TA *bows.*] Is Shen Te in?

SHUI TA. No.

YANG SUN. I guess you know our relationship? [*He is inspecting the stock.*] Quite a place! And I thought she was just talking big. I'll be flying again, all right. [*He takes a cigar, solicits and receives a light from* SHUI TA.] You think we can squeeze the other three hundred out of the tobacco stock?

SHUI TA. May I ask if it is your intention to sell at once?

YANG SUN. It was decent of her to come out with the two hundred but they aren't much use with the other three hundred still missing.

SHUI TA. Shen Te was overhasty promising so much. She might have to sell the shop itself to raise it. Haste, they say, is the wind that blows the house down.

YANG SUN. Oh, she isn't a girl to keep a man waiting. For one thing or the other, if you take my meaning.

SHUI TA. I take your meaning.

YANG SUN [*leering*]. Uh, huh.

SHUI TA. Would you explain what the five hundred silver dollars are for?

YANG SUN. Want to sound me out? Very well. The director of the Peking airfield is a friend of mine from flying school. I give him five hundred: he gets me the job.

SHUI TA. The price is high.

YANG SUN. Not as these things go. He'll have to fire one of the present pilots—for negligence. Only the man he has in mind isn't negligent. Not easy, you understand. You needn't mention that part of it to Shen Te.

SHUI TA [*looking intently at* YANG SUN]. Mr. Yang Sun, you are asking my cousin to give up her possessions, leave her friends, and place her entire fate in your hands. I presume you intend to marry her?

YANG SUN. I'd be prepared to.

[*Slight pause.*]

SHUI TA. Those two hundred silver dollars would pay the rent here for six months. If you were Shen Te wouldn't you be tempted to continue in business?

YANG SUN. What? Can you imagine Yang Sun the flyer behind a counter? [*In an oily voice.*] "A strong cigar or a mild one, worthy sir?" Not in this century!

SHUI TA. My cousin wishes to follow the promptings of her heart, and, from her own point of view, she may even have what is called the right to love. Accordingly, she has commissioned me to help you to this post. There is nothing here that I am not empowered to turn immediately into cash. Mrs. Mi Tzu, the landlady, will advise me about the sale.

[*Enter* MRS. MI TZU.]

MRS. MI TZU. Good morning, Mr. Shui Ta, you wish to see me about the rent? As you know it falls due the day after tomorrow.

SHUI TA. Circumstances have changed, Mrs. Mi Tzu: my cousin is getting married. Her future husband here, Mr. Yang Sun, will be taking her to Peking. I am interested in selling the tobacco stock.

MRS. MI TZU. How much are you asking, Mr. Shui Ta?

YANG SUN. Three hundred sil—

SHUI TA. Five hundred silver dollars.

MRS. MI TZU. How much did she pay for it, Mr. Shui Ta?

SHUI TA. A thousand. And very little has been sold.

MRS. MI TZU. She was robbed. But I'll make you a special offer if you'll promise to be out by the day after tomorrow. Three hundred silver dollars.

YANG SUN [*shrugging*]. Take it, man, take it.

SHUI TA. It is not enough.

YANG SUN. Why not? Why not? Certainly, it's enough.

SHUI TA. Five hundred silver dollars.

YANG SUN. But why? We only need three!

SHUI TA [*to* MRS. MI TZU]. Excuse me. [*Takes* YANG SUN *on one side.*] The tobacco stock is pledged to the old couple who gave my cousin the two hundred.

YANG SUN. Is it in writing?

SHUI TA. No.

YANG SUN [*to* MRS. MI TZU]. Three hundred will do.

MRS. MI TZU. Of course, I need an assurance that Miss Shen Te is not in debt.

YANG SUN. Mr. Shui Ta?

SHUI TA. She is not in debt.

YANG SUN. When can you let us have the money?

MRS. MI TZU. The day after tomorrow. And remember: I'm doing this because I have a soft spot in my heart for young lovers! [*Exit.*]

YANG SUN [*calling after her*]. Boxes, jars and sacks—three hundred for the lot and the pain's over! [*To* SHUI TA:] Where else can we raise money by the day after tomorrow?

SHUI TA. Nowhere. Haven't you enough for the trip and the first few weeks?

YANG SUN. Oh, certainly.

SHUI TA. How much, exactly.

YANG SUN. Oh, I'll dig it up, even if I have to steal it.

SHUI TA. I see.

YANG SUN. Well, don't fall off the roof. I'll get to Peking somehow.

SHUI TA. Two people can't travel for nothing.

YANG SUN [*not giving* SHUI TA *a chance to answer*]. I'm leaving *her* behind. No millstones around *my* neck!

SHUI TA. Oh.

YANG SUN. Don't look at me like that!

SHUI TA. How precisely is my cousin to live?

YANG SUN. Oh, you'll think of something.

SHUI TA. A small request, Mr. Yang Sun. Leave the two hundred silver dollars here until you can show me two tickets for Peking.

YANG SUN. You learn to mind your own business, Mr. Shui Ta.

SHUI TA. I'm afraid Miss Shen Te may not wish to sell the shop when she discovers that . . .

YANG SUN. You don't know women. She'll want to. Even then.

SHUI TA [*a slight outburst*]. She is a human being, sir! And not devoid of common sense!

YANG SUN. Shen Te is a woman: she *is* devoid of common sense. I only have to lay my hand on her shoulder, and church bells ring.

SHUI TA [*with difficulty*]. Mr. Yang Sun!

YANG SUN. Mr. Shui Whatever-it-is!

SHUI TA. My cousin is devoted to you . . . because . . .

YANG SUN. Because I have my hands on her breasts. Give me a cigar. [*He takes one for himself, stuffs a few more in his pocket, then changes his mind and takes the whole box.*] Tell her I'll marry her, then bring me the three hundred. Or let her bring it. One or the other. [*Exit.*]

MRS. SHIN [*sticking her head out of the back room*]. Well, he has your cousin under his thumb, and doesn't care if all Yellow Street knows it!

SHUI TA [*crying out*]. I've lost my shop! And he doesn't love me! [*He runs berserk through the room, repeating these lines incoherently. Then stops suddenly, and addresses* MRS. SHIN.] Mrs. Shin, you grew up in the gutter, like me. Are we lacking in hardness? I doubt it. If you steal a penny from me, I'll take you by the throat till you spit it out! You'd do the same to me. The times are bad, this city is hell, but we're like ants, we keep coming, up and up the walls, however smooth! Till bad luck comes. Being in love, for instance. One weakness is enough, and love is the deadliest.

MRS. SHIN [*emerging from the back room*]. You should have a little talk with Mr. Shu Fu, the barber. He's a real gentleman and just the thing for your cousin. [*She runs off.*]

SHUI TA.

A caress becomes a stranglehold
A sigh of love turns to a cry of fear
Why are there vultures circling in the air?
A girl is going to meet her lover.

[SHUI TA *sits down and* MR. SHU FU *enters with* MRS. SHIN.]

SHUI TA. Mr. Shu Fu?

SHU FU. Mr. Shui Ta.

[*They both bow.*]

SHUI TA. I am told that you have expressed a certain interest in my cousin Shen Te. Let me set aside all propriety and confess: she is at this moment in grave danger.

SHU FU. Oh, dear!

SHUI TA. She has lost her shop, Mr. Shu Fu.

SHU FU. The charm of Miss Shen Te, Mr. Shui Ta, derives from the goodness, not of her shop, but of her heart. Men call her the Angel of the Slums.

SHUI TA. Yet her goodness has cost her two hundred silver dollars in a single day: we must put a stop to it.

SHU FU. Permit me to differ, Mr. Shui Ta. Let us, rather, open wide the gates to such goodness! Every morning, with pleasure tinged by affection, I watch her charitable ministrations. For they are hungry, and she giveth them to eat! Four of them, to be precise. Why only four? I ask. Why not four hundred? I hear she has been seeking shelter for the homeless. What about my humble cabins behind the cattle run? They are at her disposal. And so forth. And so on. Mr. Shui Ta, do you think Miss Shen Te could be persuaded to listen to certain ideas of mine? Ideas like these?

SHUI TA. Mr. Shu Fu, she would be honored.

[*Enter* WONG *and the* POLICEMAN. MR. SHU FU *turns abruptly away and studies the shelves.*]

WONG. Is Miss Shen Te here?

SHUI TA. No.

WONG. I am Wong the water seller. You are Mr. Shui Ta?

SHUI TA. I am.

WONG. I am a friend of Shen Te's.

SHUI TA. An intimate friend, I hear.

WONG [*to the* POLICEMAN]. You see? [*To* SHUI TA:] It's because of my hand.

POLICEMAN. He hurt his hand, sir, that's a fact.

SHUI TA [*quickly*]. You need a sling, I see. [*He takes a shawl from the back room, and throws it to* WONG.]

WONG. But that's her new shawl!

SHUI TA. She has no more use for it.

WONG. But she bought it to please someone!

SHUI TA. It happens to be no longer necessary.

WONG [*making the sling*]. She is my only witness.

POLICEMAN. Mr. Shui Ta, your cousin is supposed to have seen the barber hit the water seller with a curling iron.

SHUI TA. I'm afraid my cousin was not present at the time.

WONG. But she was, sir! Just ask her! Isn't she in?

SHUI TA [*gravely*]. Mr. Wong, my cousin has her own troubles. You wouldn't wish her to add to them by committing perjury?

WONG. But it was she that told me to go to the judge!

SHUI TA. Was the judge supposed to heal your hand?

[MR. SHU FU *turns quickly around.* SHUI TA *bows to* SHU FU, *and vice versa.*]

WONG [*taking the sling off, and putting it back*]. I see how it is.

POLICEMAN. Well, I'll be on my way. [*To* WONG:] And you be careful. If Mr. Shu Fu wasn't a man who tempers justice with mercy, as the saying is, you'd be in jail for libel. Be off with you!

[*Exit* WONG, *followed by* POLICEMAN.]

SHUI TA. Profound apologies, Mr. Shu Fu.

SHU FU. Not at all, Mr. Shui Ta. [*Pointing to the shawl.*] The episode is over?

SHUI TA. It may take her time to recover. There are some fresh wounds.

SHU FU. We shall be discreet. Delicate. A short vacation could be arranged. . . .

SHUI TA. First of course, you and she would have to talk things over.

SHU FU. At a small supper in a small, but high-class, restaurant.

SHUI TA. I'll go and find her. [*Exit into back room.*]

MRS. SHIN [*sticking her head in again*]. Time for congratulations, Mr. Shu Fu?

SHU FU. Ah, Mrs. Shin! Please inform Miss Shen Te's guests they may take shelter in the cabins behind the cattle run!

[MRS. SHIN *nods, grinning.*]

SHU FU [*to the audience*]. Well? What do you think of me, ladies and gentlemen? What could a man do more? Could he be less selfish? More farsighted? A small supper in a small but . . . Does that bring rather vulgar and clumsy thoughts into your mind? Ts, ts, ts. Nothing of the sort will occur. She won't even be touched. Not even accidentally while passing the salt. An exchange of ideas only. Over the flowers on the table—white chrysanthemums, by the way [*he writes down a note of this*]—yes, over the white chrysanthemums, two young souls will . . . shall I say "find each other"? We shall NOT exploit the misfortune of others. Understanding? Yes. An offer of assistance? Certainly. But quietly. Almost inaudibly. Perhaps with a single glance. A glance that could also—also mean more.

MRS. SHIN [*coming forward*]. Everything under control, Mr. Shu Fu?

SHU FU. Oh, Mrs. Shin, what do you know about this worthless rascal Yang Sun?

MRS. SHIN. Why, he's the most worthless rascal . . .

SHU FU. Is he really? You're sure? [*As she opens her mouth.*] From now on, he doesn't exist! Can't be found anywhere!

[*Enter* YANG SUN.]

YANG SUN. What's been going on here?

MRS. SHIN. Shall I call Mr. Shui Ta, Mr. Shu Fu? He wouldn't want strangers in here!

SHU FU. Mr. Shui Ta is in conference with Miss Shen Te. Not to be disturbed.

YANG SUN. Shen Te here? I didn't see her come in. What kind of conference?

SHU FU [*not letting him enter the back room*]. Patience, dear sir! And if by chance I have an inkling who you are, pray take note that Miss Shen Te and I are about to announce our engagement.

YANG SUN. What?

MRS. SHIN. You didn't expect that, did you?

[YANG SUN *is trying to push past the barber into the back room when* SHEN TE *comes out.*]

SHU FU. My dear Shen Te, ten thousand apologies! Perhaps you . . .

YANG SUN. What is it, Shen Te? Have you gone crazy?

SHEN TE [*breathless*]. My cousin and Mr. Shu Fu have come to an understanding. They wish me to hear Mr. Shu Fu's plans for helping the poor.

YANG SUN. Your cousin wants to part us.

SHEN TE. Yes.

YANG SUN. And you've agreed to it?

SHEN TE. Yes.

YANG SUN. They told you I was bad. [SHEN TE *is silent.*] And suppose I am. Does that make me need you less? I'm low, Shen Te, I have no money, I don't do the right thing but at least I put up a fight! [*He is near her now, and speaks in an undertone.*] Have you no eyes? Look at him. Have you forgotten already?

SHEN TE. No.

YANG SUN. How it was raining?

SHEN TE. No.

YANG SUN. How you cut me down from the willow tree? Bought me water? Promised me money to fly with?

SHEN TE [*shakily*]. Yang Sun, what do you want?

YANG SUN. I want you to come with me.

SHEN TE [*in a small voice*]. Forgive me, Mr. Shu Fu, I want to go with Mr. Yang Sun.

YANG SUN. We're lovers you know. Give me the key to the shop. [SHEN TE *takes the key from around her neck.* YANG SUN *puts it on the counter. To* MRS. SHIN:] Leave it under the mat when you're through. Let's go, Shen Te.

SHU FU. But this is rape! Mr. Shui Ta!!

YANG SUN [*to* SHEN TE]. Tell him not to shout.

SHEN TE. Please don't shout for my cousin, Mr. Shu Fu. He doesn't agree with me, I know, but he's wrong. [*To the audience.*]

I want to go with the man I love
I don't want to count the cost
I don't want to consider if it's wise
I don't want to know if he loves me
I want to go with the man I love.

YANG SUN. That's the spirit.

[*And the couple leave.*]

5A

In front of the inner curtain. SHEN TE *in her wedding clothes, on the way to her wedding.*

SHEN TE. Something terrible has happened. As I left the shop with Yang Sun, I found the old carpet dealer's wife waiting on the street, trembling all over. She told me her husband had taken to his bed sick with all the worry and excitement over the two hundred silver dollars they lent me. She said it would be best if I gave it back now. Of course, I had to say I would. She said she couldn't quite trust my cousin Shui Ta or even my fiancé Yang Sun. There were tears in her eyes. With my emotions in an uproar, I threw myself into Yang Sun's arms. I couldn't resist him. The things he'd said to Shui Ta had taught Shen Te nothing. Sinking into his arms, I said to myself:

To let no one perish, not even oneself
To fill everyone with happiness, even oneself
Is so good

How could I have forgotten those two old people? Yang Sun swept me away like a small hurricane. But he's not a bad man, and he loves me. He'd rather work in the cement factory than owe his flying to a crime. Though, of course, flying *is* a great passion with Sun. Now, on the way to my wedding, I waver between fear and joy.

6

The "private dining room" on the upper floor of a cheap restaurant in a poor section of town. With SHEN TE*: the* GRANDFATHER, *the* SISTER-IN-LAW, *the* NIECE, MRS. SHIN, *the* UNEMPLOYED MAN. *In a corner, alone, a* PRIEST. *A* WAITER *pouring wine. Downstage,* YANG SUN *talking to his* MOTHER. *He wears a dinner jacket.*

YANG SUN. Bad news, Mamma. She came right out and told me she can't sell the shop for me. Some idiot is bringing a claim because he lent her the two hundred she gave you.

MRS. YANG. What did you say? Of course, you can't marry her now.

YANG SUN. It's no use saying anything to *her*. I've sent for her cousin, Mr. Shui Ta. He said there was nothing in writing.

MRS. YANG. Good idea. I'll go and look for him. Keep an eye on things.

[*Exit* MRS. YANG. SHEN TE *has been pouring wine.*]

SHEN TE [*to the audience, pitcher in hand*]. I wasn't mistaken in him. He's bearing up well. Though it must have been an awful blow—giving up flying. I do love him so. [*Calling across the room to him:*] Sun, you haven't drunk a toast with the bride!

YANG SUN. What do we drink to?

SHEN TE. Why, to the future!

YANG SUN. When the bridegroom's dinner jacket won't be a hired one!

SHEN TE. But when the bride's dress will still get rained on sometimes!

YANG SUN. To everything we ever wished for!

SHEN TE. May all our dreams come true!

[*They drink.*]

YANG SUN [*with loud conviviality*]. And now, friends, before the wedding gets under way, I have to ask the bride a few questions. I've no idea what kind of wife she'll make, and it worries me. [*Wheeling on* SHEN TE.] For example. Can you make five cups of tea with three tea leaves?

SHEN TE. No.

YANG SUN. So I won't be getting very much tea. Can you sleep on a straw mattress the size of that book? [*He points to the large volume the* PRIEST *is reading.*]

SHEN TE. The two of us?

YANG SUN. The one of you.

SHEN TE. In that case, no.

YANG SUN. What a wife! I'm shocked!

[*While the audience is laughing, his* MOTHER *returns. With a shrug of her shoulders, she tells* YANG SUN *the expected guest hasn't arrived. The* PRIEST *shuts the book with a bang, and makes for the door.*]

MRS. YANG. Where are *you* off to? It's only a matter of minutes.

PRIEST [*watch in hand*]. Time goes on, Mrs. Yang, and I've another wedding to attend to. Also a funeral.

MRS. YANG [*iratelyt*]. D'you think we planned it this way? I was hoping to manage with one pitcher of wine, and we've run through two already. [*Points to empty pitcher. Loudly.*] My dear Shen Te, I don't know where your cousin can be keeping himself!

SHEN TE. My cousin?!

MRS. YANG. Certainly. I'm old-fashioned enough to think such a close relative should attend the wedding.

SHEN TE. Oh, Sun, is it the three hundred silver dollars?

YANG SUN [*not looking her in the eye*]. Are you deaf? Mother says she's old-fashioned. And I say I'm considerate. We'll wait another fifteen minutes.

HUSBAND. Another fifteen minutes.

MRS. YANG [*addressing the company*]. Now you all know, don't you, that my son is getting a job as a mail pilot?

SISTER-IN-LAW. In Peking, too, isn't it?

MRS. YANG. In Peking, too! The two of us are moving to Peking!

SHEN TE. Sun, tell your mother Peking is out of the question now.

YANG SUN. Your cousin'll tell her. If he agrees. I don't agree.

SHEN TE [*amazed, and dismayed*]. Sun!

YANG SUN. I hate this godforsaken Setzuan. What people! Know what they look like when I half close my eyes? Horses! Whinnying, fretting, stamping, screwing their necks up! [*Loudly.*] And what is it the thunder says? They are su-per-flu-ous! [*He hammers out the syllables.*] They've run their last race! They can go trample themselves to death! [*Pause.*] I've got to get out of here.

SHEN TE. But I've promised the money to the old couple.

YANG SUN. And since you always do the wrong thing, it's lucky your cousin's coming. Have another drink.

SHEN TE [*quietly*]. My cousin can't be coming.

YANG SUN. How d'you mean?

SHEN TE. My cousin can't be where I am.

YANG SUN. Quite a conundrum!

SHEN TE [*desperately*]. Sun, I'm the one that loves you. Not my cousin. He was thinking of the job in Peking when he promised you the old couple's money—

YANG SUN. Right. And that's why he's bringing the three hundred silver dollars. Here—to my wedding.

SHEN TE. He is not bringing the three hundred silver dollars.

YANG SUN. Huh? What makes you think that?

SHEN TE [*looking into his eyes*]. He says you only bought one ticket to Peking.

[*Short pause.*]

YANG SUN. That was yesterday. [*He pulls two tickets part way out of his inside pocket, making her look under his coat.*] Two tickets. I don't want Mother to know. She'll get left behind. I sold her furniture to buy these tickets, so you see . . .

SHEN TE. But what's to become of the old couple?

YANG SUN. What's to become of me? Have another drink. Or do you believe in moderation? If I drink, I fly again. And if you drink, you may learn to understand me.

SHEN TE. You want to fly. But I can't help you.

YANG SUN. "Here's a plane, my darling—but it's only got one wing!"

[*The* WAITER *enters.*]

WAITER. Mrs. Yang!

MRS. YANG. Yes?

WAITER. Another pitcher of wine, ma'am?

MRS. YANG. We have enough, thanks. Drinking makes me sweat.

WAITER. Would you mind paying, ma'am?

MRS. YANG [*to everyone*]. Just be patient a few moments longer, everyone, Mr. Shui Ta is on his way over! [*To the* WAITER:] Don't be a spoilsport.

WAITER. I can't let you leave till you've paid your bill, ma'am.

MRS. YANG. But they know me here!

WAITER. That's just it.

PRIEST [*ponderously getting up*]. I humbly take my leave. [*And he does.*]

MRS. YANG [*to the others, desperately*]. Stay where you are, everybody! The priest says he'll be back in two minutes!

YANG SUN. It's no good, Mamma. Ladies and gentlemen, Mr. Shui Ta still hasn't arrived and the priest has gone home. We won't detain you any longer.

[*They are leaving now.*]

GRANDFATHER [*in the doorway, having forgotten to put his glass down*]. To the bride! [*He drinks, puts down the glass, and follows the others.*]

[*Pause.*]

SHEN TE. Shall I go too?

YANG SUN. You? Aren't you the bride? Isn't this your wedding? [*He drags her across the room, tearing her wedding dress.*] If we can wait, you can wait. Mother calls me her falcon. She wants to see me in the clouds. But I think it may be St. Nevercome's Day before she'll go to the door and see my plane thunder by. [*Pause. He pretends the guests are still present.*] Why such a lull in the conversation, ladies and gentlemen? Don't you like it here? The ceremony is only slightly postponed—because an important guest is expected at any moment. Also because the bride doesn't know what love is. While we're waiting, the bridegroom will sing a little song. [*He does so.*]

The Song of St. Nevercome's Day

On a certain day, as is generally known,
One and all will be shouting: Hooray, hooray!
For the beggar maid's son has a solid-gold throne
And the day is St. Nevercome's Day
On St. Nevercome's, Nevercome's, Nevercome's Day
He'll sit on his solid-gold throne

Oh, hooray, hooray! That day goodness will pay!
That day badness will cost you your head!
And merit and money will smile and be funny
While exchanging salt and bread
On St. Nevercome's, Nevercome's, Nevercome's Day
While exchanging salt and bread

And the grass, oh, the grass will look down at the sky
And the pebbles will roll up the stream
And all men will be good without batting an eye
They will make of our earth a dream
On St. Nevercome's, Nevercome's, Nevercome's Day
They will make of our earth a dream

And as for me, that's the day I shall be
A flyer and one of the best
Unemployed man, you will have work to do
Washerwoman, you'll get your rest
On St. Nevercome's, Nevercome's, Nevercome's Day
Washerwoman, you'll get your rest

MRS. YANG. It looks like he's not coming.

[*The three of them sit looking at the door.*]

6A

Wong's den. The sewer pipe is again transparent and again the GODS *appear to* WONG *in a dream.*

WONG. I'm so glad you've come, illustrious ones. It's Shen Te. She's in great trouble from following the rule about loving thy neighbor. Perhaps she's *too* good for this world!

FIRST GOD. Nonsense! You are eaten up by lice and doubts!

WONG. Forgive me, illustrious one, I only meant you might deign to intervene.

FIRST GOD. Out of the question! My colleague here intervened in some squabble or other only yesterday. [*He points to the* THIRD GOD *who has a black eye.*] The results are before us!

WONG. She had to call on her cousin again. But not even he could help. I'm afraid the shop is done for.

THIRD GOD [*a little concerned*]. Perhaps we should help after all?

FIRST GOD. The gods help those that help themselves.

WONG. What if we *can't* help ourselves, illustrious ones?

[*Slight pause.*]

SECOND GOD. Try, anyway! Suffering ennobles!

FIRST GOD. Our faith in Shen Te is unshaken!

THIRD GOD. We certainly haven't found any *other* good people. You can see where we spend our nights from the straw on our clothes.

WONG. You might help her find her way by—

FIRST GOD. The good man finds his own way here below!

SECOND GOD. The good woman too.

FIRST GOD. The heavier the burden, the greater her strength!

THIRD GOD. We're only onlookers, you know.

FIRST GOD. And everything will be all right in the end, O ye of little faith!

[*They are gradually disappearing through these last lines.*]

7

The yard behind Shen Te's shop. A few articles of furniture on a cart. SHEN TE *and* MRS. SHIN *are taking the washing off the line.*

MRS. SHIN. If you ask me, you should fight tooth and nail to keep the shop.

SHEN TE. How can I? I have to sell the tobacco to pay back the two hundred silver dollars today.

MRS. SHIN. No husband, no tobacco, no house and home! What are you going to live on?

SHEN TE. I can work. I can sort tobacco.

MRS. SHIN. Hey, look, Mr. Shui Ta's trousers! He must have left here stark naked!

SHEN TE. Oh, he may have another pair, Mrs. Shin.

MRS. SHIN. But if he's gone for good as you say, why has he left his pants behind?

SHEN TE. Maybe he's thrown them away.

MRS. SHIN. Can I take them?

SHEN TE. Oh, no.

[*Enter* MR. SHU FU, *running.*]

SHU FU. Not a word! Total silence! I know all. You have sacrificed your own love and happiness so as not to hurt a dear old couple who had put their trust in you! Not in vain does this district—for all its malevolent tongues—call you the Angel of the Slums! That young man couldn't rise to your level, so you left him. And now, when I see you closing up the little shop, that veritable haven of rest for the multitude, well, I cannot, I cannot let it pass. Morning after morning I have stood watching in the doorway not unmoved—while you graciously handed out rice to the wretched. Is that never to happen again? Is the good woman of Setzuan to disappear? If only you would allow *me* to assist you! Now don't say anything! No assurances, no exclamations of gratitude! [*He has taken out his checkbook.*] Here! A blank check. [*He places it on the cart.*] Just my signature. Fill it out as you wish. Any sum in the world. I herewith retire from the scene, quietly, unobtrusively, making no claims, on tiptoe, full of veneration, absolutely selflessly . . . [*He has gone.*]

MRS. SHIN. Well! You're saved. There's always some idiot of a man. . . . Now hurry! Put down a thousand silver dollars and let me fly to the bank before he comes to his senses.

SHEN TE. I can pay you for the washing without any check.

MRS. SHIN. What? You're not going to cash it just because you might have to marry him? Are you crazy? Men like him *want* to be led by the nose! Are you still thinking of that flyer? All Yellow Street knows how he treated you!

SHEN TE.

When I heard his cunning laugh, I was afraid
But when I saw the holes in his shoes, I loved him dearly.

MRS. SHIN. Defending that good-for-nothing after all that's happened!

SHEN TE [*staggering as she holds some of the washing*]. Oh!

MRS. SHIN [*taking the washing from her, dryly*]. So you feel dizzy when you stretch and bend? There couldn't be a little visitor on the way? If that's it, you can forget Mr. Shu Fu's blank check: it wasn't meant for a christening present!

[*She goes to the back with a basket.* SHEN TE*'s eyes follow* MRS. SHIN *for a moment. Then she looks down at her own body, feels her stomach, and a great joy comes into her eyes.*]

SHEN TE. O joy! A new human being is on the way. The world awaits him. In the cities the people say: he's got to be reckoned with, this new human being! [*She imagines a little boy to be present, and introduces him to the audience.*] This is my son, the well-known flyer!
Say: Welcome
To the conqueror of unknown mountains and unreachable
regions

Who brings us our mail across the impassable deserts!

[*She leads him up and down by the hand.*]

Take a look at the world, my son. That's a tree. Tree, yes. Say: "Hello, tree!" And bow. Like this. [*She bows.*] Now you know each other. And, look, here comes the water seller. He's a friend, give him your hand. A cup of fresh water for my little son, please. Yes, it *is* a warm day. [*Handing the cup.*] Oh dear, a policeman, we'll have to make a circle round *him.* Perhaps we can pick a few cherries over there in the rich Mr. Pung's garden. But we mustn't be seen. You want cherries? Just like children with fathers. No, no, you can't go straight at them like that. Don't pull. We must learn to be reasonable. Well, have it your own way. [*She has let him make for the cherries.*] Can you reach? Where to put them? Your mouth is the best place. [*She tries one herself.*] Mmm, they're good. But the policeman, we must run! [*They run.*] Yes, back to the street. Calm now, so no one will notice us. [*Walking the street with her child, she sings.*]

Once a plum—'twas in Japan—
Made a conquest of a man
But the man's turn soon did come
For he gobbled up the plum

[*Enter* WONG, *with a* CHILD *by the hand. He coughs.*]

SHEN TE. Wong!

WONG. It's about the carpenter, Shen Te. He's lost his shop, and he's been drinking. His children are on the streets. This is one. Can you help?

SHEN TE [*to the* CHILD]. Come here, little man. [*Takes him down to the footlights. To the audience:*]

You there! A man is asking you for shelter!
A man of tomorrow says: what about today?
His friend the conqueror, whom you know,
Is his advocate!

[*To* WONG:] He can live in Mr. Shu Fu's cabins. I may have to go there myself. I'm going to have a baby. That's a secret—don't tell Yang Sun—we'd only be in his way. Can you find the carpenter for me?

WONG. I knew you'd think of something. [*To the* CHILD:] Good-bye, son, I'm going for your father.

SHEN TE. What about your hand, Wong? I wanted to help, but my cousin . . .

WONG. Oh, I can get along with one hand, don't worry. [*He shows how he can handle his pole with his left hand alone.*]

SHEN TE. But your right hand! Look, take this cart, sell everything that's on it, and go to the doctor with the money . . .

WONG. She's still good. But first I'll bring the carpenter. I'll pick up the cart when I get back. [*Exit* WONG.]

SHEN TE [*to the* CHILD]. Sit down over here, son, till your father comes.

[*The* CHILD *sits cross-legged on the ground. Enter the* HUSBAND *and* WIFE, *each dragging a large, full sack.*]

WIFE [*furtively*]. You're alone, Shen Te, dear?

[SHEN TE *nods. The* WIFE *beckons to the* NEPHEW *offstage. He comes on with another sack.*]

WIFE. Your cousin's away? [SHEN TE *nods.*] He's not coming back?

SHEN TE. No. I'm giving up the shop.

WIFE. That's why we're here. We want to know if we can leave these things in your new home. Will you do us this favor?

SHEN TE. Why, yes, I'd be glad to.

HUSBAND [*cryptically*]. And if anyone asks about them, say they're yours.

SHEN TE. Would anyone ask?

WIFE [*with a glance back at her husband*]. Oh, someone might. The police, for instance. They don't seem to like us. Where can we put it?

SHEN TE. Well, I'd rather not get in any more trouble . . .

WIFE. Listen to her! The good woman of Setzuan!

[SHEN TE *is silent.*]

HUSBAND. There's enough tobacco in those sacks to give us a new start in life. We could have our own tobacco factory!

SHEN TE [*slowly*]. You'll have to put them in the back room.

[*The sacks are taken off-stage, while the* CHILD *is alone. Shyly glancing about him, he goes to the garbage can, starts playing with the contents, and eating some of the scraps. The others return.*]

WIFE. We're counting on you, Shen Te!

SHEN TE. Yes. [*She sees the* CHILD *and is shocked.*]

HUSBAND. We'll see you in Mr. Shu Fu's cabins.

NEPHEW. The day after tomorrow.

SHEN TE. Yes. Now, go. Go! I'm not feeling well.

[*Exeunt all three, virtually pushed off.*]

He is eating the refuse in the garbage can!
Only look at his little gray mouth!

[*Pause. Music.*]

As this is the world my son will enter
I will study to defend him.
To be good to you, my son,
I shall be a tigress to all others
If I have to.
And I shall have to.

[*She starts to go.*]

One more time, then. I hope really the
last.

[*Exit* SHEN TE, *taking Shui Ta's trousers.* MRS. SHIN *enters and watches her with marked interest. Enter the* SISTER-IN-LAW *and the* GRANDFATHER.]

SISTER-IN-LAW. So it's true, the shop has closed down. And the furniture's in the back yard. It's the end of the road!

MRS. SHIN [*pompously*]. The fruit of high living, selfishness, and sensuality! Down the primrose path to Mr. Shu Fu's cabins—with you!

SISTER-IN-LAW. Cabins? Rat holes! He gave them to us because his soap supplies only went moldy there!

[*Enter the* UNEMPLOYED MAN.]

UNEMPLOYED MAN. Shen Te is moving?

SISTER-IN-LAW. Yes. She was sneaking away.

MRS. SHIN. She's ashamed of herself, and no wonder!

UNEMPLOYED MAN. Tell her to call Mr. Shui Ta or she's done for this time!

SISTER-IN-LAW. Tell her to call Mr. Shui Ta or *we're* done for this time.

[*Enter* WONG *and* CARPENTER, *the latter with a* CHILD *on each hand.*]

CARPENTER. So we'll have a roof over our heads for a change!

MRS. SHIN. Roof? Whose roof?

CARPENTER. Mr. Shu Fu's cabins. And we have little Feng to thank for it. [FENG, *we find, is the name of the* CHILD *already there; his* FATHER *now takes him. To the other two:*] Bow to your little brother, you two!

[*The* CARPENTER *and the two new arrivals bow to* FENG. *Enter* SHUI TA.]

UNEMPLOYED MAN. Sst! Mr. Shui Ta!

[*Pause.*]

SHUI TA. And what is this crowd here for, may I ask?

WONG. How do you do, Mr. Shui Ta. This is the carpenter. Miss Shen Te promised him space in Mr. Shu Fu's cabins.

SHUI TA. That will not be possible.

CARPENTER. We can't go there after all?

SHUI TA. All the space is needed for other purposes.

SISTER-IN-LAW. You mean we have to get out? But we've got nowhere to go.

SHUI TA. Miss Shen Te finds it possible to provide employment. If the proposition interests you, you may stay in the cabins.

SISTER-IN-LAW [*with distaste*]. You mean *work?* Work for Miss Shen Te?

SHUI TA. Making tobacco, yes. There are three bales here already. Would you like to get them?

SISTER-IN-LAW [*trying to bluster*]. We have our own tobacco! We were in the tobacco business before you were born!

SHUI TA [*to the* CARPENTER *and the* UNEMPLOYED MAN]. You *don't* have your own tobacco. What about you?

[*The* CARPENTER *and the* UNEMPLOYED MAN *get the point, and go for the sacks. Enter* MRS. MI TZU.]

MRS. MI TZU. Mr. Shui Ta? I've brought you your three hundred silver dollars.

SHUI TA. I'll sign your lease instead. I've decided not to sell.

MRS. MI TZU. What? You don't need the money for that flyer?

SHUI TA. No.

MRS. MI TZU. And you can pay six months' rent?

SHUI TA [*takes the barber's blank check from the cart and fills it out*]. Here is a check for ten thousand silver dollars. On Mr. Shu Fu's account. Look! [*He shows her the signature on the check.*] Your six months' rent will be in your hands by seven this evening. And now, if you'll excuse me.

MRS. MI TZU. So it's Mr. Shu Fu now. The flyer has been given his walking papers. These modern girls! In my day they'd have said she was flighty. That poor, deserted Mr. Yang Sun!

[*Exit* MRS. MI TZU. *The* CARPENTER *and the* UNEMPLOYED MAN *drag the three sacks back on the stage.*]

CARPENTER [*to* SHUI TA]. I don't know why I'm doing this for you.

SHUI TA. Perhaps your children want to eat, Mr. Carpenter.

SISTER-IN-LAW [*catching sight of the sacks*]. Was my brother-in-law here?

MRS. SHIN. Yes, he was.

SISTER-IN-LAW. I thought as much. I know those sacks! That's our tobacco!

SHUI TA. Really? I thought it came from my back room! Shall we consult the police on the point?

SISTER-IN-LAW [*defeated*]. No.

SHUI TA. Perhaps you will show me the way to Mr. Shu Fu's cabins?

[*Taking* FENG *by the hand,* SHUI TA *goes off, followed by the* CARPENTER *and his two older children, the* SISTER-IN-LAW, *the* GRANDFATHER, *and the* UNEMPLOYED MAN. *Each of the last three drags a sack. Enter* OLD MAN *and* OLD WOMAN.]

MRS. SHIN. A pair of pants—missing from the clothesline one minute—and next minute on the honorable backside of Mr. Shui Ta.

OLD WOMAN. We thought Miss Shen Te was here.

MRS. SHIN [*preoccupied*]. Well, she's not.

OLD MAN. There was something she was going to give us.

WONG. She was going to help me too. [*Looking at his hand.*] It'll be too late soon. But she'll be back. This cousin has never stayed long.

MRS. SHIN [*approaching a conclusion*]. No, he hasn't, has he?

7A

The Sewer Pipe: WONG *asleep. In his dream, he tells the* GODS *his fears. The* GODS *seem tired from all their travels. They stop for a moment and look over their shoulders at the water seller.*

WONG. Illustrious ones. I've been having a bad dream. Our beloved Shen Te was in great distress in the rushes down by the river—the spot were the bodies of suicides are washed up. She kept staggering and holding her head down as if she was carrying something and it was dragging her down in the mud. When I called out to her, she said she had to take your Book of Rules to the other side, and not get it wet, or the ink would all come off. You had talked to her about the virtues, you know, the time she gave you shelter in Setzuan.

THIRD GOD. Well, but what do you suggest, my dear Wong?

WONG. Maybe a little relaxation of the rules, Benevolent One, in view of the bad times.

THIRD GOD. As for instance?

WONG. Well, um, good will, for instance, might do instead of love?

THIRD GOD. I'm afraid that would create new problems.

WONG. Or, instead of justice, good sportsmanship?

THIRD GOD. That would only mean more work.

WONG. Instead of honor, outward propriety?

THIRD GOD. Still more work! No, no! The rules will have to stand, my dear Wong!

[*Wearily shaking their heads, all three journey on.*]

8

Shui Ta's tobacco factory in Shu Fu's cabins. Huddled together behind bars, several families, mostly women and children. Among these people the SISTER-IN-LAW, *the* GRANDFATHER, *the* CARPENTER, *and his* THREE CHILDREN. *Enter* MRS. YANG *followed by* YANG SUN.

MRS. YANG [*to the audience*]. There's something I just *have* to tell you: strength and wisdom are wonderful things. The strong and wise Mr. Shui Ta has transformed my son from a dissipated good-for-nothing into a model citizen. As you may have heard, Mr. Shui Ta opened a small tobacco factory near the cattle runs. It flourished. Three months ago—I shall never forget it—I asked for an appointment, and Mr. Shui Ta agreed to see us—me and my son. I can see him now as he came through the door to meet us. . . .

[*Enter* SHUI TA *from a door.*]

SHUI TA. What can I do for you, Mrs. Yang?

MRS. YANG. This morning the police came to the house. We find you've brought an action for breach of promise of marriage. In the name of Shen Te. You also claim that Sun came by two hundred silver dollars by improper means.

SHUI TA. That is correct.

MRS. YANG. Mr. Shui Ta, the money's all gone. When the Peking job didn't materialize, he ran through it all in three days. I know he's a good-for-nothing. He sold my furniture. He was moving to Peking without me. Miss Shen Te thought highly of him at one time.

SHUI TA. What do *you* say, Mr. Yang Sun?

YANG SUN. The money's gone.

SHUI TA [*to* MRS. YANG]. Mrs. Yang, in consideration of my cousin's incomprehensible weakness for your son, I am prepared to give him another chance. He can have a job—here. The two hundred silver dollars will be taken out of his wages.

YANG SUN. So it's the factory or jail?

SHUI TA. Take your choice.

YANG SUN. May I speak with Shen Te?

SHUI TA. You may not.

[*Pause.*]

YANG SUN [*sullenly*]. Show me where to go.

MRS. YANG. Mr. Shui Ta, you are kindness itself: the gods will reward you! [*To* YANG SUN:] And honest work will make a man of you, my boy. [YANG SUN *follows* SHUI TA *into the factory.* MRS. YANG *comes down again to the footlights.*] Actually, honest work didn't agree with him—at first. And he got no opportunity to distinguish himself till—in the third week—when the wages were being paid . . .

[SHUI TA *has a bag of money. Standing next to his foreman—the former* UNEMPLOYED MAN—*he counts out the wages. It is* YANG SUN*'s turn.*]

UNEMPLOYED MAN [*reading*]. Carpenter, six silver dollars. Yang Sun, six silver dollars.

YANG SUN [*quietly*]. Excuse me, sir. I don't think it can be more than five. May I see? [*He takes the foreman's list.*] It says six working days. But that's a mistake, sir. I took a day off for court business. And I won't take what I haven't earned, however miserable the pay is!

UNEMPLOYED MAN. Yang Sun. Five silver dollars. [*To* SHUI TA:] A rare case, Mr. Shui Ta!

SHUI TA. How is it the book says six when it should say five?

UNEMPLOYED MAN. I must've made a mistake, Mr. Shui Ta. [*With a look at* YANG SUN.] It won't happen again.

SHUI TA [*taking* YANG SUN *aside*]. You don't hold back, do you? You give your all to the firm. You're even honest. Do the foreman's mistakes always favor the workers?

YANG SUN. He does have . . . friends.

SHUI TA. Thank you. May I offer you any little recompense?

YANG SUN. Give me a trial period of one week, and I'll prove my intelligence is worth more to you than my strength.

MRS. YANG [*still down at the footlights*]. Fighting words, fighting words! That evening, I said to Sun: "If you're a flyer, then fly, my falcon! Rise in the world!" And he got to be foreman. Yes, in Mr. Shui Ta's tobacco factory, he worked real miracles.

[*We see* YANG SUN *with his legs apart standing behind the workers who are handing along a basket of raw tobacco above their heads.*]

YANG SUN. Faster! Faster! You, there, d'you think you can just stand around, now you're not foreman any more? It'll be your job to lead us in song. Sing!

[UNEMPLOYED MAN *starts singing. The others join in the refrain.*]

Song of the Eighth Elephant

Chang had seven elephants—all much the same—
But then there was Little Brother
The seven, they were wild, Little Brother, he was tame
And to guard them Chang chose Little Brother
Run faster!
Mr. Chang has a forest park
Which must be cleared before tonight
And already it's growing dark!

When the seven elephants cleared that forest park
Mr. Chang rode high on Little Brother
While the seven toiled and moiled till dark
On his big behind sat Little Brother
Dig faster!
Mr. Chang has a forest park
Which must be cleared before tonight!
And already it's growing dark!

And the seven elephants worked many an hour
Till none of them could work another
Old Chang, he looked sour, on the seven he did glower
But gave a pound of rice to Little Brother
What was that?
Mr. Chang has a forest park
Which must be cleared before tonight
And already it's growing dark!

And the seven elephants hadn't any tusks
The one that had the tusks was Little Brother
Seven are no match for one, if the one has a gun!
How old Chang did laugh at Little Brother!
Keep on digging!
Mr. Chang has a forest park
Which must be cleared before tonight
And already it's growing dark!

[*Smoking a cigar,* SHUI TA *strolls by.* YANG SUN, *laughing, has joined in the refrain of the third stanza and speeded up the tempo of the last stanza by clapping his hands.*]

MRS. YANG. And that's why I say: strength and wisdom are wonderful things. It took the strong and wise Mr. Shui Ta to bring out the best in Yang Sun. A real superior man is like a bell. If you ring it, it rings, and if you don't, it don't, as the saying is.

9

Shen Te's shop, now an office with club chairs and fine carpets. It is raining. SHUI TA, *now fat, is just dismissing the* OLD MAN *and* OLD WOMAN. MRS. SHIN, *in obviously new clothes, looks on, smirking.*

SHUI TA. No! I can NOT tell you when we expect her back.

OLD WOMAN. The two hundred silver dollars came today. In an envelope. There was no letter, but it must be from Shen Te. We want to write and thank her. May we have her address?

SHUI TA. I'm afraid I haven't got it.

OLD MAN [*pulling* OLD WOMAN*'s sleeve*]. Let's be going.

OLD WOMAN. She's got to come back some time!

[*They move off, uncertainly, worried.* SHUI TA *bows.*]

MRS. SHIN. They lost the carpet shop because they couldn't pay their taxes. The money arrived too late.

SHUI TA. They could have come to me.

MRS. SHIN. People don't like coming to you.

SHUI TA [*sits suddenly, one hand to his head*]. I'm dizzy.

MRS. SHIN. After all, you *are* in your seventh month. But old Mrs. Shin will be there in your hour of trial! [*She cackles feebly.*]

SHUI TA [*in a stifled voice*]. Can I count on that?

MRS. SHIN. We all have our price, and mine won't be too high for the great Mr. Shui Ta! [*She opens* SHUI TA*'s collar.*]

SHUI TA. It's for the child's sake. All of this.

MRS. SHIN. "All for the child," of course.

SHUI TA. I'm so fat. People must notice.

MRS. SHIN. Oh no, they think it's 'cause you're rich.

SHUI TA [*more feelingly*]. What will happen to the child?

MRS. SHIN. You ask that nine times a day. Why, it'll have the best that money can buy!

SHUI TA. He must never see Shui Ta.

MRS. SHIN. Oh, no. Always Shen Te.

SHUI TA. What about the neighbors? There are rumors, aren't there?

MRS. SHIN. As long as Mr. Shu Fu doesn't find out, there's nothing to worry about. Drink this.

[*Enter* YANG SUN *in a smart business suit, and carrying a businessman's briefcase.* SHUI TA *is more or less in* MRS. SHIN*'s arms.*]

YANG SUN [*surprised*]. I guess I'm in the way.

SHUI TA [*ignoring this, rises with an effort*]. Till tomorrow, Mrs. Shin.

[MRS. SHIN *leaves with a smile, putting her new gloves on.*]

YANG SUN. Gloves now! She couldn't be fleecing you? And since when did *you* have a private life? [*Taking a paper from the briefcase.*] You haven't been at your desk lately, and things are getting out of hand. The police want to close us down. They say that at the most they can only permit twice the lawful number of workers.

SHUI TA [*evasively*]. The cabins are quite good enough.

YANG SUN. For the workers maybe, not for the tobacco. They're too damp. We must take over some of Mrs. Mi Tzu's buildings.

SHUI TA. Her price is double what I can pay.

YANG SUN. Not unconditionally. If she has me to stroke her knees she'll come down.

SHUI TA. I'll never agree to that.

YANG SUN. What's wrong? Is it the rain? You get so irritable whenever it rains.

SHUI TA. Never! I will never . . .

YANG SUN. Mrs. Mi Tzu'll be here in five minutes. *You* fix it. And Shu Fu will be with her. . . . What's all that noise?

[*During the above dialogue,* WONG *is heard off-stage, calling:* "The good Shen Te, where is she? Which of you has seen Shen Te, good people? Where is Shen Te?" *A knock. Enter* WONG.]

WONG. Mr. Shui Ta, I've come to ask when Miss Shen Te will be back, it's six months now. . . . There are rumors. People say something's happened to her.

SHUI TA. I'm busy. Come back next week.

WONG [*excited*]. In the morning there was always rice on her doorstep—for the needy. It's been there again lately!

SHUI TA. And what do people conclude from this?

WONG. That Shen Te is still in Setzuan! She's been . . . [*He breaks off.*]

SHUI TA. She's been what? Mr. Wong, if you're Shen Te's friend, talk a little less about her, that's my advice to you.

WONG. I don't want your advice! Before she disappeared, Miss Shen Te told me something very important—she's pregnant!

YANG SUN. What? What was that?

SHUI TA [*quickly*]. The man is lying.

WONG. A good woman isn't so easily forgotten, Mr. Shui Ta.

[*He leaves.* SHUI TA *goes quickly into the back room.*]

YANG SUN [*to the audience*]. Shen Te pregnant? So that's why. Her cousin sent her away, so I wouldn't get wind of it. I have a son, a Yang appears on the scene, and what happens? Mother and child vanish into thin air! That scoundrel, that unspeakable . . . [*The sound of sobbing is heard from the back room.*] What was that? Someone sobbing? Who was it? Mr. Shui Ta the Tobacco King doesn't weep his heart out. And where does the rice come from that's on the doorstep in the morning? [SHUI TA *returns. He goes to the door and looks out into the rain.*] Where is she?

SHUI TA. Sh! It's nine o'clock. But the rain's so heavy, you can't hear a thing.

YANG SUN. What do you want to hear?

SHUI TA. The mail plane.

YANG SUN. What?!

SHUI TA. I've been told *you* wanted to fly at one time. Is that all forgotten?

YANG SUN. Flying mail is night work. I prefer the daytime. And the firm is very dear to me—after all it belongs to my ex-fiancée, even if she's not around. And she's not, is she?

SHUI TA. What do you mean by that?

YANG SUN. Oh, well, let's say I haven't altogether—lost interest.

SHUI TA. My cousin might like to know that.

YANG SUN. I might not be indifferent—if I found she was being kept under lock and key.

SHUI TA. By whom?

YANG SUN. By you.

SHUI TA. What could you do about it?

YANG SUN. I could submit for discussion—my position in the firm.

SHUI TA. You are now my manager. In return for a more . . . appropriate position, you might agree to drop the inquiry into your ex-fiancée's whereabouts?

YANG SUN. I might.

SHUI TA. What position *would* be more appropriate?

YANG SUN. The one at the top.

SHUI TA. My own? [*Silence.*]And if I preferred to throw you out on your neck?

YANG SUN. I'd come back on my feet. With suitable escort.

SHUI TA. The police?

YANG SUN. The police.

SHUI TA. And when the police found no one?

YANG SUN. I might ask them not to overlook the back room [*Ending the pretense.*] In short, Mr. Shui Ta, my interest in this young woman has not been officially terminated. I should like to see more of her. [*Into* SHUI TA*'s face:*] Besides, she's pregnant and needs a friend. [*He moves to the door.*] I shall talk about it with the water seller.

[*Exit.* SHUI TA *is rigid for a moment, then he quickly goes into the back room. He returns with Shen Te's belongings: underwear, etc. He takes a long look at the shawl of the previous scene. He then wraps the things in a bundle, which, upon hearing a noise, he hides under the table. Enter* MRS. MI TZU *and* MR. SHU FU. *They put away their umbrellas and galoshes.*]

MRS. MI TZU. I thought your manager was here, Mr. Shui Ta. He combines charm with business in a way that can only be to the advantage of all of us.

SHU FU. You sent for us, Mr. Shui Ta?

SHUI TA. The factory is in trouble.

SHU FU. It always is.

SHUI TA. The police are threatening to close us down unless I can show that the extension of our facilities is imminent.

SHU FU. Shui Ta, I'm sick and tired of your constantly expanding projects. I place cabins at your cousin's disposal; you make a factory of them. I hand your cousin a check; you present it. Your cousin disappears; you find the cabins too small and start talking of yet more—

SHUI TA. Mr. Shu Fu, I'm authorized to inform you that Miss Shen Te's return is now imminent.

SHU FU. Imminent? It's becoming his favorite word.

MRS. MI TZU. Yes, what does it mean?

SHUI TA. Mrs. Mi Tzu, I can pay you exactly half what you asked for your buildings. Are you ready to inform the police that I am taking them over?

MRS. MI TZU. Certainly, if I can take over your manager.

SHU FU. What?

MRS. MI TZU. He's so efficient.

SHUI TA. I'm afraid I need Mr. Yang Sun.

MRS. MI TZU. So do I.

SHUI TA. He will call on you tomorrow.

SHU FU. So much the better. With Shen Te likely to turn up at any moment, the presence of that young man is hardly in good taste.

SHUI TA. So we have reached a settlement. In what was once the good Shen Te's little shop we are laying the foundations for the great Mr. Shui Ta's twelve magnificent super tobacco markets. You will bear in mind that though they call me the Tobacco King of Setzuan, it is my cousin's interests that have been served . . .

VOICES [*off*]. The police, the police! Going to the tobacco shop! Something must have happened!

[*Enter* YANG SUN, WONG *and the* POLICEMAN.]

POLICEMAN. Quiet there, quiet, quiet! [*They quiet down.*] I'm sorry, Mr. Shui Ta, but there's a report that you've been depriving Miss Shen Te of her freedom. Not that I believe all I hear, but the whole city's in an uproar.

SHUI TA. That's a lie.

POLICEMAN. Mr. Yang Sun has testified that he heard someone sobbing in the back room.

SHU FU. Mrs. Mi Tzu and myself will testify that no one here has been sobbing.

MRS. MI TZU. We have been quietly smoking our cigars.

POLICEMAN. Mr. Shui Ta, I'm afraid I shall have to take a look at that room. [*He does so. The room is empty.*] No one there, of course, sir.

YANG SUN. But I heard sobbing. What's that? [*He finds the clothes.*]

WONG. Those are Shen Te's things. [*To crowd.*] Shen Te's clothes are here!

VOICES [*off, in sequence*]:
—Shen Te's clothes!
—They've been found under the table!
—Body of murdered girl still missing!
—Tobacco King suspected!

POLICEMAN. Mr. Shui Ta, unless you can tell us where the girl is, I'll have to ask you to come along.

SHUI TA. I do not know.

POLICEMAN. I can't say how sorry I am, Mr. Shui Ta. [*He shows him the door.*]

SHUI TA. Everything will be cleared up in no time. There are still judges in Setzuan.

YANG SUN. I heard sobbing!

9A

Wong's den. For the last time, the GODS *appear to the water seller in his dream. They have changed and show signs of a long journey, extreme fatigue, and plenty of mishaps. The* FIRST *no longer has a hat; the* THIRD *has lost a leg; all three are barefoot.*

WONG. Illustrious ones, at last you're here. Shen Te's been gone for months and today her cousin's been arrested. They think he murdered her to get the shop. But I had a dream and in this dream Shen Te said her cousin was keeping her prisoner. You must find her for us, illustrious ones!

FIRST GOD. We've found very few good people anywhere, and even they didn't keep it up. Shen Te is still the only one that stayed good.

SECOND GOD. If she *has* stayed good.

WONG. Certainly she has. But she's vanished.

FIRST GOD. That's the last straw. All is lost!

SECOND GOD. A little moderation, dear colleague!

FIRST GOD [*plaintively*]. What's the good of moderation now? If she can't be found, we'll have to resign! The world is a terrible place! Nothing but misery, vulgarity, and waste! Even the countryside isn't what it used to be. The trees are getting their heads chopped off by telephone wires, and there's such a noise from all the gunfire, and I can't stand those heavy clouds of smoke, and—

THIRD GOD. The place is absolutely unlivable! Good intentions bring people to the brink of the abyss, and good deeds push them over the edge. I'm afraid our book of rules is destined for the scrap heap—

SECOND GOD. It's people! They're a worthless lot!

THIRD GOD. The world is too cold!

SECOND GOD. It's people! They're too weak!

FIRST GOD. Dignity, dear colleagues, dignity! Never despair! As for this world, didn't we agree that we only have to find one human being who can stand the place? Well, we found her. True, we lost her again. We must find her again, that's all! And at once!

[*They disappear.*]

10

Courtroom. Groups: SHU FU *and* MRS. MI TZU; YANG SUN *and* MRS. YANG; WONG, *the* CARPENTER, *the* GRANDFATHER, *the* NIECE, *the* OLD MAN, *the* OLD WOMAN; MRS. SHIN, *the* POLICEMAN; *the* UNEMPLOYED MAN, *the* SISTER-IN-LAW.

OLD MAN. So much power isn't good for one man.

UNEMPLOYED MAN. And he's going to open twelve super tobacco markets!

WIFE. One of the judges is a friend of Mr. Shu Fu's.

SISTER-IN-LAW. Another one accepted a present from Mr. Shui Ta only last night. A great fat goose.

OLD WOMAN [*to* WONG]. And Shen Te is nowhere to be found.

WONG. Only the gods will ever know the truth.

POLICEMAN. Order in the court! My lords the judges!

[*Enter the* THREE GODS *in judges' robes. We overhear their conversation as they pass along the footlights to their bench.*]

THIRD GOD. We'll never get away with it, our certificates were so badly forged.

SECOND GOD. My predecessor's "sudden indigestion" will certainly cause comment.

FIRST GOD. But he *had* just eaten a whole goose.

UNEMPLOYED MAN. Look at that! *New* judges.

WONG. New judges. And what good ones!

[*The* THIRD GOD *hears this, and turns to smile at* WONG. *The* GODS *sit. The* FIRST GOD *beats on the bench with his gavel. The* POLICEMAN *brings in* SHUI TA *who walks with lordly steps. He is whistled at.*]

POLICEMAN [*to* SHUI TA]. Be prepared for a surprise. The judges have been changed.

[SHUI TA *turns quickly round, looks at them, and staggers.*]

NIECE. What's the matter now?

WIFE. The great Tobacco King nearly fainted.

HUSBAND. Yes, as soon as he saw the new judges.

WONG. Does *he* know who they are?

[SHUI TA *picks himself up, and the proceedings open.*]

FIRST GOD. Defendant Shui Ta, you are accused of doing away with your cousin Shen Te in order to take possession of her business. Do you plead guilty or not guilty?

SHUI TA. Not guilty, my lord.

FIRST GOD [*thumbing through the documents of the case*]. The first witness is the policeman. I shall ask him to tell us something of the respective reputations of Miss Shen Te and Mr. Shui Ta.

POLICEMAN. Miss Shen Te was a young lady who aimed to please, my lord. She liked to live and let live, as the saying goes. Mr. Shui Ta, on the other hand, is a man of principle. Though the generosity of Miss Shen Te forced him at times to abandon half measures, unlike the girl he was always on the side of the law, my lord. One time, he even unmasked a gang of thieves to whom his too trustful cousin had given shelter. The evidence, in short, my lord, proves that Mr. Shui Ta was *incapable* of the crime of which he stands accused!

FIRST GOD. I see. And are there others who could testify along, shall we say, the same lines?

[SHU FU *rises.*]

POLICEMAN [*whispering to* GODS]. Mr. Shu Fu—a very important person.

FIRST GOD [*inviting him to speak*]. Mr. Shu Fu!

SHU FU. Mr. Shui Ta is a businessman, my lord. Need I say more?

FIRST GOD. Yes.

SHU FU. Very well, I will. He is Vice President of the Council of Commerce and is about to be elected a Justice of the Peace. [*He returns to his seat.*]

[MRS. MI TZU *rises.*]

WONG. Elected! *He* gave him the job!

[*With a gesture the* FIRST GOD *asks who* MRS. MI TZU *is.*]

POLICEMAN. Another very important person. Mrs. Mi Tzu.

MRS. MI TZU. My lord, as Chairman of the Committee on Social Work, I wish to call attention to just a couple of eloquent facts: Mr. Shui Ta not only has erected a model factory with model housing in our city, he is a regular contributor to our home for the disabled. [*She returns to her seat.*]

POLICEMAN [*whispering*]. And she's a great friend of the judge that ate the goose!

FIRST GOD [*to the* POLICEMAN]. Oh, thank you. What next? [*To the Court, genially:*] Oh, yes. We should find out if any of the evidence is less favorable to the defendant.

[WONG, *the* CARPENTER, *the* OLD MAN, *the* OLD WOMAN, *the* UNEMPLOYED MAN, *the* SISTER-IN-LAW, *and the* NIECE *come forward.*]

POLICEMAN [*whispering*]. Just the riffraff, my lord.

FIRST GOD [*addressing the "riffraff"*]. Well, um, riffraff—do you know anything of the defendant, Mr. Shui Ta?

WONG. Too much, my lord.

UNEMPLOYED MAN. What don't we know, my lord.

CARPENTER. He ruined us.

SISTER-IN-LAW. He's a cheat.

NIECE. Liar.

WIFE. Thief.

BOY. Blackmailer.

BROTHER. Murderer.

FIRST GOD. Thank you. We should now let the defendant state his point of view.

SHUI TA. I only came on the scene when Shen Te was in danger of losing what I had understood was a gift from the gods. Because I did the filthy jobs which someone had to do, they hate me. My activities were restricted to the minimum, my lord.

SISTER-IN-LAW. He had us arrested!

SHUI TA. Certainly. You stole from the bakery!

SISTER-IN-LAW. Such concern for the bakery! You didn't want the shop for yourself, I suppose!

SHUI TA. I didn't want the shop overrun with parasites.

SISTER-IN-LAW. We had nowhere else to go.

SHUI TA. There were too many of you.

WONG. What about this old couple: Were *they* parasites?

OLD MAN. We lost our shop because of you!

OLD WOMAN. And we gave your cousin money!

SHUI TA. My cousin's fiancé was a flyer. The money had to go to *him*.

WONG. Did you care whether he flew or not? Did you care whether she married him or not? You wanted her to marry someone else! [*He points at* SHU FU.]

SHUI TA. The flyer unexpectedly turned out to be a scoundrel.

YANG SUN [*jumping up*]. Which was the reason you made him your manager?

SHUI TA. Later on he improved.

WONG. And when he improved, you sold him to her? [*He points out* MRS. MI TZU.]

SHUI TA. She wouldn't let me have her premises unless she had him to stroke her knees!

MRS. MI TZU. What? The man's a pathological liar. [*To him:*] Don't mention my property to me as long as you live! Murderer! [*She rustles off, in high dudgeon.*]

YANG SUN [*pushing in*]. My lord, I wish to speak for the defendant.

SISTER-IN-LAW. Naturally. He's your employer.

UNEMPLOYED MAN. And the worst slave driver in the country.

MRS. YANG. That's a lie! My lord, Mr. Shui Ta is a great man. He . . .

YANG SUN. He's this and he's that, but he is not a murderer, my lord. Just fifteen minutes before his arrest I heard Shen Te's voice in his own back room.

FIRST GOD. Oh? Tell us more!

YANG SUN. I heard sobbing, my lord!

FIRST GOD. But lots of women sob, we've been finding.

YANG SUN. Could I fail to recognize her voice?

SHU FU. No, you made her sob so often yourself, young man!

YANG SUN. Yes. But I also made her happy. Till he [*pointing at* SHUI TA] decided to sell her to you!

SHUI TA. Because you didn't love her.

WONG. Oh, no: it was for the money, my lord!

SHUI TA. And what was the money for, my lord? For the poor! And for Shen Te so she could go on being good!

WONG. For the poor? That he sent to his sweatshops? And why didn't you let Shen Te be good when you signed the big check?

SHUI TA. For the child's sake, my lord.

CARPENTER. What about *my* children? What did he do about them?

[SHUI TA *is silent.*]

WONG. The shop was to be a fountain of goodness. That was the gods' idea. You came and spoiled it!

SHUI TA. If I hadn't, it would have run dry!

MRS. SHIN. There's a lot in that, my lord.

WONG. What have you done with the good Shen Te, bad man? She *was* good, my lords, she was, I swear it! [*He raises his hand in an oath.*]

THIRD GOD. What's happened to your hand, water seller?

WONG [*pointing to* SHUI TA]. It's all his fault, my lord, *she* was going to send me to a doctor—[*To* SHUI TA:] You were her worst enemy!

SHUI TA. I was her only friend!

WONG. Where is she then? Tell us where your good friend is!

[*The excitement of this exchange has run through the whole crowd.*]

ALL. Yes, where is she? Where is Shen Te? [*Etc.*]

SHUI TA. Shen Te . . . had to go.

WONG. Where? Where to?

SHUI TA. I cannot tell you! I cannot tell you!

ALL. Why? Why did she have to go away? [*Etc.*]

WONG [*into the din with the first words, but talking on beyond the others*]: Why not, why not? Why did she have to go away?

SHUI TA [*shouting*]. Because you'd all have torn her to shreds, that's why! My lords, I have a request. Clear the court! When only the judges remain, I will make a confession.

ALL [*except* WONG, *who is silent, struck by the new turn of events*]. So he's guilty? He's confessing! [*Etc.*]

FIRST GOD [*using the gavel*]. Clear the court!

POLICEMAN. Clear the court!

WONG. Mr. Shui Ta has met his match this time.

MRS. SHIN [*with a gesture toward the judges*]. You're in for a little surprise.

[*The court is cleared. Silence.*]

SHUI TA. Illustrious ones!

[*The* GODS *look at each other, not quite believing their ears.*]

SHUI TA. Yes, I recognize you!

SECOND GOD [*taking matters in hand, sternly*]. What have you done with our good woman of Setzuan?

SHUI TA. I have a terrible confession to make: I am she! [*He takes off his mask, and tears away his clothes.* SHEN TE *stands there.*]

SECOND GOD. Shen Te!

SHEN TE. Shen Te, yes. Shui Ta *and* Shen Te. Both.
Your injunction
To be good and yet to live
Was a thunderbolt:
It has torn me in two
I can't tell how it was
But to be good to others
And myself at the same time
I could not do it
Your world is not an easy one, illustrious ones!
When we extend our hand to a begger, he tears it off for us
When we help the lost, we are lost ourselves
And so
Since not to eat is to die
Who can long refuse to be bad?
As I lay prostrate beneath the weight of good intentions
Ruin stared me in the face
It was when I was unjust that I ate good meat
And hobnobbed with the mighty
Why?
Why are bad deeds rewarded?
Good ones punished?
I enjoyed giving
I truly wished to be the Angel of the Slums
But washed by a foster mother in the water of the gutter
I developed a sharp eye
The time came when pity was a thorn in my side
And, later, when kind words turned to ashes in my mouth
And anger took over
I became a wolf
Find me guilty, then, illustrious ones,
But know:
All that I have done I did
To help my neighbor
To love my lover
And to keep my little one from want
For your great, godly deeds, I was too poor, too small.
[*Pause.*]

FIRST GOD [*shocked*]. Don't go on making yourself miserable, Shen Te! We're overjoyed to have found you!

SHEN TE. I'm telling you I'm the bad man who committed all those crimes!

FIRST GOD [*using—or failing to use—his ear trumpet*]. The good woman who did all those good deeds?

SHEN TE. Yes, but the bad man too!

FIRST GOD [*as if something had dawned*]. Unfortunate coincidences! Heartless neighbors!

THIRD GOD [*shouting in his ear*]. But how is she to continue?

FIRST GOD. Continue? Well, she's a strong, healthy girl . . .

SECOND GOD. You didn't hear what she said!

FIRST GOD. I heard every word! She is confused, that's all! [*He begins to bluster.*] And what about this book of rules—we can't renounce our rules, can we? [*More quietly.*] Should the world be changed? How? By whom? The world should *not* be changed! [*At a sign from him, the lights turn pink, and music plays.*]

And now the hour of parting is at hand.
Dost thou behold, Shen Te, yon fleecy cloud?
It is our chariot. At a sign from me
'Twill come and take us back from whence we came
Above the azure vault and silver stars. . . .

SHEN TE. No! Don't go, illustrious ones!

FIRST GOD.

Our cloud has landed now in yonder field
From which it will transport us back to heaven.
Farewell, Shen Te, let not thy courage fail thee. . . .

[*Exeunt* GODS.]

SHEN TE. What about the old couple? They've lost their shop! What about the water seller and his hand? And I've got to defend myself against the barber, because I don't love him! And against Sun, because I do love him! How? How?

[SHEN TE*'s eyes follow the* GODS *as they are imagined to step into a cloud which rises and moves forward over the orchestra and up beyond the balcony.*]

FIRST GOD [*from on high*]. We have faith in you, Shen Te!

SHEN TE. There'll be a child. And he'll have to be fed. I can't stay here. Where shall I go?

FIRST GOD. Continue to be good, good woman of Setzuan!

SHEN TE. I need my bad cousin!

FIRST GOD. But not very often!

SHEN TE. Once a week at least!

FIRST GOD. Once a month will be quite enough!

SHEN TE [*shrieking*]. No, no! Help!

[*But the cloud continues to recede as the* GODS *sing.*]

Valedictory Hymn

What rapture, oh, it is to know
A good thing when you see it
And having seen a good thing, oh,
What rapture 'tis to flee it

Be good, sweet maid of Setzuan
Let Shui Ta be clever
Departing, we forget the man
Remember your endeavor

Because through all the length of days
Her goodness faileth never
Sing hallelujah! Make Shen Te's
Good name live on forever!

SHEN TE. Help!

EPILOGUE

You're thinking, aren't you, that this is no right
Conclusion to the play you've seen tonight?°
After a tale, exotic, fabulous,
A nasty ending was slipped up on us.
We feel deflated too. We too are nettled
To see the curtain down and nothing settled.
How could a better ending be arranged?
Could one change people? Can the world be changed?
Would new gods do the trick? Will atheism?
Moral rearmament? Materialism?
It is for you to find a way, my friends,
To help good men arrive at happy ends.
You write the happy ending to the play!
There must, there must, there's got to be a way!

°*At afternoon performances:*
We quite agree, our play this afternoon
Collapsed upon us like a pricked balloon.

ALTERNATE ENDING FOR GERMAN PRODUCTION

FIRST GOD.
And now . . . [*He makes a sign and music is heard. Rosy light.*] let us return
This little world has much engaged us.
Its joy and its sorrow have refreshed and pained us.
Up there, however, beyond the stars,
We shall gladly think of you, Shen Te, the good woman
Who bears witness to our spirit down below,
Who, in cold darkness, carries a little lamp!

Good-bye! Do it well!

[*He makes a sign and the ceiling opens. A pink cloud comes down. On it the* THREE GODS *rise, very slowly.*]

SHEN TE. Oh, don't, illustrious ones! Don't go away! Don't leave me! How can I face the good old couple who've lost their store and the water seller with his stiff hand? And how can I defend myself from the barber whom I do not love and from Sun whom I do love? And I am with child. Soon there'll be a little son who'll want to eat. I can't stay here! [*She turns with a hunted look toward the door which will let her tormentors in.*]

FIRST GOD. You can do it. Just be good and everything will turn out well!

[*Enter the witnesses. They look with surprise at the judges floating on their pink cloud.*]

WONG. Show respect! The gods have appeared among us! Three of the highest gods have come to Setzuan to find a good human being. They had found one already, but . . .

FIRST GOD. No "but"! Here she is!

ALL. Shen Te!

FIRST GOD. She has not perished. She was only hidden. She will stay with you. A good human being!

SHEN TE. But I need my cousin!

FIRST GOD. Not too often!

SHEN TE. At least once a week!

FIRST GOD. Once a month. That's enough!

SHEN TE. Oh, don't go away, illustrious ones! I haven't told you everything! I need you desperately!

[*The* GODS *sing.*]

The Trio of the Vanishing Gods on the Cloud

Unhappily we cannot stay
More than a fleeting year.
If we watch our find too long
It will disappear.

Here the golden light of truth
With shadow is alloyed
Therefore now we ask your leave
To go back to our void.

SHEN TE. Help! [*Her cries continue through the song.*]

Since our search is over now
Let us fast ascend!
The good woman of Setzuan
Praise we at the end!

[*As* SHEN TE *stretches out her arms to them in desperation, they disappear above, smiling and waving.*]

Edward Albee (b. 1928)
THE SANDBOX

CHARACTERS

THE YOUNG MAN, *25, a good-looking, well-built boy in a bathing suit*
MOMMY, *55, a well-dressed, imposing woman*
DADDY, *60, a small man; gray, thin*
GRANDMA, *86, a tiny, wizened woman with bright eyes*
THE MUSICIAN, *no particular age, but young; would be nice*

Note: When, in the course of the play, MOMMY *and* DADDY *call each other by these names, there should be no suggestion of regionalism. These names are of empty affection and point up the presenility and vacuity of their characters.*

The Scene: A bare stage, with only the following: Near the footlights, far stage-right, two simple chairs set side by side, facing the audience; near the footlights, far stage-left, a chair facing stage-right with a music stand before it; farther back, and stage-center, slightly elevated and raked, a large child's sandbox with a toy pail and shovel; the background is the sky, which alters from brightest day to deepest night.

At the beginning, it is brightest day; the YOUNG MAN *is alone on stage, to the rear of the sandbox, and to one side. He is doing calisthenics; he does calisthenics until quite at the very end of the play. These calisthenics, employing the arms only, should suggest the beating and fluttering of wings. The* YOUNG MAN *is, after all, the Angel of Death.*

MOMMY *and* DADDY *enter from stage-left,* MOMMY *first.*

MOMMY [*motioning to* DADDY]. Well, here we are; this is the beach.

DADDY [*whining*]. I'm cold.

MOMMY [*dismissing him with a little laugh*]. Don't be silly; it's as warm as toast. Look at that nice young man over there: *he* doesn't think it's cold. [*Waves to the* YOUNG MAN] Hello.

YOUNG MAN [*with an endearing smile*]. Hi!

MOMMY [*looking about*]. This will do perfectly . . . don't you think so, Daddy? There's sand there . . . and the water beyond. What do you think, Daddy?

DADDY [*vaguely*]. Whatever you say, Mommy.

MOMMY [*with the same little laugh*]. Well, of course . . . whatever I say. Then, it's settled, is it?

DADDY [*shrugs*]. She's *your* mother, not mine.

MOMMY. I know she's my mother. What do you take me for? [*A pause*] All right, now; let's get on with it. [*She shouts into the wings, stage-left*] You! Out there! You can come in now.

[*The* MUSICIAN *enters, seats himself in the chair, stage-left, places music on the music stand, is ready to play.* MOMMY *nods approvingly.*]

MOMMY. Very nice; very nice. Are you ready, Daddy? Let's go get Grandma.

DADDY. Whatever you say, Mommy.

MOMMY [*leading the way out, stage-left*]. Of course, whatever I say. [*To the* MUSICIAN] You can begin now.

[*The* MUSICIAN *begins playing;* MOMMY *and* DADDY *exit; the* MUSICIAN, *all the while playing, nods to the* YOUNG MAN.]

YOUNG MAN [*with the same endearing smile*]. Hi!

[*After a moment,* MOMMY *and* DADDY *re-enter, carrying* GRANDMA. *She is borne in by their hands under her armpits; she is quite rigid; her legs are drawn up; her feet do not touch the ground; the expression on her ancient face is that of puzzlement and fear.*]

DADDY. Where do we put her?

MOMMY [*the same little laugh*]. Wherever I say, of course. Let me see . . . well . . . all right, over there . . . in the sandbox. [*Pause*] Well, what are you waiting for, Daddy? . . . The sandbox!

[*Together they carry* GRANDMA *over to the sandbox and more or less dump her in.*]

GRANDMA [*righting herself to a sitting position; her voice a cross between a baby's laugh and cry*]. Ahhhhhh! Graaaaa!

DADDY [*dusting himself*]. What do we do now?

MOMMY [*to the* MUSICIAN]. You can stop now. [*The* MUSICIAN *stops. Back to* DADDY] What do you mean, what do we do now? We go over there and sit down, of course. [*To the* YOUNG MAN] Hello there.

YOUNG MAN [*again smiling*]. Hi!

[MOMMY *and* DADDY *move to the chairs, stage-right, and sit down. A pause.*]

GRANDMA [*same as before*]. Ahhhhhh! Ah-haaaaaa! Graaaaaa!

DADDY. Do you think . . . do you think she's . . . comfortable?

MOMMY [*impatiently*]. How would I know?

DADDY [*pause*]. What do we do now?

MOMMY [*as if remembering*]. We . . . wait. We . . . sit here . . . and we wait . . . that's what we do.

DADDY [*after a pause*]. Shall we talk to each other?

MOMMY [*with that little laugh; picking something off her dress*]. Well, *you* can talk, if you want to . . . if you can think of anything to *say* . . . if you can think of anything *new*.

DADDY [*thinks*]. No . . . I suppose not.

MOMMY [*with a triumphant laugh*]. Of course not!

GRANDMA [*banging the toy shovel against the pail*]. Haaaaaa! Ah-haaaaaa!

MOMMY [*out over the audience*]. Be quiet, Grandma . . . just be quiet, and wait.

[GRANDMA *throws a shovelful of sand at* MOMMY.]

MOMMY [*still out over the audience*]. She's throwing sand at me! You stop that, Grandma; you stop throwing sand at Mommy! [*To* DADDY] She's throwing sand at me.

[DADDY *looks around at* GRANDMA, *who screams at him.*]

GRANDMA. GRAAAAA!

MOMMY. Don't look at her. Just . . . sit here . . . be very still . . . and wait. [*To the* MUSICIAN] You . . . uh . . . you go ahead and do whatever it is you do.

[*The* MUSICIAN *plays.* MOMMY *and* DADDY *are fixed, staring out beyond the audience.* GRANDMA *looks at them, looks at the* MUSICIAN, *looks at the sandbox, throws down the shovel.*]

GRANDMA. Ah-haaaaaa! Graaaaaa! [*Looks for reaction; gets none. Now . . . directly to the audience*] Honestly! What a way to treat an old woman! Drag her out of the house . . . stick her in a car . . . bring her out here from the city . . . dump her in a pile of sand . . . and leave her here to set. I'm eighty-six years old! I was married when I was seventeen. To a farmer. He died when I was thirty. [*To the* MUSICIAN] Will you stop that, please? [*The* MUSICIAN *stops playing*] I'm a feeble old woman . . . how do you expect anybody to hear me over that peep! peep! peep! [*To herself*] There's no respect around here. [*To the* YOUNG MAN] There's no respect around here!

YOUNG MAN [*same smile*]. Hi!

GRANDMA [*after a pause, a mild double-take, continues, to the audience*]. My husband died when I was thirty [*indicates* MOMMY], and I had to raise that big cow over there all by my lonesome. You can imagine what *that* was like. Lordy! [*To the* YOUNG MAN] Where'd they get *you?*

YOUNG MAN. Oh . . . I've been around for a while.

GRANDMA. I'll bet you have! Heh, heh, heh. Will you look at you!

YOUNG MAN [*flexing his muscles*]. Isn't that something? [*Continues his calisthenics.*]

GRANDMA. Boy, oh boy; I'll say. Pretty good.

YOUNG MAN [*sweetly*]. I'll say.

GRANDMA. Where ya from?

YOUNG MAN. Southern California.

GRANDMA [*nodding*]. Figgers; figgers. What's your name, honey?

YOUNG MAN. I don't know. . . .

GRANDMA [*to the audience*]. Bright, too!

YOUNG MAN. I mean . . . I mean, they haven't given me one yet . . . the studio . . .

GRANDMA [*giving him the once-over*]. You don't say . . . you don't say. Well . . . uh, I've got to talk some more . . . don't you go 'way.

YOUNG MAN. Oh, no.

GRANDMA [*turning her attention back to the audience*]. Fine; fine. [*Then, once more, back to the* YOUNG MAN] You're . . . you're an actor, hunh?

YOUNG MAN [*beaming*]. Yes. I am.

GRANDMA [*to the audience again; shrugs*]. I'm smart that way. *Anyhow,* I had to raise . . . *that* over there all by my lonesome; and what's next to her there . . . that's what she married. Rich? I tell you . . . money, money, money. They took me off the *farm* . . . which was real decent of them . . . and they moved me into the big town house with *them* . . . fixed a nice place for me under the stove . . . gave me an army blanket . . . and my own dish . . . my very own dish! So, what have I got to complain about? Nothing, of course. I'm not complaining. [*She looks up at the sky, shouts to someone off stage*] Shouldn't it be getting dark, now, dear?

[*The lights dim; night comes on. The* MUSICIAN *begins to play; it becomes deepest night. There are spots on all the players, including the* YOUNG MAN, *who is, of course, continuing his calisthenics.*]

DADDY [*stirring*]. It's nighttime.

MOMMY. Shhhh. Be still . . . wait.

DADDY [*whining*]. It's so hot.

MOMMY. Shhhhhh. Be still . . . wait.

GRANDMA [*to herself*]. That's better. Night. [*To the* MUSICIAN] Honey, do you play all through this part? [*The* MUSICIAN *nods*] Well, keep it nice and soft; that's a good boy. [*The* MUSICIAN *nods again; plays softly*] That's nice. [*There is an off-stage rumble.*]

DADDY [*starting*]. What was that?

MOMMY [*beginning to weep*]. It was nothing.

DADDY. It was . . . it was . . . thunder . . . or a wave breaking . . . or something.

MOMMY [*whispering, through her tears*]. It was an off-stage rumble . . . and you know what *that* means . . .

DADDY. I forget . . .

MOMMY [*barely able to talk*]. It means the time has come for poor Grandma . . . and I can't bear it!

DADDY [*vacantly*]. I . . . I suppose you've got to be brave.

GRANDMA [*mocking*]. That's right, kid; be brave. You'll bear up; you'll get over it.

[*Another off-stage rumble . . . louder.*]

MOMMY. Ohhhhhhhhhh . . . poor Grandma . . . poor Grandma. . . .

GRANDMA [*to* MOMMY]. I'm fine! I'm all right! It hasn't happened yet!

[*A violent off-stage rumble. All the lights go out, save the spot on the* YOUNG MAN; *the* MUSICIAN *stops playing.*]

MOMMY. Ohhhhhhhhhh. . . . Ohhhhhhhhhh. . . .

[*Silence.*]

GRANDMA. Don't put the lights up yet . . . I'm not ready; I'm not quite ready. [*Silence*] All right, dear . . . I'm about done.

[*The lights come up again, to brightest day; the* MUSICIAN *begins to play.* GRANDMA *is discovered, still in the sandbox, lying on her side, propped up on an elbow, half covered, busily shoveling sand over herself.*]

GRANDMA [*muttering*]. I don't know how I'm supposed to do anything with this goddam toy shovel. . . .

DADDY. Mommy! It's daylight!

MOMMY [*brightly*]. So it is! Well! Our long night is over. We must put away our tears, take off our mourning . . . and face the future. It's our duty.

GRANDMA [*still shoveling; mimicking*]. . . . take off our mourning . . . face the future. . . . Lordy!

[MOMMY *and* DADDY *rise, stretch.* MOMMY *waves to the* YOUNG MAN.]

YOUNG MAN [*with that smile*]. Hi!

[GRANDMA *plays dead. (!)* MOMMY *and* DADDY *go over to look at her; she is a little more than half buried in the sand; the toy shovel is in her hands, which are crossed on her breast.*]

MOMMY [*before the sandbox; shaking her head*]. Lovely! It's . . . it's hard to be sad . . . she looks . . . so happy. [*With pride and conviction*] It pays to do things well. [*To the* MUSICIAN] All right, you can stop now, if you want to. I mean, stay around for a swim, or something; it's all right with us. [*She sighs heavily*] Well, Daddy . . . off we go.

DADDY. Brave Mommy!

MOMMY. Brave Daddy! [*They exit, stage- left.*]

GRANDMA [*after they leave; lying quite still*]. It pays to do things well. . . . Boy, oh boy! [*She tries to sit up*] . . . well, kids . . . [*but she finds she can't*] . . . I . . . I can't get up. I . . . I can't move. . . .

[*The* YOUNG MAN *stops his calisthenics, nods to the* MUSICIAN, *walks over to* GRANDMA, *kneels down by the sandbox.*]

GRANDMA. I . . . can't move. . . .

YOUNG MAN. Shhhhh . . . be very still. . . .

GRANDMA. I . . . I can't move. . . .

YOUNG MAN. Uh . . . ma'am; I . . . I have a line here.

GRANDMA. Oh, I'm sorry, sweetie! you go right ahead.

YOUNG MAN. I am . . . uh . . .

GRANDMA. Take you time, dear.

YOUNG MAN [*prepares; delivers the line like a real amateur*]. I am the Angel of Death. I am . . . uh . . . I am come for you.

GRANDMA. What . . . wha . . . [*Then, with resignation*] . . . ohhhh . . . ohhhh, I see.

[*The* YOUNG MAN *bends over, kisses* GRANDMA *gently on the forehead.*]

GRANDMA [*her eyes closed, her hands folded on her breast again, the shovel between her hands, a sweet smile on her face*] Well . . . that was very nice, dear. . . .

YOUNG MAN [*still kneeling*]. Shhhhhh . . . be still. . . .

GRANDMA. What I meant was . . . you did that very well, dear. . . .

YOUNG MAN [*blushing*]. . . . oh . . .

GRANDMA. No; I mean it. You've got that . . . you've got a quality.

YOUNG MAN [*with his endearing smile*]. Oh . . . thank you; thank you very much . . . ma'am.

GRANDMA [*slowly; softly—as the* YOUNG MAN *puts his hands on top of* GRANDMA'*s*] You're . . . you're welcome . . . dear.

[*Tableau. The* MUSICIAN *continues to play as the curtain slowly comes down.*]

Part Five

Writing about Literature

We have spent much of our time in this book thinking about how readers participate in producing the meaning of works of literature. Rather than thinking of readers as passive consumers, we have emphasized that readers are active. They are engaged in the complex process of turning marks on a page into stories that move us, or poems that challenge us, or plays that ask for our sympathy. Without active readers, literary works remain just those marks on a page, full of potential but never fulfilled. Accepting the challenge of reading calls for rich emotional and analytical responses from readers in every phase of its process.

Exercising the Power of Language

Writing about literature can be considered as the final step in the reading process. Reading produces meaning, but writing about literature allows you to produce a carefully thought out and detailed interpretation of what you've read. The act of scanning the marks on the page and turning them into meaningful language does not allow us much time to reflect on the meanings we've produced. When we get the opportunity to write about our reading, however, we can organize our thoughts, reread more slowly, see how various passages of the text relate to one another, reflect on what the text has put us through. When we write about literature we display how we made sense of the text.

The reading process is so various that it doesn't make sense to think about looking for a single correct interpretation of a text. Literary texts, as we have seen, tend to multiply meaning rather than narrow it down. They also tend to disrupt our ordinary expectations about language and life. As readers we are often disoriented, trying to make sense of difficult language and a strange fictional world. In this complex process, various readers will make sense of the text differently. A poem that uses the word *light,* to take a common example, sets loose many different denotative and connotative possibilities that can be read legitimately in many different ways. Literary texts also call for an emotional response from readers, but they often present a scene without comment, leaving it up to readers to decide *how* to respond. A story about a drunk, for example, may elicit sympathy from a reader who is a reformed drinker, whereas it elicits scorn from a reader who condemns all drinking. The purpose of writing about literature is not to come up with the *correct* reading of a text but rather to *explain the validity* of your own reading. Writing requires readers to take final responsibility for their reading.

Taking the Responsibility

The meaning of a work of literature is not something that can be decided in the way that the correct answer to a math problem can be.

When you read you don't *find* a correct meaning already hidden in the work; you *produce* meaning as you read. You ask questions, make connections, mark out patterns. You imagine the scene, the look and sound of the characters, the actions. You make judgments and bring your own value systems into play. Each reader produces his or her own text by playing this active role. Writing about literature allows you to present your argument for the meaning you have produced.

Now, that doesn't mean that all readings are equally valid. There may be no such thing as the one "correct" meaning, but we can still make judgments about which readings have the most *power*. To be sure, there *are* incorrect readings. If a reader isn't competent in the language system, for example, he or she might well be completely lost, unable to generate meaning at all. Or suppose a reader did not understand the significance of a certain gesture that is referred to in a story. That reader's processing of the story would be incomplete. Most readers have to face problems like these whenever they read. Literary texts can generate so many meanings that it is almost inevitable that each of us will be at some level of ignorance as readers—there will be some possibility for meaning that we will miss. No reading is perfect; there is always more meaning to produce. In fact, one way of judging a reader's interpretation of a literary text is on the basis of how much meaning the reader has produced, and on whether that meaning makes sense.

But how do we judge that? All readers are working inside certain constraints. They live inside linguistic and cultural systems that give meaning to experience. Literary texts also exist within those constraints. Words have their meanings within the language; body movements and gestures have meanings within a given culture. As a result, readers are not free to produce just any meaning—it has to make sense within these systems. So the reader's responsibility is to make clear how his or her reading of the text comes out of those systems of communication. Does the reading take into account all of the important language of the text? Does it make sense of the messages that characters and their actions communicate?

Most literary texts produce a large number of complex messages. As a result, many valid readings of a given work are possible. In writing about literature, you have to demonstrate at least that your reading is valid within the cultural codes. But if you have done a thorough job and become involved with the work, you will want to show more—that your reading is *powerful,* that it makes sense of the text in a way that should compel other readers' agreement. When active readers write, then, they are performing an act of *persuasion*. Readings compete with one another, in this sense, and writing about literature thus enters you into that competition—so you should always present your case as powerfully as possible.

Let's look at an example of how a reading gains power. In James Joyce's "Eveline," which is reprinted in the fiction section, a young woman who lives a grim life with her repressive father is offered the chance to escape that life and find adventure with a dashing sailor who wants to marry her and take her away to Buenos Aires, Argentina. At the end of the story, just as she is about to get on the boat with Frank, she panics at the thought of the risk she is taking and returns to her narrow life. Some readers see "Eveline" as a story about a failure of nerve. Eveline cannot escape the repression that she has suffered, and she denies herself her one chance for freedom. But other readers argue that Eveline did not in fact have much of a choice. After all, if she goes with Frank to a place where she knows no one and nothing of the culture, she will be as dependent on Frank as she was on her father. To these readers, Eveline's return to her life is pitiful, but they feel that she is paralyzed by a lack of options. What seemed so adventurous, they would argue, turns out to be a repetition of her original situation.

Now, I feel strongly that both of these readings are valid within the systems of linguistic and cultural and literary codes. They both make sense. In the process of arguing for one reading or the other, readers would have to offer arguments and evidence in support of their position. Readers who see this as a story about a failure of nerve might point out that at the moment when she panics at the docks the narrator refers to her as "a helpless animal." The figure of speech here clearly suggests, such an argument would run, that she has given up her human freedom, sunken below the human level. She is now trapped in the cage that her father has fashioned. Those who see the story as a dramatization of a woman who has no choice could quote those passages in which Frank is discussed in terms that recall the characterization of Eveline's father. This line of argument might then claim that Frank offers no real alternative for Eveline. To make such arguments, you must think of the literary text as a source of evidence for your own reading of it. The stronger argument would be the one that marshaled the most evidence and argued for itself in the most effective way. In our terms, the strength of the argument would depend on how clearly you could explain how the evidence makes sense within the systems of meaning that we put into play when we read.

Another way of saying this is that writing about literature involves *rhetoric*—the success of the argument depends on the skill of the writer. Each reader makes judgments about the text, and the reader who writes best can present his or her judgments most forcefully. This achievement depends on reading the text well, of course, and on constructing a valid and powerful argument, but it also depends on writing well in the most general sense—using language effectively. Writing about literature, that is to say, needs to be well written. By writing, readers take language into their own hands. You write in response to someone else's writing, but you must be faithful to your own reading of the text, the meanings you have produced. Writing about literature is therefore putting yourself on the line. You make your writing available to others' readings, and those readers will make their own senses of your writing, just as you have made sense of the literary text. So you as a writer must work to produce language that will shape your readers' reactions. You must choose the words whose connotations will communicate your emotional response; you must construct a pattern that will communicate the logic of your argument. You want to present your reading of the text in the best light possible.

THE PROCESS OF CRITICAL WRITING

One area of almost universal agreement about writing is how to do it wrong—the worst thing you can do when faced with a writing assignment is to sit down with the topic and begin to write. "Off the top of the head" just doesn't work in writing about literature (or in almost any other kind of writing). Good writing almost always comes out of a disciplined process, one that involves preparation for writing as well as a commitment to rewriting. The process I describe below may seem somewhat mechanical to you, but it separates the task out into a series of steps that will lead to a finished product. By keeping the steps separate, you can worry about one thing at a time. While you're writing a first draft, for example, it makes sense to have a plan already worked out, and it makes sense to worry about grammar and details later on.

These steps may be mechanical, but they are a good starting point. For many good writers, the writing process is intuitive rather than mechanical—no one exactly follows the steps outlined below. But these same good writers will nevertheless accomplish all the goals that these steps describe, from the first reading of the literary text to the final draft of the critical essay. These goals emphasize that writing about literature is integrally related to the process of active reading. In fact, critical writing is the fulfillment of active reading. It is the reader's opportunity to work out completely an interpretive idea, so that it can achieve a form that will persuade other readers. What follows, then, is a description of the steps you as a reader can take to turn your readings into effective writings of your own.

Read the Text Thoroughly

Successful writing about literature depends on active reading. No one who has not mastered the language of the text, for instance, can hope to write well about it. And since the language of literature is often difficult, even this basic requirement can be a challenge. In fact, many readers do not accept this challenge; if the language is too difficult, they will simply abandon the text. But if you are willing to be challenged, there is virtually no text that you cannot master. There are dictionaries, to make an obvious point, that will help you make sense of the language. There are encyclopedias and other reference works that will help you identify historical figures and events mentioned. There are historical works that will fill in the context that a work refers to. A reader who is willing to put out some effort can at least succeed in a basic comprehension of any text.

But there is more to even a good first reading than that. Dictionaries, for example, can only go so far in helping you make sense of the language. They do not tell you much, for instance, about the connotative meanings of words, which depend in great part on the verbal context. To get the connotation of a word, you must be *looking for* such meanings. You must bring to the text the expectation that more than one level of meaning might be at work. And you need to have some experience in seeing how words can bounce off one another, altering each other's connotations. Good reading, that is, is not simply a matter of knowing what the words mean; it requires having a sense of how those words can produce an emotional effect. It also means being open to such effects.

More generally, good reading requires you to build up strong expectations about how literature works. These can be developed by learning to recognize patterns of meaning, so that you will know what to look for. In following the plot of a story, for example, you project into the future as you read, guessing at what will likely follow from the story as you know it so far. If those expectations are fulfilled, then you can speak confidently about the pattern you have helped bring into existence. If they are not fulfilled, you can talk about the breakdown of a pattern that might transform itself into a new configuration. As you gain more experience as a reader, you learn more of what to look for and expect. Your mastery of a text increases. Even a first reading can be very productive, if you are able to work effectively within the systems of meaning that make sense of the text.

Ask Good Questions

In order to transform a first reading into a coherent piece of critical writing, you must focus your thinking. No essay can cover all facets of a literary work. You must concentrate on a few good questions about the text, to see if some pattern of meaning can be produced. Good questions to start with are "How did the experience of reading make me feel?" and "What were my emotional reactions to the characters, the plot, the language itself?" The advantage of these questions is that they can be answered by any reader. After all, who is the expert on your own emotional responses? The more difficult question follows: "What caused those emotions?" Obviously, some of the answers to that question will lead right to you yourself, since each of us has typical patterns of emotional response that come out of our own habits and backgrounds. But you can also look to the text for answers to this question. There are words, for example, that have a sad feel to them, that almost any reader would associate with a mournful mood. By beginning with your emotional reactions, you can move back into the text with something to look for—the origins of those reactions.

Another source of good questions is the literary terminology that has been introduced throughout this book. You could think of each of those terms as a set of questions that can be superimposed on a text. To ask about *character,* for example, will lead to such questions as "Who is the protagonist?" "How do we get to know him or her?" "Do we have direct access to the thoughts and feelings of the character, or are we kept on the outside?" "How do the character's appearance and gestures communicate his or her personality?" Such issues can become the topics of effective critical writing. They are focused enough to allow you to organize your material. And the questions you ask will determine the features of the text to which you should attend. In a poem, for example, if you ask about *imagery,* all the sensory words will appear to be highlighted and begin to relate to one another as you reread. Coming after a careful first reading, such pointed questions will begin the process of organizing your interpretation of the text.

Sometimes, of course, readers are instructed in the kinds of questions they should ask; that is, they are given assignments, topics to pursue. In this case, part of the job has been done for you. A focus has already been superimposed, and your job is to re-examine the text in those terms. But when the topic is open, you must choose the focus—and the best guide to choosing a focus is your own response to the text. Usually what struck you as the most intriguing feature of the text is the one you should follow up. Your essay will then at least stay true to your reading. Perhaps the questions you ask won't get you anywhere, in which case you might need to rethink your response, but usually the focus you think right will serve you well. However you arrive at your focus, the next step is to allow that focus to open up the text for you.

Reread the Text, Looking for Detail

In almost all cases, a first reading of a text is not an adequate basis for good critical writing. Literary language is difficult and rich enough in meaning to call for rereading. Particularly if the second reading is armed with specific questions, you can attend to the text more closely, producing a fuller and more intense reading experience. Even if you have comprehended the text pretty well on the first reading, a rereading will open up new questions and suggest new ways of thinking about the text. There is an ancient truth of literature that the great works will stand up to repeated readings, always giving more opportunities for the production of new meaning. It is very difficult to exhaust the meanings of a literary text. Rereading is therefore essential with the writing process.

As a writer, you must make that rereading as useful as possible. It must, in other words, be a *focused* reading. If you have been assigned a topic, reread the text with the assignment in mind. If you are devising your own topic, reread the text only after you have a good sense of what you want to write about. In either case, the rereading ought to allow you to look for details from the text that are related to the issues you want to pursue. Depending on the questions you raise, you will find new patterns of meaning emerging as you reread. You should make note of those patterns, either by keeping your own notes or by marking the text in ways that will assist your memory. Many good readers mark up texts pretty thoroughly, leaving for themselves a visual reminder of the work they have done.

The results of this note-taking process will become the evidence for the argument your essay will make. What you are looking for are words, passages, and incidents from the text that you can point to in support of your reading. If you are going to claim that Eveline in Joyce's story finds herself in a situation that offers no real alternatives, you should realize that yours is one of many possible positions that could be taken on that question. So you need to be able to point to the story, to the places where your reading was generated. As a writer you need to ask yourself the simple question, "Why do I see the story this way?" The challenge is how to show a reader that it makes sense to read the story as you do. What exactly are the images in a poem, for example, that allow you to claim that its speaker is feeling alienated from nature? What outward signs does a character show that suggest that he or she is insecure? What function does a particular scene play in the comic subplot to a tragic play? Good writing always gets down to the details. So your rereading of the text should produce for you the details you need to make your argument plausible.

Organize Your Argument

Before you write a first draft, it makes sense to have some kind of plan for the entire essay. Writing is a difficult enough task—it is eased by having at least a rough idea of how the essay's argument will develop before you set pen to paper. There are a number of very different ways such plans can be formulated. For some people, a detailed and formal outline works well, in which the evidence is placed in the appropriate paragraph and the entire argument methodically worked out. For other writers, an informal procedure seems to work, in which they simply write out their ideas, allowing themselves to follow the thread of the argument without elaborating or criticizing it. This latter process may produce only a few phrases that will make their way into the final draft, but it allows you to explore your ideas freely. After all, you are not yet at the point where anyone else will see your work, so you can be free to brainstorm, to generate ideas that can later be organized more carefully. In any event, some kind of plan for the essay will make the first draft a lot easier.

The organizational plan that an essay takes can depend on the writer's purpose. One time-honored pattern is an introductory paragraph that presents the essay's main idea, followed by a series of paragraphs that each develop one of the main reasons that the writer can give for his or her belief in that idea, and ending with a paragraph that returns to the main idea, now seen in the light of the evidence that has been presented. This pattern has the advantage of providing clarity and ease for readers. It allows you to organize details logically and to make clear how the evidence supports your claims. But in many cases this format is not appropriate. To take obvious ones, you may be developing an idea that requires a comparison or contrast pattern, or you may want to re-create in a narrative format the process you went through as a reader. The bottom-line requirement here is that you devise an overall structure that will take your readers through a logical process of thought. You want your reading of the text to be presented coherently, with each of your points clearly related to all the others.

One pattern you might want to avoid is a chronological one. That is, you usually do not want to retell or summarize a story, or to paraphrase a poem. Sometimes teachers will assign such a task as a learning tool, but generally if a teacher asks for an analysis of a story, a summary or a paraphrase is not what he or she is looking for. In some cases, say if you are writing about the development of a character over time, a chronological arrangement might be appropriate, but more frequently you want to re-arrange the details of the text in order to use them effectively as evidence in your argument. The order in which details from the text appear in your essay should not depend on the order in which they appear in the text, but rather on the order in which they will best serve the purpose of your essay.

In writing about literature, you are presenting an interpretation, one among many possible. If you can work out that interpretation fully before you write the first draft, you will make your job as a writer easier, and more importantly, you will make your reader's job easier. The result of your planning will be a clearer argument for your interpretation. Your reader will be able to feel a plan being completed, so that your argument will seem compelling and well structured.

Consider Your Audience

Good writers always know their audience. Many of the decisions that writers face get resolved by keeping the audience in mind. What word should I use? Do I need to develop this point more fully? Do I need to define this term? The answers to such questions depend in great part on the writer's estimation of the audience's needs and abilities. In fact, the answers will come easier if the questions are rephrased in terms of the audience. Will the audience understand and respond to a certain word? How much does the audience already know about the point I've raised? Is the term familiar to the audience, or is it too obscure to be useful? Keeping the audience in mind does not mean that you have to abandon your ideas or water them down, but it does mean that effective writing is writing correctly aimed at its audience. Writing puts the writer into a relationship with readers, and it is important to understand the exact nature of this relationship in each piece of writing you do.

Now, who is the audience for writing about literature? For most students the answer to that question is obvious: the teacher. And what is the nature of the relationship between the writer and this audience? The answers to that question, of course, can vary widely, but at least we can say that the relationship is institutionalized and formal. It may have various personal elements as well, but students usually relate to teachers within an academic structure. Judgments are made; grades are given. This suggests that writing about literature is usually a formal kind of writing, not a purely personal writing aimed at the writer himself or herself. Teachers may assign the task of keeping an informal reading journal, in which case more personal writing is allowed, but most writing about literature that happens in the university occurs in formal papers and therefore calls for a more public form of discourse.

This does not have to mean that the writing must be dull and mechanical. But it does mean that such features as grammatical correctness count heavily, and that the reader expects a fully developed and coherent argument. A half-formulated, vague idea jotted down in fragmented form is not going to work. Writing about literature requires that the very personal experience of reading be transformed into a discourse that can be shared with others so that they gain a fully developed picture of that reading experience. The challenge of such writing is to attain this formal quality without losing the personal touch. After all, reading involves a personal commitment. You use your own imagination as you read, you make value judgments that derive from your personal beliefs, and you bring your own experiences to the work. It only makes sense, then, that your writing about literature should be animated by that same personal quality. Writing about literature, in a sense, must be directed in two ways—it must communicate formally with an audience, and it must still express the personal experience of the writer. Notice in the student essays reprinted later, that both are written in a formal, academic style, that both develop a logical and detailed argument. Yet both are lively and personal. You can hear the personalities of the writers as they express themselves in a comfortable yet serious style.

One practical outcome of keeping your audience in mind is that summary and paraphrase do not make sense. If the reader of your essay is the teacher, it is obvious that he or she has read the text you are analyzing. This audience does not need to have the plot restated, or to hear the poem translated into your own words. So unless you are specifically asked to do so, avoid summary and paraphrase. They will only bore the reader and distract you from your goal, which is to explain why you interpret the text in a certain way.

Considering the audience will also help guide you in selecting a focus for critical writing. An audience familiar with your text does not want to hear a bland and obvious reading. Its interest will be held more powerfully if your focus is on a controversial point. Most successful critical writing takes on questions that have many possible answers. Open questions thrust the writer and the reader into a debate, an argument, which gives an edge to the writing. For example, an essay that was out to prove that Eveline was trapped would not produce much controversy—the point is too obvious—but an essay that argued that there was no way out of the trap could attract some disagreement. Its writer would therefore be required to support that assertion, knowing that other readers might well disagree. Focusing the essay on a controversial point involves the audience in the writing, forcing them to judge the power of your argument.

Writing about literature can therefore take some delicate judgment. Your audience is usually a teacher who will be evaluating your work. You are usually writing in an institutional setting, which will lead to a grade and to academic credits. It therefore demands that you produce a finished piece of writing, right down to correct mechanics and footnote format. Yet despite this formality, the best writing about literature is faithful to your personal experience of the text. What you need is a way to achieve both these goals. They can in fact be treated as separate tasks, and in the next two sections I suggest that your first draft be concerned with expressing your personal response as fully as possible, and later drafts be used for worrying about the formal issues of mechanics and format.

Write a First Draft

Following the steps I've outlined here, your writing the first draft should come almost naturally. You have read and reread the text, subjected it to critical questioning, prepared an argument for your interpretation, considered your audience. The kind of first draft I'm proposing will rely on these preliminary steps to allow it to be as free-flowing as possible. The point of this draft is not to produce a finished product, but to fill out the plan for the essay that you have already constructed. The word choice doesn't have to be perfect, the punctuation doesn't have to be exact, the format doesn't have to be complete. But there does have to be a coherent argument, supported by relevant details. And there does have to be an attempt to find the language that will express your emotional response to the text, as well as your analytical interpretation.

The purpose of a first draft is to get your ideas on paper in an organized and detailed way. Writing the first draft allows you to move from a vague and unformed idea to words on a page. No doubt it is the most difficult step for many writers. This is, after all, the point when you must face the blank page, and many writers develop a paralyzing fear of taking this step. But as I said earlier, the step is easier if it has been prepared for thoroughly. If you know where the essay is going before you write, you can write any given section of the draft in the confidence that you know where it fits in your plan. Now this does not mean that you cannot be open to ideas and details that occur to you in the process of writing the draft. This is only a *first* draft, so there is plenty of opportunity for following impulses. You can evaluate them later, in the light of the plan for the essay that you have evolved.

A first draft is your opportunity to work out specifically the argument you want to make. At this stage, you will want to make sure that you have incorporated into your essay the quotes and details from the text that will help make sense of your argument. You should be aware, however, that such evidence does not speak for itself. You might quote a passage that seems to you to support your point, but a reader might see something completely different in the same passage. Therefore, you must comment on your quotations and details, making clear the function they play in your argument. There are rules about using quotes effectively, but while you are writing the first draft you need not worry about such details. They can be taken care of in the process of revision and proofreading.

In general, it is wise to write the first draft without worrying very much about editing for grammar and mechanics. If you are thinking about such issues as you write, you can easily become sidetracked or even paralyzed. Writing a good first draft is difficult enough without giving attention to whether you are spelling all the words correctly or using commas in the right places. In the formal context in which most writing about literature occurs, issues of grammar and mechanics are important, but they are best left to a rewrite stage. Separating these tasks eases the writing process. The *worst* writers, those who have the most difficulty and produce unconvincing arguments, are those who disrupt the flow of the first draft in order to worry over minute details of grammar. These writers are often overly fearful of being "incorrect," and as a result cannot get into a writing rhythm. Leaving such concerns to the last step allows the writing to proceed and the details to get the full attention they deserve.

Revise for Content/Proofread for Correctness

Just as the literary text deserves a rereading, your essay deserves a rewriting. Not only for mechanics and grammar, but also for the opportunity to read your own writing as if it were not your own. Does it have a clear focus? Does it argue its case effectively? Does its language communicate an emotional response to the text? In general, you need to revise your essay to make sure that it represents your thinking as well as possible. A revision might also allow you to incorporate into your essay ideas that have occurred to you during the writing of the first draft. You could also ask your teacher or a fellow student to read your first draft. Often another reader will see problems in argument and expression that would be invisible to the writer. Ultimately, though, you must take final responsibility for your writing.

That responsibility extends to every grammatical problem or format error that the first draft might contain. In a formal essay, such concerns are important. For one thing, such errors distract the reader's attention from what you are trying to say. For another, they may give the impression that you are careless with language, an impression that can be fatal to an essay that depends on convincing its readers that the writer is sensitive to the language of the literary text. There is no question that a well-presented essay has a better chance of affecting a reader positively. Therefore, it is necessary for good writers (about literature or anything else) to have a working knowledge of grammar, punctuation, and spelling—matters, of course, beyond the scope of this chapter. There is no tolerance for sloppiness in this area. There are dictionaries for checking spelling, and grammar handbooks for finding out if a sentence is well constructed. An essay handed in without a careful proofreading for these errors will almost always suffer as a result.

Since quotations from the literary text are used so frequently in support of critical arguments, you must learn the conventions that govern the use of quotations in writing about literature. There are a number of systems that you can use, but here is a simple and flexible set of procedures that are easy for a reader to follow.

First of all, it is essential to identify the sources of all your quotations. I suggest you use this simple method. List all the books you quote from or refer to on a separate sheet at the end of the essay. On this **bibliography** page, provide the books and articles you refer to, their authors and editors, and the place and date of their publication. The point of this procedure is to enable your readers to find the source of your quote if they want to, perhaps in order to decide independently if they agree with your interpretation of the passage. A useful pattern for listing these sources is shown in the example below:

Blake, William. The Poetry and Prose of William Blake. Edited by David V. Erdman. Garden City, N.Y.: Doubleday, 1965.

Wordsworth, William. Selected Poems and Prefaces. Edited by Jack Stillinger. Boston: Houghton Mifflin, 1965.

Note that the list is in alphabetical order by the last names of the authors, and that all the necessary facts are in the same order in each entry. In the body of your essay, each time you quote or refer to a source, follow the reference with, in parentheses, the author's last name and the page on which the passage appears. If you have listed more than one title by the same author, you might use the title of the work and then the page number. In fact, if you are referring over and over again to the same text (which you probably will be in a critical essay), you might devise an abbreviation for the title to use in your parenthetical notes.

This is a very simple system, much easier for readers to follow and for writers to use than traditional reference footnotes. The only footnotes you might need would be comments that are related to your essay but don't fit into its design. For further examples see the student essays reprinted later.

Next, there are some grammatical rules for incorporating quotations into your essay. For a brief quotation, blend the quote smoothly into your own sentence, placing the reference note immediately after the quote. As an example:

In "Eveline" Joyce describes Frank as "kind, manly, open hearted" (Dubliners 22), traits seldom shown in her father's character.

For longer passages (more than three lines of verse or fifty words of prose), the convention is to indent the entire passage seven to ten spaces:

```
Blake's concept of Innocence is illustrated

clearly in the second stanza of "The Shepherd":

    For he hears the lamb's innocent call,

    And he hears the ewe's tender reply;

    He is watchful while they are in peace,

    For they know when their Shepherd is
       nigh.

The speaker sees the shepherd's life in

completely positive terms, as perfectly at one

with the natural world.
```

Notice that this quoted passage is not in quotation marks—the indentation is the sign that the words are being quoted. In either pattern, you must show how the quote is related to the point that your own argument is making.

There are a couple of other conventions to keep in mind. If you are quoting in the midst of your sentence a short passage of poetry that happens to run over the end of a line in the poem, you indicate where the line breaks by using a slash (/):

```
In "Sailing to Byzantium" Yeats clearly feels

jealous of "the young / In one another's arms."
```

Also, if you wish to leave out unnecessary words in the midst of a quote, you can indicate their absence by the use of three dots, called an ellipsis (. . .):

```
Lawrence tells us that the doctor in "The Horse

Dealer's Daughter" fears love so much that "The
```

word cost him a painful effort. . . . the saying seemed to tear open again his newly torn heart."

There are, of course, a lot of other rules and conventions that apply to writing about literature. The few I have mentioned are basic ones I feel you need to know now. If you are writing a lengthy, formal paper, I suggest you refer to the *MLA Handbook for Writers of Research Papers* as a guide to these rules. Your instructor may also impose certain procedures and formats, in which case his or her rules should be followed.

STUDENT ESSAYS

The following two essays, written by students, take on topics in poetry and fiction that you might well encounter in an introductory course. They have the virtue of developing an argument in a formal manner while still maintaining a personal voice. They also use details from the texts effectively as evidence in their arguments. Note especially how the students incorporate quotations into their own writing.

"Jesus Loves Me, This I Know"

One of the most wonderful things about childhood is the belief that everyone and everything in your world is beautiful. When you fall down and scrape your knee, Mama will kiss it and make it better. Most children live in a warm cocoon of their parents' love, away from the cruelty of "the real world." In Blake's poem "The Divine Image," the speaker is innocent and childlike in that he believes mankind is always compassionate—even that man is Godlike. "The

Divine Image" represents the state of innocence. A more experienced person would see that man and his world have the potential for both good and bad.

The world of "The Divine Image" is Utopian. The God of Blake's Songs of Innocence is benevolent and patriarchal. He is the complete antithesis of the judgmental God the Blake of experience saw, with his churches, commandments, and priests who make a crime of love, "binding with briars my joys and desires" (Blake 111). Instead of being vengeful and restrictive, the God of innocence will always watch over his children and answer their every prayer: "To Mercy, Pity, Peace, and Love/All pray in their distress" (Blake 91). There is no need for a vengeful God. Since he created man in his own image, and since God in "The Divine Image" is perfect, so are his children, mankind: "and Mercy, Pity, Peace, and Love/Is Man, his child and care" (Blake 91).

Wouldn't it be terrific to be an adult and still be able to adhere to the innocent belief that all mankind is Godlike? Experience disillusions us about our world and shows us that people die in wars and children are abused — life cannot always be as wonderful as we would like it to be. There are times when one wonders if there can be a God at all because of all the terrible things that happen in the world. Merely turning on the evening news raises a thousand questions about exactly how "merciful" our world is. Life is not what "The Divine Image" would have it be — mankind is not perfect and neither is the world we live in.

Because man is imperfect, he doesn't generally embody the Christian ethic or spout forth mercy and love. Despite the fact that man should, as "The Divine Image" asserts, "love the human form,/In heathen, turk, or jew" (Blake 91), we are frequently prejudiced against anyone different from ourselves. All the virtues are certainly not seated in the human form one hundred percent of the time.

It is necessary to grow out of this innocent belief that one's world is always going to be idyllic. The world is neither always as cruel as depicted in the _Songs of Experience_, or as Utopian as presented in "The Divine Image" and the _Songs of Innocence_. The world is a blend of both, and the innocent views of "The Divine Image" must be abandoned before change can happen. God will not always answer our prayers for a better world -- we must learn to answer them ourselves.

Susan Shoemaker

Bibliography

Blake, William. _The Portable Blake._ Edited by Alfred Kazin. New York: Penguin Books, 1976.

Narrative Technique in "The Open Boat"

In times of trial, few men remain emotionally unmoved. The narrator of Stephen Crane's "The Open Boat" reflects the myriad emotions of men stranded at sea. The narrator's attitude towards the four prisoners of the ocean changes from one of cynicism and despair to one of hope and respect. This change in attitude is related to a change in perspective. Removed from the scene at first, the narrator later views events through the correspondent's eyes, changing point of view from third person omniscient to third person limited.

When the narrator begins his tale, the dialogue is sparse and choppy. Although one would not expect overly intellectual statements from sailors, conversation mainly consists of disjointed phrases and childlike bickering. The cook and the correspondent, differing over the exact nature of a house of refuge, find nothing better to say than "Oh, yes, they do" and "No, they don't" (Crane 142). The narrator paints the scene with an air of tension and despair, using the arguments and expletives that abound in the boat. He is but an amused witness to pointless disagreements. He does not focus on and identify with the men's thoughts. The removed perspective indicates a lack of concern, for the narrator lends the men no sympathy when watching from afar.

The narrator's cynical side is revealed by

his extensive comments on the ocean. He devotes a great deal of time to the power of the water: "after successfully surmounting one wave you discover that there is another behind it" (Crane 141). He gives pessimistic advice and comment, but gives no credit to human intelligence and determination. He never allows the reader to forget the indifferent hand of nature, waiting to smite the "four waifs [riding] impudently in their little boat" (Crane 147) with waves "most wrongfully and barbarously abrupt and tall" (Crane 140). He feels that nature is taunting the men with the hope of survival. After the men sight a remote coast with its deadly surf, he describes their rage: "If I am going to be drowned, . . . why in the name of the seven mad gods who rule the sea, was I allowed to come thus far and contemplate sand and trees?"(Crane 148). The narrator believes that nature is playing with the men, and he himself does nothing except belittle them.

As the story progresses, the narrator's harsh attitude softens. Weariness has silenced the men's mouths, so the narrator explores the thoughts of the correspondent. When the correspondent remembers and identifies with a poem about the dying soldier of Algiers, his experience is described as "no longer merely a picture of a few throes in the breast of a poet" (Crane 157). He can see the soldier dying; he can see himself dying. The narrator now recognizes the solemn struggle the men face, speculating that the dance with death would prompt one to "mend his conduct and his words" (Crane 160) if given another chance at life. By looking through the correspondent's eyes, the narrator obtains a more emotional perspective.

In contrast to his earlier diatribes against the helpless men, the narrator expresses an attitude of respect, an appreciation of the tenuousness of life. He writes that the correspondent thinks drowning "would be a shame" (Crane 160) after holding on for so long. The final effort in the surf is described in a hopeful manner, as the man on the shore who shines "like a saint" (Crane 163) pulls the correspondent from the ocean's grip. The narrator credits man for struggling and banding together to overcome nature. He states, "the wind brought the sound of the great sea's voice to the men on shore, and they felt that they could then be interpreters" (Crane 164). Nature is still indifferent, and they may have escaped by luck as well as effort, yet the narrator no longer views them as amusing pawns on a watery chessboard, but as fellow men.

The attitude of the narrator of "The Open Boat" changes from a pessimistic, cynical outlook to one of optimism and hope. The narrator begins the tale removed from the scene, but he is drawn in by the plight of his fellow humans. By identifying with the correspondent and sympathizing with the other sailors, he becomes the fifth man to ride the open boat.

Tim Cook

Bibliography

Crane, Stephen. The Red Badge of Courage and Selected Stories. Edited by R. W. Stallman. New York: New American Library, 1960.

GLOSSARY OF LITERARY TERMS

alliteration A technique for creating verbal music by repeating the same consonantal sound. In Wilfred Owen's "Anthem for Doomed Youth," he describes the "stutte*r*ing *r*ifles' *r*apid *r*attle," thus creating out of the repeated *r* sounds a music that mimics the sound of the rifles themselves. (p. 56)

anapestic A metrical unit characterized by the rhythmic pattern *unstressed, unstressed, stressed.* "In the heat of the night" is a phrase with two anapestic units. (p. 58)

antagonist In a traditional plot, the opponent of the *protagonist* or hero of the story. The antagonist may be a villain or it may be some impersonal force with which the hero must struggle. (p. 344, 912)

assonance A repetition of vowel sounds in poetry. An example from a poem by Emily Dickinson: "M*i*ne—by the R*i*ght of the Wh*i*te Election!" When two words related by assonance occur at the end of succeeding lines, they create *rhyme.* (p. 56)

ballad A story told in verse. The ballad stanza is a four-line unit, in which the second and fourth lines rhyme. Ballads have been told and sung in the folk tradition for hundreds of years, and many poets have created ballads as well. (p. 60)

bibliography A list of books and articles that served as sources for a writer's words or ideas. In writing about literature, the bibliography should include any critical works that the writer may have consulted, as well as the literary works that the writer has quoted. (p. 1446)

character The fictional people who are the agents of the actions in poetry, plays, and stories. Characters may be complex and fully developed, or they may be simple and superficial. One of the tasks of the reader is to understand how the story allows us to come to know its characters. (p. 375)

climax The point where the conflict within a plot is resolved by a confrontation between the two opposing forces. This is the moment when the protagonist has to face the antagonist in a final conflict, as when the men in "The Open Boat" must battle the surf at the end of their ordeal. (p. 912)

closed form A poetic form defined by a pre-established set of rules, such as a given stanza form, rhythm, or rhyme scheme. Examples of closed forms are sonnets, ballads, and villanelles. (p. 52) See also *open form.*

comedy A type of play or story that sets up readers or audiences to expect that the plot will end positively, and that the actions and characters of the work will be amusing or laughable. (p. 916)

complication The process in the plot by which the opposing forces are brought into conflict. The complication is the logical continuation of the *exposition* of those forces, and leads logically to the *climax.* (p. 912)

connotation An aspect of meaning that emphasizes a word's emotional power. The connotative meaning of a word shapes the reader's emotional response to the object or event being described. Calling a homeless person a *bum* imposes on that person a negative connotation. (p. 23)

couplet A two-line unit of verse, often rhymed and sometimes set off as a stanza. A couplet is the last unit of a Shakespearean *sonnet.* (p. 60)

dactylic A metrical unit characterized by the rhythmic pattern *stressed, unstressed, unstressed.* The word game "higgledy piggledy" sends you looking for double dactyls. (p. 58)

denotation The aspect of meaning by which a word names a category of objects or experiences. *Prison* and *correctional facility* have roughly the same denotative meaning—both words describe the same kind of facility—but the *connotations* or emotional associations of *prison* are much harsher. (p. 23)

denouement The outcome of the conflict in the plot. The denouement of a story shows what the effects of the conflict have been. In "Guests of the Nation," for example, the denouement is brief but suggestive. After his involvement in the killing, the main character tells us, "Anything that happened to me afterwards, I never felt the same about again." (p. 912)

dialogue The spoken language of characters in a play or story. One of the primary techniques for revealing character. Dialogue in a play allows various characters to express their points of view without authorial interruption. (p. 377, 907)

dimeter A poetic line having two metrical feet. An example of iambic dimeter from Heather McHugh's "Language Lesson, 1976": "the rich prepare/to serve, to fault." (p. 58)

end-stopped A line of poetry in which the sense of the language comes to a conclusion at the end of the line. Gives a feeling of completion and closure. (p. 59)

enjambment A situation in poetry in which the sense of the language flows over the end of the line, creating a feeling of incompleteness and expectation that hurries the reader on to the next line in order to get the conclusion of the thought. (p. 59)

exposition The introduction of the opposing forces in a plot. The story tells us what those forces are and why they are in conflict. The exposition sets out the terms from which the rest of the plot develops. (p. 912)

figure of speech Also called a *trope,* a use of language that twists or distorts the usual meaning of a word. A figure of speech applies a word to a context in which it is not proper. To call a traitor a *snake* is to use the word outside its proper or literal meaning, applying to the traitor the characteristics of the snake. (p. 31) See also *metaphor, metonymy, personification, simile.*

first-person narration A form of narration in which the teller of the story is also a character in the story. First-person narration tends to involve readers in the story as they identify with its teller. First-person narrators tend to tell stories in intense, vivid detail, and they tend to interpret events in terms of their own value systems. Sherwood Anderson's "I Want to Know Why" is an excellent example of this technique. (p. 458)

hexameter A poetic line having six metrical feet. (p. 58)

iambic A metrical unit characterized by the rhythmic pattern *unstressed, stressed.* Iambic meter is considered the closest to the rhythm of normal speech, so it is often used in verse plays like Shakespeare's. (p. 58)

image Language used to describe a sensory experience, so that the reader will be able to imagine an object or event in detail. Imagistic language can appeal to any of the senses. Visual detail is extremely important in many poems, but aural images as well as images that appeal to touch and even smell can contribute to a poem's attempt to put its readers into a particular place and moment. (p. 39)

interpretation The process by which readers make sense of a text and construct its meanings. Typically, poems and stories and plays do not directly announce their meanings; they tell a story or describe a scene. Readers must do the work of interpretation in order to get at the meanings that the literary work leaves implicit. The term *interpretation* suggests that different readers will come up with different meanings, since there is always a personal element in reading. This does not mean that any interpretation is allowable—it still must relate to the language of the literary text. (p. 10)

metaphor A figure of speech by which two different terms are asserted to be identical. If I say, "Her speech was a riot," you know that *riot* is not being used in its proper or literal sense, but rather that it suggests the extreme response that her speech received. Some metaphors are so common in our language that they become invisible ("she is a *deep* thinker"). Others, such as the elaborate metaphors of the poet John Donne, draw attention to themselves and require a serious effort on the part of readers to make sense of them. (p. 33)

metonymy A figure of speech in which an object or person is spoken of in terms of some other object that is associated with it. "The crown" is a metonymy for a king; "the White House" is a metonymy for the president in such phrases as "the White House announced . . ." (p. 34)

monometer A poetic line having one metrical foot. In William Carlos Williams's "Young Woman at a Window," most of the lines are monometer. (p. 58)

narrative style The sum total of the narrative decisions—such as who will tell the story, how much detail will be revealed, how time will be handled, how much interpretation of events will be offered—that determine exactly how the story will be told. The accumulation of these decisions gives readers a sense of the identity of the narrator's mind. In Faulkner's "That Evening Sun," for example, the fact that the story is told fifteen years later but still with intense detail suggests the continuing importance of the event in the life of the narrator. (p. 457)

narrator The teller of a story. The concept is important to counteract the commonsensical assumption that the voice telling a story is that of its author. A narrator is a fictional character, a creation of the author. The narrator may be directly involved in the story's action or may be detached, serving merely as a storyteller. (p. 457) See also *first-person narration, third-person narration, omniscient narrator,* and *unreliable narrator*.

omniscient narrator A storyteller who literally knows all the details of the story. Such a narrator has access to the thoughts and feelings of every character, and has knowledge of all the events related to the story. An omniscient narrator is an almost godlike figure who is capable of knowledge that would not be available in real experience. (p. 458)

open form Poetry in an open form is *not* poetry without form, which is a contradiction in terms, but poetry that makes up its own form for the occasion. See, for example, the poem by William Carlos Williams called "Young Woman at a Window," which does not follow the pattern of any pre-existing form but rather sets up its own rules of operation. (p. 52)

pentameter A poetic line having five metrical feet. The most common kind of line in English poetry. (p. 58)

personification A figure of speech by which an inanimate object is given human characteristics. This is a common technique in poetry—see William Wordsworth's "Lines Written in Early Spring"—and is also common in ordinary language, where we casually personify the world in such phrases as "an indifferent sky" or "an angry wind." (p. 34)

plot The arrangement of actions in a story. The term *plot* emphasizes the relationships between events, the cause-and-effect dynamics of the story. In most stories, the plot deals with a conflict between opposing forces, showing how those forces come to clash and what the results of that struggle are. Not all stories have a coherent plot, but most stories work out the implications of their conflict in a very logical manner. (p. 344)

propaganda The use of literature for political purposes, especially where all subtlety of characterization and plot is sacrificed so that the political message comes through clearly. Many—perhaps all—stories have a political dimension in the sense that they express a set of values, but propaganda begins with a set of values and constructs a story that does no more than embody them. (p. 565)

proscenium arch A type of stage in which the space for the play is separated from the audience by the plane of the curtain, hanging from the proscenium arch. That plane is also called the "fourth wall," because it can be thought of as an invisible wall through which we are able to look into the scene being presented. This type of stage is best suited for *realistic* drama, which wants to trick the audience into believing that it is watching real events. (p. 1294)

protagonist The main character in a plot; the person toward whom our interests and sympathies are directed. See also *antagonist,* which is the force the protagonist comes into conflict with. The protagonist is usually but not always a hero. In a story like "The Chaste Clarissa" by John Cheever, the protagonist, Baxter, is a cold and manipulative man, but Cheever forces us to direct our interest toward Baxter so that we can come to understand what motivates such a person. (p. 344, 912)

purgation According to Aristotle, *purgation* is the effect of tragedy. That is, tragedies incite very negative feelings, such as fear and sorrow, in order to allow us to make sense of them and get rid of their negative effects. A tragedy is therefore a kind of cleansing. It allows us to get rid of excessive negative emotions and restore ourselves to emotional balance. (p. 915)

quatrain A four-line unit of poetry, often constituting a stanza. A Shakespearean *sonnet,* for example, consists of three quatrains and a concluding *couplet.* A *ballad* stanza is also a quatrain. (p. 60)

realism A type of play or story that attempts to convince the reader or audience that the events being described are real. *Realistic* literature tries to cover over its status as an imaginative product. (p. 1291). See also *spectacular theater,* which in opposite approach draws attention to itself as a play, making no pretense of presenting reality.

rhyme A poetic device in which the last words of succeeding lines of verse are similar in sound, usually sharing the same vowel sound as well as the same consonant following the vowel. Rhyme is usually a feature of serious poetry in traditional, *closed forms.* Some forms, such as the *sonnet* or the *villanelle,* require a specific rhyme scheme, or pattern of rhyming lines. (p. 57)

rhythm The pattern of sound produced by accented and unaccented syllables. For specific patterns, see also *anapestic, dactylic, iambic,* and *trochaic.* Rhythm produces subtle effects in readers of poetry, working on their emotions even without the readers' conscious attention. (p. 58)

satire A form of comedy that arouses and directs readers' aggressions against a ridiculous target, usually a pretentious or hypocritical person who stands in the way of the happiness of the main characters. (p. 918) See also *sentimental comedy*.

script The written document produced by a playwright that forms the basis for a theatrical production. A script usually consists of *dialogue*—the language that the characters use—and stage directions, which sometimes include elaborate descriptions of the set for the drama, the costumes for the characters, and the physical actions that the characters perform. (p. 906)

sentimental comedy A form of comedy that emphasizes the happiness of characters who achieve unity with one another. Often the plot of a comedy leads to a moment of unity, and the warm feeling that this moment produces is the sentimental essence of the play. (p. 918)

setting The physical and social situation in which the action of a story or play occurs. Setting can reveal aspects of *character* in that we can understand a person by seeing the environment he or she inhabits. Setting can also affect the *plot* in that actions are changed by the situation in which they occur. (p. 408)

simile A figure of speech that asks the reader to compare two objects, people, or ideas. In a simile such as "My love is like a red, red rose," the reader is asked to think about characteristics of the rose—beauty, freshness, naturalness—and to apply them to the beloved. In extreme cases, a simile can ask the reader to compare two terms that seem to have almost nothing in common. (p. 33)

slant rhyme A poetic effect in which the last words of two succeeding lines recall each other in sound but are not exact rhymes. Exact rhymes tend to create full stops in the flow of the poetry, whereas slant rhymes create only slight pauses that allow the flow to proceed. (p. 57)

soliloquy A speech in a play delivered by a character who is alone on stage. Sometimes the speech is the private thoughts of the character, overheard by the audience, but sometimes the soliloquy is delivered directly to the audience, as though the character were admitting that he or she is in a play rather than in real life. (p. 1291)

sonnet A fourteen-line poetic form that has been one of the most frequently used forms in the history of poetry. There are two major kinds of sonnet: the Petrarchan or Italian sonnet, which has an eight-line unit called an octave and a six-line unit called a sestet; and the English or Shakespearean sonnet, which consists of three *quatrains* and a *couplet*. (p. 60)

speaker The (fictional) person who is the source of the language of a poem. In some cases, as in Thomas Hardy's "The Man He Killed," the speaker is obviously not the author but rather a character that the author has created. In all poetry, one of the tasks of the reader is to construct out of the language of the poem an image of the person who is responsible for it. (p. 67)

spectacular theater A theatrical performance that draws attention to itself as a play and does not attempt to convince its reader or audience that it is depicting reality. Such plays pursue a tactic opposite to that of *realism,* which attempts to catch its audience in the illusion that it is witnessing real life. (p. 1291)

stanza A grouping of lines in a poem. See also *couplet* and *quatrain.* The form of a given stanza may be predetermined by tradition or may be created for the occasion by the poet. (p. 60)

style An author's characteristic manner of writing. Style includes such elements as the author's typical choice of words—simple or complicated, formal or informal, familiar or strange—and how the author arranges words into sentences—simple or complex sentences, straightforward or difficult to follow. The style of a text is a powerful clue to the personality of its *narrator* or *speaker.* (p. 516)

tetrameter A poetic line having four metrical feet. The typical line of the *ballad* stanza. (p. 58)

theater-in-the-round A design for theaters in which the stage is in the midst of the audience. Unlike the situation with a *proscenium arch* stage, theater-in-the-round constantly reminds the audience that it is at a play, not observing reality. Such a design therefore serves the needs of *spectacular theater.* (p. 1294)

third-person narration A form of narration in which the person who tells the story is *not* a character in the plot. A third-person narrator tells a story in which he or she was not involved, often speaking with a sense of detachment or objectivity. Some third-person narrators are *omniscient,* able to see into the lives of all the characters; some are limited to seeing the world mainly through the mind of one particular character. (p. 458)

tragedy A play that ends with the destruction of its hero. That destruction may be brought about by fate, as in *Oedipus Rex,* or by a weakness in the character, as in *King Lear.* (p. 915) See also *purgation,* which describes the effect of tragedy on its audience.

tragicomedy A play that combines *tragedy* and *comedy,* usually out of the conviction that life also combines both emotions. Sean O'Casey's *The Plough and the Stars* is a good example. (p. 918)

trimeter A poetic line having three metrical feet. (p. 58)

trochaic A metrical unit characterized by the rhythmic pattern *stressed, unstressed.* (p. 58)

unreliable narrator A teller of a story whose interpretation of events cannot be trusted, because he or she either does not know all the facts or cannot respond to them objectively. The point of creating such a narrator is to remind readers that their view of the events of the story is always the result of the narrator's interpretation, and that interpretation can be misleading. (p. 459)

villanelle An elaborate poetic form composed of five three-line *stanzas* and one *quatrain*. The poem uses only two *rhymes*, and it repeats line one in lines six, twelve, and eighteen, and repeats line three in lines nine, fifteen, and nineteen. (p. 60) See discussion of Dylan Thomas's "Do Not Go Gentle into That Good Night" in Chapter Five of Part Two.

Copyrights and Acknowledgments

The author is grateful to the following publishers and copyright holders for permission to reprint material in this book.

POETRY

Ahsahta Press. For "The Red Fox" by Marnie Walsh. From *A Taste of the Knife*, copyright 1976 by Ahsahta Press at Boise State University.

American Poetry Review. For "Pick-Up" by Philip Booth. First published in *The American Poetry Review*. Reprinted with permission.

Appalachian Journal. For "Get In, Jesus" by Jim Webb. Copyright 1984, *Appalachian Journal*.

Star Black. For "Really" by Star Black. First published in *The American Poetry Review*, Vol. 15/No. 2, March/April 1986. Reprinted with permission.

Robert Bly. For "Waking from Sleep" by Robert Bly. Reprinted from *Silence in the Snowy Fields*, Wesleyan University Press, 1962. Copyright 1962. Reprinted with permission of Robert Bly.

Carnegie-Mellon University. For "Beached Whales Off Margate" by Stephen Dunn. Reprinted from *A Circus of Needs*, by permission of Carnegie-Mellon University Press. Copyright 1978 by Stephen Dunn.

Raymond Carver. For "Photograph of My Father in His Twenty-Second Year" by Raymond Carver. From *At Night the Salmon Move*, Capra Press, 1983. Copyright by Raymond Carver and used by permission of the author.

The David Company. For "Kitchenette Building" by Gwendolyn Brooks. Reprinted from *Blacks*, published by the David Company. Reprinted with permission of Gwendolyn Brooks.

Doubleday & Company. For "Cuttings" and "Cuttings (Later)" by Theodore Roethke. From *The Collected Poems of Theodore Roethke*, copyright 1948 by Theodore Roethke. Reprinted by permission of Doubleday & Company.

E. P. Dutton & Company, Inc. For "Decoy" from *The Double Dream of Spring* by John Ashbery. Copyright 1966, 1967, 1968, 1969, 1970, by John Ashbery. Reprinted by permission of Georges Borchardt, Inc. for John Ashbery.

The Ecco Press. For "Mirror" from *Descending Figure* by Louise Glück. Copyright 1976, 1977, 1978, 1979, 1980 by Louise Glück. Published by The Ecco Press in 1980. Reprinted by permission.

Elpenor Books. For "Four Brothers" by W. S. Di Piero. Reprinted by permission of Elpenor Books.

Lynn Emanuel. For "Frying Trout while Drunk" from *Hotel Fiesta* by Lynn Emanuel. Published by University of Georgia Press, 1984. Reprinted by permission of Lynn Emanuel.

Farrar, Straus and Giroux, Inc. Reprinted by permission of Farrar, Straus and Giroux, Inc.: "Cartography" from *Collected Poems* by Louise Bogan. Copyright 1954 by Louise Bogan. Copyright renewed 1982 by Madie Alexander Scannell. "Making Strange" from *Station Island* by Seamus Heaney. Copyright 1985 by

Henry Holt and Company. For "To an Athlete Dying Young," "Eight O'Clock," "With Rue My Heart Is Laden," and "Loveliest of Trees, the Cherry Now" from *The Collected Poems of A. E. Housman* by A. E. Housman. Copyright 1965 by Holt, Rinehart, and Winston, Inc. For "Design," "After Apple-Picking," "Out, Out—," and "Stopping by Woods on a Snowy Evening" from *The Poetry of Robert Frost* by Robert Frost, edited by Edward Connery Lathem. Copyright 1969 by Holt, Rinehart, and Winston, Inc. Copyright 1962 by Robert Frost. Copyright 1975 by Lesley Frost Ballantine. All reprinted by permission of Henry Holt and Company, Inc.

Houghton Mifflin Company. For "The Fundamental Project of Technology" from *The Past* by Galway Kinnell. Copyright 1985 by Galway Kinnell. For "She Didn't Even Wave" from *Killing Floor* by Ai. Copyright 1979 by Ai. For "The Moss of His Skin" from *To Bedlam and Part Way Back* by Anne Sexton. Copyright 1969 by Anne Sexton. For "Language Lessons" from *A World of Difference* by Heather McHugh. Copyright 1981 by Heather McHugh. All reprinted by permission of Houghton Mifflin Company.

The Kenyon Review. For "Running the River Lines" by David Baker. First published in *The Kenyon Review—New Series,* Fall 1984, Vol. VI, No. 4. Copyright 1984 by Kenyon College. Reprinted by permission of David Baker and *The Kenyon Review*.

Phoebe Lamore. For "Spelling" by Margaret Atwood. Copyright 1981 and reprinted by permission of Margaret Atwood.

Little, Brown and Company. For "An Elegy for Bob Marley" from *A Happy Childhood* by William Matthews. Copyright 1983 by William Matthews. First appeared in *Crazy Horse.* Reprinted by permission of Little, Brown and Company in association with The Atlantic Monthly Press.

Liveright Publishing Corporation. For "Buffalo Bill's Defunct" and "in Just-" from *Tulips & Chimneys* by E. E. Cummings, edited by George James Firmage. Reprinted by permission of Liveright Publishing Corporation. Copyright 1923, 1925, and renewed 1951, 1953 by E. E. Cummings. Copyright 1973, 1976 by the Trustees for the E. E. Cummings Trust. Copyright 1973, 1976 by George James Firmage.

Louisiana State University Press. For "Old Bibles" from *For the Body* by Marilyn Waniek. Copyright 1978 by Marilyn Waniek. Reprinted by permission of Louisiana State University Press.

Macmillan Publishing Company. For "After Greece" from *Water Street* by James Merrill. Copyright 1962 by James Merrill. For "Sometimes Heaven Is a Mean Machine" from *Reasons for Going It on Foot* by William Pitt Root. Copyright 1981 by William Pitt Root. Both reprinted by permission of Atheneum Publishers, an imprint of Macmillan Publishing Company. For "An Egyptian Pulled Glass Bottle in the Shape of a Fish," "Poetry," and "To a Snail" from *Collected Poems* by Marianne Moore. Copyright 1935 Marianne Moore, renewed 1963 by Marianne Moore and T. S. Eliot. For "The Mind Is an Enchanting Thing" from *Collected Poems* by Marianne Moore. Copyright 1944, renewed 1972 by Marianne Moore. For "The Fisherman" and "The Wild Swans at Coole" from *Collected Poems* by W. B. Yeats. Copyright 1919 by Macmillan, renewed 1947 by Bertha Georgie Yeats. For "Easter 1916," "A Prayer for My Daughter," and "The Second Coming" by W. B. Yeats. Copyright 1924 by Macmillan, renewed 1952 by Bertha Georgie Yeats. For "Among School Children," "Leda and the Swan," and "Sailing to Byzantium" by W. B. Yeats. Copyright 1928 by Macmillan, renewed 1956 by Bertha Georgie Yeats. For "Crazy Jane Talks with the Bishop" by W. B. Yeats. Copyright 1933 by Macmillan, renewed 1961 by Georgie Yeats. For "Lapis Lazuli," "Long Legged Fly," and "The Wild Old Wicked Man" by W. B. Yeats. Copyright 1940 by Georgie Yeats, renewed 1968 by Bertha Georgie Yeats, Michael Butler Yeats, and Anne Yeats. All reprinted with permission of Macmillan Publishing Company. For "Adam's Curse," "The Folly of Being Comforted," "The Lake Isle of Innisfree," "The Stolen Child," and "Who Goes with Fergus?" reprinted from *Collected Poems* by W. B. Yeats (New York: Macmillan, 1956). For "Hap" and "The Man He Killed" reprinted from *The Complete Poems of Thomas Hardy*, edited by James Gibson (New York: Macmillan, 1978).

Modern Poetry Association. For "The River" by Raymond Carver, from *Poetry,* June 1986; "Mother's Day" by Robert A. Fink, from *Poetry,* May 1986; "Understanding Poetry" by Marie Boroff, from *Poetry,* July 1986; "A Film" by Albert Goldbarth, from *Poetry,* November 1982; "Frying Trout while Drunk" by Lynn Emanuel, from *Poetry,* May 1983. Copyright 1982, 1983, 1986, by The Modern Poetry Association. All the above works first appeared in *Poetry* and are reprinted by permission of the Editor of *Poetry*.

William Morrow & Company, Inc. For "Sign for My Father, Who Stressed the Bunt" from *In a U-Haul North of Damascus* and "Under the Boat House" by David Bottoms. Copyright 1983 by David Bottoms. For "Ego Tripping" from *The Women and the Men* by Nikki Giovanni. Copyright 1973, 1975 by Nikki Giovanni. Reprinted by permission of William Morrow & Company, Inc.

New Directions Publishing Corp. For "Queen Anne's Lace," "Nantucket," "This Is Just To Say," "Spring and All," "The Red Wheelbarrow," and "Young Woman at a Window" by William Carlos Williams, from *Collected Poems, Volume I: 1909–1939.* Copyright 1938 by New Directions Publishing Corp. For "A Sort of Song" by William Carlos Williams, from *Collected Later Poems.* Copyright 1944 by William Carlos Williams. For "Anthem for Doomed Youth" and "Futility" by Wilfred Owen, from *The Collected Poems of Wilfred Owen.* Copyright 1963 by Chatto & Windus Ltd. For "The Sea Rose" and "Sea Poppies" by H. D. from *Collected Poems 1912–1944.* Copyright 1982 by the Estate of Hilda Doolittle. For "Heat" by H. D., from *Selected Poems.* Copyright 1957 by Norman Holmes Pearson. For "In a Station of the Metro" by Ezra Pound, from *Personae.* Copyright 1926 by Ezra Pound. For "Fern Hill" and "Do not go gentle into that good night" by Dylan Thomas, from *The Poems of Dylan Thomas.* Copyright 1952 by Dylan Thomas, 1945 by the Trustees for the Copyrights of Dylan Thomas. For "Not Waving but Drowning" and "How Cruel Is the Story of Eve" by Stevie Smith, from *Collected Poems.* Copyright 1972 by Stevie Smith. For "O Taste and See," "In Mind," "The World Outside," and "Stepping Westward" by Denise Levertov, from *Poems 1960–1967.* Copyright 1961, 1963, 1964, 1966 by Denise Levertov Goodman. "In Mind" was first published in *Poetry.* All reprinted by permission of New Directions Publishing Corporation.

New England Review. For "Starlight Scope Myopia" by Yusef Komunyakaa from *New England Review and Bread Loaf Quarterly,* Vol. 7, No. 1. For "Homage to Elvis, Homage to the Fathers" by Bruce Weigl from *New England Review and Bread Loaf Quarterly,* Vol. 5, No. 1. Reprinted by permission of *NER and BLQ.*

W. W. Norton & Company, Inc. For "Corsons Inlet," reprinted from *Collected Poems, 1951–1971* by A. R. Ammons, by permission of W. W. Norton & Company, Inc. Copyright 1972 by A. R. Ammons. For "Now That I Am Forever with Child" from *Coal* by Audre Lorde, reprinted with the permission of W. W. Norton & Company, Inc. Copyright 1968, 1970, 1976 by Audre Lorde. For "Aunt Jennifer's Tigers," "The Knight," "From a Survivor," and "Power," reprinted from *The Fact of a Doorframe, Poems Selected and New, 1950–1984* by Adrienne Rich, by permission of W. W. Norton & Company, Inc. Copyright 1984 by Adrienne Rich. Copyright 1975, 1978 by W. W. Norton & Company, Inc. Copyright 1981 by Adrienne Rich.

Gregory Orr. For "Morning Song" by Gregory Orr. Copyright 1980 and permission to reprint by Gregory Orr.

Simon Ortiz. For "Story of How a Wall Stands" from *Going for the Rain* by Simon Ortiz. Copyright 1976, Harper & Row Publishers. Reprinted by permission of the author.

The Overlook Press. For "Miami" from *The Book of Fortune* by Daniel Mark Epstein. Copyright 1982 by Daniel Mark Epstein. Published by The Overlook Press, Lewish Hollow Rd., Woodstock, New York.

Oxford University Press. For "A Consumer's Report" from *Collected Poems (1983)* by Peter Porter. Copyright Peter Porter 1983. Reprinted by permission of Oxford University Press.

Princeton University Press. For "Upon a Spider Catching a Fly" and "Huswifery" by Edward Taylor from *Political Works of Edward Taylor,* edited with an Introduction and Notes by Thomas H. Johnson. Copyright 1939 by Rockland, 1943 by Princeton University Press. For "Reading Plato," which first appeared in *American Poetry Review,* and "History," which first appeared in *Ironwood,* by Jorie Graham from *Erosion.* Copyright 1983 by Princeton University Press. For "Learning to Type," which first appeared in *Berkeley Poetry Review,* by Diana O Hehir from *The Power to Change Geography.* Copyright 1979 by Princeton University Press. For "Concepts and Their Bodies," which first appeared in *Poetry,* by Pattiann Rogers from *Expectations of Light.* Copyright 1981 by Princeton University Press. All poems reprinted with permission of Princeton University Press.

Random House, Inc., Alfred A. Knopf, Inc. For "Fast Break" and "Dawn Walk" from *Wild Gratitude* by Edward Hirsch. Copyright 1985 by Edward Hirsch. For "Anecdote of the Jar," "The Death of a Soldier," and "The Snow Man" by Wallace Stevens. Copyrights 1923 and all renewed 1951 by Wallace Stevens. For "The Idea of Order at Key West" by Wallace Stevens. Copyright 1936 by Wallace Stevens and renewed 1964 by Holly Stevens. Reprinted from *The Collected Poems of Wallace Stevens.* For "Archaeology" from *Antarctic Traveller* by Katha Pollitt. Copyright 1981 by Katha Pollitt. For "The Death of Marilyn Monroe" from *The Dead and the Living* by Sharon Olds. Copyright 1983 by Sharon Olds. For "Dream Variation" from *Selected Poems of Langston Hughes* by Langston Hughes. Copyright 1926 by Alfred A. Knopf, Inc. and renewed 1954 by Langston Hughes. All preceding excerpts are reprinted by permission of Alfred A. Knopf, Inc. For "In an Arab Town" from *The Hands of Exile* by Susan Tichy. Copyright 1983 by Susan Tichy. For "The Shield of Achilles," copyright 1952; "Law Like Love," copyright 1940 and renewed 1968; "Musée des Beaux

Arts," copyright 1940, renewed 1969; and "For What As Easy," copyright 1945; all by W. H. Auden. Reprinted from *W. H. Auden: Collected Poems,* edited by Edward Mendelson. For "The Missionary Visits Our Church in Scranton" from *Anthracite Country* by Jay Parini. Copyright 1982 by Jay Parini. For "Carmel Point," copyright 1954, and *"Hurt Hawks,"* copyright 1928 and renewed 1956, by Robinson Jeffers. Both poems reprinted from *The Selected Poetry of Robinson Jeffers.* All preceding excerpts are reprinted by permission of Random House, Inc.

Stan Rice. For "Metaphysical Shock from Watching a T.V. Cartoon" by Stan Rice. Reprinted by permission of the author.

Norman Russell. For "indian school" by Norman Russell. Copyright 1975. Reprinted by permission of N. H. Russell.

The Seal Press. For "Radiation Leak" by Jody Aliesan from *as if it will matter.* Copyright 1978 by Jody Aliesan. Reprinted with permission.

Charles Simic. For "Ford" by Charles Simic. Copyright 1967 by Charles Simic. Reprinted by permission of the author.

Kay Smith. For "Annunciation" by Kay Smith. Reprinted by permission of the author.

Gary Snyder. For "Mid-August at Sourdough Mountain Lookout" from *Riprap* by Gary Snyder. Copyright 1959 by Origin Press. For "Hay for the Horses" by Gary Snyder. First appeared in *Writing* 7 published by Four Season Foundation. Reprinted by permission of the author.

Sterling Lord Literistic, Inc. For "Preface to a Twenty Volume Suicide Note" by Amiri Baraka (LeRoi Jones) from *Black Magic Poetry.* Copyright 1969 by Amiri Baraka. For "Poem for Black Hearts" by Amiri Baraka. Copyright 1969 by Amiri Baraka. Reprinted by permission of Sterling Lord Literistic, Inc.

May Swenson. For "Bleeding" from *New & Selected Things Taking Place* by May Swenson. Copyright 1970 by May Swenson. Reprinted by permission of the author.

University of Arkansas Press. For "Unsent Message to My Brother in His Pain" from *The Drifting Away* by Leon Stokesbury. Copyright 1986 by Leon Stokesbury. Reprinted by permission of University of Arkansas Press.

University of California Press. For "The Language," "Place (There was a path)," "Some Echoes," and "The World" by Robert Creeley. Copyright 1982. Reprinted by permission of the Regents of the University of California.

University of Illinois. For "Dear John, Dear Coltrane" from *Images of Kin* by Michael Harper. Copyright 1970, 1985 by Michael Harper. Reprinted by permission of the author.

University of Pittsburgh Press. For "The Elements of San Joaquin" from *The Elements of San Joaquin* by Gary Soto. Reprinted by permission of the University of Pittsburgh Press. Copyright 1977 by Gary Soto.

Viking Penguin Inc. For "Piano" from *The Complete Poems* by D. H. Lawrence. Copyright 1971 Viking Penguin Inc. Reprinted by permission of Viking Penguin Inc.

Wake Forest University Press. For "Hen Woman" by Thomas Kinsella. Reprinted by permission of Wake Forest University Press.

Wampeter Press. For "The Sergeant" from *The Importance of Visible Scars* by Don Johnson. Reprinted by permission of Wampeter Press.

Wesleyan University Press. For "Widow's Walk" by Elizabeth Spires. Copyright 1981 by Elizabeth Spires. Reprinted from *Globe.* For "What For" by Garret Hongo. Copyright 1980 by Garret Hongo. Reprinted from *Yellow Light.* For "A Blessing" by James Wright. Copyright 1961 by James Wright. Reprinted from *The Branch Will Not Break.* For "A Dog Sleeping at My Feet" by James Dickey. Copyright 1962. Reprinted from *James Dickey Poems 1957–1967.* All works reprinted by permission of Wesleyan University Press.

West End Press. For "Delphine" from *Speaking in Sign* by Teresa Anderson. Copyright 1978, West End Press. Reprinted by permission of West End Press.

FICTION

Astor-Honor, Inc. For "Miss Leonora When Last Seen" ("Fancy Woman") by Peter Taylor. Copyright 1963. Reprinted by permission of Astor-Honor, Inc., New York, NY 10017.

James Baldwin. For "The Rockpile" from *Going to Meet the Man* by James Baldwin. Published by Dial Press. Copyright 1965 by James Baldwin. Reprinted by permission of the author.

Farrar, Straus and Giroux, Inc. Reprinted by permission of Farrar, Straus and Giroux, Inc.: "Parker's Back" from *The Complete Stories* by Flannery O'Connor. Copyright 1965, 1971 by the Estate of Mary Flannery O'Connor. "The Lottery" from *The Lottery* by Shirley Jackson. Copyright 1948, 1949 by Shirley Jackson; renewed 1976, 1977 by Lawrence Hyman, Barry Hyman, Ms. Sarah Webster, and Mrs. Joanne Schnurer. "Sarrasine" by Honoré de Balzac from *S/Z* by Roland Barthes, translated by Richard Miller. Translation copyright 1974 Farrar, Straus and Giroux, Inc. Reprinted by permission of Hill & Wang, a division of Farrar, Straus and Giroux, Inc.

Four Quarters. For "Grandfather" by Claude Koch. Originally printed in *Four Quarters* (Spring 1981). Copyright 1981 by La Salle University. Reprinted by permission of *Four Quarters.*

Harcourt Brace Jovanovich, Inc. For "Moments of Being" from *A Haunted House and Other Stories* by Virginia Woolf. Copyright 1944, 1972 by Harcourt Brace Jovanovich, Inc. For "The Petrified Man" from *A Curtain of Green and Other Stories* by Eudora Welty. Copyright 1939, 1967 by Eudora Welty. For "A Worn Path" from *A Curtain of Green and Other Stories* by Eudora Welty. Copyright 1941, 1969 by Eudora Welty. For "A Good Man Is Hard to Find" from *A Good Man Is Hard to Find and Other Stories* by Flannery O'Connor. Copyright 1953, renewed 1981 by Mrs. Regina O'Connor. For "Everyday Use" from *In Love and Trouble* by Alice Walker. Copyright 1973 by Alice Walker. For "The Star" from *The Nine Billion Names of God* by Arthur C. Clarke. Copyright 1955 by Royal Publications. For "New Wave Format" from *Shiloh and Other Stories* by Bobbie Ann Mason. Copyright 1982 by Bobbie Ann Mason. For "Mrs. Saunders Writes to the World" from *Acquainted with the Night* by Lynn Sharon Schwartz. Copyright 1984 by Lynn Sharon Schwartz. For "Through the Tunnel" from *The Habit of Loving* by Doris Lessing. Copyright 1955 by Doris Lessing. For "The Grave" from *The Leaning Tower and Other Stories* by Katherine Anne Porter. Copyright 1944, 1972. All reprinted by permission of Harcourt Brace Jovanovich, Inc.

International Creative Management, Inc. For "The Indian Uprising" by Donald Barthelme, first published in *The New Yorker.* Copyright 1965 by Donald Barthelme. Reprinted by permission of International Creative Management, Inc. For "The Skater" by Joy Williams, first published in *Esquire.* Copyright 1984 by Joy Williams. Reprinted by permission of the author.

Phoebe Lamore. For "Rape Fantasies" by Margaret Atwood from *Dancing Girls* published by McClelland and Stewart. Copyright 1977. Reprinted by permission of Margaret Atwood.

Macmillan Publishing Company. For "Babylon Revisited" from *Taps at Reveille* by F. Scott Fitzgerald. Copyright 1931, The Curtis Publishing Company; renewed 1959 by Frances Scott Fitzgerald Lanaham. For "The Undefeated" from *Men without Women* by Ernest Hemingway. Copyright 1927, Charles Scribner's Sons; copyright renewed 1955, Ernest Hemingway. For "The Bet" from *The Schoolmistress and Other Stories* by Anton Chekhov. Translated from the Russian by Constance Garnett. Copyright 1921 by Macmillan, renewed 1949 by David Garnett. Reprinted by permission of Macmillan Publishing Company.

Elaine Markson Literary Agency, Inc. For "The Loudest Voice" by Grace Paley. Copyright 1956 to 1987. Originally published in *The Little Disturbances of Man* (Doubleday, 1959). Reprinted by permission of Grace Paley.

Harold Ober Associates. For "I Want to Know Why" from *The Triumph of the Egg* by Sherwood Anderson. Copyright 1921 by B. W. Huebsch, Inc.; renewed 1948 by Eleanor C. Anderson. Reprinted by permission of Harold Ober Associates, Inc.

Penguin Books Canada, Ltd. For "Angela" from *Darkness* by Bharati Mukherjee. Copyright 1985 by Bharati Mukherjee. Reprinted by permission of Penguin Books Canada, Ltd.

Random House, Inc., Alfred A. Knopf, Inc. For "Cathedral" from *Cathedral* by Raymond Carver. Copyright 1981, 1982, 1983 by Raymond Carver. For "Guests of the Nation" from *Collected Stories* by Frank O'Connor. Copyright 1981 by Harriet O'Donovan Sheehy, Executrix of the Estate of Frank O'Connor. For "The Chaste Clarissa" from *The Stories of John Cheever* by John Cheever. Copyright 1952 by John Cheever. The preceding selections reprinted by permission of Alfred A. Knopf, Inc. For "Battle Royal" from *Invisible Man* by Ralph Ellison. Copyright 1948 by Ralph Ellison. For "A Rose for Emily" by William Faulkner. Copyright 1930, renewed 1958 by William Faulkner. For "That Evening Sun" by William Faulkner. Copyright 1931, renewed 1959 by William Faulkner. Both Faulkner stories reprinted from *Collected Stories of William Faulkner.* The preceding selections reprinted by permission of Random House, Inc.

Simon & Schuster, Inc. For "The Pardoner's Tale" by Geoffrey Chaucer, edited by R. M. Luminansky, from *The Canterbury Tales.* Copyright 1948, 1975 by Simon & Schuster, Inc. Reprinted by permission.

Vanguard Press. For "Where Are You Going, Where Have You Been?" from *The Wheel of Love* by Joyce Carol Oates. Copyright 1965, 1966, 1967, 1968, 1969, 1970 by Joyce Carol Oates. Reprinted by permission of Vanguard Press.

Viking Penguin Inc. For "Eveline" from *Dubliners* by James Joyce. Copyright 1916 by B. W. Huebsch. Copyright 1967 by the Estate of James Joyce. For "Rocking-Horse Winner" and "The Blind Man" from *The Complete Short Stories* by D. H.

Lawrence. Copyright 1933 by Viking Penguin Inc. For "The Chrysanthemums" from *The Long Valley* by John Steinbeck. Copyright 1938, renewed 1966 by John Steinbeck. All rights reserved. Reprinted by permission of Viking Penguin Inc.

DRAMA

Dodd, Mead & Company, Inc. For *Trifles* from *Plays* by Susan Glaspell. Reprinted by permission of Dodd, Mead & Company, Inc. Copyright 1920 by Dodd, Mead & Company and renewed 1948 by Susan Glaspell.

Harcourt Brace Jovanovich, Inc. For *Oedipus Rex* from *The Oedipus Rex of Sophocles: An English Version* by Dudley Fitts and Robert Fitzgerald. Copyright 1949 by Harcourt Brace Jovanovich, Inc. Renewed 1977 by Cornelia Fitts and Robert Fitzgerald. CAUTION: All rights, including professional, amateur, motion picture, recitation, lecturing, public reading, radio broadcasting, and television are strictly reserved. Inquiries on all rights should be addressed to Harcourt Brace Jovanovich, Inc., Copyrights and Permissions Department, Orlando, FL 32887. For Notes to accompany *As You Like It* and *The Tragedy of King Lear* from *Shakespeare: The Complete Works* edited by George Harrison. Copyright 1948, 1952 by Harcourt Brace Jovanovich, Inc. For *Tartuffe* by Molière, translated by Richard Wilbur. Copyright 1961, 1962, 1963 by Richard Wilbur. CAUTION: Professionals and amateurs are hereby warned that this translation, being fully protected under the copyright laws of the United States of America, the British Commonwealth, including Canada, and all other countries which are signatories to the Universal Copyright Convention and the International Copyright Union, is subject to royalty. All rights, including professional, amateur, motion picture, recitation, lecturing, public reading, radio broadcasting, and television, are strictly reserved. Particular emphasis is laid on the question of readings, permission for which must be secured from the author's agent in writing. Inquiries on professional rights (except for amateur rights) should be addressed to Mr. Gilbert Parker, Curtis Brown Ltd., 10 Astor Place, New York, NY 10003. Inquiries on translation rights should be addressed to Harcourt Brace Jovanovich, Inc., Copyrights and Permissions Department, Orlando, FL 32887. The amateur acting rights of *Tartuffe* are controlled exclusively by the Dramatist's Play Service, Inc., 440 Park Avenue South, New York, NY 10016. No amateur performance of the play may be given without obtaining in advance the written permission of the Dramatist's Play Service, Inc., and paying the requisite fee. All selections reprinted by permission of Harcourt Brace Jovanovich, Inc.

Macmillan Publishing Company. For *The Plough and the Stars* by Sean O'Casey from his *Collected Plays.* Copyright 1967 by Macmillan and St. Martin's Press.

New American Library. For *A Doll House* by Henrik Ibsen from *Complete Major Prose Plays of Ibsen,* translated and edited by Rolf Fjelde. Copyright 1965, 1970, 1978 by Rolf Fjelde. Reprinted by arrangement with NAL Penguin Inc., New York, NY.

Putnam Publishing Group. For *The Sandbox* from *The Plays: Volume I* by Edward Albee. Copyright 1981 by Edward Albee. Reprinted by permission of the Putnam Publishing Group.

University of Minnesota Press. For *The Good Woman of Setzuan* by Bertolt Brecht, translated by Eric Bentley. Originally published in *Parables for the Theatre: Two Plays by Bertolt Brecht.* Copyright 1956, 1961 by Eric Bentley. Epilogue copyright 1965 by Eric Bentley. Reprinted by permission of the University of Minnesota Press.

Viking Penguin, Inc. For *Crimes of the Heart* by Beth Henley. Copyright 1981, 1982 by Beth Henley. All rights reserved. Reprinted by permission of Viking Penguin, Inc.

INDEX TO FIRST LINES OF POETRY

INDEX TO AUTHORS AND TITLES

A 8
B 9
C 0
D 1
E 2
F 3
G 4
H 5
I 6
J 7

Teaching the Power of Language

Instructor's Manual for *Literature: The Power of Language*

Thomas Mc Laughlin

INTRODUCTION

Literature: The Power of Language is based on the premise that reading literature provides an understanding of language, which is in turn vital to an understanding of the self in society. The study of literature, then, is a way of coming to self-knowledge, in the sense that the self is situated in language, the preeminent social institution. Language acts as a framework through which we all see the world, and since literature draws our attention to language, it reminds us of the existence of that framework and its power over our perceptions. Reading well is therefore necessary to students' growth into self-awareness and social responsibility.

By "reading well" I mean reading actively, accepting responsibility as a reader for the meanings produced in cooperation with the text. Readers are not passive consumers of the text; they are active workers who turn the marks on a page into meaningful patterns, questioners who bring literary concepts and expectations to the text, reshaping it in the forms that their questions impose. Readers produce the meanings of texts out of their competence in language and in the cultural codes that they bring to the reading experience. That is to say, we all *interpret* when we read. We bring ourselves to the reading experience, and what we are shapes how we read. This is not to say that we can create any meaning we desire, since what we are reading only makes sense inside rules of language and culture that we cannot change. But it does mean that many valid meanings are possible, and that it ought to be the role of the teacher of literature to open up possible meanings rather than to close them off. Eventually, of course, the teacher may have to rule out certain incompetent readings, but the first impulse ought to be to engage students in the interpretive process and to honor their honest efforts. Even their mistakes will be instructive for them, and like it or not they are responsible for their own reading, which teachers should at least allow to be in fact their own. A teacher must resist the rush to close off meaning, even if students are eager to hear the "correct" meaning from the teacher.

Therefore, the strategy of this manual is *not* to provide the instructor with authoritative and final readings of the literary texts in the anthology. Rather, it suggests interpretive questions that instructors can pass on to students, either in classroom discussion or in assignments for writing. It also suggests how the literary readings can be fit into the structure of the textbook. Any given text, of course, could be understood in terms of many different critical concepts, so this manual suggests the concepts I feel are most useful in connection with each of the literary texts.

Note: The suggested questions either follow the interpretive paragraph here or are found in the text.

PART ONE: ACTIVE READING

e. e. cummings, "in Just-"

This poem is used in the text as an example of how ordinary words can be combined to produce a complex and unique meaning. Such phrases as "mud- / luscious" and "puddle-wonderful" can be discussed in terms of the richness of meaning they produce as the connotations of the words interact. And a discussion of suggested meaning could well end up with a focus on the "balloonman" with his goat foot as a personification of the energy of spring. That energy is also evident in the sound and the visual design of the poem, so that it could profitably be studied in a discussion of how the form of a poem becomes part of its message.

1. What is the significance of the way the poem is spaced on the page?
2. What are the feelings about spring that the poem produces? How does it do so?

3. What does the poem suggest about sexual differences? How is sexuality treated in the poem?
4. What does the "goat-footed / balloonMan" represent on the symbolic level? Can he be read as a sinister figure?

A. E. Housman, "To an Athlete Dying Young"

One useful approach to this poem would be to think of it in terms of its speaker. Although its ostensible subject is the athlete who has died, the character who emerges from the poem is that of the speaker. Why is he so moved by the athlete's death? Why is his tribute to the athlete so very formal and restrained, almost to the point that he cannot say outright that the athlete has died—he has to resort to periphrasis, elaborate ways of suggesting what he can't quite say. The extreme formality of the language, metrics, and stanza patterns in the poem makes sense as a manifestation of the speaker's feelings.

1. What image of the speaker of the poem arises out of the poem's language and poetic technique? What is the speaker's attitude toward the athlete who has died?
2. What does the poem have to say about the benefits to the athlete of his early death? Do these benefits outweigh the sorrows of death in the mind of the speaker?
3. What attitudes toward death do you bring to the poem? Does the poem challenge or reaffirm those attitudes?

PART TWO: POETRY AND THE POWER OF LANGUAGE

Chapter One: Introduction

Wilfred Owen, "Anthem for Doomed Youth"

"Anthem for Doomed Youth" is discussed in the text as a challenge to our conventional attitudes toward war. Its language forces on us a particular emotional and intellectual response. The poem could also be studied more formally as an experiment in sonnet form and as an exercise in onomatopoeia, an attempt to re-create in the language itself the sounds of the field of battle. Clearly, though, these two concerns are not separate; the metrical and verbal techniques of the poem contribute to the poem's effort to shape our response. Students should be urged to think about their own attitudes toward war and the texts that have shaped them.

1. How does this poem work as a sonnet? How is it similar to or different from traditional sonnets? Why would the poet use such a traditional form in presenting such a challenging message?
2. What are the circumstances of warfare in World War I that would have led Owen to think of soldiers as dying like cattle?
3. How does the language of the first stanza suggest the experience of modern war?

Thomas Hardy, "The Man He Killed"

A classic poem for teaching about the speaker of a poem. Here is a speaker who is radically divided within himself—he still accepts the conventional wisdom about war ("kill or be killed") while he has also realized the humanity of his enemy. Instructors can benefit from the clear difference between the voice of the speaker and the apparent intentions of the poem. But making that difference apparent to students requires interrogating the poem, looking for the places where the speaker's voice contradicts itself. As a persona poem, "The Man He Killed" is also an excellent example of language chosen to depict the character of the speaker. In this case, the colloquial language gives us a clear sense of the social standing of the speaker.

1. Thinking of the poem as a miniature narrative, what is the plot of the story? How has the speaker been changed by his experience?
2. What does the language of the poem suggest about the character of the speaker?
3. What is the effect of phrases like "just so" and "of course" in the third stanza? What do they tell us about the mental process the speaker is going through?

Randall Jarrell, "The Death of the Ball Turret Gunner"

This grim and disturbing poem has an immediate, visceral effect on most readers, but it is also true that the closer you look the odder the poem becomes. That is, the poem seems to be about the horror and finality of death—nothing could be more depressing than the last line—but the very premise of the poem suggests a more positive message. What I mean is that the speaker of the poem is speaking from an afterlife; his life as a mind has not been ended, even if his body has been turned into refuse by the violence of war. His mind still exists, able to look back on his life with a degree of calm and analytical distance. In fact, his death seems to have been an awakening. He now understands his life better than when he was alive (at which time he was mentally asleep). Nevertheless, the shocking horror of the poem remains.

1. What attitude toward war comes out of the poem? What is the significance of the word *State?*
2. How does the speaker of the poem describe himself and his war experience?
3. What does the rhyme in line five do to the poem? What effects does it have on the reader?

Yusef Komunyakaa, "Starlight Scope Myopia"

Perhaps more than any other of our war poems, this poem takes us into the mind of a soldier during the experience itself. We see what he sees, feel and think along with him. Everything is of the moment, as in a stream of consciousness. For this reason, the poem would make an excellent if complex example of *imagery* in poetry, showing how an experience is filtered through the mind of an observer. Here the scene is not just described; the speaker's feelings color the experience, so that we are getting a unique perspective on a specific event and moment. The perspective is close-up, because of the scope, but detached by distance. In every detail the poem is consistent to the point of view it sets up for the speaker.

1. How is the attitude of the speaker of this poem comparable to that of the speaker of "The Man He Killed"?
2. What is the significance of the lines "inside our skulls years / after this scene ends"?
3. Extrapolating from the end of the poem, what do you think the speaker does next? Does he shoot?

Alfred, Lord Tennyson, "The Charge of the Light Brigade"

One of the most famous poems in English, it has become one of our icons of heroism. The poem is also a powerful example of how language can control our reactions to an event. Even the poem itself admits that the charge was a mistake, but it insists on the heroism of those involved. It focuses on the gallantry and daring of the individual soldiers, even those who realized that the charge was hopeless. And that gallantry is evident in the language of the poem, and in its vivid figures of speech. The poem is one of the most memorized and performed poems of all time as well, and the rhythm deserves attention to see how the poem carries us and our emotions along.

1. What is the rhetorical effect of all the verbal repetitions in the poem?
2. The poem is very careful to follow the charge throughout its course. Why?
3. What is the effect of such metaphors as "the jaws of Death" and "the mouth of Hell"? Are they in any way comparable to Wilfred Owen's characterization of soldiers as "cattle"?

Chapter Two: Denotation and Connotation

John Milton, "On the Late Massacre in Piedmont"

Milton's poem serves in the text as an example of a highly rhetorical use of connotation, an attempt to impose on readers a particular interpretation of experience by means of carefully selected words whose connotations serve his view of events. Analogy could be drawn by the instructor to the ways that contemporary politicians attempt to exercise verbal and conceptual control over our reactions to events. Another interesting feature of the language of this poem is the aggressive tone it takes in addressing its prayer to God. The speaker seems almost angry with God for allowing this senseless slaughter. And yet all of this anger and horror is contained within a very carefully crafted and innovative sonnet form that deserves attention in itself and for its contribution to the rhetoric of the poem.

1. How does the poem characterize the two sides in this battle? Is it possible that his language simplifies the event?
2. How does the speaker address God in this prayer?
3. How does this poem function as a sonnet? What stanza forms does it use? How do the sentences as logical units interact with the stanzas as formal units?

William Wordsworth, "A slumber did my spirit seal"

This poem has long been the subject of critical debate as to whether or not Wordsworth's response to the young woman's death is a pantheistic acceptance of her transformation into an element of nature or a bitter lament at her loss of power and consciousness. The debate has continued precisely because there is no general agreement on the connotations of the poem's language. The poem can be used, that is, to support either interpretation. As a result, this is a perfect poem to stimulate interpretive debate. The interpretive issue—does the poem express hope or despair?—is simple to grasp yet difficult to close off. Students can therefore safely take either side without fear of being ruled out of court, or they can search for other possible readings that might combine, transcend, or resist the two interpretations we've discussed.

Stevie Smith, "How Cruel Is the Story of Eve"

Compression is the great achievement of this poem. Its subject is vast—the effects throughout history of the Eve story on the relationships between men and women. Yet the poem manages in a short space to treat the subject without reducing its complexity. This is possible because the language of the poem is richly suggestive of meaning; whole systems of thought and argument can be spun out of single words in the poem. Therefore the poem lends itself to study in terms of the connotative force of its language. This poem may be particularly challenging and uncomfortable for students who are offended by the notion that a story from the Bible could be criticized as an enforcer of "cruelty" and "misery." The instructor should encourage students to examine their values in the light of this poem, to see whether the poem challenges those values effectively or whether its argument must be rejected.

Robinson Jeffers, "Carmel Point"

Since this poem engages a current subject of political debate—issues of development and environmental responsibility—it is an excellent example of how the language of a poem can shape our perception of a complex reality. The poem clearly has a point of view on the relationship between mankind and nature, and it enforces that point by means of powerful word choices. "The power of language" is here demonstrated on an issue that students already have strong feelings about, so that they can see the verbal strategies that the poem employs. The poem's claim that we must "uncenter our minds from ourselves" goes against our usual habits of thought and therefore presents readers with a complex imaginative challenge.

Raymond Carver, "Photograph of My Father in His Twenty-Second Year"

The language of Carver's poem does at least double duty. The occasion of the poem involves a son looking at a picture of his father as a young man. The son (the speaker) uses language as a way of making sense of the father. The connotations of such words as "sheepish" and "limply" give us a picture of the father as the son interprets him. But since the son recognizes himself to be very much like his father, those words come round as the son's description of himself as well. The poem can therefore be studied as a revelation of the speaker as well as of the father. The difficulty of the poem is in deciding for yourself the tone that the son takes. Does he love his father as he claims, or does he hate his father for turning the son into a copy of himself? The language supports both possibilities, or better yet suggests that both are possible at the same time.

Heather McHugh, "Language Lesson, 1976"

In "Language Lesson" we have a poem explicitly concerned with language, especially with slang. The speaker seems to be fascinated by the fact that such ordinary language could produce such complex meanings. Even ordinary language plays with the conventional meanings of words, creating a complex and subtle framework for human perception. We often think of poetry as the sheer opposite of ordinary language, as though the latter were simple and only the former needed our close analysis. A poem such as this one reminds us of the complexity of "ordinary" language, which can create in its multiple meanings a kind of poetry of its own.

Chapter Three: Figures of Speech

William Shakespeare, "Sonnet 73" ("That time of year thou mayest in me behold")

This poem serves in the text as an example of figurative thinking. But what makes the poem most interesting is that its figures are deployed for a strong rhetorical purpose. That is, the poem very strongly communicates a speaker who is making an argument and a listener who is either swayed or not. Students can respond very well to this poem in the context of such questions as "Who is talking?" "To whom?" and "For what purposes?" The fact that there is no definitive answer to these questions allows for open debate, but the questions can be legitimately answered as extrapolations from the language—especially the figurative language—of the poem. Students most often have trouble with the quatrain dealing with the ashes of the fire, but critics have often argued about those difficult lines as well.

1. What is the dramatic situation in which this poem occurs? Who is speaking; who is listening? What is at stake?
2. What qualities can be ascribed to the speaker as a consequence of his metaphors? How is he like autumn, like a sunset, like a dying fire?

3. How is the poem composed as a sonnet? Is the form effective in communicating the message the speaker is sending?

Gerard Manley Hopkins, "God's Grandeur"

Hopkins's great poem of romantic spirituality argues that God is visible and active in the natural world. The metaphors of the poem attempt to describe how the grandeur of God (which is in itself spiritual, invisible) becomes visible. It "will flame out"; it "gathers to a greatness," like oil from crushed olives. There is no direct, proper way to describe God's grandeur. It surpasses the power of human language to describe it. Figurative language is, so to speak, the best we can do. We can say what God's grandeur *is like;* we can give a human or natural model that might help us to imagine what we can't literally know. These metaphors, in other words, reflect Hopkins's beliefs and desires, which means that the poem can also profitably be seen in terms of the speaker's mind. What do the metaphors tell us about him, about the way his mind makes sense of the world?

1. What does the poem have to say about the *obstacles* to perceiving the grandeur of God? How can these obstacles be overcome?
2. Are the last two lines of this poem figurative? Or does Hopkins literally believe in the Holy Ghost as a dove brooding over the world?
3. Since Hopkins's language creates a complex kind of music, how does the sound of the poem contribute to the point it is making?

John Donne, "Holy Sonnet 14" ("Batter my heart, three-personed God; for you")

This poem is constituted by a series of figures of speech that describe the relationship between God and mankind. In all the figures the human is passive; it is by God's efforts that the relationship exists at all. As the poem progresses the figures become more violent and extreme. How is the relationship between God and the individual man like a siege of a town? Even more extremely, how is that relationship like a rape ("except you ravish me")? The extremity of these figures is of course typical of metaphysical poetry, which often asks readers to engage in very unusual analogical thinking. As a result, such poetry forces us to think outside our usual categories, to think more creatively.

William Wordsworth, "Lines Written in Early Spring"

The question of personification is at issue in this poem. The speaker asserts again and again that what we might think of as personifications (the joyful flowers, the playing birds, the twigs taking pleasure in the breeze) are not figures of speech but literal descriptions of a natural world infused with a spirit that is in fact capable of those emotions. But doesn't the speaker protest too much? His very insistence reveals a doubt ("I must think, do all I can, / That there was pleasure there."). Wordsworth seems caught between a confidence that there is a spirit in the world and a nagging doubt, a suspicion that it is his own imagination that has created that spirit. Again, therefore, the poem could be seen as an episode in the life of the speaker, a moment in his spiritual quest.

Wallace Stevens, "The Death of a Soldier"

In terms of figures of speech, the most interesting part of this poem for me is the last two stanzas, which compare the death of a soldier with a very particular and recognizable moment in nature. In these six lines we have a perfect example of how the reader is asked to fill in meaning. The two events are compared, but the poem does not make explicit at all what they have in common, what we can learn about death by thinking of it in these terms. That task is left to the reader. The poem is also interesting as an exercise in tone. Just how does the speaker feel about the soldier's death? Is he as cold as he sometimes sounds (as in the first stanza)? Or is he drawing attention to the cold indifference of society, which goes on with its concerns without pausing to reflect on those who have died in its name? Is there a principled way of deciding on the basis of the poem's language which of these attitudes the poem wants us to adapt?

Richard Wilbur, "Mind"

Wilbur's poem is a perfect example of a *conceit,* an extended meditation on the consequences of a figure of speech. "The mind is like a bat." If so, what are the analogies in mental life to the cave the bat lives in, the senseless wit it flies by? What is "a graceful error," and how can it "correct the cave"? The poem does not answer these questions, but it does set up a verbal pattern that suggests some answers. Perhaps the most noticeable feature of the poem is the extremity of the simile. The poem asks us to compare two things that seem totally unrelated to each other, as though it were asking us to exercise some little-used mental muscles. I have found that students enjoy the process of working out the analogies, engaging in the "purest play" with the language of the poem.

Sylvia Plath, "Morning Song"

In this poem the figures of speech reveal the feelings of the speaker who utters them. The speaker, the mother of the child, has the entire world of language before her as a resource for finding figures of speech to describe her child. The objects she chooses to compare with the child therefore tell us more about her than about the child. And each figure of speech sends a different message. I think it would be difficult to find a common denominator under all these figures. Rather, the diversity of figures seems to me to suggest a diversity of feelings, as though the experience is too new to have allowed the mother to sort it out and speak with clarity. This seems to me to be a poem, in other words, that would be damaged by demanding that it must be consistent. The *difference* among the figures might be what is really interesting.

Chapter Four: Imagery

Imamu Amiri Baraka, "Preface to a Twenty Volume Suicide Note"

If an image is always a depiction of the world as seen through an individual mind, then the key to understanding this poem is understanding the speaker. The image of the daughter in the last stanza is a function of the mind revealed in the first two stanzas. The speaker seems to be simultaneously trapped in his madness and at least aware enough to recognize what is happening to him. It is therefore difficult—and interesting—to read the tone of the last stanza. Does it reflect a despair at his growing madness or a hope that he can return to health and human relationships?

1. What is the significance of the title?
2. What is the mental state of the speaker as he reveals it in the first two stanzas?
3. How does the speaker see the event described in the last stanza? How do you see it?

Ezra Pound, "In a Station of the Metro"

This poem serves in the text as an example of the mental work that an imagistic poem calls for from the reader. A fruitful discussion of the poem might therefore be stimulated by asking the students to begin by writing a paragraph that describes the scene as they see it. Discussion might then center on the variety of scenes the poem evokes, and on how the language of the poem evokes them. Some students' imaginings will be ruled out as the class attends to the language, but a wide variety might remain and seem valid.

John Keats, "To Autumn"

This poem deploys its images in three distinctive patterns. In the first stanza we get a quick succession of images of the season's fruitfulness, as though we are being given a quick panorama of the season. In the second stanza the images focus around a human figure who becomes a living symbol of the season as it fits into human life and work. In the third stanza the poem focuses on one moment, forcing us to attend closely to the symphony of sound that nature produces. The aural images of the last stanza are particularly challenging to readers, first because the images are complex and dense, and second because we are more used to exercising our *visual* rather than *aural* imaginations. In the last stanza there is also a challenge for the reader to interpret the tone of the scene out of the connotations of the language. How does this scene make the speaker feel? How does it make each of us as readers feel?

William Carlos Williams, "Young Woman at a Window"

In terms of imagery, this poem represents a minimal style. There is a picture presented here, but only a few details are drawn in, the speaker offers almost no emotion or perspective, and there is no clear context for the scene. The reader therefore has very little to go on, either in reconstructing the scene or in developing an attitude toward it. And yet there is a lot of room here for interpretive debate. One logical place to begin is with the context. Where are we? What larger event is this scene a part of? Several plausible scenarios can be developed, though it might be that students will claim that we don't need to know the context, that the point of the poem is that all we have in this scene is a fragment, that its poignance comes precisely from not knowing how it fits into the woman's life. There is also a lot of room for debate about what this scene is supposed to make us feel. There is almost no emotive, connotative language here that could guide us to a proper response. The language seems factual, almost cold. And yet there is an emotion here, perhaps because almost any scenario you can imagine would suggest that some tragedy has occurred. With this image we get the picture, but everything else is left up to our imagination and sympathy.

Emily Dickinson, "A Bird came down the Walk"

This encounter with nature is described in vivid detail. The bird's actions are precisely narrated, and the poem's emphasis on the look in the bird's eye suggests how closely the speaker must have been looking. The speaker constructs a narrative in this short poem. A plot emerges, a story of how the speaker perceives the foreignness of the bird (when it eats the worm), tries to make contact (by offering food), but is rejected by the bird (by flying away), so that it retains its difference, refusing to be domesticated by the speaker. A profitable approach to this poem would be to get a sense of how this story is told so concisely. This might lead to the poem's rich figurative language, which compresses ideas and feelings.

Denise Levertov, "O Taste and See"

Levertov's poem is a call for the kind of sensory attention that can make poetic images come into existence. It calls, that is, for an active, searching life of the senses that would take pleasure in perceiving the world, transforming it into the self. The poem begins with a sense that we are alienated from the world of the senses, and that it takes an active commitment and effort in order to overcome that distance. Appropriately, she describes such perception in very physical terms, using images of taste and eating in order to emphasize the physicality of all the senses. This poem, that is, can be used not only as an example of imagery but as a manifesto that places sensory life at the center of the human self.

Gary Snyder, "Hay for the Horses"

This little narrative poem presents us with quick insights into the experiences of two people in the same event. The speaker of the poem, in highly imagistic language, tells us of the sensory delights of stacking bales of hay. The truck driver with whom he shares this work, however, simply reports in straightforward, bitter terms on his disappointment at being stuck in this job. For him the work has not been an occasion for imagistic pleasure but simply a boring task to be finished as soon as possible. We therefore have the same event seen through two pairs of eyes, each account of the event colored by the experience and personalities of the two participants. The poem is therefore an excellent example of how an image is always an interpretation of reality rather than a direct presentation of reality itself.

Gary Soto, "The Elements of San Joaquin"

As in all imagistic poems, the speaker of this poem is central. He occupies a space in the midst of the natural world, organizing his perception in terms of the "elements" of that world—field, wind, sun, etc. Yet the natural world seems to give him little delight. He notices the beauty of the world, but the dominant tone of the poem is one of dissatisfaction, anger at the brutal work the speaker does as a migrant laborer. Hard work does not allow the luxury of contemplation. Obviously a different speaker might see these events differently, but this speaker's perceptions are colored by his anger. He is not indifferent to the beauty of nature but rather is bitter at having that beauty taken away from him. This set of poems is therefore a rich exercise in imagery. Each poem sees the world differently, though all are saturated with the personality of the speaker.

Chapter Five: Poetic Form and Sound

William Carlos Williams, "Young Woman at a Window"

This poem is discussed in Chapter Four as an example of imagery. In this chapter it serves as an example of a poem that sets up its own rules of formal operation. Students have responded well to simple questions along the lines of "How does this thing work?" and "What are its rules?"

See Chapter Four for further discussion.

William Blake, "The Lamb," "The Tyger"

These two poems are matched here as examples of how the sounds of poems reinforce their meaning and tone. The poems can, of course, be compared in any number of ways, in terms of their speakers, their imagery and figures of speech, and their outlooks on experience. The poems can be seen as meditations on God, creating images of the divine as it appears to first an innocent and then an experienced mind. It should be remembered that for Blake neither of these states of mind was perfect. Both have blind spots, both are overly confident that their own view of the world is absolutely accurate. The poems can therefore be played off against each other almost endlessly. In terms of this chapter of the text, the sound of the poems works well with any other oppositions between the poems that we might devise.

1. "The Lamb" consists of a series of questions in the first stanza that are answered by a series of statements in the second stanza. "The Tyger" consists of a series of questions with no answers offered. What does this difference tell us about the state of mind of the speaker of each poem?
2. What images of God do you see in "The Lamb" and "The Tyger"? How are those images of God related to the speakers of the poems?
3. How does the language of the two poems differ?
4. How does the metrical arrangement of the two poems differ?
5. Which of the two poems seems closest to you in spirit? Why?

Gerard Manley Hopkins, "The Windhover"

Hopkins's poem is a prayer occasioned by the speaker's experience of seeing a falcon in flight. The power and beauty of the bird come to symbolize Christ, who is therefore seen as a beautiful and "dangerous" figure. The verbal strategy of the poem is not just to *describe* the bird's flight but to *re-enact* it in the sound of the poem. The flowing alliterations and the propulsive rhythm suggest the swooping flight of the bird very effectively. Of course, for all the aural and verbal pyrotechnics, this is still a sonnet, carefully rhymed and crafted. For all these reasons, the poem is a perfect example of how sound and form can be manipulated for the poet's purposes.

1. Is it possible to find a rhythmic pattern under all the variations in this poem? If so, what is it? If not, is this a problem?
2. Does the rhythm of this poem succeed at the expense of meaning? Can you figure out the logical relationships in this language? Is there a grammar to the sentences?
3. What image of God is presented in the poem? If it is a prayer, what kind of prayer is it?

Allen Ginsberg, "First Party at Ken Kesey's with Hell's Angels"

Ginsberg has fashioned a poem in which the sound and rhythm perfectly match the subject matter. The rhythm changes subtly throughout the poem, at times propulsive, at times quiet. The poem is informal in tone, which makes sense since it's about the first meeting of the counterculture and the Hell's Angels, hardly a subject for formality or profundity. And yet the poem manages to give us vivid flashes of the scene very economically. The poem is therefore appropriate for use in teaching imagery as well. And the images add up to an interesting interpretation of the sixties. This is a poem that students can immediately get, but it becomes richer as they look at it more closely.

1. Is there a recognizable metrical pattern here? How does the rhythm of the poem contribute to its effect?
2. There are a number of references to rock and roll here. Would it make sense to call this a rock-and-roll poem, and if so, what would that mean?
3. How does the last picture that the poem evokes—the police—fit in with the rest of the poem?
4. This poem is, after all, about the Hell's Angels. Is there any sense of violence in this poem?

Adrienne Rich, "Power"

Rich's poem serves in the text as an example of a formal pattern devised especially for a poem. Clearly the spacing on the page has an effect on how we read the poem.

It sets up a discernible but irregular rhythm that disrupts the natural flow of the language so that we can think about each phrase carefully. The poem also provides a challenging "reading" of Curie's life, one that also raises questions about the importance of Curie to the speaker. Is there some way in which the speaker finds herself in the same condition as Curie?

1. Is there a pattern to the line breaks and typography in the poem? What does the setting of the words on the page do to how you read it aloud?
2. How are the first two stanzas related to the rest of the poem?
3. What is the significance of the last line of the poem?

William Wordsworth, "It is a beauteous evening"

The sonnet structure of the poem emphasizes that there is an important contrast between the adult and the child. The first eight lines are the adult's response to the natural world, and the last six lines are the adult's account of the mind of the child—who is not attending to the sublimities of nature but rather pursuing un-self-conscious play, and therefore coming closer to nature than the hyper-self-conscious narrator ever can, for all his sense of the sublime. The poem, especially the first eight lines, is also noteworthy for its figurative language, especially its personifications of nature. Which leads to a question common in reading Wordsworth—if nature is divine, why does it need to be personified?

1. What is it about the sea that makes it seem divine to the speaker?
2. In what ways is the sea personified? What image of God and nature arises from those figures of speech?
3. What does the poem suggest about the differences between the mind of the child and the mind of the speaker?
4. What makes the child so close to God? How does the speaker feel about the child's relationship with God?

William Shakespeare, "Sonnet 116" ("Let me not to the marriage of true minds")

This is a very tightly and logically ordered sonnet. Each quatrain is a logical unit, and in sequence they comprise a coherent argument. The argument proceeds by means of figures of speech, but it is not therefore any the less logical. The subject matter of the poem—that love can conquer time and separation—may not seem to students to call for this logical approach, but the poem is based on the premise that love and logic are not contradictory.

1. What does each quatrain add to the argument the poem proposes?
2. What is the function of the last two lines? Do they confirm the argument or undercut it?
3. Do you believe in the philosophy of love that the poem presents? Does it seem unrealistic?

Anonymous, "Sir Patrick Spens"

"Sir Patrick Spens" is one of the popular ballads, passed down in the oral tradition from generation to generation. Its story is a folk version of the lives of the aristocracy, emphasizing their tendency toward intrigue and betrayal. The ballad form is used very straightforwardly here, telling a story without much commentary or interference on the part of the narrator.

1. Why does the poem have so little to say about *why* Sir Patrick is betrayed?
2. What is the significance to the poem of the last two lines?

John Keats, "La Belle Dame sans Merci"

Keats makes direct use not only of the ballad form but of the subject matter of the traditional ballad, which often concerns itself with meetings between mortal men and spirits. In this case the spirit is a woman who completely fulfills the knight's desires, which suggests that she exists only as a projection of his desires. The interest of the poem to many students is that this story of a perfect fulfillment of a fantasy leads in the end to the destruction of the knight. That fantasy and desire might be dangerous is a difficult paradox for many students. The poem is also of interest in its psychological acuity. It is the dream inside the fantasy that wakes the dreamer up to a cold reality. In order to avoid confusion, students should be reminded that there are two speakers in the poem, with the knight taking over from a speaker-observer at the beginning of stanza four.

1. What is the state of the knight at the beginning and end of the poem?
2. As a narrative, what does this ballad emphasize most?
3. What does this poem have to say about the role of fantasies in our lives?

Dylan Thomas, "Do Not Go Gentle into That Good Night"

This poem serves in the text as an example of an extremely formal metrical pattern that still deals with deep emotion. The idea of strong emotion and careful attention to form may seem contradictory, but in this case it is as if the villanelle form served as an antidote to the extreme emotion caused by the death of the speaker's father. This poem is also famous as an example of extreme verbal complexity, especially in stanzas two through five. Students will often struggle with these lines dealing with the reactions to death of wise and good and wild and grave men, all of which the speaker wants to serve as models to his father of the resistance to death. In fact, the speaker's need for his father to resist death suggests that the poem is more about the state of mind of the speaker than about the father's struggle.

1. Is the villanelle form appropriate to the subject matter of the poem?
2. What relationship between the speaker and his father comes out of the poem?
3. Why do wise men, good men, wild men, grave men resist death so fiercely? Do you agree that they do resist death? Isn't acceptance of death one sign of wisdom?

Chapter Six: The Speaker of the Poem

William Carlos Williams, "This is just to say"

This is used in the text as an example of a poem that does not directly present its own dramatic context but rather requires the reader to construct the speaker and his context. Classroom discussion might well turn up a large number of valid reconstructions of the event, all of them legitimate extrapolations of the language of the poem. What everyone might agree on, though, is that the words of the poem comprise a meaningful gesture inside some kind of relationship. This poem, within whatever dramatic situation we invent, is an *action* that sends a complex message. Close attention to the language of the poem could also lead to a discussion of its form, especially its metrics and line structure. In this poem, the exact presentation of the message obviously contributes to the meaning of the gesture within the relationship.

1. What is your image of the speaker and the situation inside which this message is sent?
2. How does the poem suggest that context?
3. What are the formal rules of this poem? Describe the stanza and line formations.

William Shakespeare, "Sonnet 18" ("Shall I compare thee to a summer's day?")

Shakespeare's poem also takes us into the midst of a relationship. The poem takes the form of a compliment, which suggests that we could construct an image of the speaker who gives the compliment and the listener who receives it. The poem would therefore be a symptom of their relationship. My own reading of the poem is that the relationship is more complex than it first seems, largely on account of the egotism of the speaker. The poem can also be read profitably as an example of the sonnet form, especially in terms of how the sections of the poem interact.

Robert Browning, "My Last Duchess"

This poem is an obvious selection for this section of the text, but the poem deserves its classic status as a revelation of character through language. The Duke's intricate rhetoric reveals more of himself than he intends, and the poem allows us the detachment necessary to take in the Duke's point of view and yet retain our own, letting us come to our own judgment of his actions. Students can move from the poem's language and rhetoric to the mind of the Duke, and they can get at the Duke's destructive attitude toward his duchess. The poem is an extended argument in verse, with the Duke attempting to force his listener to see events as the Duke sees them. We catch the Duke at the process of putting a meaning on his own life, which allows us the distance to put our own meaning on it. The fact that we can see the Duke attempting to utilize the power of language allows us to be critical of his account.

Alfred, Lord Tennyson, "Ulysses"

The speaker of the poem is Ulysses himself, now caught in what seems to him the boring regularity of life in Ithaca after the adventures of the Odyssey. The poem presents Ulysses' feelings and his life situation very clearly, so that students can work back from the poem to the speaker. The poem is also noteworthy for its powerful rhetoric, directed at the mariners in order to persuade them to join Ulysses in his adventure. The poem is therefore interesting as a revelation of the character of its fictional audience. In this case, who is being spoken to is as important as who is speaking. Ulysses' rhetoric is directed specifically at the mariners who, he hopes, share his restlessness, his sense that life without adventure is not worth living.

Theodore Roethke, "My Papa's Waltz"

In this descriptive poem, there is no overt judgment. The speaker of the poem does not reflect—he only remembers. And yet the language of the poem is richly evocative not only of an action but of the emotions that surrounded it. The language is far from objective. It is emotional, but not simply so. The connotations of its language suggest a complex emotional state in the speaker. There is therefore a lot of room for debate on the question of the speaker's attitude toward the father. To say that the speaker is ambivalent would be only to begin an answer. All of the father's actions can be interpreted in various ways, and the poem registers a wide variety of emotional responses. The poem is also interesting as a highly compressed narrative in verse. There is a very strong plot, developed characters, a vivid setting, and a coherent point of view. In fact, the speaker of this poem could better be called the narrator, so that we could focus on how he reconstructs the story.

Marnie Walsh, "The Red Fox"

This poem attempts to present a moment of experience that has stayed vividly alive in the memory of the speaker. The question of why the event is so important could lead to a useful discussion of the poem. The image of the fox fits into the speaker's account of her state of mind at the moment she saw it. The poem suggests that the fox is a message that comments on the speaker's life, but it leaves the content of that message unsaid, up to the reader to discern. Is the fox a rebuke, a sign of hope, part of an instructive opposition? Or can we leave it a random event, not a message but a coincidence? This is a poem that leaves the reader a lot of options.

Chapter Seven: Poems in Relationship to Other Poems

Poems in a Book

William Blake's *Songs of Innocence and of Experience* provide the instructor with a great deal of flexibility. Each poem can be studied separately, or matching poems from each section can be studied together, or poems from within one section can be compared in order to show the range included under the concept, for example, of Innocence. "The Lamb" from *Innocence*, to take an obvious case, matches well with "The Tyger" from *Experience*, but it is also interesting to compare "The Lamb" with a poem from *Innocence* such as "Holy Thursday," whose speaker seems to be clinging too late to an Innocence that the speaker of "The Lamb" possesses naturally. The poems are all interesting with regard to their speakers. Each poem suggests a slightly different speaker. Some of the speakers in *Experience*, for example, seem new to the state and startled by the harshness of reality, whereas other speakers in this state seem to have developed a tougher skin. Each poem develops its own characteristic verbal strategies and styles, consistent with the speaker of the poem. The differences between *Innocence* and *Experience* are easy to describe in the abstract, as I do briefly in the text, but once you start to look closely at the poems, the definitions become less secure and more flexible. In my comments on these poems I hope to suggest how they could be related to others in the book, and how each poem develops its own speaker.

Songs of Innocence

"Introduction"

Blake's "Introduction" to *The Songs of Innocence* constructs a miniature myth to explain the creative origins of these poems. The speaker of the poem claims that his inspiration was a spirit-child who dictated the subject of his poem ("Pipe a song about a Lamb!") and its mediums of expression (*pipe, sing, write*). The very fact that the child gets exactly what it wants in this poem suggests the simple, uncomplicated spirit of Innocence. There is, however, one word in the poem with negative connotations, "stain'd," which is associated with writing and which suggests that the writing of the songs is somehow impure, that they could only exist in complete purity if they were spoken or sung rather than written. Despite this one negative, the poem is otherwise an uplifting and simple message that sets the tone for the rest of *The Songs of Innocence.*

1. What is the relationship between the piper and the child? Who is in control?
2. Is there any significance in the sequence of orders that the child gives to the piper—*pipe, sing, write?*
3. How is writing described in the poem?

"The Shepherd"

In this poem the lambs and the Shepherd symbolize for the speaker the state of Innocence. They live in utter confidence that the Shepherd will take care of them, and the Shepherd just as simply fulfills his role and protects them. From the perspective of Innocence, such simple relationships are possible. In fact, the "call" and "reply" between the lambs and the ewes are a good image for the state of Innocence itself. In Innocence every call gets an answer and every Shepherd is completely reliable. It is interesting to note, however, that even in this most innocent poem, there is a hint of danger, if only in the realization that there is something out there that requires protection for the lambs. That "something" cannot be spoken by this speaker, but it looms silently behind the poem.

1. What is the significance of the word "strays" as it applies to the Shepherd?
2. Does the Shepherd of this poem recall the "good shepherd" of the Bible? How does such imagery fit into the state of Innocence?
3. What image of the speaker arises from the poem?

"The Ecchoing Green"

This poem depicts an almost Edenic scene of natural beauty, childlike play, and gracefully aging, nurturing adults. In the first stanza the description of the natural scene is full of personifications that give the impression that nature is fully unified with mankind. In the second stanza, the old folk seem accepting of their aging and they look back wistfully but not bitterly on their childhood. The third stanza does, however, suggest a darker side to life with its image of night coming and children gathering for protection around their mothers. The speaker in this poem is a child for whom the world is a safe and nurturing place where children can play as securely as the lambs in "The Shepherd."

1. In what ways is nature personified in the first stanza?
2. What image of aging does the poem suggest?
3. What is the effect of having the word "darkening" replace "ecchoing" in the last line of the last stanza?

"The Lamb"

As I suggested earlier, this poem matches interestingly with "The Tyger" from *Experience*. Both poems ask questions dealing with creation. "The Tyger" asks the troubling question of what kind of god could have created such a fearsome creature. But in "The Lamb" there are no such difficult matters. The speaker of the poem is a child who has all the answers. For him the world is symbolized by the lamb—it is an innocent and mild world. He is equally sure that the god of that world is a meek and mild god, a divine version of the lamb and of the child himself. In contrast with "The Tyger," which consists completely of questions, this poem poses questions only to answer them immediately, with certainty. What makes the poem particularly interesting is how consistently it expresses the simple metaphysics of the child. Its metrics and form are as simple as its worldview. The poem has an almost singsong quality that perfectly captures the simplicity of the child speaker.

1. What image of the lamb's life comes out of the first stanza?
2. What qualities do the lamb, the child, and Christ share?
3. How does the god of this poem contrast with the god suggested by "The Tyger"?

"The Little Black Boy"

This is one of the most intricate of the *Songs of Innocence*. Blake, whom one critic has called a "prophet against empire," believed that imperialism attempted to diminish the humanity of those it dominated, and this poem shows in intimate detail how the imperialist mind-set affects a child who grows up inside it. The child has already learned to hate himself because he is black, and his mother's kindly protection offers little help. She tries to teach him to deal with his second-class status by arguing that the body is temporary and separate from the soul, so that the suffering he experiences here on earth will be rewarded by joy in the next life. For Blake, such teachings deny his belief in the unity of soul and body and in a heaven that is here now and not to be waited for in some sweet by-and-by. Nevertheless, the child is capable of seeing the injustice of his situation, and he and his mother have at least imagined a world in which such injustice does not exist. So the poem presents two people who are learning from Experience but trying to hold on to Innocence in the face of an evil system.

1. What does it suggest about the black child that he believes that although his body is black his soul is white?
2. What does the child's mother teach him about how to survive in the cruel world he inhabits?
3. What kind of relationship does the black child anticipate he will have with the white child in Heaven?
4. In what sense is the speaker of this poem innocent?

"The Blossom"

This cryptic poem leaves almost everything up in the air. Is the speaker the Blossom itself or some observer? What is the difference between the merry sparrow and the sobbing robin? What is the Blossom's response to these different emotions? How does the simple, childlike verse relate to the complex emotional and even sexual connotations of the language? This poem gives so few strong clues that it serves almost as a Rorschach test in which the reader can see whatever he or she projects.

1. How does the second stanza repeat the first? How does it differ?
2. What is the effect of personification in the poem?
3. What is the significance of the fact that the Blossom is happy whether it observes happiness or sorrow in others? Is the Blossom's response innocent or cold?

"The Chimney Sweeper"

This poem is one of the most often debated of the *Songs of Innocence.* The debate centers around the tone of the last line of the poem, "So if all do their duty they need not fear harm." The speaker of the poem is one of the sweepers who is helping Tom, the new boy, to adjust to the hard life of the chimney sweeper. Sweepers in early industrial England were often very young children, usually orphans who were kept in church-run orphanages and used to clean the huge, labyrinthine industrial chimneys, in whose narrow chambers sweepers were often injured or killed. The last line of the poem follows on Tom's dream of liberation from the sweeper's dark life, in which an Angel tells him " if he'd be a good boy, / He'd have God for his father, and never want joy." Some critics see the last line as a pathetic irony, in the sense that the boys may convince themselves that obedience will preserve them and be rewarded in Heaven, whereas the reality is that obedience will almost certainly end in their destruction. Other critics feel that the boys can use their innocent faith in God as a real shield against the pains of their life, so that, in a complex irony, their naiveté turns out to be truer than our experienced cynicism. The openness of this point at the end of the poem can lead to interesting student discussion and writing.

1. How does the speaker try to console Tom for the loss of his beautiful hair?
2. What is the significance of Tom's dream? In what ways does the dream make sense in the lives of chimney sweepers?
3. Do you agree with the speaker's assertion in the last line?

"The Little Boy Lost"

This poem may seem ill-suited as a song of *Innocence.* In this poem the world is certainly not the secure and nurturing place it is in "The Ecchoing Green" or "The Shepherd." It is a terrifying and truly dangerous place in which the little boy has been abandoned. But there are two ways the poem makes an interesting comment on the state of Innocence. The poem could be thought of as a nightmare of Innocence, in which the dependent status of Innocence is brought harshly to light. The child is going through one of the primal childhood fears, abandonment by the father in a nightmare landscape of mire and dew. And when you connect this poem with "The Little Boy Found," which stresses the fact that it is the mother who has been seeking the boy, it seems that Blake may be suggesting that the psychology behind Innocence is much more complex than we might think. Also, the poem belongs in *Innocence* in the sense that the speaker of the poem empathizes with the child so strongly, suggesting the speaker's innocent state of mind.

1. How would you describe the rhyme scheme of this poem? What is the effect of the strong rhyme in the second stanza?
2. How much difference is there between the language of the first stanza, which is spoken by the lost boy, and the language of the second stanza, which is spoken by an observing narrator?

"The Little Boy Found"

The immediacy of this response to "The Little Boy Lost" confirms the Innocence of the speaker of the poems. That is, the second poem is so obviously a wish fulfillment generated by the fears of the first, that one can only think of the speaker as an innocent who sees the world as a place in which all suffering is relieved, in which all calls are answered. The poem also confirms the psychological complexity that "The Little Boy Lost" suggests. The little boy is saved by God, who takes the place of the missing father and leads the boy to the loyal, grieving mother. In these poems "father" seems to represent the cold, uncaring world of Experience, whereas "mother" represents the nurturing world of Innocence. What this suggests to me is that Blake saw this conventional psychological structure as an indication of the simplifying mind of Innocence.

1. What does it suggest about Innocence that God takes the place of the father in this poem?
2. Why does Blake take two poems to tell this story? Why not tell the lost and the found together?
3. What other characters in Innocence does the mother in this poem resemble?

"Laughing Song"

It is hard not to think of Blake as laughing at the expense of Innocence in this silly poem. The chorus of "Ha, Ha, He!" is almost too much to take—it sounds hysterical rather than innocent. And the poem is so loaded with personifications—the woods laugh, the stream laughs, the air and the hill and the meadows and the grasshoppers and the birds all laugh along with the speaker—that the speaker's tendency to personify the world seems almost psychotic. This poem, along with others, suggests that Innocence is a state that must eventually be left behind if the person is to achieve a coherent vision of the world. At the same time, it must be remembered that the *vision* here, of a world unified with mankind, is the goal of Blake's writing career. He felt, though, that only by giving up Innocence and entering Experience could one later regain an innocent state that does not deny the harsher realities of life.

"A Cradle Song"

For me, the speaker of this poem is the center of interest. It is the mother of a sleeping baby who speaks, praying for her child's Innocence. She seems to me to be aware of the dangers of the world, but she wants to shield her child from them as long as possible. In the last three stanzas, however, the speaker seems to shut out that awareness of danger by returning to a more innocent view of the world as the benign creation of a childlike God. She seems to offer her naive theology as a defense against her more experienced recognition that the world is not so secure (or else why would she weep over her child?). Blake's perspective on Innocence in this poem, then, is to see it as a quality that can be lost but still called on as a reassurance.

1. What is the effect of repetition in this poem? What patterns do the repetitions form? Are there significant deviations from the pattern? What effects do they produce?
2. What is the significance of the word "beguiles," which is used three times in the poem?
3. How and why does the poem associate the sleeping baby with the Christ child?

"The Divine Image"

This poem suggests the complexities of Innocence that lie under its simple surface. On one level the speaker of the poem seems innocent in the negative sense—naive, oversimplifying. We all know, in our experienced state, that there is more to mankind than "Mercy, Pity, Peace, and Love." So it is easy for us to look down on this speaker. However, the speaker is also articulating a powerful vision of what human beings and their relationships could be. He is acting as a prophet in Blake's sense, one who sees what can only be imagined. The concluding message of the poem, that we need to see the god in all men and to respect their religious practices, is one that Blake can respect as a truth that only Innocence can reveal.

1. What does the poem suggest about the relationship between human beings and God?
2. What does this poem have to say about religious diversity, especially in the last two stanzas?
3. How do the abstract nouns ("Mercy, Pity, Peace, and Love") function in this poem? Are they personified?

"Holy Thursday"

This poem is obviously best studied in relationship to its companion poem in *Experience*. Both poems "cover" the same event, a ceremonial procession of orphan children supported by the Church. The speaker of this poem sees the procession in completely positive terms. He sees the beauty of the children as a spectacle and he trusts implicitly in the wisdom of the children's caretakers. In the matching poem in *Experience* we get a more critical view of the procession, stressing the exploitation of these children by their masters in the name of religion. Comparing the two poems makes the speaker of this poem seem extremely naive, a willing follower of the party line. But there is a sense in which this innocent speaker is closer to the mind-set of these children and can therefore see their joy and their potential power ("like harmonious thunderings"). The speaker in *Experience*, however, can see only the children's suffering and cannot feel their—temporary—joy.

1. What figures of speech does the speaker use to describe the children? What do these figures tell us about his attitude toward them?

2. What image of the speaker does the poem convey?
3. How does the metrical practice of the poem differ from other poems in *Innocence?*

"Night"

In this poem Innocence expresses itself in two—perhaps contradictory—images. The first is a fanciful image of night in which angels stand guard over and bring solace to all of God's creatures, so that the world seems to be the benign place that Innocence so often depicts it. The poem then pivots around the image of the attacking predators who shatter that peace. In the second image of Innocence, that peaceful world is then projected into the future, after the souls of the victims are received into Heaven, where the lion lies down with the lamb and recognizes their common creator. But if the world is a benign place, why do we need the solace of Heaven? Or is the depiction of the angels who keep watch over the night simply a wish fulfillment?

1. How is nature depicted in the poem?
2. What role does the poem give to the angels?
3. What is the image of Heaven that the poem depicts?
4. How does the violence of the predators fit into the poem's innocent vision?

"Spring"

On one level this is one of the simplest of the *Songs of Innocence.* Through a series of aural images, the speaker connects the sound of the flute, the sound of the birds, and the sound of the baby, suggesting the themes of natural unity and benevolence so common in these poems. But when you think about the speaker, you get a more complex poem. The language and the metrics of the poem suggest that a child is speaking, but the speaker is in fact an adult observing children. The discontinuity between the language and the speaker is unsettling. As a reader, I find it difficult to imagine an adult speaking these words. And if I think of the speaker as an adult, I have to find the last stanza downright creepy. Is Blake suggesting that an adult who holds on to Innocence too long can become pathetic—even simpleminded?

1. What are the metrical rules for the stanzas in this poem?
2. How does the poem unify human beings and the natural world?

"Nurse's Song"

This poem is almost the sheer opposite of "Spring." It is much more realistic. We are presented with a believable speaker in a recognizable situation, a nurse calling in the children from their evening play. Her interactions with the children are part of the ordinary give and take of the day: with the children delaying as long as possible and the nurse giving in, perhaps realizing that they should be allowed to enjoy their Innocence as long as possible. Some readers hear a different tone in the poem, suggesting that the nurse's response is spiteful, that she is aware of the dangers of the night (perhaps suggesting Experience) and still allows the children to be exposed to those dangers, perhaps out of her own bitterness at the harshness of Experience. It seems to me that the poem supports either reading, and that the question therefore would make an interesting writing assignment.

1. What is the nurse's state of mind as she describes in the first stanza the children playing on the green?
2. In what way is she affected by the coming of night, described in the second stanza?
3. What argument do the children offer in the third stanza in order to keep their play going?
4. Why does the nurse respond as she doe sin the last stanza?

"Infant Joy"

The themes that dominate *Innocence* are presented beautifully here. The poem centers on the loving unity between parent and child. It enacts an imaginary conversation between parent and child, in which the parent intuits the name of the child, Joy. It is as though the name of a child were not assigned by the parent but rather that the identity of the child somehow speaks itself to the parent and demands a name. What is presented here, then, is in a sense an "innocent" view of language as the set of proper names for objects in the world, rather than as a set of categories imposed on the world by the human mind. This poem of course contrasts very sharply with "Infant Sorrow" from *Experience*. There, the baby's experience is not one of unity but of conflict.

1. What is the effect of repetition in the poem?
2. How is the "conversation" between parent and child handled in the poem?

"A Dream"

This poem presents a dream of Innocence. In the dream, the speaker sees an ant who is lost, hears her anguish over her children's sorrow, and sympathizes with the ant's suffering. What makes this an innocent dream is that the speaker feels this sympathy for such a "humble" representative of nature, and especially that the speaker's sympathy magically saves the ant from its predicament. To the innocent mind, all sorrow can be relieved, as it is in "Night," for example. But clearly the speaker of this poem is not completely innocent, at least in the realization that suffering is a reality. The world of this poem may ultimately be benign, but it has its dangers as well.

1. What is the significance of the image of the shade that the speaker uses to describe the dream?
2. Why does Blake present this vision of an innocent world as a *dream?*

"On Another's Sorrow"

The structure of this poem is built around a series of questions and answers. The questions constitute a poetic argument, an attempt to convince the reader (and maybe the speaker himself) of God's benevolence. The argument itself is curious, in that it uses the benevolence of mankind as a basis for arguing for the benevolence of God. For the speaker, all the poem's questions are rhetorical, asked only so that they can be answered. But they can also be read as open, serious questions. After all, is the answer to the question "Can a father see his child / Weep, nor be with sorrow fill'd?" so self-evident, as though their were no malevolent fathers? Nevertheless, the last three stanzas of the poem are a powerful vision of the god of Innocence, a sympathetic, sacrificing god who wants to destroy human suffering and create a perfect home for mankind.

1. What is the relationship between parent and child in the poem?
2. What is the relationship between God and mankind in the poem?
3. What is the effect of the metrical pattern of the poem—stanzas of rhymed couplets?

Songs of Experience

"Introduction"

In this poem we hear the difficult voice of Blake's prophetic works. For Blake, the prophet (or Bard, as in this poem) speaks out of an imaginative power that comes from his acceptance of the divine power that dwells within him. Here the Bard is calling to the Soul of mankind and to nature to arise out of their separateness and reunify. Obviously they have lost the simple unity that they enjoyed in Innocence. In the state of Experience, human beings are not at home in a benevolent world. In Experience there is conflict and denial, as we see in the last stanza, where the Earth turns away from the Prophet's plea. Unlike in Innocence, his call receives no satisfying reply. A comparison of this poem with its match in *Innocence* will show even at a glance how much more complex and demanding the vision of Experience is.

1. The voice of the poem is identified in the poem as a Bard. On the basis of his language and poetic strategies, what can you say about the mental state of the Bard?
2. What does the second stanza suggest about the power of the human Soul?
3. What does the Bard offer to the Earth in the last two stanzas?

"Earth's Answer"

Earth's reply to the Bard is expressed in overtly sexual terms, as she explains her inability to answer his offer in terms of repression and jealousy. A mythic father figure keeps her in chains, denying her the freedom to love. This theme of sexual repression and its spiritual consequences is common throughout the *Songs of Experience.* If we read this poem on an allegorical level, is Blake suggesting that the unity between mankind and nature is lost because we repress our ability to love and therefore lose our Innocence? These first two poems in *Experience* are probably the most difficult in the book, and yet they do introduce the themes of the book on a mythic level, and therefore deserve students' attention, even if the poems are puzzling and frustrating.

1. What do the images of cold and darkness do in the poem?
2. What is the role of "the father of men" in the relationship between the Earth and the Bard?
3. What is the effect of the rhetorical questions in the fourth stanza?

"The Clod and the Pebble"

This poem presents an allegorical debate about the nature of love. The Clod articulates an extremely innocent vision of love as a completely selfless emotion, seeking only the happiness of the other. The Pebble, however, presents a grimmer view, seeing love as a selfish desire for power and control. Who is right? In the eyes of the speaker, the Pebble is right, I think. To the speaker, the Clod's attitude gets him "trodden" down, whereas the Pebble's beliefs are, in the speaker's words, "meet" or correct. Which means that the speaker is in the state of Experience, in which human desires appear not to cooperate in search of unity but rather to compete with each other in a selfish conflict. For Blake, I think, the fact that such a view is "realistic" is terrible, and this selfishness is a result of restraints on desire that become a major theme of the book.

1. How do the speeches of the Clod and the Pebble differ from each other? How are they similar?
2. What are the strengths and weaknesses of each view?
3. Is it possible to get a sense of the speaker from the little that we see in the second stanza?

"Holy Thursday"

This poem has its exact match in *Innocence*, and a comparison of the two poems can serve pedagogically as a compact introduction to the *Songs*. The poems provide us with a situation in which we have two very different speakers observing the same event, so that we can see Innocence and Experience sharply and richly contrasted. But that does not mean that the speakers are sheer opposites. Within Experience there is as much variety in the mental states of speakers as there is in Innocence. In this poem I feel that the speaker's outrage at the plight of these orphans is so raw that he could be seen as new to Experience, still holding on to the purity of the innocent vision, even as it is betrayed in front of his eyes. This speaker knows that the orphans are exploited—he has no illusions of a benign social order—but he is still shocked by the revelation. And his outrage blinds him to the joy that lives in these still innocent children. Obviously this speaker's personality can be read in other ways, but none of those ways would be simple. The speakers of these poems cannot be defined by category, for each poem constructs a different identity for its speaker.

1. How would the speaker answer the questions posed in the first two stanzas? Is it possible to answer them differently?
2. What does the nature imagery of the third stanza tell us about the speaker's view of the orphans' lives?
3. What does the last stanza suggest about the speaker's personality?

"The Little Girl Lost"

With the following two poems the interconnections between poems become extremely complex. That is, "The Little Girl Lost" must be read in terms of "The Little Girl Found," as well as in connection with the "Little Boy" poems of *Innocence* and with "A Little Boy Lost" and "A Little Girl Lost" from *Experience*. Obviously, this whole group of poems would make an interesting project for a class or a writer. In this poem, the story of Lyca lost in the desert is told in terms that might recall Innocence. That is, despite her fears, she is saved by a benevolent natural order. However, the sexuality suggested by the lion and lioness place us in the world of Experience. Realization of sexuality is one of the events that form the transition from Innocence to Experience. Lyca moves outside the control of her parents and is initiated into the mysterious world of sexuality, which is associated in the poem with natural drives, and in the next poem even with spirituality. Lyca is therefore a figure who we can see making the transition into Experience and thus helps to display its differences from Innocence.

1. How are the first two stanzas of the poem related to the story of Lyca?
2. What is the setting for Lyca's story? What kind of world does she inhabit?
3. How are the images of unity between human beings and nature in this poem different from the images of unity in *Innocence?*

"The Little Girl Found"

The completion of Lyca's story again might seem to belong in *Innocence*—Lyca's parents prove faithful to her, as parents do in Innocence, and they find her in a natural paradise that they choose to live in forever. But as a continuation of Lyca's story, the poem helps to define Experience by completing the logic of Lyca's introduction to sexuality. The first poem associates sex with nature, and this poem connects both to the world of spirit. That is, it denies the distinction between body and spirit, seeing sexuality as a spiritual act. Blake's state of Experience involves an awareness and acceptance of sexuality, and Lyca's story could therefore be seen as a successful transition into Experience. As other poems show, there is a harsher side to Experience, but this story of Lyca presents the state very positively.

1. How are Lyca's parents presented in the story? Are they changed by their experience?
2. In some ways this story resembles a fairy tale. How is it similar and how is it different from typical fairy tales?
3. What is the significance of the ending of the poem? Is this a vision of Innocence?

"The Chimney Sweeper"

The speaker of this poem provides a striking contrast to the speaker of "The Chimney Sweeper" in *Innocence,* the little boy who consoles his friend with the belief that "if all do their duty they need not fear harm." The child who speaks here is almost completely cynical, abandoned by his parents and convinced that they abandoned him *because* of his happiness. He blames his parents and along with them "God & his Priest & King" for his exploitation. For this child there is no benevolence in the world, as there is in Innocence. He gets no protection from family, from society, even from religion. He has found through bitter Experience that the innocent vision is inadequate to the complexities of the world.

1. What is the significance of the color imagery in the first line?
2. What does the poem suggest about the relationship between the child and his parents?
3. What is the child's attitude toward religion?

"Nurse's Song"

This poem provides a relatively simple version of the dark side of Experience. The speaker here can be contrasted with her matching figure in *Innocence*, who watches lovingly over the children's play. In this poem the speaker is made bitter by the children's joy, which reminds her of her own losses. Her attitude is summed up in the bitter last lines, and the flat, straightforward style of the poem reinforces that attitude as well.

1. How does the last line fit into the rest of the first stanza?
2. How does the nurse in this poem differ from the nurse in *Innocence?*
3. What does the speaker mean by the word *disguise* as a description of adulthood?

"The Sick Rose"

This poem seems in some ways the opposite of the Lyca poems, which are a positive depiction of a young girl's introduction into sexuality. For here the sexual language of the poem takes on a negative connotation, in that it is associated with conflict and death. That is, the destruction of the flower by the worm is described in sexual terms, thus associating sexuality with violence and death. The notion that love, especially "dark secret love," can destroy is clearly far from the innocent version of love as benevolent unity. But it is also darker than Lyca's story, in which sexuality is accepted but is presented in an idyllic style. Here we fully inhabit the harsh world of Experience, where love can be used to destroy.

1. What is the effect on the poem of the "howling storm" that surrounds the destruction of the flower?
2. Why is it important that the worm's is a "dark secret love"?

"The Fly"

This poem uses the language and metrics of Innocence to deliver an Experienced message. The speaker of the poem realizes that what he has in common with the natural world is that he is subject to death. Like the fly, he is vulnerable to the power of a force he cannot control. What is perhaps most interesting about that discovery is that it happens only after the speaker has played the role of that higher power to the fly. Being in power leads to an awareness of one's own victimization. The language of the poem is also of interest, recalling the simplicity of the style of *Innocence.* As a result, it is difficult to imagine a speaker this simple in his language and this complex in his thought.

1. What does the poem suggest that the man and the fly have in common?
2. Can you paraphrase the "if . . . then" reasoning of the last two stanzas?

"The Angel"

This poem of Experience tells a tale of sexual denial and repression. It is the fact that the Queen hides her sexuality that leads to her isolation at the end. In Experience, we encounter sexuality, but we also encounter the fears and rules that deny sexuality. As a result, the Queen defends herself against sexuality, unwilling to risk the complexities of sex in Experience. It is also of interest that it is a woman who denies in this poem, for Blake felt that the repression of sexuality by society fell especially hard on women, who were required to deny their own sexual energy.

1. Is it important that the story told here is a dream?
2. What do you make of the line "Witless woe was ne'er beguiled!"?
3. What is the result for the Queen of her denial?

"The Tyger"

The contrasts between this poem and "The Lamb" are so striking and consistent that they make an excellent introduction to the entire book. Where "The Lamb" is simple, verbally and metrically, "The Tyger" is complex. The poems sound different and provide clearly different reading experiences. In this poem we have a speaker who asks questions, who has none of the certainty of Innocence. What kind of being could have produced the tiger? And could it have been the same god who created the lamb? Such questions cannot be answered with certainty in Experience, a state in which we recognize complexity and find few satisfying explanations. The speaker does speculate, ending up with an image of a winged god, working at a mental forge in order to produce the tiger out of fire. But the speculation is just that, an admitted guess at an answer to a question that is beyond our comprehension.

1. What are "the forests of the night," and what does the phrase suggest about the tiger being described in the poem?
2. To whom is the speaker speaking? Is it important that the poem is a direct address?
3. What image of the god who created the tiger comes out of the poem?
4. What kind of god would be capable of creating both the lamb and the tiger? Why would this be an important concern in these songs?

"My Pretty Rose-tree"

This is one of the many allegorical stories told in *Experience.* Here a dramatic event inside a relationship is narrated in terms of flowers and trees and thorns. The story is very complex, like all stories in Experience. Each character's response confounds expectations. The speaker surprises himself by refusing the flower, the Rose-tree surprises the speaker by being jealous despite his fidelity, and the speaker surprises us at the end by expressing his "delight" at the pain she inflicts on him. The very strategy of employing allegorical language suggests that this relationship is too complex and intense to be directly described. Reading a second level on to this allegorical story, as I have done and as I think students should be encouraged to do, should be done speculatively, realizing that the poem authorizes many different readings. The point is to encourage debate on the complex psychology that the poem suggests.

1. In the allegory, what does the flower represent? The rose-tree? The speaker?
2. Why does the speaker use allegorical language to tell this story?
3. Is the outcome of this story predictable, or is it a surprise?

"Ah! Sun-flower"

In this poem the allegorical language is extremely complex. Clearly the poem asks for a second-level reading, a translation of the story into a meaning. But that meaning is not at all simple. The second stanza of the poem, which could be read as a reading of the allegory in the first, is verbally confusing. How can these youths aspire to go where they already are? Or is there another way to read the logic of this stanza? One reading of the little story might be that the "sweet golden clime" that the sun-flower desires is a world exempt from time, which is also what the young lovers might desire. But how would living in a timeless realm remove the restraints that keep them apart? It seems to me that any reading of the story would run into similar complexities.

1. Why would a sun-flower be weary of time?
2. What is the "sweet golden clime" that the sun-flower seeks?
3. What do the Youth and the Virgin desire? How is their desire similar to that of the sun-flower?

"The Lilly"

"The Lilly" seems in some ways like a song of *Innocence*, in that it rejects conflict and complexity in favor of defenseless simplicity. Both the Rose and the Sheep in this poem are complex creatures, apparently mild but in fact well-defended. The Lilly, however, is what it appears to be, mild and defenseless. But as a result, *it* will find love and retain its pristine beauty. My sense is that the poem does belong in *Experience*, though, in that the speaker is weary of the complexity of Experience and longs nostalgically for the simplicity of Innocence. Perhaps this is Blake's way of dramatizing the old saw that if you scratch the surface of a cynic, you find a hidden sentimentalist.

1. How is the Lilly different from the Rose and the Sheep? What does that suggest in the poem's presentation of Love?
2. In what sense could a threat "stain" the beauty of a creature?

"The Garden of Love"

If entering Experience involves becoming aware of sexuality, it also involves learning that there are limits imposed on sexuality. The speaker here is, I would say, new to Experience, in that he is surprised by the complexity of love, in which what is most desired is most denied. The force that disciplines love is identified here as organized religion, which is described as killing the spirit and abusing the body. There is even the hint that such abuse gives the priests pleasure, denying in others what they have denied in themselves. Like many of the *Songs of Experience*, this poem is critical of religion, but only in the name of a more personal and interior spiritual experience. This poem can be read profitably in connection with such poems as "The Clod and the Pebble," "The Little Girl Lost," "The Little Girl Found," "The Sick Rose," "The Angel," "My Pretty Rose-tree," and "The Lilly" as a compound portrait of sexuality in the state of Experience.

1. How is the Garden of Love different now than it was for the speaker in the past?
2. What is the significance of the graves that now appear in the Garden?
3. What is suggested by the graphic image in the last line of the poem?

"The Little Vagabond"

The poem presents us with a clear dramatic situation. The speaker is the vagabond, and he is speaking to (or at least addressing—she may be absent) his mother. His experienced wisdom has led him to the paradoxical conclusion that the Ale-house is better for him than the Church. The Ale-house is a place of warmth and acceptance, whereas the Church is a place that does not sustain children (they are crippled and hungry) but rather disciplines them with violence (the birch). The child's cosmic vision of a reunification of God and the Devil suggests that he is a young version of the Bard who speaks in the first poem in *Experience*, one who can prophesy the imaginative future.

1. What does the Ale-house offer that the Church does not?
2. How should we judge the speaker of the poem? Is he naive or visionary?
3. What would be the result of a reconciliation between God and the Devil?

"London"

One of Blake's greatest and most complex short poems, "London" is at once a powerful attack on Church and State and commerce, and an insightful analysis of the psychology of the speaker. The speaker is a wandering observer of the city and its culture, and he is horrified by what he sees: a Church that exploits children, a State that exploits its soldiers, a sexuality so restricted by Church and society that it breeds prostitution, which in turn infects the institution of marriage. More spiritually, the speaker sees human beings who have imposed limits on themselves ("mind forg'd manacles") that will eventually destroy them. The rich and difficult last stanza suggests that sexual rules lead to their own undoing, and that society is being corrupted by its own hypocrisy. But the speaker of the poem is so absolute in his tale of woe that he undermines his own authority as an observer. That is, *everything* he sees confirms his predisposition, which suggests that he suffers from a bitter blindness to any human innocence and happiness. The poem doesn't therefore dismiss his criticisms of society, but it does suggest the costs that being constantly in opposition can incur on a person in Experience.

1. What kind of person finds "marks of woe" in every face he meets?
2. What kind of vision of London does the poem give you?
3. How does the poem suggest that prostitution and marriage are related?

"The Human Abstract"

This poem opens with a rejoinder to its matching poem in *Innocence*, "The Human Image," which identifies "Mercy, Pity, Peace, and Love" as the qualities that bind people together and connect them with God. In this poem, Pity and Mercy come from guilt, Peace comes from fear, and Love is selfish. What follows is a narrative in which the actors are the "abstract" words that the title refers to—"Cruelty, Humility, Mystery, Deceit." It is a story in which mankind humbles and deceives itself into believing that the truth is a mystery it cannot solve. The story is intricate, and can be read in various ways. How those abstractions relate to one another is a complex question, but I do feel that all answers point to the end of the poem, "the Human Brain," as the source of these self-deceptions. If we live our lives through these abstractions we can miss the significance of the specific events of life, which should not be pushed into such categories.

1. Do you agree with the speaker's analysis of Pity and Mercy in the first stanza?
2. What is the story told in the second through fifth stanzas?
3. What is the significance of the fact that the tree of Mystery grows in the human brain?

"A Poison Tree"

This is an allegorical story from Experience about personal relations. They can turn, the story suggests, into complex and violent conflicts. The poem first lays its theme out in a proverbial style, and then follows the consequences of the figure of speech that ends the first stanza, "my wrath did *grow*." The rest of the poem takes that ordinary metaphor seriously, describing wrath growing like a tree, producing a poisoned but beautiful apple, killing the foe who steals it, and allowing the speaker to gloat in his triumph. The state of the speaker's mind is an interesting question here: Has he learned the wisdom he speaks in the first stanza, or is he still feeling the elation he describes in the last stanza?

1. How does the metaphor of anger as a tree develop? How does the tree grow? What does it produce?
2. How does "the foe" get tricked? Why does he steal the apple?
3. What has the speaker learned from the experience he describes?

"A Little Boy Lost"

The first two stanzas of this poem sound like a song of *Experience* in themselves. They are a cynical questioning of the pieties of family love. But the interest of this poem is in how society responds to these harsh insights. The Priest accuses the child of holding reason above faith and then condemns him to death. It is as though society wants to enforce an innocent acceptance of its truisms, so that it sees bitter Experience as a threat to social stability. The poem is also of interest because its figures of Innocence are adults, whereas its Experienced figures are children.

1. What does the second stanza suggest about the nature of family love?
2. In what sense could a person who upholds reason be a "fiend"?
3. How does the fact that his parents weep for him relate to the child's cynical view of family love?

"A Little Girl Lost"

This poem expresses an Experienced outrage at the repression of sexual desire, and it prophesies a time when love will be freed from guilt. Sexuality in the poem is presented as the play of children, natural and innocent except in the eyes of the girl's father, who makes it into a matter of fear and sin. The description of sexuality emphasizes its holiness; the children play openly in the daylight, with nothing to hide. Within the *Songs*, this poem is also interesting for its five-line stanza form, since most of the poems have either four- or eight-line stanzas. The result is a less regular but more extended rhythm.

1. What does the word "indignant" from the first stanza tell you about the tone of this poem?

2. What is the time and place of the children's innocent love? Why do these details matter?
3. Why does Ona's father react so strongly?

"To Tirzah"

Blake wrote and added this poem to the *Songs* some ten years after the rest. "To Tirzah" shows signs of Blake's later poetic development, in that it makes sense only inside the imaginative universe that Blake created in his prophetic poems. Tirzah, in that world, is the symbol of Nature unredeemed, unconnected with the divine. Tirzah was the capital of the northern kingdom of Israel, the lost tribes, as opposed to Jerusalem, the capital of the redeemed tribes. Tirzah therefore becomes for Blake a symbol of Nature seen as separate from mankind with its senses and its imagination. The poem depicts sexuality as part of that natural world, part of what must be transcended. Blake is not condemning sexuality, but rather attacking a concept of sexuality that divides it from the spiritual. The body for Blake is an emanation of the spirit, and thinking of it as separate from the spirit degrades sexuality itself.

1. Why does the speaker want to free himself from Nature, symbolized by Tirzah?
2. What does the poem have to say about sexuality and sexual difference?
3. What does the death of Jesus set the speaker free from? Is Jesus the opposite of Nature?

"The Schoolboy"

This is another of the *Songs of Experience* that seems to harken back to Innocence. The speaker here is a boy who feels that school steals his innocence. The first stanza evokes the pleasant world of natural innocence, but that world is shattered by the adult world of school and discipline. The schoolboy is described as a caged bird and as a bud nipped before it can grow into healthy maturity. The poem suggests that the innocence of children must be protected, so that it can serve as the foundation for a healthy experience of the harsh moments in life. The language and techniques of the poem seem too mature for an innocent speaker. What we have is a speaker who has already lost his innocence in the harsh schoolroom, and who is angry at the loss and nostalgic for his simpler early life.

1. What is the relationship between the speaker and the natural world in the first stanza?
2. How does the experience of school differ from that experience in nature?
3. How do the figures of speech comparing the schoolboy to a growing plant work in the last two stanzas?

"The Voice of the Ancient Bard"

Here we return to the "Introduction" of *Experience*, which called us to "Hear the Voice of the Bard." In this poem, the Bard is calling on youth to reject reason in favor of a visionary experience of the truth. Reason leads to doubt and dispute and folly, and to an arrogant certainty that it has found the truth. For Blake, reason has usurped imagination as the controlling power in mankind, and it is the goal of his writing to remind us of our imaginative power. Reason is equated in this poem with folly, constructing an endless mental maze that does not lead to the truth. In Blake's longer poems we find that the problem with reason is that it accepts appearances as reality and assumes reality is separate from the human mind. For Blake, reality is a function of the mind, which creates it through imaginative power.

1. What does the phrase "clouds of reason" suggest? Why is it an unusual phrase?
2. How does the poem suggest we can reach truth, if not through reason?

"A Divine Image"

Blake omitted this poem from *Experience*, probably because it does much of the same work as "The Human Abstract," that is, it serves as an answer to "The Divine Image" of *Innocence*. "The Human Abstract" tells an allegorical story of how human beings can pervert "Mercy, Pity, Peace, and Love," whereas this poem replaces these virtues with cruelty, jealousy, terror, and secrecy as characteristics of mankind. The last stanza here also revises the third stanza of "The Divine Image," which argued that mankind's virtues are visible on each person's outward form, by claiming that mankind's outward appearance is a function of the fiery energy of the soul in the passion of Experience. Each of the lines in the last stanza deserves close attention as commentary on human behavior. The poem is a rich summary of the world as it appears to the perspective of Experience.

1. What can you make of the statement "Cruelty has a Human Heart"?
2. What image of the divine comes out of the first stanza?
3. How is dress related to form, and face related to heart in the last stanza?

Poems in a Career

This selection of poetry from the works of William Butler Yeats is designed to bring out the continuities and changes in Yeats's poetic career. Classroom discussion and critical writing can be directed toward seeing each of these poems in terms of the others. A growing familiarity with the works of a poet generates a set of questions that a reader can bring to a text that cannot be asked if the text is read in isolation. A reader can look for common imagery and symbolism, and typical figurative and metrical patterns. Or the reader can look for changes in these techniques over time. Out of reading a number of works by the same author, it is possible for a reader to construct a sense of the mind at work behind the poems, just as we can construct the speaker of an individual poem. As long as we remember that this mind is the product of our interpretive process, such a construct can be used to connect texts to one another in fruitful ways.

"The Stolen Child"

This early Yeats poem comes out of Yeats's fascination with the Irish folklore that he encountered as a young man in the rural west of Ireland. The poem is spoken by the faeries, the spirit folk of Irish legend, who are here trying to lure a human child away to their band. They offer him a life of play and sensory delight, a deliverance from human suffering and death. It seems to me, though, that the tone of the faeries' voices changes in the last paragraph to reveal the darker side of their offer, that is, that the child will lose contact with the human world of love and relationship. The poem is also very interesting metrically, especially in its use of a refrain, almost in the manner of a folk song.

1. What do the faeries offer the child if he joins them in the spirit-world?
2. What is the significance of the refrain? What does it offer the boy?
3. How does the last stanza differ from the rest of the poem? What has happened to cause that change?

"The Lake Isle of Innisfree"

This is one of Yeats's most famous poems, and is worthy of attention for its beautiful verbal music, its rich imagery and figurative language, and its clear depiction of the speaker's desire to escape the daily world. All we know about the speaker's current situation is that he is in an urban environment, far from the peace and simplicity of Innisfree. For the speaker, Innisfree is an image of natural perfection. It possesses all the qualities now missing in his life—peace, solitude, beauty. What matters in this poem is the speaker's *desire*. Innisfree is an imaginary place in which all desires are satisfied. It recalls the terms of the offer the faeries make to the young boy in "The Stolen Child," in that it is a land where he can escape from "a world more full of weeping than he can understand." The speaker's desire is expressed in luxuriant imagery that can absorb an entire discussion in itself.

1. What kind of life and activity does the speaker foresee for himself on the island? Why is it attractive to him?
2. What visual and aural images does the speaker evoke in his description of the island?
3. What do we know about the speaker's current life that would explain his desire for the life of Innisfree?

"Who Goes with Fergus?"

Yeats drew in this poem on his knowledge of Irish mythology, in which Fergus is a king who gives up his power and position in order to live as a wanderer in the forest in search of spiritual wisdom. Fergus is therefore a symbol of the desire to leave ordinary life behind, to search for another, better world. Fergus even calls on young men and women to give up love in favor of an ecstatic contemplation of nature. The last three lines of the poem present pictorially the changing, momentary world that fascinates Fergus. We again see Yeats's contrasting the human world with a world of imagination and desire.

1. What does the world of Fergus offer to the young man and woman that the speaker is addressing?
2. How does the speaker describe the natural world?
3. What is "love's bitter mystery," and how can Fergus deliver the young man and woman from it?

"Easter, 1916"

This poem is one of Yeats's meditations on war, in this case the Irish rebellion of 1916 against British rule, which eventually resulted in the formation of the Irish Republic. Yeats knew many of the leaders of the rebellion, and as the second stanza suggests he had at best mixed feelings about them. But the point of the story is that their bold actions, ending in their deaths, have transformed them into timeless heroes. As the last stanza suggests, Yeats doubts the practical results of their sacrifice, but he still cannot deny that they have achieved a higher level of existence. They have escaped their ordinary, limited lives and become timeless symbols of the heroic. The difficult third stanza of the poem turns away from the specifics of the political situation to a more abstract consideration of heroism. Its rich imagery and figurative language can engage a class in a productive discussion.

1. What did the speaker of the poem think about these heroes before their heroic deaths?
2. How have they been changed by their actions?
3. What does the third stanza suggest is the cost of heroism to a hero?

"The Fisherman"

This is an unusual poem in which a poet considers directly the nature of his audience. The speaker presents us with his image of the perfect audience for his poems. That audience is not the sophisticated crowd mentioned with contempt in the first stanza, but rather, suprisingly, a simple fisherman, an austere, skillful man who the speaker clearly sees as a kindred spirit. The speaker considers him to be the perfect audience for the "cold / And passionate" poems he hopes to write.

1. How does the speaker characterize the audience that he has had in the past?
2. In what ways does the fisherman resemble a poet? Why does the speaker consider the fisherman to be the perfect audience?
3. How can the words *cold* and *passionate* go together?

"Adam's Curse"

"Adam's Curse" is a poem about poetry and about love, two activities that seem to be spontaneous and effortless but that in fact require intense labor. As the speaker says, "to articulate sweet sounds together" does not occur naturally but requires imaginative work. Love can also be seen in this way, although the poem suggests that such a love might be doomed to failure. In fact, the ending of the poem is so gloomy that it seems to undercut the notion that love can be gained by effort. Still, the poem itself shows that the hard effort of constructing beautiful poetry is worthwhile, in that the poem's fluid and conversational tone is clearly the product of intense poetic work. As a result, poetry and love seem less similar than the poem at first suggests. The poem is also of interest because of its clearly dramatized speaker, who skillfully reconstructs the poetic situation, including the speeches of the other characters.

1. In the speaker's mind, why is the poet so often thought of as an idler, even though poetry is such hard work?
2. In what sense does a woman need to "labour to be beautiful"?
3. What is the speaker referring to when he talks about those who would love out of books?
4. In the last stanza, how do the poem's reflections on labor come to apply to the speaker's own love relationship?

"The Folly of Being Comforted"

One of Yeats's complex, enigmatic love poems, "The Folly of Being Comforted" makes it difficult for the reader to understand the speaker's attitude toward his beloved. The debate between the friend who speaks in the first stanza and the speaker's heart, which speaks in the second, is clear enough. The friend suggests and the heart denies that the beloved's aging will cool his love. But what of the final couplet? Does it suggest that the friend is right or that the speaker's heart is right? The open question can be the source of constructive student discussion and writing. The poem is also interesting as an experiment with the form of the sonnet.

1. What is the advice given by the friend in the first stanza?
2. What is the speaker's response in the second stanza?
3. Does the last stanza resolve the conflict between the first two?
4. What is the image of the speaker that emerges from the poem?

"The Wild Swans at Coole"

This is Yeats in a Wordsworthian mode, reflecting on nature, using it as a matrix in which to understand himself. The poem is built upon the contrast between the unchanging swans—at least they seem unchanging to the speaker—and the changing, aging speaker himself. The swans have come to symbolize for the speaker a force that resists time and change while the speaker is subject to them. Swans continue to be a major figure throughout Yeats's poetry, and as such they provide a basis for comparing various poems.

1. What is the significance of the time of day and time of year in the poem?
2. How has the speaker changed since the first time he saw the swans?
3. Does the depiction of the swans' life given in stanza four seem realistic to you?
4. Does this poem give you a clear picture of its speaker?

"The Second Coming"

Considering the fact that this poem makes full sense only inside of Yeats's esoteric theory of history, students are surprisingly able to deal with this vision of the end of one age and the beginning of a new age. Perhaps this is because current students are all too comfortable with the thought of nuclear holocaust, eco-disaster, and the Christian version of the second coming. Yeats's poem is based on the theory that history proceeds in two-thousand-year cycles and that the transition from cycle to cycle is necessarily violent. He therefore interprets the violence and disorder of modern life as signs of the coming of a new era. Those signs are described in memorable language in the first stanza; the second stanza presents Yeats's image, drawn from an almost Jungian collective unconscious ("*Spiritus Mundi*"), of the god of the era that is to come. As the image suggests, the new god that is to replace the god of Bethlehem will be anything but a god of peace. Rather, it will be a god of death, indifferent to its victims. In this poem we see Yeats as prophet, offering a visionary version of the future that accounts for the disorders of the present.

1. In the first stanza, what are the signs that convince the speaker that "some revelation is at hand"?
2. What is the image of the new god that appears in meditation to the speaker?
3. How does Yeats's "Second Coming" compare with the Christian prophecy of the second coming?

"A Prayer for My Daughter"

This poem comes out of the same sense of the chaotic nature of modern life that we saw in "The Second Coming." The speaker presents us with a violent world that he fears will become even more violent ("dancing to a frenzied drum"). His desire for his daughter, therefore, is for a more stable and secure world, one in which courtesy and tradition can survive. The speaker's desires for his daughter are for protection, security, ceremony—traditional values that may not fit into more recent feminist visions of the future. But for the speaker it is the absence of these values that has allowed the chaotic violence of our time. The poem is noteworthy for its intense imagery and for its manipulation of stanza form.

1. What is the significance of the nature imagery in the poem?
2. Why does the speaker want his child not to be given too much beauty?
3. What does the daughter need to be defended from?
4. What does it mean to say that the soul is "self-delighting"?

"Sailing to Byzantium"

This poem is one of Yeats's great meditations on aging and death. It presents in graphic imagery the pleasures of the body that the old man has lost and the horrors of the body as it decays toward death. The speaker of the poem desires an escape from that body into a timeless form. He wants to be transformed into a work of art that will never decay and never be tormented by desire. In this desire the poem recalls such early Yeats poems as "The Stolen Child" and "The Lake Isle of Innisfree," which also came out of a desire to escape the sorrows of this world into an unchangeable imaginary world. This later poem is more difficult than the earlier ones, in part because of its references to Byzantium and its culture. Byzantium represented for Yeats a world of artistic achievement and a commitment to abstract, timeless form. Discussion of the poem might therefore be enhanced by showing students photographs of Byzantine mosaics. But the difficulties of this poem should not overshadow the very simple human situation they arise from. The speaker's horror of physical decay and his desire for endless life are far from obscure.

1. How does the speaker portray the physical, natural world?
2. Why does he admire "monuments of unaging intellect"?
3. Why does the speaker depict the human body as "a tattered coat upon a stick" and "a dying animal"?
4. What would the speaker gain by going through the transformation he desires?

"Leda and the Swan"

Like "The Second Coming," "Leda and the Swan" is part of Yeats's myth of history. The moment depicted in the poem is the beginning of the classical cycle of history, in that Leda is the mother of Helen of Troy, over whom the Trojan war is fought, which in turn is the subject for Homer, whose works could be considered the beginning of Western civilization. But the poem depicts this moment of the divine conception of Helen as a personal as well as historical event. It does so by the intensity of its imagistic language. The actual sexual contact between the god in the form of a swan and the human Leda is told from the perspective of Leda, in the sense that the speaker of the poem is trying to imagine what contact with a divine force would do to the human being. The question that ends the poem seems to me to be open-ended. The speaker simply does not know if Leda experienced a spiritual and intellectual union with the god. The poem is also interesting as a modern sonnet, using the form but willing to vary it for emphasis and emotional effect.

1. Why does the poem begin in such an abrupt way?
2. What emotional changes does Leda go through as the poem progresses?
3. What is the "knowledge" that the god possesses that the speaker wonders if Leda gained?
4. Why is the speaker interested in Leda? What does she represent to him?

"Crazy Jane Talks with the Bishop"

This poem is one of the many great works of Yeats's old age. Many critics have noted that in his later poems Yeats attained a stylistic simplicity that contrasts sharply with the difficult poems of his middle years. In this case the simplicity comes from the choice of speaker—Crazy Jane is a vagrant, probably one who appears crazy enough to have earned her name. But in this poem she is the source of wisdom; through the simplicity of her language she arrives at a complex truth. It is interesting to note that the debate between Crazy Jane and the bishop concerns the relationship between the spirit and the body, a concern that we have seen throughout Yeats's career. In this case, the idea that the body should be escaped is denied in favor of a belief in the unity of body and spirit. Paradoxically, in his old age Yeats seems to have come to an acceptance of the body and of the life-in-time that seemed so horrible to him in his youth and middle age.

1. What values does the bishop represent in his debate with Crazy Jane?
2. What values does Crazy Jane uphold?
3. What is the significance of the fact that the poem supports the views of a homeless, insane woman rather than those of a powerful, respectable man?

"Lapis Lazuli"

This poem relies on a wide variety of references that students might find daunting. The speaker alludes to William of Orange in the first stanza, Shakespearean tragic heroes in the second, and the Greek sculptor Callimachus (virtually all of whose works have been lost) in the third. The poem is also challenging in that it changes directions frequently and without much warning. Nevertheless, the poem is worth the work because it is a perfect example of a poem based on a paradox—the idea that tragedy can be a source of joy. Yeats claims that even Hamlet and Lear, who suffer so much, feel joy because they have experienced "Heaven blazing into the head." They have experienced a heightened sense of life that is part and parcel of the suffering they have endured. This same paradox is featured in the speaker's description of the carving in lapis lazuli that ends the poem. Almost hypnotically, the speaker leads us to the eyes of the characters in the carving, so that we can see in them the mixture of tragedy and joy that they experience.

1. Why does the speaker say that the actors who play tragic roles "Do not break up their lines to weep"?
2. What are the connotations of the word "gay" in the poem? How do they differ from contemporary meanings of the word?
3. What is the effect in the last two lines of the word "eyes"?

"The Wild Old Wicked Man"

This poem, with its "coarse old man" speaker, recalls "Crazy Jane" in its strategy of placing wisdom in an unlikely source. The speaker's message in the poem is aimed at a young woman that he is trying to seduce. This situation, which some students might find offensive, brings out the old man's wise realization that he has learned the truths of the body without falling into despair. This is the poem of an old man who has accepted his physical decay and who will not deny his body. The poem is therefore interesting as a dramatic monologue, with a clearly depicted speaker and listener and a complex dramatic situation. Trying to get at the character of the speaker would be a good starting point for student discussion.

1. What does the old man claim that he can give to a young girl that no young man can give?
2. Why is he rejected by the girl?
3. What does the speaker tell us about himself with his claim that he can "make a cat laugh"?
4. What does the speaker have to say about human suffering?

"Long-Legged Fly"

In this poem the speaker reflects on the creative lives of three prominent figures in Western cultural history: Julius Caesar, Helen of Troy, and Michelangelo. In each case the creative act is seen to require an intense stillness, so that the mind of the creator can achieve complete concentration. Also in each case the poem characterizes the creative act in terms of a simile—the creative mind is compared to a "long-legged fly," a simile that brings together two entities seeming to have little in common. There is therefore a lot of room for students to explore the implications of the simile and construct for themselves the theory of creativity that the poem suggests but does not make explicit.

1. What visual image does the first stanza give us of Julius Caesar?
2. Why is it important that Helen of Troy "thinks . . . that nobody looks" when she practices her dance?
3. What effects does the poem describe of the portrayal of Adam that Michelangelo painted on the Sistine Chapel ceiling?

Poems in Conversation

The goal of this section of the text is to see these poems in relation to one another. I have grouped them together because they seem to me to be engaged in an extended discussion, or argument, with one another. Each poem in the sequence, I am suggesting, could be seen as a response to those that came earlier. Of course, this grouping is not the only possible arrangement of poems in the volume that could work along these lines—other instructors might construct completely different arrangements. The point is that such arrangments get students to think about how poems differ from and resemble other poems. This section, therefore, lends itself to comparison/contrast assignments, using any of these poems in combination.

William Wordsworth, "Tintern Abbey"

Wordsworth's poem is one of the most famous nature lyrics in our language. The speaker places himself in a natural scene, and meditates on the thoughts that nature produces in him. Nature is the teacher; the mind of the speaker is the learner, acquiring lessons about morality, human suffering, and spiritual growth. Nature reveals to the speaker a spiritual principle of order that lives in nature and in the mind of mankind. The speaker seems to be sustained by nature, finding in it the wisdom necessary to survive in the complexities of human life. There are moments when the speaker seems to question these beliefs, wondering if these lessons aren't produced by his own imagination rather than by the spirit of nature. But these doubts are overcome and the speaker confirms himself as a "worshipper of Nature." It teaches him the meaning of human life and the place of human life inside a larger reality that unifies mankind and nature.

1. How is the speaker different on this visit from what he had been five years earlier?
2. What are the effects of these experiences with nature at those times when the speaker is *not* in the midst of nature?
3. What is the "presence" (l. 94) that the speaker finds in nature?
4. What is the role of the speaker's sister in the poem?

John Keats, "Ode on a Grecian Urn"

The speaker of this poem is in a situation both similar to and different from that of "Tintern Abbey." Here the speaker is confronted with a work of art, not a natural scene, but he responds to the ancient urn in ways similar to the earlier speaker's response to nature. That his, he treats it as his teacher, a source of wisdom and self-knowledge. The urn has survived for centuries, and the speaker is struck by its painted decorations that tell an enigmatic story, one that has captured a moment of time and preserved it forever. The lesson that the speaker seems to get from the urn is that living outside of time (as the characters on the urn do) saves the characters from disappointment and decay. The speaker seems almost envious of these characters, caught as he is in the world of time and death. Unlike the speaker of Wordsworth's poem, he does not receive a reassuring message about the unity of body and spirit. Rather, we hear the longing of the spirit to escape time and the body into the timeless world of art. The message of the urn is made explicit at the end in the famous and enigmatic last lines. Critics have been debating the import of that message for years, even down to how the last lines should be punctuated. Students therefore have a wide field to play in with regard to the message that comes to the speaker from the work of art. What is the urn's message? How is it different from the message that nature has to offer in Wordsworth's poem?

1. What is the scene depicted on the urn?
2. Why are unheard melodies sweeter than heard melodies? Why is the unrequited passion depicted on the urn superior to "All breathing human passion"?

Matthew Arnold, "Dover Beach"

In this famous poem we return to the situation of the speaker in "Tintern Abbey," but with different results. The speaker of this poem is struck by the beauty and then the sadness of a natural scene, as well as by the lesson it can teach him. But in this case the lesson is unpleasant: mankind's faith in God is disappearing, and life without God is empty, chaotic, violent. Nature is a teacher in this poem, but it teaches a lesson that throws the speaker into despair. Instead of revealing a fullness that human beings are part of, nature reveals an emptiness in the midst of human life. Arnold lived in the midst of the scientific challenge to traditional religion that characterized the European nineteenth century, and "Dover Beach" depicts the speaker's sense of the consequences of a loss of religious faith.

1. How does nature appear to the speaker at the beginning of the poem?
2. What changes his emotional reaction? What turns his attention to human sadness?
3. What does the natural scene teach him about human beings?
4. What does the poem suggest that life would be like without religious faith?

William Butler Yeats, "Among School Children"

One aspect of Yeats's poem that is illuminated by comparing it with "Ode on a Grecian Urn" is its concern with human life in time and the desire for timelessness. Keats's meditation begins with the urn, a work of art that seems to have transcended time. With Yeats, the occasion for the meditation is his visit to a schoolroom where he becomes sharply conscious of his advancing age. The poem then turns to a consideration of the role of images in human life. Yeats sees these timeless images as "self-born mockers of man's enterprise." They are glimpses of a timeless perfection that human beings cannot attain. The two poems make for another interesting comparison, in that both end with famous and enigmatic final lines. An interesting discussion could compare the question at the end of Yeats's poem with the aphorism that ends Keats's poem. The poem also relates interestingly with "Tintern Abbey" in that both poems seem to enact a search for unity.

This difficult poem will require a great deal of explanation. Its structure is not easy to follow because it amounts to a stream-of-consciousness technique, following the associations between images in the speaker's mind. It also refers to a wide range of the classical tradition, including Leda, the mother of Helen of Troy, with whom Yeats often associated his lifelong love, Maud Gonne. A workable way to approach this poem is to try to follow its associative logic, speculating on how one image leads to the next.

1. What effect does the setting of this poem in a schoolroom have on the speaker?
2. How does the attention of the speaker's mind flow from one image to the next?
3. How do you interpret the meaning of the question that ends the poem?

Wallace Stevens, "The Idea of Order at Key West"

This complex poem can be made accessible to students if the dramatic situation of the poem is made clear. The speaker and a friend are walking on the beach, listening to the song of a woman against the background of the sound of the sea. Out of this experience the speaker meditates on the relationship between human art and nature, seeing art (the song) as "beyond the genius of the sea." Unlike Wordsworth's speaker in "Tintern Abbey," who found a transcendent unity in the natural world, this speaker sees the human mind *imposing* a unity on nature, "Arranging, deepening, enchanting night." Stevens is one of the great twentieth-century poets who returned to questions of the relationship between mankind and nature that had dominated

Romantic poetry. Students can be asked to consider how the speaker depicts the woman's song and its relationship to the sound of the sea.

1. How does the speaker describe the song of the woman singing by the sea?
2. What does her singing do to the way the speaker perceives the ocean?
3. In the last two stanzas, how has the speaker's way of looking at the world changed?

A. R. Ammons, "Corsons Inlet"

Ammons's poem is clearly in the same tradition as "The Idea of Order" and "Tintern Abbey," in that all are composed of the thoughts brought to the speaker's mind by an encounter with nature. Ammons's speaker is taking a walk on an ocean beach around a point into an inlet. Unlike Stevens's speaker, who sees humanly imposed order, this speaker is able to enjoy the constantly shifting and changing natural world. He is not looking for a final meaning to life, but rather is willing to flow along with the changing patterns he perceives. This speaker therefore contrasts interestingly with the speaker of "Tintern Abbey" as well, in that he is not looking for a transcendent unity within nature. This poem might be useful as practice in following the fluid movements of the speaker's mind. Those movements are intricate, but they are narrated in a fairly accessible language that gives the student a good chance of following the speaker's mind.

1. The speaker says, "I allow myself eddies of meaning." What does this tell us about how the poem will progress?
2. What does the speaker mean when he says, "Overall is beyond me"?
3. What is the significance of the last line of the poem?

Anthology of Poetry

Anonymous, "Get Up and Bar the Door"

This little narrative of domestic wit is an excellent example of how the ballad form lends itself to the telling of a story. Because of the compression that poetry allows, we get two complex characters and a complicated plot in a very brief poem. The husband and wife are caught up in a test of nerves and will—one that has probably been going on for a long time. They are so caught up in the game that they can't stop playing it even in the midst of danger. Clearly the contest is about who is to have power in the marriage. The man asserts it, the woman resists it, and at least for this round the woman wins it. This is one of the popular ballads that have been told and sung in England for hundreds of years. The word *popular* should be taken seriously, because it indicates that these poems were group creations, changing each time they were told, adapting to new environments and times. We can see in this poem, then, a kind of communal wisdom from folk culture about the struggles for power that go on inside relationships.

1. How would you chracterize the relationship between husband and wife in the poem?
2. What makes this a comic story? How does the comedy relate to the point of the poem?

Edmund Spenser, "Sonnet 75" ("One day I wrote her name upon the strand")

This poem makes for an interesting comparison with Shakespeare's "Shall I compare thee to a summer's day," in that both make the claim that they can immortalize the woman they are directed to in a timeless poetic universe. In this poem, however, the woman gets to speak, and she reminds the poet of the vanity of his endeavor, since she will die as surely as the letters the poem has written upon the strand. But her intervention does not affect him, and in the last six lines of the poem he renews his claim that his poetry can immortalize her. The poem can therefore be read ironically, as a revelation of the poet's pretenses, or straightforwardly, as a traditional claim for poetic immortality, in spite of the woman's more rational point of view. The poem is also interesting as a sonnet, in that it seems metrically to be a Shakespearean sonnet (three quatrains, a concluding couplet), but its logic follows the form of the Petrarchan sonnet (an eight-line unit, then a six-line unit).

1. What do the first four lines suggest about the immortality of poetry?
2. Why does the woman that the sonnet is directed to consider the poet to be a "Vayne man"?
3. In the last six lines, how does the speaker respond to the woman's criticism?

Christopher Marlowe, "The Passionate Shepherd to His Love"

One of the great pastoral lyrics in the language, Marlow's poem is an invitation to the beloved to become part of a natural paradise. The lovers will be surrounded by nature, even clothed by it, enjoying its bounty and the pleasures of life in nature. The poem also creates a clear dramatic context—a speaker, a listener, a motive. One interesting way to approach the poem would be as a piece of rhetoric, an attempt at emotional and rational persuasion. The poem is also of interest for its metrics, and for its vivid imagery.

1. How does the speaker attempt to persuade his beloved to join him in his natural paradise?
2. What kind of relationship with nature does he offer her?
3. Is the appeal he makes to her materialistic, or does it have a spiritual dimension?

William Shakespeare, "Blow, Blow, Thou Winter Wind"

This lyric is from *As You Like It,* Act 2, Scene 7, lines 174ff. The poem is built on a comparison of the pains caused by winter's wind and cold with the pains caused by human unkindness. The speaker of the poem, in fact, is so disheartened by human beings that he feels that "Most friendship is feigning, most loving mere folly." The rough and unusual metrical style of the poem is also interesting, and can be related to the thematic concerns of the poem.

1. What is the significance of the fact that the wind cannot be seen? How does this make its pains less keen?
2. Why are the pains caused by human beings more sharp than those caused by nature?

Shakespeare, "Hark! Hark! The Lark"

This lyric is from *Cymbeline.* It is a brief but elaborate praise of morning, spring, and love. The poem's mythological reference, to Phoebus, the god of the sun, suggests that this morning scene is an almost archetypal human experience of natural beauty. And the speaker is quick to connect that natural beauty to the beauty of the beloved, who is urged to join in the experience, to enjoy and in fact to become a part of the natural scene.

1. What does the poem suggest that the beloved has in common with the natural scene he describes?
2. What is the desire of the speaker that motivates these lines?

Ben Jonson, "On My First Daughter"

This is a poem of consolation, spoken by a father on the death of his infan daughter. The consolation seems to be made possible by his belief that only her body has died, and that her soul will live forever in heaven. He is also self-consoled by the inevitability of death and by the fact that she died an innocent, and will remain so as part of the Blessed Mother's "virgin-train." I am not completely convinced that the consolation here is successful. The speaker still seems not to accept her death fully. He is particularly struck by the division of body (in the grave) and soul (eternally in heaven), which the last lines suggest is a division that he cannot accept.

1. What is suggested by the phrase, "all heaven's gifts being heaven's due"? How does this idea serve as a consolation for her death?
2. Why is the speaker so concerned with the daughter's innocence?
3. Why does the speaker ask the earth to cover the girl *lightly?*

John Donne, "The Canonization"

This famous and complex poem is very challenging but also very rewarding for students. The challenge comes mainly from the compression and intricacy of the poem's language, and from the poem's allusions, especially to the myth of the phoenix. It is rewarding because students *can* eventually figure the poem out, if they engage very fully with its language and its arguments. For the poem is an argument, a speech in an implied drama, a response on the part of the speaker to the criticism he has been hearing about his new love. As a result of this dramatic quality, the poem has a rough, conversational quality to it, even though it is structured within a very formal metrical pattern. The speaker's argument in his own behalf takes many turns, beginning with an attack on his own attacker—"Don't you have anything better to do?"—continuing with a denial that his love injures anyone, and then turning to a series of images that establish his love as an almost religious experience. In this argument, the phoenix plays a major role, as a symbol of the eternity of his love, which returns even after it has been fulfilled. The culmination of the poem is the speaker's "canonization" of himself and his beloved as saints in the religion of love, models for future lovers to copy. The verbal complexity of the poem requires that it be covered slowly and in detail. The poem is also a complex exercise in figurative language, as the lovers are compared to a series of items that emphasize the eternal passion they are involved in.

1. What does the speaker suggest in the first stanza that his attacker should do with his time?
2. How does the speaker answer the rhetorical question that begins the second stanza?
3. How do the images of flies, eagles, doves, and the phoenix work together in the third stanza?
4. How is the speaker's love like a sonnet (l. 32)?
5. How do the images of eyes work in the last stanza?

Donne, "Holy Sonnet 10" ("Death, be not proud")

The last two lines express directly the confidence that flows throughout this poem. The poem could be thought of as a series of arguments, directed at "Death," that prove that human beings are stronger than death itself. The argument is made within a strong religious faith that there is a life that follows death, and that therefore escapes its power. The point is also argued by analogy (sleep and rest are like death and are pleasant, so death should be even more so), by reference to folk wisdom ("soonest our best men with thee do go"), and by an odd logic (charms can put us into as deep a sleep, so why should "Death" be proud?). All this inside a very careful and skillful use of the Shakespearean sonnet form. Still, if the speaker is so confident, why does he have to argue so strongly? Is it possible to think of this as a poem that is about the weakness of death precisely because of the speaker's experience of the power of death? Is he convincing himself?

1. What is the effect of the fact that the poem is addressed directly to "Death"?
2. Lines 9–12 of the poem seem to demean "Death." Why would the speaker want to do so?
3. Is this a poem that could only have been written by a believing Christian?

Andrew Marvell, "To His Coy Mistress"

If you're in as much of a hurry as the speaker of "To His Coy Mistress," you could summarize the poem in the common phrase *carpe diem* (seize the day). But that would be to miss the rich imagery and figurative language as well as the clever logic of this great poem. There is a very strong logic to the argument here, as the speaker urges his coy mistress to action. If we had time, he says, I would take time, but we do not have all time, so we must seize the time we have. And that basic logic is argued in a profusion of imagery, figurative language, exaggeration, wit, and high style. The second stanza of the poem, which makes the argument that time is running out on the lovers, evokes a picture of death that makes the entire argument much more serious than it first seems. A phrase like "let us sport us while we may," which might otherwise sound like a cheap, overused line, in this context becomes a serious response to the chilling picture of death that the speaker has just created. Love comes to seem the only powerful human response to death, which it cannot conquer but can at least defy.

1. What does the first stanza say about how the speaker wishes he could love the woman he addresses?
2. How does the speaker describe the effects of death?
3. Does the phrase "Deserts of vast eternity" suggest an antireligious viewpoint?
4. What is the relationship between love and time that is described in the last stanza?

Marvell, "Bermudas"

This poem comes out of the European experience of the New World, which is pictured here as a paradise that God has given to these adventurers. The soul of the poem for me lies in its sumptuous description of the Bermudas as an island of plenty and in its confidence that this world was created expressly for the English. The notion that God has *given* this paradise to the Europeans, which Marvell ratifies by calling the sailors' song "An holy and a cheerful note," provides a clear if naive mandate for colonization and imperialism. But Marvell's interest seems to me to be less political than imaginative, as he tries to evoke this new place with all of its physical bounty.

1. What have the sailors endured in order to arrive at the Bermudas?
2. How do the sailors explain their fortune at landing safely?
3. What does this new land have to offer them?
4. How do the sailors express their religious devotion? How is it related to their adventure?

Robert Herrick, "Delight in Disorder"

The explicit meaning of this poem is not hard to put together, once you know that *lawn* is a kind of linen and that a *stomacher* is a decorative cloth worn around the abdomen. The poem is in praise of disorder, which is seen as a sign of passion. What makes the poem interesting is the question of whether the poem itself is an example of the disorder it praises. Does it have the "wild civility" that he admires in women, or is it "too precise in every part," like the art he says he disdains? The answer to that question is far from simple, because the metrical and verbal art of the poem is at once casual and precise. This is clearly a judgment call that should be left to the individual reader.

1. What does the speaker see in the disordered clothes he describes?
2. What is the speaker's attitude toward the women wearing the clothes he describes?
3. In the speaker's mind, what is wrong with too much precision?

Herrick, "Corinna's Going A-Maying"

This is a difficult but rewarding poem for students. Its difficulty comes from its classical allusions, its complex language, and its folkloric origins, which are foreign to most students. The poem is set inside the ritual of "Maying," a rite of natural religion that celebrates spring, fertility, and human sexuality. The speaker of the poem is hurrying on his sleepy partner, reminding her of the pleasures of the day. The moment is evoked through the allusions to Apollo, the god of the sun, and Aurora, the goddess of the dawn, and through a dazzling set of images dealing with the beauties of the dawn, the dew, the green earth. At the end of the poem the mood darkens with the realization that time passes, youth is lost, and death is a reality where "all delight / Lies drowned with us in endless night." So if the message of the speaker is that staple of so many seductions, "seize the day," he has at least earned the right to make that claim by facing squarely what the passing of time means.

1. What does the speaker ask us to notice about the dawn?
2. What senses are involved in the imagery of the poem?
3. What arguments does the speaker use to persuade the woman to join him in the rite of spring?
4. Is it possible to speculate about why the woman is slow to join the party?
5. How is the speaker's lack of belief in an afterlife related to his worship of nature?

Herrick, "To the Virgins, to Make Much of Time"

This poem is perhaps best studied as a companion piece to "Corinna's Going A-Maying." For one thing, this poem could serve as a less complicated way of getting at the combination of awareness of death and the desire to enjoy the present that is so central to "Corinna." And the two poems provide an interesting contrast, in that although they could be said to deal with the same concerns, they do so in very different verbal styles. Where "Corinna's Going A-Maying" is elaborate, complex, and rich in imagery, this poem is spare, straightforward, and full of an almost proverbial wisdom. Which of the poems deals with its concerns more effectively would make a topic for an interesting discussion or writing assignment.

1. How would you describe the speaker's attitude toward life?
2. How does the language and poetic style of the poem reflect that attitude?

Herrick, "Neutrality Loathsome"

This is one of the poems in the book that can be used to illustrate the compression that poetry can attain. In these four lines, Herrick suggests an entire philosophy of moral life. And it is a demanding philosophy, not allowing the comfortable middle ground that most of us frequently occupy. This poem can also be read profitably in connection with the other Herrick poems printed here. Does the *carpe diem* philosophy of "Corinna's Going A-Maying" fit in with this moral imperative?

1. How does the metrical technique of the poem contribute to its meaning?
2. Why would God prefer evil to neutrality?

George Herbert, "Virtue"

Herbert's poem "Virtue" would be interesting to read in connection with Herrick's poems on the passage of time and the need to "seize the day." That is, in this poem there is a very strong sense that time is passing, but instead of calling for us to enjoy the time we have, this poem calls for a devotion to virtue as the only way to escape the ravages of time. The poem is built around the contrast between nature, which is caught in time, and the spiritual side of mankind, which will live forever. It therefore makes use of natural imagery, not to celebrate nature but to differentiate mankind from it.

1. The first three stanzas of the poem are addressed directly to the day, a rose, and the spring. Why these items? What do they have in common?
2. What distinguishes "a sweet and virtuous soul" from the natural world?

Herbert, "Easter Wings"

This poem is famous for the fact that it takes the shape of what it describes. The poem is also ingeniously crafted in that as the lines narrow, the fall of mankind (in the first stanza) and the fall of the speaker (in the second) are narrated, and as the lines grow, salvation is the topic. The metrics of the narrowing and widening lines are also of interest.

1. According to this poem, what causes the fall of mankind, and what the salvation?
2. Does the visual display of the poem seem like a gimmick to you, or does it contribute to the overall effect of the poem?

Thomas Carew, "A Song"

This elaborate compliment would make a good text for studying figurative language. For all the stanzas of the poem are based on an extended metaphor that the color of the rose or the light of the day or the sound of the nightingale live in the beloved. Literally, of course, they do not. But connecting the beloved with these natural beauties, which fade in nature but abide in the beloved, makes for an attractive and complex compliment. The poem is also interesting to examine metrically, in that each stanza utilizes the same framework, but fills it in differently, almost like a theme and variation pattern.

1. What is the significance of the fact that the beloved is compared to a series of natural objects?
2. How do each of the stanzas make use of the same pattern? What are the variations?

Richard Lovelace, "To Althea, from Prison"

This poem is famous for the opening lines of the final stanza, "Stone walls do not a prison make, / Nor iron bars a cage." But it has more to offer than those lines. The poem argues that even a man in prison (where Lovelace spent some of his life) can retain an inner freedom, if his spirit is upheld by love, or by friendship, or by patriotism. Any of these bonds, these connections with life and with moral ideals, can allow the speaker to feel a freedom in his soul. The poem also uses an interesting formal structure, in that each of the stanzas of the poem is based on the same metrical and rhetorical pattern.

1. In each stanza, how does love, or friendship, or patriotism give the speaker an experience of freedom?
2. Can you believe the speaker's assertions of his freedom of spirit, or is he trying to compensate for the pains of his imprisonment?

John Milton, "When I Consider How My Light Is Spent"

This great sonnet, in which Milton meditates on his blindness, is remarkable both for its courageous acceptance of God's will and for its forceful use of the sonnet form. The speaker is frustrated because of his loss of one of the human powers by which we can do God's will. He fears that because of his handicap he will not be able to serve as the steward of God's gifts. But the last six lines suggest that those who accept God's will are those who serve him best. The speaker therefore works his way from bitterness to acceptance. As a sonnet, the poem exhibits a subtle and clever rhyme scheme, and an interesting run-on line that connects the octave with the sestet. The poem does not therefore fall into halves. The consolation is very strongly linked to the bitterness it answers.

1. Why is the speaker so concerned about being able to serve his master?
2. What is the significance of the fact that it is "Patience" who speaks the lines of acceptance that end the poem?
3. Why does God not need mankind's works?
4. How do those who "stand and wait" also serve God?

Aphra Behn, "The Willing Mistress"

Aphra Behn was the first woman professional writer in the English language. This song, which is from her play *The Dutch Lover,* is a frank statement of female sexual desire. The speaker describes the ease with which she was seduced, because her own passion led her to go against what she feels is her society's expectation that a woman will resist all sexual feeling. Despite this frankness, in some ways the poem is as interesting for what it does not say as for what it does. The sexual act itself is not described but only coyly alluded to, which suggests that the speaker is a woman who, despite her open sexuality, still lives inside the codes of behavior in force in her society. She is free enough to enjoy sex, but too polite to talk about it—and too enmeshed in the codes of her culture to question the male-dominated nature of the sexuality she accepts. The poem is also interesting for its witty, elegant rhyme scheme and metrics, in which it resembles much of the male erotic poetry of the period.

1. What kind of natural environment does the poem describe?
2. What do we hear about the sexual encounter? Who is in control?
3. What is the significance of the last lines of the last two stanzas?

Anne Bradstreet, "A Letter to Her Husband"

This poem lends itself to the study of figurative language. It makes use of a series of metaphors to describe the relationship between the speaker and her husband. The most important of these depicts the husband as the sun and the speaker as the earth, missing the warmth of the sun (the husband who is traveling). The consequences of this metaphor are worked out in such detail that the figure could be considered a conceit, and the poem could well be utilized to illustrate that term. The metaphor focuses the speaker's attention on the husband, the sun-center of her universe, but it is interesting to note that the speaker seems to be managing without him, and that, in this period, the very act of writing could be considered a revolt against the subordination of women.

1. What is the figure of speech used in the first six lines to describe the relationship between husband and wife?
2. How fully is the metaphor of the sun worked out in the poem?
3. How would you describe the relationship between the speaker and her husband?

Bradstreet, "The Author to Her Book"

This poem comes out of the circumstance that Bradstreet's poems were published without her permission. In this witty, self-deprecating poem she describes her book in metaphors of motherhood and child care. In this conceit, the book is the child of the creative mother, but it is an unkempt child who shows the imperfect care of the mother. The speaker therefore seems at once self-deprecating (in lamenting the state of her "child") and proud (in claiming the child as her own). As the metaphor of the writer as mother is worked out, such details of child care as washing the child and repairing clothes are used to suggest the process of revision and polishing the poems. The poem therefore makes an interesting example of figurative language, especially as it reveals the speaker's self-concept as a writer.

1. What is there about writing that would make it similar to mothering?
2. What is the speaker's feeling about her own writing?
3. How is writing like stitching?
4. What is the significance of the fact that these poems do not have a "father"?

Edward Taylor, "Upon a Spider Catching a Fly"

This poem narrates a story from nature, and then provides its own allegorical interpretation. That is, it tells a story of spiders and wasps and flies, a story that clearly exists in order to illustrate a moral point, and then, instead of letting the reader make sense of the story, the speaker provides the point himself—the spider is the devil, entrapping people like flies in his webs. The poem tries to limit the possible interpretations of it, forcing the reader to accept the speaker's reading. In this poem, the reader's freedom is in the decision whether or not to accept that interpretation. The reader is also free to interpret the story differently, but only in the awareness that he or she is going against the will of the speaker.

1. How does the spider treat the wasp differently from the fly? How does that difference fit into the speaker's interpretation of the story?
2. Does the speaker's interpretation seem convincing to you? Can you come up with another one?

Taylor, "Huswifery"

This poem is built upon a conceit, an extended metaphor, which describes the relationship between God and mankind in terms of the relationship between the spinner and the spinning wheel. The distaff, flyers, spools, reels, looms, and mills associated with spinning all appear in the poem as ways to describe how the speaker wishes God to *use* him, make him an instrument. He wants his entire human identity (see the first three lines of the second stanza) to be taken over, so that his entire life will glorify God. What is unusual about the figurative language here is that God is depicted by means of a task traditionally associated with women—spinning—and that the soul is also depicted in traditionally feminine imagery, as passive in the hands of a powerful female God. The meaning and importance of this imagery is not clear, but the poem's figurative language does present a concept of God unusual within the Christian system, which tends to see God in masculine images.

1. How closely do we need to read the spinning metaphors? Is it helpful to know what *quills* and *fulling mills* are?

2. What is the significance of being "clothed in holy robes for glory"?
3. How does the weaving in this poem relate to the spider's weaving in "Upon a Spider Catching a Fly"?

Anne Finch, "Friendship between Ephelia and Ardelia"

Finch has cast this poem in the form of a classical dialogue, giving the two speakers classical names and having them engage in a complex, dialectical exchange. The dialogue, which features two women speakers, concerns the question of friendship. Ephelia is looking for a definition, and finds that the attempts that Ardelia makes are either too simple or overinflated. Ardelia ends up with a statement that words are inadequate to define friendship, which can only be acted upon, not defined. This brief dialogue suggests a rich relationship between the two speakers, although the specifics of that relationship are left to the imaginative work of readers who follow the moves of the argument.

1. What are Ephelia's criticisms of Ardelia's attempts to define friendship?
2. How do the two speakers react to each other emotionally in the exchange?

Finch, "To the Nightingale"

In this poem we get a poet thinking about her own writing. In this case the speaker is musing on the sound of a nightingale, hoping that her own poetry could be as beautiful as the bird's song but still be meaningful as well. The nightingale's song seems to serve as a poetic ideal that the speaker despairs of reaching. As a result, she turns her anger on the bird, accusing it of wasting its own and her time. But the poem ends with the realization that such anger simply covers over the poet's disappointment at her inability to match the natural beauty of the bird's song. This brief poem therefore narrates a story that suggests a complex psychology of writing—that poems come out of the poet's frustration at creating perfect poetry.

1. Why do "wild" poets who do not aim to please the reader end up pleasing most fully?
2. Why would a bird be capable of producing purer poetic music than a poet?
3. Why do poets "criticize" and "censure" great poetry?

Samuel Johnson, "On the Death of Dr. Robert Levet"

Dr. Levet was a friend of Johnson's and a physician to the poor. In this response to his friend's death, Johnson memorializes Levet as a good man who did not aspire to greatness, but rather lived morally in the ordinary world. The language of Johnson's description is unusually rich in connotation. The language seeks to be at once exact and suggestive in its praise. A useful exercise with this poem would be to ask students to characterize Levet and then show how Johnson's language accounts for that characterization.

1. What is the significance of the following words and phrases, and how do their connotations contribute to the portrait of Dr. Levet: "delusive," "officious," "obscurely wise," "coarsely kind," "vigorous," "modest," "narrow."
2. Does Levet's death seem appropriate to his life?

Thomas Gray, "Elegy Written in a Country Churchyard"

Thomas Gray's justly famous poem is a reflection on death that seems to flow naturally from the speaker's situation, standing in the evening in a country churchyard, imagining the lives of the ordinary folk buried beneath his feet. His reflection is based on the premise that death is the great leveler: class and wealth do not count for much as we face mortality. Out of such considerations, the poem becomes a reflection on the potential in ordinary people that is limited by the class system within which they develop. The famous line of the poem that speculates on the possibility that there might be a "mute inglorious Milton" buried here, one whose poetic gift was never allowed to develop, is symptomatic of this point. The last nine stanzas of the poem seem to connect Gray with these ordinary people (though the "thee" to whom these lines are addressed is not clear). The speaker seems to be anticipating his own death and the reactions it will bring. And he seems to hope that in death he will be remembered as a quiet, unpretentious man who may not have achieved fame but who lived a decent, honest life.

1. What is the natural setting in which the poem is spoken?
2. What kinds of lives did those who are buried there lead?
3. What has kept these ordinary people from gaining positions of power?
4. What does "The Epitaph" tell us about the speaker's vision of himself?

Phillis Wheatly, "On Being Brought from Africa to America"

At first it might seem that this poem by America's first important black poet is an acceptance of servitude and the "white man's god." Although I won't deny that these attitudes lie behind the poem, there is also a strong sense that the "white man's god" might be in a sense turned against him, used to show that blacks are worthy as the children of that god of the same kind of treatment that white people accord each other as Christians.

1. Why does the speaker consider herself to have had a "benighted soul"?
2. What does it mean for humans to be "refined," in order to become a part of god's company?

Charlotte Smith, "Pressed by the Moon, Mute Arbitress of Tides"

This almost surreal poem dramatizes the speaker as a person tormented by life, jealous of those who have found rest in death. The powerful imagery of the poem, evoking the storm that empties a graveyard of its corpses, describes the storm in vivid terms. Particularly the description of the bones of the dead on the beach, "with shells and seaweed mingled," gives a graphic impression of the power of nature and death, a power that the speaker feels acutely and wishes she could escape. The poem is also interesting as a sonnet, playing off the Shakespearean version of the form, achieving a formality appropriate to its subject.

1. Does the poem personify nature in its description of the storm?
2. How does the speaker feel about her own death and life?
3. With regard to the last line of the poem, it is possible to envy something that is "gloomy"?

Robert Burns, "A Red, Red Rose"

This short lyric is a rich example of figurative language. It uses similes, of course, as in the famous first line, but also a series of traditional exaggerations that describe the intensity of his love. It might be interesting to students to see the history of poetic language behind the popular songs of today, which often promise the same ideal love. The simple similes at the beginning of the poem are of particular interest, because, simple as they are, they illustrate the complexity of any figurative language. That is, they do not say *how* the loved one is like a rose or like a melody. That work must be done by the reader, and the work is not simple at all.

1. How is the beloved like a rose? Like a melody? What does the poem give you to go on in order to allow you to answer that question?
2. What is the point of claiming that love will endure for the impossible lengths of time that the poem describes? This is a familiar move in love songs, but why?

William Wordsworth, "Nutting"

"Nutting" is one of the narrative poems in which Wordsworth describes the process by which he came to realize that "there is a spirit in the woods." Wordsworth tells many stories from his childhood that are concerned with his growing faith in a religion of nature, a belief that a divine spirit inhabits the natural world and can be perceived by human beings in it. The poem is therefore of interest as a *narrative,* with a coherent plot, a well-developed character, a powerfully evoked setting, a personal point of view, and a strong moral commitment. Students tend to associate narrative only with short stories, so it would be useful to get them thinking of a poem in these terms. Perhaps what is most interesting about this narrative of spiritual growth is that the speaker learns about the "spirit in the woods" by defiling it (the figurative language of the poem suggests, in fact, that he has *raped* the forest). He learns from his own guilt. The logic seems to be that if the forest can be defiled, there must be some spirit within it.

1. How does the speaker describe the forest in which he gathers nuts?
2. How does he describe his feelings on seeing the scene?
3. How does he describe the act of taking the nuts?
4. How does he feel after he has taken them?

Wordsworth, "Resolution and Independence"

This is another very strong *narrative* poem from Wordsworth, this one concerning the speaker's encounter with another character, an old man whose work is to collect leeches for medical use. His is a lonely and awful job, wandering the moors and collecting leeches from cold and isolated ponds. The role he plays in the speaker's mind comes from the fact that the old man is not dehumanized by his task, but rather maintains a dignified and religious manner that serves to the speaker as a model of resolution, of dealing with the harsh facts of life. The encounter with the old man is timely for the speaker, who is caught up in a self-pitying reflection on the sufferings of poets (thinking especially of Thomas Chatterton, a promising poet of the generation before Wordsworth who committed suicide at the age of seventeen). The old man obviously lives a life that makes such poetic suffering seem tame in comparison, and the speaker is therefore taught a useful lesson. Again, this poem is best studied as a story, in this case a story of education, but it is also of interest as a poem that devises a stanza form useful for storytelling and attractive in itself.

1. What is the speaker's mood at the beginning of the story? How does it change?
2. What is the significance of the leech-gatherer's appearance and style of talk?
3. What does the speaker gain from his meeting with this old man?

Samuel Taylor Coleridge, "Kubla Khan"

Coleridge's great poem can be studied on several levels. It is, for example, a beautiful descriptive poem, evoking in rich images the imaginary palace of Kubla Khan. But it is also a complex meditation on creativity, as the last stanza makes clear. There the poet is depicted as a holy madman who has had contact with the divine and who therefore has wisdom that makes him seem insane in the eyes of normal people. Moving from that last paragraph, the description of the chasm and fountain in the palace grounds can be seen as an allegorical description of the creative act, emphasizing its power and energy. The language of that section suggests that such energy is sexual in nature, though if you read these lines (12–24) in this way you come up with a very complex notion of the sexual energy behind creativity.

1. What kind of space does the poem describe Kubla Khan creating for himself?
2. In what sense are the chasm and the fountain described in the second stanza "holy and enchanted"?
3. How does the poem describe the ecstatic poet at the end of the third stanza?

Coleridge, "Frost at Midnight"

This is in a sense a meditative poem. It follows the workings of a mind engaged in solitary thought. We follow a chain of associations, from the soot that burns on the grate of the stove (called a "stranger" in Coleridge's time because it was thought to be a sign that a visitor was coming) to the speaker's memories of being at school (seeing this same glow, and hoping that a visitor might come for him) to the speaker's happiness that his child will live a life in nature rather than in a city school. Since we as readers are following the speaker's thought process, we get a privileged glimpse into his character. Student discussion and writing could profitably center around the character of the speaker as it is revealed in the poem.

1. Twice in the poem the action of the frost is called a "secret ministry." How does this phrase work in the poem? How is the word "ministry" being used here?
2. The speaker describes his mind at work as "Echo or mirror seeking of itself." What does this phrase tell us about how he thinks?
3. What benefits does the speaker hope his child will receive from close contact with nature?

Coleridge, "The Rime of the Ancient Mariner"

Coleridge's great imaginative travel narrative is full of marvels and spectacular effects. It takes readers on a voyage to a world in which magic and miracle are possible. But the world of this poem is also much like ours, especially in the issues it faces. The poem is therefore not just a marvelous narrative, but also the story of a moral and spiritual quest. The central issue of the story seems to be the relationship between mankind and nature. The Mariner's killing of the albatross brings about a crisis in that relationship, and his refound ability to see the holiness of nature (narrated in Part IV) only begins the healing process. The image of the Mariner we are left with recalls the image of the mad poet at the end of "Kubla Khan." He is a man who is compelled to tell his story, and who seems mad to those he captures with his "glittering eye." But the Mariner seems mad only because he has experienced spiritual wisdom that lies beyond the normal span of life. Coleridge tells this story in brilliant ballad stanzas, altered to suit his needs. The poem therefore makes a good example of how a story can be told effectively in verse.

1. What is the state of the ship and the crew before and then after they see the albatross? Does this help explain why the Mariner kills the bird?
2. How is the Mariner punished for his sin? Is the punishment appropriate to the crime?
3. How is the Mariner saved? How does his relationship with nature change?
4. Why is the Mariner's penance a requirement that he tell his story over again and again?

Percy Bysshe Shelley, "Ozymandias"

This extremely condensed poem makes a strong moral statement. The arrogance of power is revealed in the irony of Ozymandias's claim for immortality, surrounded as it is by the forces of nature that destroyed him. The interest of the poem for me lies in the fact that it is often the claim of poetry that it can achieve the kind of immortality that Ozymandias desired. Does the critique of power that this poem provides apply to poetry as well? The poem is striking in its unusual use of the sonnet form. It also manages to create a clear and evocative image of the desert in which the statue of Ozymandias lies, in spite of the fact that there are few specific details.

1. Why do we have a speaker who quotes a "traveller from an antique land"? Why not have that traveler simply be the speaker of the poem?
2. What does the face of the statue tell us about Ozymandias?
3. What makes the words on the statue seem ironic?

Shelley, "A Song: 'Men of England'"

This angry, political poem has a very strong sense of audience; it is addressed directly to the workers of England, urging them to take control of the industries they work in, to claim the profits of their own labor. The poem makes this point powerfully, by means of a striking figure of speech (working people as worker bees, their bosses as drones) and by a memorable rhetorical pattern that dominates the fifth and sixth stanzas (i.e., "The seed ye sow, another reaps" and "Sow seed—but let no tyrant reap"). The rhetoric of the poem is very thorough. The rich are "Tyrants," "drones," "impostors," "the idle." The poem is therefore useful to look at as an example of how language can be used to impose a certain meaning and feeling on experience. In this poem language does political work, characterizing the bosses and the workers in such a way as to unify the workers in their hatred of the rich.

1. Why do the first four stanzas contain so many questions?
2. What is the political message the poem delivers? Is it convincing?
3. What is the speaker's attitude toward his audience of working people?
4. How does the last stanza fit in with the rest of the poem?

John Keats, "On First Looking into Chapman's Homer"

This is one of the great poems about the experience of reading poetry, in this case Keats's first encounter with Homer, through the translation by the Elizabethan poet George Chapman. The poem is based on a figure of speech depicting literary works as expanses of land ruled by the poets. The speaker compares his encounter with a new poem with an explorer's first view of a new territory. In this case the speaker compares himself with Cortez as he discovers the Pacific. In fact, it was Balboa who first saw the Pacific, but the comparison still has poetic force. The idea of a text as new territory to explore can make for an interesting discussion of the value of reading.

1. What tells us that "the realms of gold" are literary texts?
2. What relationship does the poem suggest between poets and Apollo, the god of poetry?
3. What does the phrase "a wild surmise" suggest about adventure—and about reading?

Emily Brontë, "No Coward Soul Is Mine"

The speaker of this poem is engaged in an argument against the fear of death. Death need not be feared because God is immortal, and He has given human beings the gift of eternal life in Him. The last two stanzas extend the argument from the personal to the cosmic—all humans will exist in God even after the entire physical universe has disappeared. God "pervades" time and space, and so nothing is ever finally destroyed. The argument is elaborate and powerful. What the poem does not make clear is to whom the argument is addressed. Is the speaker trying to convince herself? It is interesting to note in the third and fourth stanzas that what might provoke doubt are the "thousand creeds" of mankind; it is the sheer existence of other forms of faith that might cause the speaker to doubt.

1. What are the figures of speech that the speaker uses to describe God and His actions?
2. What does the word *animates* suggest in this poem? What is the etymology of the word?
3. In line five, God is "within my breast"; in the last three stanzas he is described as pervading all of time and space. How do these two descriptions go together?

Brontë, "Tell me, tell me, smiling child"

In this dialogue between an adult questioner and a wise child, the child's answers are richly figurative. Instead of answering the questions directly, the child answers in metaphor, and leaves it to the questioner—and the reader—to figure out how the natural scenes provide a description of the past, the present, and the future. Each metaphor answers the question in ways that suggest strong and complex emotions. But all of that is suggested rather than stated directly. It is left to the reader to make the feelings explicit.

1. How does the metaphor that the child offers answer each of the questions that the adult asks?
2. What would you anticipate that the adult's reaction to these answers would be?

Ralph Waldo Emerson, "The Rhodora"

In some ways this poem makes an interesting contrast with a Wordsworth poem like "Nutting" or "Resolution and Independence." In Wordsworth, nature seems to exist in order to teach mankind about God, whereas here the natural world seems sufficient unto itself. Nature does not serve mankind but rather exists in its own beauty for its own sake. Of course, the speaker has seen the previously unseen flower, and he can only reflect on the fact that it has the same creator as he has, but the center of the poem for me lies in the speaker's awareness that the flower has existed for a long time in a place that no human being saw. Its beauty existed independent of any practical concern. It did not have to serve mankind but rather existed simply as a monument to divine creation. The speaker seems to be trying not to impose a meaning on the flower but to let it exist on its own terms.

1. What kind of natural scene do the first eight lines of the poem depict?
2. Does the last line of the poem identify the man with the flower? Is mankind as well a simple part of nature?
3. Does the word "Power" in the last line take the place of the word "god"?

Emerson, "The Snow-Storm"

This poem is driven by a very strong personification—the wind as a mason, a "fierce artificer" who creates beauty out of the pattern of snow fallen on the human world. The poem also includes a number of remarkable verbal combinations—"tumultuous privacy" and "frolic architecture" are two good examples—that make the poem useful in the study of connotative meaning. The "Parian wraths" are snow figures that remind the speaker of marble from the Greek island of Paros. The notion of nature as an artist is not unusual, but the idea that something as organized as "architecture" could be produced by the "mad wind" makes for an interesting paradox.

1. What kind of atmosphere does the speaker describe in the first stanza?
2. What kind of art does the wind create?
3. What does the phrase "frolic architecture" tell us about the beauty of nature?

Alfred, Lord Tennyson, "Break, Break, Break"

There is an interesting relationship between the speaker of this poem and the world he describes. His feelings don't match what he sees. What's going on around him is the joy and energy of life, but he is fixated on death and sorrow. He can see but cannot feel the joy. The only joy he desires is a joy that is irrevocably lost, and so he is trapped outside of the pleasure of experience. But at least he can see it, which suggests that it might eventually heal him of his sorrow. This poem would be interesting to use in dealing with the psychology of the speaker or as a funny kind of imagistic poem in which the images don't affect the person who perceives them.

1. How do lines thirteen and fourteen differ from lines one and two? What does the difference tell us about the speaker?
2. What are the connotations of the words *stately* and *haven* in the third stanza?
3. What is the mood created by the last two lines?

Tennyson, "Tears, Idle Tears"

The structure of this poem is provided by a series of similes that express the speaker's feelings about "the days that are no more." Each of the similes expresses a very specific emotion. Articulating what those emotions are would be a demanding task; they are not simple to name. The similes may well be the only way to express them adequately. In this poem perhaps the role of the reader is to feel the emotions that the similes suggest and to see what they add up to as a portrait of the speaker's state of mind. It is also important to listen to this poem aloud, in order to hear its stately rhythm and its complex verbal echoes.

1. Why are the tears the speaker sheds "idle tears"?
2. What does each of the similes in the poem tell us about the speaker's feelings for the past?

Tennyson, "Crossing the Bar"

This poem is based on working out the particulars of a comparison of death with leaving port and heading out to sea. Various aspects of the figurative comparison play a part in the poem: the tide, the sound of the water on the sandbar, the Pilot who will guide the voyage out. Death, then, is not to be feared or mourned, since it is not the end but the beginning of a voyage, and it is a gentle and safe beginning, under the guidance of God. As a consolation about death, this poem could profitably be read in connection with Emily Brontë's "No Coward Soul Is Mine."

1. To whom is this poem addressed? What is the speaker's message to that audience?
2. Why is putting out to sea an appropriate comparison to the moment of death?

Christina Rossetti, "Symbols"

This poem tells an evocative story about the relationship between human beings and nature. The speaker expresses a dramatic disappointment with the fragility of nature. Its beauty—the beauty of a rose or a bird's egg—is open to danger; the rose withers and so often the egg is abandoned. The beauty of nature is transitory, unreliable. But as the poem develops, we find that the speaker's anger comes from a disappointment in herself rather than in nature. She feels that she has not been fruitful, not brought her own potential worth to full growth. Whether the failure that the speaker feels has to do with childlessness (as some of the imagery suggests) or with a general sense of frustration, what is important is that she takes out her anger on those images that remind her that hopes are not always fulfilled. The speaker seems to have learned a lesson from the story she narrates; it is an episode in her moral education.

1. What do the flower in stanza one and the eggs in stanza two have in common?
2. How do the victims of her vengeance respond to her acts of violence?

Rossetti, "In an Artist's Studio"

This poem could profitably be read in terms of the relationships it implies among its characters. The speaker is reporting on the relationship between an artist and his model, and it would be interesting to get students thinking about how she characterizes that relationship. Does she feel that the artist's fixation on this model is an unhealthy obsession or a romantic devotion? What do his paintings do to the model? How do they change her? The speaker suggests but does not give definitive answers to these questions, leaving them for the work of the reader.

1. In what sense is a painting a mirror, as it is described in line four? How does that metaphor relate to the last line of the poem?
2. What does the speaker feel about the painter's fixation on this model?
3. Is the painter interested only in an illusion?

Robert Browning, "Porphyria's Lover"

Like many of Robert Browning's poems, "Porphyria's Lover" presents the reader with a very powerful and complex speaker. The chapter of this textbook titled "The Speaker of the Poem" features Browning's most famous poem in this mode, "My Last Duchess." In both of these poems the reader must achieve some distance from the speaker, not take the speaker's version of events as the authoritative account. The reader must produce his or her own interpretation of the events that the speaker presents. In this case, the poem is from a collection that Browning called *Madhouse Cells,* and we are given a speaker who seems to have committed a murder and who has lost any sense of the seriousness of what he has done ("I am quite sure she felt no pain"). The speaker is able to give a detailed account of the events of the murder as well as a quick suggestion of the relationship he had with Porphyria. As readers, we need to remember that his account is a self-serving interpretation, but it is still brilliant in its descriptive detail and psychological analysis.

1. What kind of portrait of the speaker does the poem build up?
2. What does the speaker think was the nature of his relationship with Porphyria? Do you see it differently?
3. Why did the speaker kill Porphyria?
4. Why is it important to him to claim that she felt no pain and that she has gotten her deepest wish?

Elizabeth Barrett Browning, "Grief"

This poem seems to spin out the consequences of its parodoxical first line: "I tell you, hopeless grief is passionless." Where we would usually think of grief as a violent emotion, the speaker asserts that *true* grief is silent, "like a monumental statue." The first line is a paradox rather than a contradiction, though, in that the opposition between "grief" and "passionless" is only apparent. The burden of the poem is to show that the paradox is true. The psychology of the poem seems to be based on the premise that any emotion that can be expressed in human languages (in words or in gestures, for example) is relatively superficial compared to an authentic emotion—which is always silent, unspeakable.

1. What does the phrase "incredulous of despair" tell us about people who do not experience true grief?
2. What does the metaphor of the desert in line five tell us about true grief?
3. What does the last line tell us about the relationship between grief and weeping?

Barrett Browning, "Hiram Powers' 'Greek Slave'"

This sonnet takes the form of a meditation on a work of art, a statue by Hiram Powers, an American sculptor who was a friend of the Brownings'. The poem does not emphasize the beauty of the statue (though that is of course recognized) but rather concerns itself with the social impact of that beauty. That is, this ideal beauty is possessed by a slave, a being that many would like to think of as subhuman. Her beauty is a rebuke to the institution of slavery, and the speaker is convinced that this work of art can therefore play a role in ending slavery by raising people's awareness of the humanity of its victims. The poem therefore suggests an activist view of the arts, that they can change social beliefs and values. The poem is also of interest for its rich figurative language. The first half of the poem, for example, depends on the figure of "The house of anguish," as the statue seems to emerge from the shadows of that house in order to deliver its rebuke.

1. The first two lines contain a bit of what the speaker identifies as common wisdom that "ideal beauty cannot enter / The house of anguish." Why would that be? How does the speaker show that the common wisdom is not true?
2. What can "ideal beauty" do to "confront man's crimes"?

Barrett Browning, "When our two souls stand up erect and strong" ("Sonnet 22" of *Sonnets from the Portuguese*)

In some ways this poem recalls seventeenth-century love poems like those of John Donne. That is, its expressions of love and passion are also witty figures of speech and verbal play. In this case the poem is built on the fanciful notion that the two lovers have become so perfect that they consider leaving this world for heaven. They seem to decide, though, that this world is more appropriate for them, in that it will at least leave them alone with each other. There is a cost, though, as the last line suggests, in staying in this world—the lovers will have to face decay and death. As the speaker suggests, their love will be their only defense against such pain. The poem is an interesting example of an Italian or Petrarchan sonnet, in that it divides neatly as a poem into eight-line and six-line units, but the sense of the poem does not follow this division, thus creating an interesting tension between the sound and the sense of the poem.

1. In the first four lines of the poem, how does the speaker describe their love?
2. Why is earth more attractive than heaven to the speaker?
3. Why would ordinary men "recoil away / And isolate pure spirits"? What do they have against spiritual purity?

Barrett Browning, "A Curse for a Nation"

This is Barrett Browning's attack on American slavery in 1860. The poem divides itself into two parts, "Prologue," in which the speaker tries to avoid the duty of delivering the second part, and "The Curse," which accuses the United States of betraying its own democratic ideals by its continuing acceptance of slavery. In the first part the speaker offers her love of America, her sense of her own nation's wrongs, and her female gender as excuses that would free her from the duty of condemnation. But the angel she is conversing with answers each of her arguments, claiming that it is exactly these difficulties that make her the right person to deliver the curse. The second section of the poem accuses America of betraying its own ideals and thus disqualifying itself as a friend of freedom throughout the world. This highly political poem, then, flies in the face of the common assumption that poetry is not political. It has a strong moral point to make, and it uses various poetic techniques to make it as effectively as possible.

1. What sins does the speaker accuse *England* of as disqualifications for her to send a curse against America?
2. Why does the speaker think her gender disqualifies her? Why does the angel disagree with her?
3. How is slavery, according to the speaker, a betrayal of American ideals?
4. What effects does slavery have on the standing of America in the world community?

Emily Dickinson, "I felt a Funeral, in my Brain"

In this poem the speaker seems to be imagining her own death, as though she had retained consciousness after her death and was able to see and hear the reactions of the mourners. The funeral itself seems to be depicted as an affront to reason: the mourners must engage in an endless repetition, "treading—treading" and "beating—beating" on the drum that the speaker uses as a simile for the funeral service. Only after the funeral does the soul achieve some release, freeing her into solitude and then into a complete separation from this world. Or at least that's how I'm able to make sense of this cryptic poem. But the poem leaves out so much—its language is suggestive rather than conclusive—that it's up to the reader to read into the poem in order to fill in the gaps. As a result, the pleasure of the poem is in the interpretive activity it sparks in the reader.

1. Why does the funeral service numb the speaker's brain?
2. What is the sound that is described in the third and fourth stanzas?
3. Is the fall described in the last stanza a terrifying fall or a liberating one?
4. Why has the speaker "Finished knowing" at the end of the poem? Is that good?

Dickinson, "Much Madness is divinest Sense"

Compared with the often indirect and difficult language of Dickinson's poetry, this is a fairly straightforward presentation of what is, nevertheless, a radical idea. That is, it is unsettling to think that sanity might be a matter of consensus, that thinking with the majority puts us into the category of sanity, whereas thinking against the majority makes us insane. We would like to think that there is an abstract and timeless rule of reason by which we can judge whether an action or belief is sane or insane. If sanity is a matter of consensus, are all breakthrough thinkers insane? Does our notion of sanity force us into familiar patterns of thinking?

1. How can madness be *"divinest"* sense? Can it bring you closer to God?
2. In what way can "sense" in fact be "madness"? Can you think of a current example of something that is widely accepted as true that you think is irrational?
3. Is there a tyranny of the majority in judgments about sanity and insanity?

Dickinson, "I like a look of Agony"

This little poem takes a tone of hard-won wisdom. The speaker seems to have encountered a great deal of falsehood in human relationships, enough to make her feel that the only true emotions that human beings express are emotions of agony and anxiety. To "like a look of Agony" is to be desperate for authenticity, to value the direct expression of emotion so highly that one can overlook the pain that at least allows those emotions to be expressed. It is, finally, to value death most highly, since it is "impossible to feign." This poem takes on these questions in an unusually direct manner, with little imagery or figurative language, except for the interesting last two lines that play on the double meaning of "beads" in order to talk about how anguish or the fear of death leaves its mark on mankind.

1. Do you agree with the assertions in the first stanza? Does the poem convince you of their truth?
2. Why is death "impossible to feign"?

Dickinson, "Apparently with no surprise"

This poem seems to me to be concerned with one of the oldest questions in human thought—how can a divine power allow the existence of evil? In this case it is the destruction of the flower that "an approving God" looks down on without remorse. But this poem makes the point of nature's indifference to loss and death in an unusual way, that is, by personifying the natural world. It would seem that if you wanted to show the indifference of nature to the destruction of individuals that you would carefully avoid personification, and all the emotional associations that this tactic activates. What the poem says about God and nature, then, is somewhat at odds with how God and nature are described. Logical contradiction or rich paradox?

1. What personifications are at work in the first stanza?
2. What is "the blond assassin"?
3. How is the measuring function of the sun related to the destruction the poem describes?

Dickinson, "The Brain—is wider than the Sky"

This poem would make sense as part of a study of figurative language. In each stanza the human brain is discussed in terms of comparisons with other entities that help define its scope and its powers. In each case the strategy seems to be to compare the brain with some huge power that it nevertheless controls. In the last stanza the power of human thought is elevated to divine status, almost identified with the creative power of God. But the last line of the poem suggests a more complex point. The difference between "Syllable" and "Sound," which is offered in the poem as no difference at all, seems to me to be a real and substantial difference—one between a finished human product and a raw material. What this last line suggests about the rest of the comparisons in the poem is a question that readers could pursue with profit.

1. In what sense is the brain wider than the sky, deeper than the sea? What do these comparisons tell us about the brain?
2. In what ways does the poem equate the brain with God? In what ways does it point out the differences between them?

Dickinson, "I never lost as much but twice"

Another poem of interest because of its figurative language, which in this case explicitly identifies God with "Burglar! Banker—Father!" This strange trio of terms produces a wide variety of suggestions about the speaker's attitude toward God. The poem takes the form of a prayer from a creature who feels that God has twice before taken away something precious and then provided some compensation. She therefore hopes in the midst of her feelings of loss that the same pattern can be repeated again. Also, this poem, as with any Dickinson poem, is of interest for its metrical strategies, apparently simple verse that on closer inspection turns out to be quirky and complex.

1. If the speaker sees herself as a beggar, what does the logic of the figure suggest about God?
2. What are the implications of each of the terms in the second stanza that are used to identify God? What does each figure tell us about the speaker's feelings toward God?

Dickinson, "These are the days when Birds come back"

It would be interesting to read this poem in conjunction with "To Autumn" by John Keats, since both are concerned with almost the same time of year and with the same emotional response to it—that it's a trick to make you feel that summer will endure forever. This poem makes use of a more religious discourse than the Keats poem does. Here the references in the last two stanzas to the "Sacrament of summer days" and to the "Last Communion" suggest that the poem is about more than a time of year. And when you connect these two reverent stanzas to the earlier remark in the poem that this time of year is a "fraud," you get a complex notion of the speaker's feelings about religion.

1. In the second stanza, what does the phrase "sophistries of June" suggest? What is a "blue and gold mistake"?
2. What keeps the speaker from giving her "plausibility" to the moment of late summer?
3. In what sense are summer days a "Sacrament"?

Walt Whitman, "Once I Passed through a Populous City"

In terms of metrics, this poem makes for an interesting contrast with any of the Dickinson poems. The lines of her poems are so compact and careful, whereas Whitman's line is long and flowing. How do these metrical patterns suit or not suit the points that the poets want to make? The speaker of this poem is also of interest. His main concern in life is suggested by the fact that a visit to the city, with all its sheer size and institutional diversity, is memorable to him only because of a relationship he has there. In fact, by the end of the poem we have attended to the relationship so much that the city seems to be forgotten, even though at first it absorbed the speaker's attention.

1. How does the first line of the poem relate to the rest?
2. What specific details does the speaker remember about his relationship with the woman?

Whitman, "When I Heard the Learn'd Astronomer"

This is a very compressed narrative poem that is structured around a strong contrast. The feelings of the speaker as he listens to the astronomer contrast sharply with his feelings as he gazes up into the stars. What accounts for that difference is made pretty clear in the narrative details—the difference between "charts and diagrams" and "the mystical moist night air" makes the speaker's sympathies clear. It is also clear that an entire theory of education—not just of astronomy—can be read into these lines. They even suggest some of the limitations of literary criticism, which often subjects to analysis what should best be experienced in solitary, mystic ecstasy.

1. When the speaker becomes "tired and sick," is it really as "unaccountable" as he says?
2. Why is it significant that he gazes up at the stars "in perfect silence"?

Whitman, "I Saw in Louisiana a Live-Oak Growing"

This poem seems to tell the narrative of its own writing. The speaker tells the story of being in a natural setting that sends him a message about his own state of life, then taking home a memento of the place and returning to the same insight whenever he looks at it. The next logical step in the sequence would be writing the poem that comes out of the insight. The insight deals with his *need* for love; the tree seems to him to be capable of a self-sufficiency that he lacks. But why the inability to live without others is seen as a problem is not clear. Isn't what makes a tree not human that it is unconscious, incapable of emotional need? The speaker seems to be scolding himself for being human, setting up complete isolation from others as an ideal. In any event, the poem is interesting as a revelation of the character of its speaker.

1. What qualities does the speaker see in the tree that remind him of himself?
2. How does he see the tree as being different from himself?
3. What is the purpose of the twig he has brought home?
4. What does the speaker mean by "manly love"? Why does the tree remind him of it?

Lewis Carroll, "Jabberwocky"

This poem is often described as "nonsense verse," but that is only part of the story. For certainly what is more interesting is that this poem, despite all the nonsense words, makes a heck of a lot of sense. And why it does so can tell us a lot about language and poetry and fiction. In fact, this poem could well be used as a way of talking about the theory of language and culture that this text is based on. That is, the fact that this poem makes sense at all is a testament to the power of the language system. Some of the words may be nonsense, but they are embedded inside grammatical structures that do make sense. The word order is right, and the nonsense words take the form of recognizable English words. As a result, we *almost* know what's going on, especially if we recognize the kind of poem this is—a narrative of heroic action. All the signs are there: the hero, the opponent, the conflict, the triumph of the hero. Inside this strong narrative structure, we can make sense of this nonsense as a story. And part of the fun of the poem is that although the poem seems lighthearted, it is in fact quite bloodthirsty. The Jabberwocky is slain, beheaded, and gloated over. Still, there is strong nonsense here, and the poem is a funny and insightful joke on we readers who *need* to make sense.

1. About what percentage of the words in the poem are nonsense? How do they relate to the legitimate words?
2. What is it in the poem that allows us to follow the narrative? Could you summarize the events of the story?
3. Why does the last stanza repeat the first?

Thomas Hardy, "Hap"

This poem is notable for its very formal style and unusual diction. At the end of the poem especially the wording becomes very elaborate. "Crass Casualty" seems to suggest sheer luck, and the "purblind Doomsters" of the next to last line could be loosely translated as "half-blind gods or judges." The entire poem seems to seek out unusual patterns of language that do not allow us as readers to rest easy in our usual expectations. This poem has to be worked for. The speaker is concerned with the question of suffering, claiming that the concept of an evil god as the source of suffering would be more acceptable than what he sees as the truth, that suffering occurs at random, not because it is deserved. God is not evil, just indifferent, which is even worse, the speaker says.

1. Why is the image of a vengeful god preferable to an indifferent god?
2. What images of God come out of the last stanza?
3. How does the poem work as a sonnet?

Gerald Manley Hopkins, "Spring and Fall"

This poem would make a good comparison with "Jabberwocky." Lewis Carroll's poem is a lighthearted, clever joke on readers, whereas this poem, which is almost as difficult to manage verbally as "Jabberwocky," seems to set itself much more serious goals. In Hopkins's poem language is used in an innovative way, combining familiar words into new words and into unusual sentence patterns. We are forced to slow down, attend closely to the language. But after all that work, the last two lines are surprisingly direct. The narrator tells Margaret that she does not grieve over the coming of fall; she grieves because she foresees her own death.

1. Can you make sense of the words that Hopkins creates out of two separate words: "Goldengrove," "wanwood," "leafmeal"?
2. Is it possible to disentangle the syntax of the poem's sentences?
3. What do you think of the speaker, who forces the "young child," Margaret, to see the world so darkly?

A. E. Housman, "With Rue My Heart is Laden"

In this brief and delicate poem, each word makes a serious contribution. If we were to paraphrase the poem, we could come up with something very simple such as, "I'm sorry for my friends who have died." But that would miss the specific effects of the poem, which come out of such words as "golden," "rose-lipt," "lightfoot," and "fade." The poem connects by its imagery the death of the speaker's friends and the natural process of decay and death. But that connection does not seem to be a consolation; the sorrow of the beginning of the poem remains the dominant tone throughout. This poem therefore would make an interesting example in a discussion of poetic language, in that the connotations of its words—if they are attended to by an active reader—produce a strong emotional effect.

1. What do the words *rose-lipt* and *lightfoot* tell us about the speaker's feelings for his friends who have died?
2. What is the significance of the fact that the "lightfoot boys" are buried "By brooks too broad for leaping"?
3. What does the last line of the poem tell us about the speaker's state of mind?

Housman, "Eight O'Clock"

This poem would be interesting for students to discuss in terms of the temporal process of reading. That is, the first stanza sets up expectations that the second overturns. The first stanza by itself seems pastoral, depicting the gentle passage of time in a pleasant place. But when we find in the second stanza that the "He" of the first stanza who is listening to the tolling of the bells is a condemned criminal waiting for the time of his execution, we need to go back and reread the first stanza with our new information. Thus the poem involves the reader in the unfolding of its meaning. The poem requires an active reader who is alert to changing interpretive situations.

1. What is the connotative effect of such words as *sprinkle* and *tossed* in the first stanza?
2. How do the last two lines of the poem play with normal syntactic patterns?
3. Does this poem hold together, or are the two stanzas heading in radically different directions?

Housman, "Loveliest of Trees, the Cherry Now"

This is a light and elegant poem about a dark topic. The speaker of the poem, though a very young person, seems obsessed with the passing of time and with death. He feels the need to enjoy nature's beauty *now*, while there is still time. Of course, such statements in the poem are in a sense a hyperbole aimed at praising the beauty of the trees by stressing how often they deserve to be seen, but the dark tone of the speaker's concern with time passing is still powerful. The poem is therefore of interest as a sketch of its speaker's personality, and also as an example of elegant metrical form.

1. What seems to bring thoughts of death into the speaker's mind?
2. Is it significant to the meanings of the poem that the trees are blooming at Easter?
3. What is the connotative force of the last word of the poem, *snow?*

Wilfred Owen, "Futility"

What is perhaps most remarkable about this poem is that it was written in the midst of combat, with death occurring all around, and yet the speaker of the poem seems to have held on to a sense of surprise and outrage at the death of a human being. The poem is built around images of the sun. The speaker seems to be holding on to a notion that he recognizes as irrational—that the sun can return his dead friend to life. The sun has such powers in the cosmos, bringing planets to life, but the speaker realizes that it has no such power over human life. Death is simply not reversible, and not even the power of the sun can intervene.

1. In the first stanza the sun is called "the kind old sun." In the second there is the phrase "fatuous sunbeams." What has happened to change the speaker's feelings about the sun?
2. What does it say about human beings to refer to them as "the clay [grown] tall"?
3. Does the speaker have an answer to the question that ends the poem?

T. S. Eliot, "The Love Song of J. Alfred Prufrock"

One of the most famous poems of modern literature, "Prufrock" typifies early twentieth-century poetry both in its formal strategies and its analysis of modern life. The poem follows the workings of the speaker's mind in what could be called a stream of consciousness manner. The poem consists of the speaker's remembered events, visual and aural imagery, self-reflections, and comments on life, all connected in an associative logic, as though we were following the speaker's mind as it jumps from thought to thought. The jumps are not always announced or explained, so that the reader is left to wonder about the connections. Nevertheless, there is at least the framework of a narrative, as a man prepares himself to go to a social gathering, describes the streets he passes through, anticipates his arrival and the nature of the party, remembers an afternoon with a woman, and reflects on his unromantic, limited life. The speaker seems indecisive, self-conscious, wary of others—in these ways and others the typical modern hero (or anti-hero). The vision of modern life in the poem emphasizes the difficulty of personal relations, the inauthenticity of so much of our social communication. Prufrock's monologue gives us a very clear but very complex sense of how his mind works, and students might well benefit from attempting a character sketch of Prufrock using the evidence of his own language.

1. What are the implications of the famous simile in the first three lines? What does it tell us about Prufrock?
2. How does Prufrock feel about the streets and neighborhoods he describes in the first twenty-three lines?

3. What does Prufrock anticipate about the party he is going to? How does he expect to relate to the other people there?
4. What does the phrase "eyes that fix you in a formulated phrase" suggest about human relationships?
5. What kind of relationship does he describe in lines 75–110? What happens between Prufrock and the woman?
6. What do the concluding lines dealing with mermaids tell us about Prufrock's state of mind at the end of the poem?

Eliot, "Journey of the Magi"

This is a poem with a very definitely dramatized speaker, one of the Magi who visited the Christ child. He narrates the events of the journey, his expectations, the moment of seeing the child, and its effect on the rest of his life. This sequence seems quite logical, but before they see the child, they see all around them signs of the suffering and death of Christ, still far in the future. As a result, the birth of the child is connected to thoughts of death. Christ's death, after all, is the point of his human life. The poem is therefore about a man encountering a mystery, an event that seems full of meaning but still resists reason. As such, the poem would fit well into a study of the speaker in a poem.

1. How does the speaker describe the journey to the Christ child? Why does he spend so much time on it?
2. How does the speaker weave references to the story of the Crucifixion into the second stanza?
3. What is the significance of the last line of the poem?

D. H. Lawrence, "Piano"

This poem traces out the relationships between a present event and the memories it evokes. For me, the scenario can be sketched as follows: The present event is an erotic one—a woman is singing to the speaker in the dusk. But the memory the event evokes is from the speaker's childhood, a memory of his mother and his warm family. The result seems to be the end of the erotic moment. Instead of attending to the woman who is with him, he "weep[s] like a child for the past." Other scenarios are certainly possible. But whatever the narrative you construct out of the poem's clues, you will still have to deal with the rich and complex language of the poem, which serves in its connotative power to communicate the speaker's feelings about the moment and about the memory. The poem is therefore appropriate to the study of connotative language.

1. What is the significance of the following words from the poem: *softly, boom, tingling, poised, insidious, mastery, betrays, cozy, tinkling, clamor, appassionato, glamour, flood.*
2. How does the speaker feel about the memories the music evokes?
3. How does the memory affect his present life?

H.D. (Hilda Doolittle), "Heat"

This poem would obviously be appropriate to a section on images. The point of the poem is to suggest in words the sensory experience of extreme heat and the desire for escape from it. What is also interesting is that the poem attempts to produce this effect through its complex and incisive figures of speech. The wind is a knife or scissors, the heat a stifling fabric. The air is thick enough to hold fruit up on the tree. By these figures we get a sense of the experience itself. Language seems to be able to use its resources to perform the difficult task of communicating a sensory experience to another person.

1. What does the poem do to try to communicate the feel of heat on the skin?
2. What is the significance of the fact that the poem is addressed directly to the wind itself?

H.D., "Sea Rose"

This poem seems to alternate between descriptions of the harsh and meager life of the sea rose and assertions of its great value and beauty. How those two kinds of responses go together is not made explicit, but is left to the reader to consider. Why is a "meagre" flower so "precious"? The poem is also significant for its sharp imagery, especially in the third stanza, which describes the harsh environment in which the rose must survive. The poem ends with a difficult and cryptic question that again seems to imply the superiority of the "stunted" sea rose.

1. How does the speaker describe the sea rose in the first stanza?
2. What does this rose have that the hothouse rose does not?
3. What kind of environment does the sea rose survive in?

H.D., "Sea Poppies"

This is another poem by H. D., in praise of the beauty of the marginal. The sea poppy, the poem tells us, thrives in the margins, in places where our eye does not expect beauty. It is therefore even more beautiful than the meadow-flower that thrives in more accommodating terrain. Is there another layer of meaning to the poem? Does the sea poppy "stand for" something or someone? The poem does not say. But readers are free to build an allegorical reading, as long as they are able to explain why they see the flowers as "standing for" another entity, and as long as they are willing to accept that the poem doesn't authorize any particular second level. Is the poem about a woman poet who is ignored in favor of more publicized males? Is the sea poppy the poem in the harsh modern world, rather than the poems that have flourished in more tranquil and supportive times? These and other possibilities can be argued for.

1. How does the first stanza establish the flower as a "treasure," as it is called in line five?
2. How does the flower contrast with its surroundings?
3. What is the effect of the repetition of the word *leaf* in the last two lines?

Robert Frost, "Stopping by Woods on a Snowy Evening"

This famous poem has been written about by countless critics and students. I only hope to make a few observations that might spark some ideas for students. It is useful to remember that the poem is a narrative—it tells a story. But it is a curious story. The speaker seems to be on some business, but the story is not about that business, it is rather about an interruption, an event that seems not to be part of a larger narrative pattern. And the poem focuses on tiny details of that event—the horse's impatience, the sound of its bells—rather than concerning itself explicitly with the significance of the event. How the event is significant is suggested but not stated. The poem therefore requires a reader who will explore that significance, question why such an "unimportant" event gets all of this attention. As a narrative, the poem is also an example of an effective use of present-tense verbs as a way of creating the illusion that the action of the narrative is happening in the present, before the speaker's and the reader's eyes.

1. Why is the speaker concerned about the fact that he will not be seen as he watches the snow?
2. Why does the speaker focus on the horse's reaction?

3. What is the significance of the darkness of the scene?
4. Why are watching the snow and the "promises" the speaker refers to seen as opposites in the poem?

Frost, "Design"

Frost's brilliant sonnet on natural destruction can be read usefully from many different perspectives. It is interesting as a sonnet, making use of the form to describe and then reflect on the significance of the scene. It is a richly imagistic poem, producing a powerful visual impression. It make use of complex figurative language. It reveals a speaker whose musings on this scene define him as a character. In describing this small event, the poem manages to raise central questions: Is there design in the universe? If so, is that design benevolent? I have found that students respond strongly to this poem. They find it baffling at first, with its complex syntax and its open-ended questions, but they also find it challenging, verbally and thematically.

1. What is the significance of the whiteness of the creatures in the scene?
2. Why does the speaker call the animals and plants "characters" of death and blight?
3. Does the poem answer the questions it raises in the second stanza?

Frost, "Out, Out—"

The title of this poem points us to Shakespeare's *Macbeth*, to Macbeth's speech on the death of his wife:

> Out, out, brief candle
> Life's but a walking shadow, a poor player
> That struts and frets his hour upon the stage
> And then is heard no more. It is a tale
> Told by an idiot, full of sound and fury,
> Signifying nothing.

We can use these lines as a commentary on the event that the poem narrates, which is the story of a simple accident that leads to tragic consequences. The poem speculates on the causes of the event, but no real explanation is offered. The event seems to have come out of nowhere and to have had minimal consequences, except for the boy himself (see the last two lines). Does this event suggest that there is design in the universe? Like "Design," the poem does not offer an answer, but it raises the question in a dramatic and affecting manner.

1. What is the significance of the "five mountain ranges" that stand behind the scene of the event?
2. Why does the speaker speculate that the boy "must have given the hand" to the saw?
3. What is the significance of the doctor's indifference at the end of the poem?

Frost, "After Apple-Picking"

In this poem it's not the event that matters, but the reverberations of the event in the speaker's mind. The day of apple-picking becomes an event in his memory, in his dreams. The poem evokes his bodily memory of the event, as well as his emotional response to it (guilt at the waste he has caused?). That memory is communicated by strong imagery—the sights and sounds of the day as they would appear in a dream. Again the significance of the event is not made explicit. Rather, the poem attends to the imagistic details of the event. The significance of the event is suggested by the last lines, as the speaker wonders whether the sleep that is to come will be an animal or a human sleep. The connections between the events of the day and the responses they evoke are not made absolutely clear, but rather are left to the work of the reader.

1. Why does the speaker talk about what he has *not* accomplished in his task?
2. What does the speaker remember most vividly from the day?
3. What is the importance of the apples that fall to the ground?
4. What do the last four lines suggest about the similarities and differences between humans and animals?

Wallace Stevens, "The Snow Man"

One interesting way into this poem might be to note that it is made up of one extremely complex sentence. In fact, if students can see and understand it as a sentence, they are well on the way to making sense of the poem. This complex sentence seems to be about perception, about how the mind of the perceiver shapes what is perceived. If you have a "mind of winter," the cold wind does not make a sound of "misery." The meditation on perception ends in a kind of riddle, in which the word *nothing* gets punned on and applied both to the perceiver and to the world he perceives. Making sense of these last three lines is made difficult by their abstract and complex language. Is it that only the listener who can free himself from preconceptions can perceive that the world has no emotion to it except what we impose on it, that it exists in brute form, indifferent to human feelings? Still the riddle remains, challenging our ability to make sense in the first place.

1. How is this sentence structured? Why would the poet choose to construct this complex sentence?
2. How does the word *nothing* change in meaning in each of its three uses at the end of the poem?

Stevens, "Anecdote of the Jar"

As an anecdote, this poem tells a brief story. The speaker places a jar on a hill, and reports that nature seems to rearrange itself around the jar. The jar is a human product, and its placement makes it serve as a focal point to the human eye. The natural world, therefore, subjects itself to the artifact of man, taking on an order that it did not have before. But is this a good thing? The language of the poem seems to give a complex answer. The wilderness is "slovenly," the jar takes "dominion," which suggests a positive attitude toward the power of the jar. But the jar is also lifeless, unlike what it dominates. It is "gray and bare," a mechanical product rather than a part of the organic process. The poem would therefore be very interesting as a study in connotative language. There is little disagreement about what story the poem tells, but there is plenty of room for argument about what attitude the poem wishes us to take toward the events it narrates.

1. We are given almost no information about the "I" who speaks this poem. Can we speculate about the character of this speaker on the grounds of the poem's language?
2. What kind of relationship between mankind and nature does the poem suggest?
3. What is the significance of the fact that the place named is Tennessee?

William Carlos Williams, "A Sort of a Song"

This is a poem explicitly about figurative language ("through metaphor to reconcile / the people and the stones"). It also makes use of many figurative phrases. Words are personified as "sharp / to strike, quiet to wait." "Saxifrage" is a flower that grows in the cracks of rocks, and has therefore been given its name, which means "rock splitter." Even the name of the flower is a figure of speech. These and other figures combine to make this a difficult and challenging poem, but they also make it an excellent vehicle for teaching figures of speech.

1. Does the first stanza suggest that the snake and writing are somehow comparable? If so, how?
2. What does the phrase "No ideas / but in things" tell us about the speaker's theory of human thought?
3. What do the words *compose* and *invent* tell us about writing?

Williams, "Queen-Ann's-Lace"

This is another exploration of figurative language, in which the consequences of comparing the body of a woman to a field of flowers are worked out. The comparison is at first based on color, but it also suggests other connections between the woman and the flowers. The poem is also interesting as an example of an open verse form. There is no pre-established form here; rather, Williams has fashioned a flexible form that suits his purpose in this one poem.

1. Can you define the "rules" of the poetic form for this poem? How many beats per line? Any discernible rhythm?
2. What do the last nine lines tell us about the relationship between the man and woman in the poem?

Williams, "The Red Wheel Barrow"

This poem gives a very clear picture. Things stand clear—the wheelbarrow, the chickens. The poem produces a simple image, but one that does not seem charged with emotional associations. And yet the poem asserts that "so much depends upon" these objects. Why? What is at risk? Questions also can be raised about the format of the poem. Why these line breaks? Aren't they arbitrary? What effects do they produce? What these questions suggest is that this is a quite successful minimalist poem. With very few words it raises very many questions. The picture it creates is clear, but the significance of the picture is not.

1. What is the effect of dividing the words "wheel / barrow" and "rain / water"?
2. Why are the colors of the objects in the scene important?
3. What *does* depend on these objects? What is at stake?

Williams, "Nantucket"

This poem can obviously be used in teaching the concept of imagery. It gives a clear and specific picture of a place. In fact the poem almost follows an observing eye as it moves from the view out the window, following a ray of light into the room, describing the objects that the light touches. What is interesting about the poem is its spareness. The language is direct and generally low in connotative value. There is very little emotional language and very little narrative context. Those are left to the reader. There is a strong impulse with this poem to fill in the gaps it leaves. Why is this room important? What should we feel about it? How does it fit into the speaker of the poem's life? These matters can be pursued in the imagination of the reader, following the clues of the poem. Like all Williams's poems, this poem is also of interest in its handling of the line. Line breaks give emphasis to the phrases they interrupt, and they produce a syncopated but controlled rhythm.

1. What is the significance of the sequence of objects that the poem focuses on?
2. What are the connotations in this context of the word *immaculate?*

Williams, "Spring and All"

In this poem the imagery is given something of a context. The first line of the poem puts us in a context of disease and death, so that the images of the rest of the poem, images of a barren land returning to life in spring, have to be seen in terms of that context. Do the images of nature offer consolation for the human suffering that the opening of the poem evokes? Do they suggest that life goes on, and that human death is part of the same cycle that brings new life? Surely none of this is stated by the poem, but it does seem to ask us to make some such connection between the nature imagery and its human context.

1. How is nature described in the first two stanzas of the poem?
2. Why is spring called "sluggish" and "dazed" in the poem?
3. In the fourth stanza, are the new growths of spring personified?
4. What is the significance of the fact that the last word of the poem is *awaken?*

Marianne Moore, "To a Snail"

In this poem the basic strategy seems to be metaphorical. The speaker describes the snail in order to praise a "style," presumably a writing style, that seems to resemble the beauty and efficiency of the snail. The poem is also challenging in its vocabulary, and students might benefit from some dictionary work with such words as *contractility, adorn, incidental, concomitant,* and *occipital.* It might be interesting to try to identify the kind of writing that the poem endorses, and then to check if the style of the poem itself possesses the same qualities.

1. What does the quote in the first line tell us about why the speaker admires the snail?
2. Why does the poem assert that style is not an adornment or an incidental?
3. In what way does the snail's "occipital horn" show a "knowledge of principles"?

Moore, "Poetry"

This poem might be a good way to conclude the section of the course dealing with poetry. It begins with what might seem like a startling statement for a poet to make: "I, too, dislike it." But it goes on to suggest that poetry is a legitimate way to search for the genuine in life, which the speaker seems to define as vivid sensory experience. The poem is most famous for its cryptic phrase, "imaginary gardens with real toads in them," which gets at the combination of the imaginative and the genuine that the poem praises. If students can work through to what this poem has to say about poetry, they might well benefit from a discussion of this poem as a commentary on the other poems they have read. Judged by this poem's standards, which poems that they have read seem to get at what the speaker calls the "genuine" in life? And what does that word *genuine* mean in the poem anyway?

1. What does the speaker dislike about poetry?
2. What is the "raw material of poetry" that is referred to in the stanza?
3. Do you agree that "we / do not admire what / we cannot understand"?
4. What does the speaker men by the "The genuine"?

Moore, "An Egyptian Pulled Glass Bottle in the Shape of a Fish"

This poem on its own modest scale recalls poems such as Keats's "Ode on a Grecian Urn," in that it is a poet's meditation on a work of art. In this case it is perhaps the striking contrast between the model for the work of art (the "nimble" fish) and the medium of the work (glass, which would seem to be but is not "brittle"). It's as though the artist has managed a minor miracle—a successful representation of the "spectacular" fish in a medium that seems ill-suited to capturing the essence of a living thing. This achievement is presented in the poem as a prime example of art, which brings out the essentials of its raw materials.

1. Why does the speaker see "thirst" in this work of art?
2. What do the bottle and the fish have in common? Why is the bottle a successful representation of the fish?

Marianne Moore, "The Mind Is an Enchanting Thing"

This challenging poem would be interesting to teach in terms of its figures of speech. Much of the poem is organized around a series of similes, by which the mind is compared to an insect's wing, a musical performance, a gyroscope, a bird, and so on. What these similes have in common is left to the work of the reader, who might also conclude that they lead in different directions rather than to a common goal. There are other figures of speech used in the poem: some very rich metaphors, some of which are offered as "explanations" of the similes, and some extremely paradoxical language, such as the phrase "conscientious inconsistency," a phrase in which each word seems to be straining in a different direction. I would recommend this as a poem that will challenge even the best students, particularly those who have to "figure out" every detail of a poem. This one won't let them.

1. How is the mind like "the glaze on a / katydid-wing"?
2. What is "the / mist the heart wears"? And what effect does the mind have on it?
3. What does the last line tell us about the mind?
4. How does this poem compare with "Mind," by Richard Wilbur?

e. e. cummings, "Buffalo Bill's"

In a discussion of poetic form, this poem could serve as an excellent example of a poem with a form of its own, not formless, but using a form, a pattern of language, constructed for the occasion. Discussion of such features of the poem as line breaks and words run together graphically could get at the strategies behind these verbal techniques. Thematically, the poem seems to be built around the contrast between Buffalo Bill's past vitality and his current status as the possession of "Mister Death." The speaker seems to be awed by the fact that such a powerful figure as Buffalo Bill could be conquered by death.

1. There are three proper names in the poem: Buffalo Bill, Jesus, and Mister Death. How are they related to one another?
2. Why are the words in line six printed so that they run together?
3. What is the effect of leaving the words "Mister Death" as a line by themselves?

W. H. Auden, "For What as Easy"

This poem is an excellent example of the complexities that poems can achieve, even when they are composed of extremely simple language. There is not a single challenging or unusual word here, but the poem is still puzzling, largely because of how the words are arranged in unusual syntactic patterns. There also seem to be gaps in the poem, phrases that are not clearly related to what goes before or comes after them. This might make a good poem to study early on in the poetry section of the course, in that students could define what keeps them from understanding the poem immediately and then discuss how they could approach the task of getting beyond that immediate reaction and making sense of the fragments and odd combinations of words. The poem seems to deal indirectly with a love relationship, suggesting in the last stanza that feelings endure when they are openly expressed.

1. Why is the relationship described in the poem called "easy"? What makes it so?
2. How are the lines "The data given, / The senses even" connected to the rest of the poem?

Auden, "Law Like Love"

This witty poem casts the speaker against those who are certain that they know what law is. To the gardener the law is the sun, to the old it is their wisdom, to the young their senses, to the judge the law is The Law. Unlike all of these, the speaker has no definition, only a "timid similarity." Law is like love, the last stanza declares, drawing out of the comparison some perhaps unexpected similarities. The poem is also interesting for its colloquial style and its informal, witty rhymes. The stanza on the judges, for example, succeeds in drawing a funny portrait of pompous self-certainty.

1. How does each of the people in the first half of the poem define law? How does each definition serve that person's own interests?
2. What is the "idiot's" theory of the law?
3. How is law like love?

Auden, "Musée des Beaux Arts"

Auden's famous poem can be seen in the same category as poems such as Keats's "Ode on a Grecian Urn," meditations sparked by works of visual art. In this case the painting is Pieter Bruegel's "Icarus," which is in the collection of the Musée des Beaux Arts in Brussels, and which depicts the death of Icarus, the son of Daedalus, who fashioned wings so that they could fly to their escape from the Labyrinth. Icarus disobeyed his father, flew too close to the sun, and fell to his death in the sea, which is the moment depicted in Brueghel's painting. The point that Auden draws out of the painting, of course, is that suffering takes place in the midst of ordinary life, ignored by those who are not suffering. The poem was written in 1938, and part of its power comes from its anticipation of the suffering of World War Two and the Holocaust.

1. Why is the title of this poem "Musée des Beaux Arts" instead of "Icarus," after the title of the painting it reacts to?
2. What is the "miraculous birth" that the speaker says the aged are waiting for?
3. Why does the speaker wait until the end of the poem to describe the painting?
4. What attitude toward suffering does the poem affirm?

Auden, "The Shield of Achilles"

This poem could well be a part of the series of poems on war that appear in the introduction to the poetry section of this book. The speaker of the poem is able to make his commentary on modern war by implicitly comparing it with the ancient ideas of war expressed on the shield of Achilles. Achilles' shield in the *Iliad* is made for him by Hephaestus, the god of fire, and it depicts the grandeur of the classical world and the heroism of war. In this version of the story we see Thetis, the divine mother of Achilles, watching the creation of the shield, which now depicts the horror of modern war, with its faceless armies and concentration camp horrors. What is particularly striking about the poem is that it places the depravity of modern war inside the context of the emptiness of modern life. The last three stanzas especially give the sense that we live in a time of dehumanizing violence, of which war is only a symptom.

1. What does Thetis expect to see on the shield? What is in fact depicted?
2. What image of modern war does the poem depict?
3. What happens to individual responsibility in such a war?
4. How is the "ragged urchin" of the last two stanzas related to the theme of war that dominates the poem?

Dylan Thomas, "Fern Hill"

Thomas's enthusiastic but ironic tribute to childhood could be taught very profitably in the section of the course dealing with the sound of poetry. The fluid rhythm, the alternation of long and short lines, the alliteration and assonance all make this an almost textbook example of the aural power of poetry. The poem is also rich in imagery, in its depiction of boyhood in the country. The end of the poem casts a new color on these images, as the speaker realizes that his joy in those times was destined to give way to the sorrow of aging and death.

1. How is "time" personified in the poem?
2. How does the poem depict the natural world?
3. What has allowed the speaker to realize that his youth was "heedless" of time?
4. What is the significance of the last line of the poem?

Langston Hughes, "Dream Variation"

This poem seems to succeed on two levels simultaneously. It is first of all a description of the joys of natural life—dancing in the sun, resting in the evening, luxuriating in the night. But the poem is also a racial allegory. The speaker identifies the day as white and the night as "Black like me." What the speaker is therefore saying about himself is left implicit, left up to the work of the reader. There seems to be little question about the night, which seems comfortable, tender, and gentle in its similarity to him. But what of the day, and his desire to dance his way through it? What does this tell us about his life in the "white world"?

1. How does the poem characterize day, evening, and night?
2. How does the speaker want to live in the day? Can we guess at how he does live?
3. What does the second stanza add to the first?

Louise Bogan, "Cartography"

This poem proceeds on the basis of a precise figurative logic. The arteries and veins on the hand are compared to a map of great rivers. The visual similarity is the basis for an emotional comparison, in the sense that the blood vessels trace back to the heart of the other, whereas the rivers trace back to a place that is "Beyond our fate / And distant from our eyes," which suggests that the heart of the other is equally distant, unknown to the speaker. The blood vessels, then, are a map that leads to an unknown source. For all the intimacy of the moment—watching someone sleep and looking close enough on the sleeping body to see the pattern of veins and arteries—this poem seems to suggest a failure of knowing rather than a moment of understanding.

1. How do the words *strength* and *gaunt* relate in this poem?
2. How is a "brand" like a "chart"?
3. What does the speaker feel for the person she is observing?

Theodore Roethke, "Cuttings" and "Cuttings (later)"

These poems could be thought of as different "takes" on the same idea—thinking of the contrast between the withered appearance of cuttings newly replanted and the active life going on under the soil as new growth seeks the sun and air. These new beginnings grow right up through the old plant—the "musty sheath"—and so their growth is a struggle, which the poet describes in microscopic detail. Is this description of plant growth a metaphor for other kinds of growth, human and emotional? The poem doesn't say that, but since the plant is almost personified in the description of its growth, it would be possible to read into the poem a description and analysis of personal change.

1. This description of the growth of the plant is full of words with rich connotations. What are the connotative meanings of *drowse, droop, sugary, intricate, delicate, coaxing, bulge, nub, nudges, pokes, musty, pale,* and *tendrilous?*

Gwendolyn Brooks, "kitchenette building"

Is it possible to dream of a better life while you are engaged constantly in the daily struggle with life in poverty? That is the question this poem seems to ask, and it gives a complex answer. On the one hand, it seems to say no, that "dream" is too weak a word for this harsh world. And yet the very act of bringing up the question suggests that the dream survives, even if it gets pushed aside by more mundane concerns, like getting to the bathroom while there is still warm water. After all, the word "hope" appears in the last line of the poem, which suggests that the desire for a better life is still at work. This poem would work well in a consideration of speakers, since it suggests so much about the life situation of the speaker of the poem.

1. What are the connotations of the word *giddy* in the first stanza?
2. How does the color imagery work in the first two stanzas?
3. What do we learn about the speaker's daily life from the poem?

Randall Jarrell, "Eighth Air Force"

This extremely condensed poem focuses on the details of life for airmen between missions in World War Two. The men are singing, playing with a puppy, hoping to get out of the war alive. And yet they are involved daily in death and destruction; they are, as the speaker says, "murderers," but that word doesn't begin to do justice to their lives, which are a mixture of innocence and violence. The speaker's attitude toward the men—his crewmates—lies somewhere between what "murderers" suggests and the judgment of innocence that the last line utters. Man is both the wolf and the playful puppy, and that dual nature is what torments the speaker. In this poem, the details that the speaker notices about the other men tell us more about his emotional state than about the men themselves.

1. The speaker describes himself in the last two stanzas in language that recalls Pontius Pilate, the judge of Christ. Why would the speaker think of himself in these terms?
2. What details does the speaker notice about the men? What do these details have in common?

Robinson Jeffers, "Hurt Hawks"

This complex reflection on the relationship between mankind and nature could profitably be read in connection with Jeffers's "Carmel Point," which deals with the question on a larger scale. Here the relationship is personal. The hurt hawk builds up a personal contact with the speaker, who seems almost able to read the hawk's mind. In terms of poetic technique, this identification of the speaker with the hawk is achieved by means of personification. The hawk is asserted to have feelings and responses that we would associate with human beings. But in this poem the technique is not a trick; it is an assertion that this bird *does* have its own form of consciousness, that it can predict the future and remember the past. The speaker therefore feels humanly justified in killing the hawk, which came to him "asking for death," fully aware of the message it was sending. Together with "Carmel Point," this poem can open up the question of the relationship between mankind and nature in a provocative and personal way.

1. What is your reaction to the idea that the hawk dreams of freedom? Does this seem to you to humanize the bird unrealistically?
2. What does this line tell you about the speaker: "I'd sooner, except the penalties, kill a man than a hawk"?
3. The speaker describes shooting the hawk in these terms—"I gave him the lead gift." What does this phrase tell you about the speaker's feelings?

Robert Lowell, "The Public Garden"

This poem takes the form of a report on the speaker's sensory and emotional experiences in Boston's Public Garden. The garden's famous swanboats make an appearance, along with its fountains, its ducks, and its trees with careful Latin identifications. The speaker also remembers another visit to the garden, that time in summer, making a strong contrast with the autumn setting of the current visit. The poem would make a good example in a study of the figure of the speaker in poetry, as we get to follow in this speaker's language his emotional reactions to what he sees. There is little direct commentary on the speaker's emotions, but the poem definitely produces a mood, an emotional atmosphere out of its connotative language.

1. Who do you think is the "you" mentioned in the second line? Are there any clues as to the relationship between this person and the speaker?
2. Is there any pattern that emerges out of the objects and events that the speaker notices in the garden?
3. How do you react to the contradictory phrases in lines nineteen and twenty: "And now the moon, earth's friend, that cared so much / for us, and cared so little, comes again."

Richard Wilbur, "The Death of a Toad"

This poem could well be matched with Robinson Jeffers's "Hurt Hawks," since both narrate the death of an animal, which for some reason has arrested the attention of the speaker. In this case the animal is a lowly toad rather than a majestic hawk, but there is still a grave dignity to this death. This poem is also of interest for its language rich in connotations. If we are to make sense of why this seemed to the speaker a significant event, we must attend to the language with which he describes it.

1. Discuss the connotative meanings of the following words in the context of this poem: *final, original, wizening, gutters, banded, monotone, ebullient, emperies, antique, castrate, haggard, steer.*
2. What do these words tell us about why the speaker is fascinated by the death of the toad?

Denise Levertov, "The World Outside"

This poem is very rich in imagery, as the speaker reports on what she can hear and see in the tenement. The first stanza focuses on the visual—the birds and their "swift pilgrimage," and the light of the setting sun. The next two stanzas emphasize the aural—the sounds of the Greek immigrant playing the music of his homeland, the suffering and rejoicing voices of the other inhabitants of the tenement. The poem reports on, that is, "the world outside," and the title of the poem draws our attention to the position of the speaker. Is the speaker aloof from what she sees and hears—is it "outside" her? Or does she feel herself to be a part of the world she describes?

1. What is the significance of the word *pilgrimage*, used to describe the flights of the pigeons?
2. What does "the goatherd upstairs" get out of playing his music?
3. How does the speaker use the word *counterpoint* in the last stanza?

Levertov, "In Mind"

This poem seems to be built around a contrast with which the speaker cannot be comfortable. The contrast is between two women—one who seems to have achieved a simplicity in her life, but who pays for that simplicity with a lack of imagination; and one who is driven by imagination, but who pays for her gift with a self-absorption that does not allow her to be kind to others. For a poet, this opposition is unpleasant to consider. Does it mean that she can only attain poetic power by denying her connections with others? Or does this speaker manage to combine the qualities of both women—that is, is she imaginative yet kind, energetic yet simple?

1. How do all the enjambed lines work in this poem?
2. What do we learn about the first woman when we hear that she "wears / a utopian smock or shift"?
3. What do we learn about the second woman when we hear that she is a "turbulent moon-ridden girl"?
4. What sense of the speaker do we build up out of the poem? Which of these women does she most resemble?

Levertov, "Stepping Westward"

This poem is a meditation on gender, on what it means for this speaker to be a woman. To be a woman is nothing simple, it seems. It is to be "faithful to / ebb and flow," but also to be "steady / in the black sky." And yet the speaker announces a comfort in her identity as a woman and as a person, accepting these oppositions. She also seems to accept the burdens of being a woman, as in the wonderful last seven lines in which burdens are transformed into bread that "closes me / in fragrance." She also accepts her identity as a shadow, constantly changing and growing. What is interesting here is that the speaker seems to accept some of the conventional definitions of womanhood and to transform them into positive elements of her identity.

1. What is the significance of the word *muscadine* in the first stanza?
2. What does the speaker suggest by saying that her happiness in being a woman is "sweet," and "salt"? Do the tastes go together?
3. If she is a "shadow," what is the sun?

Sylvia Plath, "Lady Lazarus"

This is a poem that cannot easily be detached from the life of its poet. Sylvia Plath attempted suicide several times and finally succeeded some six months after writing this poem, which clearly comes out of a fixation on death and an awareness of how her suicide attempts affected her and those who cared for her. The speaker describes her death in terms of the Holocaust, comparing herself to the Jewish victims and comparing her doctor and finally God and Satan to the Nazis. She seems to have a sense of her suffering as a spectacle that these powerful men enjoy, and she feels anger and at the end a desire for revenge on those who have observed her suffering. This poem could therefore make an interesting study in terms of the concept of the speaker, both because the poem depicts a dramatic moment in the life of the speaker and because the distinction between the speaker and the author is hard to draw in this situation.

1. To whom is the "I" of the poem talking? For what purposes?
2. How does the speaker now feel about her earlier attempts at suicide?
3. What does the ending of the poem suggest about the speaker's state of mind?

Plath, "Edge"

This poem is a testament to the work of the reader. So much is left unsaid. Who or what the speaker is talking about is not made explicit, the figurative language is rich and strange, and the poem seems to be an enigma waiting to be unraveled by the reader. Still, some things are clear: the woman and children are dead, and their deaths seem to the speaker to be part of some natural process. This poem needs an active and imaginative reader to fill in what is left implicit. The poem could be used in a section on figurative language or in an examination of line length and breaks in open-form poetry.

1. Is the woman in the first line "perfected" *because* she is dead?
2. How is the woman like a rose?
3. How does the moon function in this poem? What does the last line suggest about the moon?

Allen Ginsberg, "A Supermarket in California"

This poem presents us with the speaker's lively fantasy that he sees the nineteenth-century poet Walt Whitman in a supermarket (along with the Spanish writer García Lorca, who had died twenty years earlier). Whitman is clearly Ginsberg's model for what a poet is—in the last paragraph he calls Whitman *father*—so to see this almost ideal figure in the supermarket is a comic fantasy that humanizes Whitman. He and Whitman are lonely outsiders, enjoying the vitality and variety of the world, but never really becoming a part of it. The poem would also be interesting to look at in terms of its poetic form, which is printed like prose but reads with a powerful poetic rhythm.

1. What does the word *enumerations* mean in the context of the second paragraph?
2. Why does the speaker of the poem think of himself as resembling Whitman?
3. Why does the speaker feel "absurd" about the fantasy?
4. Why does the speaker describe Whitman's death in terms borrowed from Greek mythology: *Charon, Lethe?*

Ginsberg, "A Strange New Cottage in Berkeley"

This is an account of a day spent fixing up a new place. But this simple event is described in flashes of detail that communicate the pleasure taken in tasks completed, rewards accepted. The poem also gives us an indirect portrait of its speaker by presenting his reactions to these simple events. He gives us a series of images that evoke the day. The images add up to a mood; as the last line suggests, we might see the activities of the day serving as distractions from the unhappiness of a "lovelorn" man. A good poem for showing how imagery can reveal the emotional state of the speaker of a poem.

1. What do the events of the day as they are described in the poem have in common? How are they different?
2. How does "hid my marijuana" fit into the activities of the day?
3. What is the reward for his labors? How does he describe it?

Robert Creeley, "The Language"

This poem would make an interesting experiment in reading if students were to read the poem's sentences, trying to make sense of them as statements, and then read the poem's *lines*, trying to see what meanings are added by the juxtaposition of words in the same line. In the case of this poem, it's particularly appropriate to work toward multiple meanings, since it is a poem about language itself, and since it says contradictory things about language. At one point words seem to fill in an emptiness—they "say everything." But later in the poem words are "full / of holes / aching." They seem empty in themselves. Does saying "I love you" communicate a clear emotion and meaning, or does it communicate an infinite desire, a lack that it cannot hope to represent fully?

1. Can you work out the contradictory statement in the lines: "you / want so / much so / little"?
2. How do words relate to the "emptiness" that the poem describes?
3. What does the last sentence of the poem tell us about language?

Creeley, "Some Echoes"

The title and first line of this poem seem strange to me, in that the poem is full of visual images, not aural ones. The "echoes" here are not sounds that are repeated over time, but visual images that have stayed in the speaker's memory, repeating themselves over time. These fragmented memories seem to serve as symbols of a past relationship, suggesting the nature of the emotions the speaker felt. In this sense, the last line of the poem seems surprisingly negative. Before that the memories seem positive, but the last line throws the rest of the poem into a new light.

1. What does the poem suggest about the relationship between the speaker and the "you" of the poem?
2. How could you describe the rules by which the form of the poem is constructed?

Creeley, "Place"

This poem reads almost like an entry from a journal or diary, keeping an account of the ordinary events of a life. There is no grand drama or violent emotion here. The emotions that do live in the poem are muted, quiet. The poem is informal in its language, suited to the dailiness of its concerns. Nevertheless, the poem does follow some formal rules. It has regular stanzas, and it sets strict limits on line length and rhythm. Perhaps those rules set up a discipline that allows for a more acute observation of a moment of experience.

1. How does the word "still" function in the third stanza?
2. What do the last two lines of the poem tell us about the emotional state of the speaker?

Creeley, "The World"

This poem could be read as a very compressed narrative. There are characters—the speaker, his lover, the ghost of her brother. There is a plot—the ghost appears, there is a subtle conflict over the woman between the speaker and the ghost. There is a shadowy setting that brightens at the end in a new day that seems to suggest that the brother's ghost has been laid to rest. This short narrative manages to give believable characteristics to its protagonists and to suggest the complexities of their relationships. It is also interesting to note how well the short lines so characteristic of Creeley's style work as a narrative form.

1. What do the first two stanzas tell us about the speaker's feelings for the woman?
2. What does the ninth stanza tell us about the woman's brother?
3. What do the last three stanzas suggest about how the woman will deal with her brother now?

Ted Hughes, "Examination at the Womb-Door"

This poem and the next are part of a cycle of poems dealing with Crow, who is Hughes's perfectly adapted observer of modern life. As this poem suggests, Crow knows about the certainty and the power of death, but he is not deterred by it. Death is his natural element, which makes him, as I said, comfortable in this bloody century. This poem takes the form of a catechism, a test of faith that Crow must pass in order to enter the world. The questions suggest a very physical definition of human life—a person is a body, and therefore subject to death—and a sense of despair in the face of death's power. At the end, Crow claims a power greater than death's, but whether his power is akin to the human resistance to death or to a demonic disdain for death is not clear.

1. Who do you imagine is asking the questions that Crow must answer in the poem?
2. What kind of picture of Crow do you get out of the questions in the first stanza?
3. What gives Crow the confidence to claim that he is stronger than death?

Hughes, "Crow Alights"

This poem depicts how the world looks to Crow. Crow is not the speaker of the poem, but all that the speaker does is to tell us what Crow sees and feels. What he sees is horror. At first it is an almost cosmic horror, as the whole world is described in terms of violence and suffering. Next he turns his eyes to a wasteland of a moor, where he sees only garbage. And then he turns to a domestic setting, a scene of silence and loneliness that seems to match with the empty and depressing world that surrounds it. This poem is therefore an excellent example of how a given mind can see and describe the world in a way that reflects that mind's characteristic state. Crow sees what Crow is.

1. What does the figurative language in the first stanza telll us about how the world looks to Crow?
2. What is the significance of the shoe in the second stanza?
3. In what sense is what Crow sees "evidence"? Evidence of what? What is in question?

Hughes, "The Thought-Fox"

This is a poem that claims to describe the moment of its own creation. The poem is not describing the past, but rather the present moment of the writing itself. The result is a sense of immediacy, as though the event were happening in the moment of reading. The poet is also clear that this is an *imaginative* event, one that he has conjured up in order to get himself to write. And that writing seems to happen at the moment when the spirit of the fox enters into the speaker. At the end of the poem "The page is printed," because the fox and the speaker have fused into one.

1. Why does this poem use rhyme?
2. What does the speaker notice about the fox he has imagined into existence?
3. Does the speaker of the poem write in the same way that the fox moves (see lines 11–14)?

Stevie Smith, "Not Waving But Drowning"

This is a poem about misunderstanding. The dead man complains that his calls for help were mistaken for playful waves, and that his entire life, in which he has always felt at risk, was seen by others as "larking." Is there not a desperate need to have fun all the time, which only thinly masks an emptiness that the fun is supposed to fill up? The poem is also of interest because the speaker can "hear" the dead man's message while everyone else misses it. It is as though the speaker had magical or psychic powers. At least she is capable of perceptions and understandings that others ignore. The poem, then, succeeds in presenting a clear if brief portrait of the speaker as well as the dead man.

1. What makes it possible for the speaker to hear what no one else can?
2. What does the dead man mean when he says that "it was too cold always"?
3. Do you know anyone who is "not waving but drowning"?

Imamu Amiri Baraka, "A Poem for Black Hearts"

This elegy for Malcolm X is a poem that calls for action. Malcolm is described in heroic terms, as a great man who was killed for telling the truth. The speaker describes Malcolm, not just as a verbal exercise or as a vague flattery, but as a call for an active response from readers, a call to live as Malcolm would have wanted. The speaker calls Malcolm the "black god of our time," and clearly this is one of those poems that serves the function for a given community of creating the heroes after whom the members of the community should model themselves. Baraka's poem is a rallying cry for the black community. It is poetry serving a public purpose.

1. What characteristics of Malcolm X does the speaker emphasize?
2. How do the rhythm and form of the poem fit the call for action?
3. What kind of actions does the poem call for from its readers?
4. How do you react to the poem's use of the word *faggot* in the next to last line?

Anne Sexton, "The Moss of His Skin"

In this poem the poet tries to imagine herself into the mind of one of the "young girls in old Arabia [who] were often buried alive next to their dead fathers," according to Sexton's scholarly source. Imagining herself into that situation forces the speaker of the poem to contemplate some very unpleasant realities. The father's dead body is described graphically, which makes the admission at the end of the poem seem even more horrible. Allowing the girl to function as the speaker of the poem also adds to the intensity of the story. She speaks from inside that horror, reporting her sensory responses to the decay of the father. In this case the poet allows the girl to be the speaker of the poem in order to make heard a voice in the world that deserves to express itself, especially because no doubt the young girls to be sacrificed were expected to accept their fate quietly, without complaint.

1. What is the speaker's attitude toward her fate?
2. How is the father described in the poem?
3. What do the last lines tell us about the speaker?

Adrienne Rich, "The Knight'

These three stanzas are carefully calibrated to lead the reader to a logical conclusion. First we get what the knight looks like from the outside. We see the traditional splendor of the knight on horseback. Then we get with no transition the knight as he is inside the armor, sweating, frightened, all but dead. The conclusion, then, is that the knight is imprisoned in his armor, that what he thinks defends him in fact entraps him. He must be freed, either in friendship or in anger. The logic here is so strong that we can read the poem as an allegorical story, a plot that acts out one of the culture's truths. The knight *stands for something.* What that "something" is, is exactly what the poem does not say, and it is the work of the reader in participating in the poem to fill in that second level. Does the knight stand for people who are always behind a mask, presenting a face to the world that hides their emotions? Or for men in their relationships with women? Or is he about the costs of heroism in war? We could certainly come up with other possibilities. What matters is that the "second level" makes sense in terms of the first, that it accounts for the specifics of the text.

1. How does the imagery of light work in the first stanza?
2. How does the second stanza communicate the experience of being under the armor?
3. What options does the speaker offer in terms of how the knight can be freed from his imprisonment?

Rich, "Aunt Jennifer's Tigers"

The contrast that drives this poem is between the tigers in Aunt Jennifer's woven panel and Aunt Jennifer herself. The tigers are fearless, sure of themselves. Aunt Jennifer is weak, "mastered" by her husband and by her life. And yet she made the panel. She was able to create in her imagination what she lacked in her own life. The poem articulates a theory of creativity. Weaving for Aunt Jennifer was a way of expressing her desire. What she made reflected how she wanted to be. The poem also makes clear that what opposes Aunt Jennifer's desire to be powerful is her subservience to Uncle. Because she accepted the subservient role, she could only feel power in her weaving. And yet she did the weaving, desired the power, in other words kept her spirit alive even in her limited role. It is also interesting to note in this poem how its form relates to its concerns. It is a tight and disciplined form, two rhymed couplets matched in each stanza. Do the lines have the "sleek chivalric certainty" that the speaker sees in the tigers?

1. How does the speaker present the tigers in Aunt Jennifer's weaving?
2. How is Aunt Jennifer characterized in the poem?
3. How does the speaker of the poem compare to Aunt Jennifer?

Rich, "From a Survivor"

We find in line eighteen of the poem that it is addressed to someone who is dead. The speaker regrets that the man has not lived to experience the changes that have revolutionized her life. The work of the reader with this poem would have to include some thought about the speaker's attitude about the man she addresses. That attitude is never expressed directly; there is no overt evaluation of the man. But as readers we can work from the poem's language and style of thought to a sense of the unexpressed emotions of the speaker. I say "style of thought" because the poem seems very analytical to me. The speaker is trying hard to *make* sense of her experience—why her relationship with the man failed, how she feels about him now, how her life has changed. On a more formal level, it might be interesting to investigate the stanza form of the poem, to ask if there is any pattern to the length of the stanzas.

1. What does the speaker mean by the phrase "the failures of the race" in line five?
2. How have the speaker's feelings about this man changed over time?
3. What is the significance of the phrase "wastefully dead" in line eighteen?
4. What does the phrase "a succession of brief, amazing movements" tell us about the life the speaker is living now?

Thomas Kinsella, "Hen Woman"

Thomas Kinsella is one of the leading contemporary Irish poets. In "Hen Woman" he seems almost to have achieved a suspension of time. He takes many lines to describe an event that took only a second. The moment itself, the speaker tells us, seemed to freeze time. During the moment when the egg is emerging, the speaker finds time to notice tiny details about the world around him—"time stood still," he tells us. Time also seems to be suspended by the fact that this moment has retained its freshness in the speaker's memory over many years. He remembers it now as though it were happening before him. But the poem is quick to remind us that time does not in fact stand still. The egg falls "in a comical flash," and the illusion of eternity is over. Does this also serve as a reminder that time has not stood still for the speaker, that even if it feels as though he is still in that moment, time has passed, taking him closer to his end than to the beginning that this experience represents? The intensity of descriptive detail here would make this an interesting poem to teach in a section on imagery.

1. Why has this moment stayed with the speaker so long and with such power?
2. How is the beetle that the speaker sees related to the hen that he has been watching?
3. What does the fourth section of the poem tell us about memory?
4. How does the old woman's reaction to the event relate to the speaker's reaction?

Elizabeth Bishop, "In the Waiting Room"

This poem could be taught in tandem with Kinsella's "Hen Woman." Both are childhood memories that continue to define the adult speakers. Both events seemed to the speakers at the time to have meanings that they could not grasp, and that they are still working on in the present. In this poem the speaker's memory is very unsettling. In the midst of a very ordinary experience, waiting for her aunt at the dentist's office, reading *National Geographic*, the young girl undergoes an experience she cannot explain: she feels and expresses her aunt's pain. This disorients her sense of personal identity. What are the boundaries of the self? Where does she stop and others begin? Does her experience set her off from all others? At the end of the poem she is returned from her disorienting reverie, back to the "real world" of ordinary experience.

1. Why does the memory of this event stay in the mind of the speaker?
2. What role does the *National Geographic* play in the girl's experience?
3. How does the experience of feeling her aunt's pain affect how the girl thinks of herself?
4. What is the significance of the fact that "The War was on," as the speaker mentions in the last stanza?

Bishop, "The Fish"

One of the things that poetry can do well is to re-create a moment in all of its sensory detail. Here we get a very detailed account of the fish the speaker has caught—its size and weight, its "homely" appearance, its eyes, and especially its mouth, where "five old pieces of fish-line" hang. The poem is very intense in its imagery. We aren't merely told the outline of a story, we are shown the event in rich sensory detail. It is the evidence of the battles that the fish has won, though, that impresses the speaker most, that engages her emotions. What that emotional response is and why she lets the fish go are not explicitly described, and so these questions must be answered by an active reader.

1. Why is it important that the fish did not fight against being caught?
2. What does the speaker learn about the fish by looking in its eyes?
3. Why does the speaker let the fish go? Were you surprised by this ending?

James Dickey, "A Dog Sleeping on My Feet"

This is a poem about the process of its own creation. The dog sleeping on the speaker's feet seems to him to be the source of the poem. The images of the fox and the hunt emanate from the dog, or at least they are asserted to in the metaphor of the poem, "Beginning to move / Up through my pine-prickling legs." In the scene that the speaker remembers or imagines, his own role is as the stumbling, awkward human pursuing the graceful animal. The speaker seems to want to be like the animals, to speak "The hypnotized language of beasts," but he is all too aware of the differences between him and the animals. He seems to feel caught in the ordinary human world, and to desire the intensity of the hunt as a way of getting back to the animal within him.

1. What does this poem suggest about how poems are written?
2. What does the fox represent to the speaker?
3. How does the experience of writing fit into the speaker's life?

Robert Bly, "Waking from Sleep"

One way to approach this poem would be as an example of figurative language, especially because it works out in detail the implications of its central figure, describing the process of waking in terms of boats, harbors, and the like. What is perhaps most interesting in these terms is the last line of the poem, which suggests the results of the metaphor, a feeling of freedom from restraint. But who or what is the "master" referred to in the last line? The poem is also of interest for its rich evocation of the sounds and sights of the harbor, which exists, of course, only as a comparison for the speaker's state of mind. These images sharpen and enrich the figure that is the basis for the poem.

1. How does the second stanza of the poem fit in with the rest?
2. Why does the speaker refer to himself as "we"?
3. How is the body like "a harbor at dawn"?

Charles Simic, "Fork"

The key word in this poem is *strange*. In describing the fork, the poem is attempting to "make it strange," to use the language of formalist critics. It takes an ordinary object that would hardly ever attract our attention and describes it in terms that allow us to look at the object freshly. The poem does so by comparing the fork to the foot of a bird. The result seems to me almost macabre, as the poem transforms the fork, and by extension the person who uses it, into a small but horrible monster. This poem is a good example of what I feel is one of the chief functions of poetry: it takes us out of our normal patterns of perception and allows us to see the world in a new way. The subject may seem trivial, but the process of thought that the poem puts us through is very important.

1. What does the phrase "stab it into a piece of meat" suggest about human eating habits?
2. How does the poem change your perception of the fork?

Peter Porter, "A Consumer's Report"

One function this poem might serve for students is to show that poetry can have a sense of humor. Most poems concern themselves with weighty matters in a serious style. This one is light in tone, working on the premise that life is a product on which the speaker has been asked to report as a consumer. Within this framework, the poem manages to make some telling points about the complexity and difficulty of life, but it does so without losing the light touch. The poem is also of interest in its consistent working out of its premise. The poet has set himself a framework to work within, and that limitation makes the wit and insight of the poem possible.

1. What are the implications of the line, "I had it as a gift"?
2. What is the "embarrassing deposit" referred to in line eight?
3. What overall sense of life emerges from the poem?
4. How do you read the phrase "I think / we should take it for granted"?

Seamus Heaney, "Making Strange"

This poem could be taught in relationship with Charles Simic's "Fork," in the sense that both are concerned about the process of "making strange." Simic's poem takes an ordinary object and makes us see it in an extraordinary way. Heaney's poem dramatizes a moment in which that perceptual experience can take place. As I read it, the poem presents us with a speaker who is showing off his own home place to a traveler. The speaker no longer lives in the place (he has gone through "departures you cannot go back on"), but he still loves its, and finds at the end that he can show it to the traveler. But in the process he finds that the familiar place has been made strange to him. In a sense he is seeing it through the traveler's eyes, as though he were a complete outsider. My sense is that this is a positive experience for him—it increases his pride in the place and allows him to see it freshly. Many poems achieve the same effect. They force us to see the world in a new way, to break out of habits of perception that blind us to the complexity and beauty of the world.

1. Who is the "unshorn and bewildered" man in the second stanza?
2. What is the voice that the speaker hears beginning in stanza three?
3. That voice tells him that he must "Go beyond what's reliable" if he is going to understand this familiar place. How is this advice related to the concept of "making strange"?

James Merrill, "After Greece"

The structure of this poem seems to be a "stream of consciousness," as we follow the thoughts of the speaker as he remembers his time in Greece, recounts his current state, and imagines the Graces, Furies, and Fates of Greek mythology come back to find out about modern life. The speaker seems dissatisfied with his life—in Greece he experiences only "old ideas / Found lying open to the elements," whereas back at home he finds bitter relationships and no sense of meaning. What he desires are "Essentials," basic truths that could "hold up heaven," but what he is left with are questions; neither Greece nor home has given him the comforting truths he desires. This poem could be taught in a section dealing with the speaker of the poem, in that the concerns and emotions of this speaker are the main issues in this narrative.

1. What does the speaker remember about his time in Greece?
2. How does "home" compare with the experience of Greece?
3. How do the Greek figures he calls up in his imagination react to modern life?
4. What are the "meanings" of Greece and of the modern world that the speaker refers to in the last line? Why does he need to "survive" them?

Gary Snyder, "Mid-August at Sourdough Mountain Lookout"

If you considered only the first stanza of this poem, you would see it as a highly imagistic description of a place at a certain moment. The visual detail is precise and evocative. But the second stanza adds another dimension. The speaker reflects on himself as well as on what he sees. He tells us that "I cannot remember things I once read / A few friends, but they are in cities." He is caught up in the moment of experience, drinking cold water, looking down on the forest. But is his forgetfulness positive or negative? Has he lost something—alienated himself from his own past and from other people—or has he gained something—a concentration on the moment that he has learned from living in the natural world? A reader's answer to that question would have to deal with the details of the poem as they produce a certain emotional tone, but the answer would also reflect the reader's own values. The poem asks us to respond to the speaker's situation, and readers will respond in very different ways.

1. What details about the mountain does the speaker notice most sharply?
2. Is the view a pleasant or unpleasant one?
3. How is the speaker's forgetfulness related to this moment of experience?

Wendell Berry, "The Wild Geese"

One way to think about this poem is that it is a prayer in a natural religion. It is Sunday morning, and as the speaker and his companion ride through the fields, they think of those who have died, and offer a prayer that they might regain "the ancient faith." That faith is not in a god or an afterlife, but in the conviction that "what we need is here." That is, it is a faith in nature, especially in natural rebirth, symbolized by the persimmon tree that lies potential in its seed. One key to the poem is the word *abandon*, which is used as a noun, in the sense of the ability to give up control, to allow larger forces to direct our fate. The wild geese symbolize that abandon, and the speaker longs for it. The larger force in this case is nature, and the speaker seeks in nature for an explanation of death. He prays for understanding.

1. What is the significance of the time of day and the time of the year?
2. What does the phrase "time's maze" suggest?
3. What is the state of the speaker's emotions at the end of the poem?

James Wright, "A Blessing"

My own interpretation of this poem would be to see it as an exercise in personification. But I also feel that the speaker would see it differently. When he talks about the loneliness and shyness of the horses, I see it as imposing human characteristics onto the animals. But the speaker, I think, would deny this, claiming that the horses do in fact possess these emotions. He clearly makes a claim in the poem that he has understood their state of mind, and that he has communicated with them across the gap between species. Isn't that the reason for his ecstatic state at the end of the poem? But if the status of the figurative language describing the horses is at question—whether he is speaking literally or figuratively—what is the status of the last three lines? Is this statement figurative, or is there any sense in which he could be speaking literally?

1. In what ways does the speaker personify the horses? Do these phrases seem literal or figurative to you?
2. Why does this event mean so much to the speaker?
3. What is the speaker saying about himself in the last three lines?

John Ashbery, "Decoy"

The title of this poem seems to me to refer, among other things, to the poem's own strategies. After reading the first stanza, you think you are reading a very strange poem about industrial policy. But the second stanza makes a transition into more familiar poetic topics—memory and emotional conflict. The last stanza lets us know that the first is a kind of metaphor, an indirect way of talking about love. We end up with a husband and wife who seem to be suffering the same kind of "ostracism" that the first stanza sees as typical of modern economic life. Thus we have been "decoyed" by the poem, taken to its true topic by means of an elaborate detour. The poem is also of interest because of its unusual language, especially in the first stanza, where the language is extremely abstract and analytical, unlike the concrete and imagistic language of many poems.

1. What are the economic conditions described in the first stanza?
2. How are they related to the relationship described in the third stanza?
3. What is the significance of the change in wording between the last two lines?

Audre Lorde, "Now that I Am Forever with Child"

The dramatic situation of this poem is made very clear. That is, it has a well-defined speaker and a well-defined audience—a mother and her daughter. The message being sent has to do with the experience of carrying and birthing the child. The speaker seems to be trying to communicate the feelings she felt while she was pregnant, the ties that bind her so closely to her daughter. The poem expresses a kind of woman's wisdom, coming out of the experience of the female body, and predicting for the daughter the experience she might well go through in her own life. I think the poem would work well as a way of talking about how poems can create their own characters and suggest the relationship between them.

1. How are the speaker's memories of pregnancy organized in the poem?
2. What kind of figurative language does the speaker use to describe the experience of birth?
3. What does the last stanza tell us about the speaker's feelings for her daughter?

Michael Harper, "Dear John, Dear Coltrane"

This poem, written in memory of the great jazz saxophonist John Coltrane, ought to be read aloud in order to be fully appreciated. It produces its own music; in many cases the phrases follow each other more as musical effects than as logical relationships. The poem would make a very good example of how a poem can produce verbal music, which of course in this case is appropriate to—or even a tribute to—the subject matter of the poem. The poem also articulates a colloquial theory of creativity—Coltrane's music came out of his suffering. "Your diseased liver gave / out its purity," the speaker tells us. This is an old and honored way of thinking about artists. Their art is a way for them to exorcise the demons, to turn their suffering into a beautiful experience that can bring joy to others. For all the violent imagery of death and disease in the poem, the result is "a love supreme."

1. After reading the poem aloud, how does the music of the poem affect you?
2. What do we learn about Coltrane's life from reading the poem?
3. What is the effect of the question-and-answer section of the poem in the fifth stanza?

May Swenson, "Bleeding"

The feature of this poem that immediately strikes the eye is its typography. This dialogue between a knife and a cut has in fact a cut inscribed in the poem itself, inscribed in the spaces left in every line. This visual cut should perhaps remind us that all writing is cutting, in the sense that the physical process of writing involves cutting into a page. Therefore the dialogue here could be read, among other things, as a commentary on writing itself. Perhaps there is an element of violence in all writing, and especially in such emotional writing as poetry. The dialogue could also be read as a story about sexuality, with the male knife and the female cut involved in an urgent debate over the damage done by male power. Or it could be read as a comment on a particular relationship that is based on a complex exchange of power. There is undoubtedly a wide range of possible "second level" readings we could produce. The point is that the poem seems to ask for such productive activity on the part of the reader. It tells a story in rather fanciful terms—knives and cuts with feelings and thoughts—and the story seems to "stand for" something. That "something" is not defined, but left to the productive work of the reader.

1. How would you describe the relationship between the cut and the knife?
2. Does there seem to be a system or principle involved in where each line is cut?
3. Do either the cut or the knife change in any way over the course of the dialogue?

Jody Aliesan, "Radiation Leak"

Aliesan's poem is a dramatic example of how poetry can engage with political questions. What gives it its urgency, I think, is that it brings into confrontation a traditional farm culture that "know[s] about trouble" and a highly technological culture that produces "trouble" that no one knows how to deal with. When even the food is dangerous, when the water brings death, there are no folk remedies, no traditional wisdom that will help. The ending of the poem is particularly effective in the way that it transforms a simple gesture of worry (holding your head in your hands) into a horrible sign of the power of the radiation. The poison has entered the speaker's body and already done its secret damage. The poem thereby succeeds in making a political issue personal, so that the issue no longer seems huge and impersonal.

1. What does the first stanza tell us about the speaker and the culture she comes from?
2. What are the signs of the radiation damage that the poem describes?
3. How is the last stanza related to the images of nature in the third stanza?

Galway Kinnell, "The Fundamental Project of Technology"

This meditation on nuclear destruction begins at a museum that commemorates the dropping of an atomic bomb on Japan. The speaker dramatizes the human destruction that occurred on that day by drawing our attention to objects transformed by the blast and by attending to the old men and children who are visiting the museum, as they recall in their innocence the victims of the blast. But as the title suggests, the speaker is not so much concerned with the past as with the present and future. That is, he feels that this kind of destruction is not accidental, but is the logical outcome of technology itself. In the fifth stanza he tells us that technology aims at the destruction of death and the fear of death, and so, perversely, its only hope of success is to "eliminate / those who die." And in the last stanza he seems to suggest that the future holds the fulfillment of that technological desire—a time when "no one lives." This poem would be useful to teach in order to show that poetry need not be otherworldly, but can be concerned with the problems of our time. It also succeeds in producing some horrific images of nuclear destruction, images that are intended to frighten and educate readers.

1. What do the objects listed in the first stanza communicate?
2. How do the old man and the children in the second and third stanzas function in the poem?
3. What does the speaker think is "the fundamental project of technology"?
4. Does the poem end in despair or in some kind of hope for the future?

Stephen Dunn, "Beached Whales off Margate"

For me, what is striking about this poem is its concluding image, "an aerial shot" as if from a film, which shows the community of human beings that had been brought together by the whales dissolving into individuals again, retreating back into their "large, inconsiderate houses." The poem suggests that "the humans [we] used to be" were more communal, less individual than we are now, and that we have lost a sense of belonging to something larger than ourselves. But the poem also seems to suggest that we can be brought back together, and that the focus for that sense of community could be our realization that we are part of the natural world.

1. What does the phrase "two hundred people usually hurt / what they touch" suggest about the political views of the speaker?
2. Why does the speaker call the houses of these people "inconsiderate"?

Edward Hirsch, "Dawn Walk"

This poem could be taught in terms of the character of the speaker. We learn a lot about his habits of thinking and feeling, as well as about how he sees the world. The narrative of the poem is simple enough, following the speaker as he gets up out of an anxious sleep and takes a walk around the quiet town on a snowy morning. The walk seeks to reassure him and return him to his home without the anxiety he had been suffering. But what does he see on that walk that is so reassuring? The answer to that is in the poem's imagery, its description of the sleeping town that seems to be protected by a blanket of snow. The speaker's emotions and needs color his description of the town, and so in reading about the place we are indirectly reading about the speaker himself.

1. What role do the speaker's dead parents play in the poem?
2. What kind of language does the speaker use to describe the clock downtown in lines twenty-two through twenty four?
3. In the last four lines, what do we learn about how the speaker's walk has changed him?

Hirsch, "Fast Break"

I find this poem to succeed admirably in describing in words a very quick and complex movement that would in fact have taken much less time to occur than it takes to be described. The action is described very accurately, in language that simultaneously communicates the event and the speaker's emotional reaction to it. But what is particularly interesting about the poem is that it is written in memoriam, as the subtitle declares. The only indication that the poem deals with death is in the last three stanzas, which deal with the "wild, headlong" fall of the forward who makes the lay-up off the fast break. The speaker seems to be remembering an almost perfect moment that epitomizes the life of his friend who has died. It is a moment of cooperation and communication in which five people have brought about a perfect play. And it is that moment that the speaker feels would be a fitting monument for his friend, who I would guess is the forward who scores the basket.

1. What details of the fast break does the speaker notice?
2. Why did the poet choose to construct the two-line stanzas that make up the poem?
3. What does the speaker suggest by describing the forward as loving basketball as he loves his country?

Gregory Orr, "Morning Song"

In this poem the point of interest for me is the concluding image of the light in the barn as the boy comes to feed the wounded deer. The image is very effective, producing a vivid and recognizable portrait of the place. What makes the image work is a striking simile: the light resembles swords in a magician's box. In addition to helping the image come precisely clear, this simile also calls up feelings of danger survived, which are appropriate to the situation of the deer in the poem, whose song is "I lived." The deer's frightening predicament in the field is also evoked powerfully, giving a sense of entrapment that becomes the dominant emotional tone of the poem. After all, even though the deer was freed from that trap, it is still kept in the barn. And it is certainly not a coincidence that the last word of the poem is "box."

1. What is the effect of the word *spidery* in line three?
2. Why is the boy so interested in the deer?
3. What is the significance of the fact that it is morning?

Bruce Weigl, "Homage to Elvis, Homage to the Fathers"

This is a memory poem that begins in the present and then takes us back into two memories that the speaker wants to relate to each other. The more general memory is of life in a steel-mill family—the speaker now takes in "the slag stink air of home." The more specific memory is of seeing Elvis Presley at a local record store, an event that seems to have been the beginning of the speaker's adolescence. But how are these two memories related? The speaker tells us that even as he and his friends were learning to imitate Elvis, "our fathers died / Piece by piece among the blast furnace rumble." Is the moment of seeing Elvis the moment at which the speaker began to remove himself from his home and family, so that now he feels "unwelcome" in his own home? My guess is that the last four lines of the poem tell us what he learned from Elvis's supercharged music, and that these lessons made it impossible for him to stay within an ordinary, day-in-day-out existence. Nonetheless, the speaker seems to look back on his past with nostalgia, as if he has lost as much as he has gained by leaving it.

1. How does the speaker remember his childhood in this place?
2. What does the speaker notice about Elvis when he sees him?
3. How was he affected by seeing Elvis?
4. How does the speaker now feel about the place where he grew up?

William Matthews, "An Elegy for Bob Marley"

In this elegy for Bob Marley, the great Jamaican reggae musician, the speaker contrasts Marley's belief in a future political and spiritual liberation—"Soon come"—with the finality of his death. In the face of death, elegies for artists often offer the consolation that at least we have their works, which will endure beyond the death of their creators. But the speaker of this poem seems to be aware of this conventional idea, and to reject it. For him, even what we hope will survive the body is only temporary. Marley's death seems to convince the speaker that death is all-powerful. Even a man of such energy and creative force can be brought down. The speaker's pessimism stands in strong contrast to Marley's optimism, and this contrast might explain why the speaker is drawn to Marley as a topic in the first place.

1. How does the speaker connect poetry and music and death with time?
2. What does the speaker tell us about Marley? What does he assume we already know?
3. How does this poem differ from a traditional elegy?

Albert Goldbarth, "A Film"

Despite the poem's official division into three parts, I think we can identify two very different sections. Parts One and Two of the poem deal with the experience of being in a drive-in theater, and especially with the contrast of size between the "enormous" life that goes on in the film and the ordinary lives of the audience. Part Three, however, abruptly turns our attention to a cult waiting in the desert for the end of the world, for the rapture that will take them to paradise. The only connection that the poem explicitly offers is that the cult members are nearby. But clearly there are more serious connections suggested. Perhaps the cult gets out of its apocalyptic hopes what the audience gets out of the film, a sense of drama and grand scope that their lives otherwise do not offer. Clearly there is an implied comparison here, and it is up to the reader to fill in the terms of the comparison.

1. How does the speaker feel about the film that is showing at the drive-in?
2. How does he feel about the cult members in the desert?
3. How are the two experiences similar? How are they different?

Ai, "She Didn't Even Wave"

This poem is an imaginative re-creation of the death of Marilyn Monroe's mother. The poem is spoken by Monroe herself, and as such it would make for a good poem to use in a section on poetic speakers. The center of the poem for me is the visual image of the woman being struck by lightening. The speaker tells us, "I'd never seen anything so beautiful." For me, the connection between suffering and beauty seems an insightful comment on Monroe's career. In the poem the mother is warning Monroe not to get married (she married at 16), because "In ten years, your heart will be eaten out." But doesn't Monroe's brilliance have something to do with her vulnerability to suffering? It's as though, the poem suggests, the "beautiful" death of her mother set the direction for Monroe's own life.

1. Why did the poet choose to make Marilyn Monroe the speaker of the poem?
2. How does Monroe react to the death of her mother at the funeral?
3. How is the mother's death related to Monroe's marriage?

Sharon Olds, "The Death of Marilyn Monroe"

As the second poem in the anthology dealing with Marilyn Monroe, this poem could be read profitably in connection with Ai's "She Didn't Even Wave." We have here two contemporary women poets dealing with the same general subject, so that we could look at how two different poetic sensibilities react to the same situation. Olds takes the approach of focusing on the ambulance men who took Monroe's dead body to the hospital. She briefly describes the event itself, concentrating on the horrible physical closeness they experienced with what was no longer Monroe herself. And she then tells us how those men's lives were changed by the experience. Each of the men is changed in ways that tell us a lot about the public force of Monroe as a film star and about the men themselves.

1. What does the poem tell us about the experience of the men taking away Monroe's body?
2. Why is it that, afterwards, "they could not meet / each other's eyes"?
3. How are the changes that occur in each man's life related to the experience of Monroe's death?

Susan Tichy, "In an Arab Town"

This is a poem whose subject is a conversation about poetry. The conversation crosses the boundaries of nation, culture, and gender, as an American woman poet discusses "Persian verse" with Arab men who believe that women are incapable of writing poetry but are superior to men in the courage and silence necessary for sabotage. We see here a curious reversal of our own cultural stereotypes, which would define poetry as feminine and assume that martial courage was beyond the grasp of women. The speaker therefore finds herself as a woman poet in the position of being a contradiction in terms to these men. They can think of her only in sexual terms, as they do of the Arab women who appear in the fourth stanza. But if she is entrapped in their categories, barred by definition from writing, is she also in some sense liberated by the Arab notion of the coolly heroic woman who can joke while she carries bombs to their targets? This poem in a sense depicts how language and culture define our thinking. By habit of thought and language, we can much more easily connect *woman* and *poetry* than we can *woman* and *battle*, but in this poem the speaker encounters a culture in which these connections are reversed. We can therefore see that these connections are cultural rather than natural, an instance of the power of language.

1. How does the speaker feel about the men she is talking with in the café?
2. According to the men, what keeps a woman from writing poetry?
3. What is the significance of the fact that the Arab women in the poem cannot read?
4. Why are women the "most dangerous"? What gives them the ability to be cool in secret combat?

Katha Pollitt, "Archaeology"

The quote that begins this poem—"Our real poems are already in us and all we can do is dig"—suggests that this poem about archaeology is also about writing poetry. The poem, that is, sets up an implied metaphor that identifies writing and digging in the earth for fragments of history. Does this mean that writing poetry comes out of a search for the poet's own past? At the end of the poem, the comparison comes clearer. In this section the speaker emphasizes the imaginative labor involved in archaeology, moving from the fragments found in the dig to a mental picture of the world from which those fragments must have come. The task of the archaeologist is to reassemble the whole in which the parts that he has found would make sense. Similarly, the poem suggests, the poet has to create a whole world out of the fragments he or she has experienced. And we could extend the pattern to the reader, who has to construct a meaning for the poem, which never says all that it means, but rather always leaves things unsaid, so that the whole of its meaning is always larger than the words of the poem themselves.

1. How does the speaker of the poem feel about the archaeologist?
2. What kind of world does the speaker think the archaeologist will reconstruct?

Norman H. Russell, "indian school"

Although this poem is written in present tense, the last two lines suggest that it is a recollection of an earlier time in the speaker's life, a time when he did not understand his experience as well as he does now. In that earlier time, the speaker seems to be overwhelmed by the newness of his experience as an Indian boy in a white man's school. None of what he sees makes sense to him, or to put it in his own terms as he describes his teacher, "i am not wise enough to know / gods purpose in him." He can only see his new experience in terms of his old frameworks. A book is "leaves of words / from dead mens mouths"; the teacher must be "dumb and blind" because the speaker as a child is not yet capable of understanding him. But the last two lines suggest that the speaker has come to realize that he can benefit from this experience—not that he must abandon his own identity, but that he can find in his new experience what he can use and grow from.

1. What does the speaker have to say about the walls of the school?
2. How do the similes in the third stanza work?
3. Why does the teacher seem so ugly to the speaker?

Rita Dove, "Dusting"

This is another memory poem, in which an old woman named Beulah looks back on fragments of her life while she is in the middle of dusting. In the midst of this ordinary action, she remembers an unusual, dramatic moment in her life—a boy, a kiss, his gift of a fish in a bowl that she frees from the "locket of ice" that has developed as she brought it home on a winter night. The memory seems to recall a time when there were possibilities in her life. Fresh experiences, the freedom to explore a new world. Now her life is much more constricted, and we see her straining to reconstruct this earlier event that reminds her of a freer and more intense time. She succeeds at the end in remembering the boy's name, and she seems to feel the satisfaction of memory in the midst of her ordinary, old woman's life.

1. How does the speaker describe Beulah's dusting? Does the speaker respect Beulah?
2. What does the fish that the boy gives her represent to Beulah?
3. What is the significance of the meaning of Beulah's name?

Teresa Anderson, "Delphine"

The claim that this poem makes is that the past continues to exist in the present. In daytime reality, the farm the poem describes has fallen into disrepair. The farmers have been defeated by nature, which is now reclaiming the farm. But in nighttime (dreams?) the past lives on; the farmers are vital, sexual young people caught up in the romance of the prairie. The person who makes this claim, and who imagines the nighttime past, is the speaker of the poem. We could therefore look at the poem as a reflection of the speaker's character. Why does the speaker need to restore this past in her imagination? Is the present too painful to dwell on—or is it somehow a betrayal of the past? And why does she focus on an erotic moment in that past? What does the poem tell us about her interest in this place and its past?

1. What image of the prairie does the poem create?
2. How does the poem describe the abandoned farm?
3. What does the scene at the end of the poem tell us about Louis and Delphine Desaire?

Jay Parini, "The Missionary Visits Our Church in Scranton"

This is a poem that not only uses imagery to communicate its point but is *about* imagery itself. That is, the centerpiece of the poem is the speaker's description of the missionary's slides, fleeting images of a foreign land. The images form a stark contrast. The natives in their poses right off the pages of *National Geographic;* the converted natives in "makeshift" clothes. But how does the speaker react to those images? How does the poem want us to react? Are we seeing progress from barbarity to civilization or are we seeing the destruction of a native culture? The poem does not answer that question directly, but the quirky, clever ending at least suggests that some strange cross-cultural exchange is occurring.

1. How does the speaker feel about the missionary himself?
2. How does the congregation react to the slides?
3. How does the sound of the last two lines work? Do they work well as an ending to the poem?

Robert Morgan, "Bricking the Church"

This poem is extremely rich in figurative language. The concluding passage describes the church as if it were a plant, growing each of the new walls that the congregation has built. There is also the opening stanza, which implicitly compares the church to a ship, pulling "a wash of gravestones west." And in the second stanza, the speaker describes the congregation as *burying* the wood in brick, and describes the white wood as "wooden snow." There are many other metaphors and similes in the poem. As the ones I've mentioned suggest, the implications of the figures don't always fit clearly together. Thinking of the brick as a tomb for the church is not the same as thinking of the brick as its latest growth. The figures proliferate meaning if you think of them seriously and in terms of one another. Each figure suggests a slightly different answer to the question of how the speaker feels about the changes in the church, and even the concluding figure seems ambivalent.

1. What does the fourth stanza tell us about the speaker's feelings about the church?
2. How and why has the church changed over time?
3. How exactly does the last figure work? What is the connection between the doctrine and the appearance of the church?

William Pitt Root, "Sometimes Heaven Is a Mean Machine"

The figurative language of this poem is an attempt to convey the experience of riding a motorcycle, apparently the kind of "mean machine" we associate with hard-core bikers. The poem creates a sense of menace by comparing the machine to a lion, a bull, a unicorn, to death itself. The pleasure of riding seems to be the mastery of this menace, the sense that death can be controlled or transcended. In these terms, it is legitimate to compare the bike to a religion, as the title suggests, since religion is based exactly on the premise that it conquers death. Like Robert Morgan's "Bricking the Church," this poem talks about religion in figurative terms, and the two poems could well be compared and contrasted in their use of figures of speech.

1. What do the similes dealing with the motorcycle have in common?
2. What does the phrase "the road informing you" suggest?
3. What is the significance of the last line?

Marilyn Waniek, "Old Bibles"

In describing these old Bibles, this poem in effect describes the speaker to whom they mean so much. Some parts of the poem suggest that she keeps them out of superstition, or out of fanciful fear, whereas others suggest a more thoughtful reason. The last stanza seems to suggest a serious religious commitment on the speaker's part, yet other parts of the poem are light-hearted or comic. What the poem poses, then, is a question of tone. How does the speaker feel about these Bibles and about the religion they represent?

1. In what sense is the word *euthanasia* used in the first stanza?
2. What does the word *kosher* tell us about the speaker's feelings about the Bibles?
3. What is "the great collection" described in the third stanza?

Diana O Hehir, "Learning to Type"

The occasion for this poem is the fact that, as the poem tells us, "A laboratory chimpanzee has been taught to communicate by means of a symbol-keyed typewriter." What this allows the poet is a meditation on language and communication. The speaker of this poem *needs* language. She is faced with the death of her father, and she is searching for a languge adequate to that painful fact. She imagines herself sitting at the keyboard where the chimp sits, trying to find a symbol that will make sense of her sorrow—what she calls "symbols for leave-takings." In this poem the speaker seems to look to language as a source of frameworks that will make sense of emotion. But as the last line of the poem suggests, "the dangerous keys" of the typewriter do not give solace, they rather serve to call up those emotions with increasing intensity. It might be nice to have a neutral, objective language by which we could master experience, but what language seems to do is to open us up to experience and the pain that goes with it.

1. What is the significance of the word *arbitrarily* in line two? What does it tell us about the relationship between the symbols on the keyboard and their meanings?
2. How is the death of the speaker's father related to the monkey's symbolic keyboard?
3. What is "the difference between make and give," and how does that difference work in the poem?
4. Why are the keys on the keyboard "dangerous"?

Stan Rice, "Metaphysical Shock while Watching a TV Cartoon"

Poems often come out of the most ordinary experience. If you have ever watched Saturday morning TV cartoons, you have undoubtedly seen exactly the phenomenon that the speaker of this poem describes. Actions in cartoons come from nowhere and have no consequences. As the speaker tells us, a cat is shaved in one shot, and back to normal in the next. What makes this poem possible is the intensity of attention that the speaker gives to this phenomenon. All of a sudden it seems to him to say something about his own origins and about the origins of his art. Where does he come from, and where does his work come from? These ordinary cartoons have disturbed his habits of thinking about himself and opened up new possible patterns of thought.

1. How does the first line of the poem gain significance as the poem progresses?
2. What do the examples from cartoons that the poem mentions have in common?
3. How does the speaker's perception of these cartoons change the way he looks at himself?

Star Black, "Really"

This is a good example of a poem made out of ordinary language. Students often feel that poems are in another language, but this one is colloquial, even slangy. It reads as if you are listening to a person speaking. It takes the kind of associative leaps we're used to in speech; it seems rambling. But in fact it is not rambling at all; its destination is the graveyard that the speaker focuses on in the last two stanzas. Death is on the speaker's mind, and she entertains the superstition that holding your breath as you walk past a graveyard is good luck, only to realize that there is no charm that will work against death. On the way to that graveyard, the speaker reflects on her relationship with a "contorted" man, a man with an inner suffering that she shares, and that pushes her into her colloquial meditation on death. In this informal, talky poem, then, the stakes are high and the concerns are serious.

1. The slang expression "spaced out" is used in the first stanza. How is its meaning changed by its context in this poem?
2. How would you describe the relationship that the poem discusses?
3. How does the phrase "I like lies" work as an ending to this poem?

Jorie Graham, "History"

This poem beings with history and ends with fairy tales, and it suggests that the differences between the two are profound. Fairy tales simplify the world and make it seem safe and manageable. History, however, has to remember all—even the horrible—and make some sense of it. The "History" that this poem is concerned with is the Holocaust, which the speaker brings up because some want to deny its very existence. She offers as proof a horrible photograph that depicts the unthinkable suffering and the easy indifference that characterized the Nazi horror. And she demonstrates how that history continues quite materially into the present in her story of the grenade exploding years later and bringing the suffering right down to our time. The ending of the poem suggests by metaphor that there is now no way "home" for us—no way back to an innocent view of human beings now that we have seen ourselves perpetrate the torture that the photograph depicts.

1. How is history different from "the eye," as it is described in lines seven through eleven?

2. What does the photograph tell us about the history that the speaker is concerned with?
3. How does the story of the hand grenade relate to the photograph from the Holocaust?
4. Why does the poem end with some thoughts about fairy tales?

Graham, "Reading Plato"

The story that this poem tells seems to have nothing to do with the title; it is simply about a man who makes flies for fishing. He uses the hair of deer, "because it's hollow / and floats." The poem follows the men out on to the river fishing with those flies, and it then asks us to imagine the deer that the material for them came from. The deer we imagine, the speaker tells us, is somehow more alive than the real deer. It is this issue that connects the poem to Plato, one of whose concerns was the question of *mimesis* or representation—that is, the question of the relationship between art and the world it copies. This issue is also behind the act of making flies, making a believable copy of the real-world insects. The poem makes very clear how someone could become obsessed with this craft, with the desire to make as perfect a copy as possible. But the end of the poem suggests the impossibility of any man making a perfect copy of nature. Human beings, the ending suggests, are, by virtue of their very ability to copy nature, no longer a part of it. The poem, then, can be seen as a meditation on the relationship between mankind and its works on the one hand and nature on the other.

1. What is the "beautiful / lie" that the speaker mentions in the first stanza?
2. What does the poem tell us about why the man is so obsessed with making flies?
3. In the eighth stanza, the constellations are described as "the stars still connect-up / their hungry animals." How does this description fit into the concerns of the poem?
4. Why are the fishermen at the end of the poem "trying to slip in / and pass / for the natural world"?

Pattiann Rogers, "Concepts and Their Bodies"

This poem manages to make a sophisticated philosophical argument in relatively simple language. The argument deals with the relationships between abstractions ("concentricity," "persistence") and concrete instances (the eye of the turtle, the mouth of the caterpillar). As a result, the poem is almost necessarily rich in imagery, attempts to put into words the physical reality of the concrete instances. The descriptions of the bullfrog's leap or the dandelion blowing in the wind are as specific and sensory as the speaker can make them. The point of the poem, after all, is that we cannot understand abstractions unless we see them embodied in real experiences. When we do, we can rightly claim to possess those concepts, and the last stanza of the poem suggests that this possession constitutes human freedom. We are then masters of language rather than its slaves.

1. In what sense do the "five amber grasses" embody "civility"?
2. In the boy's mind, do the concepts come first or the experiences?
3. How is the concept of "freedom" related to the rest of the poem?

Kay Smith, "Annunciation"

Although there are not a large number of spectacular figures of speech in this poem, it seems to me that it is based on a metaphor, in the sense that the speaker compares her own situation to the scene she sees in the painting, or better, sees her own situation *in terms of* the painting. This is particularly true in the ending of the poem, in which the speaker puts herself in the position of Mary—"Between the angel and the book." The difference, though, is that Mary made her decision, choosing the angel, whereas the speaker seems suspended between the two choices. The poem therefore might be a good example to teach what you might call metaphorical or figurative *thinking*—thinking in terms of comparisons and contrasts. That is, figures are not just verbal patterns, but habits of thought.

1. In terms of the choice the speaker is faced with, what do the angel and the book represent?
2. What do we learn about the speaker by her saying that she believed she "could ignore / All messages"?
3. What are the consequences for the speaker of choosing "the space between"?

Simon Ortiz, "A Story of How a Wall Stands"

This poem is a story of how a wall stands, of course, but it is also a story of the relationship between a father and son. The speaker, the son, is taking in a lesson from the father. There are some differences between them—the father "works with stone," whereas the speaker works with words. But there are also connections—the son seems to respect the father's traditional wisdom, his knowledge of how the thing is done. And if we transfer this knowledge of engineering to the question of how a poem holds together, we get a sense that a poem, like a wall, is held together by the craft of its maker. The words may proliferate meaning, threatening to disrupt the poem, but a skillful maker will hold those energies together, creating a coherent poetic construction.

1. What is the father's explanation of how the wall stands?
2. What do we learn about the father from this poem?
3. What do we learn about the son from this poem?
4. Why does the third stanza repeat so much of the second?

David Baker, "Running the River Lines"

The simple story that the poem tells is surprisingly effective. The incident has stayed in the speaker's mind, and I find that it has the same power over me as a reader. The story is told straightforwardly, with only some slight personification (the bird is "utterly amazed" at its inability to escape). The speaker does not directly express his own emotion at the event, and yet it has clearly affected him. There is an occasion here for guilt, fascination, and pleasure at the bird's eventual escape, but the poem is very understated. The speaker lets the events speak for themselves.

1. Why do you think the incident has stayed with the speaker?
2. What does the last line tell us about the speaker's reaction?

Raymond Carver, "The River"

Another fishing poem, which might well go along with Baker's "Running the River Lines." In Baker's poem there is guilt that the fisherman has accidentally victimized the bird; in this poem the victim is at least potentially the fisherman himself. The speaker of this poem undergoes an experience I associate with wading in water, a sense of being in an alien environment, a place where the human animal does not belong. It therefore seems to me just right that the speaker is not sure what touches his boot—the point is that it is invisible, in its element. And because of his experience in the river, the speaker no longer feels he belongs in nature at all—it all becomes fearsome to him. The poem narrates this story with strong imagistic language. We get the sense of what the speaker sees and hears and feels.

1. How does the speaker describe the feel of the water on his legs?
2. What is the effect of the phrase "the furious eyes of king salmon"? Is it a personification to call the salmon "furious"?
3. What does the last line tell us about the speaker's reaction to the experience?

Christopher Gilbert, "Charge"

The interesting question about this poem, I think, is who is speaking. It is someone who is attempting to articulate what Willie, the ballplayer, is feeling. Willie expresses his philosophy of life in his play—"His catalogue of moves represents / his life." If Willie's style of play is a language, a set of movements that have a meaning, then this poem is in essence a translation, from the language of basketball to the language of American English. My sense of the speaker's interpretation of Willie is that Willie's play communicates a desperate intensity. He's playing against "Death and Uniformity," playing for his soul. It's important to note that in pick-up basketball if you lose you don't get to play. My interpretation of him is that he's playing out of control, that it means so much to him that he can't play within the game. He's concerned too much about himself and too little about the game. Your interpretation of him will certainly be different, depending on the values and beliefs you bring to the act of "reading" him. But the poem offers him to us—filtered through the mind of the speaker, yet still available to us for our own readings.

1. How does the character of the speaker as it emerges from the poem compare to the character of Willie?
2. Do you feel that the speaker has "translated" Willie's style of play well? Could you offer another explanation?
3. What does the repeated phrase in the poem—"Gimme the ball"—tell you about Willie?

William Heyen, "Mantle"

This is a good example of a contemporary poem with a strong rhythmic quality. A metrical analysis of the poem would draw attention to its music. Note the last stanza, where the music speeds up for the fastball and slows down around the line break for the curve. The other point of interest for me in the poem is the speaker's investment of emotion in Mantle. Mantle's whole life span, from youthful hope to complete success, through self-imposed injury to tacky celebrity, seems to take on an almost mythic quality to the speaker, as though there is a lesson to be learned from his story. The exact lesson is not made explicit, but is left to the interpretation of readers.

1. How does the speaker evaluate Mantle's life?
2. What is the significance of the shape the poem is printed in?
3. How would you describe the poem's rhythm?

David Bottoms, "Under the Boathouse"

This would be an excellent poem for teaching the imagistic power of poetry. The speaker's narration of his near-drowning is obviously intended to put us through the experience, in strict sequence, as the speaker himself went through it. The reports of sound and sight and feeling are precise and intense. I particularly like the fun of the fact that, instead of his life passing before his eyes, his groceries pass before his eyes. You could also profitably examine the connotative language of the poem as it communicates the emotions of the moment.

1. What is the connotative force of the following words in the poem: *naked, wedged, sprang, hinge, junked, clawed, fog, confusion, flailed, buoy, effigy, curiosity, bait, angel, quivering, shower, leaves, heavenly, litter, splintered, suffocating, hovering, dangerously, bobbed.*

Bottoms, "Sign for My Father, Who Stressed the Bunt"

Like Simon Ortiz's "A Story of How a Wall Stands," this poem is the story of the relationship between a father and son. In both poems, the speaker, the son, learns something from the father. In this case the learning situation is baseball. The father wants the son to learn to bunt, but the son wants to go for the home run. The poem succeeds in talking about the lesson that the father was trying to teach in terms of the language of the game. Of course, that's made a bit easier by the fact that a bunt is often a "sacrifice," which is also the name of the virtue the father is trying to teach to his ego-centered son. And just as you "lay down" a bunt, the father was "laying down" a lesson that it took years for the son to make sense of. And just as a player gives a sign to the coach to communicate that he has understood the coach's sign, so this poem is a "sign" to the father that the lesson has been learned.

1. What is the significance of the phrase "that whole timesome pitch" in terms of our understanding of the speaker's attitude?
2. How does this poem relate to the old cliché that "sports builds character"?
3. How does the language of baseball work as a way of talking about human relationships?

Jim Webb, "Get In, Jesus"

This poem reads almost like a tall tale. The wild talk and the wild ride are right out of an American tradition of stories that take you out of ordinary experience into a more intense world. Part of the fun of this hippie-meets-redneck story is that there seems to be a lot of potential for violence or danger, but none of that happens. The driver of the car and the hippie he calls Jesus (the speaker) seem to have in common the kind of wit that turns an offhand comment—"Get in, Jesus"—into a semi-serious consideration of the very idea of God become man. Of course, all of this is done in a very offhand style. The language is slang and dialect, the form is loose, the tone is light. But the issues are real—the death of Christ, the community of strangers. "Get in, Jesus" would be a good poem to teach to students who think that poetry has to be serious, musty, and dull.

1. What do we learn about the characters in this very short story?
2. How does the Appalachian setting affect the story?
3. What kind of poetic form does the poem devise for itself?

Philip Booth, "Pick-Up"

You could almost characterize this piece as "found poetry," in the sense that it takes full advantage of the color and energy of language that's already out there, in this case the language of pick-ups and their specialized options: "4 × 4 Ram," "dual tube bumpers," "daylite Off-Roaders," "Hooker roll-bars," and so on. Too often we contrast poetry with "ordinary language," forgetting that sometimes ordinary language isn't so ordinary. Sometimes, as in the language of trucks or the language of sports or the language of dance, there is a poetry in the language itself. Many contemporary poets are interested in the poetry of the normal American idiom. And in this poem a little slice of that language is brought to our attention and honored.

1. How do the fragments of popular songs work in this poem?
2. How are the last three lines of the poem related to the rest?
3. Can you tell how the speaker of the poem feels about the guys he's describing and their interests?

Nikki Giovanni, "Ego Tripping"

Nikki Giovanni performs her poetry very dramatically, like a singer who understands the music in the words. This poem therefore needs to be read aloud in order to hear the ironic humor of her "ego-tripping" boasts. In this poem she seems at different times to be speaking as all women, as black women, as the goddess of the earth itself. She speaks as an originator of life, a creative force. The irony is that her "ego-tripping" comes about by claiming an identity larger than herself, by affiliating with a vast female spirit that the poem claims to be the source of the earth itself. But all of this is done in fun; the poem seems to take pleasure in its own exaggerations.

1. In reading the poem aloud, what kind of verbal units emerge from the poem?
2. What do the claims that the speaker makes in the poem have in common?
3. Who are the sons and daughters of this primal female, and what do they tell us about her?

Louise Glück, "The Mirror"

This is another poem *about* imagery, in this case the image in a mirror, and more importantly, a person's image of another who has his own image of himself. The speaker sees this man as beautiful, but he sees himself as "A man bleeding," and he seems to want to destroy his own beauty, as though it keeps other people from seeing his real life. This desire for self-mutilation is communicated in the poem's most striking image, the description of the man shaving: "how you scrape the flesh away / scornfully and without hesitation." The speaker of the poem seems to be aware of how our image of others can disfigure them, as he realizes he has been seeing "the reflection I desire."

1. Is it possible to see a person "correctly," as the man wants the speaker to do, or do we always see what we desire?
2. How would you characterize the relationship between the speaker and this man?

Elizabeth Spires, "Widow's Walk"

This poem would be good to use as a contemporary example of a dramatic monologue. The speaker of the poem is a woman from eighteenth-century Nantucket, left at home to wait for her captain husband to return from the sea. As the quote that begins the poem suggests, that waiting happens with the aid of opium, and perhaps the tone of the poem makes sense in that light. The speaker describes herself as "Vaporous and drowsy," and the images that she relates have the intensity and radiance of a drugged perception. But what comes through most clearly here is the sense of loss that would lead someone to the use of opium as a way of making the time bearable.

1. What does the poem tell us about the character of the speaker?
2. What are the most vivid images in the poem?
3. What do the last three lines tell us about how the speaker feels about herself?

Garret Kaoru Hongo, "What For"

The title of this poem suggests its concerns. The speaker is reflecting on his boyhood, remembering what he lived for—his Hawaiian language, his family, the ocean, and the ocean air. He especially reflects back on his memories of his father, coming home from work so tired and sore that he could barely toss a ball with his son. All these memories get communicated to us by means of powerful imagery. The place and the culture that the speaker grew up in and the harsh life of his father are described in vivid sensory detail. The sections dealing with the father are particularly vivid, and they seem to depend on the speaker's ability to live inside his father's experience, feel the pain "that work / and war had sent to him." What these images dealing with the father suggest is just how important he was to the speaker as a child. The son wants to heal the father, to allow him the leisure and health to enjoy his life.

1. What details from the speaker's boyhood stand out in the poem?
2. What do we learn about the father's past and present life?
3. What does the phrase "a doctor of pure magic" tell us about the speaker's feelings for his father?

Margaret Atwood, "Spelling"

This poem begins with a simple event that leads to some complex speculations. The speaker begins by describing her daughter at play with plastic letters, the kind that hang on refrigerators all over America. But for the speaker, this play is the beginning of a significant event, that is, it is the entry of her daughter into language, particularly writing. And the speculations that follow are concerned with women and language, or more specifically with the efforts made by men to keep women from gaining power within language. The speaker reflects on women who have had to choose between writing and motherhood, and on those women who have suffered from the effort to control their bodies and their language. Perhaps the central figure of the poem is the witch, representing the ancient power of women, who is killed, and even (or especially) at the moment of her death is forcibly barred from language. The daughter, then, is not only entering into language, but entering into the power struggles that surround language and begin with "your first word."

1. What is the connection between "spelling" and "how to make spells"?
2. In the third stanza the speaker makes a strong distinction between the child and a poem, but she ends with the word *however.* How does this stanza work?
3. How is the "woman caught in the war / & in labor" related to the concerns of the poem?
4. What is the connection between witchcraft and language?

Leon Stokesbury, "Unsent Message to My Brother in His Pain"

It would be interesting to teach this poem in tandem with Dylan Thomas's famous "Do Not Go Gentle into That Good Night." Both poems present us with similar dramatic situations—the speaker is addressing someone who is facing death, trying to convince the person that he should resist, fight to live. But each poem uses a distinctive rhetorical strategy in its context. How do you convince someone that life is worth fighting for? One speaker demands rage; the other asks his brother to attend to the beauty and variety of experience. Students could benefit from comparing the rhetorical strategies in terms of the personalities of the characters and the nature of their relationships.

1. How does the figurative language work in the speaker's description of the storm?
2. What effect does "we will cook with wine" have within the overall rhetorical strategy of the poem?
3. What can we infer about the relationship between the speaker and his brother on the basis of this "message"?

W. S. Di Piero, "Four Brothers"

What will probably strike students first about this poem is that "Four Brothers" has three parts. This is because, of course, the fourth brother is dead. But his death has made him a powerful force. He is present in the horrible lives of each of the other brothers, and, to bring us back to the poem itself, he is present in each of the stanzas. Each stanza tells the story of one of the brothers, showing it to be a function of their guilt and shame at their brother's death. The poem deals with the violent and even gruesome details of the brothers' lives, but it does so in a formal and understated style that does not overemphasize the lurid details, but rather gets us thinking about exactly how the trauma of their brother's death brought about those events.

1. What do we learn throughout the poem about the death of the youngest brother?
2. How is each brother's life related to the death of the youngest?
3. How does the speaker of the poem feel about these people?

Lynn Emanuel, "Frying Trout while Drunk"

The speaker of this poem is looking back on the past, trying to understand her mother, and in the process trying to understand herself. When she thinks back, she recalls images, scenes that seem to explain her mother's lifelong devotion to a man who hurt her and to the drink that soothed the pain. The real issue of the poem seems to be expressed with these words: "When I drink I am too much like her." The speaker sees her own life in terms of or as a repetition of her mother's. So the desire to make sense of the mother's life has an urgency that drives the poem.

1. What do we learn in the poem about the relationship between the mother and the father?
2. What do we learn about the speaker's feelings for these two people?
3. What do the words "The knife in one hand and in the other / The trout with a belly white as my wrist" tell us about the speaker's state of mind?
4. How does the last image of the poem fit in with the rest of what we have learned about these characters?

Daniel Mark Epstein, "Miami"

This poem would make a good example of the decisions a poet working without a preordained form must make about length of line. Should the line coincide with the sense of the words, or should it break up the sense into rhythmic units? In this poem there is an interesting variety of rhythmic effects brought about by the interaction of the sense of the words and the composition of the lines. The poem is also of interest as a portrait of the father. His fear seems inexplicable and unacceptable to the son, who perhaps sees his own possible future in his father.

1. What does the poem suggest about the source of the father's fears?
2. What does the last stanza tell us about the speaker's feelings for the father?

Robert A. Fink, "Mother's Day"

The speaker of this poem would be the focus of my teaching strategy. He narrates for us a memory that seems to symbolize his relationship with his mother. My sense of the significance of the memory is that the boy is taking a chance, having an adventure that turns out to be too difficult for him, and that the mother is offering reassurances that both know to be false. The title of the poem suggests to me that you could read it as an ironic Mother's Day card, but I do also feel that the relationship between the speaker and his mother is only suggested, not defined by the poem.

1. How are the first two stanzas of the poem connected to the last two?
2. What is the speaker's emotional reaction to the memory he narrates?

Don Johnson, "The Sergeant"

In this poem you can feel the speaker at work making sense of his past experience through the process of writing. The experience that he is working on comes out of his childhood in the wake of the Second World War. His father, he tells us, was in charge of an honor guard that attended the burials of soldiers killed in the war, so that for the boy, death, even if only in its ceremonial aspects, was a constant presence in his life. The key to this experience is the film that he describes in the last section of the poem. In it he sees the dead and dying in the German concentration camps, and he becomes haunted by the image of a boy, "thinner than any mountain stray," that he sees in the film. This image has obviously stayed with him as a reminder of the horror that he had only a glimpse of and that his father had to deal with every day. This poem, then, is an episode in the life of the speaker, and we could profitably discuss the relationship between this remembered episode and the adult speaker that we come to know through the poem.

1. Can you tell from the first two sections of the poem how the speaker feels about his father's duty?
2. How does the speaker react to the film that his father shows?
3. Why is it the image of the boy in the film that continues to haunt the speaker?

Marie Boroff, "Understanding Poetry"

Obviously this poem ought to be taught in tandem with John Donne's "Death be not proud," which it mentions by name. Both poems are concerned with death, but their messages about it are different. Donne claims a religious victory over death; Borroff realizes, for all her achievements, that death will finally triumph. The poems are also comparable in that both are sonnets, though this one is a very informal version of the form. What the poem seems to say about "understanding poetry" is that, for all the "razzmatazz" of poetic techniques, great poems always come down to simple concerns, like the acceptance of death.

1. How does this poem as a sonnet differ from Donne's "Death be not proud"?
2. What attitude toward death does this poem suggest?
3. What attitude toward poetry does the poem suggest?

Carolyn Forché, "The Colonel"

This poem could be taught in a section on poetic form, in that it is a prose-poem, and as such stretches the definition of what a poem is. I feel that the poet chose to use prose here because she wanted to create an effect of familiarity and ordinary life before the startling and horrible facts of the colonel's life are introduced. The poem is also interesting from the perspective of its speaker, who seems almost embarrassed at writing something as refined as a poem about such a grim reality. She has the sense that the colonel is performing for her, but that does not lessen the horror of what he has done or of his pride in displaying his trophies. This is poetry that comes directly out of the harsh realities of our time: there is nothing otherworldly about it. Its aim is to bring vividly before us a fact that we would rather forget.

1. What details of the colonel's life help to create the mood of familiarity?
2. What gets the colonel angry enough to reveal his crimes to the speaker?
3. What do the last sentences about the ears suggest?

PART THREE: FICTION AND CULTURAL CODES

Chapter One: The Function of Fiction

Myth from Togoland, "The Eye of the Giant"

This story has been included in this chapter because it is a clear example of the kind of work fiction can do. The story is rich and intriguing in itself, but it also does important cultural work. It is a story of origins; it explains to the people of its culture the origins of death—how it came into the world, how it affects human beings, why it is that death takes us one at a time rather than all at once. A listener who hears this story told is being entertained on one level, but on another level he or she is getting an explanation of how the world works. The story works to make sense of otherwise inexplicable experiences. It is also important to note, I think, how difficult it is for us to get exactly the message about death that the story sends out. That is, its message is so deeply intertwined with the habits of thinking of its culture that it is difficult for those of us outside it to participate fully in creating the meanings of the story.

Jakob and Wilhelm Grimm, "Little Red-Cap"

The Grimms collected folk and fairy tales, often taking the freedom to change and invent details. This is only one of many versions of the story; in fact, any class could come up with different details and especially endings that they have heard for this story. Still, in all of the versions a set of strong moral messages emerges. The little girl in the story disobeys her parents, trusts the wrong person (the wolf), gets into mortal trouble, and is saved by a strong male figure. As I note in this chapter of the text, the story has survived because it keeps the interest of the children who hear it and the parents who tell it, but it also stays alive because it does powerful cultural work, teaching children, especially young girls, the perils of straying off the path, of not listening to adult wisdom. In our cultural situation, those messages might not serve the needs of parents and of young girls who have to learn the values of independence, but in many cases the story is told without much awareness of its message, and so it does its cultural work without the conscious consent of those who tell it. In any case the story is an excellent example of how fiction can reinforce cultural values.

Geoffrey Chaucer, "The Pardoner's Tale"

This story from the *The Canterbury Tales* seems simple at first but gets complicated in its context, some of which we have supplied here. The story the Pardoner tells, of three evil men who kill each other out of greed, is a classic of simple, ingenious storytelling. It really does exemplify the Pardoner's moral—*Radix malorum est cupiditas,* or "Greed is the source of all evil." In this sense it is a simple example of the way in which fiction can reinforce an important cultural value. But the story of the Pardoner himself complicates the situation. A Pardoner in Chaucer's time was a seller of relics and pardons from the Pope, almost always false relics and worthless pardons. His only motive, he tells us openly, is greed. So he tells a story of greed in order to produce guilt in his greedy listeners, who will then give him money for a pardon for this sins. He preaches against greed in order to satisfy his own greed. What this story therefore suggests in the context of our chapter is that fiction has the power to bring a moral lesson to life, but it can also be manipulated by a storyteller who understands the power of fiction to sway its audience's feelings. While the Pardoner tells us a story of how greed destroys men, Chaucer tells us a story about a man who has destroyed himself morally by his own greed and by his perversion of the moral power of fiction.

Anton Chekhov, "The Bet"

Unlike some of the other stories in this chapter, "The Bet" does not simply dramatize a cultural belief or value. It tells the story of a man who has given up what many of us would consider the prime value—freedom—and who comes to question and even reject all that seems valuable. In his years of study and reading in his cell, the lawyer has come to the conclusion that all of man's valued possessions and beliefs are pointless in the face of death and destruction. He has, in his own eyes, risen above all values and beliefs. He is now able to question all of them, including, of course, the value of the millions he would earn by keeping his agreement. The story therefore seems to me to be a way for readers to examine their own values, to see if any of their most cherished beliefs could withstand the intense questioning that the lawyer would submit them to. One interesting twist in the story is that the lawyer, who has rejected all values, acts on principle. His gesture of rejecting the money is one that we would associate with high moral values. The lawyer seems to reject all values, but he retains the belief that we should act in accordance with our beliefs. What the story shows us in the context of this chapter is that many modern stories do not simply dramatize values, but rather draw our attention to values, bringing them into critical question.

Sherwood Anderson, "I Want to Know Why"

For the boy who is the main character and the narrator of this story, all that is valuable in life is caught up in the world of horse racing. He loves the sights and sounds and smells of the barns and the tracks. He admires the strength and courage of the horses. And he assumes that anyone who is a part of this world will act out of a purity of motive that matches the purity of the horses as they race. The boy's relationship with Jerry Tillford, therefore, leads to a crisis in his youthful beliefs. When the boy sees Sunstreak win the race, he also sees the horse's trainer, Tillford, sharing the purity of that moment.The boy tells us that he liked Tillford at that moment even more than his own father. But later, when he sees Tillford in a whorehouse, and more importantly, when he hears Tillford bragging and taking credit for Sunstreak's win, all this does not compute. In the boy's view, no one who is part of the racing world could be so impure. The question that is the title of the story points to the anguish that the boy feels in seeing his values destroyed. The world turns out to be more complex than he has wanted to believe.

Chapter Two: Plot

Nathaniel Hawthorne, "Young Goodman Brown"

Obviously this story could be taught from any number of perspectives: it is an interesting character study of Young Goodman Brown, it is richly symbolic, it is told from an interesting point of view. I have chosen to place it in the chapter on plot because it seems to me to be an interesting variation of the basic plot structure that I discuss in the chapter. That is, Young Goodman Brown, the protagonist, sets off on a journey into a strange land (the forest) and there meets his antagonist, Satan. Satan then tries, as the plot becomes more complicated, to seduce the young man into his service. The climax of the conflict occurs at the initiation ritual, where Young Goodman Brown refuses to join the worship of the devil. The outcome of that conflict is interesting as well, in that Young Goodman Brown isolates himself from all of mankind, convinced that they are all corrupt. He cannot accept the notion that humans are both good and evil. He sees all of their goodness as hypocrisy, now that he has seen them serving the devil in the forest. The plot of the story is simple enough, but to many readers the grim ending may seem an odd outcome for a character who has chosen "virtue."

Among the many other interesting features of this story, the forest setting calls for special attention. From the very beginning the forest is described as the place of the magical and the demoniac. Since Hawthorne is writing about a time when colonial settlements have not yet tamed the wilderness, it is not surprising that this place of danger should also be thought of as a place of evil. As a result, the primitive forest contrasts sharply with the civilized town, and it makes an apt setting for Young Goodman Brown's adventures.

Frank O'Connor, "Guests of the Nation"

The plot of this story involves bringing a character to a point of choice, and then observing the effects of that choice. The main character here, who has the nickname Bonaparte, is faced with the decision of whether or not to participate in an execution of hostages with whom he has become friends. The difficulty of the choice is highlighted by the first-person narration, which allows us to focus on Bonaparte's emotional response to the atrocity. Through his eyes we see the ordinary human relationships that grow up between the prisoners and their captors, and through him we feel the conflict brought about by the order to execute them. Bonaparte does in fact participate, giving a finishing shot to one of the prisoners.

The last paragraph of the story does a remarkable job giving a concise summary of how this event will affect Bonaparte. He feels detached from everything going on around him. In the last sentence he tells us, "Anything that happened to me afterward, I never felt the same about again." In a sense, we have to see the events of this story as a turning point in the larger plot line of Bonaparte's life. The story looks back on a time when his life changed irreparably—a time when youth and innocence were lost and when the harshness of human life came clear to him.

Doris Lessing, "Through the Tunnel"

Jerry, the young boy who is the protagonist of this story, faces an antagonist in the natural rather than the human world. He chooses to prove his own manhood or maturity to himself by swimming through an underwater cave, a feat he has seen accomplished by older, local boys. Part of the challenge for him seems at first to be gaining acceptance in this group of boys, but it soon becomes clear that the challenge is internal, a desire on his part not to be considered a child (or to consider himself so). The cave provides a serious challenge. It requires a long and difficult underwater swim, forcing the boy literally to risk his life. The story does a particularly good job reporting Jerry's moment-by-moment experience in the cave, his emotions and his efforts to swim through. What is at stake in this effort is Jerry's ability to claim adulthood. The beach where his mother swims presents no challenge and so Jerry thinks of it as a beach for children. His own desires take him to a harsh challenge that will prove he is no longer a child but a man. About the results of this challenge we hear only a little, but we do know that this event serves as a turning point in the boy's life. He is strangely subdued afterwards, as though he had to allow the effects of what he has done to sink in.

Chapter Three: Character

John Steinbeck, "The Chrysanthemums"

We readers learn a lot about Elisa Allen in the brief progress of this story. We get some idea of how she feels about herself and her life, and especially how she feels about her garden of chrysanthemums. And one of the most powerful ways we learn about her is through the narrator's descriptions of her. When we first see her she is dressed for gardening, in a man's hat, heavy work gloves, a bulky sweater, and the like. All the signs suggest manliness, or at least a disregard for appearance. That is, if clothes are signs that communicate a message, the message that Elisa sends out about herself in her outfit is of a serious, hardworking person who cares more for the task at hand than for the impression she might make on people. But after her encounter with the tinker, she changes the signs she displays. She washes, makes herself up, dresses in her most flattering dress. The passion that she had felt in talking about her flowers has changed the way she thinks about herself and therefore changed the way she dresses and presents herself. We get to know her from her outward signs, as well as from her actions and emotions.

The ending of the story is also worthy of note. After she sees her flowers dumped on the road, she goes through a series of emotional responses that are narrated very effectively in a very short time. What is especially interesting is her interest, instantly repressed, in seeing a boxing match—she goes out of her way to describe what she imagines it would be like in gory detail. This desire seems to suggest her resentment at men in general, and her repression of that desire seems to seal her fate as a woman who has let life go past her. The ending is powerful emotionally and also as a suggestion of the larger social issues that the story engages.

Virginia Woolf, "Moments of Being"

In this story we have dramatized for us the process by which one person tries to come to know another. Fanny Wilmot takes off from one ordinary comment made by Julia Craye, her piano teacher, "Slater's pins have no points—don't you always find that?" This remark surprises Fanny, for she thinks of Miss Craye living in the abstract world of music and so cannot quite comprehend her making such an offhand, ordinary remark. But the comment opens up to Fanny a world of imaginative possibility. All of a sudden she finds herself imagining what Miss Craye's childhood and young womanhood must have been. She is guided slightly by what little she knows about Miss Craye, but mostly she allows her imagination to create the past. When she emerges from her imaginative revery, Julia sees Miss Craye in ecstacy, and then Miss Craye kisses her. How this event is connected to the imagined past and what the kiss tells us about the relationship between the two women is left to the reader. By the end of the story we are not sure whether Fanny has come to know or understand Miss Craye at all. After all, it is only Fanny's account of Miss Craye that the story gives us. In a way, I feel that the truth of Fanny's imaginings is not the point. What Woolf is interested in is the *process* of trying to know another, not the truth or falsity of the results.

The story is also interesting as an experiment in the narrative control of time. The events of the story happen almost instantaneously. All of the imagining that the story describes happens in the moment in which Fanny bends down to retrieve the fallen pin. But that moment is an extraordinarily rich one, and thus deserves the expansion that the story provides.

Joyce Carol Oates, "Where Are You Going, Where Have You Been?"

In the introductory section of this text, I make use of this story as an example of how reading assumes our knowledge of culturally defined signs. The character of Arnold Friend, I argue, is made up of signs taken from popular culture—the design of his jalopy, the style of his clothes, his choice of music. And these signs communicate an impression of his character because they are part of a complex cultural code by which we generate and interpret signs. But Arnold Friend is not the only interesting character in this story. The protagonist, Connie, is the focus of the story; Arnold Friend serves as the antagonist, an uncanny character who takes Connie out of her ordinary, teenage life. Connie is also made up as a character out of the signs of her teen culture. She has the right look, listens to the right music, uses the right facial expressions. But in the case of Connie, we also get to know her from the inside. We hear what she feels, how the world looks to her. We also get to know about her family, her dreams, her sense of herself. In this way she contrasts strongly with Arnold Friend, about whom we know nothing but what we see and hear. This sense of mystery is deepened by Arnold's almost magical powers and his hypnotic control over Connie. Is he simply a perverted older man? a demon? a projection of Connie's desires? Those questions are suggested by the story, but Arnold Friend's identity is exactly what is not defined. Connie is a person from our world, but in her encounter with Arnold Friend she moves into a world that neither she nor we as readers can define.

Chapter Four: Setting

Flannery O'Connor, "Parker's Back"

"Parker's Back" is used in the text as an example of how the meaning of an action is altered by its context. When Parker has a tattoo of Jesus put on his back, the action takes on a profound meaning for him—I think you could say that it helps him gain his salvation. But within the context of his family and his community, the action takes on a different meaning. His wife, Sarah Ruth, sees his action through the prism of the extremely fundamentalist beliefs that she shares with much of her rural Southern community. Within this context, Parker's action is idolatrous. According to Sarah Ruth, he has placed his faith in an image rather than in the person of Christ. And the result for Parker is that he has to suffer for what seems to him a valid religious act.

The story is also of interest, of course, as a study of Parker's character. He is a person who often finds himself engaged in actions that he seems not to have chosen. The prime example is his courtship and marriage of Sarah Ruth, who seems consciously to him to be everything he does not want. Similarly, the face of Christ that he has tattooed on his back seems to compel him to choose it. In all of these actions, Parker seems to be moving himself toward his own religious awakening without his full awareness. My sense of the story is that O'Connor sees his salvation as valid, even if it comes out of the comic act of having Jesus tattooed on his back. Parker has simply found his own appropriate path to God.

James Joyce, "Eveline"

It might be useful to know that James Joyce described the theme of *Dubliners*, from which "Eveline" has been selected, as "paralysis." Joyce felt that the constraints of the Irish society of his time kept people from making valid personal decisions. We get a sense of this stifling environment in several ways in this story. One of the most effective is in the description of the house and neighborhood that Eveline lives in. Her physical surroundings seem to suffocate her just as much as the social surroundings. Also, her family is described in ways that emphasize the powers that oppose her freedom. Her insane, self-sacrificing mother, her brutal father, and most important, her own sense that she owes both of them a debt of loyalty keep her dutifully within the family structure. The importance of physical and social setting in the story is emphasized again at the end of the story, when Eveline, after she has refused to join Frank on the boat, finds herself physically fenced in, "like a helpless animal." Eveline chooses the restricted life that she has known all along.

Stephen Crane, "The Open Boat"

In this story, the setting, the sea, serves as the antagonist in the plot. The sea is the force that the characters must struggle against; it defines them, bringing out their loyalty, their determination. It is also interesting to see how the characters think of the sea. At first, they think of it as a malevolent force that is out to get them. But later they come to a grim realization of the sea's indifference to their fates. They cannot be angry at it because it has no feelings for them. Nevertheless, this indifference does not diminish their struggle. Up until the end of the story, the characters must fight every moment against the sea. If a plot traces a conflict, then in this story the conflict with the sea never ends. There are dangers to be overcome even as safety seems within reach. One interesting outcome of this struggle is the growing bond among the sailors in the open boat. Finding themselves pitted against a common enemy, the men come closer together. This is most interesting in the case of the correspondent, who would probably otherwise be an outsider, an observer. In this situation, against this nonhuman opponent, the correspondent gives up his detachment and joins in the communal struggle for survival. His own conflict with the sea makes him a better person in the end.

Donald Barthelme, "The Indian Uprising"

The world of this story is an amalgamation of the familiar and the strange. As a result, it is difficult to know how to take the story. Many of the rules that govern our daily reality seem suspended here, but in some ways this world seems uncomfortably familiar. The very idea of Comanches attacking New York takes us into an unreal world, but there is, however, nothing unfamiliar about the notion of modern society under attack from terrorism or the violence of the underclass. The idea that the New Yorkers would make a barricade out of sherry bottles, ashtrays, and flutes takes us into the fantastic, but the idea that what stands between the civilized and their enemies are possessions makes sense in our world. In the world of this story the "civilized" are as capable of brutality as their opponents—again a reminder of our troubled world. My general point is that even in a story like this that seems to occur in a world very different from our own, a world that many students would reject as silly or meaningless, there are lessons to be learned about our own society.

Chapter Five: Narration

Ralph Ellison, "Battle Royal"

This story is a good example of the intensity that a first-person narrative can create. Because we get the events from the perspective of the boy, we are forced to feel along with him, to experience his humiliation, his fear, his careful triumph. One of the best examples of this narrative intensity is in the description of the fight itself. We get to experience that fight second by second, as if we were caught up in it ourselves. We hear the sounds, feel the blows, see the blurs and dim shapes through the blindfold. Because of the first-person narration, we also have access to the boy's mind. We understand the feelings and expectations that he brings to the event; we get a direct experience of his disappointment; we hear about his dreams and hopes.

The decision to write this story in first-person clearly had political implications for Ellison. Whoever reads the story is forced to experience the racism and brutality of the event as a black person experiences it. Of course, no white reader can completely give up his or her own experience in reading, but by being put in the position of the black boy, any reader has to identify strongly with the "I" of the story.

Arthur C. Clarke, "The Star"

In this story the use of first-person narration is appropriate because the events of the story are an episode in the spiritual life of the protagonist. He tells us directly of the crisis of faith that was brought about by his discovery that the star of Bethlehem was a supernova that destroyed a civilization of astonishing achievement and morality. His faith seems to be destroyed by the discovery, in that it convinces him of the cruelty—or indifference—of God. We could not hear this spiritual change unless the priest himself were telling the story. Besides, he is probably the only member of the crew who would fully understand the significance of the discovery. He is both scientist and priest, pointing with pride to his articles in scientific journals and to his portrait of the founder of the Jesuit order. Because he is both, he can feel the significance of the scientific data. And because we see the event from his point of view, we can feel it too.

Honoré de Balzac, "Sarrasine"

This is one of the more complex stories in the anthology in terms of its narrative technique. You could describe this story as a "framed" narrative. The story of Sarrasine and La Zambinella is framed within the story of the telling of the story. The "I" who tells the story of Sarrasine also tells us why he told that story, in order to hold the attention and gain the affection of Mme. de Rochfide, the Marquise that he has brought to the party where they see La Zambinella. He tells the story in order to satisfy the Marquise's curiosity, which has been provoked by the extreme age of La Zambinella and by the overprotectiveness of the family. In telling the frame narrative, the story gives us a first-person narrator, one who can only guess at the feelings of the people he describes. He is shut out particularly from the mind of the Marquise, whose response he cannot read with confidence. But when he tells the story of Sarrasine, he speaks as a third-person narrator—and an omniscient one. He knows the feelings of Sarrasine especially, and he can even see into the mind and feelings of La Zambinella. Their story is more distant, and so he can tell it almost like a legendary tale. But the story of the party that inspires the story is more immediate, and so he can narrate it only from within its midst.

The story of Sarrasine is a story of obsessive and blind love. Sarrasine's infatuation with La Zambinella renders him ignorant of the world, and most especially of the fact that sopranos in the Italian theaters of the time were always castrated men. Sarrasine is therefore humiliated and destroyed by his own blindness. What is interesting is that the frame narrative repeats in a more moderate form the same general story. That is, the narrator of the story is in love with the Marquise, who at times seems as unapproachable as La Zambinella. And the story that he tells seems particularly ill-suited as a way of gaining her affection. At the end of the story we find that she has been profoundly disconcerted by the story, and the narrator seems to have failed in his attempt to win her.

John Cheever, "The Chaste Clarissa"

It seems to me that Cheever is very careful in constructing the narrative strategy of this story. He gives us a third-person narrator, but one who sees the events of the story as they are filtered through one character, Baxter, the predatory male whose prey is "the chaste Clarissa." It is important for us as readers to see the world through Baxter. It is also unsettling. Baxter is so completely amoral and manipulative that it makes us squirm as readers to be put in his position. But because Baxter himself does not tell the story, we are able to detach ourselves from him and judge his actions and beliefs. Cheever wants us to understand how Baxter operates but still be able to distance ourselves from him.

The story is also of interest in its depiction of the relationship between Baxter and Clarissa. Baxter's basic working premise is that he should flatter a woman not for what she is but for what she would like to be, what she imagines herself to be. Flattering Clarissa for her beauty only bores her, but flattering her for her (imaginary) intelligence reaffirms for her a quality that she desires and doubts in herself. This premise seems to work perfectly for Baxter, but Cheever seems to work hard to allow us the distance to see the immorality of his actions.

Chapter Six: Language and Fiction

Ernest Hemingway, "The Undefeated"

Hemingway has long been thought of as a master of economy and clarity in writing. In this story, the descriptions of the bullfight are prime examples of these qualities. The writing in those passages draws our attention to every important detail of the fight in the sparest possible language. The writing does not draw our attention to itself, but to the story it is telling. Nevertheless, if we *do* attend to the writing, we can see the power of language at work. That is, Hemingway does have a system of values through which he examines the actions of his characters, and we can see those values in the language he chooses. Zurito, the picador, who is the locus for many of Hemingway's values, is always described in the most positive terms. When he fights, his skill and dedication to the task require him to risk his own safety rather than sacrifice his horse or the matador, as some of the other picadors are willing to do. Zurito's actions are described in language that pulses with energy, as though Hemingway were trying to emulate Zurito's virtues in his own writing. It is also interesting to note that Zurito's virtues are not limited to the bullring. He is also the person who is willing to make Manuel face the fact that his days as a matador are done. His physical courage is the outward manifestation of a moral courage, just as Hemingways's clean, spare language is an outward manifestation of his values.

Edgar Allan Poe, "The Fall of the House of Usher"

If you can get students to respond honestly to their reading of this story, they will often complain about the difficulty of Poe's style, especially his vocabulary. Partly this is an historical difficulty; some of Poe's language is simply unfamiliar to a modern reader used to more utilitarian prose. But part of the students' problem comes from the fact that Poe does want to draw our attention to language. His is not the economical, spare prose of Hemingway. He seems to take pleasure in the richness of the words themselves: *dilapidation, countenance, cadaverousness, luminous, cataleptical.* I am not suggesting that Poe is being self-indulgent, but rather that part of his strategy as a writer is to draw our attention to language, to make us realize how our experience of life is always filtered through the mind and its language. Poe is not so much interested in what happens as in how those events work on a character's mind. And his language always reminds us that events get reshaped and given their meaning by the human mind.

Another interesting effect of the language of the story is that it gives us a sense of the character of the narrator. After all, the narrator, rather than Usher, is the protagonist of the story. The experience with Usher is an episode in *his* life. And it seems to me that the language of the story presents us with a narrator who is trying desperately to make rational sense of Usher, fit him into a category. But the events of the story refuse to allow a reasonable explanation, and they leave the narrator with no settled system of beliefs that will explain them for him.

James Baldwin, "The Rockpile"

For me, the interesting quality of the language of this story is the difference between the language of the characters and the language of the narrator. The characters speak in an informal, uneducated street language, whereas the narrator speaks in a highly formal, educated style. As a result, I feel a distance between the narrator and the events he describes. It's as though the narrator is presenting us with a slice of life from a world that he no longer inhabits. I see the narrator as John grown up. Even within the story John is a detached observer, and the narrator seems to me even more detached. He wants to show us the dynamics of this family and this community so that we will understand where he came from, but where he came from is no longer where he is.

The story is very interesting as an analysis of a particular family. The brothers' relationship is clearly presented—John is older, more worried about parents' reactions. Roy is freer, more willing to rebel. The parents also relate to their children differently, mainly because John is not the son of this father. And the parents' own relationship is subtly drawn, with the wife fearful of but willing to fight back against a very dominant husband. What all this adds up to is a rich and complex portrait of characters in interaction, defining themselves in terms of these complex relationships.

Chapter Seven: Fiction and Society

Joseph Conrad, "An Outpost of Progress"

Like many of Joseph Conrad's stories, this is a story of imperialism and its effects on those who serve the empire. Kayerts and Carlier come to Africa with a sense of their cultural superiority and with a desire to produce as much profit as possible. But they find their moral stability and energy undermined by the heat, the loneliness, and the sheer, sublime size of the land they are supposed to master. In this story Conrad seems clearly to be suggesting that civilization is a thin veneer that can easily be removed by harsh conditions. What makes the story work, I think, is the comic quality of the conflict between the two men. Both of their deaths, after all, are brought about by a conflict over whether they should be allowed to have sugar in their coffee. Not over slavery, which they have accommodated themselves to, not over issues of economic and political power, which they never consider critically, but over sugar, which becomes for them a symbol of what they have lost in leaving their comfortable European lives. The great civilizing colonialists, theoretically in control of all they survey, are destroyed by their own petty rivalries, and the ironic contrast gives the story the comic energy that drives home its message.

Bharati Mukherjee, "Angela"

The title character of this story is a refugee from Bangladesh, a victim of horrific violence that the story gives us a strong taste of in its last paragraph. The story itself is concerned with a particular moment in this girl's life in America. Her adopted sister is in a coma from a traffic accident; she is trying to deal with a marriage proposal from an Indian doctor who works at the local hospital; she is trying to forget the terror of her past. Her story, in other words, engages with real social issues of our time. But there is no propagandizing here. It would be difficult to reduce this story to a definite political position. It takes on political issues by focusing on some people who are living through them, not by announcing a solution or a doctrine. Nevertheless, the story does take on those issues. After you read about Angela, the abstract question of how immigrants from areas of political violence and terror can adjust to American culture will seem less abstract. This story embodies those issues and engages its readers with them on a more personal level.

Alice Walker, "Everyday Use"

How do you honor the past? How do you connect it to the present? In this story the bit of the past that is under dispute is a quilt, one that has been made by two generations of black women following patterns passed down in the folk tradition for hundreds of years. The impulse of Wagnero, the daughter who has gone off to be educated and who has taken on the history of her people as an academic discipline and a political cause, is to display the quilt as a work of art. Her mother's impulse, and that of her sister Maggie, is to put the quilt to "everyday use," to use it for the purpose that those who made it intended. Which impulse honors the past more validly? Since we see the issue through the eyes of the mother, who is the narrator of the story, we tend to agree with her, and to see Wagnero as arrogant in her desire to appropriate it for her own use, in effect to steal it from her sister. But the story does not set up a simple conflict in which the mother is right and Wagnero is wrong. Wagnero's recognition of the beauty and significance of the quilt comes out of a sincere desire to connect with black history and to find the richness of black culture. She is insensitive to the reality of her family's life, but she is not an easy-to-dismiss villain.

Alice Walker's story brings some very complex cultural issues down to the terms of a family quarrel. How should black people encounter their past—often a past of poverty and suffering? Does freedom require a rejection of that past, or does it require a lived connection with it? Wagnero seems to want to leap back past the suffering and regain the African heritage that white America attempted to destroy. But to do so is to reject her family, who live richly in the folk culture that Wagnero wants to forget or transform into decorative art. In this story it seems to me that our sympathies are clearly directed to the mother and sister, who have found dignity and strength in a black culture that affirms their human desires for connection and community. Which is, ironically, exactly what Wagnero is looking for.

Margaret Atwood, "Rape Fantasies"

It seems almost impossible that there could be a funny story about rape that would not simply be grossly offensive, but this story manages to be funny and at the same time to engage seriously with the issue of rape from a feminist perspective. The narrator of the story moves smoothly from telling about a lunchroom conversation among some women who work together who, under the influence of articles in women's magazines, begin to tell their rape fantasies, into telling her own fantasies, which are touching and funny and a bit frightening. In her fantasies, the rapists are always pitiful rather than dangerous, and she is always able to find in the men a core of human feeling to which she can appeal. She is always finally in control of the situation, and the rape itself never occurs. What is frightening about the story is that we find out at the end that she is telling her fantasies to a man she has met in a bar. I think of this story as a perfect example of how a reader can be left with little guidance as to how to respond to events. How are we supposed to feel about this woman? Is she naive to the point of endangering herself? Or is she so much in control of life that she can laugh at the very idea of being out of control? And what does the story have to say about the idea of rape in the lives of women? It doesn't seem at all like a laughing matter, but the story seems to succeed in making fun without becoming callous. Perhaps it comes down to the sensitivity and toughness of the narrator. Atwood has fashioned a believable character by creating a believable speaking voice, a character who confronts the possibility of rape as she does all of life, with a powerful, optimistic energy.

ANTHOLOGY OF FICTION

Washington Irving, "Rip Van Winkle"

"Rip Van Winkle" is a story that is well-known in our country, but too little read. What most people recognize is that Rip is the character who sleeps for twenty years, reappearing with a long, white beard. But the story involves much more than that. Rip's character is more fully developed, and his story takes place within a carefully described social and political setting.

The story would be worth studying in the "character" section of the course because of how Rip's character is developed and because of the experiences he encounters. In fact, Rip's character is not so much developed as announced. The narrator of the story simple *tells* us what kind of person Rip is: good-hearted, poor, incapable of profitable work, henpecked. Unlike stories in which the character's personality is revealed gradually through their actions, in this story the character of Rip is set from the beginning and never changes. Rip's character is also interesting because he undergoes a fantastic experience that is nevertheless familiar to us. That is, because he sleeps for twenty years under the spell of the mountain's ghosts, he returns to a world that has changed radically and in which Rip no longer feels at home. He is disoriented and alienated from his surroundings to the point that he doubts his own identity. Because his surroundings have changed, he can no longer locate himself within them. In this sense his story is curiously modern and familiar, in that the experience of feeling alienated in what should be a comfortable world has become a common theme in modern fiction.

The story is also very successful in depicting Rip's family and social surroundings. During his sleep, America has been born, changing from the loyal colony that Rip knew to an independent nation in which Rip feels like an outsider. This change from bondage to freedom is mirrored in Rip's family situation. Rip's wife had dictated his life to him, but during his long sleep she has died, and Rip finds himself at the end of the story freed from her domination. It is this personal freedom that is most meaningful to Rip, who remains mostly indifferent to the political changes. I find the depiction of the wife to be offensive in its misogyny; Irving seems to assume that a woman with a strong will is unnatural. But Irving is obviously not out to make this point; it is, rather, a part of the value system of his time. The value that the story seems out to demonstrate is the value of freedom, and Rip is delivered from a twofold dictatorship.

1. What is the significance to the story of the fact that Rip cannot bring himself to do profitable work?
2. How is the physical surrounding of the story described?
3. Do we as readers know what is happening to Rip before he does?
4. What events bring about Rip's feeling that he has lost his identity?
5. Why does Irving try to demonstrate the truth of his story in the prologue?

Mary Shelley, "The Mortal Immortal"

Mary Shelley's story is a good example of first-person narrative. In fact, it would almost *have* to be a first-person narrative, since it is the life story of a man who has lived for over three hundred years. As a narrator, "Winzy" tells his story beginning with its end, in the sense that we learn from the very beginning that he has lived so long and is immortal. The story then takes us back to the moment at which he received the "Elixir of Immortality," and then forward again to the place where we began. As a result of this narrative structure, there is no possibility of suspense in the story. The death of Bertha and the continuing suffering of the immortal hero are inevitable, looming over the story from the very beginning.

Another angle for teaching the story might be to discuss the degree of success with which Mary Shelley was able to inhabit the mind of a male narrator. Is the language of the story believable as a male's language? Does Shelley convince you as a reader of the psychology of her male character?

1. Why does the narrator concentrate only on the early part of his long life?
2. Is the narrator's explanation of his decision not to commit suicide convincing?
3. Why is it appropriate that, at the end of the story, the narrator is heading into an arctic climate?

Nathaniel Hawthorne, "Rappaccini's Daughter"

If stories are a way for a culture to express its values, this story could be thought of as a cautionary tale, a warning about the dangers of science and human pride. It could therefore be compared to Mary Shelley's "The Mortal Immortal," in that both stories show the human consequences of the passionate desire for truth—for human power over nature. Rappaccini's desire for knowledge and power has led him to transform his daughter into the object of his experiments. He has turned her into a monster in the name of the desire for wisdom. Hawthorne was writing at the time of the rise of modern science, and he articulates the criticism of science that has become common in our century—that it pursues truth without regard for the human consequences of its efforts.

Another interesting feature of the story is its concern with dualities. The flowers in the garden are medicines, but they are also poisons. Beatrice is beautiful but deadly. Rappaccini himself is devoted to science but ignorant of its results. The world that Hawthorne creates in this story is a world in which opposites coexist. At one point Giovanni says of Beatrice, "What is this being? Beautiful shall I call her, or inexpressibly terrible?" The answer, of course, in this story, is both. Everything in the story, including Giovanni himself, has a dual nature. And the final duality is that of body and soul. When Beatrice dies, she is certain that her soul will "ascend" out of her corrupt body. There is a sense, then, in which Hawthorne's story is an embodiment of traditional Christian beliefs about body and soul. The story exaggerates and dramatizes the idea of the corruption of the flesh and the potential purity of the soul.

1. What is the nature of Giovanni's feelings about Beatrice? How does this become important at the end of the story?
2. Is there a villain in this story?
3. What is the significance of the fact that Rappaccini's garden is compared at the beginning of the story to the Garden of Eden?
4. What is the state of the protagonist at the end of the story? Is the story left unresolved?

Edgar Allan Poe, "The Purloined Letter'

Poe is one of the founders of the modern detective story. In this story, which is famous for the fact that the letter in question is hidden in plain sight, the skill of the detective lies in reading the mind of his adversary. The police have searched for the letter in a rigorous and scientific manner, but Dupin, the detective, works on the premise that the minister who has stolen the letter would anticipate such a search and therefore hide the letter in a place the police would never look—in plain sight. The skill of the detective, then, is like the skill of the psychologist, an ability to predict human behavior on the basis of a knowledge of a person's mental habits. In this context, one of the most interesting passages of the story become Dupin's account of the schoolchild's game of guessing in which hand the stone is hidden.

The story is also of interest as a study of character motivation. Dupin seems to be involved in the story out of sheer interest in the problem it presents, but it becomes clear that he has other, more personal, interests. The character of Dupin emerges as the story goes along, revealing new aspects of his personality.

1. Who is the narrator of the story, and what is his role?
2. Why is the letter important to each of the characters involved?
3. Why does the police search for the letter fail?
4. What do we learn about the character of the minister?
5. What is the significance of the note that Dupin leaves for the minister at the end?

Herman Melville, "Bartleby the Scrivener"

Although this story will be perceived by many students at "weird," it's important that they see the simplicity of the plot. The protagonist is the narrator, the lawyer who tells the story of Bartleby but makes himself its hero. Bartleby is the antagonist in the story, the opponent that the protagonist has to face. The two come into conflict. Bartleby's sheer presence forces the narrator-lawyer to look at himself differently, to re-examine his life. The conflict is moral rather than physical, and the outcome of the conflict could be debated for hours, but the basic lot that underlies so many stories in our culture is at work even in this strange narrative.

What makes the story weird for students is, of course, the character of Bartleby. His actions make so little sense that they are easy to dismiss as insane, but I feel that the narrator is convincing in his attempt to make us feel that Bartleby's actions—or rather, his inaction itself—force us to ask ourselves serious questions about the nature of the will, our responsibility for our actions, and our duty to others. One way of getting at what Bartleby's character is about would be to have students compare and contrast him with the narrator. Bartleby just doesn't make sense inside the highly organized world of the lawyer. He brings everything into question. He *is* weird. That's the point.

1. What role do the other scriveners in the office, Turkey and Nippers, play in the story?
2. Does Bartleby's character change over the course of the story?
3. How does Bartleby's job, copying legal manuscripts, suit his character?
4. In what ways are the lawyer's actions affected by public opinion?
5. What does the last paragraph of the story, in which we find out that Bartleby once worked in the "Dead Letter Office," add to the story?

D. H. Lawrence, "The Blind Man"

This is a classic triangular story: the woman Isabel brings together two very different men, her husband Maurice and her friend Bertie. The story can be seen as a study of the relationships among these three characters, and especially of the conflicts between the two men. The narrator of the story lays out the characters of the three people very efficiently. Maurice has been blinded in the war, and is now finding a physical peace in the farm tasks that he can still perform. Bertie is all mental—a writer and lawyer whose quick and sensitive mind seems to detach him from the physical world. Isabel feels the physical strength and peace of her husband, but longs for the intellectual life that her friend offers. The climax of the story comes about when the blind man asks Bertie to touch his face and to allow his own face to be touched. And the results are ironic. Maurice feels that their friendship has been ratified by the touch, whereas Bertie is emotionally destroyed by the intimacy. Although Maurice feels they have been brought together, what he cannot see is the horror that the narrator and Isabel see on Bertie's face. By the end of the story the relationships among the three characters are even more complex than at the beginning. The climax of the plot does not seem to have brought about any resolution of the conflicts.

1. How would you describe the relationship between Isabel and Maurice?
2. How would you describe the relationship between Isabel and Bertie?
3. What is Maurice's motive for asking Bertie to touch his scarred face?
4. How is Bertie affected by the experience?

Lawrence, "The Rocking-Horse Winner"

One of the interesting ways to teach this story would be to discuss how it combines a "real" world with fantastic events. Lawrence creates a world in the story that seems to be the world of everyday reality. There is a family, a house, troubles, and family problems. But within that normal world there are inexplicable events. First is the whispering of the house. "There must be more money," it says. At first the narrator seems to use the term "whispering" figuratively, but as the story goes on we find out that at least Paul, the young boy, literally hears those whispers. And the boy, of course, has an almost occult ability to pick winners in horse races. He rides his rocking horse, almost maniacally, until he "knows" the winner of an upcoming race. As in many great stories of the supernatural, the events in this story happen in a world that Lawrence convinces us is ours.

The other point of interest in the story is the psychology of the boy's mania. The mother is disappointed in the father, who she sees as "unlucky," and the boy takes it upon himself to replace the father as the source of income for the family. His death at the end of the story would suggest that he was too young for such a responsibility. The pressure of producing money drove him over the edge. And what makes his death so poignant is that we know, and he knows, that his mother is ultimately cold to him, centered as she is on herself. The story does an excellent job in making the psychology of Paul's character clear.

1. How does Paul act when he is riding the rocking-horse?
2. What role does the uncle play in the story?
3. What is the significance of the uncle's final comment on Paul at the end of the story?
4. Do you feel comfortable with the supernatural elements of the story, or do you want there to be natural explanations for all that happens?

William Faulkner, "A Rose for Emily"

The "plot line" of this story concerns itself with the process of coming to know something. In this plot the narrator is the protagonist, and "Miss Emily" is the antagonist, the person he needs to know about. The narrator presents himself (herself?) as a representative of the townspeople. They are all obsessed with knowing the story of Emily, precisely because they have seen so little of her and know only the externals. They know her family, and that is part of their interest in her, since her family connects her with the traditions of the old South, which the modern town is otherwise leaving behind. They know about her narrow upbringing, with her father chasing away all possible suitors. They know of her madness at the death of her father. They know of her romance with Homer Barron, and of his disappearance. But thereafter, they know almost nothing, except for the odd bad smell and her refusal to pay taxes. When Emily dies, then, they have their chance to fill in the empty spaces in her story, and they discover a truth that none of them could possibly have imagined. On this level, the plot of the story is simple. It moves from a desire to know to a knowledge that the narrator and the rest of the town would rather not have.

The discovery that the townspeople make, that Emily has murdered and held on to the body of Homer Barron, is also the completion of the story of Emily, whose life provides a second plot for the story. We can see at the end how her insane life makes sense in terms of what the story tells us about her father's repression of her sexual life. As the narrator sees it: "We remembered all the young men her father had driven away, and we knew that with nothing left, she would have to cling to that which had robbed her, as people will." This insight makes sense of her refusal to accept her father's death, and later her "clinging to" Homer, who had robbed her of happiness. The story of Emily, for all its strangeness, holds together logically.

The story is also of interest as social commentary, in the sense that Emily represents to the town the virtues of the old South but she turns out to be corrupt and insane. The setting of the story reinforces this theme, especially in the description of Emily's ornately Southern house, which is also corrupt and decaying. Faulkner does not preach a social message in the story, but the plot and characters suggest that there is more than a personal story going on here.

1. How do the descriptions of Emily and the descriptions of her house compare?
2. What is the significance of the imagery of dust that recurs in the story?
3. What is the role of the black servant in the story?
4. How do the townspeople's feelings about Emily change over time?
5. What do we learn about the character of the narrator from how the story is told?

Faulkner, "The Evening Sun"

The narrative technique of this story is interesting, in that the narrator, Quentin, is looking back on an event that happened fifteen years earlier, and yet he narrates it with an intensity that makes it seem like he is experiencing it in the present. He also shows very few signs of the maturity that must have come with those fifteen years. He doesn't analyze the situation much or try to make sense of it in terms of what he must have learned about the world during that time. He tells it in such a way that he preserves the effects that the event would have on a child. In this context, the character of his sister Caddy becomes important, in that she is the one who asks the childlike but insightful questions that often bring out the significance of events.

The story is also a brilliant depiction of the power relationships that existed within Southern society. Race, class, and gender obviously play powerful roles in these relationships. Jesus has a physical power over Nancy. The children's father holds racial power over Jesus. He also holds power over his wife. Even the children, as whites protected by the law and by tradition, hold a kind of power over Nancy and even Jesus. Power in this society flows in complicated streams, depending on the race and gender of the people involved.

Another point of interest in the story is the psychological portrait of Nancy, who is so certain that Jesus is out to kill her that she almost frightens herself to death. She is an excellent fictional portrayal of a person whose guilt and fear almost destroy her. Whether or not Jesus is lurking in the dark, ready to kill her, Nancy suffers from her own emotions.

1. What role does Caddy play in the story?
2. How would you describe the relationship between the children's mother and father?
3. Who is the protagonist of this story?
4. How are you affected by the repeated use of the word *nigger* in the story?
5. How does race affect each of the major characters in the story?

F. Scott Fitzgerald, "Babylon Revisited"

Fitzgerald's story offers an interesting example of the interaction between setting and character. The setting of the story is Paris, just *after* the twenties, the decade of "the lost generation" of American expatriates. The story occurs after the crash in the stock market that ended the high life of the twenties. Charlie Wales, the protagonist of the story, had been a part of that high life. Lifted up by money earned in the bull market of the twenties, he spent most of his time dissipating what he had earned. His life was a perfect mirror of the times, even to the point of his experiencing his own "crash" in the death of his wife. Now, in the more sober social environment of the thirties, Charlie has returned to work and to the kind of sober life that he feels entitles him to regain custody of the child he lost at the death of his wife. His wife's sister, Marion, who now has custody of the child, will not let him forget that earlier time, and she will not accept that he has changed along with the times. The story illustrates well how actions that seem natural and acceptable in one era may seem immoral and irresponsible in another. Charlie has changed, but even more profoundly, his society and environment have changed.

1. How much do we learn about Charlie as a person? How do we learn it?
2. How do his version of the past and Marion's version differ?
3. Can we completely trust Charlie's personal changes?
4. How do Lorraine and Duncan function in the story?

Katherine Anne Porter, "The Grave"

This is a classic story of a young girl's rite of passage into maturity. All the elements are present—death, sexuality, birth—and they take on a powerfully physical form that makes the experience unforgettable. In fact, the story ends with a description of a moment when the memory of the childhood incident floods back. In the incident itself, Miranda is forced to consider herself in a new way. She thinks of herself perhaps for the first time as a female; she clearly feels both a sense of horror and of kinship with the rabbit. And this moment comes on top of her enjoyment of the gold ring her brother had found in the graveyard, which itself had made her reconsider the overalls she habitually and happily wore. Events conspire to bring her to a new way of thinking about herself. This is therefore the kind of story with which most students can immediately connect, since many of them have only recently gone through such experiences themselves. The rite of passage that Miranda goes through is not hers alone—it is a passage through which we all must go.

The ending of the story is particularly interesting, in that we see how Miranda's memory reorganizes the event, trying to make sense of it in her current life. She remembers the physical horror of seeing the dead rabbit and its dead babies, but she also remembers her brother's delight at the treasure she found for him. What that memory tells us about Miranda the adult is not made explicit in the story and is therefore a subject for the reader's speculation.

1. What does Miranda go through in the story around the issue of proper dress?
2. How would you describe the relationship between Miranda and Paul?
3. What is the significance of the trade that the two children make?
4. How do each of the children react to the rabbit that Paul kills?
5. What do we learn about the mature Miranda from the last paragraph of the story?

Shirley Jackson, "The Lottery"

What drives this story is the contrast between the ordinary, small-town American setting and the "primitive" ritual that surrounds the lottery. Jackson does all she can to convince us that this story involves ordinary folks, even to the point of keeping her characters fairly bland, so that they will seem like "average" people. But these ordinary folks are capable of ritualized murder, and they take to the task at the end of the story with real enthusiasm. The *reason* for the lottery ritual is never made precisely clear. Many of the townspeople have forgotten its origins, but they make themselves part of the ritual simply because it is traditional. The expectation of the group is enough to require their involvement. Some of the individuals in the town seem to react to the event differently from others, but none radically questions the necessity for the ritual. We could therefore see the lottery as a way of affirming communal bonds, even if it requires the sacrifice of one member of the community. By requiring all of the townspeople to involve themselves in an act of violence, the lottery draws them all together in their shared emotions.

Jackson's story seems to be making serious statements about human community, the need for ritual, and the practice of offering one member of the community as a scapegoat that will ensure the survival of the community as a whole. I also get a sense of her outrage at how willingly the community sacrifices one of its members. There is no regret or horror. The gruesome murder gains everyone's assent. It is interesting to note that fundamentalist groups have urged the censorship of this story for high-school students. Students might be interested in trying to figure out why this story is considered dangerous for them.

1. How much personal identity do each of the townspeople achieve in the story?
2. Who is the narrator of the story, and how does the narrative technique effect the story?
3. How does each of the townspeople react to the lottery?
4. Can you think of any contemporary event that seems comparable to the lottery?

Peter Taylor, "The Fancy Woman"

This story takes place at the point where sexuality, race, and class intersect. And that is a volatile point, a point of conflict. Josephine, the fancy woman, is George's plaything. He keeps her for his enjoyment, and he takes pleasure in the power he has over her. Part of that power comes from the class difference between them. George is part of Memphis upper-class society, whereas Josephine is a shop-girl looking to move up. There is plenty of conflict between them, since Josephine is not a willing victim of George's desire for power, but the conflict comes to a climax when George's upper-class friends and later his two sons arrive on the scene. These reminders of George's status make Josephine feel acutely her lower-class origins and her less than respectable current occupation. She certainly does not fit in with these people, and she does not fit in with the servants either. In fact, by the end of the story, Josephine is completely isolated. The story could therefore be used as an example of the effects of social setting on individuals. Both George and Josephine are constantly reacting to the social situation they find themselves in. Are the servants around? His friends? His children? How they act is a function of who they're with.

1. What do we know about Josephine's past?
2. What is the basis of the conflict between George and Josephine?
3. What role do the two sons play in the story?
4. How does Josephine change when George's friends and family arrive?
5. What effects does Buddy's rejection of Josephine have on her?

Eudora Welty, "A Worn Path"

This story displays all the elements of the classic heroic story. Phoenix Jackson sets out on a quest, a journey through a perilous landscape in search of a valuable object that will serve not her own desires but the needs of someone she loves. She has to overcome obstacles such as the dog who bumps her into the ditch, the scarecrow that tricks her into thinking she sees a ghost, the hills and other dangers of the path she follows. And she does this for her ailing grandson, who is completely dependent on her heroism for his survival. The only element of the story that doesn't fit the heroic scheme is Phoenix herself, and that is one of the story's major points. Whereas most of us would think of a "hero" as young, male, vigorous, rich, white, and strong,

Phoenix is old, female, weak, poor, and black. Clearly, Welty wants to remind us that heroes come in all shapes and sizes, and that our stereotypes of the hero can blind us to the more complex reality of our society.

Another interesting quality of the story is the language that Welty gives to Phoenix. Her language is perfectly natural to her, but it also has a simple dignity that is appropriate to her heroic nature. And although the narrator of the story is not Phoenix, we still see the events of the story through her eyes. The result is that we readers get to take on a perspective that is not our own. We see the world from a new angle.

1. What is the significance of Phoenix Jackson's name?
2. How does she respond emotionally to the difficulties on her journey?
3. How does Phoenix interact with the white people she meets?
4. Why does the narrator hold off until the end of the story the reason for Phoenix's travels?

Welty, "Petrified Man"

The most striking feature of this story is its dialogue. The narrator of the story plays a relatively minor role. It is the characters themselves, Mrs. Fletcher and especially Leota, who are responsible for the telling of the story. The two of them work together to tell the story of Mrs. Pike and the petrified man. Leota is a gifted gossip, and Mrs. Fletcher is mad enough at Mrs. Pike to be eager for the details.

The story they tell is unsettling—there has been a rapist living among them while the carnival is in town—but they block out that issue by concentrating on the unfairness of Mrs. Pike winning the reward. The story starts out as what we might call "idle gossip," but it ends up concerning itself with some serious issues. Of course, Welty herself seems to be playing the story for laughs, but the humor—as comedy often does—deals with some dark reality. Underneath the story runs an anger at men: complaints about shiftless husbands and bratty boys, anger at the petrified man's trickery and brutality. And the anger comes out at the end, in the comic but sharp scene when Billy Boy gets paddled in front of all the women in the beauty shop.

Part of the comic effect of the story depends on its setting in the shop. The customers and beauticians are lower class and uneducated, but they use a fake genteel speaking style that produces a lot of the story's fun. And the very idea of gossip in a beauty parlor provides a rich source of comic possibilities. Nevertheless, Welty is out to show, I think, that these gossips are engaged in the same task that she is—telling a story. They may be telling a story that has more meaning than they can handle consciously, but they tell the story well, in a complex collaboration. Professional writers, the story suggests, aren't the only storytellers. And stories often mean more than their tellers know.

1. How does Leota's gossip get around to the story of the petrified man?
2. What is the significance of the petrified man in the story?
3. What does the story have to say about pregnancy and childbirth?
4. What role does Billy Boy play in the story?
5. What do we learn about the character of Leota by observing her tell this story?

Bernard Malamud, "The Magic Barrel"

One way to teach this story would be to concentrate on the character of Leo Finkle, who is so well drawn that he exemplifies how characters can be presented. We know Leo from the outside in; we see where he lives, how he dresses, what he eats. We also know him from the inside; we see his daydreams and hear directly his innermost feelings. And the plot of the story involves a change in Leo's character.

At the beginning he is withdrawn, living in a world of books. By the end he is taking a huge emotional risk, attempting to make real contact with a woman who could either redeem him in love or destroy his career and his life. What brings about this change is his encounter with Salzman, the marriage broker. Salzman, who seems to possess magical powers, leads Leo out of himself and into relationship with other people. He may do this by an old-fashioned method, brokering arranged marriages, but he is dedicated to love, to uniting people. And in this case he arranges a meeting that brings Leo into authentic contact with the world, even if it is at great risk.

Two other interesting features are the power of the social setting of the story and its admission of magic into the real world. Leo is studying to become a rabbi, and his story makes sense only within Jewish-American culture. Salzman is a part of the history of that culture, representing the old ways that are being challenged in the modern age. And although Leo is embarrassed by Salzman as an outmoded part of the heritage, it is Salzman who makes Leo's very "modern" decision possible. Salzman also seems to bring with him some of the magic of the "superstitious" past, with his impossibly quick movements and his mind reading. Malamud does a great job integrating that magic into the real world of New York, so that the magic seems almost natural and believable.

1. What is Leo's stated motive for looking for a wife? What do you think is his real motive?
2. What does Leo see in Stella, Salzman's daughter?
3. What do you think are the prospects for the relationship between Stella and Leo?
4. What is Salzman's reaction to their meeting?

Grace Paley, "The Loudest Voice"

This would be an excellent story to teach in the section of the course dealing with setting. The action of being in a Christmas pageant at school changes its meaning when it is performed in the public school in a Jewish neighborhood. It is interesting to see how the various people in the neighborhood react to the pageant: they are angry at having another religion preached at them in school, and proud that their children have a good part, and concerned at what the experience will teach their children. The narrator, Shirley, who is involved in the play, seems to have a purely dramatic interest in the proceedings, getting caught up in the rehearsals and execution of the play. And the last paragraphs of the story suggest that she has at least survived the experience, if not learned a lesson from it.

Shirley also provides an interesting focus for discussing the story, both in thinking about how her character changes and in analyzing how she tells the story. She seems to be telling it from an adult perspective, looking back on her childhood in a neighborhood culture that no longer exists, but she tells the story with tremendous immediacy, describing the sights and sounds and impressions of the experience.

1. What is the function in the story of all the references to quiet and to loudness?
2. How do each of Shirley's parents feel about the pageant? What are the reasons for their feelings?
3. What do we learn about Shirley the adult narrator from the way she tells the story?
4. What effects does the pageant seem to have had on Shirley?

Flannery O'Connor, "A Good Man Is Hard to Find"

The plot structure of this story is simple and effective. All that's required of the plot is that it bring together the Grandmother, who I would say is the protagonist of the story, and the Misfit, who is her antagonist. From early on in the story when we hear about the escaped convict, we are expecting him to show up, and the plot contrives to bring him into contact with the Grandmother and her family. For me the Grandmother represents respectability, family, following the rules. The Misfit represents questioning the rules, acting outside the law. Such opposed forces are destined to clash. But the interesting outcome of the conflict is that the Grandmother feels that she has some common nature with the Misfit. She even thinks of him as her own son. She has heard his philosophy of life, felt the suffering it must have come out of, and sympathized with his situation. Her reward for this act of love is to be killed, and O'Connor seems to be suggesting that such an affirmation often gets you into trouble in a harsh world.

It's also important to note that these serious issues are dealt with in the story in a very funny way. The Grandmother is the butt of a lot of the jokes, with her prim traveling outfit, designed to impress anyone who might see her after an accident that she is a lady, and her silly manipulations of the grandchildren. And the climax of the comedy, if I can put it so, occurs at the moment when the Misfit shoots her and then comments, "She would of been a good woman if it had been somebody there to shoot her every minute of her life." O'Connor manages to deal with serious issues in a comic style that does not at all trivialize the story.

1. What do we learn about the family at the beginning of the story?
2. What role does the scene at Red Sammy's, and especially the monkey in the chinaberry tree, play in the story?
3. How would you describe the Misfit's philosophy of life? In what sense is his nickname appropriate?
4. How does the narrator describe the deaths of the family? What effects do those murders have in the story?
5. Before her death, is the Grandmother changed by her encounter with the Misfit?

Claude Koch, "Grandfather"

The focus of this story is obviously on the relationship between the Grandfather and Andrew. From the Grandmother's perspective, Andrew gives him the uncritical attention to his fantasy life that he needs, and Andrew gets in return a heroic and larger-than-life world that gives color to his own ordinary experience. The details of the Grandfather's characterization are fun. Repeatedly we hear about projects left unfinished, repairs neglected, gardens begun with enthusiasm but forgotten and allowed to run wild. Yet the narrator as well as Andrew seems to enjoy rather than deplore the Grandfather's loose style. The same is true for the Grandfather's incessant lies. He claims to have been with Dewey at the battle of Manila Bay; the wood in his fireplace comes from India; he has single-handedly saved daylight by petitioning the governor to establish Daylight Savings Time; he claims that his Knights of Columbus coat and sword are his uniform from Dewey's navy. Andrew's father is driven wild by these lies, but since we are concentrating on the relationship between the boy and his grandfather, they seem to us like harmless fantasies that enrich the boy's world and bind him to his grandfather.

One of the prime lessons that the Grandfather passes down to the boy is a knowledge of such communication codes as semaphore and Morse code, methods for communicating from afar. The ending of the story turns this shared interest into a poignant moment as the Grandfather and the boy try to communicte across the separation imposed by the hospital. The Grandfather is facing a reality he cannot imagine himself out of, and the boy is beginning to understand the truth as well. Their gestures of communication, then, seem a desperate attempt to maintain a connection that time is destroying.

1. What do the descriptions of the Grandfather's house tell us about his character?

2. What does the narrator contribute to the story? Why did the author choose to use a third-person narrator?
3. What do we learn about the relationship between Andrew and his father? How does the Grandfather affect that relationship?

Raymond Carver, "Cathedral"

The obvious story in this anthology with which "Cathedral" could be compared is D. H. Lawrence's "The Blind Man." The basic situation is very close, except in this case the blind man is the wife's friend rather than her husband. In fact, I think you could see this story as a conscious rewriting or revision of Lawrence's story. In "The Blind Man," the sighted person is emotionally destroyed by the touch of the blind man. But here, the husband seems to learn something, to open himself up to experience in a way that he never has before. He describes himself as a person who dopes himself up and watches TV to anesthetize himself every night. The blind man, in getting him to draw the cathedral, forces him to use mental powers that he has never used before. The husband is able to overcome his discomfort with the man's blindness and his jealousy at the other's relationship with his wife in order to make some contact.

Part of the effect of the story comes from the fact that it is narrated by the husband. As a result, we can track the changes he goes through. He begins bitterly, resisting any mention of the blind man, but we see him slowly becoming more open to this new experience and almost fascinated by the ways in which the blind man has adapted to his life. Even though the experience may be more complex than the husband can articulate (his only comment on the experience is, "It's really something"), we can see the significance of the event for him because he is telling his own story, the story of an event that seems to have changed his life.

1. What sense do you get of the character of the husband from the way he narrates the story?
2. In what ways is the blind man different from what the husband expected?
3. What is the significance of all the drinking, eating, and smoking that goes on?
4. How is the conversation between the two men about cathedrals related to the question that the blind man asks the husband about his religious beliefs?

Bobbie Ann Mason, "A New-Wave Format"

The strength of this story is in its details. The characters come alive to us because of the foods they eat, the clothes they wear, the houses they live in, the music they listen to, the TV shows they watch. All of these details are signs that point to the personality of the characters who live in the midst of them. Music, of course, is particularly important, both as a way for us to understand Edwin and as a force in the plot. The music that Edwin plays on the bus is always a clue to his mental state, and it is his change to new-wave music that brings about one of his riders' convulsions. Music also tells us a lot about Sabrina, who is equally comfortable with the latest new-wave record as well as with the songs from *Oklahoma*.

These details of the character's environment also communicate a lot about their social standing. Sabrina works at McDonald's and aspires to community theater stardom. Edwin watches *WKRP in Cincinnati* and plays DJ on his school bus route. They are part of the American working class, which is mostly neglected by American writers. Mason seems to take them seriously; she sees the comedy in some of their desires and aspirations, but she also understands that as much is on the line in their problems as would be if they were people of wealth and power.

Another point of interest in the story is the characterization of the retarded students on Edwin's bus. Each person is drawn in a specific way, so that they are not simply interchangeable. Each character is briefly given a distinctive personality. And just like the main characters, they define themselves by their habits, their musical tastes, their clothing and appearance.

1. What is the basis of the relationship between Edwin and Sabrina?
2. What is the narrator's attitude toward Sabrina's ambition in the theater?
3. How does Edwin's feeling about the students on his bus change throughout the story?
4. What is the significance of the last line of the story?

Joy Williams, "The Skater"

I would describe this story as simple in the best sense of the word. The situation is simple: parents taking their daughter around to visit schools she might attend. Their emotions are dominated by one event—the absurd death of their oldest daughter. The language of the story is simple: ordinary words combined in short, simple sentences. The reason for the simplicity, I think, is the power of their emotions. The death of the daughter has made them incapable of any fancy observations or reactions. They are paying all their attention to details, trying to forget what is most on their minds. And the author is trying to match that simplicity in her language.

The story is also noteworthy for the speed and understatement of its characterizations. In this brief story we come to know the three main characters very well. We see them react to the world they observe, and we hear directly about the suffering they are going through. They are only sketched, but the sketches are insightful.

1. Why is the story set in the winter?
2. What do we learn about the schools they visit?
3. What does Molly think is her parents' motivation for sending her away to school? What do her parents think is the motive? Which is right?
4. What is the significance of the picture of Jimmy Watkins in the story?
5. Is the ending of the story positive or negative?

Lynn Sharon Schwartz, "Mrs. Saunders Writes to the World"

This story is notable for the clarity of the main character's motivation. Mrs. Saunders writes her name on walls. She is the world's oldest graffiti artist. But if her actions are strange, they make perfect sense in her emotional life. She is simply so alone in the world that she never hears her own name used by another person. As a result she feels as though she is disappearing. Writing her name is a way of confirming and announcing her existence.

The story also has an interesting ending. When her friend Jill asks her her first name, Mrs. Saunders feels the need to lie, to cover up her writing activities. As a result, she realizes, she ensures the isolation she had feared. But she also comes to a moment of personal understanding: she realizes that her longing for contact is not as strong as her need for respectability, and that makes her understand that her isolation is chosen, an integral part of her identity.

1. What is Mrs. Saunders's emotional reaction to her writing adventures?
2. How does the community view Mrs. Saunders?
3. What does this story suggest about the motivations behind writing in general?

PART FOUR: DRAMA AND THE READER'S RESPONSE

Tragedy

Sophocles, *Oedipus Rex*

Oedipus Rex virtually defines the genre of tragedy. It is not the first of the Greek tragedies, but it is the play that Aristotle probably had most in mind when he wrote the enduring definition of tragedy that appears in his *Poetics* and it continues to crystallize for our culture the essence of the tragic experience. If tragedy requires the downfall of a hero, then this play provides us with an almost divine hero who falls into an unspeakable horror. Oedipus has saved his country from the terrors of the Sphinx, and he has become the respected ruler of the land, looked up to as the man who knows the minds of the gods and who acts righteously out of that knowledge. What Oedipus finds out about himself in the course of the play is that, despite his status, he is guilty of the most horrible crimes his culture can imagine—patricide and incest.

The plot of the play involves Oedipus's efforts to discover who is responsible for the plague that has devastated his country. He goes about the search in a very logical manner, almost like a detective. He follows the clues, investigates the witnesses, draws the logical conclusions. But what his logic leads him to is a truth that he cannot accept—that he has caused the plague by killing the king his father and marrying his own mother, the queen. The fact that he has done so unknowingly makes no difference within the belief system of his society. The deeds have been done, and as a result an almost physical infection of evil has overwhelmed the land. These horrors have occurred despite Oedipus's best efforts, but he has been fated by an ancient curse of the gods to destroy himself and his family. Oedipus was aware of this curse and took steps to avoid his father and mother, but no matter how hard he struggles against his fate, it will out.

The tragedy of Oedipus is brought about by the gods, that is, by a power too great for him to resist. For some audiences, this means that his suffering is too great for his sins, which were not committed with his knowledge. But within Oedipus's own value system, his destruction makes perfect sense. It is the will of the gods, and it is a just punishment for his transgressions. Oedipus tries to escape his fate, but his people, personified in the chorus, realize that if he escapes, his success will bring into question the power of the gods on which the Greek religion rests. Oedipus's destruction, then, is a reaffirmation of the power of the gods and of destiny. As in all great tragedies, the suffering of Oedipus is painful for the reader, but it is not meaningless suffering. It makes sense.

It is also important to note that the story of Oedipus was well known to Greek audiences. The play, therefore, holds no suspense. Oedipus is fated from the beginning. The play has also continued to fascinate readers and audiences throughout the history of our culture. It provided for Freud in our time the framework that he needed to talk about what he called "the Oedipus complex," the young man's unconscious desire for the mother and rivalry with the father. Freud's use of the play is a testimony to its enduring relevance literally thousands of years after its composition.

1. Within the whole life-span of Oedipus, what period of his life does the play itself depict? Why?
2. How does Iokaste talk about the prophesies of Oedipus's fall?
3. What is at stake for the community in the fate of Oedipus?
4. What role does Kreon play in the plot?
5. Why does it take so long for Oedipus to understand the truth?
6. Why is blinding himself an appropriate act of self-destruction for Oedipus?

William Shakespeare, *King Lear*

This tragedy is much closer in spirit for a modern reader in that the fall of the hero is a result of his own character and actions. Everything that happens makes sense on the human scale. Lear is destroyed, not by the actions of a god but by his own weakness and vanity, and by the evil of his daughters and their co-conspirators. Nevertheless, his destruction is equally inevitable. By the very fact that this is a tragedy, we as readers know that Lear will be destroyed, and so the first scene of the play, in which Lear demands elaborate expressions of loyalty and love from his daughters, begins a process of self-destruction from which we know Lear will not escape. What is surprising, however, is the thoroughness of that destruction, which brings down almost all of the major characters in the play, including such sympathetic characters as Cordelia. The tragedy here extends beyond Lear and includes almost his entire society.

The destruction begins, though, within that smallest of social units, the family. The aging Lear, too weak to continue to rule, wants to give up his power and, in his weakness, he needs the reassurance of his daughters' love and loyalty. The inflated rhetoric of Goneril and Regan covers up their essential coldness toward Lear, whereas Cordelia's straightforward honesty allows Lear to underestimate her true love for him. After he banishes Cordelia, Lear leaves himself in the control of the daughters who feel nothing for him and care only for themselves. I feel that this family conflict can be the point of contact for today's students, who may otherwise feel unconnected to the concerns of the play. Their own feelings about their parents, whether positive, negative, or ambivalent, can help them connect with the daughters in the play and with Lear's suffering at their hands.

But it is not only Lear who suffers in the play. The destruction of Lear and his family infiltrates out into the entire society. Shakespeare is able to dramatize this by his masterful use of subplots. The conflict between Lear and his daughters is mirrored and extended by the conflict between Gloucester and his sons. Just as Lear is confused about the loyalty of his various daughters, so Gloucester is taken in by Edmund's trickery and becomes convinced that his loyal son Edgar has betrayed him. The very existence of the subplot suggests that Shakespeare feels the problems within Lear's family are not specific to it, but rather that they are symptomatic of problems that all families face.

The play is also noteworthy, even for a Shakespeare play, for the variety and richness of its language. Of course, for many students this richness is a problem rather than a benefit. Shakespeare's language is so foreign to us that it requires footnote translations, but I feel that students need to understand how much of his language is the ordinary and even colloquial language of his time, which is precisely why so much of it is unfamiliar. Shakespeare was writing for the public of this time, not for a learned and elite audience. We need to recognize Shakespeare as a popular writer and to convince students that his concerns are not esoteric. But the language of this play is not only strange, it is also rich. It includes the language of madmen and men pretending to be mad, the wild language of fools, the empty language of inflated rhetoric, the language of deception and trickery. Within such an untrustworthy linguistic environment, it is not surprising that Lear does not recognize the truth when he hears it. In this play, the truth is almost lost amidst all these wild perversions of language.

1. What keeps Cordelia from performing like her sisters when her father demands professions of their love?
2. In what ways does Gloucester mirror Lear?
3. What does Lear learn through his suffering at the hands of nature in his night in the storm on the heath?
4. Is it necessary to the plot for Cordelia to die at the end? Why does she die?

5. Is there anyone left to restore order at the end of this play?
6. Are Lear's suffering and destruction explained fully in the play? Does his death make sense?

Sean O'Casey, *The Plough and the Stars*

This play tests the limits of the definition of tragedy, in that there is no character in the play who fits easily into the category of hero. Most of the characters are at best would-be heroes; others are fake heroes or outright cowards and opportunists. The closest that the play comes to a hero is Mrs. Burgess, whose kindness and concern for others leads to her death. But she is far from the main character in the play. Perhaps O'Casey called the play a tragedy because he had in mind the failure of the uprising that the play depicts. The "hero" who is destroyed is not an individual, but the idealism that began a rebellion that ended in looting and defeat.

O'Casey's play is set just before and in the midst of the Easter 1916 rebellion of the Irish against English rule. The rebellion was defeated in the short term, but it began the process by which the south of Ireland became an independent republic. As such, the rebellion is often depicted as a romantic and heroic struggle, but O'Casey focuses his attention on the ordinary people caught in the midst of the battle. Many of them are hostile or indifferent to the rebellion, and all are terrified by the battle going on around them. O'Casey seems to be out to deflate our notions of heroism, depicting war as a bleak and messy affair in which the innocent are the most likely victims. Although the play is set in these particular historical circumstances, O'Casey's anti-war theme speaks to a more general concern.

Perhaps this interest in deflating heroism accounts for the large dose of comedy in this tragic play. Fluther, Mrs. Gogan, Peter, and the Covey are broadly comic characters, too full of themselves to have much common sense. They speak in an inflated rhetoric that does not succeed in covering up the commonplace nature of their lives. And when the action does turn tragic in the deaths of Clitheroe and Mrs. Burgess and in the suffering of Nora, these comic characters seem almost pathetic, swept up in events that they cannot control or comprehend.

The language of this play is a central concern. It is written in dialect, and students might encounter trouble with O'Casey's rendition of Dublin English. *Th* often takes the place of *t*, for example. But once the difficulty with the dialect is overcome, students will discover a cast of characters who delight in language, playing with it in exaggerated rhetoric, elaborate attacks, and wild comedy. Each character has a particular verbal style, and the style tells us a lot about the person. Nora's genteel style suggests her desire to escape the slums. The Covey's Marxist jargon places him politically, and reveals how little he knows about Marxism itself. O'Casey is a master at characterization by dialogue. How these characters talk tells us the kind of people that they are.

1. What details of the play tell us about the social ambitions of the Clitheroes?
2. How does the rhetoric of the political speakers at the rally compare with the language of the characters in the pub in Act II?
3. What are the politics of Mrs. Burgess? Why is it significant that she is one of the few heroes in the play?
4. Does Nora fit the definition of a tragic hero?

Comedy

William Shakespeare, *As You Like It*

In the chapter on comedy I make the point that this play shares many features with the Shakespeare tragedy anthologized here, *King Lear*. That is, both are based on family conflicts and betrayals. In this play, brother betrays brother in both of the main plots, and daughter and niece are banished from the kingdom because of their loyalty to the betrayed and rightful Duke. These conflicts may not seem like the material for *comedy*, but like many comedies *As You Like It* deals with some very unsettling issues inside of a structure that assures us that all the issues will be settled, all the conflicts resolved. That is, because the play is a comedy, its audiences and readers come to it with the expectation of a happy ending, and this play does not disappoint them. In fact, it offers *many* happy endings—lovers are brought together, mistakes are cleared up, brothers are reunited, the political order is returned to stability. The ending of the play is a multiple marriage, a ritual of unity that resolves all the tensions of the play.

The plot of the play involves delaying that unity by a complex series of misunderstandings, lies, masquerades, tricks, and confusions. Two of the main characters—Rosalind and Celia—are in disguise much of the play, hiding their true identity. Other characters are confused by the intensity of their love, and others must hide their feelings because of the conflicts that open the play. But the comic expectations that the play sets up reassure us through all these misadventures that the truth will be revealed and that justice will prevail. And further, each of the characters, particularly Orlando and Rosalind, are better off because of the comic ordeal they have endured.

One of the great achievements of the play is the character of Rosalind, one of the great female characters in Shakespeare. Rosalind is witty, strong-willed, and warmly human. She enjoys the play that her disguise allows her, but you never get the feeling that she is toying with Orlando. Rather, she is in a sense educating him, teaching him how to control and refine his passion for her. She almost takes on the role of the playwright within the play, arranging the actions of the other characters and making sure that the comic conclusion brings all of the characters together.

1. What is the significance of the wrestling match in Act I?
2. Is it believable that Orlando would not recognize Rosalind in disguise?
3. What role does the melancholy Jacques play in the comedy?
4. Does the ending strain too much to bring about all the forms of unity it presents?
5. What is the significance of the fact that the conflicts of the play are resolved in the forest rather than in the court?

Molière, *Tartuffe*

For all of its verbal wit and complexity, *Tartuffe* is a simple play. The sole intent of its plot is to bring about the destruction of Tartuffe. Like many comedies, the play ends in a reunion of lovers, but the emphasis is not on their joy but on the destruction of Tartuffe's plans. To be sure, Tartuffe deserves the scorn we feel for him. He is that worst kind of moral hypocrite who goes out of his way to accuse others of crimes he readily commits himself. He turns on his benefactor at the first opportunity. At the end of the play, in fact, we find out that he is simply a con man who has played the same trick on many victims. But even if our scorn for Tartuffe is justified, it is interesting to note that the main response from the audience that this comedy seeks is scorn, not the joyful laughter of sentimental comedy.

The ending of the play is somewhat uncomfortable formally, in that the final destruction of Tartuffe comes from outside the plot. Tartuffe is foiled not by the cleverness of one of the characters but by the acumen of the King, whose representative arrives just in the nick of time to prevent Tartuffe's triumph. This seems to some readers like an awkward and unjustified ending. But I think it is important to remember that Tartuffe is dangerous not just to these individuals but to the entire social order. He attacks the family, the smallest and perhaps most powerful social unit. He disrupts the legitimate transfer of wealth and property. He mocks the moral order, turning it into an opportunity for his trickery. His victims are not just these people but the social systems on which they rely for order in their lives. It is therefore appropriate that he is brought to justice by the King as a representative of that order. As a comedy, therefore, this play is extremely conservative, in the sense that its victim is the man who questions order and social law.

1. Why is Orgon so blind to Tartuffe's true nature?
2. What is the significance of the fact that Dorine, the lady's-maid, is so outspoken in her attacks on Tartuffe?
3. What can we learn about the family structure of Molière's time by reading this play?
4. Who is the protagonist of this play?

Beth Henley, *Crimes of the Heart*

This very contemporary comedy is also very traditional in its structure. Like many of our plays, it focuses on family conflicts, in this case the problems encountered by three sisters. But it is again like most traditional comedies in that we can work safely in reading the play on the premise that these problems will be overcome. Perhaps one sign of the contemporaneity of this play is that its happy ending does not promise perfect bliss forever after. It offers a *moment* of unity and peace in the midst of lives that have not and probably will not experience such emotions frequently.

The problems that each of the sisters encounters have to do with a failure to make connections. Lenny, the oldest, seems to have an almost pathological fear of contact with men. Meg, the middle sister, drifts in and out of relationships and lives in a world of fantastic hopes. Babe, the youngest, is estranged from her husband (to put it mildly), and the one authentic connection she does have—with Willie Jay—is not possible within her society. The most enduring connection that any of the sisters has is with one another, and the play succeeds in presenting that connection as healthy, affirming, and loving. The sisters do each other wrong and engage in heated battles, but always within the context of love and concern. The moment—Henley calls it a "magical moment"—at the end of the play in which all of the sisters are unified in spirit is a convincing symbol of their love for one another.

It is important to understanding the tone of the play to remember that this optimistic story of the sisters occurs against a very dark background. Their mother committed suicide in a lurid and dramatic fashion, largely because of her estrangement from their father. Their grandfather suffers a stroke during the play. There is violence and disloyalty in the background. The pleasure of the comic plot, then, is hard-earned. Henley seems to suggest that the pleasures of life are rare, and that they must therefore be savored all the more intensely.

1. How much effect does the Southern setting of the play have on the plot and characters?
2. What role does the sisters' cousin Chick play in the comedy?
3. Why is the character of Doc Porter important in the play?
4. What keeps Babe from committing suicide at the end of the play?
5. Does any one of the three sisters emerge as *the* main character?

Realism

Henrik Ibsen, *A Doll House*

Ibsen's play is one of the founding classics of realistic theater. It engages with a pressing social question—the institution of marriage and the status of women—and it presents us with an event that, for the time of the performance, we are supposed to see and react to *as if* it were real. Every aspect of a production of this play—the set, the lighting, the costumes, the acting—would be designed to ensnare us in the illusion that we are looking in on real events.

The plot of the play involves Nora's growing realization that she is trapped in a social world that both privileges and restrains her. She has money worries, but not nearly on the order of those that threaten her friend Mrs. Linde. Her material welfare is taken care of by her husband and by her household staff. But the cost of that care is her own autonomy. She is obligated by the terms of her relationship to defer to her husband. If she takes independent action, it must be in secret. And when she rebels against that restraint, she realizes that the cost must be the privileges she enjoys. Her decision to leave the doll house is a choice of independence. It comes out of a desire to have control over her own life.

In this play, dialogue is particularly important. We get to know these characters by what they say and how they say it. We can see in his choice of words, as I mention in the chapter, how Torvald thinks about Nora. And we can also see her acquiescence to his power. She can play the same verbal games that he can, but we can also see in Nora's dialogue a growing awareness of her own capabilities and a growing guilt and frustration at her situation. In this play, the characters use language to maintain power over others and to acquire it for themselves. Nora's dramatic announcement of her plans at the end of the play is devastating and perhaps even illuminating for Torvald. Language is a form of action and a manifestation of power.

1. What role does Mrs. Linde play in the development of Nora's character?
2. What role does Dr. Rank's death play in the plot?
3. In the reader's response to Nora's decision to leave, how do the children enter in to the considerations?
4. What does Ibsen's description of the Helmers' house tell us about them?
5. How do concerns about money affect each of the characters?

Susan Glaspell, *Trifles*

This play is included in the Realism section of the book because it is a believable depiction of an event that could well happen in our world. And the play does not draw attention to itself as a play, but rather tries to convince us that the action it depicts is in fact occurring before us. The issues that the play raises are urgent ones in our time—gender differences, male power, female resistance—and the play raises them in a dramatic and provocative form that forces us to face these issues squarely. The play is a detective story, an investigation of a murder. And like most such stories, it moves from a mystery to a solution, although in this case the solution is not part of the official investigation and does not lead to the punishment of the murderer. The crime and the characters' reaction to it occur within a recognizable setting, and we react to the characters as though they were real people making real-world decisions.

The conflict in the play obviously centers around the different responses to the crime experienced by the male and female characters. The men have come to this house on the "serious," official business of finding the murderer. The women have come along to collect some of the belongings of the woman who is being held in jail under suspicion. As the title suggests, the women are after "trifles," and the men do not miss a chance to remind them of it. The men seem to be filled up with the seriousness of their task, and they have nothing but scorn for the women's concerns. The irony of the play, of course, is that it is the women who discover the truth of the matter, and they discover it precisely because of their concern with "trifles," the day-to-day details of home life that communicate clearly to them the kind of lives that Mr. and Mrs. Wright led. Glaspell seems to be suggesting that the texture of life is what matters—not the grand gesture or the dramatic event, but the daily worries, the habits of ordinary interaction. And the women in the play are infinitely more perceptive about such matters.

What Mrs. Hale and Mrs. Peters *do with* their discovery produces the tension in the play. When they find the bird that Mr. Wright has killed by wringing its neck, they immediately understand how and why Mrs. Wright committed the crime. But although they know who the murderer is, they do not share their knowledge with the men who represent legal authority. The "trifle" they have found communicates poignantly the kind of life Mrs. Wright has had to face over the years, a life with a man who denied her the right to her only pleasure, singing, and who killed the bird that reminded her of that joy. The two women can feel along with Mrs. Wright so strongly that they cannot use their knowledge to condemn her. The ending of the play is therefore unsettling, first of all in the sense that it goes against our usual expectation that a mystery or detective story will end with the apprehension of the criminal, and more importantly because we are asked to sympathize with the covering up of a murder. The ending puts us in a sharp moral crisis. Mrs. Wright, after all, has strangled her husband in his sleep, and yet we feel along with the women who discover her crime the emptiness and daily cruelty she had to face.

1. What details do the women notice that tell them about Mrs. Wright's life?
2. Why do the men pay so little attention to such details?
3. What kind of life did Mrs. Wright lead?
4. Is there an element of revenge in the women's decision not to reveal what they have discovered?

Theater of Spectacle

Bertolt Brecht, *The Good Woman of Setzuan*

If Ibsen is one of the founders of modern realism, Brecht is one of the beginners of the modern reaction against it. Brecht believed that a play should remind its audience that they are attending a play, so that they can understand how the play manipulates their reaction. In this play the illusion of reality is broken by the character of Wong, who performs the function of a narrator, speaking directly to the audience, almost like the teller of a moral fable. The literal presence of the gods and the frequent songs are other reminders that we are not dealing with a depiction of ordinary reality. As readers or as an audience, we know all the time that we are looking at a spectacle, a theatrical production that is out to illustrate a moral point in an entertaining fashion.

But the fact that the play does not claim to depict reality does not mean that it claims no connection to our lives. After all, the spectacle concerns itself with one of the most common questions that anyone has to face—how to survive economically in a harsh world while still holding to basic moral standards. The gods in the play are looking for a good person, and what makes their task so difficult is that people must struggle against one another in a world of limited resources and so do not have the luxury of treating others with compassion when their own survival is at stake. The society of this play is filled with self-centered opportunists who are eager to take advantage of others' weaknesses. They are all engaged in a harsh competition for survival, and moral questions are rarely raised. Brecht's fable may admit that it is fiction, but it nevertheless presents us with a world that we can recognize and learn from.

The exception to the rule of cold competition is Shen Te, the good woman of Setzuan. Her goodness does not bring her happiness and properity; in fact, she has to create an alter ego for herself in the form of her cousin, Mr. Shui Ta, in order to protect herself from those who would take advantage of her virtue. Nevertheless, Shen Te does hold on to her moral values, refusing to exploit others for her own enrichment. Even in the guise of Shui Ta, who becomes a prosperous factory owner, she does not grind down those who work for her. She maintains her innocence and impulsiveness, and her belief in the power of love. At the end of the play she is left in the harsh world, trying to hold on to her goodness but needing to survive in the midst of those who have no such restraints. Shen Te is a rich and complex character who serves as a symbol for the difficulties and possibilities in human life.

1. Why does the play present the gods in such a comic fashion?
2. How do you respond to Shen Te's enduring love for Yang Sun?
3. Why did Brecht choose a prostitute for the role of the "good woman"?
4. How do you react to Mr. Shui Ta, Shen Te's "cousin"?
5. Which of Brecht's endings do you think works best?
6. How does the music function within the play?

Edward Albee, *The Sandbox*

This is a play that goes out of its way to draw attention to itself as a play. The characters think of themselves and present themselves as theatrical creations. They talk to the tech crew, ordering the lights to dim. They talk about "off-stage rumbles"; they ask the musician—who is right on stage—to adjust the music. The actor who is playing the Angel of Death identifies himself as an actor playing the Angel of Death. Everything is done to emphasize the theatricality of the events presented.

And yet the play succeeds in many of the ways a realistic play would hope to succeed. It creates believable characters and relationships. Mommy and Daddy's callous attitude toward Grandma's old age and death is unpleasantly familiar. And Grandma's anger and final acceptance of her death are quite recognizable. Even this play, which could be described as "absurd," presents us with a perspective on real experience.

But the play calls attention to its own theatricality so often that we cannot mistake what is presented for reality. The characters—not just the actors—in the play seem to be following a preordained script. They know the parts they are playing and the lines that are expected of them. Take for example Mommy's clichéd reaction to Grandma's death, one that Grandma herself mocks. It's as though Albee is suggesting that much of human life is scripted, that we follow out our roles without thinking about them. The play suggests that there is an element of theatricality—of role-playing—in all experience. In a funny way, then, his play is not so unrealistic after all.

1. What kind of relationship do Mommy and Daddy have?
2. Why does Albee make the Angel of Death a *bad* actor?
3. What would it be like to be in the audience of a play in which the actors talked to the stage crew?
4. How does the set for the play relate to its "absurd" actions?

A 8
B 9
C 0
D 1
E 2
F 3
G 4
H 5
I 6
J 7